Dictionary of Literary Biography

1 *The American Renaissance in New England,* edited by Joel Myerson (1978)

2 *American Novelists Since World War II,* edited by Jeffrey Helterman and Richard Layman (1978)

3 *Antebellum Writers in New York and the South,* edited by Joel Myerson (1979)

4 *American Writers in Paris, 1920-1939,* edited by Karen Lane Rood (1980)

5 *American Poets Since World War II,* 2 parts, edited by Donald J. Greiner (1980)

6 *American Novelists Since World War II, Second Series,* edited by James E. Kibler Jr. (1980)

7 *Twentieth-Century American Dramatists,* 2 parts, edited by John MacNicholas (1981)

8 *Twentieth-Century American Science-Fiction Writers,* 2 parts, edited by David Cowart and Thomas L. Wymer (1981)

9 *American Novelists, 1910-1945,* 3 parts, edited by James J. Martine (1981)

10 *Modern British Dramatists, 1900-1945,* 2 parts, edited by Stanley Weintraub (1982)

11 *American Humorists, 1800-1950,* 2 parts, edited by Stanley Trachtenberg (1982)

12 *American Realists and Naturalists,* edited by Donald Pizer and Earl N. Harbert (1982)

13 *British Dramatists Since World War II,* 2 parts, edited by Stanley Weintraub (1982)

14 *British Novelists Since 1960,* 2 parts, edited by Jay L. Halio (1983)

15 *British Novelists, 1930-1959,* 2 parts, edited by Bernard Oldsey (1983)

16 *The Beats: Literary Bohemians in Postwar America,* 2 parts, edited by Ann Charters (1983)

17 *Twentieth-Century American Historians,* edited by Clyde N. Wilson (1983)

18 *Victorian Novelists After 1885,* edited by Ira B. Nadel and William E. Fredeman (1983)

19 *British Poets, 1880-1914,* edited by Donald E. Stanford (1983)

20 *British Poets, 1914-1945,* edited by Donald E. Stanford (1983)

21 *Victorian Novelists Before 1885,* edited by Ira B. Nadel and William E. Fredeman (1983)

22 *American Writers for Children, 1900-1960,* edited by John Cech (1983)

23 *American Newspaper Journalists, 1873-1900,* edited by Perry J. Ashley (1983)

24 *American Colonial Writers, 1606-1734,* edited by Emory Elliott (1984)

25 *American Newspaper Journalists, 1901-1925,* edited by Perry J. Ashley (1984)

26 *American Screenwriters,* edited by Robert E. Morsberger, Stephen O. Lesser, and Randall Clark (1984)

27 *Poets of Great Britain and Ireland, 1945-1960,* edited by Vincent B. Sherry Jr. (1984)

28 *Twentieth-Century American-Jewish Fiction Writers,* edited by Daniel Walden (1984)

29 *American Newspaper Journalists, 1926-1950,* edited by Perry J. Ashley (1984)

30 *American Historians, 1607-1865,* edited by Clyde N. Wilson (1984)

31 *American Colonial Writers, 1735-1781,* edited by Emory Elliott (1984)

32 *Victorian Poets Before 1850,* edited by William E. Fredeman and Ira B. Nadel (1984)

33 *Afro-American Fiction Writers After 1955,* edited by Thadious M. Davis and Trudier Harris (1984)

34 *British Novelists, 1890-1929: Traditionalists,* edited by Thomas F. Staley (1985)

35 *Victorian Poets After 1850,* edited by William E. Fredeman and Ira B. Nadel (1985)

36 *British Novelists, 1890-1929: Modernists,* edited by Thomas F. Staley (1985)

37 *American Writers of the Early Republic,* edited by Emory Elliott (1985)

38 *Afro-American Writers After 1955: Dramatists and Prose Writers,* edited by Thadious M. Davis and Trudier Harris (1985)

39 *British Novelists, 1660-1800,* 2 parts, edited by Martin C. Battestin (1985)

40 *Poets of Great Britain and Ireland Since 1960,* 2 parts, edited by Vincent B. Sherry Jr. (1985)

41 *Afro-American Poets Since 1955,* edited by Trudier Harris and Thadious M. Davis (1985)

42 *American Writers for Children Before 1900,* edited by Glenn E. Estes (1985)

43 *American Newspaper Journalists, 1690-1872,* edited by Perry J. Ashley (1986)

44 *American Screenwriters, Second Series,* edited by Randall Clark, Robert E. Morsberger, and Stephen O. Lesser (1986)

45 *American Poets, 1880-1945, First Series,* edited by Peter Quartermain (1986)

46 *American Literary Publishing Houses, 1900-1980: Trade and Paperback,* edited by Peter Dzwonkoski (1986)

47 *American Historians, 1866-1912,* edited by Clyde N. Wilson (1986)

48 *American Poets, 1880-1945, Second Series,* edited by Peter Quartermain (1986)

49 *American Literary Publishing Houses, 1638-1899,* 2 parts, edited by Peter Dzwonkoski (1986)

50 *Afro-American Writers Before the Harlem Renaissance,* edited by Trudier Harris (1986)

51 *Afro-American Writers from the Harlem Renaissance to 1940,* edited by Trudier Harris (1987)

52 *American Writers for Children Since 1960: Fiction,* edited by Glenn E. Estes (1986)

53 *Canadian Writers Since 1960, First Series,* edited by W. H. New (1986)

54 *American Poets, 1880-1945, Third Series,* 2 parts, edited by Peter Quartermain (1987)

55 *Victorian Prose Writers Before 1867,* edited by William B. Thesing (1987)

56 *German Fiction Writers, 1914-1945,* edited by James Hardin (1987)

57 *Victorian Prose Writers After 1867,* edited by William B. Thesing (1987)

58 *Jacobean and Caroline Dramatists,* edited by Fredson Bowers (1987)

59 *American Literary Critics and Scholars, 1800-1850,* edited by John W. Rathbun and Monica M. Grecu (1987)

60 *Canadian Writers Since 1960, Second Series,* edited by W. H. New (1987)

61 *American Writers for Children Since 1960: Poets, Illustrators, and Nonfiction Authors,* edited by Glenn E. Estes (1987)

62 *Elizabethan Dramatists,* edited by Fredson Bowers (1987)

63 *Modern American Critics, 1920-1955,* edited by Gregory S. Jay (1988)

64 *American Literary Critics and Scholars, 1850-1880,* edited by John W. Rathbun and Monica M. Grecu (1988)

65 *French Novelists, 1900-1930,* edited by Catharine Savage Brosman (1988)

66 *German Fiction Writers, 1885-1913,* 2 parts, edited by James Hardin (1988)

67 *Modern American Critics Since 1955,* edited by Gregory S. Jay (1988)

68 *Canadian Writers, 1920-1959, First Series,* edited by W. H. New (1988)

69 *Contemporary German Fiction Writers, First Series,* edited by Wolfgang D. Elfe and James Hardin (1988)

70 *British Mystery Writers, 1860-1919,* edited by Bernard Benstock and Thomas F. Staley (1988)

71 *American Literary Critics and Scholars, 1880-1900,* edited by John W. Rathbun and Monica M. Grecu (1988)

72 *French Novelists, 1930-1960,* edited by Catharine Savage Brosman (1988)

73 *American Magazine Journalists, 1741-1850,* edited by Sam G. Riley (1988)

74 *American Short-Story Writers Before 1880,* edited by Bobby Ellen Kimbel, with the assistance of William E. Grant (1988)

75 *Contemporary German Fiction Writers, Second Series,* edited by Wolfgang D. Elfe and James Hardin (1988)

76 *Afro-American Writers, 1940-1955,* edited by Trudier Harris (1988)

77 *British Mystery Writers, 1920-1939,* edited by Bernard Benstock and Thomas F. Staley (1988)

78 *American Short-Story Writers, 1880-1910,* edited by Bobby Ellen Kimbel, with the assistance of William E. Grant (1988)

79 *American Magazine Journalists, 1850-1900,* edited by Sam G. Riley (1988)

80 *Restoration and Eighteenth-Century Dramatists, First Series,* edited by Paula R. Backscheider (1989)

81 *Austrian Fiction Writers, 1875-1913,* edited by James Hardin and Donald G. Daviau (1989)

82 *Chicano Writers, First Series,* edited by Francisco A. Lomelí and Carl R. Shirley (1989)

83 *French Novelists Since 1960,* edited by Catharine Savage Brosman (1989)

84 *Restoration and Eighteenth-Century Dramatists, Second Series,* edited by Paula R. Backscheider (1989)

85 *Austrian Fiction Writers After 1914,* edited by James Hardin and Donald G. Daviau (1989)

86 *American Short-Story Writers, 1910-1945, First Series,* edited by Bobby Ellen Kimbel (1989)

87 *British Mystery and Thriller Writers Since 1940, First Series,* edited by Bernard Benstock and Thomas F. Staley (1989)

88 *Canadian Writers, 1920-1959, Second Series,* edited by W. H. New (1989)

89 *Restoration and Eighteenth-Century Dramatists, Third Series,* edited by Paula R. Backscheider (1989)

90 *German Writers in the Age of Goethe, 1789-1832,* edited by James Hardin and Christoph E. Schweitzer (1989)

91 *American Magazine Journalists, 1900-1960, First Series,* edited by Sam G. Riley (1990)

92 *Canadian Writers, 1890-1920,* edited by W. H. New (1990)

93 *British Romantic Poets, 1789-1832, First Series,* edited by John R. Greenfield (1990)

94 *German Writers in the Age of Goethe: Sturm und Drang to Classicism,* edited by James Hardin and Christoph E. Schweitzer (1990)

95 *Eighteenth-Century British Poets, First Series,* edited by John Sitter (1990)

96 *British Romantic Poets, 1789-1832, Second Series,* edited by John R. Greenfield (1990)

97 *German Writers from the Enlightenment to Sturm und Drang, 1720-1764,* edited by James Hardin and Christoph E. Schweitzer (1990)

98 *Modern British Essayists, First Series,* edited by Robert Beum (1990)

99 *Canadian Writers Before 1890,* edited by W. H. New (1990)

100 *Modern British Essayists, Second Series,* edited by Robert Beum (1990)

101 *British Prose Writers, 1660-1800, First Series,* edited by Donald T. Siebert (1991)

102 *American Short-Story Writers, 1910-1945, Second Series,* edited by Bobby Ellen Kimbel (1991)

103 *American Literary Biographers, First Series,* edited by Steven Serafin (1991)

104 *British Prose Writers, 1660-1800, Second Series,* edited by Donald T. Siebert (1991)

105 *American Poets Since World War II, Second Series,* edited by R. S. Gwynn (1991)

106 *British Literary Publishing Houses, 1820-1880,* edited by Patricia J. Anderson and Jonathan Rose (1991)

107 *British Romantic Prose Writers, 1789-1832, First Series,* edited by John R. Greenfield (1991)

108 *Twentieth-Century Spanish Poets, First Series,* edited by Michael L. Perna (1991)

109 *Eighteenth-Century British Poets, Second Series,* edited by John Sitter (1991)

110 *British Romantic Prose Writers, 1789-1832, Second Series,* edited by John R. Greenfield (1991)

111 *American Literary Biographers, Second Series,* edited by Steven Serafin (1991)

112 *British Literary Publishing Houses, 1881-1965,* edited by Jonathan Rose and Patricia J. Anderson (1991)

113 *Modern Latin-American Fiction Writers, First Series,* edited by William Luis (1992)

114 *Twentieth-Century Italian Poets, First Series,* edited by Giovanna Wedel De Stasio, Glauco Cambon, and Antonio Illiano (1992)

115 *Medieval Philosophers,* edited by Jeremiah Hackett (1992)

116 *British Romantic Novelists, 1789-1832,* edited by Bradford K. Mudge (1992)

117 *Twentieth-Century Caribbean and Black African Writers, First Series,* edited by Bernth Lindfors and Reinhard Sander (1992)

118 *Twentieth-Century German Dramatists, 1889-1918,* edited by Wolfgang D. Elfe and James Hardin (1992)

119 *Nineteenth-Century French Fiction Writers: Romanticism and Realism, 1800-1860,* edited by Catharine Savage Brosman (1992)

120 *American Poets Since World War II, Third Series,* edited by R. S. Gwynn (1992)

121 *Seventeenth-Century British Nondramatic Poets, First Series,* edited by M. Thomas Hester (1992)

122 *Chicano Writers, Second Series,* edited by Francisco A. Lomelí and Carl R. Shirley (1992)

123 *Nineteenth-Century French Fiction Writers: Naturalism and Beyond, 1860-1900,* edited by Catharine Savage Brosman (1992)

124 *Twentieth-Century German Dramatists, 1919-1992,* edited by Wolfgang D. Elfe and James Hardin (1992)

125 *Twentieth-Century Caribbean and Black African Writers, Second Series,* edited by Bernth Lindfors and Reinhard Sander (1993)

126 *Seventeenth-Century British Nondramatic Poets, Second Series,* edited by M. Thomas Hester (1993)

127 *American Newspaper Publishers, 1950-1990,* edited by Perry J. Ashley (1993)

128 *Twentieth-Century Italian Poets, Second Series,* edited by Giovanna Wedel De Stasio, Glauco Cambon, and Antonio Illiano (1993)

129 *Nineteenth-Century German Writers, 1841-1900,* edited by James Hardin and Siegfried Mews (1993)

130 *American Short-Story Writers Since World War II,* edited by Patrick Meanor (1993)

131 *Seventeenth-Century British Nondramatic Poets, Third Series,* edited by M. Thomas Hester (1993)

132 *Sixteenth-Century British Nondramatic Writers, First Series,* edited by David A. Richardson (1993)

133 *Nineteenth-Century German Writers to 1840,* edited by James Hardin and Siegfried Mews (1993)

134 *Twentieth-Century Spanish Poets, Second Series,* edited by Jerry Phillips Winfield (1994)

135 *British Short-Fiction Writers, 1880-1914: The Realist Tradition,* edited by William B. Thesing (1994)

136 *Sixteenth-Century British Nondramatic Writers, Second Series,* edited by David A. Richardson (1994)

137 *American Magazine Journalists, 1900-1960, Second Series,* edited by Sam G. Riley (1994)

138 *German Writers and Works of the High Middle Ages: 1170-1280,* edited by James Hardin and Will Hasty (1994)

139 *British Short-Fiction Writers, 1945-1980,* edited by Dean Baldwin (1994)

140 *American Book-Collectors and Bibliographers, First Series,* edited by Joseph Rosenblum (1994)

141 *British Children's Writers, 1880-1914,* edited by Laura M. Zaidman (1994)

142 *Eighteenth-Century British Literary Biographers,* edited by Steven Serafin (1994)

143 *American Novelists Since World War II, Third Series,* edited by James R. Giles and Wanda H. Giles (1994)

144 *Nineteenth-Century British Literary Biographers,* edited by Steven Serafin (1994)

145 *Modern Latin-American Fiction Writers, Second Series,* edited by William Luis and Ann González (1994)

146 *Old and Middle English Literature,* edited by Jeffrey Helterman and Jerome Mitchell (1994)

147 *South Slavic Writers Before World War II,* edited by Vasa D. Mihailovich (1994)

148 *German Writers and Works of the Early Middle Ages: 800-1170,* edited by Will Hasty and James Hardin (1994)

149 *Late Nineteenth- and Early Twentieth-Century British Literary Biographers,* edited by Steven Serafin (1995)

150 *Early Modern Russian Writers, Late Seventeenth and Eighteenth Centuries,* edited by Marcus C. Levitt (1995)

151 *British Prose Writers of the Early Seventeenth Century,* edited by Clayton D. Lein (1995)

152 *American Novelists Since World War II, Fourth Series,* edited by James R. Giles and Wanda H. Giles (1995)

153 *Late-Victorian and Edwardian British Novelists, First Series,* edited by George M. Johnson (1995)

154 *The British Literary Book Trade, 1700-1820,* edited by James K. Bracken and Joel Silver (1995)

155 *Twentieth-Century British Literary Biographers,* edited by Steven Serafin (1995)

156 *British Short-Fiction Writers, 1880-1914: The Romantic Tradition,* edited by William F. Naufftus (1995)

157 *Twentieth-Century Caribbean and Black African Writers, Third Series,* edited by Bernth Lindfors and Reinhard Sander (1995)

158 *British Reform Writers, 1789-1832,* edited by Gary Kelly and Edd Applegate (1995)

159 *British Short-Fiction Writers, 1800-1880,* edited by John R. Greenfield (1996)

160 *British Children's Writers, 1914-1960,* edited by Donald R. Hettinga and Gary D. Schmidt (1996)

161 *British Children's Writers Since 1960, First Series,* edited by Caroline Hunt (1996)

162 *British Short-Fiction Writers, 1915-1945,* edited by John H. Rogers (1996)

163 *British Children's Writers, 1800-1880,* edited by Meena Khorana (1996)

164 *German Baroque Writers, 1580-1660,* edited by James Hardin (1996)

165 *American Poets Since World War II, Fourth Series,* edited by Joseph Conte (1996)

166 *British Travel Writers, 1837-1875,* edited by Barbara Brothers and Julia Gergits (1996)

167 *Sixteenth-Century British Nondramatic Writers, Third Series,* edited by David A. Richardson (1996)

168 *German Baroque Writers, 1661-1730,* edited by James Hardin (1996)

169 *American Poets Since World War II, Fifth Series,* edited by Joseph Conte (1996)

170 *The British Literary Book Trade, 1475-1700,* edited by James K. Bracken and Joel Silver (1996)

171 *Twentieth-Century American Sportswriters,* edited by Richard Orodenker (1996)

172 *Sixteenth-Century British Nondramatic Writers, Fourth Series,* edited by David A. Richardson (1996)

173 *American Novelists Since World War II, Fifth Series,* edited by James R. Giles and Wanda H. Giles (1996)

174 *British Travel Writers, 1876-1909,* edited by Barbara Brothers and Julia Gergits (1997)

175 *Native American Writers of the United States,* edited by Kenneth M. Roemer (1997)

176 *Ancient Greek Authors,* edited by Ward W. Briggs (1997)

177 *Italian Novelists Since World War II, 1945-1965,* edited by Augustus Pallotta (1997)

178 *British Fantasy and Science-Fiction Writers Before World War I,* edited by Darren Harris-Fain (1997)

179 *German Writers of the Renaissance and Reformation, 1280-1580,* edited by James Hardin and Max Reinhart (1997)

180 *Japanese Fiction Writers, 1868-1945,* edited by Van C. Gessel (1997)

181 *South Slavic Writers Since World War II,* edited by Vasa D. Mihailovich (1997)

182 *Japanese Fiction Writers Since World War II,* edited by Van C. Gessel (1997)

183 *American Travel Writers, 1776-1864,* edited by James J. Schramer and Donald Ross (1997)

184 *Nineteenth-Century British Book-Collectors and Bibliographers,* edited by William Baker and Kenneth Womack (1997)

185 *American Literary Journalists, 1945-1995, First Series,* edited by Arthur J. Kaul (1998)

186 *Nineteenth-Century American Western Writers,* edited by Robert L. Gale (1998)

187 *American Book Collectors and Bibliographers, Second Series,* edited by Joseph Rosenblum (1998)

188 *American Book and Magazine Illustrators to 1920,* edited by Steven E. Smith, Catherine A. Hastedt, and Donald H. Dyal (1998)

189 *American Travel Writers, 1850-1915,* edited by Donald Ross and James J. Schramer (1998)

190 *British Reform Writers, 1832-1914,* edited by Gary Kelly and Edd Applegate (1998)

191 *British Novelists Between the Wars,* edited by George M. Johnson (1998)

192 *French Dramatists, 1789-1914,* edited by Barbara T. Cooper (1998)

193 *American Poets Since World War II, Sixth Series,* edited by Joseph Conte (1998)

194 *British Novelists Since 1960, Second Series,* edited by Merritt Moseley (1998)

195 *British Travel Writers, 1910-1939,* edited by Barbara Brothers and Julia Gergits (1998)

196 *Italian Novelists Since World War II, 1965-1995,* edited by Augustus Pallotta (1999)

197 *Late Victorian and Edwardian British Novelists, Second Series,* edited by George M. Johnson (1999)

198 *Russian Literature in the Age of Pushkin and Gogol: Prose,* edited by Christine A. Rydel (1999)

199 *Victorian Women Poets,* edited by William B. Thesing (1999)

200 *American Women Prose Writers to 1820,* edited by Carla J. Mulford, with Angela Vietto and Amy E. Winans (1999)

201 *Twentieth-Century British Book Collectors and Bibliographers,* edited by William Baker and Kenneth Womack (1999)

202 *Nineteenth-Century American Fiction Writers,* edited by Kent P. Ljungquist (1999)

203 *Medieval Japanese Writers,* edited by Steven D. Carter (1999)

204 *British Travel Writers, 1940–1997,* edited by Barbara Brothers and Julia M. Gergits (1999)

205 *Russian Literature in the Age of Pushkin and Gogol: Poetry and Drama,* edited by Christine A. Rydel (1999)

206 *Twentieth-Century American Western Writers, First Series,* edited by Richard H. Cracroft (1999)

207 *British Novelists Since 1960, Third Series,* edited by Merritt Moseley (1999)

208 *Literature of the French and Occitan Middle Ages: Eleventh to Fifteenth Centuries,* edited by Deborah Sinnreich-Levi and Ian S. Laurie (1999)

209 *Chicano Writers, Third Series,* edited by Francisco A. Lomelí and Carl R. Shirley (1999)

210 *Ernest Hemingway: A Documentary Volume,* edited by Robert W. Trogdon (1999)

211 *Ancient Roman Writers,* edited by Ward W. Briggs (1999)

212 *Twentieth-Century American Western Writers, Second Series,* edited by Richard H. Cracroft (1999)

213 *Pre-Nineteenth-Century British Book Collectors and Bibliographers,* edited by William Baker and Kenneth Womack (1999)

Documentary Series

1 *Sherwood Anderson, Willa Cather, John Dos Passos, Theodore Dreiser, F. Scott Fitzgerald, Ernest Hemingway, Sinclair Lewis,* edited by Margaret A. Van Antwerp (1982)

2 *James Gould Cozzens, James T. Farrell, William Faulkner, John O'Hara, John Steinbeck, Thomas Wolfe, Richard Wright,* edited by Margaret A. Van Antwerp (1982)

3 *Saul Bellow, Jack Kerouac, Norman Mailer, Vladimir Nabokov, John Updike, Kurt Vonnegut,* edited by Mary Bruccoli (1983)

4 *Tennessee Williams,* edited by Margaret A. Van Antwerp and Sally Johns (1984)

5 *American Transcendentalists,* edited by Joel Myerson (1988)

6 *Hardboiled Mystery Writers: Raymond Chandler, Dashiell Hammett, Ross Macdonald,* edited by Matthew J. Bruccoli and Richard Layman (1989)

7 *Modern American Poets: James Dickey, Robert Frost, Marianne Moore,* edited by Karen L. Rood (1989)

8 *The Black Aesthetic Movement,* edited by Jeffrey Louis Decker (1991)

9 *American Writers of the Vietnam War: W. D. Ehrhart, Larry Heinemann, Tim O'Brien,*

Walter McDonald, John M. Del Vecchio, edited by Ronald Baughman (1991)

10 *The Bloomsbury Group,* edited by Edward L. Bishop (1992)

11 *American Proletarian Culture: The Twenties and The Thirties,* edited by Jon Christian Suggs (1993)

12 *Southern Women Writers: Flannery O'Connor, Katherine Anne Porter, Eudora Welty,* edited by Mary Ann Wimsatt and Karen L. Rood (1994)

13 *The House of Scribner, 1846-1904,* edited by John Delaney (1996)

14 *Four Women Writers for Children, 1868-1918,* edited by Caroline C. Hunt (1996)

15 *American Expatriate Writers: Paris in the Twenties,* edited by Matthew J. Bruccoli and Robert W. Trogdon (1997)

16 *The House of Scribner, 1905-1930,* edited by John Delaney (1997)

17 *The House of Scribner, 1931-1984,* edited by John Delaney (1998)

18 *British Poets of The Great War: Sassoon, Graves, Owen,* edited by Patrick Quinn (1999)

19 *James Dickey,* edited by Judith S. Baughman (1999)

See also DLB 210

Yearbooks

1980 edited by Karen L. Rood, Jean W. Ross, and Richard Ziegfeld (1981)

1981 edited by Karen L. Rood, Jean W. Ross, and Richard Ziegfeld (1982)

1982 edited by Richard Ziegfeld; associate editors: Jean W. Ross and Lynne C. Zeigler (1983)

1983 edited by Mary Bruccoli and Jean W. Ross, associate editor Richard Ziegfeld (1984)

1984 edited by Jean W. Ross (1985)

1985 edited by Jean W. Ross (1986)

1986 edited by J. M. Brook (1987)

1987 edited by J. M. Brook (1988)

1988 edited by J. M. Brook (1989)

1989 edited by J. M. Brook (1990)

1990 edited by James W. Hipp (1991)

1991 edited by James W. Hipp (1992)

1992 edited by James W. Hipp (1993)

1993 edited by James W. Hipp, contributing editor George Garrett (1994)

1994 edited by James W. Hipp, contributing editor George Garrett (1995)

1995 edited by James W. Hipp, contributing editor George Garrett (1996)

1996 edited by Samuel W. Bruce and L. Kay Webster, contributing editor George Garrett (1997)

1997 edited by Matthew J. Bruccoli and George Garrett, with the assistance of L. Kay Webster (1998)

1998 edited by Matthew J. Bruccoli, contributing editor George Garrett, with the assistance of D. W. Thomas (1999)

Concise Series

Concise Dictionary of American Literary Biography, 7 volumes (1988-1999): *The New Consciousness, 1941-1968; Colonization to the American Renaissance, 1640-1865; Realism, Naturalism, and Local Color, 1865-1917; The Twenties, 1917-1929; The Age of Maturity, 1929-1941; Broadening Views, 1968-1988; Supplement: Modern Writers, 1900–1998.*

Concise Dictionary of British Literary Biography, 8 volumes (1991-1992): *Writers of the Middle Ages and Renaissance Before 1660; Writers of the Restoration and Eighteenth Century, 1660-1789; Writers of the Romantic Period, 1789-1832; Victorian Writers, 1832-1890; Late-Victorian and Edwardian Writers, 1890-1914; Modern Writers, 1914-1945; Writers After World War II, 1945-1960; Contemporary Writers, 1960 to Present.*

Concise Dictionary of World Literary Biography, 20 volumes projected (1999-): *Ancient Greek and Roman Writers.*

Dictionary of Literary Biography® • Volume Two Hundred Thirteen

Pre-Nineteenth-Century British Book Collectors and Bibliographers

Dictionary of Literary Biography® • Volume Two Hundred Thirteen

Pre-Nineteenth-Century British Book Collectors and Bibliographers

Edited by
William Baker
Northern Illinois University
and
Kenneth Womack
Penn State Altoona

A Bruccoli Clark Layman Book
The Gale Group
Detroit • San Francisco • London • Boston • Woodbridge, Conn.

Printed in the United States of America

The paper used in this publication meets the minimum requirements of American National Standard for Information Sciences–Permanence Paper for Printed Library Materials, ANSI Z39.48-1984. ∞™

Library of Congress Cataloging-in-Publication Data

Pre-Nineteenth-Century British book Collectors and Bibliographers / edited by William Baker and Kenneth Womack
p. cm.–(Dictionary of literary biography: v. 213)
"A Bruccoli Clark Layman book."
Includes bibliographical references and index.
ISBN 0-7876-3107-8 (alk. paper)
1. Bibliographers–Great Britian Bibliography Dictionaries. 2. Book Collectors–Great Britian Bibliography Dictionaries. 3. Bibliography–Great Britian–History Bibliography. 4. Book Collecting–Great Britian–History Bibliography. I. Baker, William, 1944– .II. Womack, Kenneth. III. Series.
Z1003.8 .P74 1999
010'.92'241–dc21 99–16782
[B] CIP

10 9 8 7 6 5 4 3 2 1

For our parents, who first shared the magical worlds
of books and reading with us

Contents

Plan of the Series

... Almost the most prodigious asset of a country, and perhaps its most precious possession, is its native literary product—when that product is fine and noble and enduring.

Mark Twain*

The advisory board, the editors, and the publisher of the *Dictionary of Literary Biography* are joined in endorsing Mark Twain's declaration. The literature of a nation provides an inexhaustible resource of permanent worth. We intend to make literature and its creators better understood and more accessible to students and the reading public, while satisfying the standards of teachers and scholars.

To meet these requirements, *literary biography* has been construed in terms of the author's achievement. The most important thing about a writer is his writing. Accordingly, the entries in *DLB* are career biographies, tracing the development of the author's canon and the evolution of his reputation.

The purpose of *DLB* is not only to provide reliable information in a convenient format but also to place the figures in the larger perspective of literary history and to offer appraisals of their accomplishments by qualified scholars.

The publication plan for *DLB* resulted from two years of preparation. The project was proposed to Bruccoli Clark by Frederick G. Ruffner, president of the Gale Research Company, in November 1975. After specimen entries were prepared and typeset, an advisory board was formed to refine the entry format and develop the series rationale. In meetings held during 1976, the publisher, series editors, and advisory board approved the scheme for a comprehensive biographical dictionary of persons who contributed to North American literature. Editorial work on the first volume began in January 1977, and it was published in 1978. In order to make *DLB* more than a reference tool and to compile volumes that individually have claim to status as literary history, it was decided to organize volumes by topic, period, or genre. Each of these freestanding volumes provides a biographical-bibliographical guide and overview for a particular area of literature. We are convinced that this organization—as opposed to a single alphabet method—constitutes a valuable innovation in the presentation of reference material. The volume plan necessarily requires many decisions for the placement and treatment of authors who might properly be included in two or three volumes. In some instances a major figure will be included in separate volumes, but with different entries emphasizing the aspect of his career appropriate to each volume. Ernest Hemingway, for example, is represented in *American Writers in Paris, 1920–1939* by an entry focusing on his expatriate apprenticeship; he is also in *American Novelists, 1910–1945* with an entry surveying his entire career, as well as in *American Short-Story Writers, 1910–1945, Second Series* with an entry concentrating on his short stories. Each volume includes a cumulative index of the subject authors and articles. Comprehensive indexes to the entire series are planned.

Since 1981 the series has been further augmented by the *DLB Yearbooks,* which update published entries and add new entries to keep the *DLB* current with contemporary activity. There have also been *DLB Documentary Series* volumes which provide biographical and critical source materials for figures whose work is judged to have particular interest for students. One of these companion volumes is devoted entirely to Tennessee Williams.

We define literature as the *intellectual commerce of a nation:* not merely as belles lettres but as that ample and complex process by which ideas are generated, shaped, and transmitted. *DLB* entries are not limited to "creative writers" but extend to other figures who in their time and in their way influenced the mind of a people. Thus the series encompasses historians, journalists, publishers, book collectors, and screenwriters. By this means readers of *DLB* may be aided to perceive literature not as cult scripture in the keeping of intellectual high priests but firmly positioned at the center of a nation's life.

DLB includes the major writers appropriate to each volume and those standing in the ranks behind

**From an unpublished section of Mark Twain's autobiography, copyright by the Mark Twain Company*

them. Scholarly and critical counsel has been sought in deciding which minor figures to include and how full their entries should be. Wherever possible, useful references are made to figures who do not warrant separate entries.

Each *DLB* volume has an expert volume editor responsible for planning the volume, selecting the figures for inclusion, and assigning the entries. Volume editors are also responsible for preparing, where appropriate, appendices surveying the major periodicals and literary and intellectual movements for their volumes, as well as lists of further readings. Work on the series as a whole is coordinated at the Bruccoli Clark Layman editorial center in Columbia, South Carolina, where the editorial staff is responsible for accuracy and utility of the published volumes.

One feature that distinguishes *DLB* is the illustration policy–its concern with the iconography of literature. Just as an author is influenced by his surroundings, so is the reader's understanding of the author enhanced by a knowledge of his environment. Therefore *DLB* volumes include not only drawings, paintings, and photographs of authors, often depicting them at various stages in their careers, but also illustrations of their families and places where they lived. Title pages are regularly reproduced in facsimile along with dust jackets for modern authors. The dust jackets are a special feature of *DLB* because they often document better than anything else the way in which an author's work was perceived in its own time. Specimens of the writers' manuscripts and letters are included when feasible.

Samuel Johnson rightly decreed that "The chief glory of every people arises from its authors." The purpose of the *Dictionary of Literary Biography* is to compile literary history in the surest way available to us–by accurate and comprehensive treatment of the lives and work of those who contributed to it.

The *DLB* Advisory Board

Introduction

Dictionary of Literary Biography 213: Pre-Nineteenth-Century British Book Collectors and Bibliographers, the third in the three-volume survey that includes *DLB 184: Nineteenth-Century British Book Collectors and Bibliographers* and *DLB 201: Twentieth-Century British Book Collectors and Bibliographers,* explores the lives and works of thirty-nine individual collectors from the fourteenth through the eighteenth centuries. The life of the earliest collector treated in the volume, Humphrey, Duke of Gloucester (1391–1447), coincides with the early Renaissance, before the widespread establishment of print culture. Gloucester was revered as a patron of letters who brought Italian scholars to England, and his career as a collector exemplifies the emergence and growth of humanism. The volume also includes five entries that focus on the historical evolution of a specific library or a collecting family: the entries on the brothers Sir James and Sir Andrew Balfour; the Bridgewater Library, which was formed and developed by the Egerton family; father and son Robert and Edward Harley, the first and second Earls of Oxford; the brothers Thomas and Richard Rawlinson; and the Sotheby family.

Knowing full well that a survey covering more than four hundred years can make no claim to comprehensiveness, the editors, while regretting the omission of notable figures, have attempted to select subjects that suggest the importance and range of book collecting and bibliography as cultural activities. Three major sources were drawn upon for the contents of *DLB 213:* Seymour De Ricci's *English Collectors of Books and Manuscripts* (1930), William Younger Fletcher's *English Book Collectors* (1902), and nineteenth-century bookseller Bernard Quaritch's *Contributions toward a Dictionary of English Book-Collectors and also of Some Foreign Collectors Whose Libraries Were Incorporated in English Collections or Whose Books Are Chiefly Met with in England* (1892). Attempting "to draw a sketch of the history of book-collecting in England from the year 1530," De Ricci stresses the importance of King Henry VIII's dissolution of the monasteries in the 1520s, for the remnants of the old monastic libraries "formed the nucleus of several important gatherings of manuscripts." Fletcher provides "short histories of the lives of the collectors, and some description of their libraries," and also endeavors "to show what manner of men the owners of these collections were." His work is particularly valuable for his inclusion of a chapter on royal collectors. Quaritch provides selective listings of the "chief books" in the libraries of the collectors he covers.

Bibliographers and book collectors demonstrate similar behavioral patterns that transcend cultures, historical periods, political events, religious transformations, technological revolutions, and social and economic conditions. As the entries in *DLB 213* reveal, the interests of book collectors and bibliographers are symbiotic. Three studies published in the 1990s–Nicholas A. Basbanes's *A Gentle Madness: Bibliophiles, Bibliomanes, and the Eternal Passion for Books* (1995), Susan M. Pearce's *On Collecting: An Investigation into Collecting in the European Tradition* (1995), and *Cultures of Collecting* (1994), edited by John Elsner and Roger Cardinal–have shed light on the nature and variety of collecting as a cultural activity.

Arguing that the passion for books reaches back nearly two thousand years to the ancient library of Alexandria, Basbanes in *A Gentle Madness* attempts "to show that however bizarre and zealous collectors have been through the ages, so much of what we know about history, literature, and culture would be lost forever if not for the passion and dedication of these driven souls." Indeed, Sir Robert Bruce Cotton, one of the most notable collectors included in *DLB 213,* was a nationalist who hoped his collection would contribute to the construction of an English identity. On the other hand, collectors such as George Thomason had more modest goals. Thomason was concerned with preserving the record of a specific, limited period in history through which he had lived–the era of the English Civil Wars.

Like Cotton, many of the other collectors in *DLB 213* were motivated by a desire to preserve a sense of national heritage. The interests of Robert Vaughan, the sole Welsh representative in the volume, were historical rather than literary. He transcribed manuscripts, focusing on their Welsh heritage, and collected heraldic materials. He created his collection for Wales and once remarked that a "love of my contrey and our ancestors drives me." Vaughan, though, did preserve the major work of Geoffrey Chaucer, regarded by many as the father of English literature. The *Hengwrt Chaucer,* once in Vaughan's collection, is regarded as the earliest text of *The Canterbury Tales.* Other collectors notable for their love of country include

David Steuart, who was preoccupied with Scottish history and mythology, and Sir Roger Twysden, who had an abiding desire to locate his Kentish roots and Anglo-Saxon antecedents. The two Irish representatives in *DLB 213*, Archbishop Narcissus Marsh and James Ussher, were both clergymen and thus were more interested in religious issues than cultural nationalism. Marsh, however, founded the first Irish public library.

In *On Collecting* Pearce examines "collecting as a set of things which people do, as an aspect of individual and social practice which is important in public and private life as a means of constructing the way in which we relate to the material world." Collecting provides its practitioners with an avenue for self-expression and offers "a chance to create changes in the way we view the visible and tangible world." For Pearce, the activity is "a gesture of self-assertion with a dynamic potential." The library became a powerful means of patronage for a great political family such as the Harleys, who along with collectors such as Humphrey, Cotton, the Egertons, Sir Thomas Bodley, Thomas Howard, and Charles Spencer, third Earl of Sunderland, gained social prestige through their collecting. Collections became part of a social cachet, and the maintenance of a collection demonstrated a collector's potential as a cultured individual. John Dee, for example, was able to gain access to Queen Elizabeth I through his reputation as a collector as well as a published author. In contrast, John Ker, third Duke of Roxburghe, who was born into great wealth and privilege, evidently turned to the world of his books for solace after being disappointed early in love.

In *Cultures of Collecting* Elsner and Cardinal are less interested in those "for whom building a collection of things is inseparable from building up wealth and prestige" than in "the less-publicized stories of those less-perfect collectors whose vocation sends them across the confines of the reasonable and the acceptable." Of the two Rawlinson brothers, Thomas, whom Thomas Dibdin called the "leviathan of book collectors," accumulated so many books and manuscripts that he was forced to sleep in a passageway and accumulated enormous debts. His brother Richard practiced the motto "I collect and I preserve." He did not specialize but collected universally to ensure that posterity would not be deprived of the primary materials needed to satisfy historical studies. He was a hoarder who attempted to save single pages from the "waste-paper mongers" of his time. Anthony à Wood, who grew up during the English Civil Wars and the Commonwealth era, was noted for his irascibility, for his deafness, for his violin playing, and for living in a garret by Merton Gate–a house filled with assorted records, books, and manuscripts.

Noting the strong interconnection between collecting and classification, Elsner and Cardinal observe, "If classification is the mirror of collective humanity's thoughts and perception, then collecting is its material embodiment." With the development of printing in the fifteenth and sixteenth centuries, literature left the confines of the cloisters and moved into general society. The proliferation of print created the awareness of the need to record what was being produced and of arranging it for reference. In 1613, Elizabethan soldier and author Barnaby Rich observed that "one of the diseases of this age is the multiplicity of books; they . . . so overcharge the world that it is not able to digest the abundance of idle matter that is . . . brought forth." In *Systematic Bibliography in England, 1850–1895* (1967) Boyd Rayward cites the example of Martin Despois, a seventeenth-century French scholar who wrote a Latin complaint called "Too Many Books." As Rayward observes, the poetic lament expresses the "futility of bibliographical control without some matching effort to insure that what is recorded is preserved":

> Their labours have been in vain. They are forgot.
> Their books have perished; nought remains
> Except their titles in a catalogue.

A consequence of the invention of printing and the enormous growth in available materials was a growing interest in bibliography itself as a subject for scholarly endeavor. As Theodore Besterman points out in *The Beginnings of Systematic Bibliography* (1934), Conrad Gesner, a bibliographer whose principal works appeared between 1545 and 1555, "was not only the first universal bibliographer: he was also the last whose efforts of achieving universality had a chance of being reasonably successful." By the time John Harley published his eight-volume *Catalogus Universalis* (1699), the amount of published material was so great that his work was doomed to failure. Limited in their effectiveness as individuals, scholars more and more began to seek out one another and to cooperate in bibliographic projects. The Royal Society, the oldest learned society in Britain, was founded at the Restoration of Charles II in the 1660s, and the Society of Antiquaries was formed in 1707.

As print culture developed, scholars and collectors became aware of the importance not only of the earliest published books as examples of fine printing but also of the value for study of subsequent editions of a given work. In his *Essays on the Thirty-Nine Articles of Religion* (1715) Thomas Bennet used "typographical evidence (such as the spacing and damage of types)" to order sixteenth-century editions and, specifically, the 1571 edition of the "Thirty-Nine Articles of Religion." In the editing of William Shakespeare's work during the eighteenth century, attention was devoted to the details of specific printed editions. The scholar Edward Capell, whom David Garrick employed to catalogue his collection of "old English plays," studied Shakespearean texts closely, transcribing printed title pages and "indicating line endings and imitating type styles." These examples illustrate an interest in the details of artifacts, not simply mere antiquarianism. As G. Thomas Tanselle observes in a 1992 *Studies in Bibliography* essay, "A Description of Descriptive Bibliography," "The evolution of bibliophily from the collecting of *works* (that is, any copies of the texts of selected works) to the collecting of *texts* (that is, specific copies) is at once the triumph of antiquarianism and the prerequisite for the serious study of the transmission of verbal works."

According to John Carter in *Taste and Technique in Books* (1948), "by the end of the seventeenth century book collecting was in full swing" throughout Europe. Collectors were caring for and preserving materials that otherwise would have perished from neglect. Such figures as Thomason, the Harleys, Cotton, and Matthew Parker were "preservers of books and contributors to the progress of scholarship." As Carter observes, one of the collector's most important functions was "to anticipate the scholar and the historian, to find some interest where none was recognized before, to rescue books from obscurity, to pioneer a subject or an author by seeking out and assembling the raw material for study, in whatever its printed form."

As David Pearson points out in *Provenance Research in Book History* (1994), the first recorded English book auction was held in London in 1676, with the sale by William Cooper of the library of Lazarus Seaman. The English practice of sale by auction was established soon thereafter as the primary means for disposing of a late collector's private collection. Book auctions seemed to have been an import from Holland, where they had been taking place since the 1590s. In 1744 Samuel Baker established what become known as Sotheby's, the distinguished London auction house. Its rival, Christie's, was established in London in 1766 and probably began selling books in 1770. Christie's auctioned the library of Samuel Johnson in 1785. The Harleian tracts and pamphlets were sold by Thomas Osborne, a London book-selling firm, in five catalogues from 1747 to 1748.

As John Milton wrote in *Areopagitica* (1644), "And yet, on the other hand, unless wariness be used, as good almost kill a man as kill a good book; who kills a man kills a reasonable creature, God's image; but he who destroys a good book, kills reason itself, kills the image of God, as it were, in the eye. Many a man lives a burden to the earth; but a good book is the precious life-blood of a master-spirit, embalmed and treasured up on purpose to a life beyond life." In their own ways, the book collectors and bibliographers included in the three-volume *Dictionary of Literary Biography* survey illustrate the meaning of Milton's powerful dictum through their understanding of and reverence for books and manuscripts as the true "life-blood" and "master-spirit" of culture.

–Kenneth Womack

Acknowledgments

This book was produced by Bruccoli Clark Layman, Inc. Karen L. Rood is senior editor for the *Dictionary of Literary Biography* series. George P. Anderson was the in-house editor.

Production manager is Philip B. Dematteis.

Administrative support was provided by Ann M. Cheschi, Tenesha S. Lee, and Joann Whittaker.

Accounting was done by Angi Pleasant.

Copyediting supervisor is Phyllis A. Avant. Senior copyeditor is Thom Harman. The copyediting staff includes Ronald D. Aiken II, Brenda Carol Blanton, Worthy B. Evans, Melissa D. Hinton, William Tobias Mathes, Jennifer Reid, and Michelle L. Whitney.

Editorial assistant is Margo Dowling.

Editorial trainee is Carol A. Fairman.

Indexing specialist is Alex Snead.

Layout and graphics supervisor is Janet E. Hill. Graphics staff includes Zoe R. Cook.

Office manager is Kathy Lawler Merlette.

Photography editors are Charles Mims, Scott Nemzek, Alison Smith, and Paul Talbot. Digital photographic copy work was performed by Joseph M. Bruccoli.

SGML supervisor is Cory McNair. The SGML staff includes Tim Bedford, Linda Drake, Frank Graham, and Alex Snead.

Systems manager is Marie L. Parker.

Database manager is Javed Nurani. Kimberly Kelly performed data entry.

Typesetting supervisor is Kathleen M. Flanagan. The typesetting staff includes Karla Corley Brown, Mark J. McEwan, Patricia Flanagan Salisbury, and Kathy F. Wooldridge. Freelance typesetter is Delores Plastow.

Walter W. Ross and Steven Gross did library research. They were assisted by the following librarians at the Thomas Cooper Library of the University of South Carolina: Linda Holderfield and the interlibrary-loan staff; reference-department head Virginia Weathers; reference librarians Marilee Birchfield, Stefanie Buck, Stefanie DuBose, Rebecca Feind, Karen Joseph, Donna Lehman, Charlene Loope, Anthony McKissick, Jean Rhyne, and Kwamine Simpson; circulation-department head Caroline Taylor; and acquisitions-searching supervisor David Haggard.

Dictionary of Literary Biography® • Volume Two Hundred Thirteen

Pre-Nineteenth-Century British Book Collectors and Bibliographers

Dictionary of Literary Biography

Thomas Baker

(14 September 1656 – 2 July 1740)

Frans Korsten
University of Nijmegen

Thomas Baker (The Durham Dean and Chapter Library)

CATALOGUES: *A Catalogue Of a Curious and Valuable Collection of Books Of Divinity, History, Philosophy, Physick, And Classick Authors; Chiefly Collected by the Reverend and Learned T. Baker, B.D. late of St. John's College, Cambridge. Which Will be Sold by Auction, at the Great Room at the Wrestlers Inn, near Christ's College; beginning on Monday November the 9th, 1741, at One o'Clock in the Afternoon. Catalogues are delivered by W. Thurlbourn, Bookseller; at all the Coffee-Houses, and at the Place of Sale* (Cambridge, 1741);

Frans Korsten, *A Catalogue of the Library of Thomas Baker* (Cambridge: Cambridge University Press, 1990).

BOOKS: *Moestissimae ac Laetissimae Academiae Cantabrigiensis Affectus Decedente Carolo II Succedente Jacobo II Regibus Augustissimis, Serenissimis Clementissimisque,* by Baker, Matthew Prior, Charles Montagu, and others (Cantabrigiae: Ex Officina Joan. Hayes, Celeberrimae Academiae Typographi, 1684 or 1685);

Reflections upon Learning; Wherein is shewn the Insufficiency Thereof, in its several Particulars; In order to evince the Usefulness and Necessity of Revelation. By a Gentleman, anonymous (London: Printed for A. Bosvile, 1699);

History of the College of St. John the Evangelist, Cambridge, 2 volumes, edited by John E. B. Mayor (Cambridge: Cambridge University Press, 1869).

OTHER: John Fisher, *The Funeral Sermon of Margaret, Countess of Richmond and Derby, Mother to King Henry VII and Foundress of Christ's and St. John's College in Cambridge, With a Preface, containing some further account of her charities and foundations. Together with a Catalogue of her Professors both at Cambridge and Oxford, and of her Preachers at Cam-*

bridge, edited, with a preface, by Baker (London: A. Bosvile, 1708).

Although Thomas Baker published little, he was an important figure in the world of historical and antiquarian learning in the first forty years of the eighteenth century. Operating behind the scenes, he played a central role in the scholarly milieu of his day. A bibliophile, book collector, bibliographer, and historical and antiquarian scholar, he was valued by many friends and acquaintances, from the Tory bishop and wit Francis Atterbury and the leading Whig bishop Gilbert Burnet to Archbishop William Wake and the antiquary Humfrey Wanley. The collection of printed books, manuscripts, and transcripts that he amassed during the course of about half a century was large and remarkable by the standards of his time. Many of the printed books and most of the manuscripts and transcripts have been preserved. The material he collected bears witness to the scholarship and piety–the two are clearly connected–of this quiet and unassuming man.

Baker, the second son of Margaret Forster and George Baker, was born on 14 September 1656 at Crook Hall, Lanchester, in the northern county of Durham. His grandfather, Sir George Baker, was recorder of Newcastle and a staunch supporter of Charles I in the turbulent days of the Scottish invasion in 1639. There were four boys and two girls in the Baker family: George, Thomas, Ralph, Francis, Margaret, and Elisabeth; the family owned the Elemore estates and had the profits of some leases of coal mines in northeastern England.

Baker went to the Free School in Durham, where he came under the supervision of the Reverend Thomas Battersby. He was admitted on 13 June 1674 to the University of Cambridge, where he was a pensioner of St. John's College. He became a Hugh Ashton scholar on 6 November 1676. (Ashton, one of the early benefactors of the college, founded four scholarships and four fellowships.) He received his B.A. and M.A. degrees in 1678 and 1681, respectively, and was elected an Ashton Fellow on 31 March 1680. Having been ordained deacon in December 1685, he was then ordained priest on 9 December 1686 by Thomas Barlow, bishop of Lincoln.

A splendid career then appeared to be lying before him. In 1685, on the occasion of Charles II's death and the succession of James II, Baker was one of the select group of Cambridge scholars that included Matthew Prior and Charles Montagu (later, the earl of Halifax) who were asked to contribute a poem for a memorial volume, *Moestissimae ac Laetissimae Academiae Cantabrigiensis Affectus* (1684–1685). Baker declined the offer of Thomas Watson, a graduate of St. John's College who had been appointed bishop of St. David's, to become his domestic chaplain in 1687 but accepted the same position from Bishop Crew of Durham shortly after. Baker was also appointed to the rectory of Long Newton in June 1687, and more prestigious ecclesiastical posts, the rectory of Sedgefield and a prebend stall at Durham Cathedral, were soon associated with him.

In April 1688 Baker refused to read King James's Second Declaration of Indulgence–an edict designed to promote Roman Catholicism–in the Bishop's Chapel at Auckland, much to Bishop Crew's chagrin. When James II was deposed in the Revolution of 1688, however, Baker did not take the oaths to the new king, William III, because he was loyal to the Stuart line. On 1 August 1690 he officially became a nonjuror for his refusal to take such an oath and was forced to surrender the rectory of Long Newton. He then returned to his fellowship at St. John's College in Cambridge, where he lived with few interruptions for the next half a century till his death in 1740. In 1699 his elder brother, George, died, and the management of the estate and the family business devolved upon Baker and his fellow executors, his younger brother Francis and his friend Montagu. In this capacity he made regular visits to northeastern England, which he always tried to combine with research in the Durham libraries and archives. Before 1717 he also took occasional trips to London, for instance to the State Paper Office in the summer of 1709, where he had gone to transcribe original documents.

On 21 January 1717 Baker was expelled from the fellowship at St. John's because he refused to take the oath of Abjuration, requiring him to abjure loyalty to the House of Stuart. The expulsion was a shattering blow for the sixty-year-old Baker, whose loyalty and devotion to the college had been the mainspring of his actions. From that moment onward Baker suffered from a deep sense of disgrace and bitterness. Although in practical terms the change for Baker after January 1717 was not great, as he was allowed to live on in the college as a commoner-master, he felt stigmatized and saw his expulsion in dramatic terms. He went through all his printed books and manuscripts and marked them bitterly and defiantly with the phrase "Thomas Baker Collegii Johannis Socius Ejectus."

Always an admirer of the founders and early benefactors of the college, Baker idealized the glorious past of the institution and seems to have strongly identified with its heroes in his *History of the College of St. John the Evangelist, Cambridge* (1869). He started work on it in the early years of the eighteenth century but gave up the project before his expulsion because he met with obstruction from the archivist of the State Paper Office in London. Baker rated John Fisher, a man who was

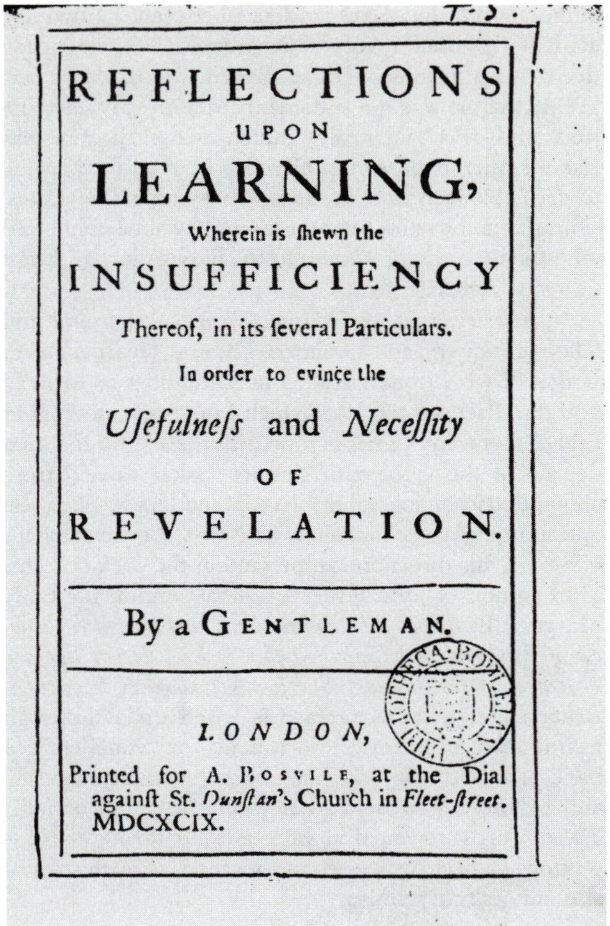

REFLECTIONS
UPON
LEARNING,
Wherein is ſhewn the
INSUFFICIENCY
Thereof, in its ſeveral Particulars.
In order to evince the
Uſefulneſs and *Neceſſity*
OF
REVELATION.

By a GENTLEMAN.

LONDON,
Printed for A. Bosvile, at the Dial againſt St. *Dunſtan's* Church in *Fleet-ſtreet.* MDCXCIX.

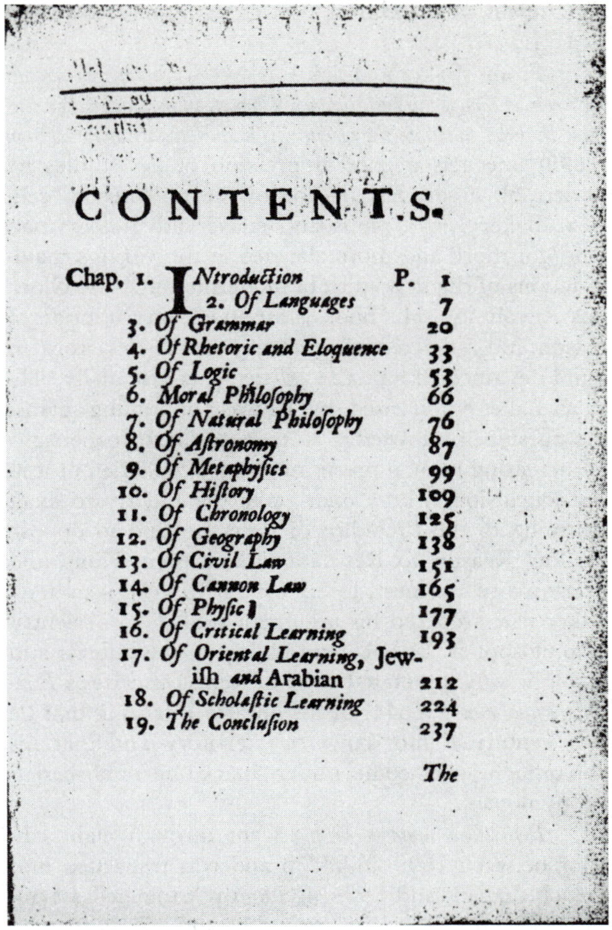

CONTENTS.

The

Title and contents pages for Baker's 1699 book, in which he argues that it is a mistake to "exalt Learning to the Prejudice of Religion"

instrumental in the founding of the college, more highly than Sir Thomas More in one respect. Commenting on the two men who refused to repudiate papal authority at the behest of King Henry VIII, he writes of Fisher in a letter of 29 January 1727 to John Lewis: "he did not article with the King, as S^r^. Tho: More did, to no great purpose"; unlike More, according to Baker, Fisher was not afraid of shame. Baker's descriptions of some of the later masters of the college show the same kind of admiration for consistency and integrity of behavior.

In an undated letter to White Kennett, the Whig bishop and antiquary, written some time after his expulsion, Baker ruefully wrote: "it is some affliction to me y^t^ it has put me out of any Capacity of doing any service to ye public." In the years subsequent to 1717 Baker only left the college for research visits to other Cambridge libraries and for an occasional visit to the coffeehouse. He lived a sober and ascetic life, arising every day at four. In the college and the university he had a small circle of friends, whom he saw regularly: Francis Dickins, William Baker, Conyers Middleton, Philip Williams, and John Tunstall. He also kept in contact with many other scholars through a regular correspondence, and in this way he retained an important position in the world of historical and antiquarian learning. Edward Harley, second Earl of Oxford, regularly tried to get Baker to come to Wimpole—not far from Cambridge—but Baker always politely declined the invitation on the grounds that he was not fit for such grand company. Baker died a few days after a grandnephew of his, George Baker of Durham, had come up from Eton to St. John's College at the end of June 1740. There were obituaries in *The London Evening-Post* and *The Daily Post,* and in the latter paper also appeared a poem in commemoration of "the Ornament of Cambridge," as Richard

Rawlinson called him in a letter to Thomas Rawlins of 15 July 1740.

From Baker's book *Reflections upon Learning; Wherein is shewn the Insufficiency Thereof, in its several Particulars; In order to evince the Usefulness and Necessity of Revelation* (1699) one gets a good impression of the studies he undertook in the last decade of the seventeenth century. Baker was a pious and conservative clergyman who got more and more alarmed at the various manifestations of the new spirit of modernity after the Glorious Revolution. His book is an attack on the pride of reason and a defense of revelation as the only rock to build on, since all human knowledge is essentially deficient. Baker emphasized that he was not arguing against the pursuit of knowledge as such but against the signs of increasing human presumptuousness. As he put it in his conclusion, where men "take the Liberty to exalt Learning to the Prejudice of Religion, and to oppose shallow Reason to Revelation, it is then Time, and every man's Business, to endeavour to keep it under." Baker had prepared his argument well. Not a scientist or philosopher, he had read widely in these fields and had a heavily annotated copy of René Descartes's *Principia Philosophiae* (1644) in his library. Realizing that he was venturing into dangerous territory and that his book might well come under attack, he published it anonymously.

Reflections upon Learning went through eight editions between 1699 and 1758 and was translated into French, Italian, and Latin. Evidently it touched a sympathetic chord with the orthodox and all those who were concerned about the rise of deism and latitudinarianism. As Baker had anticipated, however, there were adverse reactions as well. In *Reflections upon Learning* the French philosopher and critic Jean Le Clerc was one of Baker's bêtes noires; in fact Le Clerc was for Baker the embodiment of the dangerous tendencies of the age. Le Clerc was stung by Baker's criticism, and his answer, published in the index to the fourth edition of his *Ars Critica* (1712), was sharp and dismissive. He referred to the "intolerable insolence" of the anonymous author and to his strictures as "little better than indigested effusions, the observations of a man who writes without giving himself the trouble of thinking."

The reaction of John Woodward, a professor at Gresham College, was even more disconcerting for Baker. Angered by a mildly critical passage on his *Essay toward a Natural History of the Earth* (1695), Woodward forced Baker to leave out the passage in his second edition. Woodward's reaction was disproportionate, and it was the vehemence of his touchy and overbearing opponent that greatly disturbed the meek Baker. Moreover, Woodward accused Baker of cowardice and childishness in persisting in his denials that he was the author. From the correspondence between the two it is evident that Baker very much regretted having been drawn into a confrontation. Baker was made to feel keenly that he was not sufficiently at home in these subjects and was not really suited for such quarrels. Baker's often expressed preference later on for keeping to verifiable facts and his shying away from the expression of opinions and hypotheses may well be connected with the unsettling response to the publication of *Reflections upon Learning*.

In a letter of 22 October 1728 to his friend and fellow antiquary and nonjuror Thomas Hearne, Baker wrote: "I wish I had engaged in Antiquities as early as you did. I set out too late (which I now repent of) after I had spent my time in other Studies." In the first decade of the eighteenth century Baker turned from contentious religious and scientific matters to historical and antiquarian scholarship. The first specimen of his efforts in this direction can be seen in the preface to his 1708 edition of John Fisher's funeral sermon for Lady Margaret Beaufort, *The Funeral Sermon of Margaret Countess of Richmond and Derby, Mother to King Henry VII and Foundress of Christ's and St. John's College in Cambridge*. Baker states that his preface is based on a thorough examination of historical documents, or "vouchers": "I have produc'd my Vouchers for every thing material, and by these Vouchers I am willing to stand or fall." These words, repeated in various ways throughout his writings, reflect his credo and method as an historical and antiquarian scholar.

In the preface Baker announces his plan to write the history of St. John's College, and he requests others to take their college records seriously as an act of piety and gratitude because he believed that such documents of the "glorious past" were too often neglected by scholars. Even after 1717 loyalty and devotion to St. John's remained an important factor in his activities as a scholar and a book collector. Early in 1708 he told John Strype, the ecclesiastical historian and biographer, that he had collected seven or eight volumes of material chiefly relating to the University of Cambridge. For many years Baker thought of writing an "Athenae Cantabrigienses" after the model of Anthony à Wood's *Athenae Oxonienses* (1691–1692), but although he gathered a phenomenal amount of material, he gave up the idea in the early 1730s. Much of Baker's work as a book collector and a bibliographer was determined by this ambition.

Baker also had a keen interest, characteristic of most nonjurors, in the beginnings and the crucial moments and periods of the Anglican Church. After all, it always remained his church. He was intrigued by the attempts of the Anglican Church to define its position doctrinally, liturgically, and otherwise vis-à-vis the

Church of Rome. He was interested too by its dealings with the Puritans when they attacked Anglican practice. Baker's vital concern with the history of the church also played a large part in his bibliographical work and in the building up of his library.

In the world of traditional scholarship Baker's position was such that he could play a major role. Although a nonjuror, he was a peacemaker and served as a bridge between scholars from ideologically opposite camps. Baker was one of the few nonjurors who had a good word to say about Gilbert Burnet, the bishop of Salisbury, and the respect was clearly mutual. Burnet had been instrumental in putting William and Mary on the throne, and after the Glorious Revolution he was one of the most outspoken supporters of the new settlement. Among Baker's close friends were heterodox clergymen such as Conyers Middleton and William Whiston, and he amicably corresponded with Whigs and Tories alike. In a letter to John Ward of 18 May 1735 Baker described the difference between Hearne and himself as follows: "Mr Hearne . . . is so high in principle that he could do nothing for one that differs from him." In the scholarly world of his day Baker acted with delicacy and tact, smoothing out frictions and bringing about cooperation between scholars where that had seemed inconceivable before. In a letter of 12 January 1723 Kennett wrote to Baker: "I meet y^{o} almost in every treatise of o^{r} history & Antiquities as a gr^{t} encourager & helper of every writer." There was also the more practical point that Baker, in order to achieve his great ambition of composing an Athenae Cantabrigienses, needed all the help he could get, whether from Whigs, Puritans, or from his own people, the nonjurors.

Baker had easy access to all the Cambridge libraries and archives, and he had a thorough knowledge of their contents. He was on good terms with most librarians and was often allowed to take books and manuscripts to his rooms for a longer period than usually permitted. Baker had a special relationship with Edward Harley, and he could borrow anything he liked from the vast Harleian collections. After the enormous library of printed books and manuscripts of John Moore, bishop of Ely, had come to Cambridge in 1715, Baker was often to be found there, and he frequently answered queries from other scholars about the collection. Because he was so well informed about all matters relating to books and so conveniently placed, Baker was consulted by a great many scholars from all over the country.

Baker had a library of at least five thousand printed books, tracts, and pamphlets and more than one hundred manuscripts, a large collection for an amateur of modest means in the first half of the eighteenth century. Yet, he never at one time in his life owned all this material together: from early on he had freely presented others with books and manuscripts, and he went on buying books until the end of his life. For Baker there was no real distinction between printed works and manuscripts, and the crucial questions were always whether the material was authentic and historically relevant.

The largest single portion of Baker's library–1,500 books–is housed at St. John's College. During his life Baker gave hundreds of books to the college, and in his will, dated 15 October 1739, he stipulated that "To St. John's College Library I leave all such Books Printed or MSS as I have & are wanting there." Moreover, in the years since his death a few hundred Baker books have been sold or donated to St. John's College. Apart from the books in the library of his college, nearly 400 books from Baker's collection have been traced, with the Bodleian Library, the British Library, and the libraries at Cambridge University and Durham University as the chief repositories.

In November 1741 a considerable part of Baker's library was sold by auction at Cambridge by William Thurlbourn. There are 1,425 items in this sale catalogue, but the difficulty is that the Cambridge bookseller tried to dispose of books from other collections under Baker's flag. The title page of the sale catalogue reads: "Chiefly Collected by the Reverend and Learned T. Baker." It remains a matter of speculation how many of the 1,425 items had actually belonged to Baker, but counting the explicit references to his ownership in the catalogue and the books that are referred to in his correspondence or his bibliographical works and taking into account his tastes and interests, the number of Baker items in this catalogue can safely be put at 1,000 at the least. The exact fate of Baker's large collection of tracts and pamphlets upon his death is not known, but at the 1829 London sale of the extensive library of Samuel Heywood, Baker's collection of tracts and pamphlets, which had apparently survived en bloc in the intervening period, was bought by the London bookseller Thomas Thorpe. Between 1829 and 1842 Thorpe offered more than 1,500 Baker items in his catalogues. Finally, there is the large but diffuse category of Baker's references in his correspondence and in the margins of his bibliographical works to books he owned that have not been traced and of the many unspecified items in the Cambridge sale catalogue ("A bundle of Octavo Pamphlets") and the Thorpe catalogues ("Forms of Prayer–A Collection of–from the year 1689 to 1723").

Because of the incomplete record of the collection, it is impossible to be precise about Baker's library

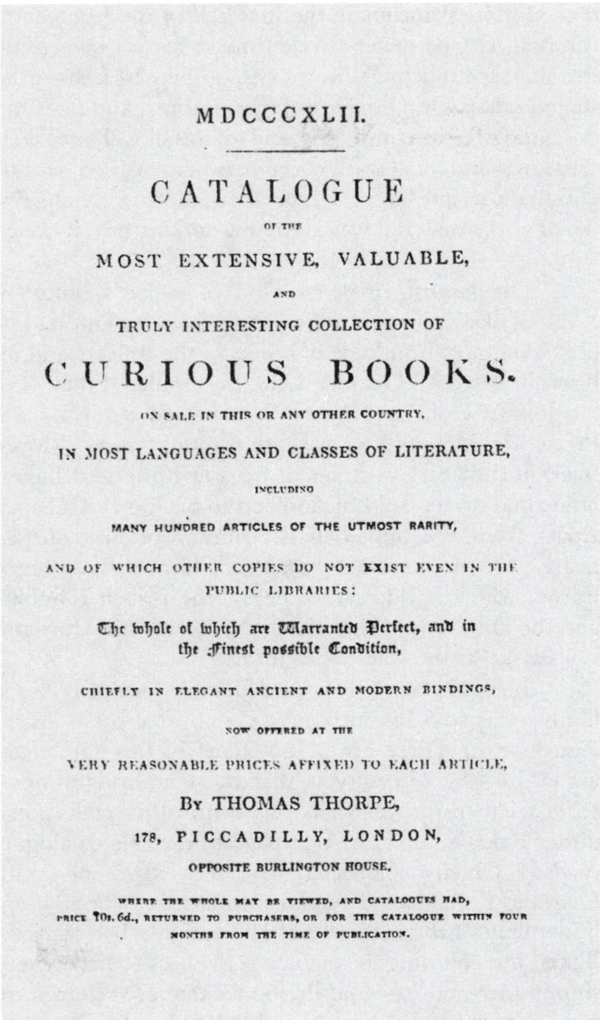
MDCCCXLII.

CATALOGUE

OF THE

MOST EXTENSIVE, VALUABLE,

AND

TRULY INTERESTING COLLECTION OF

CURIOUS BOOKS.

ON SALE IN THIS OR ANY OTHER COUNTRY,

IN MOST LANGUAGES AND CLASSES OF LITERATURE,

INCLUDING

MANY HUNDRED ARTICLES OF THE UTMOST RARITY,

AND OF WHICH OTHER COPIES DO NOT EXIST EVEN IN THE PUBLIC LIBRARIES:

The whole of which are Warranted Perfect, and in the Finest possible Condition,

CHIEFLY IN ELEGANT ANCIENT AND MODERN BINDINGS,

NOW OFFERED AT THE

VERY REASONABLE PRICES AFFIXED TO EACH ARTICLE,

BY THOMAS THORPE,

178, PICCADILLY, LONDON,

OPPOSITE BURLINGTON HOUSE.

WHERE THE WHOLE MAY BE VIEWED, AND CATALOGUES HAD, PRICE 10s. 6d., RETURNED TO PURCHASERS, OR FOR THE CATALOGUE WITHIN FOUR MONTHS FROM THE TIME OF PUBLICATION.

Title page for a sale catalogue of the London bookseller Thomas Thorpe, who acquired and sold some 1,500 of Baker's tracts and pamphlets between 1829 and 1842

of printed books. In *A Catalogue of the Library of Thomas Baker* (1990) Frans Korsten lists 4,290 items, some hundreds of which possibly never belonged to Baker. All the 1,425 items of the 1741 Cambridge sale catalogue are included as in many cases there was no way of distinguishing between Baker and non-Baker books. On the other hand there are doubtless hundreds, if not thousands, of items Baker owned but that cannot be certainly identified.

Baker bequeathed seventy-five manuscripts to St. John's College, and most of the remaining manuscripts ended up in the Harleian Collection in the British Library. Half of the Baker manuscripts at St. John's College were bought by him from Thomas Wagstaffe, a fellow nonjuror and St. John's man who died in 1712 and who wished his collection to be lodged in a public library. At least ten manuscripts were presented to him by friends. Many of the manuscripts have Cambridge associations through authorship (Robert Fairfax, John Cowell, or Henry Smith), subject matter (legal questions concerning the County of Cambridgeshire), or provenance (formerly owned by Miles Blomefield and William Cecil, Lord Burghley, one of Baker's heroes). Baker greatly valued the Puckering Collection–manuscripts and papers amassed by Sir John Puckering, lord keeper of the great seal under Queen Elizabeth–especially its extensive material on sixteenth-century Puritans such as John Udall, which he sold, along with several other manuscripts, to Robert Harley in 1714. On MS L12 at St. John's College, "The Order of the King's Coronation as it was observed Feb. 2 1625," a present from William Lloyd, the nonjuring bishop of Norwich, Baker noted: "This was Bp: Laud's own Book, the same that he made use off, at the Coronation of King Charles the first, when he acted as a subdean or Deputy to the Dean of Westminster. It is a Rarity & deserves our Care."

In addition to the printed books and manuscripts Baker diligently transcribed in his own hand more than forty folio volumes of material, from both printed and manuscript sources, which were to be the building stones for the long-cherished project of the Athenae Cantabrigienses. The volumes of transcripts are to be found partly in the Harleian Collection and partly in Cambridge University Library. All these volumes of transcripts would have stayed in Cambridge if at the end of 1716, when Baker's expulsion from his fellowship was imminent, Humfrey Wanley, Harley's librarian, had not slyly exploited the situation of Baker's disillusionment with the college.

Baker transcribed material from all the Cambridge collections, from the episcopal registers at Ely, and from the many collections that were lent to him by friends and colleagues such as Hearne, Strype, Kennett, John Anstis, Francis Peck, and Lloyd. In this way he gathered a complete file of letters to and from the University of Cambridge, and he acquired copies of all the considerable wills proved at Cambridge since the Reformation. On the basis of all this material he drew up lists and registers, such as a catalogue of all those who had ever donated books to Cambridge University Library. About one item in a volume of transcripts sold to Harley, "A Return from the Bp: of Landaff to the Archbp of Cant," Baker commented that "This is of use, to give a view of the State of the Church & Clergy at the beginning of the Reformation under Queen Eliz. For tho' this were a Welsh Diocess, yet some of the English were not in much better Condition."

All his life Baker had an incurable passion for books, yet there were clear limits to what he could afford. In an undated letter to Hearne, Baker sighed: "I am forc't (as you are) to be content with Imperfect Copies of old books." While his lament is perhaps overstated, about one-fourth of the traced pre-1550 books in *A Catalogue of the Library of Thomas Baker* are flawed. Just after the sale of one of the portions of Thomas Rawlinson's library, Baker, who had put in an order for John Purvey's *A compendious olde treatyse, shewynge howe that we ought to have ye scripture in Englysshe* (1530), wrote to Richard Rawlinson: "Had I been a moneyed man, I should have offer'd more than a Guinea." Baker told Hearne in a letter of 26 May 1724 that "Count Brienne's Collection makes indeed a noble Catalogue, but the prices are only for Men of Quality."

Baker of course bought extensively at sales. He was knowing and alert about prices and the differences between the various editions of a book. Several friends and acquaintances looked out for books and executed commissions for him: John Bagford, George Paul, Hilkiah Bedford, and George Ballard. Baker ordered books on a large scale from the Rawlinson collection; for the sale of March 1734 he marked as many as eighty-two items. In London he also had good relations with the booksellers Alexander Bosvile and John Wyatt, and their shops served as go-between addresses for Baker and other scholars.

Many books were presented to Baker by authors in grateful acknowledgment of the assistance he had given them. Archbishop William Wake gave Baker the nonjuror a copy of his own *The State of the Church and Clergy of England in their Councils* (1703), which he annotated and supplemented himself, as a small return for all the services Baker had rendered him and the French priest Pierre François Le Courayer. Baker also acquired many works through subscription, the practice of underwriting the work of others by purchasing copies before publication. All of Hearne's and Strype's books found their way to Baker's library through subscription, another indication of the close, supportive relationship he enjoyed with his colleagues.

The main emphases in Baker's library are religion, ecclesiastical and political history, Cambridge and St. John's College, and the history of printing and bibliography. Baker constantly searched for authentic historical documents, which explains why his library contains so many ephemeral pieces such as proclamations, proposals, forms of prayer, and newspaper cuttings. The man who was accused by John Woodward of adopting a completely skeptical position in *Reflections upon Learning* fervently adhered to authentic records as the only way to arrive at the truth about the past, albeit the truth from a High Anglican Tory point of view.

Baker had the historical and antiquarian scholar's disdain for less "serious" studies. There is more than a touch of irony in a 5 November 1717 letter to Hearne in which he remarks that he has heard that Matthew Prior has already received more than 2,000 guineas in subscriptions for the folio edition of his poems and adds, "I have not done my self that honor; Guil. Neubrigensis [the Latin name of William of Newburgh, the medieval English historian] will be of more use to me." Yet, in his turn Baker was well aware of how scholars of his stamp were viewed by the Augustan cultural elite. When offering notes to Richard Rawlinson on 12 July 1728 Baker told him: "What I now send . . . has so much of the Dunciad, that I doubt it will want your pardon." Baker was not a fact-monger; for him even the collecting of snippets was always related to wider issues such as his religious and political convictions and his loyalty to the college and the university.

When Wanley was negotiating with Baker in Cambridge over the sale of the volumes of transcripts in December 1716, he was much impressed by Baker's library of printed books, and he bought a select parcel of them on the spot for 20 guineas. Triumphantly he reported to Harley in a letter of 6 December 1716: "They are worth more by far." Baker owned at least ninety incunabula, and the number of fifteenth- and sixteenth-century books together amounts to nearly one thousand.

Apart from the eighty-five mainly sixteenth-century Protestant editions of Bibles, Testaments, epistles and gospels, Baker's library was strong on publications illustrating the beginnings and early development of the Anglican Church. Besides John Calvin, Martin Luther, Phillip Melanchton, and Théodore de Bèze, the chief English actors in the turbulent events surrounding the birth and growth of the Anglican Church are all present. Baker had three copies apiece of Matthew Parker's *De Antiquitate Britannicae Ecclesiae* (1572) and *The Life of the 70. Archbishopp off Canterbury presentlye Sittinge* (1574). There are eight copies of Walter Travers's book on ecclesiastical discipline–"that Directory to the Puritans" as Baker called it in the notes to one of his copies: five of the Latin edition and three of the English one. Miles Coverdale, John Bale, John Frith, William Fulke, and Nicholas Ridley are each represented by four or more works. Baker was keenly interested in the exact wording and all the variants of the successive editions of the Thirty-nine Articles, the doctrinal statements of the Church of England, and he owned many of them. On the other hand, the main Catholic controversialists of the late sixteenth century are represented as well, with as many as fifteen copies of works by Robert Parsons.

Baker often bought separate tracts, pamphlets, and sermons to build up thematically coherent collections. He formed large collections on historically central events and periods such as the Gunpowder Plot, the opposition against Laud, the execution of Charles I, the reign of James II, and–somewhat less centrally–the controversy in Cambridge surrounding Richard Bentley in 1719–1720. More unexpected, perhaps, are the collection of works by the early sixteenth century grammarian Robert Whittinton and many tracts on coinage, but by and large there are not many oddities in Baker's library. In his case the library can be confidently pronounced to reflect the known tastes and interests of the man.

Baker sometimes bought defective or incomplete books and manuscripts, and in many cases he repaired and supplemented them neatly and painstakingly. Some of the sixteenth-century Bibles in his library have title pages and other parts supplied by him in manuscript. One of the main reasons why Baker bought duplicates was that they enabled him to perfect defective copies. Baker's copy of Scot's Tables, a manuscript account by John Scot of the University of Cambridge and of each of the sixteen colleges, dated March 1617, was completed by him from another manuscript copy. In several of his books Baker drew up indexes or extended the existing ones. If there is one work that illustrates Baker's skills, it is Maunsell's catalogue (1595)–now in Cambridge University Library–which he evidently cherished and valued as a key work. In a letter of 12 July 1711 Baker told Strype that he had an interleaved copy of Maunsell's catalogue, annotated successively by Samuel Harsnett, archbishop of York, by a friend of his, and by himself, and he generously offered Strype assistance from it. All of Baker's care for the physical aspects of his books and manuscripts sprang from the wish to have effective tools of learning at his disposal.

Baker's familiarity with such rich collections as those of Harley, Bishop Moore, and Thomas Rawlinson and his frequent contacts with men such as Bagford, Wanley, Hearne, John Lewis, and Richard Rawlinson made him one of the prime bibliographers of the day. Bagford and Baker exchanged information on early printers, and Baker sent Bagford lists of all the incunabula in Cambridge libraries. Baker presented Bagford with William Caxton's folio edition of *The Canterbury Tales* (1477 or 1483), and Bagford handed over to Baker all his papers on the history of printing, papers that Baker gave to Hearne in 1724, after making copies of them that he lent to Joseph Ames in the 1730s.

Baker had an impressive collection of bibliographical reference works, both English and foreign, and the annotations in his books and manuscripts show that he was familiar with many more such works. At the age of eighty-three he got hold of *Catalogue des Livres Imprimés en Bibliothèque du Roy* (1739), and in the last year of his life he entered many references from this work into his books. His library contained as many as sixty sale catalogues of the period 1678–1700, most of which he believed had belonged to Edward Millington, the first specialized auctioneer in England. In a letter of 23 April 1732 he asked Richard Rawlinson to present a complete set of all the Rawlinson catalogues to the university library in Cambridge.

After Baker's death his friend Zachary Grey for a time intended to publish a selection from Baker's extensive annotations in his books and manuscripts, but in the end the plan came to nothing. These annotations form a distinctive and integral part of Baker's collection. In some of his books, such as Wood's *Athenae Oxonienses* (1691–1692), Francis Godwin's *De Praesulibus Angliae Commentarius* (1616), Thomas Tanner's *Notitia Monastica* (1695), and André Chevillier's *L'Origine de l'Imprimerie de Paris* (1694), Baker's notes almost exceed the printed text, and such books are therefore now often preserved among the manuscripts in the libraries that house them. The annotations fall into three main categories–bibliographical, biographical, and historical–and were often naturally influenced by Baker's interest in his Athenae Cantabrigienses project. In the incunabula and early- sixteenth-century books the notes chiefly concern the printers and the physical aspects of the works. From the Reformation onward the annotations become largely biographical and historical. Baker went on adding notes to his books and manuscripts all his life, and they were clearly meant to enhance the usefulness of these works not only for himself but also for future scholars. Baker's annotations contributed much toward making his library a lasting monument to the scholarship and piety of its owner.

Biographies:

Robert Masters, *Memoirs of the Life and Writings of the Late Rev. Thomas Baker B.D.* (Cambridge: J. Merrill, 1784);

Horace Walpole, "Life of the Rev. Mr. Thomas Baker of St John's College," in *The Works of Horatio Walpole,* nine volumes (London: G. G. and J. Robinson & J. Edwards, 1798–1825), II: 339–363.

References:

James Alsop, "A Letter Relating To Thomas Baker's Cambridge University Collections," *Proceedings of the Cambridge Antiquarian Society,* 77 (1988): 151;

Joseph Ames, *Typographical Antiquities,* 2 volumes (London: Printed by W. Faden and sold by J. Robinson, 1749);

D. C. Douglas, *English Scholars, 1660–1730,* second edition (London: Eyre & Spottiswoode, 1951);

B. J. Enright, "The Later Auction Sales of Thomas Rawlinson's Library 1727–34," *Library,* fifth series, 11 (1956): 23–40, 103–113;

Enright, "Richard Rawlinson, Collector, Antiquary, and Topographer," dissertation, Oxford University, 1956;

Thomas Hearne, *Remarks and Collections of Thomas Hearne,* eleven volumes, edited by C. E. Doble, D. W. Rannie, and H. E. Salter (Oxford: Oxford Historical Society, 1885–1921);

P. L. Heyworth, ed., *Letters of Humfrey Wanley* (Oxford: Clarendon Press, 1989);

Frans Korsten, "The 'Remarks And Collections' of Thomas Baker (1656–1740)," *LIAS,* 19 (1992): 255–270;

Korsten, "Thomas Baker And His Books," *Transactions of the Cambridge Bibliographical Society,* 8 (1985): 491–513;

Korsten, "Thomas Baker's *Reflections Upon Learning,*" *Studies in Seventeenth-Century English Literature, History and Bibliography,* edited by G. A. M. Janssens and F. G. A. M. Aarts (Amsterdam: 1984): 133–148;

Joseph M. Levine, *Dr. Woodward's Shield. History, Science and Satire in Augustan England* (Berkeley & London: University of California Press, 1977);

J. E. B. Mayor, *Cambridge under Queen Anne* (Cambridge: Deighton, Bell / Bowes & Bowes, 1911);

Gerald R. Miller, "Thomas Baker: A Sceptic's Attack on Rhetoric," *Western Speech,* 27 (1963): 69–76;

[J. J. S.], *Index to the Baker Manuscripts. By four members of the Cambridge Antiquarian Society* (Cambridge: Cambridge Antiquarian Society, 1848);

C. E. Wright and Ruth C. Wright, *The Diary of Humfrey Wanley 1715–1726,* 2 volumes (London: The Bibliographical Society, 1966).

Papers:

The letters of Thomas Baker are in the Bodleian Library (MSS Ballard, Rawlinson, Smith, Tanner); the British Library (Additional MSS and MSS Lansdowne, Loan, Stowe); Cambridge University Library (MSS Add. and Mm., Baumgartner Papers); St. John's College, Cambridge (MSS K28, N27, O54, S64, S27); Christ Church, Oxford (MS Arch. W. Epist.); and Durham University Library (Baker Papers). The British Library and Cambridge University Library have a large collection of manuscripts and transcripts. The bulk of Baker's manuscripts and the manuscript catalogues of the books he left to his college are in St. John's College, Cambridge.

Sir James Balfour
(1600 - 1657)

and

Sir Andrew Balfour
(18 January 1630 - 10 January 1694)

Richard Ovenden
National Library of Scotland

CATALOGUES: *Bibliotheca Balfouriana, sive catalogus liborum, in quavis lingua & facultate insignium illustris viri D. Andreae Balfourii M.D. & Equitis Aurati; quorum auctio habebitur Edinburgi in aedibus Balfourianis, anno 1695; quarto die mensis februarii* (Edinburgh: Ab hæredibus ac successoribus Andreae Anderson, 1695);

A Catalogue of Curious Manuscripts, being Historical, Political, Theological, Juridical, Physical, and Philosophical, with some Poets and Creators, their Writings, Ancient and Modern. Collected by Sir James Balfour of Kinaird Knight-Baronet, and Lyon King at Arms, kept in his famous study of Denmilne and now exposed to sale (Edinburgh: Printed by the heirs and successors of Andrew Anderson, 1698);

*Catalogus selectissimorum in quavis lingua & facultate librorum, quorum maxima pars pertinebat ad clarissimos fratres D.D. Balfourios, Jacobum, de Kinnaird Equitem, Leonem, Reqem Armorum: et Andream quorum auctio habebitur duodecimo die Junii 1669 [*sic*] in aedibus, in vico vulgo dicto high street, e regione templi cathedratis* (Edinburgh, 1699).

BOOKS: *The Form and Order of the Coronation of Charles the Second; King of Scotland, England, France, and Ireland: As it was Acted and Done at Scoone, the First Day of Ianuarie 1651,* by Sir James Balfour, edited by Robert Douglas (Aberdeen: Printed by James Brown, 1651);

Letters written to a Friend by the learned and judicious Sir Andrew Balfour, M.D. containing excellent directions and advices for travelling thro' France and Italy. With many curious and judicious remarks and observations made by himself, in his voyages thro' these countrey. (Edinburgh, 1700);

The Historical Works of Sir James Balfour . . . Published from the Original MSS. Preserved in the Library of the Faculty of Advocates, edited by James Haig, 4 volumes (Edinburgh: Printed by W. Aitchison, 1824–1825).

OTHER: Sir James Balfour, "Coenobia Scotica," in *Monasticon Anglicanum, sive pandectae coenobiorum Benedictinorum Cluniacensium Cisterciensium Carthusianorum . . . per Rogerum Dodsworth . . . Gulielmum Dugdale,* 3 volumes (London, 1655–1673), II: 1051–1057;

Ballads and Other Fugitive Poetical Pieces, Chiefly Scottish; from the Collections of Sir James Balfour, compiled by James Balfour (Edinburgh: Printed by Alex. Lawrie, 1834).

The brothers Sir James and Sir Andrew Balfour were among the most significant collectors of books in Scotland during the seventeenth century. Although neither man was a major writer, each was important in the cultural life of the nation. As collectors they made significant contributions to Scottish intellectual progress during a century more notable for its strife and bloodshed than for scholarly or cultural achievement. Sir James was an antiquarian and collector of medieval and early modern manuscripts–many crucial to the emerging discipline of Scottish history–and to a lesser extent of printed books. Sir Andrew was primarily a botanist and collector of plants, skills that led him to play a major role in establishing a botanical garden in Edinburgh, the equal of any in Europe. His collection of printed books was the most extensive source of medical and scientific works in the country. The dispersal of both collections at the end of the seventeenth century was a major factor in the early development of what are now Scotland's most important institutional library collections: The National Library of Scotland and The Library of The Royal Botanic Gardens.

Sir James Balfour was the eldest son of Sir Michael Balfour of Denmilne, comptroller of the household of Charles I, and of Jane, daughter of James Durham of Pitkerrow. He was born in the family home of Denmilne, near Newburgh in Fife, in 1600. Denmilne, a ruin since the eighteenth century, was a substantial fortified dwelling built in the sixteenth century on lands granted to the Balfour family. Balfour was educated at home and then at St. Andrews University, where he was admitted to St. Salvators College in 1610, and he was elected M.A. in 1614. He traveled abroad in his early years before settling to his life of antiquarian and historical studies in which he cultivated friendships with scholars and antiquarians. John Leech praised his learning in a 1626 poem.

In the late 1620s Balfour traveled to London in order to study heraldry at the College of Arms. By the 1620s the college had been transformed from the somewhat moribund state it had come to in the late sixteenth century into one of the institutions where historical scholarship was able to develop. A key event in the transformation was the appointment of William Camden as Clarenceux King of Arms in 1597. The serious historical debate between Camden and Ralph Brooke, York Herald, about Camden's major work, *Britannia* (1594), raised historical scholarship to new heights, and these standards, based on both documentary research and personal observation, led the college to place a greater emphasis on heraldic surveys. Balfour was therefore present at the college during a particularly golden period in its history, and he came into contact with its principal officers: Sir William Segar, Garter King of Arms; Sir Henry St. George, Richmond Herald; Sir William Penson, Lancaster Herald; John Philpot, Somerset Herald; and the great collector and antiquary Sir William Le Neve, York Herald. Balfour also knew Sir William Dugdale and Roger Dodsworth, for whom he wrote sections on Scottish Augustinian houses for their magisterial work, the *Monasticon Anglicanum* (1655–1673), the first comprehensive account of monastic life in Britain in the Middle Ages.

A volume dated 1628 survives in the National Library of Scotland and provides an account of the sort of studies that Balfour had to show competence in to gain the title of a herald, which he was awarded on 4 December 1628. The volume is a certificate and attestation of proficiency and includes the dated signatures of all the officers of the college along with their painted armorials, beginning with those of Segar. In it is recorded the testimony of Balfour's "insight and knowledge in diverse languages, hes also singular good experience and knowledge in all antiquities and forraine histories but especiall in those concerning the Illand of Great Britaine and Irland." He was thus qualified "to be ane expert and graduate herauld in Blasing of Mottoes, armorials inventing of Crests and Supporters in searching of genealogies and dissents in Marshalling of funeralls triumphs and inaugurations . . . and in all ceremonies whatsoever perteining to honour or armes."

Balfour returned from London and began using his newly acquired title to engage in genealogical and heraldic research. As is recorded in a manuscript now in in the British Library, he provided services to George Seton, third Earl of Winton, "for the prouffe of his antiquitie" in 1628. He also searched the "Charter Kist of the Burgh of Perth," providing a genealogy for the earl of Erroll, and copied charters from the manuscripts in the charge of the clerk register in Edinburgh. He was appointed the principal herald in Scotland, Lyon King of Arms, on 8 June 1630 and crowned at his inauguration by the king's commissioner in the presence of the nobility and officers of state after an appropriate sermon in the Chapel Royal.

The event that dominated the early part of Balfour's tenure was the coronation in Scotland of Charles I in 1633, for which Balfour acted as a kind of stage manager. He was quick to act on the problems that arose soon after he took office. The reigns of James I and of Charles I were dominated by the increasing use of patronage as a strategic political tool. In the struggle for position within English and Scottish society, heralds were placed in the difficult position of arbiters of qualification to noble titles. In July 1630 Balfour was forced to appeal to the Privy Council in Scotland for powers to combat what is termed in *Register of the Privy Council of Scotland* (1901) the growing band of "painters, goldsmiths, gravers, cutters, and others" who issued coats of arms to those who were not privileged to wear them. Parallel problems were being faced by the English heralds at the same time.

In addition to his duties at the coronation and as a herald, Balfour was charged by the Scottish Parliament to produce "an old monument concerning the entailments of the crown [of Scotland] by King Robert the Bruce" for the assistance of the Convention of Estates, which he completed in 1650. He continued his antiquarian interests, collecting manuscripts and producing copies of state and private papers for his own collection. To facilitate such work he was admitted to use the University Library at Edinburgh on 2 July 1646.

Having made useful contacts during his period in London, Balfour was anxious to keep them up after his appointment as Lyon King of Arms. In 1630, after his appointment, he wrote to Sir Robert Cotton and Segar,

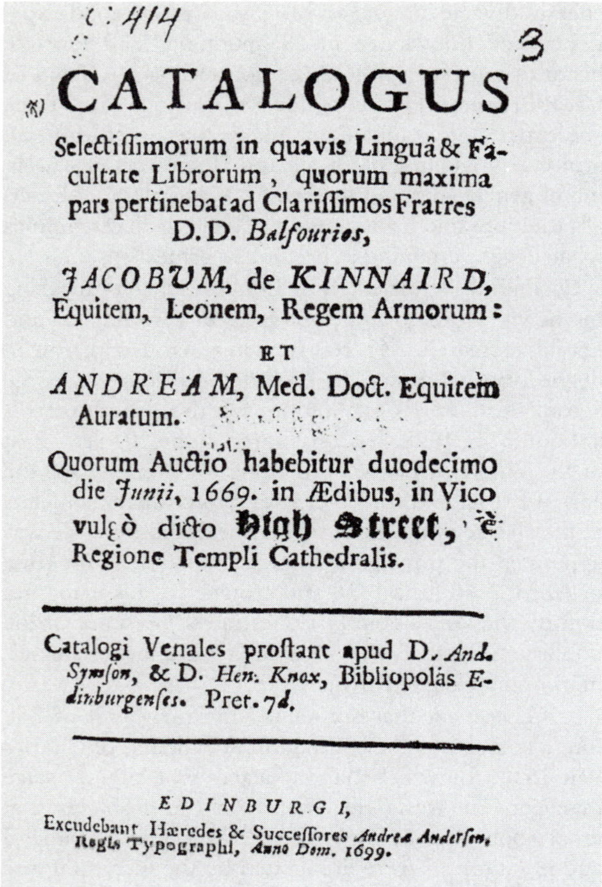

C: 414

3

CATALOGUS

Selectiſſimorum in quavis Linguâ & Facultate Librorum, quorum maxima pars pertinebat ad Clariſſimos Fratres D.D. *Balfourios*,

JACOBUM, de *KINNAIRD*, Equitem, Leonem, Regem Armorum:

ET

ANDREAM, Med. Doct. Equitem Auratum.

Quorum Auctio habebitur duodecimo die *Junii*, 1669. in Ædibus, in Vico vulgò dicto High Street, è Regione Templi Cathedralis.

Catalogi Venales proſtant apud D. *And. Symſon*, & D. *Hen. Knox*, Bibliopolás *Edinburgenſes*. Pret. 7*d*.

EDINBURGI,
Excudebant Hæredes & Succeſſores *Andreæ Anderſon*, Regis Typographi, *Anno Dom.* 1699.

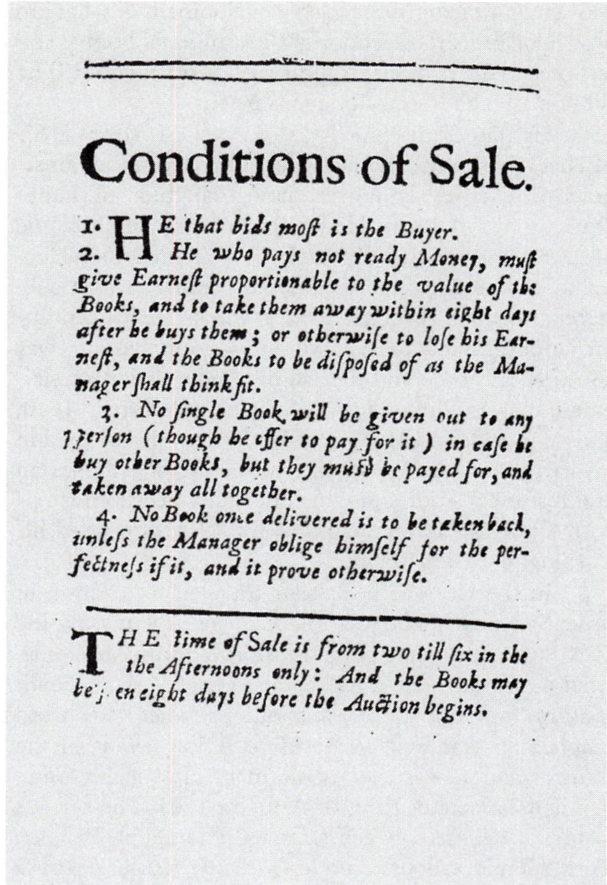

Conditions of Sale.

1. *HE that bids moſt is the Buyer.*

2. *He who pays not ready Money, muſt give Earneſt proportionable to the value of the Books, and to take them away within eight days after he buys them; or otherwiſe to loſe his Earneſt, and the Books to be diſpoſed of as the Manager ſhall think fit.*

3. *No ſingle Book will be given out to any Perſon (though he offer to pay for it) in caſe he buy other Books, but they muſt be payed for, and taken away all together.*

4. *No Book once delivered is to be taken back, unleſs the Manager oblige himſelf for the perfectneſs if it, and it prove otherwiſe.*

THE time of Sale is from two till ſix in the Afternoons only: And the Books may be ſeen eight days before the Auction begins.

Title page, advertisement, and last pages of the 1698 catalogue listing Sir James Balfour's manuscripts, which were bought by the Faculty of Advocates after a unanimous vote

Garter King of Arms at the time. Knighted in 1630, Balfour was granted the lands and barony of Kinnaird in 1631, thanks to the support and patronage of George Hay, Earl of Kinnoull, chancellor of Scotland. The grant was confirmed by Parliament in 1634. In 1652 his father died and he inherited the house and estates of Denmilne, and he seems to have moved there from Kinnaird. In the five years before his death in 1657, he renumbered his manuscripts, giving them "Denmilne" numbers.

Although Sir James acquired a substantial collection of printed books, it is his collections of manuscripts, in particular medieval manuscripts and contemporary state papers, that mark him as a collector of major importance in the first half of the seventeenth century. Like his more famous English contemporary Cotton, Balfour was motivated by his antiquarian and historical interests to collect and preserve materials from the relatively recent past as well as from the Middle Ages. Like Cotton and other collectors, he was not solely interested in originals and had copies made of materials that he was unable to acquire. He collected papers of the General Assembly of the Church of Scotland; also papers on the bishops of St. Andrews, on the English war with Spain, and on many issues relating to Scottish political history of the late sixteenth and early seventeenth centuries, most of which he used as source material for his "Annales of Scotland," which remained in manuscript until it was edited by James Haig and published in four volumes as *The Historical Works of Sir James Balfour* (1824–1825).

Balfour is remembered today principally as a collector of medieval manuscripts. His collection was naturally strong in Scottish material, including a thirteenth-century Bible from the Collegiate Church of St. Giles in Edinburgh and a volume containing texts by Eutropius and Suetonius that had been given to King's College, Aberdeen, in the early sixteenth century by Hector Boece. A *sammelband,* or miscellaneous collection of treatises, containing texts by Joannes de Hildesheim and

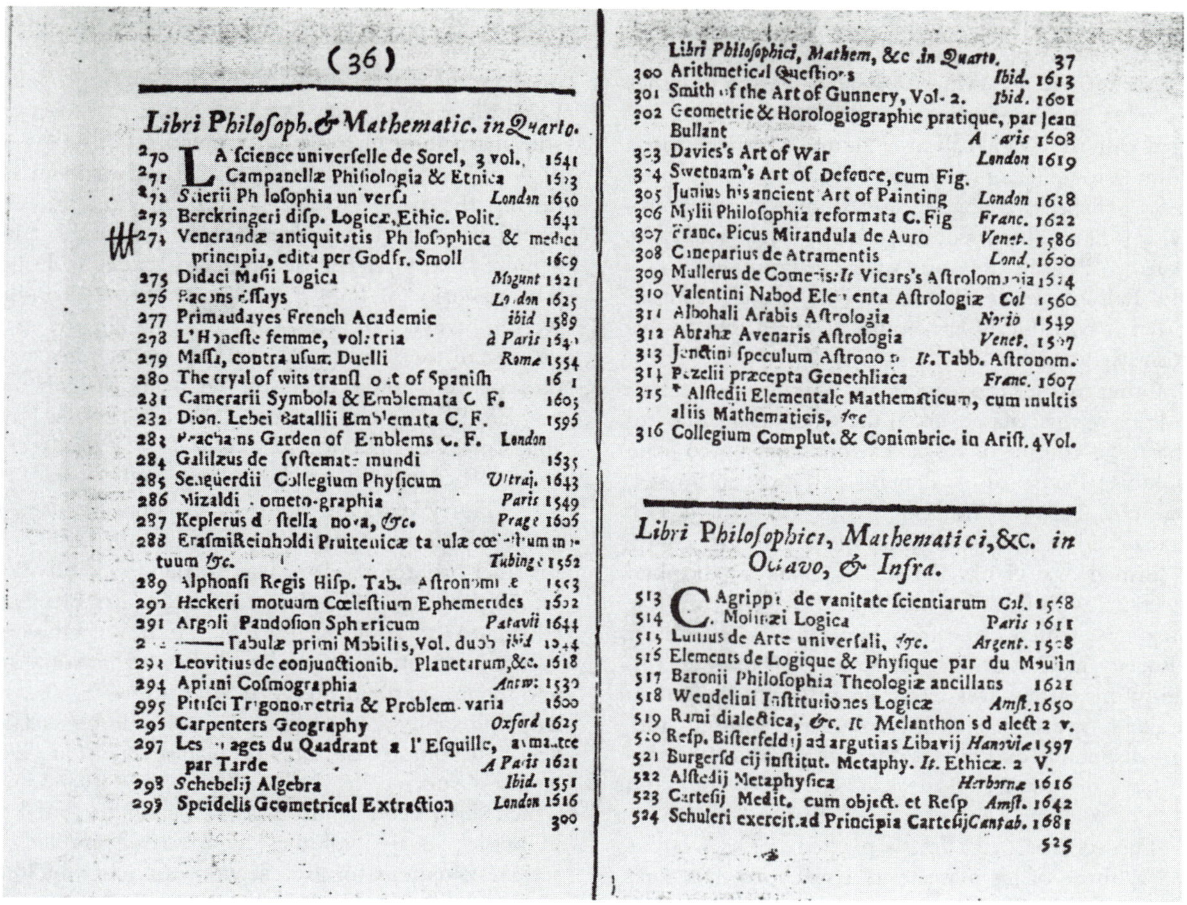
(36)

Libri Philosoph. & Mathematic. in Quarto.

270 La science universelle de Sorel, 3 vol. 1641
271 Campanellæ Philosophia & Ethica 1623
272 Sverii Philosophia universa London 1630
273 Berckringeri disp. Logicæ, Ethic. Polit. 1642
274 Venerandæ antiquitatis Philosophica & medica principia, edita per Godfr. Smoll 1609
275 Didaci Masii Logica Mogunt 1621
276 Bacons Essays London 1625
277 Primaudayes French Academie ibid 1589
278 L'Honeste femme, vol. tria à Paris 1641
279 Massa, contra usum Duelli Romæ 1554
280 The tryal of wits transl. out of Spanish 1611
281 Camerarii Symbola & Emblemata C. F. 1605
282 Dion. Lebei Batallii Emblemata C. F. 1595
283 Peachams Garden of Emblems C. F. London
284 Galilæus de systemate mundi 1635
285 Senguerdii Collegium Physicum Ultraj. 1643
286 Mizaldi Cometographia Paris 1549
287 Keplerus de stella nova, &c. Pragæ 1606
288 Erasmi Reinholdi Pruitenicæ tabulæ cœlestium motuum &c. Tubingæ 1562
289 Alphonsi Regis Hisp. Tab. Astronomicæ 1553
290 Heckeri motuum Cœlestium Ephemerides 1662
291 Argoli Pandosion Sphæricum Patavii 1644
292 ——— Tabulæ primi Mobilis, Vol. duo ibid 1644
293 Leovitius de conjunctionib. Planetarum, &c. 1618
294 Apiani Cosmographia Antw. 1530
295 Pitisci Trigonometria & Problem. varia 1600
296 Carpenters Geography Oxford 1625
297 Les usages du Quadrant à l'Esquille, augmentee par Tarde A Paris 1621
298 Schebelij Algebra Ibid. 1551
299 Speidels Geometrical Extraction London 1616

Libri Philosophici, Mathem, &c. in Quarto. 37

300 Arithmetical Questions Ibid. 1613
301 Smith of the Art of Gunnery, Vol. 2. Ibid. 1601
302 Geometrie & Horologiographie pratique, par Jean Bullant A Paris 1608
303 Davies's Art of War London 1619
304 Swetnam's Art of Defence, cum Fig.
305 Junius his ancient Art of Painting London 1638
306 Mylii Philosophia reformata C. Fig Franc. 1622
307 Franc. Picus Mirandula de Auro Venet. 1586
308 Caneparius de Atramentis Lond. 1660
309 Mullerus de Cometis; It Vicars's Astrolomania 1624
310 Valentini Nabod Elementa Astrologiæ Col. 1560
311 Albohali Arabis Astrologia Norib. 1549
312 Abrahæ Avenaris Astrologia Venet. 1507
313 Junctini speculum Astronomiæ It. Tabb. Astronom.
314 Pezelii præcepta Genethliaca Franc. 1607
315 * Alstedii Elementale Mathematicum, cum multis aliis Mathematicis, &c
316 Collegium Complut. & Conimbric. in Arist. 4 Vol.

Libri Philosophici, Mathematici, &c. in Octavo, & Infra.

513 C. Agrippæ de vanitate scientiarum Col. 1568
514 C. Molinæi Logica Paris 1611
515 Lullius de Arte universali, &c. Argent. 1598
516 Elements de Logique & Physique par du Moulin
517 Baronii Philosophia Theologiæ ancillans 1621
518 Wendelini Institutiones Logicæ Amst. 1650
519 Rami dialectica, &c. It Melanthon's dialect 2 v.
520 Resp. Bisterfeldij ad argutias Libavij Hanoviæ 1597
521 Burgersd cij institut. Metaphy. It. Ethicæ. 2 V.
522 Alstedij Metaphysica Herbornæ 1616
523 Cartesij Medit. cum object. et Resp Amst. 1642
524 Schuleri exercit. ad Principia Cartesij Cantab. 1681

Dionysius Periegetes also came from Aberdeen. A volume abridging the *Scotichronicon* of John of Fordun and Walter Bower had originally been in the library of the Charterhouse at Perth. A manuscript of Andrew Wyntoun's *Orygynale Cronykil of Scotland* had been owned by Henry Sinclair, bishop of Ross, in the sixteenth century. Balfour particularly valued medieval cartularies and registers. His collection included two cartularies from Arbroath and single cartularies from the Cistercians of Balmerino in Fife, the Praemonstratensians of Dryburgh in the Borders, the Benedictine Abbey of Dunfermline, the Lindores in Fife, and the Augustinian Abbey of Scone in Perthshire. A volume of rentals of the bishopric of Moray, a copy of the *Regiam Maiestatem,* and a missal with Irish associations that was owned by the Sinclairs of Roslin in the sixteenth century are among items in the collection, although which specific religious house produced them is unknown.

Balfour also collected some materials with distinguished English medieval provenances. Several of his volumes were most probably from English monastic libraries, although they no longer bear any marks that can positively identify them with any particular house. Several volumes were acquired from the Old Royal Library, most probably through the agency of fellow Scot Patrick Young, Royal Librarian, who is known to have assisted in the removal of books from the royal collections, most notably to James Ussher and Cotton. Balfour acquired at least three manuscripts from his this source, including Thomas Wall's translation of Ramon Lull's *L'Ordre de chevalerie* (c. 1530), which had been sequestered by Henry VIII from the collection of George Rochford, the brother of Anne Boleyn. Although there is no evidence of correspondence between Young and Balfour, given that the latter was in London at the time that Young was actively "lending" manuscripts from the royal collection, it is almost certain that he acquired the volumes from the royal librarian.

Another manuscript Balfour may have acquired through the offices of Young is an English copy of the Statutes of the Order of the Garter (circa 1558), which had been in the collection of John, Lord Lumley, one of the great collectors of the period. Lord Lumley's library had passed to Henry, Prince of Wales, the son of James I, and when the prince died in 1612, the collection was merged with the Royal Library. Young, who supervised the joining together of these great libraries, was responsible for selling, exchanging, and simply giving books away. It is likely that a volume such as this would have appealed to Balfour, a young man newly qualified as a herald (Balfour's ex libris is dated 1630), and it is probable that it was one of the books given to him by his Scottish friend.

Other manuscript items in Balfour's collection include three miscellanies from the Cathedral Priory of Rochester, a volume of works by Johannes Vasco from the Cluniac Priory of St. Pancras at Lewes in Sussex, and a book from the monastic priory at Durham. Balfour acquired three manuscripts from the large collection formed by Henry Savile of Banke, who had connections with Camden and John Dee. One of these manuscripts, which came from the Benedictine Abbey of Thorney in Cambridgeshire and had been given to Savile by his father, was either acquired by Balfour in three parts, or else he split the volume up himself, adding his distinctive ex libris at different dates, as the volumes have his ownership marks dated 1630, 1637, and 1654.

The sources of Balfour's printed books were as varied as those of his manuscript collections. His copy of Jean Le Feron's *Catalogue des noms, surnoms, faits et vies, des connestables* (1598), now in the National Library of Scotland, was acquired from the library of Sir Augustine Vincent, Windsor Herald, a brilliant antiquary who provided assistance to many historians and antiquaries. The Le Feron book had the added attraction of having Vincent's heraldic book stamp on the front cover, a feature that alone likely would have been enough to persuade Balfour to spend the £6 Scots required to secure it. Other printed books came from significant Scottish pre-Reformation collections. One volume was in the library of the Priory at St. Andrews; at least two books are known to have been owned by James Beaton, the last cardinal archbishop of Glasgow before the Reformation. Other volumes were once owned by John Sinclair, bishop of Brechin; Archibald Crawford, rector of Eaglesham; Sir James Balfour of Pittendreich, jurist and president of the Court of Session; and Edward Henryson, judge.

More-immediate sources for Balfour's printed collections can be grouped into four categories. He acquired many books new and in sheets, such as the copy of John Weever's *Ancient Funerall Monuments* (1631), which he purchased for £6 13s. 9d. Scots in London three years after it was published. Some of his books have Continental provenance and are still in their original bindings, indicating that Balfour bought them secondhand, either on the Continent or more probably in London or Edinburgh. A volume that has the ownership inscription of Johannes Helvius from Beauvais in 1576 was bought by Balfour for £3 10s. Scots in 1629, during the period when he was in London. Other books have English provenance and were most likely acquired through the secondhand trade in London. The majority of books that he acquired secondhand were, however, from Scottish libraries. In the second quarter of the seventeenth century, collections such as those of Sir Thomas Nicolson of Cockburnspath, a civil lawyer of King's College Aberdeen; Sir Thomas Henryson, Lord Chesters; John Lindsay, Lord Balcarres; and Robert Richardson were being dispersed.

Thirty years the junior of Sir James, Andrew Balfour was the youngest son in the Balfour family. Like his elder brother, Andrew was born in the family home, on 18 January 1630. On completing his elementary education he proceeded to St. Andrews University, where his brother acted effectively as a personal tutor and mentor in philosophy. At St. Andrews he also studied philosophy and arithmetic under Thomas Glegg, and two volumes of notes on Ramus taken at Glegg's lectures survive in Edinburgh University Library, which show even at this early age a sophisticated taste in books, as the volumes have been compiled with scribal colophons for each section, some of which have used stamped printer's ornaments to decorate the pages.

Andrew Balfour graduated with an M.A. at St. Andrews and soon after moved south to London. In 1650 he met the physician Sir William Harvey and found himself a position as pupil to Sir John Wedderburn, a fellow Scot, at that point physician to the King. In 1651 he went to France and visited Robert Morison, another Scot, then director of the gardens of the duke of Orléans at Blois. He then moved to Paris, attended lectures, visited hospitals, and spent time in the botanical garden. He traveled again, returning briefly to Yorkshire before visiting France again, where he attended the University of Caen, obtaining the degree of bachelor of medicine for his dissertation titled *De Venae Sectione in Dysenteria.* He then returned to London, where he obtained a position as governor to the young John Wilmot, Earl of Rochester, with whom he traveled to Italy in 1667. Rochester later recorded his debt to Balfour: "next to his parents, he thought he owed more than to all the world."

Balfour collected much on his travels and studied natural history, laws, customs, and antiquities. On returning to St. Andrews he brought with him a large library with great strengths in natural history and medicine. He also brought his collection of antique medals, modern medallions, pictures, arms, vestments, ornaments, mathematical instruments, and surgical instruments. With these he performed dissections in surgery previously unknown in Scotland. He also collected a range of medicinal and other plants as well as animals and fossils.

In 1667 or 1668 he moved to Edinburgh and entered medical practice. From this time he made his collections of books and objects freely available. He also planted a small botanical garden next to his house and received seeds from correspondents, including the Scots Morison at Oxford, John Watts in London, Marchant in Paris, Hermann in Leiden, and Spotswood at Tangiers. During this part of his life he became acquainted with the great physician, historian, and scientist Robert Sibbald, who was instrumental in organizing the College of Physicians, founded in 1681, and who later became the biographer of the Balfour brothers. Sibbald became the second president of the college in 1684, and Sir Andrew Balfour, who had been knighted by the duke of York in 1682, became the third president in 1684. Balfour's career as a professional physician was certainly distinguished, with such eminent figures as the King's Physician, Sir Charles Scarburgh, consulting him for medical opinions. Scarburgh wrote to Balfour in 1691, for example, asking for his opinion on the condition of the duke of Lauderdale. Balfour replied, giving a detailed account of the duke's unpleasant condition and advising on certain courses of action to be taken to cure him.

Sibbald and Balfour, who shared interests in medicine, botany, natural history, and book collecting, became friends with Patrick Murray, the Laird of Livingstone. Murray, who died on a European tour in Avignon in 1671, was also a prolific collector of books, many of which were acquired on his Continental tour at places suggested by Balfour. Balfour's *Letters written to a Friend by the learned and judicious Sir Andrew Balfour, M.D. containing excellent direction and advices for travelling thro' France and Italy* (1700), an account of his travels on the Continent in which he mentions all the curiosities in the gardens he visited, was originally intended as advice for Murray. In 1670 Sibbald and Balfour leased a small garden near Holyrood and stocked it with plants from their own gardens and from Murray's, soon establishing a collection of between eight and nine hundred plants. James Sutherland was appointed by them to maintain the garden, funded by the Chirurgeon Apothecaries. In 1675 the garden had to be moved because it had outgrown the space available.

Balfour's extensive collections of "Rarities" were called the "Museaum Balfourianum" by contemporaries. His collections were eventually bought from his heirs by the town council of Edinburgh for the use of the university. Among the natural history collections were included "The Rattle-Snake of Virginia," "A crocodile adorned with ribbands, suppos'd to have been an Indian pagod," "Piece of the Thigh Bone of a Giant," "Concha imbricata minor," "Murex Rhomboidalis, tuberosus maximus," and "A Jesuit's Cap."

Much less is known about the sources of Sir Andrew's collection of books than about those for his brother, mainly because Andrew appears to have been less assiduous in placing his marks of ownership–bookplates, armorial binding stamps, and ex libris marks–on his books, making it harder to identify them in modern collections. Two books that were given by James Sutherland to the Library of the Faculty of Advocates in 1707, now held in the National Library of Scotland, bear few marks of provenance, although an inscription on one of the books, a copy of *Adami Zaluzanii a Zaluzaniis Methodi herbariae libri tres* (1604), indicates that Balfour acquired it from a bookseller in Montpelier in 1672.

From his posthumously published *Letters to a Friend,* it is apparent that Sir Andrew was familiar with some of the senior figures in the London book trade. He refers his friend to "Mr. Scott a book-seller, dwelling in Little-Britain by whose means you may be furnished with any book that may be had in London; and I think as reasonably as else-where: notwithstanding you will doe well to see other shops, as particularly Mr. Bees and Mr. Pulleyns, both of them in Little Britain." Likewise in Paris, the reader is directed to "A la Rue St. Jacques; for new Books at the Palace; for French books, as Romances, &c. A la Place de Sorbone; as also at the end of the new bridge about nostre Dame church, also at the postern gate of the Palace and upon the Mont St. Hiller, for old books of all sorts." At Lyons he recommended his reader to "Forget not to take with you your Catalogue of Books, for there are many Booksellers in this place, that have great Magazins of Books, and have great traffick with all Germany, Switzerland and Italy, and it is very like, you may come by books here that you missed at Paris; for so it happened to my self." In *Memoria Balfouriana* Sibbald comments that Andrew read catalogues of books from throughout Europe, possibly referring to the Frankfurt Book Fair catalogues that certainly circulated in Britain in the seventeenth century; that he was keen on acquiring unpublished autographs, although no evidence survives to support this claim; and that he collected anything written by a Scot.

Sir Andrew Balfour died 10 January 1694. The testament of 28 March, executed by his son Michael Balfour of Northbank, refers generally to his "liberarie of bookes together with the curiosities in his studie,"

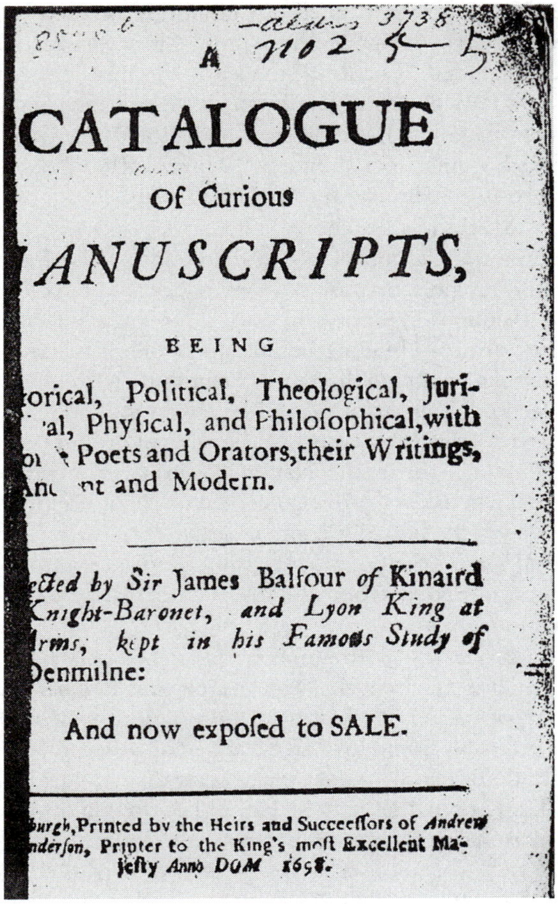
A
CATALOGUE
Of Curious
ANUSCRIPTS,
BEING
orical, Political, Theological, Juri-
al, Physical, and Philosophical, with
Poets and Orators, their Writings,
and Modern.

ected by Sir James Balfour of Kinaird
Knight-Baronet, and Lyon King at
rms, kept in his Famous Study of
Denmilne:

And now exposed to SALE.

urgh, Printed by the Heirs and Successors of Andrew
nderson, Printer to the King's most Excellent Majesty Anno DOM 1698.

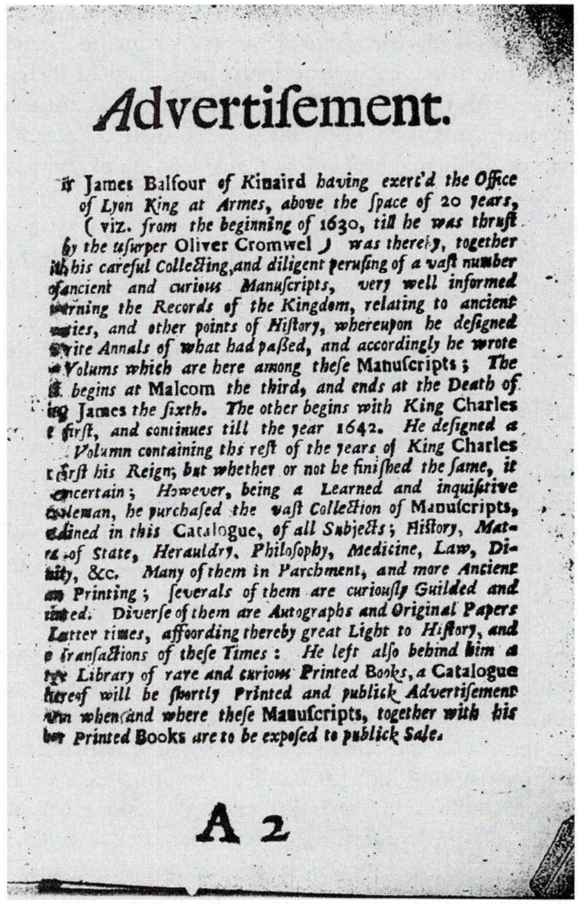
Advertisement.

ir James Balfour of Kinaird having exerc'd the Office of Lyon King at Armes, above the space of 20 years, (viz. from the beginning of 1630, till he was thrust by the usurper Oliver Cromwel) was thereby, together with his careful Collecting, and diligent perusing of a vast number of ancient and curious Manuscripts, very well informed cerning the Records of the Kingdom, relating to ancient ities, and other points of History, whereupon he designed write Annals of what had passed, and accordingly he wrote Volums which are here among these Manuscripts; The begins at Malcom the third, and ends at the Death of ing James the sixth. The other begins with King Charles first, and continues till the year 1642. He designed a Volumn containing the rest of the years of King Charles first his Reign; but whether or not he finished the same, it uncertain; However, being a Learned and inquisitive tleman, he purchased the vast Collection of Manuscripts, tained in this Catalogue, of all Subjects; History, Mat- of State, Herauldry, Philosophy, Medicine, Law, Di- nity, &c. Many of them in Parchment, and more Ancient Printing; severals of them are curiously Guilded and ted. Diverse of them are Autographs and Original Papers Latter times, affoording thereby great Light to History, and Transactions of these Times: He left also behind him a Library of rare and curious Printed Books, a Catalogue hereof will be shortly Printed and publick Advertisement when and where these Manuscripts, together with his Printed Books are to be exposed to publick Sale.

A 2

Title page and interior pages of the catalogue of the sale of Sir James and Sir Andrew Balfour's printed books

estimated to be worth thirty-three marks. His library was sold in 1695, and a printed catalogue, *Bibliotheca Balfouriana, sive catalogus librorum, in quavis lingua & facultate insignium illustris viri D. Andreae Balfourii M.D. & Equitis aurati,* was produced in order to sell the substantial collection.

The catalogue divided the collection into the conventional subject categories that were to be found in most auction catalogues of the period. The collection as it stood at his death therefore comprised: "Miscellanei & humaniorum litterarum scriptores," in four sizes, 921 items; "Libri numismatici cum iconibus & picturis illustrium virorum," in three sizes, 91 items; "Libri philosophici & mathematici," in four sizes, 192 items; "Libri theologici," in four sizes, 162 items; "Libri medici, pharmaceutici, chirurgici anatomici, chymici, botannici & naturalis historiæ scriptores," in four sizes, 1,473 items; "Livres Francois," in four sizes, 325 items; "Libri Italici," in four sizes, 209 items; "Libri Hispanici," in three sizes, 15 items; "English books," in three sizes, 82 items; and "Libri Manuscripti," in three sizes, 31 items. The sale of such a large and important library would have been an important event in Edinburgh in the 1690s, and with such a predominance of medical books, the vast majority of which were by Continental authors, the sale attracted members of the medical profession in particular, and not just in Scotland. Michael Balfour donated a copy of the sale catalogue to the newly established library of the Faculty of Advocates, although it is not known whether any items were acquired by the Faculty at the auction.

Sir James Balfour's manuscripts were sold in 1698 by auction, for which a printed catalogue was produced, *A Catalogue of Curious Manuscripts, being Historical, Political, Theological, Juridical, Physical, and Philosophical, with some Poets and Creators, their Writings, Ancient and Modern. Collected by Sir James Balfour.* The collection was acquired by the Faculty of Advocates on 2 December 1698 for £1800 (Scots), £150 sterling. The official record of the Faculty's deliberations concerning the

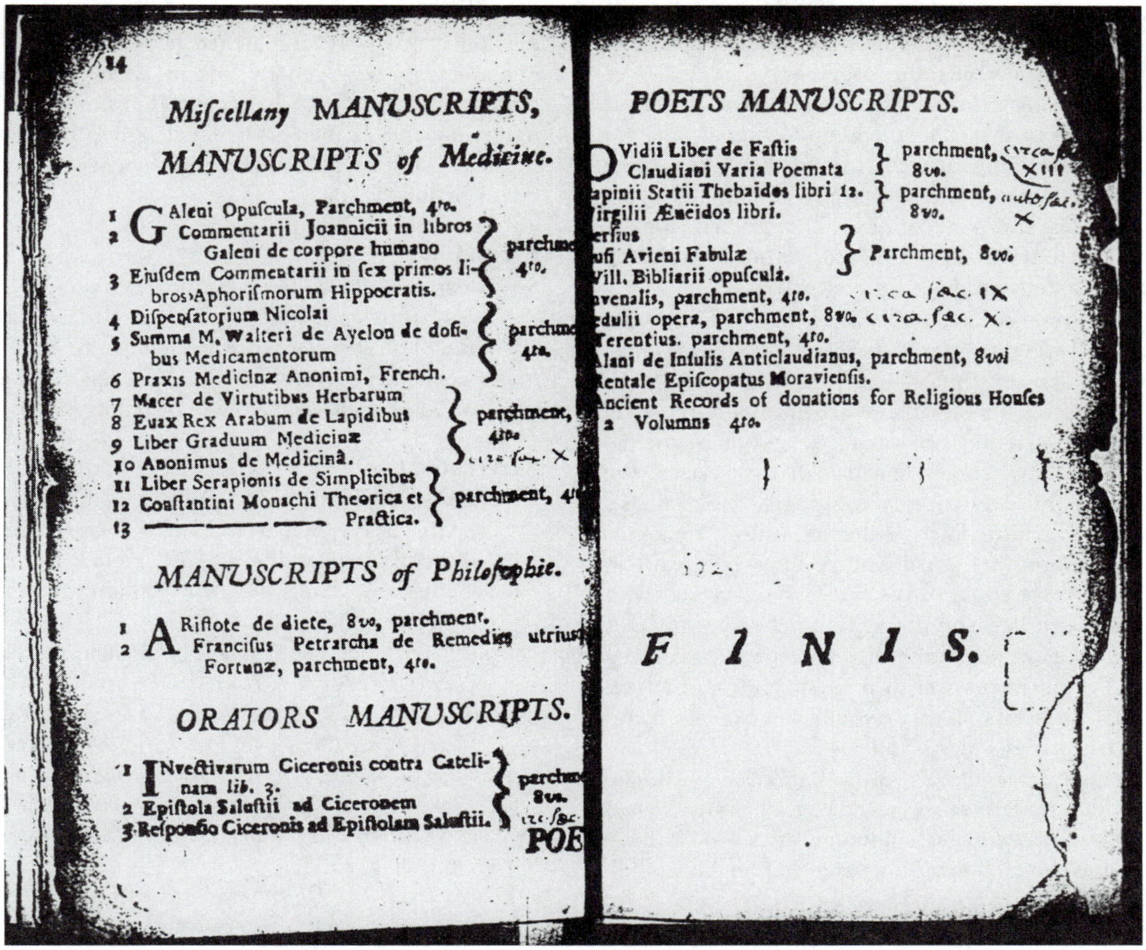
14

Miscellany MANUSCRIPTS,

MANUSCRIPTS *of* Medicine.

1 GAleni Opuscula, Parchment, 4to.
2 Commentarii Joannicii in libros Galeni de corpore humano
3 Ejusdem Commentarii in sex primos libros Aphorismorum Hippocratis. } parchm 4to.
4 Dispensatorium Nicolai
5 Summa M. Walteri de Ayelon de dosibus Medicamentorum
6 Praxis Medicinæ Anonimi, French. } parchm 4to.
7 Macer de Virtutibus Herbarum
8 Euax Rex Arabum de Lapidibus
9 Liber Graduum Medicinæ
10 Anonimus de Medicinâ. } parchment, 4to. circa sæc. X
11 Liber Serapionis de Simplicibus
12 Constantini Monachi Theorica et
13 ——— Practica. } parchment, 4t

MANUSCRIPTS *of* Philosophie.

1 ARistote de diete, 8vo, parchment.
2 Franciscus Petrarcha de Remediis utriusque Fortunæ, parchment, 4to.

ORATORS MANUSCRIPTS.

1 INvectivarum Ciceronis contra Catelinam *lib.* 3.
2 Epistola Salustii ad Ciceronem
3 Responsio Ciceronis ad Epistolam Salustii. } parchm 8vo. circa sæc.

POE

POETS MANUSCRIPTS.

OVidii Liber de Fastis
Claudiani Varia Poemata } parchment, 8vo. circa sæc. XIII
[P]apinii Statii Thebaidos libri 12.
[V]irgilii Æneidos libri. } parchment, 8vo. auto sæc. X
[P]ersius
[R]ufi Avieni Fabulæ
Will. Bibliarii opuscula. } Parchment, 8vo.
[Ju]venalis, parchment, 4to. circa sæc. IX
[S]edulii opera, parchment, 8vo. circa sæc. X.
Terentius. parchment, 4to.
[A]lani de Insulis Anticlaudianus, parchment, 8vo.
[R]entale Episcopatus Moraviensis.
Ancient Records of donations for Religious Houses 2 Volumns 4to.

F I N I S.

acquisition indicates the importance of the collection, even forty years after the death of Sir James:

> It being also represented by the Curators of the Library and the Library keeper that there was a curious collectione of manuscripts concerning the publick and priovat affairs of the kingdome collected by Sir James Balfour of Denmilne sometyme King at Arms, and which were to be exposed to sale by his heirs and that a purchase thereof was very proper to enrich their Library, it was thought that the printed catalogue of the samyne manuscripts should be delyvered to each of the Faculty and that free inspectione may be granted to any who desyred to see these books. . . . And haveing heared the opinions and reports of sundry of the members who had taken inspectione and considered the books themselves, they unanimously agreed that the said purchase should be made. And for that effect did nominat and appoint the Dean of Faculty, Mr William Aikman, Mr Charles Gray, Mr William Calderwood, the Curators of the Library, thesaurer and Clerk or any three of them a Committee to consider the value of the saids books, and to take the opinion of Sir James Dalrymple ane of the principall Clerks of Sessione who hes knouledge in the antiquities of the kingdome with pouer to the said Committee to treat and agree with the proprietar of the saids books or any others haveing warrant to sell the same for such a pryce as shall be thought reasonable to be given.

Sir James Balfour's printed books were sold with those of Sir Andrew Balfour in 1699 by the Edinburgh booksellers Andrew Symson and Henry Knox. The printed catalogue, *Catalogus selectissimorum in quavis lingua & facultate librorum, quorum maxima pars pertinebat ad clarissimos fratres D.D. Balfourios, Jacobum, de Kinnaird Equitem, Leonem, Reqem Armorum: et Andream,* sold a combined total of 2,742 lots. The books sold were divided into the following categories: Theology, History, Chronology, Politics, Antiquities, Heraldry, Philology, Philosophy and Mathematics, Law and Politics, Medicine, and Miscellaneous. Also included in the sale were a small group of manuscripts that had not been included in the sale of Sir James's manuscripts the previous year. Many of James's surviving printed books were bound in simple contemporary brown calf, largely undecorated, save for a pair of blind-stamped fillets around the edges. Some books were bound in limp vellum, with silk ties, again normally plain and undecorated, although occasionally they can be found with the Balfour armorial and with Sir James's initials on the front cover.

The presence of Sir Andrew's name on the title page of the 1699 catalogue of his brother's books is puzzling, given that the 1695 sale offered what was in itself a comprehensive library. There are not many books in common between the two catalogues, so it is not the case that Andrew's books failed to find buyers at the first sale and then were offered together with Sir James's books. What is more likely is that as Andrew took custody of his brother's great library after his death in 1657, there were some of his books interspersed with those of his brother, and the appearance of both names on the catalogue indicates either a desire for accuracy on behalf of the auctioneer or possibly a form of advertising, as Andrew's library would have been better known than James's in the 1690s.

Neither James nor Andrew Balfour were bibliophiles in the modern sense of the term. Neither owned large collections of what contemporaries would have described as "fine" books. It is true that Sir James Balfour did acquire several manuscript volumes that were exceptional examples of medieval illumination, most notably the *Bohun Psalter,* but this and other illuminated books were acquired for reasons other than aesthetic enjoyment or ostentatious display. The book-collecting activities of both men were part and parcel of their intellectual life. Both men needed books for their professional activities: Sir James's heraldic collections and Sir Andrew's medical library were both especially significant in Scotland. Both also acquired books to assist their own private researches and interests. In the case of Sir James his collections of materials relating to Scotland's medieval history and literature did connect with some of his professional duties, but the motivation behind such a distinguished collection went clearly beyond the call of duty. Likewise Sir Andrew was not a professional botanist but a physician. Naturally the two disciplines complement each other, but few physicians collected botany on the scale of Balfour, and certainly his collections were unmatched in Scotland. His interests in science were general, and his collections of books on natural history and of natural history specimens mark him out as one of the small group of men who regarded serious collecting as an essential adjunct to their scientific work.

Biography:

Sir Robert Sibbald, *Memoria Balfouriana sive Historia rerum pro Literis promovendis gestarum a clarissimis fratribus Balfouriis DD. Jacobo barone de Kinnaird equite, Leone rege armorum, et DD. Andrea M.D. equite aurato, a R. S., M.D. equite aurato, 1699* (Edinburgh, 1699).

References:

Ian C. Cunningham, "The Manuscript Collections to 1925," in *For the Encouragement of Learning: Scotland's National Library 1689–1989,* edited by Patrick Cadell and Ann Matheson (Edinburgh: HMSO, 1989), pp. 119–138;

Harold R. Fletcher and William H. Brown, *Royal Botanic Garden Edinburgh 1670–1970* (Edinburgh, 1970);

James I, *Letters to King James the Sixth from the Queen, Prince Henry, Prince Charles, the Princess Elizabeth and her husband, Frederick, King of Bohemia, and from their son, Prince Frederick Henry. From the originals in the Library of the Faculty of Advocates* (Edinburgh: Printed by T. Constable, 1835);

J. D. Mackie, *The Denmilne Manuscripts in The National Library of Scotland* (Edinburgh: History Association of Scotland, 1928);

James Maidment, ed., *Letters and State Papers during the Reign of King James the Sixth. Chiefly from the Manuscript Collections of Sir J. Balfour of Denmyln* (Edinburgh: Printed by Edinburgh Printing, 1838);

Manjil V. Matthew, *The History of the Royal Botanic Garden Library Edinburgh* (Edinburgh: HMSO, 1987);

John Macpherson Pinkerton, *The Minute Book of the Faculty of Advocates,* volume 1 (Edinburgh, 1976), pp. 190, 192–194;

J. H. Stevenson, *Heraldry in Scotland,* 2 volumes (Glasgow, 1914);

Sir Anthony Wagner, *Heralds of England: A History of the Office and College of Arms* (London, 1967);

Andrew G. Watson, *The Manuscripts of Henry Savile of Banke* (London, 1969).

William Beckford

(29 September 1760 – 2 May 1844)

Virginia T. Bemis
Ashland University

See also the Beckford entry in *DLB 39: British Novelists, 1660–1800.*

CATALOGUES: *A Catalogue of a Valuable and Elegant Collection of Books . . . Being a portion of the library of a very distinguished collector, brought from his seat in Wiltshire . . . which will be sold by auction, by Leigh and S. Sotheby . . . on Thursday 9th June, 1808, and two following days, at 12 o'clock . . .* (London, 1808);

A Catalogue of a Portion of the Library of William Beckford, esq. Of Fonthill . . . which will be sold by auction, by Mr. Sotheby . . . on Tuesday, May 6, 1817, and two following days, at 12 o'clock . . . (London: Wright & Murphy, 1817);

Valuable Library of Books, in Fonthill Abbey. A catalogue of the magnificent rare, and valuable library, (of 20,000 volumes) . . . which will be sold by auction, by Mr. Phillips, at the abbey, on Tuesday, the 9th of September, 1823, and nine following days, on Friday, the 3rd of October, & four following days, and on Thursday, 23rd October, 1825, & four following days (London, 1823);

A Catalogue of the Costly and Interesting Effects of Fonthill Abbey (London, 1823);

Catalogue of . . . the Beckford Library, removed from Hamilton Palace, which will be sold by auction by Messrs. Sotheby, Wilkinson & Hodge . . . (London: J. Davy & Sons, 1882–1883);

Catalogue of Valuable Books Returned from the Sales of the Beckford & Hamilton Libraries, having been found to be imperfect. Which will be sold by auction by Messrs. Sotheby, Wilkinson, & Hodge . . . on Tuesday, July 8, 1884 (London: Wm. Clowes, 1884).

BOOKS: *Biographical Memoirs of Extraordinary Painters* (London: Printed for J. Robson, 1780);

Dreams, Waking Thoughts and Incidents, in a Series of Letters from Various Parts of Europe, anonymous (London: Printed for J. Johnson & P. Elmsly, 1783);

William Beckford (portrait by John Hoppner; Salford Art Gallery)

Letters and Observations, Written in a Short Tour Through France and Italy. By a Gentleman (Salisbury: Printed by E. Easton, 1786);

An Arabian Tale, from an Unpublished Manuscript, with Notes Critical and Explanatory, translated by Samuel Henley from Beckford's *Vathek* (London: Printed for J. Johnson, 1786; Philadelphia: M. Carey, 1816); republished as *The History of the Caliph Vathek* (London: Sampson Low, Son & Marston, 1868; New York: J. W. Lovell, 1868);

Vathek (Lausanne, Switz.: Isaac Hignou, 1787; London: Clarke, 1815);

A Descriptive Account of the Island of Jamaica (London: T. & J. Egerton, 1790);

Modern Novel Writing; or the Elegant Enthusiast; and Interesting Emotions of Arabella Bloomville: A Rhapsodical Romance; Interspersed with Poetry, as the Right Hon. Lady Harriet Marlow, 2 volumes (London: Printed for G. G. & J. Robinson, 1796; New York: Garland, 1974);

Azemia: A Descriptive and Sentimental Novel, Interspersed with Pieces of Poetry, as Jacquetta Agneta Mariana Jenks, 2 volumes (London: Printed by & for Sampson Low, 1797; New York: Garland, 1974);

The Story of Al Raoui: A Tale from the Arabic (London: C. Whittingham for C. Geisweiler, 1799);

A Dialogue in the Shades (London: J. F. Dove, 1819);

Epitaphs, Some of which have appeared in the Literary Gazette of March and April, 1823 (London: C. Hullmandell, 1825);

Italy; with Sketches of Spain and Portugal, by the Author of Vathek, 2 volumes (London: Bentley, 1834; Philadephia: Key & Biddle, 1834);

Recollections of an Excursion to the Monasteries of Alcobaca and Batalha (London: Bentley, 1835; Philadelphia: Carey, Lea & Blanchard, 1835); republished as *Recollections of an Excursion to the Monasteries of Alcobaca and Batalha, with his Original Journal of 1794,* edited by Alexander (Sussex: Centaur Press, 1972);

The Episodes of Vathek, translated by Sir Frank T. Marzials (London: Swift, 1912; Philadelphia: Lippincott, 1912);

The Travel-Diaries of William Beckford of Fonthill, edited by Guy Chapman (Cambridge: Cambridge University Press, 1928; Boston: Houghton Mifflin, 1928);

The Vision [and] *Liber Veritatis,* edited by Chapman (Cambridge: Cambridge University Press, 1930; New York: Smith, 1930);

The Journal of William Beckford in Portugal and Spain, 1787–1788, edited by Boyd Alexander (London: Hart-Davis, 1954; New York: J. Day, 1955);

The Transient Gleam: A Bouquet of Beckford's Poesy, edited by Devendra P. Varma (Upton, U.K.: Aylesford, 1991);

Vathek and Other Stories: A William Beckford Reader, edited by Malcolm Jack (London: Pickering, 1993).

OTHER: J. C. A. Musaeus, *Popular Tales of the Germans,* translated by Beckford (London: Murray, 1791).

William Beckford, author of the Gothic novel *Vathek* (1787), was an eccentric and enthusiastic collector of books and art. Famous for commissioning the construction of Fonthill Abbey, the most remarkable building of the English Gothic revival, he was also known as a decorator and popularizer of oriental and Gothic styles and as the focus of scandal. The books, paintings, and art objects he owned testify to his well-deserved reputation as a connoisseur.

William Beckford was born 29 September 1760 at the Beckford family home on their Fonthill estate in Wiltshire. His father, William Beckford, was a wealthy and prominent political figure. A large fortune from properties in the West Indies allowed him to cultivate a taste for art and to build a handsome Palladian mansion on the Fonthill estate. The elder Beckford was an alderman of London, twice served as lord mayor of London, and was a radical Member of Parliament for the City of London. Both his enthusiasm for art and his willingness to speak his mind–he once denounced George III to his face in a public speech–were qualities he bequeathed to his son. Beckford's mother, Maria Hamilton, was the daughter of the Hon. George Hamilton and granddaughter of the sixth earl of Abercorn. It was through her that Beckford could claim noble descent and from her that he inherited a hot temper.

Beckford's father died when young William was nine, leaving to him the family fortune, a sum of £1,500,000; the West Indian inheritance, which gave him an annual income of £70,000; and the estate at Fonthill. This inheritance was to lead George Gordon, Lord Byron to refer to Beckford as "England's wealthiest son." His mother, who distrusted schools, had Beckford educated at Fonthill by private tutors. In later life Beckford told the painter Benjamin West that he regretted not having gone to school. At public school he would have learned to "make his way among others, taking the consequences of things as they might happen." Instead, "Incense was offered to him and flowers strewed in his way, wherever he went" and "he had not experienced those checks which are useful." Beckford grew up spoiled, capricious, and extravagant, but he was an apt student and was interested in all things aesthetic and artistic. While not a musical genius, he was gifted and received piano lessons from the young Wolfgang Amadeus Mozart, who at nine years of age was four years older than his pupil. His first tutor, Robert Drysdale, reported that in 1767 Beckford could already speak and read French, having done so since the age of four, and had begun Latin at the age of six.

An important influence on Beckford was his drawing teacher Alexander Cozens, who, born and raised in St. Petersburg, fed the boy's imagination with exotic tales of Russia. Cozens, though actually the child of an English shipbuilder employed by the tsar, was believed by some to be an illegitimate son of Peter the Great. Young Beckford preferred the legend of imperial ances-

Beckford's coat of arms

try, which fit in with his taste for the exotic and sense of his own importance. In addition to drawing and painting, Cozens introduced his student to *The Arabian Nights* and to magic, both of which were to fascinate Beckford throughout his life. He also owed his lifelong fascination with Persia and oriental lore to Cozens.

Disapproving of his exotic tastes and desire to write, Beckford's mother, whom he referred to as "the Begum" because of "her strong tendency to a sort of oriental-like despotism," did her best to convert him into a conventional English gentleman with interests in politics, hunting, shooting, and fishing. She also hoped to instill in him a serious religious attitude and a sober way of life. Her efforts, even when seconded by a new tutor, the Reverend John Lettice, a fellow of Sidney Sussex College, Cambridge, proved fruitless. Beckford absorbed Latin, Greek, and philosophy, particularly the thought of John Locke, from Lettice, but his character and tastes were already formed. By his mid teens Beckford was a self-centered dreamer and aesthete.

Beckford's mother was as prejudiced against universities as she was against schools, so Beckford, accompanied by his tutor, was sent off in 1777 on a Grand Tour. He completed his informal education in Geneva, a city chosen by a council of family and advisers who decided that it was safer than Paris or Rome for a young man whose character needed forming. Beckford passed his time adding Italian, Spanish, and Portuguese to the languages he had already mastered. He also studied law, physics, and the natural sciences, besides reading widely in travel books on China and Arabia and the works of Ludovico Ariosto, Torquato Tasso, and Plutarch.

In Geneva, Beckford wrote "The Long Story" and "Hylas," exotic tales found in fragments among his papers that were published in 1930 under the title *The Vision* [and] *Liber Veritatis.* He also came into contact with many of the leading European intellects, including François Huber, the naturalist, and H. Benedict de Saussure, an early Alpine explorer. A highlight of his sojourn was an audience with Voltaire, who praised his liberal political views. His mother, however, was not pleased with his freethinking contacts, which were reported by the Reverend Lettice.

Returning home in 1778 at his mother's behest, Beckford traveled around England, visiting country houses and beginning to work at translating the Wortley Montagu Arabian manuscripts. He was assisted by his Arabic teacher, an elderly Arab named Zemir, supposedly a native of Mecca. Beckford did not publish any of these translations, but they remained among his papers and testify to several years of effort that helped lay the groundwork for *Vathek.* In 1779, during a stay at Powderham Castle, he met William Courtenay, then eleven years old, and fell deeply in love with the boy he nicknamed "Kitty." The obsessive, romantic passion he carried on through years of letter-writing and diary-keeping was typical of Beckford and earned him the permanent hostility of Courtenay's family. As Robert J. Gemmett observes, "The precise nature of this relationship may be subject to varying interpretations, but there can be little doubt about its disturbing psychological effect."

Written in 1777, Beckford's first publication was the satire *Biographical Memoirs of Extraordinary Painters* (1780), in which he ridiculed the standard biographies of distinguished painters and set forth his preference for the flamboyant and romantic in art. He was ahead of his time as the Romantic movement was just then in its incipient stage. The book shows a sense of humor seldom found in Beckford's other works as he discusses with pseudosolemnity such imaginary worthies as Aldovrandus, Og of Basan, Sucrewasser of Vienna, Watersouchy of Amsterdam, and Blunderbussiana of Venice.

Beckford spent much of 1780 in France, partly to allow scandal to die down, and toured Holland, Germany, Italy, and France. Not only was his infatuation with Courtenay a source of family concern and outside gossip but also he had made matters worse by his involvement with Louisa Beckford, wife of his cousin Peter. As intense as his involvement with Courtenay, this affair had a different character since he could treat Louisa as a confidante and share with her his ideas on art, architecture, and the life of the emotions. His letters to her cover a wide range of topics: what he was writing, what books he was buying, his feelings for Courtenay, and his various emotional crises. While on the Continent, he added to his library and art collection. After his elaborate coming-of-age celebrations, which were held at Fonthill in September 1781 and featured tableaus and theatrics, he had access to his entire fortune to buy books and pictures and to live the flamboyant life that suited him.

About this time Beckford formed a friendship with the Reverend Samuel Henley, an archaeologist, orientalist, writer, and traveler who was then tutor to Beckford's cousins Alexander and Archibald Hamilton. Henley's taste for the exotic and admiration for Beckford's descriptive powers, particularly his Italian letters, may have encouraged Beckford to write *Vathek.* So similar were the two in interests that Henley's *History of Al-Raoui* has often been attributed to Beckford.

In January 1782 Beckford began to write *Vathek.* Although he liked to foster the story that he wrote the book in a three-day and two-night intense spurt of inspiration, it is likely that polishing the manuscript took a good deal longer. His letters from Rome in June of 1782 suggest that he was still working on *Vathek* about six months after his first three-day surge in January. The next book he published, though, was *Dreams, Waking Thoughts and Incidents, in a Series of Letters from Various Parts of Europe* (1783), the authorship of which was suppressed under pressure from his family. Much of this material was published again later in his life in the first volume of the two-volume book *Italy; with Sketches of Spain and Portugal, by the Author of Vathek* (1834). Beckford's travel writings are perhaps his best work, marked by an observant eye, felicitous turn of phrase, and a connoisseur's attitude to landscape and history. His *An Excursion to the Grande Chartreuse in the Year 1778,* privately printed in 1783 but not published until it was included in *Italy,* details his fascination with the gloomy and striking landscape, and the strong impression made on him by the ancient monastic architecture, which he was later to try to re-create at Fonthill.

Beckford married Lady Margaret Gordon, daughter of the earl of Aboyne, on 5 May 1783. His mother had selected her as a suitable daughter-in-law, and Beckford appears to have been sincerely fond of her. They lived mainly in Switzerland and had two daughters, Maria Margaret Elizabeth, born 23 July 1785, and Susan Euphemia, born 14 May 1786.

During a stay in Paris in early 1784 Beckford spent many happy days buying books at the Duc de la Valliere's sale. In a letter to Louisa he remarked that he had "the glorious misfortune" of having to compete with the Emperor and his Christian Majesty for the books he wanted: "Yesterday I bought a rare manuscript in spite of their royal teeth–glittering with gold letters and curious miniatures where amongst other nonsensical figures shine Jupiter and Juno married by a Catholic priest before the image of our Redeemer." Beckford, who knew a rare and desirable book when he saw one, bought many that year. He also displayed intense hostility toward anyone who mishandled his precious books.

Beckford had ambitions to follow his father in a political career and became a Member of Parliament for Wells, a seat his grandfather had once held, in 1784. On an October visit that Beckford and his wife made to Powderham, he was found in young Courtenay's bedroom. The scandal, followed by a press campaign against him orchestrated by Courtenay's family, drove him from England early in 1785 and finished his hopes of political distinction and a peerage. Only his mother and Lady Margaret defended Beckford; his mother suggested that the best way to end the gossip was for Beckford to be seen picking up women in Covent Garden. Biographer Guy Chapman suggests that Beckford did not defend himself or bring libel actions against newspapers because to do so would have meant admitting to anti-Christian practices and oriental magic, a crime which still carried the death penalty in England.

Lady Margaret died of puerperal fever on 7 June 1786, and Beckford never remarried. A family council decided he was an unsuitable parent, and his daughters were taken from him to live in a house on the grounds of Fonthill under the guardianship of Lettice and Beckford's mother. Beckford was ostracized from society, and his hermitlike lifestyle after the death of Lady Margaret, the only person he seems to have truly cared for, was not entirely of his own choosing.

In June 1786 Beckford suffered another blow when Henley published *An Arabian Tale, from an Unpublished Manuscript,* his English translation of Beckford's *Vathek,* without crediting the author. Beckford was angry at Henley for taking such a step without his permission and brought out the original French version, titled *Vathek,* in Lausanne before the end of the year (the title page is dated 1787). Inspired in part by Beckford's reading about Persia and other parts of the Near East, the novel is an Eastern romance, set in an imagined Arabian or Turkish kingdom. Beckford apparently modeled the protagonist, the Caliph Vathek, a blend of human and demon, on Alderman Beckford and himself and used family and friends as models for other characters. Vathek indulges his sensual appetites, pursues the beautiful Nouronihar, faces djinns and genii, and eventually winds up damned to eternal torment in the halls of Eblis.

While it received favorable reviews, *Vathek* was slow to attract the reading public. Nonetheless, it eventually became an influential work. The flavor of the orient in the exotic, mysterious tale influenced many other writers, among them Byron, who wrote of Beckford's work in a footnote to *The Giaour* (1813) that "for correctness of costume, beauty of description, and power of imagination, it far surpasses all European imitations." Other writers who were affected by *Vathek* include Benjamin Disraeli, who consulted Beckford while writing his *Contarini Fleming* (1832), Nathaniel Hawthorne in *The Scarlet Letter* (1850) and some of his shorter works, and George Meredith in *The Saving of Shagpat* (1856). Edgar Allan Poe, Stéphane Mallarmé, and Algernon Charles Swinburne were admirers as well.

After Lady Margaret's death, Beckford traveled in Portugal, Spain, and France. Originally he had planned to visit his properties in Jamaica but found the ship so distasteful and vermin-ridden that he decided on Lisbon as a better and closer destination. He kept a journal that was edited by Boyd Alexander and published as *The Journal of William Beckford in Portugal and Spain, 1787–1788* in 1954. During his lifetime Beckford reworked and published the material in *Italy, with Sketches of Spain and Portugal.* Beckford's description of scenery, architecture, and odd incidents show the keen eye for detail that was making him a successful art collector.

Beckford continued traveling in Europe, amassing pictures and books, with longer sojourns at Fonthill after Lord Courtenay's death, which made a return to England safer. As well as improving the grounds with trees and new vistas, he walled in the park to ensure the privacy he now craved. He retained the seat for Wells until 1790, then was M.P. for Hindon from 1790–1794. He then retired from public life until 1806, when he was re-elected for Hindon and kept the seat until 1820. He made no political mark, preferring to devote his time to art and architecture. He also passed time with his books. In 1791 he anonymously translated the German fairy tales of J. C. A. Musaeus as *Popular Tales of the Germans.*

The worsening political scene in France did not deter him from living in Paris, witnessing the fall of the Bastille and buying up as many books as he could from the libraries of French aristocrats pushed to sell their possessions after the Revolution. Though rich, he had an eye for a bargain, and bargains were to be found. Among the prizes he acquired were specimens of fine bindings by Padeloup and Eve, old manuscripts and illuminations from the libraries of princely families, and a fine selection of furniture, including items from the Louvre palace, as well as paintings and art objects. Among these were a Meissen dinner service made for the Stadtholder William

Admission ticket for the 1822 sale of Beckford's Fonthill estate and its furnishings (Collection of Edmund Esdaile, Esq.)

V and a lacquer box decorated with Japanese scenes that had once belonged to Madame de Pompadour, whom Beckford revered as a connoisseur. As political conditions worsened, Beckford left for the country and a safer life first in Savoy and then in Switzerland, taking with him twenty-four musicians, formerly of the Garde du Roy, to play for him during meals and perform his own compositions.

Little is known of Beckford's movements and activities from November 1792 until May of 1793, though he seems to have returned to Paris, probably to buy pictures. During the Reign of Terror he hid in Paris, helped out by his bookseller, Chardin, and is said to have spent time disguised as a clerk, working in the well-known bookstore Merigot. Since Beckford gave Chardin a pension of 2,400 francs a year for the rest of his life, he apparently felt he owed him a debt of gratitude beyond the typical relationship of bookdealer and client.

While in Lausanne in 1792 Beckford had been insulted by the historian Edward Gibbon, who supported the Courtenays and soundly snubbed anyone who dared to mention Beckford's name. After Gibbon died, leaving a famous library that he wanted to be used by scholars, Beckford had his revenge. In 1796 he bought Gibbon's library to prevent anyone from using it. He visited the collection in 1802 and read its contents for six weeks. He eventually gave the entire collection to his Swiss friend and agent, Dr. Scholl. Buying up the treasures of his enemies was a pleasure Beckford often indulged.

Beckford also took pleasure in writing satire and publishing it either anonymously or under pseudonyms. In 1796 he published *Modern Novel Writing; or the Elegant Enthusiast; and Interesting Emotions of Arabella Bloomville: A Rhapsodical Romance; Interspersed with Poetry,* using the pen name of Right Hon. Lady Harriet Marlow. The book pillories the excesses of contemporary popular fiction, from absurd plots and overblown language to the use of ghosts to the excessive sentimentality of heroines such as Arabella and "the matchless Amelia." In 1797 he published *Azemia: A Descriptive and Sentimental Novel, Interspersed with Pieces of Poetry,* as Miss Jacquetta Agneta Mariana Jenks. In this stirring and entirely improbable tale of a Turkish girl who is captured by the British Navy and has adventures in England, Beckford particularly targets Prime Minister William Pitt but also attacks almost every aspect of the English scene.

After again traveling to Portugal, where he met Byron and wrote the letters later published as *Recollections of an Excursion to the Monasteries of Alcobaca and Batalha* (1835), Beckford settled at Fonthill and soon began an extravagant course of rebuilding on a grand scale. He had his Palladian home razed and began a new building on a Gothic and quasi-monastic plan of his own, hoping to eclipse Horace Walpole's Strawberry Hill in taste and magnificence. Architect James Wyatt exhibited his drawings of Fonthill Abbey in 1796 at the Royal Academy. Fonthill came to be one of the most documented great houses of England. Beckford kept plans, drawings, paintings of the house, and even a wooden scale model. Books were written about the house and its treasures. It influenced many architects of the day, and traces of its design survive in other buildings, though the only remains of the original are a terrace and a few walls.

The outstanding feature of the new Fonthill was an octagonal tower, three hundred feet high, which fell down in a spring gale in 1797, soon after its last stone was placed. Beckford had it replaced with another tower, built with a new type of cement, which lasted until 1825, after he had sold the house and moved to Bath. Contruction at Fonthill continued for years and included extensive improvements in the grounds. Beckford preferred native plants in natural settings, irregular and varied topography and plantings, and disapproved of the ordered gardens of the previous age. The abbey was also notable for its stained-glass windows, including some adapted from those at Batalha Abbey, and a transept with turrets copied from the fourteenth-century monastery of St. Augustine at Canterbury. Among the assorted cloisters and galleries, St. Michael's Gallery housed the library. Beckford kept some of the more precious volumes in an oak cabinet below his sitting room. When Fonthill Abbey was ready for occupancy in 1807 it was hailed as a sublime piece of Gothic design. Even people who disliked Beckford had to admire it as a fit setting for his collections of furniture and art, among which could be found works by Breughel, Rembrandt van Rijn, and Raphael.

Beckford entertained occasionally–he hosted Sir William and Lady Hamilton and Lord Nelson in 1800–but he lived mainly a solitary existence, especially after his 1800–1803 attempts to obtain a peerage were unsuccessful, preferring to devote himself to his book and art collections. Although a wonder of design, Fonthill Abbey was not easy to live in. The chimneys smoked; the rooms were cold; the bedrooms were tiny and cramped. Even Beckford's own apartments were uncomfortable and inconvenient. The only major events during this period of Beckford's life were the marriages of his daughters. Susan Euphemia, his favorite, married her cousin, Alexander Marquess of Douglass, later the duke of Hamilton, on 26 April 1810, and Maria Margaret eloped with Colonel James Orde on 16 May 1811. Beckford found much in common with his noble son-in-law, also a book collector, though he was never able to persuade him to use his influence to get him the peerage for which he had hoped. He never forgave Maria for her elopement, but he did reconcile with her shortly before her death in 1818 and settled a small amount of money on her young daughters.

When Beckford's library was to be sold in 1882, Henry G. Bohn, his bookseller since 1834, described him in a letter to *The Times* (London) as "the greatest book enthusiast I ever knew, who preferred Aldines and other early books bearing insignia of such as Francis I, Henri et Diane [de Poitiers] and de Thou, and especially choice old morocco bindings by Dessueil, Pasdeloup and Derome." Beckford had begun collecting seriously with the Edward Wortley Montagu oriental manuscripts, some of which he bought soon after his twenty-first birthday. By the time he left Fonthill in 1822, he had eight hundred illuminated manuscripts ranging from the ninth to the sixteenth century. His interest in art books also extended to more recent works, such as William Blake's *The Marriage of Heaven and Hell* and *The Book of Thel.*

He was a clever and alert purchaser, often buying through agents so that it would not be known that Beckford was bidding, which might have driven prices beyond what he was willing to pay. He was also one to seize an opportunity and once placed a winning bid on a copy of Jean Froissart's *Chronicles* when the Persian ambassador passed by the auction rooms and most of those present rushed to the window to see him in his splendid robes.

Beckford preferred fine bindings and sometimes had books rebound to his own designs, working with the best binders of the day. From 1787 to 1804, his bookbinder was Christian Samuel Kalthoeber. Then he used several different binders, until settling on Charles Smith in 1815; Charles Lewis was his binder from 1826 to 1836. Lewis was so popular that he had to turn down or delay some of Beckford's orders, but Beckford described him as "the first artist in this line that Europe can boast of. His works alone are worthy to range in the Tower of Lansdown [Beckford's home in Bath] with the Pasdeloup, de Soeil, de Rome, etc."

Beckford worked with booksellers who knew his interests and looked out for special items of antiquarian interest. In England he used first Theophilus Thornton, and after his death in 1796 he used George and William Clarke of New Bond Street. When William Clarke died in 1830, Beckford began to deal mainly with Henry G. Bohn, who helped to catalog his library after his death for the Hamilton Palace sale of 1882. Beckford the bibliophile seldom resisted visiting a bookstore and called at Bohn's shop almost every day during his visits to London. When at Fonthill or in Bath, he was in constant correspondence with Bohn about sales and searches.

Beckford's spending on books and art, coupled with a lack of attention to business affairs, depreciation of the West Indian properties, and a series of unfortunate lawsuits, depleted his resources. He was £145,000 in debt and was losing much of the Jamaican property to his agents, the Wildman brothers, who had filed Chancery suits against him. His dwindling income and continued extravagance forced him to sell Fonthill and much of its contents in 1822. The sale was to be an auction, with a catalogue by Christie's of which 72,000 copies were printed. Public viewings of the house and its contents before the sale drew eager curiosity seekers from all ranks of society. Then, two days before the auction, Beckford sold the entire estate privately. Mr. John Farquhar, a merchant, bought the estate for £330,000; he resold a good deal of the contents the next year in a sale lasting thirty-seven days. Those who saw that sale criticized Beckford for his poor taste, not knowing that he had taken the choicest items, and his library, to Bath. Many of the substandard items were duplicates or even entirely extraneous items added by Phillips, the auctioneer, trying to capitalize on the Beckford reputation for taste. Beckford took advantage of this sale to buy back some of his books for less than he had sold them for originally.

Beckford moved to Bath, where he purchased a house at 20 Lansdown Crescent with a view of the Cotswolds over unspoiled country. He quickly bought the house next door, 1 Lansdown Place, and built a bridge connecting the two, lining the passage with bookcases. When he later sold 1 Lansdown Place, he blocked off the connecting door. His book and art collection proved too large for one house, so he bought 19 Lansdown Crescent in 1837 and altered it to suit his taste. As well as the two adjoining houses, he bought a large tract of land so that he could exercise his fondness for landscape architecture. He again indulged his love of rare plants from the Alps and America, creating a wild landscape that seemed to be entirely natural rather than a planned arrangement.

In *Views of Lansdown Tower,* Edmund English records Beckford's response when he was asked what reconciled him most to his new life:

> Extending his arms and elevating his voice, as if excited by "the poet's fire," he exclaimed, "*This!*–This!–the finest prospect in Europe!" pointing to the vast panoramic view around, to the countless hills near, the far Welsh mountains, the blue fading distance, and then to the most beautiful of our ancient cities, which at that moment slept beneath, enveloped in the rich purple mist of a summer sunset.–"This!" he repeated. Beckford had found a natural picture, a landscape to rival those he had loved in France and Portugal.

The landscape itself became his treasure.

Beckford still had activities to occupy his mind and new projects to undertake. These included achieving his long-standing hope of building a tower that did not fall down. Lansdown Tower, completed in 1828, is still standing. Built in a style best termed Italo-Greek, the tower contained a small residential suite, a set of rooms for art treasures, and a library. The main tower, 130 feet high, rises to a belvedere where Beckford often sat admiring the view and reading, and the whole is topped by a lantern adapted from an Athenian original. The tower was completed up to its originally planned height in twenty-eight days, but Beckford impulsively decided to add the belvedere. Not content with that, he again told his builder, "Higher!" and the lantern was added, bringing the whole edifice to a height of 154 feet. Beckford designed the furniture and did the decorating. *Lansdown Tower* (1844), a volume with color engravings prepared by the auctioneer and art dealer E. F. English, shows what it was like in Beckford's day. Beckford supervised the production of the book before his death.

For the rest of his life Beckford continued to collect books and pictures, never again parting with a book, though occasionally selling some of his art collection. He was an enthusiastic collector of watercolors and drawings

Beckford's "Grecian Library" at 19 Lansdown Crescent in Bath

by such artists as Prout, J. R. Cozens, and Crome the younger, and of contemporary paintings by Gainsborough, Etty, Landseer, and Turner. He bought extensively in old masters, specializing in Italian primitives. Twenty pictures from Beckford's collection are now in the National Gallery.

He also spent much time looking through his papers and the writings he had either put aside or been forced to suppress. In 1824 he brought out a new edition of his youthful satire, *Biographical Memoirs of Extraordinary Painters.* In 1834 he republished the letters his family had made him suppress in 1783 and added his letters and travel diaries from Spain and Portugal to create the critically acclaimed two-volume collection *Italy; with Sketches of Spain and Portugal, by the Author of Vathek.* Beckford followed it in 1835 with *Recollections of an Excursion to the Monasteries of Alcobaca and Batalha,* the last book he published in his lifetime, which was also well received. Other works appeared posthumously. *The Episodes of Vathek,* a translation by Sir Frank T. Marzials of additional episodes Beckford had composed for the novel, appeared in 1912. *The Vision* [and] *Liber Veritatis,* edited by Guy Chapman and published in 1930, combined the youthful work of 1777 with a late manuscript attacking the pretensions of the new aristocracy.

Beckford took good care of his books but did not keep them in systematic order. At the "Grecian Library" at Lansdown Crescent, he carefully kept his books out of direct sunlight and forbade oil lamps, lest smuts and stains mar the books. His bookcases were open for ventilation, with brass wire trellises in the doors. Beckford also had the temperature and dryness in his library controlled as strictly as possible, thus doing his best to fight two of the greatest enemies of the collector, damp and mold. He apparently did not shelve his books according to a system. Both Fonthill and Lansdown Terrace were filled with books, piled everywhere, on tables and on the floor, with no order discernible by an outsider. Yet, Beckford seemed to know exactly where any book was and would "flit across the room and pounce upon it accurately like a bird of prey." Apparently a speed-reader, he read almost every book he owned, and John Britton tells of him finishing an octavo volume during breakfast.

Beckford's collection included works by Giovanni Boccaccio and Torquato Tasso bound for Marguerite de Valois, Pierre Corneille's *Rodogune* from Mme. de Pompadour's library, accounts of the voyages of Captain James Cook, and *Coryats Crudities* (1611), inscribed by Thomas Coryate. He had books owned by or associated with Louis XIII, James I, Cosimo de Medici, the Duc de Richelieu, the Duc de Montmorency, Henry III, and Henry IV. He also had an extensive gathering of contemporary poetry and novels.

In 1842 Beckford was much interested in the sale of Walpole's library and effects at Strawberry Hill. Walpole and Beckford had never been friends, and Walpole had, in fact, tried to leave his treasures in such a way that Beckford could not buy any of them. Beckford, however, had outlived Walpole's direct heirs and could not be prevented from bidding at a public sale. Beckford was dissatisfied with the first sale catalogue and with the publicity intended to drive up the prices, decrying what he called "the egregious follies committed at this High Puff sale." Still, with the assistance of book dealer H. G. Bohn, he purchased many books and manuscripts. Bohn spent three days at Strawberry Hill looking at the collection before the sale and establishing prices as a basis for bidding on the lots Beckford was interested in. He also checked the condition of each lot and item, since Beckford was not interested in anything he considered a flawed work.

Beckford died on 2 May 1844 of a severe attack of influenza. His original resting place was in Lyncombe Vale Cemetery, since the tower grounds were not consecrated. Beckford left his books and art to his daughter, the duchess of Hamilton. At the time of his death Beckford owned 9,837 books, most of which were from the sixteenth to eighteenth centuries. His taste ranged widely. He had volumes dealing with witchcraft, magic, and demonology. He also focused on the Greek and Latin classics, architecture, painting, and poetry. In 1844 Henry Bohn valued the library at £30,000. The duchess moved the art and the library to Hamilton Palace and the house, the tower, and the rest of the contents were sold in 1845 in a sale lasting six days. In 1848 his daughter repurchased Lansdown Tower and some of its grounds, gave the land to Walcot parish as a cemetery, and had Beckford entombed there, in a pink granite tomb he designed himself, with bronze plaques bearing his coat of arms. He is buried near the tower and the grave of Tiny, his favorite spaniel.

Beckford's library remained in Hamilton Palace until 1882, when the duchess's grandson had it sold at Sotheby's. The contents of Beckford's library are chiefly known through the catalogue of the 1882 Hamilton Palace sale. The library was eagerly sought by collectors and brought in £73,551. Many of the books show annotations and marginalia in Beckford's hand. As one might expect, his remarks are often caustic, malicious, and entertaining. Books with his annotations are more valued by collectors than those without, and the notes also provide a most useful overview of his literary standards and personal dislikes.

A few of Beckford's custom bound rare books

Few of his contemporaries escape unscathed, and most come in for acid criticism. Byron, John Keats, and Percy Bysshe Shelley are all denounced. Blake's "Tyger, Tyger burning bright" is "trash, stolen from the walls of Bedlam." Mary Shelley's *Frankenstein* is "the foulest toadstool that has yet sprung up from the reeking dunghill of the present time." Reading the words of the archaeologist who excavated the pyramids at Gizeh, Beckford comments, "the thirstiest desert is not drier than Colonel Vyse's narrative."

The "Caliph of Fonthill" did leave an impact on English history and culture. His careful selection of books, enthusiasm for art, and unwillingness to go along with accepted canons of taste were his legacies to the world of art and letters. As a writer, he remains a minor, though interesting, figure. He undoubtedly would be mightily surprised to find *Vathek* bound together with Walpole's *The Castle of Otranto* (1764) in a standard collection of Gothic tales. His true contribution to the world was as a collector, for he saved books and art from damage and outright destruction, whether by climate or revolution, and made it possible for others to admire genius as he had done. The mere association with Beckford made items once his more valued by collectors, and this in turn helped art survive. His patronage of artists of the day, from Blake to Turner, shows that he was no backward-looking amasser of things simply because of their aura of antiquity. His appreciation of Blake put Beckford almost a century ahead of literary scholars and in company with those contemporaries who recognized Blake's engravings as works of genius. In art and in music Beckford was ahead of his time, able to appreciate the new not for novelty alone but for quality. His love of the shocking coupled with his trained eye for the finest work made him an influential critic.

Beckford's Fonthill Abbey is in ruins and his art and book collections are dispersed, but his legacy remains. All who study medieval manuscripts and Italian old masters or any of the other areas in which he collected have much for which to thank him. Had he succeeded in politics, he could have been little more than a minor figure, but through collecting he made a valuable contribution to the common store of culture.

Letters:

Lewis Melville, *The Life and Letters of William Beckford of Fonthill* (London: Heinemann, 1910);

Life at Fonthill, 1807–1822, with Interludes in Paris and London, translated and edited by Boyd Alexander (London: Hart-Davis, 1957).

Bibliographies:

Guy Chapman and John Hodgkin, *A Bibliography of William Beckford of Fonthill* (London: Constable, 1930);

Robert J. Gemmett, "An Annotated Checklist of the Works of William Beckford," *Papers of the Bibliographical Society of America,* 61 (Fall 1967): 243–258;

Gemmett, "William Beckford: Bibliographical Addenda," *Bulletin of Bibliography,* 25, no. 3 (1967): 62–64;

Dan J. McNutt, *The Eighteenth-Century Gothic Novel: An Annotated Bibliography of Criticism and Selected Texts* (New York & London: Garland, 1975), pp. 265–310.

Biographies:

Cyrus Redding, *Memoirs of William Beckford of Fonthill,* 2 volumes (London: Skeet, 1859);

J. W. Oliver, *The Life of William Beckford* (London: Oxford University Press, 1932);

Brian Fothergill, *Beckford of Fonthill* (London & Boston: Faber & Faber, 1979).

References:

Boyd Alexander, *England's Wealthiest Son: A Study of William Beckford* (London: Centaur Press, 1962);

Guy Chapman, *Beckford* (New York: Scribners, 1937; London: Hart-Davis, 1952);

James Lees-Milne, *William Beckford* (Montclair, N.J.: Allanheld, Osmun, 1979).

Papers:

The largest collection of William Beckford's unpublished manuscripts is owned by B. H. Blackwell of Oxford. Other important collections of Beckford's papers are at the Yale University Library, the British Library, and the Victoria and Albert Museum.

Sir Thomas Bodley

(2 March 1545 – 28 January 1613)

K. A. Manley

Institute of Historical Research, University of London

CATALOGUE: Thomas James, *Catalogvs librorvm bibliothecae pvblicae qvam . . . Thomas Bodlevcs eques auratus in Academia Oxoniensi nuper instituit: continet autem libros alphabetice dispositos secundum quatuor facultates: cvm qvadrvplici elencho expositorum e. ecripturae, Aristotelis, juris vtriusq[ue] [et?] principum medicinae, ad vsum alinae Academiae Oxoniensis* (Oxford: Josephum Barnesium, 1605); republished as *The First Printed Catalogue of the Bodleian Library 1605: A Facsimile: Catalogus librorum bibliothecae publicae quam vir ornatissimus Thomas Bodleius eques auratus in Academia Oxoniensi nuper instituit* (Oxford: Clarendon Press, 1986).

BOOKS: *The Life of Sir Thomas Bodley, the Honourable Founder of the Publick Library in the University of Oxford. Written by Himself* (Oxford: Printed by Henry Hall, printer to the University, 1647);

Reliquœ Bodleianœ; or, Some Genuine Remains of Sir Thomas Bodley. Containing his Life, the First Draught of the Statutes of the Publick Library at Oxford, (in English) and a Collection of Letters to Dr. James, &c., edited by Thomas Hearne (London: John Hartley, 1703).

Thomas Bodley, 1598 (portrait by Nicholas Hilliard; Bodleian Library, Oxford)

The name of Sir Thomas Bodley remains one of the best known in British library history, thanks entirely to his founding one of the greatest libraries in England, which by royal decree will always bear his name. The Bodleian Library in the University of Oxford was established in 1598 and, owing to Bodley's connections and enthusiasm, rapidly built up its stock of books to become the most significant "public" library available to scholars in England. The securing of the right of legal deposit of new books, which was promoted by Bodley though not originally his idea, was the key to the early importance and fame of the library.

In his own time Bodley was well known as a diplomat and spent several years in the Low Countries, though he eventually found this to be a fruitless and unsatisfactory calling. By training he was a Hebrew scholar, and his endowment in his retirement of the means of academic study in Oxford, where lay a significant part of his own personal educational roots, was a fitting legacy. Much of what is known of his life and career stems from his own autobiography, *The Life of Sir Thomas Bodley, the Honourable Founder of the Publick Library in the University of Oxford* (1647). Although brief and lacking excitement, *The Life of Sir Thomas Bodley* deserves consideration in its own right because it represents virtually the earliest published work in England of autobiographical writing of its kind, the classic *apologia pro vita*.

Bodley was born in Exeter, Devon, on 2 March 1545; his parents were both members of well-established, wealthy Devonshire families. His mother, Joan, was the heiress of Robert Hone, a rich merchant from Ottery St. Mary. She and her four sisters all married well, one of her brothers-in-law being a member of Par-

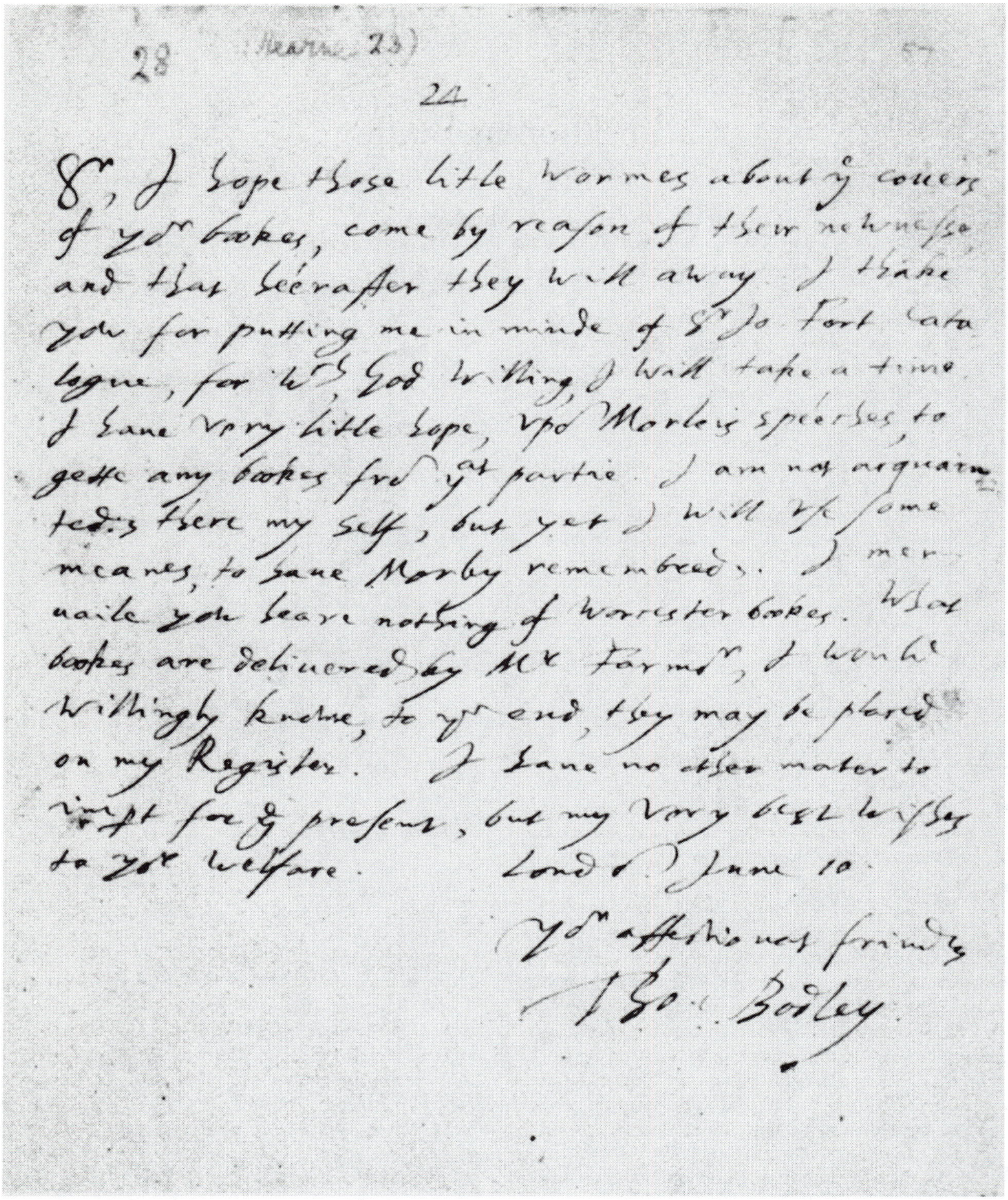

28 (Hearne 23) 57

24

Sr, I hope those litle wormes about ye couers of yor bookes, come by reason of their newnesse and that heerafter they will away. I thanke you for putting me in minde of Sr Jo. Fort. Cata logue, for wch, God willing, I will take a time. I haue very litle hope, vpon Morleis speeches, to gette any bookes from yt partie. I am not acquain ted there my self, but yet I will vse some meanes, to haue Morley remembred. I mer uaile you heare nothing of Worcester bookes. What bookes are deliuered by Mr Farmor, I would willingly knowe, to yt end, they may be placed on my Register. I haue no other mater to write for ye present, but my very best wishes to yor welfare. London June 10.

Yor affectionat frinde,

Tho. Bodley.

A 10 June 1602 letter from Bodley to Thomas James, keeper of the Bodleian Library, one of more than two hundred extant letters that Bodley wrote to James regarding the care of the collection (Bodleian Library, Oxford)

liament for Exeter. Thomas's father, John, also came from Exeter, and many members of the Bodley (or Bodleigh) family were to be found in this part of the county. (The *Dictionary of National Biography* errs in referring to the Bodleys as being descended from an "ancient family" of the village of Dunscombe; the latter were a different branch of his family.) Among Thomas's five younger brothers, Laurence studied at Oxford, became a minister in Devon and a canon of Exeter Cathedral, and was awarded the degree of doctor of divinity. His connection to Exeter Cathedral presumably accounts for the donation by the Exeter dean and chapter of many of their manuscripts to the newly founded Bodleian Library in 1602. Thomas's brother Josias served as a soldier in Poland and the Low Countries before crossing to Ireland in 1598. He was subsequently knighted. There were also six sisters, about whom little is recorded.

It is clear that the Bodley family was well connected and prominent in Exeter affairs during a particularly troublesome time in its history. In 1549 the city was under siege from rebels who objected to the efforts being made in the name of the boy king, Edward VI, to ban Catholic masses. Troops sent by the king only succeeded in lifting the siege after receiving a substantial sum of money from three wealthy Protestant merchants, namely John Bodley and two of his relations. In 1553 the Catholic Queen Mary ascended the throne, and as other so-called heretics were being burnt at the stake, John Bodley found it prudent to absent himself from the country. He traveled first to Wesel in Germany, where his friend, Miles Coverdale, bishop of Exeter, had already fled. He was joined there by most of his family, including Thomas, but they soon moved to Frankfurt to join a small congregation of like-minded exiles. Even in this community there was religious dissension, and in 1557 the Bodley family moved to Geneva, where a much larger colony of English exiles had gathered under the guidance of John Calvin.

At Geneva, John Bodley found there was no outlet for him as a merchant, and he turned to printing instead. A translation of the Bible was undertaken by several members of the English congregation, and it was for his part in printing the so-called Geneva Bible that Bodley's name became known. When the death of Queen Mary in 1558 led to the return of the exiles to England, Bodley settled in the city of London and was subsequently admitted to the Drapers' company. In 1561 Queen Elizabeth granted Bodley a royal patent to print the work for seven years. He became extremely wealthy and on his death in 1591 left his eldest son, Thomas, the huge sum of £1,000.

Young Thomas Bodley acquired his first taste for learning and classical scholarship in Geneva at the age of twelve. He studied Hebrew under the distinguished Antoine Chevalier and divinity under Calvin and Théodore de Bèze. He also studied Greek with Mathieu Beroard and read Homer privately under Robert Constantin. In 1560 Bodley entered Magdalen College, Oxford, and studied under Laurence Humphrey, a friend of his father and also an exile during the reign of Mary Tudor. After graduating with a bachelor of arts degree in 1563, Bodley moved to Merton College, becoming a fellow in 1564 and subsequently holding the university posts of proctor and deputy public orator. He took the degree of master of arts in 1566 and delivered lectures on Greek and natural philosophy.

Bodley continued to study Hebrew, his particular interest, chiefly with his friend and fellow pupil of Chevalier, Johann Drusius (Jean van der Driesche), who later became professor of oriental languages at Oxford. Merton College led the way at Oxford by promoting the study of newer subjects, including Hebrew, over the traditional divinity, law, and medicine. Although Bodley did not become a distinguished Hebraist, his study of the subject was crucial in his later determining that the Bodleian Library should act as an encouragement to all academic studies. In 1573 he did contribute an interesting poem in Hebrew to a memorial volume dedicated to Bishop John Jewel, showing that his talents in that respect were significant and unusual for the period.

Bodley was not content with a purely academic life, and in 1576 he set out abroad, spending four years traveling in France, Italy, and Germany, and studied those languages as well as Spanish. Apparently resolved on a public career, he returned to England and became gentleman usher to Queen Elizabeth I. He stood unsuccessfully for Parliament in 1584 but later in that year served as member of Parliament for Plymouth; he also served as a representative for St. Germans, Cornwall, in 1586, though there is no evidence that he took an active part in parliamentary affairs. In 1585 he was commissioned to undertake a diplomatic service to Denmark and then among the Protestant principalities of northern Germany with the intention of forging an alliance between them and England to assist Henry, king of Navarre (the future Henry IV of France), and the French Huguenots. He subsequently undertook a secret mission to France, completely unaccompanied, to the unpopular Catholic King Henry III, who was assassinated in the following year.

Bodley's most significant diplomatic role commenced in 1589 when he arrived as Queen Elizabeth's representative in Holland, or as then known, the United Provinces. The Protestant United Provinces were seen as a counter to the expansionist activities of Catholic Spain, especially important considering the

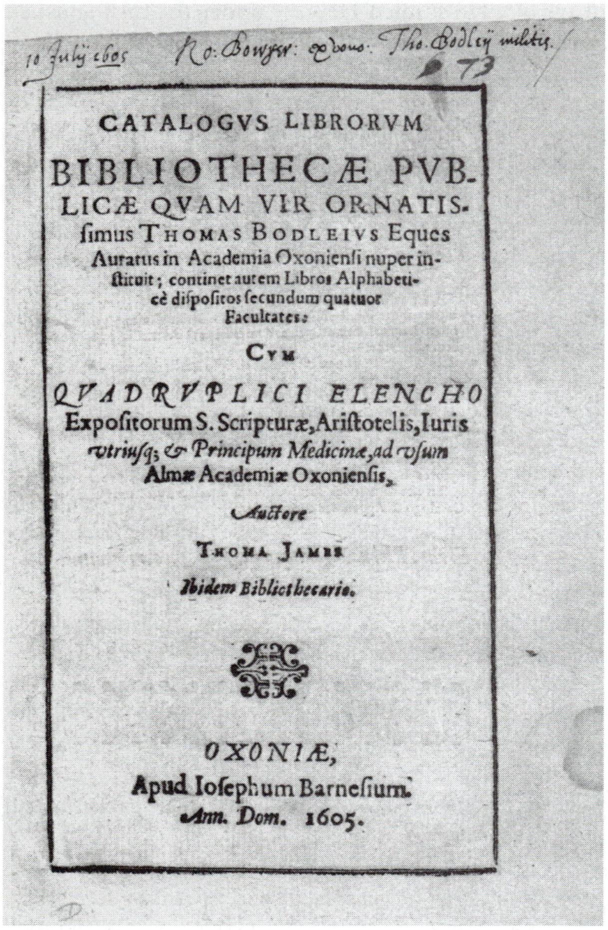
CATALOGVS LIBRORVM
BIBLIOTHECÆ PVB-
LICÆ QVAM VIR ORNATIS-
simus THOMAS BODLEIVS Eques
Auratus in Academia Oxoniensi nuper in-
stituit; continet autem Libros Alphabeti-
cè dispositos secundum quatuor
Facultates:
CVM
QVADRVPLICI ELENCHO
Expositorum S. Scripturæ, Aristotelis, Iuris
utriusq; & Principum Medicinæ, ad usum
Almæ Academiæ Oxoniensis,
Auctore
THOMA JAMES
Ibidem Bibliothecario.
OXONIÆ,
Apud Iosephum Barnesium.
Ann. Dom. 1605.

Title page for the first catalogue of the Bodleian Library, one of the earliest general library catalogues (Bodleian Library, Oxford)

dangers posed by the Spanish armada. Under a treaty of 1585 England maintained an army in the United Provinces and was allowed to place representatives on the ruling council of state. The United Provinces, however, were not as united as might be supposed, and there was much fighting by factions who were opposed both to the Spaniards and to the English troops.

Bodley sat with Count Maurice of Nassau and other leaders in The Hague but soon realized the hopelessness of trying to bring so many warring and jealous partners to agreement. The queen was intent on dictating to the United Provinces how they should act, but increasingly the states resented being told what to do while also being expected to pay for the English troops quartered in their country. Bodley recognized that the quarrelsome states were unlikely to reach a peace treaty with Spain–Elizabeth's worst fear–and reported to the queen to this effect, but for several years he had the unenviable task of ensuring that the tenuous harmony between the Protestant countries was held together despite factional fighting in the Low Countries and in Elizabeth's own court between William Cecil, Lord Burghley and Robert Devereux, second Earl of Essex. In his autobiography Bodley writes that he acted with "diligence and care . . . for which I received from her Majesty many comfortable Letters of her gracious acceptance." Nevertheless, there came a time when a particular diplomatic ploy by Bodley failed, and it became known that the Queen "wished Mr. Bodley had been hanged" in consequence. During this period of diplomatic service, Bodley married Ann Ball, the wealthy widow of a merchant of Totnes, on 19 July 1586.

Bodley asked to be recalled several times and was at last permitted to give up his ambassadorial tasks in 1596. Although he was favored by Lord Burghley for the post of secretary of state, Bodley desired a family life and steadfastly refused to undertake public office again:

> I resolved thereupon to possesse my soule in peace all the residue of may daies, to take my full farewell of State imployments, to satisfie my mind with that mediocrity of worldly living that I had of my owne, and so to retire me from the Court.

Renting a house near Smithfield in London, Bodley had a comfortable income and was in a position to use his wealth for causes close to his heart. He made the decision, as he writes in his autobiography,

> to set up my Staffe at the Library doore in Oxford; being thoroughly perswaded, that in my solitude and surcease from the Common-wealth affaires, I could not busy my selfe to better purpose, than by reducing that place (which then in every part lay ruined and wast) to the publique use of Students.

The original university library, famously augmented by Humphrey, Duke of Gloucester, 150 years earlier, had ceased to exist in the 1550s, apparently due to an excess of puritanism by Edward VI's emissaries, who had dispersed or destroyed all the books.

On 23 February 1598 Bodley wrote to the vice chancellor with an offer to restore the library, "assoone as timber can be gotten" for bookshelves and seats and to assure its continuance. He proposed to provide an income from rents of property "to be disboursed every yere in buing of bookes, in officers stipends," in the "preservation of the place, and of the furniture of it." As he modestly explained, he hoped that his planned library might "perhaps in tyme to come, proue a notable treasure for the multitude of volumes: an excellent benefit for the vse and ease of studentes: and a singuler ornament in the Vniuersity." The offer was eagerly accepted.

Bodley immediately ordered the preparation of timber supplied to him by his old college of Merton. The new bookshelves were almost certainly based on designs for the book presses at Merton, whose warden, Sir Henry Savile, Bodley frequently consulted. Bodley was ideally equipped to monitor the progress of his plans, recognizing that what was needed "was some kinde of knowledge, as well in the learned and moderne tongues, as in sundry other sorts of scholasticall literature" allied to "purse-ability" as well as a "great store of honourable friends to further the designe" and "speciall good leisure to follow such a worke."

Once shelves had been erected, Bodley directed his efforts toward persuading his friends and connections to donate books, both printed and manuscript, and money. Robert Devereux, second Earl of Essex; John, Lord Lumley; Sir Robert Sidney; and Sir Walter Ralegh figure prominently among early donors. Essex's gift included books that had been looted from Cadiz, Spain, in 1596. Bodley's brother Laurence persuaded the dean and chapter of Exeter Cathedral to donate many of their manuscripts and books. Major medieval manuscripts were acquired from a variety of sources. The most important acquisitions as well as the names of many of the donors are listed in William D. Macray's *Annals of the Bodleian Library* (1890). Bodley maintained a register of benefactors as an important way of encouraging others to add their names. The larger books were placed on open shelves, though they were chained for security; smaller books were kept in locked cases. The bookcases, erected at right-angles to walls, were arranged to form stalls, with desks for readers on either side of the shelves.

The new library was celebrated even before its opening. As Macray records in *Annals of the Bodleian Library,* the poet Samuel Daniel praised

> this goodly Magazine of witte,
> This Storehouse of the choicest furniture
> The world doth yeelde, heere in this exquisite
> And most rare monument, that doth immure
> The glorious reliques of the best of men.

Bodley did not attend the ceremonial opening on 8 November 1602 of the library, which at the time had two thousand volumes on its shelves. In 1604 he was knighted by King James I, who decreed that thereafter the library would be known by the name of its founder.

At its opening the library comprised what is still known as Duke Humphrey's Library, and the positioning of the furniture and fittings remains largely unchanged since 1602. The Arts End, a large rectangular annex for books that became the entrance to the original library, was added during Bodley's lifetime, and further extensions were begun shortly after his death. In these later additions the bookcases were placed against the walls, rather than jutting out as in Duke Humphrey's Library; it was the earliest example of this shelving practice for a public library in England.

The general overseeing of the library was left to a group of six delegates, who were heads of colleges or friends of the benefactor. As for the day-to-day administration, Bodley presented the university with a fait accompli by employing the young Thomas James as the first keeper of the library, an appointment officially ratified in 1602 at the less than princely salary of £20 per annum. He soon asked for an increase, especially as he found to his dismay that he was expected to work far longer hours than he had anticipated, and in 1602 was grateful to become rector of St. Aldate's, Oxford, for a little extra income. James, "esteemed by some a living library," had already edited several scholarly works, including Richard de Bury's famous bibliophile treatise, *Philobiblion* (1599); he dedicated this edition to Bodley with a fulsome eulogy of the latter and his benefaction. He had previously been employed in cataloguing the manuscripts contained in the college libraries of Oxford and Cambridge, published in his *Ecloga Oxonio-Cantabrigiensis* (1600). He donated to the Bodleian many important manuscripts, which, it was alleged, he had been able to remove from some colleges because of the indifference of their wardens.

It has often been stated that Bodley saw his library as a Protestant weapon against the Catholics, but this view seems a gross exaggeration. Bodley, unusually for his time, was clearly and genuinely interested in collecting books representing all kinds of knowledge, not just those representing one faction. From the start, for example, the Bodleian was pre-eminent as regards Hebrew manuscripts, and he took active steps to acquire books from Spain and the Near East, hardly bastions of the Protestant faith. Indeed, three of the delegates were not just personal friends but also Catholic sympathizers, particularly Thomas Allen, who had influential contacts and who donated many important manuscripts.

The Protestant zeal of Thomas James–an ardent anti-Catholic, the son of Protestants who suffered exile during the reign of Mary Tudor and well known as a pamphleteer–has often wrongly been taken as a reflection of Bodley's views. James's lifetime work was to be a collation of texts of the church fathers to prove that Roman Catholic editors had altered such writings for their own ends. Bodley supported James's efforts in principle, but his realization that the project was a largely wasteful, never-ending exercise in splitting doc-

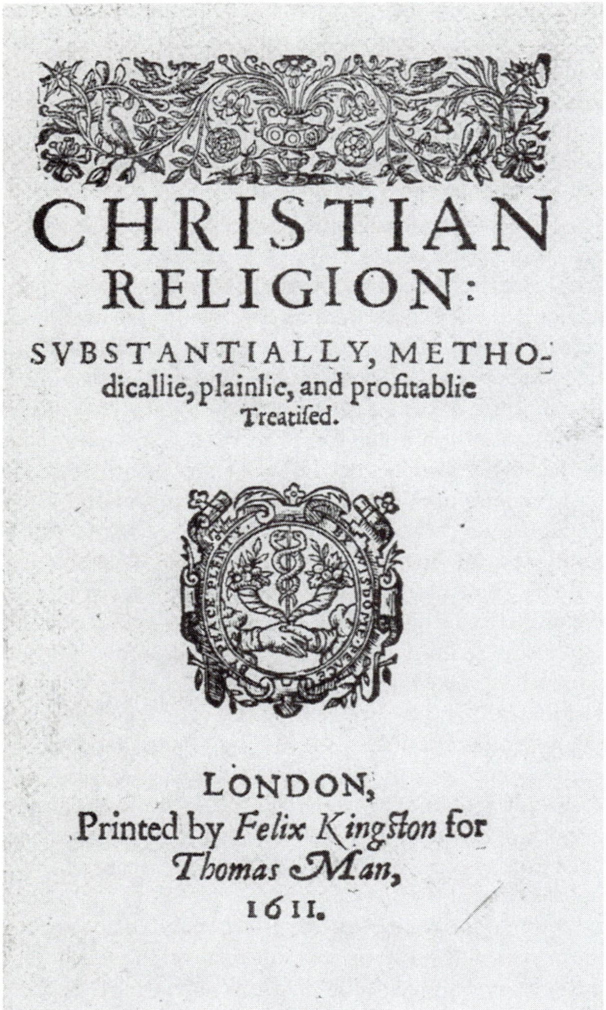

CHRISTIAN
RELIGION:
SVBSTANTIALLY, METHO-
dicallie, plainlie, and profitablie
Treatised.

LONDON,
Printed by *Felix Kingston* for
Thomas Man,
1611.

Title page for the first book deposited at the Bodleian Library as a result of the 12 December 1610 agreement by the Stationers' Company to send newly published works to the library

trinal hairs resulted in some friction between the two men. In 1610, having failed to gain support for his collation project from the university, James received some assistance from the archbishop of Canterbury. The immediate outcome was the publication of James's *A Treatise of the Corruption of Scripture, Councels, and Fathers, by the Prelates of the Church of Rome* (1611), an important work for its time. James retired in 1620 to devote his last years to similar tasks of collation and the publication of further works of "evidence" against the Catholic Church.

Bodley was always concerned about the future needs of scholars; in 1607, for example, he acquired books in Chinese, even though no one then in Oxford could understand them. He did show a reluctance to collect books in English, especially plays, believing them to be of ephemeral interest. He called them "riffe raffe books" and believed they "will but proue a discredit to our Librarie." Regarding Latin as the lingua franca of scholars, Bodley always preferred to buy a Latin text over an English translation. Not even the translation of the Roman historian Tacitus by Bodley's friend Sir Henry Savile was to find its way into the library in Bodley's lifetime. Similarly, he did not acquire many foreign publications in vernacular languages. Many scholars, of course, did not want their work to become available to the vernacular-speaking masses, although, equally, at this period Latin and, to a lesser extent, Greek were the only common languages that educated Europeans could employ to communicate directly with each other.

Although Bodley was far from a professional librarian in the modern sense, he held strong views on how his library was to be conducted. He maintained a constant and detailed correspondence with his librarian; no fewer than 231 letters to James were subsequently collected and printed. Bodley's letters are full of opinions on the relative merits of books, based on his extensive firsthand knowledge. The books themselves usually were collected in London and sent to Oxford on the twice-weekly wagon or occasionally by barge along the River Thames. An agent, John Bill, scoured western Europe for appropriate books; "his commission was large," wrote Bodley in a letter to James, "his leasure very good, and his paiment sure at home." Another bookseller, John Norton, regularly imported books from the Frankfurt book fairs for Bodley.

Bodley drew up statutes for the strict running of the library, "for as much," so he wrote in their first draft "as this Magazine of Books, was founded altogether for the Publick and Perpetual Commodity of Students." The library was to be open for six hours per day, Sundays excepted. James regularly consulted him on even the smallest of details in the regulations, from the mode of cataloguing to be employed down to the "inconuenience of spitting." Only once did Bodley waive his rules for James, and then only with much bad grace, when James announced his wish to marry. Bodley frequently found fault, as when he criticized notices written by James for the bookcases, since "your writing is both ill to be read, and vnderstood, by reason of sundrie letters but half drawen, when your paper taketh not the inke, which causeth obscuritie." Yet, when James in 1607 seemed to hint that he was unhappy with his lot and might resign, Bodley was able to soothe ruffled feathers and assured James that "your neerest frindes and kinfolkes, can neither desire, nor tender your welfare and good contentment, more than my self."

James was responsible for cataloguing the books, a tedious chore for him. The books were arranged in the bookcases according to the four faculties of theology, medicine, law, and arts. The publication in 1605 of the first catalogue, compiled by James and following that order, was a major event despite the omission of many books, probably because of the widespread practice of binding books together to save money. With the possible exception of the catalogue for the Leiden University Library, in the Netherlands, James's catalogue was the first general library catalogue of any comparable "public" library in Europe.

James evidently prepared the catalogue by gathering together the shelflists that he was obliged to affix to the end of each bookcase. The arrangement was alphabetized by author, which Bodley had insisted upon, though James had originally preferred listing the books in title order. Only the barest details of author, title, and place and date of publication were provided. Bodley was particularly upset to find that there were many errors in the printing of the Hebrew entries, and a list of some of the corrections had to be added. Interestingly, the catalogue, though published only weeks before King James visited the library, was dedicated not to the king but to his son and heir, Henry, Prince of Wales, who even at the age of eleven was already seen by many as a future patron of learning.

Macray prints a contemporary account of King James's visit to the library on 30 August 1605 in *Annals of the Bodleian Library:*

> The Bookes that are conteined within this Lybrarie, are verie rare, straunge and scarce, seldome or not at all to be heard of or seene in any place but there. All of them verie richlie guilded, and many of them bossed either with Siluer or Golde.
>
> All these are so fairelie kept and maintained, as if the Goddesse of Wisdome hadde selected and reserued it a Paradice to entertaine the Muses. . . .
>
> This object being presented vnto the sight of his Maiestie, did so sensiblie discouer his delight therewith, that he reported it a most admirable ornament to the Vniuersitie: and gratiouslie promised himselfe, a royal friend and Patron for euer.

Bodley was indefatigable in cultivating benefactors from his extensive network of influential friends, including fellow collectors such as Sir Kenelm Digby and Sir Robert Cotton, and never allowed an offered donation to remain merely an offer, lest the donor should "open the poake when the pigge is presented." The success of his proselytizing on behalf of his own foundation is one of the reasons why he figures so prominently as a benefactor in the annals of library history. One profound disappointment to him was that he could never persuade James I, who had once referred to him as Sir Thomas Godly, to redeem a pledge to donate manuscripts from the Royal Library. Throughout history royal promises have often amounted to little, even one that, like James's promise to Bodley, had been promulgated by a royal decree in November 1605.

Although use of the library was restricted to graduates and members of the House of Lords–who were admitted without question, their honesty being taken for granted–the number of users was steadily rising, including also visiting foreign students. Expansion of the library was soon necessary, both for books and readers, and in 1610 Bodley was able to proceed with the building of the Arts End extension. The cost was high, and Bodley was forced temporarily into financial difficulties; the new building was not completed until late in 1612.

In 1609 Bodley had purchased property in London and Maidenhead, whose rents were made over to the library for its future endowment. Until then he had paid bills directly himself. The most significant endowment was the agreement signed on 12 December 1610 between Bodley and the Stationers' Company, whereby the latter, "out of their zeale to the advancement of learninge," promised to send one perfect copy of every new book printed by their members to the library, though they were allowed to borrow back any such book if a reprint was needed. This contract–actually suggested by Thomas James–predated by half a century the earliest law in the British Isles on legal deposit and proved to be the basis for all future copyright legislation in the country. Bodley wrote to James on 26 February 1611 that the Stationers' agreement was "to be accounted, a gift of good moment: & I thinke I had hardly thought vpon it, if yow had not moued the mater at first: for the effecting whereof, I haue found notwithstanding many rubbes & delaies."

The Stationers' Company, many of whose members did their best to evade their new responsibility, were frequently tardy in supplying books, but an important principle had been established that has been maintained for nearly four hundred years. During Bodley's lifetime the books were delivered to him in London, and there is little doubt that he exercised considerable vetting before forwarding them to Oxford. Although foreign plays and poetry were acquired, Bodley had strong views on the value of English books, the common run of which he held in low esteem. He would not give room to any book or play thought worthless, including the works of his contemporary William Shakespeare.

Bodley's final act was to secure the future physical needs of his library. He wanted to ensure funds to

The Arts End of the Bodleian Library, with globes given by Bodley standing at the entrance to Duke Humphrey's Library (engraving in David Loggan's Oxonia illustrata, *1675)*

restore the buildings of the ruined quadrangle outside the library and to erect a third floor on top of them to provide for a picture gallery. He also specified a new wing to be built at the opposite end of the library to the Arts End. The addition, Selden End, was not completed until 1640. Bodley's statutes for the administration of the library, though drafted in 1602, were not approved by the university convocation until 1610 and not finally ratified until 1613. Only after Bodley's death did the delegates appointed to look after the interests of the library have real power to influence the institution and direct its keeper; until then Bodley kept all power to himself and continued to direct James on every matter of administration, however small.

Sir Thomas Bodley died on 28 January 1613 and was buried in Merton College Chapel on 29 March. The foundation stone of the new quadrangle was laid on the following day, and the new buildings were erected by masons employed by Bodley's old friend Sir Henry Savile. Indeed, the Bodleian tower is similar to Savile's tower at Merton. Bodley, who had left more than £660 to be spent by the college on mourning, was buried with much pomp, and two volumes of celebratory Latin verses were published. In his will Bodley bequeathed £7,000 to the library for the various building projects he had specified, and only minor bequests were made to family, friends, and servants. His wife had died in 1611, and there was considerable criticism of him, especially by his wife's family. As Macray reports, one old friend, John Chamberlain, was enraged that Bodley "was so carried away . . . with vanity and vaion glory of his Library, that he forgat all other respects and duties," though this was rather an exaggeration since he did make many small bequests.

Time has shown that his foundation was destined to become one of the chief repositories of learning in England, truly serving the "republic of letters" in the broadest interpretation of that phrase. The road ahead was not smooth, but Bodley's actions had secured the future of the library. Although the agreement with the Stationers' Company constantly had to be enforced and in some years almost dwindled away to nothing, the contract was probably Bodley's most important achievement. The finances of the library suffered during the century ahead, but the underlying strength of Bodley's endowment ensured that the library was able to continue and expand.

For his own literary memorial, Bodley wrote his autobiography in 1609 when he was in his sixty-fifth year, though it was not published until thirty-four years after his death. Only a little more than fifteen pages in length, the small octavo comprises a straightforward and rather dry account of Bodley's life and public works, dwelling on his diplomatic service, and can be interpreted as both encomium and apologia. Considering that he had forsaken the world of diplomacy through dissatisfaction, especially with the constant court intrigues around him, it is to be expected that a man whose ambition to serve was thwarted after little more than a decade should seek to write a self-justificatory memoir. He portrays himself as an honest, direct, and guileless Englishman, innocent of intrigue and driven by an ideal of public service. *The Life of Sir Thomas Bodley* is a carefully crafted construction of rhetoric rather than literature, yet it attains significance as being one of the earliest autobiographies written in English.

The publication of *The Life of Sir Thomas Bodley* at the press in Oxford in 1647 may have had political overtones. It was published in the period immediately following the first Civil War, when King Charles I had surrendered to the army, and Oxford, formerly a royalist stronghold, was in disarray. Bringing out the memoir of a disappointed diplomat who had been undermined by intrigue and forced out of the public arena might have been intended as a parallel to other events. Otherwise, the printing of Bodley's autobiography at this particular date has to be considered as curious.

A mere two pages of the autobiography are devoted to the Bodleian Library, probably because the great project was still in its infancy and many of his plans had yet to reach fruition. Bodley evidently realized in the conclusion to his autobiography however, that the library, rather than his own words, would stand as his memorial:

> But how well I have sped in all my endeavours, and how full provision I have made for the benefit and ease of all frequenters of the Library, that which I have already performed in sight, that besides which I have given for the maintenance of it, and that which hereafter I purpose to adde, by way of enlargement to that place (for the project is cast, and whether I live or dye it shall be, God willing, put in full execution) will testifie so truly and aboundantly for me, as I need not be the publisher of the dignity and worth of mine owne Institution.

As the philosopher Francis Bacon wrote to his friend Bodley in 1605, "You, having built an ark to save learning from deluge, deserve propriety in any new instrument or engine whereby learning should be improved or advanced." The continued existence of the library that bears his name is tribute enough to the vision of a man who was fortunate to possess the means, the self-regard, and the courage to plan a vast undertaking and live to see it embark on a prosperous course into the future.

Letters:

G. W. Wheeler, ed., *Letters of Sir Thomas Bodley to Thomas James* (Oxford: Clarendon Press, 1926);

Wheeler, ed., *Letters of Sir Thomas Bodley to the University of Oxford 1598–1611* (Oxford: Oxford University Press, 1927).

References:

Donald G. Davis Jr., "Problems in the Life of a University Librarian: Thomas James, 1600–1620," *College and Research Libraries,* 31 (1970): 43–49;

The First Printed Catalogue of the Bodleian Library 1605 (Oxford: Clarendon Press, 1986);

Sidney L. Jackson, "Bodley and the Bodleian: Collections, Use and Administration," *Library Quarterly,* 39 (1969): 253–270;

William D. Macray, *Annals of the Bodleian Library, Oxford,* second edition (Oxford: Clarendon Press, 1890), pp. 14–50;

Ian Philip, *The Bodleian Library in the Seventeenth and Eighteenth Centuries* (Oxford: Clarendon Press, 1983);

Cecil Roth, "Sir Thomas Bodley, Hebraist," *Bodleian Library Record,* 7 (1966): 242–251;

Frances B. Troup, "Biography of John Bodley, Father of Sir Thomas Bodley," *Report and Transactions of the Devonshire Association,* 35 (1903): 167–197;

Troup, "The Pedigree of Sir Thomas Bodley," *Report and Transactions of the Devonshire Association,* 35 (1903): 713–745;

R. B. Wernham, "The Mission of Thomas Wilkes to the United Provinces in 1590," in *Studies Presented to Sir Hilary Jenkinson,* edited by J. Conway Davies (London: Oxford University Press, 1957), pp. 423–455;

Warren W. Wooden, "Sir Thomas Bodley's *Life of Himself* (1609) and the Epideictic Strategies of Encomia," *Studies in Philology,* 83 (1986): 62–75.

Papers:

Most of Sir Thomas Bodley's surviving personal papers and letters are in the Bodleian Library, Oxford. Many miscellaneous letters are in the British Library, London.

The Bridgewater Library

Stephen Tabor
William Andrews Clark Memorial Library, UCLA

CATALOGUES: John Payne Collier, *A Catalogue, Bibliographical and Critical, of Early English Literature; Forming a Portion of the Library at Bridgewater House, the Property of the Rt. Hon. Lord Francis Egerton, M.P.*, 2 volumes (London: Thomas Rodd, 1837); republished as *A Bibliographical and Critical Account of the Rarest Books in the English Language, Alphabetically Arranged, which, During the Last Fifty Years, Have Come under Observation of J. Payne Collier, F.S.A.* (2 volumes, London: Joseph Lilly, 1865; 4 volumes, New York: David G. Francis/Scribners, 1866);

Description of the Renowned Library at Bridgewater House, London. The Property of... Earl of Ellesmere... with a Detailed Catalogue . . . Sotheby, Wilkinson & Hodge (London: Dryden Press, J. Davy & Sons, 1916);

Catalogue of Early and Modern English Literature Part VII Selections and Duplicates from the Library of Mr. Henry E. Huntington, sale 1333, 4–6 February 1918 (New York: Anderson Galleries, 1918);

Catalogue of English Literature Including First Issues of Shakespeare's Quartos and the First Edition of Milton's "Comus" from the Library of Mr. Henry E. Huntington, sale 1351, 24–26 April 1918 (New York: Anderson Galleries, 1918);

English Literature from the Library of Henry E. Huntington, sale 1365, 6–7 November 1918 (New York: Anderson Galleries, 1918);

Americana from the Library of Henry E. Huntington, sale 1406, 6 March 1919 (New York: Anderson Galleries, 1919);

English Literature Duplicates and Selections from the Library of Henry E. Huntington (Part Eleven), sale 1460, 28–30 January 1920 (New York: Anderson Galleries, 1920);

Early French Literature Mostly French Drama (from the Bridgewater Library) Early English Literature and Americana Duplicates and Selection from the Library of Henry E. Huntington (Part Twelve), sale 1477, 11–12 March 1920 (New York: Anderson Galleries, 1920);

English Literature Early & Modern Duplicates from the Library of Henry E. Huntington To be Sold by His Order, sale 1884, 2 December 1924 (New York: Anderson Galleries, 1924).

The Bridgewater Library, the oldest large family collection in England to survive intact into modern times, was begun by Sir Thomas Egerton, a high government official under Queen Elizabeth and King James I. Rich in English literature and history, the library was augmented as the Egertons were created successively earls and dukes of Bridgewater and earls of Ellesmere. In 1917 Henry Huntington bought the library, still substantially complete, from the family; it now forms the core of the Elizabethan and early Stuart collection at the Huntington Library in San Marino, California.

The founder of the Bridgewater Library was the illegitimate son of Sir Richard Egerton of Ridley, Cheshire, and Alice Sparke, a maidservant. Thomas Egerton was born in Dodleston, a village south of Chester, circa 1540. The fortune of bastards in Elizabethan England was famously variable. Thomas was lucky enough to be raised in his father's household, and his abilities were recognized early by those in a position to help him advance. A neighbor, Thomas Ravenscroft, is credited with the discovery of the boy's ability and drive. After schooling at home he was sent to Brasenose College, Oxford, in 1556. He left in three years without taking a degree–a common practice for those pursuing a career in public service–and entered Lincoln's Inn to study law.

The administration of English law in this period was in transition. The chancery courts were growing into an independent source of redress, a rival of the common law courts such as the King's Bench and Common Pleas. They had exclusive jurisdiction in matters of mortgage and trust and were a source of appeal from the sometimes excessively rigid application of the common law. Egerton was called to the bar in 1572 and quickly began to establish his name as a lawyer in chancery. He became widely known for his fairness, integrity, and knowledge. It is said that in 1582 Queen Elizabeth heard him plead a case against the Crown and was so impressed that she declared, "By my troth, he shall never plead against me again." He was named solicitor general that year and spent the remainder of his life in service to the Crown.

Early in his career he made something of a specialty of prosecuting or aiding the prosecution of Catholics and religious dissidents, including Edmund Campion, Mary Queen of Scots, and Philip Howard, Earl of Arundel. Honors and advancement followed. He was promoted to attorney general in 1592, knighted the next year, appointed chamberlain for Chester, and raised to the bench as master of the rolls. His greatest triumph under Elizabeth was being named keeper of the privy seal in 1596, the fifth highest officer of state. He approved all charters and patents that required the great seal and gave authority for disbursements from the exchequer. With this position came a seat on the privy council. His most important legal contribution during this period was a codification of the Poor Laws, completed in 1601.

Egerton married Elizabeth Ravenscroft, the daughter of his father's neighbor. By her he had two sons and a daughter. In 1599 he suffered the death of his wife and of his elder son, who was killed in the wars in Ireland under the earl of Essex's command; the younger son, John, survived to found the Bridgewater line. Egerton began to acquire vast tracts of land in the west and southwest of England. He was enabled to do this largely by the fees and land grants he received for his services to the state, but he also had a nose for a good deal.

As he rose in power, Egerton also emerged as a substantial supporter of learning and religion. He was already a benefactor of his alma mater, Brasenose, and in 1610 added the chancellorship of Oxford University to his state duties. As keeper of the privy seal, a position he continued to hold under King James, he had power as the king's deputy to present clergy to benefices worth up to £20 a year; therefore, his help was sought by up-and-coming men of the cloth. Authors looked to him for support in a period when the system of patronage was starting to decline; he became probably the foremost lay patron of his time. Eighty-one authors are known to have benefited from his direct support, and thirteen books by other authors are dedicated to him.

Among Egerton's beneficiaries was William Lambarde, the legal historian, whom he knew from Lincoln's Inn. Lambarde dedicated the second edition of his most famous work, *Eirenarchia* (1588), to Egerton and wrote a personal presentation letter in Egerton's copy. Francis Bacon, whose attainments never came even with his ambitions, rode to such success as he enjoyed in public life largely on Egerton's coattails. In a 10 May 1596 letter to the earl of Essex, Bacon said, "I do find in an extraordinary manner, that his lordship doth succeed my father almost in fatherly care of me, and love towards me." Largely through Egerton's influence Bacon eventually succeeded to the position of attorney general. The Bridgewater collection contains a manuscript of Bacon's *Certeine Considerations Touching the Plantations in Ireland* (1609), probably presented by the author. Other writers whom Egerton supported included Francis Thynne and the poet John Davies of Hereford, who lived with the Egertons for a time and taught penmanship to his children. Sir John Davies (not the Davies of Hereford), crediting Egerton with all characteristics of an ideal chancellor, dedicated *Orchestra or A Poeme of Dauncing* (1596) to him; the presentation copy has a special dedication leaf with a manuscript sonnet. Egerton's son John met John Donne in the Irish wars and recommended him to his father. Donne served as secretary to Sir Thomas from 1597 until 1601, and the family continued its association with him as he rose to the deanship of St. Paul's.

Thomas Egerton, Viscount Brackley (Henry E. Huntington Library and Art Gallery)

Egerton's position placed him near the center of several crucial Elizabethan historical events. He was one of the few eyewitnesses in 1598 when Essex insulted the queen and she boxed his ears. When Essex took up arms, Egerton was one of those briefly detained by him as a hostage. After the rebellion failed, Egerton subordi-

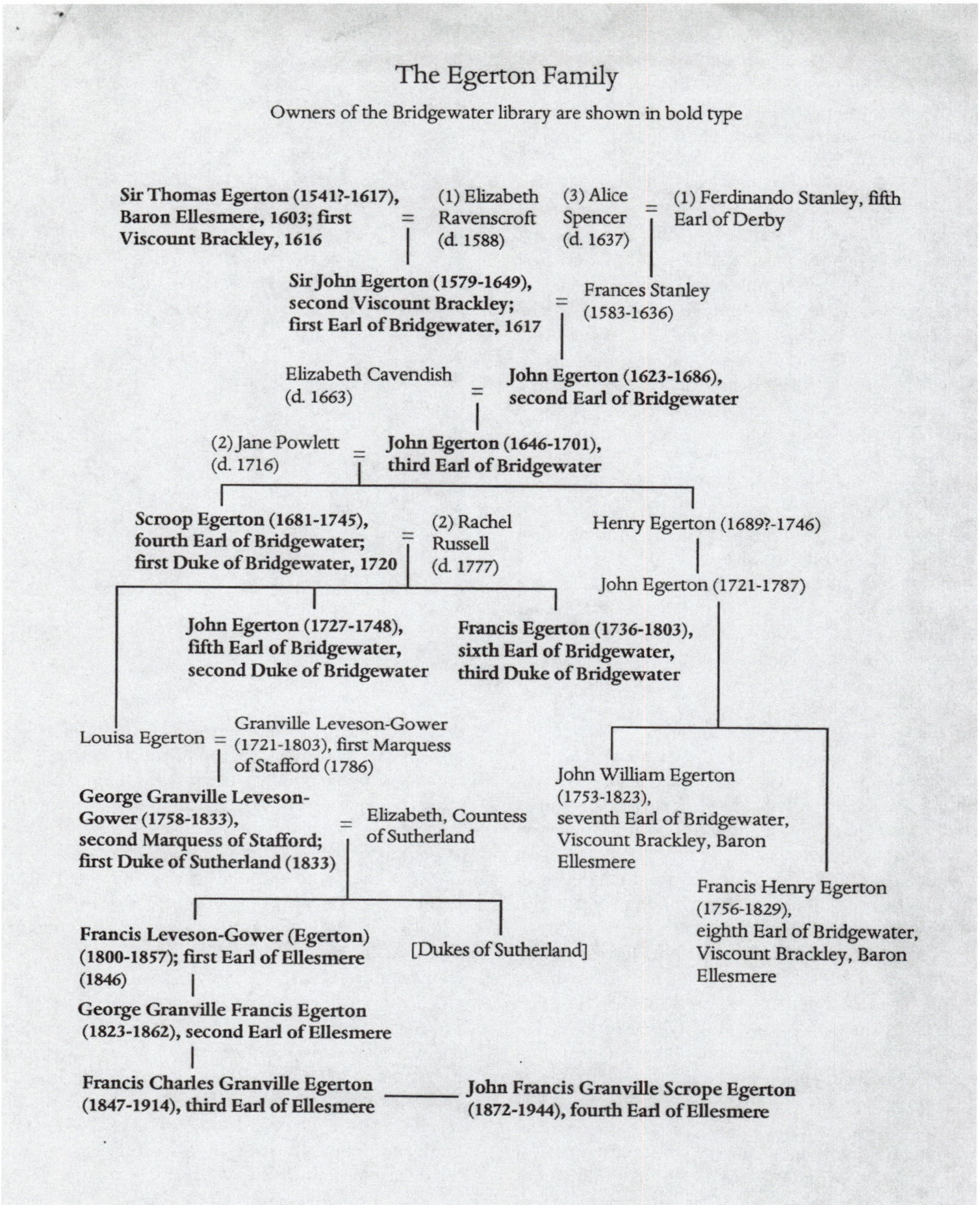

Family tree for the owners of the Bridgewater Library (Stephen Tabor)

nated friendship to duty and took a prominent part against him in the treason trial.

In 1600, after a second marriage again left him a widower, Egerton married Alice Spencer, known as the dowager countess of Derby, the widow of Ferdinando Stanley, Earl of Derby, formerly known as Lord Strange. The countess brought with her some potent literary ties. Her first husband had sponsored one of the most famous Elizabethan theater companies, and his circle included Thomas Nash and Robert Greene. The countess had become a noted patroness with close connections to Edmund Spenser. She was animated, ambitious, strong willed, and came with attractive properties, Derby family manuscripts, and two or three hundred books that augmented Egerton's already noteworthy collection. Ever alert to strategic alliances, she engineered the marriage of her daughter Frances to Egerton's surviving son; thus the stepmother also became the mother-in-law and retained control, if not ownership, of the Derby inheritance.

As Elizabeth lay dying in 1603, it was Egerton who had the task of gently eliciting her wishes as to her successor. When the Crown was settled on James I, Egerton resorted to extremes of flattery to advance his position. James's views of divine right and royal prerogative suited Egerton's temperament and beliefs, and James soon appointed him lord chancellor and made him baron Ellesmere. Egerton took his place as head of the court of star chamber and accumulated further government posts and responsibilities. In 1604 Egerton bought the estate of Ashridge in Little Gaddesden, Hertfordshire, formerly a medieval monastery and college, which served as his primary country home. The purchase netted him some older volumes from the former college. From this western property his lands eventually stretched through the midlands to his principal residence, York House in London.

The new lord chancellor justified James's expectations with his continued good work and loyalty. In his most important judgment, the so-called post-nati case, he ruled that those born in Scotland prior to the Act of Union with England (1607) were subjects of the Crown and therefore able to inherit English estates. This ruling was his only published work. (Several others published posthumously were attributed to him but are probably spurious.) Egerton was uniformly praised by his contemporaries, and authors continued to benefit by his patronage. Ben Jonson wrote three epigrams in his honor; Samuel Daniel wrote him an epistle in verse, and Joshua Sylvester, a sonnet. Francis Bacon dedicated *The Advancement of Learning* (1605) to him. In 1607 John Marston was commissioned to write a masque to honor Egerton's wife, the manuscript of which found its way into the Bridgewater Library.

While marriage with the dowager countess brought its advantages, Egerton soon found that they were incompatible. The Bridgewater papers contain an extraordinary manuscript in his hand, dated 26 August 1610, titled "An unpleasant declaration of things passed between the Countess of Derby and me since our marriage." In it he excoriated her "cursed railing and bitter tongue" as well as her extravagance and greed. "I thank God I never desired long life nor never had less cause to desire it than since this my last marriage, for before I was never acquainted with such tempests and storms." Doubtless an age difference of twenty-one years was partly to blame for this, but also around this time Egerton's health, hearing, and memory began to fail. As early as 1613 he offered to retire, but James would not have it. Honors and success continued to follow him.

One of the jewels of Egerton's library came from a nonliterary source. In 1615 a barrister named William Hakewil presented Egerton with a "traveling library": forty-four small volumes of standard works, all bound in vellum, in a wooden case small enough to be carried by one person. Egerton, then in his mid seventies, was not in a position to make much use of it, and it was kept in fine condition. As a survival of an extremely rare type, it is now kept by the Huntington Library in a bombproof vault along with its greatest treasures.

The competition between the common law courts and chancery reached a crisis in 1616 when Egerton went head to head with Sir Edward Coke, the great advocate of the common law and chief justice of the Court of King's Bench. On the force of a legal opinion cowritten by Bacon and Egerton, King James and the privy council made a declaration affirming the supremacy of the chancellor's decree. Coke was removed as chief justice; Egerton was created viscount Brackley, which supporters of Coke pronounced "Break-law." His energy, however, was spent, and James finally allowed him to retire as lord chancellor in 1617. Physical dissolution followed rapidly. Bacon and Lord Buckingham came to him with a message of comfort from James, with the promise of an earldom and a pension of £3,000 a year, but Egerton shook his head, saying that "all these things were to him but vanities," and died shortly afterward on 15 March 1617.

Egerton left a chancery both strengthened and streamlined and a family rich in money and property. It is difficult to estimate the extent of his library at his death, for it was much augmented by his heirs,

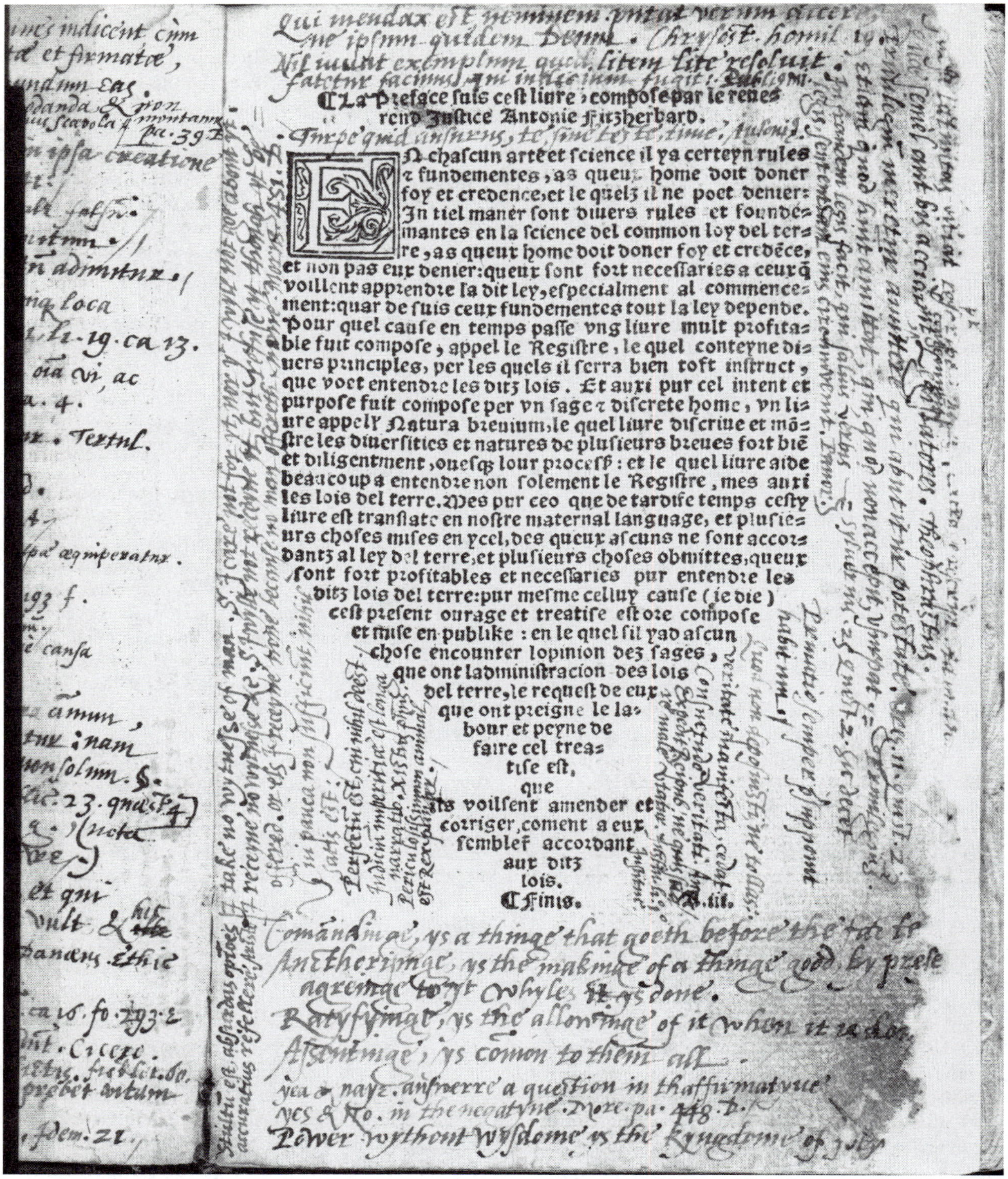

La Preface suis cest liure, compose par le reuerend Justice Antonie Fitzherbard.

En chascun arte et science il ya certeyn rules et fundementes, as queux home doit doner foy et credence, et le quelz il ne poet denier: In tiel maner sont diuers rules et foundemantes en la science del common loy del terre, as queux home doit doner foy et credece, et non pas eux denier: queux sont fort necessaries a ceux que voillent apprendre la dit ley, especialment al commencement: quar de suis ceux fundementes tout la ley depende. Pour quel cause en temps passe vng liure mult profitable fuit compose, appel le Registre, le quel conteyne diuers principles, per les quels il serra bien toft instruct, que voet entendre les ditz lois. Et auxi pur cel intent et purpose fuit compose per vn sage et discrete home, vn liure appelle Natura breuium, le quel liure discriue et monstre les diuersities et natures de plusieurs breues fort bien et diligentment, ouesque lour process: et le quel liure aide beaucoup a entendre non solement le Registre, mes auxi les lois del terre. Mes pur ceo que de tardife temps cesty liure est translate en nostre maternal language, et plusieurs choses mises en ycel, des queux ascuns ne sont accordantz al ley del terre, et plusieurs choses obmittes, queux sont fort profitables et necessaries pur entendre les ditz lois del terre: pur mesme celluy cause (ie die) cest present ourage et treatise est ore compose et mise en publike: en le quel sil yad ascun chose encounter lopinion dez sages, que ont ladministracion des lois del terre, le request de eux que ont preigne le labour et peyne de faire cel treatise est, que ils voilsent amender et corriger, coment a eux semblet accordant aux ditz lois.

Finis.

Thomas Egerton's notes on a page from the 1553 edition of Anthony Fitzherbert's La nouelle natura breuiu *(Henry E. Huntington Library and Art Gallery)* but in a period when large personal collections numbered in the hundreds of volumes, Egerton's could certainly be counted as significant. By the quality of its contents, his library was the equal of any in England.

Born in 1579, Egerton's son John gained his knighthood in the same Irish wars in which his brother was killed, and he succeeded the latter as baron of the exchequer of Chester. Under the pseudonym "J.E." he may have written *Letter from a Souldier of Good Place in Ireland, to His Friend in London* (1602). He was elected member of Parliament for Shropshire in 1601, and when James I acceded in 1603, he was named knight of the Order of the Bath on the strength of his father's position. As the stepson and son-in-law of the imperious countess, Sir John bore the brunt of her personality along with his father. The harried lord chancellor found it necessary to draft "Some notes and remembrances for preserving the continuing of quietness between my wife and my son after my death." Sir John's family at first lived chiefly at Ashridge, two hours' fast drive from the countess's seat at Harefield, but from around 1617 they also had a house in Aldersgate Street in the Barbican, London, then a fashionable neighborhood.

Sir John succeeded his father as viscount Brackley in 1617. Thanks to King James's regard for his father and a £20,000 bribe to the duke of Buckingham he was soon created earl of Bridgewater (actually "Bridgwater," a spelling seldom used). Around this time he became a member of the council of Wales, and after fourteen years he became its president, which amounted to the viceroyalty of Wales. Sir Henry Chauncy, quoted in *The Historical Antiquities of Hertfordshire* (1826), described the earl: "He was a person of middling stature, somewhat corpulent, had black hair, a round visage adorn'd with a modest and grave aspect, a sweet and pleasant countenance, a comely presence, and allowed free access to all persons who had any concerns with him; he was a learned man."

The first earl of Bridgewater was even more of a bibliophile than his father, though not as active as a patron. John Vicars dedicated *Babels Balm* (1624), his translation of George Goodwin's *Melissa religionis pontificiae,* to him; and Robert Codrington, the translator of Seneca's *Ad Marciam* (1635), had a special dedication leaf printed for the earl's copy. John Donne preached at solemn occasions celebrated by the family. The earl continued to augment his father's library with books both new and rare. His bold signature "JBridgewater" appears at the foot of many title pages. The first surviving inventory of a portion of the library dates from this time: "A catalogue of my Ladies Bookes at London, taken October 27th 1627," with more entries added in 1631 and 1632. The manuscript lists more than two hundred titles. Probably before 1620 either the earl or his father acquired the finest item in the collection, a manuscript of Geoffrey Chaucer's *Canterbury Tales* written within a decade or so of the author's death and considered the most reliable as well as the most beautifully illustrated text of that work. It is, arguably, the most important English manuscript in existence.

The earl played an important role in launching the literary career of John Milton, though it is not certain that the two men ever actually met. The countess, having buried two husbands and seen her three daughters each married to an earl, was now a revered matriarch. In the early 1630s it was decided to have a masque performed in her honor, the music to be written by Henry Lawes, who had taught music to the Egerton children. Lawes selected Milton to write the words for the few songs, titled *Arcades.* Performed probably in 1632 or 1633 with the earl's children in some of the roles, it brought "Spenser and Milton picturesquely together within one length of Time's outstretched hand," in the words of David Masson in his edition of Milton's *Poetical Works* (1874).

When the earl of Bridgewater was to be officially installed as president of the council of Wales a year or two later, another masque, with extensive spoken parts, was written by Lawes and Milton. Later titled *Comus, a Maske Presented at Ludlow Castle, 1634: on Michaelmasse night, before the Right Honorable John Earl of Bridgewater, Lord President of Wales* after it was first published without a title in 1637, the work is regarded as Milton's first mature poetical work and his first masterpiece. A legend has grown up that the plot was based on an actual incident in which the Bridgewater children were benighted in the forest of Heywood while returning from a visit to relatives. It is more certain that at least three of the earl's many children took roles in the scaled-down version first performed. When the full work was published, Lawes dedicated it to the future second earl; the Bridgewater copy has manuscript corrections, possibly in Milton's hand.

The general breakdown of order attending the onset of the civil wars rendered the earl of Bridgewater's governorship of Wales increasingly ineffectual. When he turned down a loan request from Charles I, the king relieved him of his office. He spent the remainder of his life mostly in retirement at Ashridge, where at least part of the library was then housed. In 1643 Royalist troops broke into and vandalized the home while he was away; however, the library, much of which was shelved in a semihidden room, was spared. Bridgewater died 4 December 1649 and was buried in the church at Little Gaddesden.

Thomas Egerton's traveling library, a wood and leather box about the size of one large folio volume that holds forty-four small volumes bound in vellum (Henry E. Huntington Library and Art Gallery)

Born in June 1623, John Egerton, second Earl of Bridgewater, was bred to literary connections. At the age of twelve he took part with the King Charles I in a performance of Thomas Carew's masque *Coelum Britannicum.* He probably performed in the masque *Arcades,* and he played the Elder Brother in the first performance of Milton's *Comus.* At age nineteen he married Elizabeth Cavendish, a descendant of the famous Bess of Hardwick. Although the Cavendish family had many ties to the literary world–Thomas Hobbes served for twenty years as the family tutor–the marriage was also a true love match.

At twenty-six, he succeeded to the earldom "environed with a multitude of troubles left upon me by my late father," as reported by Bernard Falk in *The Bridgewater Millions* (1942). Compounding an £80,000 debt resulting from risky speculations, the family's Royalist background was well known. In 1651 the second earl of Bridgewater was briefly imprisoned; he was released on bail when he agreed not to do anything prejudicial to the Protectorate. His private feelings are clear enough; when in the same year Milton published his republican manifesto *Pro Populo Anglicano Defensio,* the earl wrote an angry note on the title page: "Liber igne, author furcâ dignissimi" (a book most worthy of the fire, and the author of the gallows). When *Comus* was reprinted in a 1673 collection, the dedication to the erstwhile Elder Brother was deleted.

Bridgewater spent the interregnum in retirement, much of it at Ashridge, where he added to the library and is said to have compiled a manuscript catalogue of it. (No copy of this is known.) His often blustering comments in a distinctive handwriting, the letters bent as if stepped on, are found in many volumes.

After the Restoration, the earl was free to enter politics. He served with the earl of Clarendon and the bishop of London as manager of the conference between the houses of Parliament on the new Act of Uniformity and served on the privy council from 1666. As lord lieutenant of Buckinghamshire and Hertfordshire he persecuted Quakers and other dissidents, following in his illustrious grandfather's footsteps. He also continued the family tradition of patronizing authors and served as high steward for Oxford University. He did not invariably support Charles II's policies. Samuel Pepys in his diary entry for 30 December 1667 speaks of Bridgewater and several others on the privy council being out of favor, and after this year he was not employed on any special commissions.

In 1663 his wife died, a blow from which he never recovered. His epitaph claims he

> desired no other memorial of him but only this, that having . . . . married the Lady Elizabeth Cavendish . . . he did enjoy . . . all the happiness that a man could receive in the sweet society of the best of wives, till it pleased God in the 44th year of his age to change his great felicity into as great misery, by depriving him of his truly loving and intirely beloved wife . . . after which time . . . he did sorrowfully wear out 23 years, 4 months and 12 days. . . .

Piously he made a manuscript compilation of his wife's religious meditations and prayers. The second earl died in Bridgewater House in the Barbican on 26 October 1686 and was buried with his forebears in the church at Little Gaddesden.

The third in the line of John Egertons was born 9 November 1646. He was much more active in politics than his father. As viscount Brackley he was made a knight of the Order of the Bath and was elected to the House of Commons. He succeeded his father as lord lieutenant of Buckinghamshire. His highest offices were first lord of the admiralty and lord justice, the latter capacity requiring him to preside over the House of Lords in the absence of the lord chancellor. Bridgewater married the daughter of Charles Paulet, first Duke of Bolton. The couple was touched by tragedy in 1687 when a fire started by a drunken tutor burned Bridgewater House and killed two of their sons. The earl sold the property to Sir Christopher Wren, and the site, on the east side of Aldersgate Street, was afterward formed into Bridgewater Square. The family resettled in Red Lion Square, Holborn, and in 1700 the earl bought Cleveland House–sometimes thereafter referred to as Bridgewater House–in Cleveland Row, just north of St. James's Palace. These events did not affect the main Bridgewater Library, which by now was safely housed at Ashridge. Before his death on 19 March 1701, the third earl of Bridgewater made some additions to the library, but the great period of its growth was over.

The fortunes of the library were affected by the grandson of the third earl of Bridgewater, Francis Egerton. Born in 1736, he claimed the title of the sixth earl of Bridgewater; he was also the third duke of Bridgewater. As he built canals to carry his coal cheaply, the duke closed down all of his houses except for two austere lodgings near the works. As a consequence, Ashridge and the library it contained languished; the buildings became decrepit, and some of the books sustained damage from neglect. The canals eventually yielded him £80,000 a year, and by the end of his life he was legendarily rich. The Bridgewater name resounded in faraway places long after his death. Mark Twain has one of his con men in *The Adventures of Huckleberry Finn* (1885) pose as the lost heir to the dukedom of Bridgewater.

In 1795 through 1797 the duke remodeled Cleveland House, partly to accommodate his growing collection of art, valued at £150,000. At the same time, he was dismantling Ashridge, most of which had decayed beyond repair. He had some idea of the value of the library and consulted with his first cousin once removed, John William Egerton (later the seventh earl of Bridgewater), on its relocation. Egerton recommended the services of the Reverend Henry John Todd, a scholar with a knowledge of rare books who was becoming a leading editor of Milton. Todd was accordingly engaged to pack the books and manuscripts and move them to Cleveland House.

Todd proved both a blessing and a bane to the library. On the one hand, the material was now securely housed and well tended. On the other hand, Todd saw fit to "improve" the collection by disposing of duplicates and some items held in only one copy in three auction sales held by Thomas King on 27 April and 8 June 1802 and 26 May 1804. He had much of the remainder rebound in brown calf with the Bridgewater crest stamped on the sides. He gave a thematic rearrangement to the tract volumes that jumbled the order originally assigned by the second earl of Bridgewater. According to Isaac Disraeli in *Curiosities of Literature* (1873 edition), the collection suffered more severely at the hands of the duke, who, evidently ashamed of the illegitimacy of his ancestor the lord chancellor Ellesmere, burned or bricked up many family papers. "It is said he declared that he did not choose that his ancestors should be traced back to a person of mean trade."

Being anxious for the perpetuation of the Egerton line, the duke stipulated that the income from his canals should go to his nephew and fellow art collector, George Granville Leveson-Gower, though their administration would be left in the hands of a trust. Along with this income went Cleveland House, with the library and paintings. He also directed that Leveson-Gower's second son, Francis, should inherit these things in turn, on condition that he adopt the surname Egerton.

Although he did not inherit the library, the eighth and last earl of Bridgewater deserves mention as a collector. In Francis Henry Egerton the strain of eccentricity in the family line reached a high point. Schooled as a clergyman, he aspired to a life of scholarship. He had full access to the Bridgewater papers, on which he based short biographies of his father (John Egerton, Bishop of Durham) and Lord Chancellor Egerton. The latter was published in several editions, mostly in France, where the earl lived in his later years, with increasingly voluminous and irrelevant footnotes dealing with continental affairs. The final edition ran to 508 pages, unfinished, and bankrupted its printer. The earl was famous for dressing up his cats and dogs and dining with them or taking them out for drives. The eight "Bridgewater Treatises," by various authors, were financed by his bequest of £8,000 given for the best work "on the Goodness of God as manifested in the Creation." He had a valuable collection of sixty-seven volumes of manuscripts and nintey-six charters, mostly on French and Italian literature and politics, which he bequeathed to the British Museum with a substantial endowment for their curatorship and augmentation. These manuscripts are distinct from the Bridgewater

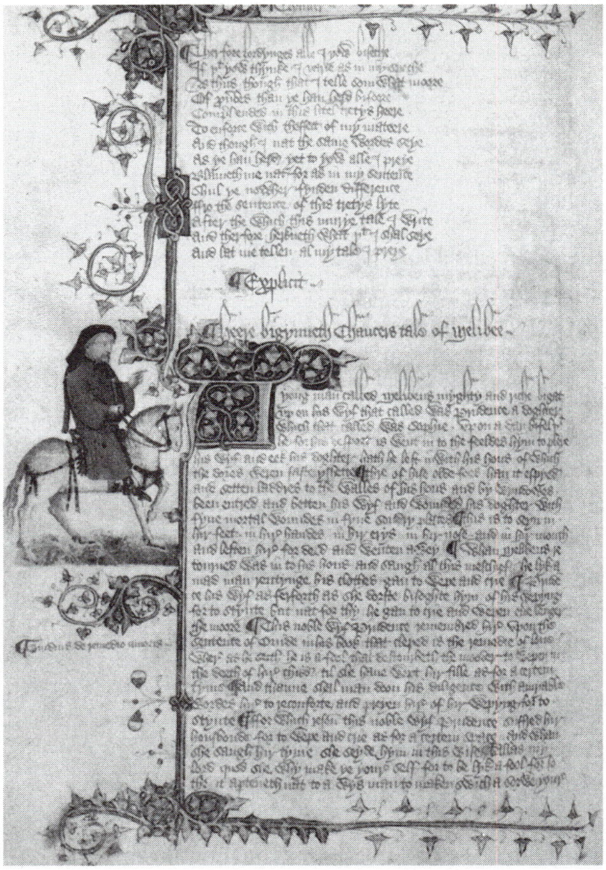

The first page of "The Tale of a Melibee" in the Ellesmere manuscript of Geoffrey Chaucer's The Canterbury Tales, *the most important manuscript in the Bridgewater Library (Henry E. Huntington Library and Art Gallery)*

Library collection. With Francis Henry Egerton the earldom died.

The heir to the Bridgewater Library, Leveson-Gower, was a politician like his father, the marquis of Stafford. He was a privy councilor, but the most important post he achieved was the ambassadorship to France in the 1780s. Through marriage and inheritance he gained vast properties, of which the Bridgewater canals and estates were not the least. He continued to supplement the paintings he had bought and inherited, which during his lifetime were known as the Stafford Collection. Beginning in 1806 he allowed public viewings in a new gallery at Cleveland House, becoming one of the first collectors in London to do so. The cartoonist James Gillray commemorated his benefactions to art and literature with an etching titled "The Modern Maecenas," but he appears to have taken little interest in the famous library in his care. In the last year of his life he was named duke of Sutherland; the title passed to his eldest son and continues to the present day.

Francis Leveson-Gower, born on New Year's Day in 1800, was three years old when he was designated the heir by entail of the duke's canal properties and the Bridgewater Library. The younger Leveson-Gower followed his father into politics, filling various posts, including member of Parliament and privy councillor. He served as a trustee of the National Gallery, chancellor of Oxford University, and president of the Camden, Royal Asiatic, and Royal Geographical Societies.

In 1833, on the death of his father, Leveson-Gower took his granduncle's surname and inheritance. He took his responsibilities to his tenants seriously, living part of the year among them in wet and grimy Worsley. The library underwent more improvements during his ownership than at any time since the seventeenth century, chiefly because of the interest taken in it by John Payne Collier. The Shakespearean scholar, who was librarian to the duke of Devonshire, obtained an introduction to Egerton and was soon given the run of the Bridgewater Library, partly on the understanding that he was working on a biography of Lord Chancellor Ellesmere and an edition of his papers. Thanks to connections in the book trade he was able to recover many items that Todd had sold, including a fine copy of William Shakespeare's *Sonnets* (1609). He also acquired, and sold to Egerton, the splendid Larpent collection of around 2,500 manuscript plays from the eighteenth and early nineteenth centuries that had been submitted for licensing before their first performances. He aided Egerton in the formation of a separate collection devoted to Shakespeare and the early English stage. Collier published his selection of the Egerton papers in 1840 and a catalogue of "high spots" among the printed books in 1837.

Although he benefited the library in many respects, Collier also seeded it with many of the Shakespeare-related forgeries for which he is notorious. The Bridgewater First Folio bears thirty-two manuscript corrections that Collier claimed dated from the reign of Charles I but were in fact his own. A sheet of accounts contains a record of payment by the Lord Strange to Richard Burbage's players for a performance of *Othello* at Harefield in 1602–a revelation that delighted Egerton, but was unfortunately a Collier forgery. Collier is known to have fabricated or tampered with eight manuscripts in the muniment room at Cleveland House, and other forgeries may remain undiscovered. Not long after he published his "findings," they came under suspicion, and their author spent the rest of his long life in controversy and discredit.

In 1840 or 1841 Egerton pulled down Cleveland House, which had become structurally unsound, and hired Sir Charles Barry, the architect of the houses of Parliament, to design a new Bridgewater House on the same site. The construction was not completed until 1854. In 1846 Egerton was created viscount Brackley and earl of Ellesmere, partly in recognition of his support of free trade and industrial reform. He was appointed chairman of a royal commission to examine the state of the British Museum Library, where the head of the printed books department, Antonio Panizzi, was fighting to establish controversial new procedures and cataloguing rules. Collier served as secretary to this commission, which, after four years and a series of hearings, vindicated Panizzi and paved the way for his advancement to principal librarian.

Despite his many successes and his obvious good heart, the first earl of Ellesmere struck some contemporaries as lacking in decisiveness. "He gave me the impression of being a shy man, and there was about him an air of pensive gravity which was peculiar," wrote the duke of Argyll. The earl of Granville said, "If he had had a little more devil in him, he would have been a very remarkable man." Collier, less kindly, called him "a poor weak man" in his unpublished autobiography. Upon his death on 18 February 1857 and burial at Worsley, his tenants and employees genuinely mourned him. He had left his lands and his library greatly improved and the nation in his debt.

The financial fortunes of the earl's family suffered in the latter half of the nineteenth century, leading John Francis Granville Scrope Egerton, fourth Earl of Ellesmere, to decide in 1916 to send the Bridgewater Library to be auctioned by Sotheby, Wilkinson, and Hodge. The material was being catalogued when Henry Huntington, acting through his agent, George D. Smith, made an offer of $1 million on the lot, which Ellesmere accepted. Huntington signed the contract on 21 February 1917, and in April the collection of books and manuscripts, packed in 101 wooden cases, was secretly shipped across the U-boat-infested Atlantic. The Egerton family retained about 1,600 miscellaneous manuscripts, the most important being the manuscript of *Comus.* These are still owned by a collateral relation, the earl of Sutherland, but the Huntington Library has photostat copies. There was also a residue of continental books described by Sotheby at the time as "of no commercial value" that were not part of the sale.

What Huntington got for his million dollars were around 4,400 printed books of outstanding overall quality. Not counted in this figure were many pamphlets and early newspapers, many of which are unique. The books included three Caxtons, all four Shakespeare folios and many of the quartos, and famous rarities of sixteenth- and seventeenth-century English drama and verse. Added to this was a rich trove of twelve to fourteen thousand manuscripts both literary and historical, including more than 350 sixteenth- and seventeenth-century manuscript books presented by their authors, an early-fifteenth-century illuminated manuscript of John Gower's *Confessio Amantis,* and the crown jewel, the Ellesmere Chaucer.

Sotheby, for publicity purposes, issued a small edition of a catalogue of 107 of the library's high spots, but there had never been a complete inventory of the library, and Huntington did not bother to have one made after the purchase. In fact, he was so little concerned with the library's integrity that he and his librarian, George Watson Cole, shortly began weeding duplicates. From 1918 to 1924 Anderson Galleries held a series of sales of Huntington's duplicates, including hundreds of Bridgewater items. The great collector was acting prudently according to the conventions of his time, but even then some of his decisions were inexplicable. For instance, he chose to sell the presumed presentation copy of the first edition of *Comus* instead of the run-of-the-mill copy he already owned. This was gratefully scooped up for $9,200 by Herschel V. Jones and is now in the Pforzheimer collection at the University of Texas.

Because of these sales, those by Todd in the early nineteenth century, and certain items not sold to Huntington in 1917, some Bridgewater books have escaped to the market. These may have any of several characteristics: (1) the distinctive Bridgewater bookplate, inserted in the first half of the nineteenth century, which came in two sizes; (2) a handwritten number at the upper right corner of the title page of shorter works, enclosed in a three-sided frame (these are probably in the hand of the second earl of Bridgewater and indicate the binding order in pamphlet volumes); (3) a printed label, placed at top left of the front paste-down, bearing a rule separating two lines of letters and/or numbers (sometimes only the rule is printed and the remaining information added by hand); (4) a signature of one of the family, such as "Tho. Egerton Lyncoln" (later the lord chancellor), "Brackley" (his son or grandson, before they became earls), or "JBridgewater" (as earls), and "E Bridgewater," probably the wife of the second earl of Bridgewater; (5) a binding, usually dull brown calf or red straight-grain morocco, stamped with the Bridgewater crest, a lion on its hind legs holding a spear pointing-down; or (6) a limp vellum binding, probably done for the lord chancellor, using distinctive tools.

No complete inventory of the Bridgewater Library has been attempted. George Smith made a list at the time of sale of about 3,660 titles, including many from the tract volumes. All of the Bridgewater printed material at the Huntington Library is now catalogued, but the catalogue provides no access by provenance. The manuscript collection came with a ten-volume typewritten calendar of its contents, but a compiler of a new finding aid would certainly unearth some unsuspected treasures. Further papers pertaining to the Egerton family may be found in the Northamptonshire record office.

References:

James Brindley, *The History of Inland Navigations. Particularly those of the Duke of Bridgwater* (London: Printed for T. Lowndes, 1766; enlarged, 1769; enlarged, 1779);

W. N. C. Carlton, *Notes on the Bridgewater House Library* (New York: Privately printed, 1918);

Francis Henry Egerton, "The Life of Thomas Egerton, Lord Chancellor of England," anonymous, in *Biographia Britannica,* volume 5 (London: Printed by John Nichols, for T. Longman and others, 1793), pp. 562–581; enlarged (London, 1798?); enlarged as *A Compilation of Various Authentick Evidences, and Historical Authorities Tending to Illustrate the Life and Character of Thomas Egerton* (Paris: Printed by Didot l'aîné, 1812);

Benard Falk, *The Bridgewater Millions: A Candid Family History* (London: Hutchinson, 1942).

John Cosin

(30 November 1595 – 15 January 1672)

A. I. Doyle
University of Durham

See also the Cosin entry in *DLB 151: British Prose Writers of the Early Seventeenth Century.*

BOOKS: *A Collection of Private Devotions: In the Practise of the Ancient Church, Called the Houres of Prayer. As they were after this maner published by Authoritie of Q. Eliz. 1560. Taken Out of the Holy Scriptures, the Ancient Fathers, and the divine Service of our own Church,* anonymous (London: Printed by R. Young, 1627);

A Scholastical History of the Canon of the Holy Scripture; or, The Certaine and Indubitate Books thereof, as they are received in the Church of England (London: Printed by R. Norton for T. Garthwait, 1657);

Historia Transubstantiationis Papalis. Cui præmittitur, atque opponitur, tùm S. Scripturæ, tùm Veterum Patrum, & Reformatarum Ecclesiarum Doctrina Catholica, de sacris symbolis, & præsentiâ Christi in Sacramento Eucharistiae. Hanc autem Disquisitionem Historicam ante Annos XIX scribebat, & demùm instanti multorum rogatu excudi permisit paulo ante Obitum Joh. Episcopus Dunelmensis (London: Printed by Thomas Roycroft for Henry Brome, 1675); translated by Luke de Beaulieu as *The History of Popish Transubstantiation. To which Is Premised and opposed, The Catholick Doctrin of the Holy Scripture, The Ancient Fathers and the Reformed Churches, About the Sacred Elements, and Presence of Christ in the Blessed Sacrament of the Eucharist. Written Nineteen years Ago in Latine, by John, Late Lord Bishop of Durham, And allowed by him to be published a little before his Death, at the earnest request of his Friends* (London: Printed by Andrew Clark for Henry Brome, 1676);

The Works of the Right Reverend Father in God John Cosin, Lord Bishop of Durham: Now First Collected, 5 volumes, edited by J. Sanson, The Library of Anglo-Catholic Theology (Oxford: Parker, 1843–1855).

Editions: *The Durham Book, being the First Draft of the Revision of the Book of Common Prayer in 1661,* edited by G. J. Cuming (London: Oxford University Press, 1961);

A Collection of Private Devotions, edited by P. G. Stanwood and Daniel O'Connor (Oxford: Clarendon Press, 1967).

OTHER: "Scotia alloquitur Angliam," in *Epicedium Cantabrigiense, in Obitum Immaturum, Semperque Deflendum Henrici, Principis Walliae* (Cambridge: C. Legge, 1612), pp. 106–107;

"Ad Serenissimam Reginam de Partu & Libro Hoc Academico," in *Carmen Natalitium ad Cunas Illustrissimae Principis Elisabethae* (Cambridge: Cambridge University Press, 1635), sig. A3v;

Voces Votivae ab Academicis Cantabrigiensibus pro Novissimo Caroli & Mariae Principe Filio Emissae, Latin dedication and verses to the king by Cosin (Cambridge: R. Daniel, 1640), sig. A3r–v, H4v;

A Forme of Prayer, used in the King's Chappel, upon Tuesdayes. In these Times of Trouble & Distresse, anonymous (Paris, 1649);

Articles of Inquiry Concerning Matters Ecclesiastical, Exhibited to the Ministers . . . Within the Diocese of Durham, in the First Episcopal Visitation; & Articles of Inquiry . . . in the Second Episcopal Visitation (London: T. Garthwait, 1662, 1665);

An Answer to Certain Printed Reasons for Knights and Burgesses in the County Palatine of Durham (London, 1667);

Latin letter to H. Grotius, 20 Jun. 1621, in *Praestantium ac Eruditorum Virorum Epistolae Ecclesiasticae,* edited by C. Hartsoeker & P. a Limborch, second edition (Amsterdam: H. Wetsten, 1684), pp. 659–660;

The Right Reverend Doctor John Cosin, late Lord Bishop of Durham, his Opinion, when Dean of Peterburgh, and in Exile, for Communicating Rather with Geneva than Rome (London: Printed by F. Leach for Nich. Woolfe, 1684); republished as *Two Letters of the Right Reverend Father in God Doctor John Cosin . . . with Annotations on the Same . . . by R. Watson* (London: Printed by F. Leach for Nich. Woolfe, 1686);

The Differences in the Chief Points of Religion, Between the Roman Catholicks, and the Church of England, in Several

John Cosin, bishop of Durham, in his library (Episcopal library, Durham)

Letters, by George Hickes (London: R. Sare, 1705), app. iv;

"Regni Angliae Religio Catholica, Prisca, Casta, Defoecata . . . Omnibus Christianis . . . Ostensa . . . Anno MDCLII," in *Vitae Quorundam Eruditissimorum et Illustrium Virorum,* by Thomas Smith (London: D. Mortier, 1707), section 2, pp. 31–54;

"Additional Notes on the Common Prayer," in *A Comment on the Book of Common Prayer,* by William Nicholls (London: R. Bonwicke, 1710) part 2, pp. 1–71;

"An Additional Letter . . . to Mr. Cordel, who scrupled to communicate with the French-Protestants, upon some of the Modern Pretences," in *The Judgment of the Church of England in the Case of Lay Baptism . . . 2nd edition,* by William Fleetwood (London: A. Baldwin, 1712), pp. 51–57.

One of the leaders of the reaction against Calvinism in the Church of England, John Cosin championed the adoption of features of Catholic ritual and imagery under King Charles I that were based on his wide reading of patristic, medieval, and later theological works. He was a constant collector of such writings and became one of the most important English collectors of his time. Cosin was also a chief contributor to the 1662

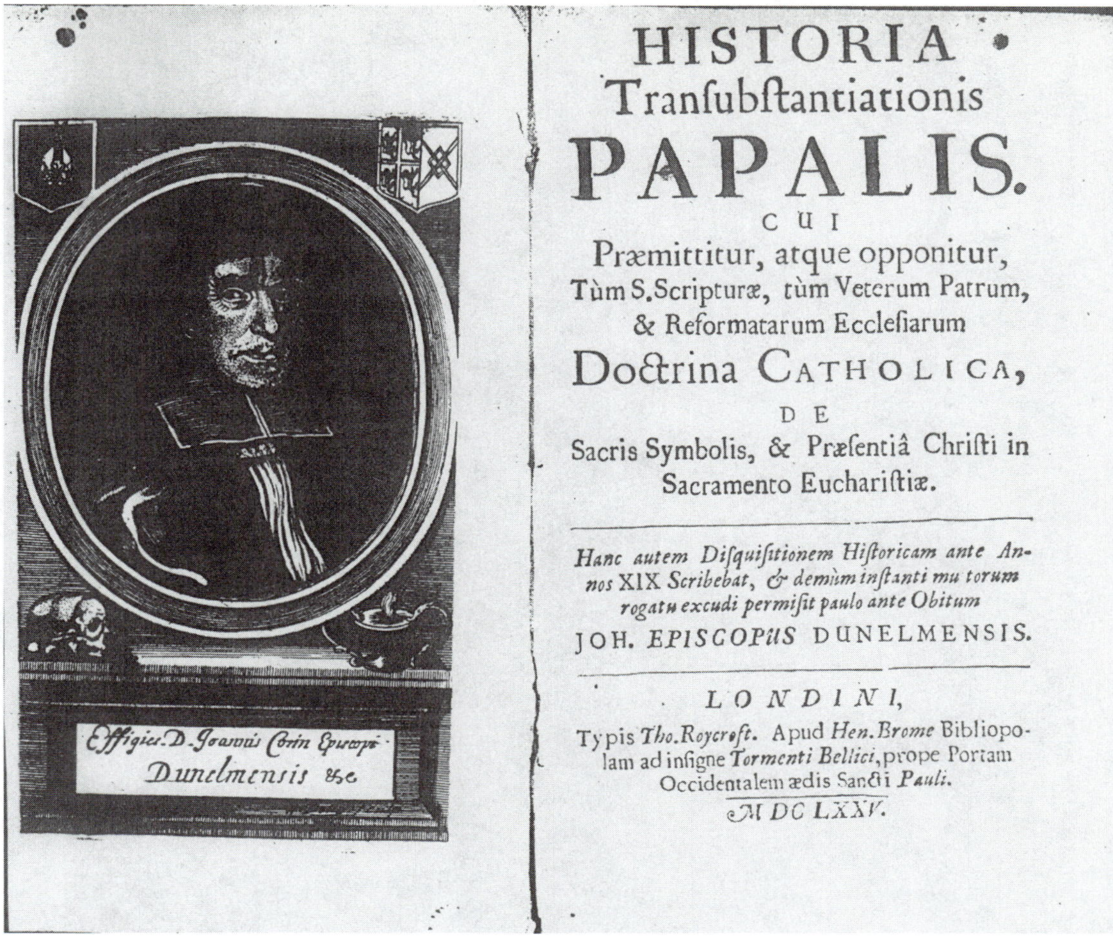

Frontispiece and title page for Cosin's 1675 book, which he consented to have published shortly before he died

revision of *The Book of Common Prayer,* and as a rector and later as bishop in County Durham he was responsible for the distinctive designs of various architectural work in the diocese, especially the cathedral city, including the Episcopal library he founded in 1669 that is named after him. He gave the library the majority of the books he had accumulated during the course of a half century; he also gave many works to Peterhouse, Cambridge, and to the cathedral library in Durham.

Cosin was born in Norwich on 30 November 1595. The eldest son of an established tradesman, he was educated at the grammar school there and on a scholarship attended Gonville and Caius College, Cambridge, taking the degree of B.A. in 1614. In about 1616 he was invited to look after the libraries in London of Lancelot Andrewes, then bishop of Ely, and of John Overall, bishop of Lichfield. Both bishops were Cambridge alumni and were associated with the reaction against Calvinism that was hostilely labeled Arminian, after the Dutch theologian Jacobus Arminius, who advocated the importance of free will and the importance of works along with faith. Through these bishops Cosin had dealings with the arch-Arminian, Hugo Grotius, who gave him an anonymously published treatise of his (1622).

Cosin returned to Cambridge as a fellow of Gonville and Caius from 1620 to 1624 but continued to be much in London as chaplain to Richard Neile, bishop of Durham, who made him a canon of that cathedral in 1624. The same year he also received the rectories of Elwick and Brancepeth in Durham through the influence of William Laud, then bishop of St. David's, and George Villiers, first Duke of Buckingham, Charles I's favorite. Cosin wrote out the king's text for his coronation service.

When the prayer books of the ladies-in-waiting of King Charles's Catholic consort Henrietta Maria inspired a demand for an Anglican counterpart, Cosin

Cosin's Library, Durham

compiled *A Collection of Private Devotions,* largely from Catholic models. Published anonymously in London in 1627, it caused immediate Puritan pamphleteering and protests in Parliament. Cosin made some alterations in the two subsequent editions that were published in 1627. Eight more editions were brought out during the seventeenth century, most of them anonymously. Cosin's authorship was first acknowledged in the edition of 1676, after his death.

In 1628 Cosin settled in his benefices in Durham. Although he was soon denounced for his use of vestments in the cathedral by a fellow canon, Cosin was able to take in hand the revival of the cathedral library. He apparently administrated the library himself until 1633 and also reorganized its archives. Cosin had been acquiring books since his early days in Cambridge and London, new and secondhand, and both during the time of his canonry and later as bishop he gave many books to the cathedral library, some of them duplicates of what he kept.

In 1634 he was elected master of Peterhouse, Cambridge, though he maintained his Durham benefices and residence, returning there for weeks at a time. Under his direction the Peterhouse library was given new bookcases, and as vice chancellor in 1639–1640 he revived plans for a new university library. His embellishments of the college chapel and choral services, however, excited further hostility from Puritan polemicists. The seizure of Northumberland and Durham by the Scots in 1640 during the second Bishops' War curtailed the collection of funds and cut off Cosin's income from Durham. In part as compensation for this loss he was made dean of Peterborough, but the Long Parliament supported his adversaries' attacks, and he was expelled from the mastership and deanery in March 1644 after sending the college silver to the king's mint at York. Cosin then fled to France, leaving his books at Peterhouse, though some possibly also in Durham and Peterborough.

The books left at Peterhouse were sequestered by the Parliamentary regime, and a summary catalogue was compiled of about 1,050 volumes valued to a total of £247. 10s., with 40 more books listed in an addendum. All of these books were entrusted to the college, where at first they were listed as Doctor Cosin's; eventually they were integrated into the shelving system of the library and its distinctive pressmarks written into them. Such marks serve to identify items now in Durham that Cosin had acquired by 1644. The detailed knowledge evident in Cosin's correspondence in the 1650s with John Evelyn, whom he met in France and later unsuccessfully tried to sell a large number of his books, shows that he was an expert collector and well aware of the value of his books.

Cosin spent nearly fifteen years in France, where he ministered to fellow Anglican exiles and had sympathetic relations with the Huguenots. In Paris, with financial help from friends, he acquired a fresh collection of new and old books, including many items in French on contemporary religious controversies, especially from the Huguenot point of view. A few books were presented by their authors. He also bought English works, which he may have had sent to him from across the English Channel. He employed probably more than one workshop to put some of his acquisitions into sheep, calf, or goatskin covers with fashionable gold tooling.

On his return to England with the Restoration of Charles II in 1660, Cosin recovered his benefices and was named bishop of Durham. The Peterhouse library returned Cosin's books, and in subsequent years he continued to support the library there, claiming in his correspondence to have given "1031 volumes of good bookes, fairely and well bound, which cost him about £300," many of which the library had held during his absence. Cosin's reclaimed books initially were taken north by installments to Bishop Auckland, one of the bishop's palaces, where most of them remained until they were moved to the Episcopal library founded by Cosin on Palace Green adjacent to the castle in Durham in 1669. He also kept a private library in his house at Brafferton in the North Riding of Yorkshire, from which he donated more gifts to the cathedral library in 1670.

The cathedral library was the private library of the dean and chapter, whereas the Episcopal library was to be a public library for the clergy and educated laity of the diocese and palatinate of Durham. The building, adjoining the palatine exchequer and chancery, was specially erected for the purpose and was furnished entirely with wall shelving and lighted by high windows on three sides, in the manner of the Bibliothéque Mazarine established during Cosin's stay in Paris. The Episcopal library was possibly the first large English library to be designed wholly on those lines, apart from the Arts and Selden Ends of the Bodleian in Oxford. On the precedent of the frieze round the upper rooms of the Bodleian and smaller sequences in other European libraries, Cosin selected portraits of authors, each trio representing a subject group, to be placed over the corresponding bookcases. The Low Countries painter, John Baptist van Eersell, worked from engravings found in the books.

Toward its opening in 1669 and until his death in 1672, Cosin strove to increase the stock of the Episcopal library beyond his earlier collecting. He bought books in London and, through his agents in Durham, requested gifts of books or cash from tenants wanting leases of the bishopric or palatinate of Durham or renewals of them. Many authors and friends gave gifts freely. In 1671 he claimed in his will that the building had cost £500 and the books £2,000 "and the care of above five and fifty yeares together." There were likely some four thousand items in the Episcopal library at the time. He had given the libraries of the cathedral and Peterhouse more than another thousand before his death.

Cosin was not primarily an antiquarian collector. His handful of medieval manuscripts and incunabula included the chief copy of Symeon's *Historia ecclesiae Dunelmensis,* a history of the see of Durham from its establishment at Lindisfarne in 635 to 1104, and H. Schedel's *Liber Cronicarum Nuremberg* (1493). Among the printed works after 1501 is the first edition of Sir Thomas More's *Utopia* (1516). Cosin did acquire fine printing, bindings, and illustrations, but he was first of all interested in collecting sources for study: Scripture, commentaries, and patristics; works on liturgy, canon law, Reformed and Counter-Reformation theology, and ecclesiastical history; Greek and Latin classics; and books on secular history, political theory, geography, natural history, and medicine. Before 1644, probably before 1632, he acquired his First Folio of William Shakespeare's works, the only copy to have remained continuously in the same collection since it was published. He also owned books by Samuel Daniel and Ben Jonson and miscellanea of all sorts, in Latin, French, and Italian as well as English.

There is a good deal of evidence about when and where Cosin got his books. In his correspondence in the 1620s and 1670s he mentions London booksellers. Many of the books he collected have Cambridge bindings of the late sixteenth and early decades of the seventeenth century, some with notes indicating what he paid for them. Other books have French bindings of the mid seventeenth century and the names or insignia of previous owners. Some of the places and dates of sales at which Cosin bought books are known. The origins of many books given to him as gifts are known through inscriptions, often from the authors. Cosin also, obtained some works–such as Sir Henry Vane's copy of William Dugard's printing of John Milton's 1651 defense of the execution of Charles I–through confiscations. The exemplary preservation of so many of Cosin's books and their various and widespread origins makes the story of his book collecting of unusual interest.

Letters:

George Ornsby, ed., *The Correspondence of John Cosin . . . Together with Other Papers Illustrative of His Life and Times,* 2 volumes, Publications of the Surtees Society, 52, 55 (Durham: Andrews, 1869–1872).

Biographies:

Isaac Basire, *The Dead Man's Real Speech. A Funeral Sermon . . . Together with a Brief of the Life, Dignities, Benefactions, Principal Actions, and Sufferings; and of the Death of the . . . Bishop* (London: J. Collins, 1673);

Thomas Smith, *Vitae Quorundam Eruditissimorum et Illustrium Virorum* (London: D. Mortier, 1707), section 2, pp. 1–62;

Percy H. Osmond, *A Life of John Cosin Bishop of Durham 1660–1672* (London: A. R. Mowbray, 1913);

M. Johnson, ed. *John Cosin: Papers Presented to a Conference* (Durham: Turnstone Ventures, 1997).

References:

A. I. Doyle, "John Cosin (1595–1672) as a library maker," *Book Collector,* 40 (1991): 335–357;

E. Dubois, "La bibliothéque de l'évque Cosin à Durham et sa collection de livres français de théologie et de spiritualité protestantes des XVIe et XVIIe siècles," *Bulletin de la Société de l'Histoire du Protestantisme Français* (1982): 175–188;

A. Hobson, "English Library Buildings of the 17th and 18th Centuries," *Wolfenbütteler Forschungen,* 2 (1977): 63–74;

J. G. Hoffman, "John Cosin, Prebendary of Durham Cathedral and Dean of Peterborough, 1624–43," *Durham University Journal,* 78 (1985–1986): 1–10;

A. Lawes, "Cosin's post-Restoration Correspondence–A Re-assessment," *Durham University Journal,* 77 (1984–1985): 141–147;

D. Pearson, "Cambridge Bindings in Cosin's Library, Durham," in *Six Centuries of the Provincial Book Trade in Britain,* edited by P. Isaac (Winchester: St. Paul's Bibliographies, 1990), pp. 41–60;

D. G. Ramage, "Portraits in Cosin's Library," *Transactions of the Architectural & Archaeological Society of Durham & Northumberland,* 11 (1958–1965): 65–74;

P. G. Stanwood and A. I. Doyle, "Cosin's Correspondence," *Transactions of the Cambridge Bibliographical Society,* 5 (1969): 74–78.

Papers:

The main collections of John Cosin's papers are at the Durham Cathedral Library; the Durham University Library; the Bodleian Library, Oxford; and the British Library, London.

Sir Robert Bruce Cotton

(22 January 1571 – 6 May 1631)

Thomas N. Hall
University of Illinois at Chicago

Sir Robert Bruce Cotton

CATALOGUES: Thomas Smith, ed., *Catalogus librorum manuscriptorum bibliothecae Cottonianae* (Oxford: E Theatro Sheldoniano, 1696); republished as *Catalogue of the Manuscripts in the Cottonian Library 1696,* edited by Colin G. C. Tite, annotations by Humfrey Wanley (Cambridge: D. S. Brewer, 1984);

Samuel Hooper, ed., *A Catalogue of the Manuscripts in the Cottonian Library. To Which Are Added, Many Emendations and Additions. With an Appendix, Containing an Account of the Damage Sustained by the Fire of 1731; and also a Catalogue of the Charters Preserved in the Same Library* (London: Samuel Hooper, 1777);

Joseph Planta, ed., *A Catalogue of the Manuscripts in the Cottonian Library, Deposited in the British Museum* (London: L. Hansard, 1802);

A Guide to a Select Exhibition of Cottonian Manuscripts in Celebration of the Tercentenary of the Death of Sir Robert Cotton, 6 May 1931 (London: British Museum, 1931).

BOOKS: *A Short View of the Long Life and Raigne of Henry the Third, King of England. Presented to King James* (London, 1627); republished as *The Troublesome Life and Raigne of King Henry the Third* (London: Imprinted for George Lindsey, 1642); republished as *A Brief Survey (Historical and Political) of the Life and Reign of Henry the III, King of England* (London: Printed for James Vade, 1680);

The Danger wherein the Kingdome now Standeth, & the Remedie (London, 1628);

Serious Considerations for Repressing of the Increase of Iesuites, Priests, and Papists, without Shedding of Blood (London, 1641); republished as *A Treatise against Recusants, in Defence of the Oath of Alegeance. With Executions of Consideration, for Repressing the Encrease of Papists* (London: Printed by R. Hearn, 1641);

An Abstract out of the Records of the Tower, Touching the Kings Revenue: and How They Have Supported Themselves (London: Printed for G. Tomlinson, T. A. and A. C., 1642);

The Forme of Governement of the Kingdome of England: Collected out of the Fundamental Lawes and Statutes of This Kingdome (London: Printed for Tho. Bankes, 1642);

Cottoni Posthuma: Divers Choice Pieces of That Renowned Antiquary Sir Robert Cotton, Knight and Baronet, Preserved from the Injury of Time, and Exposed to Publick Light, for the Benefit of Posterity, edited by James Howell (London: Printed by Francis Leach for Henry Seile, 1651);

An Answer Made by Sr. Robert Cotton, at the Command of Prince Henry, to Certain Propositions of Warre and Peace,

Delivered to His Highnesse by Some of His Military Servants (London: Printed by Roger Daniel for William Sheares, 1655); republished as *Warres with Forreign Princes Dangerous to Our Common-Wealth; or, Reasons for Forreign Wars Answered* (London: Printed for William Sheares, 1657); republished as *An Answer to Such Motives as Were Offered by Certain Military-Men to Prince Henry Inciting Him to Affect Armes More than Peace* (London: Henry Mortlock, 1665); republished as *A Discourse of Foreign War . . . Formerly written by Sir Robert Cotton Barronet, and now published by Sir John Cotton Barronet* (London: Henry Mortlock, 1690);

A Discourse of Foreign War: With an Account of all the Taxations upon This Kingdom, from the Conquest to the End of the Reign of Queen Elizabeth (London: Printed for Henry Mortlock, 1690);

A Collection of Curious Discourses Written by Eminent Antiquaries upon Several Heads in Our English Antiquities, by Cotton and others, edited by Thomas Hearne (Oxford: Printed at the Theater, 1720).

At the end of the seventeenth century, looking back on the achievements of Sir Robert Cotton several decades earlier, the biographer and antiquary Thomas Smith characterized Cotton as a man of consummate learning, a pious defender of the English church, a model of gentlemanly virtue, and a skilled parliamentarian who advised the crown on historical precedents of state matters. According to Smith, however, the main reason for Cotton's renown was without question his extraordinary collection of ancient and medieval manuscripts, "a library whose fame has travelled not only through all England but through the Christian world wherever literary studies flourish." Visitors to the Cotton library, Smith wrote, "will find literary treasures beyond price exceeding all their hopes and expectations, and as they consult and make use of the manuscripts, convinced by experience of the solid learning of these volumes, they will never cease to praise and applaud the name of Cotton."

Smith's adulation for the Cotton name is to be expected given that he was employed as librarian to Cotton's grandson Sir John Cotton and had been commissioned to write his biography, but his glowing assessment of the value of the Cotton manuscripts has been echoed by scholars in succeeding centuries. Quite apart from his prominence as a statesman and his kinship to King James I, Cotton is best remembered as the greatest English book collector of the Tudor and Stuart eras, as a prime mover of the English antiquarian movement, and above all as the man behind one of the three founding collections of the British Library. Through the whole of the seventeenth century his library served as the leading resource for scholarly inquiry into British antiquities–most particularly the study of medieval English literature and history–and his name has ever since been synonymous with the rarest of books and artifacts pertaining to pre-Conquest England.

Robert Cotton was born 22 January 1571 in the village of Denton, some three miles from his family's ancestral home of Conington Castle in northern Huntingdonshire, about eight miles southeast of Peterborough. He was the eldest son of Thomas Cotton, a wealthy gentleman who traced his ancestry back through a maternal line to Robert the Bruce and Elizabeth Shirley Cotton, daughter of Francis Shirley of Staunton-Harold, Leicestershire. As a young boy Cotton attended Westminster School in west London, where he was a favorite pupil of the learned antiquarian William Camden and a schoolmate of Ben Jonson and Hugh Holland, who would both later share his fascination with British antiquities.

In 1581 at the age of ten, Cotton, entered Jesus College, Cambridge, where he received a B.A. in 1585. Three years later he studied law at the Middle Temple, where he established fast friendships with Henry Spelman, John Selden, and John Davies. At the age of about twenty-two he married Elizabeth Brocas, the eldest daughter of William Brocas of Thedingworth, Leicestershire, and they had one child, Thomas, born in 1594.

By his early thirties Cotton had begun signing his name Robert Bruceus Cotton in order to emphasize his royal Scottish blood and take advantage of his distant kinship with James I, who is known to have addressed him on occasion as "cousin." Almost immediately upon James's accession in March 1603, Cotton presented him with "Discourse of His Majesty's Descent from the Saxon Kings," a document that circumvented the traditionally held view that the English and Scottish kings were descended from the Trojan knight Brutus and instead affirmed James's right to the throne on the basis of his true ancestry, which Cotton had been able to reconstruct using his personal collection of genealogical and heraldic records. James clearly admired the gesture, for he knighted Cotton on 11 May 1603.

While still in his teens, Cotton developed a serious interest in the kinds of historical research that would occupy him for the rest of his life. In about 1586, the year in which the first edition of Camden's *Britannia* was published, Cotton joined forces with Camden, James Ley, and Spelman to found the Elizabethan Society of Antiquaries, a group dedicated to scholarly inquiry into the origins of English customs and institutions. As the first systematic attempt at a survey of Roman Britain, Camden's *Britannia* was a landmark of Renaissance historical scholarship and a touchstone of

Two of Cotton's book stamps

the antiquarian movement; Cotton made important contributions to *Britannia* in its later editions.

During its twenty-odd years of existence, the Elizabethan Society of Antiquaries waxed and waned, but it eventually grew to include Lancelot Andrewes, Richard Carew, Selden, Francis Tate, William Fleetwood, and other learned men who shared a passionate interest in English history. In the early years of the society Cotton was most keenly interested in delving into the origins of English offices and titles. He produced papers on the antiquity of the offices of constable, earl marshal, and high steward of England that were in part etymological. Cotton demonstrated for instance that the title *constable* derives from the Continental Latin term *comes stabuli* and that the office must therefore have come to England as a result of the Conquest.

In an account of the formation and dissolution of the society written in 1614, Spelman recalls that the group's practice was to congregate every Friday at a designated place to dine together and entertain discussion of two questions that had been settled on the previous week. For a long time this designated meeting place was Derby House, Sir William Dethick's residence in the College of Heralds in Paul's Wharf Hill, but there is reason to believe that at some point the group moved to Cotton's house to take advantage of the resources of his burgeoning library, which was then beginning to gain the attention of the learned world.

Cotton was without question a driving force behind the activities of the society, even though he was only about fifteen when it was founded. In the lengthy Latin "Life of Sir Robert Cotton" prefacing his 1696 catalogue of the Cotton library, Smith lists the titles of twenty-seven papers presented at meetings of the society, including eleven authored by Cotton. These include papers on the antiquity of the laws of England, on the division and boundaries of parishes, on the custom of funerals, on the antiquity of moats, on the history of the privileges of the inns of court and chancery, on the antiquity of the Christian religion in Britain, on the origin of the term "sterling money," and on the histories of various family coats of arms. Cotton never saw any of these papers into print, though nine of his contributions were eventually collected and published by Hearne in *A Collection of Curious Discourses* (1720), one of the few published records of the society's debates.

One important result of the success of the Elizabethan Society of Antiquaries was that it inspired Cotton to aim his research at an ever wider audience and to promote the idea of a national school for historical research. In about 1602 he petitioned Queen Elizabeth to establish an "Academy for the Study of Antiquity and History founded by Queen Elizabeth," offering to donate his own manuscript collection as the founding core of what he envisioned as England's first national library, but Elizabeth showed little interest in the

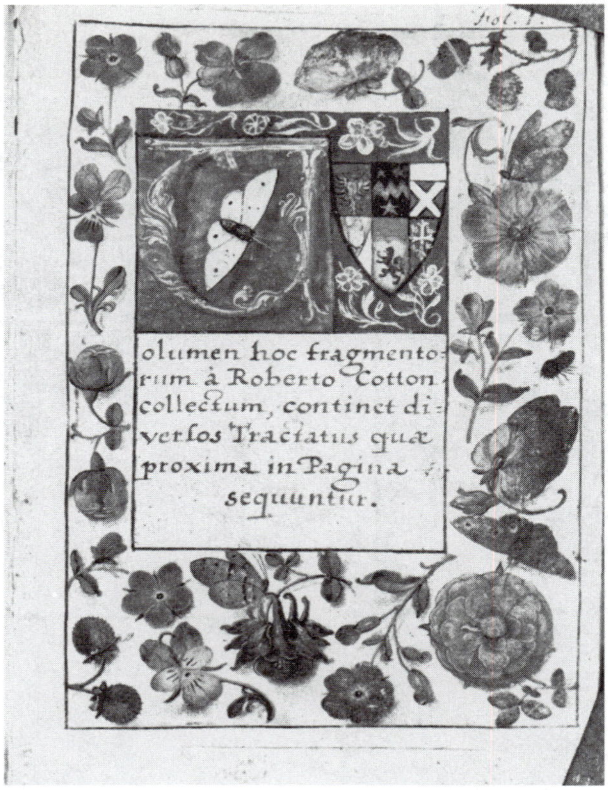

A title page created by Cotton for a collection of manuscripts (British Library)

project, and it never got off the ground. The society continued to meet for several years after that, but its activities ceased around 1607 after James expressed serious disapproval of the society's investigations into the antiquity of English common law and parliamentary rights that were at odds with the king's royal prerogative.

A formative event in Cotton's youth was the six-month archeological tour he undertook with Camden in 1600 to the environs of Hadrian's Wall–then known as the Picts Wall–to survey the Roman ruins and to inquire among the locals about the survival of British and Roman monuments. Together they scoured the area for any signs of graves, coins, building remains, or stone inscriptions; much of the information they gathered went into the 1607 edition of Camden's *Britannia,* which included a greatly augmented discussion of the topographical history of the region and reproduced many of the coins and inscriptions they had found. In the chapter on Cumbria, for instance, Camden describes an altar he had happened upon and remarks that "the whole altar and each of its sides were vividly described by the hand of Robert Cotton of Conington, knight, a great student of antiquity when we travelled together through this district delightfully nourishing our minds in a common desire to throw light on our native land."

Cotton arranged for a large number of artifacts to be transported back to Conington, where he erected a long gallery and terrace for the purpose of displaying his collection of altars and inscriptions, and it was on the basis of this collection that he wrote a series of studies of Roman epitaphs, which were published in Hearne's *Collection of Curious Discourses.* (His altars and inscriptions were donated by a descendant to Trinity College, Cambridge, in 1750; they are housed today in the Museum of Archeology in Cambridge.) Cotton's collection of British, Roman, and Anglo-Saxon coins, which during his lifetime was rivaled only by that of Henry, Prince of Wales, likewise became a national treasure that was much admired by Cotton's contemporaries before it was absorbed into the British Museum. Engravings of many of his British and Roman coins were printed in John Speed's *History of Great Britaine* (1611 and 1614), which concludes with an expression of gratitude to "that worthy Repairer of eating Time's Ruins, the learned Sir Robert Cotton, Kt. Baronet, another Philadelphus in preserving old Monuments and ancient Records; whose Cabinets were unlocked, and Library continually set open to my free access."

The field trip with Camden was of inestimable value in Cotton's intellectual development. It fired his historical imagination and expanded his range of interests as a private collector. Most important, it instilled in him the conviction that material remains are every bit as crucial as the documentary record in reconstructing the past. Guided by a strong archeological impulse and an intuitive feel for the historical method, Cotton had a remarkably forward-thinking attitude toward antiquarian research.

Cotton's passion for collecting medieval manuscripts was already evident by 1588, when he began gathering materials for a history of his native county of Huntingdonshire, a project that he periodically returned to during the course of his life, although he never published anything from it. He was already in possession of a book pertaining to the history of Ramsey Abbey, located just a few miles east of Conington, as well as three other manuscripts that may represent his earliest efforts at constructing a library. These include a tenth-century collection of Anglo-Saxon penitential texts and a fifteenth-century *Polychronicon,* both now in the British Library, and a fifteenth-century copy of Giles of Rome's *De regimine principium,* now in the Bodleian Library. Each of these manuscripts is inscribed with Cotton's name, the year 1588, and his age at the time, seventeen.

During the next several decades Cotton's collection grew steadily as he hired agents to purchase manuscripts for him both in England and abroad, and as it became customary for friends and peers to send him books as gifts. Tate gave Cotton a manuscript of Anglo-Saxon laws; James Ussher, archbishop of Armagh, presented him with the famous Samaritan Pentateuch in 1627 in appreciation for Cotton's help with his research into the history of the British church. The holdings of his library increased dramatically in the second decade of the seventeenth century when Cotton benefited, either through purchase or inheritance, from the dispersal of the libraries of several prominent collectors who died between 1609 and 1614. In this way he obtained books from the estate of Lord John Lumley and from the libraries of Prince Henry; Robert Cecil, Earl of Salisbury and lord treasurer and principal secretary under James I; William Dethik, the Garter king of arms; Henry Howard, Earl of Northampton, one of his earliest patrons; and Arthur Agarde, the keeper of the records. Cotton also acquired about eighty books from the library of Henry Savile of Banke, provost of Eton, whose library was sold upon his death in 1617. In the mid 1620s Cotton purchased about thirty manuscripts that had once belonged to the Elizabethan mathematician and astrologer John Dee.

How other books came into Cotton's hands is sometimes difficult to say, but that his reputation as a collector long carried with it an aura of sensationalism and intrigue can be gathered from an apocryphal story current in the eighteenth and nineteenth centuries about how he supposedly discovered one of his most treasured documents. As reported in *Curiosities of Literature* (1791) by Isaac D'Israeli, who came upon the story in a collection of anecdotes about the seventeenth-century Anglo-French scholar Paul Colomiès, one day Cotton paid a visit to his London tailor and found him measuring garments with a great sheet of parchment. Cotton immediately recognized the value of the document, offered to purchase the sheet at any price, and returned home that day with one of only four extant copies of the Magna Carta, complete with original signatures and seals, for just two pence. The story is regrettably fictional, since it is known that Cotton received both of his copies of the Magna Carta as gifts, the best known from Sir Edward Dering in 1630. A similarly fantastic story is related by John Aubrey, who claims in his *Brief Lives* (1898) that he was told by Meredith Lloyd that the famous conjuring books of Dee had been buried upon Dee's death in 1608 but that Cotton had caught wind of their attempted destruction and bought the field so he could dig them up and add them to his library.

Many questions persist about the formation and early history of Cotton's collection, but the physical arrangement of the library as it stood in Cotton House in the late 1620s can be deduced in part from the scheme he was in the process of devising for assigning pressmarks to the manuscripts shortly before the library was closed in 1629. In 1622 Cotton purchased a residence in the heart of the palace at Westminster, between Westminster Hall and St. Stephen's Chapel to the east and the old House of Lords to the west, where he set aside a narrow room on the second floor to house his manuscript library. This room stood immediately adjacent to the Painted Chamber, where the Commons and Lords frequently met, and according to a tradition going back at least to the eighteenth century it had once been a royal chapel for Edward the Confessor. The room was only six feet wide but was about thirty-eight feet long, with arched windows at either end and a series of niches or embrasures along the walls suitable for enclosing book presses or cabinets of varying heights and widths.

The manuscripts were placed in fourteen presses, or *scrinia,* each set back into one of the embrasures and surmounted by the brass bust of a Roman emperor or imperial lady. Six presses, those dominated by like-

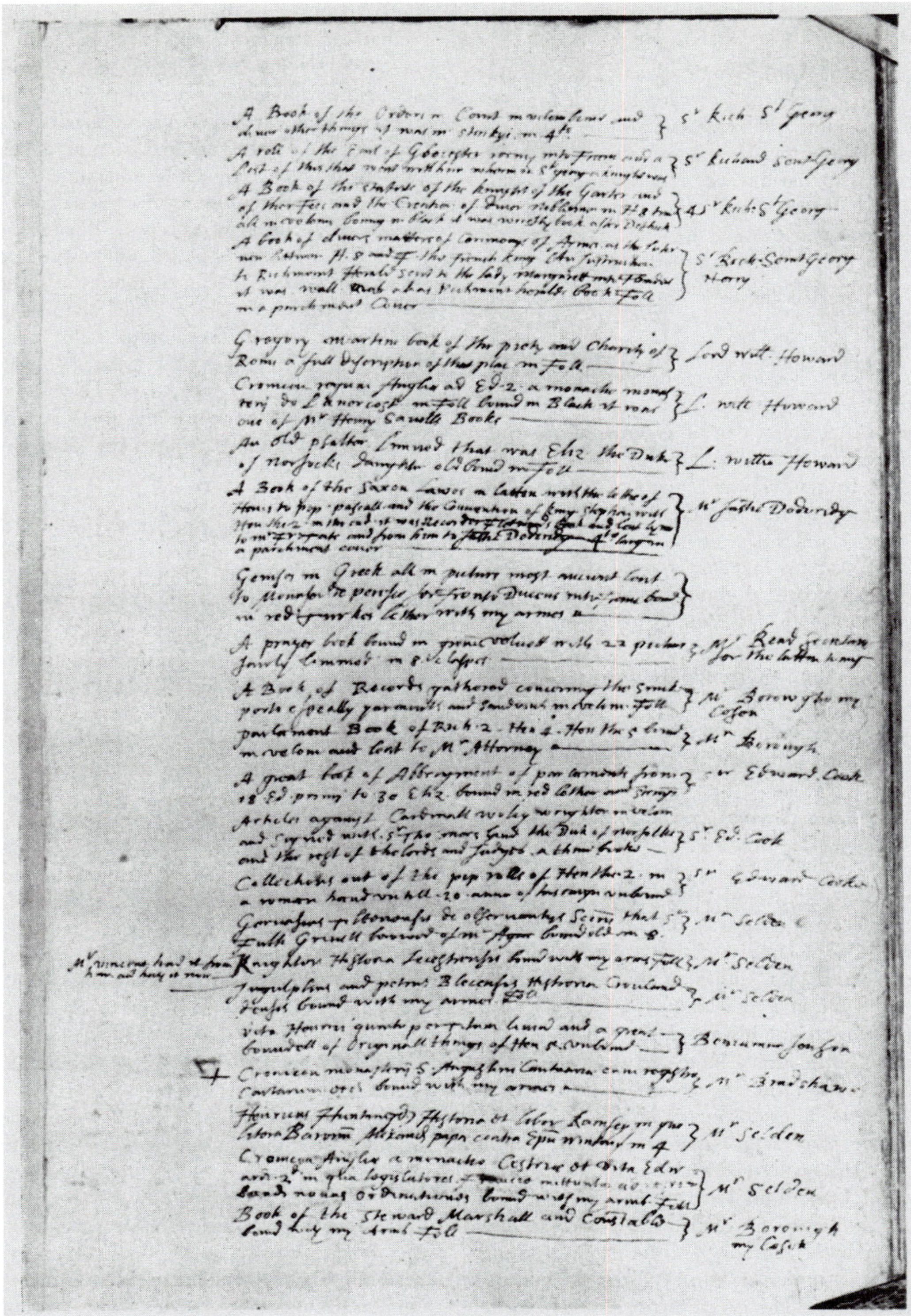

A list of books loaned by Cotton (British Library)

nesses of Julius, Vitellius, Vespasian, Titus, Cleopatra, and Faustina, contained six shelves or *classes* of books. Another six presses, those for Tiberius, Caligula, Claudius, Nero, Galba, and Otho, had five. The Domitian books occupied a single shelf located probably over the only door that entered the room, perhaps directly across from the Julius press. The Augustus books were likewise situated on a single shelf, though judging from the large number of charters and maps that survive with Augustus pressmarks, the Augustus bookshelf must have sat atop or within a sizable cabinet where loose documents and parchment rolls were stored. With its mixed arrangement of books, charters, and assorted odds and ends, the Augustus press may have held the antiquarian treasures that Camden refers to admiringly in the 1610 edition of *Britannia,* the "famous Cabinet, whence of his singular courtesie, he [Cotton] hath oftentimes given me great light in these darksome obscurities."

Several of the presses must also have contained drawers or boxes full of the precious coins, seals, medals, and other curiosities that Cotton was renowned for collecting. In 1635 when the papal legate Gregorio Panzani took a tour of the library in the company of Cotton's son, Sir Thomas Cotton, he was shown some letters pertaining to Henry VIII's divorce, a papal bull written by Clement VII, and a portion of St. Thomas à Becket's skull, presumably the fabled corona that had long been on display as a relic at Canterbury Cathedral until the Becket shrine was demolished by Cromwell in the 1530s. When Richard Lapthorne visited the Cotton library in 1692, he reported seeing a variety of rarities, including the alchemical instruments once owned by Dee and the sword of Hugo Lupus, an earl of Chester who came to England with William the Conqueror.

Precisely why Cotton chose these fourteen emperors and imperial ladies to adorn the presses in his library is not fully understood, but the plan clearly reflects an arrangement appealing to the tastes of a classically trained Renaissance gentleman. Colin G. C. Tite in his 1994 monograph *The Manuscript Library of Sir Robert Cotton* makes the intriguing suggestion that Cotton's choice may have followed from King Charles I's purchase in 1628 of a set of twelve portraits of these same caesars, eleven painted by Titian. The plan seems not to have been fully realized until after Cotton's death, however, since none of the inventories of Cotton's collection drawn up during his lifetime makes use of the imperial shelfmarks.

Within a decade of Cotton's death and well before Smith's catalogue of 1696, each manuscript was assigned a pressmark that incorporated three pieces of information: the name of the imperial figure above the press, a letter representing the shelf on which the book sat, and a Roman numeral indicating the book's position on the shelf. The *Beowulf* manuscript, for instance, was marked Vitellius A. XV, the fifteenth book from the left-hand side of the top shelf of the Vitellius press; the Lindisfarne Gospels, Nero D. IV, occupied the fourth position from the left side of the fourth shelf of the Nero press. Because the Domitian and Augustus presses consisted of only one shelf each, the pressmarks for these books stop at A, and the letter is sometimes simply omitted. Thus, the *Liber Vitae* of Durham was designated Domitian VII, the seventh of a total of eighteen books that Cotton assigned to the emperor Domitian. Within this scheme there appears to have been little effort to arrange books by content or even language. The enormous number of state papers that Cotton accumulated from the reigns of Henry VIII through James I were kept primarily in the Caligula, Nero, and Galba presses, and smaller manuscripts throughout the library were as a rule kept on top shelves.

At the time of Cotton's death in 1631, the library probably contained between 800 and 900 manuscripts. Cotton took it upon himself to compile an inventory of his library beginning in 1621, a task that was carried forward by his personal librarian, Richard James, who upon his appointment in 1624 began entering a list of contents on the flyleaf of each manuscript he worked with. Although this catalogue lists only 413 volumes, many manuscripts are not accounted for that are known to have already been part of the library at the time. When Smith catalogued the library in 1696, a full sixty-five years after Cotton's death, he listed 930 volumes that he divided into six categories: (1) manuscripts in Old English; (2) monastic registers or cartularies; (3) books of the Bible and collections of saints' lives; (4) genealogies and heraldic material; (5) histories, annals, and chronicles, chiefly of early British history; and (6) records of state. Smith's tally, however, takes into account all the manuscripts that had been added to the library since Cotton's death, including, to take one notable example, a book of statutes from the reigns of Edward I through Richard III that came into the collection in 1631 as a gift to Sir Thomas Cotton. At the time of the fire in Ashburnham House in 1731, the library had grown to 958 volumes–surely larger than it had ever been during Cotton's lifetime.

What is important to realize is that it was never the size of Cotton's library that mattered so much as the rarity and distinctiveness of its contents, which had no real parallel anywhere. Even at an optimistic estimate of 900 manuscripts, Cotton's library was considerably smaller than that of his contemporary Henry Percy, the earl of Northumberland, who owned between 1,500 and 2,000 books, and only a fraction of the size of the

A fragment of Cotton's fifth-century Greek manuscript for the Old Testament book of Genesis, which was almost completely destroyed by fire in 1731 (British Library)

library of Cotton's friend and fellow bibliophile Selden, who amassed an impressive 6,256 books in several exotic languages. Yet, the bulk of the Northumberland and Selden libraries consisted of printed books that could be had in multiple copies, whereas Cotton specialized in unique and hard-to-obtain items, including hoards of ancient and medieval manuscripts that had been rescued from the dissolved monasteries and were already centuries old.

Only Cotton possessed the sole-surviving texts of *Beowulf,* the Old English *Martyrology,* and Asser's *Life of King Alfred,* and only Cotton had multiple versions of the Anglo-Saxon *Chronicle* and Bede's *Ecclesiastical History.* Cotton's was the only library anywhere that contained the ninth-century Utrecht Psalter, the sole copy of *Sir Gawain and the Green Knight,* the only manuscript of Photius's Greek *Lexikon* known to scholars before the nineteenth century, and a fifth-century Greek Genesis that had once belonged to Origen. Cotton alone possessed the two surviving manuscripts of Layamon's *Brut* and copies of all three versions–English, French, and Latin–of the *Ancrene Riwle.* His library also had become home to the papers of the Tudor antiquaries John Bale, William Lambarde, John Leland, Laurence Nowell, and Francis Thynne, meaning that many of the choicest fruits of sixteenth-century English historical scholarship were in his sole possession. In addition, all the seventeenth-century editions of chronicles relating to the Norman Conquest were made from Cotton manuscripts. In an attempt to stock his library with the best Middle English poets, Cotton built the finest collection of manuscripts of Geoffrey Chaucer, John Gower, Thomas Hoccleve, and John Lydgate in existence. The library was in its time the premier repository of literary manuscripts in the British Isles, and in the words of Samuel Pepys, "one of the jewels of the Crown of England."

For most of Cotton's adult life, but particularly in the 1610s and 1620s when the manuscripts were located in London, his library was a formidable center of intellectual activity. Eminent figures routinely called on Cotton for assistance with research that only he could provide. Ben Jonson, who was Cotton's neighbor in Blackfriars for some years and who spent parts of 1603 and 1604 visiting with Cotton at Conington while the plague was ravaging London, consulted him on details of Roman geography for one of his masques. The chapter on Roman Britain in Speed's *History of Great Britaine* was produced under Cotton's direct editorial supervision. William Lisle's pioneering studies of Anglo-Saxon language and literature, culminating in his 1623 edition of Ælfric's *Treatise on the Old and New Testaments* and his *Divers Ancient Monuments in the Saxon Tongue* (1638), were almost wholly undertaken in the Cotton library. While imprisoned in the Tower of London, Sir Walter Ralegh wrote to Cotton to request books he needed to write his *History of the World* (1614).

Cotton similarly made his collections available to John Weever, whose *Ancient Funerall Monuments* (1631) praises Cotton's descent from the same noble lineage as King James and includes a full-page woodcut of the brass memorial to Sir Robert's great-great-great-grandfather, William Cotton, in the parish church of St. Margaret's in Westminster. The preface to Weever's book even includes a fulsome Latin elegy to Cotton, who died shortly before the book went to press. The erudite Selden, who spent years plumbing the contents of Cotton's library and who dedicated his *Historie of Tithes* (1618) to his friend, writes in the preface to his edition of Eadmer's *Historia Novorum* (1623) that "the manuscripts to whose evidence without reference or title we give our approval were all supplied (including that from which the present work is derived) from the well-equipped and priceless library of that noble and learned man, my friend Robert Cotton, knight and baronet, who has deservedly won immortal fame both abroad and at home not only from his collection of books and manuscripts of the choicest sort acquired at vast expense but also through his kindness and willingness to make them available to students of good literature and affairs of state." Sir Francis Bacon likewise acknowledged Cotton's help in furnishing materials for his *Historie of the*

Raigne of King Henry the Seventh (1622), addressing Cotton as "a worthy Preserver and Treasurer of rare Antiquities from whose Manuscripts I have had much light for the finishing of this Work."

One of the most distinguished visitors to the Cotton library was Archbishop Ussher, who made periodic visits to London during the course of about twenty years to work in the library while writing his monumental history of the Christian church in the British Isles. When an interim volume of the project appeared in 1623, Ussher sent a copy to Cotton taking special pains to mark all the manuscripts he had consulted in Cotton's collection with an asterisk. In the preface to the final volume, *Britannicarum Ecclesiarum Antiquitates,* published eight years after Cotton's death, Ussher explains that "my most abundant supplies of manuscripts came from that noble Cotton library, which alone gives more help to the achievement of a history of the British nation than all others combined. These were formerly made available by the great kindness, which for my part I reciprocate, of my friend Robert Cotton, whom Britain will always celebrate as keeper and dispenser of her antiquities."

That Cotton not only assisted other scholars with their research but had an intimate knowledge of the contents of his own books, including those in Greek, Hebrew, and Old English, is apparent from his readiness to answer questions and to direct inquiring visitors to particular texts. His early papers for the Society of Antiquaries drew from records in his possession, as did many of his parliamentary tracts produced in the 1620s. His detailed notes on books that he had loaned out to friends and his extensive compilations of materials toward a history of the English church and a history of Huntingdonshire likewise reveal a thorough knowledge of his materials. As Clement Rayner remarks in his *Apostolatus Benedictinorum in Anglia* (1626), a study of the Benedictine mission in Britain written largely in the Cotton library, Cotton "does not treat his books as Erasmus jestingly says that the Spaniards do, as ornamental cover for the walls, but he himself turns their pages so diligently that he has at the tip of his tongue whatever they contain worthy of memory about ancient history so that he becomes a living library himself." His encyclopedic grasp of English heraldry also marked him as an indispensable resource for courtiers and nobles who had questions about heraldic and genealogical matters that could not be readily answered by the College of Arms. In addition to charting his own family pedigrees, he helped Sir Thomas Howard, Earl of Arundel, trace his family history and aided Sir Kenelm Digby in locating precedents for his claim of knighthood.

In spite of the extraordinary depth of his learning, however, Cotton never published a single paper on any of the antiquarian subjects that so engrossed him. He instead seems to have been content with the role he forged for himself as England's leading orchestrator and facilitator of antiquarian studies. Perhaps at least in part because his proposal to Queen Elizabeth to found a national academy and library had failed, he worked increasingly hard in the 1610s and 1620s to promote his own library as a state archive and center for research, relocating it in 1622 to Westminster in the midst of Parliament and allowing admittance to anyone who wished to consult his books.

Cotton's zeal in acquiring manuscripts to enhance his own library was matched by his eagerness to make his books available to a wider public and to endow other libraries. In 1602 at the request of Sir Thomas Bodley, who had begun to devote his energy and influence to the improvement of the library at Oxford, Cotton donated twelve manuscripts to the fledgling project. These include the precious seventh-century Italian "Gospels of St. Augustine"; a twelfth-century collection of sermons in Latin and Old English; a twelfth-century set of Origen's Homilies on Genesis, Exodus, and Leviticus; a commentary on the Canticles; a thirteenth-century copy of Gregory the Great's *Pastoral Care;* a fourteenth-century copy of Jacobus de Voragine's *Golden Legend* from Christ Church, Canterbury; a fifteenth-century collection of theological treatises from Syon Abbey; a fifteenth-century copy of Lactantius's *Divine Institutions* from Italy; a late-fifteenth-century copy of Werner Rolewinck's *Paradise of Conscience;* a partial Old Testament in Hebrew with a table of contents in Cotton's hand; a Hebrew miscellany including grammars and fables; and a collection of Hebrew prayers. Five of these manuscripts bear an *ex dono* inscription with a date of 1602 indicating Cotton as donor, and another four are inscribed with Cotton's name. Eleven are listed in the Bodleian's Register of Benefactors under the year 1603, and only one is no longer at Oxford, having passed first into the library of Edward Stillingfleet, bishop of Worcester, thence into Robert Harley's private collection in 1707, and at length into the British Museum.

The gift to Bodley's project was in all likelihood Cotton's first donation of books his own, but it was certainly not his last. Several other manuscripts migrated from Cotton's collection into the Bodleian during the first three decades of the seventeenth century, among them an eleventh-century copy of the Old English Hexateuch, followed by Ælfric's homily on Judges, which had originally belonged to the Royal Library. How Cotton acquired this manuscript is unknown, but between 1603 and 1606 he excised one of its contents,

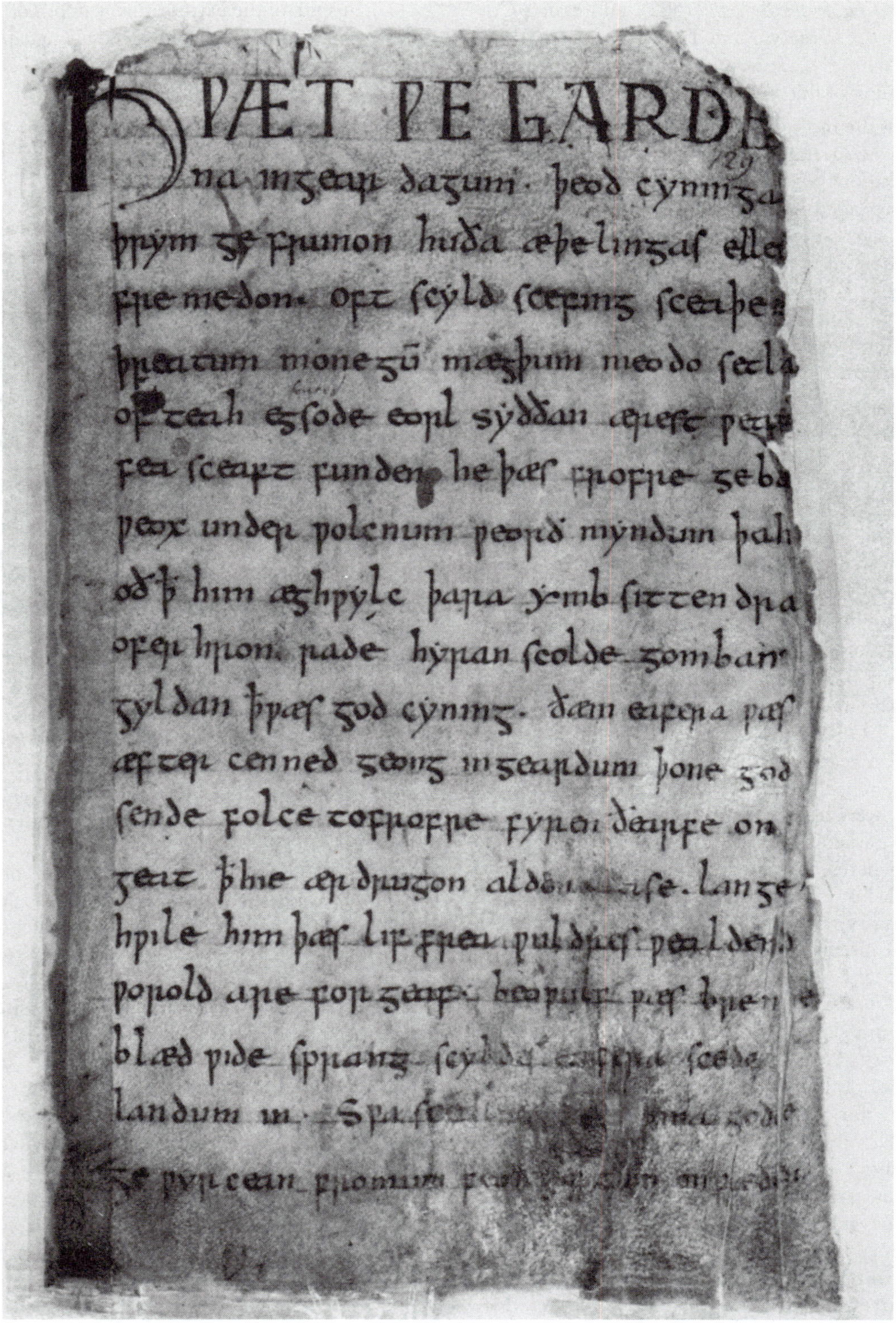
HWÆT WE GARDE
na in gear dagum. þeod cyninga
þrym ge frunon hu ða æþelingas elle
fremedon. oft scyld scefing sceaþe
þreatum monegū mægþum meodo setl
of teah egsode eorl syððan ærest wear
fea sceaft funden he þæs frofre geb
weox under wolcnum weorð myndum þah
oð þ him æghwylc þara ymb sittendra
ofer hron rade hyran scolde gomban
gyldan þ wæs god cyning. ðæm eafera wæs
æfter cenned geong in geardum þone god
sende folce to frofre fyren ðearfe on
geat þ hie ær drugon aldor ase. lange
hwile him þæs lif frea wuldres wealdend
worold are for geaf. beowulf wæs breme
blæd wide sprang scyldes eafera scede
landum in.

First page of Cotton's Beowulf *manuscript, which escaped serious damage in the 1731 fire (British Library)*

an Old English life of St. Guthlac, and inserted it into a new composite manuscript. The dismembered Hexateuch manuscript found its way into the hands of the Cambridge Saxonist Lisle, who in turn seems to have lent it to Archbishop William Laud, who donated the book to the Bodleian in 1639. Another three of Cotton's manuscripts were at some point acquired by Sir Kenelm Digby, who entrusted them to the Bodleian in 1634.

In some cases Cotton's generosity worked against him, as when he sent books out on loan that never were returned. Camden borrowed so many books from Cotton that he stipulated in his will that upon his death Cotton should be allowed to search his quarters for missing books. In the late 1620s Cotton loaned several exquisite manuscripts to his good friend the earl marshal, Thomas Howard, Earl of Arundel, that he never saw again and that for the most part now bear the pressmarks of other libraries. These include the most lavishly illustrated manuscript of the ninth century, the Utrecht Psalter, held by Utrecht University Library, and the Lovel Lectionary and the fifth-century Cotton Genesis–which was repurchased by Sir John Cotton a half-century later for thirty guineas, only to suffer severe damage in the 1731 fire–both now the property of the British Library. Through an involved series of exchanges with Patrick Young, the Royal librarian, eight of Cotton's manuscripts found their way into the Royal Library after 1616, and other manuscripts once owned by Cotton have since entered libraries around the world, including the Folger Shakespeare Library in Washington, D.C., the National Library of Wales in Aberystwyth, and the National Library of Australia in Canberra.

During the years that his library was in the process of achieving international acclaim, Cotton was actively involved in court politics and parliamentary debate. As a member of Parliament under James I, he wrote tracts on questions of church discipline and administrative reform and assisted Bacon in drafting a strategy for uniting England and Scotland. In 1608 he was appointed special counsel to the commission charged with investigating abuses in the Royal Navy, and the commission, headed by the earl of Northampton, regularly met at Cotton's house in Blackfriars. In 1611, in an attempt to rescue the troubled finances of the exchequer, Cotton authored a report on the revenues of the Crown that included a proposal to James to found a new honorary order of baronets that he envisioned as a revival of the medieval order of the knights banneret. Eager to spur revenues through the sale of new titles, James seized at the idea, and Cotton became one of the first bearers of the title of baronet on 29 June 1611.

In the mid 1610s Cotton's favor at court began to decline, partly because of his increasing opposition to Stuart methods of taxation and his open criticism of the abuses of royal power and partly because of a growing concern that the large number of state documents Cotton possessed should not be in private hands. In October 1615 Cotton was arrested for attempting to protect his patron Robert Carr, the Earl of Somerset, who had been charged with the murder of Sir Thomas Overbury, and many of Cotton's papers were carted to Whitehall for examination. After eight months in prison he was pardoned without a formal trial. In 1621 Cotton's support for the antiroyalist faction came out in the open when he wrote a tract arguing that on historical as well as ethical grounds the king was obliged to consult Parliament and council on issues concerning "marriage, peace, and warre." In 1624, near the end of James's rule, Cotton was asked to investigate the history of Anglo-Spanish political relations and produce a set of legal precedents that could be used to charge the Spanish ambassador with misconduct in office. The result was Cotton's tract "A Remonstrance of the Treaties of Amity and Marriage of the Houses of Austria and Spain with the Kings of England" and a second tract addressed to George Villiers, Duke of Buckingham, on "Proceedings against Ambassadors who have Miscarried Themselves."

In August 1625 Cotton circulated in the House of Commons an elaborate set of notes on precedents for parliamentary criticism of military officers that Sir John Eliot fashioned into an eloquent essay attacking the duke of Buckingham and threatening his impeachment. When Buckingham discovered Cotton's part in this affair, he sought revenge by orchestrating a snub of Cotton. In February 1626 the earl of Arundel arranged for the barge transporting King Charles I down the river from Whitehall to Westminster for his coronation ceremony to land at the steps leading to Cotton's garden. The plan was that Charles would disembark in the shadow of Cotton House, where he would be greeted by Cotton, who would be holding the "Gospels of Æthelstan," a manuscript in his collection onto which centuries of English monarchs had supposedly placed their hands while taking the coronation oath. Buckingham, however, ordered the barge to pass by Cotton's landing, in full view of Cotton and his chagrined entourage.

Despite his sour relations with Charles and Buckingham, Cotton continued to be consulted on important historical questions. In 1628 the council sought Cotton's advice on the mounting displeasure with the king and Buckingham following the disastrous expedition to La Rochelle and the war with Spain. Cotton took this opportunity to air his views publicly by issuing a short tract titled *The Danger wherein the Kingdome now Standeth, & the Remedie* (1628), the only piece of writing he ever published under his own name. In it he argued that the duke should take his rightful place among his peers on the privy council and should convey to the people the king's renewed commitment to serve the nation. In typical Cottonian fashion he grounded his argument in historical precedent by recalling the fates of Edward II, Richard II, and Henry IV, and he urged Charles and Buckingham to become reconciled to their enemies.

Although Cotton had produced a devoutly patriotic and ultimately pro-Royalist tract, he was not restored to Charles's good graces. His house was widely known to be the meeting place for members of the opposition party, including Selden and Eliot, and the feeling was widespread that the oppositionists' strength emanated directly from the Cotton library. Cotton's final undoing came some months later in 1629, when an allegedly seditious document, "A Proposition for His Majesty's Service to Bridle the Impertinency of Parliaments," was found among his papers. Charles and his councillors chose to interpret the article as a parody of the king's policies. Although Cotton denied any knowledge of this tract, which was later shown to be written by Sir Robert Dudley, he was arrested and charged with treason and his library was closed by order of the privy council. For more than a year he appealed to Charles to be allowed to revisit his books, but his requests were repeatedly denied. Cotton died on 6 May 1631 at the age of sixty, reportedly of grief over the confiscation of his precious library.

Following Cotton's death, the library passed into the hands of his son, who continued his father's policy of allowing open admission to any and all who wished to pursue research in the collection. The library remained in the Cotton family until 1702, when upon the death of Sir John Cotton it became national property, as his grandfather had long intended. In 1730 the library was relocated, along with the royal collection, to Ashburnham House in Little Dean's Yard, Westminster, where on 23 October 1731 a fire broke out in a room immediately below the library. Before the fire could be contained, thirteen Cotton manuscripts were utterly consumed and many others were either reduced to a handful of charred fragments or damaged beyond repair, including the fifth-century Cotton Genesis, the manuscript containing the *Battle of Maldon,* and the cartulary of Lenton Priory. The *Beowulf* manuscript escaped with a thorough singeing around the edges that destroyed the calf binding and obliterated a portion of the outermost text.

The remaining collection was then transferred to the Old Dormitory of Westminster School, where some repairs were attempted on the books damaged by fire and water. In 1753 the library was finally given a permanent resting place when it was incorporated into the British Museum as a founding collection. A new catalogue of the Cotton manuscripts was drawn up by Samuel Hooper in 1777, and yet another was published by Joseph Planta in 1802, but neither provides comprehensive coverage of the manuscripts owned by Cotton or accounts fully for the state of the fragments that survived the fire. A thorough and reliable catalogue of the entire Cotton library providing complete information about the contents, provenance, and subsequent history of each manuscript has yet to be accomplished.

Although his library is without question his most enduring achievement, Sir Robert Cotton deserves recognition for his many contributions to historical scholarship and political debate in the early decades of the seventeenth century. He was a catalyst for groundbreaking humanistic research on many subjects and a powerful advocate for parliamentary rights. He was an inspiration to students of local history and archeology and a guiding spirit behind the Society of Antiquaries and the British Library. His private collections furnished the basis for modern studies of British numismatics and medieval English poetry, and his tracts on the Continental origins of English offices and the history of English political relations with France and Spain initiated an important tradition of comparative legal study. A prolific correspondent with scholars across Europe and the supervisor of countless editorial projects undertaken in his own library, Cotton did more to further literary and historical scholarship than anyone of his era.

Biographies:

Edward Edwards, "The Founder of the Cottonian Library," in his *Lives of the Founders of the British Museum; with Notices of Its Chief Augmentors and Other Benefactors. 1570–1870* (London: Trübner / New York: J. W. Bouton, 1870), pp. 48–152;

Hope Mirrlees, *A Fly in Amber, Being an Extravagant Biography of the Romantic Antiquary Sir Robert Bruce Cotton* (London: Faber & Faber, 1962);

Thomas Smith, "The Life of Sir Robert Cotton, Knight and Baronet," in his *Catalogue of the Manuscripts in the Cottonian Library 1696,* edited by Colin G. C. Tite (Cambridge: D. S. Brewer, 1984), pp. 25–46.

References:

Janet Backhouse, "Sir Robert Cotton's Record of a Royal Bookshelf," *British Library Journal,* 18 (1992): 44–51;

James P. Carley, "The Royal Library as a Source for Sir Robert Cotton's Collection: A Preliminary List of

Acquisitions," *British Library Journal,* 18 (1992): 52–73;

Carley and Colin G. C. Tite, "Sir Robert Cotton as Collector of Manuscripts and the Question of Dismemberment: British Library MSS Royal 13 D. I and Cotton Otho D. VIII," *Library,* sixth series, 14 (1992): 94–99;

R. C. B. Gardner, "Sir Robert Cotton, a Great Collector," *Chambers Journal,* seventh series 14 (1924): 782–784;

Elisabeth M. C. van Houts, "Camden, Cotton and the Chronicles of the Norman Conquest of England," *British Library Journal,* 18 (1992): 148–162;

David Howarth, "Sir Robert Cotton and the Commemoration of Famous Men," *British Library Journal,* 18 (1992): 1–28;

Roger B. Manning, "Antiquarianism and the Seigneurial Reaction: Sir Robert and Sir Thomas Cotton and Their Tenants," *Historical Research,* 63 (1990): 277–288;

Manning, "Sir Robert Cotton, Antiquarianism and Estate Administration: A Chancery Decree of 1627," *British Library Journal,* 18 (1992): 88–96;

Graham Parry, "Cotton's Counsels: The Contexts of *Cottoni Posthuma,*" *British Library Journal,* 18 (1992): 29–43;

Parry, "Sir Robert Cotton," in *The Trophies of Time: English Antiquarians of the Seventeenth Century* (Oxford: Oxford University Press, 1995), pp. 70–94;

Kevin Sharpe, *Sir Robert Cotton 1586–1631: History and Politics in Early Modern England* (Oxford: Oxford University Press, 1979);

E. C. Teviotdale, "Some Classified Catalogues of the Cotton Library," *British Library Journal,* 18 (1992): 74–87;

Colin G. C. Tite, "A Catalogue of Sir Robert Cotton's Printed Books?" *British Library Journal,* 17 (1991): 1–11;

Tite, "The Cotton Appendix and the Cotton Fragments," *Library,* sixth series 15 (1993): 52–55;

Tite, "The Early Catalogues of the Cotton Library," *British Library Journal,* 6 (1980): 144–157;

Tite, "'Lost or Stolen or Strayed': A Survey of Manuscripts formerly in the Cotton Library," *British Library Journal,* 18 (1992): 107–147;

Tite, *The Manuscript Library of Sir Robert Cotton* (London: British Library, 1994);

A. G. Watson, "Sir Robert Cotton and Sir Simonds D'Ewes: An Exchange of Manuscripts," *British Museum Quarterly,* 25 (1961–1962): 19–23;

C. E. Wright, "The Elizabethan Society of Antiquaries and the Formation of the Cottonian Library," in *The English Library Before 1700,* edited by Francis Wormald and C. E. Wright (London: Athlone Press, 1958), pp. 176–212;

C. J. Wright, ed., *Sir Robert Cotton as Collector: Essays on an Early Stuart Courtier and His Legacy* (London: British Library, 1997).

Papers:

The personal papers of Sir Robert Bruce Cotton–consisting primarily of correspondence, antiquarian notes, family records, tracts and discourses on various subjects, and a collection of materials toward a history of the English church–are held principally in the British Library, London; the Bodleian Library, Oxford; and the Public Record Office, London. Other manuscripts are preserved in the Inner Temple Library, London; the library of Magdalene College, Cambridge; Cambridge University Library; the Cambridge County Record Office; the Huntingdonshire County Record Office; the Northumberland County Record Office; the Taunton Record Office, Somerset; Eton Hall, Peterborough; Alnwick Castle, Northumberland; Port Eliot, St. Germans, Cornwall; Holkham Hall, Norfolk; and the Houghton Library, Harvard University.

Thomas Cranmer

(2 July 1489 – 21 March 1556)

Emily Smith Riser
Southwest Texas State University

See also the Cranmer entry in *DLB 132: Sixteenth-Century British Nondramatic Writers, First Series.*

BOOKS: *An Exhortation vnto Prayer . . . to be Read in Euery Church afore Processyons. Also a Letanie with Suffrages to be Said or Song in the Tyme of the Said Processyons* (London: Printed by T. Berthelet, 1544);

Certain Sermons, or Homilies, Appoynted by the Kynges Maiestie, to be Declared and Redde, by all Persones, Vicars, or Curates, euery Sonday in their Churches, where thei haue Cure, by Cranmer and others (London: R. Grafton, 1547);

The Order of the Communion (London: R. Grafton, 1548);

The Booke of the Common Prayer and Administracion of the Sacramentes, and other Rites and Ceremonies of the Churche: after the Use of the Churche of England (London: E. Whitchurch, 1549); revised as *The Boke of Common Prayer, and Administracion of the Sacramentes, and Other Rites and Cerimonies in the Churche of Englande* (London: E. Whitchurch, 1552);

A Defence of the True and Catholike Doctrine of the Sacrament of the Body and Bloud of our Saviour Christ, with a Confutation of Sundry Errors concernyng the Same (London: R. Wolfe, 1550);

An Answere Against the False Calumniacions of D. Richarde Smyth who Hath taken vpon him to Confute the Defence (London: R. Wolfe, 1551);

An Answer of the Most Reverend Father in God Thomas Archebyshop of Canterburye Primate of all Englande and Metropolitane, unto A crafty and Sophisticall Cauillation deuised by Stephen Gardiner Doctour of Law, Late Byshop of Winchester, agaynst the Trewe and Godly Doctrine of the Moste Holy Sacrament of the Body and Bloud of Our Sauiour Iesv Christe. Wherin is also, as occasion serueth, Answered such Places of the booke of D. Rich. Smyth, as may Seeme any thyng Woorthy the Aunsweryng (London: R. Wolfe, 1551);

Articles Agreed upon by the Bishoppes and Other Learned and Godly Men, in the Last Convocatio at London, in the Yeare . . . MDLII (1553);

All the submyssyons, and recantations of Thomas Cranmer, Late Archebyshop of Canterburye, Truely set forth both in Latyn and Englysh. Agreable to the Originalles, Wrytten and Subscribed with his Owne Hande (London: John Cawood, 1556);

The Copy of Certain Lettres Sent to the Quene and also to Doctour Martin and Doctour Storye, by . . . Thomas Cranmer of Canterburye from Prison in Oxforde: who after Long and Most Greuous Strayt Emprisoning and Cruell Handlyng most Constauntly and Willingly Suffred martirdome ther for the True Testimonie of Christ in Marche 1556 (Emden: E. van der Erve, 1556?);

A Confutation of Unwritten Verities, both bi the holye Scriptures and Moste Auncient Autors, and also Probable Arguments, and Pithy Reasons, with Plaine Aunswers to Al (or at the least) to the Moste Part and Strongest Argumentes, which the Aduersaries of Gods Truth, either Haue or Can Bryng Forth for the Profe and Defence of the same Vnwritten Vanities, Verities as They Woulde Haue Them Called (Wesel?: Joost Lambrecht?, 1557?);

Reformatio Legvm Ecclesiasticarvm, ex Avthoritate primum Regis Henrici 8 . . . (London: John Daij, 1571).

Editions and Collections: *A Short Instruction into Christian Religion, being a Catechism set forth by Archbishop Cranmer in MDXLVIII: together with the same in Latin, translated from the German by Justus Jonas in MDXXXIX,* edited by Edward Burton (Oxford: Oxford University Press, 1829);

Writings of the Rev. Dr. Thomas Cranmer, Archbishop of Canterbury, and Martyr, 1556 (London: Printed for the Religious Tract Society, 1830?; Philadelphia: Presbyterian Board of Publication, 1842);

The Remains of Thomas Cranmer, 4 volumes, edited by Henry Jenkyns (Oxford: Oxford University Press, 1833);

The Works of Thomas Cranmer, Archbishop of Canterbury, Martyr, 1556, 2 volumes, edited by John Edmund Cox (Cambridge: Printed at the University Press, 1844, 1846);

The Reformation of the Ecclesiastical Laws as Attempted in the Reigns of King Henry VIII, King Edward VI, and Queen Elizabeth, edited by Edward Cardwell (Oxford: Oxford University Press, 1850);

The Work of Thomas Cranmer, edited by G. E. Duffield (Appleford, U.K.: Sutton Courtenay Press, 1964).

OTHER: Prologue, *The Byble in Englyshe, . . . This is the Byble Apoynted to the Vse of the Churches* (London: E. Whitchurch or R. Grafton, 1540); republished as *The Judgment of Archbishop Cranmer concerning the Peoples Right to, and Discreet Use of the H. Scriptures,* edited by Edward Gee (London: Printed for John Taylor, 1689);

Catechismus, that is to say, a Shorte Instruction into Christian Religion for the Synguler Commoditie and Profyte of Childre and Yong People, translated by Cranmer (London: Printed by N. Hyll for G. Lynne, 1548).

Thomas Cranmer's library is one of the best-known collections of books and manuscripts to have survived in some form from the early Tudor period. Few private collections of Cranmer's day contained more than 200 books and manuscripts. In 1530, the university libraries at Cambridge and Oxford contained 500 to 600 volumes, but as a result of censorious royal acts and proclamations during the reigns of King Henry VIII, King Edward VI, and Queen Mary I, the collections of these libraries dwindled to fewer than 175 volumes by 1557. Cranmer's collection, according to David G. Selwyn in *The Library of Thomas Cranmer* (1996), contained more than 700 printed books. Only some of the monastic libraries were larger.

A scholar by nature and an important political figure by chance, Cranmer obtained books not for the sake of collecting them but because he was interested in their contents. He was a passionate annotator and seldom read without a pen in hand. Many of the extant texts are filled with annotations by Cranmer and his secretaries, making them a boon for scholars interested in understanding the thought processes of a key figure in the English Reformation. Additionally, the variety of books proves the breadth of Cranmer's interests and his lifelong pursuit of religious and philosophical truths. He read the early church fathers, the medieval scholastics, Christian humanists, and the writings of both sides of the Reformation debate. Few of his Protestant books survive, however, and the absence of certain texts makes it clear that his collection was affected by political purgings. Since his death Cranmer's library has been scattered among at least sixty-five locations including Pembroke College, Oxford; Durham University; Ushaw College; Corpus Christi College, Oxford; Newcastle University; St. Andrews University; and Lambeth Palace Library. The largest single collection is found at the British Library, which holds 334 printed books and 51 manuscripts from Cranmer's library.

The history of Cranmer's collection follows the history of his life. Thomas Cranmer was born at Aslockton in Nottinghamshire on 2 July 1489, the middle of three sons of Agnes Hatfield Cranmer and Thomas Cranmer, the squire of Aslockton. He was probably sent to school around age seven. At age fourteen he entered the seven-year-old Jesus College at Cambridge.

During his undergraduate years Cranmer was trained in logic as well as moral and natural philosophy. As a result of the Cambridge arts course readings, which consisted of the medieval scholastics that generations of students had studied before him, the first books in Cranmer's fledgling library were medieval scholastic textbooks, obtained mostly secondhand. Selwyn has identified Peter of Spain's *Summulae Logicales* (1500), Peter Tartaret's commentary on Aristotle's logic and philosophy, and works by Ptolemy, Abu Bakr ibn al-Kasil, John Holywood, and Nicolaus Wollick. Two copies of the Duns Scotus 1497 biography of Aristotle also appear in the library. The margins of these early books contain Cranmer's annotations, including the Arabic numeral notations that also appear in his later books.

Cranmer received his B.A. in July 1511. The next three years he worked on his M.A., during which time he studied Jacques Lefèvre, Desiderius Erasmus, and a selection of Latin authors. Cranmer's library expanded to reflect this new humanist perspective. He obtained a collection of commentaries on the New Testament Gospels and Catholic Epistles by the humanist Lefèvre, seventeen volumes of Erasmus, and texts by Rudolphus Agricola, Philipp Melancthon, Sir Thomas More (including his 1516 work *Utopia*), and Polydore Virgil. He received his M.A. in 1515, and sometime around this date he was awarded a fellowship from Jesus College.

Cranmer was forced to give up the fellowship shortly thereafter, however, because of his marriage to a young woman named Joan; celibacy was required even of unordained fellows. Many scholars have seen his marriage as exhibiting an uncharacteristic lack of caution on Cranmer's part. As a result of losing his fellowship, Cranmer was forced to take a low-paying job as a teacher at Buckingham College, a much less prestigious position than the fellowship. He lodged his wife at the Dolphin Inn in Cambridge; however, he evidently lived elsewhere, perhaps at Buckingham College. Cranmer's critics claim that the marriage lasted less than a year–implying a marriage necessitated by pregnancy–while his supporters assert that it was longer than this. Not long into the marriage, Cranmer lost his wife and child in childbirth. More than thirty-five years later at Cranmer's trial, his wife was scorned as "black Joan of the Dolphin," though Cranmer's admirers attempted to elevate her reputation by claiming that she was the daughter of a gentleman.

After the death of his wife, Cranmer was readmitted to his fellowship at Jesus College, and his studies took the distinct direction that he would follow in the future. Cranmer devoted three years to religious study, with particular attention to the scriptures. He earned his doctor of divinity degree in 1526. At the time doctoral study at Cambridge entailed the study of theology, and the only subject matter of the lectures at Jesus College was the Old and New Testaments. Cranmer took holy orders around 1520 and subsequently was named one of the preachers at Jesus.

Little is known about Cranmer's religious outlook and reforming sympathies during his almost thirty years at Cambridge. He was certainly aware of the humanist reformers, but it appears that his religious outlook was quite conservative in the early years; in fact, his ideas appear to have been aligned with those of his later rival, Stephen Gardiner. Contrary to what some historians have claimed, Cranmer did not join the White Horse Tavern reformers–a group with Lutheran tendencies that met at a tavern in Cambridge–nor did he openly resist the Catholic Church. Later, his critics attempted to prove that his antipapal sympathies extended back into the 1520s; however, there is little hard evidence to back up this claim.

Some evidence of Cranmer's opinions on religious issues during the controversies of the 1520s can be found in his book annotations. He makes some telling notes, for example, in his copy of John Fisher's *Assertionis Lutheranae Confutatio* (1523), a refutation of Luther's *Assertio Omnium Articulorum* (1520). In the margins of the book are annotations in black and in red; bibliographers have determined that Cranmer first made the black annotations and added the red annotations later. Writing in black, probably in the late 1520s and definitely before 1532, he expresses horror at many of Luther's arguments as recounted by Fisher as well as agreement with several of Fisher's refutations. In red, though, Cranmer added criticisms of Fisher and crossed out some of his earlier annotations regarding Luther.

During his early years at Cambridge, Cranmer was a fledgling biblical humanist, as he insisted on the importance of a personal knowledge of the Bible. John Foxe in *The Book of Martyrs* writes that as a biblical examiner at the divinity school, Cranmer

> would never admit any to proceed in divinity, unless they were substantially seen in the story of the Bible: by means whereof certain friars, and other religious persons, who were principally brought up in the study of school authors without regard had to the authority of Scriptures, were commonly rejected by him; so that he was greatly, for that his severe examination, of the religious sort much hated, and had in great indignation.

There was at the time no perceived incompatibility between orthodoxy and belief in the central importance of biblical authority.

In addition to books by Christian humanists, Cranmer obtained in his early years at Cambridge many texts by the church fathers–including a large number of Greek texts from antiquity, lexical and grammatical guides, and works by St. Basil of Caesarea, Eusebius, St. Gregory of Nyssa, and St. John Chrysostom, altogether more than 110 patristic texts. Later, in his debates with opponents and in his own developing position on Reformation issues, he used the early Greek and Latin authors as central texts to support his understanding of Scripture. Between the 1520s and 1530s Cranmer continued to read Latin authors but did not ignore the medieval scholastics. He acquired medieval manuscripts and books, especially scholastic commentaries on biblical texts by Peter Lombard, Thomas Aquinas, and Dionysius de Leuwis.

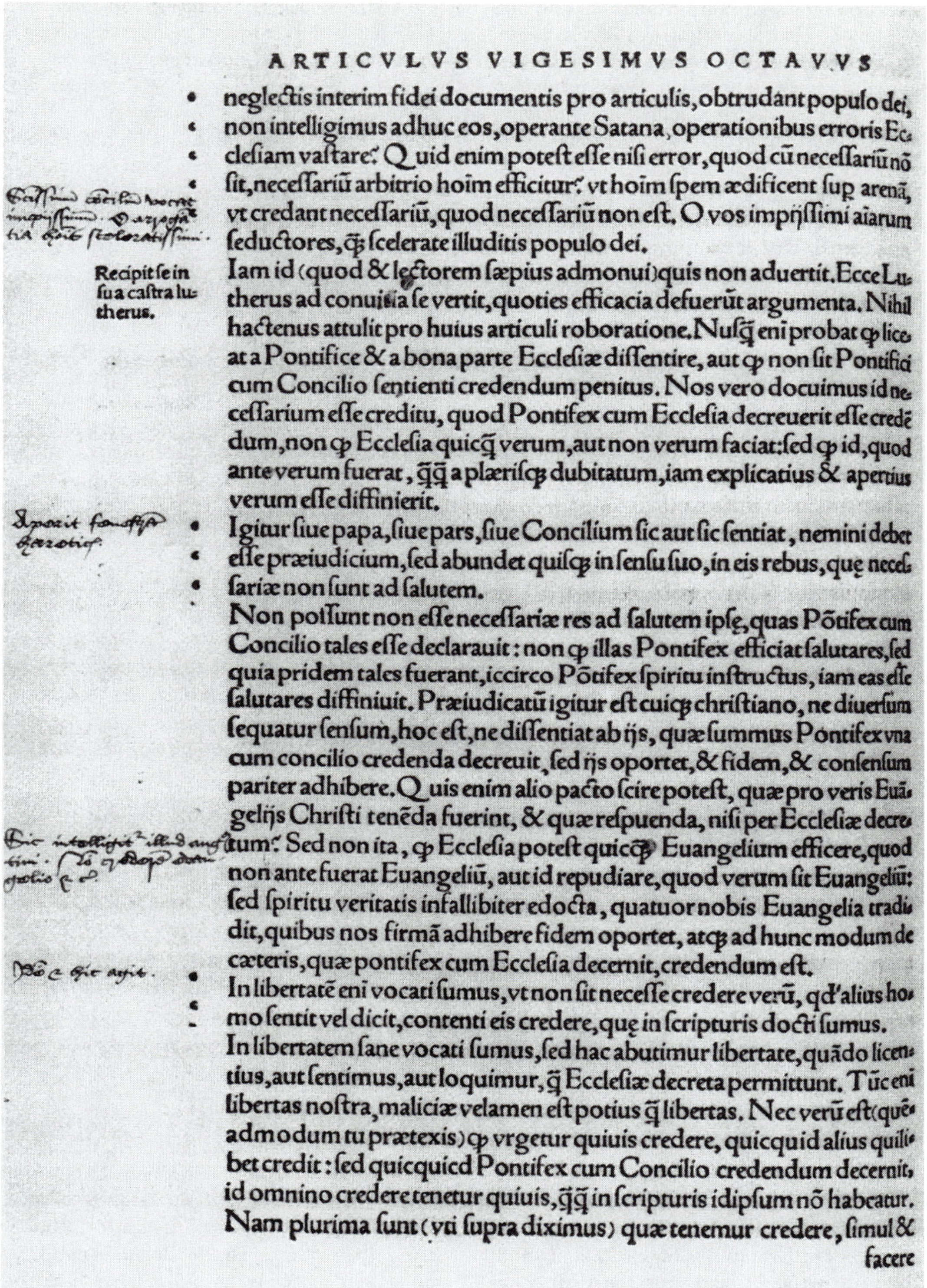

ARTICVLVS VIGESIMVS OCTAVVS

neglectis interim fidei documentis pro articulis, obtrudant populo dei, non intelligimus adhuc eos, operante Satana, operationibus erroris Ecclesiam vastare? Quid enim potest esse nisi error, quod cũ necessariũ nõ sit, necessariũ arbitrio hoĩm efficitur? vt hoĩm spem ædificent sup arenã, vt credant necessariũ, quod necessariũ non est. O vos impijssimi aĩarum seductores, qꝫ scelerate illuditis populo dei.

Recipit se in sua castra lutherus.

Iam id (quod & lectorem sæpius admonui) quis non aduertit. Ecce Lutherus ad conuitia se vertit, quoties efficacia defuerũt argumenta. Nihil hactenus attulit pro huius articuli roboratione. Nusq̃ enĩ probat qꝫ liceat a Pontifice & a bona parte Ecclesiæ dissentire, aut qꝫ non sit Pontifici cum Concilio sentienti credendum penitus. Nos vero docuimus id necessarium esse creditu, quod Pontifex cum Ecclesia decreuerit esse credẽdum, non qꝫ Ecclesia quicq̃ verum, aut non verum faciat: sed qꝫ id, quod ante verum fuerat, q̃q̃ a plærisqꝫ dubitatum, iam explicatius & apertius verum esse diffinierit.

Igitur siue papa, siue pars, siue Concilium sic aut sic sentiat, nemini debet esse præiudicium, sed abundet quisqꝫ in sensu suo, in eis rebus, quę necessariæ non sunt ad salutem.

Non possunt non esse necessariæ res ad salutem ipsę, quas Põtifex cum Concilio tales esse declarauit: non qꝫ illas Pontifex efficiat salutares, sed quia pridem tales fuerant, iccirco Põtifex spiritu instructus, iam eas esse salutares diffiniuit. Præiudicatũ igitur est cuiqꝫ christiano, ne diuersum sequatur sensum, hoc est, ne dissentiat ab ijs, quæ summus Pontifex vna cum concilio credenda decreuit, sed ijs oportet, & fidem, & consensum pariter adhibere. Quis enim alio pacto scire potest, quæ pro veris Euãgelijs Christi tenẽda fuerint, & quæ respuenda, nisi per Ecclesiæ decretum? Sed non ita, qꝫ Ecclesia potest quicq̃ Euangelium efficere, quod non ante fuerat Euangeliũ, aut id repudiare, quod verum sit Euangeliũ: sed spiritu veritatis infallibiter edocta, quatuor nobis Euangelia tradidit, quibus nos firmã adhibere fidem oportet, atqꝫ ad hunc modum de cæteris, quæ pontifex cum Ecclesia decernit, credendum est.

In libertatẽ enĩ vocati sumus, vt non sit necesse credere verũ, qđ alius homo sentit vel dicit, contenti eis credere, quę in scripturis docti sumus.

In libertatem sane vocati sumus, sed hac abutimur libertate, quãdo licentius, aut sentimus, aut loquimur, q̃ Ecclesiæ decreta permittunt. Tũc enĩ libertas nostra, maliciæ velamen est potius q̃ libertas. Nec verũ est (quẽadmodum tu prætexis) qꝫ vrgetur quiuis credere, quicquid alius quilibet credit: sed quicquid Pontifex cum Concilio credendum decernit, id omnino credere tenetur quiuis, q̃q̃ in scripturis idipsum nõ habeatur. Nam plurima sunt (vti supra diximus) quæ tenemur credere, simul & facere

Cranmer's marginal notes on a passage by Martin Luther in the 1523 edition of John Fisher's Assertionis Lutheranae Confutatio *(British Library)*

Cranmer took the sharp turn from scholar to politician as a result of a chance meeting in 1529. A plague outbreak in Cambridge had forced two of his students–sons of Master Cressey, whose wife was related to Cranmer–back to their father's house at Waltham. Cranmer went with the boys and was there in August when Henry VIII was in the immediate vicinity. With the king were Gardiner, his secretary, and Edward Fox, his almoner, both of whom had been college friends of Cranmer. Gardiner, Fox, and Cranmer met on 2 August, and the conversation naturally turned to the issue of Henry's marital situation. Since 1527 the king had been looking for a way to free himself from his wife, Catherine of Aragon, to marry Anne Boleyn. Cranmer suggested to Gardiner and Fox that the king had the right to divorce because Catherine was the widow of his brother, and he argued that the king ought to refer to theologians for support in his position rather than relying on the ecclesiastical courts to decide on the matter.

Upon hearing of Cranmer's stand, Henry summoned him and ordered that he write a book supporting the king's position with Scripture, the writings of the church fathers, and the decrees of general councils. Cranmer's ascendancy to power then proceeded quickly. In 1530 Henry appointed him to a delegation to Rome. Cranmer was soon appointed archdeacon of Taunton, and in January 1532 he was sent to Germany as an ambassador to Charles V, the Holy Roman Emperor. There he met and married Margaret, the niece of the theologian Andreas Osiander, who later bore him a son, Thomas, and a daughter, Margaret. In 1533 Henry recalled Cranmer to England and appointed him the archbishop of Canterbury. Obliging the monarch, Cranmer and the court at Dustable voided the marriage of the king and Catherine and declared valid the marriage of the king and Anne Boleyn. Subsequently, Cranmer acted to free Henry from his marriages to Boleyn in 1536, Anne of Cleves in 1540, and Catherine Howard in 1542. While Cranmer seems to have done Henry's bidding in these cases, it seems unlikely that his opinions differed greatly from those of the king.

Cranmer's role in the reconstructed English church was extremely important. With Henry's principal adviser, Thomas Cromwell, he encouraged the publication of an English Bible, which was then required in the parish churches in Cromwell's injunctions of 1538. In 1544 Cranmer wrote a litany for the Church of England, published as *An Exhortation vnto Prayer . . . to be Read in Euery Church afore Processyons. Also a Letanie with Suffrages to be Said or Song in the Tyme of the Said Processyons,* which is still in use. His leanings became more and more Protestant with time, and in 1548 he abandoned the Catholic belief in transubstantiation. Several plots were hatched to convict Cranmer of heresy, but Henry defended his archbishop in each instance.

Cranmer's books on the Protestant Reformation are often revealing. Only two of Cranmer's books from the Protestant perspective, both by Martin Bucer, have survived. Bucer's commentary on Romans, *Metaphrases et enarrationes perpetuae epistolarum pauli apostoli* (1536), which is housed at Colfe Library in London, is dedicated to Cranmer. His copy of *Gratulatio ad ecclesiam Anglicanam* (1548), now at the Cambridge Library, contains annotations in which he takes issue with Gardiner's ideas. In contrast, works hostile to the Protestant Reformation by Johann Maier von Eck, Alphonsus à Castro, Josse Clichtove, Johann Haner, and George Witzel have been located. Cranmer's copy of Eck's *Apologia* (1542) against Bucer is heavily annotated on many issues; at one point, Cranmer reacts to Eck's argument by writing, "Hoc est absurdum maxime."

Cranmer played a key role after Edward VI became king in 1547 and Protestantism for England was pushed by his guardians–first, Edward Seymour, Duke of Somerset, and then John Dudley, the Duke of Northumberland. Cranmer published a book of homilies, *Certain Sermons, or Homilies, Appoynted by the Kynges Maiestie, to be Declared and Redde, by all Persones, Vicars, or Curates, euery Sonday in their Churches, where thei haue Cure* (1547); the first Book of Common Prayer (1549), which he revised in 1552 to show a stronger Protestant strain; and his Forty-Two Articles in 1553, published as *Articles Agreed upon by the Bishoppes and Other Learned and Godly Men, in the Last Convocatio at London, in the Yeare . . . MDLII,* which defined the Church of England's positions on religious issues of the day.

Cranmer's library contained many texts on the topic of liturgy, though many of them were probably purged when his collection fell into Catholic hands. Those that remain include Clement Maideston's *Sarum Directory for Priests* (1501), William Durandus's *Rationale* (two editions, 1506 and 1508, one of which has Cranmer's annotations), and the *Deliberatio* (1545) of Archbishop Hermann; in addition, Cranmer's manuscript drafts for the reform of the Breviary have been located. His *Reformatio Legvm Ecclesiasticarvm, ex Avthoritate primum Regis Henrici 8* (1571), contained his ideas on how to revise the canon law of the Church of England, and was published well after his death. Although his proposal was not enacted, the document was nevertheless influential in the history of the Church of England.

During the reigns of Henry VIII and Edward VI, Cranmer successfully enacted many changes in church doctrine and liturgy based on his own developing ideas on religious issues, but his career ultimately ended in ruin. In July 1553 as he was nearing death, Edward VI

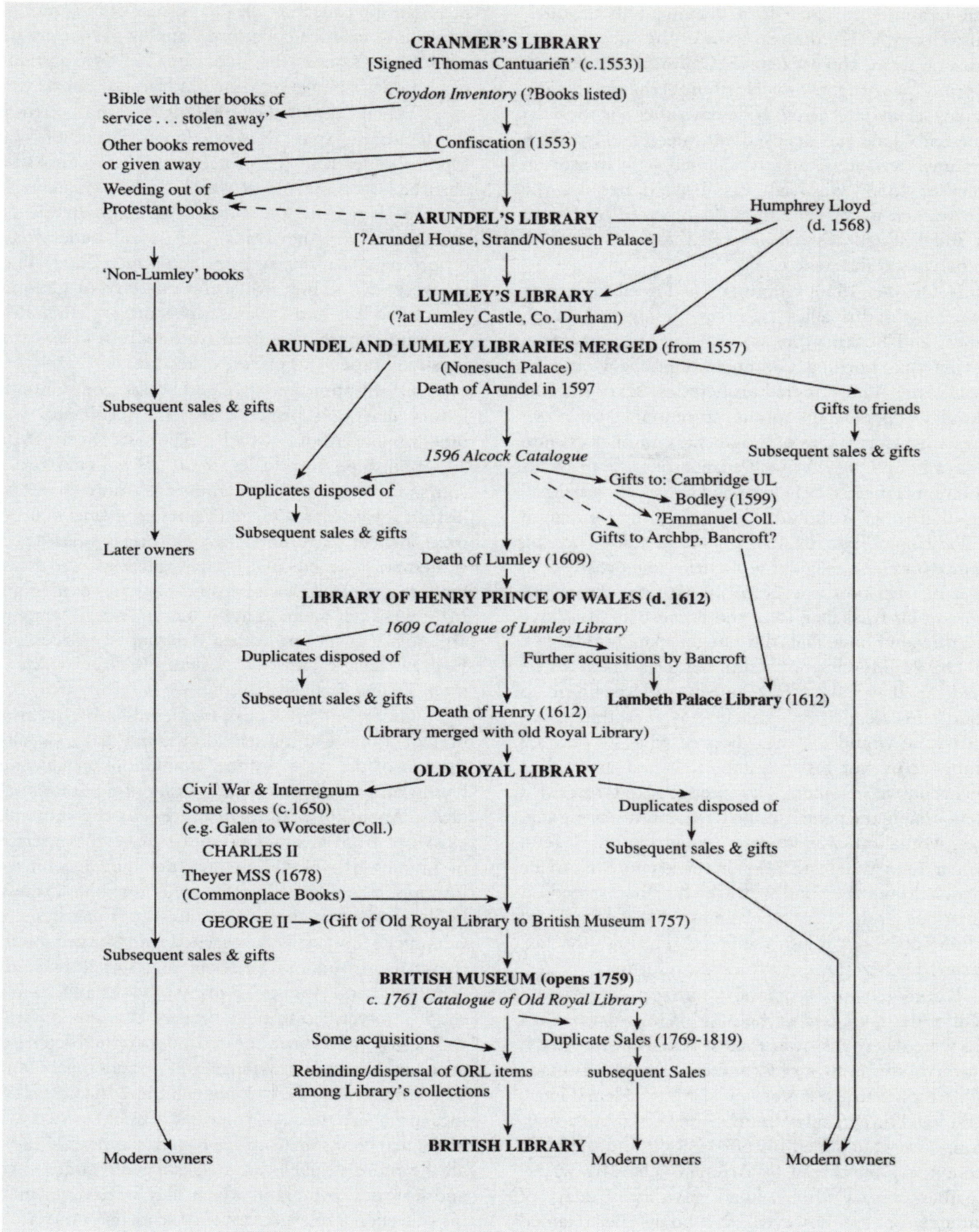

Chart of the history of Cranmer's library (from David G. Selwyn's The Library of Thomas Cranmer, *1996)*

forced Cranmer to agree to a document that would, against Henry VIII's desires, transfer the succession to the throne from Mary, Henry's Catholic daughter by Catherine of Aragon, to Northumberland's daughter-in-law, Lady Jane Grey. Nine days after she took the throne Lady Jane was deposed and succeeded by Mary I. Cranmer was subsequently charged with treason in November 1553. His trial was delayed because the queen wanted to reinstate the laws repealed by Henry VIII and Edward VI that allowed the government to burn heretics at the stake.

In October 1555, Cranmer was forced to witness the burning of his allies Nicholas Ridley and Hugh Latimer, and he knew he was to face the same fate. Believing that burning Cranmer in public would be more effective if he admitted his heresies, Mary's agents proceeded to persuade Cranmer to renounce his previous statements as errors of judgment. Cranmer eventually gave in and signed five "recantations." Four of his recantations repeated beliefs he had consistently held all along–that subjects should always obey their monarch and Parliament–but in the last recantation he did renounce his entire religious and intellectual progression. Such a renunciation was probably extracted from him because of his weakened state and because he may have held a thread of hope that Mary might spare his life.

On 21 March 1556 Cranmer was taken to be burned at the stake. The queen ordered him to announce his recantation publicly; however, the knowledge that he would die regardless of what he said led Cranmer to recant his recantation. When ordered to make his public statement, Cranmer shocked the crowd by denouncing the power of the Pope and declaring that transubstantiation was untrue. According to legend Cranmer then ran to the fire in which he was to be burned, held out the hand with which he had signed his recantations and, after proclaiming that "This hand hath offended," put it into the flame. Through this act, he inspired generations of Protestant reformers.

Fortunately for scholars, Cranmer's library did not suffer the same fate as the man. While many of his books were destroyed or lost, most survived. Ironically, the survival of so much of Cranmer's library was made possible by a staunch supporter of Mary, Henry Fitzalan, the twelfth earl of Arundel. After Cranmer's martyrdom, Mary auctioned his possessions, and the book collection was purchased by Arundel. The earl, whose sympathies were Catholic, likely gave away many of Cranmer's books; however, the books he retained included the Canterbury "Bosworth Psalter," from the tenth or eleventh centuries, still in its original binding; Peter Lombard's *Sentences* (1546); and a Venice folio edition of Apuleius's *The Golden Ass* (1510). When Arundel died in 1579, his son-in-law, John, Lord Lumley, acquired the collection. In the process of integrating the books into his own collection, Lumley gave away those of Cranmer's books that duplicated his own. Still, many of Cranmer's books remained in Lumley's library.

When Lumley died in 1609, his library went into the hands of James I's son, Henry, Prince of Wales. Upon the death of the prince in 1612 the books were absorbed into the old Royal Library, which in 1757 George II gave to the British Museum. In the nineteenth century the British Museum undertook an unfortunate fundraising project in which duplicate copies were sold. Thus, while the majority of Cranmer's extant books and manuscripts are in the British Museum, others have been scattered elsewhere in university libraries and private collections.

Of the approximately 400 books from Cranmer's library that have been located, the theological works predominate. About 130 of the books concern the arts and philosophy, most of them relevant to the arts course Cranmer took at Cambridge; more than 60 are historical works, dealing with political events that range from ancient to recent times; 35 are on classical and contemporary medicine; 14 are legal texts; and 7 books fall into the categories of cosmography and geography. Most works of the texts are in Latin, and the remaining are divided among other languages: Greek (60), Hebrew (20), English (6), Italian (3), French (2), German (1), and Spanish (1).

Cranmer's books can be identified by his inscription "Thomas Cantuarien" on the title page, usually at the top of the page, by the annotations in Cranmer's handwriting, or by the handwriting of one of his secretaries. About 90 percent of the books that are still in existence from Cranmer's library have the inscription of Lumley as well. Those that do not have Lumley's inscription include all of Cranmer's extant Protestant books–giving further proof to the hypothesis that Cranmer's library was searched and purged of these books by Arundel or by someone else before Arundel acquired them. About 585 printed books and 70 manuscripts are verified to have been in Cranmer's library–they have either been located or identified from references in Cranmer's writings and commonplace books. The library most likely contained more theological writings in English than it is currently possible to verify. The annotated books that survive from Cranmer's library are all the more valuable for suggesting the larger cultural and historical context in which they were used, making his collection a treasure trove for scholars of the era.

Biographies:

John Strype, *Memorial of the Most Reverend Father in God Thomas Cranmer. . . .* (London: Printed for Richard Chriswell, 1694);

Charles Hastings Collette, *The Life, Times, and Writings of Thomas Cranmer, D. D.: The First Reforming Archbishop of Canterbury* (London: George Redway, 1887);

A. F. Pollard, *Thomas Cranmer and the English Reformation, 1489–1556* (London: Putnam, 1926; Hamden, Conn.: Archon, 1965);

F. E. Hutchinson, *Cranmer and the English Reformation* (London: English Universities Press, 1951);

G. W. Bromiley, *Thomas Cranmer, Theologian* (Oxford: Oxford University Press, 1956);

T. Maynard, *The Life of Thomas Cranmer* (London: Staples Press, 1956);

Jasper Ridley, *Thomas Cranmer* (Oxford: Clarendon Press, 1962);

C. H. Smith, *Cranmer and the Reformation Under Edward VI* (Westport, Conn.: Greenwood Press, 1970);

Peter Newman Brooks, *Cranmer in Contest* (Minneapolis: Fortress, 1989);

Paul Ayris and David G. Selwyn, *Thomas Cranmer: Churchman and Scholar* (Woodbridge, Conn.: Boydell Press, 1993);

Diarmaid MacCulloch, *Thomas Cranmer: A Life* (New Haven: Yale University Press, 1996).

Bibliography:

David G. Selwyn, *The Library of Thomas Cranmer* (Oxford: Oxford Bibliographical Society, 1996).

References:

Pamela M. Black, "Matthew Parker's Search for Cranmer's 'Great Notable Books,'" *Library: A Quarterly Journal of Bibliography,* 29 (1974): 312–322;

Ronald B. Bond, "Cranmer and the Controversy Surrounding Publication of *Certayne Sermons or Homilies* (1547)," *Renaissance and Reformation, Renaissance et Reforme,* 12 (1976): 28–35;

Julia Houston, "Transubstantiation and the Sign: Cranmer's Drama of the Lord's Supper," *Journal of Medieval and Renaissance Studies,* 24 (1994): 113–130.

Papers:

Thomas Cranmer's manuscripts are held by the Public Records Office, London; the Lambeth Palace Library; the British Library; and the university libraries of Oxford and Cambridge.

John Dee

(13 July 1527 – ? December 1608?)

Anthony G. Medici
Northern Illinois University

See also the Dee entry in *DLB 136: Sixteenth-Century British Nondramatic Writers, Second Series.*

CATALOGUES: *Lists of Manuscripts Formerly Owned by Dr. John Dee, with Preface and Identifications by M. R. James* (Oxford: Oxford University Press, 1921);
Julian Roberts and Andrew G. Watson, *John Dee's Library Catalogue* (London: Bibliographic Society, 1990).

BOOKS: *Joannis Dee Londinensis, de prœstantiorbus quibusdam naturœ virtutibus* (London: Printed by Henry Sutton, 1558); revised as *Propaedeumata Aphoristica* (London: Printed by Reyner Wolfe, 1568);
Monas Hieroglyphica Ioannis Dee (Antwerp: Printed by William Sylvius, 1564; Frankfurt am Main: Printed by Johann Wechel and Peter Fischer, 1591);
Parallaticae commentationis praxeosqu; nucleus quidam (London: Printed by John Daye, 1573);
General and Rare Memorials Pertayning to the Perfect Arte of Navigation: Annexed to the Paradoxal Cumpas in Playne: Now first Published: 24. Yeres, After the First Inuention Thereof (London: John Daye, 1577);
A Letter, Containing a Most Briefe Discourse Apologeticall, with a Plaine Demonstration, and Feruent Protestation, for the Lawful, Sincere, Very Faithfull and Christian Course, of the Philosophicall Studies and Exercises, of a Certaine Studious Gentleman: An Ancient Seruant to her Most Excellent Maiesty Royall (London: Printed by Peter Short, 1599); enlarged as *A Letter, Nine Yeeres Since, Written and First Published: Containing . . . Gentleman: A Faithfull Seruant to Our Late Queene and (Anno 1603. Aug. 9) Sworne Seruant to the King* (London: Printed by Emma Short, 1603);
A True & Faithful Relation of What Passed for Many Yeers between Dr. John Dee . . . and Some Spirits: Tending (Had it Succeeded) to a General Alteration of Most States and Kingdomes in the World, edited by Meric Causabon (London: Printed by David Maxwell for Timothy Garthwait, 1659);
The Private Diary of Dr. John Dee, and the Catalogue of his Library of Manuscripts, from the Original Manuscripts in the Ashmolean Museum at Oxford, and Trinity College Library, Cambridge, edited by James Orchard Halliwell (London: Printed for the Camden Society by J. B. Nichols, 1842);
Diary for the Years 1595–1601, of John Dee, Warden of Manchester from 1595 to 1608, edited by John Eglington Bailey (N.p., 1880).

Editions: *The Hieroglyphic Monad,* translated, with a commentary, by J. W. Hamilton-Jones (London: J. M. Watkins, 1947);
John Dee on Astronomy, edited by Wayne Shumaker (Berkeley: University of California Press, 1978).

OTHER: John Feild, *Ephemeris Anni.1557. Currentis iuxta Copernici et Reinhaldi canones. Supputata ac examinata ad meridianum Londinensem,* with a preface by Dee (London: Printed by Thomas Marshe, 1556);
Robert Record, *The Ground of Artes Teachyng the Worke and Practise of Arithmetike. Now of Late Ouerseen & Augmented,* revised and enlarged by Dee (London: Printed by Reyner Wolfe, 1561);
"Mathematical Preface," in Euclid, *The Elements of Geometrie of the Most Auncient Philosopher Euclide of Megara,* translated by Henry Billingsley (London: John Daye, 1570);
Joannes, monk of Glastonbury, *Chronica, sive historia rebus Glastoniensis,* edited by Thomas Hearne (Oxford: Sheldonian Theatre, 1726)–includes Dee's "Compendius Rehearsall" and "Supplication."

John Dee represents many of the vital currents of scientific study in the Elizabethan Renaissance as well as some of its most notable weaknesses. Called by John Aubrey "one of the ornaments of his Age," Dee was an accomplished and influential figure in the fields of mathematics, astronomy, chemistry, geography, navigation, natural philosophy, and mechanics. Yet, while he was an associate, adviser, and tutor to many of the most important figures of his time in learned and political cir-

John Dee

cles, he was also deeply caught up in astrological, alchemical, hermetic, and occult practices, including crystal-gazing and spirit-calling. He developed among his contemporaries a reputation as a sorcerer and conjuror, which did much to harm his reputation, both during his time and to posterity.

Dee declined university positions, choosing instead to maintain himself as an independent scholar and teacher. His published writings, while significant, were not extensive, and his cramped style when he wrote in English did little to further their dissemination among educated readers; he left many more unpublished manuscripts. Dee has been the subject of greatly increased scholarly attention during the last half century. Many view him as an Elizabethan "magus," a philosopher-magician who embraced within himself the realms of natural and supernatural studies; others see him foremost as a scientist who collaborated with the leading minds of his time in a variety of fields to accomplish significant scientific, cultural, and even political ends.

While the estimate of Dee's real accomplishments is still evolving, there is general agreement that Dee formed the largest and most significant private library in Renaissance England. He ranks as one of the great book collectors in bibliophilic history, and he pursued his collecting in a time when the collection and maintenance of books and manuscripts attracted relatively little interest or concern. Dee's library provided not only a repository for many books and manuscripts that might otherwise have been lost but also a valuable intellectual resource for fellow scholars in their researches.

By his own account, John Dee was born in London on 13 July 1527 (although others have placed his birth in Radnoshire). He was the son of Johanna Wild and Rowland Dee, a gentleman server to Henry VIII. Dee later drew an elaborate genealogy that traces his descent from the ancient family of the Dees of Radnorshire and from Roderick the Great, Prince of Wales. He attended Chelmsford Grammar School and in November 1542 was enrolled at St. John's College, Cambridge. Early in 1546 he obtained a B.A. and was admitted as a foundation fellow of Trinity College in December 1546. Dee recorded that as a student he spent eighteen hours each day studying, leaving four hours for sleep and two for eating and recreation. Even allowing for some hyperbole, Dee's study habits seem to have been prodigious. Such single-minded application, bordering or crossing over into obsession, was illustrative of his character as a scholar, spiritualist, and book collector.

While he was a fellow at Trinity College, Dee's involvement in the mounting of a performance of Aristophanes' *Peace,* for which he constructed an ingenious flying machine that caused a sensation, contributed to his reputation as a magus. Early in his career Dee knew that he could astound spectators through the knowledgeable use of hydraulics, weights, string, springs, and other devices, based on mathematical formulas and calculations. Later, in his "Mathematical Preface" to *The Elements of Geometrie of the Most Auncient Philosopher Euclide of Megara* (1570), Dee cited similarly ingenious mechanical devices produced by such scientific forebears as Archites, Agrippa, Ctesibus, and Hero. He designates the art of making such machines "thaumaturgike," defining it as "that Art Mathematicall, which giveth certain order to make straunge workes, of the sense to be perceived, and to men to greatly wonder at."

Dee's contemporaries, who believed that such an illusion could only be the result of the diabolical, associated Dee with black magic. Although he vigorously denied any charge of black magic throughout his life, he nevertheless encouraged such speculation through his later consuming interest in occult matters. Dee's attitude toward his celebrity status seems to have been ambivalent; he clearly enjoyed the recognition and tangible rewards that came to him as a result of his abstruse knowledge, even when such recognition placed him in less than ideal contexts.

Dee's book collecting began in earnest as an undergraduate. His earliest known acquisitions include a work by Tacitus, ex libris Beatus Rhenanus, and a Greek grammar by Theodorus Gaza. He purchased both books in 1544 from the Cambridge stationer Nicholas Spierinck. Dee also received a copy of Roman military expert Flavius Vegetius Renatus's *De re militari* (1535) as a gift, possibly from Spierinck's wife, who was widowed in the latter part of 1545.

In 1547 Dee made his first trip to the European continent, traveling to the Low Countries in May to meet with other scholars for several months. He continued to purchase books, including Arrian's *Periplus Maris Erythrai* (1533) on commerce and navigation in the Erythrean Sea, a translation of the "periplus maris erythruei" by an anonymous writer and partly Arrian's account of the voyage to Nearkhes. Other purchases were a copy of the Roman architect Vitruvius Pollio's *De architectura* (1522) and Ermolao Barbaro's *Compendium scientiae naturalis* (1547). All of these carry Dee's signature and some form of annotation, even if just the date of acquisition, a practice he followed regularly in the early part of his career but later neglected. From this trip abroad, Dee also returned with the astronomer's instruments designed by Gemma Frisius and two globes constructed by the famed geographer, Gerard Mercator. He later donated these items to Trinity College, probably in 1547 or 1548.

In midsummer 1548, the year he began his studies for the M.A., he made another trip to the Continent. He studied civil law and the sciences at Louvain, remaining there until July 1550. He became a friend of Mercator and also tutored Sir William Pickering. It was during this trip that he bought one of his first two identified manuscripts, a fifth-century copy of the *Summa naturalisum* of Albertus Magnus. He also acquired astronomical texts by Johannes Campanus of Novara and Johannes de Muris, a Strabo geography (1549), commentaries on Pliny, and a 1544 Archimedes volume. On 15 July 1550, Dee left Louvain, arriving five days later in Paris, where he lectured at the College of Rheims on Euclid, mathematics, and physics. He was well received and was offered a professorship at the University of Paris, which he declined.

Dee began buying books in Paris soon after his arrival. He also obtained a notable manuscript, a copy of a Greek commentary believed to be from 1548 on Ptolemy's *Tetrabiblos.* On the manuscript, Dee wrote in his own hand, "Ex bibliotheca regia," indicating its putative French royal provenance. Jacques Goupyl, an eminent doctor, presented Dee with a copy of Ganivet's *Amicus medicorum* (1496). Even after his return to England in 1551, he continued to buy books from sources on the Continent.

Upon his return to England, King Edward VI granted him an annual pension of £100 per year, which was exchanged on 19 May 1553 for the living of the rectory of Upton-upon-Severn, Worcestershire. In 1554 he declined a substantial annual stipend to lecture on mathematics at Oxford, apparently preferring to maintain his independence of place and activity. Dee served as tutor in the households of the Sidneys and the Dudleys, prominent noble families, while establishing himself as an independent teacher of mathematics, astronomy, and navigation in London. The books he obtained for his library included Nicholas Copernicus's *De lateribus et angulis triangulorum* (probably 1542), Scheubelius's *Algebra* (1551), Averroes's *Destructio destructionum* (1527), and a 1533 Greek text of Euclid's writings.

Following the accession of Queen Mary I, Dee was arrested at Hampton Court on or about 26 May 1555. The charges included conjuring, casting the king's and queen's nativities, thus gaining occult knowledge or power over the royal family, and plotting

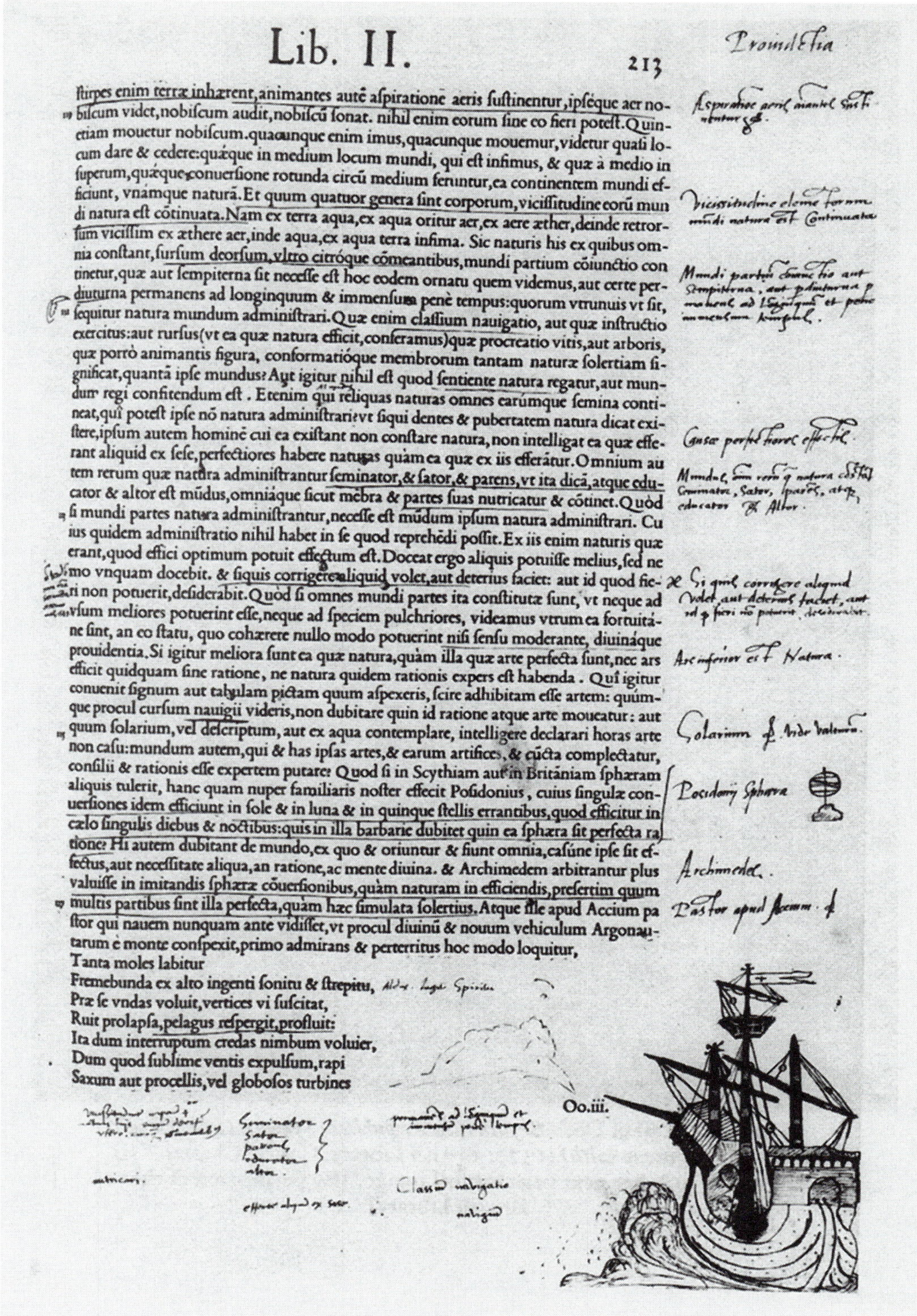

Lib. II. 213

stirpes enim terræ inhærent, animantes autẽ aspiratione aeris sustinentur, ipséque aer nobiscum videt, nobiscum audit, nobiscũ sonat. nihil enim eorum sine eo fieri potest. Quin etiam mouetur nobiscum. quacunque enim imus, quacunque mouemur, videtur quasi locum dare & cedere: quæque in medium locum mundi, qui est infimus, & quæ à medio in superum, quæque conuersione rotunda circũ medium feruntur, ea continentem mundi efficiunt, vnamque naturã. Et quum quatuor genera sint corporum, vicissitudine eorũ mundi natura est cõtinuata. Nam ex terra aqua, ex aqua oritur aer, ex aere æther, deinde retrorsum vicissim ex æthere aer, inde aqua, ex aqua terra infima. Sic naturis his ex quibus omnia constant, sursum deorsum, vltro citróque cõmeantibus, mundi partium cõiunctio continetur, quæ aut sempiterna sit necesse est hoc eodem ornatu quem videmus, aut certe perdiuturna permanens ad longinquum & immensum penè tempus: quorum vtrunuis vt sit, sequitur natura mundum administrari. Quæ enim classium nauigatio, aut quæ instructio exercitus: aut rursus (vt ea quæ natura efficit, conferamus) quæ procreatio vitis, aut arboris, quæ porrò animantis figura, conformatióque membrorum tantam naturæ solertiam significat, quantã ipse mundus? Aut igitur nihil est quod sentiente natura regatur, aut mundum regi confitendum est. Etenim qui reliquas naturas omnes earúmque semina continet, qui potest ipse nõ natura administrari? vt siqui dentes & pubertatem natura dicat existere, ipsum autem hominẽ cui ea existant non constare natura, non intelligat ea quæ efferant aliquid ex sese, perfectiores habere naturas quàm ea quæ ex iis efferãtur. Omnium autem rerum quæ natura administrantur seminator, & sator, & parens, vt ita dicã, atque educator & altor est mũdus, omniáque sicut mẽbra & partes suas nutricatur & cõtinet. Quòd si mundi partes natura administrantur, necesse est mũdum ipsum natura administrari. Cuius quidem administratio nihil habet in se quod reprehẽdi possit. Ex iis enim naturis quæ erant, quod effici optimum potuit effectum est. Doceat ergo aliquis potuisse melius, sed nemo vnquam docebit. & siquis corrigere aliquid volet, aut deterius faciet: aut id quod fieri non potuerit, desiderabit. Quòd si omnes mundi partes ita constitutæ sunt, vt neque ad vsum meliores potuerint esse, neque ad speciem pulchriores, videamus vtrum ea fortuitáne sint, an eo statu, quo cohærere nullo modo potuerint nisi sensu moderante, diuináque prouidentia. Si igitur meliora sunt ea quæ natura, quàm illa quæ arte perfecta sunt, nec ars efficit quidquam sine ratione, ne natura quidem rationis expers est habenda. Qui igitur conuenit signum aut tabulam pictam quum aspexeris, scire adhibitam esse artem: quúmque procul cursum nauigii videris, non dubitare quin id ratione atque arte moueatur: aut quum solarium, vel descriptum, aut ex aqua contemplare, intelligere declarari horas arte non casu: mundum autem, qui & has ipsas artes, & earum artifices, & cũcta complectatur, consilii & rationis esse expertem putare? Quod si in Scythiam aut in Britãniam sphæram aliquis tulerit, hanc quam nuper familiaris noster effecit Posidonius, cuius singulæ conuersiones idem efficiunt in sole & in luna & in quinque stellis errantibus, quod efficitur in cælo singulis diebus & noctibus: quis in illa barbarie dubitet quin ea sphæra sit perfecta ratione? Hi autem dubitant de mundo, ex quo & oriuntur & fiunt omnia, casúne ipse sit effectus, aut necessitate aliqua, an ratione, ac mente diuina. & Archimedem arbitrantur plus valuisse in imitandis sphæræ cõuersionibus, quàm naturam in efficiendis, præsertim quum multis partibus sint illa perfecta, quàm hæc simulata solertius. Atque ille apud Accium pastor qui nauem nunquam ante vidisset, vt procul diuinũ & nouum vehiculum Argonautarum è monte conspexit, primo admirans & perterritus hoc modo loquitur,

Tanta moles labitur
Fremebunda ex alto ingenti sonitu & strepitu,
Præ se vndas voluit, vertices vi suscitat,
Ruit prolapsa, pelagus respergit, profluit:
Ita dum interruptum credas nimbum voluier,
Dum quod sublime ventis expulsum, rapi
Saxum aut procellis, vel globosos turbines

Oo.iii.

Page from Dee's copy of Cicero's De Natura Deorum, *with Dee's marginal annotations (Royal College of Physicians)*

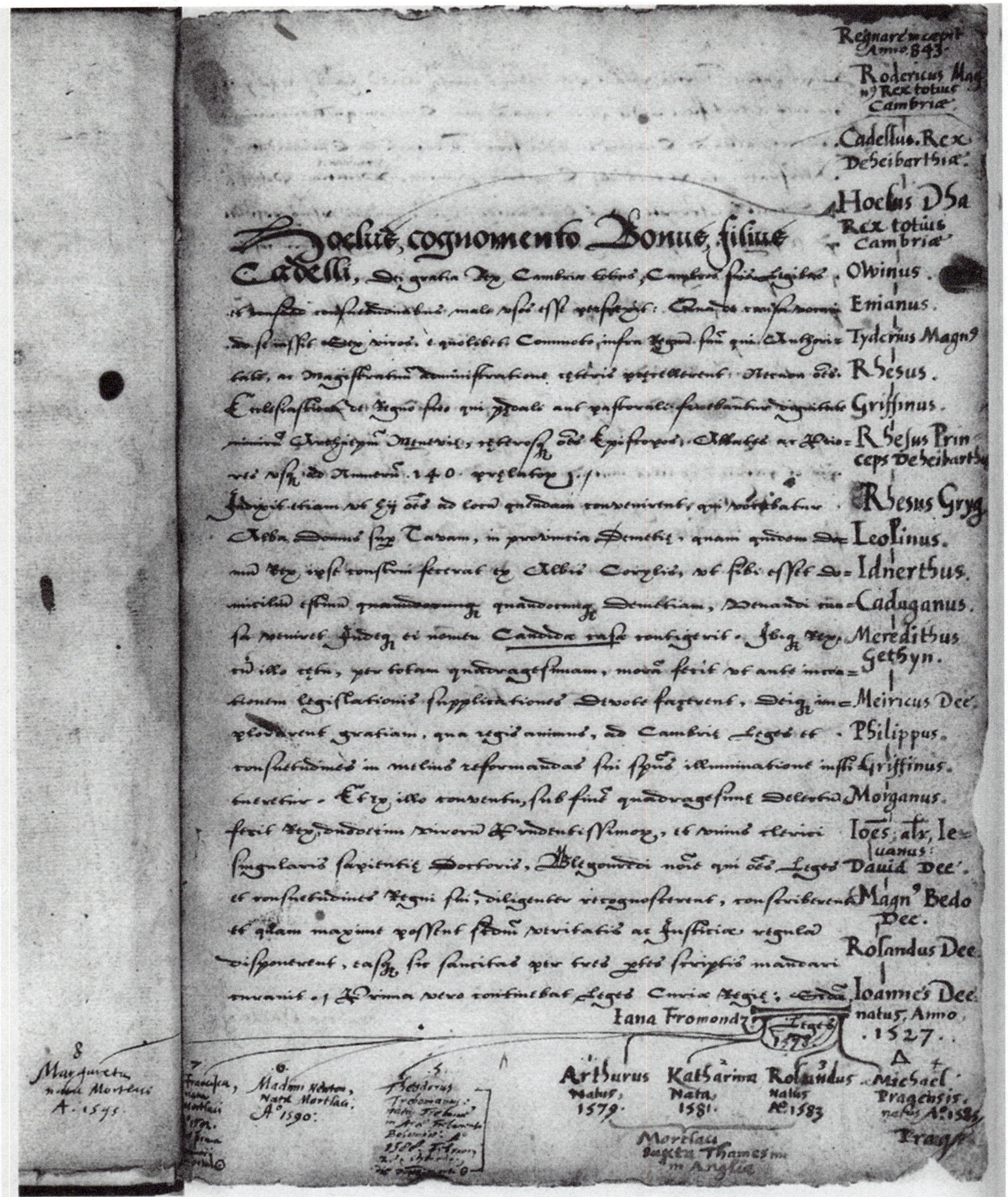

Page from Dee's manuscript copy of the laws of the Welsh king Hywel Dda. The marginal annotations, in Dee's hand, trace his lineage from King Hywel (Merton College, Oxford).

against the queen on behalf of Elizabeth. After being examined at some length and tried by the court of the star chamber, Dee was cleared of wrongdoing and released from confinement on 29 August 1555 into the custody of Edmund Bonner, Bishop of London, who ascertained his religious orthodoxy. Again able to resume book buying, Dee bought Galeatus Martius's *De doctrina promiscua,* Leone Battista Alberti's *Elementa Picturae* (1540), and Proclus's work on Ptolemy's *Tetrabiblos* before the end of the year.

Despite his prior difficulties with the court, Dee in January 1556 presented to Queen Mary his "Supplication for the recovery and preservation of ancient writers and monuments," which was collected by Joannes, monk of Glastonbury, in *Chronica, sive historia rebus Glastoniensis* (1726). Dee begins by lamenting "the subverting of Religious houses," a point perhaps designed to placate the queen, and then goes on to discuss what certainly was his more immediate concern: the "spoile and destruction of so many and so notable" books and manuscripts. Dee advises the queen that "many a pretious jewel and ancient monument did utterly perish" as a result of the dissolution of the monasteries. Observing the parlous condition of scholarly libraries, he notes that "now no one student, nor any one college, hath half a dozen of these excellent jewels, but the whole stock and store thereof drawing nigh to utter destruction." Dee requests that Mary establish a national library to permanently maintain these books and manuscripts.

The supplication proper is followed by five specific articles. The first article recommends the establishment of a commission to search out significant works, take possession of them for the Royal Library, and, should their owners request their return, make copies of the materials prior to returning them. In his second, third, and fourth articles Dee calls for the disbursement of funds to support the project and to obtain the necessary library furnishings, recommends prompt action lest materials be lost or hidden away, and suggests the establishment of a temporary holding place for the material. In the fifth article Dee requests that he be authorized to travel abroad for the purpose of visiting all "the notablest Librarys beyond the sea, (as in Vaticanna at Rome, S. Marci at Venice, and the like at Bononia, Florence, Vienna, etc.)," in order to copy out the works of "excellent Authors" for the queen's library.

While there may have been a degree of self-interest in Dee's proposal and his assurance that books "shall be gotten in wonderfull abundance," his supplication is also a true assessment of the deplorable condition of books, manuscripts, and libraries generally in England at that time. The significance of the supplication also lies in the assertion of the importance of books to the national sense of identity, history, and culture. Dee was ahead of his time in pointing to the vital role that would be played by major scholarly research collections, both at universities and in national libraries and museums. He was farsighted, too, in suggesting that a truly significant collection of books would contain the notable works of both domestic and foreign writers and of both modern and classical culture. Although the queen declined to act on his proposal, Dee himself took action, continuing his fervid pursuit of books for the library he was to assemble at his home in Mortlake, a library perhaps eventually equal to the one projected in his supplication.

At least some of Dee's acquisitions came into his possession because he apparently did not always return all the materials he borrowed. He is known to have borrowed various manuscripts and bound volumes from Corpus Christi College, Oxford, and Peterhouse, Cambridge, with a pledge to return them; however, it is uncertain that they in fact were returned, as some were still listed in the holdings of his library in 1583. Dee also seems to have borrowed books or manuscripts from faculty members at Oxford and Cambridge.

Dee also copied important texts for his collection. These included manuscripts such as Thomas Norton's *Ordinal of Alchemy,* Urso's *De effectibus qualitatum primarum,* and Ramon Lull's *Liber experimentorum.* Some of these he seems to have copied himself; others were copied for him. Dee apparently obtained many more manuscripts from the several college libraries at Oxford and Cambridge over the years, either through copies or through borrowing.

Dee was especially active in acquiring manuscripts from dissolved monasteries. The largest number of these came from the dissolved St. Augustine's Abbey at Canterbury. Dee seems to have obtained these through John Twyne, a schoolmaster and local worthy at Canterbury, who collected monastery manuscripts. In *Compendius Rehearsal!,* a 1592 autobiographical account and apologia that was published in *Chronica, sive historia rebus Glastoniensis,* Dee describes acquiring monastery manuscripts as "in manner out of a dunghill, in the corner of a Church, where very many were utterly spoiled by rotting." Most of these manuscripts deal with scientific subjects, an indication that Dee was not merely engaged in antiquarian pursuits but rather in the assembly of a working library to support his scholarly interests. His diaries occasionally show him on the alert for other possible sources of manuscripts as he notes those people said to have possession of significant manuscripts or books. For example, in his diary entry for 8 October 1581, Dee writes, "I had newes of the chests of bokes fownd by Owndle in Northamptonshire . . . but I found no truth in it."

Dee followed the method of operation he recommended to Queen Mary, collecting valuable books through rescue, purchase, borrowing, and copying. Although his motives were sometimes self-serving, his actions always benefited society. It is likely that many of the books and manuscripts he obtained, even from the college libraries, might have otherwise perished, either through neglect, vandalism, or carelessness.

In or about 1557 Dee prepared an eight-page list of his printed books and some of his manuscripts. The handwriting is difficult to read, the arrangement is imprecise, and the bibliographical detail is sparse. Only the date of the first book is given; the dates of others are not recorded. About 320 printed books and 32 manuscripts are listed. Notable among these are works by Copernicus (*De lateribus et angulis triangulorum* and, possibly, *De revolutionibus*), Aristotle, Ptolemy, Euclid, Pythagoras, Heraclitus, Plutarch, Cicero, Averroe, Vitruvius, Galen, and several works of Ramon Lull. The library is that of a scholar, directed mostly toward classical learning, mathematics, and the sciences, particularly astronomy and its closely related field of astrology. The works of contemporary astronomers such as Antoine Mizauld, Guillame Postel, Paschasius Hamellius, and Johannes Fernelius are represented. Dee's later interest in alchemy, cabala, and the occult are not yet reflected in his holdings. Already then a substantial bibliophilic achievement, the library grew almost tenfold in the next several decades.

Following the accession of Elizabeth on 17 November 1558, Dee began to perform astrological work for the new queen, including the casting of the most auspicious day for the coronation. He remained on generally good terms with Elizabeth, who made several visits to his home at Mortlake and frequently gave him money for his services. Dee's needs usually exceeded his income, and Elizabeth, who often promised more than she was able or willing to deliver, did not solve his financial problems. Still, Dee's connections with the queen and members of the court undoubtedly helped him to sustain himself, to travel, and to conduct his scientific and occult experiments. Curiously, Dee did not repeat his formal proposal for a national library to Elizabeth when she succeeded Mary. Perhaps her patronage of Dee constituted an implicit adoption of the scheme. The library at Dee's home, Mortlake, near London, became the *Bibliotheca Mortlacensis,* a place of consultation and research for itinerant scholars, privy council members, commercial explorers, philosophers, and even Elizabeth herself on a couple of notable occasions.

In 1562 Dee traveled to Antwerp and Louvain. While continuing to pursue his interests in astrology and mathematics, he also began to collect books in the fields of alchemy, Hebreica (cabala and Hebrew grammars), and Orientalia. He acquired or made a copy from a manuscript of Johann Tritheim's *Steganographia,* the earliest full treatise on writing in cipher. He also bought cryptographic works such as Jacques Gohorry's *De usu & mysteriis notarum* (1550) and Jacopo Silvestri's *Opus novum* (1526) and began to practice writing in cipher. Dee also traveled through Switzerland and on to Padua, Venice, and Urbino. He met the noted Swiss bibliographer and physician Conrad Gesner, some of whose bibliographies Dee had in his library. Dee probably discussed Paracelsus with Gesner. Dee's interest in Paracelsian literature grew increasingly strong and came to represent a sizable segment of his library. Dee also traveled to Hungary in order to present his work, *Monas Hieroglyphica Ioannis Dee* (1564), a Hermetic treatise reflecting his interest in the occult, to the Emperor Maximilian II, to whom it was dedicated. The work had been printed at Antwerp under Dee's supervision. Dee returned to England in June 1564.

Although Dee had brought books and manuscripts back to England from his earlier trips abroad, since 1534 it had been illegal to import foreign books into England, to buy a book that had been bound abroad, or to buy a book retail from an alien. Dee's accounts indicate large purchases from the London shop of Birckmann of Cologne, which was managed by Andreas Fremonsheim. Dee visited the shop shortly after his return to England in 1564 and may have arranged for the importation of the books that he had purchased on his travels. Dee may have bought some of his books, then and later, from those offered at the Frankfurt Fair, which first began printing book catalogues in 1564. Dee's library included catalogues from the fairs held in 1573 and 1574. Fremonsheim is known to have extended a sizable amount of credit to Dee, much of which apparently was not repaid as there were still efforts to collect the amount due as late as 1595. Dee's specific book-buying activities after his return are rather vague, as he no longer made a practice of dating his acquisitions. Nevertheless, he remained extremely active as a collector in the 1570s both at home and abroad.

The preface Dee wrote for Henry Billingsley's English translation of Euclid's writings on geometry, dated 9 February 1570 from his home at Mortlake, might be seen as marking a point of transition in his life. In rebutting the popular prejudice against him as a sorcerer, Dee argues that his skills in mathematics and the sciences do not make him "a companion of the hell-hounds, and a caller, and a conjuror of wicked and

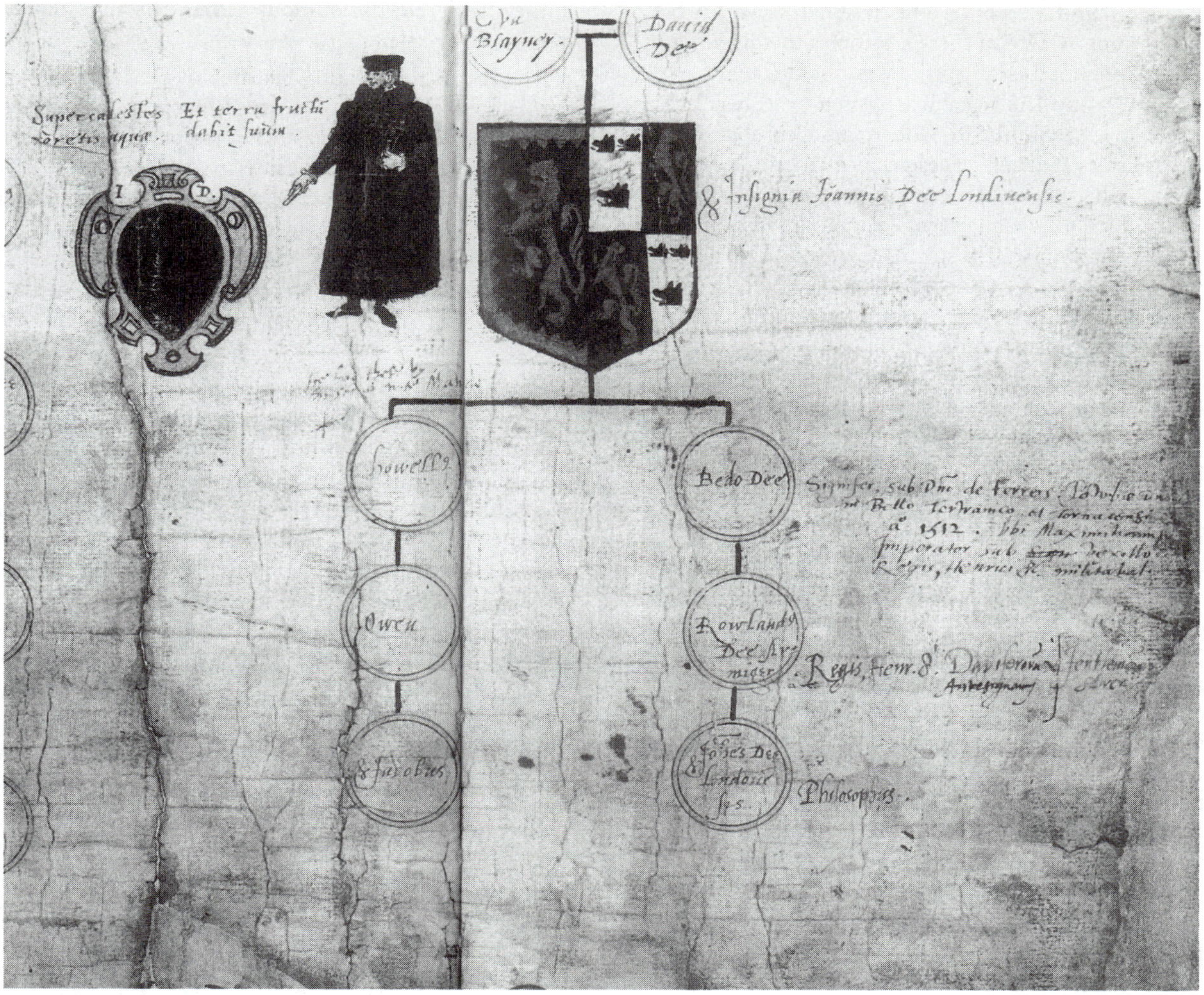

Part of Dee's genealogical roll, showing his immediate ancestry, a self-portrait, and his rendering of his coat of arms (British Library)

damned spirits." The preface, however, is a retrospective effort summing up his interests in mathematics and the sciences. While the charges against Dee were not then justified, his subsequent activities gave credence to his critics.

Dee's turn from scientific work to occult and cabalistic activities may have been prompted in part by frustrated ambition. In a letter of 3 October 1574 Dee complains to William Cecil, Lord Burghley that "in zeale to the best lerning and knowledg, and in incredible toyle of body and mynde, very many yeres, therfore onely endured, I know most assuredly that this land never bred any man, whose account therein can evidently be proved greater than myne." Revealing an almost Faustian hubris, he proceeds to offer Elizabeth the discovery of rich gold and silver mines–undoubtedly as the result of his alchemical and geographic skills–in exchange for her granting him certain proprietary rights to them. Nothing came of Dee's offer, and Elizabeth continued to use Dee to cast horoscopes for her and to consult on matters of geography and exploration. On 5 February 1578 Dee married Jane Fromond.

Engaging in occult studies and practices in earnest, Dee conducted many alchemical experiments at Mortlake after 1581. These experiments led to crystal gazing and the summoning of spirits. For his "skryer" or seer, the medium through whom intercourse with the spirits was conducted, Dee settled on the controversial and malevolent twenty-eight-year-old Edward Kelly, a convicted forger whose ears had been lopped off as punishment. Kelly joined Dee at Mortlake and soon became indispensable to him. Dee seems to have believed in all the spirit contacts described to him by Kelly. The spirits were of various sorts, both good and evil, angels and demons. The fascinating, disturbing accounts kept by Dee of these sessions show his intense, all-consuming interest in spiritual traffickings.

On 31 July 1583 Dee was visited by Albert Laski, the palatine of Siradz in Bohemia, accompanied by Robert Dudley, earl of Leicester, a courtier and favorite of Elizabeth whom Dee had tutored. Laski was intrigued by Dee's alchemical experiments and saw in them the possibility of restoring his own fortune. Dee accepted Laski's offer to host him and Kelly in Bohemia while they continued their experiments because he saw it as an opportunity to relieve his pressing financial situation. Richard Deacon and others argue that Dee was acting as a secret agent on behalf of Elizabeth, that his trips to the Continent were part of an elaborate intelligence service, and that the alchemical experiments served as an elaborate cover. In any event on 21 September 1583 Laski, Kelly, and Dee left for Poland.

Sometime prior to the time of his departure, Dee undertook to catalogue his collection of books at Mortlake, a process that appears to have continued right up to the time of his departure. Although Dee probably took part in the actual cataloguing of the books and manuscripts, it appears that the bulk of the bibliographic work and the preparation of the catalogues was done by Fremonsheim. Two catalogues of the collection, both dated 6 September 1583, are extant; they differ slightly in some matters of text and arrangement but both appear to be fair copies, bibliographically accurate and consistent, with few corrections or errors. In both catalogues all Greek titles have been translated into Latin.

Although they are superior in many ways to the list prepared in 1557, the 1583 catalogues have some interesting deficiencies. No books dated 1583 and few from the preceding couple of years appear in the catalogues. Another peculiarity is that the printed books are more fully catalogued than the manuscripts, the number of which seems surprisingly small, well below Dee's later estimates. One explanation for these flaws in the catalogues is that there simply may have been insufficient time to examine and catalogue the recent acquisitions and the manuscripts. Perhaps Dee intended to catalogue the manuscripts himself as he had done before. Another likely explanation for the lack of recent listings may be that Dee's financial straits had slowed his collecting. It is also possible that Dee was reluctant to list books and manuscripts that he had borrowed and not returned. Despite the probable gaps in the listing of the contents, however, the library is still quite impressive: 2,292 printed books and 200 manuscripts. There were probably another 160 manuscripts not listed. The 1583 catalogues represent the high point of Dee's collecting activities; following his departure for Poland, his library suffered diminution, either through damage, loss, theft, or sale.

One of the striking features of Dee's collection is the lack of theological texts. One who could serve under the Catholic Mary and Protestant Elizabeth must have been, even leaving aside his hermetic and occult interests, of a flexible and dispassionate theological temperament. Clearly, his interests were more mystical than theological. Although there were Bibles in several foreign languages, there were none in English, nor were there any English devotional works or biblical commentaries.

Interestingly, being that of a former student of the civil law at Louvain, the collection is rather poor in works on the law, and those that are listed seem more closely connected to Dee's domestic legal affairs than to any scholarly studies. Aristotle is well represented and Plato is somewhat less so. Books on logic and dialectics were a large part of the library, with some several dozen volumes devoted to that subject area. The Neoplatonists are quite evident, with works by Proclus, Porphyry, Iamblichus, and the Christian Pseudo-Dionysius. The Italian Neoplatonists and hermeticists, Pico Della Mirandola and Ficino, are also present; many of their texts bear extensive annotations by Dee. Renaissance magic is represented in the works of Pico Della Mirandola, Petrus Pomponazzi, Pontus de Tyard, Giovanni Francesco Pico, Thomas Erastus, and Jean Bodin.

Dee's collection of Hebrew books was unmatched in sixteenth-century England. There were a large number of Hebrew grammars, primers, and dictionaries, as well as Hebrew Bibles and postbiblical writings and cabalistic works. Despite the strength of this part of his collection, Dee evidently was not proficient in Hebrew and often made use of Latin translations. Much of Dee's interest was directed toward his preoccupation with the cabala.

Dee was clearly deeply interested in areas related to the occult and spiritualistic, apart from strictly Hermetic and Paracelsian studies. Dee's interest in angelology formed a notable part of the collection. Dee had a 1556 Venetian edition of *Coelestis hierarchia* by Pseudo-Dionysius, Johann Tritheim's *Liber octo quaestionum* (1534) and his *De septem secundeis* (1545), and works by Richard of St. Victor, Pomplius Azalus, and J. Rivius. The collection also contained a dozen books on witchcraft, nine books on demonology, four books on dreams, and sixteen on prognostication. Dee possessed a copy of the *Malleus Maleficarum* of Jacob Sprenger and Heinrich Kraemer; Johann Wier's *De praestigiis daemonum* (1517); Girolamo Menghi's *Flagellum daemonum; fustis daemonum;* and a Latin translation of Jean Bodin's *De la demonomanie des sorciers* (1581).

Dee's collection of Euclid was also quite strong, with a comprehensive listing of Euclidean titles and editions. Significantly, most of these seem to have been acquired prior to the 1570s; Dee's neglect of later editions and commentaries might reflect his diminishing interest in mathematics in favor of occult and alchemical studies. A copy of Andreas Alexander's textbook, *Mathemalogia* (1509), heavily annotated by Dee, is still extant. Generally, the mathematical works that remain from his library typically are not significantly annotated. Although Dee's interest in pure mathematics might have waned, his library did contain some sixty-five volumes related to mathematics, algebra, geometry, and trigonometry, certainly a substantial collection.

Dee had a large collection of books by or related to Ptolemy and to astronomy in general, amounting to some seventy-five books and manuscripts. He owned two copies of Copernicus's *De revolutionibus* (1543) as well as two or more copies of the *De lateribus et angulis triangulorum.* He also had many books concerning such contemporary astronomical events as the Cassiopeia Nova of 1572, which caused general consternation among the public.

Related to Dee's interest in astronomy was his interest in astrology, and he drew on both the Hellenistic and Arabic schools of astrological study. He had a substantial collection of editions of the *Almagest* and the *Quadripartitum* of Ptolemy and a heavily annotated copy of the *Centiloquium.* One copy of the *Quadripartitum* has a loose-leaf bound in with a long note in Dee's hand regarding the relation of an astral body to a person's nativity and fortune. Dee signed and dated "1568" his volume of Paulus Crusius's *Doctrina revolutionum* (1567), which contains a detached flyleaf, bound in afterward, with quotations in Dee's hand about the sun; Dee also added to the title page notes regarding the meridians of several European cities. Other works include Julius Firmicus Maternus's *Astronomica* (1533) and a manuscript copy of Vettius Valens's *Anthologia,* a treasured item for Dee. The Arabic tradition is represented in such works as his heavily annotated copy of Messahala's *De elementis et orbibus caelestibus* (1549), bound with his annotated collection of Messahala's *Astrologica* (1532). Dee also had three manuscript copies of the *De radiis stellarum* by the ninth-century Arab philosopher Alkundus, as well as the works of many other Arabic astrologers in manuscript form. Dee's astrological collection of some seventy volumes contained many of the important works on astrology then extant.

Dee's collection of alchemical works, including about ninety books and sixty manuscripts, are perhaps the most consistently annotated of all his volumes. Most of the alchemical works seem to have been bought during the 1560s and 1570s, although there were earlier signs of interest. Ramon Lull is well represented, and the collection included such key writers as Arnaldus de Villa Nova, Johannes de Rupescissa, Bonus Lombardus, and Ortulamus. Thomas Norton, George Ripley, and John Dastin represent the involvement of the English in alchemy. Dee's collection reflects his involvement in all aspects of alchemy: historical, experimental, theoretical, and personal.

Perhaps related to Dee's fascination in alchemy is his interest in metallurgy and mining, which was suggested by his promise to Elizabeth to discover gold and silver mines for her. Dee's diary entry for 13 March 1583 indicates that he had a financial interest in a mining venture in Devonshire. Of his mining books, Dee's most recent bibliographers, Julian Robers and Andrew G. Watson, have noted that the collection was "extraordinarily comprehensive, that he kept it up to date, and that he took nearly all of it abroad with him in 1583." Dee had Agricola's standard, *De re metallica,* as well as several others of his works; Lazarus Ercker's important *Bergwerck* (1533); John Mathesius's *Bergpostilla* (1578); Zachary Lockner's *Probierbüchlein* (1564); and rare assay books by C. Schreitmann and Samuel Zimmerman.

Dee's eighty books on medicine form a significant part of his collection. The works of Aristotle, Galen, and Hippocrates are complemented by a substantial mixture of later scientific works, such as Jean Ganivet's *Amicus medicorum* (1496). A large number of the medical books were more recent still, with many purchases made soon after publication. There are many works by Gerolamo Cardano, whom Dee had met personally. The most significant work in the collection was probably the *Anatomical Epitome* of Andreas Vesalius of 1543. His copy of Galen's *Prognostica de decubitu infirmorum,* acquired in 1551, contains notes by Dee on certain illnesses and the treatments he administered for them. Other important works included Jean François Fernel's *Medica Universa* (1555), Volcherus Coeiter's *Anatomicae exercitationes* (1513), and Amatus Lusitanus's *Curationum medicinalium centuria* (1556). In his manuscript copy of Johannes de Mirfield's *Breviarum Bartholomaei,* which Dee acquired in 1573, he continued to note remedies and treatments through the next two decades.

Dee's medical books show an emphasis on herbal remedies and were complemented by a variety of botany books, mostly of recent date. Dee owned William Turner's *Herbal* of 1568, as well as several works dealing with the plant life of the New World. He heavily annotated his illustrated copy of Gesner's *Thesaurus de remediis secretis* (1555). Dee's interest in plants seems to have been directly related to his occult experiments and cabalistic practices, rather than due to any particular appreciation of natural history.

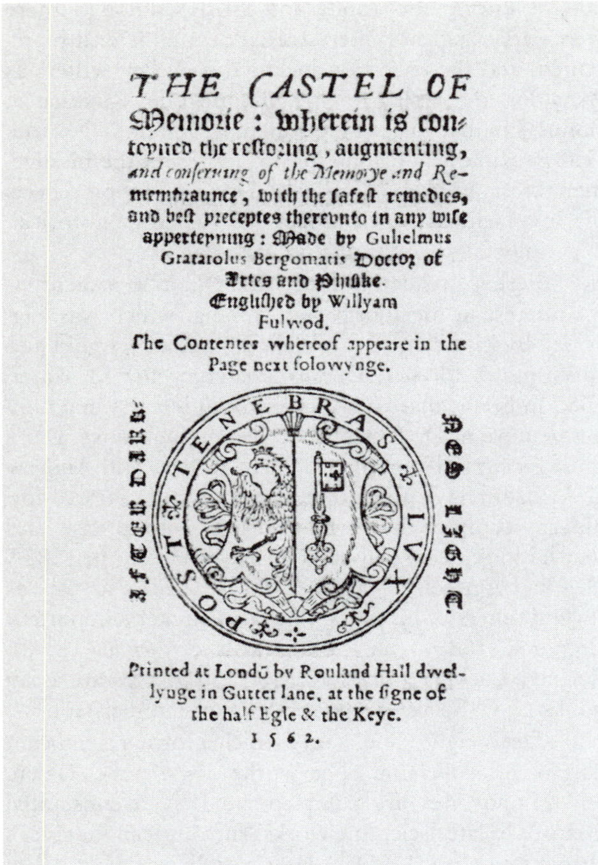

THE CASTEL OF
Memorie: wherein is conteyned the restoring, augmenting,
and conserving of the Memorye and Remembraunce, with the safest remedies,
and best preceptes therevnto in any wise
apperteyning: Made by Gulielmus
Gratarolus Bergomatis Doctor of
Artes and Phisike.
Englished by Wyllyam
Fulwod.
The Contentes whereof appeare in the
Page next folowynge.

Printed at Londō by Rouland Hall dwellynge in Gutter lane, at the signe of
the half Egle & the Keye.
1562.

Title page for one of several books in Dee's collection on the subject of memory

By far the largest section of Dee's library related to his Paracelsian texts: Dee had 157 copies of 92 editions of Paracelsus's works. He also gathered many books by followers of Paracelsus such as Gerard Dorn, Petrus Severinus, Michael Toxites, and Alexander Suchten. Of course, Paracelcus's works encompass the fields of alchemy, chemistry, and metallurgy, so that when one considers the Paracelsian holdings in conjunction with the many related works in the library, Dee's bibliophilic concentration in these fields is extraordinary.

History was another major area of interest for Dee. Although he owned books on the history of Greece and Rome and ancient history generally, the emphasis of the collection was on contemporary European history, with more than one hundred volumes concerning the subject. Dee's interest in history was consistent and extended through his collecting career; many of these books include his annotations. Historical works on most European countries are present, with an emphasis on France and Germany. There are some thirty histories of France. The works on Germany tend to be on particular regions or cities. In his annotations on European history Dee typically assumes a British imperialistic or hegemonic viewpoint. John Aubrey claims that Dee coined the phrase "British Empire."

About twenty-five of Dee's books deal substantially with British history. Dee was especially interested in works dealing with the roles of the legendary figures of Brutus and Arthur in English history, a subject of considerable contemporary interest as parallels to the heroic past were drawn to legitimate imperialist ambitions of the Tudor regime. The significant works in the collection included Matthew of Westminster's *Flores Historiarum* (1570), containing genealogies of famous men and Mercator's discussion of Arthur; John Bale's chronological encyclopedia of English history with material on Arthur (1549 and 1558); and Geoffrey of Monmouth's *Britanniae vtriusque regum origo* (1517), an influential source on Arthur and British history generally, in which Dee adds notes on his Welsh relations to the flyleaves.

Dee's collection of geography and navigation books contained many influential works. The range of the collection is indicated by books such as Levinius Apollonius's *De rebus peruvinis* (1567), Benjamin Tudelensis's *Itinerarium* (1573), Hierosius Benzoni's *Histoire du noveau monde* (1579), Monarchus Brocardus's *Novus Orbis* (1332), Ambrosio Contarini's *Viaggio nella Persia* (1559), Thomas Cooper's *Chronicles* (1565), Jacobus Navarchus's *Epistola Asiatica* (1570), and Nicolas de Nicolai's *Peregrinationes et navigationes* (1573?) and *Les navigations et peregrinations* (1577). Dee was heavily involved with the geographers and explorers of his time and traveled extensively himself. His library served as an informational resource for many of the English explorers and colonizers. Dee's library also numbers some thirty volumes on military science, gunnery, and related topics, including William Bourne's *Art of Shooting in Great Ordinance* (1578) and Robertu Valturius's *De re militaria* (1532).

While respectable, Dee's collection in the arts and literature does not compare to his holdings in the sciences. His collection of classical authors is limited, and English literature is poorly represented; for example, the only Geoffrey Chaucer is a partial manuscript copy of *Treatise on the Astrolabe.* Dee's collection of literature in foreign languages, especially French, German, and Italian, is much stronger. There are some books on architecture and engineering, including Albrecht Dürer's *De urbibus condendis* (Paris, 1535), Hans Blum's *Quinque columnarum descriptio* (1550), Silvio Belli's *Della proportione e proportionalità* (1573), Martino Bassi's *Dispareri in materia d'architettura* (1572), and works by Vitruvius.

Dee's collection also reflected his interest in books on the art of memory. He possessed Thomas Murner's

Logica memorativa (1508), Gulielmus Gratarolus Bergomatis's *Castel of Memorie* (1562), Matthew of Verona's *De arte memorandi,* included in a manuscript with several other works, and some half dozen other treatises on the subject. The library also contains relevant material in the works of such philosophers as Cicero, St. Thomas Aquinas, Lull, and Ramus.

Dee's library was housed at Mortlake, in a house that had belonged to his mother, where he settled in 1564. The house provided Dee with a settled, suitably large location for his books. Contemporary sources describe the library as being distributed through four or five rooms in the house, with perhaps a smaller group of books in Dee's private study. The books were generally arranged by size, although significant subject areas were grouped by interest, and bound and unbound books were arranged separately. Many of the books were shelved fore-edge facing out, and Dee often wrote the titles of the books vertically up or down along the fore-edge.

Dee's books were not distinguished by their scarcity or their ornate bindings. The bindings were typically of the simplest sort; indeed, many books remained the same as they came from the printer, perhaps because Dee was indifferent or because he did not wish to pay more than was necessary for his books. Some of the books he purchased were in contemporary bindings, some in medieval bindings. Those Dee had bound himself were typically bound in plain calf bindings or limp vellum.

Dee often signed his books, usually as "Joannes Deëus." He also occasionally wrote his name in Greek or French. In place of his name, he sometimes used a distinctive triangle and sometimes the astrological sign for the planet Jupiter, either in conjunction with his signature or alone. The unaccompanied Jupiter mark appears in about twenty-five to thirty of his manuscripts. The marks are typically found on the flyleaf or first page of the text. Dee also used a small ladder mark with three crossbars, usually placed at the top left hand corner of the first page of text or on a preliminary leaf, in about fifty of his manuscripts.

Dee's handwritten annotations in his books and manuscripts are readily identifiable though not dramatically distinctive. The annotations take various forms: personal notes; repetition of key words or phrases from the original text, summaries of key passages, and supplemental notes. Dee rarely takes issue with points made in the text in his marginal notes. Dee also annotated by use of such figurative devices as the "pointing hand" and the "flower sign" in the margin and by underlining. Most of his annotatations occur in books from the earlier period of Dee's collecting. After the 1570s, annotations and signatures become less common.

The depth and extent of Dee's holdings in so many diverse areas of human knowledge would make it remarkable in any era; under the circumstances in which it was assembled, it was an extraordinary bibliophilic achievement. Dee had in fact done what he had asked Queen Mary to do: create a library of national importance, one that could sustain scholarship and learning on an extensive scale. The collection was important for more than its size, however; it was actively used by a succession of scholars and students, which doubtless accounts for the many duplicate items in the collection.

Dee was a leading figure in many fields of Elizabethan science and was accordingly sought after as a teacher and adviser in such fields as geography, exploration and navigation, mathematics, mechanics, alchemy, and hermetics. He was teacher or adviser to such figures as Sir William Pickering, Thomas Digges, William Bourne, William Camden, Richard Hakluyt, Martin Frobisher, Richard Chancellor, Steven and William Borough, Humphrey and Adrian Gilbert, and Sir Walter Ralegh. Dee also served as tutor in several important families, notably to the duke of Northumberland's children, among whom were the future earl of Leicester, Robert Dudley. Dee also served as tutor to the earl's nephew, the poet Philip Sidney. Dee became a part of the Sidney "circle," which included such figures as Gabriel Harvey and Edmund Spenser. His library thus became an institution for research, analysis, and development. It performed the functions of a university library. The books were necessary sources of reference and guidance for the most important activities of the time.

Based on markings in the catalogues, it appears that some eight hundred volumes accompanied Dee on his trip to the Continent with Kelly and Laski. He took many of the important hermetic and cabalistic works, two-thirds of the bound alchemical titles, 85 percent of the bound Paracelsian titles, and about 40 percent of his semitic collection, many medieval scientific texts, and a scattering of European histories, including that of Bohemia. Dee also took with him copies of his own books. His books and personal effects were carried on three large wagons.

On 3 February 1584, Dee, Kelly, and Laski arrived at Laskoe, the palatine's principal castle, near Cracow. By the middle of the following year, the palatine had become disenchanted with Dee and Kelly and forced their departure. They went on to Prague to the court of Emperor Rudolf II, who also rejected them. After various difficulties, they found some temporary support from William Ursinus, Count Rosenberg, chief

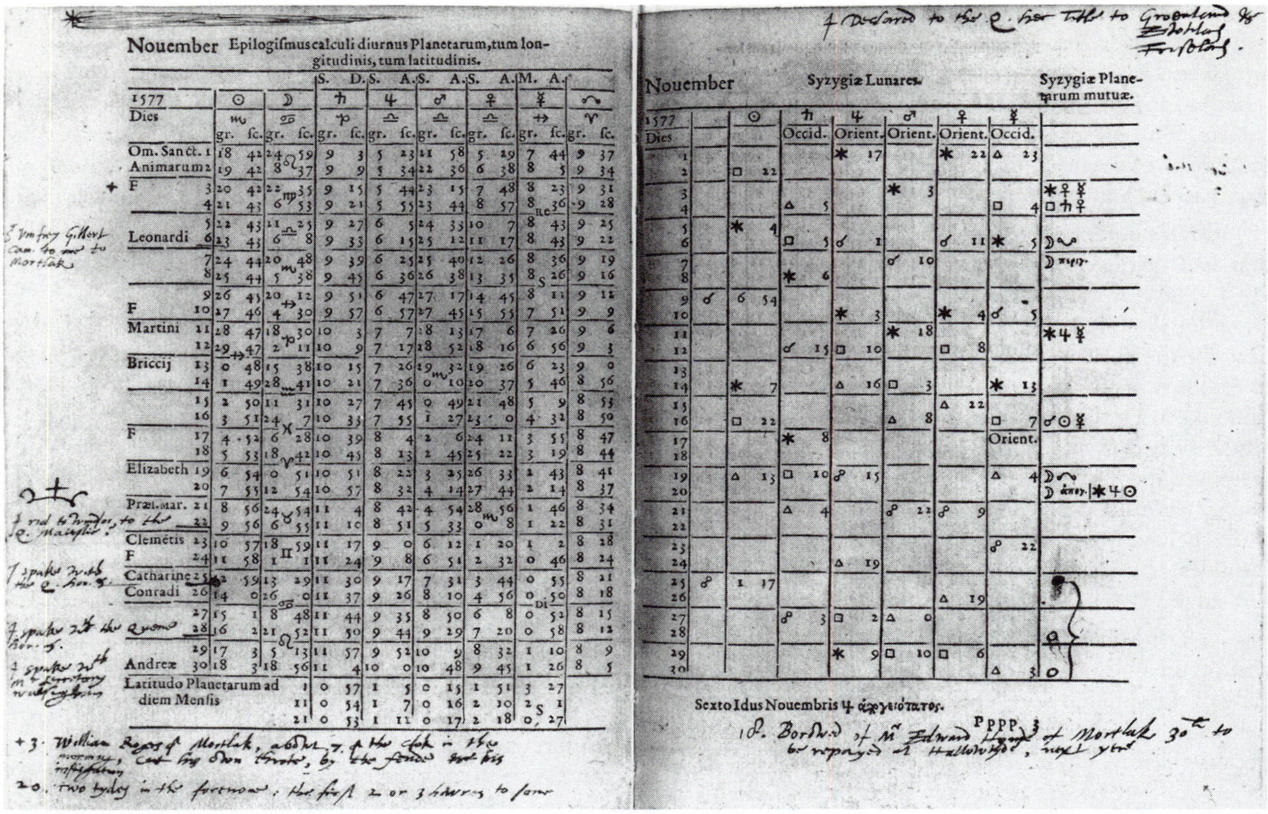

Dee's diary entries for November 1577, in the margins of his copy of Joannes Stadius's Ephemerides novae. *The note in the top right corner records a meeting with Queen Elizabeth (Bodleian Library, Oxford).*

burgrave of Bohemia. Throughout this time, Dee and Kelly maintained and intensified their alchemical and occult experiments. Dee even attempted to involve his eight-year-old son, Arthur, in the experiments as a skryer. Dee and Kelly's relationship grew increasingly complex and problematic. On 18 April 1587, Kelly informed Dee that one of the spirits with which they had been communing directed that they hold all things in common, including their wives, though it is unclear if this actually occurred. Quarrels racked their relationship, culminating in the final breakup on 4 February 1588. Dee gave Kelly his "powder, the bokes, the glas, and the bone" that they used for their experiments.

On 16 February 1588, Kelly left for Prague, and Dee began the long return journey home. In a revealing entry in his diary for 2 August 1589, Dee recorded a "terrible dream that Mr. Kelly wold by force bereave me of my bokes, toward daybreak." Dee was received by the queen on 19 December 1589 and arrived at Mortlake on Christmas Day. Although he apparently did not acquire any significant number of books or manuscripts while on his journey, Dee brought back the bulk of the books he had taken. He discovered, however, that his library at Mortlake had been partially plundered and destroyed during his absence.

According to Thomas Smith, Dee's first biographer, the destruction of Dee's library was carried out by a crowd of Mortlake residents angry with Dee for his alchemical and occult practices. In later versions of the story, the Mortlake crowd became a London mob destroying the lair of a conjuror. Yet, while the destruction or removal of books and instruments was significant, an enraged mob would hardly have been so constrained in its actions.

The selective destruction and plundering seem to point to a group of individuals of mixed motivations. One of the plunderers was probably Nicholas Saunder, who likely was connected with Dee through astronomical, navigational, and mechanistic studies. The contents of Saunder's own library included many of the stolen books and manuscripts from Dee's collection. Another thief appears to have been Fremonsheim, Dee's longtime bookseller and cataloguer of the library, who may have been exacting some repayment for Dee's prolonged failure to repay his book-buying debts. Adrian Gilbert, a chemist whom Aubrey described as a buffoon, was yet another looter, who came to Dee soon after his return to offer repayment for some of the books and instruments. Dee eventually effected the return of nearly three-fourths of his books, an indication that he had knowledge of those responsible.

Dee's own statement of the loss suffered at Mortlake is contained in his *Compendius Rehearsall.* Claiming to have amassed three thousand books and one thousand manuscripts–numbers that may have overstated the case, particularly in regard to manuscripts–Dee puts the value of his collection at £2,000 and complains that some five hundred of his books had been lost. He does not enumerate the lost books but gives much more detail about the non-book items that had been destroyed or taken. These included "some rare and exquisitely [made] instruments Mathematical," such as a quadrant made by Richard Chancellour; a "*radius Astronomicus*" ten feet in length; and two globes fashioned by Mercator. Dee also describes a "sea-compasse of diverse sorts" and "an excellent watch clock." One curious item mentioned by Dee was a "great bladder" filled with about four pounds of "a very sweetish thing, like a brownish gun," purified thirty times. He estimates his total loss at about £400.

The most intriguing loss Dee claimed was two sets of manuscripts and documents. Dee states that kept in "a great case or frame of boxes" were "some hundreds of very rare evidences of divers Irelandish territories, provinces, and lands" produced under the auspices of "ancient Irish princes." The other set of documents related to "divers evidences antient of some Welsh Princes and Noblemen, their great gifts of lands to the foundations or enrichings of sundry Houses of Religious men." The exact nature of these documents has not been determined; they do not appear in his library catalogues. Elizabeth once more helped Dee with a gift of money, though not enough to entirely or permanently remove him from financial difficulties.

Despite receiving gifts of money from friends, and perhaps fees from pupils, Dee's financial problems continued. In 1595, through Elizabeth's patronage, Dee obtained the wardenship of Christ Church, Manchester College. Dee was fortunate to have obtained this position as his reputation as a sorcerer persisted. Dee found it necessary to send a letter to the archbishop of Canterbury asserting his Christian beliefs. On 4 June 1604 Dee petitioned the new monarch, James I, to have him tried for sorcery in an effort to put an end to charges that he was "a conjurer, or caller, or invocator of divels." Perhaps fortunately, James ignored Dee's request. Continued opposition to Dee ultimately forced him to resign the wardenship in 1605. The death of his wife, shortly before his resignation, had left him with seven surviving offspring.

Dee returned to Mortlake where, with the assistance of a Bartholomew Hickman as skryer, he once again took up his occult practices and communication with spirits. His poverty increased until he was forced to sell his plate, his wife's jewelry, and the books from his library in order to subsist. Dee's autobiographical records show that he feared being turned out of his home because of his debts. The great library he had assembled for the use of scholarship became a means for bare survival. Ownership records indicate that books and manuscripts from Dee's collection found their way during this time into the hands of a wide variety of collectors.

Although the date and place of Dee's death are unknown, it appears most likely that he died at the end of December 1608 at Mortlake; he was buried in the chancel of the church near his Mortlake residence.The dispersal of the largest private library in Renaissance England did not take place immediately. Dee's final intentions regarding his estate were developed as a result of a "scrying" session with Hickman, wherein a John Pontois was named by an angel as the person who should receive and dispose of the books and appurtenances. Although some of Dee's books and personal manuscripts passed to his son Arthur, it appears that Pontois moved the majority of the library to his own house in London. Upon Pontois's death in 1624, the library passed into the possession of Patrick Saunders and John Woodall, whose relationship to Dee was tangential at best, although they might have shared an interest with him in Paracelsian philosophy.

The dispersal of the library began in earnest in 1625 as books and manuscripts were sold off mainly through London booksellers. The great collector, Robert Cotton, acquired many of the manuscripts. According to Aubrey, he purchased the land around Mortlake on the supposition that Dee had buried some rare texts in the ground. Sir William Boswell acquired many important manuscripts, as did Brian Twayne, the son of the Canterbury antiquarian, who donated many of them to Corpus Christi College, Oxford, which today has the largest surviving collection of Dee manuscripts. Dee manuscripts were also to be found in the collections of such notable later collectors as John Selden, Elias Ashmole, Henry Fowler, and Samuel Pepys. The famous Puritan, John Winthrop, an important collector in his own right, was a keen collector of Dee's manuscripts and books, some of which he brought to the New World with him. Through attrition, loss, theft, and private and public sale, Dee's library finally was widely dispersed. It has not been possible to trace the route that many of the books and manuscripts took. The largest current holding of Dee's printed books is to be found in the library of the Royal College of Physicians. Dee's famous occult crystal is in the British Museum, as are the cakes of wax used in his occult ceremonies.

The study of Dee's life and activities is tantamount to the study of the scientific milieu, with all its strengths and weaknesses, of Elizabethan England. Dee helped redefine the role of the private library, turning it from mere antiquarianism or personal recreation into the tool of scholars and the locus of applied research. Mortlake was part personal collection, part institutional library, part research organization, and part museum. The library that Dee assembled created the grounds for further scholarship as well as for flights of the imagination and spirit. In some ways Dee made all subsequent book collectors part of the tradition of the magus.

Biographies:

Thomas Smith, *Vitae quorundam eruditissimorum et illustrium vivorum* (London, 1707); translated by William Alexander Ayton as *The Life of John Dee* (London: Theosophical Society, 1908);

Thomas Frognall Dibdin, *Bibliomania; or Book-Madness,* 2 volumes (London: Henry G. Bohn, 1842), II: 261–265;

Isaac Disraeli, "The Occult Philosopher, Dr. Dee," *Amenities of Literature* (London: A. C. Armstrong, 1880; New York: Greenwood Press, 1969), II: 285–312;

John Aubrey, *"Brief Lives," Chiefly of Contemporaries, Set Down by John Aubrey, Between the Years 1669 & 1696,* 2 volumes, edited by Andrew Clark (Oxford: Clarendon Press, 1898), II: 210–215;

Charlotte Fell-Smith, *John Dee: 1527–1608* (London: Constable, 1909);

Gertrude M. Hort, *Dr. John Dee: Elizabethan Mystic and Astrologer* (London: W. Rider, 1922).

References:

Nicholas H. Clulee, *John Dee's Natural Philosophy: Between Science and Religion* (London & New York: Routledge, 1988);

Richard Deacon, *John Dee: Scientist, Geographer, Astrologer and Secret Agent to Elizabeth I* (London: Muller, 1968);

Peter J. French, *John Dee: The World of an Elizabethan Magus* (London: Routledge & Kegan Paul, 1972);

David Gwyn, "John Dee's *Arte of Navigation,*" *Book Collector,* 34 (Autumn 1985): 309-322;

S. C. McCulloch, "John Dee: Elizabethan Doctor of Science and Medicine," *South Atlantic Quarterly,* 50 (1951): 72–85;

William H. Sherman, *John Dee: The Politics of Reading and Writing in the English Renaissance* (Amherst: University of Massachusetts Press, 1995);

E. G. R. Taylor, *Tudor Geography 1485–1583* (London: Methuen, 1930; New York: Octagon Books, 1968), pp. 75–139;

Walter I. Trattner, "God and Expansion in Elizabethan England: John Dee, 1527-1583," *JHI,* 25 (January–March 1964): 17–34;

Francis A. Yates, *The Occult Philosophy in the Elizabethan Age* (London: Routledge & Kegan Paul, 1979), pp. 79–108;

Yates, *Theatre of the World* (Chicago: University of Chicago Press, 1969), pp. 1–41.

Papers:

The largest collection of John Dee's manuscripts are in the college library of Christ Church, Oxford University. The largest collection of printed books from Dee's library are held by the library of the Royal College of Physicians, London. The British Library has a collection of Dee's holograph letters, as well as a large number of his manuscripts. Other significant collections are in the Bodleian Library and Cambridge University Library.

William Drummond of Hawthornden

(13 December 1585 – 4 December 1649)

Joseph Rosenblum
University of North Carolina at Greensboro

See also the Drummond entry in *DLB 121: Seventeenth-Century British Nondramatic Poets, First Series.*

CATALOGUES: *Avctarivm Bibliothecae Edinbvrgenae, five Catalogus Librorum quos Guilielmus Drummondus ab Hawthornden Bibliothecae D. D. Q. Anno 1627* (Edinburgh: Printed by the heirs of Andro Hart, 1627);
Robert H. MacDonald, *The Library of William Drummond of Hawthornden* (Edinburgh: Edinburgh University Press, 1971).

BOOKS: *Teares on the Death of Meliades* (Edinburgh: Printed by Andro Hart, 1613);
Poems (Edinburgh?, 1614?); revised as *Poems: Amorous, Funerall, Diuine, Pastorall, in Sonnets, Songs, Sextains, Madrigals* (Edinburgh: Printed by Andro Hart, 1616);
Poems (Edinburgh: Andro Hart, 1616);
In Pious Memorie of The Right Worthie and Vertuous Euphemia Kyninghame, Who in the Prime of Her Youth Died the 23. Of Iulie, 1616 [half sheet] (Edinburgh: Printed by Andro Hart, 1617);
Forth Feasting: A Panegyrick to the Kings Most Excellent Majestie (Edinburgh: Andro Hart, 1617); revised and published in *The Mvses Welcome to the High and Mightie Prince James* (Edinburgh: Printed by Thomas Finlason, 1618);
A Midnights Traunce: Wherein Is Discoursed of Death, the Nature of Soules, and Estate of Immortalitie (London: Printed by G. Purslow for J. Budge, 1619); revised and republished as *A Cypresse Grove* in *Flowres of Sion* (1623);
Flowres of Sion. By William Drvmmond of Hawthorene-denne. To which is adjoyned his Cypresse Grove (Edinburgh?: Printed by the heirs of Andro Hart?, 1623; revised and enlarged edition, Edinburgh: Printed by the heirs of Andro Hart, 1630);
The Entertainment of the High and Mighty Monarch Charles King of Great Britaine, France, and Ireland, into His Auncient and Royall City of Edinburgh, the Fifteeth of Iune, 1633 (Edinburgh: Printed by Iohn Wreittoun, 1633);
To the Exequies of the Honovrable, Sr. Antonye Alexander, Knight, &c.: A Pastorall Elegie (Edinburgh: Printed in King James his College by George Anderson, 1638);
Polemo-Medinia Inter Vitarvam et Nebernam (Edinburgh?, 1645?); republished as *Polemo-Middinia. Carmen Macaronicum. Autore Gulielmo Drummundo, Scoto-Britanno* (Oxford: E Theatro Sheldoniano, 1691);
The History of Scotland, from the Year 1423 until the Year 1542 (London: Printed by Henry Hills for Richard Tomlins and himself, 1655);
Notes of Ben Jonson's Conversations with William Drummond of Hawthornden (London: Printed for the Shakespeare Society, 1842).

Editions and Collections: *Poems by That most Famous wit, William Drvmmond of Hawthornden,* edited by Edward Phillips (London: Printed for Richard Tomlins, 1656); republished as *The most Elegant and Elabourate Poems Of that Great Court-Wit, Mr William Drummond* (London: Printed for William Rands, 1659);
The Works of William Drummond of Hawthornden, edited by Bishop John Sage and Thomas Ruddiman (Edinburgh: Printed by James Watson, 1711);
The Poetical Works of William Drummond of Hawthornden With 'A Cypresse Grove,' 2 volumes, edited by L. E. Kastner (Edinburgh & London: Printed for the Scottish Text Society by W. Blackwood, 1913);
Conversations, in *Ben Johnson,* 22 volumes, edited by C. H. Herford and Percy Simpson (Oxford: Clarendon Press, 1925–1954), I: 128–178;
William Drummond of Hawthornden Poems and Prose, edited by Robert H. MacDonald, The Association for Scottish Literary Studies, 6 (Edinburgh & London: Scottish Academic Press, 1976)–includes the text of the "Memorialls."

OTHER: *Mavsolevm; or, The Choicest Flowres of the Epitaphs, Written on the Death of the Neuer-too-much*

William Drummond of Hawthornden, 1623 (portrait by an anonymous artist; from Robert H. MacDonald, ed., The Library of William Drummond of Hawthornden, *1971)*

Lamented Prince Henrie, includes two sonnets and an epitaph by Drummond (Edinburgh: Printed by Andro Hart, 1613).

In his book collecting as in his poetry, William Drummond was conservative and imitative. As reported in *Notes of Ben Jonson's Conversations with William Drummond of Hawthornden* (1842), Jonson said that Drummond's verses were good, "Save that they smelled too much of the Schools, and were not after the fancie of the time." In an undated letter to Dr. Arthur Johnston, Drummond expressed his objections to innovations in poetry:

> In vain have some Men of late (Transformers of every Thing) consulted upon her Reformation, and endeavoured to abstract her to Metaphysical Ideas and Scholastical Quiddities, denuding her of her own Habits, and those Ornaments with which she has amused the world some Thousand Years. . . . What is not like the ancient and conform to those rules which hath been agreed unto by all Times, may (indeed) be something like unto Poetry but it is no more Poetry than a Monster is a Man.

His book buying was informed by this same retrospective attitude.

As Robert H. MacDonald, who has made the most comprehensive study of Drummond's library, observes, "He looked for accepted opinion, and though he knew the latest ideas still he valued the old." His collection therefore serves as a guide to what contemporaries of William Shakespeare and Jonson were reading. It also shows how a man of moderate means living in a relatively isolated part of Britain acquired his books.

Because Drummond relied so heavily on his reading in composing both his poetry and his history, an examination of his library provides a biography of his intellectual life.

The son of John Drummond, first Laird of Hawthornden, and his wife, Susannah Fowler Drummond, William Drummond was born at Hawthornden on 13 December 1585. In 1590 John Drummond was appointed Gentleman-Usher to King James VI of Scotland, to whom the Drummonds were distantly related, and about the same time Drummond's uncle William Fowler was made private secretary to Queen Anne. Drummond thus grew up in a courtly, sophisticated atmosphere. In his father's library were many books of a practical nature on law, medicine, and agriculture but also Sir Philip Sidney's *Arcadia* (1590), John Lyly's *Euphues* (1579), the anthology *England's Parnassus* (1600), edited by Robert Allot and containing popular poems of the day, and Arthur Golding's English translation of Ovid's *Metamorphoses* (1567), a work that influenced Shakespeare.

Drummond attended Edinburgh's High School, and in 1600 he entered the humanity class, a preparatory year at Edinburgh University, from which he graduated with an M.A. in 1605. He gave early evidence of his literary bent. He records in his memorials, sketchy and irregular journal entries published in *William Drummond of Hawthornden Poems and Prose* (1976), that in September 1602, "By reading Heliodorus and other bookes the 17 yere of my age I had a pain in myne eyes for the space of eight dayes" and nearly went blind. This episode did not alienate Drummond from the author of the *Ethiopica,* since his library contained a copy of the work. Drummond's academic experiences influenced his tastes: the works he studied are well represented on his shelves.

In the humanity class Drummond doubtless read Horace, Juvenal, Plautus, and Cicero. He studied rhetoric from a text by Omer Talon, a student of the French philosopher Petrus Ramus. As a first-year college student, Drummond read the New Testament, Isocrates, Homer, and Theocritus in Greek and studied logic from a Ramian text. Second-year students studied rhetoric by reading Cassander, Cicero, and Demosthenes and logic through Aristotle's *Organon* in Latin and Porphyry's *Categories.* The curriculum for the third year included more logic, Hebrew grammar, Aristotle's *Posterior Analytics,* his *Ethics,* and the beginning of his *Physics.* In their fourth year students finished the *Physics,* read Aristotle's *De anima,* studied astronomy and science from Joannes de Sacro Basco's thirteenth-century *Sphaera mundi* and geography from Joannes Honterus's *Rudimentorum cosmographicorum,* first published in 1530.

In 1606 Drummond went to England and then to France, where he visited Paris before attending the university at Bourges to study law. In these years he laid the foundations of his library. According to MacDonald, by the time Drummond returned to Scotland in 1608 he had purchased nearly 400 volumes, 323 in France and 76 in England. Included here were 18 Italian books from England and 39 from France. He purchased 20 Greek books in France, 11 in England; 5 Hebrew books in France; 14 law books in France; 27 philosophy books in France, 10 in England; 30 poetry books in France, 6 in England; 69 other prose works in France, 11 in England; 102 French books in France; 10 theological works in France. Books were better printed on the Continent; they also were less expensive. Drummond's French books cost a total of 2,399 sous (about £10.18s.), his English books £6.13s.6d.

In the first decade of the seventeenth century the average price of a book in London was a halfpenny a sheet, though law books, music books, books with illustrations, erotica, and popular books cost more. The most expensive book that Drummond bought in England was Johann Scapula's *Lexicon graeco-latinum,* first published in 1580. The book cost 10s. and indicates Drummond's continuing interest in improving his Greek. How much progress he made is unclear because most of his Greek texts contain Latin translations and notes, indicating that he may have needed assistance with the language. Perhaps, though, these were the texts that were available and affordable, since Drummond bought many of his books secondhand.

Various factors influenced the prices Drummond paid for his books. For example, he paid 7s. for the relatively recent *Works* (1602) of Samuel Daniel, a high price because of the recent publication date and the popularity of the poems. Also, the book may have been nicely bound and therefore expensive. In 1827 the scholar and antiquarian David Laing had all of Drummond's books in Edinburgh University rebound, thus destroying evidence of what these books looked like when Drummond bought them. For 6s. Drummond secured his own copy of the *Arcadia;* his copy of Edmund Spenser's *Faerie Queene* (1590–1596) cost the same. For Bartholomew Yong's translation of Jorge de Montemayor's *Diane* (1561), with the Alonso Pérez continuation (1568) and Gaspar Gil Polo's *Diana enamorado* (1564) Drummond paid 7s. Spenser's *Shephearde's Calendar* (1579), *Amoretti and Epithalamion* (1595), and *Fowre Hymnes* (1596) cost 4d. each, probably because they were secondhand copies. For a second quarto of Shakespeare's *Romeo and Juliet* (1599), again probably secondhand, Drummond paid 6d. Such purchases show his interest in English literature. When he began writing, he chose English rather than Scots, and he took as

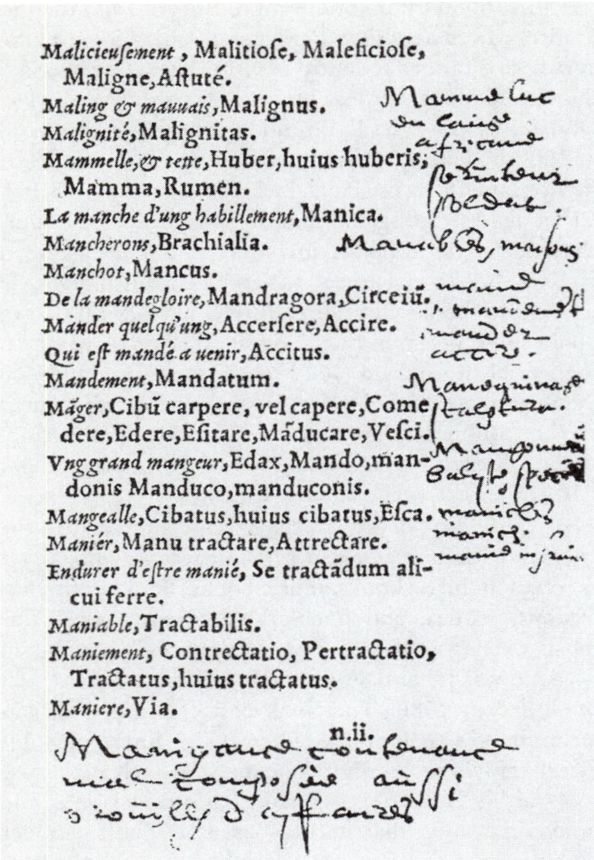
Malicieuſement, Malitioſe, Maleficioſe, Maligne, Aſtutè.
Maling & mauuais, Malignus.
Malignité, Malignitas.
Mammelle, & tette, Huber, huius huberis; Mamma, Rumen.
La manche d'ung habillement, Manica.
Mancherons, Brachialia.
Manchot, Mancus.
De la mandegloire, Mandragora, Circeiū.
Mander quelqu'ung, Accerſere, Accire.
Qui eſt mandé a uenir, Accitus.
Mandement, Mandatum.
Mãger, Cibū carpere, vel capere, Comedere, Edere, Eſitare, Mãducare, Veſci.
Vng grand mangeur, Edax, Mando, mandonis Manduco, manduconis.
Mangealle, Cibatus, huius cibatus, Eſca.
Maniér, Manu tractare, Attrectare.
Endurer d'eſtre manié, Se tractãdum alicui ferre.
Maniable, Tractabilis.
Maniement, Contrectatio, Pertractatio, Tractatus, huius tractatus.
Maniere, Via.
n.ii.

Drummond's marginal notes on a page from a French-Latin dictionary for children (Edinburgh University Library)

his models the Elizabethans rather than his Jacobean contemporaries.

Books in France cost about half what they did in England. In 1607 for 60 sous (about 6s.) Drummond bought a copy of Justinian I's sixth-century *Corpus juris civilis,* still the basis of legal practice in the seventeenth century. Though Drummond had gone to France to study law–Scotland had no law schools at the time–his purchases reveal his true interests. His most expensive acquisition in France, and the one he placed first in his 1611 catalogue of his French books, was Simon Goulart's Protestant *Memoire de l'estat de france, sous Charles neufiesme,* probably the 1576 edition in three volumes. Drummond paid 6 livres (120 sous or 12s.) for this secondhand book with a handsome binding. For Plutarch's *Lives* in Latin he paid 40 sous; Joannes Despauterius's *Grammatica* cost 30 sous and Ariosto's *Le Roland furieux* (or Phillipe Desportes's imitation with the same title) 20 sous. For Christopher Clavius's edition of *Sacro Bosco,* one of the school texts that Drummond added to his library, he paid 48 sous. Paris was a major printing center, and most of the books that Drummond bought in France were printed there. The capital was also a center of the book trade, importing works from the presses of Venice and Lyons, Geneva and Heidelberg, Leipzig, Antwerp, and Frankfurt.

After about two years in Scotland, Drummond returned to England in 1610, where he added more volumes to his library. In that year his father died, leaving an estate of £14,085 Scots together with lands and a house. Drummond received the house, lands, and a third of the money–not the fortune it may appear because the Scottish pound was worth only one-twelfth of the English; his father also left debts of £9,900 Scots. With this legacy Drummond was able to rebuild his house and buy about 1,600 books during the course of his life; at his own death he left £3,935 Scots. The value of the library he amassed was probably about £90 English, not a large sum. His was neither the only nor the finest collection in the Lowlands; its importance lies in what it reveals about the intellectual temper of the man and his times.

In 1611 Drummond compiled a catalogue of his 546 books, largely literary and scholarly titles. Of these, about 130 volumes survive. The catalogue reveals what Drummond owned, how he organized his library, where he bought his books, and what he paid for them. He recorded prices for 401 titles; the others were mostly inherited or given to him. The list includes some 250 works in Latin, 120 in French, 61 in Italian, 50 in English, 11 in Hebrew, 8 in Spanish, and more than 30 in Greek.

Drummond organized his catalogue first by language and then by subject, a system that was common at the time. Thomas James employed such a system for the 1605 Bodleian Library catalogue, and the German bibliographer George Draud used it in his *Bibliotheca classica* (1611). Drummond divided his Latin books into five categories: theology, philosophy, law, poetry, and miscellaneous prose. He grouped medicine and geography with philosophy because he had too few medical and geographical titles to warrant individual divisions. Also, at Edinburgh University geography was taught as a branch of philosophy. Each of the other languages received separate listings.

After 1611 Drummond increased his holdings in belles-lettres, buying poetry and drama in English, Italian, French, and Spanish. As the conflicts between the monarchy and Parliament intensified, he began buying polemical pamphlets and books that he used in composing his own monarchist tracts, which he circulated in manuscript. He added popular works such as accounts of voyages, travel guides, books on astrology, satirical writings, and neo-Latin poetry by his fellow Scots. Late in life he began a study of Scotland from King James I through James V. Research for this book, published posthumously as *The History of Scotland, from the Year 1423 until the Year 1542* (1655), prompted him to increase his holdings in history. Age also fostered an interest in medical and spiritual titles such as Joannes Fernel's *Vniuersa medicina* (1578) and Thomas Aquinas's thirteenth-century *Summa theologica,* for which he paid 8 livres (16 s.) in 1625 when he ordered the book from a friend going to Paris.

That same request included a dictionary by John Misheu, Giovanni Battista Marino's *L'Adone* (Drummond wanted the edition that was published in either Venice or Paris in 1623), and Famianus Strada's poems. For each title Drummond indicated the price he expected to pay. Such detailed information suggests that Drummond consulted catalogues that he could have found at the shop of Andro Hart, his publisher in Edinburgh. Paris publishers advertised regularly in the catalogues of the Frankfurt Fair, an annual book fair that attracted booksellers from all over Europe. The heirs and successors of Guillaume Rouillé of Lyons issued catalogues in 1604 and 1621, and other Continental and English publishers did the same. On 3 January 1616 the "Latin stock" of the Stationers' Company was established to export English books, import works published abroad, and to reprint the latter if demand justified. The Latin stock issued semiannual catalogues from the autumn of 1622 to the autumn of 1626. Drummond could thus keep up with the latest books despite his relative isolation.

Based on Drummond's lists and on surviving volumes, MacDonald reconstructed a catalogue of Drummond's library, *The Library of William Drummond of Hawthornden* (1971). Because Drummond continued to add to his collection and to give away books, the titles in McDonald's list were not all on Drummond's shelves at the same time. Still, the catalogue reflects what Drummond was buying and reading, since he acquired his books to read, not to display. The library reveals Drummond's interest in philosophy. MacDonald notes that Drummond's collection was rich not only in Aristotelian texts but also in books inspired by the work of Petrus Ramus, a French philosopher who simplified Aristotle's approach to logic:

> Philosophy was the mainstay of the Edinburgh curriculum, and Aristotle the chief support of philosophy. Drummond had the main Aristotelian texts, he had the commentaries of the important scholars, he had compendia. He had Ramist interpretations, and anti-Ramist interpretations; he had tracts from the Middle Ages and the latest synthesis of the day–but almost all of his collection described, supplemented or criticized the books of the Aristotelian canon.

Drummond owned twenty-two editions of Aristotle, the focus of scholastic education, in Greek or Latin, lacking only the *Metaphysics* and the *Poetics.* The latter omission may seem curious given Drummond's poetic output, but neither of these works was taught at the university where so large a part of Drummond's literary tastes was formed.

While Plato's philosophy did not supplant Aristotle's in the Renaissance curriculum or worldview, Plato's views on love were influential and were reflected in books that Drummond bought. These include the 1562 edition of Baldassare Castiglione's *Il Cortegiano,* Leone Ebreo's *Dialoghi d'amore,* Giovanni Battista Gelli's *La Circé* (1550), which Drummond bought in Paris in 1607, and Torquato Tasso's *Aminta,* which Drummond owned in French and Italian. He also had Marsilio Ficino's Latin translation of Plato (1551), also acquired in Paris in 1607, and Macrobius fifth-century Platonic commentary on Cicero's *Somnium Scipionis,* Martianus Capella's *De nuptii philologiae,* and Boethius's *De consolatione philosophiae.* Drummond's *A Midnights Traunce: Wherein Is Discoursed of Death, the Nature of Soules, and Estate of Immortalitie* (1619) draws heavily on Christian Platonism.

Drummond's conservatism is evident in his selection of works in science. He owned no books by Nicholas Copernicus, Johannes Kepler, Tycho Brahe, William Gilbert, or Galileo Galilei, though their works were available. Robert Recorde and Thomas Digges wrote books in English presenting the new scientific discoveries, but these, too, were absent from Drummond's shelves. Instead, he owned Aristotle's *Physics,* a school text, in Greek and Latin. He had Sacro Bosco's *Sphaera mundi,* another text he had studied in school that was based on Aristotelian-Ptolemaic cosmography. He had Seneca's *Naturalis quaestiones,* Philo's *De mundo,* and works by Aristarchus, Cleomedes, and Ptolemy as well as two later writers who accepted the classical worldview, Alessandro Piccolomini and Joannes Ferrerius.

Drummond, though, did keep abreast of explorations. His 1509 edition of Ptolemy's *Cosmographiae introductio* included accounts of Amerigo Vespucci's four voyages. He owned John Smith's *A Map of Virginia* (1612) and *Description of New England* (1616) and Sir Robert Gordon of Lochinvar's *Encouragements, for Such as Shall Have Intention To Bee Vnder-takers in the New Plantation of Cape Briton, Now New Galloway in America* (1625).

Drummond's library included about thirty medical books, indicating a concern for his health and a recognition that the doctors of the time were largely ineffective. In November 1620 Drummond wrote to Sir William Alexander, "For these eight weekes I have beene languishing in sicknesse, and that more by the ignorance of physicians (which, being no where good,

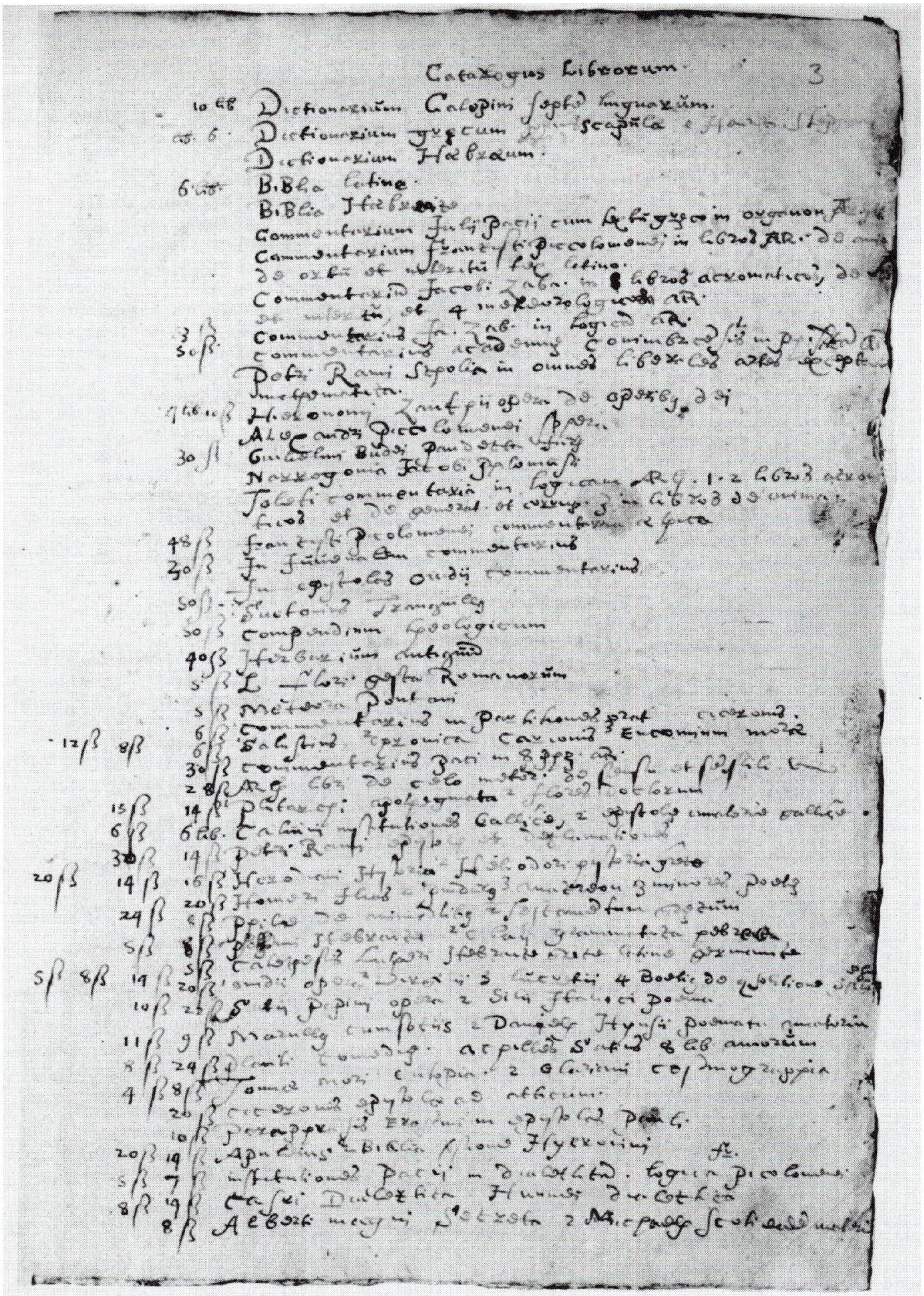

First page of a rough list Drummond made of his library, 1611 (Edinburgh University Library)

are heere naught), than any defect of nature: for my disease being a paine of the syde, they can not tell to what to adscriue the cause, nor how to help mee." In addition to Fernel's *Vniuersa medicina,* the most important medical text of the day, Drummond had two French versions of works by Galen of Pergamum, *Lanatomie des os du corps humain* (1541) and *De la raison de curer par euacuation de sang* (1542), Serenus Sammonicus's *De re medica* (1540), Albertus Magnus's *De secretis mulierum,* Michael Scott's *De secretis naturae,* a work on poisons by Arnauld of Villanova, and Sir John Harington's *The Englishmans Doctor. Or the Schoole of Salerne,* a translation of *Regimen sanitatis salernitanum* that Harington first published in 1607.

Drummond's copy of Claude Dariot's *A Briefe and Most Easie Introduction to the Astrologicall Iudgement of the Starres* (1598) included *A Briefe Treatise of Mathematicall Phisicke* by George Coombe, which indicated the auspicious time for bleeding, depending on which humor predominated. Drummond was melancholic and so, according to Coombe, should be bled under Virgo, when the melancholic humor was in the ascendant. Given the frequency of plague, Thomas Cogan's *The Hauen of Health* is not a surprising addition to Drummond's collection. Cogan warned readers to flee "from the place infested, abide farre off, and returne not soone againe." Despite his melancholy disposition Drummond did not apparently own Robert Burton's *Anatomy of Melancholy,* first published in 1621, nor did he have a copy of William Harvey's work on the circulation of the blood. He had John Hester's 1590 English translation of Joseph Du Chesne's *Sclopotarie of Iosephus Quercetanus, Phisition. Or His Booke Containing the Cure of Wounds Receiued by Shot of Gunne or Such Like Engines of Warre,* but he lacked Ambroise Paré's modern approach to the subject. Du Chesne's text reflects a curious side of Drummond. He hated war, but on 29 September 1626 he received a patent on sixteen devices, most of them military, including Glasses of Archimedes for setting ships afire at sea. He apparently did not actually produce any of these devices.

Like many other learned men of the time, including Dr. John Dee and Henry Percy, Earl of Northumberland, Drummond owned works dealing with the occult. In addition to Seneca he had Censorinus's *Liber de die natale* (1568), with a section on astrology. Martianus Capella's popular medieval *De nuptiis philologiae* was present in Drummond's library in the 1539 edition, and he had a copy of John of Seville's twelfth-century translation of Alcabitius's *Ad magisterium iudiciorum astrorum isogage* with a fourteenth-century commentary by John of Saxony (1521). In his collection were Messahala's ninth-century *De elementis et orbibus coelestibus* (1549) and the works of more contemporary authors on astrology and alchemy such as Girolamo Cardano, Marsilio Ficino, and Joannes Pontanus. Two notable books in this regard were Jofrancus Offusius's *De divina astrorum facultate* and Timothy Willis's *The Search of Causes. Containing a Theophysicall Inuestigation of the Possibilitie of Transmutatorie Alchemie* (1616).

Drummond never practiced law, but his books on the subject reflect the modern approach to the subject taken at Bourges, just as his approach to philosophy and science mirrors the conservatism of the early seventeenth century curriculum at Edinburgh University. Guillaume Budé struck the first blow against the medieval methods of teaching the Justinian Code, and Drummond owned a copy of Budé's *Annotationes* (1524), first published in 1508. Budé argued that Franciscus Accursius, whose thirteenth-century work *Glossa ordinaria* had been a key text for the medieval law student, had examined "neither histories or annals" and had not answered "such questions as when did jurisconsults, legislators, or emperors live, or who among these were contemporaries." Budé studied Justinian's Code in its historical context. Erasmus called Budé, Ulrich Zasius, and Andreas Alciatus the three great reformers of legal education. Drummond had no works by Zasius, but he owned a 1543 edition of Alciatus on dueling. Canon law still played an important role in seventeenth-century jurisprudence. Drummond owned a fine copy of Gratian's *Decretals,* printed by Christopher Plantin in 1573.

The books by scholars at Bourges in Drummond's collection provide a direct indication of the importance of Drummond's schooling in his intellectual development. Drummond owned a copy of *Paratitla in libros quinquaginta digestorum seu pandectarum imperatoris Iustiniani,* a commentary on Justinian, by Jacobus Cujacius, an important humanist legal scholar at Bourges. Cujacius also edited legal texts, such as Julius Paulus's *Receptarum sententiarum ad filium,* present in Drummond's library. Francis Hotman at Bourges sought to carry the reformation of legal studies still further by stressing the practical. Drummond owned his *Partitiones iuris civilis elementariae* and his commentary on Justinian's *Institutiones.* In sum, according to MacDonald, Drummond's small but impressive selection of

> law books show humanism in practice as it reached the student lawyer. From among only a modest number of titles nearly every name of the humanist revolution in law is represented–and usually by his most important work. . . . [T]aken together, this is a most up-to-date collection of law books.

About a sixth of Drummond's collection was theological. Although the figure may seem high, it is

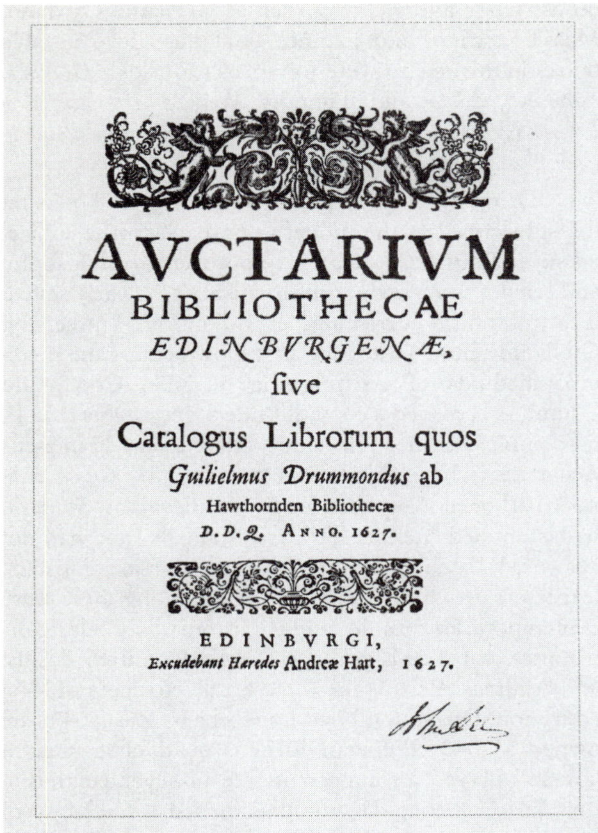
AVCTARIVM
BIBLIOTHECAE
EDINBVRGENÆ,
ſive
Catalogus Librorum quos
Guilielmus Drummondus ab
Hawthornden Bibliothecæ
D. D. Q. ANNO. 1627.
EDINBVRGI,
Excudebant Hæredes Andreæ Hart, 1627.

Title page for Drummond's catalogue of the books and manuscripts he gave to Edinburgh University in 1626 (Edinburgh University Library)

lower than might be expescted in an age when more than a third of books published dealt with religion. Also surprising is the eclectic nature of these works. Drummond owned Bibles in Latin, Greek, and Hebrew, though not in English, even though he suggested some readings that were adopted in the King James version of the Psalms. He owned a copy of the Acts of the Council of Trent (1563) codifying Catholic doctrine and Innocent Gentillet's attack on those acts. He had Jean Crispin's *Acta martyrum,* a Protestant martyrology, John Calvin's *Institutes* in French and his catechism in Greek and Hebrew.

Drummond's library included John Bale's *The First Part of the Actes of English Votaries* (1560), which attacked Catholicism and the papacy, as did John Napier's *A Plaine Discouery of the Whole Reuelation of Saint John,* present in Drummond's library in a 1602 French edition as well as in English. Yet, Drummond also owned works that were pro-Catholic. He had John Hamilton's defense of transubstantiation, *Ane Catholik and Facile Traictise, . . . to Confirme the Real and Corporell Praesence of Chrystis Pretious Bodie and Blude in the Sacrament of the Alter* (1581) as well as James Gordon's and John Hay's defenses of Catholicism. He had St. Ignatius Loyola's *Exercita Spiritualia* (1586), William Warford's Catholic *A Briefe Instruction . . . Concerning the Principall Poyntes of Christian Religiæ* (1604), and St. Peter Canisius's catechism translated into Scots by Adam King, who taught philosophy and mathematics at the University of Paris. His catalogue lists Catholic service books: two Books of Hours, an ordinary and a breviary.

Drummond may even have translated some prayers for a 1619 Catholic prayer book, *The Primer or Office of the Blessed Virgin Mary.* In his standard edition of Drummond's poetry, *The Poetical Works of William Drummond of Hawthornden* (1913), L. E. Kastner places these hymns among the "Poems of Doubtful Authenticity." They were, however, included in the 1711 folio edition of Drummond's works edited by the poet's son, and Kastner concedes that "on the whole, the evidence is in his favour." As Kastner observes and Drummond's library illustrates, "The Scottish poet was a very broad-minded man and a Protestant of a type very different from the normal Scottish Protestant of his days."

Despite Drummond's reverence for the ancients, less than a quarter of his Latin poetry is classical, even though by 1600 virtually every classical author was available, usually in an inexpensive edition. Virgil continued to be regarded in the Renaissance as the greatest Latin poet, as he had been viewed in the Middle Ages and, indeed, during the Roman Empire. Drummond owned the 1545 Aldine edition of Virgil and a 1598 Latin edition of the *Georgics.* He also had a translation of the *Aeneid* by Gavin Douglas (1553), Richard Stanyhurst's translation of the first four books, and Abraham Fraunce's English version of the *Georgics* and *Buccolics* (1589). Drummond also collected Ovid, who retained his medieval ranking as the second greatest Latin poet. He owned a copy of Ovid's works printed in Lyons about 1506, pirated from the Aldine edition. His library also contained a separate edition of the *Heroïdes* (1571) and a 1595 Spanish edition of the *Metamorphoses,* translated by Jorge Bustamento. In English he had the translations by Arthur Golding (inherited from his father) and George Sandys (1626).

Horace was represented in Drummond's library only by *Carmen seculae* in Greek and Latin (1600). He also owned books by Juvenal, Lucan, Lucretius, Silius (highly regarded in the Renaissance), and Statius, but, again reflecting contemporary taste, he apparently did not own Martial, Catullus, Tibullus, or Propertius. In 1560 Thomas Bacon described the latter authors as "wanton and unhonest," and they were not taught in Renaissance schools.

The humanist reverence for the classics found expression in neo-Latin poetry, with Petrarch here as in so many other areas serving as the Renaissance model. He was crowned poet laureate in Rome in 1341 for his *Africa,* a Virgilian imitation, a copy of which was on Drummond's shelves. Drummond collected the complete works of the Christian epics in Latin of Vida and Jacopo Sannazarro, the latter in a 1603 edition purchased in Edinburgh in 1610. He owned the neo-Latin love lyrics of Joannes Jovianus Pontanus (1531), Philip Beroaldus's works in prose and poetry, Joannes Secundus's poems to Julia (1541), and works by Daniel Heinsius, influenced by Secundus. He collected the works of Joannes Salmonius and Nicolaus Borbonius, whom the French considered modern Horaces. Of Scottish neo-Latinists Drummond had works by Hercules Rollock, Thomas Dempster, William Hegate, Mark Alexander Boyd, Andrew Melville, John Johnston, Arthur Johnson, John Leech, Sir Robert Ayton, John Barclay, and George Chalmers.

Drummond's library was rich in Latin prose, works that taught not just history, philosophy, rhetoric, or politics but also a style. Classical authors were the models; grammars and dictionaries served as keys for reading. Drummond owned seven titles by Cicero, who was to prose what Virgil was to poetry: the great precursor and archetype. His *Sententiae Ciceronis* probably dates from his school days, as likely does his *Partitiones oratoriare.* Drummond acquired Cicero's *De lege agraria contra P. Seruilium Rullum* (1561) in Paris in 1607. Drummond also owned the *Epistolae ad Atticum* and the important *Epistolarum ad familiares.* Drummond bought the *Insitutionum oratoriarum* (1585) by Quintilian, the leading authority on rhetoric for the Renaissance, in Paris in 1607.

In 1619 Ben Jonson told Drummond that "Petronius, Plinius Secundus, Tacitus spoke best Latine." Drummond's Pliny was printed by Estienne in Geneva. Dated 1611, it is the 1599 edition with a new title page. His *Satyricon* by Petronius is dated 1596. If Drummond owned a copy of Tacitus it has not survived, nor has his Livy. He certainly read the latter, since Drummond's *History of Scotland* is modeled on that Roman historian. He had Caesar and Sallust, Plutarch (in Latin) and Suetonius (*De vitae XII Caesarum*), this last printed in Trevisa by Joannes Rubeus in 1480. The third-century Roman historian Dio Cassius and Josephus were among Drummond's books, as was that classical collector of gossip Aulus Gellius.

Drummond's holdings in more recent history must also have been extensive. When the marquis of Douglas in 1639 invited Drummond to use his library for genealogical research, Drummond replied, "Being nearer manye historyes in diuerse languages in myne own studye, I can more conuientlie peruse them than in your L. [Lordship's] Castell, where I will be but like an artizan without tooles."

Drummond's catalogues, gifts, and poetry show extensive reading in the French literature of the sixteenth century: Jean le Maire de Belgers, Clément Marot, François Habert, Marguerite de Navarre, Nicolas de Herberay, Pontus de Tyard, Peletier du Mans, Jean de la Péruse, Joachim Du Bellay, Pierre de Ronsard, Jan Antoine de Baïf, Jean de la Taille, Odet de la Noue, Philippe Desportes, Jean Passerat, Guillaume de Salluste Du Bartas, Guy de Faur de Pibrac, Étienne Jodelle, Robert Garnier, Jean de Beaubrueil, and Pierre de Larivey. His knowledge and holding of–and borrowings from–Italian Renaissance poets are equally extensive: Petrarch, Benedetto Zino's Petrarchan imitations, Lodovico Ariosto, Sannazarro, Pietro Bembo, Giovanni della Casa, Lodovico Paterno, Tasso, Giovanni Battista Guarini, Muzio Manfredi, Francesco Contarini, Cesare Rinaldi, Mauritio Moro, and Girolamo Casone. Kastner concluded that "a full third of Drummond's compositions are translations or close paraphrases. . . . The rest are best described as adaptations from foreign models."

Drummond's greatest literary debt in English was to Sir Philip Sidney. Drummond transcribed *Astrophil and Stella* (1591), and Kastner claims that "practically all the outstanding verses of *Astrophil and Stella* can be paralleled in Drummond's sonnets." He read Sidney's *Arcadia* in 1606 and again in 1609, copied long extracts into his manuscripts, and listed it first among his English books in his 1611 catalogue. The second entry was Edmund Spenser's *Faerie Queene,* which he recorded reading in 1610, and the third was *The Shephearde's Calendar.*

The poet Michael Drayton was among Drummond's closest friends. In an undated letter Drummond wrote to him:

> Your great learning first bred in mee admiration, then love, which if not alwhere and allwayes I professe, testifie, I were not only an euill esteemer of you, but also of letters and all learning and poesie. . . . When first I looked on your Heroicall Epistles, I was rapt from my selfe, and could not containe my selfe from blazing that of you, which both your worth, merit, and my loue deserued, required; although, whatever I can say of you is farre vnder your ingine and vertue.

Drayton repaid the compliment in "To My Most Dearely-loued Friend Henry Reynolds Esquire, of *Poets & Poesie* (1627), as he refers to "my dear *Drummond,* to whom much I owe / For his much love, and proud I was to know / His Poesie." Drummond paid 2 s. for "Draton's Workes," either the *Poems Lyrick and Pastorall* (1606) or *Poems* (1608). MacDonald records seven Drayton

Drummond's note of donation to Edinburgh University at the bottom of the title page for his copy of Raphael Thorius's poem in praise of tobacco (Edinburgh University Library)

titles in Drummond's collection, and Drummond's list of reading includes Drayton's *The Owle* (1604) in 1606 and 1613, *Englands Heroicall Epistles* (1597), *Barrons Wars* (1603), *Legends* in 1612, and *Poly-olbion* (1612) in 1613.

Drummond enjoyed contemporary drama and read plays by George Chapman, Thomas Dekker, Jonson, John Marston, Shakespeare, and Thomas Middleton. His "List of Comedies," covering the range of Elizabethan and Jacobean drama, includes fifty-seven titles that he read and probably owned. One volume of particular significance among his English books is his 1616 edition of Ben Jonson's *Works.* Jonson visited Drummond at Christmas, 1618, and stayed two or three weeks. Drummond preserved their literary discussions in a manuscript, now lost, but a transcription was published by the Shakespeare Society in 1842. Drummond also recorded some of Jonson's comments in the folio *Works,* almost exclusively in the "Epigrammes" section. These offer important clarifications, such as the fact that epigrams 68 and 69 are about Marston.

Most of Drummond's book purchases came before 1626. Late in that year he donated more than 360 books and manuscripts to Edinburgh University. Previously, he had given a copy of Petrus Ramus's *Arithmeticae* (1599) to his alma mater upon graduating in 1605, and in 1620 he gave Sir John Scot a 1607 edition of Aristophanes' work for Scot's newly established class library at St. Andrews. The large 1626 gift is surprising and may have been made at the request of the principal of the college, John Adamson, a friend of Drummond, to encourage similar gifts from others. The donation was well publicized through a catalogue that Drummond prepared himself, *Avctarivm Bibliothecae Edinbvrgenae, five Catalogus Librorum quos Guilielmus Drum-*

mondus ab Hawthornden Bibliothecae D. D. Q. anno 1627 (1627). Drummond made further gifts to the university over the next decade; most of these have survived and in 1827 were placed in a separate collection by David Laing.

Others of Drummond's books are now at the University Library, Dundee. In 1630 Drummond married Elizabeth Logan. They had nine children, but only one survived him. In 1760 the Reverend William Abernethy married Drummond's great-great-granddaughter and last lineal descendant, Barbara Mary. Abernethy gave Drummond's manuscripts to the Society of Antiquaries of Scotland in 1782, and after his death in 1809 some seven hundred volumes from Hawthornden went to the bishop of Brechin. These books were housed in the Episcopal Chapel at Laurencekirk in Kincardineshire, and in 1961 they were moved to Queen's College, Dundee, with the other books from the Scottish Episcopal diocese of Brechin. The rest of Drummond's books probably were dispersed shortly after 1809; they appear in the catalogues of booksellers and auctioneers in the nineteenth century and have enriched public and private libraries in Europe and America.

A study of Drummond's library reveals the literary tastes of the time. It also reflects the emerging trade in secondhand books and indicates where books of the period were printed and sold. Drummond's books illustrate the growing importance of the vernacular but also indicate that Latin remained the language of scholarship. Taken together, his catalogues and surviving copies serve as a monument to the interests of the man and his age.

Biographies:

"The Life of William Drummond of Hawthornden," attributed to Bishop John Sage, in *The Works of William Drummond, of Hawthornden,* edited by Sage and Thomas Ruddiman (Edinburgh: Printed by James Watson, 1711), pp. i–xi;

David Masson, *Drummond of Hawthornden: The Story of His Life and Writings* (London: Macmillan, 1873).

References:

J. R. Barker, "A Pendant to Drummond of Hawthornden's *Conversations,*" *Review of English Studies,* new series, 16 (1965): 284–288;

French Rowe Fogle, *A Critical Study of William Drummond of Hawthornden* (New York: King's Crown Press, Columbia University, 1952);

David Laing, "A Brief Account of the Hawthornden Manuscripts in the Possession of the Society of Antiquaries of Scotland; with Extracts, Containing Several Unpublished Letters and Poems of William Drummond of Hawthornden," *Archaeologia Scotica,* 4 (1831–1832): 56–116, 225–270;

Thomas I. Rae, "The Historical Writings of Drummond of Hawthornden," *The Scottish Historical Review,* 54 (1975): 22–66.

Papers:

The major collection of William Drummond's papers are housed at the Society of Antiquaries of Scotland, Edinburgh.

David Garrick

(19 February 1717 – 20 January 1779)

John C. Ross
Massey University

See also the Garrick entry in *DLB 84: Restoration and Eighteenth-Century Dramatists, Second Series.*

CATALOGUES: *A Catalogue of the Library, Splendid Books of Prints, Poetical and Historical Tracts, of David Garrick, Esq., removed from his Villa at Hampton, and House on the Adolphi Terrace, with the Modern Works added thereto by Mrs. Garrick. Which will be sold by auction, by Mr. Saunders, at his Great Room, "The Poets' Gallery," no. 39, Fleet Street, on Wednesday, April 23rd, 1823, and 9 following days, (Sundays excepted,) at half past twelve o'clock precisely* (London, 1823);

George M. Kahrl and Dorothy Anderson, *The Garrick Collection of Old English Plays: A Catalogue with an Historical Introduction* (London: The British Library, 1982).

BOOKS: *The Lying Valet; In Two Acts. As it is Performed Gratis, at the Theatre in Goodman's-Fields* (London: Printed for and sold by P. Vaillant, 1742);

Mr. Garrick's Answer to Mr. Macklin's Case (London, 1743);

An Essay on Acting, in which will be consider'd the Mimical Behavior of a certain fashionable faulty actor, and the laudableness of such unmannerly as well as inhumane proceedings. To which will be added a short criticism on his acting Macbeth (London: W. Bickerton, 1744);

Lethe or, Esop in the Shades. As acted at the Theatres in London, with Universal Applause [unauthorized edition] (London: Printed by J. Cooke, 1745); republished as *Lethe. A Dramatic Satire. By David Garrick. As it is Performed at the Theatre-Royal in the Drury-Lane, By His Majesty's Servants* [authorized edition] (London: Printed for & sold by Paul Vaillant, 1749);

Miss in her Teens: or, The Medley of Lovers. A Farce. In Two Acts. As it is Perform'd at the Theatre-Royal in Covent-Garden (London: Printed for J. & R. Tonson & S. Draper, 1747);

Romeo and Juliet. By Shakespear. With Alterations, and an additional Scene: By D. Garrick. As it is Perform'd at the Theatre-Royal in Drury-Lane (London: Printed for J. & R. Tonson & S. Draper, 1750, 1753);

David Garrick; portrait by Benjamin Van der Gucht, 1769 (New York Public Library)

Every Man in his Humour. A Comedy. Written by Ben Jonson. With Alterations and Additions As it is Perform'd at the Theatre-Royal in Drury-Lane (London: Printed for J. & R. Tonson & S. Draper, 1752);

An Ode on the Death of Mr. Pelham (London, 1754);

The Fairies. An Opera. Taken from A Midsummer Night's Dream, Written by Shakespear. As it is Perform'd at the Theatre-Royal in Drury-Lane. The Songs from Shakespear, Milton, Waller, Dryden, Lansdown, Hammond, &c. The Music composed by Mr. Smith (London: Printed for J. & R. Tonson & S. Draper, 1755);

Catharine and Petruchio. A Comedy, In Three Acts. As it is Perform'd at the Theatre-Royal in Drury-Lane. Alter'd from Shakespear's Taming of the Shrew (London: Printed for J. & R. Tonson & S. Draper, 1756);

The Tempest. An Opera. Taken from Shakespear. As it is Performed at the Theatre-Royal in Drury-Lane. The Songs from Shakespear, Dryden &c. The Music composed by Mr. Smith (London: Printed for J. & R. Tonson, 1756);

Lilliput. A Dramatic Entertainment. As it is performed at the Theatre-Royal in Drury-Lane (London: Printed for Paul Vaillant, 1757);

The Male-Coquette: or, Seventeen Hundred Fifty-Seven. In Two Acts. As it is Performed at the Theatre-Royal in Drury-Lane (London: Printed for Paul Vaillant, 1757);

Isabella: or, The Fatal Marriage. A Play. Alter'd from Southern. As it is Now performing at the Theatre-Royal in Drury-Lane (London: Printed for J. & R. Tonson, 1757);

Florizel and Perdita. A Dramatic Pastoral, In Three Acts. Alter'd from The Winter's Tale of Shakespear. By David Garrick. As it is performed at the Theatre-Royal in Drury-Lane (London: Printed for J. & R. Tonson, 1758);

The Gamesters: A Comedy. Alter'd from Shirley. As it is Perform'd, By His Majesty's Servants, at the Theatre-Royal in Drury-Lane (London: Printed for J. & R. Tonson, 1758);

The Guardian. A Comedy of Two Acts. As it is perform'd at the Theatre-Royal in Drury-Lane (London: Printed for J. Newberry & sold by R. Bailye at Litchfield, J. Leake & W. Frederick at Bath, B. Collins at Salisbury, & S. Stabler at York, 1759);

Enchanter; Or Love and Magic. A Musical Drama. As it is performed at the Theatre-Royal in Drury-Lane. The Music composed by Mr. Smith (London: Printed for J. & R. Tonson, 1760);

The Fribbleriad (London: J. Coots, 1761);

The Provok'd Wife. A Comedy. As it was acted at the Theatre-Royal in Drury-Lane (London: Printed for J. Brindley, 1761);

Cymbeline. A Tragedy. By Shakespear. With Alterations (London: Printed for J. & R. Tonson, 1762);

The Farmer's Return From London. An Interlude. As it is Performed at the Theatre-Royal in Drury-Lane (London: Printed by Dryden Leach for J. & R. Tonson, 1762);

Hamlet, Prince of Denmark: A Tragedy. As it is now acted At the Theatres Royal in Drury-Lane, and Covent-Garden (London: Printed for Mess. Hawes & Co., B. Dodd, J. Rivington, S. Crowder, T. Longman, B. Law, T. Caslon, T. Lownds & C. Corbett, 1763);

A Midsummer Night's Dream. Written by Shakespeare: With Alterations and Additions, and Several new Songs. As it is Performed at the Theatre-Royal in Drury-Lane (London: J. & R. Tonson, 1763);

The Sick Monkey, A Fable (London: Printed for J. Fletcher, 1765);

The Clandestine Marriage, A Comedy. As it is Acted at the Theatre-Royal in Drury-Lane, by Garrick and George Colman the Elder (London: Printed for T. Becket & P. A. De Hondt, R. Baldwin, R. Davis & T. Davis, 1766);

Neck or Nothing, A Farce. In Two Acts. As It Is Performed At The Theatre Royal in Drury-Lane (London: Printed for T. Becket, 1766);

The Country Girl, A Comedy, (Altered from Wycherley) As it is Acted at the Theatre-Royal in Drury-Lane (London: Printed for T. Becket & P. A. De Hondt, L. Davis & C. Reymers, and T. Davies, 1767);

Cymon. A Dramatic Romance. As it is Performed at the Theatre-Royal in Drury-Lane (London: Printed for T. Becket & P. A. De Hondt, 1767);

A Peep Behind the Curtains; or, The New Rehearsal. As it is Now Performed at the Theatre-Royal in Drury-Lane (London: T. Becket & P. A. De Hondt, 1769);

An Ode upon Dedicating a Building, and Erecting a Statue, to Shakespeare, at Stratford upon Avon. By D. G. (London: T. Becket & P. A. De Hondt, 1769);

Songs, Choruses &c. Which are Introduced in the New Entertainment of The Jubilee. At the Theatre-Royal in Drury-Lane (London: Printed for T. Becket & P. A. De Hondt, 1769);

The Songs, Choruses, and Serious Dialogue of the Masque Called The Institution of the Garter, or, Arthur's Round Table restored (London: Printed for T. Becket & P. A. De Hondt, 1771);

The Irish Widow. In Two Acts. As it is Performed at the Theatre-Royal in Drury-Lane (London: Printed for T. Becket, 1772);

The Chances. A Comedy. With Alterations (London: Printed for the proprietors & sold by T. Becket, 1773);

King Lear, A Tragedy, By Shakespeare, as performed at the Theatre-Royal, Drury-Lane (London: Printed for John Bell & C. Etherington at York, 1773); revised edition: *King Lear, A Tragedy: Altered from Shakespeare by David Garrick, Esq. Marked from the Variations in the Manager's Book; at the Theatre-Royal in Drury-Lane* (London: Printed for C. Bathurst, J. F. & C. Rivington, L. Davis, W. Owen & Son, B. White & Son, T. Longman, B. Law, C. Dilly, T. Payne & Son, J. Nicholls, T. Cadell, J. Robson, G. G. J. & J. Robinson, T. Bowles, R. Baldwin, H. L. Gardner, J. Bew, J. Murray, W. Stuart, S. Hayes, W. Lowndes, S. Bladon, G. & T. Wilkie, W. Fox, Scatcherd & Whitaker, R. Faulder, J. Barker, T. & J. Egerton, D. Oglivy & E. Newbery, 1786);

Macbeth, A Tragedy, by Shakespeare, as performed at the Theatre-Royal, Drury-Lane (London: Printed for John Bell & C. Etherington at York, 1774);

A New Dramatic Entertainment, Called a Christmas Tale. In Five Parts. As it is Performed at the Theatre-Royal, in Drury-Lane (London: Printed for T. Becket, 1774);

Bon Ton: or, High Life above Stairs. A Comedy. In Two Acts. As it is performed at the Theatre-Royal, in Drury-Lane (London: Printed for T. Becket, 1775);

May-Day: or, The Little Gipsy. A Musical Farce, of One Act. To Which is added the Theatrical Candidates. A Musical Prelude. As They are both performed at the Theatre-Royal, in Drury-Lane (London: Printed for T. Becket, 1775);

Three Plays by David Garrick, Printed from hitherto unpublished mss., edited by Elizabeth P. Stein (New York: William Edwin Rudge, 1926)–comprises *Harlequin's Invasion, The Jubilee,* and *The Meeting of the Company; or, Bayes Art of Acting;*

The Diary of David Garrick, Being a Record of His Memorable Trip to Paris in 1751, Now First Printed from the Original Ms., edited by Ryliss Clair Alexander (New York: Oxford University Press, 1928);

The Journal of David Garrick, Describing His Visit to France and Italy in 1763, Now First Printed from the Original Manuscript in the Folger Shakespeare Library, edited by George Winchester Stone Jr. (New York: Modern Language Association of America, 1939).

Collections: *The Poetical Works of David Garrick, Esq.*, 2 volumes, edited by George Kearsley (London: Printed for George Kearsley, 1785);

The Dramatic Works of David Garrick, Esq., 3 volumes (London: Printed for A. Millar, 1798; facsimile, N.p.: Gregg International Publishers, 1969);

The Plays of David Garrick, 7 volumes, edited by Harry William Pedicord and Frederick Louis Bergmann (Carbondale & Edwardsville: Southern Illinois University Press, 1980);

The Plays of David Garrick, 4 volumes, edited by Gerald M. Berkowitz (New York & London: Garland, 1981).

PLAY PRODUCTIONS: *Lethe; or Esop in the Shades,* London, Theatre Royal in Drury Lane, 15 April 1740;

The Lying Valet, London, New Theatre, Ayliffe St. Goodman's Fields, 30 November 1741;

Macbeth, adapted from William Shakespeare's play, London, Theatre Royal in Drury Lane, 7 January 1744;

The Provok'd Wife, alteration of John Vanbrugh's play, London, Theatre Royal in Drury Lane, 16 November 1744;

Miss in Her Teens; or, The Medley of Lovers, London, Theatre Royal in Covent Garden, 17 January 1747;

Romeo and Juliet, adapted from Shakespeare's play, London, Theatre Royal in Drury Lane, 29 November 1748;

Every Man in His Humour, altered but mostly edited version of Ben Jonson's play, London, Theatre Royal in Drury Lane, 29 November 1751;

Catharine and Petruchio, afterpiece altered from Shakespeare's *The Taming of the Shrew,* London, Theatre Royal in Drury Lane, 18 March 1754;

The Chances, altered from adaptation by George Villiers, second Duke of Buckingham, of John Fletcher's play, London, Theatre Royal in Drury Lane, 7 November 1754;

The Fairies, opera based on Shakespeare's *A Midsummer Night's Dream,* libretto by Garrick, music by John Christopher Smith, London, Theatre Royal in Drury Lane, 3 February 1755;

Florizel and Perdita, afterpiece altered from Shakespeare's *The Winter's Tale,* London, Theatre Royal in Drury Lane, 21 January 1756;

The Tempest, An Opera, adapted from Shakespeare's play, libretto probably by Garrick, music by Smith, London, Theatre Royal in Drury Lane, 11 February 1756;

King Lear, adapted from Nahum Tate's adaptation of Shakespeare's play, London, Theatre Royal in Drury Lane, 28 October 1756;

Lilliput, London, Theatre Royal in Drury Lane, 3 December 1756;

The Male Coquette; or, Seventeen Hundred Fifty-Seven (originally titled *The Modern Fine Gentleman*), London, Theatre Royal in Drury Lane, 24 March 1757;

Isabella; or, The Fatal Marriage (or *The Fatal Marriage; or, The Innocent Adultery*), alteration of Thomas Southerne's *The Fatal Marriage,* London, Theatre Royal in Drury Lane, 2 December 1757;

The Gamesters, alteration of James Shirley's play, London, Theatre Royal in Drury Lane, 22 December 1757;

The Guardian, London, Theatre Royal in Drury Lane, 3 February 1759;

Harlequin's Invasion; or, A Christmas Gambol, London, Theatre Royal in Drury Lane, 31 December 1759;

The Enchanter; or, Love and Magic, libretto by Garrick and music by Smith, London, Theatre Royal in Drury Lane, 13 December 1760;

Cymbeline, altered and adapted version of Shakespeare's play, London, Theatre Royal in Drury Lane, 28 November 1761;

The Farmer's Return from London, London, Theatre Royal in Drury Lane, 20 March 1762;

The Clandestine Marriage, by Garrick and George Colman the Elder, London, Theatre Royal in Drury Lane, 20 February 1766;

The Country Girl, alteration of William Wycherley's *The Country Wife,* London, Theatre Royal in Drury Lane, 25 October 1766;

Neck or Nothing, London, Theatre Royal in Drury Lane, 18 November 1766;

Cymon, London, Theatre Royal in Drury Lane, 2 January 1767;

Linco's Travels, London, Theatre Royal in Drury Lane, 6 April 1767;

A Peep Behind the Curtain; or, The New Rehearsal, London, Theatre Royal in Drury Lane, 23 October 1767;

The Jubilee, London, Theatre Royal in Drury Lane, 14 October 1769;

The Institution of the Garter; or, Arthur's Roundtable Restored, London, Theatre Royal in Drury Lane, 28 October 1771;

The Irish Widow, London, Theatre Royal in Drury Lane, 23 October 1772;

Hamlet, London, Theatre Royal in Drury Lane, 18 December 1772;

A Christmas Tale, by Garrick, with music by Charles Dibdin, London, Theatre Royal in Drury Lane, 27 December 1773;

The Meeting of the Company, London, Theatre Royal in Drury Lane, 17 September 1774;

Bon Ton; or, High Life above Stairs, London, Theatre Royal in Drury Lane, 18 March 1775;

The Theatrical Candidates, by Garrick, music by William Bates, London, Theatre Royal in Drury Lane, 23 September 1775;

May Day; or, The Little Gipsy, libretto by Garrick, music by Thomas Arne, London, Theatre Royal in Drury Lane, 28 October 1775.

For David Garrick, the acquiring and reading of books were sidelines to a strenuous professional life as the most outstanding English actor and theater manager of the eighteenth century. His many-sided genius extended to writing 23 dramatic pieces; he substantially adapted 26 others and had a lesser hand in 18 more. He composed at least 459 items of minor verse. He also kept up a prolific correspondence, with letters surviving to as many as three hundred people. As his career prospered he developed a vigorous social life, gaining acceptance as a member of a wide range of social circles.

His first biographer, Thomas Davies, in *Memoirs of the Life of David Garrick, Esq.* (1780), opined that

> his knowledge was much greater than could be expected from a man so beset with various business. . . . A mind like his was continually improving from the company with which he was constantly surrounded. His house was a rendezvous for excellence of every kind; for lights of the church, and guardians of the laws; for the learned, the elegant, the polite, and the accomplished in arts and sciences, so that he was continually drawing from the great fountains of wisdom and knowledge.

It was from such well-read and intellectually trained companions, Davies claimed, that Garrick's mind, "strong in its own natural force, received a large accession of the most extensive and useful knowledge, and an exhaustless treasure of topics for conversation."

While there is no doubt some truth in Davies's claim, the manifest extensiveness of Garrick's library, and his many references to his reading in his correspondence, provide evidence that he was a knowledgeable, wide-ranging, and discerning reader not only of works in English and French but also, to one degree or another, of texts in Italian, Spanish, Latin, Greek, and German. Although as a professional actor he could never be completely either a scholar or a gentleman, he became cultivated enough to earn warm respect from both kinds of men. Moreover, his mastery of the arts of the theater was based in part on his wide and thoughtful reading. Garrick's activities as a bookman have been neglected by most biographers, with the exception of George Winchester Stone Jr. and George M. Kahrl in *David Garrick: A Critical Biography* (1979).

Garrick's library is significant, first, in itself as an English eighteenth-century library reflecting many interests but with a strong slant toward drama and theater. It also has great interest in its relation to the activities and mind of one of the key people in the cultural life of his century. Garrick's holdings included a distinguished collection of pre-1700 English drama, which even during his lifetime served as a vital resource for scholars and scholarly publishers. At his death, the drama collection was bequeathed to the British Museum and has since continued to be of central importance for scholarship in this field.

David Garrick was born on 19 February 1717 in the Angel Inn in Hereford, the second son of Peter Garrick, an army officer of Huguenot parentage, and Arabella Garrick, née Clough. He grew up in Lichfield; his education included some years at the Lichfield Grammar School, followed by about six months at the school conducted by the young Samuel Johnson at Edial. Even as a child he delighted in performing before an audience.

Garrick's interest in languages was encouraged by Gilbert Walmesley, the registrar of the ecclesiastical court linked to the local cathedral, who presented to him on 3 July 1732 the first book he is known to have retained: a copy of the 1719 Paris edition of *Le Jardin des Racines Grecques* by Claude Lancelot and L. J. Le Maistre de Sacy. The book provides an alphabetical listing of Greek roots, with the accompanying text in French.

Cover of the anonymous Hyckescorner *(circa 1515), the earliest play in Garrick's collection (British Library)*

Garrick's copy of it reportedly bears holograph notes by him in Latin. Although it was listed in the catalogue for the 1823 sale of Garrick's library, a note in ink in the British Library copy of the catalogue indicates it was "Withdrawn," perhaps because of its personal associations.

In 1737 Garrick and Johnson traveled to London to make careers for themselves in the metropolis. Initially Garrick tried to settle into more "respectable" vocations, in the law or in the wine trade, but in 1741 his talents and inclinations drew him to venture on to the professional stage, first at Ipswich in July, then at Henry Giffard's Goodman's Fields Theatre. He had already written the first of many farces, *Lethe; or Esop in the Shades,* which premiered at the Theatre Royal in Drury Lane in April 1740 and was published in an authorized edition in 1749. Acting also at Drury Lane, at Smock Alley in Dublin, and at Covent Garden, Garrick rose with remarkable speed to the head of his profession. On 9 April 1747 he entered into a partnership with James Lacy to purchase the patent for the Theatre Royal, Drury Lane; he remained the manager and leading actor of this theater for nearly twenty-nine years, until he retired in January 1776.

On 22 June 1747 he married the young Viennese ballet dancer Eva Maria Veigel. Although Garrick loved children, the couple had none of their own, and he became devoted to his brother George's sons and daughters. The Garricks lived for the first part of their marriage at 27 Southampton Street; in 1754 he acquired a country villa at Hampton, facing the Thames, and in 1771 a more stylish London house at Adelphi Terrace. They filled these houses with elegant furnishings, numerous paintings and engravings, and, of course, books.

In May–June 1751 the couple traveled to Paris for a month. In his diary of this excursion Garrick records visits to the theaters, social contacts, and some book buying. On 8 June, for example, he bought "Voltair's Works 11 vols. . . . Rousseau's Lettrs 5 vols . . . Plays & Operas" and the next day two books for "Ld Hunting." Thereafter he purchased many books through his Parisian contacts, particularly the theatrical director Jean Monnet, whom he had first gotten to know in London in 1748, and his banker Charles Selwin.

Between September 1763 and April 1765 the couple undertook a more protracted tour through France, Italy, Austria, and Germany, and then back to Paris, taking longer than intended because of their need to convalesce from serious illnesses. A journal Garrick kept that covered part of this excursion includes lists of "one hundred and eighty odd books," mainly in Italian, purchased in Padua and Venice. Stone notes in *The Journal of David Garrick, Describing His Visit to France and Italy in 1763, Now First Printed from the Original Manuscript in the Folger Shakespeare Library* (1939) that "only a small handful" of these books were listed in the 1823 sale catalogue and contends that he may have bought them primarily for profitable resale to English collectors such as Topham Beauclerk. Nonetheless even a limited search reveals that quite a few others were retained by members of the family.

During the final six months of their tour, Garrick and his wife resided in Paris, often visiting its three major theaters, the Opéra-Comique, the Comédie Française, and the Comédie Italienne. They also frequented the salons of Michael Etienne Pelletier and of Paul Henry, Baron d'Holbach. Garrick made many friends, especially with members of the Holbach circle, and also with the journalist Jean-Baptiste-Antoine Suard and the novelist Madame Marie Jeanne Riccoboni, née Marie Jeanne Laboras de Mézières (de Heurles), the estranged wife of the son of Luigi Riccoboni, who was the director of the Comédie Italienne. Jean François Marmontel gave him an inscribed copy of his *Contes Moraux* (1765), and Carlo Goldoni presented him with a copy of his *Lettre du Chevalier M*** a Milord K***, 1765, la Veuve Rusée Comédie* (Paris, 1761).

During this period Garrick bought many books for himself or for friends, and the contacts he retained were helpful in purchasing other works. For example, while the ten volumes of the *Encyclopédie* were being published, from 1758 to 1772, with the accompanying twelve volumes of plates, he sent an order for it to its co-editor, Denis Diderot, and they were dispatched to him by Baron Friedrich-Melchior Grimm, both men being members of the Holbach salon. Other friends also purchased books for him or presented works to him as gifts or exchanged books with him. According to Frank A. Hedgcock in *A Cosmopolitan Actor: David Garrick and his French Friends* (1912), he and Madame Riccoboni carried on a lively exchange of their published writings and other books while also discussing proposals for translations and indulging in literary and theatrical chat.

In his subsequent correspondence with his French friends, Garrick maintained a keen interest in the leading actors and the latest production trends in the Parisian theaters. Stone and Karhl argue in their biography that Garrick's technical innovations at Drury Lane–especially in the 1770s when he was assisted by the painter, Jean Phillipe de Loutherbourg, with more sophisticated and attractive modes of lighting and of scenery–show him to be an artist who was constantly seeking to achieve higher production values. Five of his own plays were based upon French works, and two of those he adapted were translations of plays by Voltaire. According to Stone and Karhl, careful examination of his "emendations" to Aaron Hill's *Zara,* a translation of Voltaire's *Zaire,* "shows careful reading of the original."

Garrick was devoted to the drama of William Shakespeare. He staged twenty-seven Shakespearean plays at Drury Lane, often playing the male leads, which were among his most important stage roles. He took special care in preparing the scripts for his theater; scholars report that he frequently worked with acting versions and restored some authentic passages that had previously been cut or botched. In this work he relied upon his own collection of early quartos and folio editions of Shakespeare's works as well as those gathered by the scholar Edward Capell, whom Garrick engaged shortly before 1756 to compile an inventory of the "old English plays" he owned at that time. Among the eighteenth-century editions of the complete plays he owned were those edited by Nicholas Rowe (1709), now in the Folger Shakespeare Library; Alexander Pope and William Warburton (1747), which Warburton presented to him; Capell (1768), now in the Folger; Sir Thomas Hanmer (second edition, 1771); and Hugh Blair (1771), which Blair dedicated to Garrrick. John Baskerville presented Garrick a copy of the handsome edition he printed and published in 1768.

Garrick's copy of the seventh volume of Pope and Warburton's edition of Shakespeare's works, comprising *Timon of Athens, Coriolanus, Julius Caesar,* and *Antony and Cleopatra,* has a personal inscription signed "Maria Garrick," in which she recalls the couple's trip to the Althorp House, the home of Lord and Lady Spencer: "This book went with us to Athorp [*sic*] in Decr the 30: 1778. My hus^d never Traveld without some Work of Shakespeare." Alexander Dyce, who acquired the book for the Dyce Collection in the National Art Library in the Victoria and Albert Muesum, added a note beneath Maria Garrick's inscription: "The vol. was doubtless endeared to Mrs Garrick from having been almost the last book her husband had read–for he died in Jany 1779." (All other volumes of his set of this edition are now in the Folger Shakespeare Library; their previous owners include Augustin Daly and Clement Scott.)

The apogee of Garrick's championing of Shakespeare was his initiating and organizing the Shakespeare Jubilee at Stratford-upon-Avon on 6 to 8 September

Ticket to the September 1769 Shakespeare Jubilee, organized by Garrick to honor the playwright (Harvard Theatre Collection)

1769. Even though some of the events planned for the second and third days were rained out, this enterprise, which Garrick officiated as steward, was generally a success, and attracted prodigious public attention. It spawned a flurry of pamphlets and verses, including Garrick's own *An Ode upon Dedicating a Building, and Erecting a Statue to Shakespeare, at Stratford upon Avon,* published in the same year.

Following his retirement in 1776 from the intense pressures of acting and theater management, Garrick lived only three more years. He led a busy social life for a man suffering from gout and other illnesses. He died on 20 January 1779 and was buried with great honor in Westminster Abbey.

Biographers Stone and Kahrl observe that nowhere in Garrick's voluminous correspondence or in his recorded conversations did he describe a systematic book-buying policy or his methods of assembling his library. Although Garrick's father was not well-to-do, his uncle and his elder brother were successful merchants and were generous to him, so that from the outset of his career Garrick had money to spend on books. Evidence of his book buying is patchy, but probably by 1743 he was already on good terms with several booksellers, among them Isaac and Paul Vaillant, Somerset Draper, Thomas Becket, Robert Dodsley, Thomas Davies, and Henry Clements, and was ready to spend substantially to procure items he wanted. Too busy during the theatrical season "to attend the late-afternoon book auctions" himself, he engaged others to act as his agents. As his career progressed he cultivated good relations with eminent book collectors of his era.

No general catalogue of Garrick's library was ever compiled, though Capell's manuscript catalogue of the plays Garrick collected up until 1756 does survive in the British Library. The auctioneer's catalogue put together in 1823–*A Catalogue of the Library, Splendid Books of Prints, Poetical and Historical Tracts, of David Garrick, Esq., removed from his Villa at Hampton, and House on the Adolphi Terrace, with the Modern Works added thereto by Mrs. Garrick. Which will be sold by auction, by Mr. Saunders, at his Great Room, "The Poets' Gallery," no. 39, Fleet Street, on Wednesday, April 23rd, 1823, and 9 following days, (Sundays excepted,) at half past twelve o'clock precisely*–is valuable as far as it goes, but many of its entries are not informative; it includes many books acquired after Garrick's death by his widow; and it leaves out many books retained by his relatives or by his executors. Moreover, while Garrick pasted his distinctive bookplate in many of his books, he evidently did not do so in more minor items; and he seems to have signed them only when recording donations. Thus, Garrick's library can be only partially reconstructed.

Garrick's interests, as suggested by the records of his collection that do survive, were impressively catholic. Beyond the expected emphasis on drama and theater–classical, English, French, and Italian–he was keenly interested in the visual arts, as he collected books of engravings, engraved reproductions of paintings, and volumes on other topics that contain many fine plates, notable among them works in folio relating to Roman ruins. Judging from his books Garrick was also evidently fascinated by such topics as the nature and uses of English and other European languages, history and travels, and poetry and prose.

Although it cannot be determined how or when Garrick acquired the majority of books known to have been in his library, the provenance of some can be deduced through references in correspondence, their inclusion in subscription lists, or evidence identifying earlier owners such as inscriptions or bookplates or signatures. The evidence of provenance for items in the "old English plays" collection has been extensively investigated by Dorothy Anderson and Kahrl in *The Garrick Collection of Old English Plays: A Catalogue with an Historical Introduction* (1982). Through the resources of the Book Subscription List Project–including F. J. G. Robinson and P. J. Wallis's *Book Subscription Lists: A Revised Guide* (1975) and P. J. and Ruth Wallis's *Book Subscription Lists: Extended Supplement to the Revised Guide* (1996)–sixty-seven books can be identified that Garrick obtained through subscription.

Of the books acquired by subscription in the Garrick sale catalogue, the earliest was the first volume of Henry Fielding's *Miscellanies* (1743) and the last of them was Thomas Sheridan's *A General Dictionary of the English Language* (1780), which was published a year after Garrick's death. His subscriptions included eighteen volumes of poetry and also William Rufus Chetwood's *A General History of the Stage* (Dublin, 1749) as well as his *Memoirs of the Life and Writings of Ben. Jonson* (Dublin, 1756), the first volume of works of Jonson as edited by Peter Whalley (1756), Philip Massinger's *Dramatic Works* as edited by Thomas Coxeter (1759), and the first volume of Shakespeare's plays as edited by Francis Gentleman and published by J. Bell (1773). Garrick also subscribed to works on music, including scores, and he owned the first volume of Charles Burney's *A General History of Music* (1776). Another particular interest was travel, but otherwise the topics range widely.

Garrick had hopes of writing a history of theater and drama and of publishing a collection of English prologues and epilogues, and he gathered together resources for these projects. Before 1776, however, he was generally too busy to proceed with them and after his retirement too ill. Published posthumously in four volumes, *A Collection of more than Eight Hundred Prologues and Epilogues from the Following Authors . . . . Together with all the Prologues and Epilogues Written by the late D. Garrick, Esq. With a Preface and Notes, by R. Griffith, Esq.* (1779) presumably drew upon the materials he had collected.

In addition to his interest in old plays, Garrick collected contemporary plays, though there is some question as to which plays he acquired for his own library and which texts, either printed or in manuscript, that he acquired for the Theatre Royal, Drury Lane, while he was manager. The extant copies of his own plays that bear performance licenses probably belong in the latter category. He also acquired items that were in effect reference works for contemporary book collectors, including sale catalogues of the libraries of eminent predecessors, such as John Bridges, Richard Mead, and Thomas Rawlinson.

Garrick was specific as to the dispersal of his library in his will, naming his brother George's eldest son, Carrington, as one of his beneficiaries:

> I Give and bequeath . . . all my Collection of old English plays to the Trustees of the British Museum for the time being for the Use of the Publick I Give all the rest of my Books of what kind soever (except such as my Wife shall chuse to the value of One Hundred pounds which I give and bequeath to her) unto my nephew Carrington Garrick, for his own use . . . .

Garrick's collection of plays was transferred to the British Museum in 1780, although certain valuable books were deliberately withheld and others evidently remained behind simply because they could not be located. What happened with "all the rest" of Garrick's books is more obscure. While some books bear the bookplates of both Garrick and his nephew and thus certainly were handed over to Carrington Garrick, the bulk of the library was held on to by his wife, who is believed to have made some kind of payment to her nephew for his interest in it. It may be that Carrington Garrick, who had been ordained and installed as the vicar of Hendon in 1776, could simply not accommodate a large collection, whereas Maria Garrick, left in sole possession of two large houses, had ample shelving.

Maria Garrick was evidently loath to part with anything that had intimate associations with her husband or that might have much financial value. In *Garrick* (1948) Margaret Barton notes that three years after the will had been probated some financial bequests remained unpaid. Maria Garrick was amply provided for and had no reason for parsimony; however, she was financially inexperienced and believed she was a poor woman. She outlived her husband by forty-three years, and eventually died on 16 October 1822 at the age of 98. Under the terms of her will, as noted in the 1823 sale catalogue, Carrington Garrick's son Christopher Philip Garrick was to receive "the greater part of the Greek and Latin Classics, together with her numerous and highly valuable Italian books." Her executors, the Reverend Thomas Rackett and George Frederick Beltz, Lancaster Herald, were to receive books to the value of £150. The remainder were to be sold, for the financial benefit of her heirs. There are two manuscripts relevant to the dispersal of the collection in the Folger Shakespeare Library: "Appraisals of the libraries of David Garrick at the Adelphi and at Hampton amounting in all to

£770, Jan. 13, 1783," presented by Thomas Evans, and a letter from Mrs. Garrick to Christopher Garrick, undated but written circa 1809, that "tells him there are 3 large bags of books for him."

Despite its deficiencies, the primary document for Garrick's general collection is the sale catalogue of 1823, which was compiled by the auctioneer Robert Saunders. It lists 2,678 lots, 38 lots of which were listed as addenda. The arrangement is roughly alphabetical, with the lots for each day in three sequences, "octavo et infra" (quarto and folio). The paintings, loose prints, and the household effects were sold in separate auctions.

A copy of the catalogue in the British Library has the prices paid for items and the names of purchasers added in ink, and the catalogue was subsequently republished with this information supplied. Many of the purchasers were book dealers, but it is noteworthy that both of the executors, Beltz and Rackett, bought some lots and that on the tenth day "C. Garrick" (presumably Christopher Garrick) bought ten lots, among them one that included "*Voltaire, _uvres de, plates after Gravelot's designs,* 39 vols, *half bound, gilt,* 1775," for three guineas. (Volume 32 of this set is held in the Garrick Club library in London.)

For the auctioneer, the outstanding items were evidently the folio volumes containing many plates. For example, the lot listed as "HOGARTH'S (W.) WORKS, consisting of 106 *plates,* BRILLIANT IMPRESSIONS," including "a bill for prints, with Hogarth's signature," realized £100.16.0, the highest price for any lot. A signed bill for prints, which may or may not be the same, is in the Garrick Club library. "RUBENS'S (P. P.) WORKS, *consisting of* 413 *Engravings, by Eminent Artists after his Paintings . . . forming* 8 LARGE VOLS., *russia,*" realized £58.16.0. By comparison, the lot including Shakespeare's First Folio (1623) sold for £34.2.6.

The collection includes an impressive number of sixteenth-century works, many of them in black letter (Gothic type) and often noted by the cataloguer as rare or very rare. Most of them are bound in composite volumes. At least three of the items are manuscripts: a "Missale Romanum, very small size, MS. on vellum;" a quarto "MISSALE ROMANUM, MS. on VELLUM;" and "Histoire des Bordels et Putains de Paris, Dedié [*sic*] a Mons. Rich," described in a note as "A singular work, apparently written about the year 1740."

The sale catalogue varies greatly in its informativeness. The majority of lots comprise individual titles and are identified by author, shortened title, place of publication if not London, and date. Other lots, however, are more complicated and involve runs of periodicals; composite volumes in which some titles are named and the rest simply noted as "and others"; pamphlets listed either in numbers of items (for example, "25 Miscellaneous, Prose") or in terms of numbers of bound volumes; unidentified plays, again listed either as numbers of bound volumes ("Plays, various, 4 vols.") or as bundles of numbers of items ("Plays, &c. 44 single, by various authors"); and numbers of "odd volumes" (presumably, from broken sets). The least informative listing of all is for lot 2,678: "A bundle of loose pamphlets, &c."

Out of 3,020 identifiable items (counting identified items within composite volumes), 134 were published after 1779 and thus must have been acquired by Maria Garrick after her husband's death. She also, of course, probably bought some of the works that had been published earlier, but these cannot be identified. Excluding the works published after 1779–109 in English, 21 in French, 3 in Latin, and 1 in German–a rough count indicates that 1,509 were in English, 1,046 in French, 229 in Latin, 75 in German, 49 in Italian, 7 in Greek, 4 in Spanish, 4 in Dutch, and 20 polyglot. The collection is notable for its linguistic variety and the prominence of French works. Quite a few of the items comprised translations, and in some cases combined two languages.

Significantly underrepresented in this enumeration are works in Latin, Greek, and Italian, some of which had gone to Christopher Philip Garrick, or in some identified instances to Carrington Garrick and then to his son, or to the executors. Particularly noteworthy was a sixty-four-volume set of Greek and Latin classics published by the Scottish printer Robert Foulis that was given to Garrick by the Reverend Thomas Beighton. The set was passed on by Christopher Philip Garrick to his executor Henry Elliot. Thirty-two volumes, presumably all from this set, were offered for sale on 18 November 1912 in the Tregaskis catalogue 733; fourteen volumes of it–all bearing Garrick's bookplate and a few also bearing Carrington's–are now in the Folger Shakespeare Library.

Many Italian titles passed into the family before the 1823 sale. Four titles in Italian bearing Garrick's bookplate or inscriptions that may have been among the "numerous and highly valuable Italian books" bequeathed to Christopher Philip Garrick are in the Garrick Club library in London: *Hieronymi Fracastorii Veronensis Poemata Omnia* (1718); Anton Francesco Doni's *Mondi Celesti, Terrestri et Infernali* (1568), which is bound with his *Filosofia Morale* (1567); and *Dottor Langlat di Fresnoy, Metodo per Istudiare la Storia* (1716), translated from French. Six other Italian titles are in the Dyce Collection in the National Art Library in the Victoria and Albert Museum. Ten more Italian works were among the twenty-three books bearing Garrick's bookplate in Charles James Sawyer Ltd.'s sale catalogue no. 91

(1928) that had belonged to "the late Major Henry Edward Trevor (*great great nephew of the Actor*)." Among these is Carlo Goldoni's *Nuovo Teatro Comico* (1757), in ten volumes octavo. An additional Trevor book, *Delle Opere di Dante Alighieri* (1741), is held in the Folger Shakespeare Library. Sotheby, Wilkinson and Hodge's sale catalogue, 19–22 February 1896 lists *Petrarca con la Spositione di M. Giovanni Andrea Gosvaldo, et Trionfo* (1553) as well as *Xenophontis Opera* (Vinegia, 1547) and the three-volume *Nouveau Théâtre Italien* (1773) in Italian and French, a copy inscribed by Garrick as given to him by George Garnier. Garnier also gave him a copy of Luigi Riccoboni's *Nuovo Teatro Italiano* (Parigi, 1733), which is now in the Folger Shakespeare Library.

Eight out of the twenty-three items in the 1928 Sawyer catalogue bear Carrington's bookplate in addition to Garrick's, and five "have a small blue printed label" with the text, "'The gift of her father to his daughter Catherine or Eva, May 1st, 1843,' the title of the book, and signature, C. P. Garrick." Non-Italian items include the Bible in royal folio (Baskerville Press, 1764), the family Bible bearing Garrick's and his son's bookplates and an inscription by an unidentified member of the family, and also the edition of the *Book of Common Prayer* published by John Baskerville in 1762.

A few of the books that came from Maria Garrick to her executors can also be identified. Beltz pasted a printed label into the front papers of books thus bequeathed to him. Examples identified include the third edition of James Beattie's *An Essay on the Nature and Immutability of Truth* (1772) and the fourth edition of Charles Pineau Duclos's *Considerations sur les M_urs de ce Siècle* (1764), which were listed in *The Rothschild Library: A Catalogue* (1954); Edward Moore's *Fables for the Female Sex* (1744), now in the Henry E. Huntington Library; and John Hammond's *Love Elegies* (1743), now in the Dyce Collection. Books in the Folger Library that passed through Beltz's hands include John Donne's *Poems* (1669), Thomas Sheridan's *A Plan of Education* (1769), which was bound with James Ralph's *The Case of Authors* (1762), and William Scott's *An Essay* (1765).

A collection of items associated with Garrick that had belonged to the Reverend Rackett were put on sale at Sotheby's on 18 June 1928 and three following days. The holograph items included three letters, seven poetical epigrams, and eight theatrical manuscripts (prologues, epilogues, and two drafts of *Cupid and Damon*). These had been the property of G. E. Solly, of Bells House, Wimborne, Dorset, described as "a direct descendant of Mrs Samuel Solly, only daughter of Thomas Rackett." Also sold at this time were some Garrick manuscripts and relics belonging to M. A. Carew, of Combe Hill, Lustleigh, Devon.

MR. WILLIAM
SHAKESPEARES
COMEDIES,
HISTORIES, &
TRAGEDIES.
Publiſhed according to the True Originall Copies.

LONDON
Printed by Iſaac Iaggard, and Ed. Blount. 1623.

Title page of the First Folio edition of Shakespeare's plays. Garrick's copy was sold at auction in 1823 (Henry E. Huntington Library and Art Gallery, San Marino, California).

A group of Rackett's books, presumably deriving from another sale at about that time, were offered for sale in catalogue 118, October 1950, by Elkin Matthews Ltd., of Takeley, Bishops Stortford. A dozen items are directly linked to Garrick and some others may be. Items evidently bequeathed include: "a short MS Diary and Account Book, kept by him . . . *ca.* 1741"; F. H. Barthelemen's *Six Petits Sonates pour le Piano Forte,* and *Six Lessons . . . Opus V* (ca. 1775); an original manuscript of a song by F. Giardini, presented to Garrick; Garrick's *The Irish Widow* (1772), possibly his own copy; Ben Jonson's *Every Man in his Humour,* with Garrick's "alterations and additions" (1755), and two further lines added in manuscript in his hand; Shakespeare's *King Lear,* as adapted by Garrick (1773), with his bookplate and manuscript alterations; *Romeo and Juliet,* as adapted by him (1756), bearing a textual correction in his hand; *The Original Songs, Airs and Choruses which were Introduced into the Trag-*

edy of Macbeth [by] Matthew Locke (ca. 1771), dedicated to Garrick and "almost certainly" his copy; and Denis Diderot's *Lettre sur les Aveugles* (1749) and *Pensées sur l'Interpretation de la Nature* (1754), with notes in his hand.

The Elkin Matthews catalogue also lists several of the items that Rackett bought at the 1823 sale, including Burney's four volumes of *A General History of Music* (1778–1789), with Garrick's bookplate in the first volume, Pierre Brumoy's *Le Théâtre des Grecs* (1763), John Walker's *Exercises for Improvements in Elocution* (1777), and Laurence Sterne's *Sterne's Letters to his Friends on Various Occasions* (1775). The second edition of Sterne's *A Sentimental Journey* (1768) and Benjamin Victor's *Original Letters, Dramatic Pieces, and Poems* (1776) had also probably been Garrick's copies.

The presence in later listings of works written or adapted by Garrick contrasts with their startling absence in the 1823 sale catalogue, in which there are only two such items: single copies of the Shakespeare Jubilee *Ode* (1769) and of the posthumously published *The Poetical Works of David Garrick, Esq.* (1785). Garrick's own works along with books with strong personal associations were doubtless part of his library in 1779 and probably also in 1822 but such works were likely to be retained by members of the family. Clearly then, extensive though it is, the 1823 sale catalogue represents only a portion of Garrick's library. Absent are not only the bequests to Rackett, Beltz, and Christopher Garrick but also a substantial body of titles that had already gone to Carrington Garrick in or about 1779. Also presumably missing are a group of works written or adapted by Garrick, or with other personal associations, that the family chose to hold on to at the time of the 1823 sale.

As has been shown, some of Garrick's books, passing from one generation of collectors and sellers to the next, have ended up in the collections of major libraries. Several of his works, including a 1547 edition of Terence's *Andria* and *History of the Mediterranean Fleet* (1745), are held in the Norman A. Philbrick Library of English and American Drama and Theater within the Stanford University libraries. His first volume of Herbert Lawrence's two-volume *The Life and Adventures of Common Sense: An Historical Allegory* (1769) is held by the William Andrews Clark Library in Los Angeles. His copy of John Home's *Douglas. A Tragedy* (1757) was one of the works that passed into the Henry E. Huntington Library. Works owned by Garrick that are held by the Rothschild Library include an undated copy of *An Arithmetical Copy-book, Containing the Fundamental Rules of Practical Arithmetick;* Home's *The Seige of Acquilea. A Tragedy* (1760); and a Garrick manuscript, a single leaf, "To Mr. Gray on his odes" (1757). Notable titles in the British Library include John Brownsmith's *The Theatrical Alphabet* (1767), and in the manuscript department *Relazione della Congiura di Alfonso della Gueva,* a work originally written in 1618 and copied in 1727. The Garrick Club has in all thirteen printed books that had been owned by Garrick, his two-manuscript "Time Books," folders of Garrickiana, and various memorabilia. Other noteworthy memorabilia are in the British Theatre Museum.

Notwithstanding the inherent interest of Garrick's general collection, it is his collection of pre-1700 English plays–admirably documented in Kahrl and Anderson's *The Garrick Collection of Old English Plays: A Catalogue with an Historical Introduction*–that has been of exceptional importance. The cultural prestige of postclassical West European drama had traditionally been relatively low, and consequently only a few British book collectors had concerned themselves with preserving dramatic texts. Garrick's enthusiasm in the mid eighteenth century led him to secure clusters of items that had descended through several important predecessors; he also stimulated others to build up invaluable collections, among them Capell, George Steevens, John Philip Kemble, and, later, Edmund Malone. Texts that had survived thus far were thereby preserved and in due course lodged in institutional libraries for the benefit of posterity.

The most important single acquisition by Garrick was undoubtedly the body of texts he was able to secure in about 1743 from the sale of the library that had belonged to Edward Harley, second Earl of Oxford. In the area of drama the large and important Harleian library included the collections of such notable figures as Humphry Dyson and Richard Smith. Bookseller Thomas Osborne's *Catalogus Bibliothecæ Harleianæ* (1743) includes substantial groups of English drama, "*Plays,* QUARTO" and "*Plays, and relating to the Theatre,* OCTAVO." Many of these titles correspond to works in the Garrick collection or to those in the 1823 sale catalogue; at least four of Garrick's books bear Harley bookplates. Garrick also secured hundreds of plays from the bookseller Robert Dodsley. A manuscript note by Garrick in his copy of Gerard Langbaine's *Lives and Characters of the English Dramatic Poets* (ca. 1695), as recorded in the 1823 catalogue, states, "All the Plays marked thus * in this Catalogue I bought of Dodsley."

In his lifetime Garrick actively encouraged the free use of his collection by scholars, notably in the preparation of Capell's edition of Shakespeare (1768), of Peter Whalley's edition of the works of Ben Jonson (1756), and of the edition of the works of Philip Massinger initiated by Thomas Coxeter and brought through to publication in 1759 by Henry Dell. His regard for his collection is evident in his hiring Capell to inventory and preserve his "old English plays." In his catalogue Capell lists 1,651 titles (the total is inflated by the listing of all constituents of collected editions) in a numbered sequence, with duplicates numbered separately. He had nearly all of the single plays bound in 242 composite volumes (they were individually rebound in 1841–1846). Capell also identified deficiencies in the collection, especially of Shakespearean quartos, and endeavoured to fill them, recording some later acquisitions in an addenda list. As Stone and Kahrl note, he perfected "nearly fifty quartos" by "the inserting of some missing leaves in manuscript."

When Garrick's plays were transferred to the British Museum in 1780, his executors convinced the trustees of the museum that only those works on Capell's lists should be involved, excluding later purchases. Even so, some items on this list were noted by the trustees as missing. Certain plays that were not located at the time were eventually sold in 1823. A probable example was the second copy of Lodowick Carlell's *The Passionate Lover* (1655). The copy of the play that went to the British Museum was mistakenly sold as a duplicate, and eventually replaced by a Thomason copy.

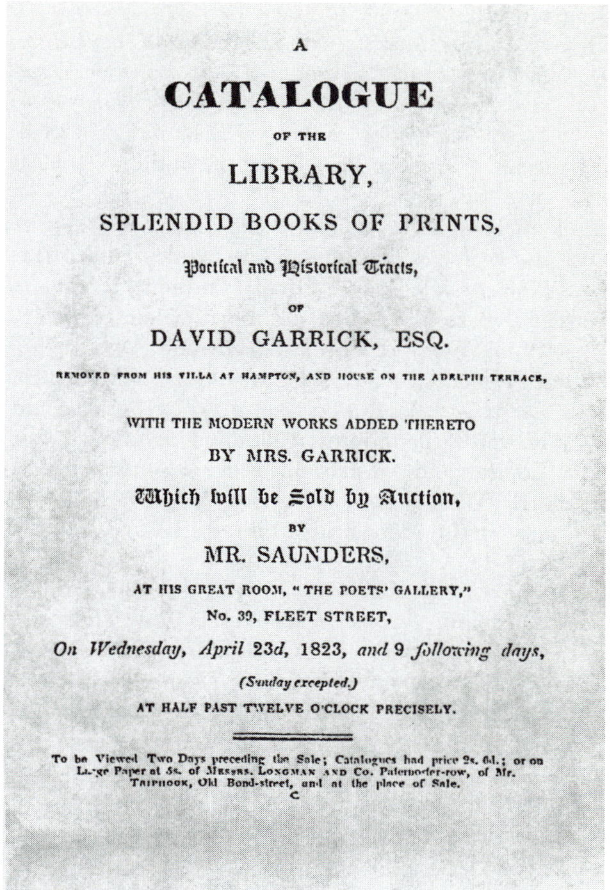
A

CATALOGUE

OF THE

LIBRARY,

SPLENDID BOOKS OF PRINTS,

Poetical and Historical Tracts,

OF

DAVID GARRICK, ESQ.

REMOVED FROM HIS VILLA AT HAMPTON, AND HOUSE ON THE ADELPHI TERRACE,

WITH THE MODERN WORKS ADDED THERETO

BY MRS. GARRICK.

Which will be Sold by Auction,

BY

MR. SAUNDERS,

AT HIS GREAT ROOM, "THE POETS' GALLERY,"

No. 39, FLEET STREET,

On Wednesday, April 23d, 1823, *and* 9 *following days,*

(Sunday excepted.)

AT HALF PAST TWELVE O'CLOCK PRECISELY.

To be Viewed Two Days preceding the Sale; Catalogues had price 2s. 6d.; or on Large Paper at 5s. of MESSRS. LONGMAN AND CO. Paternoster-row, of Mr. TRIPHOOK, Old Bond-street, and at the place of Sale.

C

Title page of the catalogue for the sale of Garrick's collection

Despite the protests of museum trustees in May 1781 and again on 9 November 1822, several valuable collected-works editions were deliberately withheld from the museum and sold in 1823. These included copies of the Shakespeare First Folio of 1623, which was acquired in 1850 by Queen's College, Oxford, and of Francis Beaumont and John Fletcher's *Fifty Comedies and Tragedies* (1679). The two-volume copy of Ben Jonson's folio *Works* (1616, 1640), although not recognized as missing, was also evidently withheld. On the other hand, eleven copies of Elizabethan romances were mistakenly included with the plays that were transferred originally to the museum.

The Garrick collection, the only substantial body of pre-1700 dramatic texts that the British Museum then possessed, became the core of a collection that gradually grew by accretion. *The Garrick Collection of Old English Plays* lists 1,312 titles. Kahrl and Anderson, though, list some items that were part of Garrick's original collection, according to Capell, but that did not come to the British Museum. Others that did come were injudiciously sold off by the trustees in 1788 or in 1805, in sales of duplicates or supposed duplicates. Several others are assumed to have been mislaid and lost within the museum by the early nineteenth century. Of those that survived into the twentieth century, some had leaves removed from them by the bibliographical criminal Thomas J. Wise to perfect defective copies, either for his own private Ashley Library or for sale to such American collectors as John Henry Wrenn.

Despite the depredations to which it was exposed, the Garrick Collection in the British Museum remains an invaluable resource. Many of its earlier texts are quite rare, and at least sixteen works are regarded as sole surviving copies of an edition. Even where other copies survive in other research libraries, the central position of the British Museum Library, now the British Library, to literary scholarship in Britain and in the English-speaking world, has meant that it has often been the Garrick copies that have been the most accessible and hence have received the most use for scholarly investigations.

Letters:

The Letters of David Garrick, 3 volumes, edited by David M. Little, George M. Kahrl, and Phoebe de K. Wilson (Cambridge, Mass.: Belknap Press of Harvard University Press, 1963; London: Oxford University Press, 1963).

Biographies:

Thomas Davies, *Memoirs of the Life of David Garrick, Esq.: Interspersed with Characters and Anecdotes of His Theatrical Contemporaries. The Whole Forming a History of the Stage, Which Includes a Period of Thirty-six Years,* 2 volumes (London: Printed for the author & sold at his shop, 1780);

Frank A. Hedgcock, *A Cosmopolitan Actor: David Garrick and his French Friends* (London: Stanley Paul, 1912; New York & London: Benjamin Blom, 1969);

Margaret Barton, *Garrick* (London: Faber & Faber, 1948; Westport, Conn.: Greenwood Press, 1978);

George Winchester Stone Jr. and George M. Kahrl, *David Garrick: A Critical Biography* (Carbondale and Edwardsville: Southern Illinois University Press; London and Amsterdam: Feffer & Simon, 1979);

Helen R. White, *David Garrick 1717–1779: A Brief Account* (London: British Library, 1979).

References:

David Pearson, *Provenance Research in Book History: A Handbook* (London: British Library, 1994);

Norman Philbrick, *Of Books and the Theatre. . . . Being an Introduction to his Library and this Exhibition. Together with an Essay by Dr. John Loftis: Garrick & the Rise of Theatrical Scholarship* (Stanford, Cal.: Stanford University Libraries, 1989);

F. J. G. Robinson and P. J. Wallis, *Book Subscription Lists: A Revised Guide* (Newcastle upon Tyne, U.K.: Harold Hill & Son for the Book Subscriptions List Project, 1975);

Nathaniel Mayer Victor Rothschild, Baron Rothschild, *A Catalogue of the Collection of Eighteenth-century Printed Books and Manuscripts Formed by Lord Rothschild,* 2 volumes (Cambridge: Privately printed at the University Press, 1954);

Johanne M. Stochholm, *Garrick's Folly: The Stratford Jubilee of 1769 at Stratford and Drury Lane* (London: Methuen, 1964);

Wallis, *Book Subscription Lists: Extended Supplement to the Revised Guide,* completed and edited by Ruth Wallis (Newcastle upon Tyne, U.K.: Project for Historical Biobibliography, 1996).

Papers:

The major body of David Garrick's verse manuscripts, family documents, and letters, with some dramatic manuscripts, including promptbooks, is in the Folger Shakespeare Library, Washington, D.C. The outstanding collection of dramatic manuscripts, including applications for licenses to perform, is in the Larpent Manuscripts collection in the Henry E. Huntington Library, San Marino, California. Other significant caches of family documents, literary manuscripts, and letters include those in the British Library; the Garrick Club, London; the British Theatre Museum, London; and the Forster Collection, National Art Library, Victoria and Albert Museum, London.

George III, King of Great Britain and Ireland

(4 June 1738 - 29 January 1820)

Jill D. Barker
University of Luton

CATALOGUES: Sir Frederick Augusta Barnard, comp., *Bibliothecae: Regiae catalogus,* 5 volumes (London: G. Bulmer & G. Nicol, 1820–1829);

Catalogue of Maps, Prints, Drawings, etc. Forming the Geographical and Topographical Collection Attached to The Library of His Late Majesty King George the Third (London: Printed by The Order of The Trustees of The British Museum, by G. Woodfall, 1829);

G. K. Fortescue, R. F. Sharp, R. A. Streatfield, and W. A. Marsden, *Catalogue of the Pamphlets, Books, Newspapers and Manuscripts Relating to the Civil War, the Commonwealth and Restoration Collected by George Thomason, 1640–1661,* 2 volumes (London: British Museum, 1908);

Sir George F. Warner and Julius P. Gilson, *Catalogue of Western Manuscripts in the Old Royal and King's Collections,* 4 volumes (London: British Museum, 1921);

William Barclay, *Catalogue of the King's Music Library,* 3 volumes (London: British Museum, 1927–1929);

T. J. Browne and Margaret Scheele, *The Old Royal Library* (London: British Museum, 1957).

SELECTED PERIODICAL PUBLICATIONS–UNCOLLECTED: "On Mr. Ducket's Mode of Cultivation," *Annals of Agriculture,* as Ralph Robinson, 7, no. 37 (1787): 65–71;

"Further Remarks on Mr. Ducket's Mode of Cultivation," *Annals of Agriculture,* as Robinson, 7, no. 40 (1787): 332–336.

George III (portrait by John Zoffany; Collection of Her Majesty the Queen)

George III succeeded to the British throne on the death of his grandfather, George II, a considerable book collector himself who formed the collection that became known as the Old Royal Library. George III collected books in a more systematic and scholarly manner than his grandfather, gathering a substantial collection with particular strengths in the areas of literature, especially drama, as well as maps, scientific textbooks, and contemporary pamphlets. In addition to contemporary works, he also valued incunabula. George III fostered book collecting as an historical and aesthetic activity. George III's was an early attempt at systematic and comprehensive collecting; under his leadership, the vision of a library as a national research resource began to be realized. There is, of course, a difficulty in distinguishing between the king's personal efforts and what others, such as librarians and agents, accomplished in his name. Certainly there were many influences on the formation of the collection, but given George's reputation as a manager and his love of books one cannot rule out direct personal involvement.

George III was born George William Frederick in London on 4 June 1738, the eldest son of Frederick Louis, Prince of Wales, and Augusta, daughter of Frederick II, Duke of Saxe-Gotha. As a child he was taught by Dr. Francis Ayscough, who later became dean of Bristol Cathedral. Apart from a series of tutors and preceptors, young George had little contact with the outside world. His later love for the theater and for collecting scripts of plays was fostered by the childhood performances in which he participated with other children at his home, Leicester House. After the death of his father in 1751, his father's trusted supporter, John Stuart, third Earl of Bute, became George's main instructor and, soon, his constant companion and confidant.

In September 1761 George married Charlotte Sophia, younger sister of Adolphus Frederick IV, Duke of Mecklenburg-Strelitz. They had fifteen children over a twenty-one-year period–the oldest, the future George IV, born in 1762, and the youngest, Amelia, born in 1783. They settled into a life of complete domesticity, going out, it is said, only to the theater. Theatrical performances were one of the king's great passions, but he is recorded as judging William Shakespeare harshly: "Was there ever such stuff as great part of Shakespeare–only one must not say so?" The Shakespearean plays he saw had, in many cases, been extensively rewritten to accord first with Restoration and then with eighteenth-century taste. The 1681 Nahum Tate version of *King Lear* (ca. 1605) was performed throughout the eighteenth century with a happy ending, while *The Tempest* (ca. 1611) had appeared in eight different forms by the end of the century. George had a good ear for music and was a lifelong devotee of the opera, appreciating the music of George Frideric Handel above all. This combination of musical and theatrical interests forms a coherent theme in the books he collected.

As a result of George II's generous gift of his library–the Old Royal Library–to the British Museum, his grandson had no official royal library when he came to the throne in 1760. He resented the loss of the royal library not because he begrudged its public use but because he thought a fine library was a necessary adjunct to a royal palace. The library he went on to build was made accessible to scholars at all stages of its existence, thus functioning from its inception as a research resource. George loved books primarily as objects rather than for their content, reflecting his broader aesthetic admiration for complex practical achievement. The king was a competent farm manager, and his only publications were on farming subjects. Under the pseudonym "Ralph Robinson" he wrote two articles for the *Annals of Agriculture* in 1787.

While it is clear that George collected his books systematically and with taste and discrimination, standards of a remarkably scholarly nature also influenced his acquisitions. His thorough antiquarian methods anticipated what Moelwyn I. Williams describes as the "canons of nineteenth-century philological scholarship, according to which the earlier texts of a particular discipline, and the typographical antiquities of a particular country are as indispensable to the scholar as the encyclopaedic coverage of current texts." Although much of the collecting was conducted by the king's librarian, Frederick Augusta Barnard, with advice from Samuel Johnson, the king's involvement was essential to initiate the project and to ensure its progress. George's pleasure in his collections was well known. Edward Edwards recounts the possibly apocryphal story of the king's delight that his copy of William Caxton's translation of Raoul Le Fèvre's *The Recuyell of the Historyes of Troye* (Bruges: William Caxton & Colard Mansion, 1474), the first book printed in English, was rarer than the copy owned by the renowned collector John Ker, third Earl of Roxburghe (some pages in the royal copy were incorrectly ordered, a printing mistake that was corrected in later copies of the same edition).

Such were the opportunities for acquiring early books in the eighteenth century that wealthy noble collectors were joined by the professional middle classes and academics. Joseph Smith, the British consul in Venice, had assembled a fine collection of incunabula–choice editions of the classics and Italian history and literature–for which George III paid £10,000 in 1765. This purchase formed the basis for his later collecting, and Edwards says that for some years "the shops and warehouses of English booksellers were also sedulously examined, and large purchases were made from them. In this labor Dr. Johnson often assisted, actively, as well as by advice." In 1768 Barnard made an extensive journey to the Continent, successfully following Johnson's advice that one must visit a country to find not only its best literature but also its finest and most characteristic works of political theory, theology, and philosophy:

> In Italy you may, therefore expect to meet with abundance of the works of the Canonists and the Schoolmen; in Germany with store of writers on the Feudal Laws; in Holland you will find the booksellers shops swarming with the works of the Civilians. Of Canonists a few of the most eminent will suffice. Of the Schoolmen a liberal supply will be a valuable addition to the King's Library. The departments of Feudal and Civil Law you can hardly render too complete. In the Feudal Constitution we see the origin of our property laws. Of the Civil Law it is not too much to say it is a regal study.

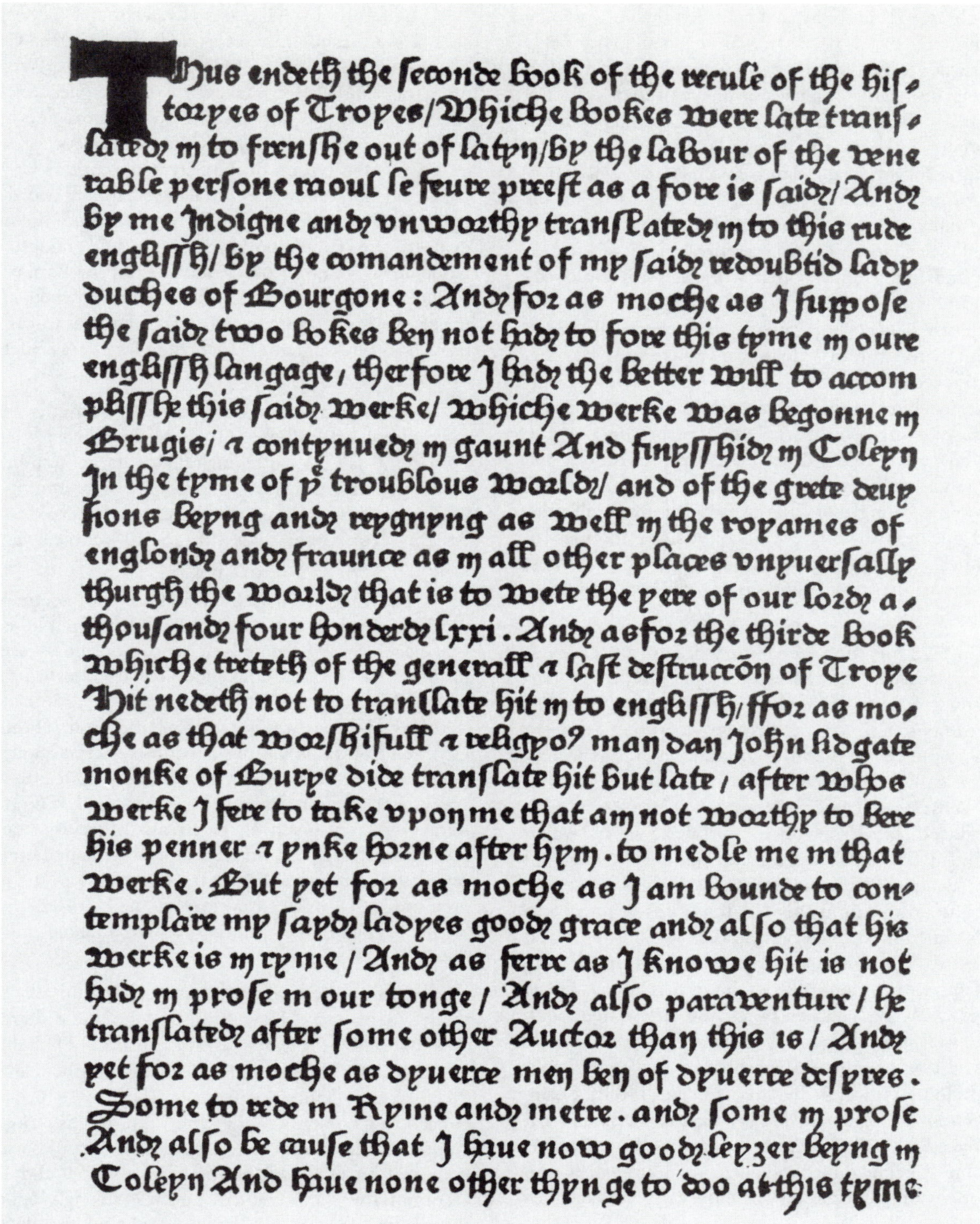
Thus endeth the seconde book of the recule of the his-
toryes of Troyes/Whiche bookes were late translated in to frenshe out of latyn/by the labour of the vene
rable persone raoul le feure preest as a fore is saide/And
by me Indigne and vnworthy translated in to this rude
englissh/by the comandement of my saide redoubtid lady
duches of Bourgone: And for as moche as I suppose
the saide two bokes ben not hade to fore this tyme in oure
englissh langage, therfore I hade the better will to accom
plisshe this saide werke/ whiche werke was begonne in
Brugis/ & contynued in gaunt And finysshid in Coleyn
In the tyme of yͤ troublous world/ and of the grete deuy
sions beyng and reygnyng as well in the royames of
englond and fraunce as in all other places vnyuersally
thurgh the world that is to wete the yere of our lord a-
thousand four honderd lxxi. And as for the thirde book
whiche treteth of the generall & last destruccōn of Troye
Hit nedeth not to translate hit in to englissh/ffor as moche as that worshipfull & religyous man dan Iohn lidgate
monke of Burye dide translate hit but late, after whos
werke I fere to take vpon me that am not worthy to bere
his penner & ynke horne after hym. to medle me in that
werke. But yet for as moche as I am bounde to con-
templaire my sayd ladyes good grace and also that his
werke is in ryme / And as ferre as I knowe hit is not
hade in prose in our tonge / And also parauenture / he
translated after some other Auctor than this is / And
yet for as moche as dyuerce men ben of dyuerce desyres.
Some to rede in Ryme and metre. and some in prose
And also be cause that I haue now good leyzer beyng in
Coleyn And haue none other thynge to doo at this tyme

Page from William Caxton's translation of Raoul Le Fevre's The Recuyell of the Histories of Troy (1479), *the first book published in English, which George III received as a gift from Jacob Bryant*

George III and Barnard intended the library to be as comprehensive as possible, embracing all major fields of knowledge. They had a particular interest in English literature and early English printing, but they collected in all other fields of the liberal arts, including classics, philosophy, fine arts, and foreign languages. During the fifty years following the Smith purchase, several collections formed by scholars and bibliophiles came up for sale, usually upon the death of the collector. As Seymour de Ricci notes, the king secured many of the best books and manuscripts, often working with the booksellers known as "Messrs Nicol" in England and with "one Horn of Ratisbon, a great despoiler of German convents," to acquire valuable incunabula in Europe. Edwards records the king's ethical instructions to Barnard not to bid against scholars or against any "known Collector of small means." Thus, the presence of the king's agent at a sale did not necessarily mean that the king would obtain anything he desired. Heeding Johnson's warning that the purchase of entire libraries would mean acquiring an inconvenient number of duplicates, Barnard focused on the earliest, the most exquisite, or the most useful edition of any given standard work.

In 1773 the sale of the library of James West, who had been treasurer of the Inner Temple and president of the Royal Society, afforded the king an important opportunity to add to his collection. West had formed a widely known collection of coins and pictures as well as a library containing thirty-six works printed by Caxton. From West's sale came the foundation of George III's unparalleled collection of the printer's early works including Jacob de Cessolis's *The Game and Playe of the Chesse* (Bruges: William Caxton & Colard Mansion, 1475), the only item in this sale that Caxton printed in Bruges and with a partner (around 1476 Caxton moved his press to Westminster, where he printed the remainder of his works alone); G. de Tiqnonville's *Dictes and Sayinges of the Philosophers* (1477), the first dated book printed in England; Geoffrey Chaucer's *Canterbury Tales* (1477); *The Mirrour of the World* (1481); *Godfrey of Boloyne* (1481); John Gower's *Confessio Amantis* (1483); Chaucer's *Troilus and Criseyde* (1484); *Paris et Vienne* (1485); and *Royal Booke* (1487?). West's friend and rival collector John Ratcliffe, a chandler from Southwark who developed an appreciation for fine early books, purchased several at West's sale. The sale of Ratcliffe's library in 1776 included around fifty Caxtons; the king purchased twenty of these, including *Boecius de Consolacione Philosophie* (1478?), *Reynarde the Foxe* (1481), Jacobus de Voraigne's *Golden Legende* (1483), *Curial* (1483), and *Speculum Vitae Christi* (1484), which was attributed to St. Bonaventura.

Dr. Anthony Askew, a physician and a considerable classical scholar, had traveled widely on the Continent and collected many Greek classical texts. George's offer of £5,000 for Askew's whole collection was refused; it went to auction in 1775 and attracted many buyers, including the king. George, however, bought only a small selection of the best items. In this way the collection now known as the King's Library was developed, with many fine historical bindings from the medieval to the contemporary period. Old books with woodcuts were also prized and collected by Barnard. In its early stages the King's Library was housed at the palace at Kew, but about 1759 a large portion was moved to Buckingham Palace, then known as Buckingham House.

One of the library's particular strengths was a magnificent collection of English plays. George Steevens's sale in 1800 included a large number of Shakespearean quartos; George III was among the major purchasers, together with the earl of Roxburghe. At the Roxburghe sale in 1812 George's agents acquired many more early plays.

The king's musical inclinations–not to mention the fashion of an age when every major public event was celebrated by a popular new composition–resulted in the formation of a considerable collection of printed music. The nucleus of the King's Library's music collection had been brought to England from Hanover; George's librarians had instructions to buy antiquarian items along with new music, so many sixteenth- and seventeenth-century scores are represented. The music library was not given to the British Museum with the rest of the King's Library but was augmented steadily over the years, remaining in the possession of the monarch until it was placed on loan to the British Museum in 1911. The music collection was donated fully in 1957.

Among the foreign-language collection are 2,085 works of Danish, Norwegian, and Icelandic literature assembled by Professor Grimr Jónsson Thokelin of Copenhagen. The pamphlet collection numbers around 30,000 items, dating from about 1550 to 1810, and is concentrated mainly on French and English political subjects. Within this collection is a group of sermons compiled by Francis Letsome between 1730 and 1760. George III was anti-Catholic and was strongly opposed to any parliamentary bill that sought to liberalize the social or professional position of Catholics. Partly for this reason and partly because of Barnard's priorities, the King's Library, though containing unsurpassed collections on the Church of England and on the Reformation, was less strong on Catholic recusancy and British nonconformity.

On his continental purchasing tour Barnard made a point of collecting local maps at every town, however small. He thus laid the foundation for George's topographical library, which housed the finest collection of maps of its day. This collection included the world atlas with the largest and best Dutch printed maps, which had been presented to Charles II by Johan Klencke of Amsterdam in 1660. There were also many atlases of the North American colonies and the theaters of war in America and in the East. Further titles included Moses Pitt's four-volume *The English Atlas* (Oxford: Printed at the Theatre for Joh. Jansonius a Waesberge and Steven Swart, 1680–1683) and the English translation of Gerardus Mercator's *Atlas,* 2 volumes (Amsterdam: J. Hondius & J. Johnson, 1635). There was a rich collection of maritime maps, including seventeenth-century Dutch and eighteenth-century English and French sea atlases. Williams notes a particularly beautifully colored copy of Joseph F. W. Des Barres's *The Atlantic Neptune: Published for the Use of the Royal Navy of Great Britain* (London, 1781). The maritime collection was given by George IV to the Admiralty in 1828 and eventually found its way to the British Museum.

George III's widely known bibliophilia meant that his collection was regularly enhanced by gifts of important books and manuscripts. Among the most notable of these gifts were two Caxtons donated by Jacob Bryant, a tutor to the duke of Marlborough: Le Fèvre's *The Recuyell of the Historyes of Troye* and the *Doctrinal of Sapience* (1489), by Guy de Roye, the only known copy of the latter to be printed on vellum. A second Caxton, from the Hewett estate, was the only known *Fables of Aesop* (1484). De Ricci narrates the circumstances of one of these gifts, the original manuscripts of a selection of the Paston letters. They had been sold by William Paston, second Earl of Yarmouth, to Peter Le Neve and passed from him to Thomas Martin, then to Thomas Worth of Diss and finally to Sir John Fenn. Fenn printed a large proportion of the collection in five volumes (1787), then bound the originals of the first two printed volumes in three volumes and presented them to the king. They did not, however, form part of the later gift to the British Museum, and the process by which they moved from George's library to that of E. G. Prettyman of Orwell Park, Suffolk, where they were eventually discovered in 1889, is a subject for further research.

As well as collecting on his own behalf, George III was involved in the collection of books for the British Museum in consultation with his fellow bibliophile Stuart, third Earl of Bute, his tutor and close friend from his youth. Although Bute had been secretary of state in 1761–1762 and even prime minister in 1762–1763, he was highly unpopular with the London populace and was forced to resign from the latter office.

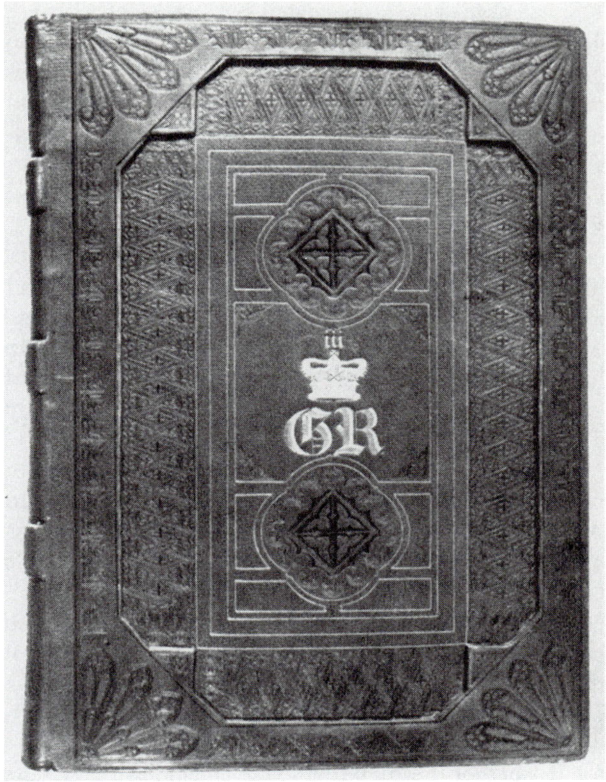

George III's brown morocco library binding, by the Buckingham Palace bindery, circa 1815

From 1765 until his death in 1792 Bute withdrew from court and devoted himself to scientific pursuits and patronage of the arts. While still in favor at court he was ideally suited to advise on book purchases, in particular on the collection of sixteenth-century London bookseller George Thomason, which came up for sale in 1762. George paid £300 to buy it for the British Museum. De Ricci notes that Thomason's collection consisted of "nearly 23,000 ephemeral tracts, pamphlets, news sheets and other broadsides mainly of a political or satirical nature," while Edwards claims that it contained 33,000 items. The Thomason collection also included some fifty plays. The whole, when rebound in chronological order in 1762, formed a library of more than 2,000 volumes known as "the King's Tracts." With the exception of reprints and Quaker tracts, Thomason had collected a high proportion of the output of the period, including, according to Edwards, "the most ponderous theological quartos that ever came from an English press as well as the tiniest handbill, or the fugitive circular which called together a 'Committee of Sequestrators' at Wallingford House." The Thomason collection was catalogued by G. K. Fortescue and others in 1908.

George was incapacitated by attacks of insanity, now thought to be due to the then unknown condition of porphyria, beginning in 1788; from 1811 until his death on 29 January 1820 he was only occasionally and briefly lucid. Arthur Bryant describes his situation movingly: "The old, blind king was irrevocably mad–immured with his medical attendants in a wing of Windsor Castle, 'with long, unkempt milk-white beard,' talking incessantly, of the dead." Instructions given to his book-buying agents remained in force, however, and purchases continued to be made regardless of the state of the king's mind–or, for that matter, of his purse. On his death, the library consisted of 65,250 volumes and more than 19,000 unbound tracts and was cared for by a staff of six.

After George III's death George IV attempted to realize the value of the library by offering it for sale to Alexander I, the emperor of Russia. The public was outraged, and Parliament found the means to persuade George IV to "donate" the library to the British Museum in the 1820s. The sum of money required to change his mind, doubtless obtained from the lords of the treasury, is not known, and no official sale took place. He retained a few especially choice books, which de Ricci describes as a "valuable library," at Windsor for the use of the monarch. They include three of the final tally of thirty-nine Caxtons in George III's library: *Recuyell of the Historyes of Troye, Fables of Aesop,* and *Doctrinal of Sapience.*

Hundreds of the King's Library volumes housed in the British Museum were destroyed during the bombing in World War II. Through diligent purchasing, however, most volumes have been replaced.

Letters:

The Correspondence of King George the Third from 1760 to December 1783, Printed from the Original Papers in the Royal Archives of Windsor Castle, 6 volumes, edited by Sir John Fortescue (London: Macmillan, 1927–1928);

The Later Correspondence of George III, 5 volumes, edited by A. Aspinall (Cambridge: Cambridge University Press, 1962–1970).

Biography:

John Brooke, *King George III* (London: Constable, 1972; New York: McGraw-Hill, 1972).

References:

Janice Anderson, *The British Library: The Reference Collections* (London: British Library, 1983);

T. A. Birrell, *The Library of John Morris: The Reconstruction of a Seventeenth-Century Collection* (London: British Museum Publications for the British Library, 1976);

Arthur Bryant, *The Age of Elegance, 1812–1822* (London: Collins, 1950);

Edward Edwards, *Lives of the Founders of the British Museum, with Notices of Its Chief Augmenter and Other Benefactors, 1570–1870,* 2 volumes (London: Trübner / New York: Bouton, 1870), pp. 464–486;

Arundell Esdaile, *The British Museum Library* (London: Allen & Unwin, 1946);

Howard M. Nixon, *English Restoration Bookbindings* (London: Published for the British Library by British Museum Publications, 1974);

Seymour de Ricci, *English Collectors of Books and Manuscripts (1530–1930) and Their Marks of Ownership* (New York: Franklin, 1930), pp. 54–70;

Moelwyn I. Williams, ed., *A Directory of Rare Book and Special Collections in the United Kingdom and the Republic of Ireland* (London: Library Association, 1985), pp. 112–136.

Robert Harley, first Earl of Oxford

(5 December 1661 – 21 May 1724)

and

Edward Harley, second Earl of Oxford

(2 June 1689 – 16 June 1741)

Richard Maxwell
Valparaiso University

CATALOGUES: Samuel Johnson, William Oldys, and Michael Maittare, comps., *Catalogus Bibliothecae Harleianae, In Locos communes distributus cum Indice Auctorum,* 5 volumes (London: Apud Thomas Osborne, 1743–1745);

Oldys, ed., *The Harleian Miscellany, or a Collection of Scarce, Curious, and Entertaining Pamphlets and Tracts, as well in Manuscript as in Print, found in the late Earl of Oxford's Library. Interspersed with Historical, Political, and Critical Notes. With a table of Contents, and an Alphabetical Index,* 8 volumes, preface by Johnson (London: Printed for T. Osborne, 1744–1746); enlarged, with additional notes by Thomas Park, 10 volumes (London: Printed for John White, John Murray, and John Harding, 1808–1813);

Humphrey Wanley and others, comps. *A Catalogue of the Harleian Collection of Manuscripts: Purchased by authority of Parliament: and Preserved in the British Museum* (London, 1759);

A Preface and Index to the Harleian Collection of Manuscripts, Published by Order of the Trustees of the British Museum, 2 volumes (London: Printed by Dryden Leach, and sold by L. Davis and C. Reymers, 1763).

BOOKS: *Faults in the Fault-Finder, or, A Specimen of Errors in the Pamphlet entitul'd Faults on Both Sides,* attributed to Robert Harley (London: Printed and to be sold by A. Baldwin, 1710);

Faults on both sides, or, An essay upon the original cause, progress, and mischevious consequences of the factions of this nation: shewing that the heads and leaders on both sides have always impos'd upon the credulity of their respective parties . . . : sincerely intended for the allaying the heats and animosities of the people . . . : by way of answer to The Thoughts of an honest Tory, by Simon Clement, attributed to Robert Harley (London: Printed and sold by the booksellers of London and Westminster, 1710);

A View of the Taxes, Funds, and Publick Revenues of England: Total Moneys Voted by Parliament during the Course of this War, attributed to Robert Harley (London: Printed for Tim. Childe, 1712);

To be given gratis to the buyers of the halfsheet, entituled, A view of the taxes, funds, and publick revenues of England, attributed to Robert Harley (London: 1712);

The Answer of Robert Earl of Oxford, and Earl Mortimer, to the Articles exhibited by the Knights, Citizens, and Burgesses in Parliament Assembled: in the name of themselves, and of all the Commons of Great Britain, in Maintenance of their Impeachment against him for High Treason and other High Crimes and Misdemeanors, supposed to have been by him committed (London: Printed for John Morphew, near Stationers-Hall, 1715);

The Tryal of Robert, Earl of Oxford and Earl Mortimer upon the Impeachment of the House of Commons: Exhibited against him for High Treason, and other High Crimes and Misdemeanours: begun in Westminster-Hall on Monday the 24th day of June, 1717, and from thence continued, by several adjournments, to the first day of July following: with the proceedings relating to the said Tryal, by Robert Harley and others (London: Printed for Jacob Tonson, 1717);

Articles of impeachment of high-treason and misdemeanors, against Robert Earl of Oxford and Earl Mortimer. July 9. 1715. With his Lordship's answer, paragraph by paragraph. To which is added, A short state of the late war and peace (London: printed for J. Roberts, A. Dodd, E. Nutt, and N. Blandford, 1727);

Robert Harley (after a portrait by Sir Godfrey Kneller; National Portrait Gallery) and his son, Edward (portrait by G. Vertu; collection of Dr. A. N. L. Munby, King's College, Cambridge)

An essay upon public credit: being an enquiry how the public credit comes to depend upon the change of ministry or the dissolutions of parliaments . . . : with an argument proving that the public credit may be upheld and maintained in this nation . . . / by Robert Harley, Daniel Defoe with Robert Harley (London: Printed for W. Baynes: J. S. Jordan, 1797).

Together, Robert Harley, first Earl of Oxford, and his son Edward Harley, second Earl of Oxford, assembled an enormously significant collection of books and manuscripts. After the death of the second earl, the printed collection, including some 50,000 books and 350,000 pamphlets, was sold to the bookseller Thomas Osborne and through him scattered throughout the world; fortunately, the manuscripts were sold en masse to the British Museum, where they form a crucial part of its holdings. Although the two Harleys were often the inspiration for the writing of others, they were not important writers for publication. Various pamphlets of the time were attributed to the Harleys, especially Robert, usually without much reason.

Born in London on 5 December 1661, Robert Harley was the eldest son of Sir Edward Harley and his wife, Abigail. Privately educated, he was admitted as a member of the Inner Temple in 1682 though he was never called to the bar. During the Glorious Revolution of 1688, the twenty-seven-year-old Harley helped take possession of Worcester for William III, an action and allegiance that suggests the traditionally Presbyterian and Whig sympathies of his family. On 2 June 1689 his first wife, Elizabeth, gave birth to his only son, Edward. Robert Harley is primarily remembered as a politician. In 1690 he represented New Radnor in Parliament, ascending quickly to a position of considerable responsibility. Harley's allegiance gradually shifted to the Tories, though he continued to cultivate his Whig connections, a tactic that enhanced his power with both sides of the House of Commons. He was elected speaker of the House of Commons in 1701. During the reign of Queen Anne from 1702 to 1714, Harley exerted enormous influence over both the queen (whose favorite, Lady Abigail Masham, was his cousin) and, more generally, over the policies of the government.

Harley's power was such that some historians regard him as, in essence, the first prime minister, though a prime minister whose sway was founded on deception. His biographers often point to his capacities for intrigue as fundamental to his character, but machinations were probably essential to sustain his political power. Harley was created earl of Oxford and made lord treasurer and Knight of the Garter in 1711, partly as a reaction to an assassination attempt that created public sympathy and affection for him. His downfall was precipitated by his role in the secret negotiations for peace he carried on during the War of the Spanish Succession and in the signing of the Treaties of Utrecht in 1713, which rebounded against him after the accession of George I the following year. The object of a motion for impeachment on the grounds of "high treason and other high crimes and misdemeanors," Harley spent from 1715 to 1717 in the Tower of London. After impeachment proceedings stalled and had to be dismissed, he appears largely to have withdrawn from political affairs.

Harley's connections with literature and learning were deep. His family had a long-established practice of book collecting, though most of the family library had been lost during the civil war when Royalist forces sacked Brampton Bryan Castle in 1643. Harley continued the tradition of book collecting on a scale much larger than that of his ancestors. In his *History of the Four Last Years of the Queen* (1758) Jonathan Swift commented of Harley, "I believe there are few Examples to be produced in any Age, of a Person, who hath passed through so many Employments in the State, endowed with so great a Share both of Divine and Human Learning." Harley was invited by Swift and Alexander Pope to join the Scriblerus Club, a British literary group devoted to writing satire that was founded in 1713 by Swift, Pope, John Arbuthnot, Matthew Prior, and Jonathan Gay. Harley was an important literary patron, but there is no evidence he ever wrote anything for the group.

Harley was fortunate to secure the services of one of the great scholars and librarians of the age, Humfrey Wanley, who oversaw the development of the Harley collection for both Robert Harley and his son. Wanley's professional diary covers the years 1714 through 1726, with a gap between August 1715 and January 1720, perhaps due to the political crisis in which Harley was involved. The diary is the source for much that is known about the compilation of this great collection. In *Fontes Harleiani: A Study of the Sources of the Harleian Collection of Manuscripts Preserved in the Department of Manuscripts in the British Museum* (1972) Cyril Wright analyzes the Wanley diary and traces the formation of their library.

Wanley's first major purchase on behalf of Harley was the collection of Sir Simonds D'Ewes, who had died in 1650. Wanley acquired D'Ewes's books and manuscripts, along with various coins and art objects, for £450 in October 1705. Although there is no doubt that D'Ewes was an outstanding antiquarian scholar of his generation, opinions on the worth of his library have varied. In his entry on Robert Harley in the *Dictionary of National Biography* George Baker judges that its quality is somewhat mixed: "The collection is very miscellaneous, embracing even such trifles as his school exercises, a large number of letters to his sisters and family, and a great deal else that is really worthless." Some material, though, was invaluable. D'Ewes had been a great transcriber of cartularies and other historical documents, the originals of which often no longer exist. He also owned medieval manuscripts and, as Wright notes, had bought the collections amassed by previous antiquaries such as Ralph Starkey. The D'Ewes collection now numbers roughly as Harley 1 to Harley 600 in the British Library holdings.

Other important acquisitions soon followed. The second major purchase, manuscripts from the library of Edward Stillingfleet, bishop of Worcester, was made in the spring of 1707. Between 1708 and 1710 Harley and Wanley acquired much heraldic material. In 1708 and 1711 several items were purchased from the historian John Strype, who was studying Harley's recently acquired Stillingfleet papers. Wanley obtained from him the papers of John Foxe, author of *The Book of Martyrs* (1563). The third large collection, added sometime before the end of 1712, was a donation from Henry Worsley, a member of Parliament and a diplomat.

In 1712 an extraordinary purchase by Wanley demonstrated that book collecting can involve both larceny and foreign policy. Jean Aymon, described in P. L. Heyworth's *Letters of H. Wanley* as a "french renegade priest and adventurer," stole manuscripts from the Royal Library in Paris, taking them with him to Holland in 1707. In a 3 January 1713 memorandum Wanley observed, "Now I considering their great Rarity, Antiquity, and other Matters of Curiosity pertaining unto them: as also, that by securing them, divers Weapons will be taken out of the Hands of Deists & Papists: & much additional strength accrue to the Protestant Religion; do think them worth the said 1625 Guilders or even 100 Pounds Sterling more." Harley returned some of the collection to Paris in exchange for 242 volumes of transcripts of state papers originally made by the command of Jean-Baptiste Colbert, controller general of finance and secretary of state for the navy under King Louis XIV of France. In 1729 Edward Harley returned to France the invaluable sixth-century biblical manuscript *Codex Claromontanus*. Another batch of papers was returned by the chief librarian of the British Library, Edward Bond, in 1878.

By 1715 Harley had accumulated three-thousand manuscripts, one-thousand rolled parchments, and thirteen-thousand deeds inclusive of many unbound papers. In a 27 July 1715 memorandum Wanley wrote proudly that the collection was the best in England, "excepting only that of Sir Robert Cotton." During Harley's sojourn in the Tower of London, the process of accumulation might well have been interrupted had the father not had a son even more intent on the building of a great library. After 1715, the supervision of the library and of Wanley's work was largely his son's responsibility.

Edward Harley attended Westminster School and matriculated at Christ Church, Oxford, in 1707. During his undergraduate years, he was a mediocre student. He spent too much money on books, a vice that proved a lifetime weakness. In 1711 Edward was elected minister of Parliament for Radnorshire. In 1713 he married a rich woman, Lady Henrietta Cavendish-Holles, daughter of the duke of Newcastle. Although Henrietta's mother opposed the marriage because she stood to lose much of her wealth in its wake, the couple was undeterred.

The marriage proved to be not altogether happy. The fabulous family library drew literati of all description to the Harleys' home. In many cases Edward had inherited the friendships of these writers from his father. Swift, a frequent guest, once wrote in a letter to Harley: "I am the only man since the first Villiers Duke of Buckingham that ever succeeded in favour from a father to son." Henrietta hated most of her husband's circle of friends, and they returned the feeling in kind. Her relationship with Pope, Edward's idol, was especially bad. She did, however, sustain a long friendship with Prior, who, of all her husband's literary friends, appears to have been the most sympathetic to her.

Harley, meanwhile, was engaged in spending his wife's fortune on books and art objects as well as to support various writers, artists, and scholars. According to Bishop William Warburton of Gloucester, Edward was "the most distinguished patron and friend of letters" of his age. The fame of Harley and his family extended to the Continent. In January 1728, during his visit to London, Voltaire wrote to Harley: "Tho I am a traveller unknown to Lordship, the name of 'Harlay' [*sic*] has been for many centuries, so glorious among us french . . . that you must forgive the liberty of this letter."

After financial disasters in 1738, Robert Harley had a harder time living and collecting on the scale to which he had become accustomed. His book collection of fifty thousand volumes housed at Wimpole had to be sold in 1740. Weakened by a lifetime of heavy drinking as well as by monetary cares, Harley died at age fifty-two on 16 June 1741. In *Earls of Creation* (1963) James Lees-Milne offers this sardonic postscript: "His widow when the first transports of mourning were over viewed the course of her husband's past life dispassionately, and allowed her justifiable grievances to overcome any desire to perpetuate his memory in stone or marble."

Edward Harley never sought the political limelight that his father had so forcefully occupied. Partly on this account, the second earl of Oxford is often characterized as indolent. Although there is considerable evidence to support such a judgment, it needs qualification. Like Horace Walpole, the son of the great Whig politician Robert Walpole who dominated British politics, after Robert Harley's fall he evidently reacted against living his life in the public sphere. In each case, a father who lived in the world of politics was succeeded by an offspring of aesthetic and scholarly inclinations, an heir almost too willing to spend the family fortune on such pursuits. Secondly, even if Edward Harley had desired a public career, the long Whig ascendancy–lasting until Robert Walpole's resignation in 1742–dimmed prospects for his political success since Edward, like his father, was an ardent Tory. The elder Harley had seized an opportunity whose time had come; he had thus done much to define the structure of British politics in the eighteenth century, when power decisively devolved from monarchs to ministers. Edward chose the path that most obviously presented itself when he in his turn achieved majority: he carried on the family tradition of collecting and became a major patron of the arts.

Although Harley had a tendency to make occasional random impulse purchases, he had inherited from his father not only his relationships with Swift and Pope but with Wanley as well. The librarian influenced Robert Harley to collect consistently and supervised the expansion of the collection up until his death in 1724. He bore responsibility not only for hard, behind-the-scenes bargaining with scores of sellers but also for receiving visitors, from the casual to the scholarly; for working with binders and restorers; and, of course, for cataloguing. Harley probably would have squandered much more money than he did had it not been for Wanley's careful husbanding of his resources.

On several occasions Harley had the opportunity to buy up large groups of books and manuscripts from the estates of deceased bibliophiles. In 1720, a high point in his acquisitions program, he bought manuscripts from John Warburton, Somerset herald; Archdeacon John Batteley; and Peter Séguier, chancellor of France. The next year was almost as eventful, for Harley added volumes from the libraries of Thomas Grey, second Earl of Stamford; Robert Paynell of Belaugh, Norfolk, and Gray's Inn; and John Robartes, first Earl of Radnor.

Generally, though, the number and quality of estate libraries for sale had declined, and bargaining–to judge from Wanley's diary and correspondence–became ever trickier. Harley sought to close deals with owners of desirable books but, often, these deals did not work out. In 1715, for example, Harley waxed enthusiastic about the collection of John Covel, Master of Christ's College, Cam-

Bookplates of Robert Harley

bridge. Covel wrote tantalizingly: "And whereas, a Greek Manuscript containing certain of ye works, of Athanasius; a Small Tract, containing Some Hymns of ye Greek Church; and my whole Collection of Original Letters from learned Men, Greek and others, are now either Mislaid, or not ready to come at; I promise, that I will make due, and Speedy Search for ye Same; and deliver them up to ye Said Lord Harley, as soon as I conveniently may, or they Shall come to my Hands." The second earl of Oxford had a lifelong interest in Greek manuscripts, and Covel led him and Wanley a fine chase over many years. Some of his important Greek material did end up in Harley's library; much of it, however, did not arrive at the British Library until the nineteenth century.

Though Harley and Wanley continued to bid for significant English collections arriving on the market, they more and more began to seek abroad for much of their material. Gradually they came to rely on book agents in Italy, France, and Germany as well as a variety of diplomatic and ecclesiastical functionaries stationed in the Levant and the Near East. Wanley evidently also encouraged scholars who used the Harleian library to look out for potential acquisitions or to donate their own acquisitions to the collection. By cultivating these many connections, Wanley and Harley gave the library a much broader scope, geographically, than it had previously boasted. As Cyril E. Wright notes, the collection eventually contained manuscripts in such languages as Hebrew, Arabic, Persian, Turkish, Armenian, Aramaic, Samaritan, Syriac, Sanskrit, Gujarati, Malayan, and Jaina-Prakit (a single instance of the latter). There were also a few examples of Chinese and Japanese manuscripts. The Harleys' initial focus on English history and lore thus evolved to comprehend an extraordinarily wide variety of cultures. The Harleian Library came to reflect not just the new culture of the Grand Tour, not just the new scholarship shaped, as Wright observes, by the paleographical triumphs of Jean Mabillon and Bernard de Montfaucon, but a truly international range of interests.

With the death of Edward Harley, the third and in some ways most crucial phase of the existence of the Harleian Library began. His wife, Henrietta, sold the collection of printed books to Thomas Osborne, bookseller of Gray's Inn, for less than £13,000, probably less than the bindings alone had cost. *Catalogus Bibliothecae Harleianae, In Locos communes distributus cum Indice Auctorum* (1743–1745), Osborne's five-volume sale catalogue, was planned by Michael Maittare, author of *Annales Typographici ab Artis Inventae Origine ad Annum MD* (1719–1741), a work that had been made possible largely by Maittare's studies in the

Harleian Library. (The second volume of the *Annales Typographici* is dedicated to Edward Harley.) The descriptions of the books were prepared largely by William Oldys, who had been Harley's literary secretary since 1738, and Samuel Johnson provided an anonymous introduction.

Johnson includes a eulogy of the two earls of Oxford, exhorting members of the nobility to follow their examples in preferring "books and manuscripts to equipage and luxury, and to forsake noise and diversion for the conversation of the learned, and the satisfaction of extensive knowledge"; however, he does not express great hopes that such a way of life will catch on. He also provides a striking overview of the collection, which, in Johnson's account, is held to cover the following subjects: ecclesiastical and theological books (subdivided in a great many categories); "Topographical Description and Antiquities of Britain"; "Heraldical and Armorial Books"; "Register Books, Chartularies"; "Ceremonials, Pomps, and Solemnities"; Wales; Scotland; Ireland; "ancient copies of the Greek and Latin Classics and Historians"; "Lexicons, Glossaries and Dictionaries"; Chronicles of France, and other Countries; "Histories of Popes"; "Poems, Essays, Ditties, Ancient Ballads, Plays"; "Musical Compositions"; "Books of Architecture"; "Natural History, Agriculture, Voyages, Travels"; "Astronomy, Cosmography, and Geography"; "Alchymical . . . and Medical Tracts"; "Letters"; and "Illuminated Manuscripts."

The manuscripts were retained by the Harley family until 1753, when a debate in the House of Commons on Sir Hans Sloane's bequest of his collections to the nation inspired an interest in the collection. Sloane's gesture helped transform the structure of knowledge in Great Britain. Nearly two centuries had passed since John Dee on 15 January 1556 had supplicated Queen Mary "for the recovery and preservation of ancient Writers and Monuments," proposing the formation of a "Library Royal" to which Dee himself would contribute. His proposal, like a similar one from Robert Cotton, was not accepted. The idea of a great state library had not elicited much enthusiasm from the rulers of England. In 1753, however, that long-standing attitude changed.

The Harleian manuscripts were purchased by the state for the somewhat nominal figure of £10,000 and became a foundational collection of the British Museum. The surviving portion of the Harleian Library along with Cotton's collection were thus absorbed into the kind of institution that Renaissance intellectuals had long before envisioned. Under the supervision of William Norris, secretary of The Society of Antiquaries, a two-volume catalogue of the manuscripts appeared in 1763, *A Preface and Index to the Harleian Collection of Manuscripts, Published by Order of the Trustees of the British Museum,* with an important anonymously written preface in which the contents of the collection, a national treasure, are analyzed.

Although there is no full overview available of the influence and cultural significance of the Harleian Library, William Weber's 1989 specialized study, "Thomas Tudway and the Harleian Collection of 'Ancient' Church Music," illustrates one dimension of such an accounting. Weber treats the Harleian manuscripts whose first of six volumes is titled "A Collection of the Most Celebrated Services and Anthems used in the Church of England, from the Reformation to the Restauration of K. Charles II. Composed by the Best Masters, and Collected by Thomas Tudway, D. M. Musick–Professor to the University of Cambridge, A.D. MDCCXV." According to Weber, the nearly three-thousand-page collection, assembled between 1715 and 1720, is "one of the landmarks in the study of English church music of the sixteenth and seventeenth centuries."

On the whole, the English did not collect music systematically, unless for the immediate purpose of performance, until the end of the eighteenth century. Tudway, a Tory organist with Cambridge connections, had started working under Wanley in 1714. By November 1715 he reported his acquisition of a score from 1532, "wch is before Tallis or Bird; I hope it will be valuable on many accounts." Tudway's concept of what he was doing soon broadened, for by late 1715 he made reference to "my great Collection of Church Musick." Weber suggests that Tudway's project shows a deepening historical and scholarly consciousness: "The idea of a national musical tradition in church music provided Tories such as [Robert] Harley with a means of exerting a broad sort of leadership with national themes." Weber's speculation provides a useful clue as to the nature of the Harleian collections. They were not just the product of mere acquisitiveness but were a manifestation of a large-scale idea of the nation, a conception grounded in an historical consciousness that could be established only with a proper scholarly foundation. Thus, Tudway's project–one of many such associated with the Harleian Library–serves as an example of how collecting can become intertwined with political and nationalistic aspirations.

A similar point could be made in regard to Oldys's eight-volume edition of papers, *The Harleian Miscellany, or a Collection of Scarce, Curious, and Entertaining Pamphlets and Tracts, as well in Manuscript as in Print, found in the late Earl of Oxford's Library. Interspersed with Historical, Political, and Critical Notes* (1744–1746). Johnson set out the rationale for this immense production in his *Proposals for the Miscellany,* published in *The Gentlemen's Magazine* for 1743: "It has been for a long Time, a very just Complaint, among the Learned, that a Multitude of valuable Productions, published in small Pamphlets, or in single Sheets, are in a short Time, too often by Accidents, or Negligence, destroyed." Johnson goes on to say that the Harleian Library contains "a greater Number of Pamphlets and small Treatises, than

Page from Solomon ibn Alzuk's Misneh Torah, *written in 1471–1472, which was acquired for Edward Harley in 1725 (British Library)*

were, perhaps, ever yet seen in one Place; Productions of the Writers of all Parties, and of every Age." Perhaps the most widely distributed and widely known of all such miscellanies, *The Harleian Miscellany* makes available an extraordinary range of fugitive documents, proclaiming, in their entirety, a commitment to the study of history, conceived as an essential part of national consciousness and political health–particularly in England, where freedom of inquiry and speech are taken to be unusually well developed, indeed a central feature of the body politic. (Weber makes a further association with Oldys's 1731 *A Dissertation upon Pamphlets;* the interest in pamphlet collecting was apparently deeply rooted in Harleian circles.)

A look at the first volume alone shows the range of material. It begins with the royal declaration that made Robert Harley a peer, proceeds to a "modest vindication" of the Glorious Revolution, and from thence to a sheaf of similar polemics, diverges to a history of Edward II (deposition still the connecting theme), a Scottish declaration of loyalty to Robert Bruce, a "Complaint of the Plowman unto Christ," and a great variety of historical narratives, suggesting a special interest in political assassinations, successful or not. Later volumes diverge into an even greater range of subjects–accounts of fires and earthquakes, handbooks for marriage, discourses on Machiavelli, a study of taxes in France, an "elegy on the death of trade," a diary of the Siege of Limerick, "a description of the library of Cardinal Mazarin, Before it was utterly ruined," a consideration from Cromwellian times on whether the Jews should be allowed to return to England, and a conversation between the ghosts of Henry VIII and Charles I. Much of this material must have entered the Harleian Library at an extremely low cost. There was a systematic intent not only of saving great manuscripts, famous printed books, and heraldic collections–the material of an aristocratic collection par excellence–but also of preserving documents that might otherwise have gone into the trash. Such material makes possible a "thick description"–in Clifford Geertz's phrase–of a particular history and culture.

During the transfer of the manuscript collection to the state Margaret Bentinck, Duchess of Portland and daughter of the second Earl, wrote as follows to the speaker of the House of Commons:

> Though I am told the expense of collecting them was immense, and that, if they were to be dispersed, they would probably sell for a great deal of money, yet, as a sum has been named, and as I know it was my Father's and is my Mother's intention that they should be kept together, I will not bargain with the Publick. I give you this trouble therefore to acquaint you that I am ready to accept of your proposal upon condition that this great and valuable Collection shall be kept together in a proper repository, as an addition to the Cotton Library, and be called by the name of the Harleian Collection of Manuscripts.

That the Harley Library, like the Dee or Cotton collections before it, was formed with more than private enjoyment in mind seems difficult to deny. Long before its absorption into the British Museum, the Harleian collection–initiated by a man who was at one time, practically speaking, the most powerful person in the realm–had a substantial public dimension. As Weber notes in his essay, "the library became a powerful means of patronage, a channel by which a wide variety of people offered gifts of their books or ancient objects and in return established important links to the great family."

Robert Harley was never a disinterested collector–quite the reverse–and was certainly among those who saw the connection between the realm of letters and the realm of power. He probably grasped the place of literary culture in public life better than had most previous politicians. The range and depth of the Harleys' collecting activities in the context of English culture and history, broadly speaking, awaits deeper exploration.

References:

Sheila Biddle, *Bolingbroke and Harley* (New York: Knopf, 1974);

David Hayton, "Robert Harley's 'Middle Way': The Puritan Heritage in Augustan Politics," *British Library Journal,* 15 (Autumn 1989): 158–172;

James Lees-Milne, *Earls of Creation* (New York: London House & Maxwell, 1963);

William Weber, "Thomas Tudway and the Harleian Collection of 'Ancient' Church Music," *British Library Journal,* 15 (Autumn 1989): 187–206;

Cyril E. Wright, *Fontes Harleiani: A Study of the Sources of the Harleian Collection of Manuscripts Preserved in the Department of Manuscripts in the British Museum* (London: British Museum, 1972);

Wright and Ruth Wright, *Humfrey Wanley and the History of the Harleian Library: A Reprint of the Introduction to The Diary of Humfrey Wanley 1715–1726* (London: London Bibliographical Society, 1966).

Papers:

The main repository for the papers of Robert and Edward Harley is the British Library, London.

Gabriel Harvey

(July 1550? - 7 February 1631)

Robert A. Shaddy
University of Toledo

See also *DLB 167: Sixteenth-Century British Nondramatic Writers, Third Series.*

BOOKS: *Ode natalitia, vel opus eius feriae, quae S. Stephani protomartyris nomine celebreta est. In memoriam P. Rami* (London: Thomas Vautrollerius, 1575);

Gabrielis Harueii Ciceronianus, vel oratio habita Catabrigiae (London: Henry Bynneman, 1577);

Gabrielis Harueii rhetor, vel duorum dierum oratio (London: Henry Bynneman, 1577);

Gabrielis Harueii Valdinatis; Smithus, vel musarum lachrymae; pro obitu T. smithi, equitis. (R. Harveij lachrymae) (London: Henry Bynneman, 1578);

Gabrielis Haruij gratulationum Baldinensium libri quatuor (London: Henry Bynneman, 1578);

Three Proper, and Wittie, Familiar Letters, bound together with *Two Other, Very Commendable Letters of the Same Men's Writing, Both Touching the Foresaid Artificial Versifying and Certain other Particulars, More Lately Delivered unto the Printer* (London: Imprinted by Henry Bynneman, 1580);

Three letters, and Certaine Sonnets: Especially Touching Robert Greene (London: Imprinted by John Wolfe, 1592); republished as *Foure Letters, and Certaine Sonnets* (London: John Wolfe, 1592);

Pierces Supererogation or a New Prayse of the Old Asse (London: Imprinted by John Wolfe, 1593);

A New Letter of Notable Contents. With a Straunge Sonet, Intituled Gorgon (London: Printed by John Wolfe, 1593).

Editions: *Letter-Book of Gabriel Harvey, A.D. 1573–1580,* edited by Edward John Long Scott (London: Camden Society, 1884; New York & London: Johnson Reprint, 1965);

The Works of Gabriel Harvey, D.C.L., 3 volumes, edited by Alexander B. Grosart (London: Huth Library, 1884–1885; New York: AMS Press, 1966);

Gabriel Harvey's Marginalia, edited by G. C. Moore Smith (Stratford-upon-Avon: Shakespeare Head, 1913);

Gabriel Harvey; portrait by an unknown artist (British Museum)

Four Letters and Certain Sonnets, edited by G. B. Harrison (London: Bodley Head, 1922; New York: Barnes & Noble, 1966);

Ciceronianus, Latin/English edition, translated by Clarence A. Forbes, Studies in the Humanities 4 (Lincoln: University of Nebraska Press, 1945);

"Rhetor: The First Lecture by Gabriel Harvey," Latin/English edition, translated and edited by Robert M. Chandler, *Allegorica,* 4 (Summer–Winter 1979): 146–290.

OTHER: "G. H. po eodem," in *Posies,* by George Gascoigne (London: Imprinted for Richard Smith, 1575);

"De Discenda Graeca Lingua Greeke," in *Lexicon Graeco-Latinum, repurgatum studio E. Grant,* by Jean Crespin (London: Henry Bynneman, 1581);

Academiae Cantabrigiensis lachrymae tumulo nobilissimi equitis, D. Philippi Sidneii sacratae per Alexandrum Nevillum (London: Printed for Alexander Neville, 1587)–includes Harvey's "Academiae Cantabrigiensis lachrimae, in obitum clarissimi Equitus, Domini Philippi Sidneii"; "De subito et praematuro interitu Nobilis viri, Philippi Sydneii, utriusque militiae, tam Armatae, quam Togatae, clarissimi Equitus: officiosi amici Elegia"; and "Ad illustrissimum Dominum Leicestrensem protheoreticon."

Gabriel Harvey was a poet and a writer who generated enough controversy that he was forced out of public life and into a thirty-year retirement. It was difficult for even Harvey's friends and admirers to get along with him, but all who knew him, including his enemies, respected his intellect and his learning. During his life Harvey developed a collection of books and manuscripts, covering a wide range of topics that exceeded many collections of the era, which provided him the means for a lifetime of intellectual stimulation and satisfaction. Although Harvey's books were scattered after his death, scholars have meticulously researched public and private library collections to virtually reassemble the collection. Harvey's marginal annotations reveal his interests and record perceptive observations on rhetoric, mathematics and navigation, astrology, medicine, his contemporaries, and literature. Harvey stands as one of the foremost bibliophiles of the Elizabethan period.

Sources usually place the date of Gabriel Harvey's birth at either 1545 or 1550. The Elizabethan poet was the eldest son of John Harvey, a successful and prosperous yeoman farmer and rope maker of Saffron Walden, Essex, who raised five other children along with Gabriel. The elder Harvey was strong willed and determined to improve his station in life and that his children should do likewise. Gabriel and his brothers received a traditional education at the local grammar school that was rigorous but yielded rich results, as many of its students went on to universities or Inns of Court. The school's curriculum was patterned after that of Eton, and emphasis was placed on Latin, grammar, and "higher learning." Years later, Gabriel Harvey recalled the long hours and strict discipline he endured at grammar school: "Good bringing upp, we call breaking, as well in children, schollars, and Servants, as young coultes &c. which cannot be withowt sum mixture of severity." Harvey was completely absorbed in learning and its pursuit and quickly proved himself to be something of a prodigy. Even his earnest enemy Thomas Nashe sketches a prose portrait of an individual who possessed literary and linguistic talents that were recognizable early in his life. Gabriel was not the only one in his family to benefit from his father's interest in success and education for his children. Three of John Harvey's sons were sent to Cambridge, and Gabriel fondly remembered his father as a man who "bore the chiefest office in Walden with good credite" and as one "whose honesty no neighbour can empeach."

Harvey matriculated at Christ's College, Cambridge, in 1566 and received a B.A. in 1569–1570. He was elected a fellow of Pembroke Hall in 1570, and while there he became a good friend of Edmund Spenser. Harvey served as Spenser's tutor and exercised great influence over the poet, although their friendship lasted longer than did their tutor-student relationship. Harvey was considered a good scholar and was attracted to classical forms–he claimed to be the father of the English hexameter. Harvey is noted (negatively) for having tried to persuade Spenser to follow the hexameter schema in *The Fairie Queene* and judging an early version of Spenser's masterpiece as "Hobgoblin runne away with the Garland from Apollo." There seems to have been no ill will generated, since Spenser immortalized Harvey in his *Shepheardes Calender* under the name of "Hobbinol," and Harvey admitted in a series of letters to Spenser the difficulties of writing English verse in classical meters.

Harvey's college life was marked by frequent association with colleagues who held dissimilar views, and, by temper and by nature, he was ill-suited for close cooperation with many of them. He has been described as a man of arrogant and reproachful spirit who was far more concerned with promoting himself and his own considerable abilities rather than recognizing the merits of others. Thomas Neville, who held a fellowship at Pembroke at the same time as Harvey and who afterwards was the master of Trinity College, believed that Harvey "could hardly find it in his heart to commend of any man." Indeed he seems to have been perpetually at war with many of the other fellows. As a result, when Harvey initially stood for his M.A. degree in 1573, he was refused the necessary "grace" from the college, although the degree was finally awarded some three months later. Shortly thereafter, Harvey was appointed college tutor, but his relations with the other fellows were permanently embittered.

For a brief time, Harvey studied rhetoric at Cambridge and sought a readership in that field. He became a reader in rhetoric about 1576. To promote his candidacy for such a position, he wrote *Gabrielis Harueii rhetor, vel duorum dierum oratio* and *Gabrielis Harueii Ciceronianus, vel oratio habita Catabriqiae,* both

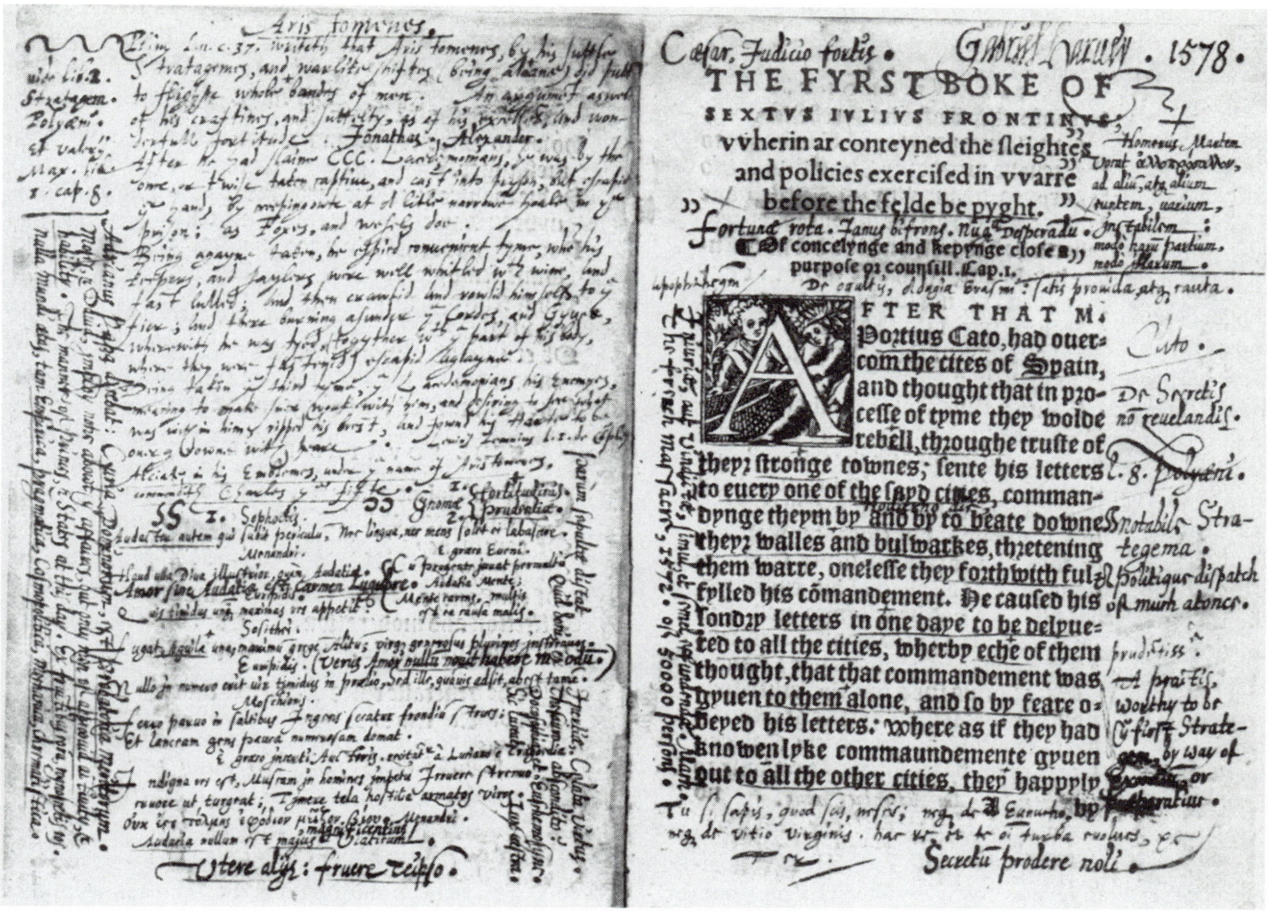
THE FYRST BOKE OF
SEXTVS IVLIVS FRONTINVS,
vvherin ar conteyned the sleightes
and policies exercised in vvarre
before the felde be pyght.
Of concelynge and kepynge close
purpose or counsill. Cap. i.
AFTER THAT M. Portius Cato, had ouercom the cites of Spain, and thought that in processe of tyme they wolde rebell, throughe truste of their stronge townes; sente his letters to euery one of the sayd cities, commandynge theym by and by to beate downe their walles and bulwarkes, thretening them warre, onelesse they forthwith fulfylled his comandement. He caused his sondry letters in one daye to be delyuered to all the cities, wherby eche of them thought, that that commandement was gyuen to them alone, and so by feare obeyed his letters: where as if they had knowen lyke commaundemente gyuen out to all the other cities, they happyly

Pages from Harvey's copy of the 1539 edition of Frontinus's The Strategemes, Sleyghtes, and Policies of Warre, *including Harvey's autograph annotations (Houghton Library, Harvard University)*

published in 1577, and sought the support of Sir Thomas Smith, Earl of Leicester. In a letter to the earl, Harvey wrote that he sought the readership in order that he might study rhetoric rather than teach the subject. By August 1578, Harvey's fellowship at Pembroke College was soon to expire, and the earl of Leicester again sought to help his friend. However, his appeal to the master and fellows was unsuccessful, and Harvey was required to find another position.

Harvey applied for a fellowship at Christ's College, with a possible view to the ministry, but he was rejected. He turned to Trinity Hall and received a fellowship in December 1578 after having received the support of its master, Henry Harvey (to whom Gabriel claimed to be related). Although Gabriel Harvey was now required to study law, he continued to focus some of his energies on writing poetry. In 1579 he accused his friend Spenser of publishing some of his English verse (designated by Harvey as his "Verlayes") against his wishes. Nashe declared that Harvey sent them to the printer himself: "I durst on my credit undertake Spenser was no way privie to the committing of them to print." They were printed and distributed, however, and they landed Harvey in a fair amount of literary controversy. Sir James Croft and Edward de Vere, the earl of Oxford, were quite displeased with the poet, believing that his verse contained satirical allusions to members of court, and Oxford seemed to be satirized as an "Italinated Englishman" in the "Mirror of Tuscanismo." Serious consequences were averted when Harvey provided the proper explanations. On the satire directed at Oxford, the poet indignantly denied any intentions at offending a man who had served as his patron ever since "in the prime of gallantest youth he bestowed angels upon me in Christes Colledge in Cambridge." However, the incident left a lasting blemish on Harvey's career and kept him from reaching the highest levels of the university's administration.

Yet around 1578, the year he composed his "Gratulationes Waldenses" and presented them to

Queen Elizabeth I during her visit to the duke of Norfolk at Audley End, Harvey's attainments and great ability were generally recognized. He began to study civil law at this time, and he completed his doctorate in the field at Oxford University. At the Cambridge commencement of 1579 Harvey was appointed one of the contenders for honors in philosophy. Early in 1581 he was a candidate for the office of public orator, but he was defeated by Wingfield of Trinity. Harvey remarked, "Mine owne modest petition, my friendes diligent labour, our high chauncellors [Burghley's] most honourable and extraordinary commendation, were all peltingly defeated by a slye practise of the olde Foxe." From May to October 1583 Harvey served in the office of junior proctor to fill a vacancy created by a retirement, and in 1585 he was elected to succeed Henry Harvey as Master of Trinity Hall. His election was quashed at court, and Preston won the position. Preston died in 1598, and Harvey was again a candidate for the mastership; he appealed to Sir Robert Cecil for royal assistance, but once more his application was unsuccessful.

Harvey possessed an immoderate estimate of his achievements and aptitudes, and these traits, combined with his disappointed ambitions, apparently made him contentious and touchy. His "paper warfare" in a series of pamphlets with Robert Greene and Nashe was especially virulent and eventually drove Harvey from his college and into retirement. The acrimonious exchange was instigated by Greene, one of the most popular English prose writers of the sixteenth century, in response to writings by Harvey's brother Richard that offended Greene and his friends. To Richard Harvey's works *Plaine Percivall* and *Lamb of God* (1592) Greene retorted by publishing *Quip for an Upstart Courtier* (1592), which included scathing remarks–the exact nature of which are now lost due to their being expunged from all later editions–on both Richard and Gabriel, particularly regarding the Harveys' humble parentage and including offensive references to their father's trade.

Outraged, Gabriel Harvey assailed Greene in his *Foure Letters, and Certaine Sonnets* (1592), in which he revealed with venomous fullness the miserable details of Greene's later years. Greene died in 1592, but Harvey kept up the assault, thereby prompting Nashe to enter in support of his dead friend. Nashe's stinging replies overwhelmed Harvey, who could not match the wit of his antagonist. After several publications, the conflict was concluded by the archbishop of Canterbury, who in 1599 ordered each man's books to be gathered up and burned: "all Nashes bookes and Dr. Harvey's bookes [should] be taken wheresoever they may be found, and that none of the same bookes be ever printed hereafter." After this episode, coupled with his failure to gain the mastership of Trinity Hall in 1598, Harvey retired to his native town of Saffron Walden, where he most likely lived in virtual obscurity until his death in February 1631, probably practicing medicine.

Despite his reputation as a quarrelsome and spiteful intellectual, Harvey was nevertheless a talented scholar and literary stylist. He aimed to introduce the classical hexameter into English poetry (but fell short). His printed works–apart from those related to his literary vendetta with Greene and Nashe–were few. They comprise two lectures on rhetoric, elegies and other verses in Latin, and several elegantly styled letters between himself and Spenser. Harvey's library, though, was exceptional in size and scope, and he is noted for the marginalia he committed to the pages of his books. Like other Renaissance men (for example, the printer Henri Estienne, Ben Jonson, and John Milton), Harvey annotated his books, but his marginalia is distinctive and noteworthy for its abundance, variety, artistry, and consistency. The inscriptions found throughout the books of his impressive collection stand as significant barometric readings that record the inner man and his thoughts, his mood changes, his views of himself and others, self-admonitions and precepts, his methods of scholarship, and his unrelenting efforts towards self-improvement.

As for his collecting strategy, Harvey's objective seems to have been nothing less than the acquisition of the sum total of human knowledge. He was not interested in learning for its own sake, rather he was directed toward more pragmatic purposes: he wanted, as he pursued his studies, to be able to have handy any and everything that might be of use. He utilized the materials for his extensive research and interacted with it–as physical objects and as conduits for intellectual stimulation–energetically and intimately, as an analysis of his extensive marginalia illustrates.

Books identified as from Harvey's library reflect his wide-ranging intellectual and practical interests. The majority of these books were in the vernacular and constitute the working library of a learned man vitally connected to many subjects. History, government, law, languages, medicine, science, and literature were all in his collection. The marginalia found on the pages of these books reveals the importance he attached to those subjects. In terms of size and monetary value, though, the Harvey collection competes favorably with the libraries held by others of his day, such as the collections of Lord John Lumley, Andrew Perne, and John Dee. It has been estimated that Lumley's library comprised 2,675 volumes, with 88 percent in Latin, and the majority dealing with theological subjects.

Perne's collection held approximately 2,000 books and manuscripts, according to a 1589 inventory. Dee, a great English mathematician, astronomer, and magus, held a magnificent scientific library that covered many other fields as well. Dee estimated his books and manuscripts to number "neere 4000." The poet William Drummond of Hawthornden owned a library comprising approximately 1,700 titles. By comparison with these private libraries, in 1582 the University Library at Cambridge had only about 450 books and manuscripts.

Unfortunately, a catalogue of Harvey's books and manuscripts was never prepared, although scholars have attempted to locate and catalogue the collection. W. Carew Hazlitt, in Bernard Quaritch's *Contributions Toward a Dictionary of Book Collectors* (1899), lists 25 printed books and one manuscript commonplace book. In 1913 G. C. Moore Smith published *Gabriel Harvey's Marginalia* and, using Hazlitt's research and his own, Smith lists 53 printed books and 9 manuscripts. Virginia F. Stern's *Gabriel Harvey: His Life, Marginalia, and Library* (1979) includes an annotated "Catalogue of Harvey's Books," which lists 180 printed books, a broadsheet, a folio sheet, and 10 manuscripts known to be from Harvey's collection.

This research, of course, only analyzes the books proven to be from Harvey's library. As for the total size of the collection, one can only estimate. Nashe reports in *Have with You to Saffron-Walden* (1596) that Harvey told his friends that he had "a Library worth 200 pounds." At the time Harvey was about forty-six years old and had several more years of collecting ahead of him. Stern calculates that Harvey's collection could have comprised from 1,300 to 3,500 titles. At the time of Harvey's death, the total number of volumes might have been much greater. However, as mentioned above, Harvey was not moving in the world of scholarship in his final years, and his collection may have been reduced or slowed in growth as a result.

Like other collectors, Harvey was proud of his library and evidence of that pride appears in his published writings. In a passage from *Ciceronianus,* Harvey expresses this feeling:

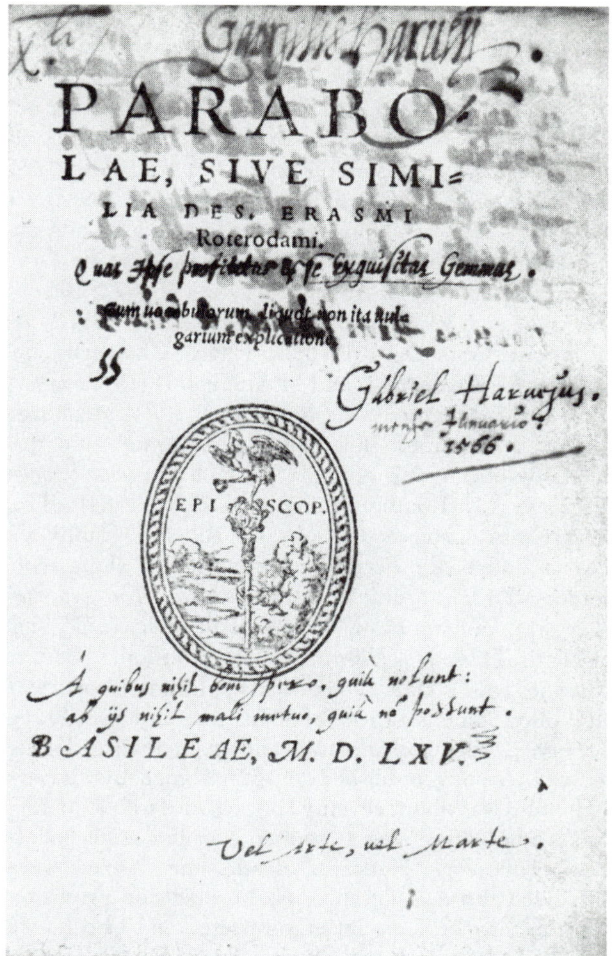

Title page for Desiderius Erasmus's Parabolae, *including autograph annotations by Harvey (Folger Shakespeare Library)*

> In my Tusculan villa . . . I have so spent my leisure that I did not seem altogether without occupation in my idleness nor without leisure amid my occupation. Often there lay at my hand . . . your friend Cicero; sometimes the champions among the historians, Caesar and Sallust (what great men were those!); or the most illustrious [Latin] poets . . . Virgil, Horace, and Ovid, writers whom I had long neglected. To tell the truth, I also had by me some of the newer writers, men who are not only lamps of the present age but ornaments of all posterity, Sturmius, Manutius, Osorius, Sigonius, and Buchanan, all of them thoroughly polished from the very school of eloquence and on so many accounts most dear to me. The rest of the more cultivated and humane authors, including all the Greeks, I left at home, caged up, as it were, in the library, as books reserved for more serious studies.

His books "uttered conversation that [he] thought delightful, and indeed nothing less than pure delight."

Harvey was no miser with his collection–it was his habit to circulate these books among his friends so that they also might benefit from them. Although the Cambridge satiric comedy *Pedantius,* which premiered on 6 February 1580, portrays Harvey as a character who had to sell many of his books when in financial trouble, Stern concludes that there is no reason to believe such an event ever really occurred. Harvey collected widely in a variety of subjects and his books were for the practical purpose of "equipping him to function in the world of his day."

In addition to the titles that reflect his major interests, he collected other books that were of use to him. For contemporary events on the European continent, he acquired three 1571 tracts by George Buchanan on Mary, Queen of Scots (*Ane admonition direct to the trew Lordis mantenaris* . . . [London: John Day, 1571], *De Maria Scotorum Regina* . . . [London: John Day, 1571, *Ane Detectioun of the duinges of Marie Queene of Scottes* . . . [London: John Day, 1571]); Roger Ascham's discourse on Germany and Charles V (*Report and Discourse of The Affaires and State of Germany and the Emperor Charles, His Court.* [London: John Day, 1570?]); David Chytraeus on Charles V, Ferdinand I, and Maximilian II (*De tribus nostrae aetatis Caesaribus Augustis, Carlo V* [Wittenburg, 1583]); and Francis Billerbege on Amurathe and the methods of Turkish diplomacy (*Most Rare and Strange Discourses* . . . [London: Thomas Hackett, 1584]). The library also contained books on the topography of France and of the Scandinavian countries, along with Jerome Turler's guide for the traveler, *The Traveller* (London: William How for Abraham Veale, 1575), and William Thomas's *Historie of Italie* (London: Thomas Marshe, 1561). Harvey kept himself informed of scientific developments throughout his life, and his library contained scientific, medical, and mathematical books as well. A book published in 1626, signed by Harvey (when he was about seventy-six), testifies to his longevity as a bookman who continued to enhance his collection. Following Harvey's death, the books were dispersed through sale because he made no provision for them to be kept intact or preserved. The books today are scattered in more than twenty-five libraries in England and America.

An analysis of Harvey's marginalia can help in understanding how he achieved his prodigious scholarship and in further characterizing his library. Harvey's earliest annotations are found in a copy of Desiderius Erasmus's *Parabolae* (Basle, 1565), which was acquired in January 1566, when Harvey was about sixteen and entering Christ's College, Cambridge. Most likely used as a college text, it collected parables and quotations from classical authors such as Plutarch, Seneca, Aristotle, Pliny, and Theophrastus. These types of books were widely used in Harvey's day and continued to be popular into the early twentieth century. As he grew older, Harvey studied the original writings of most of the great thinkers and authors, but he nonetheless treasured collections such as the *Parabolae,* because they evidently aroused his own thought. Most of these volumes in his library are heavily annotated with his comments. The *Parabolae* is clearly inscribed with Harvey's name and date in black ink, a practice he followed throughout his life with all of his books. In an immature but decorative hand, he wrote: "Gabriel Harvejus. mense Januario: 1566" and added on the title page: "A quibus nihil boni spero, quia nolunt: ab iis nihil mali metuo, puia no[n] possunt" (From those whom I hope nothing good, because they are unwilling: from these I fear nothing evil because they are unable). The volume also includes another signature of Harvey's in a large florid humanist style and a comment: "Quae ipse profitetur esse exquisitas Gemmas" (He declares that they are exquisite jewels), which is written in his later rounded italic script (probably around 1580).

In the 1560s and the early 1570s Harvey's letter formations (in English secretary, humanist, or italic script) are more angular and pinched; pen strokes are usually narrower, and there is less evenness of script and less judicious spacing than is subsequently found; from the late 1570s there is a gradual development toward greater control. Examples of this type of hand are found in the Sloane manuscript and are quite a contrast to the beautiful and decorative 1580 inscriptions of his Livy or the 1598 Geoffrey Chaucer inscriptions. Harvey's later marginalia is typified by broad pen strokes, rounded, free-flowing forms, deep intensity of ink, and usually an italic script, providing a truly ornamental appearance on the page. After about 1579 Harvey adopted a more permanent type of black ink that has resisted the ravages of time and is still relatively easy to read.

Harvey used both a secretary and an italic hand throughout his life, but the secretary is found more frequently in his early marginalia and was used primarily in his class notes written upon university texts. His beautiful italic was used almost exclusively for summarizing remarks on the flyleaves at the end of his university texts, or for observations of a generalized or philosophical nature, and in nearly all of his annotations after 1582. His handwriting is moderately large, although at times it becomes minute; the size being determined by page dimensions or other spatial limitations, but Harvey typically used an extra-large hand in order to emphasize a point. Favorite books were read and annotated several times. On the same Erasmus mentioned above one of the signatures contains a note in a firm, assured secretary hand: "Relegi mense Septembri. 1577: Gabriel Harveius," indicating a common practice of signing and dating rereadings of his books. That 1577 hand is found throughout the volume in several marginal notes. His Livy folio bears marginalia from perusals in 1568, 1580, and 1590, with each illustrating the evolving hand described above. A similar sequence of secretary or humanist followed by italic is found on pages of Sextus Julius Frontinus's *Strategemes* (1539) and Gualterus Bruele's *Praxis Medicinae Theorica* (1585).

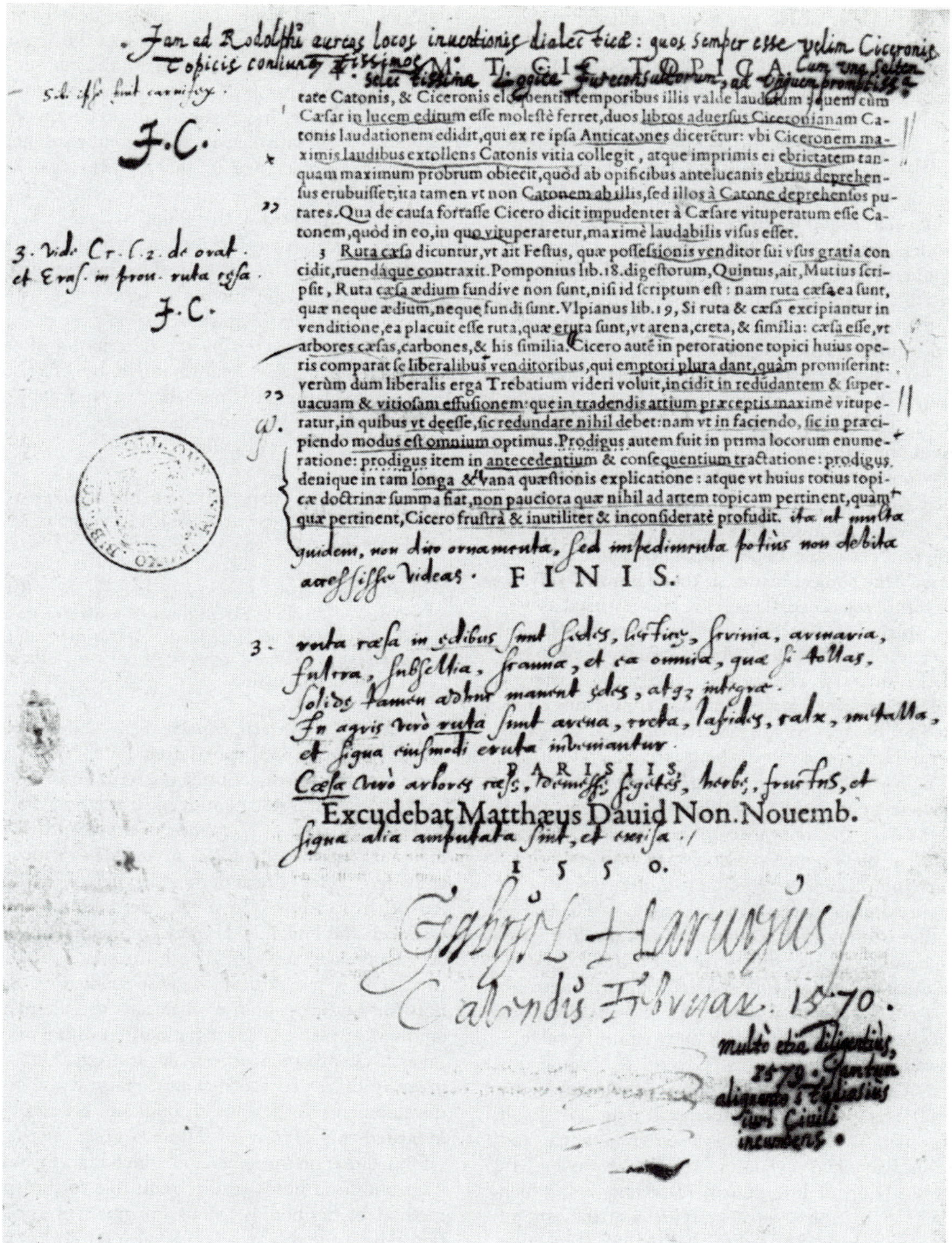

M. T. CIC. TOPICA.

tate Catonis, & Ciceronis eloquentia temporibus illis valde laudatum sequenti cùm Cæsar in lucem editum esse molestè ferret, duos libros aduersus Ciceronianam Catonis laudationem edidit, qui ex re ipsa Anticatones diceretur: vbi Ciceronem maximis laudibus extollens Catonis vitia collegit, atque imprimis ei ebrietatem tanquam maximum probrum obiecit, quòd ab opificibus antelucanis ebrius deprehensus erubuisset, ita tamen vt non Catonem ab illis, sed illos à Catone deprehensos putares. Qua de causa fortasse Cicero dicit impudenter à Cæsare vituperatum esse Catonem, quòd in eo, in quo vituperaretur, maximè laudabilis visus esset.

3 Ruta cæsa dicuntur, vt ait Festus, quæ possessionis venditor sui vsus gratia concidit, ruendáque contraxit. Pomponius lib. 18. digestorum, Quintus, ait, Mutius scripsit, Ruta cæsa ædium fundive non sunt, nisi id scriptum est: nam ruta cæsa ea sunt, quæ neque ædium, neque fundi sunt. Vlpianus lib. 19, Si ruta & cæsa excipiantur in venditione, ea placuit esse ruta, quæ eruta sunt, vt arena, creta, & similia: cæsa esse, vt arbores cæsas, carbones, & his similia. Cicero autē in peroratione topici huius operis comparat se liberalibus venditoribus, qui emptori plura dant, quàm promiserint: verùm dum liberalis erga Trebatium videri voluit, incidit in redūdantem & superuacuam & vitiosam effusionem: quę in tradendis artium præceptis maximè vituperatur, in quibus vt deesse, sic redundare nihil debet: nam vt in faciendo, sic in præcipiendo modus est omnium optimus. Prodigus autem fuit in prima locorum enumeratione: prodigus item in antecedentium & consequentium tractatione: prodigus denique in tam longa & vana quæstionis explicatione: atque vt huius totius topicæ doctrinæ summa fiat, non pauciora quæ nihil ad artem topicam pertinent, quàm quæ pertinent, Cicero frustrà & inutiliter & inconsideratè profudit. ita ut multa quidem, non dico ornamenta, sed impedimenta potius non debita accessisse videas.

FINIS.

PARISIIS,
Excudebat Matthæus Dauid Non. Nouemb.
1550.

Gabriel Harueius
Calendis Februar. 1570.

Last page of the 1550 edition of Cicero's Topica, *including marginal annotations by Harvey (courtesy of the Warden and Fellows of All Souls College, Oxford)*

Many studies of Harvey's marginalia have been conducted, including that of Smith in 1913. Smith listed 53 extant books of Harvey's and published selected annotations from 26 of them together with notes from two Harvey-owned manuscripts, thus providing a good sampling of the writings. In 1948 Harold S. Wilson described Harvey's well-organized system of annotation illuminating his use of particular symbols or comments to classify subjects and his careful cross-referencing. Harvey also used chalklike markings (usually red or green) throughout the text of several of his books, but the meaning of these marks is not known. Some have suggested they represent sections studied or passages assigned to his students, but these explanations do not account for all of the markings. For serious bibliographical analyses of some of the books from Harvey's library, one should turn to publications on one or more individual annotated volumes by Caroline Ruutz-Rees, Gregory Smith, Caroline Bourland, John Lievsay, and Eleanor Relle.

Harvey's comments are roughly of three types. First, there are concise notations or marginal symbols that classify the subject matter to make it quickly available for future reference. Generally, Harvey used abbreviations, planetary, and diagrammatic symbols. For example, the symbol for Mars designated matters related to military affairs or strategy; an asterisk denoted astronomy; a large and small contiguous circle was used for controversy; a bisected circle for the earth or natural history; the sun for kingship.

The second type is made up of Harvey's critical and supplementary comments on ideas in the text, sometimes revealing the relevance to historical or current problems. In Sir Thomas Wilson's *Art of Rhetorike . . .* (London: Jhon Kingston, 1567), the author wrote (with italics representing Harvey's underlinings): "He *hath no fellowe,* ther is none such, I thinke he will not live long, he is so honest a manne; the more *pitye that suche good fellowes shoulde know what death meaneth.* But it maketh no matter, *when he is* gone, all the *worlde will speake of hym,* his name *shall never dye,* he is so well knowen universallie.*" By the asterisk, Harvey notes "Greene, & Nash at this instant." Another page of the same text discusses the power of jesting and the greater harm that may result when a man is wrongfully accused in a witty and humorous way. Harvey notes: "Nash the rayler." In Harvey's edition of Frontinus's *The Strategemes,* which he bought in 1578, he added marginalia at the time of purchase, again in 1580, and finally in 1588. The book treats military maneuvers used in classical times and compares them to contemporary military problems in the Netherlands or relates them to situations of the English and Spanish forces during the time of the Armada. In one section, Frontinus discusses various stategies used to gain entry into a heavily fortified enemy camp, one being the donning of the apparel of a slain enemy leader. Harvey wrote in the margin: "How easely might Sr Humfry Gilbert, of Captain Forbusher, or Captain Drake, have gained sum lyke opportunity? The Spaniards with bribes, have greatly advancid his [Philip II's] procedings in the low cuntrys, & other places. Corruption, the great strategem of Philip of Macedonia: and now of this Philip of Spain." Further in the text, Harvey reacts to the account of Cassius's setting fire to several of his own ships and sending them into the midst of the enemy by writing: "Owr Inglish pollicy against the Spanish Armada, this other day." Another note, triggered by the description of the capture of a formidable Spanish town by Cato's forces (made possible by traveling what was normally a four-day journey in only two days, thus surprising the enemy) was written in Latin:

> At nihil tale feci. Ad polyhistorem, ista aliquid: sed quid ad Gabrielem Harveium? Nihil loci communes, sine propria Industria.
>
> But nothing of the sort have I accomplished. [I have progressed] to some extent towards a man of learning but what [have I accomplished] towards the man Gabriel Harvey? Without industry of one's own there are no topics for discussion.

In A. P. Gasser's *Historiarum, et Chronicorum Totius Mundi Epitome* (1538), purchased by Harvey in 1576, there are brief manuscript characterizations of some of the historical figures mentioned in the text. For example, Harvey writes: "*Tamerlane* of a lusty stowt Heardman, a most valiant & invincible Prynce," and elsewhere, "Georg Scanderbeg, Prynce of the Epirotes. An other Pyrrhus." In a text describing "Swedland, Gotland, and Finland," Harvey comments on the "Swecian Language" next to "The Lordes Prayer" in Swedish: "The same radical of owre Inglish, & Scottish: notwithstanding sundrie dialects, or idioms, even amongst owrselves." Near the bottom of the prayer, he notes: "Ut prosodia differt, sic orthographia" (As the prosody differs so the spelling). Harvey also followed developments in science throughout his life. This is indicated in his copy of Thomas Hill's *Schoole of Skil* (1599), a text on the sphere, in which Harvey observed: "Astronomical notes readily reducible to the spherical method of Scribonius, or to Freigius's physical questions about the sphere. [This is] also the sort of practice of our Blundevill in his clear tract on the sphere, recently published."

The third type of annotation consists of personal reflections, introspections, and precepts. As Stern recognized, "From the first and second kind of annotation, classification of subject matter, and critical and supplementary comments on the text, one derives an understanding of Harvey's scholarly methods and erudition, but it is from the second and third kind that one learns particularly of his attitudes and feelings." For example, an Italian publication of short anecdotes, Lodovico Domenichi's *Facetie, motti, et burle, di diversi signori et persone private* (1571), prompted Harvey to provide a number of thoughtful reflections. In terms of subject matter, Harvey's notes can be organized into nine categories, with books from each category that contain extensive annotations.

Throughout his marginalia, Harvey utilized six personae to present his views and represent himself. Axiophilus represents the poet, the "lover of the worthwhile": Angelus Furius, the Italianate Harvey, is "angelic in speech and a fury in action"; Eutrapelus, the most frequent persona, portrays the "eloquent orator, teacher of rhetoric, persuasive man in speech (and in writing) and one who engages in witty jesting and very often in irony"; Eudromus is "the pragmatic, hurrying competitive man of the world . . . constantly striving to excel"; Chrystechus refers to "the man with the golden skill" in a field, most often law; and Euscopius, a persona of Harvey's later years, represents "the sharp-sighted man" whose sensible perception provides the means for him to benefit amid frustration. As Wayne Erickson notes, Harvey's personae appear most abundantly in marginalia written between the late 1570s and at least 1608 in his editions of Lodovico Domenichi's *Facetie, motti, et burle, di diversi signori et persone private, Motti Diversi Raccolti* by Thomas Porcacchi (1574), and Ludovico Guicciardini's *Detti et Fatti* (1571). These private writings record Harvey's "ingenuous psychotherapeutic excursions into his own vulnerabilities." More specifically, the marginalia can be grouped into several units: oratory and eloquent written expression, history and politics, modern languages, gentlemanly learning, jurisprudence, cosmology and other sciences and pseudosciences, medicine, literature, and philosophical outlook and personal observation.

Included in the category of "Oratory and Eloquent Written Expression" is: a tiny, vellum-bound volume of selections from Demosthenes, *Gnomologiae* and *Similia* (sayings extracted from his speeches and epistles); spiritual sententiae of Bishop Gregory Nazianzen; the *Arithmologia Ethica;* and excerpts from Isocrates and others. A comment on one of the signatures indicates Harvey may have carried this volume with him frequently: "One of my pockettings, and familiar spirits." He wrote that so long as he had this book he would miss none of the other Greek writers if suddenly their books were no longer available. The Demosthenes volume possessed the strength and charm of the Greek language. Comparing Demosthenes to Cicero as an orator, the former was, Harvey felt, more concise and vigorous. Harvey also praised the eloquence of Epictetus, Isocrates, Dion, the "Hymn to Apollo," Julian's *Misopogon,* Eunapius, Philostratus's *Sophistae,* and the "exquisite judgement of Dionysius of Halicarnassus on Thucydides and on Demosthenes himself." Dating from the late 1570s is marginalia written in Harvey's copy of *Parabolae* that indicates his conception of good and poor oratory: "Nothing more pleasing than a brilliant and facile speech; than an affected and officious one, nothing more disagreeable. The sweetest eloquence flows smoothly but it should have neither too much honey nor too much salt." In his copy of M. Fabius Quintilian's *M. Fabii Quintiliani oratoris eleoquentissimi . . .* (Paris: Rob. Stephanus, 1542), Harvey comments that Chaucer, Thomas More, and John Jewel are very vivacious talents and that John Heywood, Philip Sidney, and Spenser are three "natural geniuses." Other illustrious English talents noted are Thomas Smith, Roger Ascham, Thomas Wilson, Leonard Digges, Thomas Blundeville, and Richard Hakluyt. A long note on the last printed page of his Quintilian concerned the Italian writer Pietro Aretino: "He is a simple orator that cannot mount as high as the quality or quantity of his matter requireth. Vain and fantastical amplifications argue an idle brain. But when the very majesty and dignity of the matter itself will indeed bear out a stately and haughty style, there is no such trial of a gallant discourser and right orator. Always an especial regard to be had of decorum, as well for orators and all manner of parleys as in other actions."

Harvey was a lifelong student of classical history and politics and his copy of Titus Livy's *Romanae Historiae Principis . . .* (Basle: Jonnes Heruagios, 1555) is profusely annotated with dated signatures implying his use of the work in 1568, 1580, and 1590. The hands span the secretary and italic, and, among many references to contemporary English political figures, Harvey mentions that Sir Edward Dyer and Sir Edward Dennie thanked him for information. Harvey's volume on Livy contains frequent memoranda on recommended readings in the field of Greek and Roman history. He believed that a knowledge of classical history brings together for the learned man a connected chain of events in uninterrupted succession and that such a chain facilitates a better understanding of the present–the sources of that chain begin with Herodotus, then move on to Xenophon, Dionysius of Halicarnassus, Polybius, Livy, and so on. Along with Tacitus, Harvey admired Livy's writing style, his knowledge of Roman jurisprudence, and his reverent treatment of subject matter. He also believed Livy's work to be packed with useful information on civil law and felt the same about Tacitus and Frontinus. He was, it is not surprising, quite demanding in his assessment of historians and

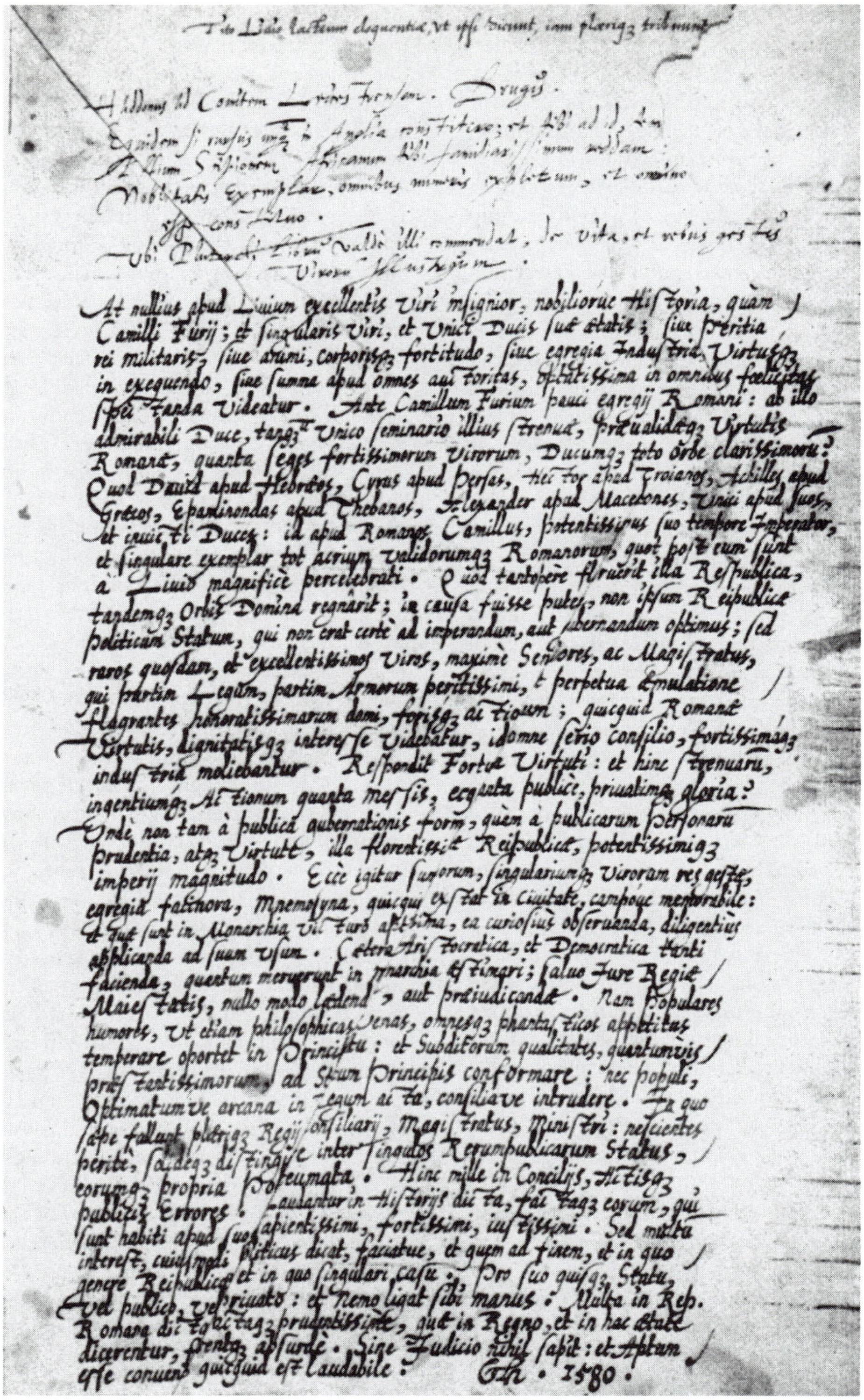

Flyleaf from a 1555 folio edition of Livy's Romanae Historiae Principis, Decades Tres, *including autograph comments by Harvey (from Virginia F. Stern,* Gabriel Harvey: His Life, Marginalia and Library, *1979)*

commented on the second-rate ones he encountered in his day:

> But today there are many asses who dare to compile histories, chronicles, annals, commentaries as, for example, Grafton, Stowe, Holinshed, and a few others like them who are not cognizant of law or politics, nor of the art of depicting character, nor are they in any way learned. How long shall we yearn for the British Livy? . . . Or when will there emerge a British Tacitus or Frontinus? We abound in petty things but how dry is our record of matters of pragmatic or military import. Almost the only men who approach former art and industry are More and Ascham. After all, even Camden, Hakluyt, . . .

(the passage was left unfinished).

Harvey demonstrated an interest in the character traits of outstanding men and what caused them to succeed. He carefully studied those he most admired. For example, on Hannibal, Harvey commented: "Annibal a craftie Foxe & even for theise days a notable example. The finest Politicians, or Pragmaticians may find in Livie to serve their turne." For Harvey, to know Livy was to know the world and study of the historian provided a great deal of practical worldly wisdom. In fact, many examples of marginalia reveal that Livy often inspired the academician to consider foregoing the world of letters and become a man of action. Harvey's books and marginalia also reveal that he was well versed in classical and biblical history and in Renaissance events and politics. It was through such studies and historical biographies that he hoped to gain the insight and resourcefulness to become a great man himself. In his copy of Quintilian, he wrote: "Without great knowledge and enormous virtue no one is a great man, for the highest knowledge requires a loftier spirit and is animated by enduring virtue." Great men are usually gifted orators, as well–for example, Cardinal Thomas Wolsey, Prorex Thomas Cromwell, Chancellor More, Archbishop Thomas Cranmer, Sir Francis Bacon, and others are tagged by Harvey for their skills in oratory.

Harvey's notes often indicate an interest in statesmanship. In J. T. Freigius's *Mosaicus; Continens Historiam Ecclesiasticam* (Basle, 1583), a work that discusses prominent biblical figures from Adam to Moses, Harvey wrote that without religion it was impossible to find a new state or to destroy an old one. Without some divine worship, it was impossible, he believed, to sustain politically a public or private state–thereby voicing his opposition to the "Machiavellians" and "Atheists" who thought it possible to govern republics while allowing neglect and contempt of religion. On the title page of his copy of Joannis Foorth's *Synopsis Politica* (London: H. Bynneman, 1582), Harvey expresses his advocation of the active over the contemplative life. He desired to better understand the qualities that led to success in the realm of active, vigorous life. In his copy of Foorth he notes, "But fower right politiques of late memory: Wulsey, Crumwell: Gardiner: & Cicill. All the rest, children in comparison. But noovices, & pupills in pollicy. Incipients: not perficients." Comments elsewhere in the volume illustrate an interest in Stephen Gardiner arising from Sir Thomas Smith's many personal observations on the man. In John Florio's *First Fruites* (London: Thomas Dawson, 1578), Harvey filled the last thirteen pages with notes on Gardiner, perhaps with a view toward writing "The politique history of Doctor Stephen Gardiner, bishop of Winchester, & afterward L. Chancelour of Ingland." These notes are categorized as "Language, Lawe, Industrie, and confidence: temperance, & excercise. His singular perfection, experience, and cunning practis in the affaires of the world." At the top of another signature, Harvey describes Gardiner: "A man reputed singularly wise, politique, & learned: especially in *Lawe,* and matters of *state.* A man much emploied in greatest *Councells, Ambassages, Judgments,* and all Occurences of *state*: next his master, *Cardinall Wolsey*: even above his fellow, the famous Lord Cromwell: an other rare politician in his kinde, & Experimenter of Fortune, by a singular Industry, & Audacity." The marginal notes include sayings by Gardiner, quotations from his letters, and opinions from contemporaries and show Harvey's attempt to present the information as an impartial critic. His marginalia are often as revealing and illuminating as the books upon which they are written. For example, in the Florio book, Harvey writes: "As memorials of Gabriel Harvey, regal, noble, gentlemanly ones, of the people, pragmatic in every way, very much of the people but not vulgar."

Regarding the category of "Modern Languages," Florio's teaching manual for Italian conversation, *First Fruites,* includes Harvey's marginalia related to the study of modern languages (along with the comments on Gardiner). On one signature he declares, "Florio, & Eliot [teacher of French and author of *Ortho-epia Gallica,* 1593] mie new London companions for Italian, & French. Two of the best for both." In his youth, Harvey became proficient in Latin and Greek and used these two languages in his marginalia, but around 1578 he decided to study Italian and French, since these languages were important for life at court (to which he aspired). He admired the language skills of the earl of Leicester, Sir Christopher Hatton, and Sidney and he too wanted to attain their fluency in Italian. On an early signature of his Florio, Harvey lamented the fact that he did not have the same proficiency as those outstanding English courtiers. Although he learned the principles of law in three days, he wondered why was it not possible to learn the Italian language which is similar to Latin in two or three days. Queen Elizabeth had remarked that he had the face of an Italian; why could he not have the tongue of one as well? Addressing Florio, Harvey notes: "How often have you instantaneously created blossoming Italians? . . . Florio and [William] Thomas in close connection will intensely inspire me with their language. This I shall learn, for where love exists there does the eye fasten itself. . . . Repeat, repeat as the ardent trainer of a gladiator would do!" He did make progress in Italian because in 1580 he read the "First Decade" of Machiavelli's *Discorsi* and inscribed marginalia in Italian (for example, in his copies of Lodovico Guicciardini's *Detti et Fatti Piacevoli* . . . [Venice: de Zanetti, 1571], Lodovico Domenichi's *Facetie, motti, et burle* . . . [Venice: Muschio, 1571], Thomaso Porcacchi's *Motti Diversi Raccolti* . . . [Venice: Muschio, 1574], and S. Stefano Guazzo's *La Civil conversation* . . . [Venice: Perchino, 1581]). Other books used by Harvey for the study of Italian (and annotated by him) include grammars by William Thomas (1550), Scipio Lentulo (1575), and Claudius Holyband (1575).

In the late 1570s and early 1580s Harvey began to acquire and study books on the French language: Claudius Holyband's *French Littleton* (1576); Pierre Du Ploiche's *Treatise in English and French* (1578), annotated by Harvey in 1580; and *Images of the Old Testament* (1549), a volume comprising twenty-four woodcuts captioned in French and English, which Harvey acquired in 1580. Harvey read François Rabelais and other French authors in the original, but very little of his marginalia was written in French. It is likely that his command of that language never reached the level of his Italian. He also studied Spanish in the early 1590s, using Antonio de Corro's *Spanish Grammar* (1590) and Richard Perceval's *Bibliotheca Hispanica* (1591), an English, Spanish, and Latin dictionary printed as an adjunct to Corro's grammar. On a signature in his Corro, Harvey recommends several Spanish books–some of which were available only in Spanish, so he did manage to read something of the language–but there are no annotations in Spanish in his books outside of a rudimentary phrase such as "Poco, y bueno" (short and good), advice that he gave himself as he studied languages. On the proper way to master languages, Harvey wrote in his Pierre Du Ploiche: "A paradox in lerning: [By whatever more, by this the less.] Beginners must not leap over hastely, lest they overleape all. Apt & reddy pronunciation of the Alphabet, one weeks exercise." Annotations in his Spanish grammar indicate, however, that Harvey had trouble with the pronunciation of French. He believed that to speak it properly one should "heare a French man pronounce it." Harvey, the Elizabethan, recorded his admiration for his Queen's linguistic skills in his Florio: "The Queen commendid by Utenhovius [the multilingual poet] and M. Ascham, not only for her Latin, & Greek, but also for her French, Italian, & Spanish. [As accomplished in speaking as in comprehending.]"

Harvey's desire to obtain an appointment at court led him into the serious study of languages he might not otherwise have attempted. The same desire influenced his study in courtly manners and arts. In about 1580 he observed in Sir Thomas Hoby's 1561 translation of Baldassare Castiglione's *The Courtier,* "A Courtier must do, & speak everie thing aswell, as possibly he can: yet with such a dexteritie, & such negligent diligence, that all may think, he might do much better, if he woold." It seems that this negligent diligence was alien to Harvey's nature. His natural pride in learning to do anything well abounds in his marginalia, and he lists aphorisms for the courtier in *The Courtier:* "No excellent grace, or fine cumlie behavious without three cunning properties: a sound judgment to informe; an apt dexteritie to conforme; & an earnest intention to performe. The rarest men extend their utterest possibilitie, with a fine (as it were) familiar sleight: & they that do not enforce themselves to display their best, cum ever short of their reckoning." Harvey sums up Castiglione's portrayal of the desired characteristics of a courtier at the end of the translation:

> Above all things it importeth a Courtier, to be gracefull & lovelie in countenance & behaviour; fine & discreet in discourse, & interteinment; skilfull & expert in Letters, & Armes; active & gallant in everie Courtlie Exercise; nimble & speedie of boddie & mind; resolute, industrious & valorous in action as profound & invincible in execution, as is possible: & withall ever generously bould, wittily pleasant, & full of life in all his sayings & doings. His apparrel must be like himself, cumlie & handsom; fine & clenlie to avoid contempt, but not gorgeous or statelie to incurr envie, or suspicion of pride, vanitie, selfloove, or other imperfection. Both inside, & outside, must be a faire paterne of wothie, fine, & Lovelie Vertu.

Harvey comments on being nimble of body in a later signature, close to Castiglione's listing of "marciall feats both on horsebacke and a foote" and other physical activities in which a courtier should be accomplished. Near two items related to horseback riding, the hopeful courtier notes "Ars Blundevili," a reference to his much annotated copy of Thomas Blundevill's *The fower chiefest Offices belonging to Horsemanship. . . . The office of the Breeder; of the rider; of the Keeper; and of the Herrer* (1580). Also in Harvey's copy of *The Courtier* is a listing of exercises in which the courtier should be proficient, including swimming, running, vaulting, wrestling, stone casting, casting the "barr," tilting, tourneying, fighting at barriers, and flinging a spear or dart. Harvey apparently did not engage in any of the courtly manifestations of expertise, since he comments on none of them. Of interest is the fact that courtly jesting seems to have been fascinating to Harvey, and he comments in this regard in book 2 of *The Courtier* and its section on this topic. Topping one signature, he inscribed: "The Art of Jesting: pleasurable, & gratious." Elsewhere in the same volume, Harvey observes that in the art of jesting Plato was cold, Isocrates silly, and Demosthenes skilled in the art of pleasing. The quantity of marginalia in Harvey's books related to jesting is plentiful and includes writings in other books from his library, such as Thomas Wilson's *Arte of Rhetorike* (1567) and Lodovico Guicciardini's *Detti et Fatti* (1571). In the latter book, Harvey advocated the combination of urbanity and political skill: "Give me the urbane man skilled in civil affairs, as much politically oriented as elegant: the only combination of cunning wit and stratagems, one who is capable of being of best use at that moment. A hook of favour and fit occasion should always be hanging down to you." Harvey was also aware that courtesy and civility should preclude displays of anger, and comments to this effect are found in his copies of Hoby's translation of Castiglioine's *The Courtier* (London: W. Seres, 1561), and Foorth's *Synopsis Politica* (London: H. Bynneman, 1582).

Harvey's marginalia also includes comments referring to his study of the techniques of warfare. Extensive notes are found in his copies of Frontinus's *The strategemes, sleyghtes, and policies of warre gathered together* . . . (translated by Richard Morysine, 1539); Niccolò Machiavelli's *Arte of Warre* (translated by Peter Whitehorne, 1573); and Whitehorne's *Certaine wayes for ordering of Soldiours in battleray* (1573). Harvey esteemed the law as a profession, and in Latin inscriptions in Joachim Hopperus's *In veram Jurisprudentiam Isagoges* (1580) he credited jurisprudence as being the master builder, the governor of the republic, protectress of remains, queen of arts, and the kingly and imperial profession. His study of civil law rather than common law was grounded upon his aspirations to serve at court. In his edition of John Florio, he remarks that the law can be abused, and in Foorth's *Synopsis Politica,* he emphasizes the importance of keeping the law alive and healthy. Marginalia in his edition of Hopperus also presents Harvey's opinions on the law and jurisprudence. Of the twelve extant law texts owned by Harvey, most treat canon or civil law. Other books in his library and their marginalia confirm that Harvey was an avid student of cosmology and astronomy (as, for example, his editions of Joannis de Sacrobosco's *Textus de Sphaera* . . . [Paris: S. Colinaeus, 1527] and Firminus's *Firmini Reportorium de mutatione* . . . [Paris: J. Kerver, 1539]); navigation (John Blagrave's *The Mathmatical Jewel* [London: W. Venge, 1585]); and astrology (Luca Gaurico's *Lacae Gaurici Geoophonensis* [Venice: Navo, 1552]).

When Harvey became a medical fellow at Pembroke in 1584, he turned to the study of medicine. Increasingly he became aware of the limitations of astrological-oriented medicine and soon favored the theories of Bruele and the empirical practice of medicine (he owned Gualterus Bruele's *Praxis medicinae theorica, et empirica familiarissima* [Antwerp: Plantin, 1585]). He also had Hieronymus von Braunschweig's *Apothecarye,* printed in Antwerp by Birckman in 1561, and its marginalia evaluated early physicians and medical writers. Harvey preferred Bruele, however, and his notes include aides to diagnosis along with various and sundry remedies, including herbal concoctions or common sense physiological or psychological measures (some being quite fanciful by the standards of today). Medical-related marginalia are also found in nonmedical books from Harvey's library: Olaus Magnus's *Historia de gentibus Septentrionalibus* (1555), a history of the Goths, contains a page filled with Harvey's manuscript discussion of the gout and cures for it. A poem by "Axiophilus" (Harvey's name for himself as a poet and lover of poetry) is included in Harvey's copy of James VI's *Essayes of a Prentise in the divine art or poesie* (Edinburgh: T. Vautrollier, 1585); it reveals his sympathy for the mentally ill:

A charme for a mad wooman
O heavenlie Medcin, Panacea high,
Restore this raging Wooman to her health,
More Worth then hugest Summes of worldlie Wealth
Exceedingly more worth then anie Wealth.

O light of Grace, & Reason from the Skie,
Illuminate her madd-conceipted minde,
And Melancholie cease her wittes to blinde.
Cease fearful Melancholie her wittes to blinde.
Axiophilus.

Probably the best known of Harvey's marginalia are related to literature and drama. In 1598 he annotated a newly bought folio of Chaucer's life and works (along with works by John Lydgate) and most likely circulated the volume, titled *The woorkes of our ancient and lerned English poet* . . . (London: G. Bishop, 1598), among his friends, who were thereby an audience for his thoughts and opinions. Harvey's Chaucer includes black-ink underscores and brief manuscript comments related to the text and two half-pages of literary appraisals. Harvey admired Chaucer's craftsmanship and his use of imagery displaying astronomical learning. In his copy of Dionise Alexandrine's *Serveye of the World* (1592)

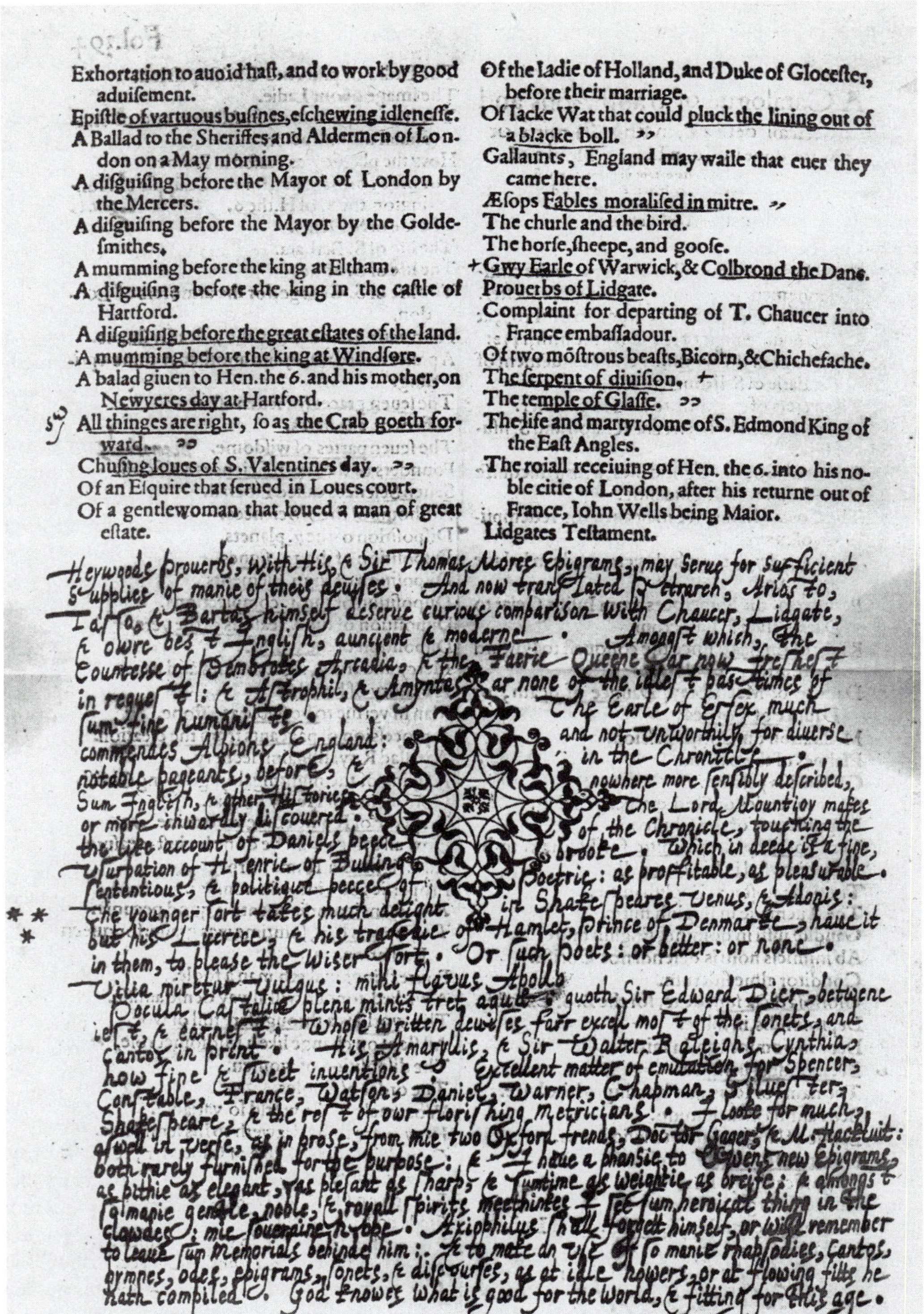

Fol. 394

Exhortation to auoid hast, and to work by good aduisement.
Epistle of vartuous busines, eschewing idlenesse.
A Ballad to the Sheriffes and Aldermen of London on a May morning.
A disguising before the Mayor of London by the Mercers.
A disguising before the Mayor by the Goldesmithes.
A mumming before the king at Eltham.
A disguising before the king in the castle of Hartford.
A disguising before the great estates of the land.
A mumming before the king at Windsore.
A balad giuen to Hen. the 6. and his mother, on Newyeres day at Hartford.
All thinges are right, so as the Crab goeth forward.
Chusing loues of S. Valentines day.
Of an Esquire that serued in Loues court.
Of a gentlewoman that loued a man of great estate.
Of the ladie of Holland, and Duke of Glocester, before their marriage.
Of Iacke Wat that could pluck the lining out of a blacke boll.
Gallaunts, England may waile that euer they came here.
Æsops Fables moralised in mitre.
The churle and the bird.
The horse, sheepe, and goose.
Gwy Earle of Warwick, & Colbrond the Dane.
Prouerbs of Lidgate.
Complaint for departing of T. Chaucer into France embassadour.
Of two mõstrous beasts, Bicorn, & Chichefache.
The serpent of diuision.
The temple of Glasse.
The life and martyrdome of S. Edmond King of the East Angles.
The roiall receiuing of Hen. the 6. into his noble citie of London, after his returne out of France, Iohn Wells being Maior.
Lidgates Testament.

Heywoods prouerbs, with His, & Sir Thomas Mores Epigrams, may serue for sufficient supplies of manie of theis deuises. And now translated Petrarch, Ariosto, Tasso, & Bartas himself deserue curious comparison with Chaucer, Lidgate, & owre best English, auncient & moderne. Amongst which, the Countesse of Pembrokes Arcadia, & the Faerie Queene ar now freshest in request: & Astrophil, & Amyntas ar none of the idlest pastimes of sum fine humanists. The Earle of Essex much commendes Albions England: and not unworthily for diuerse notable pageants, before, & in the Chronicle. Sum English, & other Histories nowhere more sensibly described, or more inwardly discouered. The Lord Mountioy makes the like account of Daniels peece of the Chronicle, touching the Usurpation of Henrie of Bullingbrooke. Which in deede is a fine, sententious, & politique peece of Poetrie: as proffitable, as pleasurable. The younger sort takes much delight in Shakespeares Venus, & Adonis: but his Lucrece, & his tragedie of Hamlet, Prince of Denmarke, haue it in them, to please the wiser sort. Or such poets: or better: or none.
Vilia miretur vulgus: mihi flavus Apollo Pocula Castaliae plena ministret aquae: quoth Sir Edward Dier, betwene iest, & earnest. Whose written deuises farr excell most of the sonets, and cantos in print. His Amaryllis, & Sir Walter Raleighs Cynthia, how fine & sweet inuentions? Excellent matter of emulation for Spencer, Constable, France, Watson, Daniel, Warner, Chapman, Siluester, Shakespeare, & the rest of owr florishing metricians. I looke for much, aswell in verse, as in prose, from mie two Oxford frends, Doctor Gager, & M. Hackluit: both rarely furnished for the purpose: & I haue a phansie to Owens new Epigrams, as pithie as elegant, as plesant as sharp, & sumtime as weightie as breife: & amongst so manie gentle, noble, & royall spirits meethinkes I see sum heroical thing in the clowdes: mie souerayne hope. Axiophilus shall forgett himself, or will remember to leaue sum memorials behinde him: & to make an vse of so manie rhapsodies, cantos, hymnes, odes, epigrams, sonets, & discourses, as at idle howers, or at flowing fittes he hath compiled. God knowes what is good for the world, & fitting for this age.

Page from Thomas Speght's 1598 edition of Geoffrey Chaucer's poems. Harvey's marginal comments provided scholars with an important clue as to the date of composition of William Shakespeare's Hamlet *(from G. C. Moore Smith,* Gabriel Harvey's Marginalia, *1913).*

Harvey praised Chaucer by writing on the verso of the second flyleaf preceding the title page, "It is not sufficient for poets, to be superficial humanists: but they must be exquisite artists, and curious universal schollers." In his edition of Chaucer, Harvey lamented the lack of writers who could match the standards of such authors as Chaucer, Lydgate, John Gower, Thomas Occleve, John Heywood, and Spenser. Harvey utilized at least three personae to express certain aspects of his own personality or interests in his marginalia: "Axiophilus," a writer or lover of worthy poetry; "Chrysotechnus" is one whose technical excellence is golden; and "Anonymus" cannot achieve recognition in his own name. Harvey also comments on his own literary efforts:

> No marvell, thowgh Axiophilus be so slowe in publishing his exercises, that is so hastie in dispatching them: being one, that rigorously censures himself; unpartially examines other; & deemes nothing honorable, or commendable in a poet, that is not divine, or illuminate, sungular, or rare; excellent, or sum way notable. I dowby not, but it is the case of manie other, that have drunk the pure water of the virgin fountaine. And Chrysotechnus esteemes a singular poet worth his weight in gould: but accountes a mean versifier a Cipher in the algorisme of the first publisher: who imitated none, but the harmonie of heaven; and published none but goulden verses. . . . More of Chaucer, & his Inglish traine in a familiar discourse of Anonymus.

The Chaucer folio also includes marginalia expressing Harvey's high esteem for Francesco Petrarch, Ludovico Ariosto, Torquato Tasso, and Seigneur du Bartas. He lists among "owre best Inglish" the "Countesse of Pembrokes Arcadia, & the Faerie Queene . . . & Astrophil, & Amyntas." Harvey comments upon Shakespeare's *Hamlet* (circa 1601) and the annotation has been used by scholars to help date this play. Three stars accompany Harvey's remarks on the popularity of various of Shakespeare's works among the "younger sort" and the "wiser sort." Harvey also mentions Shakespeare's *Richard III* (circa 1594) and *Hamlet* in marginalia found in his copy of Guicciardini's *Detti et Fatti.* Since none of Harvey's writings were published under his own name after 1593, his marginalia served as a channel for his creative and literary energies. In 1904 Gregory Smith's *Elizabethan Critical Essays* reprinted Harvey's marginalia in George Gascoigne's *Certaine Notes of Instruction* (15??), and Smith considers the notes to be evidence of Harvey's sound approach to literary criticism.

It is in the category of philosophical outlook and personal observations that Harvey most used his six personae. Moreover, most of Harvey's personal observations are found in eight books, the aforementioned volumes by Domenichi, Guicciardini, Demosthenes, Foorth, Quintilian and Chaucer, and also Joannes Ramus's *Oikonomia seu Dispositio Regularum* (Cologne: Monocerotis, 1570) and James VI of Scotland's *The Essays of a prentise in the divine art of poesie.* "Axiophilus" is the name by which Harvey refers to himself as a poet in the broad sense–one who is sensitive to the finer and nobler values of life. Original poems written by Harvey in his marginalia are most often signed "Axiophilus," and this persona acts as literary and poetic critic, most notably in the Chaucer annotations in discussions of contemporary writers and the future of English literature and poetry. "Angelus Furius," angelic in speech and a fury in action, refers to Harvey's experiences (either anticipated or actual) in Italy. In Foorth's *Synopsis Politica,* Harvey wrote: "Angelus Furius, the most eloquent Discourser, & most active Courser, not in this on Towne, or in that on Citty; but in all Italy, yea in all Christendome, yea even in the whole Universal Worlde. No on so persuasively eloquent; or so incessantly industrious."

"Eutrapelus"–one who is clever and ingenious with words–is the most frequent of Harvey's persona and, unlike "Angelus Furius," was used throughout Harvey's lifetime. In Domenichi's *Facetie* (1571), Harvey notes "Eutrapelus scornes himself, till he teaches all other, to pronounce more sensibly; to expresse more lively; to speake more effectually; to resolve & persuade more powrefully, then anie heretofore. Lett Eutrapelus excell all other in speaking, designing and doing: or lett Eutrapelus be accounted a meacock, & a base fellow." Harvey's "Eudromus" was the pragmatic, hurrying, competitive man of the world who was constantly striving to excel. According to Harvey, he "cares for the pure practical uses of arts and opportunities and wishes to be outstanding among men, in manly accomplishments."

"Chrysotechnus" was a persona used by Harvey during the period in which he was studying law; he was a man with golden skill. In the field of law, "Chrysotechnus" was "pleasing in amiable discretion as conspicuous in glorious magnificence. The golden elegance of Simon: suffused with the candour of the graces. Nor is Chrysotechnus given to hateful pride nor to begging but rather to amiable pleasantness." The persona was also presented as one skilled as a verse technician.

"Euscopius" was created by Harvey in later years: he is a sharp-sighted man who lives an energetic, full life. In his Domenichi, Harvey referred to "The indestructible core of Euscopius in many lives. But here and now is one carefully fashioned, absolutely different, and very aptly adjusted to the world." He is, as Harvey, one who lived many lives (teacher, orator, courtier, writer, and civil lawyer) who was thwarted in some way in each of them but who managed to survive and continue on.

Scholars cannot truly know why Harvey created and used these personae. Perhaps it was, as Stern suggests, a form of therapy for an often disappointed man: "His *personae* perform in a distinguished way both in discussions and negotiations. Writing of their exploits and subsequently reading about them can be considered a kind of self-therapy for Harvey to help him avoid melancholy or bitterness and maintain the cheerful demeanor for which he strove."

Harvey also found ease and comfort in his large, magnificent library, his most cherished possession. One might argue that his library presents the truest portrait of Harvey. Stern notes, "He is here revealed not by the acid pen of a contemporary but through his treasured books and voluminous records–the man of erudition who aspired to make his personal imprint upon the sands of history, left little mark, but retained indomitable spirit and health well beyond the limits of most men of his day. In addition, Harvey's marginalia constitute a unique and intimate memorial of his age. His notes tell us what he thought and felt and dreamed of. If Harvey was right in believing that each of us is a microcosm of all mankind, then this most prolific of annotators has left us a rich account of the intellectual life and interests of his times."

Letters:

The Works of Edmund Spenser: A Variorum Edition, volume 9, edited by Edwin Greenlaw and others (Baltimore: Johns Hopkins University Press, 1932–1957), pp. 1–18, 441–477;

Spenser: Poetical Works, edited by J. C. Smith and E. de Selincourt (London: Oxford University Press, 1966), pp. 609–643.

Bibliography:

The Works of Thomas Nashe, volume 5, edited by Ronald B. McKerrow (London: Sidgwick & Jackson, 1910), pp. 163–175.

Biography:

Virginia F. Stern, *Gabriel Harvey: His Life, Marginalia, and Library* (Oxford: Clarendon Press, 1979), pp. 3–134.

References:

Josephine Waters Bennett, "Spenser and Gabriel Harvey's *Letter-Book,*" *Modern Philology,* 29 (August 1931): 163–186;

Caroline Bourland, "Gabriel Harvey and the Modern Languages," *HLQ,* 4 (1940): 85–106;

Carroll Camden Jr., "Some Unnoted Harvey Marginalia," *PQ,* 13 (April 1934): 214–218.

Jardine and Anthony Grafton, "'Studied for Action': How Gabriel Harvey Read His Levy," *Past and Present,* 29 (November 1990): 30–78;

Edward George Harman, *Gabriel Harvey and Thomas Nashe* (London: Ouseley, 1923);

Henry Morley, "Gabriel Harvey," in his *Clement Marot and Other Studies,* 2 volumes (Geneva: Slatkine Reprints, 1970), 2: 229–247;

Eleanor Relle, "Some New Marginalia and Poems of Gabriel Harvey," *RES,* New Series, 23 (November 1972): 401–416;

Harold S. Wilson, "Gabriel Harvey's Method of Annotating His Books," *Harvard Library Bulletin,* 2 (Autumn 1948): 344–361;

Wilson, Introduction to Harvey's *Ciceronianus,* translated by Wilson, Studies in the Humanities, 4 volumes (Lincoln: University of Nebraska Press, 1945), 4: 1–34.

Papers:

Gabriel Harvey's letters are preserved in the British Library Sloane Manuscript 93. The British Library also holds a commonplace book by Harvey (Additional Manuscript 32,494) and a manuscript of a Harvey poem (Landsdowne Manuscript 120, folio 12). Cambridge University Library holds several letters (Baker Manuscript 36, pp. 107–114). Virginia F. Stern has identified the location of 129 volumes containing Harvey's marginalia: 29 are in the British Library; 13 in the Houghton; 10 in the Folger; 8 each in the Huntington and the Bodleian; 7 at the Rosenbach Foundation; 4 in the Newberry; 14 in collections at Cambridge; 10 in collections at Oxford; 15 in private collections; and 11 in other libraries.

Thomas Hearne

(July 1678? - 10 June 1735)

Clare A. Simmons
Ohio State University

Thomas Hearne; engraving by George Vertue, 1735

CATALOGUES: *Operum Nostrorum hactenus impressorum catalogus,* in *De vita & gestis Henrici II. et Ricardi I. E codice ms. in bibliotheca Harleiana descripsit,* by Benedict, abbot of Peterborough, 2 volumes, edited by Hearne (Oxford: Sheldonian Theatre, 1735);

Thomas Osborne, *A Catalogue of the valuable Library of . . . T. Hearne* (London, 1736);

Bibliotheca Hearneiana. Excerpts from the Catalogue of the Library of Thomas Hearne, Printed from his own Manuscript, edited by Beriah Botfield (London: Privately printed, 1848).

BOOKS: *Ductor Historicus: or, a Short System of Universal History, and an Introduction to the Study of It . . . ,* second edition, 2 volumes (London: Printed for T. Childe, 1704–1705); revised edition, 2 volumes (London: Printed by H. Clark for T. Childe, 1714); revised again, 2 volumes (London: Printed by H. Clark for J. Knapten and J. Wyatt, 1724);

A Letter containing an Account of some Antiquities between Windsor and Oxford; with A List of the several Pictures in the School Gallery adjoining the Bodleyan Library (London, 1725);

An Epistolary Letter from T[homas] H[earne] to Sr. H[ans] S[loane] attributed to Hearne (Dublin & London: T. Payne, 1729);

A Vindication of those who take the Oath of Allegiance to his Present Majestie from Perjurie, Injustice, and Disloyaltie, Charged upon them by Such as are against it. Wherein it is evidently shewed That the Common Good of a Nation is what is Primarily and Principally Respected in an Oath, and therefore when the Oath is inconsistent with that, the Persons who have taken it, are absolved from it. In Proving of which the Case of Maud and King Stephen is particularly Considered. In a Letter to a Non-Juror, edited by John Bilston and others (London, 1731);

Remarks and Collections of Thomas Hearne, 11 volumes, edited by C. E. Dobie, D. W. Rannie, H. E. Salter, and others (Oxford: Oxford Historical Society Publications, 1885–1921).

OTHER: *An Index of the Principle Passages in Sir Roger L'Estrange's Translation of Josephus into English,* compiled by Hearne (London, 1702);

Reliquiae Bodleianae; or, Some Genuine Remains of Sir Thomas Bodley, Containing his Life, the first Draught of the Statutes of the Publick Library at Oxford (in English), and a Collection of Letters to Sr. James, &c., edited by Hearne (London: John Hartley, 1703);

Plinius Coecilius Secundus, *Epistolae et Panegyricus,* edited by Hearne (Oxford: Sheldonian Theatre, 1703);

Flavius Eutropius, *Eutropii Breviarium Historiae Romanae, cum Paeanii metaphrasi Graeca,* edited by Hearne (Oxford: Sheldonian Theatre, 1703);

Indices Tres locupletissi in Cyrilli Hierosolymitiani Opera Graece-Latina, compiled by Hearne (Oxford: Sheldonian Theatre, 1703);

Index to the four parts of Dr. Edwards's Preservative against Socinianism, compiled by Hearne (Oxford: Printed for Bishop of Lichfield, 1704);

Edward Hyde, Earl of Clarendon, *The History of the Rebellion and Civil Wars in England,* 3 volumes, index compiled by Hearne (Oxford: Sheldonian Theatre, 1705–1706);

M. J. Justini historiarum ex Trogo Pompeio libri XLIV, edited by Hearne (Oxford: Sheldonian Theatre, 1705);

T. Livii Patavini Historiarum ab urbe condita libri qui supersunt, 6 volumes, edited by Hearne (Oxford: Sheldonian Theatre, 1708);

"A Discourse on an old Roman Inscription lately found near Bathe," in *The Life of Aelfred the Great,* by Sir John Spelman, edited by Hearne (Oxford: Sheldonian Theatre, 1709);

"A Discourse concerning some Antiquities lately found in Yorkshire. In a letter to Mr. Thoresby of Leeds. With an Extract of Mr. Thoresby's letter that occasioned this discourse," *Actis Philosophicis,* 322 (1710);

The Itinerary of John Leland the Antiquary, 9 volumes, edited by Hearne (Oxford: Sheldonian Theatre, 1710–1712);

H. Dodwell the Elder, *De Parma Equestri Woodwardiana Dissertatio. Accedit T. Neli Dialogus Inter Reginam Elizabetham et. R. Dudleium,* edited by Hearne (Oxford: Sheldonian Theatre, 1713);

John Leland, *De Rebus Britannica collecteana,* 6 volumes, edited by Hearne (Oxford: Sheldonian Theatre, 1715);

Acta Apostolorum Graeco-Latina, edited by Hearne (Oxford: Sheldonian Theatre, 1715);

T. Livius Foro-Juliensis, pseudonym, *Vita Henrici Quinti Regis Angliae,* edited by Hearne (Oxford: Sheldonian Theatre, 1716);

Alfred of Beverley, *Annales, sive Historia de gestis Regum Britanniae, libris IX,* edited by Hearne (Oxford: Sheldonian Theatre, 1716);

William Roper, *Vita D. Thomae Mori,* edited by Hearne (Oxford: Printed for author, 1716);

J. Rows, *J. Rossi antiquarii Warwicesis Historia Regum Angliae,* edited by Hearne (Printed for author, 1716);

William Camden, *Annales Rerum Anglicarum et Hibernicarum Regnante Elizabetha,* 3 volumes, edited by Hearne (Oxford: Sheldonian Theatre, 1717);

William of Newburgh, *Historia sive Chronica Rerum Anglicarum,* 3 volumes, edited by Hearne (Oxford: Sheldonian Theatre, 1719);

Thomas Sprott, *Chronica,* edited by Hearne (Oxford: Sheldonian Theatre, 1719);

A Collection of Curious Discourses, written by Eminent Antiquaries on Several Heads in our English Antiquities and now published chiefly for the use and service of the young Nobility and Gentry of England, edited by Hearne (Oxford: Sheldonian Theatre, 1720);

Textus Roffensis, edited by Hearne (Oxford: Sheldonian Theatre, 1720);

Roberti de Avesbury Historia de Mirabilibus Gestis Edwardi III, edited by Hearne (Oxford: Sheldonian Theatre, 1720);

Johannis de Fordun Scotichronicon Genuinum, edited by Hearne (Oxford: Sheldonian Theatre, 1722);

The History and Antiquities of Glastonbury, by an anonymous Author who entitles it, A little Monument to the once famous Abbey and Borough of Glastonbury, from an MS. never before printed, edited by Hearne (Oxford: Sheldonian Theatre, 1722);

Hemingi Chartularium Ecclesiae Wigorniensis, 2 volumes, edited by Hearne (Oxford: Sheldonian Theatre, 1723);

Robert of Gloucester's Chronicle, 2 volumes, edited by Hearne (Oxford: Sheldonian Theatre, 1724);

Peter Langtofte's Chronicle, 2 volumes, edited by Hearne (Oxford: Sheldonian Theatre, 1725);

Johannis Confratris & Monachi Glastoniensis Chronica sive Historia de Rebus Glastoniensis, 2 volumes, edited by Hearne (Oxford: Sheldonian Theatre, 1726);

Thomas of Elmham, *Vita et gesta Henrici Quinti Anglorum Regis,* edited by Hearne (Oxford: Sheldonian Theatre, 1727);

Adam of Domerham, *Historia de rebus gestis Glastoniensibus,* 2 volumes, edited by Hearne (Oxford: Sheldonian Theatre, 1727);

Liber Niger Scaccarii [The Black Book of the Exchequer], 2 volumes, edited by Hearne (Oxford: Sheldonian Theatre, 1728);

A monk of Evesham, *Historia vitae et regni Richardi II,* edited by Hearne (Oxford: Sheldonian Theatre, 1729);

Joannis de Trokelowe annales Eduardi II., Henrici de Blaneforde chronica, et Edvardi II. vita a monacho quodam [Gulielmo] Malmesburiensi fuse enarrata, edited by Hearne (Oxford: Sheldonian Theatre, 1729);

Thomae Caii . . . Vindiciae antiquitatis Academiae Oxoniensis contra Joannem Caium, Cantabrigiensem, 2 volumes, edited by Hearne (Oxford: Sheldonian Theatre, 1730);

Walter of Hemingford, *Historia de rebus gestis Edvardi I., Edvardi II., & Edvardi III.,* 2 volumes, edited by Hearne (Oxford: Sheldonian Theatre, 1731);

Duo rerum Anglicarum scriptores veteres, viz. T. Otterbourne er J. Whethamstede ab origine gentis Britannicae usque ad Edvardum IV, 2 volumes (Oxford: Sheldonian Theatre, 1732);

Chronicon, sive Annales Prioratus de Dunstaple una cum excerptis e chartulario ejusdem prioratus, 2 volumes, edited by Hearne (Oxford: Sheldonian Theatre, 1733);

Benedict, abbot of Peterborough, *De vita & gestis Henrici II. et Ricardi I. E codice ms. in bibliotheca Harleiana descripsit,* 2 volumes, edited by Hearne (Oxford: Sheldonian Theatre, 1735);

Ectypa Varia ad Historiam Britannicam Illustrandam aere olim insculpta studio et cura T. H. (Oxford, 1737).

Thomas Hearne's personal library of books and manuscripts is a remarkable achievement in itself, given the circumstances of his life. His chief claim to attention in the history of book collecting, though, is the central role that he played in creating a taste for early British literature at a time when many regarded writings in English as inferior to those in classical languages. Facts about Hearne's life and estimations of the value of his works are available from two main sources, his enemies and himself, neither of which can be considered impartial. The word applied to him by all parties alike, however, is *indefatigable.*

An antiquarian editor and nonjuror, Hearne was probably born in July 1678; in his own account of his life he records that he was born at Littlefield Green in the parish of White Waltham, Berkshire, and was baptized on 11 July of that year, although after his death his brother maintained that he was ten years older. His parents were George Hearne, clerk of White Waltham for fifty-three years, who died in 1728, and Edith, daughter of Thomas Wise of nearby Shottesbrooke, who died in 1700. There were at least four other children in the family; Thomas, the son of Hearne's brother William, was a major beneficiary in his will. Hearne's father had little money to spend on his family's education, but since he kept a small school himself, in return for which he received free accommodation at the Vicarage-House in White Waltham, he was able to educate his children at home until he sent Thomas out as a day laborer.

Young Hearne showed an aptitude for learning. He was early on interested in reading the inscriptions on gravestones, a predilection that remained with him in later life since volume forty-one of his notebooks consists entirely of transcriptions of epitaphs. Since by 1693 he was, in his own words, "much talked of for the skill he had obtained in reading and writing beyond his years," the local squire Francis Cherry secured his admittance to the Free School at Bray, three miles from his home, so that he could learn Latin. Starting behind his fellow students, Hearne soon surpassed them, claiming somewhat improbably in the notes about his life that his knowledge gave him considerable popularity among the boys.

His unusual abilities came to the attention of Henry Dodwell, who lived at Shottesbrooke. Dodwell, generally referred to by Hearne in his many references to his works and ideas as the "great" or "learned" Dr. Dodwell, was a nonjuror who had given up his ecclesiastical office rather than take the oath of allegiance to William and Mary after the expulsion of James II. Like many of his fellow nonjurors and his friend Francis Cherry, he was interested in the study of antiquities. At Dodwell's urging, Cherry took Hearne into his house in 1695 "and provided for him as if he had been his own Son," instructing him in the classics and religion. Hearne was entered in the register at St. Edmund's Hall, Oxford, in 1695, although he did not take up residence there until the following year.

Hearne's devotion to study brought him to the attention of his Oxford tutors, who employed him to collate and transcribe manuscripts. He also acted as editorial assistant for Dodwell and assisted Dr. Grabe of St. Edmund's Hall. He received his bachelor of arts degree in 1699 and considered the possibility of missionary work in Maryland. His Oxford friends, however, convinced him that this would be a waste of his antiquarian talents, and he remained at the university, reading regularly in the Bodleian Library.

The library was at this time in disarray, and the keeper appointed Hearne assistant keeper in order to improve the cataloguing. Hearne especially disapproved of the cataloguing work done by Humfrey Wanley. In *The Life of Mr. Thomas Hearne, of St. Edmund's Hall, Oxford; From his own MS. copy in the Bodleian Library* (1772), William Huddesford describes Hearne's methodical attention to detail:

> Being settled in this Employment, it is incredible what Pains he took in regulating the Library, in Order to which he examined all the printed Books in it, comparing every Volume with the Catalogue set out many Years before by Dr. Hyde: He found by this means many Books not numbered at all, and others numbered or catalogued so very imperfectly, as rendered Dr. Hyde's Catalogue in many respects very useless.
>
> He wrote down all his notes in an interleaved Copy of the said printed Catalogue, and afterwards transcribed them anew into two Volumes, entitling the Work, *Appendix Catalogi librorum impressorum Bibliotheca Bodleiana.*

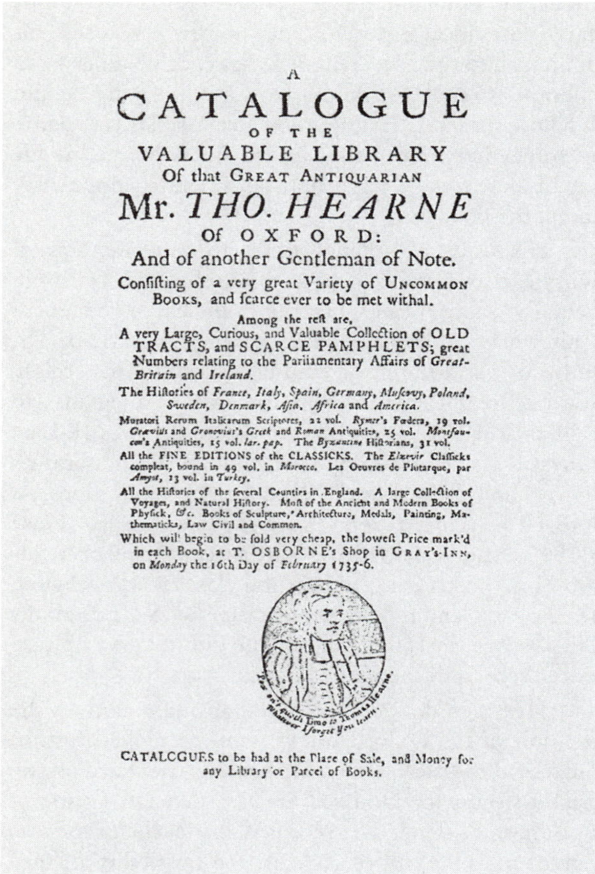

A
CATALOGUE
OF THE
VALUABLE LIBRARY
Of that GREAT ANTIQUARIAN
Mr. *THO. HEARNE*
Of OXFORD:
And of another Gentleman of Note.
Conſiſting of a very great Variety of UNCOMMON BOOKS, and ſcarce ever to be met withal.

Among the reſt are,
A very Large, Curious, and Valuable Collection of OLD TRACTS, and SCARCE PAMPHLETS; great Numbers relating to the Parliamentary Affairs of *Great-Britain* and *Ireland*.
The Hiſtories of *France*, *Italy*, *Spain*, *Germany*, *Muſcovy*, *Poland*, *Sweden*, *Denmark*, *Aſia*, *Africa* and *America*.
Muratori Rerum Italicarum Scriptores, 22 vol. *Rymer*'s Fœdera, 19 vol. *Grævius* and *Gronovius*'s *Greek* and *Roman* Antiquities, 25 vol. *Montfaucon*'s Antiquities, 15 vol. *lar. pap.* The *Byzantine* Hiſtorians, 31 vol.
All the FINE EDITIONS of the CLASSICKS. The *Elzevir* Claſſicks compleat, bound in 49 vol. in *Morocco*. Les Oeuvres de Plutarque, par *Amyot*, 13 vol. in *Turkey*.
All the Hiſtories of the ſeveral Counties in England. A large Collection of Voyages, and Natural Hiſtory. Moſt of the Ancient and Modern Books of Phyſick, &c. Books of Sculpture, Architecture, Medals, Painting, Mathematicks, Law Civil and Common.
Which will begin to be ſold very cheap, the loweſt Price mark'd in each Book, at T. OSBORNE's Shop in GRAY's-INN, on *Monday* the 16th Day of *February* 1735-6.

CATALOGUES to be had at the Place of Sale, and Money for any Library or Parcel of Books.

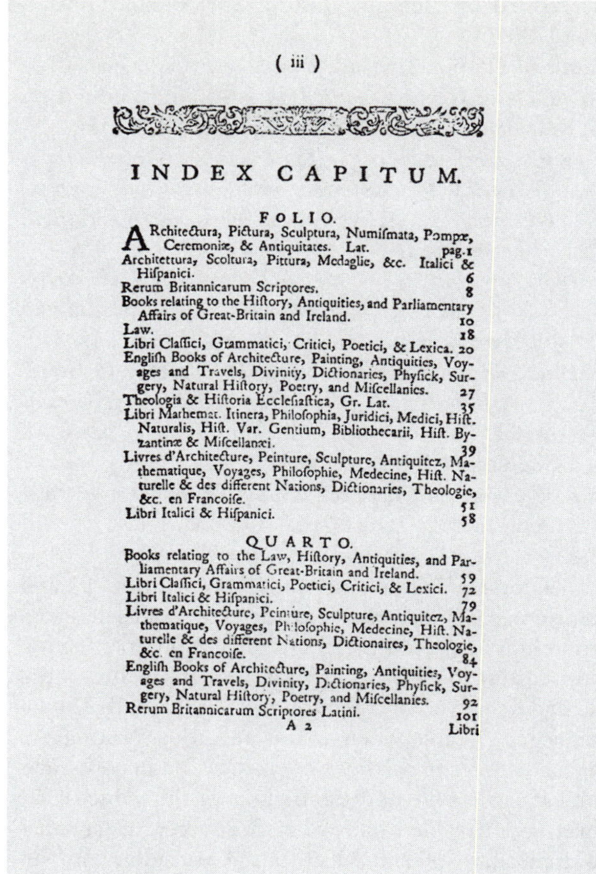

(iii)

INDEX CAPITUM.

FOLIO.

QUARTO.

A 2 Libri

Cover and first page of the index of the catalogue for the 1736 sale of Hearne's book collection

Hearne was indignant that he and other compilers received no credit when his entries were combined with the main catalogue. He also worked on the manuscript and coin catalogues.

After Hearne achieved the master of arts degree in 1703, he was offered other positions at Oxford but was obliged to decline them to retain his position at the Bodleian. By 1705 he had adopted the habit of recording anything of interest to him in a notebook, and by the time of his death, he had filled 145 notebooks; substantial selections of these were published by Philip Bliss in *Reliquiae Hearnianae: The Remains of T. H, being extracts from his MS Diaries* (1856–1857), and they were published virtually in their entirety in eleven volumes by the Oxford Historical Society as *Remarks and Collections of Thomas Hearne* (1885–1921).

Many entries from the notebooks were used in his frequent publications. The catalogue of Hearne's publications that he often attached to his later works is not entirely accurate. His first publication was probably *An Index of the Principle Passages in Sir Roger L'Estrange's Translation of Josephus into English* (1702); he also produced indexes for other works: the works of Cyril of Jerusalem, *Indices Tres locupletissi in Cyrilli Hierosolymitiani Opera Graece-Latina* (1703); and *Index to the four parts of Dr. Edwards's Preservative against Socinianism* (1704); and *The History of the Rebellion and Civil Wars in England* (1705–1706) by Edward Hyde, Earl of Clarendon. In 1704 Hearne wrote an historical compendium from the time of Christ to that of Charlemagne that was published as the second volume of *Ductor Historicus: or, a Short System of Universal History, and an Introduction to the Study of It.* Hearne also undertook the revision of the first volume, from the earliest times to the time of Christ, adding more detailed chronologies and notes on antiquities, which was published in 1705. Although Hearne states that he did not write the first edition–which had been published under the name "W.J., M.A." in 1698 when he was still an undergraduate–the first edition has nevertheless sometimes been attributed to him by later book collectors.

Hearne also produced annotated critical editions of Pliny the Younger, *Epistolae et Panegyricus* (1703); Flavius Eutropius, *Eutropii Breviarium Historiae Romanae, cum Paeanii metaphrasi Graeca* (1703); Livy, *T. Livii Patavini Historiarum ab urbe condita libri qui supersunt* (1708); and the *Acta Apostolorum Graeco-Latina* (1715). Most of Hearne's editions of old manuscripts take a similar form. After his editor's preface and the main document, he includes whatever additional material he chooses, usually other documents on a similar subject but sometimes on topics far removed from the main work. The books were published by subscription, generally in editions of 120 or less, and printed at the Sheldonian Theatre, Oxford (technically, the Sheldonian Theatre was the place of publication, and Hearne the publisher). Hearne himself seems to have collected the subscriptions. For one of his most significant works, the nine-volume edition of *The Itinerary of John Leland the Antiquary* (1710–1712), Hearne added many archeological essays and discussions of folklore by himself and others. Even in his lifetime, his supply of 150 copies was insufficient to meet the demand.

By 1712, when he was still assistant and janitor (keeper of the keys), he was made second keeper at the Bodleian at the sum of £5 a term. He insisted on keeping the keys, so that he could retain "the liberty of entering and going out as often as he pleased." According to Hearne, his troubles with the university began when he published Dodwell's *De Parma Equestri Woodwardiana Dissertatio. Accedit T. Neli Dialogus Inter Reginam Elizabetham et R. Dudleium* (1713). Because Dodwell had refused to take the oaths of allegiance to William and Mary, this publication of his work called into question Hearne's loyalty to their heir, Queen Anne, who like her sister was a committed supporter of the Protestant succession. The University of Oxford had been loyal to the Stuarts throughout the civil war years of the mid-seventeenth century, and the scholars may have feared that tacit approval of the work of a nonjuror would imply that they regretted the ousting of James II. As a result, university administrators used their authority with the university press to try to suppress Hearne's preface to the work, in which Hearne asserts that Dodwell was a more virtuous person than the conforming divines. Nevertheless, Hearne is at least somewhat mistaken in stating that Oxford was already against him early in 1713 because in January 1715 he was "very honourably, without his seeking," elected to the position of university archetypographicus (head of the press) and superior beadle in the civil law by 179 votes to 78. He did not actually assume the duties at this time but continued in the library.

When George I succeeded Queen Anne in 1714, Hearne was in a position to gain security in his career, but he refused to take the oaths of allegiance to the new monarch. As a consequence he was later accused by his enemies, notably Edmund Curll, of inconsistency because he had taken the oaths for the position of beadle during Queen Anne's reign. Yet, Hearne's notebooks reveal that he accepted Anne as a true Stuart, an Englishwoman and of the line of Charles I, who was still officially revered in Oxford as "the blessed martyr." Hearne's rejection of George I, then, seems to have been partly inspired by the religious traditionalism of the older nonjurors, by a sense of nationalism (he called George a "foreigner"), and probably by his devotion to the old ways of Oxford University.

Taking the oaths of allegiance was necessary for all university offices, so by not taking the oaths Hearne had effectively excluded himself. Even at the time of his election, the university press had made someone else "Printer overseer" so that he would gain the profits, not Hearne. On 8 November 1715, he was told that the two offices he held were mutually exclusive and that he must leave the library or resign the beadleship. Hearne refused to do either, and the locks were changed on the Bodleian, rendering his janitorial keys useless and making him a librarian without a library. Remarking that the beadleship was worth ten times as much as the sub-librarian position, Hearne explained his position in his notebook: "But I never was yet guided by Interest, so it fell out now, it being no other Principle than that of Honesty & Conscience & Regard for Learning that I went upon. I prefer my Studies to all preferment . . . ."

On 26 January 1716 Hearne directly refused to take the oaths, thus officially becoming a nonjuror like Dodwell before him. He was not even able to collect the salary owed to him in case he should be fined £500 for not taking the oath. On 3 March, Hearne was summoned to a hearing, where he asked to see the order excluding him, and enraged the vice-chancellor by ridiculing the poor spelling. Huddesford records from Hearne's notes that

> After this bad usage he retired to Edmund-Hall, and lived there very privately, carrying on his Studies in the same diligent manner he had done before, furnishing himself with Books, partly from his Study, and partly by the help of Friends.

He was now forced back on the resources of his own library. Still, he had many friends in Oxford who were willing to help him by lending him books and manuscripts and, more important, by continuing to subscribe to the editions that he produced.

Hearne encountered further troubles with the university establishment later in 1716 over remarks he made in the preface to his edition of William Camden's

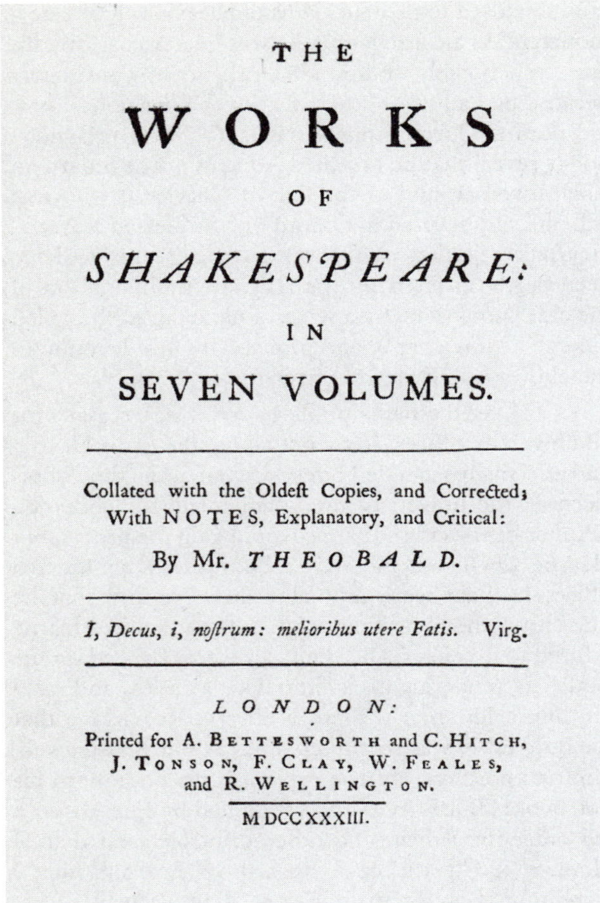
THE

WORKS

OF

SHAKESPEARE:

IN

SEVEN VOLUMES.

Collated with the Oldeſt Copies, and Corrected;
With NOTES, Explanatory, and Critical:
By Mr. *THEOBALD.*

I, Decus, i, noſtrum: melioribus utere Fatis. Virg.

LONDON:
Printed for A. BETTESWORTH and C. HITCH,
J. TONSON, F. CLAY, W. FEALES,
and R. WELLINGTON.
MDCCXXXIII.

Title page for Lewis Theobald's 1733 edition of William Shakespeare's writings. A copy of this edition was one of the few books of poetry or drama in Hearne's collection.

Annales Rerum Anglicarum et Hibernicarum Regnante Elizabetha (1717). He was prohibited from printing as a result of being prosecuted by the vice-chancellor Baron, who was influenced chiefly by Charlett, the head of St. Edmund's Hall and patron of Humfrey Wanley, as well as by Bernard Gardiner, warden of All Souls College, and John Hudson, keeper of the Bodleian Library. Hearne was also then working on an edition of William Roper's *Vita D. Thomae Mori* (1716), which had personal significance for him as the story of a nonjuror from an earlier age. The text, which clearly had political implications, appears not to have been printed at the Sheldonian. Hearne's next edition, William of Newburgh's *Historia sive Chronica Rerum Anglicarum* (1719), did not appear until after the prohibition was lifted on 25 October 1718.

Hearne considered leaving Oxford for London but did not do so because of the sufficient support from his allies. Some of his earlier works were by this time collectors' items; for example, the massive edition of Leland's *Itinerary,* which had originally cost subscribers 37 shillings, by 1724 was selling for 20 guineas. Friends such as Thomas Smith and Thomas and Richard Rawlinson lent him manuscripts to print, and he also had access to material from the Harleian and Cottonian collections. These friends were among his regular subscribers, who also included Sir Hans Sloane and Edward Harley. Toward the end of his life, he had more contacts with Jacobites, who often met with him when they visited Oxford. His later works demonstrate an interest in medieval annals, in the antiquities of Glastonbury, and always in the history of Oxford and its university. Of particular interest are his editions of the English verse chronicles, *Robert of Gloucester's Chronicle* (1724) and *Peter Langtofte's Chronicle* (1725).

Although his friends offered him constant support, Hearne also had influential enemies. Hearne would add new information to the catalogue of his works as he came across it and include it in his later editions. In one version of his catalogue, he had used the entry on Dodwell's *De Parma Equestri Woodwardiana Dissertatio* as an opportunity to contradict the findings of the recently deceased antiquarian Walter Moyle. As a consequence he was attacked in print by Moyles's publisher Curll, whom Hearne described in his notebooks as "an errant knave." Most probably, an enemy was responsible for the publication of a poem in 1729 titled *An Epistolary Letter from T[homas] H[earne] to Sr H[an]s S[loan]e,* although because in later years any work attributed to Hearne had high value, this poem appears in some bibliographies as a work by Hearne himself.

Hearne's major source of embarrassment, however, was the printing in 1731 of an essay he had written about 1700 titled *A Vindication of those who take the Oath of Allegiance to his Present Majestie from Perjurie, Injustice, and Disloyaltie, Charged upon them by Such as are against it. Wherein it is evidently shewed That the Common Good of a Nation is what is Primarily and Principally Respected in an Oath, and therefore when the Oath is inconsistent with that, the Persons who have taken it, are absolved from it. In Proving of which the Case of Maud and King Stephen is particularly Considered. In a Letter to a Non-Juror.* Hearne had sent the essay to his patron Cherry, and it had remained among his private papers. After Cherry's death his widow, Anne, donated some forty of his manuscripts to the Bodleian. Hearne was unsuccessful in his attempt to retrieve papers written by him.

Hearne's early writings fell into the hands of his enemies, who, probably led by John Bilston of All Souls College and Robert Shippen, published the embarrassing essay anonymously, taking the opportunity in the preface to ridicule Hearne's life and work:

> This is the advantageous Method he has pursued all his Life Time: He has copy'd Monuments and Inscriptions; Original Letters and venerable Ballads of Antiquity; Stories of honest John Ross and Peter Langtoft; Robert of Brun and St. Thomas Cantilupe: Men! who had not Mr. Hearne lived, might have laid forever buried in an ignoble Obscurity.

The writer of the preface points out errors in Hearne's editions but mainly makes fun of the obscurity of his subject.

Even with such criticism, Hearne's publications were successful. Although he had no income beyond them, he left at his death on 10 June 1735 more than £1,000 hidden in his rooms, as well as an impressive library. The money was shared among the members of his family, and the library went to William Bedford, the son of his old friend Hilkiah Bedford, and was auctioned in February 1736. "The valuable library of that great antiquarian Mr. Thomas Hearne of Oxford," together with some books belonging to another unidentified gentleman, were sold by Thomas Osborne of London in a total of 6,772 lots. The auctioneer's cover advertisement lists the contents as follows:

> A very Large, Curious, and Valuable Collection of OLD TRACTS, and CARCE PAMPHLETS; great Numbers relating to Parliamentary Affairs of Great-Britain and Ireland.
>
> The Histories of France, Italy, Spain, Germany, Muscovy, Poland, Sweden, Denmark, Asia, Africa and America.
>
> Muratori Rerum Italicarum Scriptores, 22 vols. Rymer's Foedera, 19 vols. Graevius and Gronovius's Greek and Roman Antiquities, 25 vols. Montfaucon's Antiquities, 15 vols. The Byzantine Histories, 31 vols.
>
> All the FINE EDITIONS of the CLASSICKS. The Elzevir Classics Compleat, bound in 49 vols. on Morocco. Les Oeuvres de Plutarques, 13 vols. in Turkey.
>
> All of the Histories of the several Counties in England. A large Collection of Voyages, and Natural History. Most of the Ancient and Modern Books of Physick, &c. Books of Sculpture, Architecture, Medals, Painting, Mathematicks, Law Civil and Common.

The most significant feature of the library is the large number of books about Britain. Works of poetry and fiction are comparatively few–a mere 157 works are listed in the category of "Poetry, Novels, and Translations"–but the catalogue includes works by Geoffrey Chaucer, Alexander Pope, and John Dryden in folio, and Lewis Theobald's edition of William Shakespeare.

In his 1985 essay "Thomas Hearne's Library" Stanley Gillam notes that much of the library was acquired through gifts and bequests, notably the bequest of Thomas Smith, who died in 1710. Smith's legacy included transcriptions of works in other collections, notably the Cottonian Library, and Hearne relied heavily on these in producing his editions, particularly in his later years when he never left Oxford. The only books that Hearne bequeathed to the Bodleian were those specifically designated for this purpose by Smith's bequest. Some catalogues compiled by Hearne survive in the Bodleian, including a list of 224 manuscripts. Hearne's papers were bought from Bedford for £105 by Richard Rawlinson, who afterward bequeathed them to the Bodleian; writings such as the notebooks that reveal so much about Hearne's personality now reside in the library that he could not enter.

In person Hearne's manner was brusque; he had some odd mannerisms, including holding up the back of his gown when he walked. He clearly judged intellectual capacity by number of publications. Although his notebooks show a preoccupation with bell ringing, he apparently did not enjoy most music and was scandalized by George Frideric Handel's visit to Oxford. His portrait, engraved by George Vertue, appears in several of his works, including *The Life of Mr. Thomas Hearne* that Huddesford compiled from his writings. It shows a solidly built, dark man standing in front of a bookshelf. Sometimes, the picture has the epigraph: "Pox on't quoth Time to Thomas Hearne, / Whatever I forget you learn"; in versions printed by his enemies, he is holding the oaths that he refused to take.

Hearne had many declared enemies of whom he in turn was critical in his notebooks. He called Charlett a "malicious, invidious prevaricator" and described John Lancaster on his appointment as Oxford vice-chancellor as "that old, hypocritical, ambitious, drunken, sot." Subsequently he took to calling him "Smoothboots." He took a disliking to Pope, who according to Curll was referring to Hearne in the following lines of *The Dunciad* (1728):

> But who is he, in closet close y-pent,
> Of sober face, with learned dust besprent?
> Right well mine eyes arede the myster wight
> On parchment scraps y-fed, and Wormius hight.
> To future ages may thy dulness last,
> As thou preserv'st the dulness of the past!

Yet, Hearne's love for study and commitment to his principles at a time when many of his peers were prepared to compromise won him many loyal friends, including Edmond Halley, who identified the comet named after him, and John Urry, whom he assisted in preparing an edition of Chaucer's works.

Hearne's contribution to the history of the book is perhaps more through his legendary reputation among later antiquarians than the quality of his editions. Although he printed many works that had before only existed in manuscript, his efforts made such texts only marginally more accessible for he published only for subscribers and largely in Latin. Nor is it clear in the case of many of the obscure annals that Hearne so loved that they deserved to be better known. His choice of works to publish was often dubious, and the supporting materials that he selected to publish with them often demonstrate his own eccentric intellectual interests (such as the antiquity of Oxford University) or seem merely included to gratify his friends. His practice was to print whichever manuscript he could obtain rather than to produce a critical edition. He took pride in his faithful transcriptions of manuscripts, noting, "I am so religious in that Affair, that I transcribe the very Faults."

Perhaps more important than Hearne's actual editions, then, are his notebooks and letters: the latter have been published only in excerpted form. While at times he simply records local gossip, for the most part Hearne includes much valuable information about himself, generally referred to as "the Writer of these matters"; the acquisition and provenance of books; many detailed descriptions of manuscripts; and extensive compilations of notes on antiquities. His papers are also a key source on the nonjuring tradition and on the personalities of early eighteenth-century Oxford, although Hearne's judgments on his contemporaries must be treated with caution since he was, more often than not, ready to believe the worst of people.

Thomas Hearne strengthened interest in antiquarianism, particularly in the English past, and he contributed to the appreciation of the indigenous historical tradition at a time when it had little or no value for many of his more classically minded contemporaries. Already increasing in value during his lifetime, his books, many of which could be considered "princeps" editions as the first printed text, were greatly prized by later book collectors, notably during the "bibliomania" of the early years of the nineteenth century, when they commanded large prices.

Biographies:

Edmund Curll, ed., *Impartial Memorials of the Life and Writings of Thomas Hearne, M.A. By several hands* (London, 1736);

William Huddesford, ed., *The Life of Mr. Thomas Hearne, of St. Edmund's Hall, Oxford; From his own MS. copy in the Bodleian Library; Also, An accurate Catalogue of his Writings and Publications, from his own MS. Copy, which he designed for the Press,* in *The Lives of those Eminent Antiquaries Anthony à Wood, Thomas Hearne, and John Leland* (Oxford: Clarendon Press, 1772);

Philip Bliss, ed., *Reliquiae Hearnianae: The Remains of T. H., being extracts from his MS Diaries,* 2 volumes (Oxford, 1856–1857); revised as *The Remains of Thomas Hearne,* edited by John Buchanan-Brown (London: Centaur Press, 1966).

References:

Stanley Gillam, "Thomas Hearne's Library," *Bodleian Library Record,* 12, no. 1 (1985): 52–64;

Walter Moyle, *An Apology for the Writings of Walter Moyle, Esq., in answer to the groundless aspersions of Mr. Hearne . . . and Dr. Woodward. . . . With a word or two concerning the frivolous cavils of Messieurs Whiston and Woolston relating to the Thundering Legion,* edited by Edmund Curll (London, 1727);

F. Ouvry, *Letters Addressed to T. Hearne* (London: Privately printed, 1874).

Papers:

Thomas Hearne's papers, including manuscript catalogues of his book collection, are mainly located in the Bodleian Library, Oxford.

Thomas Howard, second Earl of Arundel

(7 July 1585 – 24 September 1646)

Richard Ovenden
National Library of Scotland

CATALOGUES: W. P., *Bibliotheca Norfolciana, sive, Catalogus libb. manuscriptorum & impressorum in omni arte & lingua, quos illustriss princeps Henricus Dux Norfolciae, &c. Regiae societati Londinenst pro scientia naturali promovenda donavit* (London: Richard Chiswel, 1681);
Catalogue of the Arundel Manuscripts in the Library of the College of Arms, compiled by W. H. Black (London: Printed by S. and R. Bentley, 1829);
Catalogue of Manuscripts in The British Museum. New Series Part I: The Arundel Manuscripts, edited by J. Forshall (London: Printed by Order of the Trustees, 1834).

BOOK: *Remembrances of Things Worth Seeing in Italy: Given to John Evelyn, 25 April 1646, by Thomas Howard, fourteenth Earl of Arundel,* edited by John Martin Robinson (London: Privately printed for members of the Roxburghe Club, 1987).

Thomas Howard, second Earl of Arundel; portrait by Sir Peter Paul Rubens, circa 1636 (National Gallery)

Thomas Howard, second Earl of Arundel, was one of the most important collectors of art in the seventeenth century. In addition to amassing paintings, drawings, statuary, and antiquities on an almost unprecedented scale for an English nobleman, Arundel and his wife were also dedicated patrons of living artists. As a consequence of this impressive virtuosity, his book-collecting activities have received comparatively little attention. In fact, Arundel was a book collector of the first rank, and the Howard family–which can also be taken to include the Fitzalan earls of Arundel from an earlier generation–forms an impressive dynasty of book collectors.

In the sixteenth century the bulk of the Fitzalan collections passed to John Lumley, Baron Lumley, who had inherited Nonesuch Palace from his father-in-law, Henry Fitzalan, twelfth Earl of Arundel, together with a collection of paintings and a considerable library, much of which had come, sometime after 1553, from the great collection formed by Thomas Cranmer, archbishop of Canterbury. Arundel was Lumley's great-nephew, and as the sole-surviving male descendent of the Fitzalan line may have expected to inherit much of the collection. On Lumley's death in 1609, however, the estate was left to Lumley's widow, Jane, who dispersed the contents piecemeal, with the exception of the library, which was sold to King James I as a gift for Henry, Prince of Wales, in 1609. After the death of the prince in 1612 his library formally passed into the royal collection. Although partially dispersed in the seventeenth, eighteenth, and nineteenth centuries, the collection still survives to a great extent in the British Library. Lumley's widow did give Arundel some of the Lumley paintings, including a group of Holbein portraits, the genesis of his great collection of art.

Several other Howard collections had a more direct bearing on the library formed by Arundel, and these must be briefly examined. The first member of the Howard family to collect books on a serious scale was probably Thomas Howard, fourth Duke of Norfolk. He was Arundel's grandfather and lived from 1536 to 1572, when he was executed for having plotted against Queen Elizabeth I on behalf of Mary Stuart, Queen of Scots, a Roman Catholic claimant to the throne. Although some of his printed books–including sets of the works of St. Jerome (1553) and of Eusebius (1549), both published in Basle, Switzerland–survive in the library of Christ Church, Oxford University, some significant medieval manuscripts descended to Arundel through Lord William Howard, the duke's third son.

More important was the collection formed by Arundel's great-uncle and close friend Henry Howard, first Earl of Northampton, who lived from 1540 to 1614. Henry Howard was well educated, matriculating as a fellow commoner from King's Hall, Cambridge, in 1564 and taking an M.A. at Oxford in 1568. He was created earl of Northampton by King James in 1604, was appointed high steward of Oxford in 1609, and became chancellor of Cambridge University in 1612. Northampton attracted many influential men, especially antiquaries and intellectuals including Sir Robert Cotton. Throughout James's reign Northampton regularly borrowed material from Cotton's collection; for his part Cotton was able to use his position as adviser to Northampton as a means, even an excuse, to gain access to repositories of official papers.

Most of the books that survive from Northampton's library passed into Arundel's collection and thus were dispersed in the late nineteenth century. Seventeenth-century theology and history features prominently among these books, including the dedication copy of Barnabe Barnes's *Foure Bookes of Offices* (1606), now in Brasenose College Oxford, and *Antiquae liturgae arcana* (1605) and *Lidolatrie Huguenote fugurée au patron de la vielle payenne* (1608), both now in private collections. A. De Morales's *La coronica general de España 1574–7* (1586) was a presentation copy from Cotton. Some of Northhampton's books, such as a heavily annotated copy of a 1541 edition of Baldassare Castiglione's *Il libro del cortegiano,* were clearly bought while he was a young man at Cambridge. Several of the books from this period were evidently acquired secondhand in Cambridge, such as a copy of Sebastian Castilio's *Sibyllinorum oraculorum libri VII* (1555), which again is heavily annotated in Northampton's tidy italic. The collector had at least two armorial stamps cut to decorate the covers of his books (one before and one after his elevation to the earldom), and although roughly twenty-five books have been identified as belonging to him, the extent of his holdings are a matter of speculation because no catalogue of Northampton's library survives.

Although Northhampton had a significant collection of books, the second most important Howard collector to Arundel was his uncle Lord William Howard of Naworth, the third son of Thomas, fourth Duke of Norfolk. Both before and after Lord William's death in 1640, printed books and especially manuscripts were removed from the Naworth collections and placed into other Howard collections, notably those of his nephew. Lord William had married Elizabeth Dacre, an heiress of a leading border family, and came into the possession of Naworth Castle in Cumberland. Like other members of the Howard family, William was a Catholic and was imprisoned for a period in the Tower of London, 1585–1586.

Lord William's book collecting followed his religious sympathies and featured a large and impressive collection of medieval manuscripts, at least 125 volumes, many of which bore monastic provenances. He corresponded with William Camden, whom he assisted in compiling his *Britannia* (1586), the first comprehensive topographical survey of England, and with Cotton, with whom he exchanged manuscripts. Lord William also acquired manuscripts from the collection of the scientist, astrologer, and antiquary John Dee before his death in 1609, at a time when Dee was short of money and was selling books purely to stay alive. He is known to have borrowed manuscripts from Henry Savile of Banke and to have acquired at least one manuscript from Thomas Talbot, Lancaster Herald. James Ussher, archbishop of Armagh, another scholar and collector who borrowed frequently from the collection at Naworth, shared an interest with Lord William in the chroniclers Florence and John of Worcester. Lord William was the editor for a 1592 edition of the Worcester chronicle, *Chronicon ex Chronicis, ob initio mundi usque ad annum Domini,* which was based on two manuscripts then in the possession of William Lambarde the antiquary.

Other manuscripts at Naworth of great importance include an eleventh-century Gospel book associated with Queen Margaret of Scotland, now in the Bodleian Library, the Luttrell, De Lisle, Howard-Fitton and Arundel Psalters, all highly important English illuminated manuscripts, and all now in the British Library. Several manuscripts containing Anglo-Saxon were in the collection, including one that had been at Christ Church, Canterbury, in the Middle Ages. A group of twenty-three manuscripts from the Naworth collections were acquired eventually by Robert and Edward Harley and are now part of the Harleian Collection in the British Library. The group includes manuscripts from Holme Coultram, the Cluniac Abbey at Bermondsey, the Carmelite Priory at Hulne, near Alnwick, the Cistercian Abbey at Newminster, and the Benedictine Abbey at St. Albans.

Lord William also owned a substantial collection of printed books, some of which were dispersed in various auction sales from the eighteenth century onward. At least three hundred books, however, survived intact at Naworth, though many of these were badly damaged in the nineteenth century. In 1992 they were acquired by Durham University Library.

Lord William was close to his nephew, with whom he shared intellectual, cultural, and scholarly interests. When he died without an heir, a large portion of his collection of manuscripts passed to Arundel. At least thirty-eight of these eventually passed into the Arundel Collection in the British Library; twenty-three more were given by Henry Howard, seventh Duke of Norfolk, to the College of Arms, even though the majority have little to do with heraldry.

By rights Arundel should have succeeded to the dukedom of Norfolk, regarded as the senior noble title of the realm, but the title had been in abeyance since his grandfather's execution for treason in 1572. Arundel's father, Philip, had consequently been reduced in title to earl of Surrey, until the death of his maternal grandfather in 1580 had brought him the title earl of Arundel. The Howards were constantly under suspicion of treason by the crown, in part because of their staunchly held Catholic faith, and Philip was imprisoned and eventually executed in 1595. His wife, Ann Dacre, herself heir to a considerable estate, kept her children in seclusion in her rural strongholds in the north.

Thomas Howard, second Earl of Arundel, was born 7 July 1585 in Finchingfield, Essex. Little is known about his early life until his appearance at court in the early years of the reign of James I. His upbringing was likely a traditional Catholic one, and he no doubt came into contact with the clandestine Jesuits that his mother sheltered. Despite the lack of documentary evidence, it is probable that he was educated at both Westminster School and Trinity College, Cambridge. His title of earl of Arundel and Surrey, lost when his father was executed, was restored in 1604 although his dukedom and forfeited lands were not, being instead absorbed by other branches of the Howard family.

In 1606 Arundel married Aletheia Talbot, one of the daughters of Gilbert Talbot, Earl of Shrewsbury, and coheiress to the Talbot estates. The marriage at once brought Arundel new access to wealth as well as a position in the upper echelons of society. From 1606 to 1619 he regularly participated in the entertainments at court, many of which were masterminded by Inigo Jones, who became a close friend. Arundel soon came to the attention of the young Prince Henry and became

Arundel's book stamp

a member of the prince's circle of bright young noblemen. He and the prince shared a quiet, sober, and intellectual temperament. As historian Graham Parry observes in *The Golden Age Restor'd* (1981), "had the Prince lived, Arundel would doubtless have been one of his principal advisors."

Arundel was a collector, connoisseur, and patron of the arts, so much so that Horace Walpole called him "the father of *vertu* in England." His early influences may well have included his great-uncles, John, Lord Lumley, and Henry Howard, Earl of Northampton. Prince Henry, whose passions included the arts as well as science, must also have been an influence on Arundel. In *English Monarchs and Their Books: From Henry VII to Charles II* (1987) T. A. Birrell describes the prince's library–much but not entirely derived from the Lumley collection–as "an admirable mixture of the humanistic and the scientific."

Jones was certainly another important influence on Arundel. In 1613–1614 Arundel and his wife accompanied Princess Elizabeth to Heidelberg and afterward traveled on to Italy. On this trip, an example of the first flowering of "The Grand Tour," the Arundels were accompanied by Jones, the young architect, draftsman, and stage designer, who while studying ancient and modern buildings in Italy also assisted Arundel in his appreciation of the peculiarly Italian mode of the arts. In Venice and the Veneto in particular, the Arundels found the style of living to their taste, especially the role that the arts–particularly architecture–played in the lives of the nobility of the republic. Both Jones and Arundel were able to acquire some of the great architect Andrea Palladio's drawings from his pupil Vincenzo Scamozzi in Venice. Some of Arundel's printed books were acquired in Italy on the tours early in his adult life, including a copy of Vincenzo Mirabella's *Dichiarazioni della pianta dell'antiche Siracuse* (1613), which was purchased in Syracuse the year after it was published in Naples.

In Rome they studied the greatest classical ruins, Jones busily drawing them while Arundel set about excavating sites, unearthing statues that he crated up and returned to England. These statues set a fashion for antique statuary among the British aristocracy and strengthened the hold of classical culture among the nobility. On their return to England, Arundel and his wife set about creating a household marked by a cultivated neoclassicism. Arundel commissioned Jones to undertake a building program inspired by their experiences in Italy. Unfortunately, nothing survives of the two major examples of his work, Greenwich House, left to Arundel by the earl of Northampton, and Arundel House, which had been returned to Arundel from Charles Howard, Earl of Nottingham, in 1607. Nottingham was the son of William, Lord Howard of Effingham, who had taken possession of some of the Norfolk estates after the execution of Thomas Howard, fourth Duke of Norfolk, to whom he was distantly related.

Throughout his life as a collector Arundel was alert to the advances being made in scholarship and learning, and like other learned members of the English aristocracy, including his friend Prince Henry, he drew scholars and antiquarians to him to enhance the collecting experience by sharing discoveries and to continue his own education. Cotton, perhaps the most important collector of books and manuscripts in Britain in the first half of the seventeenth century, became part of Arundel's circle of antiquarian friends and advisers, especially after 1614 when Cotton was deprived of a patron by the death of the earl of Northampton. Shortly after this loss Cotton presented Arundel with a manuscript volume containing Northampton's own prayers. Arundel took advantage of Cotton's position at the center of a wide network of antiquaries–he may well have been introduced to John Selden, Camden, and Franciscus Junius through Cotton. By 1618 Cotton was collecting antiquities for Arundel, and probably books as well. In the ensuing years Arundel gave preferment to Cotton's cousin and supported Cotton in his own political career.

Politics also influenced his other antiquarian relationships. Arundel was made a privy councillor and restored to the office of earl marshall in 1616. The office of Earl Marshall was an important position in martial law and was a hereditary office held by the dukes of Norfolk. It had fallen into abeyance after the execution of the fourth duke. In part because his post as earl marshall entailed responsibility for the College of Arms, he retained a professional interest in antiquarian and genealogical research. He worked closely with Selden, who became one of his trusted circle of scholars and advisers, and acted as Selden's political patron and protector.

In 1616 the Arundel incomes, already swelled thanks to the Northampton legacy, were further boosted by the death of Lady Aletheia's father. The Arundels now had the money to indulge fully their passions for art collecting and patronage, and they were fortunate to be able to embark on their prodigious collecting round immediately as Robert Carr, Earl of Somerset, was forced to forfeit his paintings and drawings by artists such as Jacopo Robusti Tintoretto, Paolo Veronese, Tiziano Vecellio Titian, and Leonardo da Vinci, which were then given to Arundel by the king. Arundel was able to step in to purchase other Italian works that Somerset had been in the process of buying through the agency of Dudley Carleton, the Venetian ambassador. Patronage was another aspect of Arundel's passionate embrace of the arts. He brought over from Holland the portrait painter Daniel Mytens in 1618 and encouraged both Sir Anthony Van Dyck and Peter Paul Rubens to visit England. Arundel's wife was Rubin's first English subject.

In the years from 1618 to 1626 Arundel acquired some twenty-four manuscripts in five volumes from the collection of Henry Savile of Banke, whose books were sold by his executors after his death. These included manuscripts of theology and history, mainly from northern monastic libraries such as Kirkham Priory, Guisborough Priory, Fountains Abbey, Newburgh Priory, Durham Priory, Reivaulx Abbey, and Kirkstall Abbey as well as Hyde Abbey near Winchester and St. Augustine's Abbey, Canterbury.

In 1621, thanks in part to the influence of Lancelot Andrewes and William Laud, Arundel engaged Franciscus Junius as librarian and tutor to his youngest son. Junius was probably the most important member of Arundel's circle of scholars in terms of his collection of books and manuscripts. Born in Heidelberg, Junius studied philology in Leiden under Gerardus Johannes Vossius and traveled to England in search of a career that would enable him to utilize his scholarly interests.

His position with Arundel allowed Junius to continue his study of philology, basing his study on materials in Arundel's collection. Junius shared with his patron not only a deep interest in antiquarian research but also a love of painting. He managed to combine these interests in his account of painting in the classical world, *De Pictura Veterum* (1637), translated into English as *The Painting of the Ancients* (1638).

At the accession of Charles I in 1625 Arundel lost his position as a leading influence on the throne, as his rival George Villiers, first Duke of Buckingham, replaced him as favorite. Arundel even spent several weeks during 1626 in the Tower of London under suspicion of treason but was freed thanks to pressure from the House of Lords. He was still able to pursue his scholarly interests, however. The work done on the collection of marble fragments bearing inscriptions that Arundel acquired through the agency of William Petty in Turkey and Greece provides an important example of the collector's collaboration with scholars. These fragments, now known as the Arundel Marbles, were studied by the distinguished scholars Selden, Cotton, Richard James, and the royal librarian, Patrick Young. The results of their researches were published as *Marmora Arvndelliana* (The Arundel Marbles, 1628), a highly successful mix of archaeology, history, and epigraphy, and Greek and Latin learning. The book spread the fame of Arundel and his collection throughout Europe.

By the mid 1630s Arundel had recovered some of his old power and influence at court and was appointed by Charles I to undertake an embassy to Emperor Ferdinand in 1636. Junius, who had became a close adviser to Arundel, accompanied him. In May of that year Arundel was in Nuremberg, where one of the greatest private libraries of Renaissance Europe, the collection formed by Willibald Pirckheimer with the assistance of Albrecht Dürer, was offered to him for sale by Hans Imhoff, a member of a rich Nuremberg banking family that acted for both the collector and the artist. The Imhoffs had also been given works by Dürer during his lifetime and through marriage had acquired the Pirckheimer library.

The collection was of the highest order. Not only was the collection impeccably humanist–being strong in Greek and Roman classics, philosophy, philology, and history, most of which were in scholarly editions by the best Italian Renaissance editors of the late fifteenth and early sixteenth century–but also at least twenty-two of the works had been illuminated and decorated by Dürer, who had acted as an agent for Pirckheimer in Italy, even staying as a guest at the house of the great humanist printer and publisher Aldus Manutius on one of his book-buying sprees. Some of these books still bear Dürer's illuminations, often Pirckheimer's own armorials, as well as one of three book-

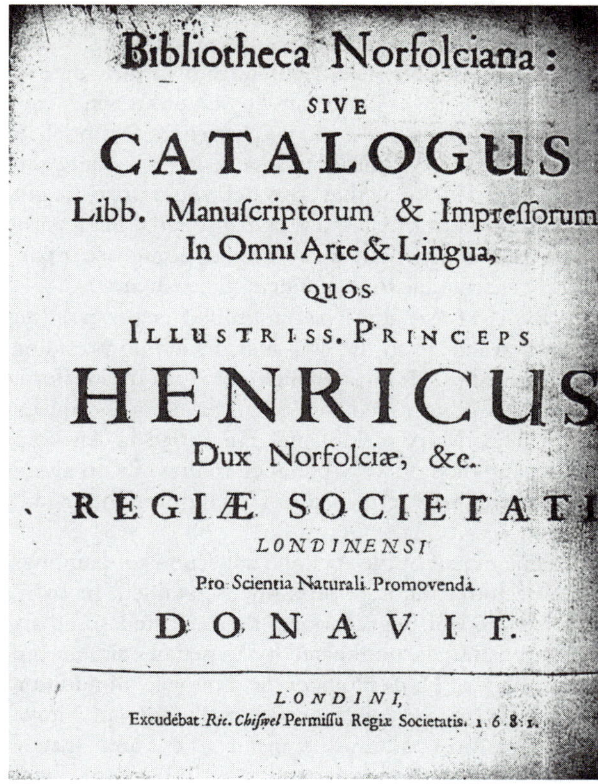
Bibliotheca Norfolciana:
SIVE
CATALOGUS
Libb. Manuſcriptorum & Impreſſorum
In Omni Arte & Lingua,
QUOS
ILLUSTRISS. PRINCEPS
HENRICUS
Dux Norfolciæ, &c.
REGIÆ SOCIETATI
LONDINENSI
Pro Scientia Naturali Promovendâ
DONAVIT.
LONDINI,
Excudebat *Ric. Chiſwel* Permiſſu Regiæ Societatis. 1681.

Cover of the catalogue compiled by William Perry to document the donation of books and manuscripts from the Arundel collection to the Royal Society

plates engraved specifically for the collection by the artist. The collection greatly enhanced Arundel's library with scholarly works of practical use to himself and his circle and also allowed him to indulge his passion for the visual arts by acquiring a large amount of work of one of the greatest artists of the Renaissance.

Arundel also made other acquisitions in Germany aside from the Pirckheimer books during his various diplomatic missions of the 1630s. In 1636 in Regensberg he bought a copy of the Nuremberg Chronicle, *Liber chronicarum* (1493), and in Nuremberg he bought a copy of Dürer's *Epitome in Divae Parthenices Mariae Historiam* (1511). While in Germany in 1636 Arundel met Wenceslaus Hollar, commencing what became by far his most important relationship with a living artist. Hollar joined Arundel's entourage and recorded the remainder of the trip in a series of watercolors. In England he documented Arundel's art collection in a series of impressive engravings and became firmly established as England's leading engraver and book illustrator.

In 1637 Arundel acquired one of the most important manuscripts in his collection–a superbly illuminated Psalter originally written in Venice in 1537 for a member of the Augustinian Convent of Santa Maria della Vergine. Although attributed from an early date to Giulio Clovio, it was illuminated by an unknown Venetian artist. The manuscript was given to Arundel in 1637 by Francesco Barberini's secretary Cassiano dal Pozzo. Barberini knew that Arundel would prize the gift because the work of Clovio was highly rated in all parts of Europe and especially by an English connoisseur particularly susceptible to the Venetian taste in art.

By 1641 Arundel was embroiled in the political events that led up to the civil war, including presiding over the trial of Thomas Wentworth, Earl of Strafford. In 1642 the king asked him to accompany the queen and Princess Mary to Holland. He settled in Antwerp in 1643 and died on 24 September 1646 while on a visit to Padua; his wife remained in Holland until her death in 1654.

The extent of the Arundel collections of paintings at their zenith cannot be certainly ascertained. In 1655, after a period of depredations, there existed some six hundred paintings, dominated by Venetian painters and by the work of Hans Holbein the Younger. In addition to the canvases, the collection also included many drawings, miniatures, albums, coins, statues, and sketchbooks. From the size, quality, and focus of these collections, and from the comments of contemporaries such as Rubens, it is clear that Arundel did not collect merely to enhance his status as a man of culture and taste. He was a passionate connoisseur who understood art.

After Arundel's death his library passed to his wife, Aletheia, who gave some of his collection away to his six sons, in particular to their fifth son, Sir William Howard, Viscount Stafford. One of the items he acquired, either before or after his father's death, was the important fifth-century manuscript of the book of Genesis in Greek, now known as the Cotton Genesis and held by the British Library. Cotton acquired the volume from Lady Stafford in the 1680s. A portion of the Arundel collection, including the marbles and works of art, passed to his eldest surviving son, Henry Frederick, and through him to his son Henry, the earl marshall, who became the sixth duke of Norfolk after that title was restored to the family in 1660.

Much of the collection was left in Arundel House in London. After Arundel's death the house had been used as a garrison, although it was returned to the sixth duke of Norfolk at the Restoration in 1660. The dispersal of the Arundel Collections is intimately bound up with the early years of the Royal Society, and the role in this organization played by Henry Howard, sixth Duke of Norfolk, his brother Charles Howard of Greystoke, and their close connection with John Evelyn, one of the leading members of the society. The Royal Society used Arundel House as a meeting place between 1666–1667 by the favor of the duke, who was elected a fellow of the Royal Society on 28 November 1666, and he, and eventually his son, Henry Howard, seventh Duke of Norfolk, played an active role in the activities of the institution.

Evelyn persuaded Henry, sixth Duke of Norfolk, to dispose of the remainder of the Arundel Collection, including the printed and manuscript books, to the Royal Society, the gift being made official on 2 January of 1667. Evelyn wrote of his influence over the duke in his diary of 29 August 1678:

> I was cald againe to London to wait againe on the Duke of Norfolck who, onely having at my request bestow'd the Arundelian Library on the Royal Society, sent to me to take charge of the Bookes & remove them; onely that I would suffer the Heraulds Chiefe Officer, Sir W: Dugdale, to have such of them as concernd Herauldry & Martials Office As bokes of Armorie & Genealogies; the Duke being Earle Marishal of England: I procured for our Society besides Printed bookes, neere 700 MSS. Some in Greeke of greate concernment; The Printed bookes being of the oldest Impressions are not the lesse valuable; I esteeme them almost equal with MSS: Most of the Fathers printed at Basil &c: before the Jesuites abused them with their Expurgatorie Indexes. There is a noble MSS: of Vitruvius: Many of these Bookes had been presented by Popes, Cardinals, & greate persons to the Earles of Arundell & Dukes of Norfolck; & the late magnificent The: Earl of Arundel bought a noble Library in Germanie, which is in this collection; nor should I for the honour I beare the family, have perswaded the Duke to part with these, had I not seene how negligent he was of them, suffering the priests, & every body to carry away & dispose of what they pleased: so as abundance of rare things are gon & irrecoverable.

Arundel apparently intended more of the manuscripts to be given to the College of Arms than eventually found their way there as Dugdale's schedule of books "given by the Duke of Norfolk to the Office of Arms" closes with a list of "Manuscripts intended by the duke of Norfolke for the Office of Armes, but taken to Gresham Colledge," presumably due to the intervention of the persistent Evelyn.

The Royal Society was understandably delighted with such a magnificent gift, which at a stroke made its collection one of the most significant in London. Samuel Pepys noted in his diary that it was a "noble gift they [the Royal Society] value at 1000£." Little was done with the books for several years, despite the council urging Robert Hooke and others to begin cataloguing, and the books remained at Arundel House even after the society was able to move back to Gresham

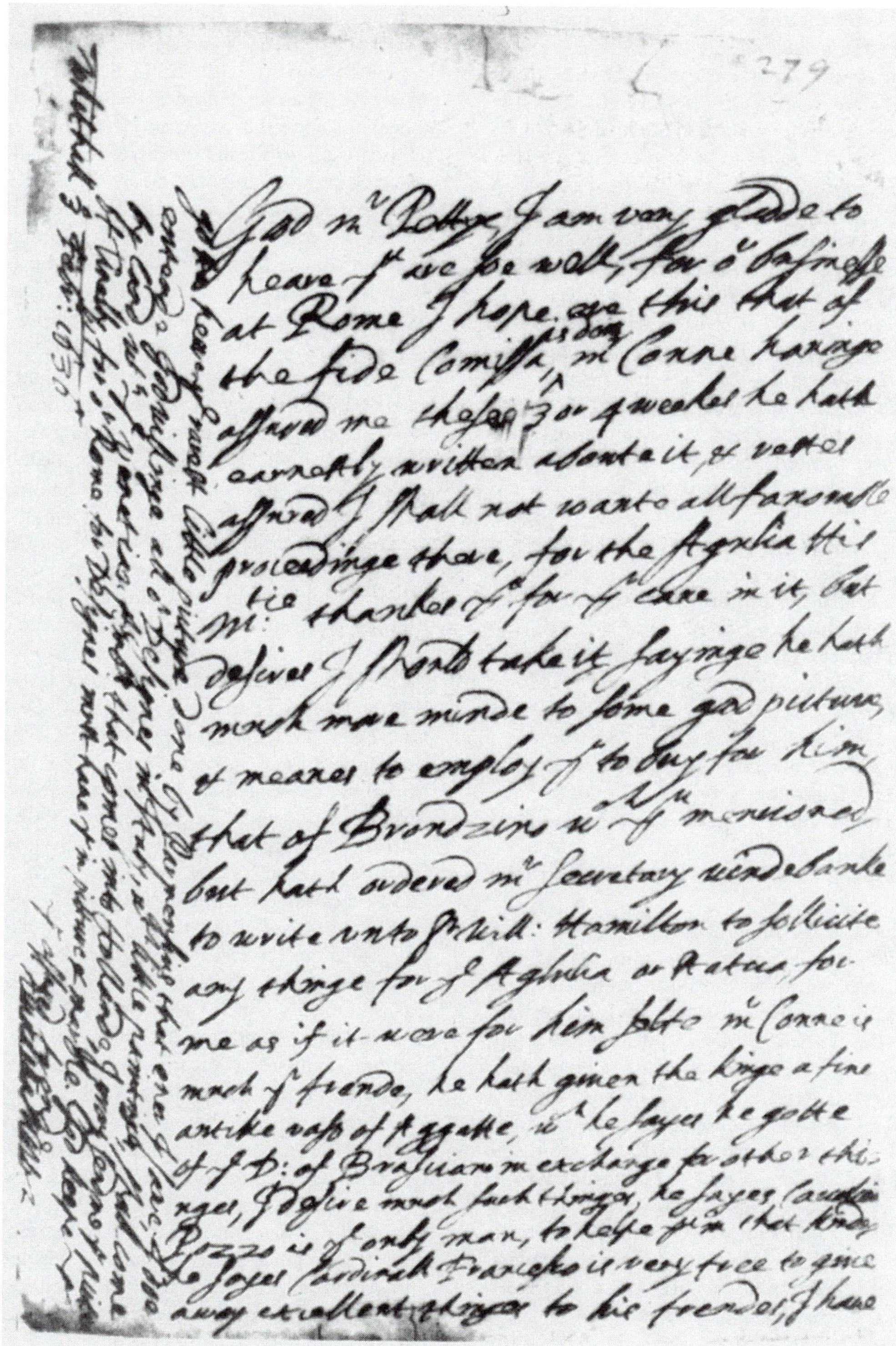

Good Mr Pettye I am very gladde to
heare yt we soe well, for or businesse
at Rome I hope ere this that of
the fide Comissa is don, mr Conne havinge
assured me these 3 or 4 weekes he hath
earnestly written about it, & rather
assured I shall not wante all favourable
proceedinge there, for the Agulia His
Matie thankes you for yr care in it, but
desires I shoulde take it, sayinge he hath
much more minde to some good pictures,
& meanes to employ you to buy for him
that of Bronzino wch you mentioned
but hath ordered mr Secretary Windebanke
to write unto Sr Will: Hamilton to sollicite
any thinge for ye Agulia or statues for
me as if it were for him selfe mr Conne is
much yr frende, he hath given the Kinge a fine
antike vase of Aggatte, wch he sayes he gotte
of ye D: of Brassiano in exchange for other thinges, I desire much such thinges, he sayes Cavalier
Pozzo is ye only man, to helpe him that kinde
he sayes Cardinall Francesco is very free to give
away excellent thinges to his frendes, I have

Letter from Arundel, dated 3 February 1636, to the scholar William Petty, who acted as Arundel's agent in the purchase of artworks in Italy (British Library)

College in 1673, prompting the duke to demand that the library be better looked after.

A committee was appointed to oversee the care of the library, and as secretary of the society Hooke made arrangements for a catalogue to be made. In 1678 he finally arranged for the books to be moved out of Arundel House to Gresham College, prior to the destruction of the old Norfolk family residence in 1678. A catalogue was compiled by William Perry, one of the professors of Gresham College, and was printed and sold by Richard Chiswel in 1681. It was titled *Bibliotheca Norfolciana, sive, Catalogus libb. manuscriptorum & impressorum in omni arte & lingua, quos illustriss princeps Henricus Dux Norfolciae, &c. Regiae societati Londinenst pro scientia naturali promovenda donavit.* The catalogue amounted to some 175 quarto pages, of which the final 26 are devoted to manuscripts. In all some 4,000 printed books and almost 500 volumes of manuscripts were given to the society in the Norfolk gift.

Arundel's manuscripts were acquired from a diverse collection of sources but were particularly rich in texts of early English historians and chroniclers, such as Geoffrey of Monmouth's *Historia regum Britanniae* (no less than seven copies), Henry of Huntingdon's *Historia Anglorum,* Ranulf Higden's *Polychronicon,* Roger de Hoveden's *Annals,* Wiliam of Malmesbury's *Gesta Regum Anglorum* and his *Historia Novella,* and Matthew of Westminster's *Flores Historiarum,* as well as works by Nicholas Trivet, Aelred of Reivaulx, Giraldus Cambrensis, and Peter of Blois. The collection was no less well represented in literary manuscripts including works by John Capgrave, Thomas Hoccleve, and John Lydgate.

The collection also included thirteen cartularies, collections or copies of charters, including a Glastonbury Abbey cartulary now in the Bodleian and a register from the same house in the British Library, and cartularies of the Hospital of St. John at Bury St. Edmunds, a register from the Cistercian Abbey of Newenham in Devon, a register from Tintern Abbey, a cartulary from St. Alban's Abbey, two registers from Christ Church at Canterbury, a cartulary from the Benedictine Abbey at Colchester, and a cartulary from the Cistercian Abbey at Sibton, all now in the Arundel Collection in the British Library. Cartularies from his collection from St. Albans Abbey and from the Augustianian Priory of Merton in Surrey are now in the Arundel Collection in the College of Arms.

There were many early printed editions in the collection, including at least 355 incunabula listed in the catalogue of the books given to the Royal Society by the sixth duke of Norfolk. As Arundel rarely inserted any marks of his own ownership into the books that he acquired there is no way of being exact about the extent of his collection. Of this part of the collection at least seventy-one volumes can be identified both from existing books and from the 1925 Sotheby's auction catalogue as being volumes from the Pirckheimer collection, acquired by Arundel in 1636. Most, but by no means all, of these books were incunabula. An illustrated edition of Cicero's *Orationes* (Venice, 1517) is now at Harvard. One of the strengths of the Pirckheimer collection was tract volumes of Reformation controversies, especially those that relate to Martin Luther, and thus Arundel owned a substantial number of controversial sixteenth-century pamphlets. Many of these works were in German, and are now exceedingly rare.

The incunabula, however, were and still are the most impressive part of the Arundel book collections. Apart from a small number of German incunabula acquired through the Pirckheimer collection–including a copy of the *Rosarium decretorum* of Guido de Baysio (Strasbourg, ca. 1473) and the *Facetiae* of Poggius Florentinus (Nuremberg, 1475)–the bulk of the collection consisted of copies of some of the most important books published in Italy in the fifteenth century. Although Venetian imprints dominate the Italian incunabula, Arundel also acquired books printed in smaller cities: from Pavia, Baldus Ubaldis's *Consilia et responsa* (1488), Felinus Sandaeus's *Super titulo De fide instrumentum* (1497) and *De exceptionibus* (1496), Laurentius de Rodolphis's *Tractatus usuarum* (1497), and Jason de Maino's *Commentaria in I infortiati veteris* (1492); from Modena, Butigella's *Pro Joanne Philippo Gambaloita Oratio* (1494); from Parma, St. Jerome's *Epistolae* (1480); and from Padua, Lanfrancus de Oriano's *De arbitris* (1498) and Franciscus Philelphus's *Invectiva in Georgiam Merulam* (1481). Some of these early books are found bound together in an interesting *sammelband* (miscellaneous collection of treatises) that contains an undated copy of Bartholomaeus Fontius's *Orationes* (Florence: Bartolommeo di Libri) together with fifteen other printed tracts and one manuscript. It came from the Pirckheimer Collection and is now in the British Library.

Aside from the incunabula the collection was particularly rich in Italian thought and literature, including works by Giovanni Boccaccio (nine different editions), Aretino, Pietro Bembo, and Dante Alighieri (seven different editions). Authors more commonly found in great Renaissance libraries, such as Desiderius Erasmus and Aristotle, are also present. It is interesting to note the presence of some rather more contemporary writing, especially on politics, the French political theorist Jean Bodin being particularly well represented, as were the theological works of several controversial English clerics, especially Andrewes. Apart from pamphlets concerning current political and theological disputes, the remainder of the works in English are legal, including

William Lambard's *Eirenarchia* (1582) and John Manwood's *Treatise on Forest Laws* (1598).

The Arundel collection as presented to the Royal Society was slowly dispersed. In 1786 the books were stamped "ex dono Henrici Howard Nofolcienses," but strays were beginning to be sold, although mainly duplicates at this early stage. As the nineteenth century progressed, the nature of the society changed and it became more closely identified with science. In 1829 a committee was appointed to examine all the manuscripts in the library with a view of exchanging with the British Museum those not considered to be relevant to the newly defined role of the society. Bernard Edward Howard, twelfth Duke of Norfolk, gave his permission for the Arundel manuscripts to be dealt with in this way, and the exchange took place in 1831. In return for handing over the manuscripts, the society received books and cash from the museum.

In 1873 many printed books were sold to fellows and booksellers, including Bernard Quaritch, who sold the cream in an October 1873 catalogue, *Bibliotheca Xylographica, Typographica, & Palaeographica,* and disposed of the humbler books in piecemeal fashion. Purchasers of books from Quaritch in 1873 included many of his regular bibliophilic customers, especially the earl of Crawford–whose acquisitions included the 1472 edition of Dante's *Liber Dantis: l'edizione principe jesina della Commedia,* published in Mantua; Robertus Valturius's *De re Militari,* published in Verona in 1472; and the Pirckheimer copy of the works of Virgil, published by the Aldine Press in 1501–Henry Huth, and the marquess of Bath. In 1920 the library committee of the Royal Library decided to dispose of the nonscientific printed books from the Norfolk collection that still remained. The British Museum was offered first choice and selected both fifteenth- and sixteenth-century books; the remainder, some 228 lots, were sold at Sotheby's in 1925.

As a collector Thomas Howard, second Earl of Arundel, must stand in the first rank. He virtually single-handedly established the standards of connoisseurship in art that dictated elite taste in Britain for almost two centuries. While his book collecting lacked the focus of his activities in collecting portrait paintings, it nevertheless took place on a serious scale, especially in the field of medieval manuscripts from the British monastic collections dispersed in the sixteenth century and in the area of Italian printed books of the fifteenth century. Arundel is remembered as a book collector of especial importance in Britain for his acquisition of the surviving portion of the library of Willibald Pirckheimer in 1636, which brought to the country one of the finest collections of books formed in early Renaissance Europe.

References:

Nicolas Barker, "The Books of Henry Howard, Earl of Northampton," *Bodleian Library Record,* 13, no. 5 (1990): 375–381;

T. A. Birrell, *English Monarchs and Their Books: From Henry VII to Charles II* (London: British Library, 1987);

Philipp F. Fehl, "Franciscus Junius and the Defense of Art," *Artibus et Historiae,* 3 (1981): 9–56;

Marie Boas Hall, *The Library and Archives of the Royal Society 1660–1990* (London: Royal Society, 1992);

Mary F. S. Hervey, *The Life Correspondence & Collections of Thomas Howard Earl of Arundel* (Cambridge: Cambridge University Press, 1921);

David Howarth, *Lord Arundel and His Circle* (New Haven & London: Yale University Press, 1985);

David Jaffé and others, "The Earl and Countess of Arundel: Renaissance Collectors," *Apollo,* 144 (August 1996): 3–31;

George Ornsby, ed., *Selections from the Household Books of Lord William Howard of Naworth Castle: With an Appendix Containing Some of his Papers and Letters, and other Documents Illustrative of his Life and Times,* Surtees Society Publications, volume 68 (Durham: Published for the Society by Andrews, 1878);

Linda Levy Peck, *Northampton: Policy and Patronage at the Court of James I* (London: Allen & Unwin, 1982);

Peck, "Uncovering the Arundel Library at the Royal Society: Changing Meanings of Science and the Fate of the Norfolk Donation," *Notes and Records of the Royal Society of London,* 52 (1), 3–24 (1998);

Kevin Sharpe, *Sir Robert Cotton 1586–1631: History and Politics in Early Modern England* (Oxford: Oxford University Press, 1979);

Colin G. C. Tite, *The Manuscript Library of Sir Robert Cotton* (London: British Library, 1994).

Papers:

The most important collections of Thomas Howard and the Howard family papers are held at Arundel Castle, the British Library, and Lambeth Palace Library. The Howard of Naworth papers are in Durham University Library.

Humphrey, Duke of Gloucester

(January? 1391 – 23 February 1447)

Virginia T. Bemis
Ashland University

CATALOGUE: *Duke Humfrey and English Humanism in the Fifteenth Century: Catalogue of an Exhibition held in the Bodleian Library, Oxford,* compiled by Albinia Catherine de la Mare and Richard Hunt (Oxford: Bodleian Library, 1970).

Humphrey, Duke of Gloucester; crayon portrait attributed to Jacques Le Boucq (Bibliothèque de la Ville d'Arras)

Humphrey, Duke of Gloucester, gained his popular title of "Good Duke Humphrey" not for his public actions and political intrigues but as a patron of learning. The grandson of John of Gaunt, Duke of Lancaster; the youngest son of the future King Henry IV; and the youngest brother of the future King Henry V, Humphrey was destined to play a part on the English political scene. As a book collector and as a sponsor of Renaissance scholarship, he did much to bring the "new learning" to England and inspired others to continue where he had begun.

Humphrey was born in 1391, the youngest son of Henry Bolingbroke, Earl of Derby, and his first wife, Mary de Bohun, daughter of Humphrey Bohun, Earl of Hereford, after whom he was named. His exact date of birth is not known, but it was probably in January or February of 1391. During Bolingbroke's exile abroad before he deposed Richard II and took the throne, Humphrey and his older brothers, Henry, Thomas, and John, remained in England, receiving the education suitable for young noblemen of the period. Little is known of Humphrey's childhood, though he spent much of his youth at Eaton Tregoes, near Ross-on-Wye, with his sisters, Blanche and Philippa. On the day before his father's coronation on 11 October 1399 as Henry IV, Humphrey was made a knight; he became a Knight of the Garter the following year. He is said to have been present at the Battle of Shrewsbury in 1403, which put down the rising of the Welsh under Edmund Mortimer and the Percy adherents in the north under Harry Hotspur. A happier note came when the young boy attended his father's second marriage, to Joanna of Navarre, widow of the duke of Brittany, early in 1403.

Tradition has it that Humphrey was educated at Balliol College, Oxford, where he studied rhetoric and "res naturae" and formed a lifelong connection to Oxford University. It is possible that young Humphrey was for a time destined for the church, a not unusual career path for younger sons of noble houses. If so, his bent for scholarship was an advantage. Certainly, he developed a taste for reading and a thirst for knowledge that later led him to gather books and patronize scholars and writers. During the course of his life he gave several gifts of books and money to Oxford University, the earliest in 1411.

Humphrey assumed a public role after his older brother's accession to the throne in 1413. Henry V created his brother duke of Gloucester and earl of Pembroke and appointed him great chamberlain of England. One of the king's chief advisers, Gloucester took part in the war with France, including the siege of Harfleur and the Battle of Agincourt. At Agincourt on 25 October 1415, Gloucester was wounded while battling the duke of Alençon and rescued by Henry V. For his services in the war, Gloucester was rewarded with lands in Wales and the positions of lord warden of the Cinque Ports, constable of Dover Castle, and lord of the Isle of Wight and Carisbrooke.

During the year 1416 Gloucester showed the dramatic tendencies that were later to be a source of difficulty for him. He rode into the sea, sword in hand, to greet King Sigismund at Dover on 30 April 1416 and made the king of Germany and Hungary promise that he would not claim jurisdiction over England. On 4 October of that year, Gloucester rode into the water again, to surrender himself to John of Burgundy as a hostage for a peace conference at Calais. Released after the conference, which had achieved nothing, Gloucester traveled with Sigismund from Calais to Dordrecht.

Gloucester proved his military ability in 1417 during Henry's second set of campaigns in France. After taking Lisieux and Cherbourg, he assisted in the siege of Rouen and was made governor of that city in 1419. Later that year Henry appointed him regent of England, replacing John, Duke of Bedford, whose services were needed in France. Gloucester stayed in England until the death of Henry V on 31 August 1422, a period in which he developed the reputation that later led the Venetian Piero del Monte to describe Gloucester as like Julius Caesar in being both active in affairs of state and a man of letters. As Kenneth H. Vickers reports in *Humphrey, Duke of Gloucester* (1907), Piero praised Gloucester for preferring study to hunting, for finding "no real pleasure aside from the reading of books."

Gloucester claimed the regency for the infant Henry VI, based partly on his brother's will, but Parliament rejected him in favor of Bedford, allowing him the secondary position of protector of the realm and chief counselor when Bedford was absent. Since Bedford was much abroad, this made Gloucester protector immediately, at a salary of 8,000 marks a year. His power, however, was limited, and a regency council of which he was but a lesser member actually ruled.

Henry V had cautioned his brother not to prefer his own interests to those of England, yet that is exactly what he did in 1422, when he married Jacqueline of Bavaria, Countess of Hainault, whose claim to the Netherlands put England in a continuing struggle with Burgundy. The marriage was irregular and may have been bigamous, since Pope Martin V did not recognize the annulment of her marriage to John, Duke of Brabant. Gloucester's efforts to reclaim his wife's inheritance in Hainault cost England lives and funds and were ultimately a failure. In 1428 Gloucester's marriage with Jacqueline was annulled, and in 1431 he married his mistress, Eleanor Cobham. She had been one of the ladies attending Jacqueline and may have been the mother of his two illegitimate children, Arthur and Antigone, the latter name an indication of the father's strong interest in the classics.

Even after Henry VI was crowned on 6 November 1429, Gloucester continued his intriguing grasp for power. After Bedford's death in 1435, which left Gloucester heir presumptive to the throne, he positioned himself as the champion of English rights in France. He denounced his nephew Henry Beaufort and others who wanted to end the constant state of war with France and repeatedly accused his opponents in council of dishonesty and treachery.

Political intrigue did not occupy all of Gloucester's time. In 1439, responding to an appeal from the university, he gave Oxford 129 books, which formed an important part of the library of the institution. While no list of his donations survives, it is likely that the books in this group included many works by Plato and Aristotle, whose work formed a great part of his collection. He is known to have given volumes by William of Occam, St. Bede, and St. Albertus Magnus as well as letters of the early church fathers. With a value of more than £1,000, the gift was "a more splendid donation than any prince or king had given since the foundation of the University." Previously, he had sponsored lectures and given grants of money toward the founding of the divinity school. Oxford at the time was not the great seat of learning it had been. Many of its buildings were closed, students were few, and books were in such short supply that most of the teaching had to be done orally. Gloucester's support helped open the university to the new learning.

Some of the books Gloucester gave to the university still exist and can be attributed to his collection. Those of his books that survive reasonably intact show his habit of inscribing them not at the beginning of the book but at the end, with the French phrase "Cest livre est A moy Homfrey duc de Gloucestre" (This book belongs to me, Humphrey, Duke of Gloucester) and a note on the donor or topic of the book. Among the books still held by the university is a copy of the letters of Nicholas de Clémanges, a French theologian who died about 1400. The last folio of the book is inscribed with Humphrey's name and the note that it was a gift to the duke from one of the canons of the cathedral at Rouen. Also part of the 1639 gift was a copy of the letters of Pliny the Younger, which Vickers asserts was

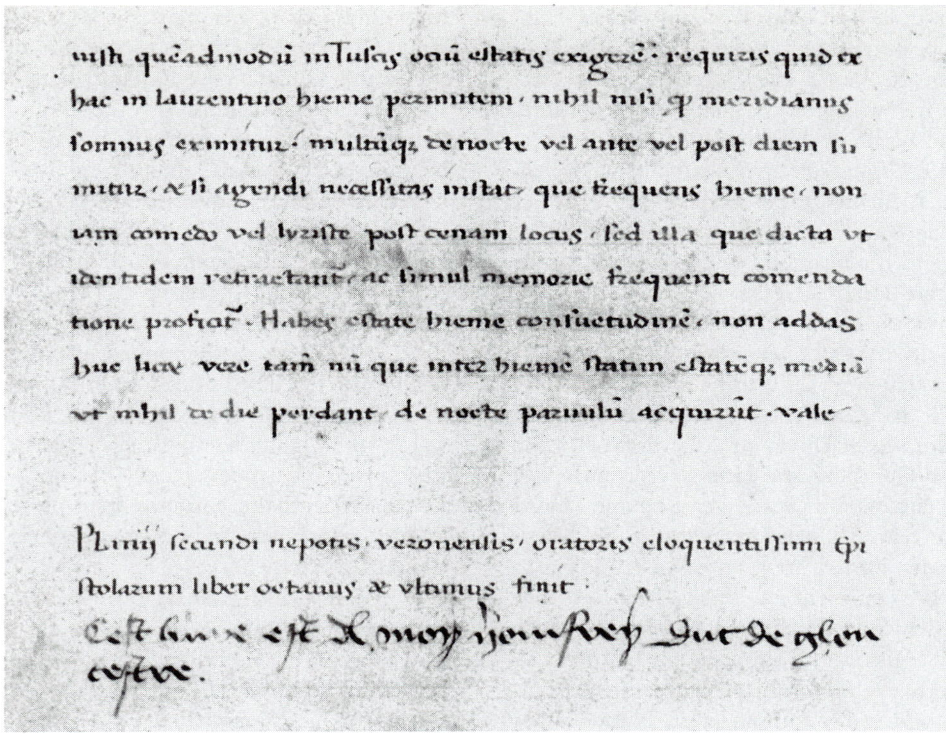

Page from a manuscript copy of the letters of Pliny the Younger commissioned by the duke, circa 1440 (Bodleian Library)

among the books sent from Italy at Gloucester's request by Pier Candido Decembrio, a translator of the Greek classics with whom he formed a scholarly connection, as well as a copy of Leonardo Aretino Bruni's translations of Aristotle's *Poetics.*

During Gloucester's lifetime, he was looked upon as a patron of letters. He brought Italian scholars to England, giving them positions in his household, and commissioned translations of the Greek and Roman classics into French and English. His friendship with Zano Castiglione, Bishop of Bayeux, brought Gloucester into contact with leading Italian writers and thinkers. Many of them either produced books for Humphrey or came to England to help him study the books he collected. His favored studies were in the Greek and early Roman classics, though he also encouraged English writers. One of the writers who translated books and sent manuscripts to Gloucester was the famed translator Lapo da Castiglionchio, whose translations of Plutarch, Demosthenes, and other Greek texts were widely admired. To Gloucester, Lapo dedicated his translation of Plutarch's *Life of Artaxerxes* and sent it to him along with the lives of Theseus, Solon, Pericles, Themistocles, and Camillus.

Gloucester is known to have had a large collection of books other than those he gave to Oxford. Because he was known as a book lover, those who sought his favor often gave him books rather than more customary gifts. He owned works by Suetonius, Flavius Josephus, Cassiodorus, and Eusebius in the historical part of his collection. His interests also included history after the classical period, as shown by the surviving illuminated volume *Chroniques des Roys de France Jusques a la Mort de St. Loys l'an 1270,* inscribed in Humphrey's hand with a notation that it was a gift from the executors of the Seigneur de Faunhere. He also owned Matthew Paris's *Historia Anglie,* originally presented by the author to the abbey of St. Albans, and possibly a gift to the duke from his close friend, Abbot John Whethamstead.

Gloucester owned many medical books and all the leading works on astronomy and astrology. His copy of Ptolemy's *Cosmographia,* which eventually made its way to the Magdalen College Library after the dispersal of the divinity school holdings, is but one of these. A treatise on surgery by the eleventh-century Arabian writer Aboo-l-Kassim testifies to the eclectic nature of Gloucester's interest in science. His scientific holdings also included Arabian works on astronomy alongside Roger Bacon's *De Celo et Mundo.* His correspondence shows orders for works on medicine by Cornelius Celsus, natural history by Pliny the Elder, architecture by Vitruvius, and agriculture by Columella.

Gloucester's holdings in philosophy and literature included Aristotle, Plato, Plutarch, Sallust, Ovid, Terence, Seneca, and all the known works of Cicero. Many of these were in translations he had commissioned. Among surviving books known to have been his at one time is a volume of philosophic treatises that includes Latin translations of Plato's *Phaedo* and *Meno*. He was reputed never to have been without his copy of Plato's *Republic*.

His commissioning of translations of Aristotle and Plato kept Gloucester in contact with many of the important scholars of Europe. His correspondence with Bruni after reading the translation of Aristotle's *Ethics* led to Bruni's doing a translation of the *Politics* and other works. As biographer Vickers asserts, Gloucester's 1439 letter to Candido upon receiving the first five books of the scholar's translation of Plato's *Republic*–a project undertaken through Gloucester's patronage–shows the duke's thorough and enthusiastic acceptance of the spirit of the Renaissance:

> We have received your longed-for letters with the books of Plato, which have given us much pleasure. Nothing could give us more pleasure, especially since they will reflect honour and glory on us, as you say. We are therefore very grateful to you for having done so much hard work in our name, whence both we and you will receive great praise. The books are of such a kind that they invite even the unwilling to read them; such is the dignity and grace of Plato, and so successful is your interpretation of him, that we cannot say to whom we owe most, to him for drawing a prince of such wise statesmanship, or to you for labouring to bring to light this statesmanship hidden and almost lost by our negligence. You have chosen a noble and worthy province which cannot be taken from you in any age, nor lost by any forgetfulness, that is, if what the wisest men say be true, and glory is indeed immortal. We have read and re-read these books, and with such pleasure that we have determined that they shall never leave our side, whether we be at home or on military service, for if your translation cannot be compared to the divine eloquence of Plato, nevertheless in our opinion it is hardly inferior. These books shall be always kept at hand, so that we may ever have something to give us pleasure, and that they may be almost as counsellors and companions for so much of our life as is left to us, as was the wisdom of Nestor to Agamemnon, and that of Achates to Aeneas. On the same page Plato and Candido can be read and admired together, and the latter, nor less than ourselves, be seen labouring to increase our dignity. We exhort, and would compel you to labour hard at the completion of the other books which we await impatiently. Do not think that anything can give us more pleasure than that which relates to learning and the cult of letters. You have and shall have whatsoever you wish from us, who have always favoured your studies. We possess Livy and other eminent writers, and nearly all the works of Cicero which have been hitherto found. If you have anything of great value, we beg of you to tell us.

After this letter, it is hardly surprising that Candido acted as Gloucester's book buyer in Italy, searching out works from lists sent to him and commissioning copies of books from libraries in Italy.

Through Candido's agency Gloucester was able to gain works by Apuleius, the elder and the younger Pliny, Cornelius Celsus, Marcus Terentius Varro, and the geographer Pomponius Mela as well as treatises on architecture and agriculture. At least thirty-one of the books Candido bought or had copied are known to have arrived safely, and many more are mentioned in terms that suggest they too reached Gloucester's collection. Gloucester evidently sent Candido a catalogue of his library that impressed the translator with its breadth and variety. It is unfortunate that, while Candido's reaction to the catalogue survived, the list itself did not.

Gloucester also served as patron of English writers and scholars, including the poet John Lydgate, from whom he commissioned several translations of Boccaccio's work, and John Capgrave, the historian monk who called Gloucester "the most lettered prince in the world" and dedicated several of his works to him. One of those books, Capgrave's *Commentary on the Book of Genesis,* written in 1437–1438, was among the last group of books given to Oxford. As Gloucester notes at the end of the book, it was presented by the author "a mon manoir de Pensherst" (at my manor of Pensherst). So well known was Gloucester as an encourager of authors that many of the surviving portrait illuminations show him with books or manuscripts. In the prologue of the translation of Boccaccio, Lydgate pays poetic tribute to Gloucester as one who "doth excel / in understanding all others of his age / and hath great joy with clerks to commune," a man who defeats sloth by diligent study of "bokis of antiquite."

Gloucester's position so near to the throne and King Henry VI's lack of a son led Duchess Eleanor to hope that she might one day be queen. She apparently resorted to fortune-telling and possibly other magic to ensure this would happen. As a result, in 1441, she was charged with heresy, witchcraft, and treason. Gloucester dared not intervene, lest he be charged himself, and she was sentenced to penance and imprisonment for life.

In his last years Gloucester had lost most political influence and spent most of his time in literary studies. He continued to collect books on the new learning and to support scholarship and maintained his connection with Oxford. In 1444 the university decided to build a new library as the upper story of the divinity school.

Duke Humphrey's Library, part of the Bodleian Library at Oxford University

Thomas Chace, former master of Balliol and chancellor of the university, who also served as chaplain to the duke, helped the negotiations to gain the duke's patronage yet again. Gloucester's pledge of £100 and the rest of his books after his death inspired them to name the new library after him. The gratitude of the university was summarized in a letter to the duke:

> By your magnificent donation, from having been well-nigh without books, this University has become richer than any other in these treasures; so that we scarcely know where to bestow them . . . Our words are too feeble to express our thanks, and we wish for a permanent memorial of your generosity. If we could place your books in a suitable chamber, separate from others, the crowding of the readers might be avoided, and for this purpose we would offer the new school now in building. The situation is retired and quiet, and we venture to suggest that the new library should be called by your name.

Under construction at the time of Gloucester's death, the building was not finally ready to receive books until forty years later. Since he died intestate, much of his final gift of books and money never arrived, but he had nonetheless started a library that was a worthy legacy.

While Gloucester had largely abandoned politics toward the end of his life, he did oppose the Beaufort-led plan to marry Henry to Margaret of Anjou, thus earning another powerful enemy and estranging himself permanently from his nephew the king. Gloucester believed that a better choice was one of the daughters of the Count of Armagnac, leading to an alliance with forces hostile to France. Because Gloucester was rumored to be raising troops in Wales in 1447 and was planning to lay claim to the throne, he was put under house arrest on 18 February. Hoping to gain a pardon for his wife, he was in fact on his way to Parliament with a small troop of Welsh horsemen when he was captured. Gloucester became ill and died on 23 February 1447, apparently of a stroke, although there were rumors that his enemies had murdered him. One of the charges the Yorkist partisans used later in the attempt to depose Henry was that his supporters had been responsible for the death of "Good Duke Humphrey."

In his history plays on Henry VI, William Shakespeare presents the legend of the "good duke" of popular mythology. Gloucester is shown as a vigorous defender of England's interests, champion of the people's liberties against intriguing clerics and tyrannical magnates such as Beaufort and Suffolk, and unfairly attacked by Queen Margaret, who saw him as a rival for control over the king. For Shakespeare, Gloucester was a victimized great leader who had dedicated his life to preserving and defending the realm, the voice of national pride and purpose. Shakespeare also makes explicit the popular belief that Gloucester was murdered at the instigation of the duke of Suffolk.

Gloucester's body was transported to St. Albans Abbey and buried there on 4 March 1447, on the south side of the shrine of St. Alban. The monks there had been his friends, even when he took the side of Oxford in a dispute with the abbey concerning student fees, and Abbot John Whethamstead, a scholar of note, had been one of Gloucester's literary advisers. His tomb can still be seen, decorated with his arms. His most lasting legacy was his gifts to Oxford and his patronage of the university. The library of which he was a patron came to be called "Duke Humphrey's Library." After being restored by Thomas Bodley in 1601, it served as the sole reading room in the Bodleian Library until 1907.

The books Humphrey left are no longer in place. Many were stolen or damaged with the passage of time, in part because of a policy of unsupervised borrowing. The Reformation also led to pillaging. By 1550 the remaining books had been removed under the Act against Superstitious Books and Images, leaving nothing in Duke Humphrey's Library save the walls and furniture. The books found their way into private collections or to booksellers. Some were broken up and used by glovers for pressing gloves and by tailors to make measures.

Three of Gloucester's original books have returned to the Bodleian, and there are others at Oriel, St. John's, and Corpus Christi Colleges. His books can be found as far afield as the British Library and the Bibliothèque Nationale. The British Library came to house his copy of Wycliff's Bible in two volumes and some translations of the minor works of St. Athanasius by Antonio di Beccaria, originally in two volumes but later rebound as one. Also to be found there are a volume of Psalms, a copy of *Le Songe de Vergier* (a discourse on spiritual and temporal power) once owned by King Charles V of France, and the Kassim surgical treatise. A collection of the letters of Cicero, originally given to Gloucester by Zano, Bishop of Bayeux; a translation of Boccaccio's *Decameron;* and a version of *Le Roman de Renard* found their way to the Bibliothèque Nationale.

Even though his library was dispersed and only a portion of the books Gloucester inscribed with "Cest livre est A moy Homfrey duc de Gloucestre" still exist, the effects of his book collecting remain. In building his collection Gloucester not only gave employment to scholars, he provided useful material for generations of future scholars. His career shows that a collector may make a contribution to history that reaches far beyond the mere physical accumulation of books.

Reference:

Vickers, Kenneth H. *Humphrey, Duke of Gloucester* (London: Constable, 1907).

Thomas James

(1572? – August 1629)

Richard W. Clement
University of Kansas

BOOKS: *Bellum papale; sive concordia discors Sixti Quinti, et Clementis Octavi circa Hieronymianam editionem* (London: G. Bishop, R. Newberie, & R. Barker, 1600);

Ecloga Oxonio-Cantabrigiensis, tributa in libros duos; quorum prior continet catalogum confusum librorum manuscriptorum in illustrissimis Bibliothecis, e duarum florentissimarum Academiarum, Oxoniae et Cantabrigiae, posterior, catalogum eorundem distinctum et dispositum secundum quatuor facultates, observato tam in nominibus, quam in operibus ipsis, alphabetico literarum ordine. Ostensum est praeterea in hoc secundo libro, quid a quoquo viro scriptum sit, quo tempore, ac postremo quot eiusdem libri exemplaria, quibus q[uod] in locis habeantur. (London: J. Bishop & G. Norton, 1600);

Catalogvs librorvm bibliothecae pvblicae qvam vir ornatissimus. Thomas Bodleivs eques auratus in Academia Oxoniensi nuper instituit; continet autem libros alphabetice dispositos secundum quatuor facultates: cvm qvadrvplici elencho expositorum e. ecripturae, Aristotelis, juris vtriusq[ue] & principum medicinae, ad vsum alinae Academiae Oxoniensis (Oxford: Joseph Barnes, 1605); republished as *The First Printed Catalogue of the Bodleian Library, 1605: A Facsimile = Catalogus librorum bibliothecae publicae quam vir ornatissimus Thomas Bodleius eques auratus in Academia Oxoniensi nuper instituit* (Oxford: Clarendon Press, 1986);

Concordantiæ sanctorum patrum, i.e. vera & pia libri canticorum per patres universus, tam Graecos quam Latinos, expositio (Oxford: J. Barnes, 1607);

The Humble Supplication of Thomas James, Student in Divinitie, and Keeper of the Publike Librarie at Oxford, for Reformation of the Ancient Fathers Workes, by Papists Sundrie Wayes Depraved (London: J. Windet, 1607?);

An Apologie for Iohn Wickliffe, shewing his Conformitie with the now Church of England; with Answere to Such Slanderous Obiections, as haue beene lately vrged against him by Father Parsons, the Apologists, and others. Collected chiefly out of diuerse works of his in written hand, by Gods especiall providence remaining in the publike library at Oxford, of the honorable foundation of Sr. Thomas Bodley Knight (Oxford: Joseph Barnes, 1608);

Thomas James (portrait attributed to Gilbert Jackson; Bodleian Library, Oxford)

Bellum Gregorianum, sive corruptionis Romanae in operibus D. Gregorii M. jussu Pontificum Rom. recognitis atq[ue] editis ex Typographica Vaticana loca insigniora, observata, a theologis ad hoc officium deputatis (Oxford: J. Barnes, 1610);

A Treatise of the Corruption of Scripture, Councels and Fathers by the Prelats, Pastors and Pillars of the Church of Rome, for Maintenance of Popery and Irreligion Together with a sufficient Answere unto James Gretser and Antonie Possevine and the Unknowne Author of The Grounds of the

Old Religion and the New (London: H. Lownes for Mathew Lownes, 1611);

The Jesuits Downefall, Threatened against Them by the Secular Priests for Their Wicked Lives, Accursed Manners, Heretical Doctrine, and more than Matchiavillian policie. Together with the Life of Father Parsons an English Jesuite (Oxford: John Barnes, 1612);

Catalogus universalis librorum in bibliotheca Bodleiana omnium librorum, linguarum, & scientiarum genere refertissimâ, sic compositus: vt non solum publicis per Europam vniversam bibliothecis, sed etiam privatis musaeis, aligsq[ue] ad catalogum librorum conficiendum vsui esse possit Accessit Appendix librorum, qui vel ex munificentiâ aliorum vel ex censibus Bibliothecae recens allati sunt (Oxford: John Lichfield & James Short, 1620);

Index generalis sanctorum Patrum, ad singulos versus cap. 5 secundum Matthaeum (London: John Haviland for P. Stephens, 1624);

Vindiciae Gregorianae, seu restitutus innumeris paene locis Gregorius M., ex variis manuscriptis, ut magno labore, ita singulari fide collatis (Geneva: P. & I. Chouët, 1625);

A Manuduction, or Introduction unto Divinitie: Containing a Confutation of Papists by Papists, Throughout the Important Articles of our Religion; their testimonies taken either out of the Indices expurgatorrii, or out of the Fathers, and ancient records; but expecially the manuscripts. (London: I. Jaggard for Henry Cripps & Henry Curteyne at Oxford, 1625);

The Humble and Earnest Request of Thomas James to the Church of England: for, and in the Behalfe of Bookes Touching Religion (Oxford: 1625?);

An Explanation or Enlarging of the Ten Articles in the Supplication of Doctor Iames, Lately Exhibited to the Clergy of England. Or, a Manifest Proofe that they are both Reasonable and Faisable within the Time Mentioned (Oxford: J. Lichfield & W. Turner, 1625);

Specimen corruptelarum pontificiarum in Cypriano, Ambrosio, Gregorio M. & authore operis imperfecti, & in jure canonico (London: G. Miller, 1626);

Index generalis Librorum Prohibitorum a Pontificiis, una cum editionibus expurgatis vel expurgandis juxta seriem literarum & triplicem classem in usum Bibliothecae Bodleianae & curatoribus eiusdem specialiter designatus (Oxford: G. Turner, 1627);

Catalogus interpretum S. Scripturae, iuxta numerorum ordinem, quo extant in Bibliotheca Bodleiana . . . In usum Theologorum concinnatus, nunc vero altera fere parte auctior redditus. Accessit elenchus authorum . . . Editio correcta. Ed. J. Verneuil. (Oxford: J. Lichfield, 1635).

OTHER: Antonio Brucioli, *A Commentary upon the Canticle of Canticles,* translated by James (London: T. Man, 1597);

Guillaume Du Vair, *The Moral Philosophy of the Stoicks, Written in French, and Englished for the benefit of them which are ignorant of that tongue,* translated by James (London: F. Kingston for T. Man, 1598);

Richard de Bury, *Philobiblon Richardi Dvnelmensis sive De Amore Librorvm, et institvtione bibliothecae, tractatus pulcherrimus. Ex collatione cum varijs manuscriptis. Editio jam secunda, cui accessit appendix de manuscriptis Oxoniensibus,* edited by James (Oxford: Joseph Barnes, 1598; republished, with dedication and appendix, 1599);

John Wycliffe, *Two Short Treatises, against the Orders of the Begging Friars, compiled by that famous Doctour of the Church, and Preacher of Gods word John Wickliffe, sometime fellow of Merton, and master of Balliol Coll. in Oxford, and afterwards parson of Lutherworth in Lecestershire. Faithfully printed according to two ancient manuscript copies, extant, the one in Benet Colledge in Cambridge, the other remaining in the publike librarie at Oxford,* edited by James (Oxford: Joseph Barnes, 1608);

Georg Witzell, *Methodus Concordiae Ecclesiasticae, cum exortatione ad Concilium; iuxta exemplar excusum apud Nicolaum Worlab 1533, cum gratia & privilegio Caesareae Majestatis. Adjectae sunt notae marginales, doctrina et vita ipsius, exalijs scriptis ejus collecta. Una cum enumeratione auctorum qui scripserunt contra squalores & errores Curiae Romanae,* edited by James (London: J. Bill, 1625).

Thomas James is best remembered for his role as Sir Thomas Bodley's first librarian. In that capacity he worked under Bodley's close supervision, and together the two men created one of the foremost libraries of Europe. James was instrumental in organizing the library and in producing the printed catalogues of 1605 and 1620, which long served as models of their kind. The adoption of mandatory legal deposit of new books in the library was his idea, though it was brought to fruition by Bodley. James was also a prolific scholar whose Protestant zeal compelled him to examine and edit the early manuscripts of the church fathers so as to return those patristic texts to their original purity. Though he never completed his editing project, he established a methodological approach to manuscripts, printed books, and the process of editing that was far in advance of his own time. As impressive as were his achievements in textual criticism, however, James's larger reputation rests firmly upon cataloguing the collections at Oxford and Cambridge and his work with Bodley in creating one of the great libraries of the world.

James was born at Newport on the Isle of Wight, probably in 1572. His parents were Marian exiles, and it may be that they knew the young Thomas Bodley and his parents in Geneva. The direction of James's future career was set in the years from 1586 to 1591 when he was a schoolboy at Winchester College. Thomas Bilson, then warden of the college and later bishop of Winchester, excited the boy's interest in the manuscripts of the church fathers when he contended that an examination of manuscripts of English provenance would expose papist corruptions and falsehoods in the current printed editions. James matriculated at New College, Oxford, in 1592 and graduated with a bachelor of arts degree in 1595. He received a master of arts degree before the turn of the century, and in 1614 was awarded the bachelor of divinity and doctor of divinity degrees. He was a fellow of the college from 1593 to 1602. His first appearance in print occurred in 1597 and 1598 with two small translations, the first from Italian, Antonio Brucioli's *Commentary upon the Canticle of Canticles,* and the second from French, Guillaume Du Vair's *The Moral Philosophy of the Stoicks.*

James's facility with manuscripts and documents was recognized early, for in 1598 he was commissioned to rearrange and transcribe the statutes of the university. In this same year he completed a treatise on the papist errors in the editions of St. Cyprian; though never published in this form it was the first in a series of similar works James published during the next thirty years. He came to wider notice with his 1598 edition of Richard de Bury's *Philobiblon,* which was republished in 1599 so that James could include a dedicatory letter to Bodley and a list of Oxford manuscripts. Building upon this first list of manuscripts, James set out to catalogue all the manuscripts at Oxford and Cambridge.

During this time Bodley began to consider James as a serious candidate for keeper of his new library. He wrote James on 24 December 1599 expressing his desire that James quickly finish his work cataloguing, as he put it, "those dusty and rusty parchment manuscripts." Although Bodley did not specifically refer to James as his choice for keeper, his detailed account of the progress of the workmen at Oxford and his solicitous manner toward James indicated his intention. James wrote to Bodley on 1 April 1600 that he was still working on the Cambridge manuscripts but when finished greatly looked forward to taking up his position at Bodley's library. James was not confirmed by Oxford University until 1602 when the library officially opened.

James's *Ecloga Oxonio-Cantabrigiensis, tributa in libros duos; quorum prior continet catalogum confusum librorum manuscriptorum in illustrissimis Bibliothecis, duarum florentissimarum Academiarum, Oxoniae et Cantabrigiae, posterior, catalogum eorundem distinctum et dispositum secundum quatuor facultates, observato tam in nominibus, quam in operibus ipsis, alphabetico literarum ordine. Ostensum est practerea in hoc secundo libro, quid a quoquo viro scriptum sit, quo tempore, ac postremo quot eiusdem libri exemplaria, quibus q[uod] in locis habeantur.* (1600) was a magnificent achievement in cataloguing that for the first time revealed the manuscript riches of Oxford and Cambridge to the scholarly world. Within the context of the times, however, the *Ecloga Oxonio-Cantabrigiensis* was much more than a pioneering union catalogue. James's purpose in beginning the work was to gain bibliographic control over a sizable corpus of manuscripts that he believed upon examination would reveal Protestant truth and Papist error. Indeed, part 1 of the catalogue includes two appendices that illustrate correct manuscript readings in St. Cyprian and St. Augustine and, conversely, demonstrate corruptions in the Catholic editions. In 1600 James also published *Bellum papale; sive concordia discors Sixti Quinti, et Clementis Octavi circa Hieronymiianam editionem,* in which he listed errors in the latest Catholic edition of St. Jerome. These works reveal James's perspective as he approached his new position as keeper at the Bodleian Library. Creating the collections and cataloguing their contents were but the first steps along the path to scholarship that would reveal the truth.

In founding his library Bodley drew up statutes for its governance that, among other strictures, forbade marriage or outside employment to his librarian. Bodley noted that "marriage is too full of domestical impeachments to affourd him so muche time from his priuat affaires, as almost euery daies necessitie of his personal presence will require." Nonetheless, James almost immediately violated both of these statutes. On 14 September 1602 he accepted the rectorship of St. Aldate's, Oxford, and then a few weeks later he married Ann Underhill. He easily was able to secure Bodley's permission to take the rectorship, but his employer was reluctant to grant his request to marry. Short of dismissing James, however, Bodley had no choice but to accept the marriage.

James was obliged to work as much as ten hours a day in the library. Because his duties were many, he often asked that Bodley provide him with an assistant. Finally, in 1606 Bodley allowed James to engage an under keeper. James was allowed four weeks of vacation in addition to holidays such as Christmas and Easter. When the keeper was absent, Bodley stipulated that his place was to "be supplied, by some learned able graduat, of whose fidelitie and truth, there was neuer any other but a publique good report." Apparently, the under keeper was not considered capable of taking charge of the library during James's absence.

Bodley had James draw up lists of potential donors and solicit books and money for the library. He was quite successful and a donations register was

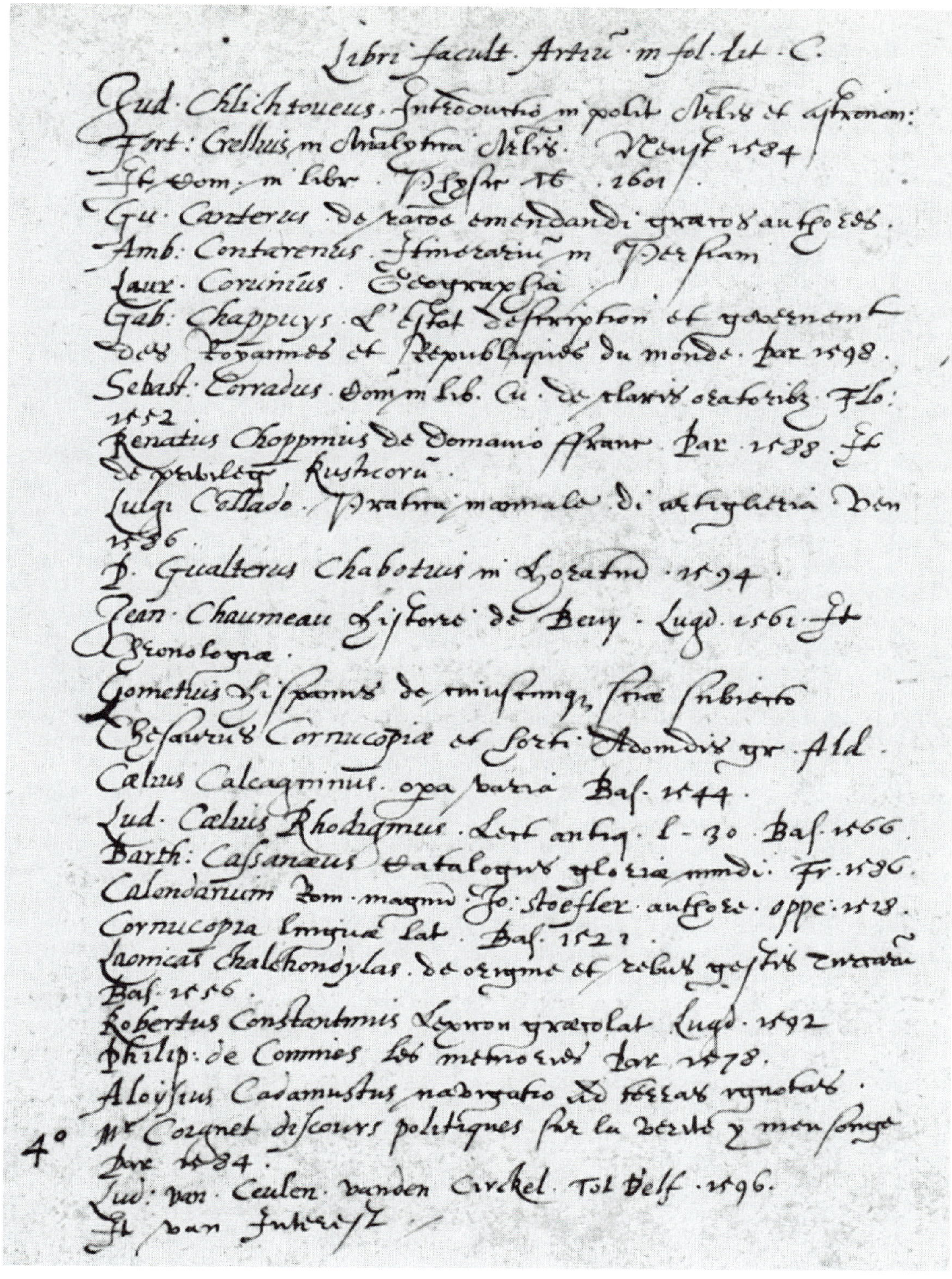

Libri facult. Artiu[m] in fol. lit. C.

Lud. Clichtoueus. Introductio in polit. Arith. et astronom:
Fort: Crellius in Analytica Arith. Norimb. 1584
It. Dom. in libr. Physic. Ar. 1601.
Gu. Canterus de ratione emendandi Graecos authores.
Amb. Contarenus. Itinerarium in Persiam
Laur. Coruinus. Geographia
Gab. Chappuys. L'Estat description et gouvernement des Royaumes et Republiques du monde. Par. 1598.
Sebast. Corradus Dom. in lib. Cic. de claris oratoribus Flo: 1552.
Renatus Choppinus de Domanio Franc. Par. 1588. It. de privilegiis Rusticorum.
Luigi Collado. Pratica manuale di artiglieria Ven. 1586.
D. Gualterus Chabotius in Horatium. 1594.
Jean Chaumeau Histoire de Berry. Lugd. 1561. It Chronologia.
Gometius Hispanus de mistionis sive subiecto
Thesaurus Cornucopiae et Horti Adonidis gr. Ald.
Caelius Calcagninus. opera varia Bas. 1544.
Lud. Caelius Rhodiginus. Lect. antiq. l. 30 Bas. 1566.
Barth: Cassanaeus Catalogus gloriae mundi. Fr. 1586.
Calendarium Rom. magnum Jo. Stoefler authore. Oppe. 1518.
Cornucopia linguae lat. Bas. 1521.
Laonicus Chalchondylas. de origine et rebus gestis Turcarum Bas. 1556.
Robertus Constantinus Lexicon graecolat. Lugd. 1592
Philip. de Commines les memoires Par. 1578.
Aloysius Cadamustus navigatio ad terras ignotas.
4° Mr Cognet discours politiques sur la verité y mensonge Par. 1584.
Lud: van Ceulen. vanden Circkel. Tot Delf. 1596.
It. van Interest

Page from James's manuscript for the first Bodleian Library catalogue, published in 1605 (MS. Rawl. Q. e. 31 [S.C. 16026], Bodleian Library, Oxford)

begun. Many of the books that were donated resulted directly in book sales, for once an edition of an author was present in the library, any other edition was considered a duplicate and sold. Usually the latest edition was preferred, and so, for instance, the First Folio of William Shakespeare's works was sold as a duplicate when the Second Folio arrived. James was far more sensitive than Bodley to the comparative value of different editions, but by selling duplicates Bodley was able to finance the binding of the many new books–which usually came unbound in sheets–acquired through the London book trade. The disposal of duplicates was evidently a sensitive issue. In the first year of the library's operation, Bodley instructed James that the books should be packed on "Sonday for that . . . there will be no repaire vnto the Librarie and I am desirous to have them conveied without any notice."

James's suggestion to Bodley that one copy of each book printed in England ought to be deposited in the library was crucial to the development of the institution and had far-reaching consequences. Bodley took up the idea and entered into negotiations with the Stationers' Company. After "many rubbes & delaies" the company agreed in 1610 to the arrangement. Subsequently given the force of law, mandatory deposit in the Bodleian Library, as well as in several other libraries in Britain, continues to the present day. Other countries followed Britain's lead and also established mandatory depositories. The practice that grew from James's idea has shaped and enriched the collections of the great libraries of the world.

James's major task was to catalogue books. When the books were received from Bodley, his agents, or donors they were classified into one of the four faculties–Theology, Law, Medicine, or Arts. They were arranged in alphabetical order according to the author and then entered on a shelflist table hung at the end of each book press. The continual acquisition of books required that the tables often be rewritten. Initially, these tables were the sole means of bibliographic control.

Recognizing the deficiencies of this system, Bodley decided in 1604 that a catalogue should be prepared and printed and, of course, most of the work fell to his keeper. James was invited at about the same time to join one of the Oxford committees for the preparation of the authorized Bible–the King James Bible–but Bodley refused to allow him to participate because of the need to prepare the new catalogue. Immediately the two men disagreed on the organization of the catalogue: James argued for an alphabetical arrangement by title, but Bodley wished to maintain the four faculties classification approach. James was unable to convince Bodley and so he prepared the manuscript sheets from the shelflist tables. When printing was under way, he read and corrected proofs. He compiled several indices to accompany the catalogue: a subject index to commentators on the Bible, a similar one to commentators on Aristotle, as well as indices to law and to medicine.

As Bodley had instructed, the books were arranged according to the subject faculties, and in each of these by rough alphabetical subdivisions; however, James did manage to get his way in part by creating an "Index Alphabeticus." The printed catalogue, *Catalogvs librorvm bibliothecae pvblicae qvam vir ornatissimus Thomas Bodleivs eques auratus in Academia Oxoniensi nuper instituit; continet autem libros alphabetice dispositos secundum quatuor facultates: cvm qvadrvplici elencho expositorum e. ecripturae, Aristotelis, juris vtriusq[ue] & principum medicinae, ad vsum alinae Academiae Oxoniensis* (1605), consisting of 8,700 entries, appeared in July 1605. In 1613, the year Bodley died, James prepared an alphabetical catalogue, abandoning the class system because of the difficulty of deciding to which category a book belonged and the inconvenience of separating the works of a single author. The alphabetically arranged second published catalogue of 1620, *Catalogus universalis librorum in Bibliotheca Bodleiana omnium librorum, linguarum, & scientiarum genere refertissimâ, sic compositus: vt non solum publicis per Europam vniversam bibliothecis, sed etiam privatis musaeis, alijsq[ue] ad catalogum librorum conficiendum vsui esse possit. Accessit Appendix librorum, qui vel ex munificentiâ aliorum vel ex censibus Bibliothecae recens allati sunt* (1620), grew out of this in-house catalogue.

As busy as James was in the early years, he continued to examine manuscripts and editions of the church fathers. During 1604 and 1605, when the first catalogue was being prepared, he convinced Bodley that a project to examine and collate the manuscripts of the church fathers was worth pursuing if they could obtain the king's patronage. It was important to have a powerful patron, as a great many manuscripts would necessarily have to be brought together: the king's warrant and his manuscript collections would greatly aid the project. Although the king originally agreed in 1605 to support the project and allow Bodley access to the royal libraries, nothing ever came of it. By late 1606 Bodley withdrew, and thereafter the project was a point of disagreement between James and Bodley, who felt that James might not fulfill his duties as keeper while occupied with the collation.

James now needed to find new patronage. In 1607 he compiled another list of papist corruptions in the Catholic editions of commentaries on the Song of Songs, *Concordantiæ sanctorum patrum, i.e. vera & pia libri canticorum per patres universus, tam Graecos quam Latinos, expositio;* and about the same time he published a broadside, *The Humble Supplication of Thomas James, Student in Divinitie, and Keeper of the Publike Librarie at Oxford, for Ref-*

ormation of the Ancient Fathers Workes, by Papists Sundrie Wayes Depraved (1607?). The first book once again demonstrated the need for his project, and the second detailed its proposed organization. To undertake the work James called for the selection of six scholars, who would be paid reasonable wages and work five or six hours a day. As the basis of the collation the scholars would use the latest Protestant editions, the latest Catholic editions, and as many manuscripts as could be obtained. He further suggested that the manuscripts be gathered together at one center, the Bodleian Library. James proposed that the scholars select four of the most ancient manuscripts for collation against the printed editions. The head of the project would be responsible for collecting and copying out those passages he judged corrupt and in need of emendation, the final printed form of the project being an index of the corruptions in the latest printed editions. James determined that the project would be completed within five years.

In 1608 James edited two tracts by John Wycliffe that attacked the Dominican and Franciscan orders, and in the same year he wrote a companion volume that demonstrated the correctness of Wycliffe's position and its conformity with the position of the Anglican church, *An Apologie for Iohn Wickliffe, shewing his Conformitie with the now Church of England; with Answere to Such Slaunderous Obiections, as haue beene lately vrged against him by Father Parsons, the Apologists, and others. Collected chiefly out of diuerse works of his in written hand, by Gods especiall providence remaining in the publike library at Oxford, of the honorable foundation of Sr. Thomas Bodley Knight.* At the same time he attempted but failed to gain the official support of Oxford University for his project. James had more success within the church. The archbishop of Canterbury, Richard Bancroft, offered James his personal support, made him one of his chaplains, and sent him manuscripts and money, though he did not give the project the official support of the church. Even so, his efforts were enough for James to begin. In early 1610 James sent a list of Oxford scholars to the archbishop for his approval. Twelve were selected and the work began on 1 July 1610.

The library of St. John's College, Oxford, holds the 1589–1591 Roman edition of St. Gregory's *opera omnia* in which James himself noted all the manuscript variants generated by the project. He also noted which manuscripts were used, the names of the collators of each day, and also who used which manuscript, each of them marked with a letter, or siglum, so that there would be no confusion between manuscripts. The collators finished with the works of Gregory on 6 December 1610, a few days more than five months after beginning the project. Halfway through Gregory's works, James rushed into print a pamphlet, *Bellum Gregorianum, sive corruptionis Romanae in operibus D. Gregorii M. jussu Pontificum Rom. recognitis atq[ue] editis ex Typographica Vaticana loca insigniora, observata, a theologis ad hoc officium deputatis* (1610), intended as a justification for the continuation of the project. The pamphlet did not adequately illustrate the significance of the variant readings; what was plain to James, immersed as he was in the project, was certainly not so to others. Bodley wrote on 30 October 1610 that unless he provided explanations and demonstrated the significance of the listed variants, James's work would "not be reputed for any special validitie." On 28 December Bodley urged James to get an enlarged volume into print before "some nimble witted felowe, will shoote his boltes against yow."

James responded with his magnum opus, *A Treatise of the Corruption of Scripture, Councels and Fathers by the Prelats, Pastors and Pillars of the Church of Rome, for Maintenance of Popery and Irreligion Together with a sufficient Answere unto James Gretser and Antonie Possevine and the Unknowne Author of The Grounds of the Old Religion and the New* (1611). As well as answering all his critics in detail in the volume, James also included what may well be the first English manual on textual criticism. It apparently came too late to reverse the negative impression caused by the publication of the *Bellum Gregorianum,* yet it has remained a valued work that was reprinted as late as the nineteenth century.

After finishing with Gregory's works, the collators evidently took up the whole of 1611 on the works of St. Cyprian, turning to the works of St. Ambrose on 27 January 1612. By this time the number of collators was down from twelve to eight, and only four of these were of the original group who began the project. The work continued regularly until 4 April and then sporadically on fourteen days spread out over a six-month period before the project was abandoned on 24 October 1612.

Wholly privately supported, the collation was the largest editing project from manuscripts undertaken in England up to that time. Aid was forthcoming from archbishop Bancroft and several like-minded bishops, with manuscripts being donated from Lambeth, Salisbury, and Winchester. By the intercession of the archbishop and the goodwill of many members of the university, the colleges of All Souls, Balliol, Corpus Christi, Lincoln, Merton, New, Oriel, Queen's, and St. John's opened their libraries to the scholars. There was never, however, any official religious or academic institutional support of the project.

One of the most significant results of the collation project was that it forced James to think through the whole process of textual editing and to put his thoughts in writing. In part 2 of *A Treatise of the Corruption of Scripture* he notes that "The best remedy for a diseased

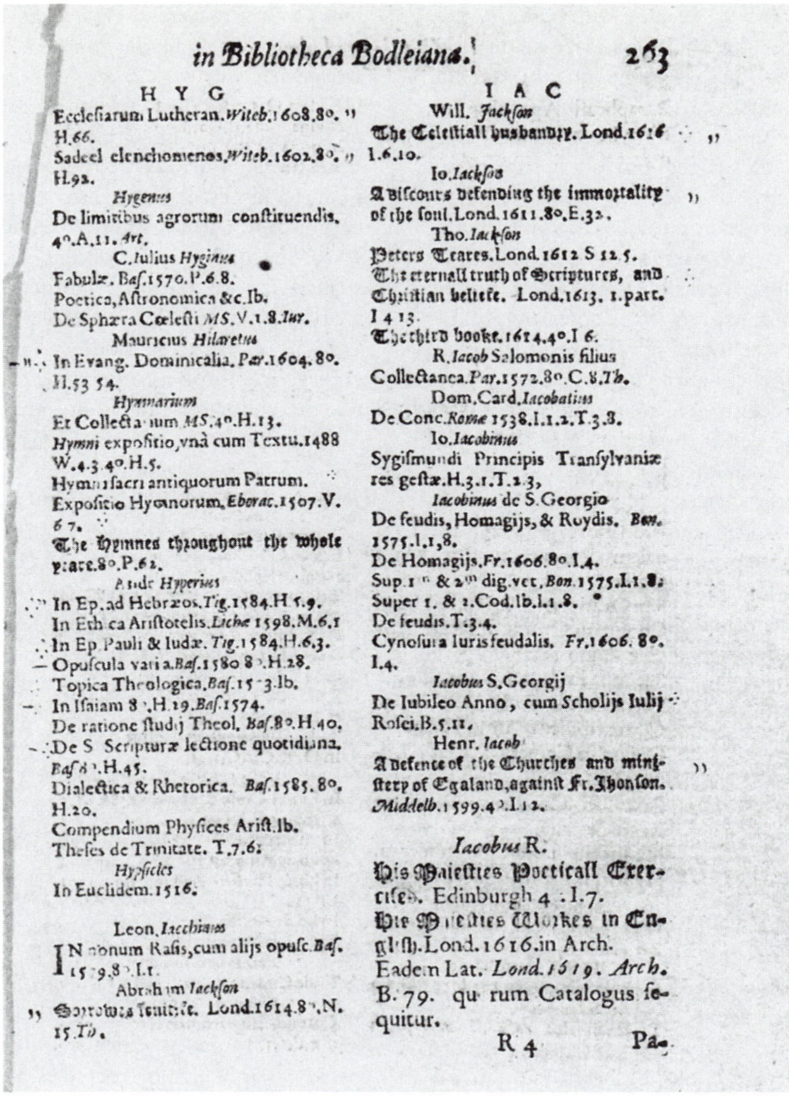

in Bibliotheca Bodleiana. 263

H Y G

Eccleſiarum Lutheran. *Witeb.* 1608. 8°. H.66.

Sadeel elenchomenos, *Witeb.* 1602. 8°. H.92.

Hygenus

De limitibus agrorum conſtituendis. 4°. A.11. *Art.*

C. Iulius *Hyginus*

Fabulæ. *Baſ.* 1570. P.6.8.

Poetica, Aſtronomica &c. Ib.

De Sphæra Cœleſti *MS.* V.1.8. *Iur.*

Mauricius *Hilaretus*

In Evang. Dominicalia. *Par.* 1604. 8°. H.53 54.

Hymnarium

Et Collectaneum *MS.* 4°. H.13.

Hymni expoſitio, vnà cum Textu. 1488 W.4.3. 4°. H.5.

Hymni ſacri antiquorum Patrum.

Expoſitio Hymnorum. *Eborac.* 1507. V. 6 7.

The hymnes throughout the whole yeare. 8°. P.62.

Andr. *Hyperius*

In Ep. ad Hebræos. *Tig.* 1584. H.5.9.

In Ethica Ariſtotelis. *Liche* 1598. M.6.1

In Ep. Pauli & Iudæ. *Tig.* 1584. H.6.3.

Opuſcula varia. *Baſ.* 1580 8°. H.28.

Topica Theologica. *Baſ.* 15 3. Ib.

In Iſaiam 8°. H.19. *Baſ.* 1574.

De ratione ſtudij Theol. *Baſ.* 8°. H.40.

De S. Scripturæ lectione quotidiana. *Baſ.* 8°. H.45.

Dialectica & Rhetorica. *Baſ.* 1585. 8°. H.20.

Compendium Phyſices Ariſt. Ib.

Theſes de Trinitate. T.7.6.

Hypſicles

In Euclidem. 1516.

Leon. *Iacchinus*

IN nonum Raſis, cum alijs opuſc. *Baſ.* 1579. 8°. I.1.

Abraham *Iackſon*

Sorrowes ſtuffe. Lond. 1614. 8°. N. 15. *Th.*

I A C

Will. *Jackſon*

The Celeſtiall husbandry. Lond. 1616 1.6.10.

Io. *Iackſon*

A diſcours defending the immortality of the ſoul. Lond. 1611. 8°. E.32.

Tho. *Iackſon*

Peters Teares. Lond. 1612 S 12.5.

The eternall truth of Scriptures, and Chriſtian beliefe. Lond. 1613. 1. part. I 4 13.

The third booke. 1614. 4°. I 6.

R. *Iacob* Salomonis filius

Collectanea. *Par.* 1572. 8°. C.8. *Th.*

Dom. Card. *Iacobatius*

De Conc. *Romæ* 1538. I.1.2. T.3.8.

Io. *Iacobinus*

Sygiſmundi Principis Tranſylvaniæ res geſtæ. H.3.1. T.2.3.

Iacobinus de S. Georgio

De feudis, Homagijs, & Roydis. *Bon.* 1575. I.1,8.

De Homagijs. *Fr.* 1606. 8°. I.4.

Sup. 1^m & 2^m dig. vet. *Bon.* 1575. I.1.8.

Super 1. & 2. Cod. Ib. I.1.8.

De feudis. T.3.4.

Cynoſura Iuris feudalis. *Fr.* 1606. 8°. I.4.

Iacobus S. Georgij

De Iubileo Anno, cum Scholijs Iulij Roſci. B.5.11.

Henr. *Iacob*

A defence of the Churches and miniſtery of Eglande, againſt Fr. Ihonſon. *Middelb.* 1599. 4°. I.12.

Iacobus R.

His Maieſties Poeticall Exerciſes. Edinburgh 4°. I.7.

His Maieſties Workes in Engliſh. Lond. 1616. in Arch.

Eadem Lat. *Lond.* 1619. *Arch.* B.79. quorum Catalogus ſequitur.

R 4 Pa-

A cancel leaf in James's second Bodleian Library catalogue, published in 1620 (Bodleian Library, Oxford)

book . . . is 4 or 5 old Manuscripts . . . compounded together, and the best of them distilled through the limbeck of a good Divines brain that is of a sound judgement and unpartial temper." His thoughts on editing are laid out comprehensively in part 5, where he asserts that there are two types of corruption: "the forging of false Treatises, or corrupting the true." He briefly considers the authorship of "False Treatises, which lurk up and down in corners, and are thence fetched to gain credit to the Popish Religion being gilded over with the names of the Ancient Fathers." As examples, he notes tracts that had supposedly been found "in a Cave . . . and of late, some few years since . . . of a Council held in the time of the Apostles, written in the Arabic or Ethiopian tongue, found on the top of a mountain in Spain." Skepticism, James clearly believed, was a first requirement of the textual critic.

The textual restoration of new books, according to James, is a straightforward matter. The corruptions in texts occur in three ways: by addition, deletion, or transposition of words, sentences, and books. Although he maintains that a competent critic can unmask forgeries and false treatises, he asserts that the emendation of corrupt works requires "industry"–that is, the collation of manuscripts–as well as "judgment." James was the first textual critic to make the sound observation that, contrary to common belief, the latest edition is often the most corrupt and so therefore several editions of a single work must be consulted in order to establish the most reliable text.

James's real interest, of course, was not in modern authors and their works, but rather in the church fathers and the English manuscripts that contained their writings. Although the bulk of what James says in the manual is not original to him, he combines his expert firsthand knowledge of manuscripts with his thorough acquaintance with the works of such humanists and editors as Angelo Poliziano, Erasmus, and Joseph J. Scaliger, and he made available for the first time in English a comprehensive and up-to-date summary of textual criticism. As James indicates in the notes of *A Treatise of the Corruption of Scripture,* he was familiar with the editions of many humanist scholars. In addition he drew upon two theoretical works of textual criticism: Franz Modius's *Novantique lectiones* (1584) and Caspar Schoppe's *De arte critica* (1597). Part 5 of *A Treatise of the Corruption of Scripture* is not a derivative imitation of a Continental model, but rather it is a pragmatic adaptation of current textual theory in the Politian mode (which emphasizes the collation of manuscripts) furthered by his own experiences with manuscripts.

James notes five reasons for scribal corruption: ignorance of language, ignorance of script, negligence, purposeful change, and marginalia incorporated into the text. He also notes three types of printing errors: lack of comparison with manuscripts before printing the text, alteration of the text by the compositors, and papist alterations of the text under the guise of having been collated with manuscripts. James may well have been the first theoretical textual critic to apply the concepts of textual corruption–heretofore applied only to manuscripts–to printed texts.

James next turned to the remedies for texts plagued with these various types of errors: "only two manner of ways [are the texts] to be corrected: either without, or with Manuscripts; that is upon probable conjecture, or sufficient authority. The first of those Remedies is dangerous, & seldom to be used; only in case of necessity: the other, common, and for the most part more certain, but, to be used with great discretion, both in regard of the choice, and orderly comparing of the Manuscripts." Older manuscripts are to be preferred to more recent copies. He asserts that one can distinguish older codices because they "are written in the Lombard or Saxon letter: or lastly, in a set hand in great letters, without points or abbreviations." Such manuscripts antedate the Norman Conquest of 1066; those that postdate the invasion are "in a small letter, full frought with sundry abbreviations." In later manuscripts scribes "use many abbreviations: which being not well understood of every one . . . oftentimes gave occasion of very foul mistakings."

James sets out several admonitions to be observed in editing texts from manuscripts. The good editor must be diligent, accurate, and cautious. He must diligently collate the whole text and not just a few passages. He must accurately note all "the differences, be they good or bad, seem right or wrong." He must exercise caution and not rush to emend "although there seem never so important reasons."

Next James considers the actual procedures to be followed. He places great emphasis on including all the manuscript variants. For example, "when we see a manifest error, in citing one Author for another, . . . the most that we can do, is to note the error in the margin. Without sufficient warrant of the Manuscripts, nothing is to be changed." James found one of the great faults of Erasmus to be his failure to note all the variant readings. James also stresses that each manuscript used must be carefully identified and each variant identified by a manuscript siglum. Again Erasmus was singled out for not following this procedure. If the text exists in both print and manuscript, "we are bound to follow [the manuscript copies], rather then the printed Copies; although the other reading may seem more probable." Although the oldest manuscripts are to form the basis for collation, the later manuscripts must not be completely neglected. "They shall be set aside, or . . . admitted as far forth as they agree with the older Manuscripts, and not otherwise."

James briefly discusses recensions and archetypes. In claiming supreme authority for manuscripts, especially the more ancient, he notes that they often disagree among themselves: "they are found often times very faulty and diverse. . . ." If all the manuscripts agree, then they must descend from a single archetype, or as James puts it, "they were all written out of one book." He continues that if the manuscripts differ in small "slight circumstances" but agree in "all material places," then "they were not written all at one time, or by one Copy." He asserts, though, that manuscripts that agree in "all material places" descend from an archetype. James's distinction was that manuscripts that exhibit small differences are unlikely to have been produced together (which is not very likely in any case) but that they do nonetheless have a recensional relationship.

In the main, James's manual is not unlike those of his continental predecessors, but in several points it represents an advance upon them. James was one of the first to realize the unreliability of the printed *textus receptus.* As an English critic, James could not but have noted the Saxon script, which he considered as the English equivalent of the continental Lombard. He went further, however, and distinguished what is almost certainly uncial, "a set hand in great letters," and gothic, "a small letter, full fraught with sundry abbreviations." James's greatest contribution to textual criticism was his insistence on the complete collation of all manuscripts. In addition, he insisted that all variants must be noted and considered. The combination of systematic methodological collation and a neutral inclusion of all variants, even "errors," gave James the potential for full-scale *recensio* far in advance of any of his contemporaries.

In most of the editions produced in the sixteenth and seventeenth centuries, editors tended to ignore the canons of contemporary textual criticism. Indeed, even the authors of manuals on the subject were known to have ignored their own theoretical strictures when faced with the practical task of editing. James's proposed editions–or indices of corruptions, as he originally conceived them–of the church fathers were never completed. Nevertheless, James and his coworkers did collate all of Gregory, all of Cyprian, and much of Ambrose, which allows a comparison of his editorial procedures to his theoretical tenets.

Because of his wide-ranging experience with manuscripts, James's paleographical skills must have been good. The scripts of the manuscripts collated ranged from the earlier insular uncial, insular pointed and square minuscule, and Carolingian minuscule to the various gothic textura and Anglicana book hands of the later Middle Ages. Certainly, in systematically collating these widely varying manuscripts, James fulfilled his major theoretical tenet: all of the variants–no matter how small–were to be noted. Each variant was accompanied by its manuscript siglum and each day the names of collators and their manuscripts were noted. The collation was certainly a model of methodological exactness. He had completed all the necessary steps, although no evidence exists to show that he carried out a recensional analysis. As the project began and ended with the collation, one cannot certainly say how James might have used the resulting large body of variants. Had he followed his critical precepts–and there is no reason to suppose he would not have–he would have produced the first true variorum editions.

With Bodley's death in January 1613, the whole administration of the library fell to James, though he now had to contend with a board of delegates, some of whom were not at all sympathetic toward him. The cessation of Bodley's letters to James closed an invaluable window on the day-to-day workings of the library. James's routine duties undoubtedly continued as before, probably leaving him little time for much else. In 1613 he completed the first draft of the alphabetically organized revised catalogue, which no doubt kept him occupied as it was periodically revised until it was finally published in 1620, the year James retired from the library. During this period James frequently attempted to restart his editorial project, but to no avail. Running a large academic library with but a single assistant was a full-time occupation, and it is not surprising that James's active publishing program ceased from the time of Bodley's death until several years after his retirement from the library. Indeed, James's main reason for leaving the library in 1620 was so that he might pursue his scholarly projects, though he was not in good health. After retirement he continued working in the library on the last of his four subject catalogues. This final catalogue, comprised of subject entries to the books of the Arts Faculty, was intended to help undergraduates use the library. No doubt James also spent a great deal of time in the library on his editorial project.

By 1623 James was again actively promoting his project for new editions of the works of the church fathers based upon a continued collation that would pick up where the old project had ended. The new project was essentially the same as the old one except that James now envisioned new editions rather than sets of indices along the lines of the ill-fated *Bellum Gregorianum*. James nevertheless finished a full-scale version of *Bellum Gregorianum* in 1623, *Vindiciae Gregorianae, seu restitutus innumeris paene locis Gregorius M., ex variis manuscriptis, ut magno labore, ita singulari fide collatis,* which was published in Geneva in 1625. He produced a similar list of variants for the works of Cyprian in 1626, *Specimen corruptelarum pontificiarum in Cypriano, Ambrosio, Gregorio M. & authore operis imperfecti, & in jure canonico,* but the volume for the works of Ambrose was not published.

James found a sympathetic patron in James Ussher, archbishop of Armagh, and an antiquarian scholar of great repute. James wrote to Ussher on 28 January 1623: "I am not so far gone in years as in sicknesses; yet my body is not so weak, but my mind is so strong, and my zeal great. . . . I would not doubt but to drive the Papists out of their starting-holes: But alas, my Lord, I have not encouragement from our bishops! Preferment I seek none . . . only 40 to 60£ per annum for others." James was financially secure himself but required funds to pay his collaborators. He also wrote to Ussher's secretary, Caesar Calendrine, on 23 May 1624 that he wished to involve the University of Cambridge in the project, and at the same time was hard at work preparing several works which "shall be fitted against the Parliament." Thus, in his attempt to find support for his project, James was moving on several fronts simultaneously: he was preparing for the upcoming meeting of Parliament in Oxford in 1625 while he sought help through the church and the universities with Ussher's assistance. In spite of what he termed "discontent and discouragement from our great ones," in a letter to Ussher 27 February 1625, James once again managed to gain the support of sympathetic churchmen but not the official support of the church. The bishop of Lichfield, Thomas Morton, was to head the project, with Ussher's close consultation.

With Bishop Morton acting as a figurehead and Ussher actively working behind the scenes, James and his assistants–one of whom was his nephew Richard James, who later became Sir Robert Bruce Cotton's librarian–set to work to prepare for the opening of Parliament. In 1625 James published *A Manuduction, or Introduction unto Divinitie: Containing a Confutation of Papists by Papists, Throughout the Important Articles of our Religion; Their testimonies taken either out of the Indices expurgatorii, or out of the Fathers, and ancient records; but especially the manuscripts,* a general treatise that demonstrated the corrupt nature of the Catholic editions of the writings of church fathers and so illustrated the need for the proposed new editions. At about the same time he published the actual proposal, *The Humble and Earnest Request of Thomas James to the Church of England; for, and in the Behalfe of Bookes Touching Religion* (1625?). James evidently believed that his proposal needed further elucidation as he soon published *An Explanation or Enlarging of the Ten Articles in the Supplication of Doctor Iames, Lately Exhibited to the Clergy of England. Or, a Manifest Proofe that they are both Reasonable and Faisable within the Time Mentioned* (1625).

The proposed project collapsed despite the combined effect of the lobbying of Parliament by Ussher, Morton, James, and others and of James's three printed works. James compiled two more lists of papist corruptions, but he seems to have accepted his not seeing to publication any new editions of the works of the church fathers. He turned over his material from the collation project on Gregory, Cyprian, and Ambrose to one of his former assistants, Jeremy Stephens, who went on to produce editions of Gregory's *Regulae pastoralis liber* (1629), as well as Cyprian's *De unitate ecclesiae* (1632) and *De bono patientiae* (1633). James died in August 1629 and was buried in the chapel of New College, Oxford.

Perhaps because so little seemed to come from James's great scholarly exertions, due in no small part to their having been cast in polemical terms, the significance of his achievement in textual criticism has been somewhat obscured. In retrospect, James first pioneered the modern approach to textual criticism in England, more than a century ahead of his time. His writings on texts and indeed his handling of the collation project demonstrate his fidelity to coherent method and scholarly rectitude.

Thomas James's greatest and most long-lasting contributions were to the library founded by Sir Thomas Bodley. Bodley and James made the Bodleian a functioning library for senior scholars, and James expanded its use by undergraduates. As part of his work as librarian, James in effect laid the bibliographical foundation upon which much of the scholarship of the next century was built. His catalogue of manuscripts at Oxford and Cambridge was only superseded in the nineteenth century, and his catalogues of the Bodleian became standards by which all others were measured across the learned world and remained so through the seventeenth century and beyond. Finally, perhaps James's most significant contribution was his concept of mandatory legal deposit, which has been adopted around the world.

Letters:

Richard Parr, *Life of . . . James Ussher* (London: Nathaniel Ranew, 1686);

George W. Wheeler, *Letters of Sir Thomas Bodley to Thomas James, First Keeper of the Bodleian Library* (Oxford: Clarendon Press, 1926);

Wheeler, *Letters Addressed to Thomas James* (Oxford: Oxford University Press, 1933).

References:

Richard W. Clement, "Librarianship and Polemics: The Career of Thomas James (1572–1629)," *Libraries & Culture,* 26 (1991): 269–282;

Clement, "Thomas James's *Ecloga Oxonio-Cantabrigiensis:* An Early Printed Union Catalogue," *Journal of Library History,* 22 (1987): 1–22;

Donald G. Davis Jr., "Problems in the Life of a University Librarian: Thomas James, 1600–1620," *College & Research Libraries,* 31 (1970): 43–49;

Neil Ker, "Thomas James's Collation of Gregory, Cyprian, and Ambrose," *Bodleian Library Record,* 4 (1952): 16–30;

William D. Macray, *Annals of the Bodleian Library with a Notice of the Earlier Library of the University,* second edition (Oxford: Clarendon Press, 1890);

J. N. L. Myers, "Oxford Libraries in the Seventeenth and Eighteenth Centuries," in *The English Library before 1700: Studies in Its History,* edited by Francis Wormald and C. E. Wright (London: Athlone, 1958), pp. 236–255;

Ian Philip, *The Bodleian Library in the Seventeenth and Eighteenth Centuries* (Oxford: Clarendon Press, 1983);

Trecentale Bodleianum: A Memorial Volume for the Three-Hundredth Anniversary of the Public Funeral of Sir Thomas Bodley March 29, 1613 (Oxford: Clarendon Press, 1913);

George W. Wheeler, *The Earliest Catalogues of the Bodleian Library* (Oxford: Clarendon Press, 1928);

Wheeler, "Thomas James: Theologian and Bodley's Librarian," *Bodleian Quarterly Record,* 4 (1923): 94–95.

Papers:

Most of Thomas James's surviving personal papers and letters are in the Bodleian Library, but a few letters are in the British Library and a few manuscripts are in Lambeth Palace Library.

Samuel Johnson

(18 September 1709 – 13 December 1784)

Joseph Rosenblum
University of North Carolina at Greensboro

See also the entries on Johnson in *DLB 39: British Novelists, 1660–1800; DLB 95: Eighteenth-Century Poets, First Series; DLB 104: British Prose Writers, 1660–1800, Second Series;* and *DLB 142: Eighteenth-Century British Literary Biographers.*

Samuel Johnson, circa 1775 (portrait by Sir Joshua Reynolds; Courage Limited)

CATALOGUES: *A Catalogue of the Valuable Library of Books, of the Late Learned Samuel Johnson, esq.; LL.D. Deceased; which will be Sold by Auction, (By Order of the Executors) by Mr. Christie, at His Great Room in Pall Mall, on Wednesday, February 16, 1785, and Three Following Days* (London, 1785); republished as *Sale Catalogue of Dr. Johnson's Library,* with an essay by A. Edward Newton (New York: E. B. Hackett, 1925);

John David Fleeman, *A Preliminary Handlist of Documents & Manuscripts of Samuel Johnson* (Oxford: Oxford Bibliographical Society, 1967);

Donald Greene, *Samuel Johnson's Library: An Annotated Guide* (Victoria, B.C.: University of Victoria, 1975);

Fleeman, *A Preliminary Handlist of Copies of Books Associated with Dr. Samuel Johnson* (Oxford: Oxford Bibliographical Society, 1984);

Sale Catalogues of the Libraries of Samuel Johnson, Hester Lynch Thrale (Mrs. Piozzi) and James Boswell, introduction by Donald D. Eddy (Newcastle, Del.: Oak Knoll Books, 1993).

BOOKS: *London: A Poem, in Imitation of the Third Satire of Juvenal* (London: Printed for R. Doddesley, 1738);

Marmor Norfolciense: or an Essay on an Ancient Prophetical Inscription, In Monkish Rhyme, Lately Discover'd near Lynn in Norfolk. By Probus Britanicus (London: Printed for J. Brett, 1739);

A Compleat Vindication of the Licensers of the Stage, from the Malicious and Scandalous Aspersions of Mr. Brooke, Author of Gustavus Vasa. With A Proposal for making the Office of Licenser more Extensive and Effectual. By an Impartial Hand (London: Printed for C. Corbett, 1739);

A Commentary on Mr. Pope's Principles of Morality, or Essay on Man. By Mons. Crousaz (London: Printed for A. Dodd, 1739);

An Account of the Life of John Philip Barretier, Who was Master of Five Languages at the Age of Nine Years. Compiled from his Father's Letters, &c. (London: Printed for J. Roberts, 1744);

An Account of the Life of Mr. Richard Savage, Son of the Earl Rivers (London: Printed for J. Roberts, 1744);

Miscellaneous Observations on the Tragedy of Macbeth: with Remarks on Sir T. H.'s Edition of Shakespear. To which is affix'd, Proposals for a New Edition of Shakeshear [sic], *with a Specimen* (London: Printed for E. Cave & sold by J. Roberts, 1745);

A Sermon Preached at the Cathedral Church of St. Paul, before the Sons of the Clergy, on Thursday the Second of May, 1745. Being the day of their annual feast. By the Honourable and Reverend Henry Hervey Aston, attributed to Johnson (London: Printed for J. Brindley & sold by M. Cooper, 1745);

Prologue and Epilogue, Spoken at the Opening of the Theatre in Drury-Lane 1747 (London: Printed by E. Cave & sold by M. Cooper & R. Dodsley, 1747);

The Plan of a Dictionary of the English Language; Addressed to the Right Honourable Philip Dormer, Earl of Chesterfield; One of His Majesty's Principal Secretaries of State (London: Printed for J. & P. Knapton, T. Longman & T. Shewell, C. Hitch, A. Millar and R. Dodsley, 1747);

The Vanity of Human Wishes. The Tenth Satire of Juvenal, Imitated by Samuel Johnson (London: Printed for R. Dodsley & sold by M. Cooper, 1749);

Irene: A Tragedy. As it is Acted at the Theatre Royal in Drury-Lane (London: Printed for R. Dodsley & sold by M. Cooper, 1749);

A New Prologue Spoken by Mr. Garrick, Thursday, April 5, 1750. At the Representation of Comus, for the Benefit of Mrs Elizabeth Foster, Milton's Grand-Daughter, and only surviving Descendant (London: Printed for J. Payne & J. Bouquet, 1750);

The Rambler, nos. 1-208 (London: Printed for J. Payne & L. Bouquet, 20 March 1750 - 14 March 1752); republished in 2 volumes (London: Printed for J. Payne, 1753);

A Dictionary of the English Language: in which the Words are deduced from their Originals, and Illustrated in their Different Significations by Examples from the Best Writers. To which are prefixed, A History of the Language, and An English Grammar, 2 volumes (London: Printed by W. Strahan for J. & P. Knapton, T. & T. Longman, C. Hitch & L. Hawes, A. Millar, and R. & J. Dodsley, 1755);

An Account of an Attempt to Ascertain the Longitude at Sea, by an Exact Theory of the Bariation of the Magnetical Needle. . . By Zachariah Williams (London: Printed for R. Dodsley & J. Jeffries & sold by J. Bouquet, 1755);

Proposals for Printing, by Subscription, the Dramatick Works of William Shakespeare (London, 1756);

The Prince of Abissinia. A Tale, 2 volumes (London: Printed for R. & J. Dodsley and W. Johnston, 1759); republished as *The History of Rasselas, Prince of Abissinia,* 1 volume (Philadelphia: Printed by Robert Bell, 1768);

The Idler, collected edition, 2 volumes (London: Printed for J. Newberry, 1761)–first published in the *Universal Chronicle, or Weekly Gazette* (15 April 1758–5 April 1760);

The Plays of William Shakespeare, in Eight Volumes, with the Corrections and Illustrations of Various Commentators; to which are added Notes by Sam. Johnson (London: Printed for J. & R. Tonson and ten others, 1765); revised by Johnson and George Steevens (London, 1773);

The False Alarm (London: Printed for T. Cadell, 1770);

Thoughts on the Late Transactions Respecting Falkland's Islands (London: Printed for T. Cadell, 1771);

Miscellaneous and Fugitive Pieces, 2 volumes, by Johnson and others (London: Printed for T. Davies, 1773); enlarged, 3 volumes (London: Property of T. Davies & Carnan & Newbery, 1774);

The Patriot. Addressed to the Electors of Great Britain (London: Printed for T. Cadell, 1774);

A Journey to the Western Islands of Scotland (London: Printed for W. Strahan & T. Cadell, 1775);

Taxation No Tyranny; an Answer to the Resolutions and Address of the American Congress (London: Printed for T. Cadell, 1775);

Prefaces, Biographical and Critical, to the Works of the English Poets, 10 volumes (London: Printed by J. Nichols for C. Bathurst and thirty-five others, 1779 [volumes 1-4], 1781 [volumes 5-10]).

Editions: *Prayers and Meditations, composed by Samuel Johnson,* edited by George Strahan (London: Printed for T. Cadell, 1785);

The Works of Samuel Johnson, LL.D., volumes 1–11, edited by Sir John Hawkins (London: Printed for John Buckland and forty others, 1787); volumes 12 and 13, *Debates in Parliament* (London: Printed for John Buckland, 1787); volume 14 (London: Printed for John Stockdale and G. G. J. & J. Robinson, 1788); volume 15 (London: Printed for Elliot & Kay and C. Elliot, 1789);

The Lives of the English Poets [Prefaces, Biographical and Critical to the Works of the English Poets], 3 volumes, edited by G. B. Hill (Oxford: Clarendon Press, 1905);

The History of Rasselas, Prince of Abissinia, edited by R. W. Chapman (Oxford: Clarendon Press, 1927);

Samuel Johnson's Prefaces and Dedications, edited by Allen T. Hazen (New Haven: Yale University Press, 1937);

The Life of Mr. Richard Savage, edited by Clarence Tracy (Oxford: Clarendon Press, 1971);

Samuel Johnson, edited by Donald Greene, Oxford English Authors (Oxford & New York: Oxford University Press, 1984).

The Yale Edition of the Works of Samuel Johnson (13 volumes to date):

Volume 1: *Diaries, Prayers and Annals,* edited by E. L. McAdam Jr., with Donald and Mary Hyde (New

Haven: Yale University Press / London: Oxford University Press, 1958);

Volume 2: *The Idler and The Adventurer,* edited by W. J. Bate, John M. Bullitt, and L. F. Powell (New Haven & London: Yale University Press, 1963);

Volumes 3–5: *The Rambler,* edited by Bate and Albrecht B. Strauss (New Haven & London: Yale University Press, 1969);

Volume 6: *Poems,* edited by McAdam and George Milne (New Haven & London: Yale University Press, 1964);

Volumes 7 & 8: *Johnson on Shakespeare,* edited by Arthur Sherbo (New Haven & London: Yale University Press, 1968);

Volume 9: *A Journey to the Western Islands of Scotland,* edited by Mary Lascelles (New Haven & London: Yale University Press, 1971);

Volume 10: *Political Writings,* edited by Donald J. Greene (New Haven & London: Yale University Press, 1977);

Volume 14: *Sermons,* edited by Jean H. Hagstrum and James Gray (New Haven & London: Yale University Press, 1978);

Volume 15: *A Voyage to Abyssinia,* edited by Joel J. Gold (New Haven & London: Yale University Press, 1985);

Volume 16: *Rasselas and Other Tales,* edited by Gwin J. Kolb (New Haven & London: Yale University Press, 1990).

OTHER: *A Miscellany of Poems by Several Hands. Publish'd by J. Husbands,* with Johnson's Latin verse translation of Alexander Pope's *Messiah* (Oxford: Printed by Leon. Lichfield, 1731);

A Voyage to Abyssinia by Father Jerome Lobo, A Portuguese Jesuit . . . by Mr. Le Grand. From the French, translated by Johnson (London: Printed for A. Bettesworth & C. Hitch, 1735);

Catalogus Bibliothecæ Harleianæ, In Locos communes distributus cum Indice Auctorum, 5 volumes, with contributions by Johnson (London: Apud Thomas Osborne, 1743–1745);

Robert James, M.D., *A Medicinal Dictionary,* 3 volumes, written with the assistance of Johnson (London: Printed for T. Osborne & J. Roberts, 1743–1745);

The Harleian Miscellany, or a Collection of . . . Pamphlets and Tracts . . . found in the late Earl of Oxford's Library, 8 volumes, with an introduction and annotations by Johnson (London: Printed for T. Osborne, 1744–1746);

Preface and "The Vision of Theodore, the Hermit of Teneriffe," in *The Preceptor: Containing a Course of General Education* (London: Printed for R. Dodsley, 1748);

William Lauder, *An Essay on Milton's Use and Imitation of the Moderns in His Paradise Lost,* with a preface and a postscript by Johnson (London: Printed for J. Payne & J. Bouquet, 1750);

Charlotte Lennox, *The Female Quixote; or, the Adventures of Arabella,* with a dedication by Johnson, who may also have written book 9, chapter 11 (London: Printed for A. Millar, 1752);

Adventurer, with twenty-nine essays by Johnson (London: Printed for J. Payne, nos. 1–140, 7 November 1752–9 March 1754);

Lennox, *Shakespear Illustrated: or the Novels and Histories on Which the Plays of Shakespear Are Founded,* with a dedication by Johnson (London: Printed for A. Millar, 1753);

Sir Thomas Browne, *Christian Morals . . . . The Second Edition. With a Life of the Author by Samuel Johnson,* edited, with biography and annotations, by Johnson (London: Printed by Richard Hett for J. Payne, 1756);

Richard Rolt, *A New Dictionary of Trade and Commerce,* with a preface by Johnson (London: Printed for T. Osborne & J. Shipton and four others, 1756);

The Greek Theatre of Father [Pierre] Brumoy. Translated by Mrs. Charlotte Lennox, with a dedication and translations of two essays by Johnson (London: Printed for Mess. Millar, Vaillant, and six others, 1759);

Introduction on the History of Early Portuguese Exploration, in *The World Displayed; or a Curious Collection of Voyages and Travels,* 20 volumes (London: Printed for J. Newberry, 1759–1761), I: iii-xxxii;

Proceedings of the Committee Appointed to Manage the Contributions begun at London Dec. xviii, MDCCLVIIII, for Cloathing French Prisoners of War, with an introduction by Johnson (London: Printed by Order of the Committee, 1760);

John Gwynne, *Thoughts on the Coronation of His Present Majesty King George the Third, or, Reasons offered against Confining the Procession to the Usual Track, and Pointing Out others more Commodious and Proper,* much of the text written by Johnson (London: Printed for the Proprietor & sold by F. Noble and three others, 1761);

"Author's Life" and dedication, in *The English Works of Roger Ascham . . . with Notes and Observations, and the Author's Life. By James Bennet,* edited in large part by Johnson (London: Printed for R. & J. Dodsley and J. Newberry, 1761);

Reliques of Ancient English Poetry, with a dedication by Johnson, who also provided general assistance (London: Printed for J. Dodsley, 1765);

Anna Williams, *Miscellanies in Prose and Verse* (London: Printed for T. Davies, 1766)–Johnson contributed the Advertisement, a short poem, "The Ant," possibly revisions to Miss Williams's poems, and "The Fountain: A Fairy Tale";

The Convict's Address to His Unhappy Brethren. Delivered in the Chapel of Newgate, on Friday, June 6, 1777. By William Dodd, largely written by Johnson (London: Printed for G. Kearsley, 1777);

Poems and Miscellaneous Pieces, with a Free Translation of the Oedipus Tyrannus of Sophocles. By the Rev. Thomas Maurice, with a preface and possibly a dedication by Johnson (London: Printed for the Author and sold by J. Dodsley and three others, 1779);

Dedication to the King, in *An Account of the Musical Performances in Westminster-Abbey and the Pantheon . . . in Commemoration of Handel. By Charles Burney* (London: Printed for the Benefit of the Musical Fund & sold by T. Payne & Son and G. Robinson, 1785);

Sir Robert Chambers, *A Course of Lectures on the English Law Delivered at the University of Oxford 1767–1773 by Sir Robert Chambers and Composed in Association with Samuel Johnson,* edited by Thomas M. Curley (Madison: University of Wisconsin Press, 1986; Oxford: Clarendon Press, 1986).

At the Samuel Johnson Birthplace Museum is displayed a copy of Ludovico Ariosto's *Orlando Furioso,* printed at Birmingham by John Baskerville in 1773, that Johnson borrowed from his friend John Hoole. Its inscription reads, "This volume was lent by Mr. Hoole to Dr. Johnson who spilt a cup of tea on it at page 1. And stained it in the manner still visible." In *A Preliminary Handlist of Copies of Books Associated with Dr. Samuel Johnson* (1984) John David Fleeman lists this work among the "Doubtful, Erroneous, and Implausible" associations, but the inscription in any case is an indication of the common view that Johnson was careless in his handling of books, more the biblioclast than the bibliophile.

Two twentieth-century scholars, however, have offered a kinder view of Johnson's relationship with books. In his essay for *New Light on Dr. Johnson: Essays on the Occasion of his 250th Birthday* (1959) Edward Lippincott McAdam writes that "Johnson as a bibliographer and book collector was about as professional as any eighteenth century Englishman, and deserves study as well as admiration." Robert William Chapman, the editor of *The Letters of Samuel Johnson, with Mrs. Thrale's Genuine Letters to Him* (1952), claims that "Johnson had all the qualities of a book collector except greed and habits of tidiness."

At the time of his death Johnson owned between three thousand and five thousand books. Although he collected books for use, with little concern for rarity or beauty, he nonetheless possessed many important editions. His work cataloguing the Harleian Library in the *Catalogus Bibliothecæ Harleianæ* (1743–1745) and *The Harleian Miscellany* (1744–1746) demonstrates a concern with all aspects of book production, including ink, paper, and binding; and his advice to Frederick Augusta Barnard, librarian to King George III, reveals a keen knowledge of bibliography. Despite his mockery of virtuosi bookmen–for example in numbers 82 and 177 of *The Rambler*–Johnson merits inclusion in the ranks of influential collectors.

Born in Lichfield, Staffordshire, on 18 September 1709, Johnson later boasted that he was bred a bookseller. His father, Michael Johnson, sold books in Lichfield, and Michael's brother, Andrew, followed the same occupation in Birmingham. Thus Johnson, whose family lived above the bookshop, was virtually born among books. His father's stock included school texts and religious works. Of the ten books that Michael Johnson published or for which he acted as subscription agent, four were theological, one included the last words of a Lichfield murderer condemned to death, and two were reference works by Anthony à Wood: the *Athenae Oxonienses,* with its biographies of Oxford graduates, and the *Fasti,* a history of Oxford University.

The range of the stock of the family bookshop must have been wide, given the works that Johnson read there. In his 1981 essay for *Johnson Society Transactions* Herman W. Liebert lists

> romances of chivalry, Anacreon and Hesiod, Horace and Macrobius, Petrarch, Shakespeare, English poetry, the anonymous Whole Duty of Man, and [Martin] Martin's Western Islands of Scotland, foreshadowing what was to come. There were also editions of the Bible, the *Book of Common Prayer,* and at least one Latin dictionary, in which Sam wrote his name and also the date 1726.

In 1706 Michael Johnson bought the library of James Stanley, tenth Earl of Derby; the library of some 2,900 volumes had been assembled by the ninth earl, William George Richard Stanley, James' brother. Financially the purchase was a disaster because the books sold slowly, but the young Johnson thus had access to a collection far greater than that available at the time to any but the wealthiest.

The scholarly nature of Michael Johnson's stock is reflected in a letter by the Reverend George Plaxton, written from Trentham on St. Peter's Day, 1716: "Johnson, the Lichfield librarian, is now here. He propagates learning all over this diocese, and advanceth knowledge to its just height; all the clergy here are his pupils, and suck all they have from him." Robert DeMaria Jr. in his *Samuel Johnson and the Life of Reading*

Johnson's diploma for the master of arts degree conferred on him by Oxford University in 1755, the year A Dictionary of the English Language *was published (British Library)*

(1997) quotes from a catalogue of Michael Johnson's sale at the Talbot Inn, Sidbury, on 21 March 1718 describing the stock as "choice Books in all Faculties, Divinity, History, Travels, Law, Physick, Mathematicks, Philosophy, Poetry, &c. Together with Bibles, Common Prayers, Shop Books." The Cathedral Library at Lichfield was well stocked, too, offering Johnson a strong collection of secular as well as ecclesiastical history.

Johnson's father's shop was ideal for acquainting Johnson with books, but according to Hester Thrale, Johnson's friend of twenty years, it was his mother, Sarah Ford Johnson, who taught him to read, using the story of St. George and the dragon. Perhaps this experience engendered his lifelong love of romances. As reported in *Johnsonian Miscellanies* (1897), edited by George Birkbeck Hill, Johnson chided Thrale for buying John Newbury's edifying children's books for her family: "Babies do not want . . . to hear about babies; they like to be told of giants and castles, and of somewhat which can stretch and stimulate their little minds."

Johnson exempted romances from his strictures against fiction in the 31 March 1750 issue of *The Rambler,* and he read such works throughout his life. In his *Miscellaneous Observations on the Tragedy of Macbeth* (1745) Johnson demonstrated his familiarity with *Don Belianus of Greece.* Thomas Percy told Johnson's most famous biographer, James Boswell, that Johnson, when visiting in the summer of 1764, read "the old Spanish romance Felixmarte of Hircania, in folio, . . . quite through," a remarkable occurrence since Johnson claimed that he rarely read a book from beginning to end. Traveling in 1776, Johnson took with him *Il Palmerino d'Inghilterra,* an Italian translation of a Portuguese romance by Francisco de Moriñes. Johnson was reading the book to practice his Italian, but he might have chosen a more serious work. His library included Richard Johnson's *The Famous History of the Seven Champions of Christendom* (1687), Alain-René LeSage's *The Adventures of Gil Blas* (1751), a 1551 copy in Spanish of *Amadis of Gaul,* and Hoole's translation of Torquato Tasso's *Jerusalem Delivered* (1763), a presentation copy for which Johnson wrote the dedication and was listed as a subscriber, though the dedication may have served in lieu of payment.

Another early influence on Johnson's literary tastes was Gilbert Walmesley, registrar of the ecclesiastical court in Lichfield and a regular customer of Michael Johnson. In his *Life of Edmund Smith,* included in *Prefaces, Biographical and Critical, to the Works of the English Poets* (1779–1781), commonly called *The Lives of the Poets,* Johnson recalled Walmesley as "one of the first friends that literature procured me. . . . His acquaintance with books was great, and what he did not immediately know, he could, at least, tell where to find. Such was his amplitude of learning, and such his copiousness of communication, that it may be doubted whether a day now passes, in which I have not some advantage from his friendship." Walmesley's purchases from Johnson's father suggest that his library offered English literature, current periodicals, theology, science, medicine, law, philosophy, and politics.

After attending the local schools, Johnson in 1725 went to Stourbridge to visit his cousin Cornelius Ford and stayed for nine months. While Johnson's formal education lagged, he had free range of Ford's sizable library and enjoyed the company of well-educated people. In 1726 Ford secured Johnson a post at Stourbridge Grammar School as student assistant, but by November of that year Johnson was back at Lichfield. He was expected to help his father with selling books, and he also learned how to bind books.

While Johnson did not become adept at bookbinding, he did learn firsthand how a volume was put together and certainly developed an appreciation for proper binding. More than fifty years later this appreciation is evident in his correspondence with the bookseller Thomas Cadell. In a letter dated 31 March 1779 Johnson ordered copies of *The Whole Duty of Man* (1658) and Robert Nelson's *Companion for the Festivals and Fasts of the Church of England* (1704), concluding, "They must be handsomely bound being a present." When Johnson received the books he was not pleased. Complaining about either the edition or the binding, he wrote to Cadell that *The Whole Duty of Man* was "not the right." Johnson noted that the work by Nelson was "bound in Sheepskin, a thing I never saw before" and reminded Cadell, "I was bred a Bookseller, and have not forgotten my trade."

Johnson often neglected to help with the shop so he could read. According to Boswell, he later told his friend Bennet Langton that "his great period of *study* was from the age of *twelve* to that of *eighteen*" and that in the two years from 1726 to 1728 he immersed himself in "literature . . . all ancient writers, all manly: though but little Greek, only some of Anacreon and Hesiod; but in this irregular manner . . . I had looked into a great many books, that were not commonly known at the Universities, where they seldom read any books but what are put into their hands by their tutors." The consequence of this diligence was that after Johnson began attending Pembroke College, Oxford, in October 1728, the master, Dr. William Adams, told him that he "was the best qualified for the University that he had ever known come there." Even before enrolling at the university Johnson on his first visit there astonished his prospective tutor by quoting from the fifth-century Latin grammarian Macrobius. The 1521 edition, edited by Arnold Haldren of Wesel, appeared in his sale catalogue.

In addition to reading diligently, Johnson was beginning to collect books. Perhaps his first acquisition was Georgius Sylvanus's *Homeri Iliados liber primus* (1685), inscribed by Johnson with his name and the year 1724. In 1726 he acquired a volume of the work of the ancient Greek poet Anacreon (1721) edited by Joshua Barnes, Pliny the Younger's *Epistolae* (1703), Sophocles' *Tragoediae VII* (1655), and Adam Littleton's *Linguae latinae liber dictionarius quadri partitus* (1678). Littleton's Latin dictionary may have been a birthday gift since it is inscribed by Johnson with his name and his birth date, "Sept: 7th 1726" (Old Style). In 1727 he added to his library a copy of Petronius's *Satyricon* (1669).

When Johnson went up to Oxford to attend Pembroke College, he took with him a considerable collection, notable for serving his own interests rather than meeting the demands of the curriculum. On the back of an 18 May 1735 letter he wrote to Gilbert Repington, a former schoolfellow then at Christ Church College, Johnson listed these books, which he had left in charge of his longtime friend John Taylor in 1729 when Johnson was forced to leave Pembroke College for want of money. The catalogue of 115 volumes begins with Joseph Scaliger's *Poemata,* first published in 1615, and ends with Julius Caesar Scaliger's *Poetice,* a work of literary criticism that appeared in 1561. Johnson regarded himself as heir to the neo-Latin humanism of the Renaissance exemplified by the two Scaligers.

Other books in Johnson's early collection in the neo-Latin vein include George Buchanan's *Poemata* in two volumes, perhaps the 1715 edition edited by Thomas Ruddiman and published at Edinburgh that became part of the 1785 sale of Johnson's books. He also listed Erasmus's *Colloquia* and an anthology of neo-Latin poetry by Italians (1684), Julius Caesar Scaliger's *De causis linguae latinae,* a study of Latin grammar published in 1540, and Claudius Quillet's *Callipaedia* in Latin and English. First published in 1655, Quillet's book may be regarded as an early sex manual as well as a neo-Latin poem. Johnson took to Oxford scholarly editions such as Nicholas Heinsius's edition of Claudianus, published by Elzevier in 1665 and part of the 1785 sale, and Theodore Beza's Latin New Testament, first published in Geneva in 1556 and then in 1559 with Robert Estienne's Greek text. The latter may be the copy that, according to his diary, Johnson planned to read in 1771 and that he left to George Strahan in his will. Johnson's first projected literary effort was an edition of the Italian humanist Angelo Poliziano. In 1734 Robert Boyse borrowed a copy of Poliziano's work from the Pembroke College Library for Johnson to use. Johnson failed to secure enough subscriptions, so the edition did not appear; but, according to Boswell, Johnson never returned the book.

Classical literature was well represented in Johnson's early collection. He had a Heinsius edition of Virgil; at his death Johnson owned at least twelve editions of the works of the poet. He also owned works by Lucretius, perhaps the 1725 edition that John Hoole chose to keep as a memento of his friend; Theocritus; Horace in Latin and English; Seneca; Livy; Longinus; Suetonius; Quintilian (1693); Homer (1689); Ovid; Lucan; Cicero; Tacitus; Catullus; Tibullus; Propertius; and William Baxter's edition of Anacreon, probably the first edition published in 1695. The edition of Sophocles he acquired in 1726 was presented to Pembroke College in 1912 by the Reverend John Butteridge Pearson, rector of Whitestone, Essex.

Johnson's inclination toward humanist and classical works did not cause him to ignore English literature. About a third of the books that he took to Oxford fall into this category. He had works by Edmund Spenser, John Milton, Edmund Waller, and Edmund Smith. He owned copies of John Dryden's translations of Virgil and Juvenal and his *Fables,* Samuel Butler's *Hudibras,* Joseph Addison's *Works* (1721) in four volumes, Sir Richard Steele's *The Guardian* in two volumes, Richard Blackmore's *Creation,* Samuel Garth's *Dispensary,* Ambrose Philips's poems and his *Three Tragedies* (1725), Edward Young's *Poem on the Last Day* (1713), two volumes of *Miscellanies* (1727) of Alexander Pope and Jonathan Swift. Johnson's eleven volumes of Pope's translations of the *Iliad* and the *Odyssey* were almost certainly not the quarto subscription copies that cost a guinea a volume but rather the duodecimo editions. The *Iliad* appeared in that smaller format in 1720–1721 in six volumes and the duodecimo *Odyssey* in five volumes in 1725–1726. The influence of this early reading was apparent half a century later when Johnson was writing his prefaces on the English poets. For example, Johnson argued successfully to include Blackmore's *Creation* in the edition of that poet's works for which his *Life* served as preface.

Johnson brought with him no books in French or Italian, though he could certainly read the former language. At Oxford he read Joachim Le Grand's *Relation historique d'Abissime* (1728); his first book, *A Voyage to Abyssinia* (1735), was a translation of this French version of Jerónimo Lobo's Portuguese account. By 1738 Johnson also knew Italian, since in that year he began an abortive translation of Paolo Sarpi's 1619 history of the Council of Trent. Johnson had already read *Hamlet,* but he brought no works of William Shakespeare with him. Neither did he have any books about science or mathematics. Still, as Aleyn Lyell Reade writes in *Johnsonian Gleanings* (1909–1952), taken as a whole, Johnson "possessed a collection . . . that could truthfully be described as remarkable for a first year student, even had he come from a prosperous home."

The scholarly aspirations manifest in Johnson's early collection were not immediately fulfilled. As Johnson wrote in *London: A Poem, in Imitation of the Third Satire of Juvenal* (1738) in a line that he capitalized for emphasis, "SLOW RISES WORTH, BY POVERTY DEPRESS'D." The five years from 1730 to 1735 were perhaps the darkest that Johnson was to experience as he struggled to make a living mainly through writing for journals. As Walter Jackson Bate writes in *Samuel Johnson* (1977), "A measure of his paralysis was his continued failure to do anything about the books he had left at Oxford. . . . It was better to repress the thought of them, as though they had never existed, lest their return upset his effort to strangle and bury forever those exorbitant hopes they had symbolized."

Although Johnson did not seek to recover his books until 1735, he did continue to acquire neo-Latin authors. About 1731 he secured the works of Andreas Naugerius (1718), either at the sale of Elijah Fenton's library that year or from a bookseller who had bought the book there. In 1732 he purchased a copy of the works of Clement Marot (1573). He inscribed it, "Sam: Johnson. July 13, 1732," which may be the date he acquired the book.

While Johnson was forced to write as a hack, he remained a bookman. McAdam cites a passage in the *Gentleman's Magazine* of 1740, when Johnson was serving as a sub-editor for Edward Cave:

> *Strasbourg, Feb. 19.* N. S. Here was lately celebrated the third hundred Year's Feast of the noble Art and Mystery of PRINTING, discover'd in 1440, the Honour of which is claim'd by this City, which disputes it with *Mentz* and *Harlem.* It is remarkable that two other Arts were discovered in the same Century, *viz.* The Use of the Loadstone and Compass, and that of Gunpowder, which three made a total Change in the Affairs of the World, *viz.* Printing in Politicks and Divinity, the Com-

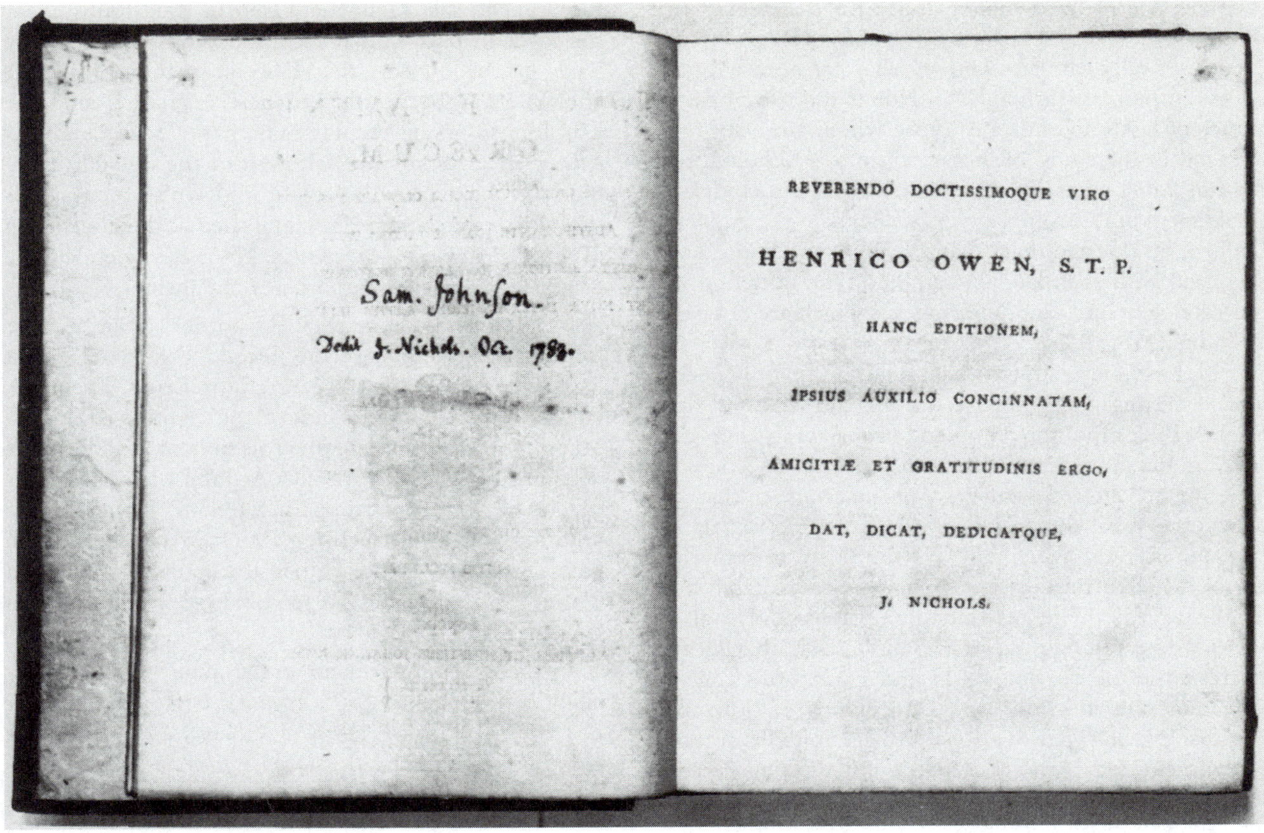

Johnson's signature and note on the verso of the title page of a copy of the New Testament presented to him by the publisher John Nichols (Maggs Bros., sale catalogue 1038, 1983)

> pass in Trade and Navigation, and Gunpowder in the Art of War.

Whether or not Johnson had a hand in the composition of this notice, he remembered the details twenty-eight years later when he wrote to Frederick Augusta Barnard.

By 1743 Johnson had demonstrated sufficient bibliographical knowledge to be hired by the bookseller Thomas Osborne, perhaps on the recommendation of Cave, to catalogue the Harleian collection. Starting about 1705, Robert Harley, who became prime minister in 1710 and the earl of Oxford in 1711, began assembling a library that at the time of his death in 1724 contained some 40,000 printed books and 6,000 manuscripts. Harley's son, Edward, the second Earl of Oxford, continued to add to the collection; when he died in 1741 it contained at least 50,000 books, 7,639 manuscripts, and 14,236 charters. His widow sold the books, for which the Harleys had spent £18,000 on bindings alone, for just £13,000 to Osborne. Michael Maittaire, author of *Annales typographiae* (1719–1726), drew up the plan of the catalogue and wrote the Latin dedication to Lord Carteret, then secretary of state.

Johnson described Maittaire as "a puzzle-headed man, with a large share of scholarship, but with little geometry or logick in his head, without method, and possess'd of little genius." Despite this unflattering judgment, Johnson owned Maittaire's *Miscellania Graecorum aliquot scriptorum carmina* (1722), a collection of Greek verse with Maittaire's Latin translations. He also owned Maittaire's copy of *Poetae Graeci principes heroici carmina* (1566), a large folio containing almost all the Greek hexameter poetry then known, which he bought at the Maittaire sale in 1749 for £12, a large sum. Johnson had received £5 for his translation of *A Voyage to Abyssinia.* In 1749, however, he was still receiving installments of the £1,575 he was paid for his *Dictionary* (1733) and so could afford the book. In his will Johnson left the work to William Windham of Felbrigg Hall.

In his *Proposals for Printing, by Subscription, the Two First Volumes of Bibliotheca Harleiana,* published in 1742 in *The Gentleman's Magazine,* Johnson justified charging 10s. for what might appear to be only a bookseller's advertisement. His defense demonstrates his understanding of the value of enumerative bibliography: "By means of catalogues only can it be known what has been written on every part of learning. . . . Nor is the use of catalogues of less importance to those whom curiosity has engaged in the study of literary history." Although he did not flatter himself with the belief that the Harleian catalogue would prompt others to emulate the earls of Oxford, he asserted that "if any man should happen to be seized with such laudable ambition, he may find in this catalogue hints and informations which are not easily to be met with."

Johnson also showed his understanding of collectors, asserting that they would be attracted to the English Bibles for "the pomp and beauty of the impression, or for the notes with which the text is accompanied, or for any controversy or persecution that it produced, or for the peculiarity of any single passage." His appreciation of the book arts is evident in his writing of "Roman missals and breviaries, remarkable for the beauty of their cuts and illuminations." He also stressed fine printing, informing his readers that those interested in the classics would find in Oxford's collection "not only the most ancient editions of [Johann] Faustus, [Nicolas] Jenson, [Johannes da] Spira, [Conrad] Sweynheim and [Arnold] Panartz, but the most accurate, likewise, and beautiful of [Simon de] Colinaeus, the Juntae, [Christopher] Plantin, Aldus [Manutius], the Stephens [Henri and Robert], and Elzevir, with the commentaries and observations of the most learned editors."

Johnson and William Oldys shared the responsibility of cataloguing Osborne's books. They worked diligently, publishing the first two volumes, describing 15,242 titles, in March 1743 and the next two, with 20,724 titles, in January 1744. Johnson's contribution to the notes is unclear. Boswell credits him with the descriptions of the Latin books and ascribes the notes on the English books to Oldys. Sir John Hawkins asserts that Johnson wrote all the descriptions in the third and fourth volumes. Whatever his role, Johnson certainly handled a vast number of rare books and learned much about the history of printing.

Johnson's curiosity or meticulousness often struck his employer as excessive, and Osborne once reprimanded him for spending too much time with a volume. When Johnson replied that he could not describe a book without looking into it, Osborne apparently claimed that Johnson was just reading for pleasure. Angered at being called a liar, Johnson seized a large sixteenth-century folio Greek Bible and knocked Osborne down with it. The volume he used is supposedly the *Biblia sacra Graece* (1597), which is listed in the second volume of *Catalogus Bibliothecæ Harleianæ* and in the Johnson sale catalogue. Osborne paid Johnson for his work in part with books, and the bookseller may have given Johnson this folio in memory of their encounter. Osborne did not bear a grudge, since he kept Johnson in his employ to prepare *The Harleian Miscellany,* an eight-volume selection of the 350,000 pamphlets in the Harley library. In Johnson's proposals for this work, which were first published at the conclusion of *The Gentleman's Magazine* in 1743, he defended the project by noting the importance of ephemera.

Another volume that Osborne certainly gave Johnson was a Shakespeare Second Folio (1632) that had belonged to Shakespeare editor Lewis Theobald, whose strictures on Alexander Pope's edition of Shakespeare's works earned him the role of hero in Pope's first version of the *Dunciad* (1728). At Johnson's sale it was purchased for 22s. by Samuel Ireland, father of the notorious Shakespeare forger William Henry Ireland. Later, Sir Henry Irving bought the book for £100, and it now resides at the Folger Shakespeare Library in Washington, D.C.

Johnson's next major undertaking was the compiling of *A Dictionary of the English Language: in which the Words are deduced from their Originals, and Illustrated in their Different Significations by Examples from the Best Writers* (1755). The task provided an incentive to acquire books for illustrative quotations and examples of word use, and the income from the booksellers who underwrote the publication made such purchases possible. Thirteen titles survive from those that Johnson marked for this project: Francis Bacon's *Works* (1740); Robert Burton's *Anatomy of Melancholy* (1676), bound with Matthew Hale's *Primitive Origination of Mankind* (1667); Samuel Butler's *Hudibras* (1726); Michael Drayton's *Works* (1748–1753); Bryan Duppa's *Holy Rules and Helps to Devotion Both in Prayer and Practice* (1675); John Norris's *Collection of Miscellanies* (1699); an edition of Shakespeare's plays edited by William Warburton (1747); Robert South's *Twelve Sermons Preached upon Several Occasions* (1694); Virgil's *Aeneid,* translated by Christopher Pitt (1740); Izaac Walton's *The Life of Dr. Sanderson* (1678); Isaac Watts's *Logick* (1745); and *The Works of the Most Celebrated Minor Poets: Volume the First* (1749). Because of their publication dates, four of these works must have been acquired as Johnson was working on the *Dictionary,* and some if not all of the others probably were as well. The book by Butler bears Johnson's signature with the date of August 1747. The work by Norris, according to an inscription in the book, belonged to John Paterson on 1 February 1734. Johnson would not have needed Pitt's translation of the *Aeneid* except for examples for his dictionary, though in the event he did not quote from Pitt's work.

In 1762 Johnson received a pension of £300 a year from the government. With the extra income Johnson was better able to indulge his love of books. One measure of his changed circumstances is the number of books to which he subscribed. Before 1762 he subscribed to nineteen; after he received his pension he subscribed to forty-eight. Johnson was working on his edition of Shakespeare in the early 1760s and may have used some of his pension to buy a second issue of the Third Folio (1664).

Though Johnson bought his books for use, his comments in the *Proposals* for the Harleian catalogue show that he appreciated their aesthetic qualities. In *The Rambler* of 26 November 1751 Johnson poked fun at Hirsutus, a collector who valued black letter, or Gothic type, above all else. Hirsutus

> had early withdrawn his attention from foreign trifles, and that since he begun to addict his mind to serious and manly studies, he had very carefully amassed all the English books that were printed in the black character. This search he had pursued so diligently, that he was able to show the deficiencies of the best catalogues. He had long since completed his Caxton, had three sheets of Traveris unknown to the antiquaries, and wanted to a perfect Pynson but two volumes, of which one was promised him as a legacy by its present possessor, and the other he was resolved to buy, at whatever price, when Quisquilius's library should be sold. Hirsutus had no other reason for the valuing or slighting a book, than that it was printed in the Roman or the Gothick letter, nor any ideas but such as his favourite volumes had supplied; when he was serious, he expatiated on the narratives of Johan de Trevisa, and, when he was merry, regaled us with a quotation from the *Shippe of Foles.*

The passage in *Ship of Fools* opens with Johnson's mockery of unlearned book collectors. Despite the satire Johnson himself, according to Boswell, "loved . . . the old black letter books."

Other references to Johnson's appreciation of books as physical objects abound. In 1757 he subscribed to John Baskerville's finely printed *Virgil.* Later he gave the book to Thomas Warton for Trinity College in appreciation for the use of the school's library in his research. On 6 January 1784 he wrote to the bookseller Charles Dilly for some titles, including "the best printed edition of [Richard] Baxter's *A Call to the Unconverted,*" first published in 1658. He was pleased that in 1784 the Royal Library secured a copy of Brian Walton's *Biblia Sacra Polyglotta,* published at Oxford in 1655–1656. In a letter of 4 September 1784 Johnson described this work as "undoubtedly the greatest performance of English typography, and therefore ought to appear in its most splendid form among the books of the king of England."

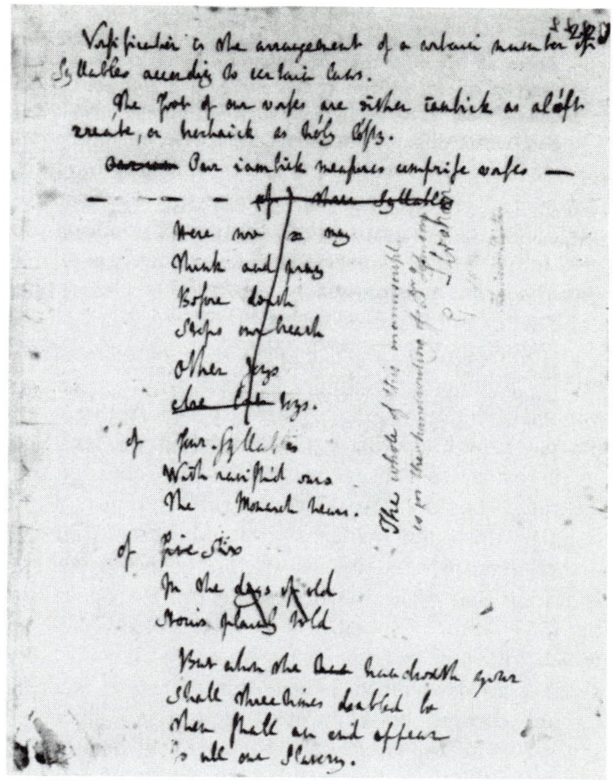

A page from the only extant manuscript for Johnson's dictionary (Houghton Library, Harvard University)

Johnson also loved libraries. He was among the earliest ticket holders of the British Museum, receiving his on 8 May 1761. He frequented Buckingham House, where George III was assembling a personal library to replace the one his grandfather George II had given to the nation, and there befriended Barnard. As Barnard was preparing to visit the Continent in search of books for his employer, Johnson sent him a lengthy letter, dated 28 May 1768, containing Johnson's principles of book collecting. He maintained that the Royal Library "should have at least the most curious [elegant] Edition, the most splendid, and the most useful" of a title. Johnson did not, however, favor collecting large numbers of copies of a work. When Boswell told him that he had seen sixty-three editions of the works of Thomas à Kempis in the Royal Library, Johnson replied, "He would have [only] the original, and all the translations, and all the editions which had any variations in the text."

On the other hand, Johnson did approve of Dr. James Douglas's large collection of Horace. He observed to Boswell that "every man should try to collect one book in that manner, and present it to a publick library." Johnson's own library contained multiple copies of various texts: at least eight editions of Homer and Horace, twelve of Virgil, nine New Testaments, and seven complete Bibles. As an editor of Shakespeare Johnson understood the need for comprehensive collections. When the Reverend George Horne was considering an edition of Izaac Walton's *Lives,* Johnson told him, "In order to do it well, it will be necessary to collect all the editions of Walton's Lives. By way of adapting the book to the taste of the present age, they have, in a later edition, left out a vision which he relates Dr. Donne had [of his wife], but it should be restored."

Johnson urged Barnard to buy as many works of the old printers as possible, and he provided bibliographical references to help Barnard identify these, "so that you may know when you have them all, which is always of use as it prevents needless searches." Early illustrated books were also desirable because "the designs were often made by great Masters." Johnson further demonstrated his knowledge of early printing by noting that while the first dated printed book was the 1457 Mainz Psalter of Fust and Peter Schoeffer (which Johnson, trusting to his memory, dated 1458), "there is great reason to believe that there are latent in obscure corners books printed before it," since he recalled from *The Gentleman's Magazine* that Strasbourg celebrated the three hundredth anniversary of printing in 1740.

Johnson informed Barnard that typographical antiquaries suspected that the Bible had been printed three times before 1462, as in fact it had been, though Johnson quoted Augustin Calmet's *Dictionnaire historique de la Bible* (1722) saying that the 1462 Bible was the earliest well-documented edition. Johnson knew that an old Bible, probably a copy of the Gutenberg, had been discovered in a monastery in 1739. He had read in an obscure poem by Gabriel Naudé, librarian to Cardinal Jules Mazarin, that Fust and Schoeffer had used a device of horns to mark their books. Johnson added that he knew of no such examples, indicating a familiarity with the work of these early printers, but he urged Barnard to watch for any such books. McAdam suggests that Naudé was referring to watermarks; however, it may be that Naudé mistook the printers' mark–a branch holding two shields–for horns.

Johnson warned against buying entire libraries because of duplication and shipping costs. "It will generally be more commodious to buy the few that you want at a price somewhat advanced," he wrote, "than to encumber yourself with useless books." He made an exception for specialized libraries, which were likely to contain "very few Superfluities." Finally, he cautioned Barnard always to collate his books and reminded the librarian of "how near we both were to purchasing a mutilated Missal at a high price."

Much of Johnson's extensive bibliographic knowledge came from his work on the Harleian collection. Much, too, came from his incessant examination of libraries. The first time he visited Charles Burney, 20 March 1777, he scrutinized the musician's books. Burney feared Johnson's reaction, but Johnson reassured him, "You are an honest man, to have formed so great an accumulation of Knowledge." Similarly, when he visited Richard Owen Cambridge on 18 April 1775, Boswell reports, "No sooner had we made our bow to Mr. Cambridge, in his library, than Johnson ran eagerly to one side of the room, intent on pouring over the backs of the books."

Johnson's interest in matters of printing is evident from his reading William Bowyer's *The Origin of Printing* (1774) shortly after it was published. While visiting at Blenheim Palace in Oxfordshire in 1774 he saw Constantine Lascaris's *Erotemata* (1476), an elementary Greek grammar that was the first book in which Greek type was used throughout. Johnson observed that it was well printed but not so well as later editions. He may have been thinking of his own more attractive Aldine Press edition of *Erotemata* (1521).

On his 1775 visit to France Johnson toured several collections, including those of the Royal Library, the Sorbonne, St. Cloud, Chartreux, and St. Germain des Près. His observations indicate his grasp of early printing and bookmaking. Examining a Gutenberg Bible, he remarked that it was "supposed to have been printed with wooden types.–I am in doubt; the print is large and fair, in two folios." He also doubted that another early book, probably William Durand's *Rationale officiorum divinorum* (1459), had been printed from wooden type. He noted that such printing "is inferred from the difference of form sometimes seen in the same letter," but he thought that these letters "might be struck with different puncheons.–The regular similitude of most letters proves better that they are metal," as of course they are. At St. Germain des Près he saw another copy of Durand's book and a 1473 *De civitate Dei* by St. Augustine. He recognized the type as the same used by Fust and Schoeffer for their 1465 Cicero *De officiis.*

McAdam summarizes Johnson's tour of French libraries:

> Although anyone reading all of the existing part of Johnson's *French Diary* knows that he did many things other than looking at early books, when his comments on these books are brought together, it becomes clear that he is not merely wandering through libraries and politely glancing at their treasures. One can readily believe that at each one he asked what early or remarkable books the library owned and then, with great interest, examined those which were handed him, com-

paring products of the same printers, remembering other books among the early incunabula, using his sound common sense about claims for the use of wooden types–in other words, acting like any other well-trained, skeptical bibliographer.

On 17 April 1778 Boswell and Johnson spoke about death. Boswell noted that Thomas Percy felt unhappy at the prospect of leaving his books. Johnson dismissed the thought. "A man need not be uneasy on these grounds, for, as he will retain his consciousness, he may say with the philosopher, 'Omnia mea meum porto'" (I carry all that is mine with me). However, some six years later Johnson sounded much like Percy. Ordered by his physician, Richard Brocklesby, to return from Lichfield to London, Johnson wrote back on 25 October 1784, "The town is my element, there are my friends, there are my books to which I have not yet bidden farewel, and there are my amusements."

On his deathbed slightly more than a month afterwards, Johnson began to bid farewell to his library. On 7 December 1784 Johnson gave William Windham a two-volume New Testament, quoting from Virgil, "Extremum hoc munus morientis habeto" (take this as my last dying gift). Two days later he added a codicil to his will, leaving some of his books to friends. To Bennet Langton he left his polyglot Bible, the typography of which he so much admired. The Reverend George Strahan, vicar of Islington, was to receive all of Johnson's Latin Bibles, two Greek New Testaments, and a Greek Bible printed by A. Wechelius. Strahan, however, did not end up with all the Bibles bequeathed to him, as the Wechelius Bible–the one with which Johnson felled Osborne–was later sold. Joshua Reynolds received a copy of Johnson's 1773 edition of *A Dictionary of the English Language* and "my great French Dictionary, by Martiniere," that is, Antoine Augustin Bruzen de la Martinière's *Le grand dictionnaire géographique et critique*. Other friends were to choose a volume as a keepsake.

The rest of the library, between three thousand and five thousand volumes, was sold on 16–19 February 1785 by James Christie. Sir John Hawkins, Johnson's executor, wanted William Paterson to prepare the sale catalogue, but Paterson was in Rotterdam. Christie assigned the task to an assistant. The result, according to Arthur Wollaston Hutton in his 1899 essay "Dr. Johnson's Library" was

> a very sorry production, sadly unworthy of the occasion that called it into existence. . . . Hardly an entry in the catalogue is free from mistakes; hardly any book is adequately described, so as to place the edition beyond doubt; some of the entries are so incomplete that a book is unrecognizable; while every lot contains a number of books that are not named at all.

The collection included one incunabulum, Boethius's *Consolation of Philosophy* (1491), and at least fifty-six books from the sixteenth century, including the Aldine Press edition of Hesychius of Alexandria's *Dictionarium* (1514) and Aeschines' *Orationes Rhetoricae Graecae* (1513), both editiones principes. Johnson also had an Aldine edition of Horace (1555), Pindar (1516), Quintilian (1512), and Macrobius (1521) as well as Apollonius Rhodius's *Argonautica* (1521), a 1534 edition of Virgil printed by Johannes Froben, and a 1575 edition of Virgil printed by Christophe Plantin.

Of the 650 lots of books, more than 200 relate to classical literature, about 130 to theology and philosophy, 80 to history and law, nearly 40 to mathematics and science, more than 20 to medicine. The medical books begin with the 1538 and 1542 editions of Galen and the editio princeps of Aretaeus of Cappadocia's *De causis morborum* (1554). Johnson owned Percivall Pott's *Chirurgical Works* (1779)–Pott attended Johnson–and George Cheyne's *English Malady* (1733), one of Johnson's favorites. Although Johnson's *The Lives of the Poets* began with writers of the seventeenth century, he owned the works of Geoffrey Chaucer and John Gower, and many English poets from Spenser onward were well represented.

The sale was heavily attended because Johnson's friends wanted mementos of the great writer. Burney bought a verse translation of Tibullus by James Grainger (1759) for 9s. 6d.; Claude Saumaise Salmasius's *Opera* in nine volumes, probably a made-up set, for 12s. 6d.; and an edition of Juvenal for 7s. 6d. Johnson's friend Langton purchased the works of Seneca for 6s. 6d. Shakespeare scholar Edmond Malone paid £1 19s. for a lot that included the first two volumes of Burney's *A General History of Music* (1776, 1777). Johnson was listed as a subscriber, and he wrote the dedication. Volume two was a presentation copy from Burney to Johnson and inscribed by the latter, "Given by the Author to Sam: Johnson May 16, 1782."

Malone also paid 9s. for a lot that included Thomas Chatterton's poems. Chatterton had claimed that the poems were the work of the fifteenth-century Bristol priest Thomas Rowley. Although Johnson did not believe in their medieval character and excluded Chatterton from *The Lives of the Poets,* he admired Chatterton's work, commenting, "This is the most extraordinary young man that has encountered my knowledge. It is wonderful how the whelp has written such things." The lot also contained a presentation copy of Thomas Tyers's *An Historical Rhapsody on Mr. Pope* (1782); Tyers was an early biographer of Johnson. The third volume in

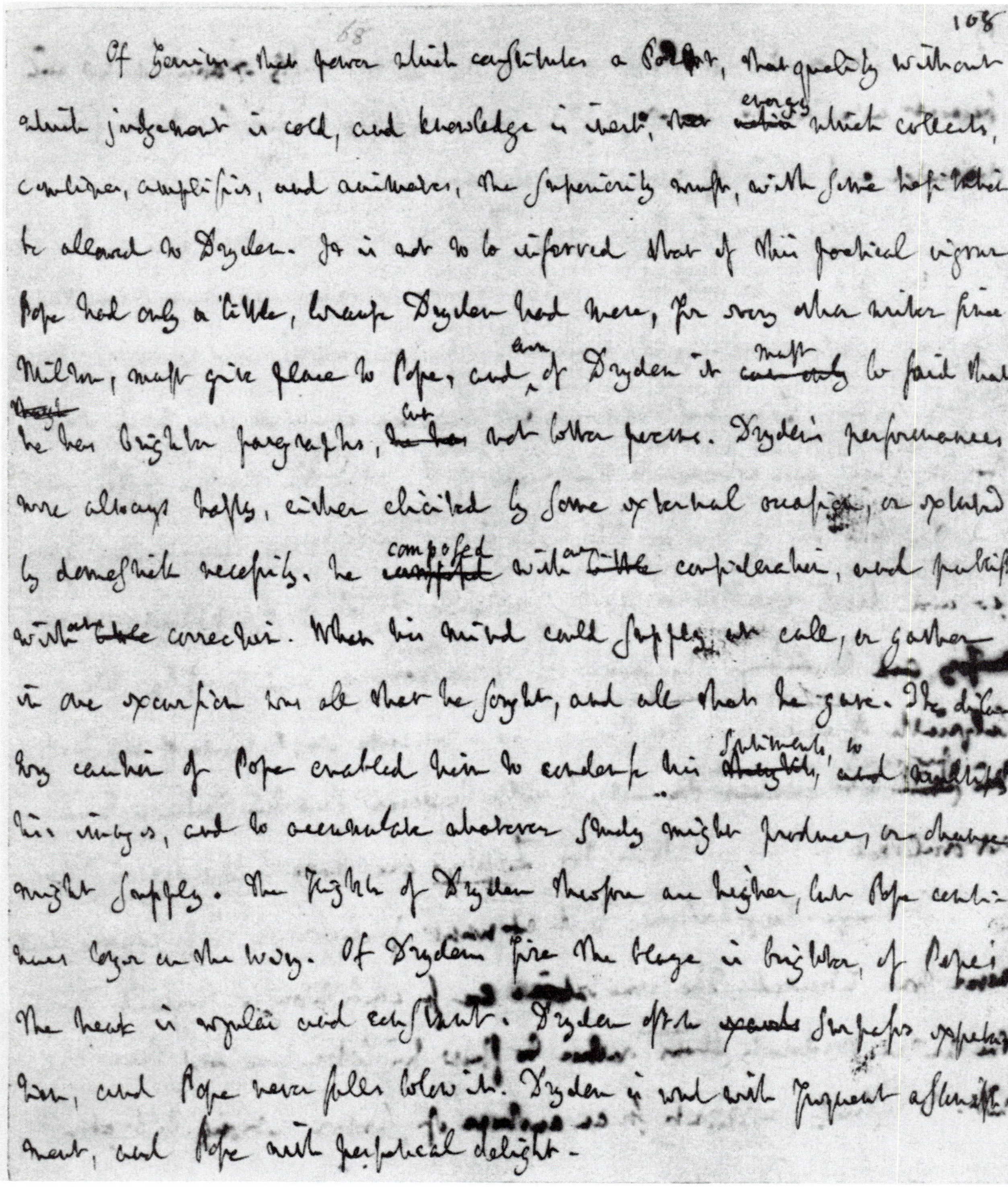

108

Of Genius, that power which constitutes a Poet, that quality without which judgement is cold, and knowledge is inert, that energy which collects, combines, amplifies, and animates, the superiority must, with some hesitation, be allowed to Dryden. It is not to be inferred that of this poetical vigour Pope had only a little, because Dryden had more, for every other writer since Milton, must give place to Pope, and even of Dryden it must be said that if he has brighter paragraphs, he has not better poems. Dryden's performances were always hasty, either excited by some external occasion, or extorted by domestick necessity. he composed without consideration, and published without correction. What his mind could supply at call, or gather in one excursion was all that he sought, and all that he gave. The dilatory caution of Pope enabled him to condense his sentiments, to multiply his images, and to accumulate whatever study might produce, or chance might supply. The flights of Dryden therefore are higher, but Pope continues longer on the wing. Of Dryden's fire the blaze is brighter, of Pope's the heat is more regular and constant. Dryden often surpasses expectation, and Pope never falls below it. Dryden is read with frequent astonishment, and Pope with perpetual delight.

A page from the manuscript for Johnson's "Life of Pope," written in 1780 (British Library)

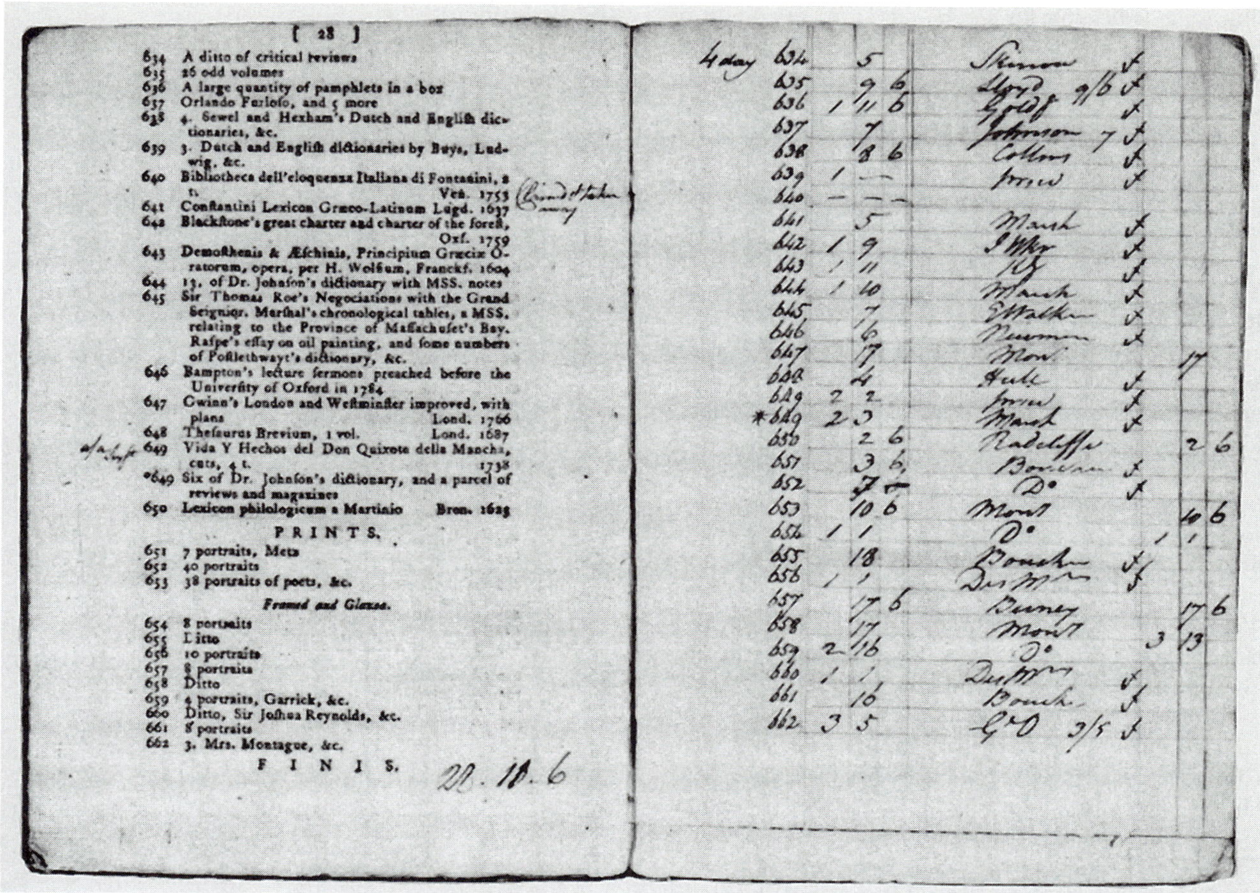

[28]

634 A ditto of critical reviews
635 26 odd volumes
636 A large quantity of pamphlets in a box
637 Orlando Furioso, and 5 more
638 4. Sewel and Hexham's Dutch and English dictionaries, &c.
639 3. Dutch and English dictionaries by Buys, Ludwig, &c.
640 Bibliotheca dell'eloquenza Italiana di Fontanini, 2 t. Ven. 1753
641 Constantini Lexicon Græco-Latinum Lugd. 1637
642 Blackstone's great charter and charter of the forest, Oxf. 1759
643 Demosthenis & Æschinis, Principium Græciæ Oratorum, opera, per H. Wolfium, Franckf. 1604
644 13. of Dr. Johnson's dictionary with MSS. notes
645 Sir Thomas Roe's Negociations with the Grand Seignior. Marshal's chronological tables, a MSS. relating to the Province of Massachuset's Bay. Raspe's essay on oil painting, and some numbers of Postlethwayt's dictionary, &c.
646 Bampton's lecture sermons preached before the University of Oxford in 1784
647 Gwinn's London and Westminster improved, with plans Lond. 1766
648 Thesaurus Brevium, 1 vol. Lond. 1687
649 Vida Y Hechos del Don Quixote della Mancha, cuts, 4 t. 1738
*649 Six of Dr. Johnson's dictionary, and a parcel of reviews and magazines
650 Lexicon philologicum a Martinio Brem. 1623

PRINTS.

651 7 portraits, Mets
652 40 portraits
653 38 portraits of poets, &c.

Framed and Glazed.

654 8 portraits
655 Ditto
656 10 portraits
657 8 portraits
658 Ditto
659 4 portraits, Garrick, &c.
660 Ditto, Sir Joshua Reynolds, &c.
661 8 portraits
662 3. Mrs. Montague, &c.

FINIS.

The last page, with handwritten price list, in a copy of A Catalogue of the Valuable Library of Books, of the Late Learned Samuel Johnson, *prepared for the 1785 sale of Johnson's library (Houghton Library, Harvard University)*

the lot was John Ogilvie's *An Inquiry into the Causes of the Infidelity and Scepticism of the Times* (1783). Malone bought two more lots, one for £1 4s. that included the eight volumes of Johann Albrecht Fabricius's *Bibliotheca Graeca* (1705–1728) and another for £1 5s. that included a volume by Roman historian Sallust, edited by the great Dutch classical scholar Siegebert Haverkamp (1742).

The bibliophile Isaac Gossett bought a dozen lots at the sale. Among these was a lot that included William Hutton's *History of Birmingham* (1781) for 7s. 6d. Malone found Johnson reading this book in March 1783 and observed that local histories tended to be dull. Johnson replied, "It is true, sir; but this has a particular merit with me; for I passed some of my early years and married my wife there."

Dr. Brocklesby bought two Robert Foulis editions of Xenephon, the *Hellenica* (1762), for 8s. and the *Anabasis* (1764) for 9s. 6d. He paid 17s. for Lucan's *Pharsalia,* edited by Franciscus Oudendorp (1728), which perhaps was the copy that Johnson had with him at Oxford, and 15s. for Baron Gerard van Swieten's *Commentaria in Hermanni Boerhaave aphorismos de cognoscendis et curandis morbis* in three volumes (1741–1742), an important medical work as well as an interesting association copy because Johnson published a brief biography of Boerhaave in 1739. He paid £1. 5s. for the lot that included a 1695 copy of the work of Juvenal, edited by Heinrich Christian Hennin, and an edition of the work of Persius, edited by Isaac Casaubon. The edition of Juvenal is an important association copy because the Latin poet inspired Johnson's two greatest poems, *London: A Poem, in Imitation of the Third Satire of Juvenal* (1738) and *The Vanity of Human Wishes. The Tenth Satire of Juvenal, Imitated by Samuel Johnson* (1749). On visits to Johnson in 1783 and 1784 Brocklesby quoted from Juvenal. On the latter occasion Brocklesby got a word wrong, and Johnson corrected him.

John Hoole paid 6s. 6d. for one of Johnson's two copies of the sermons of Samuel Clarke. Hoole also bought a copy of Giuseppe Baretti's two-volume *Dictionary of the English and Italian Language* (1760) with

Johnson's dedication for £1 1s., a variorum edition of the work of Statius (1671) for 14s., a 1663 edition of the work of Ovid for 18s., and an edition of the work of Aristotle for 4s. John Desmoulins, whose mother Johnson housed for many years, and whose grandfather, Dr. Samuel Swinfen, had been Johnson's godfather, bought two unidentified bundles of pamphlets, one in quarto for £1 12s. and one in octavo for £1 7s.

Gen. James Oglethorpe, founder of Georgia, Steevens, and Windham also secured volumes. Between gifts and purchases, Windham secured eighteen Greek and Latin works from Johnson's library. Among these were Eustathius of Thessalonica's commentary on Homer (1542) for 10s.; Pico della Mirandola's *Opera* (1573) for 8s. 6d.; Jan Gruterus's six-volume *Fax Artium Liberalium* (1602–1612), an annotated dictionary of technical terms used by the various professions, for 5s.; and the second edition of the work of Horace (1713), edited by Richard Bentley, for 9s.

The sale attracted connoisseurs such as Horace Walpole, no admirer of Johnson, William Maltby, William Hodgson, Samuel Rogers, Michael Woodhull, and Charles Marsh. Most of the books were sold to "Price" or "Money," probably code names for booksellers, who attended in large numbers. Benjamin Collins, John Cuttell, Robert Faulder (who printed Boswell's "Ode to Mrs. Thrale, by Samuel Johnson, LL.D. on their Supposed Approaching Nuptials"), Joseph Johnson, Thomas King, William Lowndes, John Nourse (who acted as Windham's agent in the sale), and Benjamin White were among those buying. Because different copies of the auction catalogue record different prices, the exact amount paid for Johnson's library remains in doubt. Boswell gave the figure £247 9s., while George Birkbeck Hill and Lawrence Fitzroy Powell cite a total of £321 15s.

Born in a bookshop, Johnson spent his life surrounded by books. Reading calmed his nervous fits, and he never left home without a book to accompany him. Never rich, he could not afford a sumptuous collection, but he acquired a large library with many notable and often handsome editions. His library and his writings testify to his extensive bibliographic interests, and his knowledge of books extended to all aspects of bibliography. To paraphrase Johnson's judgment of Alexander Pope, if Johnson be not a bibliophile, where is bibliophily to be found?

Letters:

The Letters of Samuel Johnson, with Mrs. Thrale's Genuine Letters to Him, 3 volumes, edited by R. W. Chapman (Oxford: Clarendon Press, 1952);

The Letters of Samuel Johnson, 5 volumes, edited by Bruce Redford (Princeton: Princeton University Press, 1992–1994).

Bibliographies:

William P. Courtney and D. Nichol Smith, *A Bibliography of Samuel Johnson* (Oxford: Clarendon Press, 1915);

Donald Greene, "The Development of the Johnson Canon," in *Restoration and Eighteenth-Century Literature,* edited by Carroll Camden (Chicago: University of Chicago Press, 1963), pp. 407–427;

James L. Clifford and Donald J. Greene, *Samuel Johnson: A Survey and Bibliography of Critical Studies* (Minneapolis: University of Minnesota Press, 1970);

Greene and John A. Vance, *A Bibliography of Johnsonian Studies, 1970–1985,* University of Victoria English Literary Studies, no. 39 (Victoria, B.C., 1987);

John David Fleeman, *A Bibliography of the Work of Samuel Johnson* (New York: Oxford University Press, 1999).

Biographies:

Hester Lynch Piozzi (Mrs. Thrale), *Anecdotes of the Late Samuel Johnson, LL.D. During the Last Twenty Years of His Life* (London: Printed for T. Cadell, 1786); republished, and edited by Arthur Sherbo, in William Shaw, *Memoirs of the Life and Writings of the Late Dr. Samuel Johnson,* Oxford English Memoirs and Travels (Oxford: Oxford University Press, 1974);

Sir John Hawkins, *The Life of Samuel Johnson, LL.D.,* volume 1 of *The Works of Samuel Johnson, LL.D.* (London: Printed for J. Buckland and forty others, 1787); republished (slightly abridged), edited by Bertram H. Davis (New York: Macmillan, 1961);

James Boswell, *The Life of Samuel Johnson, LL.D.,* 2 volumes (London: Printed by Henry Baldwin for Charles Dilly, 1791); republished in *Boswell's Life of Johnson, Together with Boswell's Journal of a Tour to the Hebrides and Johnson's Diary of a Journey into North Wales,* 6 volumes, edited by G. B. Hill, revised and enlarged by L. F. Powell (Oxford: Clarendon Press, 1934–1964);

George Birkbeck Hill, ed., *Johnsonian Miscellanies,* 2 volumes (Oxford: Clarendon Press, 1897);

Aleyn Lyell Reade, *Johnsonian Gleanings,* 11 volumes (London: Privately printed for the author, 1909–1952);

Joseph Wood Krutch, *Samuel Johnson* (New York: Holt, 1944);

John Wain, *Samuel Johnson* (London: Macmillan, 1944; New York: Viking, 1975);

James L. Clifford, *Young Samuel Johnson* (New York: McGraw-Hill, 1955);

O. M. Brack Jr. and Robert E. Kelley, eds., *The Early Biographies of Samuel Johnson* (Iowa City: University of Iowa Press, 1974);

Walter Jackson Bate, *Samuel Johnson* (New York: Harcourt Brace Jovanovich, 1977; London: Chatto & Windus, 1978);

James L. Clifford, *Dictionary Johnson: Samuel Johnson's Middle Years* (New York: McGraw-Hill, 1979; London: Heinemann, 1979).

References:

Greg J. Clingham and N. Hopkinson, "Johnson's Copy of the *Iliad* at Felbrigg Hall, Norfolk," *Book Collector,* 37 (Winter 1988): 503–521;

Robert DeMaria Jr., *Samuel Johnson and the Life of Reading* (Baltimore: Johns Hopkins University Press, 1997);

Donald D. Eddy and John David Fleeman, *A Preliminary Handlist of Books to which Dr. Samuel Johnson Subscribed* (Charlottesville: Bibliographical Society of the University of Virginia, 1993);

Arundel Esdaille, "Dr. Johnson the Bibliographer," *Contemporary Review,* 126 (1924): 200–210;

John David Fleeman, *The Sale Catalogue of Samuel Johnson's Library. A Facsimile Edition* (Victoria, B.C.: University of Victoria Press, 1975);

Percy Hazan Houston, *Doctor Johnson: A Study in Eighteenth Century Humanism* (Cambridge, Mass.: Harvard University Press, 1923);

Arthur Wollaston Hutton, "Dr. Johnson's Library," in *Johnson Club Papers* (London: T. Fisher Unwin, 1899) pp. 117–130;

Robert Wyndham Ketton-Cremer, "Johnson's Last Gifts to Windham," *Book Collector,* 5 (1956): 354–356;

Paul J. Korshin, "Johnson and the Scholars," in *Samuel Johnson: New Critical Essays,* edited by Isobel Grundy (New York: Barnes & Noble, 1984), pp. 51–69;

Herman W. Liebert, "Samuel Johnson, Bookseller at Uttoxeter Market," *Johnson Society Transactions* (December 1981): 29–35;

Edward Lippincott McAdam, "Dr. Johnson as Bibliographer and Book Collector," in *New Light on Dr. Johnson: Essays on the Occasion of his 250th Birthday,* edited by Frederick W. Hilles (New Haven: Yale University Press, 1959), pp. 163–175;

David McKitterick, "Thomas Osborne, Samuel Johnson and the Learned of Foreign Nations: A Forgotten Catalogue," *Book Collector,* 4 (1992): 55–68;

Sydney Castle Roberts, "Johnson's Books," in his *An Eighteenth-Century Gentleman and Other Essays* (New York: Macmillan / Cambridge: Cambridge University Press, 1930), pp. 46–66;

Arthur Sherbo, "Another Book Owned by Samuel Johnson," *Notes and Queries,* 229 (September 1984): 402–403;

Kai Kin Yung, "The Association Books of Johnson, Boswell, and Mrs. Piozzi in the Birthplace Museum," *New Rambler: Journal of the Johnson Society of London,* 12 (Spring 1972): 23–44.

Papers:

The largest holdings of Samuel Johnson manuscript material is at the Hyde-Eccles Collection, Four Oaks Farm, Somerville, New Jersey. The Yale University Library, the British Library, the Bodleian Library, Pembroke College Library, and the Johnson Birthplace Museum, Lichfield, have important manuscripts.

John Ker, third Duke of Roxburghe

(23 April 1740 – 19 March 1804)

Brian Hillyard
National Library of Scotland

CATALOGUES: *A Catalogue of the Library of the Late John Duke of Roxburghe, Arranged by G. and W. Nicol, Booksellers to His Majesty, Pall-Mall; Which Will Be Sold by Auction, At His Grace's Late Residence in St. James's Square, On Monday, 18th May, 1812, and the Forty-one following Days, Sundays excepted, at Twelve o'Clock, by Robert H. Evans, Bookseller, Pall-Mall* (London: W. Bulmer, 1812);

A Supplement to the Catalogue of the Library of the Late John Duke of Roxburghe. The Books will be Sold at His Grace's Late Residence in St. James's Square, on Monday, the 13th of July, 1812, and the Three Following Days, by Robert H. Evans (London: W. Bulmer, 1812);

A Catalogue of the Library of the Late John, Duke of Roxburghe, Which will be Sold, by Auction, in Lauder's Ball-Room, in Kelso, on Thursday, September 16, 1813 . . . (Kelso, U.K: A. Ballantyne, 1813).

The entry in Robert Chambers's *Biographical Dictionary of Eminent Scotsmen,* published in Glasgow in 1835, begins "KER, JOHN, third Duke of Roxburgh, distinguished by his eminent bibliographical knowledge, and his extensive and valuable collection of books . . . ," and many later dictionaries of biography follow suit. A duke he was, but his chief claim to fame is as a bibliophile. As such, he earned the distinction of having named after him one of the most exclusive and famous of bibliographical societies, the Roxburghe Club, which came into being at the sale of the Roxburghe Library in 1812 and still thrives. The sale of 1812 has gone down in the history of book collecting as the high point of bibliomania, when the edition of Giovanni Boccaccio's *Decamerone* (Venice: Christophorus Valdarfer, 1471) sold for £2,260, a record for a single printed book that lasted until 1884. While it may be argued that the Boccaccio was quite exceptional and the duke's library is not to be ranked alongside, for example, that of George John, second Earl Spencer, nonetheless Roxburghe books, many of them in their distinctive armorial bindings, are today treasured items in many great libraries.

John Ker, third Duke of Roxburghe

John Ker was born in Hanover Square, London, on 23 April 1740, the eldest son of Robert, second Duke of Roxburghe, whom he succeeded in that title in 1755. There is little to relate about the third duke's life. After some years at Eton (1753–1754 and 1756–1758), he traveled abroad. The story goes that while on the Continent he became attached to Christiana Sophia Albertina, eldest daughter of the duke of Mecklenburg Strelitz, but as her younger sister Charlotte married King George III in September 1761, Roxburghe avoided creating a situation in which Christiana would become the subject of her younger sister. The notice of Roxburghe's death in the *Gentleman's Magazine* for 1804 refers to this problem of etiquette: "this, operating with some other reasons, broke off the negociation." It is unclear what were the other reasons here referred to, but neither party ever married.

In reviewing Robert Pitcairn's *Trials, and other Proceedings, in Matters Criminal, before the High Court of Justiciary in Scotland* (Edinburgh, 1829–1830) in the *Quarterly Review* for 1831, Sir Walter Scott, while not specifically mentioning this episode, may well have been referring to it when he comments: "Youthful misfortunes, of a kind against which neither rank nor wealth possess a talisman, had cast an early shade of gloom over his prospects, and given to one so splendidly endowed with the means of enjoying society that degree of reserved melancholy, which prefers retirement to the splendid scenes of gaiety." The preface to the 1812 sale catalogue puts this more strongly in saying that it was the duke's "favourite plan to pass through life among his books, studiously endeavouring to conceal, from the world, his eminent talents, and his extensive knowledge. And so successful was he in this endeavour, that neither his neighbours in the country, nor his friends in the capital, seem to have been much acquainted with them."

Roxburghe remained close to George III, who, according to George Nicol, bookseller to both the king and the duke, appreciated his skills. The king awarded him various honors at court, including appointing him a lord of the bedchamber (1767), a knight of the Thistle (1768), and a knight of the Garter (1801). As a great favor the king permitted Roxburghe to combine the orders of the Thistle and the Garter, a rare distinction. His position at court required him to spend much of his time in London, after 1796 at 13 St. James's Square, where his main library was housed. His ancestral home was Fleurs (now Floors) Castle, about a mile from Kelso in the Scottish Borders. While Scott refers to "sylvan amusements" as occupying "the more active part of his life when in Scotland," he by no means abandoned his bibliophilic interests when in Scotland. He apparently lived an uneventful life until he died of an inflammation of the liver on 19 March 1804. His successor in the dukedom was William, seventh Lord Bellenden, who died in 1805 and left a disputed succession. Only when this was resolved in 1812 was the family library–in both London and Fleurs–sent to the salesrooms.

Famous though his library is, Roxburghe's collecting activities have not been examined in depth. There are two categories of evidence to be considered: what can be learned about his bibliophily from his own letters and from the writings of others who knew him and, secondly, the evidence of his library. Information about his library comes in part from examining some of the books that were once part of it (no systematic tracing of his holdings, however, has ever been done) and otherwise from the sale catalogues.

The question of when Roxburghe began to collect books seriously cannot be definitively answered. Did he turn to book collecting as a solace for his personal disappointments, or did his interests go further back? Although there is no evidence in the books examined that he acquired any of them early in life, on the other hand, he may well as a youth have had access to a family library. His grandfather John Ker, who became the first duke of Roxburghe in 1707, was described by George Lockhart of Carnwath in his *Memorial Concerning the Affair of Scotland* (1715) as "a man of good sense, improved by so much reading and learning, that, perhaps, he was the best accomplish'd young man of quality in Europe." The first duke is known to have purchased books, as the Scottish Record Office holds accounts of July 1695 – April 1697 for £102 5s. and of January–March 1699 for £181 17s. 8d. with the Edinburgh bookseller Henry Knox. Also, two states are known of his armorial bookplate dated "1703."

The first duke is most likely to have been the collector of the philosophical writings that bookseller George Nicol in *The Preface to a Catalogue of the Library of the Late John Duke of Roxburghe, Arranged by G. and W. Nicol, Bookesllers [sic] to His Majesty, Pall-Mall* (1807) claims had been acquired by earlier members of the family:

> It seems proper to say, that there is one class of books in this catalogue, among which there are some very rare ones, that were not purchased by the late possessor. They were collected early in the late century, by some of the Duke's predecessors, when free-thinking was much the fashion. William Postel, Giordano Bruno, or Benedict Spinosa, could be no favourites with the Duke of Roxburghe, who only valued philosophical writers, in proportion as they improved the morals of mankind.

As the books Nicols mention have not been traced, the identification of the first duke of Roxburghe as the third duke's predecessor must remain speculative.

In his 1831 review Scott tells a story of how Roxburghe's passion for books began. He reports that the duke's interest

> was inspired by an incident to which his grace had been witness while his father was alive. It is in such cases pleasing to trace that species of impression in youth which stamps the leading point of character on the mind in advanced age; and we may therefore give the anecdote. It seems that Lord Oxford and Lord Sunderland, both famous collectors of the time, dined one day at the house of Robert the second duke of Roxburghe, when their conversation chanced to turn upon the *editio princeps* of Boccaccio, printed at Venice, in 1471, and so rare that its very existence was doubted of. The duke

Roxburghe's bookstamp

> was himself no collector, but it happened that a copy of this very book had passed under his eye, and been offered to him for sale at a hundred guineas, then thought an immense price. It was, therefore, with complete assurance that he undertook to produce to the connoisseurs a copy of the treasure in question, and did so at the time appointed, with no small triumph. His son, then marquis of Beaumont, who never forgot the little scene upon this occasion, used to ascribe to it the strong passion which he ever afterwards felt for rare books and editions, and which rendered him one of the most assiduous and judicious collectors that ever formed a sumptuous library.

The reference, of course, is to the Valdarfer Boccaccio, the same book that caused the sensation at the 1812 sale. Although the coherence of the details of Scott's account may be challenged, there is no reason to doubt the essential point that the rare edition of Boccaccio–whether it was acquired by the second duke or perhaps more likely by his father–was in the family library and that it made an impression on Roxburghe when he was young.

Whenever his interest in books began, Roxburghe at his death left a magnificent library. The London bookselling firm G. and W. Nicol prepared the library for sale and, the sale being delayed until 1812, published *The Preface to a Catalogue* separately. Referring to the library in St. James's Square where the duke kept the greater part of his collections, Nicol writes of Roxburghe: "He spent much more than a third part of every twenty-four hours in his library, to the exclusion of all visitors, and sometimes even of his friends."

In a 25 March 1807 letter to the Edinburgh bookseller and, later, publisher Archibald Constable, his business partner Alexander Gibson Hunter describes a visit to the Roxburghe library with George Nicol:

> this indeed was a treat to me beyond anything I could possibly suppose,–so many truly curious and valuable books, and in so beautiful, perfect, judicious, and tasteful conditions. The number of curious neat little books of immense rarity, and of the earliest printers, is really wonderful, and they are done up with inconceivable taste and judgment. Perhaps the greatest curiosities of the whole are the immense Catalogues, all in the Duke's own handwriting–raisonné many of them, with remarks in red ink, extending to several immense folio volumes; and implying a degree of reading beyond belief. He always wrote these on slips of paper, and pasted them on old newspapers, bound up into loose volumes–an excellent way apparently.

In the *Preface* Nicol makes similar remarks, noting in particular the condition of the early English books:

> There are in this Library, not only the rarest, but in point of condition the most beautiful specimens that exist; and everyone knows the extreme difficulty of finding early English books in clean condition.–To the Duke of Roxburghe, who read his books, this was a great object. He used to say, "that in reading a dirty book, more senses than one were offended."

Roxburghe evidently acted as his own librarian and put his great library at the disposal of bona fide scholars. Joseph Ritson, in his *Bibliographia poetica* (1802), refers to the duke's poetical treasures as being "most liberally thrown open, to enrich the present work." Scott also found the duke helpful. For his three-volume *Minstrelsy of the Scottish Border* (1802–1803) he approached Roxburghe for relevant material and received full cooperation. It is not certain how much, if any, material he did owe to his friend, but he did want to dedicate the book to the duke. Roxburghe declined the honor, however, on the grounds that he always declined such offers. Roxburghe's letter of 23 March 1801, which seems to be his reply to Scott's initial request, reveals his generosity:

> If there is any thing in my library that will be of any use to you, I shall have great pleasure in communicating it to you. I have no librarian, and the fact is that at this moment I know not exactly what my library contains, as the person employed in making a catalogue of my books has not yet finished it. As far as my memory serves me, I do not recall any account either in prose or verse, in my possession, of any old Borderers. I have indeed a pretty large collection of old ballads, some of which were printed by Lekprevik, but yet I do not remember any, at this moment, that can properly be

> called Border Ballads. If you would send me the titles, or first line, of such as you may be in search of, I will look for them, or if you wish it, I will send you the titles, and first line, or first stanza of such as I may consider to enter within the description.

On 2 July 1803, when he had received a copy of the third volume of *Minstrelsy of the Scottish Border,* Roxburghe wrote: "I am very happy that my library afforded you any amusements, possibly, when I can get it put in order and a proper catalogue made, some things may be found which you had not time to see. At all events you shall always have free access to it whenever you wish it."

Roxburghe was always much concerned with acquisitions. His enthusiasm is evident in a letter of 9 February 1790 to an unidentified bookseller, possibly in Edinburgh, as this was written from Fleurs Castle when he was on the point of setting out for London:

> As I am possessed of 2 vols. of old ballads in Black Letter [Gothic type], which I believe were in the Oxford Collection, but which have been increased by the late Col. [Thomas] Pearson, and to which I myself have added some, which I met with by accident in Edinburgh, I shall be obliged to you if you should happen to meet with any thing of this kind if you would reserve them for me.

In a letter of 21 May 1802, on receiving a copy of the first two volumes of *Minstrelsy of the Scottish Border,* he wrote to Scott:

> I have in my library a collection of old ballads which once made part of Ld Oxford's library, to these I have added a good many more, which I have at different times picked up, and I continue to collect such as I am not posessed of. They are printed on single sheets in the Black Letter. I am also a collector of old plays. As I think it very possible, that in making your searches, you may have found both old ballads and old plays lurking in booksellers shops in the country, I shall be very much obliged to you if you will inform me if you recollect any bookseller, either in Scotland or in the North of England, that have any of the articles which I am likely to want. I think you mention a bookseller at Carlisle, I believe his name is Jollie, where you met with some M.S.S. ballads, but it is printed ones that I collect.

Roxburghe's habits of dealing with booksellers by post, which includes ordering from catalogues and making discoveries in their shops in person, are well documented. Bookseller Archibald Constable was clearly an important contact for Roxburghe in his search for Scottish books, as is clear from an autobiographical fragment included at the beginning of *Archibald Constable and his Literary Correspondence: A Memorial by his Son Thomas Constable* (1873):

> In November 1795 I published a supplement to my Catalogue, containing a good many curious articles; and it was on this occasion that I was first introduced to the acquaintance of John Duke of Roxburghe, the eminent collector. His Grace selected several rare and curious articles from my Catalogue, was henceforth a constant visitor of my shop whenever he came to Edinburgh, and I had ever afterwards a great deal of intercourse with him. He was a person of elegant and accomplished manners, of a most noble and engaging appearance, and generally visited Edinburgh twice a year, when he usually honoured me with conversation on the subject of his favourite pursuit.

Thomas Constable sums up his father's position by writing that "he was usually employed as searcher when his Grace was either in quest of literary treasures, or desired, by pillaging a duplicate, to complete an imperfect copy of some rare work." With access to correspondence between his father and Roxburghe dating from 1798 to 1803, he contends that much of it is too technical to be of general interest–a tribute, perhaps, to the duke's bibliographical expertise.

In his autobiographical fragment Archibald Constable mentions Roxburghe's interest in Scottish literature and antiquities and refers in particular to *The Complaynt of Scotland* (Paris, ca. 1559):

> Scottish literature and antiquities engaged his particular attention. I may mention here that the Complaynt of Scotland was the favourite volume of all he possessed, and that he never travelled from home without it. This copy is now in my possession, having purchased it at the sale of his Grace's library, and I need not add that I esteem it as one of my greatest literary treasures. The Duke had received it as a legacy from his friend the late David Erskine, W.S., whose autograph is still in the volume. The copy wanted several leaves, which I had afterwards the satisfaction to supply from a still more imperfect one given to me by the late Mr. John McGowan, and which was used in printing the edition edited by the late Dr. Leyden. From the same copy, now in the Advocates' Library I also gave several leaves to the British Museum. The Duke's is, however, the only one known containing the full text, and is only incomplete by the want of the title-page, of which, however, a small portion still remains.

Letters printed by Thomas Constable show Roxburghe asking to see Archibald Constable's copy to compare it with his own: the duke had leaves 84 and 85 in manuscript and received leaf 85 from Constable's copy. Roxburghe's copy of *The Complaynt of Scotland,* for which Constable paid £35 10s. in 1812, now is held by the British Library.

Frontispiece from Roxburghe's copy of the first book printed by William Caxton, his 1474 translation of Raoul Le Fèvre's Recuyell of the Historyes of Troye *(Henry E. Huntington Library and Art Gallery)*

The correspondence with Constable also reveals Roxburghe's interest in other early Scottish books. Ludovico Ariosto's *The Historie of Ariodanto and Jeneura, daughter to the King of Scottes,* translated into English verse by Peter Beverley (London, ca. 1575) is a very rare book. It had been acquired by Constable as part of the Gordonstoun Library in 1801. Constable had sold this library to John Clerk, Lord Eldin, who weeded out this particular book, which Constable then sent to the duke, though making it clear that Clerk had not yet made a final decision about it. When Clerk decided to retain the entire library, Constable had to ask Roxburghe for the return of the Ariosto, which provoked the duke:

> I am not only vexed but much surprised at the latter part of your letter respecting the little volume of poetry, which is a translation from Ariosto. Upon the good faith of the book being mine, I had it bound and my coat-of-arms put on it. I now should be sorry to part with it, and I should hope that Mr. Clerk would yield it to me. I am very willing to pay the fair price that you will put on it, or give him any book of equal value in lieu of it.

Roxburghe seems to have had his way, for there was a copy of this book in his library at his death. However, it is not clear that it was sold (perhaps its ownership was disputed and it was withdrawn), for the printed list of prices omits this as an item "passed in the original Sale, and again inserted in the Supplement," and it is not included in *A Supplement to the Catalogue of the Library of the Late John Duke of Roxburghe* (1812). A copy of the book, the only copy now known, was included in the Gordon-Stoun library when Clerk sold it in 1816, so it is possible that he may have reclaimed the duke's copy.

Another famous Scottish book owned by Roxburghe that both Archibald Constable and Nicol write about is the first collected acts of the Scottish Parliament, *The Actis and Constitutiounis of the Realme of Scotland* (Edinburgh: R. Lekpreuik, 1566), sometimes called the Black Acts made by King James I through King James V and Queen Mary. The duke owned a copy with the colophon date 28 November and, on Nicol's suggestion that he should compare this with a copy with the earlier date 12 October, borrowed one from George Chalmers and made the comparison. He found that they were not different printings but that the copies with the November date constituted the second issue and were the result of cancellation; some acts about religion had been removed and a new title leaf substituted. Nicol reports that Roxburghe reprinted these acts for the benefit of owners of the November copies as *The Acts of the Scotish Parliament, that were cancelled in the printed copies, bearing the date of November 28, 1566; now reprinted, from the perfect copy, that bears the date of October 12, 1566* (1801?); at the duke's insistence, the preface was signed G. N. (George Nicol) and the duke was nowhere mentioned. Constable was also involved in the process: in April 1800 Roxburghe thanked Constable for a list of the Black Acts "which I have not yet had leisure to compare with my copies"; in December 1801 he offered John Clerk, via Constable, a copy of "the reprinted Acts if he wants it"; and in November 1802 he sent from Fleurs two copies of "the reprinted Black Acts," one for Clerk and one for Constable.

Roxburghe was also interested in works of romance. In his *Memoirs of the Life of Sir Walter Scott, Bart.* (1837–1838) John Gibson Lockhart quotes a letter of 15 December 1807 that Scott, who in his preface to *Sir Tristrem: A Metrical Romance of the Thirteenth Century; by Thomas of Ercildoune* (1804) refers to the duke's "invaluable collection of books of chivalry," wrote to Robert Southey, probably referring back to 1803:

> The late Duke of Roxburghe once showed me some curious remarks of his own upon the genealogy of the Knights of the Round Table. He was a curious and unwearied reader of romance, and made many observations in writing; whether they are now accessible or no, I am doubtful.

Romance was one field in which Roxburghe's collecting spilled over into manuscripts, as is noted by Nicol in an interesting passage in the *Preface:*

> As to the Duke's collection of the Table Ronde, his Grace was not satisfied with the printed editions, some of which are uncommonly rare; he also collected many of them in MS. in magnificent volumes, on vellum, illustrated with beautiful illuminations. . . . These MSS. his Grace read with great facility, and with uncommon accuracy, as may be seen from a note written with his own hand, and inserted in the book it refers to, wherein he contraverts the opinion of Adrien Baillet, author of the *Jugemens des Savans,* who had called it *Le Roman du Roi Artus,* whereas the Duke has shown it to be *Le Roman du Roi Meliadus de Leonnoys.*

As well as frequenting bookshops and corresponding with booksellers, Roxburghe evidently also attended auctions in person. In *The Bibliomania; or, Book-madness* (1809) Thomas F. Dibdin tells a story concerning the First Folio of William Shakespeare:

> A friend was bidding for him in the sale-room: his Grace had retired to a distance, to view the issue of the contest. Twenty guineas and more were offered, from various quarters, for the book: a slip of paper was handed to the Duke, in which he was requested to inform his friend whether he was "to go on bidding"–his Grace took his pencil, and wrote underneath, by way of reply–
>
> ------lay on, Macduff!
> And d---d be he who first cries, "Hold, enough!"
>
> Such a spirit was irresistible, and bore down all opposition. His Grace retired triumphant, with the book under his arm.

The less important of Roxburghe's two libraries, that from Fleurs Castle, was auctioned by Alexander Ballantyne. As a general rule, the duke did not keep important books at Fleurs, and *A Catalogue of the Library of the Late John, Duke of Roxburghe, Which will be Sold, by Auction, in Lauder's Ball-Room, in Kelso, on Thursday, September 16, 1813 . . .* (1813) contains not a single incunabulum–the earliest book is an edition of Lucius Annaeus Seneca's tragedies (Basel, 1515)–and little early-sixteenth-century English poetry. But the sale catalogue is still impressive: there are 1,383 lots in all, with the last lot listed consisting of 113 folio volumes of British Acts of Parliament from 1727 to 1802. There are at least 70 sixteenth-century books, many of them by classical authors.

Notable books at Fleurs include Gavin Douglas's translation of Virgil's *Aeneid* (London, 1553), two editions of George Buchanan's *Rerum Scoticarum historia*

(Edinburgh, 1582, and "Edinburgh" [that is, Antwerp], 1583), Moses Pitt's four-volume *Atlas* (Oxford, 1680–1683), two copies of Allan Ramsay's *Poems* (Edinburgh, 1721), and Daniel Defoe's two-volume *Robinson Crusoe* (London, 1719, exact edition is uncertain). *Robinson Crusoe* is an example of the striking quality of the fiction in Fleurs library. While such works were collected from many European countries, especially from France, in particular Roxburghe had an extensive collection of novels published in London in the 1790s and from 1800 to 1803: this collection of fiction is not matched in the London library.

The Scottish books kept at Fleurs are less significant than those kept in London. Perhaps because of local interest, the duke owned five copies of George Ridpath's *The Border-history of England and Scotland* (London, 1776) and eight copies of *Essays on the Following Interesting Subjects; viz. I. Government II. Revolutions. III. The British Constitution. IV. Kingly Government. V. Parliamentary Representation & Reform. VI. Liberty & Equality. VII. Taxation and, VIII. the Present War, & the Stagnation of Credit as Connected with It* (Glasgow, 1794) by John Young, a minister of Hawick.

The Fleurs catalogue also lists some important works of bibliographical reference: the catalogues of the Gaignat (Paris, 1769) and Vallière (Paris, 1783) sales Guillaume François de Bure's seven-volume *Bibliographie instructive* (Paris, 1763–1768), and the *Catalogus Bibliothecae Harleianae,* published in five volumes (London, 1743–1745). These are all also found in the London 1812 sale catalogue, as indeed are copies of other books sold from Fleurs, including Douglas's *Aeneid* and both Buchanan editions. The extent of duplication between the two libraries has not been determined.

The most important part of Roxburghe's library, however, was sold in London, at what had been his house. *A Catalogue of the Library of the Late John Duke of Roxburghe, Arranged by G. and W. Nicol, Booksellers to His Majesty, Pall-Mall; Which will be Sold by Auction, at His Grace's Late Residence in St. James's Square, on Monday, 18th May, 1812, and the Forty-one Following Days, Sundays Excepted, at Twelve o'clock, by Robert H. Evans, Bookseller, Pall-Mall* (1812) lists 9,353 lots, an estimated 30,000 volumes. The catalogue for a follow-up sale, *A Supplement to the Catalogue of the Library of the Late John Duke of Roxburghe. The Books will be Sold at His Grace's Late Residence in St. James's Square, on Monday, the 13th of July, 1812, and the Three Following Days, by Robert H. Evans,* lists 767 lots, or about 1,280 items.

The main sale catalogue has Nicol's *Preface* reprinted, with small alterations to the title page and at the end, from the edition published separately in 1807. Nicol comments on the gaps in the duke's collection, remarking that the library was "in a progressive state." He notes that Roxburghe's approach was to go for the scarce items, assuming that he could acquire the more common ones at any time. Nicol reports that when he died the duke "was in full pursuit of collecting our dramatic authors. And when his collection of English plays are examined, and the reader is informed that he had only turned his mind to this class of literature for a few years, his indefatigable industry will be readily admired."

The scope of the library may be conveniently summarized from the contents list of the catalogue, with lot numbers following in parentheses: "Theology–to Mythology" (1–690), "Jurisprudence–to Government, Politicks, &c." (691–1175), "Philosophy–Morals–Apophthegms" (1176–1444), "Arts and Sciences–Mathematicks–to Medicine" (1445–2007), "Philology–Gram. Dictionaries, to Rhetorick" (2008–2337), "Poetry–Ancient and Modern" (2338–3541), "Dramatick Poetry–Ancient and Modern" (3542–6065), "Romances–Ancient and Modern" (6066–6420), "Criticism–Lit. Journals–Catalogues" (6421–6554), "Satires–Facetiae–Emblems–Epistles" (6555–6856), "Polygraphy–Tracts, &c." (6857–7076), "Geography–Voyages, Travels" (7077–7355), "History–Universal, and Chronology" (7356–7481), "Ancient" (7482–7785), "Ecclesiastical" (7786–7848), "Modern divided into Nations" (7849–8938), "Antiquities" (8939–9112), and "Heraldry, Genealogy, Biography" (9113–9353). In his *Contributions towards a Dictionary of English Book-Collectors* (1892–1921) Bernard Quaritch provides a long list of selected items and a descriptive account of the collection; other accounts may be found in William Clarke's *Repertorium bibliographicum; or Some Account of the Most Celebrated British Libraries* (1819) and William Younger Fletcher's *English Book Collectors* (1902). In *The Bibliographical Decameron* (1817) and *Reminiscences of a Literary Life* (1836) Dibdin describes the sale but gives few details about the books themselves.

Roxburghe's interest in early English literature led him to the collecting of the earliest English printing, which put the duke at the center of so-called bibliomania. The craze for black letter was noted by Dibdin in *The Bibliomania* as a particular feature of the fad, which he says made the collecting of English incunabula its essence. Seymour de Ricci in *A Census of Caxtons* (1909) lists fifteen William Caxton editions owned by Roxburghe, to which can be added incunabula printed by Wynkyn de Worde, Richard Pynson, and other English printers as well as a Dutch-printed English book, twenty-three items in all.

Discussing Roxburghe's main group of English incunabula (many of them from the Romances–Ancient and Modern section) brings to light some of the highlights of the collection. One of Roxburghe's most important incunabula was Raoul Le Fèvre's

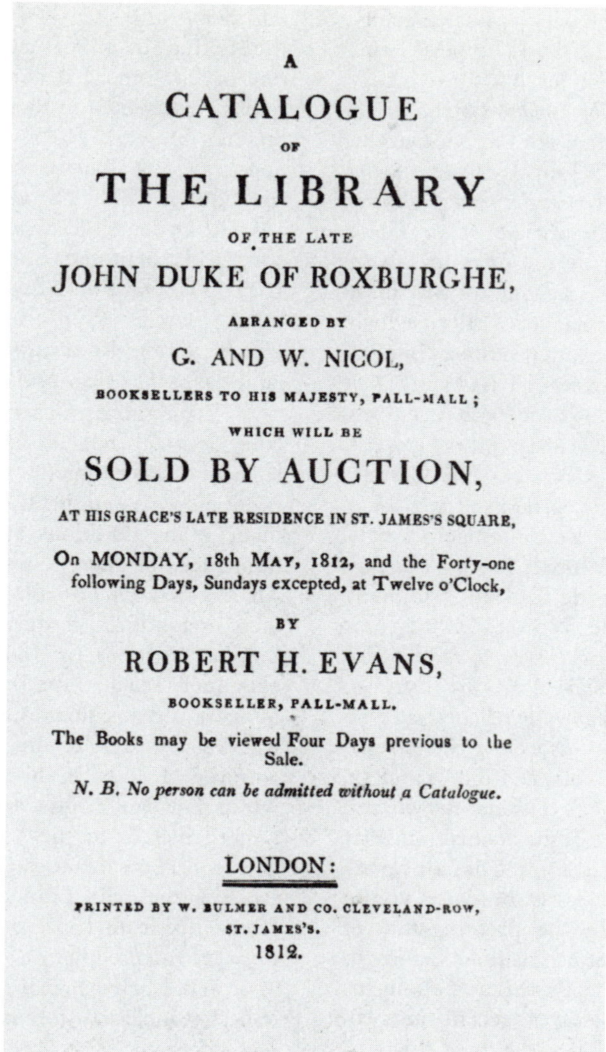
A

CATALOGUE

OF

THE LIBRARY

OF THE LATE

JOHN DUKE OF ROXBURGHE,

ARRANGED BY

G. AND W. NICOL,

BOOKSELLERS TO HIS MAJESTY, PALL-MALL;

WHICH WILL BE

SOLD BY AUCTION,

AT HIS GRACE'S LATE RESIDENCE IN ST. JAMES'S SQUARE,

On MONDAY, 18th MAY, 1812, and the Forty-one following Days, Sundays excepted, at Twelve o'Clock,

BY

ROBERT H. EVANS,

BOOKSELLER, PALL-MALL.

The Books may be viewed Four Days previous to the Sale.

N. B. No person can be admitted without a Catalogue.

LONDON:

PRINTED BY W. BULMER AND CO. CLEVELAND-ROW, ST. JAMES'S.

1812.

Catalogue for the 1812 sale of Roxburghe's London library, at which a copy of Christophorus Valdarfer's 1471 edition of Giovanni Boccaccio's Decamerone *sold for £2,260, setting a record for the price of a single printed book that stood until 1884*

Recuyell of the Historyes of Troye, translated and printed by Caxton (Bruges, 1474). As recorded in G. Goudie's *David Laing, LL.D.: A Memoir of his Life and Literary Work* (1913), David Laing–who attended the Roxburghe sale at the request of his father, the Edinburgh bookseller William Laing–watched as the book "which my father had sold to the Duke for £50 some twenty years previously" (ca. 1792) was bought for £1,050. Any copy of this edition–the first book ever printed in the English language and the first by an English printer–would be a marvellous collector's item, but this particular book, a "matchless copy" according to the 1812 catalogue, has an engraved frontispiece showing a book being presented to Margaret, Duchess of Burgundy, Caxton's patroness, to whom he presented his translation of *Recueil,* and also has an ownership inscription showing that it had belonged to Elizabeth, wife of Edward IV and sister-in-law to the duchess. In his *Preface* Nicol remarks that the duke discovered and noted a transposed sheet. The item is now held in the Huntington Library. Roxburghe also owned a later edition of *Recueil* (Bruges, ca. 1476), the earliest of the French books Caxton printed at Bruges and the first book ever printed in French. According to the 1812 catalogue the only other known copy is in the king's library; Nicol writes that Roxburghe gave eleven leaves of his copy to George III.

Other English incunabula (except where otherwise stated, these books were printed by Caxton at Westminster) include Raimundus de Vineis's *The Lyf of*

Saint Katherin of Senis (1492?), which was actually printed by de Worde with Caxton's types; Saint Bonaventura's *Speculum vitae Christi* (ca. 1490); two copies of Jacobus de Voragine's *The Golden Legend* (1483 and or 1487?–it is uncertain which edition Roxburghe owned; he may have had both); John Lydgate's *Lyf of Our Lady* (1484); *History of Blanchardin and Eglantine* (1490); Vincentius's *Bellovacensis. Myrrour of the World* (1481), which had been bought by the duke at sale of books from the Louvain Jesuits, date unknown; John Mirk's *Liber festivalis and Quatuor sermones* (1491), which previously belonged to Thomas Potter and was bought by Roxburghe at York; *Chastysing of God's Children* (1493), actually printed by de Worde with Caxton's types; Cicero's *Of Olde Age* . . . (1481); John Gower's *Confessio amantis* (1493 [1483]); Christine Du Castel's *Fayttes of Armes* (1489); Jacques Legrand's *The Book of Good Manners* (de Worde, 1498); Bartholomaeus Anglicus's *De proprietatibus rerum* (de Worde, 1495); *The Contemplation of Sinners* (de Worde, 1499); Thomas Mallory's *Le Morte d'Arthur* (de Worde, 1498); John Lydgate's *Lytell Treatise of the Horse, the Sheep, and the Goos* (de Worde, 1499?); *Abbreviamentum statutorum* (Pynson, 1499); *The Book of Hawking, Hunting, and Blasing of Arms* (St. Albans, 1486); Chaucer's *Love and Complayntes Between Mars and Venus* (Julian Notary, 1500?); and Le Fèvre's *The Veray Trew History of the Valiaunt Knight Iason* (Antwerp: G. Leeu, 1492). Some of the acquisitions that cannot be dated could, of course, come from an earlier period of his collecting, but what can be dated comes from the period after 1790. In the present state of knowledge, Roxburghe's earliest acquisitions belong to 1788, a date in keeping with Nicol's remarks about his collecting of English plays being a recent interest. Although it is generally assumed that the duke collected all his life, there is no evidence to support such an assumption.

Incunabula apart, Roxburghe owned a host of other early editions of English verse, printed mainly by de Worde and Pynson but also by others. One group of these, originally in a single volume bought in 1798 at the sale of Richard Farmer's library, is composed of Geoffrey Chaucer's *Troilus and Cressida* (de Worde, 1517); Lydgate's *Temple of Glas* (de Worde, 1506?); Thomas Feylde's *Contraverse Bytwene a Lover and a Jaye* (de Worde, 1527?/1532?–again which addition was owned by Roxburghe is uncertain); Boccaccio's *Tytus and Gesyppus,* translated by William Walter (de Worde, ca. 1525); Walter's *Spectacle of Lovers* (de Worde, 1533?); Boccaccio's *Guistarde and Sigismonde,* translated by Walter (de Worde, 1532); *Dysputacyon or Complaynt of the Herte* (de Worde, 1516?); Lydgate's *Complaynte of a Lover's Lyfe* (de Worde, 1531?); William Nevill's *Castell of Pleasure* (de Worde, 1530?); *La Conusance damours* (Pynson, 1528?); and *Beaulte of Women* (Wyer, ca. 1540). For these editions the Roxburghe copy is either the only recorded copy or one of few recorded copies. Other very rare English books represented in the Roxburghe collection include Stephen Hawes's *Pastime of Pleasure* (de Worde, 1517) and *Example of Vertu* (de Worde, 1530); *Lyf of Saynt Ursula* (de Worde, 1509?); *Example of Euyll Tongues* (de Worde, 1525?); Lydgate's *Governaunce of Kyngs and Prynces* (Pynson, 1511); Sebastian Brant's *Shyppe of Fooles* (de Worde, 1517); D. Mancinus's *Myrrour of Good Maners,* translated by A. Bercley (Pynson, 1518?/1520?–it is uncertain which edition Roxburghe owned); and Robert Copland's *Hye Way to the Spyttel Hous* (Copland, 1536?).

Even more celebrated, perhaps, is Roxburghe's collection of black-letter ballads in three volumes. The collection was originally formed by Robert Harley and eventually passed in 1773 to Thomas Pearson, who made many additions and had it bound in two volumes. Roxburghe bought it in 1788 at the sale of Pearson's library for £36 14s. 6d. He made some additions, including adding a third volume, bringing the total number of items to 1,341. It sold for £477 15s. and eventually reached the British Museum. The testimony of Scott and Archibald Constable reveals that the duke was keen to add to this collection, which was widely admired. Dibdin in his *Reminiscences of a Literary Life* wrote that Roxburghe would have preferred the collection of ballads to the Valdarfer edition of Boccaccio. The collection includes nine rare broadside ballads by Robert Sempill printed in Scotland by Robert Lekpreuik from 1567 to 1570, four of which were the only recorded copies.

The early English poetical works that Roxburghe collected included dozens of romances, many of which were derived from French writings, as H. S. Bennett indicates in his *Chaucer and the Fifteenth Century* (1947). The major manuscripts Roxburghe owned, with the exception of one fifteenth-century Book of Hours, were collections of French romantic tales concerning King Arthur and the knights of the Round Table, which suggests that his collecting was driven by his interests rather than by a desire to own fine works whatever their subject. He also collected the classical antecedents of the romance, including editions of authors such as Achilles Tatius, Eustathius, Heliodorus, Longus, Parthenius, and Xenophon of Ephesus. His ownership of Francesco Colonna's *Hypnerotomachia Polifili,* an amorous romance published by Aldus Manutius in Venice in 1499, probably resulted from this same interest.

In the area of dramatic poetry Roxburghe had a good collection of editions of Shakespeare and also some secondary works. In addition to the First, Second, Third, and Fourth Folios (1623, 1632, 1664, 1685), he owned the first quarto editions of seven of the plays that had been printed separately prior to the First Folio–*Much Ado About Nothing, A Midsummer Night's Dream, The Merchant of Venice, Henry IV Part 2* (all 1600), *King Lear* (1608), *Troilus and Cresseida* (1609), and *Pericles* (1609)–and early quarto editions of most of the others. Many of these quartos were purchased in 1800 from the library of George Steevens, bearing out Nicol's remark that dramatic poetry was a recent interest of the duke. The Roxburghe collection also contained the first quarto editions of three spurious plays that had been included in the Third Folio: *Locrine* (1595), *Sir John Oldcastle* (1600), and *Cromwell* (1602).

While the Roxburghe collection is not outstanding for the number and overall quality of its non-English incunabula, it does include some notable items. Only two copies are known of the Valdarfer Boccaccio–the Roxburghe copy, perfect, now in the John Rylands University Library of Manchester, and the other, imperfect, in the British Library. (One other edition of Boccaccio, probably printed in Florence or Naples, may predate the Valdarfer edition by one year.) In addition, there are some other choice incunabula, such as several editiones principes of classical texts, including Pliny the Elder's *Historia naturalis* (Venice, 1469); *Scriptores rei rusticae* (Venice, 1472); Aulus Gellius's *Noctes Atticae* (Rome, 1469); Macrobius's *In Somnium Scipionis,* which is published with his *Saturnalia* (Venice, 1472); Cicero's *Ad Atticum* (Rome, 1470); and Cornelius Nepos's *Vitae* (Venice, 1471).

Roxburghe, though, was evidently not a keen collector of incunabula per se. Because of the problem of undated books it is difficult to give an exact figure, but his total holdings in this area numbered about 120; the corresponding figure for William Hunter is 534, and for the second Earl Spencer it is much larger. He apparently did not own the most recent standard listing of incunabula, G. W. Panzer's *Annales typographici* (Nuremberg, 1793–1803), and his library lacks many of the choice items that were found in other great collections of the era. For example, the only pieces of early Mainz printing are the Bibles of 1472 and 1483, and it is difficult to believe that the reason why Roxburghe did not own a copy of the Gutenberg Bible was that he had been unable to acquire one. His lack of interest is also shown by the absence of a copy of the most recent specialized bibliography of early Mainz printing, Stephan Alexander Würdtwein's *Bibliotheca Moguntina* (Augsburg, 1789). The presence of only two pre-1501 Bibles in the collection and the absence of pre-1501 legal books show that he was not particularly interested in early printing as such: because of the total holdings of pre-1501 editions of the Bible and of legal works, most collectors of early printing tended to have many books falling into these categories. He may well have acquired his celebrated copy of Colonna's *Hypnerotomachia Polifili*–a prized possession for a true bibliophile–as part of his romance collection. The majority of his incunabula are classical texts, probably not because he had a compelling interest in early printing but because of his general interest in the classics, which explains his concentration of sixteenth- and seventeenth-century editions of classical texts.

Although Roxburghe prized them, his Scottish books, including *The Complaynt of Scotland, The Actis and Constitutiounis of the Realme of Scotland,* and the ballads printed by Lekpreuik, make up fewer than two hundred lots of his collection. Some of the other rare and important Scottish books the duke owned are John Rolland's *The Seuin Sages* (Edinburgh, 1578), *Ane Compendius Buik of Godly and Spirituall Sangis* (Edinburgh, 1600), *Ane Compendious Booke, of Godly and Spirituall Songs* (Edinburgh, 1621), David Lindsay's *Warkis* (Edinburgh, 1568), *The Lyfe and Actis of William Wallace* (Edinburgh, 1601), the manuscript of a Scots metrical version of part of Ariosto that had belonged to King James I, John Hamilton's *Catechisme* (St. Andrews, 1552), and *Kalendayr of the Shyppars* (Paris, 1503), a rare Scots translation of *Le compost et kalendrier des bergiers* (Paris, 1493), which Roxburghe also owned.

Among the bibliographical items Roxburghe kept in London were catalogues from which it is known he purchased material: he bought the Lekpreuk-printed ballads from the catalogue of Thomas Pearson (1788); many works printed by de Worde from Richard Farmer (1798), and Shakespeare quartos from Steevens (1800). There are also the catalogues of library sales from which it seems probable he acquired items: *Bibliotheca Croftsiana* (1783), the catalogue of Peter Antoine Crevenna (1789), *Bibliotheca Lamoigniana* (1790), the catalogue of Rev. Michael Lort (1791), *Bibliotheca Parisiana* (1791), and the catalogue of Samuel Ireland (1801). Roxburghe owned other catalogues that were well-known reference works: *Bibliotheca Heinsiana* (1682), the Robert Cotton manuscript catalogue (1696), and *Catalogus Bibliothecae Thuanae* (1679). He also owned such monographs as Cornelius à Beughem's *Incunabula typographiae* (1688) and Michael Maittaire's nine-volume *Annales typographici* (1719–1741).

A total of £23,341 was realized from the auction of the Roxburghe collection, many times more than the duke is likely to have paid for it. Dibdin gives an eyewitness account in his *Bibliographical Decameron.* Of course, the highlight in excitement was reached when the second Earl Spencer, marquis of Blandford, and William George sixth Duke of Devonshire fought over the Valdarfer Boccaccio, for which the marquis of Blandford paid £2,260, the highest price paid to that date for a single printed book; just seven years later in 1819, when the Blandford Library was sold, the copy brought less than half this price–£918 15s. In *Reminiscences of a Literary Life* Dibdin discusses the combination of factors that might explain why the prices were driven so high, among them the long wait for the sale, especially after the Nicols had published the *Preface* in 1807; the lack of good stock coming from the Continent at the time of the Napoleonic Wars; and, possibly, Dibdin's praise of the collection in *Bibliomania*. The arrival of a new buyer on the scene, William George, who had recently come of age and into a fortune, may also have contributed.

The most famous consequence of the sale was the founding of the Roxburghe Club. A week before the sale began, Dibdin arranged a dinner to take place on 17 June 1812, the day of the sale on which the Valdarfer Boccaccio was scheduled to be auctioned. At the dinner the Roxburghe Club was formed. There were eighteen at the dinner that night when the club was formed; six more members were added on the spot; and seven were added in the following year.

References:

Clive Bigham, *The Roxburghe Club: its History and its Members 1812–1927* (Oxford: Roxburghe Club, 1928);

William Chappell and Joseph Woodfall Ebsworth, eds., *The Roxburghe Ballads,* 9 volumes (Hertford: The Ballad Society, 1869–1899);

William Clarke, *Repertorium bibliographicum; or, Some Account of the Most Celebrated British Libraries* (London: W. Clarke, 1819), pp. 517–534;

Thomas Frognall Dibdin, *The Bibliographical Decameron,* 3 volumes (London: For the author, 1817), vol. 3, pp. 49–69;

Dibdin, *The Bibliomania; or, Book-madness* (London: Longman, Hurst, Rees & Orme, 1809);

Dibdin, *Reminiscences of a Literary Life* (London: J. Major, 1836), pp. 345–371;

William Younger Fletcher, *English Book Collectors* (London: Kegan Paul, 1902);

The Gentleman's Magazine; and Historical Chronicle. For the Year MDCCCIV. Volume LXXIV (London: Nichols, 1804);

James Augustus Henry Murray, ed., *The Complaynt of Scotlande,* extra series, no. 17 (London: Early English Text Society, 1872);

George and William Nicol, *The Preface to a Catalogue of the Library of the Late John Duke of Roxburghe, Arranged by G. and W. Nicol, Bookesllers [sic] to His Majesty, Pall-Mall* (London: W. Bulmer, 1807);

Bernard Quaritch, ed., *Contributions towards a Dictionary of English Book-Collectors* (London: B. Quaritch, 1892–1921);

Walter Scott, *Quarterly Review,* 44 (1831): 438–475.

Papers:

Some of the miscellaneous papers of John Ker, third Duke of Roxburghe, are held by the National Library of Scotland.

William Laud

(7 October 1573 – 10 January 1645)

John Gallagher
Northern Illinois University

CATALOGUE: *Catalogi codicum manuscriptorum bibliothecae Bodleianae* (Oxonii: E. Typographeo Academico, 1848–1862).

BOOKS: *Laud's Liturgy. The Booke of Common Prayer, and the Administration of the Sacraments for the Use of the Church of Scotland* (Edinburgh: R. Young, Printer to the King, 1637);

A Speech Delivered in the Starr-Chamber, on Wednesday, the XIVth of Iune, MDCXXXVII: at the censvre of Iohn Bastwick, Henry Burton, & William Prinn; concerning pretended innovations in the Church (London: Printed by Richard Badger, 1637);

A Relation of the Conference betweene William Lawd, then, Lrd. Bishop of St. Davids; now, Lord Arch-Bishop of Canterbury, and Mr. Fisher the Jesuite: by the Command of King James of Ever Blessed Memorie: with an answer to such exceptions as A.C. takes against it / by the sayd Most Reverend Father in God, William, Lord Arch-Bishop of Canterbury (London: Printed by Richard Badger, 1639); republished as *A Relation of the Conference between William Laud, Late Lord Archbishop of Canterbury, and Mr. Fisher the Jesuit* (London: R. Holt, 1686);

The Recantation of the Prelate of Canterbury: Being his Last Advice to his Brethren the Bishops of England: to Consider his Fall, Observe the Times, Forsake their Wayes, and to Joyne in this Good Work of Reformation . . . (London, 1641);

A Breviate of the Life of William Laud . . . Extracted (for the most part) verbatim, out of His Owne Diary, and Other Writings, Under His Owne Hand. Collected and published at the speciall instance of Sundry Honourable Persons . . . by William Pyrnne . . . (London: Printed by F. L. for Michaell Sparke, 1644);

The Archbishop of Canterbury's Speech, or, His Funerall Sermon Preacht by Himself on the Scaffold on Tower-Hill: on Friday the 10 of January, 1644 upon Hebrews 12.I, 2. Also, the Prayers which He Used at the Same Time and Place Before His Execution All Faithfully Written by John Hinde (London: P. Cole, 1644);

William Laud, archbishop of Canterbury (copy of a 1635 portrait by Sir Anthony Van Dyck; Bodleian Library, Oxford)

A Commemoration of King Charles his Inauguration. Or, A Sermon Preached at Pauls Crosse by William Laud (London, 1645);

Seven Sermons Preached upon Severall Occasions, by the Right Reverend and Learned Father in God, William Laud, late Arch-Bishop of Canterbury (London: Printed for R. Lowndes, 1651); republished as *The Sermons Preached by William Laud,* edited by J. W. Hatherell (London: Stroud, 1829);

A Summarie of Devotions, Compiled and Used by Dr. William Laud, somtime Ld Archbishop of Canterbury. Now published according to the Copy written with his Own Hand, and Reserved in the Archives of St. John Baptist's Col-

ledge Library in Oxon (Oxford: Printed by W. Hall, 1667);

The History of the Troubles and Tryal of the Most Reverend Father in God, and Blessed Martyr, William Laud, Lord Arch-Bishop of Canterbury, Wrote by Himself, During his Imprisonment in the Tower; To which is Prefixed the Diary of His Own Life . . . , a Supplement to the Preceding History, the Arch-Bishop's Last Will, His Large Answer to the Lord Say's Speech Concerning Liturgies, His Annual Accounts of His Province Delivered to the King, and Some Other Things Relating to the History (London: R. Chiswell, 1695);

The Second Volume of the Remains of the Most Reverend Father in God, and Blessed Martyr, William Laud, Lord Archbishop of Canterbury. Written by himself. Collected by the Late Learned Mr. Henry Wharton . . . (London: Printed for Sam. Keble at the Tuck's-Head in Fleet-street, Dan. Brown without Temple-Bar, Will. Heneman in Westminster-hall, Matt. Wotton near the Inner-Temple gate, and R. Knaplock at the Angel in St. Paul's church-yard, 1700);

The Works of the Most Reverend Father in God, William Laud, sometime Lord Archbishop of Canterbury, 7 volumes (Oxford: J. H. Parker, 1847–1860).

As an influential archbishop of Canterbury, William Laud's name inevitably stands out in almost any survey of Renaissance England, whether political, religious, or academic. Unfortunately for the purposes of examining his value to book collecting, most of the material written on Laud places great weight on his conservative political and religious roles in the turbulent years before the English revolution and much less on his contributions to intellectual advancement through the gathering and donating of manuscripts. Nevertheless, Laud lived in a time when the centers of learning in England were rapidly expanding, and at least in part he seems to have valued his various social positions as opportunities to contribute to that expansion.

By Laud's time, the improvement of the materials stored in university libraries–both their quality and quantity–had become of utmost importance to many scholars and benefactors. Because of the invention of the printing press, manuscripts were no longer copied by hand in monasteries. Instead, texts that had previously been unavailable to many literate individuals were widely circulated in English society. Nevertheless, the historical value of important original documents and the difficulties of paying for and obtaining adequate printings of less popular ancient texts contributed to the need for acquiring authoritative and intact manuscripts. Libraries such as the Bodleian in Oxford became in the Renaissance storehouses for texts otherwise unattainable by even the most diligent scholars in England as well as convenient sources of more available printed works.

Laud was a pioneer in the acquisition and protection of such valuable materials. Indeed, he stands out in history as a man who devoted much of his life and the lives of others under his political and personal influence to the collection and donation of valuable books as well as to their security for the sake of future scholarship. He is best known for his improvement of the study of Greek and oriental literatures in England through his gifts to St. John's College, Oxford, and to the Bodleian Library. In addition to his activities in these two fields, Laud also improved the availability of the most important works in mathematics and the other sciences. Realizing, however, that the mere presence of scholarly materials was not enough, Laud attempted to shape the discipline and diligence of the students at Oxford.

Laud was born in Reading on 7 October 1573 to William Laud, a fairly wealthy clothier, and his wife, Lucy. Once he had graduated from the Reading Grammar School, he entered St. John's College at the age of sixteen in 1589. He did this primarily through a scholarship that had been established by Sir Thomas White, the founder of the college, for young men from Reading Grammar School. White had himself been a clothier's son and a student at Reading. Indeed, White's fidelity to his own roots in founding St. John's and providing scholarships for the sons of the commoners in his hometown may well have provided an example to the young Laud of the importance of generosity and loyalty in education.

Laud clearly never forgot the debt he owed to his education. His donations to the college and more notably to the Bodleian Library attest to his sense of responsibility to and love for the university where he spent more than thirty years of his life. He earned the degrees of bachelor of arts (1594), master of arts (1598), and doctor of divinity (1608). As biographer Charles Carlton points out in *Archbishop William Laud* (1987), Laud's education at St. John's encouraged him to pursue and perfect a thorough and oftentimes obscure knowledge of different disciplines, languages, and texts. At St. John's, Laud developed a love for order and academic rigor, even, Carlton suggests, to the point of an obsession. These traits, however unpleasant to those who had to deal with Laud on a personal level, proved invaluable to him in improving the library at St. John's and eventually contributed to the remarkable quality of his private collection, which he gradually gave to the Bodleian Library.

On 29 August 1611, despite considerable opposition, Laud officially assumed the role of president at St. John's College. King James himself had to intervene in determining the outcome of the election because of accusations that Laud's supporters had forced the results through blackmail. In spite of the deep enmity of the newly appointed archbishop of Canterbury, Robert Abbot, Laud prospered as president of the college and quickly found favor with the king. According to Carlton, with the help of his powerful friend Richard Neile, bishop of Rochester, Laud on 22 January 1621 was "installed as a prebend of Westminster Abbey," a position that allowed Laud to perform many public duties that strengthened his place in the king's favor. Less than a year after Laud was made prebend of Westminster Abbey, he resigned the presidency at St. John's and accepted an appointment as bishop of St. David's in West Wales. His new role as a member of the House of Lords allowed him to show even greater support for King James than he had before, and as a result even more distaste for those who sought political and religious reform in English society.

During the turbulent time between the death of King James and the coronation of Charles I, Laud continued to prove his loyalty to the monarchy. Because of Laud's royalist sympathies in his sermons and his support of the king in the Parliament, Charles transferred him from the bishopric of Wales to that of Bath and Wells. Then, on 2 July 1628, the king appointed Laud bishop of London, a position from which the previous two archbishops had been chosen. Less than two years later, on 28 April 1630, Laud was installed as the chancellor of Oxford.

In his role as bishop of London, Laud frequently assumed tasks properly belonging to the archbishop, as Carlton makes clear:

> As the king's *de facto* minister of religion, Laud handled myriad public problems as well as his own personal concerns. At Charles's command he drafted new statutes for Norwich Cathedral and orders to be issued in Archbishop Abbot's name commanding all clergy to leave London and return to their livings unless required at court. The king charged him with the collection of contributions for the relief of Huguenot refugees, and ministers who had left the palatinate. On 9 December [1629] he held the Bible as Charles swore to uphold the treaty with Spain, a "peace disliked by everyone," as one ambassador noted.

Because of his place as a favorite of the king, Laud was widely feared in the House of Commons. His conservative religious attitudes and his often ruthless enforcement of them also made him a primary enemy of the resurgent Puritan movement. In spite of these unfavorable reactions against Laud, Charles made him archbishop of Canterbury on 29 August 1633. Less than a decade later, the political and religious opposition to

One of Laud's bookstamps, with the arms of the Archiepiscopal See of Canterbury on the left and his personal arms on the right

Laud became strong enough to obtain his arrest on the grounds of high treason in 1640. Five years later, after all attempts by Laud's few but powerful friends had failed to reprieve him, he was led from the Tower of London and executed on 10 January 1645.

Although he had made some small donations to St. John's College before 1611, it was not until Laud was made its president that his valuable work as a collector and donor of manuscripts and books truly began to take shape. As John Fuggles notes in his 1981 article "William Laud and the Library of St. John's College, Oxford," Laud left the library of St. John's in 1621 with fewer books than it had held before he took the presidency in 1611 because he had many double and triple copies sold and replaced with new acquisitions. The majority of these replacements were contemporary printings of various religious and philosophical works, as Fuggles notes:

> As might be expected many of the books bought with [the money made from the sale at St. John's] were in recently published editions, a number of the authors rather in vogue: a set of the *Systema Systematum* of Bartholomaeus Keckermannus, the works of Justus Lipsius, two volumes of Rudolt Goclenius, the Elder, and the massive three-volume commentary on the Gospels

> of Sebastianus Barradas. Works by authors already represented in the Library were acquired: another Bible commentary by the Spanish Jesuit, Juan de Pineda; a two-volume *Opera* of Marsilio Ficino; and five volumes of Denis the Carthusian, to supplement the *Opera Minora:* a number of works of the Fathers were bought, in the case of the Clement of Alexandria replacing the edition sold with the very latest.

With such acquisitions Laud hoped to bring to St. John's the most recent scholarly editions of important works.

Historians have noted the orthodox or even Catholic nature of the texts Laud had a hand in appropriating for the library, implying that his collecting of certain works may have been driven by High-Church Anglican sentiments. Indeed, Laud's interest in the Scholastics and contemporary Catholic writers certainly did not help him when he had to defend himself against accusations of being a papist. Not all of the St. John's purchases overseen by Laud, however, carried such charged religious and political ramifications but instead showed a more general scholarly interest. Some, Fuggles notes, were valuable medieval manuscripts of Aristotle with commentaries. Also, the majority of the ten manuscripts Laud is known to have contributed personally to St. John's between 1610 and 1620 reveal the beginnings of his interest in classical Greek and oriental literatures. Included in the gifts are the *Ptolemaei Geographia* (1546), *India Orientalis* (1601–1604), *Lucretius* (1514), and *Polybius* (1582).

In addition to his purchases and personal gifts, Laud during his tenure at St. John's seems to have inspired many donations, especially texts of a particularly orthodox vein. Of note are such manuscripts as the *De Concordantia Evangelistiarum* by Zacharias, a bishop of Besançon; an edition of Heliodorus; biblical manuscripts; Gregory the Great's Homilies on the Gospels from the fourteenth century; Peter Lombard's *Sentences* from the thirteenth century; and an Eton copy of St. John Chrysostom's writings. Also, an important portion of new acquisitions resulted from the gifts of books by wealthy commoners, a practice strongly encouraged by Laud. Fuggles attributes to Laud the implementation of measures that emphasized the acquisition of traditional Church writings, even works by the often unpopular medieval scholastic theologians, through monetary gifts from London merchants.

Fuggles points out that there is a pattern in the type of works bought, arguing that it "is interesting to consider such works in the light of the Royal Edicts sent to the University in 1617. The seventh of these," he continues, "ordained, 'that young Students of Divinitie be directed . . . to bestowe there time in the Fathers and Counsells, Scholemen histories, and controversies, and not insist to longe uppon Compendiums and Abbreviators.'" From early in Laud's career as a book collector, his religious or political motives intertwine with his scholarly interests, and the types of donations that flow into the institutions he supports mirror his private donations. Laud's influence as a collector of books must be examined from both perspectives, for some of his most valuable contributions to libraries were at the expense of others who had been persuaded or otherwise influenced by Laud into benefaction.

Laud's dedication to the improvement of the St. John's library did not end with his presidency in 1621. Once Laud was made chancellor of the University of Oxford, he did more for St. John's than perhaps he had been able to before. In 1630 Laud donated to the college seventeen volumes of works containing primarily orthodox liturgical materials. In subsequent years, he saw to the construction of the famous quadrangle of St. John's College and a new wing to the library. The entire quadrangle with its library was completed in 1636 at a personal cost to Laud of more than £5,000. The new library for the college had an inner room specifically designed for the keeping of rare books and other valuable objects, especially scientific instruments. He established the paid position of librarian for one of the fellows, allowing no one else to keep a set of keys, with the exception of the president. Such drastic measures were enacted by Laud presumably because he wished to keep the accessibility to the materials limited only to those who would use them well and with great care.

Laud made generous donations to this new portion of the library. Fuggles notes that among his gifts are those works dealing with mathematics, revealing Laud's desire to improve the study of this discipline at St. John's: Christopher Clavius's *Opera Mathematica,* Simon Stevin's *Hypomnemata Mathematica,* Guido Ubaldo's *De Cochlea,* and Denis Henrion's *Usage du Compas.* He also included in his gifts a large number of oriental books and manuscripts. Among these were a printed edition of the Arabic Gospels, two manuscripts of the *Koran,* a selection of Euclid's works in an Arabic manuscript, and a printing of the Melanchthon Greek Bible. All told, Laud is credited with giving some seventy-nine volumes of printed works and twenty-seven manuscripts of extremely diverse subject matter and authorship to St. John's from 1630 to the end of his career and life in the 1640s.

Laud also remembered St. John's in his will and requested that any books left in his study be given to the college library. Laud's desire was evidently not carried out, however. William Young Fletcher in *English Book Collectors* (1969) cites evidence that Hugh Peters, who was responsible for the death of Charles I, received the archbishop's books instead of St. John's

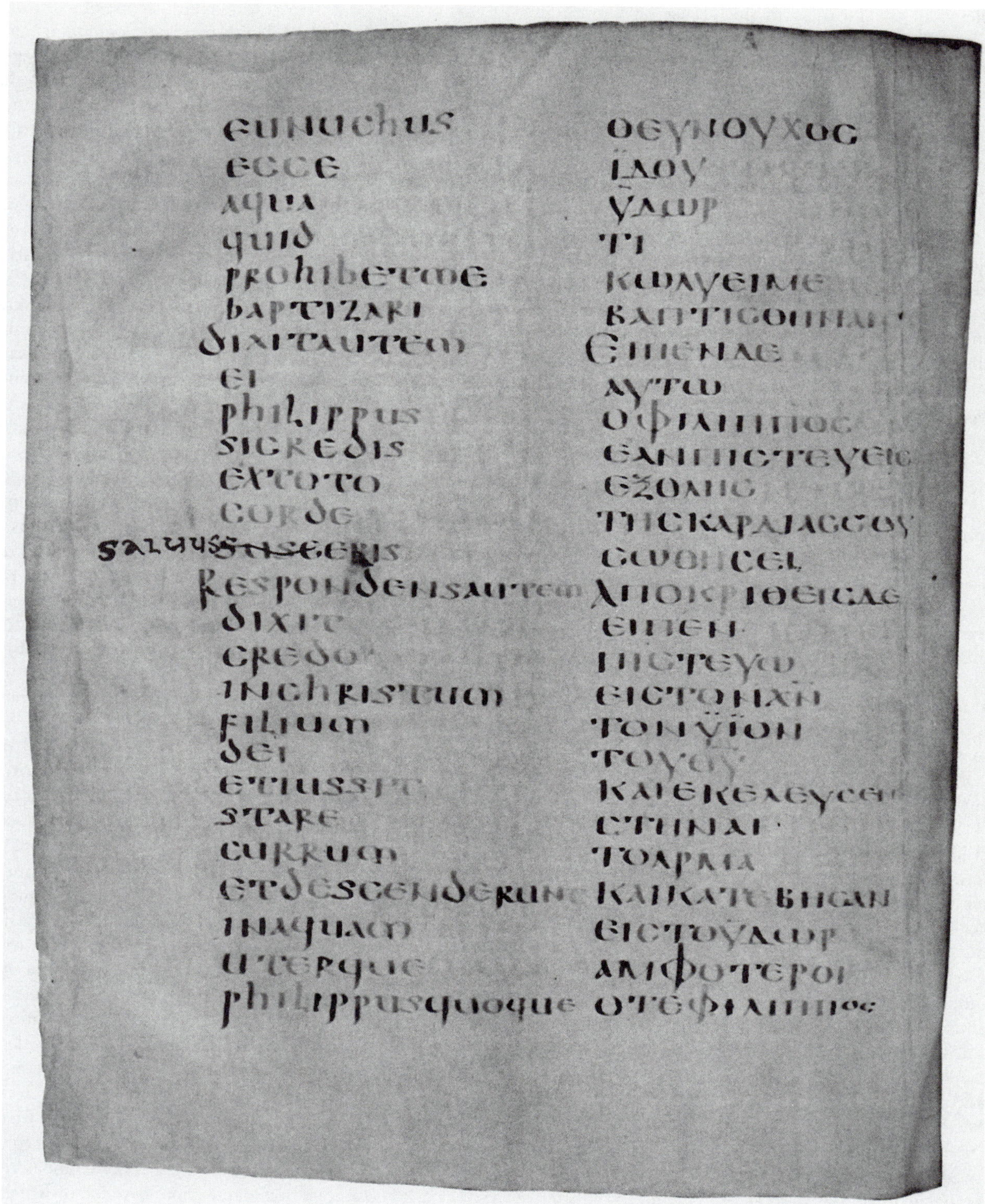

Page from the bilingual manuscript for the Acts of the Apostles *that Laud presented to the Bodleian Library in 1636. Written circa 600, the manuscript has Latin text on the left and a Greek translation on the right (MS. Laud Gr. 35, Bodleian Library, Oxford).*

College. In the Journals of the House of Commons, entries dating from 8 March to 27 June 1644 record the transaction; the entries end with the injunction, "It is this day ordered, That Mr. Peters shall have the whole Study of Books freely bestowed upon him." The value of Laud's study was appraised by the House of Commons at approximately £140, an inconsequential amount considering what he had already given in years past.

Although Laud's devotion to St. John's brought a wide variety of acquisitions to its library and led to its general development, his contributions to the college do not compare with his gifts to the Bodleian Library in volume or in value. By the time of Laud's death on the scaffold, the Bodleian Library had received from him a total of 1,250 volumes of manuscripts through personal gifts, including his own sizable library. In *The Bodleian Library in the Seventeenth and Eighteenth Centuries* (1983) Ian Philip notes that the manuscript contributions of Laud, Federico Barocci, and Digby, especially their Greek texts, made the Bodleian a crucial source of scholarship not only for England but also for the entire continent of Europe. Laud's portion of these contributions by far outweighed the rest. In addition to donating a collection of manuscripts that actually doubled the holdings of the library at the time, Laud was essential in negotiating the donation of the Barocci manuscripts by William Herbert, Earl of Pembroke. According to Philip, Pembroke had always planned to maintain the integrity of the collection of 240 Greek manuscripts by donating them all to a single recipient, believing his manuscripts "would be of more use to the church in being kept united in some public library, than scattered in particular hands." It was Laud, though, who convinced him that they would best serve the church at the Bodleian rather than elsewhere. Philip writes that Pembroke's sizable gift "was the beginning of a decade of enlightened benevolence which placed the Bodleian among the foremost centres of European scholarship."

Laud gradually became a collector of great magnitude, enlisting everyone under his sway to obtain manuscripts throughout Europe and the Mediterranean. David Rogers in *The Bodleian Library and its Treasures, 1320–1770* (1991) states that by the time he was made archbishop in 1633, Laud "owned quite a sizable collection, numbering 303 manuscripts." His donations to the Bodleian arrived in four separate installments between the years 1635 and 1640. Almost all of Laud's personal acquisitions up to 1635 made up the substance of his first gift to the Bodleian. It consisted of 461 manuscripts, and though, Rogers notes, "most of these were in Latin, there were also large and important groups in Arabic . . . and in Greek and English." These certainly were not the only languages included in the first gift. Rogers writes, "the overall scope of this donation was astonishingly wide-ranging, embracing as it did books in a total of seventeen different languages, eleven of them Oriental." Laud's next three gifts arrived at the Bodleian in the years 1636, 1639, and 1640. Each of them exhibited a range and value similar to the first. As was the case of his gifts to St. John's, the contents of these installments reflected Laud's personal intellectual interests as well as his political and religious vision for the future of English scholarship.

Laud's process of acquiring his collection reveals as much about his character as does the substance of the gifts. He repeatedly exhibited a talent for seizing upon the opportunities that chance afforded him in order to realize his goals as a collector and benefactor. In 1636, for example, Laud acquired a group of sixteenth- and seventeenth-century Latin manuscripts from the German cities Würzburg and Mainz, the first installment of a windfall of sorts arising from the Thirty Years' War, eventually amounting to more than three hundred volumes. The two cities were among those, Rogers notes, that "had fallen to the invading Swedish armies of Gustavus Adolphus in 1631." Through the English ambassadors to the area, Laud apparently gained access to the treasures of ransacked religious houses, including the "celebrated early scriptorium at Lorsch." On another occasion in 1636, Laud mentioned receiving a gift of Latin manuscripts from the earl of Arundel on his return from Vienna. Although Laud was certainly motivated in part by his desire to improve the holdings of the Bodleian Library, he also seems to have believed that he was rescuing sacred religious texts and ancient writings of the church fathers from the hands of idolatrous papists. It is ironic, then, that later the grounds for his execution stemmed in part from accusations that he was at heart a papist and an idolater.

Laud's capitalization on the devastation of Germany was not the only instance of his creative use of the misfortune of others for the benefit of the scholars of England. Carlton notes an occasion when Laud punished the royal printer Patrick Young for a typographical error he had made. Young had left out the word "not" in printing the seventh commandment in an edition of the Bible, thus rendering it, "Thou shalt commit adultery." Laud "ordered Young to atone by buying a set of Greek type and, at his own expense, publishing at least one book a year in that language." On another occasion, Laud utilized his friendship with King Charles I and convinced him to require every trading ship traveling for the Turkey Company "to bring home at least one manuscript in Arabic or Russian, the Koran excluded."

Laud's connections, however, did not always bring him success. Philip tells of a famous misadventure in 1638 when Laud sent John Greaves, the professor of geometry at Gresham College, London, to Alexandria

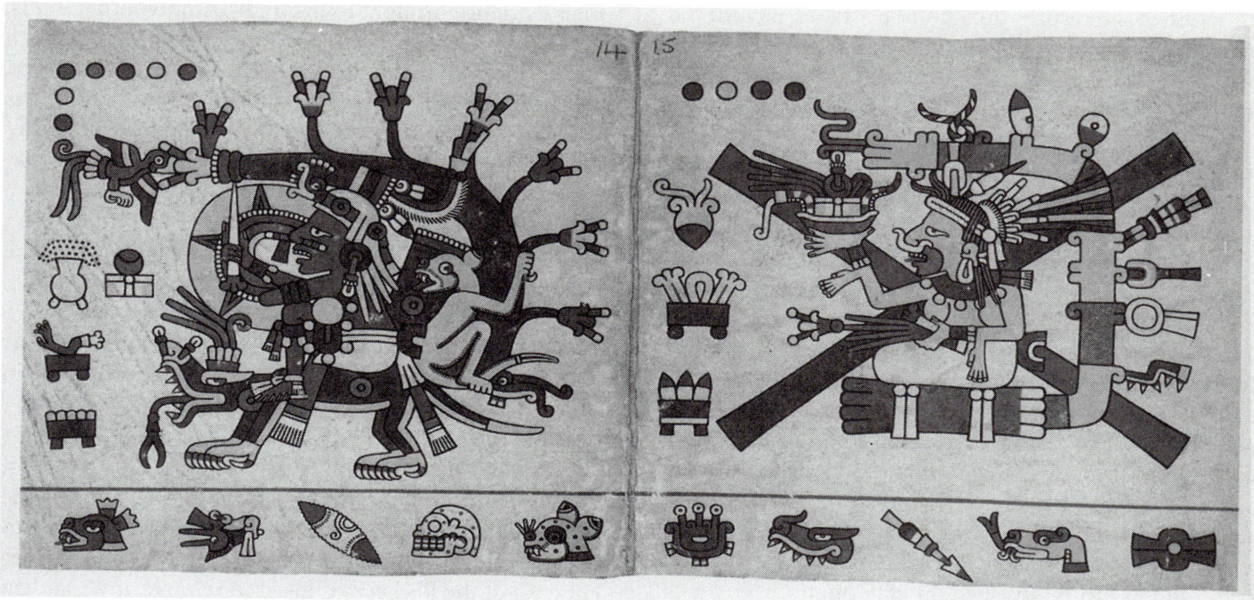

Pages from a pre-Columbian Mexican codex that Laud donated to the Bodleian Library in 1636 (Codex Laud, MS. Laud Misc. 678, Bodleian Library, Oxford)

and Constantinople in the hopes of obtaining manuscripts from the Patriarch Lucar, who had in the past been a profitable connection for Sir Thomas Roe, a famous traveler, diplomat, and benefactor of the Bodleian Library. Unfortunately for Laud, Lucar was executed as a traitor before Greaves could reach him. Greaves had been sent with gifts from Laud for Lucar, including a 1637 Greek edition of the Book of Job with "an autograph Greek inscription from the Archbishop to the Patriarch." Philip writes that as a result of the Patriarch's execution,

> Greaves had to curtail his activities. Through the Patriarch's good offices, he had, he said, already "procured out of a blinde and ignorant Monastery" fourteen good manuscripts of the Fathers, but now he had to put these back quickly and lose his money. And other more ambitious schemes had to be abandoned. Greaves reported that the Patriarch would have recommended him to Mount Athos so that he could catalogue the manuscripts of important texts which the Patriarch would then have presented to Laud "for the better prosecution of his Grace's honourable designs in the edition of the Greek authors."

The failed venture was not, however, without benefit to the Bodleian, as the library received Laud's Book of Job.

Laud had a talent for locating and appropriating valuable texts, especially ones that added to his collection of oriental manuscripts. As with his donations to St. John's College, Laud distinguished himself in his devotion to Greek and Arabic studies. While chancellor of Oxford, Laud single-handedly established Arabic studies and greatly expanded the Greek program. He was clearly aware that simply having texts for study would not necessitate an improvement in the education received by Oxford students. In fact, one could argue that Laud's extraordinary career as a book collector arose almost entirely out of his vision for the education of the clergy in the English Church. He was of the opinion that all well-educated clergymen ought to know Latin and some Greek as well as be able to consult works from other languages when the need arose.

Many valuable religious texts, often in their original language, are found among Laud's donations. One of the most notable gifts the Bodleian received from Laud is a manuscript of the *Acts of the Apostles* that provides a side-by-side Latin and Greek text. Rogers describes the manuscript: "Each page contains two parallel columns of text, Greek on the right, Latin on the left, with only a word or two in each line. To make the words match exactly . . . the word order of the Latin text (a pre-Vulgate version) has sometimes been altered." It is conjectured that those who composed the text sometime around 600 A.D. originally did so to instruct Greek-speaking readers in Latin. Many scholars and historians also believe that this is the same manuscript used by the Venerable Bede when he wrote his commentaries on the *Acts,* for, as Rogers notes, it contains textual errors similar to ones in his commentaries that have not been located in manuscripts elsewhere. Laud appears to have obtained this version of the *Acts* from one of the Würzburg installments.

Other interesting donations by Laud include an ornate Würzburg missal and the diocesan breviary of Bishop Rudolf von Scherenberg, printed in 1479 by the first printer of the city, Georg Reyser. Rogers notes that the missal and breviary represent "two of the few printed books among Laud's gifts." Laud also donated a manuscript known as the Laudian *Mahzor*. A Hebrew prayer book from the south of Germany, the *Mahzor* was probably written in the late thirteenth century. As were the other valuable religious works from his third donation to the Bodleian, this text was probably obtained from Germany during the Thirty Years' War. Rogers writes, "the manuscripts imported from Germany were almost all stripped of their covers (no doubt to facilitate packing) and irrecoverable details of provenance were thereby lost." Before Laud presented his gifts to the Bodleian, he had almost all of the manuscripts rebound, "through the agency of Richard Badger the London printer, in plain dark calf with the Archbishop's arms stamped in gilt on both covers." Laud's interest in books and manuscripts did not involve a careful concern for the physical evidence to be found in a volume's binding but simply for the unique contribution it made to the scholarship of the day.

Aside from their religious significance, many of Laud's donations to the Bodleian were of historical or literary value. Among the gifts from Laud's third and most valuable donation to the Bodleian was a version of the Anglo-Saxon Chronicle recorded at the Abbey of Peterborough through the year 1154. Fletcher mentions other contributions that deserve notice, including "an Irish vellum manuscript containing the Psalter of Cashel, Cormac's Glossary," and "Poems attributed to St. Columb-Kill and St. Patrick." Not all of Laud's collections came from the continents on his side of the Atlantic. A particularly fascinating gift, known as the Codex Laud, is the richly decorated and colorful codex from pre-Columbian Mexico, of unknown provenance, which was part of Laud's second donation. It is in excellent condition and must certainly have been a rare find in Laud's day. Perhaps most telling of Laud's broader influence on scholarship, the Codex Laud–one of the most intact specimens of its kind–attracts many modern scholars whose interests in pre-Columbian culture and literature were by no means anticipated in the seventeenth century.

Laud's library was used as evidence against him in the trials that led to his execution. George Henderson in his article "Bible Illustration in the Age of Laud" (1981) discusses the Puritan reaction to Laud's involvement in the production and distribution of copies of the Bible that allegedly encouraged Catholic sentiments. After Laud was arrested and placed in the Tower of London, his "study and books were scrutinized and their evidence brought to his trial." Among other items, Laud's accusers presented an Antwerp Missal "with many Idolatrous Pictures of Christ, Crucifixes, &c. printed within it, in Copper peeces accurately cut" as well as "A Popish Book neatly bound up in Turky Leather with guilt leaves, intituled *Imagines Vitae, Passionis & Mortis, D. N. Jesu Christi,* printed by Boetius a Bolswert, 1623, *cum gratia & Privilegio:* beginning with the Picture of the Annuntiation and concluding with the Assumption of the blessed Virgin, containing in all 74. Idolatrous Superstitious Pictures of Christ, and the Virgin Mary . . . ." Laud's books, now a lasting sign of his love for scholarship and his loyalty to Oxford, were in his own time tangible proof to his enemies of his heresy and idolatry.

By the end of his life Laud had donated almost his entire library to the Bodleian Library under the strict injunction that none of his manuscripts should ever be removed from the premises. Indeed, in 1970 the curators of the Bodleian refused to remove any Laudian manuscripts for their exhibition in America. Throughout his turbulent career as a clergyman and a politician, Laud's passion for the collection and preservation of texts and his devotion to Oxford never seemed to fade. Indeed, some of the final words he wrote expressed regret that he could not have given more to his college and his university.

References:

The Bodleian Library and its Friends (Oxford: Bodleian Library, 1970);

Charles Carlton, *Archbishop William Laud* (London: Routledge & Kegan Paul, 1987);

William Younger Fletcher, *English Book Collectors* (New York: Burt Franklin, 1969);

John Fuggles, "William Laud and the Library of St. John's College, Oxford," *Book Collector,* 30, no. 1 (1981): 19–38;

George Henderson, "Bible Illustration in the Age of Laud," *Transactions of the Cambridge Bibliographical Society,* 8 (1981): 173–204;

Richard Hunt, "Donors of Manuscripts to St. John's College, Oxford, During the Presidency of William Laud, 1611–1621," in his *Studies in the Book Trade* (Oxford: Oxford Bibliographical Society, 1975);

William Holden Hutton, *S. John Baptist College* (London: F. E. Robinson, 1898);

Ian Philip, *The Bodleian Library in the Seventeenth and Eighteenth Centuries* (Oxford: Clarendon Press, 1983);

David Rogers, *The Bodleian Library and its Treasures, 1320–1770* (United Kingdom: Bodleian Library and Aidan Publishing, 1991).

George Lawson

(April 1598 – July 1678)

Conal Condren
University of New South Wales

CATALOGUE: *Catalogus librorum in bibliothecis selectissimis doctissimorum viorum; viz. D. Georgii Lawsoni, Salopiensii D. Georgii Fawleri, Londinensis D. Oweni Stockdoni, Colcestiensis D. Thomae Brooks, Londinensis: Quorum auctio habebitur Londini apud domum Auctionariam ex adverso areae Warwicensis in vico vulgo dicto Warwick-lane, tricesimo maii, 1681* (London, 1681).

BOOKS: *An Examination of the Political Part of Mr. Hobbs, His Leviathan* (London: Printed by R. White for Francis Tyton, 1657);

Theo-politica: or, A Body of Divinity, containing the Rules of the Special Government of God, according to which, He orders the Immortal and Intellectual Creatures, Angels, and Men, to their Final and Eternal State. Being a Method of those Saving Truths, which are contained in the Canon of the Holy Scripture, and Abridged in Those Words of Our Saviour Jesus Christ . . . which were the Graound and Foundation of those Apostolical Creeds and forms of Confessions, related by the Ancients; and in particular, by Irenaeus, and Tertullion (London: Printed by J. Streeter for Francis Tyton, 1659);

Politica sacra et civilis; or A Modell of Civil and Ecclesiasticall Government. Wherein, besides the Positive Doctrine concerning State and Church in General, are Debated the Principall Controversies of the Time concerning the Constitution of the State and Church of England, tending to Righteousness, Truth, and Peace (London: John Starket, 1660);

An Exposition of the Epistle to Hebrewes. Wherein the Text is Cleared; Theopolitica Improved: the Socinian Comment Examined . . . (London: Printed by J. S. for George Sawbridge, 1662);

Magna charta ecclesiae universalis. The Grand Charter, Issued Out and Granted by Jesus Christ for the Plantation of the Christian Faith in All Nations . . . (London: Printed by G. Miller for J. Leigh, 1665).

Edition: *Politica sacra et civilis,* edited by Conal Condren (Cambridge: Cambridge University Press, 1992).

When George Lawson's library was auctioned in 1681, it was clear that his reputation as a scholar, theologian, and writer on politics was substantial. Richard Baxter, perhaps the most prolific and influential seventeenth-century nonconformist, regarded him as a major influence in his own intellectual development, and his political ideas were being popularized by John Humfrey. Lawson's prominence survived into the early years of the eighteenth century, sufficient at least for one anonymous satire, *The Prerogative of the Breaches* (1702), to make familiar allusion to him in ridiculing female pretensions to political rule. At one point it is related how some unemployed poets subdue their landlady with moral lessons on sovereignty taken from Lawson. Nowadays, Lawson is known principally as a significant early critic of Thomas Hobbes, as a possible influence on John Locke, whose own huge library contained all of Lawson's published works, and as a sophisticated political philosopher.

As a collector Lawson must be considered not only in the context of what was sold as his own library but also in connection with two other interesting seventeenth-century collections: the libraries of More Church and of Richard More of Linley (1627–1698). The head of a substantial Shropshire gentry family, More was a member of the House of Commons for Bishops Castle; upon the death of Lawson, the rector of More, More donated a large collection to the church, including some of Lawson's volumes. More's book list, now in the Shropshire County Records Office, catalogues works that may also have been part of Lawson's collection, and, as a whole, it provides the bibliographic context for the library he gave to the church. All three overlapping libraries must be taken into account in understanding the remarkably rich resources–especially important given his location in what was a peripheral and isolated part of the country–upon which Lawson drew in his writing.

George Lawson was probably born in Lancliffe, Ribblesdale, in Yorkshire in April 1598, the son of Thomas and Ellen Lawson. There is no record of his early education, but he is recorded as a sizar at Emmanuel College, Cambridge, in 1615, which suggests a modest yeoman background. He claimed a master of arts degree from Emmanuel, was ordained by the bishop of Chester in 1619, apparently reordained in 1624, and settled in southern Shropshire where he eked out a precarious ecclesiastical living as a stipendiary curate in the hamlet of Mainstone. By 1635, however, he had been licensed to preach by William Laud, archbishop of Canterbury, a circumstance that seems curious since Laud was vehemently hostile to Puritan tendencies within the Church of England and Lawson had been educated at one of the more austere reform-minded Cambridge colleges.

Laud's recognition of Lawson entangled him in ecclesiastical and royal politics being played out in Shrewsbury. In *The Carolinian State Papers, Domestic* (1637–1638), Lawson is recorded as being "a very able scholar and well read in the Fathers, Schoolmen, Councils and history of all sorts" and perhaps more importantly as being an ardent and outspoken supporter of the primate. No doubt because of this reputation, Lawson was backed for a curacy in the principal Shrewsbury church of St. Chads. It is probable, however, that Lawson's Laudian reputation was enhanced by Sir Humphrey Mackworth, a deft Shrewsbury lawyer intent on prompting Lawson. The parishioners, however, had elected Richard Poole, alleged to be both a Puritan and a pluralist (one who held several benefices), and would not be told what to do.

Lawson's life took another seemingly odd turn in 1637 when he was named the rector of the tiny village of More near Bishops Castle, an appointment he held for more than forty years until his death in 1678. Despite his apparently boisterous backing of Archbishop Laud, Lawson was given the rectorship by a member of the anti-Laudian gentry of southern Shropshire, Richard More, the Elder, (ca. 1570–1643). In many ways More seems almost to have been the stereotypical Puritan. Much involved in trade and the owner of substantial estates, he was a Hebrew scholar and a man of deep piety and fervent religious convictions. In later life he remained strongly committed to the parliamentarian cause and in 1643 translated Joseph Mede's Calvinist escatological treatise, *Clavis apocolipsin* (1632). Lawson was already living in More with his wife, Anne, and young son, Jeremiah, when More made the rectorship of the village available to him. There simply may have been little choice as to who might fill an ecclesiastical vacancy in the wilds of Shropshire. It may be also that More had been involved with Mackworth's attempt to get Lawson the position in Shrewsbury and that the offer of the rectory in his own village gave Lawson compensation and some ease to ecclesiastical tension in the region.

Whatever their disagreements, More and Lawson did share scholarly interests, and the one issue that Laud and his enemies agreed on was the need for better-educated clerics. Further, Lawson may have already made himself useful to More in helping the latter pen a defense of the area and its people after a violent attack on its "puritanism" by the Reverend Peter Studely of Shrewsbury. The pretext for the attack had been a set of gruesome murders and their aftermath, which Studely took to evidence a Puritan conspiracy. In the acknowledgments of his measured reply, *A True Relation of the Murders,* which was not published until 1641, More thanks, among others mentioned by name, an anonymous local cleric of his acquaintance for reducing his notes on the case to a methodical argument. More was succeeded by his son Samuel, a man of Lawson's generation, who rose to prominence during the civil wars. He put the education of Robert, the younger son of his second marriage, into Lawson's care. In the ecclesiastical politics of the time, Lawson's name crops up usually in concert with Samuel More's. In 1662 Samuel More died and was succeeded by his elder son, Richard, who had been about ten years old when Lawson became the rector of More.

Lawson's literary career developed late. Some manuscript material, dating from 1649–1651, survives in the unpublished "Baxter Treatises" held in the Dr. Williams Library in London. During these remarkable years of instability, the most substantial piece to survive is the "Amica dissertatio," a critique of Baxter's controversial *Aphorisms of Justification* (1649) in the form of a dialogue. Short quotations from Baxter's work are followed by Lawson's own replies to them. The work is an effective if exhausting and repetitive demolition of Baxter's handling of the concepts of sin, punishment, redemption, and divine judgment.

Despite what must have been the considerable burdens of office, Lawson had been preparing to write some original work. In 1657, however, the interest generated by Hobbes's *Leviathan* (1651) led him to publish *An Examination of the Political Part of Mr. Hobbs, His Leviathan.* The book has the same structure as the "Amica dissertatio," juxtaposing statements by Hobbes with extensive and focused critique. Given the hostility Hobbes generated, especially among clerics, Lawson is for the most part relatively unpolemical. He followed *Examination* with *Theo-politica: or, A Body of Divinity, containing the Rules of the Special Government of God, according to which, He orders the Immortal and Intellectual Creatures, Angels, and Men, to their Final and Eternal State* (1659), a wide-ranging and conventional blend of English Protestant theology and devotional care, largely elaborated from the Ten Commandments.

In 1660 Lawson published the work for which he is now studied, *Politica sacra et civilis; or A Modell of Civil and Ecclesiasticall Government. Wherein, besides the Positive Doctrine concerning State and Church in General, are Debated the Principall Controversies of the Time concerning the Constitution of the State and Church of England, tending to Righteousness, Truth, and Peace.* With methodical care and terminological precision, Lawson posits analogous concepts of church and state, each comprised of people subject to authority, and yet, also considered free and equal participants within the community. He uses the tensions arising from the individual being a subject and citizen in both church and state to explore the causes and conduct of the ecclesiastical upheaval and the civil wars. While Lawson's ostensible audience is unlearned, the work is a conspicuous display of learning, designed, one suspects, to impress as well as inform and persuade. His many allusions to names and texts provides clues to the extent of the library holdings to which he had access. Initially *Politica sacra et civilis,* probably unsuited to the increasingly oppressive atmosphere of Restoration England, seems to have fallen on deaf ears. It is significant that Lawson never proceeded with a second volume, to be published contingent upon the reception of the first; and that although he was a member of the Established Church, his ideas were taken up by those his church excluded.

If the development of Lawson's career suggests that the earlier Laudian Lawson was by 1660 a fellow traveler with nonconformity, another oddity lies in the fact that almost throughout his encumbancy he kept his records in Latin, a high church reversion from the modernizing English adopted by his predecessor and successors at More. His densest theological work, *An Exposition of the Epistle to Hebrewes. Wherein the Text is Cleared; Theopolitica Improved: the Socinian Comment Examined . . . ,* was published in 1662. In 1665 he brought out *Magna charta ecclesiae universalis. The Grand Charter, Issued Out and Granted by Jesus Christ for the Plantation of the Christian Faith in All Nations,* an attempt to render his theology more accessible, which he achieved at the high cost of a loss of conceptual discrimination. This last work was republished in 1683 by Lawson's son. In 1688–1689 James II was overthrown by William of Orange, and it was in this context that Lawson's original printer, John Starkey, republished *Politica sacra et civilis,* a work that helped provide an explanatory and descriptive framework for what was happening. Lawson's characteristic conceptual vocabulary cropped up often in polemical and pamphlet literature, and his continuing prominence may have encouraged the republication of *Theo-politica* in 1705.

Parish registers at More record Lawson's burial in July 1678. He left his wife and son a comfortable estate that included damask tablecloths, wall hangings, carpets, and, to offer yet another rub of contradiction, a horse-

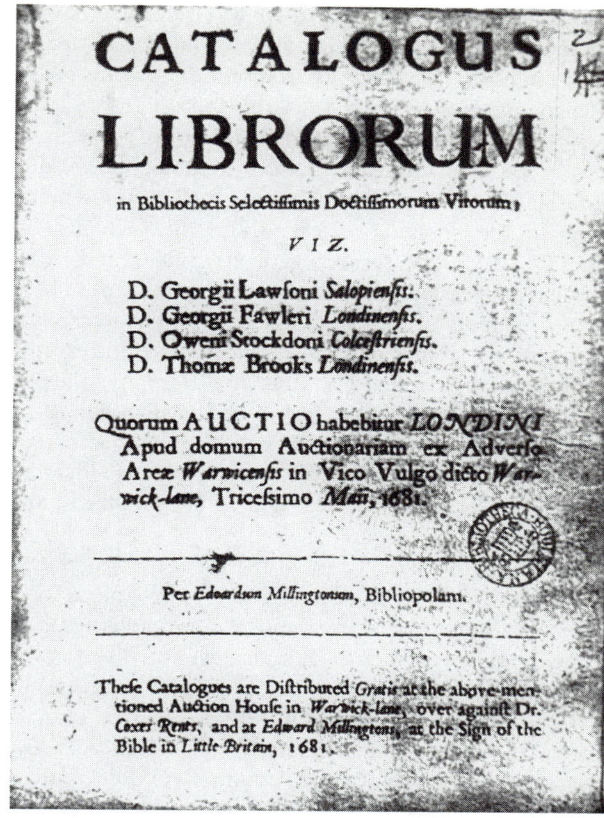
CATALOGUS
LIBRORUM
in Bibliothecis Selectissimis Doctissimorum Virorum;
VIZ.
D. Georgii Lawsoni Salopiensis.
D. Georgii Fawleri Londinensis.
D. Oweni Stockdoni Colcestriensis.
D. Thomæ Brooks Londinensis.
Quorum AUCTIO habebitur LONDINI
Apud domum Auctionariam ex Adverso
Areæ Warwicensis in Vico Vulgo dicto Warwick-lane, Tricesimo Maii, 1681.
Per Edoardum Millingtonum, Bibliopolam.
These Catalogues are Distributed Gratis at the above-mentioned Auction House in Warwick-lane, over against Dr. Coxes Rents, and at Edward Millingtons, at the Sign of the Bible in Little Britain, 1681.

Title page for the only catalogue of George Lawson's library, which intersperses descriptions of his books with those of three other clergymen without indicating ownership

hair undershirt worn specifically to encourage humility through discomfort. His own wearing "Apparill" was priced at £8, showing perhaps that Lawson was not a man to dress in rags even if a hair shirt lay next to his skin. Above all, there was a study of books valued at £150. After Anne Lawson was interred in 1680, Lawson's son, Jeremy, had the library sold by the London auctioneer Edward Millington, with part of the proceeds going toward the costs of republishing *Magna charta ecclesiae universalis.*

Lawson's library was merged with those of three otherwise quite obscure clergymen, but nevertheless it is possible to get a good sense of its size and nature. The *Catalogus librorum in bibliothecis selectissimis* (1681) is bound in with other catalogues of sale dated between 1681 and 1695, a copy of which is held in the British Library. The sixty-four-page Millington *Catalogus librorum* lists 4,592 volumes, of which 95 form an addendum, possibly a late-entry library. The works most readily associated with Lawson, or referred to or quoted by him, are in the main listing of 4,497 volumes. As Lawson is named first among the four defunct clerics and then singled out for separate mention as "a person of . . . Universal learning and general esteem," it is probable that his was the largest library. As there is no reason to think it would have been smaller than the others, it is plausible to conclude that his collection comprised at least 1,500 volumes.

All the libraries included in *Catalogus librorum* were clearly less book collections, as that term might be understood in the modern sense, than the tools of trade necessary for the pursuit of learning and the fulfillment of priestly office. The sprinkling of geographic and cartographic folios listed in the catalogue may have been used by one or more of the clerics in teaching. The intellectual range of the remainder of the stock covers theology, church history, Greek and Roman philosophy, rhetoric and drama, biblical concordances and dictionaries of the appropriate ancient languages, Chaldean and Hebrew, together with medieval logic. The catalogue also includes works on modern languages such as Italian, Dutch, and French.

The ecumenical scope of the theology and church history represented in the catalogue is striking. It may, of course, to some extent be simply the fortuitous result of tumbling different libraries in with each other, but as will be seen from the clearer evidence of the structure of the More Church Library, clerics were expected to be as familiar with the works of their enemies as their friends. At any rate, along with volumes of Theodore Beza, John Calvin, and Samuel Rutherford, there are names such as Francisco Suarez and Saint Robert Bellarmine, who were both familiar to Lawson.

Another noticeable feature is that the catalogue shows chronological continuity. Naturally, one would expect classical authors, but there is also a strong showing of medieval, pre-Reformation philosophers and theologians, including Duns Scotus, Peter Lombard, and Thomas Aquinas, who are cheek by jowl with Reformation and Renaissance figures such as Guicciardini, Pico della Mirandola, Polydore Virgil, and Erasmus. Who owned what is another matter, although the presence of multiple copies narrows the possibilities. There are three copies of Henry Spelman's *Glossarium* (1626) on which Lawson relied as well as two copies of Niccolò Machiavelli's *Discourses* (1591 and 1619) and two of Thomas Hooker's *Summ of Church Discipline* (1648)–both works Lawson certainly used. The catalogue also lists multiple copies of texts by Rutherford, Richard Hooker, and many other contemporary religious writers with whom Lawson took issue or, as in the case of Hooker, seems to have endorsed on questions of church development, without discussing.

Certain books can confidently be assigned to Lawson despite there being only single copies of them listed. Adam Contzen's *Politicorum libri decem* (1621) and Lancelot Andrewes's *Torta torturi* (1609), both rare, were praised and used by Lawson. In *Politica sacra et civilis* he quoted Francis Mason's *Vindiciae ecclesiae Anglicanae* (1638 edition) extensively in a marginal note in conjunction with Andrewes's work. Sir Thomas More's *Utopia* (1516) he also discussed in different works, but one of the editions listed in the catalogue (1680) is too late to have been Lawson's own; the other is undated. What was probably his copy of the first edition of *Leviathan* (1651) is listed, as is Marsilius of Padua's *Defensor pacis* (1324; Frankfurt, 1592), entered as "Patavini *defensor pacis*."

The work of Marsilius is especially notable because it provides an intellectual link between the Middle Ages and early modern Britain. *Defensor pacis* had been officially translated in the sixteenth century and printed in an issue of only twenty-four copies specifically for Henry VIII's bishops. It was, however, well known as an antipapal polemic in its original Latin and in a wide range of European translations. Marsilius's arguments concerning priestly equality were quite widely cited in the seventeenth century, and it has long been suspected that in other ways the Paduan was an important figure behind writers such as Hobbes and Locke. Lawson himself, from a comment in *Examination,* seems to have believed that Hobbes depended on the admired Marsilius. Lawson, though, seems to have been the major conduit in England for Marsilius's dextrous and sophisticated blend of imperialism, medieval republicanism, biblical exegesis, and Franciscan fundamentalism.

The combined libraries of Lawson and his fellow clerics were on view for a whole week and then sold with rapidity in a day. It is possible to identify Lawson's dispersed books, though, because it was evidently his practice to sign and annotate the books he owned–a point established by an examination of the portion of his library that was not sold at auction in 1681. Some of Lawson's volumes remained back in the village of More probably at Linley Hall, the home of the Mores.

Anne Lawson's death and the sale of her husband's books by her son appears to have led Richard More to give a library of some three hundred volumes to the village church. While there were eleven known parochial libraries in Shropshire at the time, More's gift was unusual because of its size and because it was not a bequest or a library accrued in an ad hoc fashion. It instead represented a considered selection from the donor's extensive holdings. As the deed of gift in the Shropshire County Record Office shows, the books were provided specifically for educational use, stipulating rules of borrowing (restricted to More and his friends) and reading. More also insisted on a system of accountability by the churchwardens, who were to answer annually to the village for the state of the library. The gift thus assumed literacy and was for the encouragement of a preaching minister. The timing, contents, and nature of the donation all suggest that it was to fill a gap left by the Lawson library. Many of the authors and some of the specific texts replicate items in the Millington catalogue.

There are signs of use, ownership, or circulation in 124 of the remaining volumes. Signatures and sometimes handwriting taken in conjunction with parish and other records give a glimpse of a literate local elite, distinct from a social elite dating back into the sixteenth century. Eight of the books had been owned by Lawson. Thomas Bilson's *The Perpetual Government of Christe's Church* (1593) is annotated appropriately for the sort of use Lawson made of it but in a distinctive ink postdating his printed references to Bilson. Erasmus's *Paraphrases* (1539–1543) was owned by one of Lawson's servants, another is marked "Mr. Ri. More his book if borrowed of Mr. Lawson"–a curious addendum unless Lawson collected by selective bibliographic amnesia. Another book carries a more peremptory inscription: "Sam: More his booke."

More's donation includes books that Lawson knew well, though to which he did not make explicit claim. Although there is no signature in the copy of Thomas Jackson's *A Treatise of the Holy Catholicke faith and Church* (1627), Jackson was a theologian that Lawson accorded considerable respect. A copy of Mauricius Helingus's *Versificatorius* (Frankfurt, 1593), possibly the only copy now extant, has both Jeremy Lawson's and Robert More's boyish signatures in it, suggesting they learned their Latin and Greek together. The collection as a whole is clearly focused on religious matters, excepting a scattering of Greek and Roman authors, most notably Aristotle's *Rhetoric* (1530), Euripides' *Tragedies* (1537), Isocrates' *Scripta* (1570), the historical and rhetorical writings attributed to Dionysius of Halicarnassus (1589), and Cicero's *De officiis* (1569)–all appropriate for good grammar-school style teaching. Caesar Baronio's *Annals of the Church* (1589–1601), a Roman Catholic catechism (1581), the works of Pope Leo I (1577), and the damaged remains of a French *politiques* tract as well as a host of reformed theologians, including Mede, Jewel, Musculus, and Calvin, attest to the theological scope Richard More expected of a preaching minister.

The collection includes five incunabula, which may well have come from the dissolved priory of Chirbury: Anglus Alexander's *Destructorium vitiorum* (1497), Petrus Dorbellus's *Sermones* (1490), Sancta Maria de Paulus's *Scrutinium scripturarum* (1470), Johann Tritheim's *Noctes sacrae* (1590), and Aquinas's *Commentaria in omnes epistolas beati Pauli* (Basel, 1495). There are also splendid first editions of English devotional and controversial texts, most notably William Chillingworth's *The Religion of the Protestants* (Oxford, 1638). It was common before and during the early days of the printing press to reuse resilient medieval velum in bindings, and bound in with some works are exquisite illuminated manuscript fragments, later identified as such by Neil Ker of Oxford. He listed the sixteen substantial fragments and singled out two leaves of an eleventh-century gospel book bound in with Bonaventure Bertramus's *Lucubrationes* (1588) and a twelfth-century fragment of Lucan in Beza's *Epsitolae* (1575). His findings were pinned to the inside of one of the book presses in the church.

Only a third of the library remains intact. It could not have operated as intended in the early eighteenth century, as at that time the church wardens were not literate, signing their names with crosses in parish registers. The Reverend W. G. Clark Maxwell made a partial catalogue of the remaining books in 1909 when they were disinterred from the church tower in poor condition. Conal Condren provides an account of the library and its foundation and social significance in the context of surviving parish and family records in *Library History* (1987). A full catalogue with details of provenance is included as an appendix. What remains of the original library was effectively saved from further deterioration by Sir Jasper and Lady More during the 1960s, but after their deaths the books were taken from the two oak book presses in which they had been locked in More Church and removed from the public domain for complete restoration.

The loss of so many books from the More Church Library may be explained in various ways, but the most obvious explanation is that the borrowing rights reserved by Richard More resulted in some books gradually being reabsorbed into his own library or that of his brother's descendants who inherited the estates. One volume carries several partially erased abbreviated titles not to be found in the church library, which may have been some sort of borrowing tally. At the end of the seventeenth century More drew up a list of his own books, now in the Shropshire County Records Office: twenty-four pages of closely written entries with marginal insertions. Not all details are clear or complete, and the aging hand in places is difficult to read. Not all items carry dates, and the details provided for those that do not sometimes make it impossible to tell what or which editions they were. One entry, for example, simply states "seven Italian books."

Even with its deficiencies, More's list is useful. It lists roughly 838 separate works, about 65 percent of which are seventeenth-century volumes or republished seventeenth-century works, leaving a considerable number of sixteenth-century texts. There is a substantial medical library, broadly defined, comprising some 360 volumes. About one-third of this classification carries sixteenth-century dates. Richard More probably inherited most of these books from his brother John, a physician who died in or about 1686. Among the medical books is the only incunabula listed, Magnini's *Regimen sanitatis* (1486). Of the remaining 480 or so volumes, about 75 were published after 1665, the year of Lawson's last publication. Thus, it is fair to say that, depending on the time of acquisition, some 400 works may have been part of Lawson's bibliographical environment. Lawson's own library, of course, was likely much larger than the More collection, but as in the Millington catalogue, one is struck by the chronological sweep of the books listed, ranging from antiquity through to the late seventeenth century.

More's catalogue is organized into sections on divinity, law, medicine, poetry, tragedy and comedy, history and geography, and miscellaneous. As with many book lists, the volume size also provides a subclassification. There is no category for *libri politici,* the classification for books specifically regarded as about politics; nor is there the standard heading for studies in philosophy, *libri philosophici*–classifications also absent from the Millington catalogue. Perhaps these cataloguers did not think in terms of the political as it is modernly understood and believed a section on philosophical works would be too broad. The title *Politique discourses upon truth and lying* (1586), for example, is classified as divinity. What might seem cognate titles are treated as history or law or are found in "Micelanea."

Under the heading of medicine one finds the sorts of books on husbandry, hawking, and riding appropriate to running a substantial estate. Among these is a listing of an otherwise unknown edition of John Fitzherbert's *Husbandry,* of which no other copy is known. A category that is alien to anything associated with Lawson's writings is poetry. There are substantial listings of English poetry including works by John Donne, Thomas Carew, Abraham Cowley, George Herbert, Edmund Spencer, Henry Vaughan, Samuel Butler, and George Withers. Also listed is Hobbes's early and popular Latin country-house poem *De mirabilibus pecci* (1638) as well as two copies of Andrew Marvell's *Miscellanies* (1681) and some of his verse satires. Most of the volumes of poetry are first editions.

Excluding the works having to do with domestic concerns, poetry, and medicine, the coincidence of interests between More's collection and Lawson's own is striking. The catalogue is replete with works on theology, church history, and what modern librarians would classify as political theory. Notable titles include Dudley Diggs's *The Unlawfulness of Subjects taking up Arms* (1647), Matthew Wren's *Monarchy Asserted* (1660), and two copies of Philip Hunton's *A Treatise of Monarchy* (1663, a possible misreading of 1643, and 1689). More also lists *Vindiciae contra tyrannos,* a controversial pamphlet from the French Wars of Religion of the sixteenth century justifying tyrannicide, which Lawson criticized for what he considered conceptual confusion. There is also Marvell's explosive *Growth of Popery and Arbitrary Government,* published anonymously and illegally just prior to Lawson's death; Italian political literature, including Machiavelli's *Opera* (1550); much legal and antiquarian material of the sort on which Lawson drew extensively, including two copies of William Camden's *Britannia* (1590); a 1580 edition of *Utopia,* which may have been the one used by Lawson; a copy of John Spotswood's *History of the Church of Scotland* (the first edition was published in 1655 but no date is cited), which Lawson also used; and George Bate's *Elenchus Motuum nuperorum in Anglia* (cited as 1649 although the first edition is recorded as Edinburgh 1650; no author listed), which Lawson attacked. At one with Lawson's interests but postdating his writing career are, for example, John Bramhall's *Works* (1676) and Benedict de Spinoza's *Tractatus theologico-politicus* (1673). Two works replicate those in the church library, Chillingworth's *Religion* (1664 edition) and the complete three-volume set of William Perkins's *Works* (1617).

The More family library continued to grow for the next two hundred years before its destruction after World War II. In his short reminiscence, *A Tale of Two Houses* (1978), the last of the Mores, Jasper, accounts for the need to disperse the library. When he returned to the family home, which had been rented out for many years, he found Linley Hall crumbling and rat-infested, its vast estates decaying and in disarray. In the process of restoration he had to sell eight tons of moldering books and manuscripts. Among those he kept was Richard More's own signed copy of Lawson's *Examination of the Political Part of Mr. Hobbes, His Leviathan.* At the time Lawson, almost forgotten for more than a century, was being rediscovered in the wake of renewed interest in Hobbes and Locke. Now, when the final traces of his world have been dispersed and the family that made his career possible is extinct, Lawson is being studied as a figure in his own right and the tensions, puzzles, and oddities of his life and works are generating controversies and books of their own.

References:

Conal Condren, *George Lawson's Politica and the English Revolution* (Cambridge: Cambridge University Press, 1989);

Condren, "More Parish Library, Salop," *Library History* (1987): 141–162;

W. G. Clark Maxwell, "The Church Library of More," *Transactions of the Shropshire Archaeological and Natural History Society,* third series, 9 (1909);

Maxwell, "On the Library of More Church, Salop," *Transactions of the Shropshire Archaeological and Natural History Society,* third series, 7 (1906): 115;

Jasper More, *A Tale of Two Houses* (Shrewsbury, U.K.: Wilding, 1978).

Papers:

The main collection of George Lawson's papers are held in Dr. Williams Library, London.

John Locke

(29 August 1632 - 28 October 1704)

Suzanne Rosenblum

See also "Eighteenth-Century Background: John Locke," in *DLB 31: American Colonial Writers, 1735–1781* and the Locke entry in *DLB 101: British Prose Writers, 1660–1800, First Series.*

CATALOGUE: John Harrison and Peter Laslett, *The Library of John Locke* (Oxford: Oxford University Press, 1965; enlarged, 1971).

BOOKS: *Epistola de Tolerantia ad Clarissimum Virum T.A.R.T.O.L.A. Scripta a P.A.P.O.I.L.A.* (Gouda: Apud J. ab Hoeva, 1689); translated by William Popple as *A Letter Concerning Toleration. Humbly Submitted, &c. Licensed Octob. 3, 1689* (London: Printed for A. Churchill, 1689);

Two Treatises of Government: In the Former, The False Principles and Foundation of Sir Robert Filmer, and His Followers, Are Detected and Overthrown. The Latter Is an Essay Concerning the True Original, Extent, and End of Civil-Government (London: Printed for A. & J. Churchill, 1690);

An Essay concerning Humane Understanding. In Four Books (London: Printed by Eliz. Holt for T. Basset, 1690; second edition, with large additions, London: Printed for T. Dring & S. Manship, 1694; fourth edition, with large additions, London: Printed for A. & J. Churchill and S. Manship, 1700; fifth edition, with many large additions, London: Printed for A. & J. Churchill and S. Manship, 1706);

A Second Letter concerning Toleration. Licensed, June 24, 1690 (London: Printed for A. & J. Churchill, 1690);

Some Considerations of the Consequences of the Lowering of Interest and Raising the Value of Money. In a Letter to a Member of Parliament (London: Printed for A. & J. Churchill, 1692);

A Third Letter for Toleration to the Author [J. Proast] *of the Third Letter concerning Toleration* (London: Printed for A. & J. Churchill, 1692);

Some Thoughts concerning Education (London: Printed for A. & J. Churchill, 1693);

John Locke, 1672 (portrait by John Greenhill; National Portrait Gallery, London)

Short Observations on a Printed Paper, Intituled, For Encouraging the Coining Silver Money in England, and After for Keeping it Here (London: Printed for A. & J. Churchill, 1695);

The Reasonableness of Christianity, as Delivered in the Scriptures (London: Printed for A. & J. Churchill, 1695);

A Vindication of the Reasonableness of Christianity, &c. from Mr. Edwards's Reflections (London: Printed for A. & J. Churchill, 1695);

Further Considerations concerning Raising the Value of Money, Wherein Mr. Lowndes's Arguments for It in His Late Report, concerning 'An Essay for the Amendment of the

Silver Coins' Are Particularly Examined, anonymous (London: Printed for A. & J. Churchill, 1695);

A Second Vindication of the Reasonableness of Christianity, &c. By the Author of the Reasonableness of Christianity, &c. (London: Printed for A. & J. Churchill and E. Castle, 1697);

A Letter to the Right Reverend Edward Ld. Bishop of Worcester, concerning Some Passages Relating to Mr. Locke's Essay of Humane Understanding; in a Late Discourse of His Lordship's, in Vindication of the Trinity (London: Printed for A. & J. Churchill, 1697);

Mr. Locke's Reply to the Right Reverend the Bishop of Worcester's Answer to His Letter, concerning Some Passages Relating to Mr. Locke's Essay of Humane Understanding; in a Late Discourse of His Lordship's in Vindication of the Trinity (London: Printed by H. Clark for A. & J. Churchill and E. Castle, 1697);

Mr. Locke's Reply to the Right Reverend the Bishop of Worcester's Answer to his Second Letter (London: Printed by H. C. for A. & J. Churchill and E. Castle, 1699);

A Paraphrase and Notes on the Epistles of St. Paul to the Galatians, I & II Corinthians, Romans, and Ephesians. To Which Is Prefix'd 'An Essay for the Understanding of St. Paul's Epistles, by Consulting St. Paul Himself,' published in parts (London: Printed for A. & J. Churchill, 1705–1707);

Posthumous Works of Mr. John Locke: Viz. I. Of the Conduct of the Understanding. II. An Examination of P. Malebranche's Opinion of Seeing All Things in God. III. A Discourse on Miracles. IV. Part of a Fourth Letter on Toleration. V. Memoirs relating to the Life of Anthony First Earl of Shaftesbury. To which is Added, VI. His New Method of a Common-Place-Book. Written Originally in French, and Now Translated into English (London: Printed by W. B. for A. & J. Churchill, 1706);

A Collection of Several Pieces of Mr. John Locke, Never Before Printed or Not Extant in His Works, edited by Pierre Des Maizeaux (London: Printed by J. Bettenham for R. Francklin, 1720).

Editions: *The Works of John Locke,* 3 volumes (London: Printed for J. Churchill & S. Manship, 1714); eighth edition, 4 volumes, edited by Edmund Law (London: Printed for W. Strahan, 1777); new edition, corrected, 10 volumes (London: Printed for T. Tegg, 1823);

An Essay Concerning the Understanding, Knowledge, Opinion, and Assent, edited by Benjamin Rand (Cambridge, Mass.: Harvard University Press, 1931)–Locke's longer and later draft of *Essay Concerning Human Understanding,* known as Draft;

An Early Draft of Locke's Essay, edited by R. I. Aaron and Jocelyn Gibb (Oxford: Clarendon Press, 1936)–Locke's earlier and shorter 1671 draft of *Essay Concerning Human Understanding,* known as Draft A;

Locke's Travels in France As related in his Journals, Correspondence and Other Papers, edited by John Lough (Cambridge: Cambridge University Press, 1953);

Essays on the Law of Nature, The Latin Text with a Translation, Introduction and Notes, Together with Transcripts of Locke's Shorthand in his Journals for 1676, edited by W. Von Leyden (Oxford: Clarendon Press, 1954);

Two Treatises of Government: A Critical Edition, edited by Peter Laslett (Cambridge: Cambridge University Press, 1960; second edition, revised, 1967);

Two Tracts on Government, edited by Philip Abrams (London: Cambridge University Press, 1967);

The Clarendon Edition of the Works of John Locke, 30 volumes (Oxford: Clarendon Press, 1975–)–includes *An Essay Concerning Human Understanding,* 1 volume, edited by Peter H. Nidditch (1975); *A Paraphrase and Notes on the Epistles of St. Paul,* 2 volumes, edited by Arthur W. Wainwright (1987); *Some Thoughts Concerning Education,* 1 volume, edited by John Yolton and Jean Yolton (1989); *Drafts of 'An Essay Concerning Human Understanding' and Other Philosophical Writings,* 3 volumes, edited by Nidditch and G. A. J. Rogers (1990–).

OTHER: *Aesop's Fables in English & Latin, Interlineary; for the Benefit of Those Who Not Having a Master Would Learn Either of These Tongues,* edited by Locke (London: Printed for A. & J. Churchill, 1703).

The library that John Locke assembled was intended for use rather than for show. Unlike Samuel Pepys, who assembled a collection of some three thousand volumes, about the same size as Locke's, he did not care for display; nor is there evidence to suggest that he, like Pepys, lost sleep over a missing volume. Still, Locke carefully listed his reading and his acquisitions, meticulously keeping a personal catalogue of his books, and arranged for their distribution after his death. About a quarter of his collection remains together at the Bodleian Library, Oxford, the 1978 gift of Paul Mellon.

By the standards of the day Locke's library was sizable, but others were building more impressive collections. John Evelyn's contained about five thousand volumes, and Dr. Thomas Plume, the vicar of Greenwich and archdeacon of Rochester, left some six thousand books at Maldon. On the other hand, Isaac Newton's library contained about two thousand books, which Newton never catalogued, nor did he leave a will stipulating the disposition of his collection (or of any other of his possessions). Locke's purchases and the catalogues he prepared indicate his interests, making a

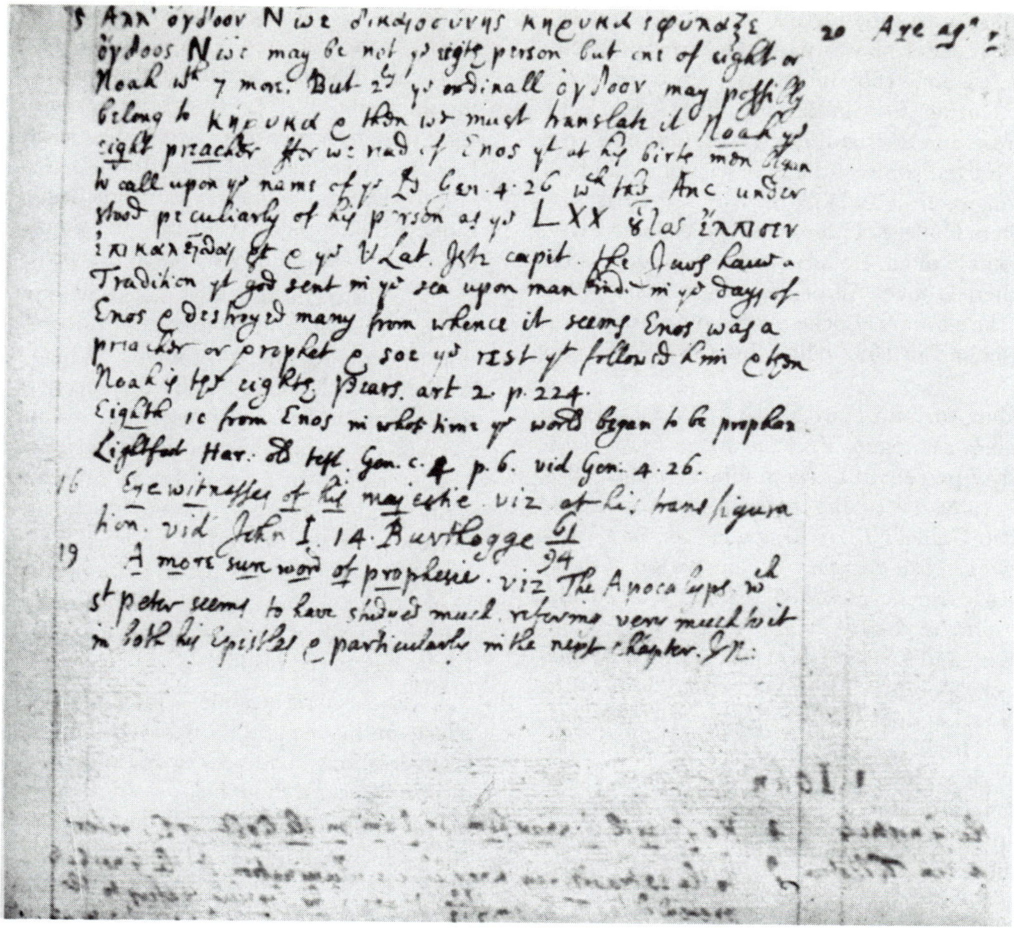

Notes by Locke in his interleaved copy of a Bible printed in London by William Bentley in 1648 (Bodleian Library, Oxford)

study of his collection an intellectual biography of one of the great minds of the seventeenth century.

The son of John Locke Sr. and Agnes Keene Locke, Locke was born at Wrington, Somersetshire, on 29 August 1632. The elder John Locke was a lawyer, clerk for justices of the peace, and agent for Alexander Popham, a neighboring justice of the peace. At the outbreak of the English Civil War, Popham became a colonel in the Parliamentary army, and the elder Locke served under him as captain. Through his father's connections with Popham, the younger Locke secured admission to Westminster School in 1647. By the time of his enrollment on 27 November 1652 at Christ College, Oxford, as a King's Scholar, Locke had already begun his lifelong collecting of books.

Though he was a brilliant student at Westminster School, he paid little attention to his studies as an Oxford undergraduate, devoting his first year there to the reading of romances. His fondness for such works persisted. The final listing of his library included Torquato Tasso's *Gerusalemme liberata* (Casalmaggiore, 1581) and *Aminta, favola boscareccia* (Venice, 1609), Aphra Behn's *Oroonoko* (London, 1688), Miguel de Cervantes's *Don Quixote,* translated into English by Thomas Shelton (London, 1652) and two copies of Filleau de Saint-Martin's French translation (Paris, 1678 and 1681), and two copies of François Rabelais's *Oeuvres* (Lyons, 1608, and another edition, printed by Elzevir, probably at Amsterdam, 1675). Cervantes was his favorite; he remarked in "Some Thoughts Concerning Reading and Study for a Gentleman," an essay included in *A Collection of Several Pieces of Mr. John Locke, Never Before Printed, or not Extant in His Works* (1720), that "Of all the books of fiction, I know none that equals Cervantes's *History of Don Quixote* in usefulness, pleasantry, and a constant decorum."

Locke received his bachelor of arts degree on 14 February 1656. After receiving his master of arts degree on 29 June 1658, Locke remained at Christ College as a fellow. On Christmas 1660 he was appointed Greek lecturer. Two years later he was named lecturer on rhetoric, and on Christmas 1663 he became censor of moral philosophy. During his studies for his M.A. Locke became interested in the natural sciences. Oxford in the 1650s had attracted some of the best scientific minds of the day, among them John Wilkins, who served as warden of Wadham College, Thomas Willis, William Petty, and, most notable of all, Robert Boyle, who took as his assistant Robert Hooke. All of these figures are represented in Locke's library. Locke owned more than sixty titles by Boyle and in 1692 edited his *General History of the Air*.

According to John Harrison and Peter Laslett in their extensive catalogue *The Library of John Locke* (1965), nearly 7 percent of Locke's library, or 242 titles, fall into the category of the natural sciences. Locke owned Galileo Galilei's *Opere* (Bologna, 1656), a work found in few English libraries of the period. On 11 November 1676 Locke recorded reading Galileo and referred to him as the "Tuscan Archimedes of our time." Harrison and Laslett list several items by Francis Bacon in Locke's library, including two editions of the *Novum organum* (Leyden, 1650, and Amsterdam, 1660). Locke owned Hooke's *Micrographia* (London, 1665), an important work on microscopy; and his copies of Isaac Newton's *Principia* (London, 1687) and *Opticks* (London, 1704) were presented to him by the author. As in the fields of philosophy, religion, medicine, and politics, Locke demonstrated an impatience with older methodology. His library illustrates his interest in the new scientific work being done across Europe.

Locke, who became a member of the Royal Society in 1668, showed an interest not only in science but also in alchemy and magic. About sixty books in his library relate to these occult topics. Among these volumes were Domenico Auda's *Breve compendio di Maraviglioso secreti* (Brief Compendium of Amazing Secrets; Torino, 1665); Alvaro Alonso Barba's *The Art of Metals* (London, 1674) as translated by Edward Montague, first Earl of Sandwich; and Joannes Fanianus Chrysippus's *De arte metallicae metamorphoseos liber singularis* (Of the Art of Transforming Metals; Basle, 1576).

His scientific inclination led Locke to study medicine, which became his first profession and an abiding interest. Locke acquired more than four hundred medical titles, comprising about 11 percent of his collection. Only theology is better represented among his holdings. Here again his library reveals his rejection of the older scholastic approach to medicine and his preference for the experimental. Locke owned William Harvey's revolutionary *De motu cordis & sanguinis circulatione* (On the Beating of the Heart and the Circulation of the Blood; Rotterdam, 1654) as well as Harvey's *Exercitationes de generatione animalium* (Of the Generation of Animals; Amsterdam, 1651). Locke befriended the noted physician Thomas Sydenham, who praised Locke in the third edition of his treatise on fevers. Locke owned eight titles by Sydenham, two by Daniel Sennert, two by Lazarus Riverius, and Jean Fernel's *Universa medicina* (1656). Even after he gave up practicing medicine for money, he kept abreast of new developments and continued to read and buy books in this field.

In his medical studies Locke worked closely with the physician David Thomas, who in July 1666 introduced him to the prominent Whig politician Sir Anthony Ashley Cooper. By the spring of 1667 Locke was living at Exeter House, the Strand, London, as Cooper's secretary and private physician. In that year Locke copied out a list of books drawn from a manuscript guide prepared for young scholars by Thomas Barlow, who had served as Thomas Bodley's librarian. Locke was to use this list as a buying guide. In 1668 Locke operated on Cooper for an internal abscess, inserting a silver drainage tube. Cooper believed that Locke had saved his life.

Locke's association with Cooper had profound effects on his life and thought and hence on his library. Conversations with Cooper and his Whig circle directed Locke's thoughts toward the political and theological questions with which he is most closely associated. Locke's pupil, Cooper's grandson, claimed that his grandfather, who became the first earl of Shaftesbury in April 1672, urged Locke to "study . . . the religious and civil affairs of the nation." Through his influence Cooper, when his faction was in the ascendant, secured government posts for Locke that enhanced his income and allowed him to augment his library. Thus, after Cooper became lord chancellor in November 1672, Locke was named secretary of presentations, a sinecure with a salary of £500 a year. On 15 October 1673 Locke was named secretary to the Council of Trade, which also carried with it a salary of £500, though Locke never received this money. When Cooper was dismissed from office at the end of 1673, he granted Locke an annuity of £100 a year.

After receiving his bachelor of medicine degree from Oxford on 6 February 1675, Locke in November of that year went to France, where he remained until April of 1679. Several explanations have been offered for his French sojourn. Gabriel Bonno suggests that Locke may have left England for health reasons. He may have been sent by Cooper, since the Whigs were secretly negotiating with the French. His main reason may have been to pursue his medical studies at Montpelier, where he stayed from 4 January 1676 to 25 March 1677. A letter to John Mapletoft dated 9 August

1677 from Paris reveals that Locke hoped to succeed Mapletoft as professor of medicine at Gresham College.

Locke's journals for this period record his readings and bookbuying. Medical matters certainly were on his mind. He met the physician Moïse Charas and bought his *Pharmacopée royale* (Paris, 1676). Locke attended the lectures of the anatomist Joseph Guichard du Verney, though he sat so far back in the hall that he could not hear. When Verney published his *Traité de l'organe de l'ouïe* (Paris, 1683), establishing the anatomy of the middle and inner ear, Locke secured a copy. He also bought the major works of the four leading French physicians of the day: François Bayle, professor of medicine at the University of Toulouse; Nicolas de Blégny, named the queen's physician in 1678; Jean-Baptiste du Hamel, first permanent secretary of the Academy of Sciences; and Jacques Chaillou, author of books on the circulation of the blood. At Aix, Locke met Claude Brouchier, professor of chemistry and physician to the archbishop Grimaldi. Brouchier recommended Paul Dubé's *Le Médicin des pauvres* (Paris, 1671), a copy of which Locke then bought. Altogether Locke bought twenty-four medical books in France, seventeen of them published in 1675 or later.

Philosophy, too, was much on Locke's mind. At Montpelier, he bought a copy of Blaise Pascal's posthumously published *Pensées;* he owned two copies of this title, one published at Lyon in 1675, another at Paris in 1678. He also acquired Filleau de la Chaise's *Discours sur les Pensées de Pascal* (Paris, 1672), intended as a preface to Pascal's work until Pascal's family substituted one by Etienne Périer. Remarks in Locke's journals regarding the littleness of people compared to the infinity of the universe and other comments about religious faith echo Pascal's thoughts. In Paris Locke lived with a "Mr. de Launay" from 10 June to 19 October 1677; perhaps this was Gilles de Launay, author of *Introduction à la Philosophie* (Paris, 1675) and *Essais de physique universelle* (1677), both of which Locke bought in France and sent back to England. On 8 August 1677 Locke catalogued in his journal "Cartesii opera omnia," a complete list of the works of René Descartes, whom he had read at Oxford about 1660. He also prepared a bibliography of forty titles relating to Descartes. During his sojourn in France, Locke secured Descartes's complete works and eleven of the forty items he listed in his secondary bibliography. In 1678 Locke hastened to procure the newly published *Abrégé de la philosophie de Gassendi* by François Bernier. Later Locke secured Bernier's *Doutes sur quelques uns des principaux chapitres de l'Abrégé de la philosophie de Gassendi* (Paris, 1681). Of nine titles by Gabriel Naudé that Locke purchased in France, two relate to philosophy: *De Augustino Nipho philosopho judicium* (Paris, 1645) and *Vita Cardani ac de eodem judicio* (Paris, 1663).

Locke's interest in ethics is indicated by his purchase of Jacques Esprit's *La Fausseté des vertus humaines* (Paris, 1678) and Cureau de La Chambre's *Les Caractères des passions* (1640–1662). Pierre Daniel Huet's *Demonstratio evangelica,* published on the eve of Locke's return to England in 1679, accompanied the Englishman when he left France. Huet, like Pascal, argued that human reason alone cannot attain complete possession of the truth. Ignace Gaston Pardies's *Discourse de la connoissance des bestes* (Paris, 1672), which Locke acquired in France, argued, as Locke would later, that animals are capable of reasoning, though not of abstractions or generalizations. While in France he acquired and translated Pierre Nicole's *Essais de morale,* of which he owned at least three copies (Paris, 1671; Paris, 1673; Paris, 1678–1679). Nicole argued that people made themselves unhappy by giving way to self-love and that, as Locke wrote in his journal for 15 August 1676, "experience vouches the weakness of our understanding."

While Locke's French visit probably most profoundly influenced his thinking about philosophy, the trip shaped him in other ways as well. He diligently studied the French language, and from this period dates his interest in French literature. He regularly attended the theater in Paris, and while he did not acquire the works of Jean Racine, he did buy those of Pierre Corneille and Molière. On 13 June 1678 he paid three livres for a copy of Montaigne's *Essais* (Paris, 1669). Other titles he added to his library during this period were Pascal's *Lettres provinciales* (undetermined edition), François VI, duc de la Rochefoucauld's *Maximes*–he owned four copies of this work–and various writings of Jean Louis Guez, Sieur de Balzac, Paul Scarron, and Vincent de Voiture. Locke's final library included at least 669 French titles, comprising about 18 percent of his collection, a high figure for English libraries of the period. Among the twenty classical works that Locke purchased in France were editions of Homer, Terence, Virgil, Sallust, Lucien, Thucydides, Herodotus, and Plutarch.

Other titles that his journals show he was reading during this period include John Lightfoot's *The Harmony of the Four Evangelists*–part 3 (London, 1650) was in Locke's library–Gabriel de Chinon's *Relations nouvelles du Levant* (Lyon, 1671), Gabriel Naudé's *Considérations politiques sur les coups d'estat* (Locke owned the 1667 Paris edition), and the first part of Pietro della Valle's *Viaggi,* of which he owned parts 1–4 (Venice, 1667). Locke probably bought these books in France; in March 1677 he listed 43 titles that he was sending back to England. Before returning to England in 1679 he sent back five cases containing an additional 151 titles.

While in Paris, Locke further visited various book collections, including the royal library. In his journals he noted seeing there a copy of Livy's *Ub urbe condita* in manuscript, the love letters of Henry IV in the king's own handwriting, and a copy of the 1462 Bible on vellum, then thought to be the first produced using movable type. What he found most fascinating, though, were eighteen large folios illustrating plants and six others of birds that he praised in his journal: "so exactly done, that whoever knew any of the plants or birds before, would then know them at first sight; they were done by one Mr. Robert, who is still employed in the same work." These folios were Nicolas Robert's illustrations commissioned by Gaston d'Orléans, brother of Louis XIII. Executed on vellum, they recorded the flora and fauna of the château at Blois. Robert's pictures are now at the Musée national d'histoire naturelle in Paris. Locke's botanical interest led him to purchase Denis Dodart's *Mémoires pour servir à l'histoire des plantes* (Paris, 1676). Later he received a copy of the second edition (1679) from Dodart himself. Other French acquisitions relating to botany were Ferrante Imperate's *Dell'Istoria naturale* (Venice, 1672) and Leonhardt Thurneisser's *Historia, sive descriptio plantarum omnium* (Berlin, 1578).

On 7 October 1677 Locke first mentioned in his journals a meeting with Henri Justel, a leading Parisian intellectual and book collector. Justel probably introduced Locke to many other French scholars and philosophers, including Huet, Charas, and Verney, as well as the physician Adrien Auzout, the author Melchisédec Thévenot, whose *Relations de divers voyages curieux* (Paris, 1663–1672) Locke bought, and Nicolas Thoynard, student of biblical chronology, whose works were on Locke's shelves. After returning to England Locke continued to correspond with some of these French intellectuals, particularly Justel and Thoynard. Often their letters dealt with books. Thus, on 9 February 1681 Locke asked Thoynard's opinion of Cristóbal de Acuña's *Nuevo descrubimento del gran rio de los Amazones* (1641). On 29 July 1682 Thoynard sent Locke the recently published *Geographica* (Paris, 1682) of Michel Anton Baudrand. Thoynard repeatedly notified Locke about forthcoming and recent Continental publications that might interest his English friend, as did Justel and Jean-Baptiste Du Bos, with whom Locke became acquainted through Thoynard; and Locke reciprocated with news about the output of the British presses. Bonno concludes that "in the intellectual biography of Locke, these four years in France represent an active period, interesting and productive." Its effects on his library were palpable and enduring.

When Parliament met at Oxford in 1681 Locke accompanied Cooper and probably spent much of the next two years there. In July 1681 Locke prepared a list of the books that he had at Christ Church. This inventory of 288 titles (305 volumes) does not reflect his complete holdings, since many of his books were in London. The list does, however, reveal Locke's wide-ranging interests and the cataloguing habits that persisted throughout his life. The arrangement was by size, as was typical for the period, but Locke was not content to group his volumes merely as folios, quartos, octavos, and duodecimos–designations that only roughly correspond to height and actually refer to the number of leaves printed on a single sheet: two for folio, four for quarto, eight for octavo, and twelve for duodecimo. Reflecting his delight in scientific precision, Locke measured all but his largest books, the folios, and grouped them by their height in inches. When he assigned shelf marks to his books in the 1690s and early 1700s, he arranged them based on this measurement.

The books listed in the Oxford catalogue reflect Locke's earliest interests. Harrison and Laslett found that about 40 percent relate to medicine as compared to 11 percent in the final listing and about 17 percent deal with science as compared to about 7 percent later. His interests in other subjects grew, as the proportion devoted to theology rose from about 7 percent in 1681 to almost 24 percent later; likewise, politics and law rose from less than 3 percent to more than 10 percent; classics, from 7 to 10 percent; and travel literature, in which Locke found particular delight, from 4 to more than 7 percent. The proportion of works in Latin declined, from 61 to 37 percent, while the proportion of French books increased, from 7 to 18 percent.

By the time Locke drew up his list in 1681 his interests had broadened because of the time he had spent in France and because of political developments in England. In the period 1679–1681 Cooper led the efforts in Parliament to exclude Charles II's brother James Stuart, Duke of York, from the succession to the throne because of James's overt Catholicism, and Locke was writing his *Two Treatises of Government: In the Former, The False Principles and Foundation of Sir Robert Filmer, and His Followers, Are Detected and Overthrown. The Latter Is an Essay Concerning the True Original, Extent, and End of Civil-Government,* which were not published until 1690, after the Glorious Revolution. He also was writing in favor of religious toleration (except for atheists and Catholics), though without attacking the Anglican establishment.

Locke's book purchases in these years are closely related to his writing. In 1680 he bought the fourth edition of William Chillingworth's *The Religion of Protestants* (London, 1674), the second edition of John Godolphin's *Repertorium canonicum: An Abridgement of the Ecclesiastical Laws of This Realm* (London, 1680), and in December the anonymous *Liberty of Conscience in Its Order to Universal Peace* (London: Thomas Parkhurst, 1681). In 1681

Locke read William Cave's *Primitive Christianity* (London, 1675), which he drew on that year in drafting a response to *Unreasonableness of Separation* (London, 1681), the attack on dissenters by Edward Stillingfleet, bishop of Worcester. He read Stillingfleet's *Defence of the Discourse Concerning the Idolatry Practiced in the Church of Rome* (London, 1676), one of seventeen works he owned by Stillingfleet, including two attacks on Locke's *An Essay Concerning Human Understanding* (1690). He also read *Naked Truth* (London, 1675), by Herbert Croft, bishop of Hereford, which he cited in his writings of the 1690s. In 1682 Locke purchased a copy of John Wilkins's *Of the Duties & Principles of Natural Religion* (London, 1675), and he recommended to Cooper the Anglican George Lawson's *Politica sacra & civilis* (London, 1660), the first part of which Locke owned.

Locke owned seven books by Samuel von Pufendorf. In June 1681 Locke was reading Pufendorf's *De jure naturae et gentium* (1672), which he had bought in France in the 1670s. Locke later gave this copy to his cousin Peter King and acquired a 1698 edition published in Amsterdam. According to John Marshall in *John Locke: Resistance, Religion and Responsibility* (1994), Pufendorf's arguments influenced the second treatise of Locke's *Two Treatises of Government:*

> Locke's reading of Pufendorf in mid-1681 and 1682 very probably provided him with some significant elements of the form of his argument on the state of nature as co-operative, and of the reasons for establishing political society because that state was also insecure, that Locke used in the Second Treatise, and it may have provided him with some elements of his theory of property.

At the same time that Locke was reading Pufendorf, he was reading Thomas Hooker's *Laws of Ecclesiastical Polity*. Locke owned three editions of this work (1632, 1666, 1676), all published in London. Hooker argued that many matters of ritual had not been divinely specified and so might be regulated by the ruler. In two drafts written in the early 1660s, one in English and the other in Latin, later published in *Two Tracts on Government* (1967), Locke argued as Hooker did, but he took a different approach in a 1667 manuscript titled "Essay on Toleration" and opposed such regulation. The first of Locke's two treatises on government is a response to the doctrines most popularly expressed by Sir Robert Filmer's *Patriarcha* (London, 1680), a copy of which appears in Locke's catalogue of books. Locke helped James Tyrrell write a response to Filmer, *Patriarcha non monarcha* (London, 1681). Locke owned two copies of this title, one of them extensively annotated by Tyrrell.

On 15 September 1682 Locke accompanied Cooper to a meeting of the Protestant conspirators involved in the plot to place the Protestant James Scott, Duke of Monmouth, on the throne. After the plot failed Cooper fled to Holland, where he died the next year. Locke was implicated in the 1683 Rye House plot to kidnap Charles II, and later that year Locke also fled to Holland. By this time, according to Harrison and Laslett, his library probably totaled a thousand volumes. Most of Locke's books–about seven hundred–were entrusted to Tyrrell and were kept at Oakley, Buckinghamshire; the rest remained in the London lodgings he rented from Mrs. Rabsby Smithsby. In November 1684, Locke was expelled from his Oxford fellowship by royal decree. During his residency in Holland he earned no money and so relied on his patrimony, his annuity from Cooper, and income from investments to finance his extensive book purchases.

In the years from 1684 to 1690 Locke acquired some seven hundred works. His correspondence indicates that one of his chief sources of books in the Netherlands was the Amsterdam bookseller Hendrik Wetstein. On 10 March 1687 Wetstein wrote to Locke to ask if he would like to purchase the mystic Pierre Poiret's *L'Oeconomie divine,* a work Wetstein had recently published. Locke apparently did not, but he did buy the *Acta eruditorum* for 1686, an important learned journal published at Leipzig. On 20 June 1688 Wetstein sent the *Acta eruditorum* for 1687 bound in calf and offered Locke a 1657 (Leipzig) Hebrew Old Testament, Greek New Testament, and Latin translation, which Locke purchased. This version was adapted from the Polyglot Bible edited by Benito Arias Montano and published by Christopher Plantin at Antwerp (1569–1573).

On 28 February 1687 Locke wrote to the scholar Johann Georg Graevius, sending him a copy of Alexander Trallianus's medical works in Greek, edited and published by Robert Estienne in 1548. Locke owned a copy in Latin published by Henri Estienne in 1567. Bound with Trallianus's writing was a book by the medieval Arab physician Rhazes on plague. In return, Locke asked for a copy of Seutonius edited by Graevius and published in Utrecht in 1672. Graevius sent a copy to Wetstein for Locke, including a bill. Wetstein offered to have the book bound if Locke wished. Locke bought the book, which he later gave to Edward Clarke when he secured a copy of the second edition (Utrecht, 1691).

Even after returning to England Locke continued to buy from Wetstein. On 23 January 1691 Wetstein wrote that he had left at the Black Boy Tavern on Lombard Street a copy of the ancient Greek philosopher Cebes's *Tabula Graece et Latine multis in locis restituta* edited by Jakob Gronovius and published at Amsterdam by Wetstein in 1689. With this letter Wetstein sent a bill for works that Locke had bought in 1689, including the *Acta eruditorum* for 1688, Bernard Le Bovier de Fon-

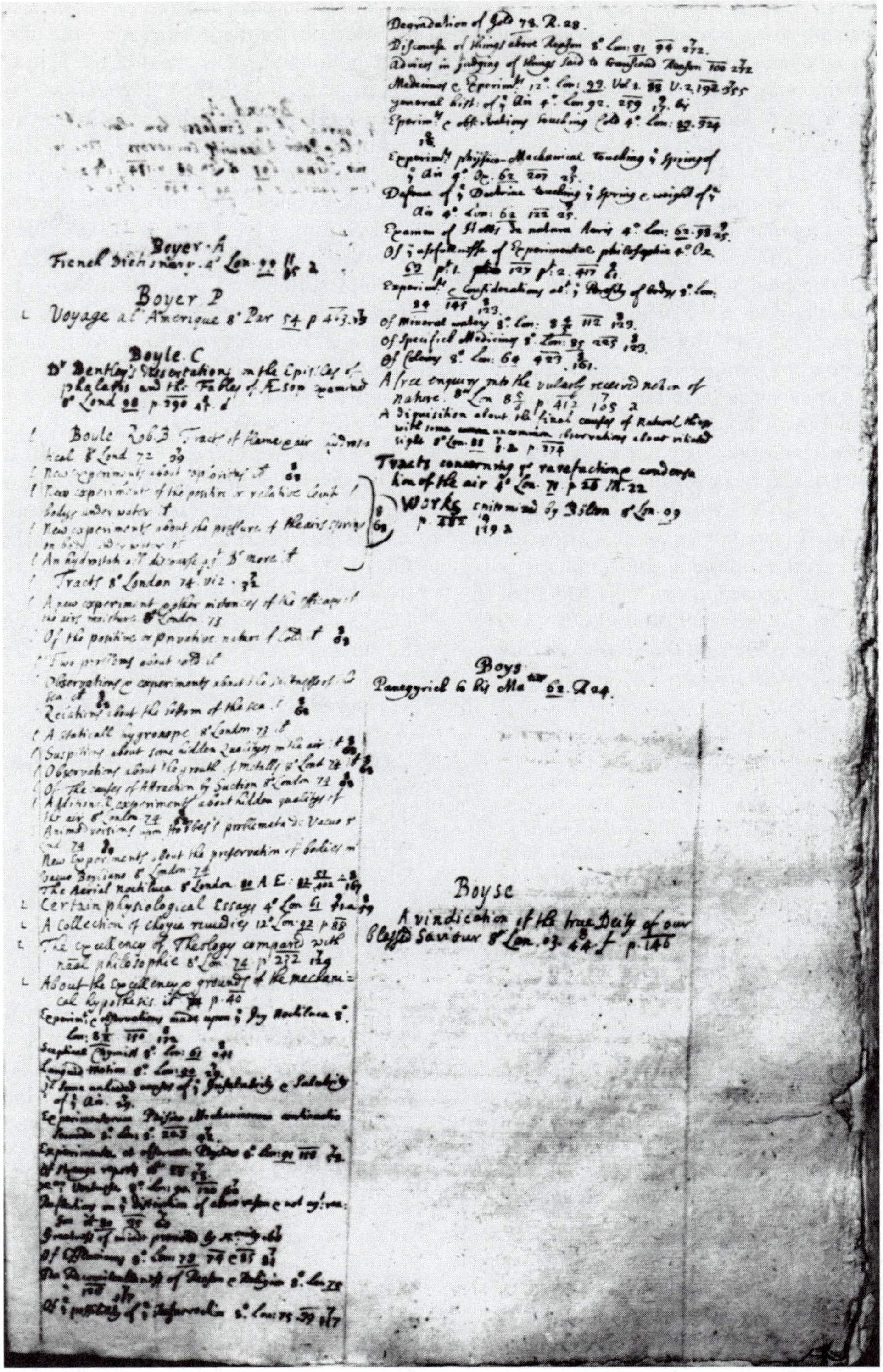

Pages from Locke's interleaved copy of Thomas Hyde's 1674 catalogue of the Bodleian Library. Locke put the initial L *next to the printed descriptions of items he owned, and on the facing blank pages he or his amanuensis wrote comments on works in his library, including many books not listed in the printed catalogue (Bodleian Library, Oxford).*

104 CATALOGUS IMPRESSORUM LIBRORUM

BOY

Prima Religionis Christianæ Rudimenta, antiquissimâ Saxonum & Alemannorum linguâ, cum Versione Latinâ. *Lug. Bat.* 1650. 8° B. 9. *Th. BS.*

Jacques BOYCEAU.

Traité du Jardinage, en 3 livres. *Par.* 1638. U. 1. 10. *Med.*

BOYCH. v. *Bohic.*

Rice BOYE. v. Edw. *Norrice.*

Philbert BOYER.

Le Stile de la Cour de Parlement, & forme de proceder en toutes les Cours Souveraines du Royaume de France. *Par.* 1602. 8° B. 15. *Jur. Seld.*

Le Stile de la Cour & Justice des Requestes du Palais, & Pratique universelle, en 4 livres. *Par.* 1601. 8° B. 16. *Jur. Seld.*

Honoratiss. Dñs Rob. BOYLEUS.

De Stylo S. Scripturæ. *Oxon.* 1665. 8° B. 18. *Art. BS.*

Seraphick Love, or Motives and Incentives to the Love of God. *Lond.* 1659. 8° B. 14. *Th. BS.*

The Origine of Formes and Qualities. *Oxon.* 1667. 8° H. 91. *Art.*

The History of Cold. *Lond.* 1665. 8° B. 16. *Art. BS.*

New Experiments touching the Spring of the Aire. *Oxon.* 1660. 8° B. 7. *Art. BS.*

A Continuation of New Experiments touching the Spring and Weight of the Aire; the first part: also a Discourse concerning the Atmospheres of Consistent Bodies. *Oxon.* 1669. 4° B. 12. *Art. BS.*

Hydrostatical Paradoxes made out by New Experiments. *Oxon.* 1666. 8° B. 17. *Art. BS.*

Discovery of the Admirable rarefaction of the Aire. *Lond.* 1671. 4° B. 58. *Art.*

New Observations about the Duration of the Spring of the Aire. *Ibid.*

New Experiments conc. the Condensation of the Aire by meer Cold, and its compression without Mechanical Engins. *Ibid.*

The Differing extension of the same quantity of Aire rarified and compressed. *Ibid.*

Several Tracts, *viz.* Cosmical Qualities, Cosmical Suspicions, of Subterraneal Regions, of Submarine Regions, and of the bottom of the Sea. *Oxon.* 1671. 8° A. 118. *Art.*

John BOYS, Theologus Anglus.

His Works. *Lond.* 1629. B. 3. 16. *Th.*

His Remaines, *viz.* Certain Sermons of his. *Lond.* 1631. 4° B. 46. *Th.*

Third part of his Postills from John Baptist's Nativity to the last Holy-day in the year. *Lond.* 1615. 4° P. 60. *Th.*

Exposition of the last Psalme. *Ibid.*

Exposition upon the Festival Epistles and Gospels in the English Liturgy. *Lond.* 1614. 4° W. 35. *Th.*

Joh. du BOYS, Pharmacopæus Parisiensis.

Observationes in Methodum miscendorum Medicamentorum Topicorum, quæ in quotidiano sunt usu; & Dilucidationes diversorum Simplicium. *Lond.* 1639. W. 1. 9. *Med.*

Jean du BOYS, Olivier, Parisiensis.

Le Portraict de Henry le Grand. *Par.* 1610. 8° D. 3. *Th. BS.*

Aux Bons François. *Ibid.*

Matthæus BOYS. v. Joh. à *Ripâ.*

Notæ ad Jacobi de San-Georgio librum de Homagiis, Operis, & Servitiis. *Franc.* 1606. 8° I. 4. *Jur.*

Monsieur de BOYS-ROBERT.

The Indian History of Anaxander and Orazia, into English by W. G. *Lond.* 1657. 8° G. 13. *Art. Seld.*

BRA

P. BOYSSAT.

Histoire des Chevaliers de l'Ordre de l'Hospital de S. Jean de Hierusalem, *vol.* 1. *Lyon* 1612. A. 2. 19. *Art. Seld.*

François de BOYVIN.

Memoires sur les Guerres en Piedmont, & Montferrat, &c. en 10 livres. *Par.* 1606. K. 4. 7. *Art.*

Jean BOYVIN.

Le Siege de la Ville de Dole. *Anvers* 1638. 4° A. 48. *Art.*

Relation du Siege & Prise de Breme. *Ibid.*

Corñ. BOYUS. v. Jac. *Catsius.*

Paolo BOZI.

Thebaïde Sacra. *Ven.* 1621. 4° B. 74. *Th.*

Thomas BOZIUS, Eugubinus.

De Signis Ecclesiæ Dei, libri 24, 2 tomis. *Rom.* 1591. B. 7. 1. *Th.*

De Ruinis Gentium & Regnorum, contra Politicos. *Col. Agr.* 1598. 8° B. 23. *Th.* Et *Rom.* 1596. 4° B. 50. *Art. Seld.*

De Jure Divino & Naturali Ecclesiasticæ Libertatis & Potestatis. *Col. Agr.* 1600. 8° B. 46. *Th.*

De Italiæ statu antiquo & novo, libri 4, contra Machiavellum. *Col. Agr.* 1595. 8° B. 39. *Art.*

De Imperio Virtutis, libri 2, contra Machiavellum. *Col. Agr.* 1594. 8° B. 81. *Art.*

De Robore Bellico, diuturnis ac amplis Catholicorum Regnis, contra Machiavellum. *Ibid.*

Franc. BOZZIUS, Eugubinus.

De Temporali Ecclesiæ Monarchiâ & Jurisdictione, libri 5, contra Politicos & Hæreticos. *Col. Agr.* 1602. 8° B. 45. *Th.*

Henr. à BRA.

De curandis Venenis per Medicamenta Simplicia & facilè parabilia, 2 lib. *Arnhemii* 1603. 8° B. 8. *Med.*

Medicamenta Simplicia & facilè parabilia, contra Calculum. *Franck.* 1591. 8° L. 12. *Med.*

Catalogus Medicamentorum contra Epilepsiam. *Arnhemii* 1605. 8° S. 20. *Med.*

BRABANTIA. v. *Barlandus.*

Theoph. BRABOURN. {v. Fr. *White.* v. John *Collings.*}

Defense of the Sabbath day, &c. —— 1632. 4° B. 2. *Th. Seld.*

Discourse of the Sabbath, *viz.* that it is not abolished, and that the Lords Day is not the Sabbath Day by Divine Institution. —— 1628. 8° B. 254. *Th.*

Joh. Andreas BRACCHUS.

Comm. in Epistolam Jacobi. *Parmæ* 1605. W. 3. 9. *Th.*

Jac. BRACELLUS, seu *Bracelius.*

De Bello Hispano, libri 5. *Haganoæ* 1530. C. 4. 5. *Art.*

Liguriæ descriptio. p. 638. *Franc.* 1600. I. 2. 1. *Art.*

De Claris Genuensibus. p. 641. *Ibid.*

Joh. BRACESCHUS. v. *Tauladanus.*

Dialogus dictus *Lignum Vitæ*, in quo etiam Geberi Philosophi expositio continetur. *Bas.* 1561. M. 5. 9. *Art.*

H. Dr. BRACHELIUS. v. *Driverus.*

Theophile BRACHET, seu *Brachetus*, Milleterius. {v. Pet. *Mulinæus.* v. A. *Rivetus.*}

Le Moyen de la Paix Chrestienne, en la Reunion des Catholiques & des Evangeliques. [quatuor partium prima, de Justificatione contra M. Daillé.] *Par.* 1635. 8° B. 264. *Th.*

tenelle's *Nouveaux dialogues des morts* (Amsterdam, 1687), and his *Entretiens sur la pluralité des mondes* (Paris, 1686). A bill from early 1695 records the sale to Locke of an edition of Cicero published at Amsterdam in 1691 and edited by Graevius, *Acta eruditorum* for 1690–1694, a decennial index of the periodical (1693), and the 1692 supplement.

Bonno's research shows that just as Locke's sojourn in France resulted in his meeting various French intellectuals, so in the 1680s Locke met various Dutch scholars, whose works became part of his collection. Pieter Guenellon, whom Locke had met in France, introduced him to Philip Limborch, a professor of theology at Amsterdam. Locke's 1695 Amsterdam edition of Limborch's *Theologia Christiana* bears the inscription "John Locke ex Dono Doctissimi et Amicissimi Authoris" (John Locke, a gift from the most learned and most dear friend the author). During the winter of 1685–1686 Limborch introduced Locke to Jean Le Clerc, and some of Locke's books by Le Clerc similarly note that they were given to him by the author. Le Clerc edited the *Bibliothèque universelle et historique* (Amsterdam), of which Locke owned a run from 1686 to 1693. In July 1686 this periodical carried the first printing of Locke's "Méthode nouvelle de dresser des recueils," which was first published in English in 1697 as *A New Method of Making Common-Place Books* (London, 1706); the January 1688 number included the first printing of part of Locke's *An Essay concerning Humane Understanding. In Four Books.* Such journals included notices and reviews of books and thus served as buying guides for Locke.

From 1687 to 1689 Locke lived in Rotterdam with the English Quaker merchant Benjamin Furly, whose library was larger than Locke's and on whose shelves Locke found titles that he then secured for himself. During this period Locke was writing to his friend Edward Clarke about the education of Clarke's son. These letters served as the basis of Locke's *Some Thoughts concerning Education* (1693), thoughts shaped in part by books Locke was reading and buying in the Netherlands. Among these were François de Salignac de la Mothe Fénelon's *Traité de l'education des filles* (Paris, 1687) and Claude Fluery's *Traité du choix et de la méthode des études* (Paris, 1686). In the pages of the *Nouvelles de la république des lettres,* edited by François Bayle, Locke followed the debates between Antoine Arnauld and Nicolas Malebranche regarding the senses, happiness, and knowledge, and he bought books by both men as well as Bayle's journal. Malebranche's *Recherche de la verité* was particularly influential on Locke's thinking, and he owned copies of the third edition (Paris, 1677–1678) as well as the fourth edition (Paris, 1678–1679).

Locke returned to England on 12 February 1689, bringing with him most of his Dutch purchases in thirteen boxes, though he left sixty-eight titles behind, either as gifts or to be sent along later by booksellers. In May 1689 he was named a commissioner of appeals at a salary of £200 per annum, and from May 1696 to July 1700 he was a member of the Council for Trade and Plantations, a post carrying with it the generous salary of £1,000 a year. Between 1689 and 1691 Locke added about two hundred books to his library, and between 1691 and 1704 this figure grew to a total between 3,000 and 3,500 volumes.

Early in 1691 Locke settled himself and his books at Oates, in the parish of High Laver, Essex, some twenty miles away from London and the city smoke that he found bothersome. The house belonged to Sir Francis Masham. Locke had met Masham's future second wife, Damaris Cudworth, in 1682 and had fallen in love with her; but while Locke was in exile she had married Masham. Locke rented two rooms where he organized most of his books in them, though about 150 remained at his London lodgings in Little Lincoln's Inn Fields, where he spent part of each summer.

To keep track of his acquisitions Locke in 1685 or 1686 bought a copy of Thomas Hyde's *Catalogus Impressorum Librorum Bibliothecae Bodlejanae in Academia Oxoniensi* (Oxford, 1674), a list of the books at the Bodleian Library. Many collectors used Hyde's work as a buying guide, but Locke had the two volumes rebound with blank leaves so that they could serve as a master catalogue for his own collection. He marked those titles he owned with an *l* or *L.* On the blank pages he wrote comments about the books he owned, including what he paid for them; and he noted down those titles that he owned that were not in Hyde's listing. The Bodleian Library at this period did not have large holdings of economics and belles lettres, nor did it contain a large number of Continental imprints. In these areas Locke's library was more comprehensive. Also, the catalogue was already a decade old when Locke acquired it and therefore he could not list recent imprints; so the printed pages contain relatively few markings. For example, Hyde lists twelve titles by Robert Boyle. Seven of these are marked with an *L,* but Locke owned fifty other titles not noted in the printed catalogue.

In this final listing of Locke's holdings, theological works predominate, with 870 titles, including thirty-one Bibles. These works indicated not only his concern for religious toleration but also his interest in the "Unitarian Controversy" that raged in England between 1687 and the beginning of the eighteenth century, in which the Trinitarians maintaining the divinity of Christ were opposed by the Unitarians, who denied it. Locke never took a clear stand on the matter, but his insistence on the compatibility of Christianity and reason and his view that Scripture presented Jesus as the

Messiah but not necessarily divine, were compatible with Unitarian doctrines. The controversy began with the publication of Stephen Nye's *Brief History of the Unitarians* (London, 1687), in which he defends the Unitarian position and discusses the biblical position which this belief rests. Locke owned a copy of this work and in 1689 sent another to Jean Le Clerc in Holland. Locke followed the controversy closely. He owned six titles by Arthur Bury, including his *Naked Gospel* (London, 1690), in which Bury condemned the Trinitarian doctrine of the equality of Christ with God the Father. Bury showed "how the primitive chastity of the gospel was defil'd with the . . . vain philosophy of the pagans; how Platonic enthusiasm was imposed upon the world of faith." This book, too, Locke sent to Le Clerc. Locke also sent Unitarian texts to Benjamin Furly. Though both Le Clerc and Furly were Trinitarians, Newton and King were not; Locke owned a copy of King's *An Enquiry into the Constitution, Discipline Unity and Worship of the Primitive Church* (London, 1691), which argued the Arian position. By 1704 Locke owned nine books by Nye, eight by Faustus Socinus; who developed the anti-Trinitarian doctrine of Socinianism; nine by John Crell, Socinus's major disciple; and two by John Volkel, Socinus's secretary. Locke's collection included Volkel's *De vera religione* (ca. 1642), a compendium of Socinus's thought, and *Bibliotheca Fratrum Polonorum* (Amsterdam, 1656), a nine-volume collection of major Unitarian texts.

At the same time Locke was acquiring important defenses of the Trinitarian view. John Tillotson gave him a copy of his moderate *Sermons of the Divinity and Incarnation of Our Savior* (London, 1693), and he owned Stillingfleet's more strenuous defense of orthodoxy. He possessed three works by John Williams, one of these a defense of Tillotson, nine titles by Edward Fowler, and a large collection of sermons and tracts by Bishop Gilbert Burnet. In 1694 Locke began a notebook that he labeled "Adversaria Theologica." He divided the pages into two columns and listed arguments for and against Christ's divinity. Stillingfleet, for one, suspected that Locke deviated from orthodox Anglicanism.

In the field of politics and law Locke owned 390 titles, nearly 11 percent of his total library. He owned more than a dozen works by Hugo Grotius and took extensive notes on Grotius's works. Niccolo Machiavelli is well represented in Italian and English. He owned two copies of Sir Thomas More's *Utopia* (Amsterdam, 1631, and Oxford, 1663), and late in life he secured copies of Algernon Sidney's *Discourses Concerning Government* (London, 1698) and James Harrington's *Works* (London, 1700). The leading political thinker of the seventeenth century was Thomas Hobbes. Locke had a copy of the first edition of the *Leviathan* (London, 1651). Robert Sanderson, John Selden, John Sadler, and John Milton were also influential political writers whose works appeared on Locke's shelves.

Nearly equaling his holdings in politics, Locke owned 366 works of classical literature. Although he was a Greek tutor, the majority of these works were in Latin, and the Greek texts are accompanied by Latin translations or glosses. Here were Homer and Hesiod, Xenophon, Herodotus, Thucydides, Theophrastus, and Demosthenes. Among the Romans Cicero was particularly well represented, with twenty-nine works. Plautus, Terence, Tacitus, Sallust, Catullus, Pliny, Ovid, Juvenal, Martial, Petronius, Quintillian, and Virgil were also present. Overall, the 1,326 Latin works, or about 37 percent of the library, nearly equaled those in English, which numbered 1,426, or about 39 percent. Locke's library was unusual in these proportions, however, for in the libraries of most seventeenth-century academics, Latin works predominated.

Locke's holdings in English literature were respectable if not extensive. John Dryden, the leading writer of the late seventeenth century, is not represented in the collection, nor did Locke possess some of the other British poets widely read and owned at the time, such as Geoffrey Chaucer and Edmund Waller. He owned only one work by Andrew Marvell, *The Rehearsal Transpos'd,* though he had copies of the first and second editions, both published in London in 1672, as well as a copy of the second part (London, 1673). He also owned only one work by Abraham Cowley, *The Cutter of Coleman Street* (London, 1663). Still, Locke owned not only Milton's *Pro populo adversus tyrannos* (London, 1689) and the poet's collected historical, political, and other prose works (Amsterdam, 1698) but also a first edition of *Paradise Lost,* secured at the 15 May 1682 sale of Dr. Richard Smith's library, one of the finest collections of the period. The title page of Locke's *Paradise Lost* bears the date 1669.

Locke's library contained the first collected edition of the plays of Francis Beaumont and John Fletcher (London, 1647), an early quarto of Shakespeare's *Henry IV* (London, 1632), and John Donne's poems (London, 1654). John Cleveland, much enjoyed in his day, is listed in Locke's catalogue in an unidentified edition. Also listed were Sir John Suckling's first edition of *Fragmenta aurea* (London, 1646), the second edition of William Congreve's *Mourning Bride* (London, 1697), six plays by James Shirley, two copies of the first collection of Ben Jonson's plays (London, 1616), and William Davenant's *Siege of Rhodes* (London, 1656). Locke's library thus indicates that he was keenly interested in drama in particular and belles lettres in general. As Richard Ashcraft, who examined more than eighty auction catalogues from the period 1676–1723, concludes,

"Locke's literary holdings are certainly not seriously deficient by comparative standards."

History and biography made up 187 titles, or about 5 percent, of Locke's library. In his posthumously published "Some Thoughts Concerning Reading and Study for a Gentleman" Locke singled out history as a means of learning the art of government and observed, "In Mr. Tyrrel[l]'s History of England, he will find all along those several authors which have treated of our affairs, and which he may have recourse to, concerning any point, which either his curiosity or judgment shall lead him to inquire into." Locke's library held Tyrrell's *General History of England* (London, 1699–1700). Locke recommended Sir Walter Ralegh and owned a copy of the first edition of his *History of the World* (London, 1614). Other historical titles present in Locke's collection included John Rushworth's *Historical Collections* (London, 1659) and François VI, duc de la Rochefoucauld's *Memoires* (two copies, both published at Cologne, in 1662 and 1664, respectively). French history was well represented, particularly those works written from a Protestant perspective.

Judging from his journals, among Locke's favorite reading were books of travel. Harrison and Laslett found that such works comprised 275 titles, or nearly 8 percent, of his collection. While many of these works related to his official positions with the Board of Trade and to his concern with political institutions and economic systems, he seems to have indulged in them for pleasure, too. Helen Campbell Hughes notes that the late seventeenth century witnessed a proliferation of travel works, and Locke appears eager to have surveyed mankind from China to Peru. He owned many classics of the genre, including two copies of Richard Hakluyt's three-volume set *Principal Navigations* (London, 1599–1600), Sir Francis Drake's *The World Encompassed* (London, 1635), Samuel Purchas's *Pilgrimes* (London, 1625) and *Pilgrimage* (London, 1626), and two editions of *Novus Orbis, id est, navigationes primae in Americam,* (Basle, 1532, and Rotterdam, 1616), which brought together early accounts of New World exploration, including those of Christopher Columbus.

Locke owned books dealing with the remoter portions of the British Isles, such as James Wallace's description of the Orkneys (two editions, 1693 and 1700), Martin Martin's account of St. Kilda and the Hebrides, and William Sacheverell's book on the Isle of Man (London, 1702). He also possessed volumes dealing with the various countries of Europe, the Levant, the Far East, and the Orient. George Psalmanazar's fabricated *Historical and Geographical Description of Formosa* (London, 1704), later revealed to be one of the great hoaxes of the eighteenth century but taken at the time of its publication as factual, must have been among his last purchases. In France he read and probably bought Garcilasso de la Vega's *La commentaire royal, ou l'histoire des Yncas du Peru* (Paris, 1633) as well as François Bernier's writings about India and China. In 1704 the London bookseller Awnsham Churchill published *A Collection of Voyages and Travels* in four folio volumes. The third edition (1744–1746) credited to Locke the preliminary essay on the history of navigation, and the 1812 edition of Locke's works accepted that attribution. Even if Locke did not compose the essay, he certainly corresponded with Churchill about the set, helped him assemble the books, and may have edited the text. The idea of the publication may have been Locke's.

In the last years of Locke's life, Churchill was a close friend and his chief supplier of new books. Churchill arranged to have Locke's books rebound, since in this period most texts appeared in temporary bindings not intended to be permanent; he also sent books as gifts at Locke's request and acted as Locke's banker, stockbroker, and postman. Locke's correspondence is filled with lists of volumes that Churchill sent to him. For example, on 24 December 1703 he supplied Samuel Clarke's *A Paraphrase on the Gospel of St. John* (London, 1703) for 3s. Locke owned Clarke's paraphrases of all four Gospels, acquired probably in conjunction with Locke's own project of paraphrasing Paul's epistles, published posthumously as *A Paraphrase and Notes on the Epistles of St. Paul to the Galatians, I & II Corinthians, Romans, and Ephesians. To Which Is Prefix'd 'An Essay for the Understanding of St. Paul's Epistles, by Consulting St. Paul Himself'* (1705–1707). John Moore, bishop of Norwich, gave Locke a copy of Clarke's *Paraphrase on St. Matthew* (London, 1701); the others Locke apparently bought. Together with the Clarke, Churchill sent a Bible for 7s.; Johannes Lewsden's *Compendium graecum novi testamenti . . . cum versione latina* (1703) for 2s. 6d.; another Greek and Latin New Testament at 6s.; three copies of *A Short History of the Revolutions that Have Befallen the Principality of Orange in the Reign of Louis XIV* (1704), published by Churchill, for 6 d. each; several almanacs; and copies of Queen Anne's recent addresses to Parliament. This same shipment contained the first sheet of a new edition of Boyle's *General History of the Air.* Locke, who had edited the 1692 edition, had declined to undertake the task again, but Churchill continued to send him proof sheets and to ask for his suggestions.

Locke's concern for his books is evident not only in his careful cataloguing but also in his provision for them in his will. On 4 April 1704 he stipulated that Dame Damaris Masham receive "any four folios, eight quartos and twenty books of less volume, which she shall choose out of the books in my Library." To his "good friend Mr. Anthony Collins of the Middle Temple" Locke bequeathed his "*Plautus* in folio in Lambin's edition" (Paris, 1577); *Bibliotheca instituta et collecta primum a C. Gesnero* (Tiguri, 1583), Conrad Gesner's attempt at a complete listing of books in Latin, Greek, and Hebrew; *Kerckringii Spicilegium anatomicum* (Amsterdam, 1670); *Catalogus librorum Bibliothecae Raphaelis Trichett du Fresne* (Paris, 1662), a bibliography of the collection of Raphaël Trichet du Fresne; *Bibliotheca Thuana* (Paris, 1679), a bibliography of the library of Jacques Auguste de Thou; *Bibliotheca Heinsiana* (Leyden, 1682), a bibliography of the library of Daniel Heinsius; and "*Wisten's Map of Tartary* that hangs up in my Study."

To his "cosen Peter King of the Inner Temple" Locke left *Harmonia Evangeliorum Toinardi,* an effort by Nicolas Thoynard to reconcile the Gospels that was not published until 1707 but printed much earlier. Thoynard gave a copy of the printed sheets to Locke, who had the book interleaved and bound. He also gave King his five-volume set of *Poli Synopsis Criticorum* (London, 1669–1676), by Matthaeus Polus; *Les memoires de Monsieur Deagent* (Grenoble, 1668); *Marci Antonii de Dominis Espistola de pace Religionis ad Josephum Hallum* (1666), a letter from Marco Antonio de Dominis to Joseph Hall relating to religious peace; and many other manuscripts and books. He also bequeathed half of his books to Francis Cudworth Masham "when he shall attain to the age of one and twenty years."

After Locke's death on 28 October 1704, Sir Peter King took about 1,800 volumes to London and then to Ockham, Surrey. In the nineteenth century William King, the first Earl of Lovelace, moved them to Horsley Towers in East Horsley. In the 1840s some of these books were sold, and Peter the seventh Lord King and, Lionel Fortescue, third Earl of Lovelace, rebound some of the books, occasionally thereby removing evidence of Locke's ownership. Nonetheless, much of the King legacy remained together, and 835 of the books left to King were found at Ben Damph Forest, one of the seats of the earls of Lovelace, in December 1951. These were acquired by Paul Mellon, who gave them to the Bodleian Library.

The Masham moiety became widely dispersed. In 1762 Samuel Masham, the second Lord Masham, grandson of Sir Francis Masham, sold off many of Locke's volumes to Robert Davis, a London bookseller, to make room for what he regarded as more entertaining books. Davis took the books with him to Barnes, from which in 1777 Edmund Law, bishop of Carlisle, rescued the manuscripts and later sold them to the British Museum. Robert Palmer of Bloomsbury was Samuel Masham's chief creditor; Palmer's bookplate in some of Locke's books indicates that he prized the volumes and took them to his seat at Holme Park. Henry Richard Fox Bourne, who published a biography of Locke in 1876, and A. C. Fraser, who edited an 1894 edition of Locke's *An Essay Concerning Human Understanding,* used Locke's books there.

In 1880 the Reverend Henry Golding, who added Palmer to his name, inherited Holme Park. He soon began dispersing Locke's books. From 29 through 31 May 1883 Hodgson's sold "Miscellaneous books, including the library of a clergyman. Many of the books were formerly in the possession of John Locke, the philosopher, and contain his autograph." Included here was Locke's copy of *An Essay Concerning Human Understanding* that he had given to Damaris Masham. In December 1894 Golding Palmer gave Locke's copies of Newton's *Principia* and *Opticks* to Trinity College, Cambridge, Golding Palmer's alma mater. When Golding Palmer died about 1898, his widow moved to Kensington and sold some of the books at Holme Park. In 1916 the contents of the Kensington house were sold by A. and C. Barber and Company of Windsor, thus completing the scattering of the Masham portion of Locke's books.

From the books that survive, from Locke's catalogues, journals, and letters, one may recognize that in religion, politics, philosophy, and science Locke sought out the newest thinking. As Ashcraft asserts, for Locke "books were useful instruments of knowledge, never objects of aesthetic value." Nevertheless, Locke built and arranged for the preservation of an important library.

Letters:

The Correspondence of John Locke, 8 volumes, edited by E. S. de Beer, the Clarendon Edition of the Works of John Locke (Oxford: Clarendon Press, 1976–1989).

Bibliographies:

H. O. Christophersen, *A Bibliographical Introduction to the Study of John Locke* (Oslo: I Kommisjon Hos Jacob Dybwad, 1930);

Roland Hall, *80 Years of Locke Scholarship: A Bibliographical Guide* (Edinburgh: Edinburgh University Press, 1983);

John Charles Attig, *The Works of John Locke: A Comprehensive Bibliography from the Seventeenth Century to the Present* (Westport, Conn.: Greenwood Press, 1985);

Jean S. Yolton and John W. Yolton, *John Locke: A Reference Guide* (Boston: G. K. Hall, 1985).

Biographies:

Peter, Seventh Baron King, *The Life of John Locke, with Extracts from His Correspondence, Journals, and Common-Place Books* (London: Henry Colburn, 1829);

Henry Richard Fox Bourne, *The Life of John Locke,* 2 volumes (New York: Harper; London: H. S. Knight, 1876);

Maurice Cranston, *John Locke: A Biography* (New York: Macmillan, 1957; London: Longmans, Green, 1957);

Kenneth Dewhurst, *John Locke. Physician and Philosopher. A Medical Biography* (London: Wellcome Historical Medical Library, 1963).

References:

Richard I. Aaron, *John Locke* (Oxford: Clarendon Press, 1937; third edition, 1971);

Peter Alexander, *Ideas, Qualities, and Corpuscles. Locke and Boyle on the External World* (Cambridge: Cambridge University Press, 1985);

Richard Ashcraft, "John Locke's Library: Portrait of an Intellectual," *Transactions of the Cambridge Bibliographical Society,* 5 (1969): 47–60;

Ashcraft, *Revolutionary Politics and Locke's "Two Treatises of Government"* (Princeton: Princeton University Press, 1986);

Gabriel Bonno, *Les relations intellectuelles de Locke avec la France* (Berkeley & Los Angeles: University of California Press, 1955);

Vere Chappell, ed., *The Cambridge Companion to Locke* (Cambridge: Cambridge University Press, 1994);

John Dunn, *The Political Thought of John Locke* (Cambridge: Cambridge University Press, 1969);

James Gibson, *Locke's Theory of Knowledge and Its Historical Relations* (Cambridge: Cambridge University Press, 1917);

John Harrison and Peter Laslett, *The Library of John Locke* (Oxford: Oxford University Press, 1965; second edition, 1971);

Helen Campbell Hughes, "John Locke's Library," *The Book-Collector's Quarterly,* 12 (October 1933): 32–40;

Sterling P. Lambrecht, *The Moral and Political Philosophy of John Locke* (New York: Columbia University Press, 1918);

John Lough, "Locke's Reading during His Stay in France (1675–1679)," *Library,* fifth series, 8 (December 1953): 229–258;

Kenneth MacLean, *John Locke and English Literature of the Eighteenth Century* (New Haven: Yale University Press; London: Oxford University Press, 1936);

John Marshall, *John Locke: Resistance, Religion and Responsibility* (Cambridge: Cambridge University Press, 1994);

William M. Spellman, *John Locke and the Problem of Depravity* (Oxford: Clarendon Press, 1988);

James Tully, *A Discourse on Property: John Locke and His Adversaries* (Cambridge: Cambridge University Press, 1980);

John W. Yolton, *John Locke and the Compass of Human Understanding* (Cambridge: Cambridge University Press, 1970);

Yolton, *John Locke and the Way of Ideas* (Oxford: Clarendon Press, 1956).

Papers:

The major collection of John Locke's papers, including most of his manuscripts, is held by the Bodleian Library at Oxford University. Some papers are held by the British Library.

Narcissus Marsh

(20 December 1638 - 2 November 1713)

Muriel McCarthy
Marsh's Library

CATALOGUE: Newport J. D. White, *An Account of Archbishop Marsh's Library, Dublin . . . With a Note on Autographs, by Newport B. White* (Dublin: Hodges, Figgis, 1926).

BOOKS: *The Charge Given . . . July 27, 1692* (Dublin: Printed by Joseph Ray, 1694);

Charge to His Clergy at His Primary Visitation June 27 1694 with His Articles of Visitation, Etc. (Dublin: Printed by Joseph Ray, 1694);

The Charge Given by . . . to the Clergy . . . of Leinster (Dublin: Printed by Joseph Ray, 1694);

Narcissus Marsh's Lyra Viol Book, edited by Leslie Hewitt, Musical Sources, no. 10 (Kilkenny: Boethius Press, 1978);

The Marsh Lute Book: C. 1595, Containing 152 Solos and Duets for 6-course Renaissance Lute, Four Solos for 7-course Renaissance Lute and Nine Pieces for 6-course Bandora, introductory note by Robert Spencer (Kilkenny: Boethius, 1981).

OTHER: "Essay Touching the (Esteemed) Sympathy between Lute or Viol Strings," in *The Natural History of Oxfordshire: Being an Essay towards the Natural History of England,* by Robert Plot (Oxford: The Theatre, 1677), pp. 289–299;

Philippe Du Trieu, *Institutio Logicae in usum Juventutis Academicae Dubliniensis,* revised by Marsh (Dublin: S. Helsham, 1681);

An Biobla Naomhtha, translated by William Bedell, Murtagh King, and Dennis Sheridan; revised by Marsh, Andrew Sall, and others (London: R. Ebheringtham, 1690).

SELECTED PERIODICAL PUBLICATIONS–UNCOLLECTED: "An Introductory Essay to the Doctrine of Sounds, Containing Some Proposals for the Improvement of Acousticks," *Philosophical Transactions,* 14, no. 156 (1684): 471;

"The Diary of Archbishop Marsh," edited by J. H. Todd, *British Magazine,* 27 (July–August 1845).

Archbishop Narcissus Marsh (Marsh's Library)

Archbishop Narcissus Marsh was the founder, in 1701, of the first public library in Ireland. He financed the building entirely from his own resources and donated his own scholarly collection to the library. Marsh also purchased Bishop Edward Stillingfleet's collection of ten thousand volumes for the library.

Marsh was born on St. Thomas's Eve, 20 December 1638, in the village of Hannington, near Highworth in the northern Wiltshire, to William and Grace Marsh, née Colburn. He had two older brothers–Epaphroditus and Onesiphorus–and two older sisters. The unusual names of the boys in the family seem to have come from the Epistles of St. Paul.

Marsh went to five local schools, "in all which schools I never was so much as once whipt or beaten," he later wrote proudly in the diary that he kept from 1690 to 1696. At sixteen he was entered as a commoner at Magdalen Hall, Oxford. In his diary he describes his studies: "Old Philosophy, Mathematics and Oriental Languages, and before Lent 1658 (when I took my degree of Bachelor of Arts) I had made good progress in them all."

Marsh was elected to a Wiltshire Fellowship at Exeter College on 30 June 1658. He took the degree of master of arts in 1660 and in 1662 was offered the living of Swindon in Wiltshire. Robert Skinner, bishop of Oxford, ordained him deacon and priest in King Henry VII's Chapel, Westminster, even though he was underage for the priesthood. Marsh wrote in his diary, "the Lord forgive us both, but then I knew no better but that it might legally be done."

Marsh was made chaplain to the bishop of Exeter, Seth Ward, and took up residence in Swindon. He then discovered to his horror that in return for his appointment he was expected to marry a friend of the persons responsible for his preferment. But Marsh refused to marry. He later said in his diary that he had had no intention of ever getting married, but at the time he offered the reason that his father was opposed to the marriage. Ward, furious, demanded Marsh's resignation as his chaplain, and Marsh returned to Oxford in 1663 to continue his studies.

In 1665 Marsh was made chaplain to Lord Chancellor Edward Hyde, first Earl of Clarendon, before whom he preached in Worcester House in May of that year and in Berkshire House the following February. In 1667 he took the degree of bachelor of divinity. In 1671 he began to study for his doctorate of divinity. These studies were interrupted when he undertook, at the request of John Fell, dean of Christ Church and bishop of Oxford, to revise the notes and supervise the printing of the translations of Theodore Balsamon and Joannes Zonaras's *Comments on the Canons of the Greek Councils,* which was then being printed at the Oxford University Press. This monumental task took almost a year.

Marsh was deeply interested in music and played the bass viol. He wrote a tract titled "Essay Touching the (Esteemed) Sympathy between Lute or Viol Strings" that was included in Robert Plot's *The Natural History of Oxfordshire: Being an Essay towards the Natural History of England* (1677).

Marsh was appointed principal of St. Alban Hall, Oxford, in May 1673 by James Butler, first Duke of Ormonde, the chancellor of the university. He was a great success in this position, leading Fell and the duke to suggest a more important appointment: the provostship of Trinity College, Dublin. Marsh was sworn and invested provost on 24 January 1679. He revised and altered Philippe Du Trieu's *Logick* (1662) and had it printed for the use of the students at the university; titled *Institutio Logicae in usum Juventutis Academicae Dubliniensis* (1681), it was used until about 1782, when it was replaced by Richard Murray's textbook.

While he was at Trinity, Marsh played a major part in the preparation for printing of Bishop William Bedell's Irish translation of the Old Testament. Bedell had supervised the translation before 1641, but it had never been printed. Marsh, with the help of Andrew Sall, a transcriber known only as Denine, and some others, prepared the transcripts, which they then sent to Robert Boyle in London. Boyle financed the publication, and the translation was printed in London in 1690.

Marsh built a new college hall and chapel; during construction the members of the college had to eat in the library, and the books were removed for safekeeping and piled in heaps in various empty rooms. When the hall and chapel were complete, Marsh began to reorganize the library. He ordered tables to be drawn up and hung at the end of each division of books, listing the shelves and the numbers and names of all the books on each shelf. There was no regular library keeper at Trinity College at that time; one of the junior fellows was chosen to fill the position each year, for which he was paid £6 annually. Marsh insisted that when a new library keeper was appointed, he should check all the books; the old library keeper would then be required to replace or pay for any missing items.

Although Marsh was able to reorganize the operation of the library, he was unable to change the statute that entitled only the provost and fellows to study there; students had to be accompanied by the provost or one of the fellows, who was obliged to remain in the library with the reader. Marsh noted, as he said later in a letter to his friend Thomas Smith, vice president of Magdalene College, Oxford, and a well-known collector of rare books, that the nearby booksellers' shops were furnished with "new Triffles and Pamphlets and not well with them also. . . . 'twas this, and this consideration alone that at first moved me to think of building a library in some other place (not in the College) for publick use, where all might have free access, seeing they cannot have it in the College."

In 1683 Marsh was appointed bishop of Ferns and Leighlin and resigned the provostship. He was one of the first members of the Dublin University Philosophical Society, founded by William Molyneux that year, and contributed a paper to the society, "An Introductory Essay to the Doctrine of Sounds, Containing Some Proposals for the Improvement of Acousticks," that was printed in the society's *Philosophical Transactions* in 1684. K. Theodore Hoppen notes that in this paper Marsh was the first scientist to use the word *microphone*. When Molyneux developed the "Dublin Hygroscope," an instrument for measuring moisture in the air, Marsh suggested the substitution of a lute string for the more fragile whipcord that Molyneux was using. Marsh also invented a lamp to illuminate a large hall or church. Other interests of Marsh included astronomy and entomology.

On 20 December 1690 Marsh was promoted to archbishop of Cashel. While he was on a visitation in Cork, he received news of his promotion to the see of Dublin. He was enthroned as archbishop of Dublin in St. Patrick's Cathedral on 26 May 1694.

Whatever his other accomplishments, Marsh is remembered today for building Marsh's Library, the first public library in Ireland, entirely at his own initiative and expense. Although he had had the idea for the library while he was provost of Trinity College, he did not have the money or the opportunity to build it until he became archbishop of Dublin. On 4 May 1700 he wrote to Smith, seeking the latter's assistance in "recommending to him choice books." Marsh told Smith that he intended to leave his oriental manuscripts to the Bodleian Library at Oxford and to construct a public library for the rest of his books. Marsh decided to build the library in the large grounds of the Palace of St. Sepulchre, the archbishop's residence. He hired as architect Sir William Robinson, the surveyor general of Ireland. The lower story of the L-shaped building was designed as a residence for the librarian, although Marsh hoped that it, too, would eventually be used as a library.

Elias Bouhéreau donated his books to Marsh's Library when he was made its first librarian in 1701. Bouhéreau was a Protestant from La Rochelle, France; he and his family had been forced to leave after the revocation of the Edict of Nantes in 1685. His collection represents a typical scholar's library of the seventeenth century: religious controversy, history, politics, science, medicine, and the classical authors are well represented. Many of his books have the signatures of previous owners, including the humanist Tanneguy Lefèbvre, the father of the classical commentator and translator Anne Dacier.

In February 1703 Marsh was promoted to the primacy of Armagh and was elected vice president of the Dublin University Philosophical Society; the first gallery and the reading room of the library were completed in midsummer of that year. After the first part of the library was erected, Marsh, wrote to Smith that he was "indeed earnestly pressed to buy Dr. Stillingfleet's library." Stillingfleet had been dean of St. Paul's Cathedral and bishop of Worcester and one of the best-known preachers and writers of his day; his controversy with the philosopher John Locke on the doctrine of the Trinity and his books against Socinians and Catholics had aroused great interest. More important for Marsh, Stillingfleet was a superb book collector who had continued to collect until a few weeks before his death in March 1699. John Evelyn, secretary of the Royal Society, described Stillingfleet's collection as the best private library in England; Richard Bentley, master of Trinity College, Cambridge, and royal librarian, tried to get William III to buy the collection, "the like of which was not anywhere else in the world." Marsh bought the collection for about £2,500. It contained books on a wide range of subjects, including theology, history, the classics, law, medicine, and travel. Many of

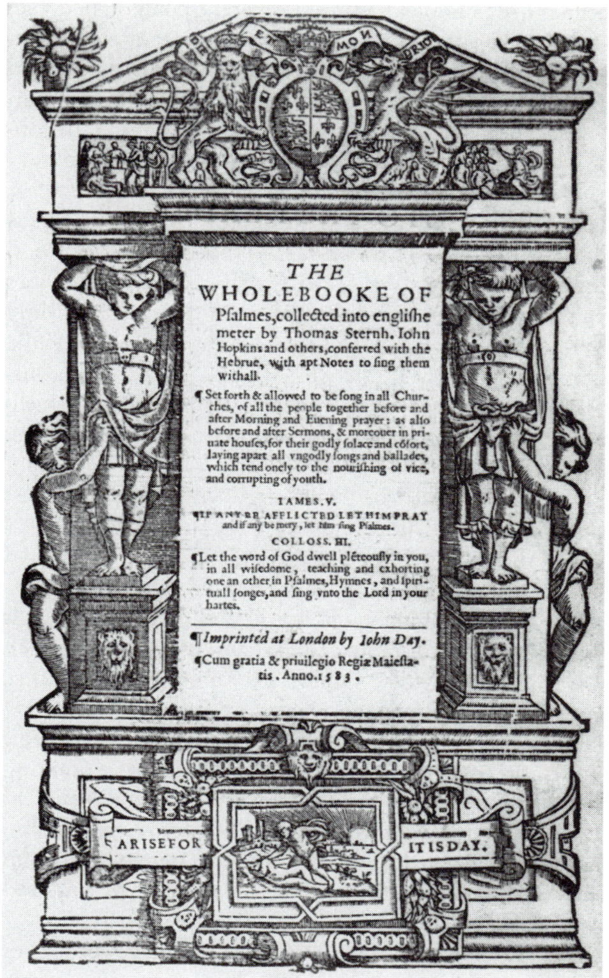
THE
WHOLEBOOKE OF
Psalmes, collected into englishe meter by Thomas Sternh. Iohn Hopkins and others, conferred with the Hebrue, with apt Notes to sing them withall.

¶ Set forth & allowed to be song in all Churches, of all the people together before and after Morning and Euening prayer: as also before and after Sermons, & moreouer in priuate houses, for their godly solace and cōfort, laying apart all vngodly songs and ballades, which tend onely to the nourishing of vice, and corrupting of youth.

IAMES. V.
¶ IF ANY BE AFFLICTED LET HIM PRAY and if any be mery, let him sing Psalmes.

COLLOSS. III.
¶ Let the word of God dwell plēteously in you, in all wisedome, teaching and exhorting one an other in Psalmes, Hymnes, and spirituall songes, and sing vnto the Lord in your hartes.

¶ *Imprinted at London by Iohn Day.*
¶ Cum gratia & priuilegio Regiæ Maiestatis. Anno. 1583.

Title page for the Marsh's Library copy of a psalter printed by John Day of London in 1583

Stillingfleet's books had been owned by famous people, including Bishop Hugh Latimer; the statesman William Cecil, first Baron Burghley; the mathematician and astrologer John Dee; the naval commander, diplomat, and author Sir Kenelm Digby; the dramatist Ben Jonson; and the poet John Donne. Donne's Italian motto, "per Rachel ho servito & no per Lea" (I have served for Rachel and not for Leah), appears in one of the books he had owned. (In medieval symbolism Rachel stood for the contemplative, Leah for the active life.) There were books with scholarly annotations by Archbishop William Laud and books that belonged to one of the heroes of classical scholarship, Isaac Casaubon, and his son, Meric. Many of the books had belonged to well-known English collectors, including Richard Smith, Humphrey Dyson, Edward Gwynn, Lazarus Seaman, and John Morris, who had bought them at the earliest book auctions held in England.

Marsh's Library was completed in 1707; it had cost Marsh £5,000, and he intended to spend another £500 on it. Having built the library and furnished it with books, he submitted to Parliament "An Act for Settling and Preserving a Publick Library for ever." Rather surprisingly, the act met with some opposition in Ireland, although in England, Marsh said, "it met with great applause, if I may say so." The act incorporating Marsh's Library as a public institution was passed in 1707. The building was exempted forever from all chimney money, hearth money, and lamp money and from all manner of taxes or charges "hereafter to be imposed by Act of Parliament."

Marsh gave strict instructions to the governors of the library as to the qualifications future librarians should have. He required the librarian to take a solemn oath promising not to give away, lend, or steal any of the books. He also laid down rules for readers, which said that "All Graduats and Gentlemen shall have free access to the said Library on the Dayes and Houres before determined, Provided They behave Themselves well, give place and pay due respect to their Betters, But in case any person shall carry Himself otherwise (which We hope will not happen) We order Him to be excluded, if after being admonished He does not mend His manners."

While the government and most of his fellow bishops respected Marsh, the dean of St. Patrick's Cathedral and great Irish satirical writer, Jonathan Swift, blamed Marsh for his lack of promotion in the Church of Ireland. In the spiteful "Character of Primate Marsh," written about three years before Marsh's death, Swift said: "Marsh has the reputation of most profound and universal learning; this is the general opinion, neither can it be easily disproved. . . . He is the first of human race, that with great advantages of learning, piety, and station ever escaped being a great man. . . . No man will be either glad or sorry at his death, except his successor."

Marsh died on 2 November 1713 and is buried in the churchyard of St. Patrick's Cathedral, beside his beloved library. He bequeathed his own collection of books to the library.

The library's fourth collection–after those of Bouhéreau, Stillingfleet, and Marsh–was bequeathed by the bishop of Clogher, John Stearne, in 1745. It is similar in scope to the other collections. Stearne said that he was giving his books to Marsh's Library "as a small token of the great regard I have, for the bountiful erector and endower of the Library." Some of Stearne's books had been purchased at the sale held by the English bookseller John Dunton in Dublin in 1698.

The design and arrangement of Marsh's Library were evidently influenced by the Bodleian Library, judging from Marsh's many references to the latter in his letters to Smith. Today one of the few eighteenth-century buildings in Dublin still being used for its original purpose, the library is furnished with dark oak bookcases, each with a carved and lettered gable topped by a miter. The first gallery is sixty feet in length, the second seventy-six feet. At the end of the second gallery are three wired alcoves, called "the cages." They were intended by Marsh for the protection of smaller and more valuable books; over the years the tradition developed that the cages were used to lock up students so that they could not steal the books. The library has changed so little internally that the books that the first librarian, Bouhéreau, catalogued and that he and the archbishop placed on the shelves in the first gallery are still in the same places, with the same shelf numbers, three hundred years later. Although the library is made up of four separate collections that reflect the individual interests of the collectors, they are homogeneous because they were all formed during the latter half of the seventeenth century by men of scholarly tastes.

The library holds about twenty-five thousand books, including approximately eighty incunabula (books printed between 1450 and 1501). About twenty books are listed in Alfred W. Pollard and Gilbert R. Redgrave's *A Short-Title Catalogue of Books Printed in England, Scotland, and Ireland and of English Books Printed Abroad, 1475–1640* (1927) as being in Marsh's Library only. There are fine examples of early English printers, including Wynkyn de Worde, Richard Pynson, Julian Notary, John Day, and Richard Grafton. The great Continental printers are also well represented and cover the golden age of French printing. There are splendid examples of books printed by the scholar-printers Aldus Manutius in Venice, Johann Froben in Basel, Josse Bade (Badius in Latin) and Robert Estienne

(Stephanus in Latin) in Paris, and Christophe Plantin in Antwerp. A particularly fine example of Estienne's printing is the Greek New Testament printed in 1550 in the Bouhéreau collection. The eleven hand-colored volumes of the *Atlas Major,* printed in Amsterdam by Johannes Blaeu (Blaevius in Latin) in 1662, are widely regarded as the most beautiful books ever produced and were the most expensive that money could buy in the seventeenth century.

While many of the books are examples of fine printing, Bouhéreau, Stillingfleet, Marsh, and Stearne were primarily interested in their contents. Marsh's Library is a scholars' library and is used mainly for research. The collections reflect their former owners' tastes: the subject of religious controversy is well represented, particularly the Reformation and Counter-Reformation, with books by Desiderius Erasmus, Martin Luther, Philipp Melanchthon, and John Calvin. Calvin's outstanding contribution to prose style can be seen in his *Institutio Christianae religionis* (Institutes of the Christian Religion, Paris: Jean le Preux, 1607). Books by the great Catholic writers Cardinals Caesar Baronius and Robert Bellarmine and Sir Thomas More are also present.

John Gee, an anti-Catholic writer, wrote *Foote out of the Snare with a Detection of Sundry Late Practices and Impostures of the Priests and Iesuites in England* (London: Printed by H. L. for Robert Milbourne, 1624); it includes a list of the names of devils, many of which William Shakespeare used for the evil spirits in *King Lear* (performed, 1605 or 1606; published, 1623). The Library also has Gee's *New Shreds of the Old Snare* (London: Printed for Robert Mylbourn, 1624), which has references to Shakespeare's *Hamlet* (performed, circa 1600–1601; published 1604) and *A Midsummer Night's Dream* (performed, circa 1595–1596; published, 1600) and Jonson's *The Alchemist* (performed, 1610; published, 1612).

Some of the books were highly controversial. Robert Parsons, the English Jesuit missionary and one of the most important and skillful men of his time, was condemned by Queen Elizabeth, and possession of his book, *A Conference about the Next Succession to the Crowne of Ingland* (St. Omer, 1594), published under the pseudonym R. Doleman, was declared high treason by Parliament. Cardinal Baronius's *Annales Ecclesiastici* was written as a reply to the Protestant Centuriators of Magdeburg, the authors of a church history that was dominated by anti-Catholic views. This copy originally belonged to Swift. Swift was not impressed by the cardinal's reply; he wrote in the first volume, printed in Antwerp in 1612: "Worst of bad writers, falsest of the false, Shallowest of the shallow. Silliest of the silly. This, when I had read twelve volumes and with ire and boredom was incensed was my considered opinion. AD. 1729 J. S." The library's copy of Hyde's *History of the Rebellion and Civil War Begun in England in the Year 1641* (Oxford: At the Theater, 1703–1707) originally belonged to Swift and is extensively annotated by him with outbursts against the Scots for the part they took in the rebellion.

Title page for the Marsh's Library copy of the 1581 edition of Andrea Palladio's influential book about architecture, printed by Barttolomeo Carampello of Venice

Writings of English and Continental philosophers include the disputes between the Arminians and Remonstrants and works by Gottfried Wilhelm Leibniz, Nicolas Malebranche, and René Descartes, the "Father of Modern Philosophy." The Stillingfleet Collection includes many books written and owned by the French Protestant and foremost Greek scholar Isaac Casaubon, as well as the first edition of Locke's *An Essay concerning Humane Understanding: In Four Books* (London: Printed by Eliz. Holt for T. Basset, 1690), the book that had inspired Stillingfleet to engage Locke in their famous controversy.

Bouhéreau's Collection, apart from being a unique source for the study of Calvinism, contains a

eroti simile. Hæc sibi in chorographia illa Septentrionali per-
nt pictores,quę tamen vera nonnulla continet,vt astarum ma
,onocrotalum satis rectè expressum,& terrestria aliquot.
De Pisce monachi habitu.
CAPVT XX.

Illustration of the "Monkfish" in the Marsh's Library copy of Guillaume Rondelet's De piscibus marinis, *printed in 1544 by Matthias Bonhomme in Lyon*

wealth of historical material relating to sectarian conflicts in seventeenth-century France. Among them is Theodore Agrippe d'Aubigne's history of the Protestants in France, *Histoire universelle* (Maillé: Printed by Jean Moussat, 1616–1620). Copies of the first edition are extremely rare, as the book was ordered to be burned. Also included is Jean Bodin's *Six livres de la Republique* (Paris: Jacques du Puys, 1576), in which he maintains that a limited monarchy is the best form of government.

The French books are not confined to controversy and religious disputes. The Bouhéreau Collection includes the medieval romance *Le rommant de la rose ou tout lart de lamour est enclose,* begun by Guillaume de Lorris and finished by Jean de Meung, printed by Galliot du Pré in Paris in 1526 in the Gothic *lettre batarde* typeface; the book is in its original binding. Pierre de Ronsard's *Oeuvres,* printed in Paris in 1609 by Barthelemy Macé with the architectural title page designed by Leonard Gaultier, and Michel de Montaigne's *Essais,* printed in Paris in 1652 by Augustin Courbé, are also in the Bouhéreau Collection.

The Italian books are fine printings from the Renaissance and include works by Giovanni Boccaccio, Dante, Petrarch, Girolamo Savonarola, and Paolo Sarpi.

The oldest book in the library was printed in Milan in 1472 by Pamfilio Castaldi: Cicero's *Epistolarum familiarum liber primus.* Printed on handmade paper and set with exceptionally wide margins, it shows the transitional stage between manuscript and print. Most of the Italian books are in Latin, but the Stillingfleet Collection holds the first edition of Cardinal Pietro Bembo's vernacular *Prose nellequali si ragiona della uolgar lingua* (Venice: Giouan Tacuino, 1525). The copy in the library of Andrea Palladio's influential *Quattro libri dell'architettura,* printed in Venice in 1581 by Barttolomeo Carampello, is a reprint of the 1570 first edition.

The books on travel and natural history are probably the best-illustrated volumes in the library. On a pilgrimage to the Holy Land, Bernard von Breydenbach, dean of the Cathedral of Mainz, was accompanied by the artist Erhard Reuwich; they produced an account of their travels, *Sanctarum peregrinationum in montem Syon ad venerandum Christi sepulcrum in Jerusalem atque in montem Synai ad divam virginem et matirem Katherinam opusculum* (Mainz: Erhard Reuwich, 1486), that includes magnificent illustrations of the cities they visited. The panorama of Venice is nearly five feet long and is an astonishing piece of early printing. The authors say that it is the first book with illustrations taken from life and not from the imagination, with "animals truly depicted as we saw them in the Holy Land." This claim is suspect, as the illustrations include a unicorn. The books on natural history include works by Ulisse Aldrovandi, Conrad Gesner, Leonard Fuchs, John Ray, and Edward Topsell. The French physician Guillaume Rondelet's *De piscibus marinis,* printed in Lyon in 1544 by Matthias Bonhomme, includes such illustrations as a "Monkfish" and a "Bishopfish" clothed in their full religious habits.

Since Marsh was deeply interested in mathematics and science, he must have been especially pleased, when he purchased the Stillingfleet collection, to discover first editions of the first great scientific work published in England, William Gilbert's *De Magnete Magneticisqve Corporibvs et De Magno Magnete Tellure Physiologia Noua Plurimis Argumentis Experimentis Demonstrata* (London: Printed by Peter Short, 1600), and of Sir Isaac Newton's *Philosophiae Naturalis Principia Mathematica* (London: Printed for the Royal Society by Joseph Streater, 1687).

The witchcraft craze of the sixteenth and seventeenth centuries is represented by a small collection that contains many of the great Continental and English writers on the subject. Although the library does not have the 1486 first edition of what became known as the encyclopedia of demonology, the *Malleus maleficarum,* it does have two later editions. The book was written by two Dominican inquisitors, Heinrich Institoris (real name: Kramer) and Jacob Sprenger. When it was first published, it bore on the title page the warning "Haeresis est maxima opera maleficarum non credere" (to disbelieve in witchcraft is the greatest of heresies). One English writer of humanitarian views, Reginald Scot, became so distressed by the number of elderly and ignorant people who were being accused of witchcraft that he attempted to end the persecution by writing *Discoverie of Witchcraft Wherein the Lewde Dealing of Witches and Witchmongers Is Notablie Detected the Knauerie of Coniurors the Impietie of Inchantors the Follie of Soothsaiers Are Deciphered* (London: William Brome, 1584). James I, who believed in witches, ordered Scot's book to be burned. It includes illustrations and descriptions of magicians' conjuring tricks and disappearances; the edition in Marsh's Library has two woodcut leaves that are missing from many copies of the book.

Considering that three of the main collections were put together by an archbishop and two bishops, it is hardly surprising that the library has particularly fine holdings of Bibles and prayer books. The first of the great polyglot Bibles, the Complutensian Polyglot, was printed in Alcalá de Henares, Spain (ancient Complutum), by Arnaldo Guillen de Brocar from 1502 to 1517. This magnificent Bible was commissioned by the Cardinal Francisco Ximenes and cost him about £25,000. The later polyglot Bibles in the library were printed in Antwerp (1569–1572), in Paris by Antoine Vitré (1629–1645), and in London (*Waltons The English Polyglot*) by Thomas Roycroft (1657) and are all in the Stillingfleet Collection. The first polyglot edition of part of the Bible to be printed with exotic types, including five versions of the Psalms, was produced in Genoa by Petrus Paulus Porrus in 1516. The title-page border is an oriental design of intersecting polygons, and the decorated initials were cut to match it. It was edited by Agostino Giustiniano, the bishop of Nebbio. Marsh had two copies of the book. There are Bibles in many languages, including Bengali, Dutch, French, Greek, German, Hebrew, Irish, Latin, Persian, Rarotongan, Slavonic, and Spanish, ranging in size from enormous folios to small pocket editions.

The books in Marsh's Library are for the most part highly serious, but occasionally a book of lighter content can be found, particularly in the medical section. Queen Elizabeth's orders against the plague include recipes for preventing sickness; one recipe advises taking a special mixture, after which the afflicted person "should go to bed and provoke yourself to sweating." A French writer, Marie Fouquet, in *Recueil de remedes faciles et domestiques* (Dijon and Paris, 1678), gives recipes for almost every imaginable illness, from apoplexy to melancholy. The recipe in chapter 42, "Contre le Miserere," includes in the ingredients a quarter bottle of white wine.

While the collections of Bouhéreau, Stillingfleet, and Stearne have been used by scholars for research purposes, Marsh's oriental collection has never been examined. Marsh began to collect these books while he was studying oriental languages and rabbinical and medieval writers at Oxford. He purchased Hebrew books from Aron Moses in London, many of them printed by Daniel Bomberg in Venice and by the well-known Jewish printers in Amsterdam. A copy of Edmund Castell's *Lexicon heptaglotton Hebraicum Chaldaicum Syriacum Samaritanum Aethiopicum Arabicum conjunctim et Persicum separatim* (London: Printed by Thomas Roycroft, 1669) was given to Marsh by Frances Guise, the widow of the Oxford orientalist William Guise, in 1690. This enormous work includes Persian and Arabic sections.

The writings of Joannes Cocceius, professor of theology at the University of Leiden, are well represented, including his *Duo tituli Thalmudici Sanhedrin et Maccoth cum excerptis ex utriusque Gemara versa annotationibus illustrata* (Amsterdam: Printed by Frederick Heinz, 1629). Petrus Cunaeus's study of the government of ancient Israel, *De Republica Hebraorum Libri III* (Leiden: Elzevier, 1632), was collected by Marsh, along with books on rabbinical and medieval Hebrew by Johannes Buxtorf the Elder, professor of Hebrew at the University of Basel. Another Basel professor, Sebastian Münster, wrote Hebrew grammars and dictionaries that Marsh collected; Marsh also had copies of Münster's *Praecepta Mosaica Sexcenta Atque Tredecim cum Succincta Plerumque Mirabili Superstitiosa Rabinorum Expositione* (Basel: Heinrich Stein, 1533) and *Cosmographiae Universalis Libri Vi in Quibus Iuxta Certioris Fidei Scriptorum Traditionem Describuntur* (Basel: Heinrich Stein, 1634).

Campegius Vitringa the Elder's account of the ancient synagogue, *De synagoga vetere Libri Tres* (Franeker: Printed by Johannis Gyzelaar, 1696), is in the library. Marsh regarded as particularly valuable a work in Hebrew by Immanuel ben Solomon of Rome, *Liber Mechabberoth seu poeticarum compositionum,* printed in Brescia in 1491 by Rabbi Gerson ben Moses of Soncino, inscribing the words "*Liber rarissimus*" on the title page. The printing historian S. H. Steinberg describes Gerson ben Moses as "the greatest Jewish printer the world has ever known."

Important religious works in eastern languages include an edition of the Koran in Arabic edited by Abraham Hinckelmann (Hamburg: Schultze-Schiller, 1694). Marsh also collected John Selden's version of the history of the Church of Alexandria by Patriarch Eutychius (London: Richard Bishop, 1642) and Ali Aguba Isthanel's *Liber de fide religionis Christianae, et de religione Mohamedicâ* in Arabic, printed in Rome in 1680.

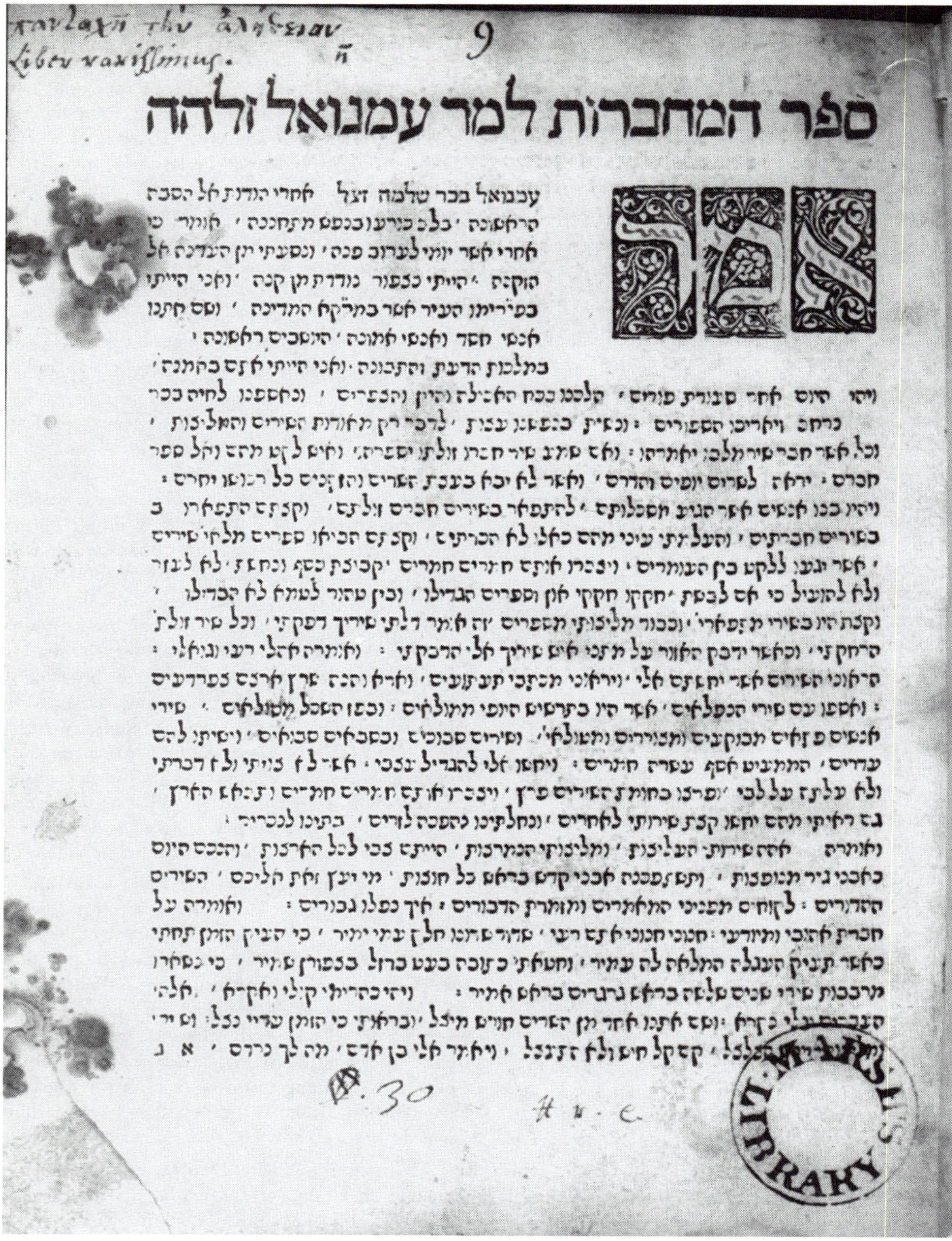

Page from Marsh's copy of the 1491 edition of Immanuel ben Solomon's Liber Mechabberoth sev poeticarum compositionum, *printed in Brescia by Gerson ben Moses of Soncino. Marsh's Greek motto, which may be translated as "Truth Everywhere," and the Latin words for "rare book" are written at the top of the page (Marsh's Library)*

The celebrated Dutch scholar Thomas Erpenius was professor of Hebrew and Eastern languages at the University of Leiden. He was also the director of a printing press that published books in Hebrew, Syriac, and Arabic. The library has an edition of his *Historia Iosephi patriarchae ex Alcorano Arabice* (1617) and an Arabic version of the Pentateuch printed by Erpinus in 1622. A New Testament in Greek, Syriac, and Latin printed by Henricus Stephanus (Henri Estienne) in Paris in 1569 that originally belonged to Erpenius is also in the Marsh Collection. Apart from his religious publications, Erpenius wrote and edited Arabic and Syriac grammars that Marsh collected.

James Golius's *Lexicon Arabico-Latinum Contextum ex Probatioribus Orientis* (Leiden: Printed by Bonaventure and Abraham Elzevir, 1653) is in the Marsh Collection. In his diary for 16 September 1695 Marsh records that he gave his friend, the English orientalist Edward Bernard, £220 to go to Holland and purchase on his behalf the choicest of Golius's manuscripts, which were then being sold. An even more important work that Marsh acquired was Anthony Gigge's *Thesaurus linguae Arabicae* in four volumes (Milan: Printed by Johann Peter Ramellat, 1632). The dictionary was compiled over a period of eighteen years and was the first Arabic book printed in Milan.

Edward Pocock the Elder, professor of Hebrew at Oxford, published books that were of great interest to Marsh. The archbishop had a copy of Pocock's elegant edition of Husain ibn 'Ali's *Lamiato 'l Ajam, carmen Tograi* (Oxford: Printed by Henry Hall, 1661) and many of his other writings. Marsh also collected the works of Christophorus Crinesius, the German divine who taught oriental languages at Wittenberg University, including his *Gymnasium Syriacum hoc est Linguae Iesu Christo Vernaculae Perfecta Institutio ex Novo Testamento Syro et Aliis Rerum Syriaearum Scriptoribus Collecta Novis et Genuinis Characteribus Adornata* (Wittenberg: Printed and sold by Johann Gormann, 1611).

While Marsh seems to have mastered various Eastern languages, it is not known whether he was able to understand an illustrated liturgy that had originally belonged to the orientalist Dudley Loftus, the great-grandson of the lord chancellor of Ireland and archbishop of Armagh, Adam Loftus. It is part missal and is in the Ge'ez language, an old liturgical form of Amharinya used by the Ethiopian Orthodox Church. It was printed in Leiden, probably in 1660. Marsh also acquired historical works and grammars in Latin and Persian by Ludovicus de Dieu the Elder, a Dutch Protestant minister and expert on oriental languages in Leiden. Marsh's Persian books included an edition of *Gazophylacium linguae Persarum Triplici linguarum clavi Italicae Latinae Gallicae nec non Specialibus Praeceptis Ejusdem Linguae Reseratum,* by Angelus à Sancto Josepho (Joseph Labrosse), published in Amsterdam by Johann Jansson van Waesberg in 1684. Another book in Latin and Persian is a copy of the Gospel of St. Matthew, *Quatuor evangelia,* dated 1652 with no place of publication given. A beautiful edition of a liturgical work in Syriac, *Virtute et Ope Trinitatis Sanctissimæ Gloriosissimae et Consubstantialis Patris et Filii et Spiritus Sancti Unius Dei Verbi Cui Gloria et Honor in Saecula Amen Officia Sanctorum Juxta Ritum Ecclesiæ Maronitarum* (Rome: Printed by the Sacred Congregation for the Propagation of the Faith, 1666), and two copies of what appear to be a Maronite *Horae* printed in Rome by Dominici Basae in 1584 are in the Marsh Collection. An Illyrian breviary, *Breviarium Romanum Slavonico Idiomate Iussu Innocentis X Papae,* edited by Raphael Levakovic and Methodius Terlecki, bishop of Chelm (Rome: Printed by the Sacred Congregation for the Propagation of the Faith, 1648), is also there. Marsh owned six books in Armenian, including *Liturgia Armenorum,* which appears to be a missal translated by Giovanni Molino, printed in Rome in 1636 by the Sacred Congregation for the Propagation of the Faith; Francisco Rivola's *Dictionarium Armeno-Latinum* (Paris: Societatis Typographicae, 1633); and Petro Paulo's *Doctrina Christiana in Linguam Armenam* (Paris: Societatis Typographicae, 1634), in Latin and Armenian verse.

Although most of the books in Arabic and other Eastern languages are religious works, Marsh also collected works in those languages that reflect his interests in mathematics and astronomy. Among these books is Euclid's *Elementorum Geometricorum Libri Tredecim ex Traditione Nasiridini Tusini,* which was printed at the Typographia Medicea in Rome in 1594 in superb Arabic letters that were probably cut by the famous French typecutter Robert Granjon. In a letter to Smith dated April 1681 Marsh gave a detailed account of his observation of a comet; when he became archbishop of Dublin, he had an observatory tower attached to his palace and library. For his astronomical collection Marsh seems to have been particularly interested in the writings of Ulugh Beg, the grandson of Tamerlane and founder of the observatory at Samarkand. He acquired two important works by Ulugh Beg that were edited by John Greaves, the Savilian Professor of Astronomy at Oxford: *Binae Tabulae Geographicae una Nassir Eddini Persae Altera Ulug Beigi Tatari* (London, 1648) and *Epochae Celebriores Astronomis Historicis Chronologis Chataiorum Syrograecorum Arabum Persarum Chorasmiorum Usitatae ex Traditione Vlug Beigi* (London: Printed by Jacob Flesher and sold by Cornelius Bee, 1650). From his friend Thomas Hyde, the Bodleian librarian, Marsh purchased a copy of Hyde's edition of Ulugh Beg's catalogue of the stars, *Tabulae Long Ac Lat Stellarum Fixarum ex Observatione Ulugh Beighi Jam Primum Luce Ac Latio Donavit Commentariis Illustravit*

Thomas Hyde Tabulae Declinationum Rectarum Ascensionum Mohammed Tizinus (Oxford: Printed by Henry Hall for Richard Davis, 1665).

The Marsh Collection includes six early Russian books in their original bindings. Four of these books probably exist nowhere else outside Russia; three of these were produced by the first Russian printer, Ivan Fedorov: *Apostol* (Liturgical Epistles, 1564), *Evangelie uchitel 'noe* (Liturgical Gospels, Belorussia, 1569), and a Psalter and New Testament (Ostrog, 1580). There is also a *Bukvar,* or elementary instruction book for children (Kuteino, Belorussia, 1653), and *Pouchenie o Morovom Yazve,* written by the Patriarch Nikon and printed in Moscow in 1656. Two copies of a devotional work on the sacraments, *O Sakramentakh,* printed at the Monastery of the Caves in Kiev in 1657, are also in the collection.

Because the collectors whose books were donated to Marsh's Library were interested in the contents rather than in the appearance of their books, the majority are bound in plain leather or vellum and have remained in surprisingly good condition. Marsh did, however, present to his library two magnificent green vellum-bound books intended for recording donations and accounts of the annual visitations. There are also examples of Continental and English blind-tooled and stamped bindings, and the cover of a copy of Jacobus Faber's *Liber Trium Virorum Hermae Uguctini F Roberti et Trium Spiritualium Virginum Hildegardis Elizabethae Mechtildis* (Paris: Henri Estienne, 1513), which originally belonged to the library of Henry VIII, probably represents the first attempt at gold tooling in England.

The library holds about three hundred manuscripts, mainly relating to ecclesiastical and historical matters. Some of the most important manuscripts dealing with Irish affairs originally belonged to Dudley Loftus. There are also some illustrated manuscript Bibles from the fourteenth century.

It has been said that Marsh's Library is an intellectual fossil, a collection of books frozen in time that remain on the same shelves where they were placed by the scholars who collected them. To study the books in the library is to explore a microcosm of Europe's great cultural heritage; Marsh's Library is a treasury of the European mind.

Letters:

"Letters from Archbishop Marsh to Dr. Thomas Smith," *Christian Examiner,* 2 (November 1833): 761–772.

References:

David C. Douglas, *English Scholars* (London: Cape, 1939);

William Young Fletcher, *English Book Collectors* (London: Kegan Paul, Trench, Trübner, 1902);

K. Theodore Hoppen, *The Common Scientist in the Seventeenth Century: A Study of the Dublin Philosophical Society, 1683–1708* (London: Routledge & Kegan Paul, 1970), pp. 33–36;

Richard Mant, *History of the Church of Ireland: With a Catalogue of the Archbishops and Bishops . . . and a Notice of the Alterations Made in the Hierarchy by the Act of 3 and 4 William IV,* volume 2: *From the Revolution to the Union of the Churches of England and Ireland, January 1, 1801* (London: J. W. Parker, 1840), I: 670; II: 6–8, 23–24, 46–48, 71–72, 107–118, 130–131;

Muriel McCarthy, *All Graduates and Gentlemen: Marsh's Library* (Dublin: O'Brien Press, 1980);

S. H. Steinberg, *Five Hundred Years of Printing,* third edition (Harmondsworth, U.K.: Penguin, 1974);

Newport J. D. White, *Four Good Men: Luke Challoner, Jeremy Taylor, Narcissus Marsh, Elias Bouhéreau* (Dublin: Hodges, Figgis, 1927).

Thomas Martin

(8 March 1696 – 7 March 1771)

David A. Stoker
University of Wales, Aberystwyth

and

Michelle Kingston
University of Wales, Aberystwyth

CATALOGUES: *A Catalogue of the Library of Mr. Thomas Martin of Palgrave in Suffolk, Lately Deceased* (Lynn: Printed by W. Whittingham, 1772);

A Catalogue of the Very Curious, Valuable, and Numerous Collection of Manuscripts of Thomas Martin . . . Which Will Be Sold by Auction, by S. Baker and G. Leigh . . . on Wednesday, April 28, 1773 (London: Baker & Leigh, 1773);

A Catalogue of the Entire Collection of Prints, Coins, &c. &c. of the Late Mr. Martin F.A.S., which he sold by Auction at the King's-Head at Diss Norfolk on Thursday the 29th and Friday the 30th and Saturday 31st of October and Monday the 2nd of November ([London?], 1772);

Bibliotheca Martiniana: A Catalogue of the Library of the Late Eminent Antiquary Mr. Thomas Martin . . . Which Will be Sold . . . Saturday June 5, by Martin Booth and John Berry (Norwich: Booth & Berry, 1773);

A Catalogue of the Remaining Part of the Library of the Late Well Known Antiquary Mr. Martin . . . Which Will be Sold, by Auction, by S. Baker and G. Leigh . . . on Wednesday the 18th of May 1774 (London: Baker & Leigh, 1774).

BOOK: *The History of the Town of Thetford, in the Counties of Norfolk and Suffolk, from the Earliest Accounts to the Present Time,* memoir by John Cullum, edited by Richard Gough (London: Printed by & for J. Nichols, 1779).

Thomas Martin (engraving by Hodgetts from an etching by Cook)

Thomas Martin was one of the most colorful book and manuscript collectors of the mid eighteenth century, and his assemblage of antiquities was immense. He was known by the nickname "Honest Tom," which was not entirely warranted in light of the questionable means by which he acquired the bulk of his collection. His character was such that he was never able to exploit the materials in his possession through publication; furthermore, he left his financial affairs in such a parlous state that the collection had to be sold quickly on his death. Nevertheless, Martin actively encouraged others to undertake historical research and was always willing to make the resources of his library available to such researchers and to assist them whenever he could.

Thomas Martin was born on 8 March 1697 in Thetford, on the border between Norfolk and Suffolk, to William Martin, rector of Great Livermore in Suffolk and curate of St. Mary's in Thetford, and Elizabeth Martin, née Burrough. Martin was largely self-taught since for several years he was the only pupil at the Thetford free school and was left to read as he pleased. It was during this period that he developed his interest in antiquities, and his leisure time was spent exploring the many ruins and other relics of the past in the area. Around 1710 Thetford was visited by the elderly antiquarian Peter Le Neve, Norroy King of Arms (a title signifying the right to grant heraldic bearings) and the first president of the recently revived Society of Antiquaries of London. Martin was introduced to Le Neve as the most suitable guide to the antiquities of the town. The relationship between the learned old man and the teenage boy grew into a friendship that lasted until Le Neve's death in 1729.

Martin's ambition to study at Cambridge and then take holy orders was thwarted by his father, who insisted that he practice law. After finishing school at Thetford, Martin took a position as a clerk in his brother's law office. Although he was a capable lawyer, Martin never enjoyed the more prosaic duties he was obliged to perform. Over the years his practice dwindled slowly but relentlessly.

Through Le Neve's recommendation Martin became a fellow of the Society of Antiquaries of London on 17 February 1719; he remained a member for fifty-three years. Around 1722 he married Sarah Cropley, a wealthy young widow with children. They moved to the village of Palgrave in Suffolk, where Martin lived for the rest of his life. Although he had been a regular purchaser of books and manuscripts since his youth, his collecting activities seem to have become serious during this period.

Contemporary accounts of Martin are replete with lively anecdotes about his heavy drinking and boisterous behavior while under the influence. The antiquarian John Fenn related a typical story in a letter to James Granger:

> An acquaintance of his one night, in London, being taken to the round-house, for some disorderly behaviour in the street, sent for his friend, Tom Martin, to extricate out of this difficulty; who immediately came, and by his humorous stories, freedom of address, and a quantum sufficit of old beer (his favourite liquor) so wrought upon the hearts and heads of the constable and his attendants, that he left them dead drunk, and not only brought off his friend, but the staves and insignia of affairs of these nightly magistrates, which he kept, and always shewed as marks of his triumphant retreat.

His contemporaries, however, also recognized Martin's extensive historical knowledge and his skills as an antiquary and calligrapher. Sir John Cullum, in his memoir prefixed to Martin's *The History of the Town of Thetford, in the Counties of Norfolk and Suffolk, from the Earliest Accounts to the Present Time* (1779), says:

> As an antiquary, he was most skilful and indefatigable; and when he was employed as an attorney and genealogist, he was in his element. . . . He had the happiest use of his pen, copying, as well as tracing, with dispatch and exactness, the different writing of every aera, and tricking arms, seals, &c., with great neatness. His taste for antient lore seems to have possessed him from his earliest to his latest days. He dated all the scraps of paper on which he made his church notes, &c. Some of these begin as early as 1721, and end but the autumn before his death, when he still wrote an excellent hand; but he certainly began his collections even before the first mentioned period.

His abilities as an archivist were recognized by the authorities of Eton College during the summer and autumn of 1724, when he was paid £30 for setting the muniment room in order and compiling a digest of many of the records there.

Martin's interest in antiquities was so diffuse, however, that it prevented him from concentrating on any one topic or period. Thus, he published nothing during his lifetime, in spite of his claim to Andrew Ducarel in a letter of 25 May 1762 of having "several things upon the anvil which I have hopes of publishing." *The History of the Town of Thetford,* his only published work, was finished after his death by Richard Gough using the notes Martin had never managed to form into a coherent whole.

Martin's collections included prints, paintings, coins, tokens, an Indian tomahawk, medieval weapons, Roman urns, lamps, spurs, horse bits, pieces of sculpture, a swordfish, seashells, fossils, petrifactions, and an ostrich egg. He is, however, primarily remembered for his library, which at its height contained about twelve thousand printed books, several thousand manuscript volumes, and many thousands of unbound documents. As a well-to-do young lawyer Martin might have been expected to own a respectable library, but he would never have been able to amass a collection on such a scale. The true origin of a large portion of Martin's collections lies not with the attorney himself, but rather with his rich, elderly friend Le Neve.

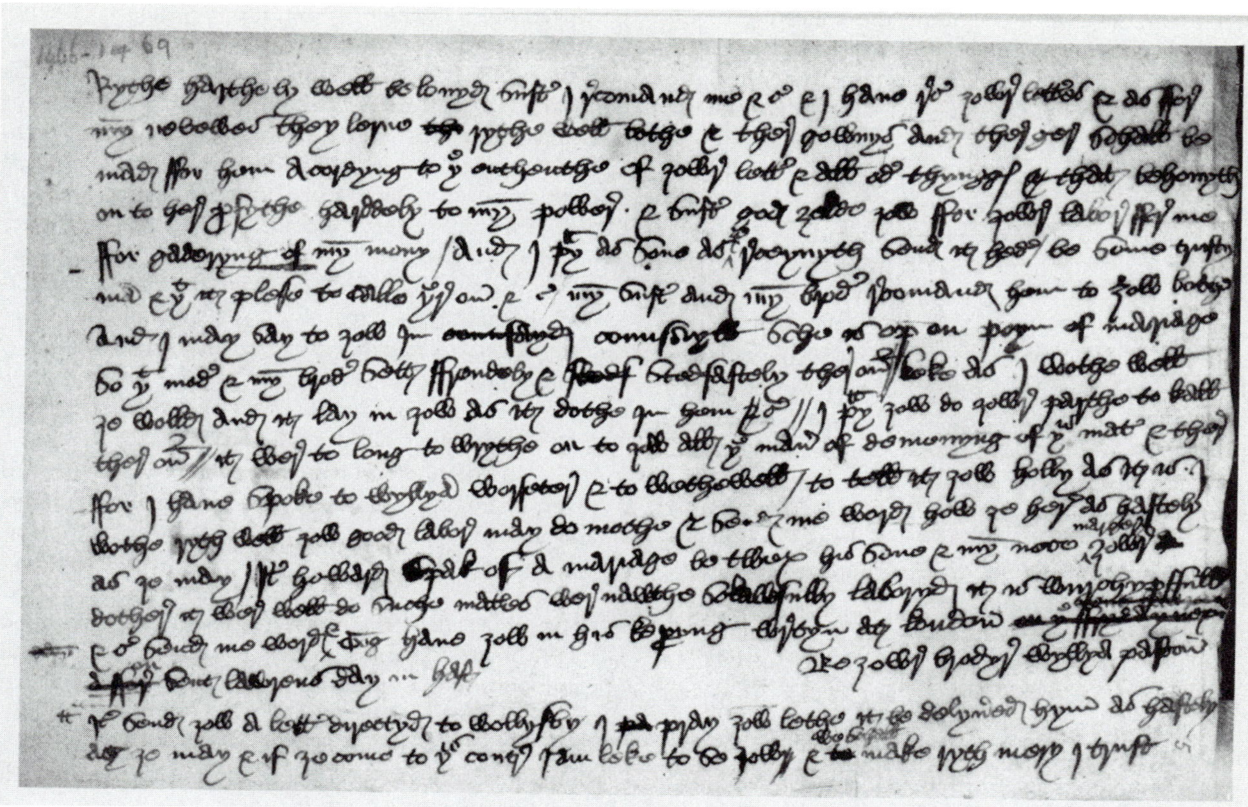

Letter written by William Paston II, probably in 1458. Martin may have acquired this and the other Paston letters from the widow of the historian Francis Blomefield (British Museum).

Le Neve had built up an enormous collection of manuscripts relating to the topographical history of Norfolk and Suffolk, described by Gough as "the greatest fund of antiquities for his native county that ever was collected for any single one in the kingdom." Le Neve intended his manuscripts to be available for public use and meant to place them in a suitable repository in Norwich. The remainder of his collection and his printed books were to be auctioned, and he appointed his friends Martin and Thomas Tanner as his executors. The disposal of the Norfolk and Suffolk manuscripts was postponed while the other manuscripts were auctioned in 1730–1731. Three events, however, ensured that the manuscripts were never placed in a public repository. Martin's wife died a few days after giving birth to twins in November 1731, leaving her husband to care for eight children. At about the same time, Tanner was appointed bishop of St. Asaph and had to leave the county. In January 1732 Martin married Le Neve's widow, Frances, and the couple moved the remaining collections to Martin's house in Palgrave.

In 1732 or early 1733 Martin persuaded the young historian Francis Blomefield to use Le Neve's Norfolk collections for a topographical history of the county. Blomefield's proposals of 1 July 1733 make it clear that he expected to be given full access to the collection, and his introduction to the work makes it apparent that he believed that Martin was only housing the collection until a suitable repository became available. Other Norfolk antiquaries interested in the collection, notably Tanner and Benjamin Mackerell, were dismayed at Martin's moving the manuscripts to Palgrave rather than placing them in a public archive. Although Tanner was pleased to see their use by Blomefield, Mackerell was upset because he had hoped to write the histories of the Norfolk towns himself, leaving the rural areas to Blomefield.

Blomefield was about to publish the third volume of his history when he died in 1752. After Blomefield's death Martin spent many months sorting out the manuscripts in Blomefield's study, which were in a greatly confused state, and he purchased substantial parts of Blomefield's collection from his widow, Elizabeth. It may have been at this time that he acquired the earliest surviving manuscript copy of Sir Philip Sidney's *The Defence of Poesy* as well as some priceless manuscripts, including the collection of fifteenth-century correspondence known as the Paston Letters. He got Charles Parkin to undertake the completion of Blomefield's work, which was eventually published in five volumes as *An Essay towards a Topographical History of the County of Norfolk* (1739–1775).

Martin is known to have assisted many reputable historians and antiquaries, including Ducarel, Browne Willis, Thomas Gale, William Cole, Sir Andrew Fountain, Joseph Ames, William Herbert, George Vertue, Richard Rawlinson, William Stukeley, Philip Carteret Webb, and Edward Rowe Mores. Many of the newer books in his library were donated by such men, including a copy of the revised edition of Tanner's *Notitia Monastica; or, An Account of All the Abbies, Priories, and Houses of Friers, heretofore in England and Wales; and also of all the Colleges and Hospitals founded before A.D. MDXL* (London: Printed by W. Bowyer, at the expense of the Society for the Encouragement of Learning, and sold by John Whiston, John Osborn, and Francis Changuion, 1744), which was donated by Tanner's brother John, who sent it with a note requesting that Martin "not speak of it lest every one whom he had any little assistance from should expect the same." Other historians of East Anglia who benefited from the Martin–Le Neve collections included Mackerell, Henry Swinden, Philip Morant, James Bentham, and Sir Joseph Ayloffe.

Martin's library appears to have been regarded as something of a tourist attraction among the learned who visited East Anglia. In his notebooks Vertue left an account of a brief stay in 1739:

> From thence wee went to see Thom: Martin at Palgrave brother Antiquary–who entertaind us with much Friendly civility. his Collections are very curious and valuable his pictures &c. Armes grants Chartularies Mss. of many kinds great collections towards the History of Suffolk & Norfolk. some rare old printed books. this collection & his own collections of Notes & remarkable deeds is very numerous. and woud require much time to consider well. all the time wee had there that evening & next morning was fully employd, to see and cursorily observe what was possible in our short stay.

After acquiring the Le Neve collection, Martin continued for the next three decades to collect books, papers, correspondence, and drawings through more usual means. He was a regular participant at auctions in Norwich and elsewhere in East Anglia and made frequent purchases from local booksellers as well as from the widows of deceased booksellers. In these ways he added large numbers of drawings, transcripts, letters, and other loose papers to Le Neve's collections. The majority were topographical or genealogical, although other packages contained notes of early printed books and political, satirical verses. His library was particularly strong in British history but also included scholarly works in Italian, French, Hebrew, Arabic, Latin, and Greek. He possessed eight hundred "black letter" titles, a significant portion of which were incunabula from the early presses of Wynkyn De Worde and Richard Pynson. These works provided valuable material for Ames and Herbert in their respective editions (1749 and 1790) of *Typographical Antiquities: Being an Historical Account of Printing in England. With Some Memoirs of Our Antient Printers, and a Register of the Books Printed by Them, from the Year MCCCCLXXI to the Year MDC.*

When sober, Martin was an orderly man who loved arranging and classifying historical documents and meticulously recorded all of his book purchases. According to Fenn's "Memoirs of the Life of Thomas Martin, Gent." (1904), Martin's manuscript collections were "all fairly transcribed with his own hand in the neatest manner." He also compiled lists and catalogues of the various parts of his collections, such as "Books in my library which relate to the antiquities and other curiosities of the city of Rome." If a complete catalogue was made during Martin's life, it does not appear to have survived, although much of the collection can be pieced together from the sale catalogues compiled after his death.

The fate of Martin's collections resulted from the flaws in his character. In 1757 he admitted to Ducarel that he knew that he should be more frugal, as he had a family to support and only a small income, "but wholly to abridge myself from buying some few books in the study I so much delight in, would be worse than imprisonment or death itself." Furthermore, as he grew older, his "dislike to the practical part of the law" increased and made him "exceedingly dilatory and remiss in his business," a circumstance made even more serious by his extravagant way of life.

The beginning of the end of Martin's collecting activities was heralded in his 1762 letter to Ducarel, in which he seeks to blame everybody but himself for his troubles:

> My eldest son has married very imprudently; that daughter . . . now is, and for two years past has been, confined, through a high disorder in her senses, without any present symptoms of ever recovering. My second son (whom I had bound out to a Surgeon and Apothecary) enlisted for a common soldier. Others in my family, either afflicted with sickness, or not behaving with that dutifulness, as to be any company in my old age. &c. &c. And, to complete my

> calamities fortune has seemed for a long while past to frown upon me. Pardon me, my dear friend, for troubling you with this ungrateful detail of my misfortune, but, in short, they have brought me under a necessity of parting with my large and expensive Collection of Books, Deeds, Coins, and various other Curiosities, in my life-time. Nor do I repine at it, as I have no child who understands any thing about them. The great hardship is the present scarcity of money, and want of friends to advise and direct me in what method to dispose of them to the best advantage. Sometimes I am thinking of finding out some Nobleman or Gentleman who would purchase them all together; sometimes of offering the most choice of them to the British Museum; and at other times of exposing them to a public sale or auction in town.

In his reply Ducarel advised Martin to dispose of the whole collection, but Martin was unable to bring himself to do so. For the remainder of his life he gradually sold his books and manuscripts as his creditors' demands became so pressing that they could no longer be ignored.

Martin described the forced sale of "many curious black letter and other books of antiquity" to the bookseller John Payne in 1769 as "driving the first nail in [my] coffin." Fenn's account of this period in his memoir of Martin shows a man desperate to cling to his treasures:

> Whilst Mr. Payne was examining his library and picking out such books as he thought proper, Mr. Martin would never come near him, though often in a morning early, whilst every one else was in bed, he would get up, go down into his library, take away and hide up such old curious books as he most valued. Many of these were found after his death hidden in various parts of the house.

Martin died in Palgrave on 7 March 1771 and was buried in the south porch of the church. In spite of his questionable method of collecting manuscripts, he was held in high esteem by his contemporaries. In a letter to Granger in November 1772, Fenn eulogized Martin's generosity in making available the resources of his library and giving unstintingly of his time to anyone interested in historical research: "He was of a very cheerful disposition, very communicative, and always ready to lend his papers, books, &c. to forward any Topographical publication." His friends and colleagues tempered their praise of Martin, however, with regret that he had not been able to fulfill his potential. According to Fenn, he had been

> A friendly and cheerful neighbour, and when sober, an instructive and entertaining companion; and would he have paid that attention to his profession that his abilities enabled him to do, and which circumstances and children required he should do, he might have possessed such a fortune as would have entitled him both to have pursued his favourite amusements with comfort and satisfaction, and to have provided for his family; but being always distressed, his mind was uneasy, and he too often sought relief from low company.

In his introduction to *The History of the Town of Thetford* Cullum summed up Martin's faults more baldly:

> Mr. Martin's desire was not only to be esteemed, but to be known and distinguished by the name of Honest Tom Martin of Palgrave, an ambition in which his acquaintance saw no reason not to gratify him. . . . Had he desired the appellation of wise and prudent, his inattention to his business, his contempt and improper use of money, and his fondness for mixed and festive company, would have debarred him, as the father of a numerous family, of that pretension. He died poor, having been little attentive to frugality and sobriety; but left behind him the character of an honest man.

Martin's family had no great attachment to the books and manuscripts that had dominated their lives and had led to their living in poverty during his old age. His eldest daughter, who was executrix of his will, let it be known that she had to dispose of the collection largely for the benefit of her father's creditors. During the first few months she sold many of the choicest items to his antiquarian friends, including Fenn and John Ives. The rest of the collection was sold to John Worth, a pharmacist in Diss, Norfolk, who immediately divided it up and sold it off. Some of the manuscripts were auctioned by Samuel Baker and George Leigh in London on 28 April 1773. The printed books were sold to Martin Booth and John Berry of Norwich, who auctioned them on 5 June 1773; Worth auctioned off the pictures and curiosity items; and Baker and Leigh sold much of the remainder of the collection on 8 May 1774. The dispersal of the rest of the library took place over the next several years. Fenn gives a detailed, although not entirely complete, account of the disposal of the collection in an appendix to his "Memoirs of the Life of Thomas Martin, Gent." (1904).

As his friends and colleagues noted, Thomas Martin's spendthrift attitude and less-than-scrupulous methods in amassing his collection show him to have been neither shrewd nor honest in his scramble to acquire the books and manuscripts he lusted after. They do, however, reveal the consuming passion of a true bibliophile, a passion that prompted Martin to be generous in allowing others to study and admire his collection.

References:

John Fenn, "Memoirs of the Life of Thomas Martin, Gent.," *Norfolk Archaeology,* 15 (1904): 233–248;

Richard Gough, *British Topography,* 2 volumes (London: T. Payne and Sons, and J. B. Nichols, 1780);

James Granger, *Letters between the Rev. James Granger, M.A. Rector of Shiplake and Many of the Most Eminent Literary Men of His Time,* edited by J. P. Malcolm (London: Longman, Hurst, Rees & Orme, 1805);

John Bowyer Nichols, ed., *Illustrations of the Literary History of the Eighteenth Century, Consisting of Authentic Memoirs and Original Letters of Eminent Persons,* 8 volumes (London: J. B. Nichols, 1858);

Nichols, ed., *Literary Anecdotes of the Eighteenth Century, Comprising Biographical Memoirs of William Bowyer,* 9 volumes (London: Nichols, Son & Bentley, 1813);

David A. Stoker, "Benjamin Mackerell, Antiquary, Librarian, and Plagiarist," *Norfolk Archaeology,* 42 (1993–1994): 1–12;

Stoker, "The Ill-Gotten Library of 'Honest' Tom Martin," in *Property of a Gentleman: The Formation, Organisation and Dispersal of the Private Library 1620–1920,* edited by Robin Myers and Michael Harris (Winchester: St. Paul's Bibliographies, 1991), pp. 90–111;

Stoker, "Innumerable Letters of Good Consequence in History: The Discovery and First Publication of the Paston Letters," *Library: Transactions of the Bibliographical Society,* 17 (1995): 107–155;

Stoker, "Mr. Parkin's Magpie, the Other Mr. Whittingham, and the Fate of Great Yarmouth," *Library: Transactions of the Bibliographical Society,* 12 (1990): 121–130;

Stoker, ed., *The Correspondence of the Reverend Francis Blomefield, 1705–1752* (Norwich: Norfolk Record Society and the Bibliographical Society, 1992);

Patrick and Felicity Strong, "The Last Will and Codicils of Henry V," *English Historical Review,* 96 (1981): 79–101;

George Vertue, *The Thirtieth Volume of the Walpole Society, 1951–1952, Volume 7: Vertue Note Books* (Oxford: Printed for the Walpole Society by Frederick Hall, 1955).

Papers:

The Suffolk Record Office, Ipswich, has Thomas Martin's personal account book for the period 1726 to 1731.

Matthew Parker

(6 August 1504 – 17 May 1575)

Kimberly Van Kampen
The Scriptorium: Center for Christian Antiquities

CATALOGUES: Jacob Nasmith, ed., *Catalogus librorum manuscriptorum quos Collegio Corporis Christi et B. Mariæ Virginis in Academia Cantabrigiensi legavit . . . Matthæus Parker, Archiepiscopus Cantuariensis* (London: G. & J. Innys, 1722);

M. R. James, *A Descriptive Catalogue of the Manuscripts in the Library of Corpus Christi College, Cambridge,* 2 volumes (Cambridge: Cambridge University Press, 1912);

R. I. Page, *Matthew Parker's Legacy: Books and Plate* (Cambridge: Corpus Christi College, 1975).

BOOKS: *An Admonition to all suche as shall intende hereafter to enter the state of Matrimony godly, and agreable to lawes* (London, 1560);

A godly and necessary Admonition of the Decrees and Canons of the Counsel of Trent, celebrated under Pius the Fourth . . . in . . . M.D. LXII and M.D. LXIII. Wrytten for Those Godlye Disposed Persons Sakes, which Looks for Amendment of Doctrine and Ceremonies to Bee Made by Generall Counsels. Lately Translated out of Latine (London: Imprinted by John Day, 1564);

A Brief and Lamentable Consideration of the Apparel now used by the Clergy of England (London, 1565);

A Brief Examination for the Tyme, of a Certaine Declaration, Lately Put in Print in the Name and Defence of Certaine Ministers of London, Refusyng to Weare the Apparell Prescribed by the Laws and Order of the Realme. In the End Is Reported, the Judgement of Two Notable Learned Fathers, M. Doctour Bucer, and M. Doctour Martir, Sometyme in Eyther Universities Here of England the Kynges Readers, and Professours of Divinitie Translated out of the Originals, Written by Theyr Owne Handes, Purposely Debatyng This Controversie (London: Richard Jugge, 1566);

De Antiquitate Britannicæ Ecclesiæ & Privilegiis Ecclesiæ Cantuariensis, cum Archiepiscopis Eiusdem 70 (London: John Day, 1572);

A Defence of Priests' Marriages . . . against a civilian naming himself Thomas Martin, etc. (London, n.d.);

Matthew Parker; from a portrait by Richard Lyne (Lambeth Palace)

Liber quorundam canonum disciplinæ ecclesiæ Anglicanæ anno MDLXXI (London, n.d.);

Articles of Enquiry within the diocese of Winchester in his Metropolitical Visitation (London, n.d.).

OTHER: *A List of Occasional Forms of Prayer and Services used during the Reign of Queen Elizabeth,* with several prayers attributed to Parker (London, 1559–1560);

The Whole Psalter translated into English Metre, which contayneth an hundred and fifty Psalmes, edited by Parker (London: Imprinted by John Daye, 1563);

Matthew of Westminster, *Flores historiarum,* edited by Parker (London, 1567);

Gildæ de excidio et conquestu Britanniae epistola, edited by Parker (London, 1567);

Abbot Ælfric, *A Testimonie of Antiquitie shewing the Auncient Fayth in the Church of England touching the Sacrament of the Body and Bloude of the Lord here publikely preached, and also receaved in the Saxons tyme, above 600 years agoe,* edited, with a preface to the sermon "Of the Paschal Lamb," by Parker (London: John Day, 1567);

The Holy Bible . . . , edited by Parker and Richard Cox (London, 1568);

The Gospels of the Fower Evangelistes, edited by Parker and John Joscelyn (London, 1571);

Matthew Paris, *Historia maior,* edited by Parker (London, 1571);

John Caius, *De Antiquitate Cantabrigiensis Academiæ,* edited by Parker (London, 1574);

Asser, *Ælfredi Regis Res Gestæ,* edited by Parker (London, 1574);

Thomas Walsingham, *Ypodigma Neustriae,* edited by Parker (London, 1574);

Articles to be enquired of within the Diocese of Canterbury . . . in the year of our Lorde God MDLIX, in *Concilia Magnae Britanniae et Hiberniae, a synodo Verolamiensi A.D. 446 ad Londiensam A.D. 1716. Accedunt constitutiones et alia ad historiam Ecclesiæ Anglicanae spectantia: a Davide Wilkins, S.T.P. collecta,* by David Wilkins, 4 volumes (London, 1737), IV: 257.

Occasionally history produces an individual who embodies the virtues of his time. Matthew Parker, archbishop of Canterbury, was not merely a product of the Renaissance and Reformation of England during the sixteenth century. He contributed, through his life of endeavor and influence, to the events and institutions that define those eras as cultural movements. In all, it is as much to Parker's credit as to any other's that the turmoil of the sixteenth century did not undo the English ecclesiastical system altogether or arrest the progress of the intellectual awakening. He was a clergyman whose practice and position took him into the political arena and an academic who applied his classical methodology to the process of rendering texts in the vernacular. His staunch support of the Reformation was both innovative and conservative, based upon historical precedent as well as the need for a contemporary compromise. His role at the time was as a shaper of the newly reformed Church of England, but his legacy today is in the library that he left to Corpus Christi College, Cambridge.

The contents of a man's library often disclose the substance of his intellect and imagination. Parker was a lover of both old and new books. His positions of authority in academic and ecclesiastical circles allowed him to be involved in two processes: the collection and conservation of the manuscript treasures of the realm and the promotion of texts to a wider audience through the flourishing print trade. His collaboration with London printers produced some of the greatest imprints of the day, while his vast collection of manuscripts established the basis for Anglo-Saxon studies and English antiquarianism. Parker's own collection contained both ancient and modern texts and illustrates Parker's greatest virtue, that is, his ability to find a common philosophical ground where extremes may coexist harmoniously. He found this ground in the contemporary interpretation of historical ideas. Blending the present with the past was Parker's primary occupation in his role of archbishop during the reign of Queen Elizabeth I, and his collection bears witness to the kind of historical continuation that he desired for Protestant England.

Matthew Parker was born at Norwich, in the parish of St. Saviour, on 6 August 1504, the son of Alice Monins Parker and William Parker, a manufacturer of cloth. His father died when Parker was twelve years old, and his mother later married John Baker. Parker had three surviving brothers, one of whom became mayor of Norwich, and a half brother, who likewise eventually became a benefactor to Corpus Christi College, Cambridge. Parker was sent to Cambridge in September 1522 at his mother's expense and was educated partly at St. Mary's Hostel and partly at Corpus Christi College. Shortly after, he was elected a Bible clerk and in 1525 was admitted to the college as a bachelor of arts student. He was ordained a priest on 15 June 1527 and in September of the same year was elected a fellow of his college. He commenced studies for a master of arts in 1528.

During this period Parker became involved with a group of young Cambridge academics who eventually became leaders of the English Reformation. Members of the group, which came to be widely known as the "Cambridge Reformers," included Thomas Bilney and Hugh Latimer. Parker's resistance to extremes is evident in even this earliest association. Although he espoused the tenets of Protestantism, he was more favorably inclined to the doctrines of the patristic writers than those of Luther's teachings, which were espoused by the Cambridge group. In times of upheaval Parker's pattern was to reject innovative theology and rely upon the foundational thought and practice of ancient Christianity. A true reformer at heart, Parker's sensibilities nevertheless often separated him from his more reactionary colleagues and his ultimate critics, the Puritan party. Parker's Protestantism was never one that favored the annihilation of the current establishment. His loyalties were to the preservation of the Church of England; his desire was to see it strengthened through the purification of reform.

During the reign of Henry VIII, Parker began his association with the court. In 1533 his popularity in the pulpit resulted in his being granted a license to preach throughout the southern province by Archbishop Thomas Cranmer, who two years later persuaded Parker to assume the office of chaplain to Anne Boleyn. With this post came the deanery of the College of St. John the Baptist at Stoke by Clare in Suffolk. For the next twelve years Parker found great contentment in this role. He brought with him his commitment to the English language for the purpose of educating the unlearned in religious matters, a commitment that was demonstrated in his earlier days of preaching and that led to his involvement in Bible translations in the later part of the century. He established a statute at the college that all lectures were to be given in Latin and English for those who were not trained in the former tongue. In Suffolk he also established long-term friendships with Nicholas Bacon and William Cecil.

In 1537 Parker was appointed chaplain to the king. The following year he earned his doctor of divinity degree, and on 4 December 1544 Parker returned to Cambridge as master of Corpus Christi College. In this capacity Parker began to exercise the sort of influence for which he eventually became known: he caused an inventory of the college to be made and directed all accounts to be preserved on parchment. Parker's inventories have survived as important pieces of evidence in the story of the college in the early modern period. In addition to the inventories, he commissioned a history of the college to be written by his secretary, John Joscelyn. Parker's lifelong collaboration with Joscelyn preserved many ancient texts and traditions that have proven invaluable to contemporary scholars.

Also during his years at Corpus Christi College, Parker learned to be a skillful moderate in the issues of the newly reformed state. He made it his personal mission to quell the spoliation of the colleges that came as a result of the new Protestant sentiment. An avid antiquarian at heart, Parker opposed the destruction of historical monuments for polemic purposes. Nonetheless, his close relationships with important Reformation figures guaranteed his connection with the court during the reign of Edward VI. Moreover, Parker's moderation did not prevent him from taking action on issues for which he retained strong convictions. His most visible issue, and the one that plagued Parker throughout his tenure as archbishop under Queen Elizabeth, was the permissibility of marriage for the clergy. Parker, like most of the reformers, felt that the Holy Scriptures did

Binding for a 1570 edition of Matthew of Westminster's De rebus Britannicis, *bound for Parker and decorated with his book stamp (All Souls College, Oxford)*

not forbid priests to marry, and indeed, at the age of forty-two Parker married Margaret Harlestone, the daughter of a prominent reformer. They were married on 24 June 1547. By this time Parker had been elected vice chancellor of Cambridge University.

In the tumult that followed Edward VI's death in 1553, Parker found himself in the dangerous predicament of having supported the accession of Lady Jane Grey over Edward's sister, Mary. When Mary assumed the throne and set about to restore the nation to its former Roman Catholic status, most of Parker's colleagues fled to the Continent and avoided Mary's vicious persecution of English Protestants. Parker remained in hiding in England, having been removed summarily from all his appointments for his support of Lady Jane and for his marriage.

At the accession of Elizabeth in 1558, Parker resumed his role of prominence in the restored Protestant nation. He returned to Cambridge to try to reinstate order in the university after the confusion of the previous five years. He was summoned away from his beloved Cambridge, however, by none other than the queen, who desired to appoint him to the see of Canterbury. The same man who reluctantly agreed to be chaplain to her mother entreated the queen to excuse him from the position. Parker claimed to be in poor health, but he no doubt was aware also of the risks involved in a position that held such political distinction, particularly in light of the queen's disapproval of a married priest. Parker's love was for his studies and for the university, and he would have led a contented life had he never re-entered the higher arena of public service. Yet, the queen was willing to overlook his marriage and persisted in her request until Parker relented.

Within seven months Parker had been elected to the archbishopric, and on 9 September 1559 the order for his consecration was given. His appointment, however, was controversial in that the consecration was conducted in a new and different manner from the former Roman ceremony. Parker, with forethought for his own credibility and his proclivity for record keeping, caused an account and defense of the occasion to be drawn up and deposited at Corpus Christi College.

Queen Elizabeth's judgment proved to be wiser than Parker's, for as archbishop he became one of the great figures of the sixteenth century, shaping the new English church and preserving the heritage of the past as the precedent for the new order. In this capacity Parker's tendency to prefer moderation became the policy of the Anglican party, which defined itself as a middle road between Roman and Puritan extremes. It retained the ecclesiastical structure and practices that had been in place before the Reformation while it espoused the major tenets of Protestantism, namely the symbolic nature of the Eucharist, the marriage of priests, and the Scriptures in the common tongue. Parker was personally responsible for the 1562 and 1571 revisions of the Articles of the Church, and he produced the first English version of the Psalms in meter in 1562. His revised prayer book for the universities retained the Roman calendar out of respect for the Catholic community in those places. A tremendous controversy that required his attention was the issue of priests' apparel. In 1565 he published his *Advertisements,* a prescription for a modified ecclesiastical garb that was intended to please the conservative tastes of the queen as well as the nonconformist sensibilities of the Puritans.

Parker's conflicts with the Puritan party became his greatest affliction. By the mid 1560s the voices of reform had moved away from unified opposition to the Roman church to disagreements between factions within Protestantism. Parker was forced to oppose the most zealous Puritans, and even though he also imposed penalties on those who refused to give up their Roman allegiances, his relationship with Cambridge became strained as the philosophical trend there increasingly favored Puritanism. Parker's attempts to diffuse Puritan influences are documented in his 1570 Constitution of the University, later known as the Elizabethan Statutes. Although the document is now seen as a milestone of the academic history of the university, it caused him to be labeled "the Pope of Lambeth" by his Puritan contemporaries.

During this time Parker also was occupied with the editorship of the Bishops' Bible, one of the great biblical monuments of the Tudor period. This version was intended to be a translation from the original languages that would avoid the controversial readings of the Geneva Bible, which was heralded by the Puritans. From 1563 to 1568 Parker was involved with this project, and although his name is not attached to any edition, it is accepted that he was one of the chief editors of the work. It was presented to the queen in 1568 with a letter from Parker imploring her to authorize this version to be read in all churches.

The end of Parker's life was characterized by continual opposition to the furtherance of nonconformist doctrines and by his own personal study into the history of the English church. In 1568 Parker was given permission to collect all literary documents that related to the history of the English nation, and this census marked the beginning of his infatuation with the Anglo-Saxon language. As the controversies of his day became more complex and irritating, Parker became more convinced that the tenets of Protestantism should conform with the pre-Roman practices of the English church. The popular idea of the day was "the return to the purity of the primitive church," as documented in the four-volume *Annals of the Reformation* (1824) by John Strype, the self-proclaimed chronicler of the Reformation and biographer of Parker. Parker's manuscripts were the last remaining records of the Anglo-Saxon period. Parker commissioned his personal staff, Joscelyn in particular, to begin to decipher the texts, written in a language that had not been spoken for more than five hundred years, for their doctrinal content. The results of these efforts in Parker's household are twofold: the preservation of endangered texts and the genesis of Old English studies.

The 1568 general letter from the Privy Council that permitted Parker to seek out and bring together manuscripts from throughout the nation is now preserved as Corpus Christi College MS 114. It relates the queen's interest in ancient records and her concern for their preservation for both the ecclesiastical state and the civil government. Parker gathered books from all over the country, but mainly from the south and west. He found his treasures in religious houses, cathedral priories, and private collections. R. I. Page's introduction to *Matthew Parker's Legacy,* the catalogue of an exhibition in 1975 of Parker's collection, lists the contents of these collected national monuments as follows: "Bibles, service books and books of devotion, theology and canon law . . . but also historical and hagiographical writings, treatises of astronomy and music, mathematics, alchemy, philosophy, politics and low, French romances, bestiaries, and works by Homer and Euripides, Cicero and Seneca, Chaucer, Langlund, and Wycliffe."

The standard inventory of Parker's manuscript holdings is M. R. James's *A Descriptive Catalogue of the Manuscripts in the Library of Corpus Christi College, Cambridge* (1912). Parker kept an inventory of his books, as did successive librarians, including his eldest son, John Parker, in a master list that came to be known as the Parker Register (MS CCCC 575). The Parker Register provides an account of the early circulation of these books during the years when the curatorial colleges lent them to scholars.

Parker's collection is best known for its manuscripts, but the larger portion of the archive was printed material. Parker understood the art of printing and collected several of the industry's first imprints. He brought together many of the incunable editions of humanist and religious works, including those by authors such as Giovanni Boccaccio, Gregory, Cicero, Vegetius, and Isadore. He also amassed an important contemporary library, with works by sixteenth-century writers such as Desiderius Erasmus and Hermann of Wied. Many of the printed books collected by Parker formerly had been owned by his friends and colleagues, including the reformers Martin Bucer, Thomas Yale, and Nicolas Robinson.

Some of the world's most important manuscripts were once in Parker's hands. MS CCCC 286, the Gospels of St. Augustine, is a sixth-century gospel book from Italy that came to England during the Anglo-Saxon period. This manuscript was one of the first biblical books to come to pagan England with Augustine, the first missionary sent there by Pope Gregory in the sixth century. Although incomplete, the manuscript retains several of its resplendent illustrations. Another monument in the Parker collection is a life of St. Cuthbert (MS CCCC 183), a tenth-century book in verse and prose that was presented to the Shrine of St. Cuthbert by King Athelstan in the 930s. The twelfth-century Bury Bible (MS CCCC 2) is one of the most lavishly illustrated bibles of the English tradition of manuscript illumination. MS CCCC 61 is a primary text for Chaucer's *Troilus and Criseyde* (circa 1382–1386), dated to shortly after the poem's composition.

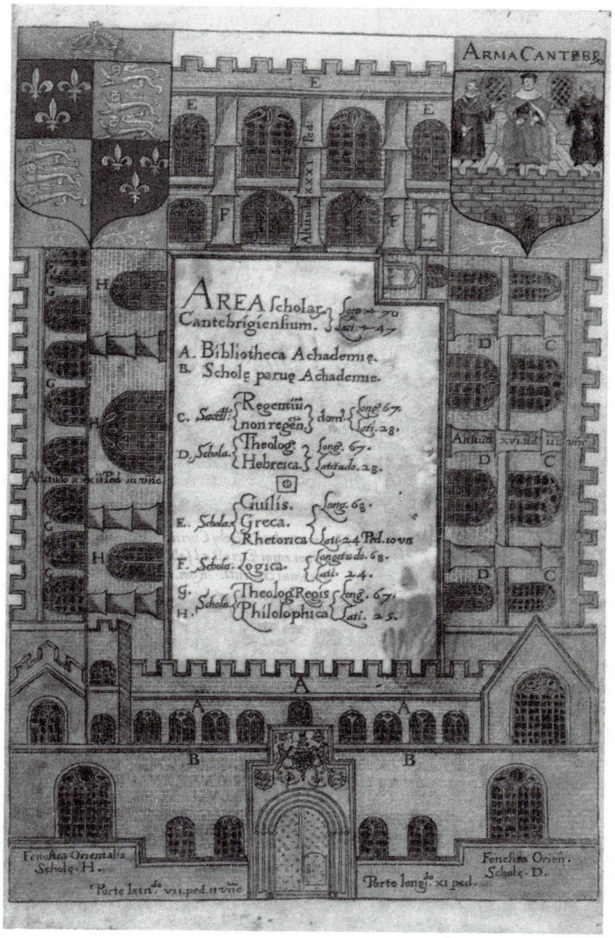

Diagram of the Quadrangle at Cambridge University from Parker's presentation copy of Catalogus cancellariorum *(1574), which lists his and others' donations to the university library (Royal Library)*

Many of the early medieval texts were unique, especially those from the period prior to the Norman Conquest. Some forty remnants of the great literary tradition of Anglo-Saxon culture were collected by Parker. These include MS CCCC 26 and 16, the autograph copy (in two volumes) of Matthew Paris's *Chronica Majora* (1235–1259), which chronicles the history of the world from Creation to 1188, as well as the homilies of Abbott Ælfric, MS CCCC 162. Parker's own study of the early Christian writings in England convinced him of an affinity of the first English church to the doctrines espoused by the Protestant cause, particularly those held by the Anglican establishment, and he became fascinated with the ancient language itself. In *The Life and Acts of Matthew Parker* (1821) Strype attributed the following comment to Parker: "It was worth ones Pains . . . to compare our Country Language, which we now use, with that obsolete and almost extinguished Speech; and while we are comparing them, to observe, how like they are, and almost the same."

Parker's household was known for its study of Old English, and from this small fraternity of scholars developed the Antiquarian Society, which met regularly until 1604. Joscelyn, Parker's secretary, is known for creating the first Anglo-Saxon lexicon, as well as being the chief editor of the texts for publication. Printing in Anglo-Saxon types was revolutionary for the period. Strype credits Parker with employing the printer, John Day, to cut the first Saxon type in brass in 1566. Four books were produced using this type, either wholly or in part: a 1567 edition of Ælfric's *A Testimonie of Antiquitie;* William Lambard's *Archaionomia* (1568); *The Gospels of the Fower Evangelistes* (1571), edited by Parker and Joscelyn; and Parker's own *De Antiquitate Britannicæ Ecclesiæ & Privilegiis Ecclesæ Cantuariensis, cum Archiepiscopis Eiusdem 70,* which he had privately printed in 1572. The significance of the Anglo-Saxon documents for the reform cause is expressed by the martyrologist John Foxe in his preface to *The Gospels of the Fower Evangelistes:*

> So likewise have we to understand and conceive, by the edition hereof, how the religion presently taught and professed in the Church at this present, is no new reformation of things lately begun, where were not before, but rather a reduction of the Church to the Pristine state of olde conformitie, which once it had, and almost lost by discontinuance of a few later years: as it is manifest to be proved, not only in this cause of the vulgar translation of the Scriptures, but in other cases also of doctrine, as transubstantiation, of Priests' restraint from marriage, of receiving under one kind, with many other points and articles more of like quality newly thruist in, and the old abolished by the clergy of Rome.

Arguably Parker's greatest publication was his *De Antiquitate Britannicæ Ecclesiæ*. Intended to be a sixteenth-century addition to the Venerable Bede's monumental work, it carried the English ecclesiastical tradition from Augustine all the way to the Anglican succession. Many of the manuscripts in Parker's collection were cited as ancient authorities in ecclesiastical matters, and the book managed to rile both the Catholic recusants and the Puritans. The work was reissued many times after Parker's death.

Parker may have been more of a polemicist than a scholar of Old English, but his efforts at salvaging what little material was left and learning the contents of the manuscripts are recognized today as the birth of Old English studies. One can hardly criticize these early scholars of Old English for having other than academic motives when it was their efforts at preservation that allowed the discipline to take hold. As well, Parker has often been criticized by modern scholars for his preservation techniques. The manuscripts that came through his household all bear marks of their sixteenth-century usage. Almost all in Parker's collection were foliated or annotated, at times into the text block, by his characteristic red crayon. Those that were prepared for publication were often edited directly on the parchment folios by typesetters. Page, in his *Matthew Parker and His Books* (1993), has illustrated where a printer's wooden block was laid across a page to hold it flat, suggesting that the manuscript itself and not a transcription was sent to the printer's shop. In addition to marking manuscripts, Parker removed and discarded defective leaves from various books and had them replaced by facsimiles, which were copied on parchment in his household by trained scribes. He also unbound certain books and rebound them with others in an order that he found more pleasing. When a text was fragmentary, he had it erased so as not to detract from the complete text that followed.

Overly critical judgment of the actions of Parker and his conservators does not take into account that Parker accomplished, to a greater degree than most present-day conservators, what he set out to do: that is, to preserve the literary monuments of a culture that had been all but extinguished in the five hundred years since its demise. The same sense of organization that motivated him to keep immaculate records also applied itself to the long-term well-being of the books he curated. It is impossible to ascertain the condition that the discarded leaves were in, but their texts were preserved as Parker intended. And while his ubiquitous red crayon may appear to reduce the beauty of a medieval page, four hundred years later scholars are looking at these sixteenth-century readers' marks with the same interest as they do the earlier text.

The general letter of the Privy Council of 1568 also required that the obscure texts that Parker collected be made known to the realm by way of publication, and Parker's efforts to this end were invaluable, particularly after the fire that destroyed much of the private collection of Sir Robert Bruce Cotton in 1731, including many of these primary texts. In addition to the Anglo-Saxon monuments, Parker brought many later medieval works to print, such as Matthew of Westminster's *Flores historiarum,* Thomas Walsingham's *Historia brevis* and *Ypodigma Neustriæ,* and Matthew Paris's *Historia maior.* He was also aware of the influence of the press and believed that the archbishop had the authority to monitor it. W. W. Greg, in "Books and Bookmen in the Correspondence of Archbishop Parker" (1935), described Parker's relationship with the press thus: "As archbishop he was in control, to some extent at least, of all official or semi-official publications of an ecclesiastical nature at a time when the Anglican settlement was perhaps the most urgent task of English statesmanship; he also kept in touch with the theological controversy of the time, and was responsible for the exclusion or suppression of unorthodox writings whether on the Roman or the puritan side."

No doubt Parker had the ability to grant privileges to printers of his choice, as was probably the case with John Day. Yet, all the while that he was controlling the trade, as Greg suggests, he was adding to his own collection of printed books, which contained some of the finest imprints produced in England or the Continent in the first one hundred years of printing.

In all, Parker left more than 450 manuscripts and several hundred books to Corpus Christi College and 25 manuscripts plus many printed books to the University Library at Cambridge. Several more manuscripts are at Trinity College, the Royal Library, and the British Library, while some stayed in Parker's family and others are lost. In addition to books are Parker's extensive records and correspondences, which trace the progress of the Reformation and the Anglican establishment throughout much of the sixteenth century. Parker's intention was for the library to remain intact, and his will instructed Corpus Christi College to take two yearly audits that were to be conducted by two other Cambridge colleges, who would stand to inherit the library should it be found that Corpus Christi was remiss in its curatorial responsibilities.

Parker died on 17 May 1575 after suffering from a long illness. He was buried in his private chapel at Lambeth. During the Interregnum, Parker's remains were disinterred and buried under a dunghill. They were returned to their original tomb by Archbishop William Sancroft after the Restoration. The library in Corpus Christi College, which now holds Parker's book collection, was named after its greatest benefactor. The Parker Library has boasted many great librarians and bibliographers who have held in trust Parker's own testimony of antiquity in order that the innovations of the future would not be made without consideration of the past.

References:

Bruce Dickens, "The Making of the Parker Library," *Transactions of the Cambridge Bibliographical Society,* 4, no. 1 (1972): 19–34;

W. W. Greg, "Books and Bookmen in the Correspondence of Archbishop Parker," *Library,* fourth series 16 (December 1935);

N. R. Ker, *Catalogue of Manuscripts Containing Anglo-Saxon* (Oxford: Clarendon Press, 1990);

Ker, *Medieval Libraries of Great Britain: A List of Surviving Books,* second edition (London: Royal Historical Society, 1964);

R. I. Page, *Matthew Parker and His Books; Sandars Lectures in Bibliography Delivered on 14, 16, and 18 May 1990 at the University of Cambridge* (Kalamazoo, Mich.: Medieval Institute Publications / Cambridge: Research Group on Manuscript Evidence, Parker Library, Corpus Christi College, 1993);

Page, introduction to *Matthew Parker's Legacy* (Cambridge: Cambridge University Press, 1975);

John Strype, *Annals of the Reformation,* second edition, 4 volumes (Oxford, 1824);

Strype, *The Life and Acts of Matthew Parker,* second edition, 3 volumes (Oxford, 1821).

Papers:

Many of Matthew Parker's writings were never published and are in manuscript in Corpus Christi College Library, now the Parker Library, Cambridge.

Samuel Pepys

(23 February 1633 - 26 May 1703)

Joseph Rosenblum
University of North Carolina at Greensboro

See also the Pepys entry in *DLB 101: British Prose Writers, 1660–1800, First Series.*

Samuel Pepys (portrait by Geoffrey Kneller; Pepys Library, Magdalene College, Cambridge)

CATALOGUES: Edward Bernard, *Catalogi librorum manuscriptorum Angline et Hiberniae in unum collecti, cum indice alphabetico,* 2 volumes (Oxford: E Theatro Sheldoniano, 1697), items 6716–6848;

Bibliotheca Pepysiana: A Descriptive Catalogue of the Library of Samuel Pepys: part I, *"Sea" Manuscripts,* by J. R. Tanner (London: Sidgwick & Jackson, 1914); part II, *Early Printed Books to 1558,* by E. Gordon Duff, with a general introduction by Frank Sidgwick (London: Sidgwick & Jackson, 1914); part III, *Medieval Manuscripts,* by Montague Rhodes James (London: Sidgwick & Jackson, 1923); part IV, *Shorthand Books,* by William John Carlton (London: Sidgwick & Jackson, 1940);

Stephen Gaselee, *The Spanish Books in the Library of Samuel Pepys,* supplement to the Bibliographical Society's *Transactions,* no. 2 (London: Printed at the Oxford University Press for the Bibliographical Society, 1921);

Robert Latham, ed., *Catalogue of the Pepys Library at Magdalene College, Cambridge,* 7 volumes to date (Cambridge: D. S. Brewer; Totowa, N.J.: Rowman & Littlefield, 1978–).

BOOKS: *Memoirs Relating to the State of the Royal Navy in England, for Ten Years, determin'd December 1688* (London: Printed for R. Griffin, 1690); facsimile, edited by J. R. Tanner as *Pepys' Memoires of the Royal Navy, 1679–1688* (Oxford: Clarendon Press, 1906);

An Account of the Preservation of King Charles after the Battle of Worcester, edited by Sir David Dalrymple (London: Printed for William Sandby, 1766);

Memoirs of Samuel Pepys, Esq., F. R. S., Secretary to the Admiralty in the Reigns of Charles II. and James II., Comprising His Diary from 1659 to 1669, Deciphered by the Rev. John Smith, 2 volumes, edited by Richard, Lord Braybrooke (London: Colburn, 1825);

Diary and Correspondence of Samuel Pepys, F. R. S., Secretary to the Admiralty in the Reigns of Charles II. And James II. . . . 3rd Edition, Considerably Enlarged, 5 volumes, edited by Braybrooke (London: Colburn, 1848, 1849);

Diary and Correspondence of Samuel Pepys, Esq., F. R. S., from His Manuscript Cypher in the Pepysian Library, 6 volumes, deciphered and edited by Reverend Mynors Bright (London: Bickers, 1875–1879);

The Diary of Samuel Pepys, 10 volumes, edited by Henry B. Wheatley (London & New York: Bell, 1893–1899);

Samuel Pepys's Naval Minutes, edited by J. R. Tanner (London: Printed for the Navy Records Society, 1926);

The Tangier Papers of Samuel Pepys, edited by Edwin Chappell (London: Printed for the Navy Records Society, 1935);

Mr. Pepys upon the State of Christ-Hospital, edited by Rudolf Kirk (Philadelphia: University of Pennsylvania Press / London: Oxford University Press, 1935);

Charles II's Escape from Worcester: A Collection of Narratives Assembled by Samuel Pepys, edited by William Matthews (Berkeley & Los Angeles: University of California Press, 1966);

The Diary of Samuel Pepys: A New and Complete Transcription, 11 volumes, edited by Robert Latham and William Matthews (Berkeley & Los Angeles: University of California Press, 1970–1983).

In a 1695 memorandum in his diary Samuel Pepys wrote that he intended for his collection of books to differ from the "Extensive, Pompous, and Stationary Libraries of Princes, Universities, Colleges and other Publick-Societies" and from the "Voluminous Collections . . . of the Professors of Particular Faculties: as being calculated for the Self-Entertainment onely of a solitary, unconfined Enquirer into Books." His goal was to assemble "in fewest Books and the least Room the greatest diversity of Subjects, Stiles, and Languages its Owner's Reading [would] bear." He wanted these books bound decently and uniformly, and he sought to catalogue them clearly and comprehensively. The three-thousand-volume library that resulted from this vision indicates its creator's diverse activities: naval administrator, competent musician, amateur scientist who served as president of the Royal Society, devoted playgoer, intelligent observer of his world–in short, a Restoration virtuoso. As Robert Latham observes in the tenth volume of *The Diary of Samuel Pepys: A New and Complete Transcription* (1983), "The library came to reflect almost as clearly as the diary itself the mind and personality of its owner." Because of Pepys's foresight, this library remains intact at Magdalene College, Cambridge University, where it has served generations of scholars, illuminated the book culture of seventeenth-century England, and provided insights into the mind of the man who assembled the collection.

The son of John Pepys, a tailor, and Margaret Kite Pepys, the sister of a butcher, Samuel Pepys was born in London on 23 February 1633. The fifth of eleven children, he was the eldest of the three that survived to adulthood. He attended Huntington Grammar School and then St. Paul's School, where he undoubtedly studied Greek and Hebrew as well as Latin. The lack in his library of books in Greek or Hebrew suggests that he did not make much progress in these first two languages, though he became fluent in French and Spanish and perhaps Dutch. On 21 June 1650 he entered Trinity Hall, Cambridge, as a scholarship student, but on 1 October he transferred to Magdalene College, a decision that would influence the final disposition of his library.

Pepys probably began his book collecting during his college years. At least one of Pepys's books was purchased from William Morden in 1654, the year after Pepys graduated from Cambridge; on 25 February 1660 he bought another book from Morden, George Bate's *Elenchi Motuum,* a defense of Charles I first published in 1650. Characteristically, Pepys replaced Bate's book with a later edition published in 1661. This tendency to prefer the latest edition prompted him to dispose of a Third Folio of Shakespeare when he acquired a copy of the Fourth (1685), but the practice was not unique to Pepys. The Bodleian Library, Oxford, withdrew its First Folio (1623) when it secured a copy of the Second (1632).

Pepys wed fifteen-year-old Elizabeth St. Michel on 1 December 1655 and in the latter part of the decade worked as a clerk to George Downing in the Exchequer and also as an assistant to Edward Mountagu, a distant relative. In February 1660 Pepys removed his books from the lodgings of Mountagu, who became the first earl of Sandwich, to Axe Yard. Pepys recorded in the shorthand diary, which he had started keeping at the first of the year, that he spent Sunday, 19 February, arranging his books, so by this time he must have had the beginnings of a library. Later that year Pepys moved again, this time to Seething Lane, and again he recorded in his diary on 17 October that he put his books in order in his closet. Organizing his collection proved to be a recurrent motif in his diary. Some of his books contain evidence of seven different arrangements. Pepys loved order, and he delighted in handling and looking at his ever-growing collection.

In 1660 Mountagu was vice admiral in charge of the fleet that sailed to the Netherlands to end the Interregnum by bringing Charles II back to England. Mountagu invited Pepys to join him as his secretary, a post he filled with such distinction that he was appointed clerk of acts to the Navy Board, the first of several government posts he would fill, culminating in his serving as secretary of the Admiralty from 1684 to 1689. On this 1660 voyage to Holland, as on all his subsequent trips, Pepys found time for book buying. On 15 May at The Hague, Pepys went "to a bookseller's and bought, for the love of the binding, three books–the French Psalms

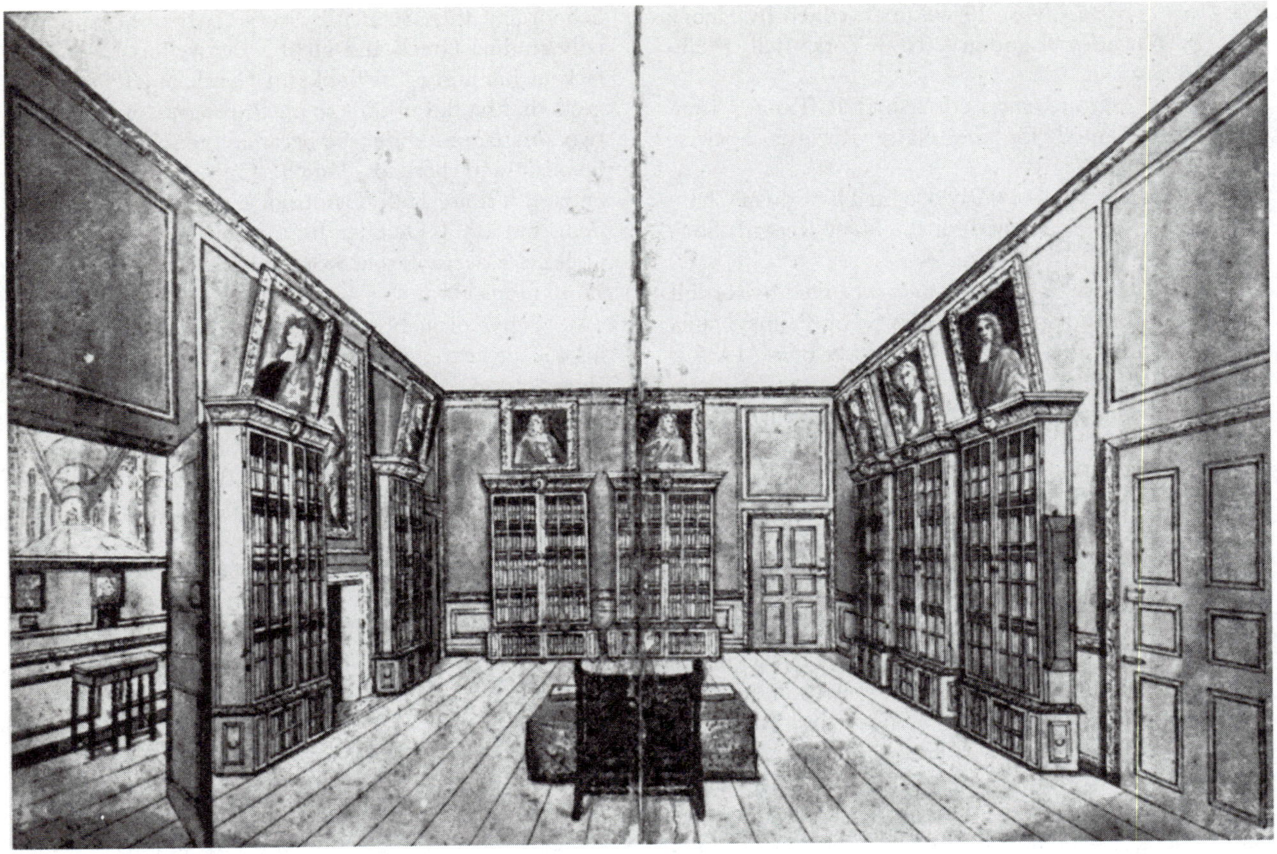

Pepys's library in York Buildings, London

in four parts–Bacon's *organon,* and Farnaby's *Rhetoric.*" The last of these is probably Thomas Farnaby's *Index rhetoricus* (Amsterdam, 1648) in a plain limp white vellum binding. Bacon's *organon* is no longer in the Pepys library. Robert Latham and William Matthews suggest in *The Diary of Samuel Pepys* that the book of Psalms also was replaced, but Pepys owned *Les pseaumes de David, mis en rime françoyse par Cl.*[ément] *Marot & Th.*[éodore] *de Beze* (1660), printed at Rotterdam. The date and place of publication argue for its being the volume Pepys secured at The Hague.

Pepys's diary, which covers the period from 1 January 1660 to 31 May 1669, contains some five hundred references to books read, examined, bought, bound, arranged, catalogued, and, occasionally, sold. Pepys liked to keep up with the latest literature. In the entry for 26 December 1662 he reported that John Battersby told him of Samuel Butler's *Hudibras.* The first part, though dated 1663 on the title page, actually was published in late November 1662 and became an instant success. Pepys rushed out to get a copy but found it so "silly" that he disposed of it for 18d. after paying 2s.6d. (30d.) for it. Two months later, on 6 February 1663, Pepys wrote in his diary, "To a bookseller in the Strand, and there bought *Hudibras,* it being certainly some ill humour to be so against that which all the world cries up to be the example of wit; for which I am resolved once more to read him, and see whether I can find it or no." He evidently could not, and when the second part appeared later that year, he borrowed a copy, not intending to buy it. Yet, on 10 December 1663 he bought a copy of both parts. This, too, he later disposed of, but his final collection includes a 1689 edition of all three parts.

On 2 February 1667 Pepys read with greater pleasure *Annus Mirabilis* by John Dryden, his distant relative and fellow graduate of Magdalene College. The poem had been licensed for publication on 21 January, so again Pepys was keeping up with the most recent products of the press. Later that year Pepys bought the newly printed *Indian Emperor* (1667) by Dryden, and on 18 January he secured a copy of Dryden's just-published *Secret Love; or, The Maiden Queen* (1668), which Pepys had seen performed on stage. Pepys grew up during the Cromwellian Commonwealth, when the Puritans closed the theaters, and he remained ambivalent about the stage. As his purchases of Dryden indicate, he overcame his scruples in this matter as he did in various others. Thus, on 20 April 1666 he records, "And I to the New Exchange, there to get a list of all the modern plays–which I entend to collect and to have them bound up together."

Pepys carried out this plan at least in part, producing two volumes of "Loose Plays," one with fourteen works published between 1638 and 1667, the other with thirteen from 1664 to 1685. Two more volumes, which Pepys titled "Old Plays," contain another twenty-seven printed between 1565 and 1617. In addition, he owned such popular works as William Wycherley's *The Plain Dealer* (second edition, 1678), Thomas Shadwell's *The History of Timon of Athens* (1678), *The Sullen Lovers* (1670), a 1692 edition of Ben Jonson's *Works,* as well as the Fourth Folio of Shakespeare.

Pepys again wrestled with his conscience regarding the salacious *L'escolle des filles,* usually attributed to Michel Millot and Jean L'Ange and first published in Paris in 1655. The book was condemned and burned in Paris in 1655; English translations were prosecuted during Pepys's lifetime in 1677 and 1688. On 13 January 1668 Pepys saw a copy at the shop of John Martin, a bookseller at Temple Bar. Pepys thought it was a romance and was going to buy it for his wife, but when he began reading he found it "the most bawdy, lewd book that ever I saw," worse even than *La puttana errante.* On 8 February Pepys returned to buy *L'escolle des filles* for himself, but he wanted it in a plain binding because he intended to burn the book after reading it, "that it may not stand in the list of books, nor among them, to disgrace them if it should be found." The next day Pepys finished reading the book and destroyed it.

On 15 February 1665 Pepys became a member of the Royal Society. Some months earlier, on 13 August 1664, he had paid £5. 10s. for a microscope, and on that day he read part of Henry Power's *Experimental Philosophy . . . Containing New Experiments Microscopical, Mercurial, Magnetical* (1664). He finished the book the following day, and on the sixteenth he collected "observations" from this early work on microscopy. On 2 January 1665 he visited Joseph Kirton at St. Paul's Churchyard; Kirton was Pepys's favorite bookseller before the Great Fire of 1666. At Kirton's shop he saw Robert Hooke's *Micrographia* (1665), which he found "so pretty" that he ordered a copy, which he took home on 20 January, presumably after having it bound. Pepys described the book as "a most excellent piece, and of which I am very proud." The next day he stayed up until 2:00 A.M. reading this "most ingenious book that ever I read in my life."

Pepys's scientific interest began early and lasted throughout his life. On 12 September 1660 he gave his brother copies of Thomas Bartholinus's *Anatomia* (fifth edition, 1651, or sixth edition, 1660; Pepys's library contains a copy of the latter) and Pierre Gassendi's *Institutio astronomica,* first published in 1647. Pepys later secured a copy of the 1683 edition. Pepys owned forty titles by the great English chemist Robert Boyle; the pre-Newtonian work on gravity by Sir Matthew Hale, *An Essay Touching the Gravitation, or non-Gravitation of Fluid Bodies* (1673); Anthony van Leeuwenhoek's *Anatomia* (1687), *Arcana naturae* (1695), and *Continuatio epistolarum* (1689); and the first edition of Isaac Newton's *Philosophiae naturalis principia mathematica* (1687), with the imprimatur signed by Pepys as president of the Royal Society.

In 1666 Pepys had John Hayls paint his portrait. In Pepys's hand is a copy of the song "Beauty Retire." Pepys composed the music and took the words from the second part of Sir William Davenant's opera *The Siege of Rhodes.* Pepys saw the second part acted on 2 July 1661 and owned a copy of the 1663 edition, in which the two parts were published together for the first time. In his typically hyperbolic fashion, Pepys called Davenant's work "the best poem that ever was wrote" and read the work repeatedly "with great delight." Pepys composed several other songs, including a musical setting for Jonson's lines beginning "It is decreed nor shall thy fate, O Rome! / Resist my vows, though hills were set on hills," from *Catiline.*

On 30 July 1666 Pepys recorded in his diary, "Music is the thing of the world that I love most." In 1661 Pepys engaged John Goodgroome to give him voice lessons for £1 a month. Pepys carried a flageolet with him and would play it whenever the mood struck him. He also played the lute, the theorbo, treble viol, bass viol, bass flute, and recorder. After listening to the music for *The Virgin Martyr* (1622) by Philip Massinger and Thomas Dekker at the King's Theatre, Pepys wrote on 27 February 1668 that he found the sound "so sweet that it ravished me, and endeed, in a word, did wrap my soul so that it made me really sick, just as I have formerly been when in love with my wife."

The diary is filled with references to his delight in listening to and in playing music, and his library contains many works in this field. On Saturday, 18 February 1660, Pepys spent "a great while at my Viall and voice, learning to sing *Fly boy, fly boy* without book." The song was printed in William Lawes's *Select Ayres and Dialogues* (1659) published by John Playford, a title which is not in Pepys's collection. Pepys may, however, have owned a copy at the time. Richard Luckett, the author of the entry on music in Latham's edition of the diary, suggests that Pepys took this volume and Henry

Some of the wooden bases Pepys had made so that his books stood at the same height on the shelves

Lawes's *Third Book of Ayres* (1658) aboard the *Naseby* when he went to Holland to retrieve Charles II. Pepys certainly owned five other books by John Playford and his son Henry. John Playford, whose shop was in the Inner Temple, was the leading publisher of music in this period.

Pepys was especially proud of his music books. On 24 February 1668 Pepys left Athanasius Kircher's *Musurgia universalis* (1650) at John Martin's to be bound. Two days earlier Pepys had paid William Shrewsbury of Duck Lane 35s. for this work, and he spent another 25s. for binding the two volumes in thick calf, with gold tooling on the spines. On 3 April 1668 he sought Marin Mersenne's *Harmonie universelle* (1633–1637) in Duck Lane. He did not find a copy but bought René Descartes's *Musical Companion* (first published in 1650). On 28 May 1668 John Martin brought Pepys a copy of Mersenne's book, for which Pepys paid £3. 2s. Despite the high price, Pepys remarked that he was delighted to have it, "expecting to find great satisfaction in it." Pepys owned Thomas Morley's *A Plaine and Easie Introduction to Practicall Musicke* (1597), which Pepys found "a very good but inmethodical book." Other music works in Pepys's collection include William Holder and Matthew Locke's *A Treatise on the Natural Grounds, and Principles of Harmony* (1694); Francis North, Baron Guilford's *A Philosophical Essay of Musick* (1677); Thomas Salmon's *An Essay to the Advancement of Musick* (1672); and Matthew Locke's 1672 response, *Observations upon a Late Book Entituled, "An Essay to the Advancement of Musick."*

On 27 October 1660 Pepys purchased for 38s. John Heinrich Alsted's *Encyclopaedia* (1630), which includes an essay on music. John Birchensha, who taught composition to Pepys, translated book 14 of Alsted's compendium as *Templum musicum* (1664). As a student Pepys had found Birchensha's system "not so useful" as his teacher believed it to be, and the two had parted on bad terms. Nonetheless, in 1667 Pepys borrowed or bought his former teacher's book. On 4 March he read the work while sailing on a barge, but he remained unimpressed. He called the *Templum musicum* "the most ridiculous book . . . that ever I saw in my life. . . . I understand not three lines together, from one end of the book to the other." The title does not appear in Pepys's final library. In 1680 the composer Cesare Morelli prepared for Pepys a guide to playing the guitar; this work Pepys did retain.

Pepys also bought much music in manuscript, even though it proved expensive because of the labor involved. Some of his manuscript music cost him nothing. When the court musician John Bannister visited him on 7 May 1668, Pepys asked him to write out the music for Shakespeare's *The Tempest* (ca. 1611) that Bannister had composed and that Pepys had enjoyed on 7 November 1667. The actress Elizabeth Knepp gave Pepys the words and music to "The Lark Now Leaves His Watery Nest."

Related to this musical interest was Pepys's pursuit of ballads. Five large albums in the Bibliotheca Pepysiana contain more than 1,800 broadsheet ballads, with about 950 of them unique. Included here is the first printed broadside ballad, "A Ballad of Luther[,] the Pope[,] a Cardinal and a Husbandman" (ca. 1535). Hyder Edward Rollins, who published 505 of Pepys's ballads in the eight volumes of *The Pepys Ballads* (1929–1932), notes their historical significance. As he writes in the preface to the third volume, "In these seventy-three ballads may be seen the ideas that were held by common reporters about the great events of their time." The ballads also reveal more mundane aspects of life, such as the hairstyles then in vogue and the conditions of the working poor. They shed light on other literature as well. "The Two Faithful Friends" (ca. 1620) preserves the plot of the lost play *Alexander and Lodowick* (1597), and "A New Song Shewing the Cruelty of Gernutus a Jew" (ca. 1610) retells the central events of *The Merchant of Venice* (ca. 1596).

Pepys collected other forms of popular literature as well. He owned 114 chapbooks, mainly twenty-four page duodecimos printed in black letter (Gothic typeface). These he bound into three volumes that he titled "Penny Merriments." Another set of four volumes contains fifty-one examples of popular literature from about 1637 to 1693. Pepys did not limit this interest in popular literature to English. One volume in his library contains seventy-one Spanish ballads; another holds twenty-six Spanish comedies. These he acquired in Seville in 1684 while traveling on a government mission to abolish the fortifications at Tangiers. In his Tangiers papers at the Bodleian Pepys describes his purchases as "Pamphlets Plays Sermons &c." and "Bundle of Ballads." He was sufficiently familiar with Spanish to use the language in his diary when he wished to mask his amorous activities.

Pepys's interest in Spanish books began early. On 11 February 1660 he records, "This morning I lay long abed; and then to my office, where I read all the morning my Spanish book of Rome," referring to Girolamo Franzini's *Las cosas maravillosas dela sancta cuidad de Roma* (1651), a pilgrim's guide to the city. His diary repeatedly speaks of his wandering through Duck Lane, where inexpensive books were to be found, in search of Spanish titles. On 24 April 1668 he found a cache of books that had belonged to Nicolas Fouquet, who had served as Minister of Finance to Louis XIV but was removed from office and imprisoned in 1661. Fouquet's extensive library of some thirty-thousand volumes was confiscated; though most of these are now in the Bibliothèque Nationale, some were sold. One of the books Pepys bought was Juan Sedeño's *Summa de varones illustres* (1590), with Fouquet's coat of arms on the back cover.

Searching Duck Lane on another occasion, Pepys in November 1668 saw a copy of Francisco de los Santos's *Descripcion breve del monasterio de S. Lorenzo el real del Escorial* (second edition, 1667) that Edward Mountagu had promised him. Although the copy of this edition in Pepys's library contains no indication that it was a gift, Pepys probably did not spend money on it. He noted that he wanted a copy, "though I took it for a finer book when he [Mountagu] promised it me."

Pepys also requested others to provide Spanish books for him. On 28 April 1669 Henry Sheeres, a miltary engineer, sent Pepys the two-volume *Historia general de España* by Juan de Mariana, first published in 1590. Pepys, who was pleased to receive the book, may have asked Sheeres, recently returned from Spain, to secure him a copy of this learned work. Pepys later replaced the edition, perhaps that of 1650, with one published at Madrid in 1678. When Pepys's favorite nephew, John Jackson, was traveling on the Continent from 1699 to 1701, Pepys asked him to buy books for the library, including books from Spain. Altogether Pepys secured 185 Spanish works.

One of Pepys's most important Spanish works is a manuscript that he called "Libro de Cargos (as to provisions and munition) of the Proveedor-General of the Spanish Armada, 1588." On each sheet of the manuscript, which is bound together in vellum, is the name of a ship, and below it are listed the provisions it carried. A circular 3/4-inch hole has been bored through the volume. Pepys may have allowed the admiralty to buy this item for him: at times he would charge personal acquisitions to the government, writing, "I think I will let the King pay for this."

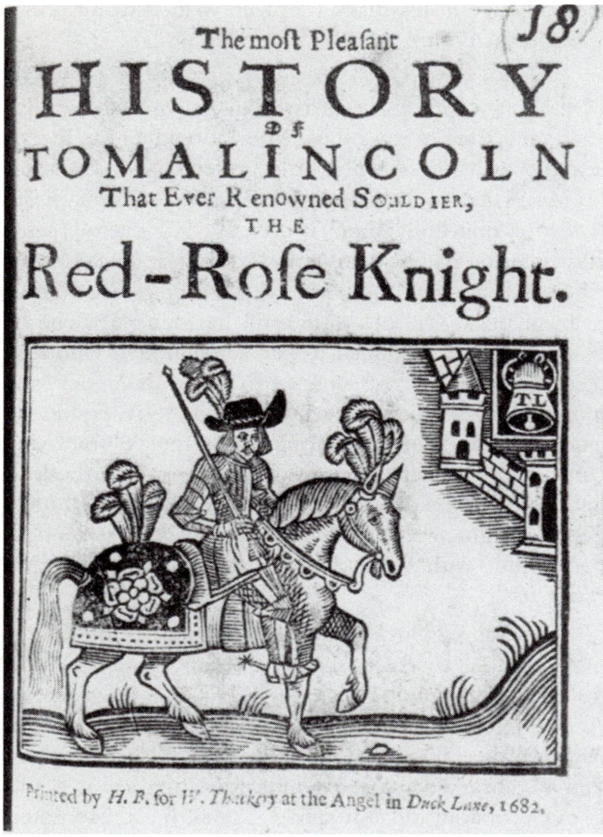

18
The moſt Pleaſant
HISTORY
Of
TOMALINCOLN
That Ever Renowned Souldier,
THE
Red-Roſe Knight.
TL
Printed by H. B. for W. Thackery at the Angel in Duck Lane, 1682.

Title page for one of the popular romances that Pepys called "Vulgaria"

Pepys's professional duties required that he have a solid knowledge of geography. He owned Dutch (1584 edition), English (1588 edition), and Latin (1591 edition) versions of Lucas Janssen Wagenaer's *Spieghel der zeevaert,* which describes and charts the seacoasts of western Europe. From the late 1660s to 1673 Pepys often visited Thomas Jenner's print shop at the south entrance to the Royal Exchange. In 1666 Pepys bought from him a collection of sixteen maps of the world and the quartermaster's map of England and Wales. These he had made into a pocket atlas. In the 1670s London had about ten shops that sold maps; by 1705 the number had risen to about fifteen. Pepys visited most of these. John Seller supplied him with sea atlases and charts; Richard Mount provided navigational books and sea atlases. William Berry, a globemaker, sold Pepys Guillaume Sanson's maps of Europe; John Burston and then John Thornton sold him manuscript charts. From Joseph Moxon he bought *Sacred Geography or Scriptural Maps* (1671). In 1693 Pepys bought from Philip Lea *The Shires of England and Wales* (ca. 1693), with forty-six engraved maps, a book that Lea produced with Christopher Saxton. In 1694 Pepys asked his nephew to write to Lea instructing the bookseller-mapmaker on the hand coloring of his *New Mapp of England* (1689).

In the 1690s Pepys considered compiling a "Bibliotheca nautica," which he described as a "catalogue of authors the [most] perfect I can yet arrive at upon the Art and Practice of Navigation." Mount sent Pepys lists of relevant works. When Joseph Hill prepared to go to Holland in 1695 Pepys gave him a list of requests, including an old copy in Dutch of Pierre Garcie's *The Rutter of the Sea,* which showed havens and harbors with soundings. Pepys had to content himself with a 1555 copy in English, in which he wrote that he knew of only one other such copy, that of the jurist and book collector John Selden at the Bodleian. While his nephew Jackson was in Italy, Pepys wrote to him on 20 July 1700 for an illuminated copy of Jan Blaeu's *Theatrum civitatem et admirandum Italiæ.* Jackson wrote back that he knew only of the Dutch edition (1663) already in Pepys's library. Jackson did add to Blaeu's atlas the first volume of *Nouveau théâtre d'Italie* (Amsterdam: Pierre Mortier, 1704) and extracts from the other three volumes, together with "a compleat sett of ye best mapps of Italy as well as originals brought back from Rome to accompany ye said vol." Most of these Italian maps were published by the Roman firm of Domenico de Rossi and date from the 1680s onward.

Pepys's primary interests in maps were in those of the British Isles, France, and Italy. He acquired Charles Pene's *Le Neptune françois, ou recueil des cartes maritimes* (1693), with twenty-nine engraved maps, and Greenville Collins's *Great Britain's Coasting Pilot* (1693). Pepys distrusted Collins's abilities, so in 1694 he asked John Thornton to compare the atlases of Collins and Pene. Thornton drew up six charts showing the coastlines for England, Scotland, Ireland, France, Holland, Denmark, and Spain. By the time of his death, Pepys owned more than 1,100 maps, charts, and plans.

Pepys also owned old and new accounts of voyages. These include Richard Hakluyt's *Diuers Voyages Touching the Discouerie of America* (1582) as well as his *The Principal Navigations, Voyages, Traffiques and Discoveries of the English Nation* (1599–1600), both lacking the maps. Among his notable books were Samuel Purchas's *Purchas His Pilgrimes* (1625) and *Purchas His Pilgrimage* (fourth edition, 1626); Jan Huygen van Linschoten's *Discours of Voyages into ye Easte and West Indies* (1598); George Best's *A True Discourse of the Late Voyages of Discouerie, for the Finding of a Passage to Cathaya, by the Northwest, vnder . . . Martin Frobisher* (1578); and William Dampier's *A New Voyage Round the World* (second edition, 1697), *A Voyage to New Holland, &c. in the Year 1699* (1703), and *Voyages and Descriptions* (1699). Even after leaving the admiralty, Pepys retained his interest in naval matters.

His naval collection holds many official papers from his years of government service. Among other manuscript items is the Anthony Roll, an illustrated record of Henry VIII's navy of about 1546, executed by Anthony Anthony, an officer in the ordnance. Charles II gave Pepys two of the three rolls, those of ships and of pinnaces and row-barges. The other roll, of galliasses (large galleys), is now in the British Library. Pepys cut up his rolls, mounted each ship on a separate piece of vellum, and had the whole sumptuously bound. Pepys also owned a nautical almanac signed "F. Drak" with a copy of a map of western Europe.

During the period covered by the diary, and perhaps throughout his life, Pepys showed the same ambivalence toward book buying as he did toward playgoing. He indulged in both but repeatedly expressed reservations. On 27 March 1663 he found some Spanish books that he wanted "but with much ado keeping myself from laying out money there." On 2 March 1666 he came home with books costing £10, "all I hope to buy a great while." A month and a half later, on 20 April, he was at the new exchange getting his list of modern plays to collect. Then he went to St. Paul's Churchyard "and there bespoke some new books." On 10 January 1668 at John Martin's he could not resist buying Georges Fournier's *Hydgrographie* (second edition, 1667) and Athanasius Kircher's *China monumentis . . . illustrata* (1667), a folio with many engravings. Pepys acknowledged that he had been spending much money on books recently, "but I think to buy no more till Christmas next." This resolution lasted until 18 January, when he bought a copy of Dryden's *Secret Love; or, The Maiden Queen.*

About the appearance of his books Pepys had no reservations. On 10 August 1663 he wrote, "Whereas before my delight was in multitude of books and spending money in that and buying always of other things, now that I am become a better husband and have left off buying, now my delight is in the neatness of everything." Though he did not in fact leave off book-buying, his desire to have his books well bound is evident in both the diary and the library. On 2 November 1660 he recorded, "In the afternoon I went forth and saw some silver bosses put upon my new Bible, which cost me 6s. 6d. the making and 7s. 6d. the silver"; the Bible itself cost 9s. 6d. On 18 January 1665 he visited Kirton "and there did give thorough direction for the new binding of a great many of my old books, to make my whole study of the same binding, within very few." The work was finished less than a month later. He reported on 10 February, "and much pleased I am now with my study, it being a beautiful sight."

Pepys evidently enjoyed watching the bookbinding process. On 27 November 1667 he watched William Richardson bind some papers. Pepys returned at least twice more, and on 31 January 1668 he mentions "observing his working and his manner of gilding of books with great pleasure." William Nott was a bookseller and binder who did much work for Lord Chancellor Edward Hyde, Earl of Clarendon. On 12 March 1669 Pepys ordered a book to be bound by Nott just to have an example of his work. The volume Pepys chose was probably Robert Parsons's *A Conference about the Next Succession to the Crowne of Ingland* (1594), which Parsons published under the name R. Doleman.

Unable to restrain his urge to accumulate books, by 1666 Pepys found his sense of order offended by the condition of his library. He noted on 23 July 1666 that his books "now growing numerous, and lying one upon another on my chairs, I lose the use, to avoid the trouble of removing them when I would open a book." Pepys therefore summoned Thomas Simpson, a joiner who worked at the Deptford and Woolich dockyards, to make two bookcases, or, as Pepys called them, presses. Simpson was not a skilled cabinetmaker. Rather, he was a joiner, trained to make paneling, staircases, doors, and chimney pieces. Instead of using walnut veneer, the wood of choice for fine carpentry of the period, Simpson used oak that had been imported for wainscoting.

Writing for the *Connoisseur* in 1930, Robert Wemyss Symonds notes that "the cornice of Pepys's library in York Buildings appears to be of the same section and design as those of the bookcases." Simpson or Pepys decided to glaze the presses, which could be assembled and disassembled. Both the glass and the portability of the presses were innovations in the 1660s and served as models for similar pieces at Cuckfield Park and Dyrham Park. Eventually Pepys owned twelve of these presses, though during the 1660s he tried to limit his library to the five hundred volumes that were the capacity of his two bookcases.

Pepys ordered the presses in July. When they were ready a month later, Simpson and Pepys assembled them, and Pepys yet again set about arranging his books. He was pleased with the results: "I think it will be as noble a closet as any man hath, and light enough, though endeed, it would be better to have had a little more light." Soon, though, the Great Fire of London, which began in the early morning hours of Sunday, 2 September 1666, forced him to remove his books. On 3 September he sent many items–including his diary–to Sir William Rider's house at Bethnal Green; three days later he sent other possessions to Sir George Carteret at Deptford.

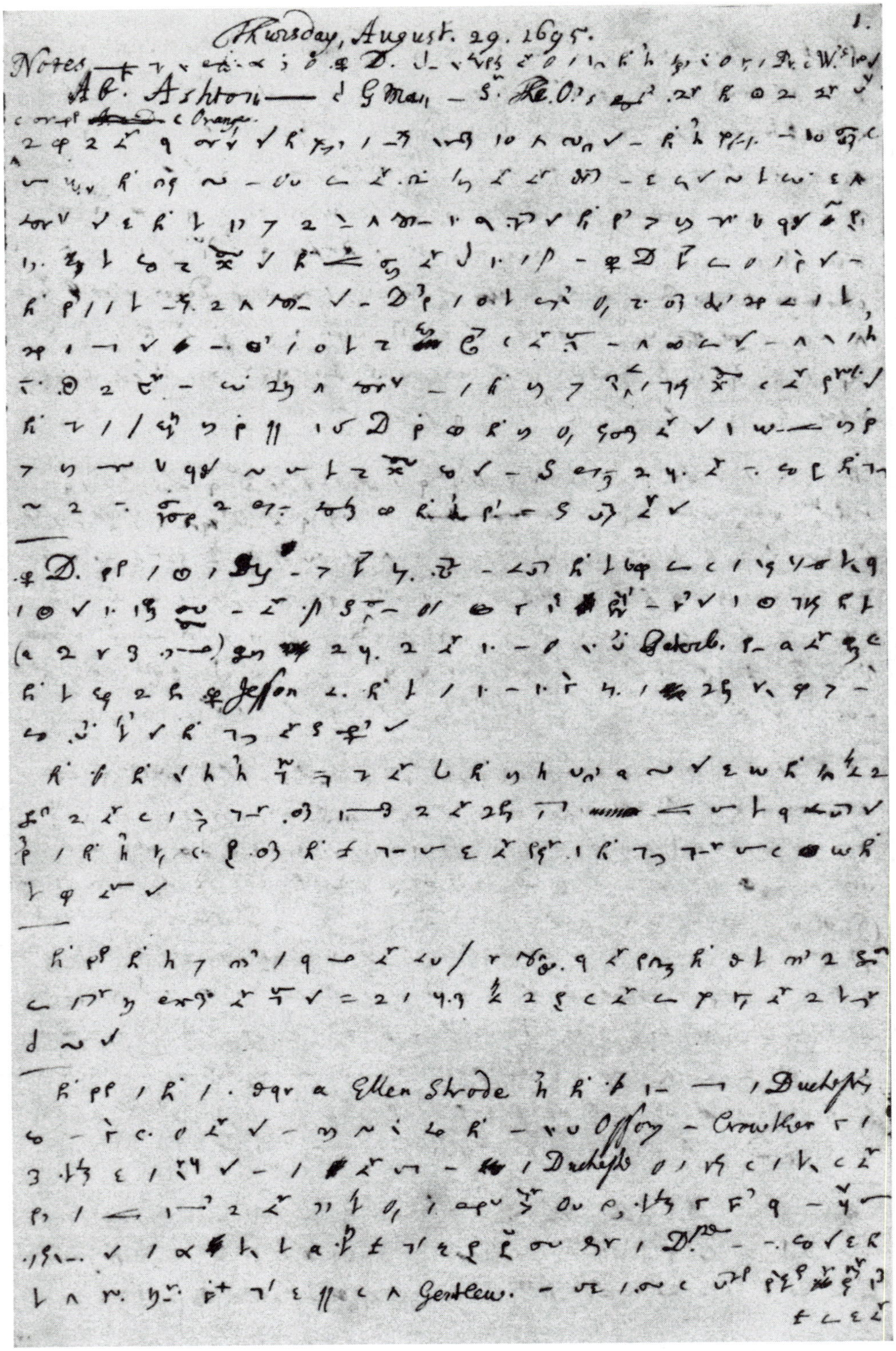

Pepys's shorthand notes, dated 29 August 1695, on an interview about the birth of the Prince of Wales (Pepys Library, Magdalene College, Cambridge)

By 19 September Pepys was once more setting up his books, "But mightily troubled, even in my sleep, at my missing four or five of my bigger books–Speed's Chronicle–and maps, and the two parts of Waggoner, and a book of Cards; which I suppose I have put up with too much care, that I have forgot where they are, for sure they are not stole." The missing books were John Speed's *History of Great Britaine* (1650) and *A Prospect of the Most Famous Parts of the World* (1631), with twenty-two engraved maps, and Lucas Wagenaer's *Mariners Mirrour* (1588) as translated into English by Anthony Ashley, all large folios. The book of cards probably was a collection of sea charts. The next day Pepys was still losing sleep over his missing books: "Up, much troubled about my books; but cannot imagine where they should be." The mystery was solved on 21 September when William Penn found an extra hamper that he thought contained wine but in fact held Pepys's volumes. Pepys gave 5s. to the boy who returned them, and he wrote in his diary, "And now I am in as good condition as I desire to be in all worldly respects."

The fire affected Pepys's world of books in other ways also, especially as it gave rise to higher prices. On 20 March 1667 Pepys found a copy of Paul Rycaut's *The Present State of the Ottoman Empire.* Before the fire the book had cost 8s. Pepys now offered 20s., the price that Lord Herbert had paid for his copy in November, 1666, but the bookseller asked 50s. Pepys paid 55s. for the 1667 edition as a memorial to the Great Fire and further rationalized his extravagance by noting that his copy was "finely bound and truly coloured, all the figures; of which there was but six books done so." The binding is acid-stained calf that has not worn well, but the colored plates remain attractive. Pepys later bought a copy of the fourth edition (1680) but kept the older one.

Before the fire St. Paul's Churchyard boasted twenty-three booksellers, including Kirton, Pepys's chief supplier, who was ruined by the fire and died the next year. He was replaced by John Starkey as Pepys's favorite bookseller. Pepys also bought from John Martin, whose shop, like Starkey's, was in the Temple; Henry Herringman of the New Exchange; William Shrewsbury in Duck Lane at the sign of the Bible, who specialized in foreign books; and Miles and Ann Mitchell of Westminster Hall, who sold new books. In the 1680s, Robert Scott of Little Britain became an important source, and later still Pepys bought from Samuel Lowndes near the Savoy. John Beresford handled the bookbinding in those last years and was sufficiently close to the collector to receive a memorial ring at Pepys's funeral.

These bookshops served as more than mere emporia. Here Pepys kept up with the latest gossip and news. For example, on 10 August 1667 at Herringman's shop he learned about the death of the poet Abraham Cowley, who had died 28 July, and also heard of "several new books coming out." These were Thomas Sprat's *History of the Royal Society,* which Pepys ordered on 16 August, a collected edition of the poems of John Denham, which Pepys also acquired, and the poetry of Katherine Philips, which he apparently did not buy.

Bibliophily was not the only attraction of the London bookshops. At Herringman's Deb Willet, a former servant with whom Pepys carried on an affair, could leave notes arranging assignations. From Shrewsbury on 10 April 1668 Pepys bought a copy of Jacobus de Voragine's *Legenda Aurea* (1527) printed by Wynkyn de Worde; he also kissed Shrewsbury's wife. Pepys bought more books from Shrewsbury on 13 July, writing in his diary that he had "a mind to" Mrs. Shrewsbury and was disappointed that she had not been in the shop when he called. The Mitchells' shop served as a meeting place for the Pepyses, but Pepys was also attracted to the Mitchells' daughter-in-law, whom he called his "wife."

The period from 1660 to 1669 is the best documented for Pepys's book purchases, but when Pepys stopped writing in his diary on 31 May 1669 because he feared for his eyesight, he owned only about a sixth of the books that would finally constitute the Bibliotheca Pepysiana. In mid 1669 Pepys owned no medieval manuscripts, no incunabula, none of his broadside ballads, no calligraphy, and only a fraction of the naval papers he eventually acquired. During the next thirty-three years he collected actively, as is indicated by the increasing number of presses in his study. By 1693 he had seven. Five years later he needed eight, and at the time of his death in 1703 he had twelve.

From mid September to mid October 1669, Pepys, his wife, and his brother-in-law Balthasar St. Michel were in Paris. Pepys visited the Bibliothèque Royale on the Rue de Vivienne, where he examined books, manuscripts, antiquities, and scientific specimens. He saw the Greek manuscript of Dioscorides, an important botanical work that served as the basis of virtually all medieval texts on the subject, and a manuscript of Aurelius Prudentius Clemes, a fourth-century Christian Latin poet whose *Psychomachia* influenced medieval writers. Another manuscript, of Paul's epistles, appeared to Pepys to be in the same hand as a copy of the Gospels at Cambridge, and he was tempted to steal the French section to reunite the two texts.

Fear for his eyesight did not prevent his frequenting the Parisian booksellers. He visited Thomas Moette on the Rue de la Vieille Boucherie, near Saint-Jacques. At the sign of the Venetian shield on the Rue Saint-Jacques Pepys looked in on Frédéric Léonard, who specialized in diplomacy and political science. Pepys tried to buy a copy of the Gombourst map of Paris and Jacques du Breul's *Théâtre des antiquitez de Paris* (1612). Both eluded him for the moment. Five years later, on 12 March 1674, Pepys wrote to John Brisbane, then in Paris, asking for a copy of the map and for a history of the city. Pepys eventually secured a 1652 copy of the Gambourst map.

In Paris Pepys went to see Louis Rossignol, an expert on codes. The subject interested Pepys, who used a form of Thomas Shelton's shorthand for his diary to protect the contents from prying eyes. Pepys owned four of Shelton's books: *A Tutor to Tachygraphy* (1642), *Tachy-graphia* (1671), *Zeiglographia* (1685), and *Tachygraphy* (1691). Shorthand fascinated scholars of the seventeenth century, among them Robert Hooke, John Locke, and Isaac Newton. Editions of Shelton's books were published by Cambridge University Press in 1635, 1641, and 1647.

Pepys's interest was both practical and academic, and he assembled one of the earliest collections of such writing systems. About 1695 he bound up five volumes of pamphlets dealing with shorthand, ranging from Timothy Bright's *Characterie* (1588) to Abraham Nicholas's *Thoographia* (1692). One item, Thomas Heath's *Stenographie* (1644), is known only because of Pepys's copy. Pepys closed his shorthand collection in 1695, but his interest in forms of writing continued. About 1700 he assembled a manuscript collection of calligraphy. Most of the examples come from sixteenth- and seventeenth-century copybooks, but some pieces go back at least to the 700s. The collection includes a leaf from an eighth-century Gospel book and six lines from an eighth-century Psalter. At Durham Cathedral the dean gave Pepys permission to remove two fragments from a Gospel Book that may have been executed as early as 679.

A decade after his visit to Paris, Pepys was accused by Colonel John Scott of betraying the navy and being involved in the so-called Popish Plot, the baseless charge that the Jesuits were planning the assassination of King Charles II. Pepys was briefly imprisoned in the Tower of London in May 1679 but was allowed to post bail on 9 July. Despite his precarious predicament, Pepys continued to think about his library. On 18 December 1679 he wrote to his brother-in-law, who had returned to Paris to gather information about Scott to help Pepys in his defense:

> I likewise pray you to looke out for and bring over with you a Book or 2 if you can find them, viz one called La Police de la Mer, another upon the same subject, respecting the Sea and Navigation writ by one Hobier, and any other you can finde relateing to the same Matters, as I am told there are Severall. There is alsoe another Book called L'Admiral de France printed, as I take it, about 80 or 90 years agoe, which I would bee glad to have.

In a letter of 5 January 1680 dealing primarily with securing witnesses for Pepys's possible trial, Pepys reminded his brother-in-law of his book order and a week later thanked St. Michel "for your Care about the Bookes." None of the three titles specified in the 18 December letter appear in Pepys's final collection, but St. Michel may have found others relating to naval matters.

Pepys assembled 238 items relating to the Popish Plot and to the Exclusion Crisis, as Parliament sought to keep Charles II's Catholic brother James from the throne. Another volume in his library contains thirty-three pieces dealing with the Second Exclusion Parliament of 1679–1681 and the Oxford Parliament of 1681. Pepys was always interested in current events, as another four volumes with 430 news pamphlets from the period 1660–1666 indicate. Pepys also apparently contemplated forming an almanac collection. He bound together thirty-two examples from 1688 in one volume, and thirteen from 1689 in another.

At least as early as 1681 Pepys was acquainted with Robert Scott, bookseller and publisher at the Princes Arms. Scott had been apprenticed to Daniel Frere at the Red Bull in Little Britain and later was a partner of William Wells. Frere, Wells, and Scott are not mentioned in the diary, but in a letter of 4 November 1681 Scott addressed Pepys as "my honored friend." Scott sold to the leading figures of Restoration England, including Charles II, Sir Christopher Wren, and Sir William Temple. He wrote to Pepys, "Without flattery, I love to find a rare book for you," and on 30 June 1688 he reported finding several. Scott wrote that he was sending Pepys *The Historie of Ireland* (1633, 12s.) by Meredith Hanmer, Edmund Campion, and Edmund Spenser; John Hardyng's *Chronicle . . . from the First Begynnyng of England* (1543, 6s.); Sir John Price's *Hystoriae Brytannicae defensio* (1573, 8s.); and a 1510 edition of Alexander Barclay's translation of Sebastian Brant's *Stultifera navis* (8s.). Scott also promised Pepys a copy of Edward Halle's *The Vnion of the Twoo Noble and Illustre Famelies of Lancastre & Yorke*. Pepys owned a copy of the 1550 edition, which may have come from Scott. Scott was an important importer of foreign books, so Pepys may have bought some of these from him as well.

After retiring as clerk of acts at the naval board in 1689 in the wake of the Glorious Revolution, Pepys devoted more time to building and organizing his library, a project for which he enlisted his nephew John Jackson and a clerk. In this undertaking he was influ-

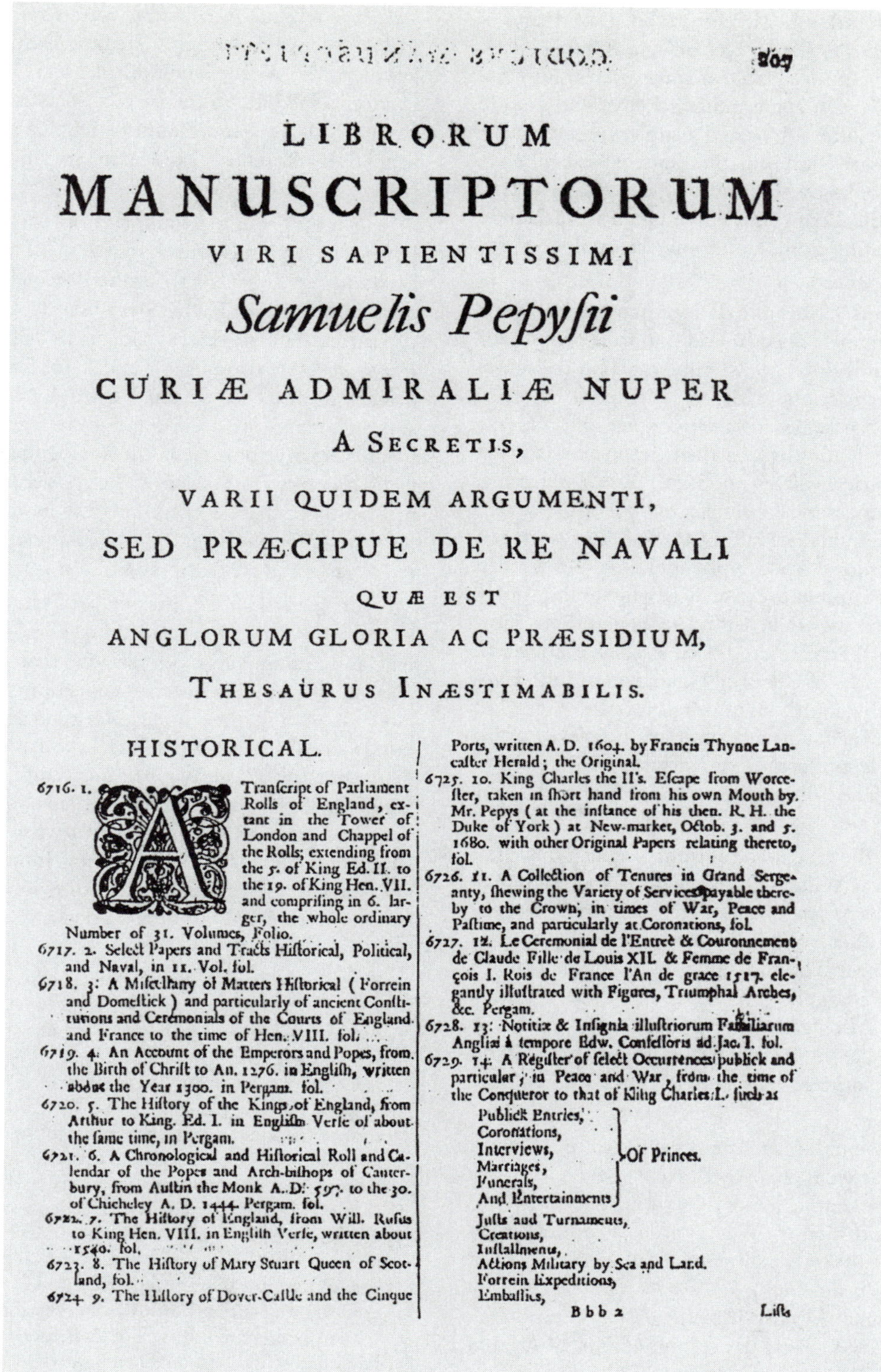

207

LIBRORUM
MANUSCRIPTORUM
VIRI SAPIENTISSIMI
Samuelis Pepysii
CURIÆ ADMIRALIÆ NUPER
A SECRETIS,
VARII QUIDEM ARGUMENTI,
SED PRÆCIPUE DE RE NAVALI
QUÆ EST
ANGLORUM GLORIA AC PRÆSIDIUM,
THESAURUS INÆSTIMABILIS.

HISTORICAL.

6716. 1. A Transcript of Parliament Rolls of England, extant in the Tower of London and Chappel of the Rolls; extending from the 5. of King Ed. II. to the 19. of King Hen. VII. and comprising in 6. larger, the whole ordinary Number of 31. Volumes, Folio.

6717. 2. Select Papers and Tracts Historical, Political, and Naval, in 11. Vol. fol.

6718. 3. A Miscellany of Matters Historical (Forrein and Domestick) and particularly of ancient Constitutions and Ceremonials of the Courts of England and France to the time of Hen. VIII. fol.

6719. 4. An Account of the Emperors and Popes, from the Birth of Christ to An. 1276. in English, written about the Year 1300. in Pergam. fol.

6720. 5. The History of the Kings of England, from Arthur to King. Ed. I. in English Verse of about the same time, in Pergam.

6721. 6. A Chronological and Historical Roll and Calendar of the Popes and Arch-bishops of Canterbury, from Austin the Monk A. D. 597. to the 30. of Chicheley A. D. 1444. Pergam. fol.

6722. 7. The History of England, from Will. Rufus to King Hen. VIII. in English Verse, written about 1540. fol.

6723. 8. The History of Mary Stuart Queen of Scotland, fol.

6724. 9. The History of Dover-Castle and the Cinque Ports, written A. D. 1604. by Francis Thynne Lancaster Herald; the Original.

6725. 10. King Charles the II's. Escape from Worcester, taken in short hand from his own Mouth by Mr. Pepys (at the instance of his then. R. H. the Duke of York) at New-market, Octob. 3. and 5. 1680. with other Original Papers relating thereto, fol.

6726. 11. A Collection of Tenures in Grand Sergeanty, shewing the Variety of Services payable thereby to the Crown, in times of War, Peace and Pastime, and particularly at Coronations, fol.

6727. 12. Le Ceremonial de l'Entreè & Couronnement de Claude Fille de Louis XII. & Femme de François I. Rois de France l'An de grace 1517. elegantly illustrated with Figures, Triumphal Arches, &c. Pergam.

6728. 13. Notitiæ & Insignia illustriorum Familiarum Angliæ à tempore Edw. Confessoris ad Jac. I. fol.

6729. 14. A Register of select Occurrences publick and particular, in Peace and War, from the time of the Conqueror to that of King Charles I. such as

Publick Entries,
Coronations,
Interviews,
Marriages,
Funerals,
And Entertainments
} Of Princes.

Justs and Turnaments,
Creations,
Installments,
Actions Military by Sea and Land.
Forrein Expeditions,
Embassies,

Bbb 2 Lists

First page of the section on Pepys's collection in Edward Bernard's 1697 catalogue of medieval manuscripts

enced by his friend John Evelyn, who gave Pepys a copy of his *Instructions Concerning Erecting a Library* (1661), a translation of Gabriel Naudé's *Advis pour dressser une bibliothèque* (1627). On some matters Pepys and Naudé disagreed, as the latter advocated a subject arrangement for books and cared little for bindings, whereas Pepys organized his books by size and showed great concern for bindings. Still, Pepys may have taken from Naudé the idea of creating author and subject catalogues for his collection.

By the end of his life Pepys had assembled a library rich in many areas. In addition to the strengths of his early acquisitions he assembled a fine collection of medieval manuscripts, which were listed in Edward Bernard's *Catalogi manuscriptorum Angliae et Hiberniae* (1697). The catalogue divided them into seven subject categories: historical, fifteen; political, fifteen; religious, seventeen; mathematical, nineteen; poetical, seven; "mixt," seventeen; and naval, thirty-nine. Pepys owned a fourteenth-century Apocalypse in Latin and French with eighty-nine miniatures; an early-fifteenth-century *Speculum humanae salvationis* with 192 pen-and-ink illustrations, some of them colored with washes; manuscript poems of the works of Geoffrey Chaucer and John Lydgate; a fifteenth-century manuscript of the poetry of Guilluame de Machaut, with some of the pieces set to music; and a late-fifteenth- or early-sixteenth-century songbook produced during the reign of Henry VII for the Prince of Wales.

Perhaps the most important manuscript that Pepys owned was Wiliam Caxton's translation of books X–XV of Ovid's *Metamorphoses.* Pepys acquired this item in 1688. The other volume, with books I–IX, became the property of Sir Thomas Phillipps in the nineteenth century. Thanks largely to the efforts of Eugene Power of Ann Arbor, Michigan, the two parts are reunited at Magdalene College. Another important manuscript now in the Bibliotheca Pepysiana is Pepys's six-volume diary.

Pepys assembled an impressive group of early printed books as well. He owned twenty-seven incunabula, including seven printed by Caxton, seven by Richard Pynson, and nine by Wynkyn de Worde. Pepys's collection holds the only extant copies of *Wednesday's Fast* (Wynkyn de Worde, 1500), *The Foundation of the Chapel of Walsingham* (Richard Pynson, 1496), *Horae ad usum Ebor* (John Wight, 1556), and the second edition of *Reynard the Fox* (Caxton, 1489). According to E. Gordon Duff in *Bibliotheca Pepysiana: A Descriptive Catalogue of the Library of Samuel Pepys,* Nicolaus Perottus's *Grammatica,* published in Paris by Nicholas de la Barre in 1498, "appears to be entirely unknown" outside Pepys's collection. Among his incunabula are the first printing of Juliana Berners's *The Book of Hawking, Hunting and Heraldry* (St. Albans, 1486), an early example of color printing, as well as Wynkyn de Worde's edition of 1496. He also owned Caxton's second, more correct, illustrated edition of Chaucer (1484), and Ranulph Higden's *Polycronicon* as printed by Caxton (1482) and Wynkyn de Worde (1495).

Among other examples of early printing in Pepys's collection is John Lydgate's *The History, Siege and Destruction of Troy* (1513), printed on vellum and in its original binding of leather over boards. Only two other copies are known. Here, too, is Lydgate's *The Fall of Princes and Princesses* (1554), and a 1515 Book of Hours printed in Paris for Simon Vostre. The latter contains seventeen large woodcuts, and each page is surrounded by an attractive border. In his catalogue of Pepys's early printed books Duff describes Pepys's copy of the missal printed by Richard Pynson in 1520 as "perhaps the finest production of the early English press and . . . a marvel of taste and typographic skill."

In June 1700 Thomas Gale, Dean of York, wrote to Pepys, "When you shall think fit to make your last will and testament, I beg of you that you would be pleased to put all your rare collections (of which you have so many), into some one good hand." Pepys's library is not mentioned in his will, dated 2 August 1701, but on 12 May 1703, in a codicil revoking his bequests to Samuel Jackson, the elder brother of John who had married against Pepys's wishes, Pepys made stipulations in regard to his nephew John and his executor, William Hewer, his clerk, with whom Pepys lived at Clapham from 1700 to Pepys's death on 26 May 1703:

> Item, I will that my nephew John Jackson have the full and Sole possession and use of all my Collections of Books and papers contained in my Library (now remaining at Mr. Hewers at Clapham or in any other place or places) during the Terme of his natural Life. And in case it shall not please God in his mercy to restore me to a Condition of prosecuting my thoughts, relating to a more particular disposal and Settlement thereof My will and desire is that my said nephew John Jackson doe with all possible diligence betake himself to the dispatch of such p[ar]ticulars as shall be remaining undone at the time of my decease towards the completion of my said Library according to the Scheme delivered to him for that purpose. . . . And that he together with my executor and such of their friends as they shall judge fittest and best qualified to advise them herein do faithfully and deliberately consider of the most effectual means of preserving the said library intire in one body, undivided unsold and Secure against all manner of deminution damages and embesselments; and finally disposed most suitably to my inclinations . . . for the benefit of posterity.

Some of Pepys's bookplates and bookstamps

Pepys also now left £20 to his servant David Milo on the condition that Milo help Jackson in the completion of the library.

Pepys wanted his collection to number exactly three thousand volumes; to reach that number additional purchases would be required, as would a new catalogue. At the end of the codicil Pepys appended his scheme for completing his library. This plan contained twelve provisions, including the building of new presses if necessary, "That my Arms or Crest or Cypher be stampt in Gold on the outsides of the Covers of every booke admitting thereof," and that the library be arranged by height.

The 12 May codicil left the final disposition of the library to Jackson's discretion, but the next day Pepys added another codicil specifying

> 1st That after the death of my said nephew my said Library be placed and for ever Settled in one of our Universities and rather in that of Cambridge than Oxford. 2dly And rather in a private College there than the publick Library. 3dly And in the Colleges of Trinity or Magdalene preferable to All others. . . .5thly That in which soever of the two it is a faire roome be provided therein on purpose for it and wholly and soly appropriated thereto. . . . 8thly That my said Library be continued in its present form and noe other books mixt therewith Save what my Nephew may add to them of his own Collecting in distinct presses.

To ensure that his conditions be followed, Pepys required that Trinity and Magdalene check on each other, and if any of the provisions were violated, the college then having the collection would lose it to the other. Magdalene received the library, and Trinity never exercised its right to inspection.

Pepys died less than two weeks after adding this second codicil. On 1 August 1705 Jackson added a note to Pepys's catalogue of books prepared in 1700 declaring that the library had been completed and the final catalogue drawn up. After Jackson's death in March 1723, Arthur Annesley, Earl of Anglesea, donated £200 to move Pepys's library from Clapham to Cambridge. The actual cost of the move was £117. Except for a five-year period (1849–1854), when the library was housed in the Master's Lodge, Pepys's books have resided on the first floor of Magdalene's "New Building," for the construction of which Pepys in 1677 had donated £60. Not all of Pepys's books went to Magdalene; some seventy volumes of manuscripts remained in York Buildings after Pepys moved to Clapham. Richard Rawlinson acquired these materials and left them to Oxford University when he died on 6 April 1755. They remain at the Bodleian Library.

Pepys's collection has been a boon to scholarship since the eighteenth century. Thomas Percy used Pepys's ballads for his *Reliques of Ancient English Poetry* (1765), and Richard Gough drew on Pepys's prints and drawings of London and Westminster for his *British Topography* (1780). John Pinkerton, who used Pepys's library for his *Ancient Scotish Poems . . . from the MS Collections of Sir Richard Maitland* (1786), described Pepys's holdings as "undoubtedly the most curious in England, those of the British Museum excepted; and . . . kept in excellent order." As Pepys ordered, his books bear his crest and name in front; arms, crest, and motto on the back.

Almost all of the books contain a bookplate with Pepys's picture from the Geoffrey Kneller portrait in the library and also an end-plate, a device of intertwined ropes and anchors with the initials "S.P." and Pepys's motto, "Mens cujusque is est quisque" (The mind of a person is that person). One might pararphrase this epigram to read, "Bibliotheca cuiusque is est quisque." As Frank Sidgwick observed in *Bibliotheca Pepysiana: A Descriptive Catalogue,*

> Were the *Diary* non-existent, and were no other source of knowledge available, a judgment of Pepys's character formed upon a consideration of the contents of his Library would reveal him to have been a man of great breadth of interest and catholicity of taste, an inquisitive scholar conversant with more languages than his own, and a person in whom a love of order and neatness in detail was paramount.

Under 26 May 1703 Pepys's friend and fellow-diarist John Evelyn recorded a lengthy tribute praising the man and his library, calling the former secretary of the Admiralty "a very worthy, Industrious, & curious person," an assessment confirmed by Pepys's diary and library.

Letters:

Private Correspondence and Miscellaneous Papers of Samuel Pepys, 1679–1703, 2 volumes, edited by Joseph Robson Tanner (London: Bell, 1926; New York: Harcourt, Brace, 1926);

Further Correspondence of Samuel Pepys, 1662–1679, edited by Tanner (London: Bell, 1929; New York: Harcourt, Brace, 1929);

Letters and the Second Diary of Samuel Pepys, edited by Robert Guy Howarth (London: J. M. Dent / New York: Dutton, 1932);

Shorthand Letters of Samuel Pepys, edited by Edwin Chappell (Cambridge: Cambridge University Press, 1933);

Letters of Samuel Pepys and His Family Circle, edited by Helen Truesdell Heath (Oxford: Clarendon Press, 1955).

Bibliography:

Dennis G. Donavan, *Elizabethan Bibliographies Supplements XVIII John Evelyn (1920–1968) Samuel Pepys, 1933–1968* (London: Nether Press, 1970).

Biographies:

Arthur Bryant, *Samuel Pepys,* 3 volumes (Cambridge: Cambridge University Press, 1933; New York: Macmillan, 1933);

John Harold Wilson, *The Private Life of Mr. Pepys* (New York: Farrar, Straus & Cudahy, 1959);

Richard Ollard, *Pepys: A Biography* (London: Hodder & Stoughton, 1974).

References:

Richard W. Barber, *Samuel Pepys Esquire, Secretary of the Admiralty to King Charles & King James the Second* (Berkeley: University of California Press, 1970);

Urban Tigner Holmes Jr., *Samuel Pepys in Paris and Other Essays* (Chapel Hill: University of North Carolina Press, 1954);

Marjorie Hope Nicolson, *Pepys' Diary and the New Science* (Charlottesville: University Press of Virginia, 1965);

John Claud Trewhard Oates, "Richard Pynson and the Holy Blood of Hayles," *The Library,* fifth series, 13 (December 1958): 269–277;

Leona Rostenberg, "The Liberal Arts: Robert Scott, Importer & University Agent," in her *Literary, Political, Scientific, Religious & Legal Publishing, Printing & Bookselling in England, 1551–1700: Twelve Studies* (New York: Burt Franklin, 1965), pp. 281–313;

Rostenberg, "A Look at Pepys," *American Book Collector,* 7 (October 1986): 17–24;

Robert Wemyss Symonds, "More about the Pepys, Dyrham Park and Sergisson Bookcases," *Connoisseur,* 85 (1930): 353–360;

Symonds, "The Pepys, Dyrham Park and Sergisson Bookcases," *Connoisseur,* 85 (1930): 275–285;

Ivan E. Taylor, *Samuel Pepys* (Boston: Twayne, 1989);

Roger Thompson, "Samuel Pepys's *Penny Merriments:* A Checklist," *The Library,* fifth series, 31 (September 1976): 223–234;

Francis McDougall Charlewood Turner, *The Pepys Library* (Cambridge: Cambridge University Press, 1950?);

Sarah Tyacke, "Samuel Pepys as Map Collector," in *Maps and Prints: Aspects of the English Booktrade,* edited by Robin Myers and Michael Harris (Oxford: Oxford Polytechnic Press, 1984), pp. 1–29;

Henry B. Wheatley, "Two English Bookmen: (1) Samuel Pepys," in *Bibliographica,* part 2 (1895): 155–162;

Edward M. Wilson and Don W. Cruickshank, *Samuel Pepys's Spanish Plays* (London: Bibliographical Society, 1980);

J. Yeowell, "The Rawlinson Manuscripts," *Notes and Queries,* second series, 112 (20 February 1858): 141–143.

Papers:

The major collections of Samuel Pepys's papers are held by the Rawlinson Collection, Bodleian Library, Oxford University; the Pepys Library, Magdalene College, Cambridge University; and the Cockerell Papers, National Maritime Museum, Greenwich, England.

Thomas Plume

(August ? 1630 – 20 November 1704)

K. A. Manley
Institute of Historical Research, University of London

CATALOGUE: S. G. Deed, comp., *Catalogue of the Plume Library at Maldon, Essex* (Maldon: Trustees of the Plume Library, 1959).

WORK: "An Account of the Life and Death of the Author," in *A Century of Sermons, Upon Several Remarkable Subjects, preached by John Hacket,* edited by Plume (London: Printed by Andrew Clark for Robert Scott, 1675), pp. i–iv; republished as *An Account of The Life and Death of . . . John Hacket,* edited by M. E. C. Woolcot (London: J. Masters, 1865).

The Reverend Thomas Plume is remembered for the establishment of the library that bears his name in the small Essex town of Maldon. He bequeathed his substantial personal library to his native town and made many generous benefactions for the education and well-being of the townspeople. His library still exists, a lasting memorial to its pious benefactor, as well as a monument to the town of his birth. He is further known for his endowment of the Plumian professorship of astronomy at the University of Cambridge. Little is known of his life other than the bare dates of his education and official appointments. No correspondence or diaries survive. Although the Plume Library contains many of his papers, these are mostly manuscript sermons and commonplace books that reveal virtually no personal information. Many of the sermons and papers belonged to others, chiefly his mentor, Bishop John Hacket. Plume seems to have led a quiet, unassuming life–wisely, perhaps, considering the dangerous and uncertain times of civil war in which he grew up and received his education.

Plume was baptized 18 August 1630 in All Saints' Church, Maldon. His father, Thomas, was an alderman of the town and a well-known local Presbyterian. His mother, Helen, was his father's third wife. The Plume family held substantial property in Essex at this time; Alderman Thomas's brother owned Yeldham Hall, which had belonged to the Plumes for almost a century.

The young Thomas Plume's education began at nearby Chelmsford Grammar School. At sixteen he entered Christ's College, Cambridge, as a pensioner in February 1646, matriculating on 11 July. This was a particularly dangerous time; though the first English Civil War between Oliver Cromwell's forces and those of Charles I was coming to an end, Puritan military forces still occupied the city; in addition, the city had fallen victim to an outbreak of plague in the spring of that year. Many Cambridge fellows of Royalist sympathies had left the university, and several heads of colleges had been ousted in the previous year, along with four fellows of Christ's College. In practice most fellows steered a middle course and did their best not to embroil themselves in politics. Most members of the college at this time were probably mildly Royalist, including Plume himself, but many prominent Puritans had also passed through its doors, including John Milton, who received an M.A. in 1632. Plume's views are revealed by a juvenile poem that survives in manuscript in the Plume Library that compares Charles I to the sun in eclipse, while the parliamentary leaders are likened to the stars in revolt, racing down the path to chaos.

The undergraduate Plume studied under Henry More, who, along with the master of the college, Ralph Cudworth, was a leader of the Cambridge Platonists, an intellectual group of theologians who were antagonistic to Puritanism. They comprised one of the most important philosophical movements of their time, and Plume can hardly have failed to have been influenced by them. He graduated in 1649 with the degree of bachelor of arts; he never proceeded to take the degree of master of arts. In the same year his tutor, More, and three other fellows of Christ's College abandoned their positions and left Cambridge. This was the period of the second Civil War, and Plume may have thought that the times were too uncertain to permit him to remain at the university in safety.

The 1650s, the decade of the Commonwealth under the Lord Protector, Cromwell, is virtually a blank page as far as Plume's life is concerned. At some period he must have taken holy orders, but bishops and dioceses were abolished under the Commonwealth, so he would have had to act surreptitiously, which could explain his virtual invisibility during this period. He clearly held Royalist leanings, though his father had been elder of the presbytery of Maldon (presbyteries replaced dioceses under the Commonwealth), and his uncle, Samuel Plume of Yeldham Hall, had served on several Essex commissions, the bodies appointed by Cromwell to conduct local affairs. It is impossible to determine whether their actions were dictated by prudence or conviction.

What is known is that by 1656 Plume was living at, or near, the nearly deserted royal Nonsuch Palace in Surrey. He had become the close friend and amanuensis of John Hacket, the prominent and strongly Royalist divine who had been deprived of all his ecclesiastical preferments except the rectory of nearby Cheam in Surrey. Hacket was a strong supporter of the Church of England and had spoken in the House of Commons against the abolition of deans and cathedral chapters. After the Restoration he was appointed bishop of Lichfield and Coventry and spent a great deal of his own money in restoring Lichfield Cathedral, which was seriously damaged during the Civil Wars. He continued his friendship with Plume and frequently asked him to buy books in London on his behalf (Hacket had vowed never to set foot in London again because it had been "polluted" by the execution of Charles I in 1649). Hacket considered Plume to be a man "of great merit" and hoped to find a position for him at Lichfield Cathedral, though this was not to materialize. On his death in 1670, Hacket bequeathed to Plume a small sum of money and his manuscript sermons. In 1675 Plume published the sermons–prefixed with a substantial, if pietistic, life of the bishop–titled "An Account of the Life and Death of the Author" in *A Century of Sermons, Upon Several Remarkable Subjects, Preached by John Hacket.* Plume publicly reveals his own political views in that publication when he refers to the "happy revolution" that led to the Restoration of 1660, and adds that "all the world would stink" of the name of Cromwell. This work is a massive folio of almost 1,100 pages and was Plume's only published work. Hacket's own library, on which Plume claimed the former had spent £1,500, was bequeathed to the University Library at Cambridge.

Preferment had already come to Plume before the Restoration in 1660, for on 22 September 1658 he was instituted as vicar of Greenwich, Kent, or East Greenwich, as it was then called. The patron of this appointment was Richard Cromwell, who had succeeded his father, Oliver, as protector. It may seem surprising that a man with Plume's sympathies should receive patronage from a republican leader, but by this period many Royalists supported Richard in the hope that his regime would be more relaxed concerning religious matters, as turned out to be the case. Plume signed the declaration of conformity to the Church of England on 28 July 1662. He spent the remainder of his life as vicar of St. Alphege's, Greenwich. In addition, in 1662 he became rector of Merston, Kent, a sinecure since there was neither church nor inhabitants, and from 1665 he was rector of Little Easton, Essex. Samuel Pepys attended the Greenwich church on many occasions; he recorded in his famous diary on 17 September 1665 that he had there heard a "very good sermon (Mr. Plume being a very excellent scholler and preacher)."

Whatever the true circumstances surrounding Plume's holy orders, he was, presumably through Hacket's influence, conferred the honorary degree of bachelor of divinity at Cambridge in 1661. This title involved no further study at the university and would have more than compensated for his not taking the M.A. degree. He became a doctor of divinity in June 1673. His only promotion–a considerable one–was to become archdeacon and prebendary of Rochester on 10 June 1679. For this post he was entitled to move to the official residence of Longfield Court, a large medieval house in the village of Longfield, Kent. He was buried in that parish's churchyard following his death on 20 November 1704. Clearly a modest man, Plume spent an unassuming life, playing no part in national affairs. He never engaged in ecclesiastical controversies. The fact that he asked to be buried in the churchyard in "a plain brick grave" rather than inside the church shows an unpretentious nature, as does his insistence that his portrait not be hung in his library at Maldon. Furthermore, he did not ask for his name to be attached to any of his benefactions; the Plume Library and the Plumian professorship are later designations.

Besides the donation of his library, the well-being of the clergy, relief for the poor, and education are the keynotes of his bequests. At this period the question of sources of income for clergy, tithes in particular, was a matter of great concern to them. Many parishes had lost a large part of their income in the time of Henry VIII, when so many church lands, and the rents and any other income deriving from them, were seized for the benefit of that monarch. As Hacket frequently complained to Plume, this loss of income prevented the poorer clergy from buying books for themselves.

Plume wished to help needy clergy. He willed small sums of money to parishes throughout Kent and decreed that his household goods in Greenwich and Rochester should be divided among any ten poor ministers. Plume was an original member of the Society for the Promotion of Christian Knowledge, founded in 1698 by Thomas Bray, the promoter of parochial librar-

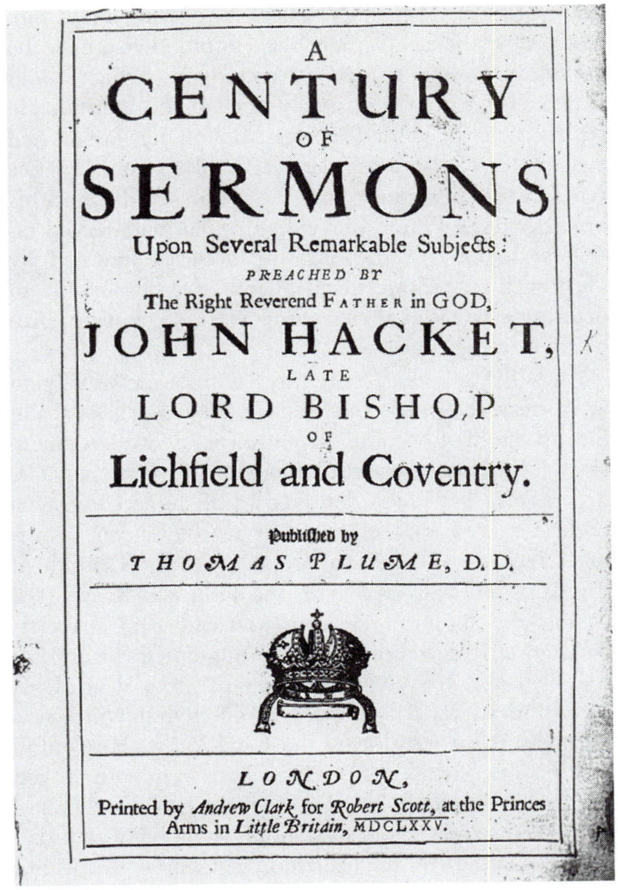

Frontispiece and title page for Thomas Plume's edition of his mentor's sermons

ies for the specific purpose of distributing complete collections of approved books to poor clergy. He left £100 toward the good works of its sister organization, the Society for the Propagation of the Gospel in Foreign Parts, and gave houses in Deptford to be used as almshouses. A confirmed bachelor himself, he left £100 to encourage the marriages of ten maids who had been in his service for seven years.

Mindful of his concern for education, Plume left £100 to Bromley College and £20 to his old grammar school in Chelmsford specifically to purchase books for a "Standing Library." His largest bequest was to leave no less than £1,902 12s. 6d. to establish a professorship of astronomy and experimental philosophy at Cambridge University. It is unclear how or why Plume became interested in astronomy. He is said to have been influenced by reading Christian Huygen's *Cosmotheoros* (an English edition was published in 1698). Other, older works on the same subject by Galileo, Johannes Kepler, and Danish astronomer Tycho Brahe were in his library. As vicar of Greenwich, Plume must have known John Flamsteed, the Astronomer Royal, who worked at the Royal Observatory erected in Greenwich Park in 1675. Plume's gift, administered by trustees, was spent on an estate in Cambridgeshire to provide the necessary income, and advice on the new foundation was sought from Flamsteed and Sir Isaac Newton. An observatory, which was built over the main gatehouse of Trinity College for the use of the new professor, was regarded by the master, Richard Bentley, as "the commodiousest building for that use in christendom," though others thought it an excrescence. The room fell into dereliction and was demolished in 1797, and a completely new observatory was erected in 1822. Plume specified that the professor should not be a fellow resident in Trinity but should live in the town to be accessible to any scholar or gentleman, whether a member of the university or not.

Plume's native town of Maldon reaped his generosity most of all. He provided for ten poor boys to study at the grammar school in the town and arranged for a scholarship to be established for one scholar to attend Christ's College, Cambridge. He also gave £200 and part of his estate to produce income for a workhouse for the poor of Maldon and surrounding villages. Plume's most obvious benefaction was made while he was still alive. Only a few years before his death he had decided to rebuild the old, ruined church of St. Peter's, Maldon, which, apart from the tower, had collapsed in 1665. He began by restoring the damaged tower, while over the ruins of the original medieval church he erected a new two-story building; the ground floor was to be used by the local grammar school, and the upper floor was to be for his library. The latter, he specified, was to be for the benefit of the local minister, as well as for the clergy of other parishes. For this purpose he bequeathed to the local corporation not only his books but also a farm in the nearby village of Mundon, without which source of revenue his plan could never have materialized. The building was probably completed by 1700. The tower was to remain the joint property of the two parishes of All Saints' and St. Peter's, while the secular part of the building was vested in trustees.

On his death Plume's library contained at least 7,400 titles in approximately 5,000 volumes, including many unbound contemporary pamphlets. It is obvious that Plume had spent considerable time planning his library and what was to happen to it after his death. What is important for posterity is that he conceived the collection as a public library, so that, as his will stated, "any Gentleman, or Scholar, who desires, may go into it, and make use of any book there, or borrow it"; in the case of borrowing, a deposit of money had to be left. Careful instructions were made as to the employment of a suitable keeper of the library. The holder had to be a scholar, with an M.A., in holy orders, and could be a local minister or the schoolmaster. He had to agree to open the library daily, Sundays excepted, for two hours in the morning and two hours in the afternoon. For these duties he was to receive the considerable sum of £40 a year, as well as the use of a nearby house. Plume also left to the library his collection of portraits, mostly of prelates; a large painting of Archbishop William Laud is still one of the prominent features. Although he asked that his own portrait not be placed in the library, the trustees have decided otherwise, as an appropriate gesture of respect.

The questions arise as to how far the existing Plume Library can be regarded as the "personal" library of Thomas Plume himself and what statement it might make about his own life and tastes. The sheer size of the collection (as well as multiple copies of some of the titles) and what little is known about his life are arguments against the library having been planned to be private. The evidence suggests that he must always have intended his library for a wider audience.

The books in the Plume Library are mainly, though not exclusively, theological, but the collection as a whole is well balanced. Plume collected books that took different sides in the religious debates of his time, suggesting that he bought books with not just himself in mind as their reader and that he had made a conscious decision to amass a wide-ranging and broad-minded selection of scholarly books. For instance, he owned six works by Andrew Marvell, accompanied by Theophilus Thorowthistle's confutation, and Marvell's response to the latter. Works by Milton and his critics are similarly found. Richard Baker's *A Chronicle of the Kings of England* (London: J. F. and E. C., sold by G. Bedell and T. Williams, 1653) is balanced by Thomas Blount's *Animadversions Upon Sir Richard Baker's Chronicle, and Its Continuation* (Oxford: Printed by H. H. for Ric. Davis, 1672). Other opposing works were often bound together. The Nonconformist Richard Baxter is represented by no less than forty-seven titles. His works, and titles such as Thomas Delaune's *A Plea for the Non-Conformists* (London: Printed for the author, 1684), show Plume's concern to take in works that did not follow one particular religious persuasion. Many anti-Catholic tracts, as one might expect, are included: Daniel Featley's *The Romish Fisher Caught and Held in His Owne Net* (London: Printed by H. L. for Robert Milbourne, 1624) and Thomas Long's *A Compendious History of All the Popish and Fanatical Plots* (London: Printed for D. Brown and T. Godwin, 1684) are typical examples. Foreign theologians are well represented, including Jean Calvin, Isaac and Meric Casaubon, the Du Moulins (Louis, Pierre the Elder, and Pierre the Younger), Samuel Desmarets, Desiderius Erasmus (fifteen titles), Johann Heinrich Hottinger, Moses ben Maimon, and Samuel von Pufendorf, though only one title of Martin Luther appears (and that is not theological but about the Turks).

There are many books or pamphlets on subjects that were most pressing to the clergy of the time, including tithes, the influence of the Quakers (such as the anti-Quaker writings of Francis Bugg), and the constitutional question of the monarchy (including the works of Charles I). The library contains eighteen editions of the complete Bible (including a volume printed in Nuremberg in 1487), as well as twenty-two New Testaments. Books on science and medicine are present, as well as law, and a sprinkling of the classic Roman and Greek texts. Some Cicero is present, but only a selection. Plume's particular interest in astronomy is shown in works by Flamsteed, Edmund Halley, and Kepler, for example. Niccolò Machiavelli is represented, as well as René Descartes, Galileo, John Locke, Thomas Hobbes, William Harvey, William Petty, William Prynne (thirty-five titles), John Selden (sixteen titles), Sir William Dugdale, and William Camden, but not authors such as William Shakespeare or Ben Jonson, whose books, few, if any, clergymen or scholars of the period would have deemed worth preserving. John Donne is represented only by his sermons. A volume of John Dryden's poems was acquired only after Plume's death. There are twenty-seven volumes of the scientific and philosophical writings of Robert Boyle. History comprises a wide-ranging section: for instance, Hector Boethius's *Scotorum historiae* (Paris, 1574) and fourteen titles of Hugo Grotius.

Many old works are present, a large number dating from the sixteenth century. When the library was recatalogued in the 1950s, at least thirty books were found that were absent from the *Short-Title Catalogue of Books Printed in England, Scotland, and Ireland and of English Books Printed Abroad, 1465–1640,* by Alfred W. Pollard and Gilbert R. Redgrave (London: Bibliographical Society, 1926 [i.e., 1927]). Most of Plume's books were probably acquired at secondhand bookshops. Plume was familiar with the London booksellers because of the purchases he made on behalf of his friend Hacket. Several of the books have ownership inscriptions revealing one or two previous owners, and it seems clear that Plume rarely bought new books, except for contemporary political tracts (the library houses about 1,700 of those pamphlets dating from the seventeenth century). Plume made little provision in his will for the increase of his library. Although he left an annual allowance of 20s. for the library keeper to spend on whatever books he might choose, this stipend was hardly likely to produce many new accessions. Furthermore, the physical extent of the bookcases that Plume erected prevented more than a small amount of future expansion.

In almost three hundred years of existence, it is hardly surprising that the library has lost books. More than one hundred have been replaced, occasionally by the original copy, aided by the formation in 1987 of the Friends of the Plume Library, who have also helped in the conservation and repair of the library. It is still open to the general public several days per week, and the books may be consulted by scholars. The Plume Library provides a rare glimpse of an educated seventeenth-century clergyman's intellect and interests and of his desire to share the fruits of his fortune with others through the medium of the printed word.

References:

Andrew Clark, "Dr. Plume as a Cambridge Undergraduate," *Essex Review,* 14 (1905): 147–148;

Clark, "Dr. Plume's Notebook," *Essex Review,* 14 (1905): 152–163, 213–220; 16 (1906): 8–24;

Clark, "Dr. Plume's Pocket Book," *Essex Review,* 14 (1905): 9–20, 65–72;

Clark, "Plume MS. Papers," *Essex Review,* 13 (1904): 30–33;

Clark, "The Plume Pamphlets at Maldon," *Essex Review,* 12 (1903): 159–165;

Frank Herrmann, "The Plume Library, Maldon: A New Chapter," in *Essex: Full of Profitable Things,* edited by Kenneth Neale (Oxford: Leopard's Head, 1996), pp. 245–252;

William J. Petchey, *The Intentions of Thomas Plume* (Maldon: Trustees of the Plume Library, 1985).

Papers:

Thomas Plume's surviving commonplace books, notebooks, and manuscript sermons are in the Plume Library, Maldon. Many of these notebooks, as well as Plume's will, were transcribed by the Reverend Andrew Clark and deposited in the Bodleian Library, Oxford.

Alexander Pope

(21 May 1688 - 30 May 1744)

Claudia Thomas Kairoff
Wake Forest University

See also the Pope entries in *DLB 95: Eighteenth-Century British Poets, First Series,* and *DLB 101: British Prose Writers, 1660–1800, First Series.*

Alexander Pope; portait by Charles Jervas, 1714 (Barber Institute of Fine Arts, The University, Birmingham)

BOOKS: *An Essay On Criticism* (London: Printed for W. Lewis & sold by W. Taylor, T. Osborn & J. Graves, 1711);

The Critical Specimen (London, 1711);

Windsor-Forest: To the Right Honourable George Lord Lansdown (London: Printed for Bernard Lintott, 1713);

The Narrative of Dr. Robert Norris, Concerning the strange and deplorable Frenzy of Mr. John Denn– (London: Printed for J. Morphew, 1713);

The Rape of the Lock: An Heroi-Comical Poem. In Five Canto's (London: Printed for Bernard Lintott, 1714; revised, 1718);

The Temple of Fame: A Vision (London: Printed for Bernard Lintott, 1715);

A Key to the Lock: Or, A Treatise proving, beyond all Contradiction, the dangerous Tendency of a late Poem, entituled, The Rape of the Lock, to Government and Religion, as Esdras Barnivelt, Apoth. (London: Printed for J. Roberts, 1715);

The Dignity, Use and Abuse of Glass-Bottles: Set forth in A Sermon Preach'd to an Illustrious Assembly, And now Publish'd for the Use of the Inferiour Clergy, sometimes attributed to Pope (London: Printed & sold by the Booksellers of London & Westminster, 1715);

A Full and True Account of a Horrid and Barbarous Revenge by Poison, On the Body of Mr. Edmund Curll, Bookseller (London: Sold by J. Roberts, J. Morphew, R. Burleigh, J. Baker & S. Popping, 1716);

God's Revenge Against Punning [single sheet] (London: Printed for J. Roberts, 1716);

A Further Account of the most Deplorable Condition of Mr. Edmund Curll, Bookseller (London: Printed & sold by all the Publishers, Mercuries, and Hawkers within the Bills of Mortality, 1716);

The Works of Mr. Alexander Pope (London: Printed by W. Bowyer for Bernard Lintot, 1717; enlarged edition, Dublin: Printed by & for George Grierson, 1727);

A Clue To the Comedy of the Non-Juror: With some Hints of Consequence Relating to that Play. In a Letter to N. Rowe, Esq.; Poet Laureat to His Majesty (London: Printed for E. Curll, 1718);

Miscellanea: In Two Volumes.–Never before Published.–Viz. I. Familiar Letters Written to Henry Cromwell Esq. by Mr. Pope. II. Occasional Poems by Mr. Pope, Mr. Cromwell, Dean Swift, &c. III. Letters from Mr. Dryden to a Lady (London, 1727 [i.e., 1726]);

The Dunciad: An Heroic Poem. In Three Books (Dublin, Printed, London Reprinted for A. Dodd [i.e., London: Printed for A. Dodd], 1728); revised as

The Dunciad, Variorum: With the Prolegmena of Scriblerus (London: Printed for A. Dod, 1729); enlarged as *The Dunciad, in Four Books. Printed according to the complete Copy found in the Year 1742* (London: Printed for M. Cooper, 1743);

An Epistle To The Right Honourable Richard Earl of Burlington: Occasion'd by his Publishing Palladio's Designs of the Baths, Arches, Theatres, &c. of Ancient Rome (London: Printed for L. Gilliver, 1731); enlarged as *Of False Taste: An Epistle to the Right Honourable Richard Earl of Burlington. Occasion'd by his Publishing Palladio's Designs of the Baths, Arches, Theatres, &c. of Ancient Rome* (London: Printed for L. Gilliver, 1731 [i.e., 1732]);

Of The Use of Riches, An Epistle To the Right Honorable Allen Lord Bathurst (London: Printed by J. Wright for Lawton Gilliver, 1732);

The First Satire Of The Second Book of Horace, Imitated in a Dialogue between Alexander Pope of Twickenham in Comm. Midd. Esq.; on the one Part, and his Learned Council on the other (London: Printed by L. G. & sold by A. Dodd, E. Nutt & the Booksellers of London & Westminster, 1733);

An Essay On Man. Address'd to a Friend.–Part I (London: Printed for J. Wilford, 1733);

An Essay On Man. In Epistles to a Friend.–Epistle II (London: Printed for J. Wilford, 1733);

An Essay On Man. In Epistles to a Friend.–Epistle III (London: Printed for J. Wilford, 1733);

The Impertinent, Or A Visit to the Court. A Satyr (London: Printed for John Wileord [Wilford], 1733);

An Epistle To The Right Honourable Richard Lord Visct. Cobham (London: Printed for Lawton Gilliver, 1733 [i.e., 1734]);

An Essay On Man. In Epistles to a Friend.–Epistle IV (London: Printed for J. Wilford, 1734);

An Essay on Man, Being the First Book of Ethic Epistles. To Henry St. John, L. Bolingbroke [Epistles I–IV] (London: Printed by John Wright for Lawton Gilliver, 1734; Philadelphia: Printed by William Bradford, 1747);

A Most Proper Reply to the Nobleman's Epistle to a Doctor of Divinity (London: Printed & sold by J. Huggonson, 1734);

The First Satire Of The Second Book of Horace, Imitated in Dialogue Between Alexander Pope of Twickenham in Com' Mid' Esq; and his Learned Council.–To which is added, The Second Satire of the same Book (London: Printed for L. G., 1734);

Sober Advice From Horace, To The Young Gentlemen about Town. As deliver'd in his Second Sermon (London: Printed for T. Boreman, 1734); republished as *A Sermon against Adultery* (London: Printed for T. Cooper, 1738);

An Epistle From Mr. Pope, To Dr. Arbuthnot (London: Printed for Lawton Gilliver, 1735);

The Works of Mr. Alexander Pope, Volume II (London: Printed for L. Gilliver, 1735);

Of The Characters of Women: An Epistle To A Lady (London: Printed for Lawton Gilliver, 1735);

Letters of Mr. Pope, and Several Eminent Persons (London: Printed & sold by the Booksellers of London & Westminster, 1735);

A Narrative of the Method by which Mr. Pope's Private Letters were procured and published by Edmund Curll, Bookseller (London, 1735);

The First Epistle Of The Second Book of Horace, Imitated (London: Printed for T. Cooper, 1737);

The Second Epistle Of The Second Book of Horace, Imitated (London: Printed for R. Dodsley, 1737);

Letters of Mr. Alexander Pope, and Several of his Friends (London: Printed by J. Wright for J. Knapton, L. Gilliver, J. Brindley & R. Dodsley, 1737);

The Sixth Epistle Of The First Book of Horace Imitated (London: Printed for L. Gilliver, 1737 [i.e., 1738]);

The First Epistle Of The First Book Of Horace Imitated (London: Printed for R. Dodsley, 1738);

One Thousand Seven Hundred and Thirty Eight. A Dialogue Something like Horace (London: Printed for T. Cooper, 1738);

One Thousand Seven Hundred and Thirty Eight. Dialogue II (London: Printed for R. Dodsley, 1738);

Letters between Dr. Swift, Mr. Pope, &c. (London: Printed for T. Cooper, 1741);

The Works of Mr. Alexander Pope, In Prose. Vol. II (London: Printed for J. & P. Knapton, C. Bathurst & R. Dodsley, 1741);

The New Dunciad: As it was Found In the Year 1741 (London: Printed for T. Cooper, 1742);

The Last Will and Testament of Alexander Pope, of Twickenham, Esq. (London: Printed for A. Dodd, 1744);

The Works of Alexander Pope Esq. In Nine Volumes Complete. With His Last Corrections, Additions, And Improvements; As they were delivered to the Editor a little before his Death; Together With the Commentaries and Notes of Mr. Warburton (London: Printed for J. & P. Knapton, 1751).

Collections and Editions: *The Prose Works of Alexander Pope,* volume 1, edited by Norman Ault (Oxford: Blackwell, 1936); volume 2, edited by Rosemary Cowler (Hamden, Conn.: Archon Books, 1986);

Memoirs of the Extraordinary Life, Works, and Discoveries of Martinus Scriblerus, by Pope, Jonathan Swift, John Arbuthnot, John Gay, Thomas Parnell, and Robert Harley, Earl of Oxford; edited by Charles Kerby-Miller (New Haven: Yale University Press, 1950);

Literary Criticism of Alexander Pope, edited by Bertrand A. Goldgar (Lincoln: University of Nebraska Press, 1965);

Selected Prose of Alexander Pope, edited by Paul Hammond (Cambridge: Cambridge University Press, 1987).

OTHER: *The Iliad of Homer, Translated by Mr. Pope,* 6 volumes (London: Printed by W. Bowyer for Bernard Lintott, 1715–1720);

William Shakespeare, *The Works of Shakespear,* 6 volumes, edited, with a preface, by Pope (London: Printed for Jacob Tonson, 1725);

The Odyssey of Homer, 5 volumes, translated by Pope (London: Printed for Bernard Lintot, 1725–1726);

Miscellanies in Prose and Verse: The First Volume, edited by Pope and Jonathan Swift, preface by Pope (London: Printed for Benjamin Motte, 1727);

"Memoirs of P. P. Clerk of This Parish," "Stradling versus Stiles," and "Thoughts on Various Subjects," in *Miscellanies: The Second Volume,* edited by Pope and Swift (London: Printed for Benjamin Motte, 1727);

Peri Bathous: or, Martinus Scriblerus. His Treatise of the Art of Sinking in Poetry, in *Miscellanies: The Last Volume,* edited by Pope and Swift (London: Printed for B. Motte, 1727);

"To The Reader" and letters, in *The Posthumous Works of William Wycherley, Esq; In Prose and Verse: The Second Volume,* edited by Pope (London: Printed for J. Roberts, 1729);

"A Strange but True Relation How Edmund Curll of Fleetstreet, Stationer, Out of an extraordinary Desire of Lucre, went into Change-Alley, and was converted from the Christian Religion by certain Eminent Jews: And how he was circumcis'd and initiated into their Mysteries" and "An Essay Of the Learned Martinus Scriblerus, Concerning the Origine of Science," in *Miscellanies: The Third Volume,* edited by Pope and Swift (London: Printed for Benj. Motte, 1732).

Alexander Pope's biographer Maynard Mack has estimated that the poet's personal library contained between 650 and 750 volumes. Such a collection would have been similar to those of other contemporary men of letters, such as Jonathan Swift, although far smaller than those of such avid and wealthy bibliophiles as Pope's friend Edward Harley, second Earl of Oxford, whose books and manuscripts eventually formed the core of the British Museum's library. Of Pope's library, only about 165 books survive; he is known, through references by himself or by contemporary witnesses, to have owned approximately 100 more titles.

Alexander Pope was born on 21 May 1688 in London to Alexander and Edith Pope, née Turner. Around 1700 the family moved to Binfield, Berkshire, to comply with laws forbidding Catholics to reside within ten miles of the capital. As an infant Pope contracted tuberculosis of the spine, most likely by drinking contaminated milk from his wet nurse. Among the devastating consequences of the disease were stunted growth and the progressive collapse of his lungs. Educated mostly at home to comply with laws forbidding Catholics to attend public schools, Pope often represented himself as virtually self-taught–particularly during adolescence, when, by his later account, he devoured untranslated versions of most great ancient and modern poetry. "Bred up at home," he says in *The Second Epistle Of The Second Book of Horace, Imitated* (1737), "full early I begun / To read in Greek, the Wrath of Peleus' Son." Of the four editions of Homer in Greek that survive in Pope's library, two could have belonged to him in his adolescence, although all might have been acquired later for the purposes of his translation. His copies of translated editions of Herodotus (*The History of Herodotus,* translated by Isaac Littlebury [London, 1709]), Lucian (*Certain Select Dialogues of Lucian,* translated by Francis Hicks [Oxford, 1663], bound with *Part of Lucian Made English,* translated by Jasper Mayne [Oxford: Printed by H. Hall for R. Davis, 1664]) and Theocritus (*The Idylliums of Theocritus with Rapin's Discourse of Pastorals Done into English,* translated by Thomas Creech [Oxford: Printed by L. Lichfield for Anthony Stevens, 1684]) also survive, as does as his Greek and Latin Pindar (Heidelberg: Jerome Commelin, 1598). He also possessed a Latin edition of Statius's *Thebaid* (Leiden: Hacke, n.d.), the first book of which he imitated at fifteen. His youthful reading formed his taste, influencing a rich body of writings described by Reuben Arthur Brower as "the Poetry of Allusion." Pope also steeped himself in the works of Protestant and Catholic controversy that constituted his father's library. These volumes have disappeared, but the poet inherited them; and they are known to have formed part of the library in his villa when he later resided in Twickenham. Perhaps from such writings he imbibed the feisty spirit that invigorates his mature, politically motivated verse.

One surviving book owned by Pope in his youth is a 1598 folio edition of the works of Geoffrey Chaucer published in London by Adam Islip, which was given to him by a Catholic neighbor when he was thirteen. The rather sparse marginalia of the text exhibits a method of indicating interest, or recalling attention, that Pope practiced throughout his life: a system of quotation marks, mostly single but some double, and an occasional cross to mark passages he found especially

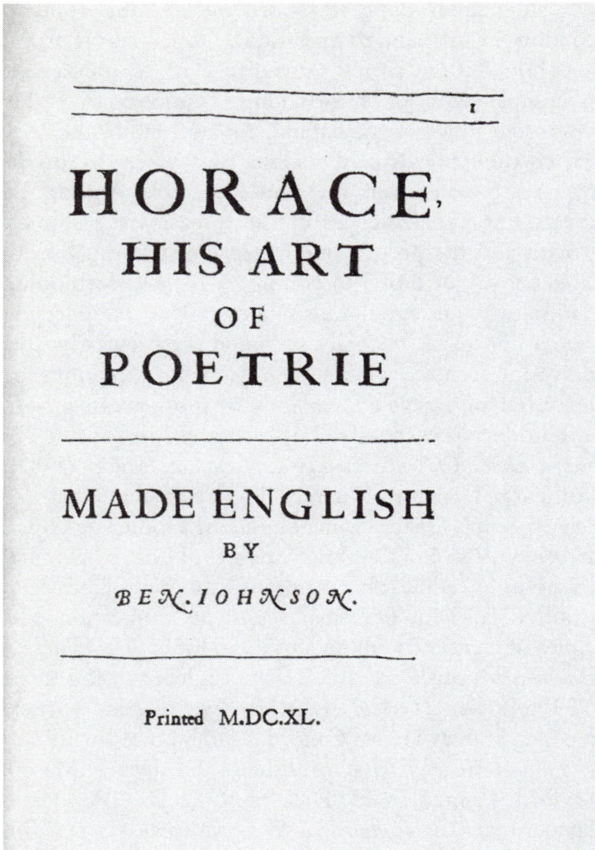
I

HORACE,
HIS ART
OF
POETRIE

MADE ENGLISH
BY
BEN. IOHNSON.

Printed M.DC.XL.

Title page for Ben Jonson's translation of the Roman poet, a copy of which was part of Pope's collection

compelling. In the Chaucer volume Mack observed passages, such as a description of lecherous clerics in Chaucer's translation of *Roman de la Rose,* indicating the young reader's susceptibility to satiric commentary. Further attesting to Pope's boyish interest in bawdy satire is his composition before 1709 of a naughty poem in imitation of Chaucer about an Irish boy who conceals a stolen duck in his breeches. (As the mature Pope acknowledged in *The First Epistle Of The Second Book of Horace, Imitated* [1737], "Chaucer's worst ribaldry is learn'd by rote.") In or about 1704 Pope selected two passages from *The Canterbury Tales* for imitation: "The Wife of Bath's Prologue," published in 1713 in Sir Richard Steele's *Miscellanies,* and "The Tale of January and May," which appeared in Jacob Tonson's *Miscellanies* in 1709. These choices suggest, in addition to his continuing interest in the prurient, that Pope had studied his copy of Chaucer with care and wished to apply what he had learned from his medieval predecessor. His decision to "translate" two Chaucer poems into heroic couplets further attests to Pope's fondness for a poet whose obsolete English rendered him obscure to current readers. By planning to rescue Chaucer from threatened oblivion, the young Pope exhibited the same fear expressed by John Dryden, Jonathan Swift, and other contemporaries that English itself might shortly become archaic.

The Islip Chaucer provides valuable insight into the adolescent Pope's mind as well as his development as a poet. Such opportunities are rare, as many of the books that Pope is known to have studied during this period–books he recalled as the shaping influences of his imagination–have been lost. Those that remain, however, indicate Pope's familiarity with most of the great Greek, Latin, Continental, and English writers to whom he alludes throughout his canon. From Theocritus and Virgil he gleaned the refined conception of pastoral that informs both his youthful pastorals published in Tonson's *Miscellanies* in 1709 and the 27 April 1713 essay in *The Guardian* in which he defined the genre. John Milton contributed a fund of phrases and images, as well as the model of English epic lurking beneath its antitype, *The Dunciad* (1728–1743). In Nicolas Boileau-Despréaux he found a model satirist, witty and urbane. Pope mentions his reading of Vincent Voiture in correspondence of 1710; the French poet suggested the gallant style he adopted for letters to ladies. Later in 1710 Pope accompanied a present to his friend Teresa Blount with the occasional poem "Epistle to Miss Blount, with the Works of Voiture." Pope bought Peter Motteux's four-volume translation of *Don Quixote* (*The History of the Renown'd Don Quixote de la Mancha: Translated from the Original by Several Hands* [London: Peter Motteux]) as soon as it was printed in 1700–1703 and, like many other English writers throughout the century, was inspired by Miguel de Cervantes Saavedra's tale of a man driven mad by his reading material.

The letters of Pope's youth and early manhood refer often to his reading and reveal him winning the friendship and respect of much older mentors by reflecting on mutually familiar authors. In fact, the friends sometimes presented one another with favorite books. A copy of Terence (*Comoediae Sex,* edited by Cornelius Schrevel [Leiden and Rotterdam: Hacke, 1669]) that was given to Pope by Henry Cromwell survives; in a letter of 17 December 1710 Pope writes of posting Cromwell a volume by the seventeenth-century poet Richard Crashaw, "who has held a place among my other books of this nature for some years." Pope's letters to Cromwell appeal to the elderly gentleman by creating a reciprocal persona compounded of the rakish man-about-town and the somber critic. "I have," he assured Cromwell on 11 November 1710, "a very good opinion of Mr. *Row's* 9th book of *Lucan:* Indeed he amplified too much, as well as *Breboeuf,* the famous *French Imitator.*" Pope's copy of Georges de Breboeuf's translation, *La Pharsale de Lucain* (Leiden: Jean Elsevier, 1658), is no longer extant, but his copy of *Lucan's Pharsalia,* translated by Nicholas Rowe (London: Printed for Jacob Tonson, 1718 [i.e., 1719]), survives, with Pope's autograph on the flyleaf. (Pope evidently was writing of a manuscript of the translation in his 1710 letter.) The Pope-Cromwell correspondence reveals the young man reading and testing the opinions of such critics as Michael Maittaire, whose *Opera et Fragmenta Veterum Poetarum Latinorum Profanorum & ecclesiasticorum* Pope owned in a two-volume folio published in 1713 (London: Printed by J. Nicholson, B. Tooke, and J. Tonson). Literary allusion remained integral to Pope's style as a mature poet.

Of Pope's surviving books, seven copies of Homer–three in Greek (Paris: Adr. Turnebus, 1554; edited by Cornelius Schrevel, Leiden: Francis Hacke, 1656; and edited by Josua Barnes, Cambridge: Cornelius Crownfield, 1711), one in Greek and Latin (edited by Stephen Bergler, Amsterdam: Henry Wetstein, 1707), two English translations by George Chapman (*The Iliad of Homer Prince of Poets* [London: Nathaniel Butter, 1611]) and Thomas Hobbes (*Iliads and Odysses* [London: William Crook, 1686]) and Anne Dacier's French version (*L'Iliade d'Homere* [Paris: Rigaud, 1711])–commemorate the lucrative translations of the *Iliad* and *Odyssey* that occupied Pope from 1713 to 1726. None of the books by the "hundred Pedants" Pope despaired of reviewing for his annotations are extant, perhaps because he persuaded learned friends to assess the writings of Dionysus of Halicarnassus and Eustathius. The Chapman and Hobbes editions, however, attest to Pope's painstaking study of his predecessors. Another book that survives to illustrate Pope's method of studying, annotating, then emulating as well as criticizing competitors is his copy of Dacier's *L'Iliade d'Homere.* As Mack observes, Pope's copy is sprinkled with comments identifying Dacier's scholarly borrowings. Milton, John Ogilby, Eustathius, and, most often, Spondanus are discerned as the sources of her opinions. Although implicitly accusing Dacier of plagiarism through these comments, Pope, in turn, borrowed copiously–and with as little acknowledgment–from Dacier's notes in his translation–especially from her notes to John Ozell's five-volume English translation of *The Iliad* (London: Printed by G. James, for Bernard Lintott, 1712), which is conspicuously absent from Pope's remaining library. Although largely unaccompanied by comment other than the stark recording of a source ("out of Spondanus verbatim," or, simply, "In Ogilby"), Pope's jottings in Dacier's Homer testify to his informed reading and competitive writing.

One more survivor from Pope's Homeric phase is his heavily marked copy of a rival publication, Thomas Tickell's version of *The First Book of Homer's Iliad* (London: J. Tonson, 1715). Commissioned by Joseph Addison and his Whig associates in hopes of capitalizing on the politicized literary climate, Tickell's version was published two days after the appearance of Pope's first volume. Pope's literary rivals had hoped that the Oxford graduate's translation would expose to ridicule Pope's inferior knowledge of Greek. The contest proved brief, as Pope's was soon universally acclaimed the stronger version. But the revelation of a concerted effort to demean his translation–the labor of years–was traumatic for Pope. His copy of Tickell's book is heavily marked, evidently in preparation for an extensive and systematic reply that he decided not to pursue.

Other books used by Pope early in his career are lost. After completing his *Iliad* (1715–1720) and *Odyssey* (1725–1726) translations, for example, he turned to editing the works of William Shakespeare. This project proved to be one of his few failures. The recovery of the early folios that Pope assembled for comparative purposes would illuminate his editorial process. In a letter to Tonson in May 1722 he describes his intention "to pass the next whole week in London, purposely to get together Parties of my acquaintance ev'ry night, to collate the several Editions of Shakespear's single Plays." Of this project, however, only Pope's copy of *Othello, the Moor of Venice* (London: Richard Bentley, 1695) survives. The book includes notes in two hands recording folio textual variants, perhaps produced during one of Pope's collating "parties."

Pope's six-volume *The Works of Shakespear* was published in 1725, only to be criticized thoroughly in Lewis Theobald's *Shakespeare Restored* (1726). Theobald's book, intended partly to "puff" his own forthcoming edition, respectfully but convincingly exposed Pope's inadequacies as a professional editor. The poet had, in fact, deliberately affected the traditional role of gentleman-scholar rather than the "modern" conception of scholarship; but despite Theobald's professed admiration of his poetry, Pope never forgave Theobald for what he perceived as an attack. While only one pamphlet co-authored by Theobald and Benjamin Griffin, a critique of John Gay's burlesque *The What D'Ye Call It* (*A Complete Key to the last New Farce The What D'ye Call It. To Which Is prefix'd a Hypercritical Preface on the Nature of Burlesque, and the Poets Design* [London: James Roberts]) survives from Pope's library, the poet soon enshrined his enemy as the King of the Dunces in the first three-book version of his satiric masterpiece, *The Dunciad* (1728).

In *The First Satire Of The Second Book of Horace, Imitated* (1733) Pope declares his intention to "pour out all myself, as plain . . . as old Montagne" [*sic*]. Two of Pope's copies of Michel de Montaigne's *Essays* survive,

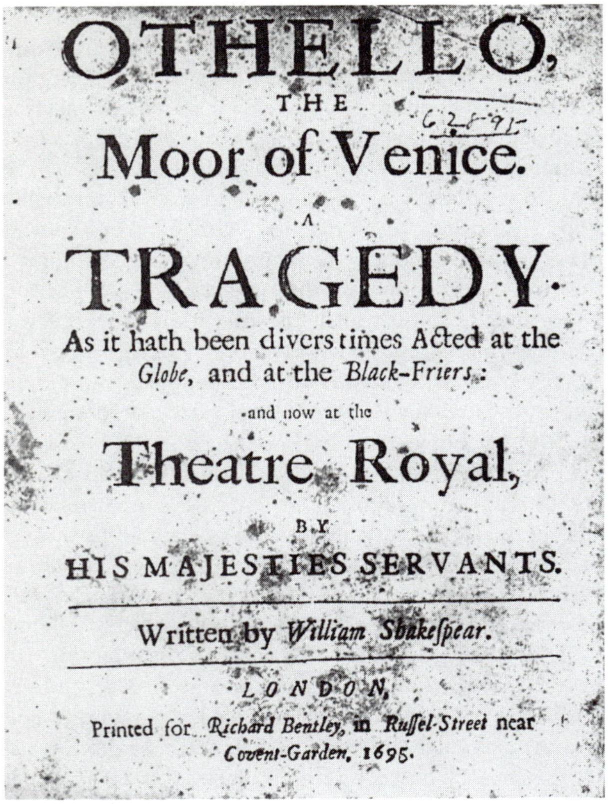
OTHELLO,
THE
Moor of Venice.
A
TRAGEDY.
As it hath been divers times Acted at the
Globe, and at the *Black-Friers*:
and now at the
Theatre Royal,
BY
HIS MAJESTIES SERVANTS.
Written by *William Shakespear.*
LONDON,
Printed for *Richard Bentley*, in *Russel-Street* near
Covent-Garden, 1695.

Title page for the 1695 printing of Shakespeare's play, a copy of which Pope used in preparing his edition of the collected plays

including the three-volume Charles Cotton translation (London: Printed for T. Basset, M. Gilliflower, and W. Hensman, 1685–1693) he purchased when he was eighteen. (The other is the "Nouvelle Edition" of the *Essais* in French, published in Paris in 1652 by Augustin Courbe.) The volumes of Robert Bruce Cotton bear the marks of Pope's attentive reading throughout, and in his later verse he often adopts Montaigne's preference for moderation. Desiderius Erasmus–whom Pope, in *An Essay On Criticism* (1711), calls "The *Glory* of the Priesthood, and the *Shame!*"–was another lifelong Pope hero of moderate principles, but no copy of his writings owned by Pope survives. Among his English predecessors, Pope owned folios of Sir Philip Sidney's *The Countesse of Pembrokes Arcadia* (London: Imprinted by H. L. [Humphrey Lownes] for Simon Waterson, 1613), Edmund Spenser's *The Faerie Queen: The Shepheards Calendar, together with the other Works of England's Arch-poët* (London: H. L. for Mathew Lownes, 1611 [i.e., 1613?]), and *The Works of Ben Jonson* (London: Printed by Thomas Hodgkin, for H. Herringman, E. Brewster, T. Bassett, R. Chiswell, M. Wotton, G. Conyers, 1692). Pope admired the satires of John Donne enough to "preserve" two of them through imitation in his twenties (they were published in 1735 as "The Second Satire of Dr. John Denne . . . versifyed" and "The Fourth Satire of Dr. John Donne . . . Versifyed" in *The Works of Mr. Alexander Pope, Volume II*), but only his copy of Donne's *Pseudo-Martyr* (London: Printed by W. Stansby for Walter Burre, 1710) was known to be extant in the twentieth century. Throughout his career Pope emulated and refined John Dryden's style; he owned copies of at least four individual plays by Dryden–*An Evening's Love, or The Mock Astrologer* (London: Printed by T. N. for Henry Herringman, 1671); *The Assignation: or, Love in a Nunnery* (London: Printed by T. N. for Henry Herringman, 1673); *Oedipus,* by Dryden and Nathaniel Lee (London: Printed for R. Bentley and M. Magnes, 1679); and *The Duke of Guise,* by Dryden and Lee (London: Printed by T. H. for R. Bentley and J. Tonson, 1683)–in addition to Dryden's *A Poem upon the Death of his late Highness, Oliver, Lord Protector of England, Scotland, & Ireland* (London: Printed for William Wilson, 1659 [i.e., ca. 1692]), *Fables Ancient and Modern: Translated into Verse, from Homer, Ovid, Boccace, & Chaucer; with Original Poems* (London: Printed for Jacob Tonson, 1700), the two-volume *Comedies, Tragedies, and Operas* (London: Printed for Jacob Tonson, Thomas Bennet, and Richard Wellington, 1701), and the third edition of Dryden's translations of Virgil in three volumes (London: Printed by Jacob Tonson, 1709).

Of Dryden's contemporaries–that "mob of gentlemen who writ with ease," as he referred to them in his imitation of "The First Epistle of the Second Book of Horace" (1737)–Pope owned editions of works by John Wilmot, Earl of Rochester; John Oldham; and probably–according to Graham Cartwright in a 1986 article–George Etherege. In the course of assembling a catalogue of the Hurd Library at Hartlebury Castle, Cartwright took the opportunity to review the evidence of Pope's ownership of more than forty volumes in the collection. He deduced that a 1704 octavo edition of *The Works of Sir George Etherege: Containing His Plays and Poems* (London: Printed for H. H. and sold by J. Tonson and T. Bennet) was probably Pope's. Cartwright also verified that a previously unrecorded edition of Sir John Denham's *Poems and Translations, with the Sophy: The fourth Edition. To which is added, Cato-Major of Old-age* (London: Printed by T. W. for H. Herringman and sold by Jacob Tonson and Thomas Bennet, 1703) was Pope's. (In "Cooper's Hill" Denham describes the Thames as "Tho' deep, yet clear; tho' gentle, yet not dull"; in *The Dunciad* Pope parodies the melodious lines to praise "Beer, / Tho' stale, not ripe; tho' thin, yet never clear.") Together, the books help to substantiate Pope's familiarity with these seventeenth-century predecessors. On the other hand, Cartwright determined that the notes in four volumes attributed to Pope by Mack in his article "Pope's Books: A

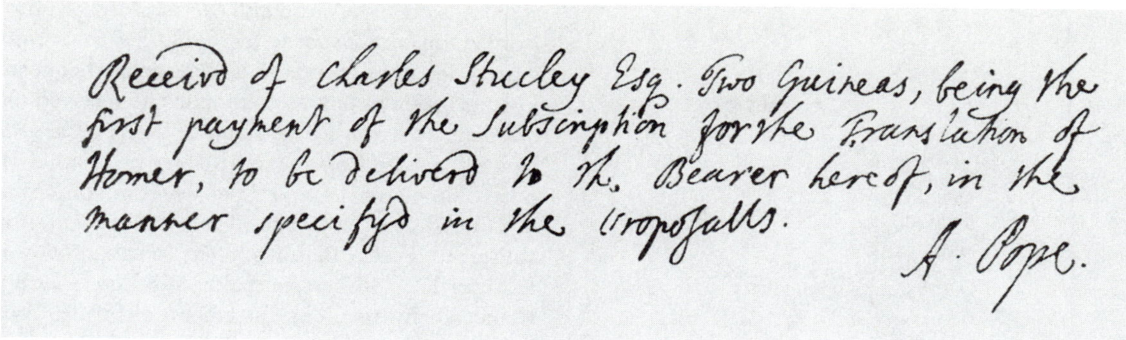

Receiv'd of Charles Stucley Esq. Two Guineas, being the first payment of the Subscription for the Translation of Homer, to be deliver'd to the Bearer hereof, in the manner specify'd in the Proposalls.

A. Pope.

Receipt acknowledging a subscriber's payment in 1756 for Pope's translation of The Iliad *(Maggs Bros.,* English Literature and History, *catalogue no. 536, part 2, 1930)*

Biographical Survey with a Finding List" (1977)–translations of Virgil and Cicero and two works by Thomas Gale–were not, in fact, in Pope's handwriting and had, therefore, most likely not belonged to Pope.

Pope's mature verse has often been compared to that of his chief classical model, Horace. Pope himself, in his "Epilogues to the Satires, published in *One Thousand Seven Hundred and Thirty-Eight, A Dialogue Something Like Horace*" (1738), imagines a friend complaining of his recent work, "'Tis all from *Horace*." As Howard Weinbrot has observed, Pope actually combined the satiric attributes of three ancient models to produce poems with the cleverness of Horace, the harshness of Persius, and the strength of Juvenal. Of these predecessors' works, four of Pope's volumes of Horace remain: a 1629 *Opera,* edited by Daniel Heins (Leiden: Elzevir); a 1640 edition of *The Art of Poetry,* translated by Jonson (London: Printed by J. Okes for J. Benson); a 1695 *Opera,* edited by Ludovicus Desprez, printed in Amsterdam, and purchased by Pope in 1707; and a 1721 *Poemata* (London [printed in The Hague]: Fratres Vaillant et N. Prevost). Pope owned two Latin editions of Juvenal, one of which (edited by Schrevel; Leiden and Rotterdam: Hacke, 1664) included the satires of Persius, and a translation of the two Roman satirists by Dryden and others (London: J. Tonson, 1693).

While replete with references to works in his personal library by authors whom he admired, Pope's mature verse is also peppered with references to writers he despised. *The Dunciad,* virtually an index of those writers Pope deemed indefensible, grew into four books to include all the figures Pope believed responsible for Britain's cultural decline. Many of the "dunces" had been provoked to attack by inclusion in Pope's *Peri Bathous* (1728), a parodic tribute to modern writing designed to evoke just such replies. Following publication of *The Dunciad, Variorum* (1729), in which their identities were clarified, many wrote additional pamphlets accusing Pope of the same vanity and greed he attributed to them. As their attacks multiplied, *The Dunciad* grew and "dunces" were added to and taken out of the poem as their relations with Pope soured or improved. Pope certainly monitored all the entrants in this "paper war." According to a well-known anecdote, Jonathan Richardson and his son called on Pope soon after publication of a particularly scurrilous attack on him by Colley Cibber. They discovered the poet studying the pamphlet, his face distorted with anguish, although he assured them that "These things are my diversion." Pope had many of the attacks bound into a four-volume octavo set; surviving among these volumes are five of John Dennis's pamphlets, including *Reflections Critical and Satyrical, upon a late Rhapsody, call'd An Essay Upon Criticism* (London: Printed for Bernard Lintott, 1711). Other bound anti-Pope salvos include Sir Thomas Burnet and George Duckett's *Homerides: or, A letter to Mr. Pope, occasion'd by his intended translation of Homer. By Sir Iliad Doggrel* (London: Printed by W. Wilkins, and sold by J. Roberts, 1715), Matthew Concanen's *A Supplement to the Profund* (London: J. Roberts, 1728), and Aaron Hill's *The Progress of Wit: A Caveat. By Gamaliel Gunson, Professor of Physick and Astrology* (London: Printed for J. Wilford, 1730). Pope's copies of Cibber's pamphlets have disappeared, but not Edmund Curll's *The Curliad: A Hypercritic upon the Dunciad Variorum* (London: Printed for the author, 1729), nor Giles Jacob's *The Mirrour: Or, Letters Satirical, Panegyrical, Serious and Humorous, on the Present Times . . . To which is added A legal Conviction of Mr. Alexander Pope of Dulnes and Scandal, in the High Court of Parnassus* (London: J. Roberts, 1733). Such careful preservation enabled Pope to quote his enemies–usually out of context and often turning their words against themselves–in the vast notes that supplemented his poem.

But while perpetuating his vendettas against enemies, Pope's library also enshrined many memorials of friendship. In this respect, his library resembled the art on the walls of his Twickenham villa, consisting mostly

Terra cotta bust of Pope by L. F. Roubiliac, 1738 (Bodleian Library)

of images of his friends–even after they ceased to be friends, as in the case of Lady Mary Wortley Montagu. Pope's shelves abounded in editions such as Edward Young's *The Force of Religion; or, Vanquished Love* (London: Printed for E. Curll and J. Pemberton, 1714) and *Ocean: An Ode occasion'd by His Majesty's late Royal Encouragement of the Sea-Service* (London: Printed for Thomas Worrall, 1728), both inscribed to Pope by the author. Pope's volumes of James Thomson's works (volume 1, London, 1730; volume 2, London: A. Millar, 1736) were both presentation copies, as was the copy of his friend Thomas Parnell's *Homer's Battle of the Frogs and Mice* (London: Printed for Bernard Lintot, 1717). Elijah Fenton (*Poems on Several Occasions* [London: Printed for Bernard Lintot, 1717]), Samuel Garth (*The Dispensary* [London: Printed for John Nutt, 1706]), John Gay (*Trivia: or, The Art of Walking the Streets of London* [London: Printed for Bernard Lintott, 1716]), Richard Glover (*Leonidas* [London: Printed for R. Dodsley, 1737]), George Granville, Lord Lansdowne (*Poems upon Several Occasions* [London: Printed for J. Tonson, 1712)], and Elizabeth Rowe (*The History of Joseph* [London: Printed for T. Worrall, 1736]) all presented Pope with their publications, as did his sometime enemy, Aaron Hill (*Alzira: A Tragedy* [London: Printed for John Osborne, 1736]). Other items commemorated deceased friends and were either bequeathed to Pope or given to him as memorials: he received his copy of Nicholas Rowe's translation of *Lucan's Pharsalia* from Rowe's widow. Pope gave his copy of Matthew Prior's two-volume *Poems on Several Occasions* (London: Printed for J. Tonson and J. Barber, 1721), itself a gift from the author, to Teresa Blount's sister, Martha, following the death in 1721 of their mutual friend. Pope's early friend Robert Digby gave him the edition of Juvenal translated by Dryden and others, while Henry St. John, first Viscount Bolingbroke, gave him a fourth-edition folio of John Locke's *An Essay Concerning Human Understanding* (London: Printed for Awnsham and John Churchill and Samuel Manship, 1700). Jonathan Swift commemorated his friendship with Pope in 1714 with a Greek and Latin New Testament edited by Erasmus (Paris: J. Roigny, 1543). Other surviving books were given by Pope to friends: to Ralph Allen, for example, he gave his two-volume edition of Cicero's *Opera* (Paris: Stephanus, 1555) in 1741, and the 1664 edition of Juvenal and Persius and the 1721 edition of Horace's *Poemata* in 1742. He made several gifts to William Warburton, his friend and editor during his final years, such as his edition of Pierre-Daniel Huet's *Demonstratio Evangelica ad Serenissimum Delphinum* (Paris: Daniel Hortemels, 1690). He bequeathed his library to Warburton and Allen, with exceptions such as the eighty-five copperplates of J. Houbraken as well as George Vertue and Thomas Birch's *Heads of Illustrious Persons of Great Britain* (1735–1744) that he reserved for Martha Blount.

Pope's poems include several portraits of ignorant book collectors. In the ascerbic "Verses sent to Mrs. T. B. with his Works," which was published anonymously in 1721 in *The Grove; Or, A Collection of Original Poems Translations, etc.* (1717), he chides Teresa Blount for choosing both men and books for their appearances. "She keeps thee, Book! I'll lay my Head, / What? Throw away a *Fool in Red:* / No, trust the Sex's sacred Rule; / The gaudy Dress will save the Fool." In *An Epistle To The Right Honourable Richard Earl of Burlington: Occasion'd by his Publishing Palladio's Designs of the Baths, Arches, Theatres, &c. of Ancient Rome* (1731) he ridicules the wealthy dilettante who hires specialists to assemble collections "he ne'er can taste" that will ultimately descend to more discriminating connoisseurs, such as Thomas Hearne, Richard Mead, and Sir Hans Sloane: such a collector purchases "Rare monkish manuscripts for Hearne alone, / And Books for Mead, and Butterflies for Sloane." The poem culminates in Pope's notorious description of "Timon's villa," where the proud owner invites the poet to admire his library:

His Study! With what Authors is it stor'd?
In Books, not Authors, curious is my Lord;

To all their dated Backs he turns you round,
These Aldus printed, those Du Sueil has bound.
Lo some are Vellom, and the rest as good
For all his Lordship knows, but they are Wood.
For Locke or Milton 'tis in Vain to look,
These shelves admit not any modern book.

Similarly, *The Dunciad* commences with a vignette in which Theobald–in the 1743 edition, Theobald is replaced by Cibber–languishes in a garret furnished with books that are either sources for plagiarism, "serve (like other Fools) to fill a room," or (those on the highest shelves) represent "The Classics of an Age that heard of none": that is, tomes of outmoded religious controversy.

Pope was often accused of hypocrisy during his lifetime, but the faults he exposes in others' libraries were not represented in his own. While he ridicules collectors such as Teresa Blount and "Lord Timon" for selecting books because of their red and gold bindings, his own was a working library and embodied the cherished learning of a man excluded from formal education. Pope evidently despised those who assembled libraries merely for show; his personal books bear the marks of his attention and analysis. As Mack observes, Pope frequently performed for himself the cross-referencing and annotation that modern readers expect in standard editions and that were then practically unknown. Such reading habits enabled Pope both to emulate the techniques and to determine the sources of his models, as well as to detect the borrowings of his enemies. While Theobald and Cibber merely chewed over and regurgitated their predecessors, according to *The Dunciad,* Pope earned the right to emulate his precursors by reconstructing their imaginative and intellectual sources. While wealthy collectors might have assembled "monkish manuscripts" or "the classics of an age that heard of none" merely to fill their vast libraries, Pope included both ancient and modern writers in his library. In *The First Epistle of the Second Book of Horace Imitated* he derided the custom that, "estimating Authors by the year," bestows "a Garland only on a Bier." Pope's library thus contained multiple editions of Milton and Dryden, as well as the works of Homer and Horace.

Pope's choice of Warburton as corecipient of his library was, in some ways, unfortunate. Warburton gave away many books from Pope's collection as mementos to his friends. Those that have been recovered bear notes, such as those in a copy of Joseph Hall's *Virgidemiarum* (Oxford: Printed for R. Clements; sold by R. Baldwin and R. Dodsley, London; and T. Merrill in Cambridge, 1753), indicating that Warburton had given it to Richard Hurd when, "looking into Mr. Pope's Library I found an edition of your favorite Satires of Hall." After Warburton's marriage to Allen's niece Gertrude, however, their two portions of the library were united and eventually accompanied the Warburtons to the bishop's palace when he was granted the See of Gloucester. Although Warburton gave some of the books away and others were sold by Gertrude after his death, many of Pope's remaining books were purchased by Hurd for his library at Hartlebury Castle. There they remain today, included in Cartwright's catalogue of the Hurd Library that is available through the Special Collections Department of the University of Birmingham Library. While Pope scholars must regret that only this fraction remains, the surviving books help to fill out the picture of Pope as an avid reader, self-taught scholar, competitive poet, dogged enemy, and devoted friend.

Letters:

The Correspondence of Alexander Pope, 5 volumes, edited by George Sherburn (Oxford: Clarendon Press, 1956).

Bibliography:

Reginald Harvey Griffith, *Alexander Pope: A Bibliography,* 2 parts (Austin: University of Texas Press, 1922, 1927).

Biographies:

George Sherburn, *The Early Career of Alexander Pope* (Oxford: Clarendon Press, 1934);

Maynard Mack, *Alexander Pope: A Life* (New Haven: Yale University Press, 1985).

References:

Reuben Arthur Brower, *Alexander Pope: The Poetry of Allusion* (Oxford: Clarendon Press, 1959);

W. J. Cameron, "Pope's Annotations on *State Affairs* Poems," *Notes & Queries,* 203 (1958): 291–294;

Graham Cartwright, "Pope's Books: A Postscript to Mack," *Notes & Queries,* 231 (1986): 56–58;

Maynard Mack, *Collected in Himself: Essays Critical, Biographical, and Bibliographical on Pope and Some of His Contemporaries* (Newark: University of Delaware Press, 1982);

Mack, "Pope's Books: A Biographical Survey with a Finding List," in *English Literature in the Age of Disguise,* edited by Maximillian E. Novak (Berkeley: University of California Press, 1977), pp. 243–305;

Valerie Rumbold, *Women's Place in Pope's World* (Cambridge: Cambridge University Press, 1989);

Howard D. Weinbrot, *Alexander Pope and the Traditions of Formal Verse Satire* (Princeton, N.J.: Princeton University Press, 1982).

Thomas Rawlinson
(25 March 1681 – 6 August 1725)

and

Richard Rawlinson
(3 January 1690 – 6 April 1755)

Robert A. Shaddy
University of Toledo

Thomas Rawlinson

CATALOGUE: *A Catalogue of Choice and Valuable Books . . . the Collection made by Tho. Rawlinson,* parts 1–6 by Thomas Rawlinson, parts 7–16 by Richard Rowlinson (London, 1721–1734).

OTHER: Poem on the death of William Henry, Duke of Gloucester, in *Exequiae desideratissimo principi Gulielmo Glocestriae Duci ab Oxoniensi Academia solutae* (Oxford: E Theatro Sheldoniano, 1700).

Richard Rawlinson

CATALOGUES: William Dunn Macray, *Catalogi Cocicum Manuscriptorum Bibliothecae Bodleiane Partis Quintae Fasciulus Primus [Quintus] Ricardi Rawlinson . . .*, 5 volumes (Oxford: E Typographeo Academico, 1862–1900);

Michael Hawkins, ed., *The Rawlinson Manuscripts* [microform] (Brighton, U.K.: Harvestor Press Microform Publications, 1981).

Richard Rawlinson (Bodleian Library, Oxford)

BOOKS: *The Life of Mr. Anthony à Wood, Historiographer of the Most Famous University of Oxford* (London: Printed for the Author, 1711);

The Jacobite Memorial: Being a True Copy of the Letter sent to Mr. Broadwater, Mayor of Oxford. With the Proceedings of that Loyal University and City relating thereunto. In a Letter from a Gentleman of Magdalen College, to his Friend in London (London: Printed for J. Roberts, 1714);

The Laws of Honour: or a Compendious Account of the Ancient Derivation of all Titles, Dignities, Offices, &c. as well Spiritual as Temporal, Civil or Military (London: R. Gosling, 1714);

A Full and Impartial Account of the Oxford-Riots. . . . In a Letter from a Member of the University to his Friend in London, as Philoxon (London: Fleetwood, 1715);

The Conduct of the Reverend Dr. White Kennet, Dean of Peterborough, From the Year 1681, to the Present Time. Being a Supplement to his Three Letters to the Bishop of Carlisle, Upon the Subject of Bishop Herks, as An Impartial Hand, second edition (London: Printed & sold by C. King, 1717);

The History and Antiquities of the Cathedral Church of Rochester (London: Printed for E. Curll, 1717);

The History and Antiquities of the City and Cathedral-Church of Hereford (London: Printed for R. Gosling, 1717);

The Inscriptions upon the Tombs, Grave-stones, &c. in the Dissenters Burial Place near Bunhill-Fields (London: Printed for E. Curll, 1717);

Proposal for Printing by Subscription "Antiquitates & Athenae Etonenses," or the History and Antiquities of the Famous College of Eton, as An Impartial Hand (London, 1717);

The History and Antiquities of the Cathedral-Church of Salisbury and the Abbey-Church of Bath (London: Printed for E. Curll, 1719);

The English Topographer: or, An Historical Account . . . of all the Pieces that have been Written relating to the Antiquities, Natural History, or Topographical Description of any Part of England . . ., as An Impartial Hand (London: Printed for T. Jauncy, 1720);

John Norden, *Speculi Britannae Pars Altera: or, A Delineation of Northhamtonshire . . .,* edited by Richard Rawlinson (London, 1720);

Pictures Rawlinsoniansis: Being a Collection of Original Paintings of Tho. Rawlinson. (London, 1734);

The Deed of Trust and Will of Richard Rawlinson, of St. John Baptist College, Oxford, Doctor of Laws, Containing his Endowment of an Anglo-Saxon Lecture, and other Benefactions to the College and University (London: Printed for James Fletcher Jr., Oxford, and sold by John & James Rivington, London, 1755).

OTHER: *The University Miscellany: or, More Burning Work for the Oxford Convocation,* second edition, corrected, edited by Rawlinson (London, 1713);

Tristram Risdon, *The Chorographical Description, or, Survey of the County of Devon, with the City and County of Exeter,* edited by Rawlinson (London: E. Curll, 1714);

Risdon, *A Continuation of the Survey of Devonshire,* edited by Rawlinson (London, 1714);

Miscellanies on Several Curious Subjects: Now first Published from their Respective Originals, edited by Rawlinson (London: Printed for E. Curll, 1714);

The Oxford Packet, edited by Rawlinson (London: Printed for J. Roberts, 1714);

Pietes Universitatis Oxoniensis on Obitum Sereniasimmae Reginae Annae at Gratulatio in Auguetiasimi Regis Georgii Inaugurationem, edited by Rawlinson (Oxford, 1714);

Exequiae Clarissimo Viro Johanni Radcliffe M. D. ab Oxoniensi Academia Salutae, edited by Rawlinson (Oxford: E Typographeo Clarendoniano, 1715);

William Lilly, *Mr. William Lilly's History of his Life and Times, from the Year 1602, to 1681,* edited by Rawlinson (London: J. Robert, 1715);

Some Memoirs of the Life of John Radcliffe M. D., includes two letters by Rawlinson (London, 1715);

Thomas Abingdon, *The Antiquities of the Cathedral Church of Worcester. . . . To which are added, The Antiquities of the Cathedral Churches of Chichester and Lichfield,* edited by Rawlinson (London, 1717);

Elias Ashmole, *Memoirs of the Life of that Learned Antiquary, Elias Ashmole, Esq: Drawn up by Himself by way of Diary,* edited by Rawlinson (London: J. Roberts, 1717);

Robert South, *Opera Posthuma Latina, Viri Doctissimi et Clarissima Roberti South, S. T. P.,* edited by Rawlinson (London: Printed for E. Curll, 1717);

South, *Posthumous Works of the Late Reverend Robert South D. D. Containing Sermons on Several Subjects,* edited by Rawlinson (London: Printed for E. Curll, 1717);

Sampson Erdeswicke, *A Survey of Staffordshire. Containing, the Antiquities of that County,* edited by Rawlinson (London: E. Curll, 1717);

Peter Abelard, *Petri Abaelardi, Abbatis Ruyensis et Heliossae, Abbatissae Parancletensie Epistise A prioris Editiones Erroribus purgatae, A cum Cod. MS.,* edited by Rawlinson (London: Printed for E. Curll & W. Taylor, 1718);

Joseph Addison, *A Dissertation upon the most Celebrated Roman Poets,* translated from the original Latin by Christopher Hayes, edited by Rawlinson (London: Printed for E. Curll, 1718);

Ashmole, *The Antiquities of Berkshire,* 3 volumes, edited by Rawlinson (London: Printed for E. Curll, 1719);

John Aubrey, *The Natural History and Antiquities of the County of Surrey. Begun in the year 1673, by John Aubrey, Esq; F. R. S. and continued to the present time,* 5 volumes, edited by Rawlinson (London: E. Curll, 1719);

Sir John Perrott, *The History of That Most Eminent Statesman, Sir John Perrott . . . Now First Published from the Original Manuscript,* edited by Rawlinson (London, 1728);

Nicolas Lenglet du Fresnoy, *A New Method of Studying History,* 2 volumes, translated, with additions, by Rawlinson (London: Printed for W. Burton, 1728);

Bernard Le Bovier Fontenelle, *A Week's Conversation on the Plurality of Worlds,* translated by William Gardiner, second edition [and] Joseph Addison, *Mr. Secretary*

Addison's Oration, made at Oxford, in Defense of the New Philosophy, edited by Rawlinson (London, 1728);

William Laud, archbishop of Canterbury, *A Speech Delivered in the Starr-Chamber, on Wednesday, the xiv of June MDCXXXVII at the Censure of John Bastwick, Henry Burton, & William Prinn; Concerning Pretended Innovations in the Church,* edited by Rawlinson (London: Printed by Richard Badger, circa 1729);

Copy of a Bull taken from the Door of St. John Baptist's Church in the City of Valletta in the Isle of Malta. Ex Autographo, edited by Rawlinson (London, 1729);

Theophilus Downes, *Viri Eruditissmi Theophili Downes, A. M. Coll. Baliol, Oxon. olim Socii, De Clypeo Woodwardiano Stricturae Breves,* edited by Rawlinson (London, 1729);

Living during the late 1600s and the early 1700s, two brothers, Thomas and Richard Rawlinson, collected books, manuscripts, art objects, and other collectibles on a virtually unrivaled scale for their time. The collection of Thomas, the elder brother, was scattered after he became a victim of poor fiscal administration and unchecked bibliomania. Richard's collection, which grew in size to eclipse his brother's magnificent assemblage, is preserved in the Bodleian Library at Oxford, where it continues to be a valuable resource for scholars. Indeed, the 1986 Oxford edition of Shakespeare's works includes a previously unattributed, anonymous poem that was found in Richard Rawlinson's collection. Cataloguing the collection took more than 150 years. The brothers' activities inspired admiration, respect, envy, and animosity. Thomas Rawlinson was the inspiration for Joseph Addison's "Tom Folio" character in *The Tatler:* "a learned idiot–an universal scholar so far as the title-pages of all authors; who thinks he gives you an account of an author when he tells you the name of his editor and the year in which his book was printed." To the renowned bibliographer and librarian Thomas Frognall Dibdin (1776–1847), Thomas was a "towering spirit" and "the Leviathan of book-collectors." Richard was known to be quarrelsome and "a bit of a crank" but also "as quintessential an antiquary as may be conceived."

Thomas Rawlinson was born in the Old Bailey (an older section of London in which prosperous middle-class families lived) in the parish of St. Sepulchre, on 25 March 1681. He was the eldest son of Sir Thomas Rawlinson (1647–1708) and Mary (1663–1725), eldest daughter of Richard Taylor of Turnham Green, Middlesex. An owner of much property, Sir Thomas was named lord mayor of London in 1705, and his eldest son received an education that reflected the family's lofty social and economic status. Thomas Rawlinson was educated at Cheam under William Day and at Eton College under John Newborough. He entered St. John's College, Oxford, on 25 February 1699 and left in 1701 without a degree to study law at the Middle Temple in London. Thomas Rawlinson was called to the bar on 19 May 1705 and then set out on a long tour through England and the Low Countries. During this Grand Tour, his taste for antiquities, manuscripts, and rare books was whetted. According to his younger brother Richard, Thomas collected widely but especially favored "old and beautiful editions of the classical authors, and whatever directly or indirectly related to English history."

Thomas Rawlinson returned to London following his tour of the Continent to devote himself to the study of municipal law, anticipating a good practice. The death of Sir Thomas in 1708 provided Thomas the means to satisfy his book-collecting inclination, and he spent the rest of his life purchasing books, manuscripts, and, to a lesser extent, pictures. For several years he lived at Gray's Inn, where his collection of books and manuscripts became so large that he had to sleep in a passageway because there was no space for him in his room. In 1716 the problem was eased somewhat by moving his library to London House in Aldersgate Street, which he leased from the bishop of London. There, as Dibdin wrote in *Bibliomania* (1809), Rawlinson was "among dust and cobwebs and bulwarks of paper" and would "regale himself with the sight and scent of innumerable black-letter volumes, arranged in sable garb, and stowed three deep from the bottom to the top of the house."

In addition to distinguishing himself as a book collector, Thomas Rawlinson was elected to the governing boards of Bridewell and Bethlehem Hospitals in 1706 and of St. Bartholomew's in 1712; he became a fellow of the Royal Society in 1713 and of the Royal Society of Antiquaries in 1724. Rawlinson published only one work during his life, a poem in a book of verses on the death of Queen Anne's eldest son, William Henry, Duke of Gloucester, in 1700.

Thomas Rawlinson allowed scholars easy access to his valuable collection. He was an intimate of antiquarian Joseph Ames, bibliophile John Murray, and "biblioclast" John Bagford. Michael Maittaire dedicated his 1716 edition of Juvenal's works (London: J. Tonson & J. Watts) to Rawlinson. Rawlinson frequently lent manuscripts to Thomas Hearne (1678–1735), an historical antiquary, author, and editor, who regarded the collector as "the most judicious and industrious of collectors." Hearne's edition of Alfred of Beverley's *Aluredi Beverlacensis Annales* (Oxford: E Theatro sheldoniano, 1716) was based on a manuscript in Rawlinson's collection.

Two of Richard Rawlinson's bookplates

Thomas Rawlinson's choice of a wife was disastrous not only for him but for the rest of his family. On 22 September 1724 he married his servant, Amy Frewin, formerly a maid at a coffeehouse and an alleged prostitute. They did not have any children, and Rawlinson died on 6 August 1725. Some accounts hint that he was poisoned by his wife; others relate that he was distraught over losing a great deal of money he had invested in the South Sea Company, which went into general collapse in 1720. He died £10,000 in debt. Although by all rights the bulk of Thomas's collection should have gone to his bibliophile brother, Richard, his wife and an accomplice, William Ford, tinkered with his will, which he signed only two days before his death. The resulting document signified for Richard Rawlinson the loss of his brother's book and manuscript collection, a loss of control over the Rawlinson family estates, and several years of tangled lawsuits with Mrs. Rawlinson and others who became entwined in the affair.

In 1930 Seymour de Ricci, a noted twentieth-century bibliographer, referred to Thomas Rawlinson's library as "the largest library as yet sold in England and, with the Heber library, the largest sold to the present day." As early as 1716, Hearne wrote to Rawlinson: "Your Collection of Books is admirable. I hope they will be kept together after your death." Thomas Rawlinson had spent most of his energies searching for bibliographical rarities rather than administering the family estates, which were left in a poor state on the death of Sir Thomas. A man with an interest in the properties could have revived them, but Thomas Rawlinson was soon immersed in considerable debt. Hoping to recoup the family fortunes, he then unwisely invested in the South Sea Company. Because of his financial difficulties, Thomas Rawlinson was forced to start selling his collection of printed books, reportedly "the largest at that time known to be offered to the public." The first sales of duplicate copies began the year after the general collapse of the company. In the margin of one of his books, in which the wealth of his collections is mentioned, Rawlinson wrote: "God knows for his sinns on sale."

According to Brian J. Enright's 1956 article on the auctions, they were well conceived, and the plan was carried out quite well. Many of the collector's creditors were also collectors and agreed to receive payment in kind. These first sales of the magnificent library realized £2,409 and, to Hearne, Rawlinson's position was far from irredeemable: "Had he lived some Years longer . . . 'tis probable he might have extricated himself, & lived comfortably. For an Estate (I am told, of six hundred Pounds per an.) came to him a few months since by the Death of his Mother, and he had begun to sell his Books in order to pay his Debts, and printed several Catalogues . . . in wch are many rare, excellent, & uncommon Books, tho' the chief of his Collection was not comprehended in these Catalogues." Since many of the best books still belonged to Rawlinson, Enright believes that the creditors would have been willing to draw interest from the collection "so long as the Rawlinson family prestige remained high" in London, leaving Thomas his beloved books and his pride.

Thomas Rawlinson's marriage to Amy Frewin, however, enraged his creditors, who lost confidence in his judgment and began pestering Rawlinson for their money, which by some accounts hastened his death. Hearne thought that they should have been "less violent" toward the collector, especially "Booksellers, for whom he had done eminent service" because "by his high bidding he strangely advanced the Prices of Books, wch he likewise did in Booksellers' shops. . . ." At the death of Thomas Rawlinson, Richard was on a tour of the Continent with their younger brother Constantine. He returned to England, where he found the Rawlinson estates in disarray and his own legacy vanished.

Richard Rawlinson, who used as his motto "I Collect and I Preserve," became a bookman of more long-lasting renown than his brother. A man somewhat behind his times who never expressed appreciation of the political, social, or cultural developments of the Age of Enlightenment, he spent many years dealing with the financial setback created by his brother and yearning for the "golden age" of his youth when his family's fortunes were bright and not the target of public ridicule. According to Enright, the collector's "constant struggle against debts and disappointments to which he was condemned accounted not only for his eccentric economies but also for much of his petulance and vindictiveness." He embraced antiquarianism, devoting his life to the scholarly traditions of the late seventeenth century. Believing in the value of primary-source materials, he accumulated old books, rare books, and manuscripts of all types with the intent of having them as "ammunition" to prove his theories and beliefs and preserving them should there come a recurrence of the civil wars and strife that had raged in England during the previous century. Thus, his ultimate contribution was providing a link between the great era of English antiquarian scholarship and a future age that might appreciate its achievements.

Richard Rawlinson was born on 3 January 1690 in London. He was educated first at St. Paul's School, London, and entered Eton in 1702. At the age of eighteen, he went to St. John's College, Oxford, and was matriculated as a commoner on 9 March 1708. In 1709, following the death of his father the previous November, he became a gentleman commoner. He graduated with a B.A. on 10 October 1711 and received an M.A. on 5 July 1713. In June 1719 Oxford awarded him a doctor of civil law degree. In 1713 Richard Rawlinson joined his brother Thomas as a governor of Bridewell and Bethlehem Hospitals, of which his father had been president. On 29 June 1714 Richard was elected a fellow of the Royal Society.

As an unreconstructed Jacobite and a nonjuror, Rawlinson supported the claims of the Stuart pretenders to the British throne and refused to swear allegiance to the monarchs who had supplanted them as heads of church and state. Anyone who refused to take the oath was excluded from positions in the government and the Church of England, a serious consequence for Rawlinson, whose education prepared him for the clergy. In autumn 1716 he was ordained a nonjuring priest and deacon in a secret ceremony and joined other clergymen of his convictions, who had set up chapels and services separate from the established church. After his ordination he devoted himself to antiquarianism and in 1718–1719 traveled in the midlands and southern parts of England.

In comparing Richard's career with that of Thomas, Enright wrote, "Richard's life was a completion and fulfilment of his elder brother's unrealized hopes. Thomas' influence on Richard's collecting and antiquarian interests was crucial." Richard had free access to his elder brother's library. Thomas took Richard to the London bookshops and taught him how to collate books. (They both used the same "C & P" mark, for "collated and perfect.") Thomas also encouraged his brother to travel in England and abroad to collect books and inscriptions, and he introduced him to other antiquaries and bibliophiles such as Hearne, whose diary documents the development of Richard's collecting activities at Oxford. While there Richard Rawlinson published anonymously a short life of Anthony à Wood, an antiquary who was Richard's hero as he developed his antiquarian collections.

After leaving Oxford, Rawlinson spent a great deal of time traveling and publishing books based on works in his brother's and his own topographical and historical collections. With the publisher Edmund Curll, Rawlinson made an extensive antiquarian tour of Oxfordshire, during which he collected tombstone and monument inscriptions and added to his library. During this time he published several books on English antiquarians, antiquities, and topography. These books are now collectors' items worth handsome prices for their lavish illustrations. In 1720 he published *The English Topographer,* an extensive survey of topographical manuscripts and books in public and private hands, which includes a summary of his earlier topographical activities and is considered a useful publication, perhaps the best before Richard Gough's *British Topography* (1768).

After a journey to France and the Low Countries during the first half of 1719, Rawlinson set sail for the Continent in June 1720 and did not return to England until April 1726. He had reason in addition to hunting for books and manuscripts for spending so long abroad. Hearne believed that Rawlinson had been on an expedition to the Jacobite courts in St. Germain and Rome to establish links and to seek royal permission for nonjuring consecrations. Rawlinson considered his arrival in Rome in 1720 in time for the birth of Charles Edward, the "Young Pretender" to the British throne, to be particularly satisfying. Rawlinson made an exhaustive tour of Continental bookshops, libraries, and ancient sites, recording his activities in his travel diaries. For example, while exploring the catacombs of Rome, he was reprimanded for picking up an artifact and was told "that to carry it off was excommunication." He also mentioned that "I lost my silk purse out of my pocket while I was looking over some books at a shop in the Corso." He braved the threat of pirates and shipwreck to travel to Sicily and Malta, areas not commonly visited by English travelers. He called one monastic library in Sicily "perhaps the only collection in this part of the world which has escaped my countrymen's money."

During this time Rawlinson acquired more than two thousand books, along with large collections of coins, medals, seals, and marbles. He also established friendly relations with many foreign scholars. Rawlinson was quite proud of his travels, his linguistic skills, and the fact that he had seen the "shores of the Mediterranean."

After his return to England in 1726, Richard Rawlinson immediately sought to break his brother's "barbarously-framed will," but he feared the delay and cost of a legal battle and reached a compromise with his brother's widow. As a result he became the administrator of Thomas's will and resumed the sale of the elder Rawlinson's book collection in order to settle the debts. It was excruciatingly difficult for a bibliophile such as Richard Rawlinson to consign to the auction room his brother's magnificent collection, one that under different circumstances would have been his, but he needed to sell the books to pay off creditors and to resume control of the family's properties. Having to deal with the troublesome interference of Thomas's widow and her new husband soured Richard on marriage. He came to believe it "spoiled the Antiquary," and he never married.

Richard Rawlinson organized ten large auctions of his brother's library, which were held between 1726 and 1733. More than fifty thousand books and in excess of one thousand manuscripts were sold. Although the sales, as well as Rawlinson's prudent and industrious management of the family's properties, eventually provided enough money to free him completely from debt by 1749, he was disappointed by the sum realized from the sale of the library. Hearne wrote to Richard, "The booksellers and others are in a combination against you." Selling so many books and manuscripts in such a short time led to a glut on the market, and prices were lower as a result. Rawlinson also compiled the auction catalogues, writing to Hearne on 15 January 1734 that he was taking special care with Thomas's manuscripts, "in whose description I have been as particular as possible that it may be of use to posterity, if they can discover into whose possession any article may come." He also republished the catalogue of Thomas's paintings after the sale, adding the prices paid for each item.

After 1749 Richard was free to develop his own collection, doing so on a grand scale. He did not specialize, rather he gathered a variety of materials on a wide range of subjects. There is no dominant thrust to the collections he donated to the Bodleian Library. The nineteenth-century cataloguer of the collection, William Dunn Macray, called its strengths the manuscripts on topography, biography, heraldry, and seventeenth-century history, but he also noted the "omnigeneous" character of the collection, which includes a range of materials from early copies of the classics and works by the church fathers to contemporary log books of sailors' voyages. During his time Richard Rawlinson was called "a Universal Collector," who liked "without breach of the Tenth Commandment" to make "collections as perfect as possible." For Rawlinson, his books were "the pleasure, I may almost say, the only pleasure of my life," and he collected widely to ensure that posterity would not be deprived of primary materials for historical studies.

Furthermore, as Enright suggested in 1953, Rawlinson's search for "stray papers" was an attempt to keep valuable materials out of the hands of "wastepaper mongers," who collected "waste" manuscripts and printed leaves of paper and sold them to shopkeepers to use in wrapping their wares. In a 13 July 1739 letter to Thomas Rawlins, Rawlinson described how Sir John Cooke's manuscripts "were sold by his nephew's widow to support pyes, currants, sugar &c., and I redeemed as many as came to 12*s.* at 3*d.* a pound, which I intend to digest and bind up." In 1741 he remarked on the discovery of Archbishop William Wake's papers "at a chandler's shop; this is unpardonable in his executors as all his Mss were left to Christ Church. But quaere whether these did not fall into some servant's hands who was ordered to burn them." In 1749 Rawlinson saved

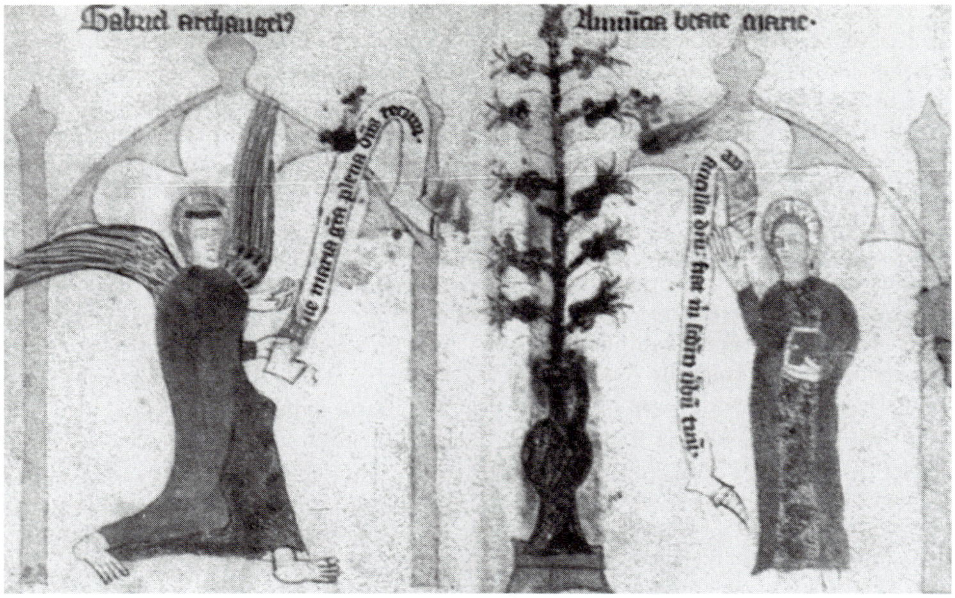

The Annunciation, an illumination in Richard Rawlinson's circa 1370 manuscript of the New Testament (MS. Rawl. D. 939, Part I, Bodleian Library, Oxford)

from destruction nearly one hundred volumes of papers once belonging to Samuel Pepys.

Rawlinson kept his collections in the saleroom blocks in which he acquired them, along with the relevant list or auction catalogue. Rawlinson was interested to a large degree in provenance and often acquired portraits or busts of former owners of the materials he bought. His living quarters, like his brother's earlier, were filled with books and manuscripts from ground floor to garrets. The collector led a quiet and retired life and was frugal in his expenditures to a fault. He did not mind spending money on his collections, however, and he was a common figure in the auction houses and salerooms of the 1730s, buying items from the libraries of Peter le Neve, Thomas Atterbury, Thomas Grainger, and his distant cousin Christopher Rawlinson. In 1740 he purchased fifty manuscripts from the sale of the library of Charles Montagu, Lord Halifax, and noted it "was garbled by Ld Sunderland, and was never improved by his late Nephew, who delighted in nothing but Horseracing, Cocking, Turd, Turnips, and Mob Elections." In 1742 he bought books and manuscripts at the sale of the collection of Edward Harley, second Earl of Oxford, although he initially resisted the urge because he did not trust the bookseller handling the sale and thought the prices to be extravagant. He relented when he "saw the books before the opening of the sale, and a beautiful sight it was. . . ." Rawlinson purchased many fine Irish manuscripts at the sale of the library of James Brydges, Duke of Chandos, some of which he bought outside the saleroom. As the years went by, Rawlinson relied on the strategy of dealing directly with other collectors or their executors, thereby obviating the need for the auction room. Through this means he gained some of antiquarian Elias Ashmole's papers and the books and papers of his friend Thomas Hearne. In 1751 Rawlinson negotiated successfully for the state papers of John Thurloe. Rawlinson was so anxious to acquire the papers of his fellow nonjurors that friends joked Rawlinson hardly waited for them to die before he moved in on their papers. He attended auctions in 1751, 1754, and 1755. His last was the sale of the library of Richard Mead, which reportedly brought to an end a period in English book sales when rarities could be obtained relatively cheaply. The bookman noted in his diary, "in general, the Articles . . . went beyond my Purse, at monstrous Rates." Rawlinson often transcribed items he could not afford. Two hundred volumes of his transcriptions are deposited in the Bodleian Library and the St. John's College Library at Oxford. He was also a bibliographer. His Eton, Oxford, and nonjuring biographical projects include bibliographical information compiled from contemporary authors themselves.

Once the sale of his brother's library was completed, Richard Rawlinson moved to London House. Nearby were the bookshops of Little London. One friend who visited Richard Rawlinson in 1742 found

> such confusion of Books and MSS that there was no end in viewing of them. It would have took me up a twelve months time to have gone through with them and in short I looked into very few of them [no] more than what he shewed me in a transient prospect for he has no conveniences to sitt down to see or write out any thing for he does not spend much time in his Chamber, but only to take his Breakfast for I went 3 or 4 times before I could be admitted for he gets up into the uppermost Rooms and there is no making him hear at the Door you enter into.

The situation was no better seven years later, in 1749, when engraver George Vertue called on the collector and found a great clutter of books and manuscripts, "many in confused heaps on the floors, stools, tables, and shelves," filling the entire house. Apparently Rawlinson's memory was sharp regarding his collections; he well knew what he had purchased and where he had stored the materials. He did, however, try to "labour hard every day to sett my books in order, which costs me much patience and sweat."

In organizing his collections Rawlinson was energetic indeed: "The better to preserve letters, and strengthen them, I putt all sizes first by dates, and then each within a single sheet of paper, and with these precautions and strong Cloths, it is to be hoped they will be of no use to Chandlers &c the sad fate of many valuables." He did not believe in the use of lavish bindings but was careful to preserve documents with the use of "a strong bind of old parchment leases" as covers. Despite his reputation for saving any sort of old manuscripts and books from the wastepaper mongers, Rawlinson recognized that "there must necessarily be a quantity of rubbish" in all collections. He once wrote, "I am digesting and putting together my M.S.S. and I'm gleaning my large collection in order to contract my compass, and throw out a great quantity of Chaff, for we collectors are insensibly overwhelmed with learned paper and dust." He devoted much time to collating books, foliating manuscripts, inserting names of former owners, identifying authors and handwriting, and looking for printed texts that differed from the manuscript form.

Through the years, Rawlinson used publication as a means to preserve and disseminate the contents of manuscripts. He also considered copperplate engraving an excellent device to preserve and publicize. About one item he was considering to purchase, he wrote: "I shall be glad to be a purchaser, and that only in order to multiply it by the Engraver's Tool." Rawlinson also collected sets of old copperplates, some of which are still used by researchers.

Seymour de Ricci once remarked, "It is a pleasant thought to discover how public-spirited English book-collectors have been in the course of the last four centuries . . . personal vanity, the mainspring of collecting, has continually given way to local and national pride." Richard Rawlinson was one such collector, dedicated to the proposition that his collection should have the greatest possible influence on contemporary scholarship. He told one congregation to which he was preaching, "all the abilities and perfections we have are given to us at that end that we might advantage others by communicating our gifts unto them." He loaned manuscripts to many authors and was indirectly responsible for several publications.

Rawlinson was also eager to support colleges, universities, and other institutions of learning and culture. In 1726 Hearne urged Rawlinson to begin thinking about how to prevent his collection from being dispersed after his death, and by 1749 the collector was thinking seriously about the disposition of his collection, particularly since London House was in danger of being sold. During the last five years of his life he considered the Society of Antiquaries and Oxford University as sites for the materials. Rawlinson, who often displayed items from his collection at meetings of the Society of Antiquaries and supported the society's program of commissioning prints of antiquities, began thinking of the Society of Antiquaries as an organization to which he could donate his collections. The society did not respond as favorably as the Bodleian Library at Oxford, which was successful in the long run because of the patience and tact of its librarian, Humphrey Owen, who managed to retain Rawlinson's favor along with his own independence. The gift was tied up with restrictions for several years, but its scope and content eased any problems associated with them. Rawlinson's manuscripts alone numbered about 5,700. While he left his books and manuscripts to the Bodleian Library, he left the bulk of his estate to St. John's College and his antiquarian collections and the family estate at Fulham to the Society of Antiquaries.

Unlike his older brother, Richard Rawlinson left his affairs in order when he died on 6 April 1755. His body was interred in St. Giles's Church, London, while his heart was enclosed in a silver vase and deposited, according to the terms of his will, in the Chapel of St. John's College, Oxford. This act was symbolic, but the long-lasting contribution of his books and manuscripts was Rawlinson's most lasting bequest. A line from his obituary for Thomas Baker may be applied as a tribute to Rawlinson himself: "tho' dead, in his Virtues and Collections will live as long as Time shall endure."

Biography:

Georgian R. Tashjian, "Richard Rawlinson: A Biographical Study," in *Richard Rawlinson: A Tercente-*

nary Memorial, by Georgian R. Tashjian, David R. Tashjian, and Brian J. Enright (Kalamazoo: New Issues Press, Western Michigan University, 1990), pp. 1–67.

References:

John Carter, *Books and Book Collectors* (Cleveland: World, 1957);

Edmund Craster, *History of the Bodleian Library* (Oxford: Clarendon Press, 1952);

Seymour de Ricci, *English Collectors of Books and Manuscripts (1530–1930) and Their Marks of Ownership* (Cambridge: Cambridge University Press, 1930);

C. E. Doble, D. W. Rannie, and H. E. Salter, eds., *Remarks and Collections of Thomas Hearne,* 11 volumes (Oxford: Clarendon Press, 1886–1915);

David C. Douglas, *English Scholars, 1660–1730,* revised edition (London: Eyre & Spottiswoode, 1951);

C. I. Elton and M. A. Elton, *The Great Book-Collectors* (London: Kegan Paul, Trench, Trubner, 1893);

Brian J. Enright, "'I Collect and I Preserve': Richard Rawlinson 1690-1755 and Eighteenth Century Book Collecting," *Book Collector,* 39 (Spring 1990): 27–54;

Enright, "The Later Auction Sales of Thomas Rawlinson's Library: 1727–34," *Library,* 11 (1956): 23–40, 103–113; republished in *Richard Rawlinson: A Tercentenary Memorial,* by Georgian R. Tashjian, David R. Tashjian, and Enright (Kalamazoo: New Issues Press, Western Michigan University, 1990), pp. 133–167;

Enright, "Richard Rawlinson and the Chandlers," *Bodleian Library Record,* 4 (1953): 216–227; republished in *Richard Rawlinson: A Tercentenary Memorial,* pp. 121–132;

Enright, "Richard Rawlinson: Collector, Antiquary, Topographer," dissertation, Oxford University, 1955;

W. Y. Fletcher, "The Rawlinsons and Their Collections," *Transactions of the Bibliographical Society,* 5 (1899): 67–84;

Georgian R. Tashjian, David R. Tashjian, and Brian J. Enright, *Richard Rawlinson: A Tercentenary Memorial* (Kalamazoo: New Issues Press, Western Michigan University, 1990).

Papers:

The Richard Rawlinson manuscripts and his unpublished diaries for 1720–1726 are in the Bodleian Library at Oxford University. The catalogues for the manuscript collection have been reproduced in Michael Hawkins, ed., *The Rawlinson Manuscripts* [microform] (Brighton, U.K.: Harvestor Press Microform Publications, 1981).

John Selden

(16 December 1584 – 30 November 1654)

Sandra Naiman
Elmhurst College

John Selden (portrait by Daniel Mytens; Bodleian Library)

BOOKS: *Jani Anglorum facies altera. Memoria nempe a primula Henrici II. adusq abitionem, quod occurrit prophanum Anglo-Britanniae Ius resipiens succincto* (London: Printed by T. S. for I. Helme, 1610);

England's Epinomis (London, 1610);

The Dvello, or Single Combat: from Antiquity Deriued into this Kingdome of England; with Seueral Kindes, and Ceremonious Formes thereof from Good Authority Described (London: Printed by G. E. for I. Helme, 1610);

Titles of Honor (London: Printed by William Stansby for John Helme, 1614);

Analecton Anglobritannicon libri duo. Quibus ea maxime, qvae ad civilem illivs, qvae iam Anglia dicitvr, Magnae Britanniae partis antiquitus administrationem, res domi publicas, sacras, prophanas, statusque catastrophas vsq; ad Normanni aduentum attinet, ex antiquis simul & neotericis depromta, temporum iuxta seriem digesta historice & arctissime componuntur (Frankfurt: Ex Officina Paltheniana, 1615);

De dis Syris syntagmata II. Adversaria nempe de numinibus commentitijs in Veteri Instrumento memoratis. Accedunt fere quae sunt reliqua Syrorum. Prisca porro Arabum, Egyptiorum, Persarum, Afrorum, Europaeorum item theologia, subinde illustratur (London: Guilielmus Stansbeius, 1617);

The Historie of Tithes; that is, the Practice of Payment of Them. The Positive Laws Made for Them. The Opinions Touching the Right of Them. A Review of It is also Annext, which both Confirmes It and Directs in Use of It (London, 1618);

De successionibus in bona defuncti, seu Iure haereditario, ad leges Ebraeorum, quae, florente olim eorum republica, in vsu, liber singularis, ex sacris literis, vtroque Talmude, & selectioribus rabbinis, id est, ex iuris Ebraici fontibus, pandectis, atque consultissimis magistris, desumtus (London: Guillielmi Stanesbeij, 1631);

Mare clausum, seu, De dominio maris libri duo. Primo, mare ex jure naturae seu gentium omnium hominum non esse commune sed dominii privati seu proprietatis capax, pariter ac tellurem, esse demonstratur. Secundo, Serenissimum Magnae Britanniae Regem maris circumflui ut individuae atque perpetuae imperii Britannici appendicis dominum esse, asseritur (London: Printed by W. Stanesbeius for R. Meighen, 1635);

De Successionibus In Bona Defuncti, Ad Leges Ebraeorum, Liber Singularis. Editio altera, correctior & multum auctior. Accedunt ejusdem De Successione In Pontificatum Ebraeorum, Libri Duo. Prior Historicus est; Pontificum ab Aharone usque ad Templi Secundi Excidium Successionem continens. Posterior est Juridicus; Legitima, seu quae in Successione Pontificali adeoque in admissione ad munus Sacerdotale apud Ebraeos Juris fuere complexus (London: Richard Bishop, 1636);

De successionibus ad leges Ebraeorum in bona defunctorum, liber singularis: in Pontificatum, libri duo. Editio ultima, ab auctore denuo aucta et emendata (Leiden: Elseiver, 1638);

De jure naturali et gentium, juxta disciplinam Ebraeorum, libri septem (London: R. Bishop, 1640);

A Briefe Discourse, Concerning the Power of the Peeres and Comons of Parliament, in Point of Judicature (London, 1640);

The Privileges of the Baronage of England, when They Sit in Parliament. Collected (and of late revised) by John Selden . . . out of the Parliament Rolles . . . and Other Good Authorities (London: Printed by T. Badger for M. Wallbanck, 1642);

Eutychii ecclesiae suae origins (1642);

De Anno Civili et Calendario Veteris Ecclesiae; seu Reipublicae Judaicae, Dissertatio (London: R. Bishop, 1644);

Uxor Ebraica; seu, De nuptiis & divortiis ex iure civili id est, divino & Talmudico, veterum Ebraeorum, libri tres: Stupenda & Christianis quasi inaudita Karaeorum seu Judaeorum scripturariorum de incestu dogmata interseruntur. Accedunt non pauca de contrahendis solvendisque matrimoniis paganorum, Mahumedanorum, atque Christianorum, idque ex jure tum Caesareo aliarumque gentium complurium, tum pontificio tam orientis quam occidentis, qua sive ex Ebraeorum moribus defluxerint, sive eis cognata videantur (London: R. Bishop, 1646);

Dissertatio ad Fletam (London, 1647);

De synedriis & praefecturis iuridicis veterum Ebraeorum, 3 volumes (London: Jacob Flesher, 1650–1655);

Judicium de decem scriptoribus Anglicanis (London, 1652);

Historiae Anglicanae scriptores X . . . Ex vetustis manuscriptis, nunc primum in lucem editi. Adjectis variis lectionibus, glossario, indiceque copioso (London: Jacob Flesher, 1652);

Vindiciae de scriptione Maris Clausi (London, 1653);

Θεάνθρωπος [Theanthropos]: *or, God Made Man. A Tract Proving the Nativity of Our Saviour to be on the 25 of December* (London: Printed by G. J. for Nathaniel Brooks, 1661);

A Brief Discourse Touching the Office of Lord Chancellor of England . . . Transcribed from a True Copy Thereof . . . (London: Printed for William Lee, 1671);

Of the Judicature in Parliaments, a Posthumous Treatise; wherein the Controversies and Precedents belonging to that Title are Methodically Handled (London: Printed for Joseph Lawson, 1681);

Tracts Written by John Selden of the Inner-Temple, Esquire. The First Entituled, Jani Anglorum facies altera, rendred into English, with Large Notes thereupon, by Redman Westcot . . . The Second, England's epinomis. The Third, Of the Original of Ecclesiastical Jurisdictions of Testaments. The Fourth, Of the Disposition or Administration of Intestates Goods. The Three Last Never Before Extant (London: Printed for Thomas Basset and Richard Chiswell, 1683);

De anno civili veterum Judaeorum & Jac. Usserius de Macedonum et Asianorum anno solari (Leiden: Petrum van der Aa, 1683);

Table-talk: Being the Discourses of John Selden Esq; or his Sence of Various Matters of Weight and High Consequence relating especially to Religion and State, edited by Richard Milward (London: Printed for E. Smith, 1689).

Editions: *Opera omnia, tam edita quam inedita,* 3 volumes, edited by David Wilkins (volume 1, London: Printed by G. Bowyer for J. Walthoe, 1726; volume 2, London: Printed by S. Palmer for J. Walthoe, 1726); volume 3 published as *The Works of John Selden* (London: Printed by T. Wood for J. Walthoe, 1726);

The Dissertation of John Selden, Annexed to Fleta, translated by Robert Kelham (London: J. Worrall and B. Tovey, 1771).

OTHER: Michael Drayton, *Poly-olbion . . . ,* edited by Selden (London, 1612);

Sir John Fortescue, *De laudibus legum Angliae,* edited by Selden (1616);

Ralph de Hengham, *Summae magna et parva,* edited by Selden (1616);

Drayton, *A Chorographicall Description of all the Tracts, Rivers, Mountains, Forests, and Other Parts of this Renowned Isle of Great Britain, with Intermixture of the Most Remarkable Stories, Antiquities, Wonders, Rarities, Pleasures, and Commodites of the Same . . . Digested into a Poem,* edited by Selden (London: I. Marriott, 1622);

Marmora arundelliana; siue Saxa Graece incisa. Ex venerandis priscae Orientis gloriae ruderibus, auspicijs & impensis herois illustriss. Thomae Comitis Arundelliae & Surriae, Comitis Marescalli Angliae, pridem vindicata & in aedibus eius hortisque cognominibus, ad Thamesis ripam, disposita. Accedunt inscriptiones aliquot veteris Latij, ex locupletissimo eiusdem vetustatis thesauro selectae, auctariolum item aliunde sumtum, edited by Selden (London: Published for Selden at I. Billium, 1629);

Fleta, seu Commentarius juris anglicani sic nuncupatus, sub Edwardo rege primo, seu circa annos abhinc CCCXL, ab anonymo conscriptus, atque e codice veteri, autore ipso aliquantulum recentiori, nunc primum typis editus: Accedit tractatulus vetus de agendi excipiendique formulis gallicanus, fet assavoir dictus. Subjungitur etiam Joannis Seldeni ad Fletam dissertatio historica, edited by Selden (London: Printed by M. F., 1647);

Marmora Oxoniensia, ex Arundellianis, Seldenianis aliisque conflata. Recensuit, & perpetuo commentario explicavit, Humphridus Prideaux Aedis Christi alumnus. Appositis ad eorum nonnulla Seldeni & Lydiati annotationibus.

Accessit Sertorii Ursati Patavini De notis Romanorum commentarius, edited by Selden (Oxford: Theatro Sheldoniano, 1676).

The son of a yeoman with an annual income of £40, Selden left an estate of £ 50,000, a library of more than eight thousand volumes, and a collection of Greek sculptures and monuments. His reputation was so distinguished that Archbishop James Ussher came out of retirement to preach the sermon at his funeral, which was attended by "all the judges and other persons of distinction" in the Temple Church, where his gravestone lies in the floor near the south porch.

Selden was a dedicated researcher and a prolific writer, a biblical scholar, a famous orientalist, and a practical philosopher. He was also a first-rate historian and one of the leading antiquaries of his day. In *Areopagitica* (1644) John Milton called him "the chief of learned men reputed in this land." Ben Jonson, a friend of Selden's youth, described him as "the law-book of the judges of England, the bravest man in all languages." In a poetical epistle addressed to Selden, Jonson wrote:

> Stand forth my object, then, you that have been
> Ever at home, yet have all countries seen;
> And, like a compass, keeping one foot still
> Upon your centre, do your circle fill
> Of general knowledge; watched men, manners too,
> Heard what times past have said, seen what ours do. . .
> What fables have you vexed! what truth redeemed!
> Antiquities searched! Opinions disesteemed!
> Impostures branded, and authorities urged!
> What blots and errors have you watched and purged
> Records and authors of! how rectified
> Times, manners, customs!

Selden's greatest personal claim on posterity is his contribution to law. In his 1994 analysis of the origins of historical jurisprudence, Harold J. Berman locates Selden's importance in that tradition:

> In the seventeenth century, leading English jurists introduced into the Western legal tradition a new philosophy of law, later called historical jurisprudence, which both competed with and complemented the two major schools of legal philosophy that had opposed each other in earlier centuries, namely, natural law theory and legal positivism. The basic tenet of the historical school is that the primary source of the validity of law, including both its moral validity and its political validity, is its historicity, reflected especially in the developing customs and ongoing traditions of the community whose law it is. Historical experience is thought to have a normative significance. This theory was adumbrated by Edward Coke, developed by John Selden, and articulated by Matthew Hale, who integrated it with the two older theories . . . Although historical jurisprudence, which predominated in Europe and the United States in the late nineteenth and early twentieth century, has been ignored or repudiated by most contemporary American legal philosophers, it continues to play an important role in the thinking of American judges and lawyers, especially in constitutional law and in areas of law in which common law tradition still prevails.

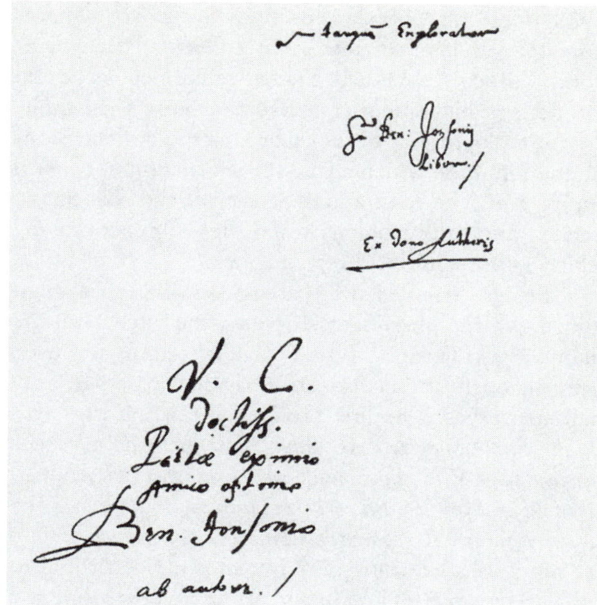

Inscriptions by Selden and Ben Jonson in a copy of Selden's De Dis Syris *(1617) from the 23 March 1925 Britwell Sale (no. 555)*

Selden was born in Sussex on 16 December 1584 in a cottage at Salvington near Worthing. The record of his baptism on 20 December 1584 names him "John, the sonne of John Selden, the minstrell." His mother was Margaret Baker, the only daughter and heir of Thomas Baker, of the knightly family of Baker of Kent. Selden received his early education at the Prebendal Free School in Chichester, where he attracted the attention of his master, Hugh Barker, who obtained a scholarship to Oxford for his pupil. At the age of sixteen Selden matriculated at Hart Hall (now Hertford College) under the tutelage of his old master's brother, Anthony Barker. After less than three years, and without receiving a degree, Selden moved to London to begin studying law at the Inns of Court. He was not called to the bar until 14 June 1612.

Selden was able to pursue his training at his own speed, enabling him to earn some money for his expenses as well as follow other interests. There is a legend that he was a copyist for Sir Robert Bruce Cotton. In any case, Cotton became Selden's mentor as well as his staunchest friend, according to Selden's biographer David Sandler Berkowitz in *John Selden's Formative Years*

(1988). Cotton's "influence on the younger scholar was more than that of an intelligent collector," Berkowitz writes, "though obviously Selden reinforced, if he did not derive, his bibliomania from Cotton's example. Cotton looked upon his collection as the indispensable foundation upon which a true reconstruction of English history could be built and the glory of the past recovered . . . and he is probably responsible for encouraging Selden's efforts in this direction."

Selden enjoyed free access to Cotton's great library, which subsequently became the nucleus of the manuscript collection of the British Museum, and used it prodigiously to become an unrivaled expert in antiquarian studies. The first product of this industry was *De dis Syris syntagmata II. Adversaria nempe de numinibus commentitijs in Veteri Instrumento memoratis. Accedunt fere quae sunt reliqua Syrorum. Prisca porro Arabum, Egyptiorum, Persarum, Afrorum, Europaeorum item theologia, subinde illustratur,* not published until 1617 but finished according to the preface in 1605. The great discoveries that are responsible for the modern understanding of Assyrian civilization had not yet been made; Selden used the Bible for his comparative analysis of the Syrian deities. Upon the publication of this work Selden became celebrated as an orientalist in mainland Europe as well as in England.

In 1607, according to the date of the preface, Selden finished *Analecton Anglobritannicon libri duo. Quibus ea maxime, qvae ad civilem illivs, qvae iam Anglia dicitvr, Magnae Britanniae partis antiquitus administrationem, res domi publicas, sacras, prophanas, statusque catastrophas vsq; ad Normanni aduentum attinet, ex antiquis simul & neotericis depromta, temporum iuxta seriem digesta historice & arctissime componuntur* (English Collections in Two Books), an attempt to summarize in chronological order everything recorded by ancient and modern writers regarding the civil government and public events in England down to the Norman invasion in 1066. Dedicated to Cotton, it was not printed until eight years later at Frankfurt and then in such a form that Selden complained he could scarcely recognize it as his own work.

In 1610 he published two treatises, one in English, *England's Epinomis,* the other in Latin, *Jani Anglorum facies altera. Memoria nempe a primula Henrici II. adusq abitionem, quod occurritprophanum Anglo-Britanniae Ius resipiens succincto* (The Reverse or Back-face of the English Janus). Both were general historical surveys of the laws and customs of the Britons, Saxons, and Norsemen. What was significant about Selden's treatment, Berkowitz asserts, is that he used Old English records to develop his thesis of the essential continuity of English legal traditions. In the same year Selden published a history of trial by combat, *The Dvello, or Single Combat: from Antiquity Deriued into this Kingdome of England; with Seueral Kindes, and Ceremonious Formes thereof from Good Authority Described* (1610), in which he concluded that in England this practice derived from the Normans.

While Selden was establishing himself as an authority on English law by the time he was called to the bar at age twenty-seven, he also was pursuing other interests. In 1612 he furnished the historical and topographical notes for the first eighteen cantos of Michael Drayton's *Poly-olbion,* and in 1613 he wrote commendatory verses in Greek, Latin, and English to William Browne's *Britannia's Pastorals.*

In 1614 Selden published *Titles of Honor,* a quarto volume of more than nine hundred pages dealing with titles, dignities, honorary attributes, and the laws of precedence. It was the prototype for *Burke's Peerage* and *Debrett's Peerage.* "With the publication of this distinguished work," Berkowitz says, "Selden registered his first serious claim to a reputation as a scholar." No doubt it also enhanced his legal career. Although Selden rarely appeared in court after being called to the bar, his practice is said to have been large and to have specialized in conveyancing–that is, the transfer of property and titles.

Through his research Selden not only became an expert on English law but also made himself the father of English legal history. He utterly scorned most of what passed for history in his day, regarding it instead as opinion. He called for a rigorous examination of the original sources, the comparison of texts, and the use of induction to arrive at historical truth. According to Berkowitz,

> Selden found history fable and left it fact, a reformation that he accomplished by regarding history as a science and endowing it with a scientific mind. The implications of this attitude for the future development of historical studies were far-reaching for both Selden's day and later times. It was obvious that analysis based on source materials would not bear fruit without considerable technical skill. The use of manuscripts could not proceed without special knowledge of palaeography, diplomatics, and philology; and Selden's net took in coins, inscriptions, and statues, necessitating familiarity with numismatics, epigraphy, and heraldry. . . . Only with such an endowment would the historian be competent to solve the difficulties presented by his materials.

Berman makes a similar assessment of Selden as an historian:

> Unlike Coke, Selden had a strong sense of chronology. Also he viewed skeptically later interpretations of previous historical developments and insisted on going back to contemporary or near-contemporary sources. He was, in that sense, in the humanist tradition of six-

The Selden End of the Bodleian Library, as depicted in David Loggan's Oxonia illustrata *(1675)*

teenth- and seventeenth-century European, and especially French, historical scholarship, with which he was, of course, familiar. Selden uses the word "synchronism" to signify the method of grouping historical events and personages according to the times and places and circumstances of their occurrence. His concern with narrative sequence and with congruence was linked to his antipathy both towards mythical interpretations of the past and towards mere antiquarianism. At the same time, humanist scholarship led him to recognize breaks in the evolution of English law. He recognized, for example, that the Norman Conquest brought substantial changes, including the introduction of feudal law and the establishment of separate church courts. He understood outside influences on English law in the twelfth century, including the influence of Roman law, as part of a general revival of learning which took place at that time throughout Western Europe. From Arab versions of ancient Greek texts, he wrote, "physics, moral philosophy, logic, medicine, and mathematics began almost simultaneously to shine out like stars that had long been obscured, and so likewise canon law and theology."

Selden's *The Historie of Tithes; that is, the Practice of Payment of Them. The Positive Laws Made for Them. The Opinions Touching the Right of Them. A Review of It is also Annext, which both Confirmes It and Directs in Use of It* (1618)–in which he traced the history of tithes from the gift of Abraham to Melchizedek down to the practice of tithing in seventeenth-century England–aroused a storm of protest from the clergy. What excited violent antipathy was the implication that the clergy did not have a "divine right" to tithes but instead received them as the result of custom, or common–that is, human–law. James I sided with the clergy because any challenge at all to the concept of divine right might be imagined to threaten the king. Selden was summoned by the lords of the high commission as well as the lords of the privy council to answer for his opinions, and the book was suppressed. He escaped other punishment by submitting in writing an apology in which, without retracting anything he had written, he expressed remorse for having given offense. Selden's old friend Ben Jonson interceded with the king on Selden's behalf, and Lancelot Andrewes, also a friend, displayed great courage by praising Selden's book.

Andrewes was one of several bishops among the friends with whom Selden shared a love of scholarship and books; Archbishop Ussher was another. Selden also made friends among the aristocracy, often as the result of being introduced by Cotton, and some of these acquaintances became valuable clients in Selden's law practice. Among them were Henry, Lord Grey and his wife Elizabeth. Their town house, White Friars, adjoined the grounds of the Inner Temple, where Selden studied law. Selden's friendship with them proved to be enormously important for the rest of his life.

Selden's active involvement in politics began in 1621, when he was thirty-seven years old. He had been engaged by the Virginia Company, first for research and counsel regarding proper laws for the colony of Virginia and later for advice about pursuing fishing rights in North America. His association with this company confirmed for King James the suspicion that Selden was involved in some kind of nefarious conspiracy. Selden had also been retained by the House of Lords to research its privileges. The lords were pleased with the information provided to them and used it to assert authority to give judgment in an impeachment proceeding brought by the House of Commons. Parliament adjourned on 4 June, and on 16 June, Selden was suddenly arrested, along with the earl of Southampton and Edwin Sandys, all of whom had worked together to advance the fortunes of the Virginia Company. Selden's papers were seized from his study, and among them was his unfinished report to the House of Lords regarding its privileges. Without being charged, Selden was confined to the home of Robert Ducie, a London sheriff. Confinement gave him the leisure for scholarship; he passed his time preparing an edition of Eadmer's *History,* published as *Notae in Eadmeri historiae novorum* in 1623.

When Selden was finally interrogated, he realized that he was suspected of being involved in the assumption by the House of Commons of the right to pass judgment against a nonmember. Bishop Lancelot Andrewes intervened in Selden's behalf, and Selden appealed for help to Bishop John Williams, who had been appointed to succeed Sir Francis Bacon as lord keeper. Williams promptly interceded on behalf of both Southampton and Selden, and all three men were soon freed. Selden's papers were not liberated for several months however, and then only after a series of negotiations in which Bishop Williams defended the king's right to seize the papers.

The chief issue was Selden's notes for his report to the House of Lords on its privileges. Eventually published in 1642 as *The Privileges of the Baronage of England, when They Sit in Parliament. Collected (and of late revised) by John Selden . . . out of the Parliament Rolles . . . and Other Good Authorities,* Selden's treatise was surely consulted in manuscript many times in the interim. In it Selden discussed the rights of barons both as individuals and collectively, as a branch of the legislature, and brought together all the precedents relating to impeachment. Almost two-thirds of the text deals with the lords' power of judicature, including their power to judge the behavior of the king's ministers. The king cannot have liked the book or another that was circulating in manuscript and that all of Selden's biographers have attributed to him, *Of the Judicature in Parliaments, a Posthumous Treatise; wherein the Controversies and Precedents belonging to that Title are Methodically Handled* (1681).

In the early 1620s Selden's time and energy were required for his law practice. He was not yet a rich man, and he did not have great leisure to pursue the research and writing that were so congenial to him. In 1623 his life changed dramatically when his friend Henry Grey became the earl of Kent. The new earl needed a solicitor and a steward; he named his friend Selden to both positions. Selden immediately became financially secure, and the Kents' country seat in Wrest, Bedfordshire, became his home away from home, where he spent pleasant summers for years to come. Given the security of his income from the Kent estate, Selden felt free to pursue his personal interests.

In 1624 Selden took a seat in the last parliament of James's reign, as a representative from Lancaster. His initial role in the struggle between Parliament and the king was to supply arguments, based on his deep knowledge of English law and precedent; later he took an active part in debates.

Selden did not sit in the first parliament under Charles I, but evidently he was eager to sit in the second, for he stood for election both at Ilchester in Somersetshire and Great Bedwyn, Wiltshire. He won in each constituency, possibly because he had close ties to the nobles who controlled those seats. He played a prominent role in Parliament's unsuccessful effort to impeach the royal favorite, George Villiers, Duke of Buckingham, and took an active part in opposing the expansion of ecclesiastical jurisdiction.

In the parliament of 1628 Selden was one of the most important speakers for individual liberty–for freedom from arrest and imprisonment without due process and for freedom from seizure of personal property. He was arrested in the first week of March 1629 and committed to the tower along with several other members of Parliament; in addition, his study was sealed. He remained under arrest until the last day of February 1635, when Charles granted Selden's request to be discharged. Whether there was a quid pro quo is not known, but Selden subsequently published *Mare clausum, seu, De dominio maris libri duo. Primo, mare ex jure naturae seu gentium omnium hominum non esse commune sed dominii privati seu proprietatis capax, pariter ac tellurem, esse demonstratur. Secundo, Serenissimum Magnae Britanniae Regem maris circumflui ut individuae atque perpetuae imperii Britannici appendicis dominum esse, asseritur* (1635), an argument for the monarch's ownership of the seas, dedicated to Charles with the motto "Pontus quousque serviet illi" (The sea will also submit to him). Selden had written the piece in 1618 for James I in an apparent effort to appease that monarch, who for diplomatic reasons did not find publication convenient.

After Charles dissolved the parliament of 1628–1629, Parliament remained suspended until 1640. During that decade Selden worked on several books regarding the practices of the ancient Hebrews. The topics included succession to property and goods, succession of religious leaders, the interpretation of natural law, and marriage and divorce; the last named was of particular interest to Milton. In the *Dictionary of National Biography* Sir Edward Fry said of these works:

> Their extraordinary erudition won much praise, and, as Selden rarely if ever attacked other writers, they offended few susceptibilities; but severe critics complained with justice of their discursiveness and occasional obscurity, and still more of the uncritical use

> made by Selden of documents of very unequal value; and indeed Selden's statements about Jewish law are more often based on comparatively modern compilations than on the original sources, to some of which perhaps he had not access; and in accepting the rabbinical tradition as a faithful account of the Israelitish state, he was behind the best criticism of his time.

Though critics differ in their estimates of Selden's scholarship, there is widespread agreement that his style of writing was entirely without appeal. Selden's contemporary Edward Hyde, first Earl of Clarendon, anticipated later readers who preferred Selden's conversation–some of which was recorded by his amanuensis, Richard Milward, in the posthumously published *Table-talk: Being the Discourses of John Selden Esq; or his Sence of Various Matters of Weight and High Consequence relating especially to Religion and State* (1689)–to his writing:

> His style in all his writings seems harsh and sometimes obscure; which is not wholly to be imputed to the abstruse subjects of which he commonly treated . . . but to a little undervaluing the beauty of style, and too much propensity to the language of antiquity: but in his conversation he was the most clear discourser, and had the best faculty of making hard things easy, and presenting them to the understanding, that hath been known.

In 1640 Selden was returned to Parliament as a representative for Oxford University. He performed many valuable services for the university, trying to protect its interests against persecution by Parliament, and for Cambridge University as well. Selden was instrumental in seeing to it that Archbishop Richard Bancroft's library went to Cambridge University (after the Restoration, however, it was reclaimed for Lambeth Palace, the official residence in London of the archbishops of Canterbury). He was also involved in securing William Laud's collection of oriental manuscripts for Oxford University. When Laud was impeached for treason, his endowment of the Arabic chair at Oxford was seized, jeopardizing the livelihood of its occupant, Edward Pococke, who was after Selden the leading orientalist of the period; Selden intervened to have Pococke reinstated, and in 1648 Pococke was appointed to the chair of Hebrew at Oxford.

In Selden's lifetime the great libraries were still private rather than public. Intimately aware of their importance, Selden helped to preserve and protect such collections as those of Robert Cotton, Charles I, Archbishop Ussher, and Edward Herbert. He also performed other services for scholarship and earned a reputation for personal generosity to scholars, providing financial as well as intellectual assistance. A letter from Meric Casaubon to Archbishop Ussher, dated London, October 1650, begins:

> I was with Mr. Selden after I had been with your Grace; whom, upon some intimation of my present condition and necessities, I found so noble, as that he did not only presently furnish me with a considerable sum, but was so free and forward in his expressions, as that I could not find in my heart to tell him much of my purpose of selling, lest it might sound as a further pressing upon him, of whom I had already received so much.

Although Selden amassed a vast library of his own, he depended upon the libraries of others for his research. Colin Tite in his 1991 article "A Loan of Printed Books from Cotton to John Selden" shows that a list that survives among the Harleian manuscripts at the British Library records a loan of printed books to Selden from Cotton on 2 February 1622. At least six of the titles on the list were absorbed by Selden into his own collection, where they can now be found at the Bodleian Library. Selden's books bear the signs of ownership by other contemporaries as well, including Thomas Crashawe; Edward Gwynne; David Gouband; Joseph Fenton; William Alabaster; Bacon; Charles Blount, Lord Mountjoy; Robert Burton; William Camden; Robert Cecil, Earl of Salisbury; Sir Kenelm Digby; Jonson; and John Donne. Selden's copy of William Camden's *Britannia* (1607) was King James's copy, according to Tite.

The eighteen volumes in Selden's library that belonged to Donne bear his signature and his motto and are all bound in contemporary limp vellum; "that this binding was given them by Donne," Tite writes, "is practically proved by the fact that in three of the books so bound fragments of the same manuscript have been used as end-papers." Among these books are: J. P. Windeck's *De theologia iureconsultorum* (1604), Paulus Comitolus's *Responsa moralia* (1609), Henningus Arnisaeus'a *De subiectione clericorum* (1612), Bartholomaeus Ugolinus's *Responsiones* (1607), Sibrandus Siccama's *Fastorum kalendarium lib. II* (1600), J. B. Persona's *Noctes solitariae* (1613), Theodorus Beza's *Tractatio de polygamia* (1568), Henry VIII and John Fisher's *Assertio septem sacramentorum* (1562), Alphonsus Alvarez's *Utriusque dignitatis . . . speculum* (1607), *Ecloge bullarum et motupropriorum sanctissimorum patrum* (1582), Carolus Molinaeus's *Opuscula* (1610), and C. Wintzler's *Observationes de collectis seu contributione Imperii* (1612).

Presentation copies in Selden's collection include John Davies's *Antiquae linguae Britannicae dictionarium* (1632); Thomas Farnaby's *Lucan* (1618), *Martial* (1615), and *Virgil* (1634); Robert Fludd's *Utriusque cosmi . . . historia* (1617); Jacobus Golius's *Lexicon Arabico-Latinum*

(1653); Constantine Huygens's *Momenta desultoria* (1644); Sir Henry Spelman's *Concilia* (1639) and *Archaeologus* (1626); *Christianus Ravius: Orthographiae Ebraicae delineatio* (1646); and Henry Parker's *The Generall Junto, or The Councell of Union* (1642). There are also presentation copies of the works of James Howell, J. F. Gronovius, Daniel Heinsius, and Joannes de Laet. Among the books in Selden's library that belonged to owners who were not Selden's contemporaries are Conrad Gesner's *Xenophon: Omnia opera* (1561), Simon Grynaeus's *Hebrew Bible* (1525–1528), Thomas Linacre's *Picus Mirandula: De providentia Dei* (1508), Guido Panciroli's *Notitia utraque dignitatum . . . et in eam Guidi Panciroli commentarium* (1593), Benedictus Pererius's *Ptolemy: Almagestum* (1515), a copy of *Paschalis Gallus: Bibliotheca medica* (1590) presented by the author to Lord Edward Zouche, and Abraham Ortelius's copies of *Atto della giustitia d'Inghilterra* (1584), *Matthaeus Hostus: Historia rei nummariae* (1580), and *Dialoghi di Don Antonio Agostini* (1592).

Selden's library contained many Hebrew and Arabic works, some of them rare. He also owned books in the Persian, Turkish, and Chinese languages as well as the languages of Europe. Thomas Lockey, the Bodleian librarian from 1660 to 1665, said there were about thirty thousand authors. There were also manuscripts in Greek and Hebrew and other oriental languages as well as many estate records.

Selden gave some oriental books to Cambridge University a few weeks before making his will. Upon his death on 30 November 1654 most of his library, except for some Arabic medical manuscripts bequethed to the college of physicians, passed to his executors–Edward Heyward, John Vaughan, Matthew Hale, and Rowland Jewks–with the instruction that they should either divide the books among themselves or give them to some institution but not "put them to any common sale." Four years after Selden's death, his executors gave what was for many years believed to be most of his collection to the Bodleian. The gift was the Bodleian's biggest accession of the seventeenth century. The executors made certain conditions. One was that copies of items that the Bodleian already owned were to be transferred to Gloucester Cathedral Library. Another was that Selden's books and manuscripts should forever after be kept together "in one distincte pile and body under the name of Mr. Seldens Library." In fact, the space they occupy in the library is known as "Selden End."

In 1947 forty manuscripts that had belonged to Selden or to his friend Matthew Hale were purchased by the Bodleian from James Fairhurst. Among them was a catalogue of Selden's library, apparently written shortly after Selden's death. It is now MS. Selden supra III in the Bodleian. The first part lists 6,256 items, consisting of historical, legal, and miscellaneous manuscripts as well as printed books; the second part, listing 1,210 items, consists of Greek, Latin, and English literary manuscripts, oriental books and manuscripts, and a few miscellaneous items such as a small collection of Dutch books.

The difficulty of describing Selden's collection from this catalogue has been summarized by D. M. Barratt in "The Library of John Selden and its Later History":

> Selden's own collectanea are included in the catalogue of his miscellaneous manuscripts, but identification of some of them from brief descriptions such as '4 Note Bookes by J.S.' would be impossible. Some were collections from particular classes of records such as patent and close rolls, others were collections for particular works of Selden, such as his 'Titles of Honour', and others, such as MS. Selden supra 125, purchased by the Bodleian in 1947, were entirely miscellaneous. Some volumes were marked with a single letter of the alphabet. In a notebook which had belonged to Selden, Hale listed the contents of eight volumes of Selden's collectanea labelled AA-HH, all of which can be traced. Five of these eight are now in Lincoln's Inn Library, bequeathed by Hale, where there are also at least two other volumes of Selden's collectanea, Lincoln's Inn MSS. xxxii and lxxxi.

Until the eighteenth century, according to Barratt, it was believed that Selden's executors gave all of his library to Oxford University, but the twentieth edition of Edward Chamberlayne's *Present State of England* in 1702 says, in describing the Selden collection, that "'tis to be lamented that his whole Library was not given by his Executors; for the Fire of London destroyed in one of their Chambers . . . 8 chests full of the Registers of Abbeys, and other Manuscripts relating to the History of England; tho' his Law Books are still safe in Lincoln's Inn." Barratt continues the account:

> The story of loss, therefore, appears to have begun only as a rumour current fifty years after Selden's death, but it is borne out by the catalogue of the library. No attempt has been made to work out what losses Selden's very large collection of printed books suffered before coming to Oxford, but it is evident that more than half of his manuscripts were never sent to the Bodleian.

Barratt also reports, however, that

> Of the one class specifically mentioned by Chamberlayne, 'Registers of abbeys', few, if any, owned by Selden can have perished in a London fire. There are a number of untraced monastic records in the catalogue, but only three entries certainly refer to cartularies. [Sir William] Dugdale,

157

LIBRORUM

MANUSCRIPTORUM

BIBLIOTHECÆ BODLEIANÆ

CLASSIS SEPTIMA

CODICES CCCLVII. DOCTRINÆ PLERIQUE ORIENTALIS

DONANTE VIRO MAGNO

JOHANNE SELDENO:

QUI HANC

ACADEMIAM MUSEO PRÆSTANTISSIMO LOCUPLETAVIT,

ATQUE ETIAM LIBRIS QUOS IPSE GENERE OMNI CONSCRIPSIT

NON MINUS ILLUSTRAVIT.

In iſto autem Catalogo parent venerabilium virorum Thomæ Lockey & Thomæ Hyde *ſedulitas ac peritia.*

Archivo A.

3134. 1. Hiſtoria *Mexicana* Hiſpanice, cum Figuris & Iconibus,& explicatione Lingua Mexicana partim, partimque Hiſpanica.
The Standard of the Roman Money digeſted into Tables.

2. Hieroglyphica *Mexicana* ſine Explicatione. Vide infra inter Rotulas, &c. Num. 3.

3136. 3. Pars דו *Machazor* Judæorum Germanorum, Hebraice.

3137. 4. Liber *Miclal Jophi*, Heb. per Auctorem דו *Makor Chajim.*

3138. 5. Liber dictus *Tractatus Medii*, qui ſunt *Euclidis Data, Archimedes de Sphæra, Autolycus de ortu & occaſu* cum ejuſdem generis aliis, quos lingua Arabica exhibet *Zin Eddin Abhari.*

3139. 6. Liber dictus *Tractatus medii*, continens eoſdem Auctores, Arabice, per *Naſſireddin Tuſæum.*

3140. 7. *Apollonius* de Sectione linearum ſecundum proportionem, cum aliis ſcriptis Mathematicis, Arab.

3141. 8. Tabulæ Aſtronomicæ, Auctore *Ibn Shatir* Damaſceno, Arab.

3142. 9. *Calendarium* pro Meridiano Conſtantinopolitano, Turcice.

3143. 10. *Calendarium*, Turcice.

2. Aliquot Tabulæ de Manſionibus & motionibus Planetarum, Arab.

3. *Ulug Beghi* Tabulæ motionum Solis in Annis Arabicis pro longitudine Samercand 99. 16. & Lat. 39. 37. 28. cum aliis tabulis de Æquatione Dierum & Noctium, & de Æquationibus Planetarum.

3144. 11. Liber dictus fundamentum Scientiæ *Aſtrorum.*

2. Liber de Formâ orbium Cœleſtium, Auctore *Coſta Ibn Luca.*

3. Liber, Aſtrologica quædam continens, Auctore *Abu-Rihan Ahmed AlBiruni.*

4. Lib. de mendis *Tabularum*, Auctore *Ali Ibn Soleiman AlHaſhemi*; Arabice omnes.

3145. 12. Liber *Ephmeridum* variarum, viz.

1. De Conſtructione 12. Domuum Cœleſtium, Perſice.

2. *Tabulæ* Apogæi & Perigæi Solis pro Annis Jeſdegjerdicis, ſcil. inter annum 300. & 700. hujus Epochæ; & Tabulæ Mediæ motionis Lunæ, Perſice.

3. *Tabulæ* compendioſæ, ſcil. Fundamenta Aſtronomiæ, Perſice: Auctore *Teſdan-bacſh Ibn Pir-Ali* celebratus Nomine *Parvi*, nempe *Pir-Ali* Parvi. Sequuntur Tab. Aſtronomicæ.

3146. 13. Comment. in *Alcoranum*, Arabice Auctore, ut videtur, *Ahmed Ibn Pherhad.*

3147. 14. Comm. in *Alcoranum*, Arabice Auctore *Ibn Salim AlAbai.*

3148. 15. Liber *Kalaid AlAkyan*, eſt ſcil. Elucidatio *Alcorani* Auctore *AlRazi.*

3149. 16. *Selim-nama*, Hiſtoria Familiæ Othomanicæ, Auctore *Salih Ephendi*, Turcice.

2. *Selim-nama*, &c.

3. Aliquot victoriæ ſeu Expugnationes *Sultan Soleiman*, eſt ſcil. Liber nonus ex eis qui vocantur Soleimanici, de rebus geſtis Imperatoris noni Chalipharum, qui dicuntur Othomanici.

3150. 17. Liber *Subh AlAſha*, &c. eſt ſcil. Polyantheæ Volumen primum ex ſeptem Arabice, Auctore *Abul'Abbas Ahmed AlKalkaſhendi.*

3151. 18. *Kalkaſhendii* pars ſecunda ex ſeptem.

3152. 19. Liber *Raudato 'lMadachir* de Primis & poſtremis: eſt ſcil. liber Hiſtoricus ab orbe condito, Arabice Auctore *Ibn Shahna.*

2. Liber Hiſtoricus Arabice, Auctore *Abul Haſan Ali Ibn Hoſein Ibn Ali Ibn Abdollah AlHudeli Almeſudi.*

3. Hiſtorai

First page of the section on Selden's collection in Edward Bernard's 1697 catalogue of medieval manuscripts

> in a list of such records and their owners in the seventeenth century, attributes to Selden cartularies of just the same three houses: Lewes, Bermondsey, and Worksop. The Lewes cartulary is now B.M.MS. Cotton Vesp.F.XV; that of Bermondsey has not been identified. The Worksop cartulary had probably belonged to the three Talbot heiresses whose estates Selden supervised for the second daughter, Elizabeth Gray, Countess of Kent. . . Selden had other later estate papers of Talbot property, including four volumes of seventeenth-century rentals and surveys purchased by the Bodleian in 1947.

When Selden died, his library was at White Friars, where he had made his home with the countess of Kent. There is a tradition that they were married, although there is no evidence of this, unless the fact that she bequeathed her estate to him is evidence. He was certainly a wealthier man after her death than before it, but he always enjoyed an elegant style of life.

The book by which Selden is most commonly known, *Table-talk: Being the Discourses of John Selden Esq,* was published three decades after Selden's death. In his *Men and Letters* (1901) Herbert Paul wrote that "except Bacon's Essays there is hardly so rich a treasure-house of worldly wisdom in the English language as Selden's *Table Talk.*" Samuel Johnson, whose conversational style may owe something to Selden's, was also a great admirer of the book.

T. A. Birrell has written an interesting account of how *Table-talk* came to be popular in his 1985 essay titled "The Influence of Seventeenth-Century Publishers on the Presentation of English Literature." Birrell's thesis is that the fate of a book is inextricably bound up with the way it is packaged by its publisher. *Table-talk,* Birrell says, was first published as a quarto pamphlet for "E Smith." According to Birrell, E. Smith was Elizabeth Smith, a Whig publisher, and Selden was a Whig saint:

> It was as a political pamphlet that Elizabeth Smith published it, in quarto, a year after the Glorious Revolution. Indeed, it was as a political pamphlet that Richard Milward had compiled it, and that was the very reason why he had never published it. The late 1650s were too unsettled, and after the Restoration it might have been fatal to his career . . .

After Smith closed her shop, Thomas Rymer suggested publication of a new edition to Jacob Tonson, who brought out an octavo edition in 1696. He published a third edition in 1716 in duodecimo with the simple title *Table Talk.* What had happened in the meantime was that in the late seventeenth century collections of pithy or wise sayings had become popular. Duodecimo was the characteristic format for these collections and was the perfect size for what a modern reader would call a pocket book. Tonson's layout of *Table Talk* is an attractive example. Birrell concludes:

> The book is presented as a charming little souvenir–and from Tonson's third edition onwards most subsequent editions have been in 12mo or 24mo (the Temple Classics edition is very small octavo, 9 x 15 cms–which goes to show that size and shape can be more important than format). The Bodleian copy of the 1716 edition has the following inscription: 'to James Boswell Esq. who is a most happy preserver of the apothegms of his friends, this collection of those of Selden is presented by his faithful servant, Thomas Percy'. What was once a hot political pamphlet has been transformed into a bijou gift book.

A man such as John Selden who valued the history of books might well have appreciated the irony.

Biographies:

Henry Roscoe, "Life of Selden," in *Eminent British Lawyers* (London: Printed for Longman, Brown and others, 1850), pp. 1–199;

David Sandler Berkowitz, *John Selden's Formative Years* (Washington, D.C.: Folger Shakespeare Library; London & Toronto: Associated University Presses, 1988).

References:

D. M. Barratt, "The Library of John Selden and its Later History," *Bodleian Library Record,* 3 (1950–1951): 128–142, 208–213, 256–274;

Harold J. Berman, "The Origins of Historical Jurisprudence: Coke, Selden, Hale," *Yale Law Journal,* 103 (May 1994): 1651–1738;

T. A. Birrell, "The Influence of Seventeenth-Century Publishers on the Presentation of English Literature," in *Historical & Editorial Studies in Medieval & Early Modern English for Johan Gerritsen,* edited by Mary-Jo Arn, Hanneke Wirtjes, and Hans Jansen (Groningen, Netherlands: Wolters-Noordhoff, 1985), pp. 170–171;

Sir Eric Fletcher, *John Selden 1584–1654: Selden Society Lecture delivered in the Old Hall of Lincoln's Inn, July 9th, 1969* (London: Bernard Quaritch, 1969);

George W. Johnson, *Memoirs of John Selden* (London: Orr & Smith, 1835);

Herbert W. Paul, "The Autocrat of the Dinner Table," in his *Men and Letters* (London & New York: John Lane, 1901), pp. 314–334;

A. L. Rowse, "John Selden and the Middle Way," in his *Four Caroline Portraits* (London: Duckworth, 1993), pp. 125–155;

John Sparrow, "The Earlier Owners of Books in John Selden's Library," *Bodleian Quarterly Record,* 6 (1931): 263–271;

Colin Tite, "A Loan of Printed Books from Sir Robert Cotton to John Selden," *Bodleian Library Record,* 13 (April 1991): 486–490.

Sotheby Family

James Sotheby
(1682 – 17 November 1742)

John Sotheby
(1740 – 1 November 1807)

William Sotheby
(9 November 1757 – 30 December 1833)

Samuel Sotheby
(14 July 1771 – 4 January 1842)

Samuel Leigh Sotheby
(31 August 1805 – 19 June 1861)

Alexis Weedon
University of Luton

See also the William Sotheby entry in *DLB 93: British Romantic Poets, 1789–1832.*

CATALOGUE: Frederick Edward Sotheby, *The Sotheby Heirlooms, Part I: Catalogue of the Highly Important Collection of English Portrait Miniatures of the 16th and 17th Centuries, Removed from Ecton Hall, Northampton, the Property of the Late Major-General F. E. Sotheby . . . on Tuesday, 11th October, 1955* (London, 1955).

William Sotheby

BOOKS: *Poems: Consisting of a Tour through Parts of North and South Wales, Sonnets, Odes, and an Epistle to a Friend of Physiognomy* (Bath: Printed by R. Cruttwell; sold by R. Faulder, London, and T. Baker, Southampton, 1790); republished as *A Tour Through Parts of Wales, Sonnets, Odes and Other Poems* (London: Printed by J. Smeeton for R. Blamir, 1794);

The Battle of the Nile: A Poem (London: Hatchard, 1799);

The Cambrian Hero; or, Llewelyn the Great, an Historical Tragedy, tentatively attributed to Sotheby (Egham: Printed by Wettons, 1800?);

The Siege of Cuzco: A Tragedy in Five Acts (London: Printed for J. Wright by W. Bulmer & Co., 1800);

Julian and Agnes; or, The Monks of the Great St. Bernard: A Tragedy in Five Acts: As it was Performed at the Theatre Royal, Drury Lane (London: J. Wright, 1801); revised as *Ellen; or, The Confession: A Tragedy in Five Acts* (London: Murray, 1816);

A Poetical Epistle to Sir George Beaumont, bart., on the Encouragement of the British School of Painting (London: Printed for J. Wright, 1801);

Oberon: or, Huon de Bordeaux: a Mask. and Orestes: A Tragedy (London: Sold by T. Cadell & W. Davies, printed by J. Mills, Bristol, 1802; facsimile, New York: Garland, 1978);

Saul: A Poem in Two Parts (London: Printed for T. Cadell & W. Davies by W. Bulmer, 1807; Boston: Printed by D. Carlisle for John West, 1808);

Constance de Castile: A Poem in Ten Cantos (London: Printed for T. Cadell & W. Davies, 1810; Boston: West & Blake, printed by Greenough & Stebins, 1812);

A Song of Triumph (London: Printed for John Murray by W. Bulmer & Co., 1814);

Tragedies, viz. The Death of Darnley. Ivan. Zamorin and Zama. The Confession. Orestes (Printed for John Murray by W. Bulmer & Co., 1814);

Ivan: A Tragedy in Five Acts (London: Printed for John Murray, 1816);

Farewell to Italy, and Occasional Poems (London: Printed by W. Bulmer, 1818); revised and enlarged as *Poems* (London: Printed by W. Nichol, 1825); enlarged again as *Italy and Other Poems* (London: Murray, 1828);

Lines Suggested by the Third Meeting of the British Association for the Advancement of Science, held at Cambridge, in June, 1833. By the Late William Sotheby . . . with a Short Memoir of His Life (London: G. & W. Nicol and Murray, 1834).

PLAY PRODUCTION: *Julian and Agnes; or, The Monks of the Great St. Bernard: A Tragedy in Five Acts,* London, Theatre Royal, Drury Lane, 25 April 1801.

TRANSLATIONS: Christoph Martin Wieland, *Oberon, a Poem from the German of Wieland* (1 volume, London: Printed for T. Cadell and W. Davies, 1798; 2 volumes, Newport: R.I.: L. Rousmaniere / Boston: J. Belcher, 1810);

The Georgics of Virgil, translated, with notes, by Sotheby (London: Printed for J. Wright, 1800; Middletown, Conn.: Printed by Richard Alsop for I. Riley, New York, 1808); revised edition, (London: Printed for John Murray by W. Bulmer, 1815); enlarged as *Georgica Publii Virgilii Maronis hexaglotta,* edited by Sotheby with the Latin of C. G. Heyne and with translations in Italian by G. F. Soave, Spanish by J. de Guzmán, German by J. H. Voss, French by Delille, and English by Sotheby (London: Printed by W. Nicol, 1827);

The First Books of the Iliad; the Parting of Hector and Andromache; and the Shield of Achilles: Specimens of a New Version of Homer (London: Murray, 1830); enlarged as *The Iliad of Homer* (London: Murray, 1831);

The Odyssey of Homer, illustrated by the designs of Flaxman (London: G. & W. Nicol and Murray, 1834).

SELECTED PERIODICAL PUBLICATION–UNCOLLECTED: "Address," *Gentleman's Magazine,* 92 (31 March 1822): 418.

Samuel Leigh Sotheby

CATALOGUES: *Catalogue of a Singularly Interesting Collection of Books, Formed by Mr. S. Leigh Sotheby, for the Publication of His Work on the Autograph Annotations by the Great Theological Reformers, Melanchthon and Luther; as Found in Copies of Theological and Classical Works Formerly in Their Possession* (London: Printed by J. Davy & Sons, 1848);

John Gray Bell, *Catalogue of a . . . Collection of Early Printed Books, with Autograph Annotations by . . . Luther and Melancthon . . . Carefully Selected from the . . . Library of the Late S. Leigh Sotheby. . . and Now Offered at the Affixed Prices* (Manchester, 1862).

BOOKS: *A List of the Original Catalogues of the Principal Libraries Which Have Been Sold by Auction by Mr. Samuel Baker from 1744 to 1774; S. Baker and G. Leigh from 1775 to 1777; George Leigh 1778; Leigh and Sotheby from 1780 to 1800; Leigh, Sotheby and Son, from 1800 to 1803; and Mr. Sotheby, from 1816 to 1828* (London: Compton & Ritchie, 1828);

Catalogue of the Entire Oriental, and Classical and Biblical Library of the Late Rev. Alexander Nicoll . . . Which Will Be Sold by Auction, by Messrs. Sotheby and Son . . . on Wednesday, January 21st, 1829, and Three Following Days (London, 1829);

Catalogue of the Very Valuable Classical, Theological, & Miscellaneous Library of the Late Right Rev. Charles Lloyd . . . Which Will Be Sold by Auction, by Mr. Sotheby and Son . . . on Tuesday, the 7th July, 1829, and Four Following Days (London, 1829);

Catalogue of the Valuable Theological and Classical Library of the Rev. Walter Birch . . . to Which Is Added the Library of a Gentleman . . . Which Will Be Sold by Auction, by Mr. Sotheby and Son . . . on Friday, the 5th of March, and Four Following Days (London, 1830);

Catalogue of the Bibliographical and Other Collections of Eminent Literary Men, forming a Most Interesting and Curious Series of Sale and Privately Printed Catalogues of Literary Property, from the Commencement of the Last Century, Collected Together with the Greatest Difficulty (London: Sotheby, 1831);

Bibliotheca Heberiana: Catalogue of the Library of the Late Richard Heber . . . Which Will Be Sold by Auction by Messrs. Sotheby and Son . . . on Thursday, April 10 . . . 1834 (London: Printed by W. Nicol, 1834);

Catalogue of the Library of Dr. Kloss of Franckfort A. M. . . . Including Many Original and Unpublished Manuscripts, and Printed Books with Ms. Annotations, by Philip Melanchthon . . . Which Will Be Sold by Auction, by Mr. Sotheby and Son . . . May 7th, and Nineteen Following Days (Sundays Excepted) (London: S. Sotheby & Son; Parker, Oxford; Deighton, Cambridge; Laing, Edinburgh; Charnley, Newcastle; and thirteen others in Dublin, Lubeck, Hamburg, Paris, Vienna, Prague, Leipzig, Augsburg, Berlin, St. Petersburg, Riga, Copenhagen & Belgium, 1835);

Catalogue of the Remaining Portions of the Libraries of Dr. Rich . . . and of Dr. Kloss . . . Which Will Be Sold by Auction, by Mr. Sotheby and Son . . . on Friday, November 27, 1835, and Following Day (London: Compton & Ritchie, 1835);

Catalogue of the Theological and Miscellaneous Library of a Clergyman, Deceased; to Which Are Added Another Collection of Books . . . Which Will Be Sold by Auction . . . July 11th, 1838 (London, 1838);

Catalogue of the Very Select and Valuable Library of a Gentleman . . . Also the Collection of Modern Books & Books of

Prints, the Property of an Engraver . . . Which Will Be Sold by Auction . . . July 17th, 1838 (London, 1838);

Catalogue of the Second and Select Portion of the Extremely Beautiful and Highly Interesting Collection of Greek and Etruscan Vases, Principally Found at Vulci, of That Distinguished Antiquarian Signor Giuseppe Bassegio of Rome: Which Will Be Sold by Auction, by Mr. S. Leigh Sotheby . . . on Friday, the 13th Day of July, 1838 (London: Printed by J. Davy, 1838);

Catalogue of a Collection of Historical, Theological and Miscellaneous Books . . . Which Will be Sold by Auction . . . August 10th, 1838 (London, 1838);

Catalogue of the Well Selected Classical, Historical, Theological, Mathematical & Miscellaneous Library of a Gentleman . . . Which Will Be Sold by Auction by S. Leigh Sotheby . . . August 15th, 1838 (London, 1838);

Catalogue of Some Valuable Books Including a Well-Selected Dramatic Library, the Property of a Gentleman. Will Be Sold by Auction, by S. Leigh Sotheby, May 16, 1838 (London, 1838?);

Observations upon the Handwriting of Philip Melanchthon: Illustrated with Fac-similes from His Marginal Annotations, His Common Place-Book, and His Epistolary Correspondence. Also, a Few Specimens of the Autograph of Martin Luther, with Explanatory Remarks (London: Printed by J. Davy, 1839); enlarged as *Unpublished Documents, Marginal Notes, and Memoranda, in the Autographs of Philip Melanchthon and of Martin Luther. With Numerous Fac-similes. Accompanied with Observations upon the Varieties of Style in the Handwriting of These Illustrious Reformers* (London: Printed by J. Davy, 1840);

A Collection of Nearly 500 Facsimilies of the Water Marks, Used by the Early Paper Makers, During the Latter Part of the Fourteenth, and Early Part of the Fifteenth Centuries, anonymous (London, 1840);

Catalogue of the Highly Valuable and Important Collection of Sanskrit Manuscripts of the Late Sir Robert Chambers . . . Chief Justice of Bengal. Which Will Be Sold by Auction, by Mr. S. Leigh Sotheby . . . on Wednesday, April 13, 1842, and Three Following Days (London, 1841);

Catalogue of the Singularly Curious, Very Interesting, and Valuable Library of Edward Skegg . . . Which Will Be Sold by Auction by Mr. S. Leigh Sotheby . . . April 4th, 1842, and Seven Following Days (London, 1842);

Catalogue of a Miscellaneous Collection of Coins and Medals, from the Cabinets of Several Collectors . . . Which Will Be sold by Auction, on Friday, 22d of April, 1842, at One O'clock Precisely (London: Printed by J. Davy & Sons, 1842);

Catalogue of the Valuable Collection of Early British, Saxon, English, Greek, Roman and Foreign Coins and Medals, of the Late Very Reverend Dean of St. Patrick . . . Which Will Be Sold by Auction, by Order of the Executrix by S. Leigh Sotheby, 10th of June, 1842 (London, 1842);

Catalogue of an Extensive Collection of Books on Angling, the Property of a Gentleman. To Which Is Added the Library of Machel Stace. Which Will Be Sold by Auction by S. Leigh Sotheby, Jan. 16th, 1843, and Following Day (London, 1843);

Catalogue of the Valuable Library of the Late Benjamin Heywood Bright . . . Containing a Most Extensive Collection of Valuable, Rare, and Curious Books, in All Classes of Literature. Which Will Be Sold by Auction, by Messrs. S. Leigh Sotheby & Co . . . on Monday, March 3, 1845, and Eleven Following Days (London: Compton & Ritchie, printers, 1845);

The Typography of the Fifteenth Century: Being Specimens of the Productions of the Early Continental Printers, Exemplified in a Collection of Fac-similes from One Hundred Works, Together with Their Water Marks. Arranged and edited from the Bibliographical Collections of the late Samuel Sotheby, by his Son, S. Leigh Sotheby (London: Thomas Rodd, 1845);

Catalogue of the . . . Original Drawings . . . by D. Maclise for the Illustrated Edition of Moore's Irish Melodies, also the Original Drawings by Maclise and Geo. Jones, for the Poetical Works of T. Moore and J. Montgomery; Together with the Original Reduced Drawings of Prize Cartoons by Cope (London, 1846);

Catalogue of the Very Important Collection of Coins and Medals the Property of a Well-Known Baronet, Comprising Choice Examples of Roman Gold and Silver (London: J. Davy & Sons, printers, 1850);

A Few Observations to the Shareholders of the Crystal Palace Company, made by proxy on the part of Mr. S. L. Sotheby at the extraordinary general meeting of the shareholders held on the 8th of February 1855 (London, 1855);

A Few Words by way of a Letter Addressed to the Directors of the Crystal Palace Company (London: Smith, 1855);

A Postscript to the Letter Addressed to the Directors of the Crystal Palace Company, December 8th, 1854 . . . Giving Verbatim the Observations of Several Shareholders Relating to the Five Resolutions Proposed by Proxy for Mr. Sotheby (London: Smith, 1855);

A Few Words by Way of a Letter Addressed to the Shareholders of the Crystal Palace Company, with Remarks on the Various Subjects Necessarily Brought under the Notice of the Committee, Appointed to Investigate . . . the Affairs of the Company (London, 1855; enlarged, 1856);

Principia Typographica: The Block-Books; or Xylographic Delineations of Scripture History, issued in Holland, Flanders, and Germany during the Fifteenth Century, Exemplified and Considered in Connexion with the Origin of Printing. To Which Is Added an Attempt to Elucidate the Character of the Paper-marks of the Period. A Work Contemplated by the Late Samuel Sotheby, and Carried out by His Son,

The poet and playwright William Sotheby, who inherited his grandfather James Sotheby's library at Ecton; portrait by Sir Thomas Lawrence (National Portrait Gallery, London)

Samuel Leigh Sotheby, 3 volumes (London: Printed for the author by W. McDowell, 1858);

Memoranda Relating to the Block-Books Preserved in the Bibliothèque Impériale, Paris, Made October, M.DCCC.LVIII., by Samuel Leigh Sotheby, Author of the "Principia Typographica" (London: Printed for the author by T. Richards, 1859);

Catalogue of the Very Important and Valuable Collection of Genealogical and Heraldic Manuscripts: and a Few Printed Books, the Property of the Late Sir William Betham, Ulster King of Arms: Which Will Be Sold by Auction (By Order of the Executors) by S. Leigh Sotheby & John Wilkinson (London: S. L. Sotheby & J. Wilkinson, 1860);

List of a Few Specimens of Art, Chiefly the Productions of English Artists, in Oil and Water-Colours: Collected during the Last Twenty-five Years, by S. Leigh Sotheby, F. S. A. Buckfast-Leigh Abbey, South Devon (London: Printed by J. Davy & Sons, 1861);

Ramblings in the Elucidation of the Autograph of Milton (London: Printed for the author by Thomas Richards, 1861).

The Sotheby name has long been associated with the firm of book and fine-art auctioneers established in 1744 by Samuel Baker on York Street, London. Three generations of Sothebys were connected with the firm from 1778, when Baker's nephew, John Sotheby, became a partner, until the death of John's grandson Samuel Leigh Sotheby in 1861. Earlier generations, however, founded the family interest in books: James Sotheby (1682–1742) was a keen collector of manuscripts and early printed books. The two branches of the family that descended from him appear to have inherited his zeal but put it to use in quite different ways: the auctioneer branch rapidly acquired and disposed of their collections, putting their bibliographical knowledge to commercial use, while the other branch preserved and enlarged James's collection at Ecton Hall, Northamptonshire.

The Sotheby family originally came from Pocklington and Birdsall in Yorkshire. In 1673 James Sotheby, a London merchant, purchased Sewardstone, on the edge of Epping Forest in Essex. The estate passed on to his son, also named James, who was born in 1682. The younger James's collection of books and manuscripts was inherited by his grandson William Sotheby, who was born on 9 November 1757, the eldest of four children of Colonel William Sotheby of the Coldstream Guards (the fourth son of James Sotheby and the grandson of the original purchaser of Sewardstone) and Elizabeth Sloane. The younger William Sotheby's brother Thomas, with whom he went on a walking tour in Wales that was immortalized in his *Poems: Consisting of a Tour through Parts of North and South Wales, Sonnets, Odes, and an Epistle to a Friend of Physiognomy* (1790), became an admiral. Their father died when William was nine, and he was left under the guardianship of Charles Yorke, fourth Earl of Hardwicke, and Hans Sloane, his maternal uncle; they sent him to Harrow. On William's marriage to Mary Isted on 17 July 1780 he acquired the property at Ecton and was able to resign his commission in the dragoons and take up a literary life. He also purchased Bevis Mount, near Southampton, and lived there until he moved to London in 1791. Later he spent much of his time at Fairmead Lodge on the Sewardstone estate, which he called "my beloved forest retreat," and he was one of the master keepers of Epping Forest, as his grandfather had been. William studied classics zealously and gained a reputation for his translations of Virgil's *Georgics* (1800) and Homer's *Iliad* (1830; enlarged, 1831) and *Odyssey* (1834). Perhaps his highest accolade was when the poet Christoph Martin Wieland expressed pleasure at Sotheby's translation from the German of Wieland's poem *Oberon* (1798).

William Sotheby's own poetry and plays met with less success. The poems he wrote on topical issues were published in *The Gentleman's Magazine;* some of his plays received private performances, but the only one to be performed before the public was *Julian and Agnes; or, The Monks of the Great St. Bernard: A Tragedy in Five Acts,* which opened at the Theatre Royal, Drury Lane, on 25 April 1801. On her exit, Sarah Siddons, who was playing one of the leading roles, accidentally hit the head of the wooden baby she was carrying on a doorpost, and the actress and audience broke into laughter. There was no second performance. Sotheby appears to have been an eloquent and sought-after speaker, and his address to the Society of Dilettanti on the death of its secretary, Sir Henry Englefield, was published in *The Gentleman's Magazine* on 31 March 1822. His oratorical and persuasive powers were employed on behalf of the Literary Fund, to which he gave his lifelong support. He was a friend of William Wordsworth; George Gordon, Lord Byron; and Sir Walter Scott, and many other literary men dined at his table.

At some point James Sotheby's library was transferred from Sewardstone to Ecton Hall and combined with works that had belonged to the Isted family; the latter included a prayer book and Bible dating from 1671 that had probably belonged to Richard Isted, who had purchased Ecton in 1712. The Ecton library was sold at auction on 24 July 1924. The forty-page catalogue of the sale has 218 lots, mainly of Western manuscripts; the title page says, "Many of these books have been in the possession of the family since they were purchased by James Sotheby towards the end of the XVIIth Century." The collection exhibits a predominant interest in English history, literature, and travel, but there were also French and Latin classics, mostly from the sixteenth and seventeenth centuries. The highest price, £3,300, was paid for an early fourteenth-century *Biblia Sacra Latina* from northern France, on thin vellum, "beautifully written in clear gothic characters . . . 48 lines to the page, double columns." It was illustrated with "Eighty-one large and exquisitely painted historiated initials in gold and colours with diaper backgrounds, and sixty-five other large initials beautifully painted," mostly on a gold background and with marginal decoration on every page, and had a seventeenth-century English red morocco binding. The quality and quantity of the illustrations–mostly of animals, grotesques, and humorous scenes–probably aided its sale. A less spectacular work was the fourteenth-century manuscript *Biblia Sacra Latina* of William III, bound with his monogram. A Latin metrical manuscript Bible on vellum from the same century was also on sale. Two first editions published by William Caxton and dating from 1480 also sold well: a black-letter *Chronicles of England* and a *Description of Britain.* A First Folio edition of William Shakespeare's works (London: Printed by Isaac Jaggard and Edward Blount, 1623) and a fourteenth-century manuscript of William Langland's *Piers Plowman* attracted attention. The sale also included a rare first edition of John Alcock's *Mons Perfeccionis, Otherwyse in Englysshe the Hyll of Perfeccon,* printed by "Wynkyn de Worde, Westminister 22 September 1496." The catalogue lists as "apparently unrecorded" *Of the tryumphe and the vses that Charles the emporour & the most myghty redoubted Kyng of England Henry the VIII were saluted with passyng through London,* printed by Richard Pynson and illustrated with a woodcut of Charles V on the title page and the royal arms of England on the verso.

Samuel Baker, founder of the auction house that became Sotheby's (Sotheby Parke Bernet, London)

According to annotations in a handwritten catalogue of the Ecton library prepared in 1920, which recorded the original prices paid for some of the books and the prices received at the sale in 1924, James Sotheby paid £2 for Pietro Santi Bartoli's *Admiranda Romanarum Antiquitatum ac veteris Sculpturae Vestigia* (Rome: Giovanni Giacomo de Rossi, 1693) and a bit less for Bartoli's *Columna Cochlis M. Aurelio Antonino Augusto Dicata, eius rebus gestis in Germanica, atque Sarmatica Expeditione Insignis ex S.C. Romae ad Viam Flaminiam Erecta.* He is also recorded as purchasing Antonio Campo's *Cremona Fedelissimo citta et nobilissima Coloniae de Romani* (1645) and Giulio Raviglio Rosso's *Historia delle Cose occorse nel Regno d'Inghilterra* (Venice: Nell'Academia Venetiana, 1558). In addition, he owned copies of Angelo Portenari's *Della Felicita di Padova* (Padua: Pietro Paolo Tozzi, 1623), George Havers's translation of *The Travels of Sig. Pietro Della Valle, a Noble Roman, into East-India and Arabia Deserta: In Which the Several Countries, Together with the Customs, Manners, Traffique, and Rites Both Religious and Civil, of Those Oriental Princes and Nations, Are Faithfully Described: in Familiar Letters to His Friend Signior Mario Schipano* (London: Printed by J. Macock, for J. Martin and J. Allestry, 1665), and Francis Willoughby's *Ornithology* (1678), which he bought for the sum of 19s. 6d.

While James Sotheby prized early English manuscripts and printed books, he also collected European classics. The Ecton library had a vellum manuscript of John Lydgate's English verse translation of Giovanni Boccaccio's *The Fall of Princes, Princesses and Other Nobles* from the fifteenth century; a printed edition of Lydgate's translation, *A Treatise Excellent and Compedious, Shewing and Declaring, in Maner of Tragedye, the Falles of Sondry Most Notable Princes and Princesses with Other Nobles, through y' Mutabilitie and Change of Vnstedfast Fortune Together with Their Most Detestable & Wicked Vices* (London: Printed by Richard Tottel, 1554), showing the coat of arms of E. V. Utterson; a French edition of the *Decameron,* translated by Antoine le Macon (Lyon: Guillaume Rouille, 1560); and a seventeenth-century edition of the latter half of the same work (Paris: Jean Guignard, 1629), illustrated with woodcuts.

An interest in voyages to places such as Russia and Peru and records of settlers in newfound lands from Tobago to North America is also evident in the collection. The library had Theodor de Bry's *A Briefe and True Report of the New Found Land of Virginia, of the Commodities and of the Nature and Manners of the Naturall Inhabitants,* translated into English by Thomas Harriot (Frankfurt: Printed by John Wechel for Theodor de Bry, 1590), and a first edition of Walter Biggs's *A Svmmarie and Trve Discovrse of Sir Frances Drakes West Indian Voyage* (London: Printed by Richard Field, 1589), with four folding maps showing St. Jago, St. Domingo, Cartagena, and St. Augustine. When it came up for auction, the latter work was purchased by the booksellers Bernard Quaritch and Son, who bought most of the Americana.

While it is doubtful that the poet William Sotheby was a serious book collector, the existence in the Ecton library of certain books that were published during his lifetime and display his interests appears to link him to the growth of the collection in the 1820s and 1830s. For example, the library contained copies of *The Anti-Jacobin or Weekly Examiner* (1799); two editions of *Poetry of the Anti-Jacobin* (London: Printed for J. Wright by W. Bulmer & Co., 1801; London: Printed for William Miller & J. Hatchard by W. Bulmer & Co., 1807); the second edition of William Tennant's *Anster Fair: A Poem in Six Cantos; with Other Poems* (Edinburgh, 1814); C. E. Dodd's *An Autumn near the Rhine; or, Sketches of Courts, Society, Scenery, &c. in Some of the German States Bordering on the Rhine* (London: Longman, Hurst, Rees, Orme & Brown, 1818); *The Angler: A Poem, in Ten Cantos,* by T. E. Lathy as "Piscator" (London, Printed for W. Wright and M. Iley, 1819); and Robert Montgomery's *The Age, Reviewed, a Satire, with the Runaways* (London: William Carpenter, 1827)–all works that a man with Sotheby's literary tastes would have read. The library had a first edition of Byron's *English Bards, and Scotch Reviewers* (London: Printed for James Cawthorn, 1809), which includes a reference to Sotheby's poetry, and another edition, illustrated, mounted in quarto, and bound in half morocco (London: Printed for J. Cawthorn, 1810)–apparently a treasured item. Also in the collection was Byron's *Hours of Idleness: A Series of Poems, Original and Translated* (London: Printed for W. T. Sherwin, 1820). From the Society of Dilettanti there were seven volumes of *The Ionian Antiquities* (1769), two volumes of *Specimens of Ancient Sculpture* (1809, 1835), one volume of *The Unedited Antiquities of Attica: Comprising the Architectural Remains of Eleusis, Rhamnus, Sunium and Thoricus* (1817), and three volumes of *Antiquities of Ionia* (1821). There were volumes of poetry by James Hogg, Robert Southey, and George Crabbe; William Cowper's Greek translations; and Sotheby's own translation of Homer's *Odyssey* with designs by John Flaxman (1834). His acquaintance with Scott may be responsible for the presence of the complete *Waverley Novels* in forty-one volumes (1823–1833) and another edition in five volumes that included Scott's poems "Marmion," "The Lady of the Lake," and others (1841). John Gibson Lockhart's seven-volume *Memoirs of the Life of Sir Walter Scott, Bart.* (Edinburgh: Cadell, 1837–1838) was also in the library.

Although the two branches of the Sotheby family kept themselves separate, works written by the auctioneer branch found a place in the Ecton library. Among these are Samuel Leigh Sotheby's *Memoranda Relating to the Block-Books Preserved in the Bibliothèque Impériale, Paris, Made October,* M.DCCC.LVIII., *by Samuel Leigh Sotheby, Author of the "Principia Typographica"* (1859) and *Ramblings in the Elucidation of the Autograph of Milton* (1861). They are apt symbols of the continuance of the bibliophilic interests of both branches of the family through the generations.

The Sothebys whose name is associated with the auction house were descended from James's illegitimate son John, who was born in 1703 and died in 1775. His wife, Anne, was the sister of Samuel Baker. Baker was the real founder of the business, building up from humble beginnings a firm that was, according to *The Times* (London) of 6 January 1842, "the first established in this country for the exclusive sale of literary property by auction." His first auction was of the valuable library of the Right Honourable Sir John Stanley, Bart., which began on Monday, 11 March 1745, and continued for ten nights in the Great Room at the Exeter Exchange, The Strand. There were 457 lots, and each book was sold separately in order of size: octavos, then quartos, and finally folios.

Baker, who had no children, became fond of his sister's family–especially his nephew John Sotheby, born in 1740, and John's wife, Elizabeth. The couple lived on Charles Street, Bloomsbury, and after Baker was widowed Elizabeth Sotheby looked after his London house and occasionally his house at Woodford Bridge, near Chigwell in Essex. Baker sometimes asked her to visit the firm in York Street and check that the business was running smoothly.

Baker published twenty-nine sale catalogues between 1744 and 1774. In 1775 he took George Leigh into partnership; in the next two years they produced five catalogues, concluding with the F. R. John and A. S. Ives sale in 1777. In that year Baker retired to his house at Woodford Bridge. When he died in 1778 he left his share of the business to his nephew. Leigh held two further sales before John Sotheby took up his partnership and the firm became Messrs. Leigh and Sotheby.

Baker's enterprise and industry were remembered fondly by his heirs. Thomas Frognall Dibdin added in a footnote to his portrait of the auctioneer in his *Bibliographical Decameron* (1817) his recollection of a conversation with John Sotheby's son:

> "But," said the forementioned Mr. Samuel Sotheby, "by all means, in your brief view of the sales of books by auction, make mention of Mr. Samuel Baker, the Father of our tribe!" "What of him, good Mr. Sotheby?" "What of *him*, Sir!–Why he was as fine a fellow as ever broke a crust of bread; and we have a *portrait* of him, up stairs, taken not long before he died, in his 60th year, and with every tooth in his head as sound as a roach!"

Leigh also appears to have been quite a colorful personality–especially on the rostrum, where he maintained the tension by opening a crumpled-horn snuffbox and carefully taking a pinch of snuff when prices were running high. John Sotheby was in charge of the administrative side of the business. Realizing the importance of the catalogue in generating interest in the sale and for purchasers unable to view the books in person, Sotheby increased the elegance of and detail in the firm's catalogues.

The Sotheby firm profited from an increase in interest in manuscripts and books at end of the eigh-

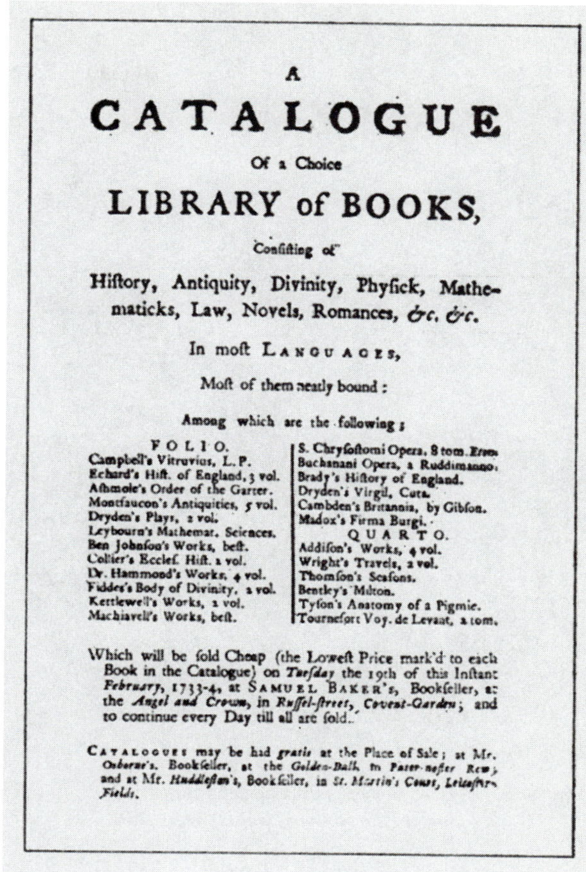
A

CATALOGUE

Of a Choice

LIBRARY of BOOKS,

Confifting of

Hiftory, Antiquity, Divinity, Phyfick, Mathematicks, Law, Novels, Romances, *&c. &c.*

In moft LANGUAGES,

Moft of them neatly bound:

Among which are the following;

FOLIO.	
Campbell's Vitruvius, L. P.	S. Chryfoftomi Opera, 8 tom. *Eton*
Echard's Hift. of England, 3 vol.	Buchanani Opera, a Ruddimanno.
Afhmole's Order of the Garter.	Brady's Hiftory of England.
Montfaucon's Antiquities, 5 vol.	Dryden's Virgil, Cuts.
Dryden's Plays, 2 vol.	Cambden's Britannia, by Gibfon.
Leybourn's Mathemat. Sciences.	Madox's Firma Burgi.
Ben Johnfon's Works, beft.	QUARTO.
Collier's Ecclef. Hift. 2 vol.	Addifon's Works, 4 vol.
Dr. Hammond's Works, 4 vol.	Wright's Travels, 2 vol.
Fiddes's Body of Divinity, 2 vol.	Thomfon's Seafons.
Kettlewell's Works, 2 vol.	Bentley's Milton.
Machiavell's Works, beft.	Tyfon's Anatomy of a Pigmie.
	Tournefort Voy. de Levant, 2 tom.

Which will be fold Cheap (the Loweft Price mark'd to each Book in the Catalogue) on *Tuefday* the 19th of this Inftant *February*, 1733-4, at SAMUEL BAKER's, Bookfeller, at the *Angel and Crown*, in *Ruffel-ftreet*, *Covent-Garden*; and to continue every Day till all are fold.

CATALOGUES may be had *gratis* at the Place of Sale; at Mr. *Osborne's*, Bookfeller, at the *Golden-Ball*, in *Pater-nofter Row*; and at Mr. *Huddlefton's*, Bookfeller, in *St. Martin's Court*, *Leicefter-Fields*.

Cover of Baker's first known auction catalogue

teenth century. Earlier in the century books rarely sold for more than £20, but prices rose in the 1780s. Frank Herrmann notes in his *Sotheby's: Portrait of an Auction House* (1980) that before 1784 the firm seldom held more than four sales a year, and that most of those took place early in the year with an occasional one in December. In 1786, however, the firm held eight sales; a decade later the number had risen to fourteen, with four in the autumn. Between 1798 and 1800 there were an average of twenty-three sales a year. In 1800 John Sotheby's son Samuel joined the firm, and its name was changed to Leigh, Sotheby and Son. At least sixty-six sales were held between 1801 and 1803. During this period the firm auctioned the libraries of the essayist Joseph Addison and the politician John Wilkes, the property of the bookseller William Browne, as well as legal libraries, prints, book stock, coins, and medals.

Leigh and John Sotheby followed Baker's example and sought to expand the basis of the business while retaining their reputation as book auctioneers. Baker had sold stationery and had published books; Leigh and Sotheby were also publishers and booksellers, and

John Sotheby, Baker's nephew, who inherited the auction house in 1778 (from Frank Herrman, Sotheby's, *1980)*

in 1799 they put out a catalogue of more than a thousand titles. Among the works they published was *Supplement to a General Synopsis of Birds* (1787–1801), by John Latham, in seven sumptuous volumes illustrated with 119 color plates; Thomas Harwood's *Annotations upon Genesis: With Observations Doctrinal and Practical* (Reading: Printed for the author by A. M. Smart and T. Cowslade and sold by Leigh and Sotheby, London, 1789) and some of his sermons; William Pole's *Collections towards a Description of the County of Devon* (London: Printed by J. Nichols, and sold by Messrs. White and Son; Robson; Leigh and Sotheby; and Payne, 1791)–Pole had died in 1635, and the book was printed from the autograph manuscript); Lady Sophia Burrell's *Poems, Etc.* (1793); Charles Buckle's *Familiar Essays on Interesting Subjects (For Use in Schools),* which sold for 3s. sewed and 3s. 6d. bound; and *Trade Displayed, Simplified and Perfected: An Entire New System of Mercantile Calculation . . . by an Old Merchant.* They also published editions of books by Oliver Goldsmith, John Locke, and Samuel Johnson.

In 1804 Leigh and John Sotheby had an altercation; as a result, Leigh and Samuel Sotheby moved to new premises at 145 The Strand, naming their business Leigh and S. Sotheby. John Sotheby held two more sales in York Street before retiring, but it appears that the former partners were never reconciled: after his death on 1 November 1807 John's books were sold not by his son but by William Richardson.

Samuel Sotheby's wife, Harriet, died shortly after his father. They had been married for five years, and Samuel was left, at the age of thirty-seven, with four children to raise. Ten years later he married Laura Smith. According to William Carew Hazlitt, it was Samuel "who impressed on the concern his powerful and enduring personality. He had a long innings, and had excellent opportunities of building up the structure which his son and successor inherited." Samuel presided over the firm during politically turbulent times; the Napoleonic Wars caused an economic depression that severely affected the book trade.

Despite these financial ups and downs, the sales continued in ever increasing numbers. Leigh and Sotheby sold the Merley Library, the collection of Ralph Willet, in 1813. It included some fine block books, early bibles, and several books printed by England's first printer, Caxton. Dibdin recalls in *The Bibliographical Decameron* that the Caxtons "brought gallant prices," in particular that George John Spencer, second Earl of Spencer, bought "Caxton's 'vii. profytes of trubylacion' for the enormous sum of 194*l.* 5*s.*!" On 7 June of the same year Leigh and Sotheby sold the collection of Reverend Isaac Gossett. It was not a large library, but it was a select one, consisting of sound, clean copies of grammars, classics, theology, and belles lettres in respectable covers. Its owner had been given the sobriquet "milk white Gosset" because of his love of books bound in vellum. The sale evidently caused some amusement, as *The Gentleman's Magazine* published a poem by "Ching-Chou" about the low prices at the sale: "When GOSSET fell, / *Leigh* rang his knell, / And *Sotheby* 'gan to vapour; / For I've been told, / That Folios sold / Indiguant for waste paper." Some sales were famous for their rarities or the oddness of the collections; others were renowned because of the person who was selling. The sale of the collection of oriental and Islamic books of Dr. Samuel Guise in July 1812 attracted attention, including that of the famous collector of manuscripts Sir Thomas Phillipps. A sale with broader appeal was that of the Talleyrand Library, which had lain three or four years in the Leigh and Sotheby warehouse before being dispersed by the firm in May 1816. Sotheby's catered to fashions, such as that of collecting autographs: in May 1819 the firm sold the autograph letters of John Thane, author of *British Autography: A Collection of Facsimiles of the Hand-writing of Royal and Illustrious Personages, with Their Authentic Portraits* (1819). Sotheby's prestige was enhanced by sales such as that on 27 July 1823 of the books Napoleon had taken to St. Helena, and bibliophiles such as the earl of Spencer sold their duplicates at the auction house. But the wars took their toll on book prices, and it was a difficult time for Sotheby's: the number of sales was rising, but, although there was a great deal of work, it was not always profitable. On 25 November 1825 there was a notice in *The Times* declaring "Samuel Sotheby, Wellington Street, Strand, auctioneer" insolvent, followed on 5 December with the dates of the proceedings at the bankruptcy court. Two years later Samuel Sotheby partially retired from the business, and his second son, Samuel Leigh Sotheby, took charge.

A sale that attracted interest as much because of its collector and its value as a national historical record as for its bibliographical merits, was that of the library of the late Frederick, Duke of York, in April 1827. *The Times* (27 April 1827) reported that the collection included some important public records, such as *The Ecclesiastical Taxation of Pope Nicholas* (1291); the *Calendarium Rotulorum Patentum, in Turri Londinensi,* the *Libri Censualis vocati Doomsday-Book Indices, The Nono Rolls;* and *The Valor Ecclesiasticus* of the time of Henry VIII. The duke also had a complete series of 136 Napoleoic medals, several hundred novels, and a large collection of newspapers and periodicals, including an almost complete run of *The London Gazette* from 1684 to 1825.

As an auctioneer, Samuel Leigh Sotheby was in a good position to build a collection of sale catalogues of the libraries of eminent collectors and literary men. Such catalogues provide a wealth of information about the items on sale, including their value and rarity. For a sale of these catalogues on 27 July 1831 Sotheby produced what Archer Taylor has called probably the "most important full-dress sale catalogue of a private collection of catalogues of private libraries," the *Catalogue of the Bibliographical and Other Collections of Eminent Literary Men, forming a Most Interesting and Curious Series of Sale and Privately Printed Catalogues of Literary Property, from the Commencement of the Last Century, Collected Together with the Greatest Difficulty* (1831). Taylor notes that

> Bibliographers have often recognised the peculiar merits of catalogues made by or for the owners of libraries, but have not, with the exception of Gustave Brunet, ordinarily listed them separately. The owners of a few collections that were sold anonymously are identified, and the authors of a few catalogues are named.

Sotheby's collection was formed "with the greatest difficulty," he says in the catalogue, "for a particular purpose, now no longer existing"–possibly a bibliography of British poets that he never completed. The sale was in 320 lots, mainly comprising English catalogues arranged in chronological order. Sotheby later gave an

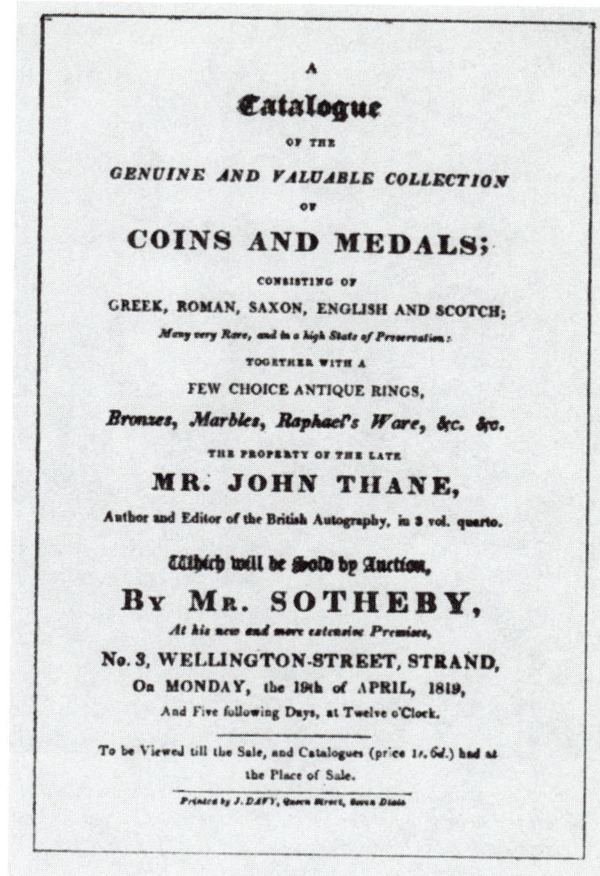

A
Catalogue
OF THE
GENUINE AND VALUABLE COLLECTION
OF
COINS AND MEDALS;
CONSISTING OF
GREEK, ROMAN, SAXON, ENGLISH AND SCOTCH;
Many very Rare, and in a high State of Preservation:
TOGETHER WITH A
FEW CHOICE ANTIQUE RINGS,
Bronzes, Marbles, Raphael's Ware, &c. &c.
THE PROPERTY OF THE LATE
MR. JOHN THANE,
Author and Editor of the British Autography, in 3 vol. quarto.
Which will be Sold by Auction,
BY MR. SOTHEBY,
At his new and more extensive Premises,
No. 3, WELLINGTON-STREET, STRAND,
On MONDAY, the 19th of APRIL, 1819,
And Five following Days, at Twelve o'Clock.

To be Viewed till the Sale, and Catalogues (price 1*s*. 6*d*.) had at the Place of Sale.

Printed by J. DAVY, Queen Street, Seven Dials

Cover of a catalogue issued by John Sotheby

almost perfect set of his own firm's sale catalogues, with prices and purchasers marked, to the British Library.

In 1835 the firm received the library of Georg Franz Burkhard Kloss, a physician and professor at Frankfurt University. While cataloguing the collection Samuel Leigh Sotheby became convinced that many of the marginal annotations in the five thousand volumes were in the handwriting of the Reformer Philipp Melanchthon, a friend of Martin Luther. In the introduction to his *Observations on the Handwriting of Philip Melanchthon: Illustrated with Fac-similes from His Marginal Annotations, His Common Place-Book, and His Epistolary Correspondence. Also, a Few Specimens of the Autograph of Martin Luther, with Explanatory Remarks* (1839) he explained what put him onto Melanchthon's track:

> When I had nearly completed the catalogue and had almost prepared it for the press, I met with the volume on the title of which appears the following manuscript note. . . "Nulla dies abeat quin linea ducta supersit." "PH. MELANCHTHON." Struck with this circumstance, I immediately referred to Dr. Kloss's manuscript

Samuel Leigh Sotheby, circa 1861, admiring a terra-cotta vase that he believed to be of ancient origin but that turned out to be a modern reproduction by Josiah Wedgwood; sketch by J. L. Tupper (from Frank Herrman, Sotheby's, *1980)*

> catalogue of his collection, and great was my surprise at finding no mention made of it. That the passage was in the autograph of the illustrious Melanchthon required very little consideration: its authenticity was at once evident.

Sotheby was so convinced by his own researches and those of the graphologists he consulted that he bought twenty-two volumes from the collection himself, most of them inscribed with what he thought were Melanchthon's annotations. His enthusiasm persuaded Dibdin, who said of the sale in his *Reminiscences of a Literary Life* (1836):

> What an extraordinary collection was the Bibliotheca Klossiana! and with what admirable talent and success has the catalogue of that collection been ushered into the world by Mr. Sotheby the Younger. When I take the introductory matter of this catalogue into consideration, I may conscientiously say that I scarcely know such a *début;* which does equal credit to the author's acumen, diligence, and gallantry of spirit–for the plates accompanying the catalogue are at once curious and abundant. I consider the Melanchthon point as fairly and fully established by the framer of the catalogue: throwing, thereby, a new light upon the marvellous talents of that most learned, most amiable, and most enviable of the Protestant Reformers.

Later bibliographers, however, have disagreed. Seymour De Ricci wrote in 1930: "A number of books bore early manuscript notes, which S. L. Sotheby ascribed, on the slenderest grounds, to the reformer Philip Melanchthon, an ascription which was emphatically contradicted by Kloss himself and a number of German scholars."

On 23 November 1836 *The Times* again carried a bankruptcy notice for Samuel Sotheby, and on 9 February 1837 his library was sold anonymously. Times had been difficult for his father, but during Samuel Leigh's term as head of the firm the financial foundations of the business become more secure. As the business recovered after the crises of 1825 and 1837, he was able to take on more staff. On 24 August 1837 Sotheby's announced the sale of duplicates from the library of William IV.

Samuel Sotheby died on 4 January 1842 and was buried in the churchyard of St. Paul's, Covent Garden, in the same tomb as Samuel Baker and others of his family. *The Times* (6 January 1842) said of him: "If amenity in the discharge of his public duties, an excellent taste, profound acquaintance with the objects of his profession, and extensive acquirements in those branches of literature and the fine arts with which it is so intimately connected, be titles to the sympathy of the public, it will not be withheld on the present occasion."As *The Gentleman's Magazine* put it in April 1842, though esteemed, Samuel was "not so happy as he deserved in realising a fortune in a very arduous profession."

In 1842 Samuel Leigh Sotheby married Julia Emma Pitcher. They had two daughters, Alicia Marian and Rosa Mary, and a son, Frederic Petit Wilkinson; another son died in infancy. After his father's death Samuel Leigh Sotheby changed the name of the firm to S. L. Sotheby & Co., signing himself S. Leigh Sotheby.

Herrmann quotes a contemporary account in the *Morgenblatt für Gebildete Leser* of the stir in the sale room on 26 April 1843 when a rare autograph of William Shakespeare came up for sale:

> among the documents was a deed relating to Shakespeare's house in Blackfriars which bore his signature. . . . When Sotheby raised the precious document the room was overflowing with interested spectators. The auctioneer himself hesitated to break the sudden silence. Finally after a short preamble he started the sale. After five minutes of bidding the sum offered reached one hundred guineas. . . . There was a long pause before the next bid. The bidders withdrew one after another. Excitement was running high and Sotheby's voice as he announced each new bid became deliberate. When he said one hundred and fifty guineas for the third time everyone held his

breath. Only when the hammer fell and the auctioneer solemnly said "gone" was the silence broken.

In 1843 Sotheby took his accountant, John Wilkinson, into partnership. According to Herrmann, Sotheby's idiosyncrasies were tempered by Wilkinson's objectivity. Hazlitt said that Wilkinson had a "tenacious resistance to the admission of any one else to a share in the conduct of the sales." Thus, he presided over the sale room while Sotheby devoted himself to the cataloguing. On 8 May 1844 the firm sold the library of Robert Southey, Poet Laureate. Describing the improvement in the firm's fortunes in the previous decade, Hazlitt noted that

> the portions of the stupendous Heber library dispersed here in 1834, owing to the prevailing depression and what Dibdin called *bibliophobia,* nearly ruined the auctioneers. They rallied from the blow, however, and have never suffered any relapse to bad times, what ever account they may be pleased to give of the very piping ones which they have known well ever since '45, when Mr. Benjamin Heywood Bright's important library was intrusted to their care. The secret of this steady and sustained progress is to be found, I apprehend, in the general confidence secured by strict commercial integrity.

The Bright sale epitomized "the firm's activities in the lifetime of the last of the Sothebys," according to Herrmann. It was in two divisions and took up more than a tenth of Sotheby's selling time in a single year. When the rival Evans firm went bankrupt in 1846, Sotheby's was able to purchase its goodwill and stock. The Wilkes sale was reported in *The Times* (15 March 1847) as "the most important sale of rare books and manuscripts that has taken place in the metropolis for several years." It included the *Biblia Sacra Latina* (1450–1455) attributed to Johannes Gutenberg that had formerly been in library of George Hibbert.

One of Samuel Leigh Sotheby's most famous auctions was the sale of the Stowe library in March, June, and August 1849. Richard Grenville, second Duke of Buckingham and Chandos, had been left debts by his father; these obligations, along with the burden of entertaining a visit by Queen Victoria and Prince Albert to his home, Stowe, had caused his financial ruin. The most important part of the library, the ancient manuscripts and state papers, were sold to Bertram, fourth Earl of Ashburnham, who paid £8,000 for the collection and bought every available copy of the catalogue.

Neither Sotheby nor Ashburnham were so fortunate on another occasion. Guglielmo Bruto Icilio Timoleone Conte Libri Carucci della Sommaia–known as

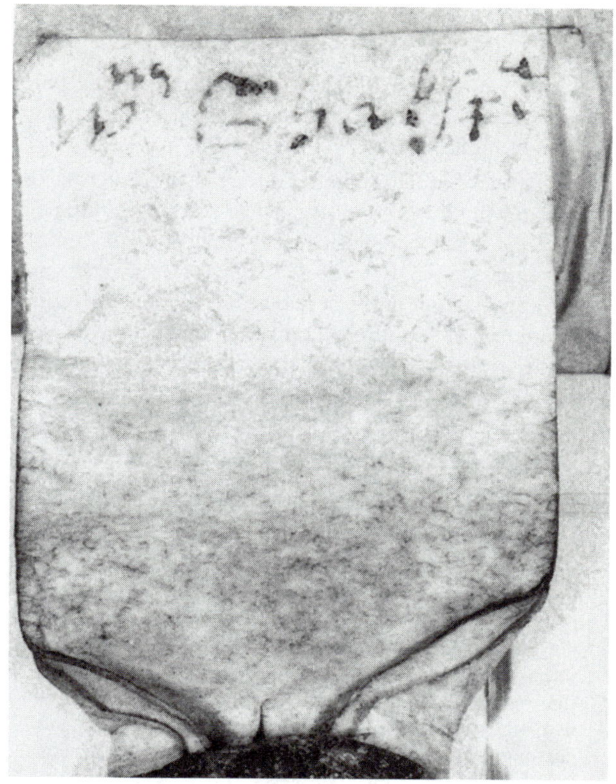

William Shakespeare's signature on a 1613 deed for his house at Blackfriars, London, auctioned by Samuel Leigh Sotheby on 26 April 1843 (British Library)

Libri–was a French nobleman who, through his role in the preparation of a union catalogue of manuscripts in French public libraries, was able to plunder the rare and valuable items. He removed or altered the marks of provenance and renewed the bindings. After rumors started in Paris in 1847 about the provenance of some of his books, Libri tried to sell abroad. Ashburnham, unaware of the rumors, bought privately from Libri's collection 1,923 manuscripts, including a pre-eleventh-century Bible, a Dante work, and ancient classics. When it was discovered that some of the items had been stolen, Ashburnham had to return them to the French government. Sotheby was also a victim. In 1849 Libri approached Sotheby's, and his first sale was held anonymously on 19 February. A series of sales followed in 1853, 1857, 1859, and–after Samuel Leigh Sotheby's death–in 1865. But Libri became dissatisfied with the prices he was getting and filed suit against the firm, even entering the premises and removing the best of his unsold books. When Libri died in 1869, Sotheby's had to pay the £1,500 cost of the lawsuit.

Sotheby and his family lived for many years at Woodlands, Norwood. The Crystal Palace, built in

Hyde Park for the Great Exposition of 1851, was re-erected near their home from 1852 to 1854. Sotheby took great interest in the structure, writing some pamphlets discussing its management and purchasing paintings on exhibition there.

Samuel Sotheby had been deeply interested in the origin and the progress of the art of printing, and at the time of his death had been researching fifteenth-century "paper-marks"–what are today called watermarks–and typography. Father and son had worked closely together, and Samuel Leigh Sotheby completed and published several books on which his father had worked. He said of his father in *The Gentleman's Magazine* (April 1842):

> From the earliest period of his introduction to business Mr. Sotheby became devotedly attached to the study of literary antiquities, and particularly to the history of the origin and progress of the art of printing, on the subject of which he had long been engaged in preparing a work for the press; an undertaking for which, indeed, the circumstances of his profession afforded him peculiar facilities. His collections for this purpose are known to have been most extensive, and were so far advanced that he anticipated, had not the hand of death arrested its progress, to have brought it before the public in the ensuing year. We have much pleasure, however, in stating that his interesting accounts and observations on the early block books, and other specimens of the infancy of printing, are, together with the numerous plates of facsimiles of these and other works of the early printers, in the course of preparation for publication under the hand of his son, Mr. S. Leigh Sotheby.

Samuel Leigh may have been exaggerating the completeness of his father's manuscript–it took him a further sixteen years to finish the work and publish it as the three-volume *Principia Typographica: The Block-Books; or Xylographic Delineations of Scripture History, issued in Holland, Flanders, and Germany during the Fifteenth Century, Exemplified and Considered in Connexion with the Origin of Printing. To Which Is Added an Attempt to Elucidate the Character of the Paper-marks of the Period. A Work Contemplated by the Late Samuel Sotheby, and Carried out by His Son, Samuel Leigh Sotheby* (1858). Nevertheless, two sections of the work–"Facsimiles of the typography of the fifteenth century" and "Paper-marks in the Early Block-books of the Netherlands and Germany"–clearly owe much to his father's scholarship. By dating watermarks, Samuel Sotheby had thought that he could throw light on the long-disputed claim of Holland to be the place where printing was invented. Samuel Leigh Sotheby says of his father in *Principia Typographica:*

> Accordingly, his attention was turned to the marks found on the paper of the various editions of the Block-Books; of the Four Editions of the *Speculum;* of the Early Editions of the Bible; of the books from the press, as believed, of Gutenberg; of those of Fust, Schoeffer, Ulric Zell, and, indeed, of all the earliest printers. At the same time he made a collection, from all available sources, of the marks on the paper of Manuscripts when *dated.*

Samuel gathered transcriptions of more than four hundred such marks for publication; between them the Sothebys illustrated the work with forty-three plates containing facsimiles of typographical samples from more than a hundred works, plus more than a score of plates of watermarks they had traced from the books illustrated. There were facsimiles of sixteen works from Strasbourg, most of them from the press of Johannes Mentellin and five from that of Henricus Eggesteyn; twenty-one from Cologne, with more than half of these from the press of Ulric Zell; eleven from Mainz and its environs, including two Gutenbergs, two Johann Fusts, and four Peter Schöffers; and twelve from printers in Venice. The earliest dated work was Johannes Balbus de Janua's *Catholicon* (1460), illustrated by a colored initial; the latest was Rodericus Zamorensis's *Speculum Humanæ Vite* (1488). In the "Summary of Contents" Samuel Leigh Sotheby says:

> while my object has been to give, as far as I have been enabled, a faithful account of the various editions of the Block-Books, I have endeavoured to shew, that, while those executed in Germany are by far the most numerous, yet some of the earliest of those works were copied from editions which had been previously issued in Holland or the Low Countries.
>
> Therefore, in asserting the justness of the claims of Holland to the origin of the art of printing by moveable type, I think that country may equally claim the invention of block-type as applied to the illustration of those xylographic productions which have formed the subject of the present work.

Sotheby's "short, slight figure" (as Hazlitt described it) was not robust, and he suffered from bouts of ill health and fainting spells. He had been too ill in the autumn of 1850 to look at some letters of Percy Bysshe Shelley that the firm had been given for sale. He was seriously ill again in 1856 and feared that he would not complete the *Principia Typographica;* he says in the introduction that he was "in so dangerous state of health that little hope was entertained of my being able to attend to the duties of my business, and much less, that I should ever live to realise the pleasure of seeing my labours in print." In the autumn of 1858 he spent ten days in the Bibliothèque Impériale in Paris examining block books but had to break off his work because he was too fatigued to continue traveling around Europe. Spurred on to publish what he had so far achieved, he

Plate from Samuel Leigh Sotheby's Principia Typographica *(1858)*

wrote in the preface to his *Memoranda Relating to the Block-Books Preserved in the Bibliothèque Impériale, Paris, Made October, M.DCCC.LVIII:* "Considering the uncertainty of life, and how extremely doubtful it is, at the present time, whether I may ever be able to accomplish my projected examination of the Xylographic treasures of the other Libraries on the Continent, I have determined, without further delay, on committing the ensuing Memoranda to the press, that they may be preserved for the use of future Bibliographers."

Seeking a more healthful climate, Sotheby rented Buckfast Abbey in the Devonshire countryside in February 1861. On the following 19 June he failed to return from a walk and was found drowned in the Dart; he had probably fainted and fallen into the river. Recording his death, *The Gentleman's Magazine* said that he was "a gentleman of amiable disposition and of good judgment in his profession." He was a fellow of the Society of Antiquaries, to which he had presented a copy of the *Principia Typographica,* as well as of the Royal Geographical, Numismatic, and other societies. He was also a keen collector of cabinet pictures. These pictures and his books were auctioned at the firm's Wellington Street premises in two sales, on 6 and 8 February 1862. Some of his early printed books with autograph annotations by Luther and Melanchthon were bought by John Gray Bell of Manchester, who published a catalogue of them.

Sotheby had written, with some relief, in the introduction to the *Principia Typographica* that with that work finished, "I shall be enabled to follow up with more zeal my 'Bibliographical Account of the Printed Works of the English Poets to 1660,' a work commenced when I was a school-boy, and towards which I have written a thousand pages." He had worked on the project for nearly forty years, drawing together the records of all copies described in sale catalogues. Although his widow continued it, it was never published. The manuscript is in the Humphrey Chetham Library in Manchester.

Samuel Leigh was the last of the Sothebys to head the auction house. The success of the firm in its first century was largely the result of the acumen and scholarship of Samuel Sotheby and his son; their interests as collectors were guided by the needs of their business, and they learned the skills of dating early books and manuscripts through watermarks, detecting misattributions and forgeries through graphology, and ascertaining the provenance and previous sale prices of valuable books that appeared in their auction room. Samuel Leigh's works found their way into the library at Ecton, and the seventeenth-century collection of James Sotheby was added to by subsequent generations until many of the most valuable works were sold in 1924. Another sale in 1956 dispersed the remains of the Sothebys' collection.

References:

William Beloe, *The Sexagenarian; or, The Recollections of a Literary Life,* 2 volumes (London: F. C. & J. Rivington, 1817);

Seymour De Ricci, *English Collectors of Books and Manuscripts (1530–1903) and Their Marks of Ownership* (Cambridge: Cambridge University Press, 1930);

Thomas Frognall Dibdin, *The Bibliographical Decameron,* 3 volumes (London: Printed for the author, 1817);

Dibdin, *Bibliomania* (London: Henry G. Bohn, 1842);

Dibdin, *Reminiscences of a Literary Life* (London: John Taylor, 1836);

William Carew Hazlitt, "My Recollections of an Auction-Room," *Bookworm: An Illustrated Treasury of Old-Time Literature,* 7 (1894): 1–7, 33–37;

Frank Herrmann, *Sotheby's: Portrait of an Auction House* (London: Chatto & Windus, 1980);

Daniel Hipwell, "W. Sotheby," *Notes & Queries,* eighth series, 8 (23 November 1895): 411;

John Bowyer Nichols, *Illustrations of the Literary History of the Eighteenth Century* (London: J. B. Nichols, 1858; New York: Kraus Reprint, 1966);

Nichols, *Literary Anecdotes of the Eighteenth Century* (London: Nichols, Son & Bentley, 1812);

Archer Taylor, *Book Catalogues: Their Varieties and Uses,* revised by William P. Barlow Jr. (Winchester: St. Paul's Bibliographies, 1986).

Papers:

The Bodleian Library, Oxford, has some correspondence of William Sotheby and a letter from Samuel Leigh Sotheby to John Bowyer Nichols. The National Library of Scotland has some poems and correspondence of William Sotheby, a few items of Samuel Leigh Sotheby's correspondence, and letters from other family members. The John Rylands Library at the University of Manchester has an autograph letter by William Sotheby. The British Library has some correspondence of family members, including William, Samuel, and Samuel Leigh Sotheby; it also has copies of the auction house's catalogues, with annotations listing prices and purchasers. The unfinished manuscript for Samuel Leigh Sotheby's "Bibliographical Account of the English Poets to the Period of the Restoration" is in the Humphrey Chetham Library in Manchester.

Charles Spencer, third Earl of Sunderland

(1674 - 19 April 1722)

Clare A. Simmons
Ohio State University

CATALOGUES: *Catalogue of Books in the Library at Blenheim Palace, Collected by Charles, Third Earl of Sunderland* (Oxford: Printed by T. Combe, E. B. Gardner, and E. Pickard Hall, 1872);

Bibliotheca Sunderlandiana: Sale Catalogue of the . . . Library of Printed Books Known as the Sunderland or Blenheim Library (London: G. Norman, 1881–1883).

Charles Spencer, third Earl of Sunderland

Charles Spencer, third Earl of Sunderland, was an early eighteenth-century statesman and bibliophile, and in both of these fields the keenest rival of Sir Robert Harley. Perhaps more than in the case of Harley, the love of classical literature reflected in Sunderland's library was mirrored in his political agenda. During a life of constant political intrigue, he managed to amass one of the finest collections of printed books of the age, which was to form the foundation of two important book collections of the succeeding century.

Sunderland was the second son of the second earl of Sunderland, Robert Spencer, and his wife, Anne Digby, a daughter of the second earl of Bristol. The first earl of Sunderland, Henry Lord Spencer, was raised to the earldom in June 1643, probably because of a loan he made to the embattled King Charles I. The following September, the first earl was killed at the Battle of Newbury, and the second earl, whose mother, Dorothy, was a member of the renowned Sydney family, succeeded to the title. The second earl married Digby in 1665. Charles Spencer was the youngest of the second earl's five surviving children. Charles's elder siblings were Robert (born in 1666), Anne (1667), Isabella (1668), and Elizabeth (1671). Charles was born in 1674, presumably in the early months of the year, since his date of birth is also given in old style as 1673.

Charles Spencer spent his early years at the family home at Althorp. His tutor was a Genevan named Pierre Flournois, alias Florival; Spencer's early demonstrations of intellectual ability caught the attention of the diarist John Evelyn, who as a close friend of the countess of Sunderland is a major source of information on the family. He described the young Spencer as a "Youth of extraordinary hopes, very learned for his age, & ingenious, & under a Governor of Extraordinary worth." Other observers also remarked on his learning and his familiarity with classical texts, and between his Genevan tutor and his readings on Athenian and Roman government, the boy seems to have developed early an intellectual interest in republicanism.

The political involvements of his family filled Spencer's childhood with uncertainty and disruption. In the reign of Charles I, his father had been identified with the "Exclusionist" faction, those who wished to preserve a Protestant succession, among whom his uncles Henry and Algernon Sydney were prominent;

Algernon Sydney was beheaded for treason in 1683 as was the countess of Sunderland's cousin Lord Russell. After the accession of James II, the second earl turned Catholic like his king, although he was suspected of being sympathetic to William of Orange. The family was always in debt, and rumors also circulated that the countess, who identified strongly with the Anglican faction, was having affairs, including one with her husband's uncle Henry Sydney.

With the death of his elder brother in 1688, Charles Spencer became heir to the title, and by courtesy Lord Spencer. After the landing of William of Orange and Mary in November 1688, his father, who had earned the distrust of Catholics and Protestants alike, fled to Holland. Although the second earl of Sunderland spent three days in a Rotterdam jail in early 1689, William extended protection to him, and in the summer the rest of the family joined him at Amsterdam. In November they moved to Utrecht so that Spencer could study Dutch politics at the university. He was now under the tutorship of Charles Trimnell, who later became bishop of Winchester.

The Sunderland family returned to Althorp in late 1691; Spencer seems to have begun collecting books soon after this date; he also spent time touring in England. When he came of age in 1695, he was sent to Parliament for two constituencies, Heydon in Yorkshire and Tiverton in Devon: he chose to represent Tiverton and remained a member of Parliament for that borough for his entire time in the lower house. He identified himself as a firm Whig, and according to Jonathan Swift, he "would often among his familiar friends refuse the title of Lord (as he hath done to myself), swear he would never be called otherwise than Charles Spencer, and hoped to see the day when there should not be a peer in England." A Whig of the following century, Lord Macaulay, commented that the party was "more than once brought to the verge of ruin by his violent temper and his crooked politics." Also in 1695, he made the first major purchase toward his library, Sir Charles Scarborough's collection of works on the sciences. Of this, Evelyn wrote:

> My lord [Spencer] shewed me his incomparable Library, now againe improved by many books bought at the same of Sir Charl Scarbrs, which was the very best collection especialy of Mathematical books that was I believe in all Europe: once designed for the Kings library at Saint James but the Queene dying (who was the greate patronesse of that design &c) it was let fall, and so miserably dissipated. . . .

Marriage was for the Sunderland family a political and commercial enterprise. In the time of King James II, the second earl had betrothed his two surviving daughters (Isabella had died in 1684) to Catholic landowners whose Jacobitism was to cause some embarrassment under William and Mary. Spencer was married on 12 January 1695 to Lady Arabella Cavendish, the daughter of the duke of Newcastle, having complicated the marriage negotiations by falling in love with her. His father settled most of his landed property on the couple but used his daughter-in-law's dowry of £25,000 to pay his debts.

In 1697 Spencer was involved in a public scandal involving his sister Elizabeth and her husband, the earl of Clancarty. She had been married to him as a child and spent most of the subsequent years living with her parents. He was captured in Ireland while fighting on behalf of James in 1690 and spent four years in the Tower of London. In 1694 he escaped to James's court at St. Germain, but in 1697 he returned to London, set up a secret meeting with his wife, and the two consummated their relationship. Spencer, who was living nearby, was alerted and arranged for his brother-in-law to be taken from his bed and arrested. The long-term result was that Elizabeth left England for exile with her husband and cut herself off entirely from her family; Spencer, however, had demonstrated his commitment to King William.

Spencer's wife Arabella died of smallpox on 4 June 1698, leaving one daughter, Frances, who was to marry Henry Howard, later the fourth earl of Carlisle. Spencer's second marriage was even more auspicious from his family's point of view and indeed seems to have been negotiated by the parents as a type of political alliance common among royalty. In autumn 1699 he married Lady Anne Churchill, the daughter and joint heiress of John and Sarah Churchill; already titled as earl and countess, they were later to achieve great power and authority as the duke and duchess of Marlborough after the accession of Queen Anne in 1702. Since the marriage was contracted without the knowledge of William and Mary, it was only celebrated publicly the following January. Although the Marlboroughs and the Sunderlands remained political opponents for about two years, the Marlboroughs' political position began to move toward the Whigs: their elder daughter, Henrietta, was married to the son of another great Whig politician, Sidney Godolphin. About this time, Spencer made another purchase of an entire library, possibly the collection of Hadrian Beverland, which is mentioned in a note on libraries by John Bagford.

On 28 September 1702 Spencer's father died, and despite his earlier republican declarations, one month later Spencer took his seat in the House of Lords as the third earl of Sunderland and immediately played a major role. Alexander Cunningham claims that

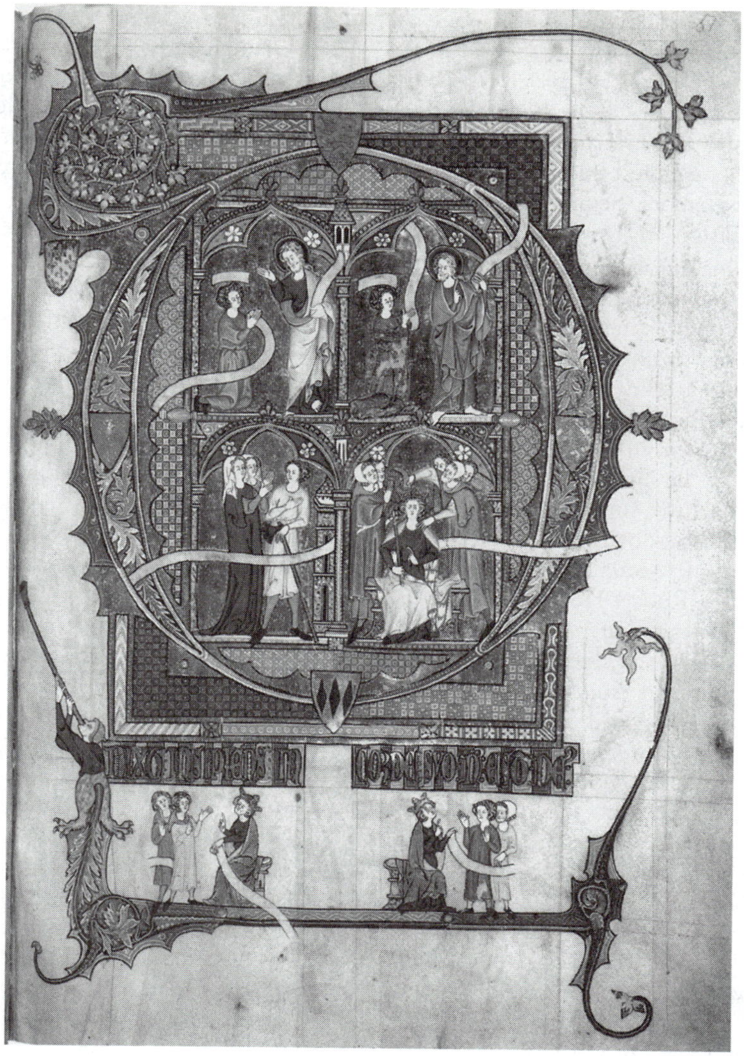

Illuminated initial for Psalm 52 in the Tickhill Psalter, one of the manuscripts Sunderland bought for his library. Attributed to John Tickhill, prior of the Augustinian monastery at Worksop, the manuscript dates from the early fourteenth century (Ms. Spencer 26, New York Public Library, Astor, Lenox and Tilden Foundations).

> in order to show how heartily he abhorred his father's faults, in the collection of books which he made for his library, he cast out the works of the holy fathers, like dregs of antiquity, and commended Machiavel as much preferable to them all; Which gave so much scandal to the clergy, that his very name became offensive to them.

In fact, the catalogue of the Sunderland-Blenheim Library, while including an impressive twenty-one editions of Niccoló Machiavelli from the sixteenth century, including a 1540 Aldine, also lists texts by church fathers such as Augustine and Boethius, and many important editions of the Scriptures. One of Sunderland's first actions on joining the Lords, to the embarrassment of the Marlboroughs, was to oppose the queen's request that a settlement of £100,000 be made on her husband, Prince George of Denmark. By 1704 Sunderland was already one of the leading political forces in the House of Lords, using his connection with the Marlboroughs and Godolphin to further his ambitions. The Marlboroughs' only surviving son had died in 1702, and the duchess seems to have centered her dynastic ambitions on her daughter Anne and Sunderland, although the duke had more reservations about his abilities.

In 1705, on the accession of Joseph I, Sunderland was sent to Vienna as envoy extraordinary to represent the British position regarding Hungary, Marlborough assuring all involved that Sunderland would be guided by his opinions. He traveled to Berlin with Marlborough in December 1705, where they were well received by the king of Prussia. By January 1706, however, the Whigs were rising politically in England, and Sunderland returned to become a member of the Whig "junto" of five, the others, all his seniors, being lords Somers, Halifax, Orford, and Wharton.

Sunderland was wholehearted to the point of unscrupulousness in his pursuit of Whig policies. He continued to demonstrate the rashness that he had earlier displayed over such matters as his sister's relationship with her husband, and according to Cunningham, Somers, "the only man to whom Sunderland would listen," thought "there was reason to fear he would bring all things into confusion by his boldness and inexperience." Sunderland also had the support of his family connections, and the Marlboroughs and Godolphin asked the queen to make him a secretary of state for the southern region, in place of Robert Harley. When she refused, they requested instead that he might replace the other secretary, Sir Charles Hedges. No love was lost between Queen Anne and Sunderland: Gilbert Burnet notes that according to Lord Dartmouth, she said that "Lord Sunderland always treated her with great rudeness and neglect, and chose to reflect in a very injurious manner upon all Princes before her, as a proper entertainment for her." Neither had she forgotten Sunderland's opposition to her husband and his connection with the Whigs, and she held out as long as she could, repeatedly asserting that she feared his temper; she finally conceded in December 1706, when Godolphin threatened to resign. This opposition to her interests on the part of her longtime friends the Marlboroughs, however, encouraged her to find supporters elsewhere, notably in Harley. Sunderland now saw Harley as his political rival and succeeded in having him dismissed from office in February 1708.

Sunderland stood against the Tories by opposing the theory of divine right, and it was this persistence against the wishes of Queen Anne, together with encouragement from Harley and Abigail Masham, which led to his own dismissal from office in June 1710. To appease Marlborough and the Whigs, who organized a meeting to protest this move, the Queen offered him a pension of £3,000 a year for life. The contemporary historian Abel Boyer records that Sunderland, "with the Generosity of an old Roman, hardly to be parallel'd in these corrupt Times, answer'd, He was glad her Majesty was satisfy'd he had done his Duty, but if he could not have the Honour to serve his Country, he would not plunder it." On the election following the dissolution of Parliament in 1710, the Tories were triumphant, and for the next few years, they sought constantly to remove Sunderland from political power on a permanent basis. He seems to have had some part in the passing of a revised version of the Occasional Conformity Bill, which, although claimed to be a measure securing the Protestant succession, in effect imposed more limitations on Protestant dissenters from the Church of England.

The next decade was marked by some significant changes. Queen Anne died on 1 August 1714, and the accession of George I was to give Sunderland the political ascendancy he had so long sought. On 29 April 1716 Sunderland's second wife died, leaving him three sons and two daughters. He married for the third time on 5 December 1717, to Judith Tichborne, who had a large fortune; the duchess of Marlborough, however, considered that the marriage settlement slighted the children of Sunderland's second marriage, and all associations between her and Sunderland ceased by 1720. Three children were born of this last union, but all died in infancy.

Sunderland was a strong supporter of the Hanoverian succession, and from before the accession of George I until his death, Sunderland wielded great influence with the king, which he often used against his political rivals (unlike most of his British contemporaries, Sunderland seems to have been able to communicate in German, a great point of advantage with George I, who spoke no English). Initially, however, he was disappointed in the reward for his loyalty. He had hoped for supreme political power in England, but was given the position of lord lieutenant of Ireland and later the sinecure of vice treasurer of Ireland for life, although he did not visit the country for a year after his appointment and seems never to have had much real power there. In August 1715 he became lord privy seal, but he still coveted the role of secretary of state, the government having been given to Robert Walpole and Charles Townshend. After the death of his second wife, Sunderland traveled in Europe and took the opportunity to meet with George I in Hanover, where he seems to have suggested to the king that his political rivals were in league with the King's despised son–the future George II. Townshend was dismissed, and in April 1717 Sunderland became secretary of state for the second time; from 1718 to 1721 he was first lord of the treasury, and along with Philip Dormer, Earl of Stanhope, finally in charge of running the country.

Among the events of the Sunderland-Stanhope ministry were the continued war with Spain, the repeal of the Schism Act, the failed Peerage Bill, and the South Sea Bubble incident. The Schism Act of 1714 had forbidden dissenting Protestants to run their own schools. While repeal of the Schism Act alleviated the political restrictions placed on Protestant dissenters, Sunderland decided that a total repeal of the Test Acts was impracticable at this time, and they continued in force for another century. The Peerage Bill was an attempt to restrict the number of peers that could be created by the monarch and to keep the total number of peers at a consistent number. Sunderland's objective was probably to limit the power available to the prince of Wales when he succeeded his father, but opinion was divided (notably between essayists Joseph Addison and Richard Steele) as to whether this would increase the power of the House of Commons or rather confirm the authority of the Lords, and the bill was finally dropped.

Sunderland was never especially interested in money, and with his chancellor of the Exchequer, John Aislabie, and his fellow secretary of state James Craggs, he agreed to the floating of stock of the South Sea Company–formed a decade earlier by Harley to have exclusive trade rights in the South Pacific–as a means of raising government revenue and repaying the national debt that had been accumulating during many years of war. When stock prices rose to huge highs and then fell so drastically that many investors were ruined, Sunderland, who himself lost money, admitted responsibility. During subsequent recriminations, Aislabie was found to have resources of £750,000, while Sunderland was accused of having accepted £50,000 in unsecured stock. He was tried for corruption but was acquitted in Parliament by 233 votes to 172, probably through the contrivance of the new rising political star Walpole, who did not wish to destroy the Whig Party. Nevertheless, Sunderland had lost public support and was forced to resign on 3 April 1721, when Walpole succeeded him as chief minister.

Although Sunderland was officially out of office, he continued to have political influence with George I. Rumors nevertheless circulated that he was not entirely committed to the Hanoverian succession. Letters in the Stuart papers confirm that about the time of Sunderland's death, the Jacobites were interested in what direction Sunderland's government might take. Other changes–such as the Pope's claim that he had proof from the duchess of Marlborough that Sunderland "had strong dealings" with James Edward, the Old Pretender, and that he "betrayed all the whig-schemes to Harley" and the Tories–are probably manifestations of the general lack of trust that he prompted rather than chicanery on the level of his father.

Sunderland showed an ambition for supremacy in his book collecting as in his politics. While he had many books at Althorp House, his main library, described by Edward Edwards in *Libraries and Founders of Libraries* (1864), was housed in his London home, Sunderland House, located near the present-day Piccadilly Circus. It consisted of five rooms extending fifty meters

Sunderland's bookstamp

in length, and in 1722 it housed about twenty thousand books. Edwards quotes a contemporary estimate that the total cost exceeded £30,000. Sunderland received advice on book collecting from the bibliographer Michael Maittaire, the author of a history of printing. He paid £1,500 in 1720 for manuscripts to Joseph Smith of Venice, thus thwarting Harley, who was also in negotiation for them. Sunderland owned only a few manuscripts, but these included an exceptional manuscript version of Dante's *Inferno* from the early fifteenth century. The collection was not particularly strong in English books, but it had a remarkable number of first editions of classical works, notably works produced by Aldine Press; it was also strong in early Italian printed books, and was particularly known for its bibles: when auctioned in the 1880s, the collection totalled 13,858 lots, which included 146 early printed bibles, more than 100 new testaments, and 65 psalters. Sunderland's political interests were also well represented in his library; at the auction, his tracts on the early history of America and on civil war–era England drew particular attention.

Although as a politician Sunderland was less acquisitive than most of his contemporaries, he was well known for his extravagance in book collecting. As early as 1703, William Nicolson, bishop of Carlisle, recorded some remarks by Richard Bentley, master of Trinity College, Cambridge. Bentley

> ridiculed the Expensive humour of purchaseing old Editions of Books at Extravagant Rates; a vanity to which the present Earl of Sunderland and the Bishop of Norwich much subject. The former bought a piece of Cicero's Works out of Dr Francis Bernard's Auction,

Sunderland's son, Charles Spencer, third Duke of Marlborough, who took part of his father's library to Blenheim Palace, where it became the basis for the Sunderland-Blenheim Library, which remained intact until the 1880s

printed about 1480 at the Rate of 3.l. 2.s. 6.d. which Dr Bentley himself had presented to that physitian, and which cost him no more than the odd half Crown.

Humfrey Wanley, who worked for Sunderland's political and bibliophilic rival Harley, disapproved of Sunderland's conspiring with booksellers such as Nathaniel Noel and Paul Vaillant to ensure that he had preferential treatment when major collections were for sale: he recorded on 22 January 1720, for example, that Alexander Cunningham had offered Noel 200 guineas "to lett the Earl of Sunderland have the Preference before all others, as to the buying of his old Books." Wanley was particularly contemptuous of the prices that Sunderland was prepared to pay for a rare acquisition. At the auction of Robert Freebairne's collection in December 1721, Wanley recorded in his diary that some books had been bought by Vaillant on Sunderland's behalf at "unaccountably high" prices; these included a printed works of Virgil from about 1472 by Antonio Zarotti, and when Vaillant completed the purchase for £46, Wanley noted sarcastically that "he huzza'd out loud, & threw up his Hat for Joy, that he had bought it so cheap." Wanley adds:

> The Booksellers, upon this Sale, intend to raise the Prices of Philological Books of the first Editions, and indeed of all Old Editions accordingly. Thus Mr Noel told me yesterday, that he ha's actually agreed to sell the said Earl of Sunderland, six duplicate Printed Books, (now coming up the River toward the Custom-house) for fifty Pounds per Book: although my Lord [Harley] give's no such Prices. They are:
>
> The Clementines, with the Gloss. Mogunt. per Fust & Schoyffer, 1460 fol. velum.
>
> Lactantius, in Monasterio Sublacensi, per Maximos, 1465 fol.
>
> The Virgil printed at Rome, by the Maximi.

Edwards nevertheless records a significant opportunity that Sunderland missed. He was offered the Christophorus Valdarfer edition of Giovanni Boccaccio's *Decamerone* (1471) for 100 guineas, but Sunderland, who had an edition missing five leaves, turned it down. When this book was offered at the Roxburghe sale in 1812, two of Sunderland's heirs bid against each other, the sale finally going to the fourth duke of Marlborough for £2,260. The bindings of Sunderland's collection are said to be not particularly fine, and he did not use a bookplate or stamp his arms on his books. While Wanley records that he visited Sunderland's library, it does not seem to have functioned as a rare-book resource in the same way that Harley's did, and the suspicion arises that Sunderland was not particularly generous in allowing others to benefit from his collection.

In 1703 Sunderland had pledged the Althorp library to Marlborough in partial payment of a loan. He never prepared a catalogue, although the bookseller Paul Vaillant produced an index. Wanley records a plan by the duchess of Marlborough to have the library catalogued in 1724; perhaps this was the trust inventory in three folio volumes completed by Bishop Hare in 1728. According to Edwards, "there is a special and partial Catalogue of early editions," probably the work of Nicholas Clagett, later bishop of Exeter; while in the nineteenth century there existed at Blenheim "a very elaborate shelf-list, with appendices, made under the direction of Mr. Vaughan Thomas, in eighty volumes, quarto."

Sunderland died unexpectedly of heart failure on 19 April 1722–so suddenly, in fact, that a post-mortem examination was carried out to ensure that he had not been poisoned (his political partner Stanhope and James Craggs and his father, all implicated in the South Sea affair, had predeceased him). Over the Marlboroughs' objections, his political papers were seized and examined by the current ministry. Wanley, using the language of the South Sea Bubble incident, noted that

> by Reason of his Decease, some benefit may accrue to this [the Harleian] Library, even in Case his Relations will part with none of his Books. I mean, by his raising the Price of Books no higher now; So that, in Probability, this Commodity may fall in the Market; and any Gentleman be permitted to buy an uncommon old Book for less than fourty or fifty Pounds.

In appearance, Sunderland was of average height and fair-complexioned; by middle age he was heavily built and unfriendly in expression. His commitment to party politics outweighed other moral considerations, yet his reserved manner when dealing with others, his hasty temper and his interest in intrigue sometimes undermined the cause of the Whigs rather than advancing it. His acknowledged learning does not seem to have been matched with an equal good sense, and although the Marlboroughs saw political advantages in their connection with him, they clearly distrusted his judgment. While Evelyn praised his early intelligence, Swift asserted that "His understanding, at the best, is of the middling size; neither hath he much improved it, either in reality, or, which is very unfortunate, even in the opinion of the world, by an overgrown library." In her old age, the duchess of Marlborough was even more blunt: "The Earl of Sunderland, it was thought, would be a fool at two and twenty: But afterward, from the favour of a weak Prince, he was cried up for having parts, though 'tis certain he had not much in him."

After Sunderland's death the complications of succession between the Sunderlands and the Marlboroughs decided the destiny of the collection. Sunderland's eldest son, Robert, born in 1701, succeeded him as earl, but he died on 15 September 1729. He was succeeded by his brother Charles, born in 1706, who also, on the death of the Marlboroughs' surviving daughter in 1733, became third Duke of Marlborough, although he did not succeed to the Marlborough estates until the duchess died in 1744. The youngest son, John, a favorite of his grandmother Sarah, the first duchess, succeeded to the Althorp property. The library was hence divided between Blenheim Palace and Althorp, where in time it formed the basis of two great nineteenth-century book collections. The Sunderland-Blenheim Library came into the possession of George Spencer, fourth Duke of Marlborough, himself an avid book collector, who formed a remarkable collection in his White Knights Library in Berkshire in the years of "Bibliomania" in the early nineteenth century. The duke, however, overextended himself financially, and was forced to disperse his acquisitions in 1819. The Sunderland-Blenheim Library remained intact until the 1880s, when it was sold at auction by Puttick and Simpson for £56,581, more than £33,000 being spent by the publisher and bibliophile Bernard Quaritch. The Althorp part of the collection descended to Sunderland's youngest son John's grandson George John, second Earl Spencer, who was to build perhaps the most distinguished book collection of the early nineteenth century at Althorp.

References:

Edward Edwards, *Libraries and Founders of Libraries* (London: Trubner, 1864; New York: Burt Franklin, 1969);

J. P. Kenyon, *Robert Spencer, Earl of Sunderland 1641–1702* (London: Longmans, Green, 1958);

Michael Kerney, "Charles Spencer, Third Earl of Sunderland," in *Contributions towards a Dictionary of English Book-Collectors,* part 2 (London: Bernard Quaritch, 1892).

Papers:

The family papers of Charles Spencer, third Earl of Sunderland, of Althorp House have been deposited in the British Library.

David Steuart

(20 September 1747 - 19 May 1824)

Brian Hillyard
National Library of Scotland

CATALOGUE: Brian Hillyard, *David Steuart Esquire: An Edinburgh Collector. The 1801 Sale Catalogue of Part of his Library Reproduced from the Unique Copy in New York Public Library with an Introductory Essay* (Edinburgh: Edinburgh Bibliographical Society in association with The National Library of Scotland, 1993).

BOOKS: *Plan for a General Bridewell* (Edinburgh, between October 1780 and July 1782);

General Heads of a Plan for Erecting a New Prison and Bridewell in the City of Edinburgh, by Steuart and Archibald Cockburn (Edinburgh, 1783);

The Historical Remembrancer; or, The Epitome of Universal History (Edinburgh: Printed at the University Press for J. Thomson & Co.; R. Baldwin, London; and J. Cuming, Dublin, 1814).

David Steuart (Edinburgh City Art Galleries)

The library of David Steuart, auctioned in Edinburgh in 1801, was described as "the most uncommon, and certainly the most valuable private library ever brought to the hammer on this side the Tweed." Admittedly it was Cornelius Elliot, the auctioneer, who thus characterized it, but Steuart's collection of early Mainz printing, which included a copy of the Gutenberg or 42-line Bible (Mainz: ca. 1455)–the first that is known for certain to have reached Scotland–is probably itself sufficient justification for his statement. Seymour de Ricci's 1911 *Catalogue raisonné des premières impressions de Mayence (1445-1467)* shows that Steuart owned more Mainz editions than any other Scottish collector. His patronage of the great Italian printer from Parma, Giambattista Bodoni, whose books were renowned for their fine typography, elegant bindings, and quality paper, further attests to Steuart's stature as a collector.

David Steuart was born in Perthshire, Scotland, 20 September 1747. He was the fifth and youngest son of John Steuart of Dalguise. The family could trace its ancestry from King Robert II (1316-1390), first of the Stewart (Stuart) sovereigns in Scotland and the grandson of King Robert I (Robert the Bruce). Little is known of Steuart's childhood, except that as a boy he wanted to go to India. An older brother, Hew, was stationed at the main settlement of the East India Company on the island of Sumatra. Hew wrote his father of the educational requirements his younger brother would need in order to prepare him for a post in India, and stated that sixteen would be a good age to come over. After Steuart finished his studies, he decided against going to India, probably as a result of parental concerns. In 1762 or 1763 he wrote his father:

> I am favored with your letter by which I see you are quite against my going to India, unless I should persist in my Resolution. I am very sensible of your Tenderness for me, & I should certainly show my self very unworthy of it if I was to do any thing that would give my Mother or you any uneasiness. I have therefore given over thoughts of it.

He chose commerce as a career and spent several years (from 1768 until 1775) on the Continent, in Barcelona, Roscoff, and Nantes. Apart from becoming prosperous, he cultivated a broad Continental outlook that helped shape the development of his tastes in books: naturally skilled in linguistics, he became fluent in Spanish and French; his interest in foreign literature and fine printing was likely fostered abroad; and it seems reasonable to assume he made the acquaintance of noted booksellers, especially in London. Though there is no evidence he began to assemble a library while away, he began to purchase many important books after returning to Scotland in 1775.

In 1776 he formed a trading company in Edinburgh with Robert Allan, but over time the business gradually moved into banking. According to S. G. Checkland in *Scottish Banking: A History, 1695–1973* (1975), the firm of "Allan & Steuart was the most important new private bank in the post-1772 period." In that same year Steuart married eighteen-year-old Anne Fordyce, who came from a large, talented, and prominent family (she had nineteen aunts and uncles, and she bore sixteen children during her marriage). Her grandfather, George Fordyce, was the eminent Provost of Aberdeen, and several of her uncles were prominent in their professions: David, an Aberdeen professor; James, a poet and author of sermons; and William, a renowned physician in London.

The 1780s were a time of great achievement and financial success for Steuart. Preferring the speculative side of business to banking, he made a great deal of money developing property and buying and selling farmland. In Edinburgh, his was the initiative that eventually led to the building of the second New Town. From 1780–1782 he served a standard two-year term as Lord Provost of Edinburgh (the official portrait owned by the city shows him with a book in his hand and books in the background). In 1785 he founded the Edinburgh chamber of commerce, served as president in 1787 and 1790 and was generally the driving force behind many of its activities. Probably most important to Steuart in this decade of prosperity was having the ability to expand and perfect his library. By the early 1780s he had become an accomplished and serious book collector. Correspondence flowed to and from prominent booksellers in Scotland and England, and in this decade and the next he spent large sums on books, a fact that later proved disastrous.

Besides being remembered as a book collector and civil servant, Steuart also deserves recognition as a humanitarian. His efforts to improve conditions for prisoners is evidenced by his serious attempts to build a new prison for Edinburgh. He published two pamphlets on the subject; *Plan for a General Bridewell* (Edinburgh, between October 1780 and July 1782) and with Archibald Cockburn *General Heads of a Plan for Erecting a New Prison and Bridewell in the City of Edinburgh* (Edinburgh, 1783). In these pamphlets he set forth his plans–which incorporated a radical, advanced design for a prison building–and appealed for funds. John Howard, the well-known reformer, visited the Edinburgh jail in 1782. Later, in his book *The State of the Prisons in England and Wales* (1784), he wrote of the conditions he found there: "I will only just mention the close confinement of poor criminals in the Tolbooth, the horrid cage in the room known by that name, and the severity practised there of chaining the condemned to an iron bar; because I found that the late Provost Mr. Steuart was using his best endeavours to get a new gaol built, which should be subject to better regulations and stand in a more airy situation." Steuart's new prison, however, was never built. Though greatly disappointed, his concern for the welfare of prisoners continued, and a few years later he offered his services again, though in a different way. In a letter to Scotland's political manager Henry Dundas in October 1790, he stated: "As it may be thought expedient to appoint a Comissary for the Prisoners of War in Scotland, I should willingly undertake the Duties of that office, which from a residence of several years in France & Spain and an intimate knowledge of the language and manners of these two nations, I flatter myself I could discharge entirely to the satisfaction of the Publick."

Steuart quit the banking firm of Allan and Steuart in 1790. He had suffered some financial setbacks but claimed at that time that his fortune was more than £20,000. The next decade brought additional financial problems for Steuart, and by the end of the century he was involved in bankruptcy proceedings (he was even jailed for a time by a Portuguese creditor for a debt of about £2,000). In 1801 his assets were sequestered by the court, and he had no choice but to send a major part of his library to auction. His business interests, while they prospered, had supported his collecting habits, but their decline brought about the dispersal of most of his books.

The primary source of information on Steuart's collection is the 1801 auction catalogue of his library: "A Catalogue of a Small but very Select Collection of Books, in which are to be Found some of the Finest

One of Steuart's bookplates

Specimens of Typography Extant, from the First Attempts on Wooden Blocks, until the Present Time." This catalogue is preserved in the New York Public Library and is believed to be the only extant copy. Although Steuart is not named anywhere in the catalogue as the owner of the books listed, it can be easily proved the collection was his. The National Library of Scotland has preserved the original front pastedown of *Real Academia Espanolano, Ortografia de la lengua Castellana,* sixth edition (Madrid, 1779), which shows one of Steuart's bookplates, as well as the lot number (10/62) for the 1801 sale. His skill as a bibliographer must account for the number of notes included in the descriptions of many of the lots. Elliot did not have access to some of the information noted–nor probably the expertise–to provide so detailed a bibliography. There can be little doubt that Steuart supplied the information. There are thirty-two references alone to Guillaume-François de Bure's seven-volume *Bibliographie instructive* (Paris, 1763–1768), thus providing precise identifications of a kind not seen even in London catalogues of the previous decade. The note on a Bodoni edition, which introduces a quotation from Bodoni with the words "the printer wrote a friend here above three years ago," almost certainly derives from Steuart, whether or not he himself is the "friend." In addition to providing additional proof that the books sold at the 1801 auction belonged to Steuart, the meticulous notes he supplied for the sale catalogue are useful in determining the characteristics of his collecting. Without these notes, nothing would be known of the importance to him of general condition, bindings, and other specific features–especially in the absence of the majority of Steuart's own copies of his books. The notes comment on original bindings: for example, *Diogenes Laertius Vitae philosophorum* (Paris, 1499), "wooden boards, original binding," and also on fine eighteenth-century bindings, such as the 1780 Madrid edition of Miguel de Cervantes's *Don Quixote,* described as "most superbly bound by Scott" (James Scott of Edinburgh).

Anonymity was only one of several unusual features of the sale. One of the "conditions of the sale" listed in the catalogue states that books could be previewed "on Friday the 15th, and Saturday the 16th May, and the mornings of the sale, excepting such articles as are marked *, which can be shewn only by particular application to Mr Elliot." Twenty-four books had the mark and were set aside. For the most part they are described as in perfect condition, though the books were not necessarily in their original bindings nor classified as scarce. No explanation is known as to why they were selected out, but it is quite possible they were simply some of Steuart's most beautiful books–those he could least bear seeing other people handle. A preview stipulation of that kind was not commonplace for an auction house, so there is little doubt that Steuart's influence was responsible for its inclusion. The wide distribution of the sale catalogue is another uncommon practice for an Edinburgh auction. The catalogue was made available, according to the title page, in London, Oxford, Cambridge, Glasgow, Aberdeen, Perth, Dundee, and Dublin. The explanation may be that collections such as Steuart's generated widespread interest and were usually sold in London–where he had sent some Bodoni editions to auction in 1798–but that the sequestration procedures prevented this in 1801. The exact date of the auction is not known for certain. Elliot first advertised a twelve-day sale for 9 March in the 28 February edition of the *Caledonian Mercury.* He then announced the postponement of the sale in the press on 2 March. It was readvertised on 25 April in the *Edinburgh Evening Courant* for Monday 18 May. Also, the title page of the catalogue states the date of the sale to be "On Monday, the 18th May, 1801, and the Eleven following Days, at Twelve o'clock." The sale may indeed have taken place on that date. An announcement appeared, however, in the 23 May edition of the *Caledonian Mercury* stating: "Mr. Elliot has been induced, from numerous and respectable applications, to alter the hour of sale of the valuable library now under his charge.–Therefore the books will be seen from 11 to 3, and the sale commence on Monday 25th May, and five succeeding evenings, at six o'clock." Since Elliot could not have been conducting two sales concurrently, it seems likely that the announcement does refer to Steuart's sale and represents yet another late change. If the auction was held on 25 May, the catalogue does not reflect the change. The shifting dates of the sale may be explained, perhaps, because Steuart, trying to avoid selling his books, petitioned the court to lift the sequestration order on his library. The biographical sketch accompanying Steuart's portrait in *A Series of Original Portraits and Caricature Etchings by the late John Kay* gives a brief account of what took place: "he exposed a part of his library to sale by auction . . . the prices not coming up to Mr. Steuart's expectation, the greater part were bought in, either by himself or his friends." The buying back of his own books reveals a desperate attempt by Steuart to prevent the wholesale disposal of the collection he so painstakingly and lovingly assembled. Over a six-day period, 958 lots were offered, though many items were not sold. How many are not known, but the Gutenberg, or 42-line, Bible, the *Biblia Latina,* and the *Brevarium Romanum* (Venice, 1473) were among them. Steuart had these in his possession after the auction and sold them privately some years later.

Steuart is not mentioned in Thomas F. Dibdin's book *Bibliomania: or Book madness; a Bibliographic Romance* (1809, 1842); even so, he exhibited most of the symptoms described. The first and second symptoms, those consisting of the acquisition of large or fine paper copies and uncut copies, are illustrated by Steuart's copies of Sir Robert Douglas's *Baronage of Scotland* (Edinburgh, 1798), "large paper, leaves uncut," and Warren Hastings's *A Narrative of the Insurrection* (Calcutta, 1782), "printed on silk paper, very scarce," not to mention the great attention given to these features in his correspondence with Bodoni. The third symptom, illustrated copies, is amply confirmed by the number of notes describing plates as "fine impressions" and "very early impressions," and of the *Don Quixote* bound by Scott it is said "This copy was selected with great care by the Count of Campomanes, and has the first set of the Plates." The fourth symptom Dibdin described as "a passion for a book which has any peculiarity about it, by . . . the foregoing methods of illustration–or which is remarkable for its size, beauty, and condition." Steuart was certainly proud of his copies of the Gutenberg Bible and Gulielmus Durandus' *Rationale divinorum officiorum* (Mainz, 1459), both, he noted, "in the most perfect preservation." The fifth symptom, copies printed on vellum, is very characteristic of Steuart, who owned vellum books such as the Jenson Breviary, which he described as "most beautifully printed on the finest vellum." He corresponded at great length with Bodoni about special printings on vellum. As for the sixth symptom, collecting first editions, many of Steuart's incunables and post-incunables are specified as first editions, so also, to name just a few examples, are copies of Samuel Johnson's *Dictionary,* George Buchanan's *History,* Pierre Corneille's *Théâtre,* Ben Jonson's *Works,* and John Milton's *Paradise Lost.* The seventh symptom, true editions, is concerned with variants and the collecting of rare states. The notes on copies of Elzevir editions of Virgil (1636) and Horace (1629) describe them as the genuine Elzevir editions. In fact, Dibdin lists this very Virgil edition among his examples under this symptom. The eighth and–in the 1809 edition of *Bibliomania*–the last symptom of bibliomania is the most famous one, which Dibdin describes as "at present the most powerful and prevailing": the passion for books printed in the black letter; for example, in Gothic rather than Roman type. Early Mainz books, of which Steuart seems to have been greatly enamored, were in black letter, but Dibdin had early English printing in mind. Steuart owned no William Caxtons, but there were two Wynkyn de Wordes included in the 1801 sale. One of them accounts for the reference to Caxton on the title page of the catalogue, the 1495 *Vitas patrum,* translated by Caxton and with Caxton's device but entirely printed by Worde.

The 1842 "new and improved edition" of Dibdin's *Bibliomania* added five further symptoms. The ninth and tenth are a passion for books printed for private distribution and books printed at a private press. Of the former there are no known examples, but the latter is present in Steuart's overwhelming enthusiasm for Bodoni's editions. The eleventh symptom, a desire for suppressed and condemned works, can be noted in his ownership of *Joyell Precios* (Barcelona, 1714), which "has passed through the hands of the Inquisition, as appears by the certificate of the Qualificator, who has erased many passages," and also of *Aventures de Télémaque* (Amsterdam, 1719), "with very curious cuts, which were prohibited in France." Symptoms twelve and thirteen–all the editions of a work and large and voluminous works–are hardly represented in Steuart's collection, and so are the two symptoms for which Steuart fails to qualify as a bibliomaniac.

Steuart's early books may not have included many English black-letter books, but he was an avid collector of incunables and post-incunables. Although there are only thirty-four incunables in the 1801 catalogue (William Hunter had 534, and George John, second Earl of Spencer, had many more), many important books, in addition to the early Mainz books, are here including the Latin edition of Breydenbach's *Peregri-*

natio; four books printed by Jenson at Venice, including Cornelius Nepos's *Vitae* (1471), Aulus Gellius's *Noctes Atticae* (1472), and the *Breviarium Romanum* (1478), on vellum; the first editions of the works of Hesiod and Theocritus, printed in one book (Venice: Aldus Manuzio, 1495); three books printed by Sweynheym and Pannartz at Rome, including the first editions of Ovid's *Metamorphoses* (1471) and his *Fasti* (1471); the first editions of Livy's *History* (1470) and Boccaccio's *De genealogia deorum* (1472), both printed at Venice by Vindelin de Spira; the first edition of Homer's works (Florence: Printer of Vergilius [C6061], not before 13 January 1489); and Thomas à Kempis's, *Sermones* (Harlem, 1472). This collection is of high quality, and one can appreciate why Steuart drew comparisons with the very best: on the Sweynheym and Pannartz edition of Ovid's *Fasti* the catalogue notation says "This edition is exceedingly scarce, there being only one other copy known in Britain–it is in the magnificent library of Earl Spencer."

Unlike Spencer and Hunter, Steuart possessed no blockbooks. The reference on the title page of the catalogue is explained by the inclusion of a copy of *Catalogue de la Bibliothèque du Duc de la Vallière* (Paris, 1783): "This book contains, among a great many other curiosities, an impression from two wooden blocks, part of the Catholicon which were in use about the beginning of the 15th century." He did not yield to Spencer and Hunter in owning the first books printed with moveable type, however. Steuart's library included the Gutenberg Bible; the second book printed with a date, the 1459 Mainz Durandus (sold in 1801, for £115; more recently at Sotheby's in New York, 12 December 1991); the 1472 Mainz Bible, a copy, as the catalogue description says, containing a duplicate leaf taken from the 1462 Mainz Bible; Peter Schöffer's 1463 edition of St. Augustine's *De civitate Dei;* and, apparently acquired after 1801, a vellum copy of the second-ever classical text–the 1466 Mainz second edition of Cicero's *De officiis.* The London-based Hunter had the first edition (1465) as well as the second edition (1466) of Cicero's *De officiis* and the 1472 Bible, but he did not have the Gutenberg Bible or the 1459 Durandus; nor did he have the 1462 Bible.

Steuart's copy of the 1472 Bible, as preserved in the National Library of Scotland, contains a letter dated 29 November 1798 from the leading London dealer of printed books and manuscripts, James Edwards. The letter reveals much about Steuart's bibliophilic tastes:

> You wished me to acquaint you whenever there was an opportunity of purchasing the Bible of 1462 by Fust & Schoeffer–There is now a copy of it *upon vellum* as clean as when it came out of the printer's hands–the vellum is also remarkably white & beautifull–it is bound in 2 vols red morocco German binding with heavy silver clasps & corners–in a very neat German Hand some former possessor has marked at the bottom of every page the contents or subject of the chapter in green & black ink and the chronological dates so that it is really a book of use as well as curiosity. It will be sold at Legh & Sothebys early next month with many other curious books and some duplicates of Lord Spencer's–I fancy it will go at between 200 & 300. If you dont chuse it for yourself it would be a treasure to your Advocates Library.

The sale took place on 20–21 December 1798, and the 1462 Bible was sold for £252. It was apparently not bought by Edwards, and so not by Steuart, though it is possible he may have been the underbidder.

Although the title page of the sale catalogue is much concerned with fifteenth- and early-sixteenth-century printers, it also refers to specimens of the finest typography of the "present time." Steuart collected books printed by the English printer John Baskerville (fifteen editions) and owned many other examples of fine, contemporary English and Scottish printing. What was exceptional, however, was for a collector in Scotland to be interested in the work of contemporary continental printers, most of all Bodoni. The 1801 catalogue contains no fewer than thirty-four Bodoni editions, and Steuart had probably sold some in London in December 1798, for Edwards's letter also states, "I think it would be a good opportunity to try a part of your Bodoni's books in the same sale–if you think so I will send *one* of each and desire Legh if there is still time to put them in," and the sale of 20–21 December 1798 also included some Bodoni editions. Steuart's holdings of Bodoni editions would merit comment even if he had come by them through normal commercial channels, but he enjoyed direct contact with the printer himself. Steuart initiated the correspondence between them in March 1791 because, he says, he found three productions of Bodoni's press so superior in their printing to anything that has previously appeared, he would like to acquire a couple of copies of all the books Bodoni is going to print, in the same taste and of the same beauty. When he adds that it does not matter what the book is, provided that the execution is as pretty as that of the three books he has seen, it becomes clear that the appeal of Bodoni's books lies in their design and printing. In the course of their

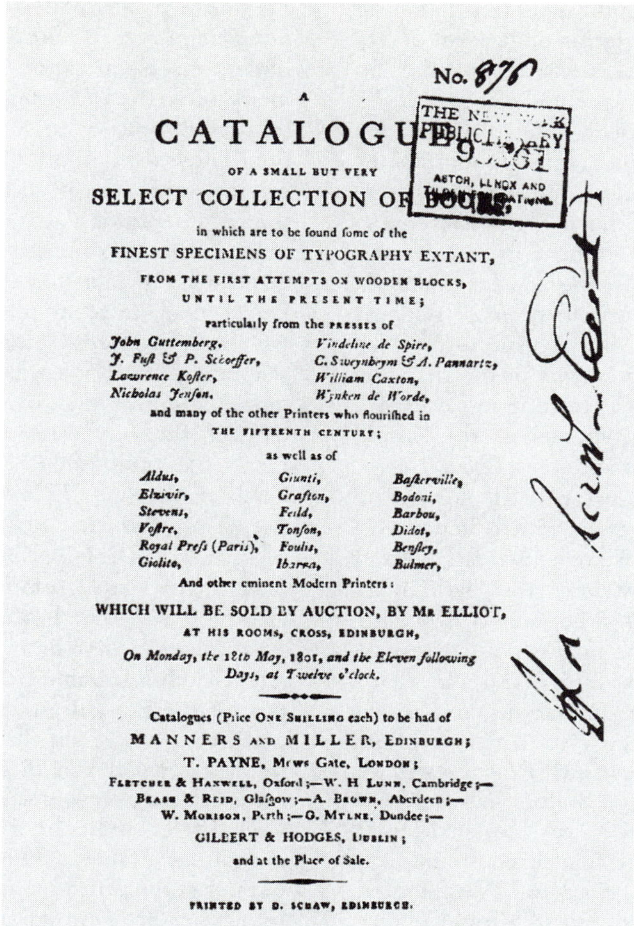

No. 876

A

CATALOGUE

OF A SMALL BUT VERY

SELECT COLLECTION OF BOOKS,

in which are to be found ſome of the

FINEST SPECIMENS OF TYPOGRAPHY EXTANT,

FROM THE FIRST ATTEMPTS ON WOODEN BLOCKS,

UNTIL THE PRESENT TIME;

particularly from the PRESSES of

John Guttemberg,	*Vindeline de Spire,*
J. Fuſt & P. Schoeffer,	*C. Sweynheym & A. Pannartz,*
Laurence Koſter,	*William Caxton,*
Nicholas Jenſon,	*Wynken de Worde,*

and many of the other Printers who flouriſhed in

THE FIFTEENTH CENTURY;

as well as of

Aldus,	*Giunti,*	*Baſkerville,*
Elzivir,	*Grafton,*	*Bodoni,*
Stevens,	*Feild,*	*Barbou,*
Voſtre,	*Tonſon,*	*Didot,*
Royal Preſs (Paris),	*Foulis,*	*Benſley,*
Giolito,	*Ibarra,*	*Bulmer,*

And other eminent Modern Printers:

WHICH WILL BE SOLD BY AUCTION, BY MR ELLIOT,

AT HIS ROOMS, CROSS, EDINBURGH,

On Monday, the 18th May, 1801, and the Eleven following Days, at Twelve o'clock.

Catalogues (Price ONE SHILLING each) to be had of

MANNERS AND MILLER, EDINBURGH;

T. PAYNE, Mews Gate, LONDON;

FLETCHER & HANWELL, Oxford;—W. H LUNN, Cambridge;—
BRASH & REID, Glaſgow;—A. BROWN, Aberdeen;—
W. MORISON, Perth;—G. MYLNE, Dundee;—

GILBERT & HODGES, DUBLIN;

and at the Place of Sale.

PRINTED BY D. SCHAW, EDINBURGH.

Cover for the only extant copy of the catalogue for the 1801 sale of Steuart's library (New York Public Library, Astor, Lenox and Tilden Foundations)

correspondence, Steuart's appetite for Bodoni editions became greater. On receiving a copy of Bodoni's Horace from Edwards, he was so pleased that he ordered ten ordinary paper—and two large paper—copies of the similar edition of Virgil, in preparation. Later, on receiving more details about the Virgil, he ordered three copies on Anonay paper and twelve on fine Parma paper. Bodoni normally made his editions available in different formats (usually folio and quarto), and on different papers (superior Annonay paper, other fine paper, and ordinary paper), and sometimes on vellum. Steuart normally wanted at least one copy of each state. Commercialism, not extreme bibliophily, was the reason he bought more copies than he wanted for his own use.

Steuart not only sought to import—whether for himself or for resale—everything Bodoni printed, he also tried to influence Bodoni's choice of titles to print. For example, he suggested a Spanish edition of *Don Quixote,* a French edition of *The Adventures of Gil Blas of Santillane* by Alain-René Lesage, Milton's *Paradise Lost,* and James Thomson's *The Seasons,* and of each he promised to take fifty copies as presents for his friends. The only one of these titles Bodoni printed was *The Seasons.* He dedicated his 1794 edition to Steuart and wrote a fulsome address in the dedication to show his gratitude for Steuart's patronage: "If I particularly wish immortality to any of my works it is to this, that the testimony of my respect and gratitude for a person of so much worth and eminence may be handed down to future ages, and remain a monument of my ardent wish to extend the fame of my Press, and of your Liberality in not confining your protection to the Printers of your own country."

The eight-year correspondence between the two men continued until January 1799 and is preserved in the Bodoni Archive at Parma. Their letters provide the background behind Bodoni's flattering tribute. The printer referred in his dedication of *The Seasons* to the many commissions given him by Steuart that enabled him to undertake work he would not otherwise have been able to afford. He needed the Scottish market because commissions from France, Spain, Germany, and England were hazardous and irregular, and his patron's encouragement was important because "tutto è in decadenza e langurre" (everything is in decline and languishing). The extent of Steuart's readiness to promote Bodoni's interests finds its climax in his suggestion–to which no response is preserved: "It seems to me that you would not fail to make a great fortune in London if you could decide to establish yourself there–I would help you with both my purse and my advice."

Bodoni's books were custom-made for bibliomaniacs, and all the passages in which Steuart discusses Bodoni's books are of great interest. A letter of special importance, however, was written to Bodoni on 18 January 1799. The date is of significance because this letter is the final extant correspondence from Steuart to Bodoni. Also, by 1799 Steuart's financial affairs were precarious, and he was on the verge of bankruptcy. Nonetheless, Stuart shows the strength of his acquisitive instincts in his postscript to the letter. He told Bodoni he would pay 25 guineas each for good copies of "Horace Mediol. 1470," in fact referring to the first printed edition of Horace (Venice, 1471–1472), and for "Virgile Ven. 1470," the second printed edition of Virgil (Venice, 1470). These editions were true bibliophilic treasures and were described in Dibdin's four-volume *Bibliotheca Spenceriana* (1814–1815) as "of such extraordinary rarity" and a "rare and truly beautiful impression."

Steuart survived his bankruptcy and the 1801 auction. He ran a wine merchant's business in Edinburgh until around 1815. During this period he sold privately to the Advocates' Library some of his most valuable books that had not been sold in 1801: the 42-line Bible for 150 guineas, in 1805 or 1806; in 1810, both the 1478 Jenson Breviary on vellum for 100 guineas, and the 1472 Mainz Bible for 50 guineas. These last two books, and presumably many others, were in his library in the summer of 1806 when a German traveler, Philip Andreas Nemnich, wrote of Steuart: "the man whom I had taken to be just a wine trader turned out to be a passionate collector of first editions, manuscripts, and fine works. His large collection of rare books from all parts of Europe amazed me."

In 1814 Steuart published *The Historical Remembrancer; or, The Epitome of Universal History*. Although the title page states "By David Steuart, Esq.," this has not generally been attributed to Steuart the bibliophile; but examination of the contents–there are many references to printers and engravers, and also to persons known to Steuart–leaves no reasonable doubt he is the author. The following, from a passage on the invention of printing, testifies to Steuart's interests: "Printing was early practised by the Chinese, in wooden blocks; this mode was invented at Strasburgh by Faust, 1440; and next it was carried so far as to make separate types of wood; metal types were used by John Gottenburgh, of Mentz, 1444, by whom the first book was printed, 1550–it is a Bible, in two volumes folio, of which there is a very perfect copy in the Advocates' Library, at Edinburgh, formerly the property of David Steuart, Esq., a merchant in that city." His pride in having owned the Gutenberg Bible is unmistakable.

In late 1814 his financial affairs seem to have been finally settled, and he left Edinburgh to live first at the home of Hugh Mair, husband to his daughter Anne; then in 1818 he moved to nearby Gretna Hall. After leaving Edinburgh he continued as joint secretary of the Edinburgh chamber of commerce, but it was not to his credit that he performed none of the duties associated with that post. He nonetheless received the whole salary attached to it, and even after 1818, contrived to receive this salary twelve months in advance. This misappropriation of funds did not go unnoticed, but any scandal was forestalled by his death, in Annan, on 19 May 1824. The body was brought back to Edinburgh for interment in St. Cuthbert's Churchyard, at the West End of Princes Street. The funeral monument can still be seen, with also the name of his wife, Anne, who died in 1828.

It was hardly to be expected that he would die with his financial affairs in order. The *Caledonian Mercury* of 3 June 1824 carries this announcement: "Notice to debtors and creditors. It is requested that all persons who may have claims against the late David Steuart Esq. merchant in, and formerly Lord Provost of Edinburgh, will lodge the same with William Dallas, writer to the Signet; and that all persons who stood indebted to Mr Steuart will make payment of his debts to Mr Dallas."

It seems likely that he was the "gentleman lately deceased" whose "private cellerage of superior and choice wines, curious old spirits, &c.," most of which had been "imported and bottled by the gentleman himself," were for sale by public auction on 23–24 June of that year. It is possible that some of his remaining books were similarly sold off. His eldest son, John Robert Steuart, the author of *A Description of some Ancient Monuments, with Inscriptions, still existing in*

Lydia and Phrygia (London, 1842), collected ancient coins, medals, and gems and owned books on numismatics, which were sold at Sotheby's 25 November 1846. This son may have had some of his father's books, but none have ever come to light with signatures of both father and son.

David Steuart was undoubtedly a significant book collector. In Edinburgh, where book collectors were usually lawyers, doctors, academics, or men of letters, his were an unusual mixture of bibliophilic and mercantile interests. Only a small proportion of the books he owned have been located.

References:

Barbara Traxler Brown, "The Northern Grand Tour: Contemporary Scottish Publishing and the Continental Tourist, 1760–1810," *Bibliotheck,* 20 (1995): 55–69;

Connie Byrom, "The Development of Edinburgh's Second New Town," *Book of the Old Edinburgh Club,* new series, 3 (1994): 37–61;

Sydney George Checkland, *Scottish Banking: A History, 1695–1973* (Glasgow: Collins, 1975);

Seymour de Ricci, *Catalogue raisonné des premières impressions de Mayence (1445–1467),* Veröffentlichungen der Gutenberg-Gesellschaft, 8–9 (Mainz: Gutenberg-Gesellschaft, 1911);

Thomas Frognall Dibdin, *Bibliomania: or Book madness; a Bibliographic Romance* (London: Longman, Hurst, Rees, & Orme, 1809);

Dibdin, *Bibliotheca Spenceriana,* 4 volumes (London: Longman, Hurst, Rees, Orme & Brown, 1814–1815), II: pp. 62–66 and 465–467;

Gilbert Goudie, *David Laing, LLD: A Memoir of his Life and Literary Work* (Edinburgh: For private circulation, 1913);

Brian Hillyard, "History of the National Library of Scotland's 42-line Bible," *Bibliotheck,* 12 (1985): 105–125;

Hillyard, "History of the National Library of Scotland's 42-line Bible: Addenda," *Bibliotheck,* 15 (1988 [published 1991]): 23–26;

Hillyard, "Parma and Edinburgh: Some Letters Relating to the European Booktrade at the End of the Eighteenth Century," *Bulletin du Bibliophile,* 2 (1992): 330–364;

John Howard, *The State of the Prisons in England and Wales,* third edition (Warrington: William Eyres, 1784), pp. 198–199;

A. Keith, "All for a Penny," *Aberdeen University Review,* 42 (1967–1968): 221–227;

Thomas A. Markus, "Buildings and the Ordering of Minds and Bodies," in *Philosophy and Science in the Scottish Enlightenment,* edited by P. Jones (Edinburgh: John Donald, 1988), pp. 169–224;

Philipp Andreas Nemnich, *Neueste Reise durch England Schottland, und Ireland [sic], hauptsächlich in Bezug auf Produkte, Fabriken und Handlung* (Tübingen: J. G. Cotta, 1807), pp. 499–500;

Henry Paton, ed., *A Series of Original Portraits and Caricature Etchings by the Late John Kay, Miniature Painter, Edinburgh; with Biographical Sketches and Illustrative Anecdotes,* 2 volumes, no. XVI (Edinburgh: H. Paton, 1837–1838), I: pp. 42–45;

Marguerite Wood, *The Lord Provosts of Edinburgh 1296 to 1932* (Edinburgh: Sir Thomas B. Whitson, 1932).

Papers:

Some of David Steuart's papers are in the Edinburgh City Archives and the Scottish Record Office.

Thomas Tanner

(25 January 1673/1674 – 14 December 1735)

David A. Stoker
University of Wales, Aberystwyth

and

Michelle Kingston
University of Wales, Aberystwyth

CATALOGUE: *Catalogi codicum manuscriptorum Bibliothecae Bodleianae, pars quarta : codices viri admodum reverendi Thomae Tanneri, Episcopi Asaphensis, complectens,* edited by Alfred Hackman (Oxford: Oxford University Press, 1860).

BOOKS: *Notitia Monastica; or, A Short History of the Religious Houses in England and Wales* (Oxford: Printed at the Theater, and are to be sold by A. & J. Churchill, London, 1695); revised and enlarged as *Notitia Monastica; or, An Account of all the Abbies, Priories, and Houses of Friers, heretofore in England and Wales; and also of all the Colleges and Hospitals founded before A.D. 1540,* edited by John Tanner (London: Printed by W. Bowyer for the Society for the Encouragement of Learning, 1744); revised and enlarged edition, edited by James Nasmith (Cambridge: J. Archdeacon, 1787);

Bibliotheca Britannica-Hibernica: sive, De scriptoribus, qui in Anglia, Scotia, et Hibernia ad sæculi XVII initium floruerunt, literarum juxta familiarum nomina dispositia commentarius: auctore . . . Thoma Tannero . . . qui non tantum scriptores quam plurinos, a Lelendo, Baleo, Pitseo, et aliis prætermissos, e codicibus mss. nunc primum in lucem protulit; sed notis etiam uberioribus, tum omissa supplevit, tum parum fideliter tradita correxit et illustravit. . . . , edited, with an introduction, by David Wilkins (London: Printed by G. Bowyer for the Society for the Encouragement of Learning, 1748).

Thomas Tanner (Christ Church, Oxford)

Thomas Tanner, bishop of St. Asaph and antiquarian, was both an important bibliographer of monastic writings and also the possessor of a large and valuable collection of printed books and manuscripts, particularly relating to the English Civil War. He published only one major work in his lifetime, but he left another in an advanced state of readiness at his death and made many contributions to other scholarly works, which sometimes went unacknowledged.

Thomas Tanner was born at Market Lavington, Wiltshire, on 25 January 1674, the eldest child and namesake of the vicar of that parish. He was initially educated at home by his father, and then spent two years at the Free School in Salisbury. Later he was a student at Queen's College, Oxford, matriculating in November of 1689 and graduating with a bachelor of arts degree in 1693. He received his master of arts degree in April 1696, and in November of that year he was elected fellow of All Souls College. In June 1710 he was awarded the degrees of bachelor of divinity and doctor of divinity. He was appointed Chapel Clerk of Queen's College in 1690 through the recommendation of Archbishop Thomas Lamplugh of York, an acquaintance of his father, and he was ordained deacon in December 1694. In January 1695, he was appointed chaplain of All Souls College by the warden, Leopold William Finch, thereby enabling him to remain in Oxford and continue his antiquarian researches. His fellowship of the following year enabled him to travel and visit collections of manuscripts, thereby laying the foundation for his later work, *Bibliotheca Britannica-Hibernica: sive, De scriptoribus, qui in Anglia, Scotia, et Hibernia ad sæculi XVII initium floruerunt, literarum juxta familiarum nomina disposita commentarius: auctore . . . Thoma Tannero . . . qui non tantum scriptores quam plurinos, a Lelendo, Baleo, Pitseo, et aliis prætermissos, e codicibus mss. nunc primum in lucem protulit; sed notis etiam uberioribus, tum omissa supplevit, tum parum fideliter tradita correxit et illustravit. . . .* (1748).

While at Queen's College, Tanner began his lifelong friendship and association with Edmund Gibson (later bishop of London), and the two men planned an edition of the works of the antiquary John Leland. In 1695, at the remarkably young age of twenty-one, he also published his *Notitia Monastica; or, A Short History of the Religious Houses in England and Wales,* which was dedicated to his friend and patron Leopold William Finch. The *Notitia Monastica* continues Roger Dodsworth and William Dugdale's *Monasticon Anglicanum* (3 volumes, 1655–1673), and provides the framework of Tanner's future studies. It included many references to manuscript works about monastic institutions and soon became a standard reference work. Apparently Tanner had prepared a second edition of *Notitia Monastica* by 1709, as copies of the original were then in great demand, but it was never published. After his death the papers relating to the new edition passed to his brother John, who subsequently edited and incorporated Tanner's notes to form an enlarged edition in 1744, which was financed by the Society for the Encouragement of Learning. A third edition, with many further additions, was edited by James Nasmith and published in 1787.

While at Oxford, Tanner had been involved in the compilation of Edward Bernard's index of historical writers, *Catalogi librorum manuscriptorum Angliæ et Hiberniæ in unum collecti* (1697), contributing materials gleaned from the collections of the seventeenth-century scholars Francis Junius and Richard James. This work probably caused him to broaden his plans for an edition of Leland's collection, which incorporated the writings of other medieval authors. Gibson had already suggested to him the idea behind the *Bibliotheca Britannica-Hibernica* in 1694, and they discussed the scope of this work throughout the year. Tanner envisaged a study in which "particular account will be given of the Lives & Writings of the Learned Men that either have been born or have had preferments in these three Kingdoms," and he published proposals around 1696. The *Bibliotheca Britannica-Hibernica* would include details of their lives, titles of their works, details of editions, and "if only in MSS. the Libraries or private Studies in wch they are preserv'd." Tanner later estimated that Leland had left out more than two thousand writers, and the accounts of some of those included were full of inaccuracies. The compilation of the *Bibliotheca Britannica-Hibernica* was therefore a massive undertaking, and gathering the necessary materials was to take him to various parts of the country.

The publication of the *Notitia Monastica* brought Tanner to the notice of John Moore, bishop of Norwich, who appointed him as his private chaplain and librarian in 1698. Tanner's friendship with Moore, whose daughter Rose he married in 1701, enabled him to make steady progress through the ecclesiastical hierarchy. He was appointed chancellor of the Norwich diocese in the same year, commissary of the archdeaconry of Norfolk in 1703, and commissary of the archdeaconry of Sudbury in 1707. Other preferments included the rectory of Thorpe Bishop's, near Norwich, in 1706, and the canonry of Ely Cathedral, bestowed by Moore, in 1713. This position he vacated in 1724, when he was installed as a canon of Christ Church, Oxford. In 1721 he became archdeacon of Norfolk and was elected as prolocutor of the Lower House of the Convocation in 1727. He was finally appointed bishop of St. Asaph in 1731 (consecrated at Lambeth, January 1732) and held the sinecure rectory of Llandrillo in Merionethshire, from 1733. From 1731 until his death he divided his time between London, Christ Church College in Oxford, and his diocese.

A bout of smallpox in 1699 that affected his eyesight for the remainder of that year, followed by his marriage and an increasing number of ecclesiastical commitments, impeded the progress of his work thereafter. However, he never ceased to collect historical materials, nor to assist others engaged upon antiquarian research; but the nonappearance of his great work during his lifetime was a subject of great disappointment to his contemporaries at Oxford, who had predicted an outstanding scholarly career. In the meantime, the assistant librarian at the Bodleian Library, Thomas Hearne, was taking an interest in Leland's collections, and in 1708, Anthony Hall, a fellow of Queen's College, was

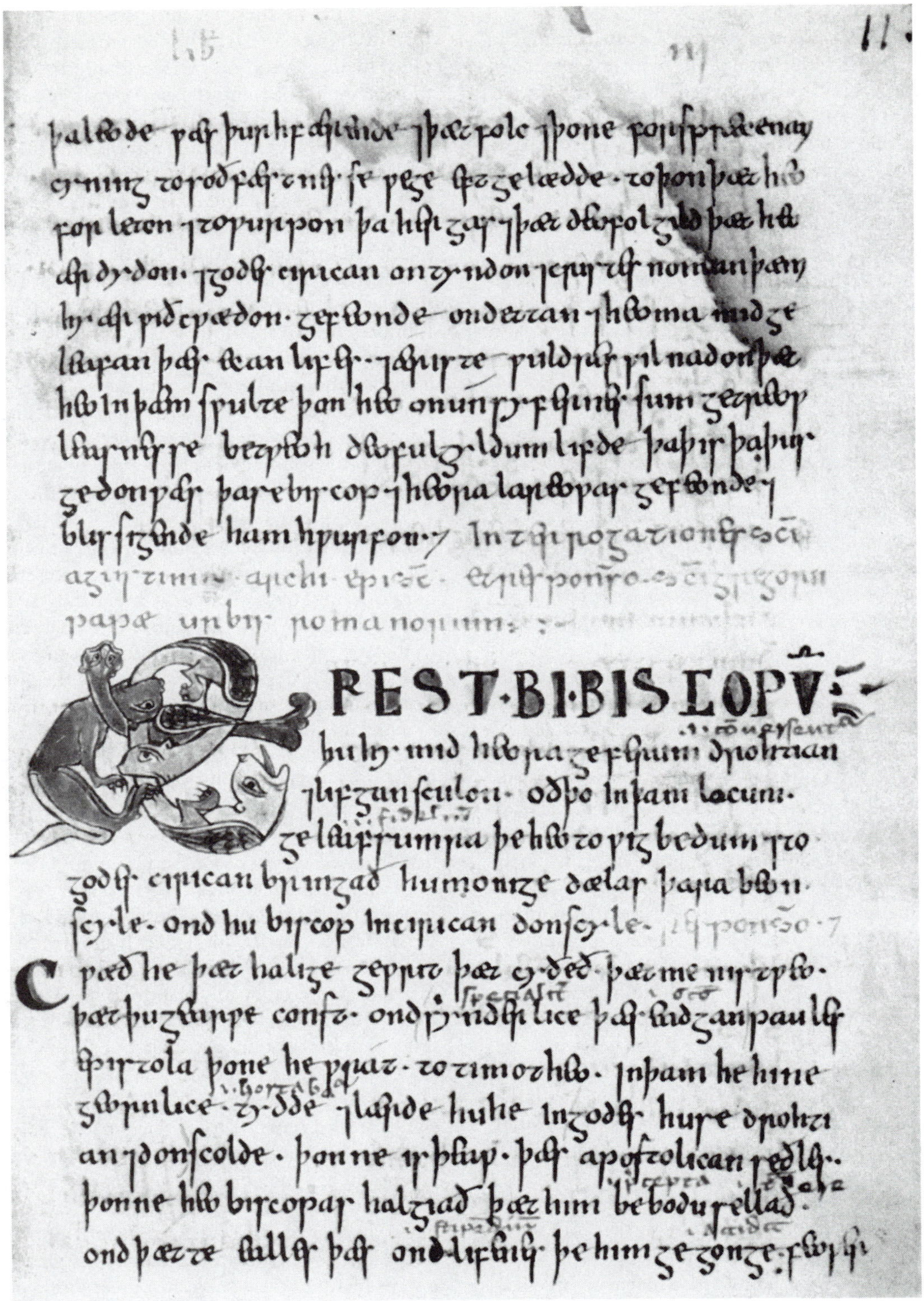

Page from the earliest Old English translation of Bede's Historia ecclesiastica gentis Anglorum, *written no later than the first decade of the tenth century, one of the manuscripts Tanner left to the Bodleian Library (MS Tanner 10, f. 58r, Bodleian Library, Oxford)*

commissioned to edit the works of Leland. Tanner's correspondence with Arthur Charlett, master of University College, shows that he was disappointed that he had not been consulted, particularly when Hall's edition appeared in 1709 and proved to be full of mistakes.

The *Bibliotheca Britannica-Hibernica,* edited by David Wilkins, was finally published in 1748, after Tanner's death. Printing expenses were paid for by the Society for the Encouragement of Learning, which had earlier paid for the second edition of Tanner's *Notitia Monastica.* The manuscripts relating to the work had been left to Tanner's brother John who together with Bishop Gibson had selected an appropriate antiquary to carry out the work. It remained a great work of authority for many years. Although the *Bibliotheca Britannica-Hibernica* was largely a revision of the work of earlier researchers, including Leland, Bale, and Pits, Tanner had examined all of the texts discussed within the work and made many additions and corrections, thus making much of the text his own.

In addition to his two works, Tanner was actively involved in several scholarly projects during his lifetime, notably those involving topographical history. In the opinion of David C. Douglas, in his *English Scholars 1660–1730* (1951), Tanner was convinced of the importance of local studies to any historical study attempting to show the development of medieval England. As a young man he therefore began collecting materials for a history of his native Wiltshire, the plans for which were announced as early as 1694. He was able to supply the Wiltshire additions for his friend Gibson's 1695 translation and enlargement of William Camden's Latin topographical history of the British Isles, *Britannia* (1586). However, according to a letter to Peter Le Neve in 1696, he postponed work pending the completion of his *Bibliotheca Britannica-Hibernica.* As the years passed Tanner continued to collect information, but his history was never completed. Ultimately the Wiltshire collections were bequeathed in part to the Bodleian Library, Oxford, in 1736, and the remainder to his son, who in turn gave them to the library in 1751. On the evidence of the collections, Douglas has suggested that Tanner's history of Wiltshire is "one of the great unwritten histories of England."

While in Norwich, Tanner became actively involved with the Norfolk antiquarian community and particularly with the antiquarian Le Neve, Norroy King-at-Arms, who during the first three decades of the eighteenth century was preparing his own topographical history of the county. In December of 1718, Tanner was elected a fellow of the Society of Antiquaries, of which Le Neve was then president. Writing to Le Neve in 1725, Tanner refers to himself, John Kirkpatrick, and Benjamin Mackerell as "a little Society of Icenian antiquaries [which] may attend you our President at Wichingham." Tanner contributed much material to Le Neve's collections and also used his influence to solicit the local clergy to assist Mackerell with the project. Upon Le Neve's death, Tanner was left as the joint literary executor, together with Thomas Martin, charged with arranging for the deposit of the collection in a suitable repository in Norwich. However, his subsequent installation to the bishopric of St. Asaph, together with Martin's unexpected marriage to Le Neve's widow, Frances, meant that the terms of the will were never carried out. Instead, Thomas Martin and his new wife moved the collection to their home at Palgrave, where it remained for the next forty years. Martin's action was undoubtedly instrumental in Tanner's decision to leave the bulk of his manuscripts to the Bodleian Library, rather than to combine them with the Le Neve collection in a public repository in Norwich, as he had originally planned.

Tanner did subsequently have the satisfaction of seeing the Le Neve Norfolk manuscripts used by the historian Francis Blomefield in preparing his five-volume *An Essay Towards a Topographical History of the County of Norfolk* (1735–1775) and was able to provide a great deal of encouragement to Blomefield. Although he had a dislike for honors, Tanner accepted Blomefield's request that his aid be acknowledged and wrote him agreeing to "submit to what I have refused many others, your dedicating it [the history] to me." Tanner's correspondence with the young historian illustrates his good nature and willingness to help others in their scholarly endeavors.

The other great project in which he was involved concerned the publication of a new edition of Anthony à Wood's biographical dictionary of notable Oxford graduates since 1500, *Athenæ Oxonienses* (2 volumes, 1691, 1692), an edition that included an additional five hundred lives together with Tanner's corrections. Tanner had been associated with Wood since 1694, and Wood, upon his deathbed in November 1695, bequeathed his manuscripts to Tanner to prepare them for publication. For years they remained unpublished, and rumors circulated that Tanner was keeping the papers for his *Bibliotheca Britannica-Hibernica.* In 1719, however, Jacob Tonson purchased the copyright of Wood's work; application was made to Tanner for the additional biographies, and they were incorporated into a new edition of Wood's work published under the editorship of Laurence Eachard in 1721. This edition was criticized by Hearne and others for several reasons, such as the delay in publication and the modifications made to Wood's memoirs.

The explanation for Tanner's reluctance to publish Wood's manuscript is revealed in his correspondence with Charlett; it was because of Wood's harsh criticisms of many at Oxford who were still living. Tanner had written Charlett at Oxford, asking his opinion on "whether one may now fairly take the liberty of leaving out now and then a hard word, or line," and Charlett had agreed that such slight omissions were reasonable. After publication Tanner regretted the fact that several scholars at Oxford were unhappy but defended his actions, arguing that he wanted to be honest to Wood's memory while not offending those still living: "I can truly say, there was not by one sentence, nor so much as one hard word added; and in the few things I omitted I believe neither Mr. Wood's memory nor truth will much suffer." Moreover, Tanner states in a 2 April 1722 letter to Arthur Charlett that the publisher never allowed him to obtain his own copy of the work: "Nor is this the only thing wherein the Booksellers have done unhandsomely by me."

Tanner also assisted John Ray in scientific works and Robert Hawes in his *History of Framlingham* in the County of Suffolk. Likewise, he provided materials to Samuel Knight for his lives of John Colet and Desiderius Erasmus, and he helped with the publication of the English works of Sir Henry Spelman in 1722. He also had a significant involvement in the preparation of *Concilia Magnae Britanniae et Hiberniae*. This four-volume work was eventually published in 1737 under the editorship of David Wilkins. Tanner's researches into the work of Spelman and the materials he contributed to William Wake's *State of the Church and Clergy of England* (1713) were of importance to Wilkins's compilation, and his advice was greatly appreciated.

Tanner's first wife died in 1706, at the age of twenty-five; their only child, Dorothy, had died in infancy. He subsequently married Frances, daughter of Jacob Preston, a citizen of London but from a Norfolk family, and had two daughters, who both died young, and a son, Thomas, who was later a canon of Canterbury Cathedral and rector of Hadleigh and Monk's Eleigh, Suffolk. Frances died in 1718 at the age of forty, leaving Tanner devastated. He remained unmarried for fifteen years, and apparently his widowed sister acted as housekeeper during this period. In May 1733 he married for a third time, to Elizabeth Scottowe, an heiress with a considerable fortune.

Tanner's correspondence with Blomefield shows that he was in poor health during the autumn of 1733, confined to his chamber for nearly three weeks. By early January 1734, he described himself in a letter to Blomefield as "scarce able to run about my study, take down and put up books as formerly" after a relapse of the fever.

Tanner died at Christ Church, Oxford, on 14 December 1735, after an illness of seven days. John Bowyer Nichols reports that there were rumors that his death had been due to taking one of "Dr. Ward's pills." He had taken one of them about two weeks before his illness, and it had appeared to work; but he took another just a week before his death, "which had so violent effect on his bowels as to produce the complaint of which he died." He is buried in the cathedral of Christ Church, and a monumental inscription was placed upon one of the cathedral pillars, written by Tanner himself. Part of this inscription (translated), reads:

> Whom late posterity shall justly praise,
> Skill'd in the monuments of antient days;
> Whose works more truly shall consign thy fame,
> Than Parian marble could preserve thy name.

His charitable bequests included £200 for Market Lavington, Wiltshire, the interest of which was to be used for teaching and other social functions, annually; £80 "to buy coats for poor men"; £100 to his college library, which was then being built; and £100 for poor vicarages. Tanner's collection of manuscripts and printed books was left to the Bodleian Library, the curators and library keeper being able to take whatever they wished to accept. Two years earlier he had given his collection of coins to the library. His papers relating to the *Notitia Monastica* and his *Bibliotheca Britannica-Hibernica* were claimed by his brother, John Tanner, and his sermon notes and other private papers and correspondence were ordered to be burned by his executor.

Tanner is today best remembered for his collections of manuscripts and printed books in the Bodleian Library. These include 467 volumes of his papers, charters, rolls, and correspondence, many of which had been collected by Archbishop Sancroft and were related to the English Civil War period, and more than 900 volumes of printed books. Some of these are in poor condition, having been damaged during transit between Norwich and Oxford. In December 1731 a barge transporting them sank at Bensington Lock, near Wallingford, and his books and papers were submerged for twenty hours. The effects of the sinking are still evident amongst many of them, although there were exaggerated reports about their condition, such as a note in James Peller Malcolm's edition of *Letters Between the Rev. James Granger . . . and Many of the Most Eminent Literary Men of His Time* (1805), which described the books as "crumbling into pieces on the slightest touch." However, certain rare volumes probably did perish, including a copy of *The Children of the Chapel Stript and Whipt* that, according to Thomas Warton, was among Tanner's books but never appeared in the Bodleian catalogue.

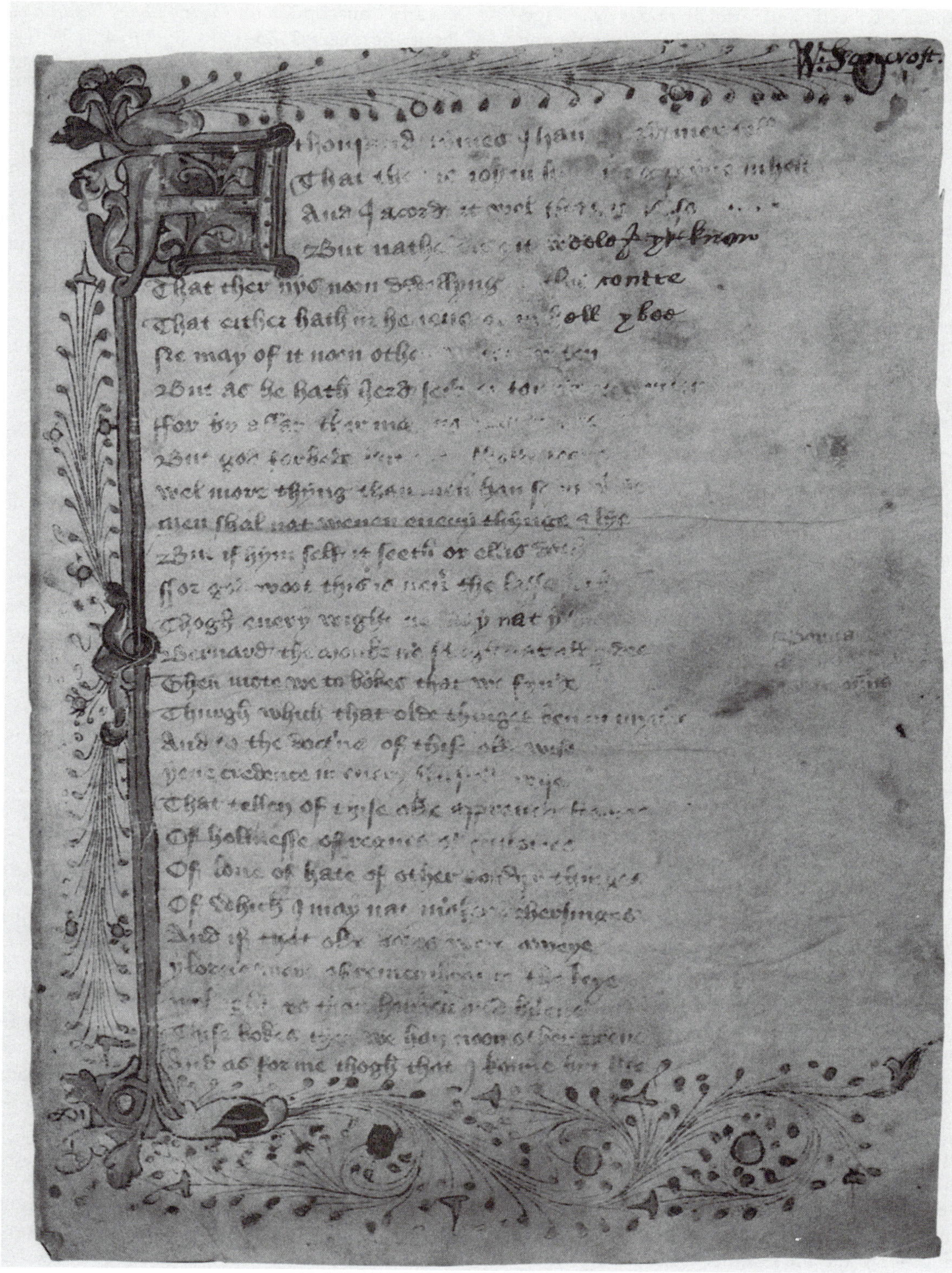

First page of the most important literary manuscript in Tanner's library, a mid-fifteenth-century collection of poems that includes works by Geoffrey Chaucer and John Lydgate (MS Tanner 346, f. 1r, Bodleian Library, Oxford)

Tanner's collection of printed books was especially strong in rare examples of English fifteenth- and early-sixteenth-century printing. Tanner's association with Bishop Moore was beneficial to his book-collecting activities. Moore had been a great book collector, and following his death in 1714, his library was purchased by George I and presented to Cambridge University Library. In common with other scholars of his time many of the books in Tanner's study had been borrowed from others and not returned. William Dunn Macray has noted that four volumes from Moore's library, which were found in Tanner's collection upon his death were returned to Cambridge in 1741. Indeed, several of the books bequeathed to the Bodleian had subsequently to be returned to their rightful owners, and some of the rolls in Tanner's collection were later found to have been borrowed from the archives of Ely Cathedral.

Many of the surviving books were, according to Macray, of "the utmost rarity in early English black-leather divinity." One such was an edition of the *Pore Helpe,* and another volume includes two tracts printed by William Caxton and others by Wynkyn de Worde and Gerard Leeu. Unfortunately, in about 1820 all the books in Tanner's collection were rebound in dark green calf, thereby removing the flyleaves and destroying valuable information about their provenance. Tanner also possessed an edition of Sallust's writing printed at Lyons in 1519 by John Marion. This copy once belonged to the library of King Henry VIII, and the interlining within the text could be in the king's handwriting. Moreover, Macray has suggested that the volume "may have been one of the school-books of Princess Mary." It was later given to the Bodleian Library by William Williams of Brasenose College.

As a young man Tanner began to collect autograph letters, some of which may have belonged to church archives. His collection increased considerably in 1718 when he purchased part of John Nalson's collection, and then in 1724 he bought most of the surviving papers of Archbishop William Sancroft from the London bookseller Christopher Bateman for 80 guineas. After Tanner's death, a claim was made upon some of the Nalson papers by the archbishop's grandson in 1737; but John Tanner argued that his brother had bought them at Ely, and the matter was dropped.

One of the most valuable parts of his manuscript collection was the historical papers relating to the late sixteenth century and the seventeenth century from the collections of Sancroft, and Nalson, who had taken many of these papers, including the correspondence of the leading figures in the civil war–Oliver Cromwell, Charles I, and Prince Rupert–from the clerk of Parliament's office. Other treasures in the collection included an early transcription of *The Itinerary of John Leland* in or about the years 1535–1543 by the Elizabethan antiquary, John Stowe, which is imperfect, but is nevertheless the best of the five manuscripts in the library, according to Macray. Tanner also owned a version of St. Bede's *Historia ecclesiastica gentis Anglorum* with medieval binding leaves, which is the earliest of the Old English manuscripts of the work. According to Janet Bately, it was probably produced no later than the first decade of the tenth century. The most important literary text is a manuscript anthology of poetry relating to courtly and chivalric experience that includes four booklets written in the mid-fifteenth century consisting of works by Geoffrey Chaucer and John Lydgate as well as the works of unknown poets; the manuscript contains one of the earliest collections of Chaucer's minor poems.

Another important part of the collection consists of seventeenth-century diocesan manuscripts, with a particularly large collection relating to the Norwich diocese; however, most of his collections relating to the ecclesiastical history of Norfolk were exempted from the bequest to the Bodleian. They were rather to be kept within the Diocesan Registrar's office unless, Tanner wrote Blomefield, a scholar were willing to finish the work and "let the profitt of my . . . pains go to the Society for Clergyman's Widows."

More than two thousand charters and rolls primarily concerned with Norfolk and Suffolk also went to the Bodleian. They included documents from the Abbies of St. Benet of Holm and St. John's at Colchester, some of which had previously been in Le Neve's collections. The collection also contained correspondence and papers of individual scholars such as Tanner's friends Charlett and Moore, and some of the manuscripts from Wood's collection, though the manuscript of the additions to *Athenæ Oxoniensis* was never deposited.

After the manuscripts arrived at the Bodleian Library in 1736, they were sorted and bound. In 1741 Thomas Toynbee, an undergraduate at Balliol, was commissioned to undertake the task of cataloguing the manuscripts, which consisted of merely placing them in chronological order without regard to content. Even before this work was finished, the manuscripts were consulted by Richard Rawlinson–who also collected Sancroft manuscripts. By the 1740s, the manuscripts were becoming widely known and used, according to Sir Edmund Craster. A catalogue of the collection was published by Alfred Hackman as the fourth volume of the general catalogue of manuscripts in 1860. It includes brief descriptions of the volumes within the main section, and the full index includes details of all letters and papers. The printed books were received too late to be included in the general catalogue of 1738. By the 1750s the books had shelfmarks, but it appears that as late as 1780, many were still in a cramped, unclassified, uncatalogued, and dusty state.

Tanner was a well-liked man who had a considerable influence upon his generation as a scholar. This influence resulted from not only his hard work, but also his good nature, avoidance of political argument, and the friendly and helpful advice he gave to colleagues and other scholars. Tanner's correspondence shows his kindness and willingness to assist younger scholars. He helped a scholar of humble origins find a suitable appointment and also aided well-known scholars such as Blomefield. According to William T. Davies, he has suffered "from the oblivion which usually befalls men who collect but do not interpret facts," and his name is now remembered primarily through his association with the manuscripts that he bequeathed to the Bodleian Library.

References:

Janet Bately, ed., *The Tanner Bede: The Old English Version of Bede's Historia Ecclesiastica, Oxford Bodleian Library Tanner 10, Together with the Mediaeval Binding Leaves, Oxford Bodleian Library Tanner 10* and the Domitian Extracts, London British Library Cotton Domitian a Ix Fol. 11,* Early English Manuscripts in Facsimile, no. 24 (Copenhagen: Rosenkilde & Bagger, 1992);

John Chambers, *A General History of the County of Norfolk,* 2 volumes (Norwich, 1829);

Sir Edmund Craster, ed., *History of the Bodleian Library 1845–1945* (Oxford: Clarendon Press, 1952);

William T. Davies, "Thomas Tanner and His Bibliotheca," *Times Literary Supplement* (14 December 1935): 856;

David C. Douglas, *English Scholars 1660–1730,* second edition (Westport, Conn.: Greenwood Press, 1951);

P. L. Heyworth, ed., *Letters of Humfrey Wanley: Palaeographer, Anglo-Saxonist, Librarian 1672–1726* (Oxford: Clarendon Press, 1989);

R. W. Hunt, "Tanner's *Bibliotheca Britannico-Hibernica,*" *Bodleian Library Record,* 2 (1949): 249–258;

William Dunn Macray, *Annals of the Bodleian Library Oxford,* second edition (Oxford: Clarendon Press, 1890);

Falconer Madan, *Collections Received During the 18th Century,* in his *A Summary Catalogue of the Western Manuscripts in the Bodleian Library at Oxford,* volume 3 (Oxford: Clarendon Press, 1895);

Manuscript Tanner 346: A Facsimile, introduction by Pamela Robinson (Norman, Okla.: Pilgrim Books, 1988);

John Bowyer Nichols, ed., *Illustrations of the Literary History of the Eighteenth Century, Consisting of Authentic Memoirs and Original Letters of Eminent Persons,* 8 volumes (London: J. B. Nichols, 1858; republished, New York: AMS Press, 1966);

Nichols, ed., *Literary Anecdotes of the Eighteenth Century, Comprising Biographical Memoirs of William Bowyer,* 9 volumes (London: Nichols, Son & Bentley, 1813; republished, New York: AMS Press, 1966);

M. J. Sommerlad, "The Historical and Antiquarian Interests of Thomas Tanner," dissertation, University of Oxford, 1962;

David A. Stoker, "Benjamin Mackerell, Antiquary, Librarian, and Plagiarist," *Norfolk Archæology,* 42 (1993–1994): 1–12;

Stoker, ed., *The Correspondence of the Reverend Francis Blomefield (1705–52)* (London: Bibliographical Society, 1992);

Stoker, "The Ill-gotten Library of 'Honest' Tom Martin," in *Property of a Gentleman: The Formation, Organisation, and Dispersal of the Private Library 1620–1920,* edited by Robin Myers and Michael Harris (Winchester: St. Paul's Bibliographies, 1991), pp. 90–111.

George Thomason

(1602? - 1666)

David A. Stoker and Michelle Kingston
University of Wales, Aberystwyth

CATALOGUES: *Catalogue librorum diversis Italiae locis emptorum, anno Dom. 1647, a Georgio Thomasono, Bibliopola Londinensi, apud quem, in Caemiterio D. Pauli ad insigne Rosae coronatae, prostant venales. (Biblia . . . quibus textus originales totius Scripturae sacrae, quorum para in editione Complutensi, deinde in Antverpiensi regiis sumptibus extat, nunc integri, ex manuscriptis toto fere orbe quaesitis exemplaribus, exhibentur.)* (London, 1647);

British Museum, *Catalogue of Pamphlets, Books, Newspapers, and Manuscripts relating to the Civil War, the Commonwealth, and Restoration, collected by George Thomason, 1640–1661,* 2 volumes, preface by G. K. Fortescue (London, 1908).

George Thomason was a bookseller and publisher who is remembered almost entirely because of the famous collection he made of tracts, newspapers, and other ephemeral materials during the civil war period. In the words of a descendant, Gordon Thomasson, this famous bookseller "both made and preserved history, having a significant personal role in religion and politics in London throughout the period, while conscientiously documenting and preserving its history at great effort, risk, and expense to himself." Relatively few details of his personal life are known, and no publications by him survive; yet, his name is held in gratitude and esteem by all historians of those turbulent years.

The exact date of George Thomason's birth is not known. He was probably born in or before the year 1602, apparently the son of George Thomason, a farmer. Different sources for his life suggest different birth places–either at Sudlow in Cheshire or Westham in Sussex. The most recent source points out that Thomason's adopted trademark for his bookselling business (a rose and a crown) forms part of the arms of the county of Sussex. However, the Stationer's Registers describe him as having come from Gostlowe, Cheshire. The bookseller had at least two brothers, William and Roger, but other siblings are unknown.

Thomason was apprenticed to Henry Fetherstone, a London bookseller and publisher, at the sign of the Rose in St. Paul's churchyard, from September 1617 to June 1626 and became a freeman of the Stationers' Company on 5 June 1626. About 1631 he married Catharine Hutton, his master's niece and ward, who was living as a member of his family. Catharine was unusually well educated and well read, having been left a large library as part of her inheritance. John Milton was a family friend, who later wrote his Sonnet XIV to her memory. The couple spent most of their married life residing in St. Paul's churchyard in London, where Thomason conducted his bookselling business.

They had at least nine children, seven of whom were still alive when their mother died in 1646. The eldest child, also named George, received a classical education and graduated from Queen's College, Oxford, in 1655; he was later rector of Halston, and became prebendary of Lincoln in 1683. Catharine was buried on 12 December 1646 in the South aisle of St. Dunstan's church, Fleet Street. Thomason never remarried, and his will of 1664 spoke of his "late dear and only wife."

There are no surviving portraits or other illustrations of the bookseller. However, in a note written in May 1660, he refers to himself as one of the ten "most grave, tall, & comely personages, well horsed and in their best array, or furniture of velvet plush or sattin & Chaine of Gold" attending the Lord Mayor's reception for the restored King Charles II.

There is contradictory evidence concerning Thomason's early career as a bookseller and regarding his relationships with his former master and various other members of the trade. Thomason's name begins to appear in the Stationers' Register as a copyright owner in November 1627, and he appears to have been in partnership with Octavian Pulleyn, although under Fetherstone's sign of the Rose, from 1637 until 1643. The partnership was dissolved in 1643, and the premises were apparently retained by Pulleyn. In the same year Thomason moved and became the sole owner of a new establishment, with the sign of the Rose and Crown, in St. Paul's churchyard, and his publishing career began in earnest. The Rose and Crown emblem subsequently figured in many of the books he published. Henry Fetherstone died in 1647, and his copyrights, stock, and the business probably passed to Thomason. However, throughout his career, Thomason's principal business was that of a retail bookseller.

There are many surviving records of Thomason as a supplier of books to the libraries of the universities of Oxford and Cambridge, to English Parliament, and to the Norwich Public Library. He was also a regular attender at the Frankfurt Book Fair and had close links with the Continental book trade. He is known to have visited the Low Countries, Germany, Italy, and Switzerland, and as an importer of books, he was fortunate in his training by Fetherstone, who (according to Gordon C. Thomasson) frequently traveled abroad and "pioneered the systematic importation and sale of foreign books through published catalogs."

During the late 1630s and the early 1640s most purchases made by the Bodleian Library were made from Thomason and Pulleyn, and in 1650 it appears that Thomason was still a regular supplier to Oxford, as in that year (according to William Dunn Macray) books to the value of £69. 10s. were bought from him. He is also well known for his part in the sale of nearly two thousand sixteenth-century and early-seventeenth-century books and manuscripts, many of which were in oriental languages. These books and manuscripts were collected during a trip to Italy following his wife's death and were offered for sale in a printed catalogue dated 21 May 1647. Thomason described the collection in his preface as "more Rabbinical and Oriental books and manuscripts than have ever before been collected together, and in addition to these the principal educational and medical writers and the chief authorities on mathematics, history and languages." Parliament authorized their purchase, and the works were transported to Cambridge University, where they formed the basis for the Oriental Collection. There is some question, however, as to whether the bookseller ever received payment for them.

Thomason's publishing activities were on a somewhat less ambitious scale. Between 1636 and 1639 he published six titles together with Pulleyn, a period that was followed by an apparent hiatus of about five years. However, in 1645 the bookseller was implicated in the anonymous publication of David Buchanan's *Truth's Manifest,* a work that attacked Parliament and was later condemned to be burned by the hangman. After publishing Philip Freher's *A Treatise Touching the Peace of the Church* in the following year, Thomason published nothing until 1659, when the first part of John Rushworth's historical collections appeared under the Rose and Crown imprint. He did, though, later acquire the copyrights of Robert Bostock in December 1656.

Thomason took an active role in the Stationers' Company throughout his working life, and his interest

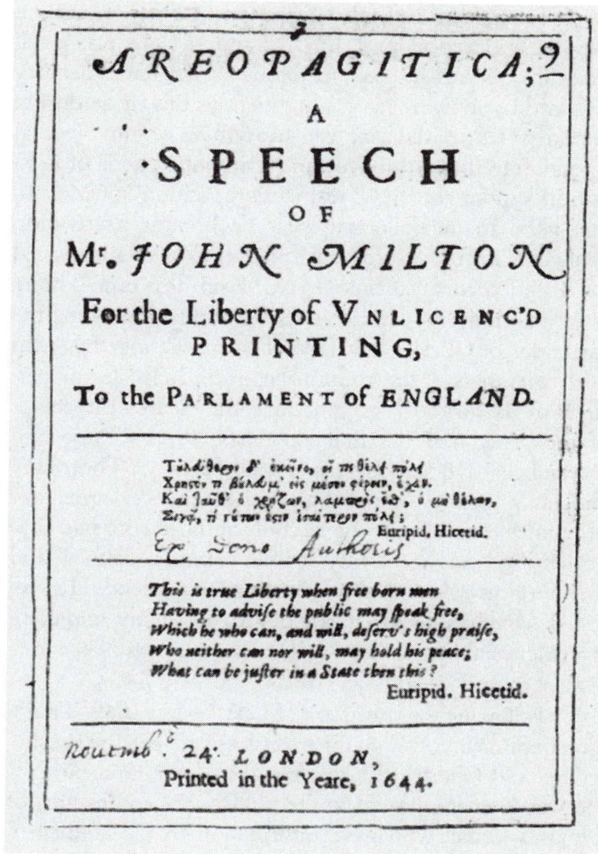

AREOPAGITICA;

A

SPEECH

OF

Mr. JOHN MILTON

For the Liberty of VNLICENC'D PRINTING,

To the PARLAMENT of ENGLAND.

Τοὐλεύθερον δ' ἐκεῖνο, εἴ τις θέλει πόλει
Χρηστόν τι βούλευμ' εἰς μέσον φέρειν, ἔχων.
Καὶ ταῦθ' ὁ χρῄζων, λαμπρὸς ἔσθ', ὁ μὴ θέλων,
Σιγᾷ, τί τούτων ἐστὶν ἰσαίτερον πόλει;

Euripid. Hicetid.

Ex Dono Authoris

This is true Liberty when free born men
Having to advise the public may speak free,
Which he who can, and will, deserv's high praise,
Who neither can nor will, may hold his peace;
What can be juster in a State then this?

Euripid. Hicetid.

Novemb: 24. LONDON,
Printed in the Yeare, 1644.

Title page for George Thomason's copy of John Milton's famous speech defending the freedom of the press (C.55.c.22[9], British Library)

probably originates from his apprenticeship with Fetherstone, who served as warden from 1635 to 1639 and master from 1641. In 1641 Thomason became active in the financial administration of the company, and in 1645 he began to play a more controversial role, together with Fetherstone, by arguing for democratic reforms within the election process. In 1651 Thomason served as an assistant warden of the company, and he became a junior warden in July 1657. In 1661 he was senior warden and played an active role in resettling the company's business following the Restoration.

George and Catharine Thomason were Presbyterians; according to Thomasson, they were "members of very select religious, literary and intellectual communities," and their friends included Milton, William Prynne, the politician Henry Parker, and the historian Rushworth. Thomason also had many close friends among the clergy–such as Edmund Calamy, leader of the Presbyterians in Parliament from 1643 through 1653; Edward Reynolds, later bishop of Norwich; and Thomas Lockey, keeper of the Bodleian Library.

Thomason was also active in politics at both a national and a local level. In 1642 and 1643 he was a collector for his parish of subscriptions for the Parliamentary Army, thus showing his commitment to this cause during the early years of the civil war. In 1646 he was involved in a petition to the lord mayor and common council of London in support of the "Presbyterian Petition" of May of that year. In the following year he became a common councillor for the Ward of Faringdon Within and served for the succeeding turbulent year. From this time Thomason was noticeably more active politically. Following the surrender of Charles I in 1647, Thomason, together with other members of the common council, called for a "personal treaty" with the king because they feared the power of the army and the independents. "Pride's Purge" of December 1648 served to justify the fears of Thomason and his associates; it was followed by the Parliamentary ordinance that forbade the election of those who had supported the "personal treaty" to the common council, and therefore his role as a councillor came to an end. He protested actively at the exclusion of the councillors, and there is evidence that he was involved in a series of protests against these measures.

Following the execution of Charles I in 1649, Thomason became involved in the overtures between the Presbyterians and Charles II known as the "Love Conspiracy." He was later implicated in the plot by the confessions of Thomas Coke, who gave information to the council of state implying that Thomason was a leading player, "delivering letters written by Charles II from Breda to the London Presbyterian Ministers." Thomason was arrested in April 1651 and spent several weeks in prison at Whitehall before being bailed out for £1000 at the end of May. His estate had been seized in April but was restored to him in June. Ultimately he was not prosecuted nor called as a witness in the trial of Christopher Love.

During the 1650s Thomason suffered bouts of illness, possibly due to the effects of his time in prison, and after 1651 he appears to have become politically inactive. Political differences between Milton and Thomason had been shown in 1649 by Milton's *The Tenure of Kings and Magistrates,* which was an indictment of the Presbyterians, but Milton and Thomason were in contact again by 1654, and Milton may have interceded on behalf of the bookseller during his imprisonment.

Thomason died at Mickleham in Surrey early in 1666 and was buried near his wife in St. Dunstan's–according to the register, on 13 February 1666. However, according to Richard Smyth, Thomason was "buried out of Stationers' Hall (a poore man)" on 10 April of that year. His will, drawn up in 1664, indicates Thomason was quite prosperous, with legacies to all of his children, servants, the Stationers' and the Haberdashers' Companies, and St. Paul's and St. Dunstan's. By the time of his death, however, he was clearly in much reduced circumstances, as is indicated by later codicils. These losses may have resulted from his political activities and also from the expense of forming his famous collection, from which he received no personal gain. In September 1666 the Fire of London destroyed the area around St. Paul's, including the Rose and Crown. The Thomason collection, however, had been moved to Oxford soon after Thomason's death. One of his apprentices, James Allesty, later appears to have taken over the business from Henry Thomason, George's son, in the late 1660s.

The remarkable collection of printed tracts and manuscripts, amassed by Thomason between 1640 and 1661, is the reason his name is so well known today. According to G. K. Fortescue, "On 3rd November 1640 the Long Parliament met; and Thomason who had already accumulated a few books published during the course of the year, systematically began his collection, acquiring, either by purchase or occasionally by presentation, every book, pamphlet and newspaper issued in London, and as many as he could obtain from the provinces or abroad."

In the opinion of Falconer Madan, Thomason's "achievement is unparalleled in its kind." The collection was described in an early-eighteenth-century manuscript prospectus as

> An exact Collection of all Books & pamphlets concerning the Revolution in England print'd from the beginning of the year 1640 to ye Coronation of King Charles ye Second 1661 with several Manuscripts relating to those times never print'd, the Whole contain'g 30,000 Books & Tracts all uniformly bound in above 2000 Volumes markt in a most exact manner, & so carefully kept, that they have received no Damage. The Catalogues of them are 12 Volumes in Folio, the whole so digested and the Volumes so markt & Number'd, that ye least Treatise may be readyly found, & ye Day, on wch they came out wrott on most of them.

When the collection was eventually catalogued by the British Museum in 1908, however, there were 22,255 items in 2,008 volumes.

The range of subjects and types of material collected was enormous; it encompassed subjects such as Parliamentary Acts, works by Milton, sermons, correspondence, and books on subjects from medicine to witchcraft, to the first edition of Isaac Walton's *Compleat Angler*. The collection is principally concerned, however, with political and religious tracts and has been the mainstay of all British historical writing relating to this period. According to Thomas Carlyle, Thomason's collection included "The whole secret of the seventeenth century." The most remarkable aspect of the collection was Thomason's foresight in forming such a collection at this time. He has been

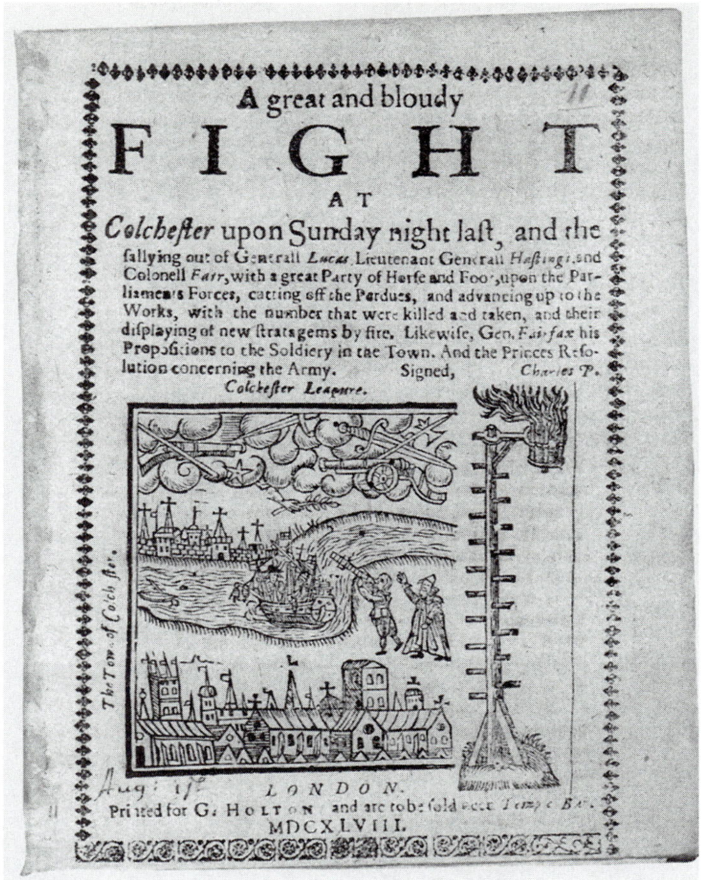
A great and bloudy
FIGHT
AT
Colcheſter upon Sunday night laſt, and the ſallying out of Generall Lucas, Lieutenant Generall Haſtings, and Colonell Farr, with a great Party of Horſe and Foot, upon the Parliaments Forces, cutting off the Perdues, and advancing up to the Works, with the number that were killed and taken, and their diſplaying of new ſtratagems by fire. Likewiſe, Gen. Fairfax his Propoſitions to the Soldiery in the Town. And the Princes Reſolution concerning the Army. Signed, Charles P.

LONDON.
Printed for G. Holton and are to be ſold neer Temple Bar.
MDCXLVIII.

Cover for an account of an incident during the 1648 siege of Colchester by the Parliamentary Army, a news pamphlet in Thomason's collection of tracts from the period of the English Civil Wars (E.456[11], British Library)

described as "a man of historical prescience and imagination, who could grasp at once the full significance of the Long Parliament." He was also in an ideal position to collect the materials, particularly during 1647–1648 when he served as a common councillor and was in receipt of a huge number of petitions and tracts that appeared at this time supporting the "personal treaty with the King." However, the collection reflects all shades of political and religious opinion at the time; the only significant weakness is the incomplete collection of "Quaker tracts" dating from 1653. This omission may have resulted from their number or, as Fortescue implies, from Thomason's viewing the movement with disdain.

Thomason began his collecting activities at a time when the strict system of censorship and controls on publication was beginning to break down and the number of titles produced was rapidly increasing. During the period in which he was collecting, only approximately 6,300 publications were legally registered, whereas four times this number remain in his collection. Ironically, while Thomason was warden of the Stationers' Company, he was collecting and preserving materials that he was required to censor. It was a dangerous time, and the bookseller undertook considerable risks both financially and politically in forming and preserving his collection for twenty years in such precarious circumstances.

The collection is remarkably comprehensive as a representation of the material circulating in London, although inevitably it is less complete for works published in the provinces, Ireland, or Scotland; he often had to rely upon reprints. He was also most systematic in his collecting habits. Each item was classified, numbered, and put into one of five categories according to size and date, and from 1642 onward Thomason made a manuscript note of the date of publication or acquisition on the title pages. These dates have proved to be invaluable in establishing the chronology of events during this period. His marginal notes on some acquisitions also both identify anonymous authors and indicate the clandestine manner in which some of the works were distributed. The whole collection was subsequently catalogued by Thomason in twelve volumes, and two manuscript copies survive.

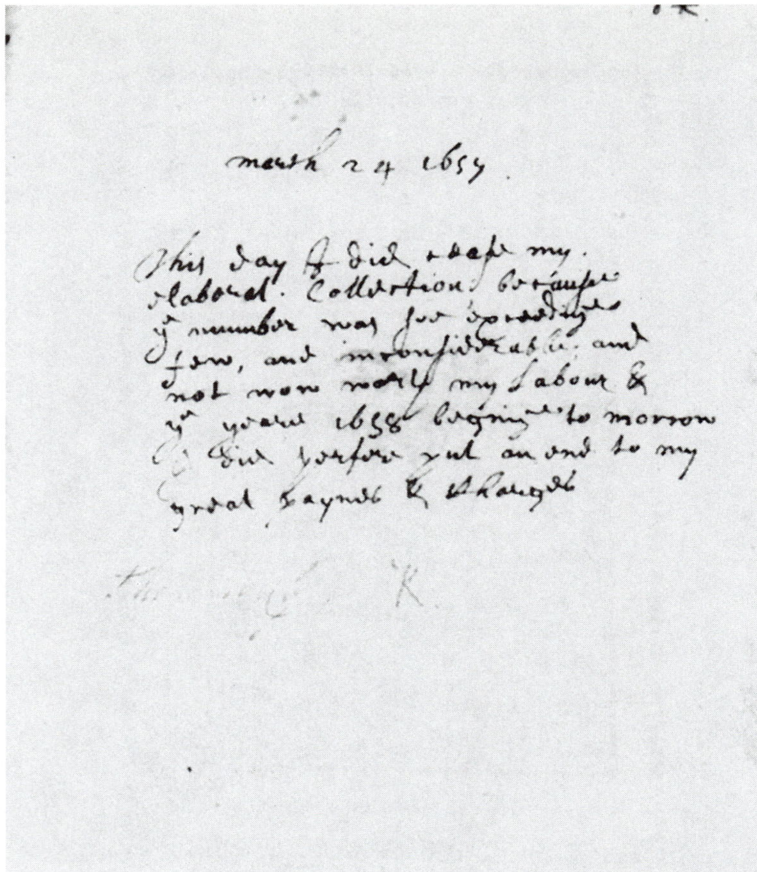
march 24 1659

This day I did cease my laboured Collection because ye number was soe [illegible] few, and inconsiderable and not worth noting my labour & ye yeare 1658 beginning to morrow I did therefore put an end to my great paynes & charges

Inscription by Thomason in one of his volumes of tracts (E.936[8], British Library)

While the overwhelming majority of the items were printed, there were also approximately one hundred original manuscripts, many of which were in Thomason's own handwriting–such as "An ordinance of the Commons of England constituting the High Court for the Trial of Charles I." These manuscripts are also of great historical significance, although there is some debate as to the extent of their subversive nature.

The bookseller's objectives in forming the collection were set out in "Mr Thomason's Note about his Collection," attached to the first volume of one of the two original manuscript catalogues. He wished to make a record of events that would "prove of greate Advantage to Posterity, and besides this there is not the like." Lois Spencer describes Thomason as "a born collector, rating the completeness o his work above all other inducements." Indeed, there was a considerable financial cost in acquiring and having the materials bound, for which the Thomason family received no payment.

According to Thomason, his collection "was so privately Carried on, that it was never knowne that there was such a Designe in hand." The precautions taken when forming the collection were described by Thomason in his note, although these may have been exaggerated in an attempt to enhance the value of the materials when he was seeking to dispose of them toward the end of his life:

> And that hee might prevent the Discovery of them when the Army was Northward hee Packt them up in Severall Truncks, and by one or two in a Weeke hee sent them to a Trusty friend in Surrey who safely preserved them, but when the Army was Westward and feareing there Returne that way hee was Faigne to have them sent back againe, and thence Safely Received them, but durst not keepe them by him the Danger was so greate, but packt them up againe and sent them into Essex, and when the Army Ranged that way to Triple Heath was faigne to sent for them back from thence and not thinking them safe anywhere in England att last tooke a Ressolucon to send them into Holland for their more Safe preservation, but Considering wth himselfe what a Treasure it was, upon Second thoughts hee durst not venture them att sea, but Resolved to place them in his Warehouses in forme of Tables round

> about the Roomes Covered over with Canvas, Continuing still without any Intermission his Goeng on nay either then when by the Usurpers Power Command hee was taken out of his Bed and Clapt up Close Prisoner att Whitehall for Seaven weekes, and above, hee still hopinge and looking for that day and time wch thankes bee to God is now come, and there hee putt a Period to that Unparalell'd Labour Charge and Paines hee had been att.

It is highly likely that during the Love Conspiracy in 1651 and Thomason's subsequent imprisonment the whole of the collection was sent to the Bodleian Library at Oxford for safekeeping, where it probably remained until his death. Presumably the items collected subsequently were transferred there at a later date. There was no gap in his collecting activities during the period of his imprisonment, and so presumably he relied upon several assistants in his work.

The existence of the collection possibly was known to the authorities on both sides, however, and after the Restoration Thomason described an incident that he claims took place in 1647 in which two courtiers requested the loan of a particular pamphlet on the king's behalf. This pamphlet was supplied and subsequently returned, together with a message from the king encouraging Thomason to continue with his project. This incident seems to have made an impression upon Thomason in favor of the Royalist cause.

The fate of the tract collection in the century after Thomason's death is described by David A. Stoker in "Disposing of George Thomason's Intractable Legacy." The collection was acquired from Thomason's descendants by Royal Bookbinder Samuel Mearne on behalf of Charles II, circa 1678, who rebound the collection. The bookbinder, however, never received payment for them, and so the collection remained in his family and that of the descendants of his daughter. During the next eighty years various members of the Mearne and Sisson family tried on many occasions to sell the collection en masse to institutional or private libraries–including the Bodleian Library, Cambridge University, and the royal family–but without success. Eventually, in 1761 the collection was sold to George III for the paltry sum of £300, a fraction of its intrinsic worth. He subsequently presented it to the British Museum in 1762.

George Thomason in his various roles as a bookseller, occasional publisher, politician, and prominent Presbyterian was ideally placed within London to undertake his enormous collection of civil war tracts. However, his foresight in beginning his collecting in 1640 was remarkable. In spite of his changing political allegiances, he collected material from both sides throughout the period and also organized the material so as to make it accessible to future generations of scholars. In "Mr. Thomason's Note about his Collection" Thomason is characteristically direct in describing the problems he faced during the twenty years of his collecting and also fully recognizes his legacy to posterity:

> All these hard Shifts and Exigents hath hee been putt unto to preserve them and preserved they are (by Providence) for the Use of Succeeding Ages wch will Scarce have ffaith to Believe that such horrid and most detestable Villanyes were ever Committed in any Christian Commonwealth since Christianity had a Name.

References:

Cyprian Blagden, "The Stationers' Company in the Civil War Period," *Library,* 5, no. 13 (1958): 1–17;

Peter W. M. Blayney, *The Bookshops in Paul's Cross Churchyard* (London: The Bibliographical Society, 1990);

William Younger Fletcher, *English Book Collectors* (London: Kegan Paul, Trench, Trübner, 1902);

William Dunn Macray, *Annals of the Bodleian Library Oxford,* second edition (Oxford: Clarendon Press, 1890);

Falconer Madan, "Notes on the Thomason Collection of Civil War Tracts," *Bibliographica,* 3 (1897): 291–308;

John J. McAleer, "The King's Pamphlets," *University of Pennsylvania Library Chronicle,* 27 (1961): 163–175;

D. F. McKenzie, *Stationers' Company Apprentices 1605–1640* (Charlottesville: Bibliographical Society of the University of Virginia, 1961);

Notes & Queries, second series 4 (1857): 412–414;

Henry R. Plomer, *A Dictionary of the Booksellers and Printers Who Were at Work in England, Scotland and Ireland From 1641 to 1667* (London: The Bibliographical Society, 1907);

John S. Smart, *The Sonnets of Milton* (Oxford: Clarendon Press, 1921);

Lois Spencer, "The Politics of George Thomason," *Library,* 5, no. 14 (1959): 11–27;

Spencer, "The Professional and Literary Connexions of George Thomason," *Library,* 5, no. 13 (1958): 102–118;

David A. Stoker, "Disposing of George Thomason's Intractable Legacy 1664–1762," *Library,* 6, no. 14 (1992): 337–356;

Stoker, "Doctor Collinges and the revival of Norwich City Library 1657–1664," *Library History,* 5 (1980): 73–84;

Gordon C. Thomasson and Elizabeth Ann Erikson Thomasson, *Thomasson Traces: Narrative of the Thomasson Family, 1677–1995,* volume 2 (Roswell, Ga.: Wolfe, 1995);

"The Will of George Thomason," *Library,* 2, no. 10 (1909): 34–43;

Francis Wormald and C. E. Wright, eds., *The English Library before 1700* (London: University of London Press, 1958).

Sir Roger Twysden

(21 August 1597 – 27 June 1672)

Richard Ovenden
National Library of Scotland

BOOKS: *The Commoners Liberty; or, the English-man's birth-right* ([London], 1648);

An Historicall Vindication of the Church of England (London: Printed by R. Daniel for Daniel Pakeman, 1657);

"The Beginners of a Monastick Life, in Asia, Africa, and Europe," in *The History and Fate of Sacrilege, Discover'd by examples of scripture, of heathens, and of Christians; from the beginning of the world, continually to this day. . . . A Treatise omitted in the late edition of his posthumous works, and now published for the terror of evil doers,* by Sir Henry Spelman (London: Printed for J. Hartley, 1698);

Certayne Considerations upon the Government of England, Camden Society Publications, no. 14 (London: Printed for the Camden Society, 1849);

The Twysden Lieutenancy Papers, 1583–1668, edited, with an introduction, by Gladys Scott Thomson (Ashford, U.K.: Printed for the Kent Archaeological Society, 1926).

OTHER: Bede,venerabilis, *Ex officina Rogeri Daniel, Prestant Londoni apud, Historiae Ecclesiasticae gentis Anglorum,* edited by Twysden (Cambridge: Cornelium Bee, 1644);

Historiae Anglicanae scriptores X, 2 volumes (London: Typis Jacobi Flesher, sumptibus Cornelius Bee, 1652);

[Sir Robert Filmer], *Questio Quodlibetica; or a Discourse, whether it may be lawfull to take use for money* (London: Printed for Humphrey Moseley, 1653);

"An Historical Narrative of the two howses of parliament and either of them, their committees and agents violent proceeding against Sr Roger Twysden their imprisoning his person, sequestring his estate, cutting down his woods, and tymber to his allmost undoing, and forcing him in the end to composition for his own." [under the title "Sir Roger Twysden's Journal"], edited by L. B. Larking, *Archaeologia Cantiana,* 1 (1858): 187–214; 2: 175–220; 3: 145–176; 4: 131–195.

Sir Roger Twysden (portrait at Bradbourne, East Malling, Kent)

Sir Roger Twysden, second Baronet, parliamentarian, antiquary, and book collector, was the eldest son of Sir William Twysden and was born 21 August 1597 at the house of his maternal grandfather, Sir Moyle Finch, in the Charterhouse in London. He inherited the family seat at Roydon Hall in Kent on the death of his mother in 1638. He had two sisters and four brothers. Of the latter, Sir Thomas Twysden (1602–1683) became a judge and a staunch royalist, and John Twysden (1607–1688) became a noted physician, despite also having trained as a barrister.

Twysden was educated at St. Paul's School in London and in 1614 entered Emmanuel College, Cambridge, as a fellow commoner, although he did not graduate, and it has been suggested that he did not fit in with the college's staunchly Puritan culture. In 1620 Twysden was knighted, since it was the privilege of a baronet to present his eldest son for knighthood. In 1623 he was admitted to Gray's Inn in London, where he continued his education. The Inns of Court were regarded in Stuart England as the "third university" and an appropriate place for young gentlemen to complete their training, as the universities were still predominantly geared toward educating future clergymen. Although Twysden was never called to the bar, nor did he practice in the courts, the Inns of Court provided him with a place to meet like-minded men and to cultivate new interests.

After his father died, Twysden inherited not only an estate but also considerable debts occasioned by his father's neglect of Roydon and passion for hawking and hunting; as a result, it was some time before Twysden felt he could afford to marry. In 1635, at the age of thirty-seven, he married Isabella, the daughter of Nicholaus Saunder, an M.P. (member of Parliament) for Penrhyn. Although he was a man of cultivated interests, especially in astronomy, and a man who was friends with important figures such as Thomas Harriot and John Dee, Saunder was a failure in business and unable to provide his daughter with a dowry. He may, however, have supplied books to his son-in-law, although only two books survive–a commentary on Solinus of 1518 (which had been owned by Dee) and a 1587 copy of *De orbe novo decades octo* by Petrus Martyr Anglerius (which had been given to Dee by Harriot)–and these books may have been acquired directly from the Dee sale by Twysden himself. The couple lived long and had six children, all of whom outlived their parents.

Twysden first entered Parliament in 1625 as member for Winchelsea. During the Parliament of 1626, with Charles I showing signs of increasing hostility toward Parliament, Twysden formed his ideas about the power of the monarchy in relation to representative assemblies and about the revival of the practice of impeachment. These thoughts later surfaced in his book *Certayne Considerations upon the Government of England* (not published until 1849). Twysden did not serve in Charles I's third Parliament of 1628–1629, choosing instead to surrender his seat to his father, and he did not sit again until 1640.

In the meantime, Twysden became increasingly involved in the government of Kent, becoming a justice of the peace, and he strongly objected to the enforced levy of ship money, although he paid the first levy. Twysden objected to extremes of all kinds in religion, finding both Calvinism and Roman Catholicism contrary to his preferences, as in his opinion they both sought to raise the power of the church above that of the state.

With Parliament at last recalled, Twysden was elected one of the two M.P.'s for Kent in the Short Parliament, although he was not returned for the Long Parliament. Instead, he reluctantly accepted the position of treasurer for the composition at the 1641 Maidstone Assizes. He played a key role in drawing up–with Sir Edward Dering and others–the Petition from Kent in 1642; this event was instrumental in forming his political ideas. As a result of the petition, Twysden and four others who had signed it, including Dering, were summoned before the House of Commons as delinquents. Twysden was released on bail but imprisoned again on the publication of *Instructions from the County of Kent to Mr Augustine Skinner,* which Twysden had drafted although not initiated. He was discovered trying to escape the country, was imprisoned again, and had his estates sequestered in 1643.

He returned to Kent in 1650 to devote himself to his antiquarian and literary interests. At the Restoration his political life received a boost when he was appointed deputy lieutenant of the county, but he remained unreconciled to the court and the government. He died on 27 June 1672 at East Peckham, Kent.

Twysden was a prolific collector of both manuscripts and printed books, but it is his collection of manuscripts, particularly medieval manuscripts, that is of special significance. Not only was he one of the great collectors of manuscripts from the former monastic collections in Britain, but he was also one in the small group of men who combined a passion for collecting with a genuine antiquarian and historical interest in medieval Britain and a curiosity to discover the origins of the country in which they lived.

Antiquarianism in the seventeenth century was a pursuit that related directly to the political and social turmoil in which the nations of Britain had become embroiled. It was also an interest that was engaged in by a small but devoted group of intellectuals and men of letters, united by a common interest, who frequently grouped themselves together in small circles known as societies, often centering on a particular individual. Thus Matthew Parker, the great Elizabethan archbishop of Canterbury and collector, was the center of a group of scholars devoted to rediscovering Anglo-Saxon Britain; and in London, Sir Robert Cotton, collector par excellence, was the focal point for virtually all those interested in pursuing antiquarian studies or just interested in collecting medieval manuscripts. In Kent the county supported a society dominated by a series of

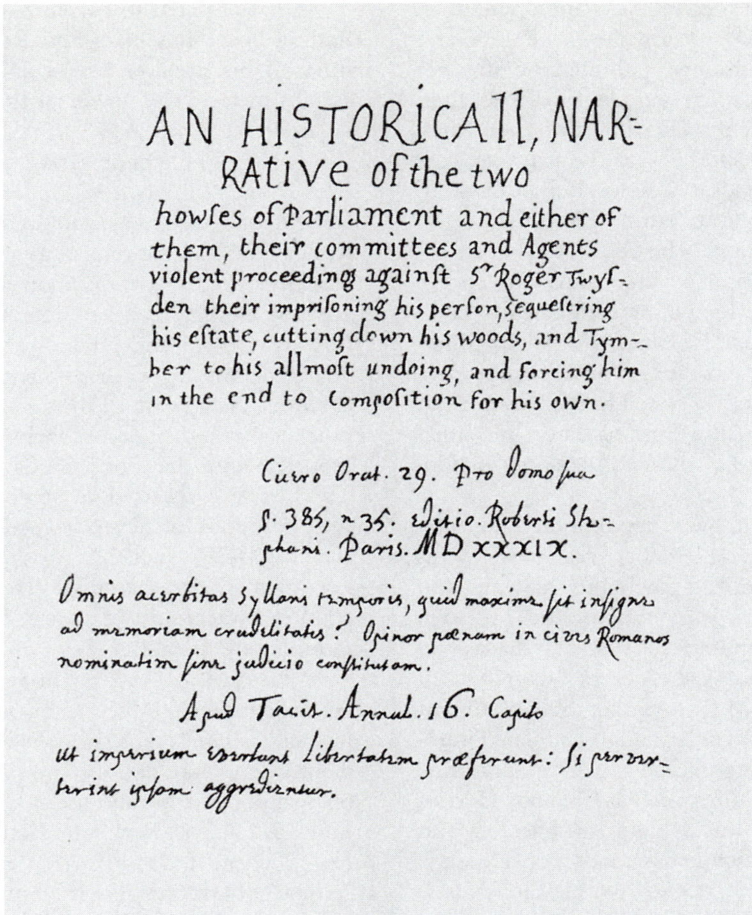
AN HISTORICALL NARRATIVE of the two howses of Parliament and either of them, their committees and Agents violent proceedings against Sr Roger Twysden their imprisoning his person, sequestring his estate, cutting down his woods, and Tymber to his allmost undoing, and forcing him in the end to composition for his own.

Cicero Orat. 29. Pro Domo sua p. 385, n 35. editio. Roberti Stephani. Paris. MDXXXIX.

Omnis acerbitas Syllani temporis, quid maxime fuit insigne ad memoriam crudelitatis? Opinor poenam in cives Romanos nominatim sine judicio constitutam.

Apud Tacit. Annal. 16. Capite

ut imperium evertant libertatem praeferunt: si perverterint ipsam aggredientur.

Title page for the journal Twysden kept during the parliamentary proceedings against him in 1642–1643 (Kent Archaeological Society)

groupings of county gentlemen, locally distinct, but interconnected by individual relationships, into what several historians have described as the "county community." Several circles of men interested in historical and antiquarian research existed for a short period in the seventeenth century. Sir Peter Manwood gathered men such as Richard Knolles and Edward Grimestone around his home near Canterbury; Sir Edward Dering engaged in serious antiquarian researches and historical debate with Sir Christopher Hatton and Sir Thomas Shirley, even going to the extent of forming a "Society of Antiquaries" of their own.

Whether Twysden was part of such a circle is unclear. Dering knew Twysden's father well; indeed, he witnessed Sir William's last will and testament in 1629. Dering and Twysden were neighbors and shared some of their book-collecting activities. In 1639 Twysden wrote to Dering inviting him to come to Roydon Hall and asking him to bring his copy of Thorne's chronicle, in return for which he promised to "shew you an old manuscript, sometyme of the same abbeys, conteyning many pretty miscellaneas, writ about Ed. 3 hys tyme, out of which perhaps Thorn took some part of hys History." But Dering never admitted Twysden to his antiquarian society, so the exact nature of their relationship cannot be determined. Twysden was also on close and friendly terms with the great antiquary Sir William Dugdale, especially as the two men were both equally concerned with the monastic houses of Britain, although Twysden was more interested in the chroniclers who lived in them. Twysden became acquainted with the antiquary and collector Elias Ashmole in 1658, possibly because Ashmole was interested in Twysden's knowledge of the records in the Tower of London. He did, however, express the opinion that two monasteries in each county should have been preserved for purposes of devotion and scholarship. Another of his close friends was the antiquary William Somner, who, although a professional physician, was principally interested in the Anglo-Saxon language and contributed a glossary of obscure words to Twysden's principal work, *Historiae Anglicanae scriptores X* (1652). The introduction describes Somner as a "most sagacious searcher into the antiquities of his country, and most expert in the Saxon tongue." Twysden was one of seventy-eight "Philologi" who contributed toward the cost of printing Somner's *Dictionarium Saxonico-Latino-Anglicum* (Oxford, 1659).

Another of Twysden's antiquarian collaborations was with Abraham Whelock–specifically on his edition of *Beda, venerabilis, Historiae Ecclesiasticae gentis Anglorum* (Bede's *Ecclesiastical History,* 1644) in the Anglo-Saxon translation attributed to King Alfred, which was published together with the *Anglo-Saxon Chronicle* in 1643 and reprinted the following year, including William Lambarde's *Ἀρχαιονομία* of 1568. Twysden played his part in the reprint, for, according to the preface to the reader, Twysden had admired the first edition so much that he persuaded Whelock "to reprint Lambarde entire, together with much of Henry Spelman's and some things in Latin from Selden's published edition of Eadmer, and some unpublished materials of his own." Twysden's additions have their own divisional title page in the volume and a preface signed by him and dated 23 August 1644, comprising the laws of William the Conqueror reprinted from John Selden's edition of the monk Eadmer's *Monachi Cantuariensis Historiae novorum sive sui saeculi libri VI* (1623) and the laws of Henry I, printed for the first time from the *Red Book of the Exchequer,* supplemented and corrected by manuscripts belonging to Selden and Twysden himself. Finally, there was a Latin–Anglo-Saxon glossary and a list of difficult Anglo-Saxon words glossed in Latin from a manuscript of ancient laws that had belonged to the Abbey of St. Augustine, Canterbury, and that had been supplied by Twysden to satisfy the printers' demand for more copy.

Although *Historiae Anglicanae scriptores X* is often assigned solely to Twysden, it was in fact a collaborative effort involving several scholars, in addition to Twysden and Somner, who provided the glossary of Anglo-Saxon terms. James Ussher and, in particular, Selden made substantial contributions, including a long introduction, and Ralph Jennynge–a Cambridge graduate who also collected manuscripts in Cambridge and London–saw the book through publication. It provided the first printed editions for many chronicles–including those of Simeon of Durham, Ralph de Diceto, and Henry Knighton–and has been called by David C. Douglas "by far the best edited of the collections of English chronicles which appeared before the Restoration." The publication of the book was initiated by the London bookseller Cornelius Bee, who suggested the publication of some "English histories, now lying hidden in private libraries." Bee's business was evidently aimed at the scholarly market, as he had taken a leading part, together with Lawrence Sadler, in importing 350 copies of Gerhard Mercator's *Atlas* from Amsterdam in 1637, was responsible for the 1660 publication of the nine folio volumes of John Pearson's *Critici sacri,* and had published in 1640 Matthew Paris's *Historia major,* edited by William Watts, evidently the spur for him to persuade Twysden to edit more early English historians for the press. Bee's involvement with Twysden actually had begun somewhat earlier, as Bee had published Whelock's revised edition of Bede with Twysden's additional material.

Twysden's reputation as an historian should not rest solely with *Historiae Anglicanae scriptores X.* His treatise *Certayne Considerations upon the Government of England* was written after reading his neighbor Sir Robert Filmer's *Patriarcha; or, The Natural Power of Kings* (1680; at that time only circulating in manuscript) and was intended as a refutation of Twysden's ideas. Although Twysden's work was never published in his lifetime, it has been described by Philip Styles as Britain's "earliest constitutional history," although the influence of Selden can be detected.

For Twysden, collecting and antiquarian research were activities that were so closely related as to be almost indistinguishable. But there were some manuscripts that he was unable to own. The Cambridge University Library copy of Simeon of Durham's *Historia ecclesiae Dunelmensis* was one of two copies of the text used in *Historiae Anglicanae scriptores X;* the other is in the Cotton Library. At Cambridge, Twysden also used a manuscript including several chronicles, among them that of a monk of the priory of Christ Church, Gervase of Canterbury. Twysden may well have used an important early-thirteenth-century volume including the texts by Radulfus de Diceto, Radulfus Niger, and Radulfus De Coggeshall (now in the Library of Trinity College, Dublin), which was at the time owned by Ussher. In November 1663 Twysden returned the manuscript of the *Textus Roffensis* to Rochester Cathedral, from which he had borrowed it with the permission of the dean and receipt of prebends. Twysden also used his circle of antiquarian friends to borrow from and lend to in return. In 1658 he wrote to Dugdale that "As for ye Ovids, I pray tell Mr. Junius he shall have them when ever you appoynt me to send them to you, and where."

Twysden took book collecting seriously, not merely as an adjunct to his interests in politics or history, because he needed the books to establish precedence, to quote from Hugo Grotius on legal matters, or to assist in his editing work. Twysden was one of the few great collectors in seventeenth-century Britain to regard his collection both as a memorial to his own life

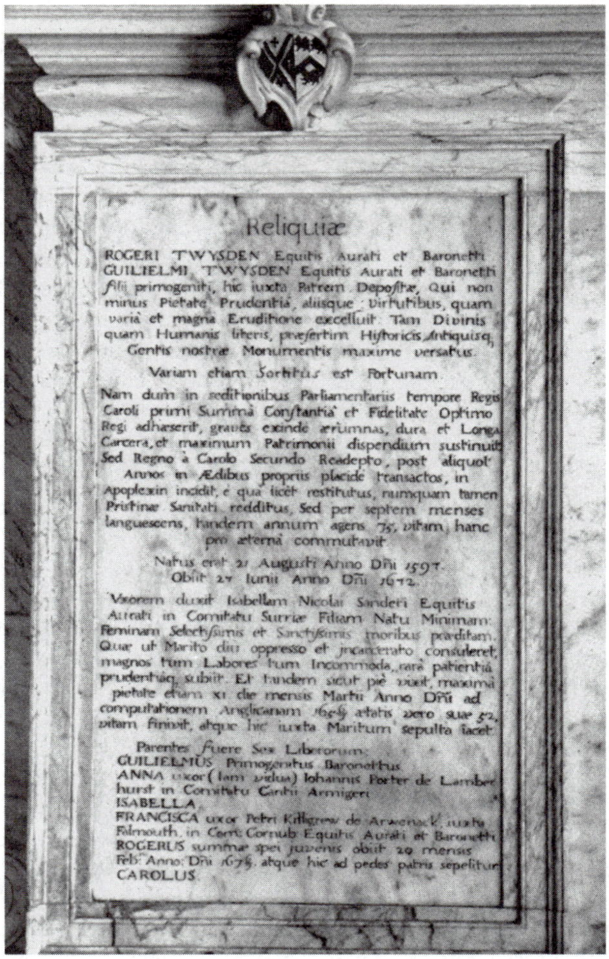

Memorial to Twysden in St. Michael's Church, East Peckham

and as a gathering of material that could not be replicated in subsequent years. As a man who evidently took great pains and care in developing his collection, he was acutely aware that many of his books would not be found again easily on the open market. He wrote in his memorandum book of his feelings toward his collection:

> I would not have them come after me sell any of my books, nay though they find I have two of one and the same sort assure himself there was somewhat why I kept them. Nay, if it so fortune I have the same edition twice, as certain works of Padre Paolo's and others printed at Venice 1606 and 1607 during the time the Republic was interdicted by Paolo Vto, yet put them not away for they are such books as not to be got, at least of that edition, nor ever will be printed again with equal authority by the approbation of the state, see the Trattato dell' interdetto printed at Venice anno 1606, not only by the allowance of the Republic but with the arms of that State, and I have two of them of that impression which I keep fearing I may lose one of them, or it might have some mischance, and one or more of another. Now for books that it may be my son cannot understand yet put them not away for some may come after us that will highly esteem them; my father was a great Hebricean and left many books of that tongue, which though I have little knowledge of yet I never parted with any of them, though I could have sold them well. So perhaps I have books of Italian, French, Spanish, and some manuscripts which my son will not regard, perhaps can not read, yet let them not be sold for perhaps his son may esteem them as much as I do. In short I would have my library for an Earthloom, or Heirloom as we call it, to the family of Twysdens for ever.

Twysden's printed books were acquired new and secondhand and were both purchased and given to him. Of the latter category, of particular interest is the copy of Manassah Ben Israel's *Vindiciae Judaeorum* (1656), which was presented to Twysden to enlist his support for the Jewish cause but also because Twysden's father had been a noted Hebraist. Twysden's interest in the monastic orders also can be seen in his possession of a manuscript of the Statutes of the Gilbertine Order, which had been in the possession of the subprior of the Church of Slaidburn in Yorkshire during the Middle Ages. More straightforward were those acquisitions such as the copy of William of Malmesbury's *De legibus Angliae,* which had been in the Library of the Hospital of St. John the Baptist at Exeter in the Middle Ages, was acquired by Twysden in 1636, and had a direct relevance to his own historical studies.

Kentish sources predominate among the earlier provenances for Twysden's collections of medieval manuscripts–and not simply because the books were more easily acquired in the neighborhood. Certainly Twysden may have had the chance to acquire volumes in Kent, but as most of the collections themselves were dispersed quite soon after the Reformation, he had to rely on other Kentish collectors. Thus, one manuscript probably came to him directly from the Lambarde family, as the volume had been owned by the scholar William Lambarde in the sixteenth century and his descendant Thomas Lambarde in the seventeenth century. Dering certainly gave him others. One manuscript, Berengaudus on the Apocalypse, came from the Abbey at Lessness in Kent, although how Twysden came to own the volume is now uncertain. Volumes of rentals and other estate documents pertaining to Kentish properties owned by the Twysden family were bound in discarded leaves from medieval manuscripts, presumably from manuscripts formerly in Kentish collections.

The most important manuscripts that Twysden owned with Kentish associations came to him through the London book trade. Indeed, Twysden's collections included manuscripts from as far afield as Scotland, Exeter, and York, indicating more a general interest in medieval manuscripts than a particular focus on Kentish associations. Twysden was no regional antiquary: the volumes he acquired from the library of William Schevez, archbishop of St. Andrews (a missal), and from William of Newburgh in Yorkshire (Newburgh's copy of Bede's *Historia Anglorum*), for example, were both acquired for the information they shed on British as opposed to Kentish history. The Schevez volume is particularly interesting; although it is of no real textual significance, it must have been of interest to Twysden for its distinguished provenance, as it was from the collection of one of the most bibliophilic of Scottish medieval prelates.

Twysden relied particularly heavily on booksellers in London to supply him with materials, both printed books and medieval manuscripts, although he may well have used his connections with other antiquaries to acquire volumes by gift and exchange as did others, such as Sir Simons D'Ewes and Cotton. Twysden's copy of William Thorne's Chronicle of the Abbey of St. Augustine, Canterbury, now in the British Library, one of the most important sources for the history of that house in the Middle Ages, and printed by Twysden in *Historiae Anglicanae scriptores X,* was acquired through the London bookseller Lawrence Sadler on 15 October 1629 for 25s.; Twysden immediately had the book rebound, for which he paid 3s. 6d. for the brown calf binding with a gilt centerpiece. Sadler was the source of many important manuscripts for Twysden, including a handsome Bible also from the Abbey of St. Augustine, Canterbury, now in the British Library, which had been acquired during the Reformation by Sir Anthony St. Leger, a Kentish grandee who had bought quantities of former monastic property in the 1530s and 1540s. Another of St. Augustine's books that passed through Sadler's hands was a thirteenth-century copy of the Italian monk Gratian's *Decretum,* for which Twysden paid 20s. also on 15 October 1629, having it rebound through Sadler's agency for 4s. Sadler was clearly an influential figure in the London book trade, or at least that part of it that served the scholarly, or "higher," end of the market. In 1637 he had joined Cornelius Bee, Twysden's publisher, in the importation of Mercator's *Atlas maior,* and in the 1640s he was supplying D'Ewes with secondhand printed books; Sadler is mentioned in the list of thirty-nine booksellers in London "who dealt in old libraries, mart books or any other" compiled by William Laud, archbishop of Canterbury, for the Privy Council in 1628.

In 1626 Twysden bought from Stephen Potts, who operated his business from Aldersgate Street in London, a manuscript of the *Legenda Aurea* of Jacobus de Voragine, which had belonged to St. Stephen's Chapel, Westminster, in the Middle Ages. Potts had given several manuscripts to the Library of St. John's College, Oxford, and, like Sadler, appeared in the 1628 list of dealers of old books; in 1633 he together with Sadler and the bookseller Francis Hill had a class catalogue of books compiled, presumably for a joint trade venture.

Twysden repeated in his will his desire that his collection should not be dispersed but should pass through the family, and accordingly he left all of his books to his eldest son, William, requiring that they remain at Roydon Hall. Thomas Twysden made similar stipulations in his will, but about 1715 the major part of the library, both manuscripts and printed books, was sold by his grandson Sir William Twysden, third Baronet, to Sir Thomas Saunders Sebright; the sale was managed by a Reverend Boraston, about whom nothing more is known. The Sebright collection was eventually dispersed in 1807 by Sir John Sebright, seventh Baronet, in what is now known as the Sebright Sale. The document of the sale, *A Catalogue of the Duplicates and a Considerable Portion of the Library of Sir John Sebright, Bart. . . . also the very curious collection of manuscripts . . . collected by Sir Roger Twysden and Mr E. Lhwyd,* indicates that the collection was auctioned by Leigh and Sotheby in a seven- day sale beginning 6 April 1807. At the Sebright sale a considerable quantity of material was purchased by the family of Surrenden-Dering, still living at Surrenden in Kent, and when that collection was sold in 1858, at least thirty-eight books were referred to in the printed sale catalogue of the Dering library as bearing the annotations of Sir Roger Twysden. Also prominent among the buyers at the sale were Sir Francis Douce, who acquired seven lots, all medieval manuscripts, of which six are now among the Douce manuscripts in the Bodleian Library; Richard Heber; and the classical scholar Charles Burney, who also acquired a clutch of manuscripts.

Twysden was one of the most accomplished scholars of the seventeenth century and the mind behind a groundbreaking volume of historical editing. One historian has described him as "in every respect the type of the seventeenth-century scholarly squire," and this scholarship was underpinned by several decades of focused collecting of medieval source material and a lifetime of purchasing the most significant secondary printed works that could be acquired in Britain. Twysden's deep knowledge of the medieval sources allowed him to comment on the work of others with critical authority. His comments written in a letter to Dugdale concerning the sometimes unquestioning acceptance of the statements made in bulls and charters used in the compilation of the great *Monasticon Anglicanum* reveal a sharp and cautious mind, one of the first truly modern historical intellects. Books dominated Twysden's life as much as politics or local government. In 1669 he wrote to his son, then at Christ Church, Oxford, asking him to copy a manuscript by Walter Maps and tried to persuade him to make the effort to copy it himself, assuring him that "as for ye being an ille hand att auld bookes, all most are so, but in writing they presently grow easy . . . ," and he went on to assure his son that when he returned to Roydon he "must not think that I shall not desire your assistance to helpe me in such things, truly I would very fayn put out an other tome of auntient writers of England, in wch I think to include Anselmes and Thomas Beckets Epistles, wch truly I doe very much desire to illustrate the story of those tymes." A man of seventy-two, he was admitting to his young son that he needed help in the physical part of historical scholarship, the laborious copying that was a feature of research in the days before the photocopier and microfilm. Twysden remained passionately devoted to historical study and the world of books that went with it until his last days.

References:

M. A. F. Borrie, "The Thorne Chronicle," *British Museum Quarterly,* 31 (1966–1967): 87–90;

A. H. Davis, ed., *William Thorne's Chronicle of St Augustine's Abbey Canterbury* (Oxford: Blackwell, 1934);

W. W. Greg, *A Companion to Arber* (Oxford: Clarendon Press, 1967);

Frank W. Jessup, *Sir Roger Twysden 1597–1672* (London: Cresset Press, 1965);

White Kennet, *The Life of Mr W. Somner* (Oxford, 1693);

J. C. T. Oates, *Cambridge University Library: A History From the Beginnings to the Copyright Act of Queen Anne* (Cambridge: Cambridge University Press, 1986);

David Rogers, "Francis Douce's Manuscripts: Some Hitherto Unrecognised Provenances," in *Studies in the Book Trade in Honour of Graham Pollard,* edited by R. W. Hunt, I. G. Philip, and R. J. Roberts, *Oxford Bibliographical Society Publications,* new series, 19 (Oxford: Oxford Bibliographical Society, 1975), pp. 315–340;

Philip Styles, "Politics and Historical Research in the Early Seventeenth Century," in *English Historical Scholarship in the Early Seventeenth Centuries,* edited by Levi Fox (London & New York: Oxford University Press, 1956);

C. H. Dudley Ward, *The Family of Twysden and Twisden: Their History and Archives from an Original by Sir John Ramskill Twisden* (London: Murray, 1939).

James Ussher

(4 January 1581 – 21 March 1656)

Suellen Mutchow Towers
Folger Shakespeare Library

CATALOGUES: *Catalogi librorum manuscriptorum Anglia et Hiberniae in unum collecti, cum indice alphabetico* (Oxford: E Theatro Sheldoniano, 1697);

Thomas Kingsmill Abbott, comp., *Catalogue of the Manuscripts in the Library of Trinity College Dublin* (Dublin: 1900);

Bernard Meehan, "The Manuscript Collection of James Ussher," in *Treasures of the Library Trinity College Dublin,* edited by Peter Fox (Dublin: Royal Irish Academy, 1986), pp. 97–110;

Marvin L. Colker, *Trinity College Library Dublin: Descriptive Catalogue of the Mediaeval and Renaissance Latin Manuscripts* (Aldershot: Published for Trinity College Library, Dublin by Scolar, 1991).

BOOKS: *Gravissimae Quaestionis, de Christianarum Ecclesiarum, In Occidentis praesertim partibus, Ab Apostolicis Temporibus ad nostram usq; aetatem, Continua Successione Historica Explicatio* (London: B. Norton, 1613);

The Substance of That Which was Delivered in a Sermon Before the Commons House of Parliament, in St. Margarets Church at Westminster, the 18. of February, 1620 (London: Printed by Felix Kyngston for John Bartlet, 1621);

An Answer to a Challenge Made by a Iesuite in Ireland. Wherein the iudgement of antiquity in the points questioned is truly delivered, and the noveltie of the now Romish doctrine plainely discovered . . . (Dublin: Society of Stationers, 1624);

A Briefe Declaration of the Universalitie of the Church of Christ: and the Unitie of the Catholike Faith professed therein: Delivered in a Sermon before His Majestie the 20th of Iune, 1624, at Wansted (London: Printed by Robert Young for Thomas Downes and Ephraim Dawson, 1624);

A Discourse of the Religion Anciently Professed by the Irish and Brittish (London: Printed by R. Y. for the Partners of the Irish Stock, 1631);

James Ussher in 1641 (Jesus College, Oxford)

Gotteschalci, et Praedestinatianae Controversiae ab Eo Motae, Historia: una cum duplice ejusdem confessione (Dublin: Ex Typographia Societatis Bibliopolarum, 1631);

A Speech Delivered in the Castle-Chamber at Dublin, the XXII. of November, Anno 1622. At the Censuring of Certaine Officers, who Refused to take the Oath of Supremacie . . . (London: Printed by R. Y. for the Partners of the Irish Stock, 1631);

Veterum Epistolarum Hibernicarum Sylloge; quae partim ab Hibernis, partim ad Hibernos, partim de Hibernis vel rebus Hibernicis sunt conscriptae (Dublin: Ex Officina Typographica Societatis Bibliopolarum, 1632);

Immanuel, Or, the Mystery of the Incarnation of the Son of God; unfolded by Iames, Archbishop of Armagh (Dublin: Printed by the Society of Stationers, 1638);

Britannicarum Ecclesiarum Antiquitates. Quibus inserta est pestiferae adversus Dei gratiam a Pelagio britanno in ecclesiam inductae haereseos historia (Dublin: Ex Officina Typographica Societatis Bibliopolarum, 1639);

A Geographicall and Historicall Disquisition, touching the Asia properly so called, the Lydian Asia (which is the Asia so often mentioned in the New Testament) the proconsular Asia, and the Asian, diocese (Oxford: Printed by H. Hall, 1643);

In Polycarpianam Epistolarum Ignationarum Syllogen Annotationes; numeris ad marginem interiorem appositis respondentes: in quibus Graecorum Ignatii exemplarium, & inter se, & cum utraque vetere Latina interpretatione, comparatione continetur (Oxford: Excudebat Henricus Hall, 1644);

The Principles of Christian Religion: with A Briefe Method of the Body of Christian Religion, shewing the Connexion, and Coherence of the Chiefe Points Thereof . . . (London: Printed by T. B. for Geo. Badger, 1644);

A Body of Divinitie, or The Summe and Substance of Christian Religion, Catechistically Propounded, and Explained, by way of Question and Answer: Methodically and Familiarly Handled. Composed long since by James Ussher . . . Whereunto is adjoyned a Tract, intituled Immanuel, or The Mystery of the Incarnation of the Son of God: hertofore writen and published by the Same Author . . . (London: Printed by M. F. for Tho. Downes and Geo. Badger, 1645);

De Macedonum et Asianorum anno solari, dissertatio, cum Graecorum astronomorum parapegmate, ad Macedonici et Juliani anni rationes accommodato (London: Typis M. Flesher, a prostant apud Cornelium Bee, 1648);

Annales Veteris Testamenti, a prima mundi origine deducti: una cum rerum Asiaticarum et Aegypticarum chronico, a temporis historici principio usque ad Maccabaicorum initia producto (London: Ex Officina J. Flesher & prostant apud L. Sadler, 1650);

De textus Hebraici Veteris Testamenti Variantibus Lectionibus ad Ludovicum Cappellum Epistola. Cui addita est et Consimilis Argumenti altera, ante annos XLV a Guilielmo Eyrio ad eundem Jacobum data, Epistola (London: Typis J. Flesher, impensis J. Crook & J. Baker, 1652);

Annalium Pars Posterior. In qua, praeter Maccabaicam et Novi Testamenti historiam, imperii Romanorum caesarum sub C. Julio & Octaviano ortus, rerumque in Asia & AEgypto gestarum continetur chronicon: ab Antiochi Epiphanis regni exordio, usque ad Imperii Vespasiani inita atque extremum templi & reipublicae Judaicae deductum (London: Typis J. Flesher, impensis J. Crook, 1654);

De graeca Septuaginta interpretum versione syntagma: cum libri Estherae editione Oigenica, & vetere graeca altera, ex Arundelliana bibliotheca nunc primum in lucem producta. Accesserunt ob argumenti cognationem, De Cainane, in Vulgata LXX editione superaddito, ex ejusdem chronologia sacra nondumedita, dissertatio: una . . . edita ad Ludovicum Capellum . . . & altera a Guilielmo Eyrio ad eundem Jacobum . . . epistola (London: Prostant venales apud J. Crook, 1655);

The Reduction of Episcopacie unto the Form of Synodical Government, received in the Ancient Church, by the most Reverend and Learned Father of Our Church, D. James Usher, late Arch-bishop of Armagh, and Primate of all Ireland, proposed in the year 1641, as an Expedient for the Prevention of Those Troubles, which Afterwards did Arise about the Matter of Church-Government (London: Printed by T. N. for G. B. and T. C., 1656);

A Method for Meditation; or, A Manuall of Divine Duties, fit for every Christians Practice (London: Printed for John Crooke, 1651);

The Annals of the World. Deduced from the Origin of Time, and continued to the Beginning of the Emperour Vespasians reign, and the Totall Destruction and Abolition of the Temple and Common-Wealth of the Jews. Containing the Historie of the Old and New Testament, with that of the Macchabees. Also all the most Memorable Affairs of Asia and Egypt, and the Rise of the Empire of the Roman Caesars, under C. Julius, and Octavianus. Collected from all history, as well sacred, as prophane, and methodically digested, by the Most Reverend James Ussher (London: Printed by E. Tyler for J. Crook and G. Bedell, 1658);

Eighteen Sermons Preached in Oxford 1640 of the Doctrine of Repentance, Speedy Conversion, and Redemption by Christ, Seasonable for These Times (London: J. Rothwell Dorchester, W. Churchill, 1659); enlarged as *Twenty Sermons Preached at Oxford, before His Majesty, and Elsewhere . . .* (London: Printed for Nathanael Ranew, 1678);

The Power communicated by God to the Prince, and the Obedience required of the Subject. Briefly laid down, and Confirmed out of the Holy Scriptures, the Testimony of the Primitive Church. The Dictates of Right Reason, and Opinion of the Wisest among Heathen Writers. By the most Reverend Father in God, James, late Lord Archbishop of Armagh, and Primate of all Ireland. Faithfully published out of the Original Copy, (written with his own hand) by the Reverend Father in God, Robert, Lord Bishop of Lincoln, with his Lordships preface thereunto . . . (London: Printed for Anne Seile, 1661);

Armachani Annales veteris et novi testamenti: a prima mundi origine deducti usque ad extremum templi et reipublicae judaicae excidium una cum rerum asiaticarum et aegyptiacarum chronico. Cum duobus indicibus quorum primus est historicus, secundus vero geographicus, qui nunc rursus prodit in lucem. Cura et studio A. Lubin ... Accedunt ejusdem J Usserii tractatus duo. I. Chronologia sacra veteris testamenti. II. Dissertatio de Macedonum et Asianorum anno solari (Paris: Tibus L. Billaine & J. du Puis, 1673);

Episcopal and Presbyterial Government Conjoyed, Proposed as an Expedient for the Compremising of the Differences, and Preventing of Those Troubles about the matter of Church-Government. Written in the Late Times by the Late Learned and Famous Ja. Usher . . . and now Published, seriously to be Considered by All Sober Conscientious Persons . . . (London, 1679);

The Protestant school; or, a Method, containing Several Forms of Prayer, Psalms, Lessons, Thanksgivings, and Graces, for the Bringing Up, and Well Grounding Children and Elder Persons in the Protestant Religion; also a Catalogue of all the English words, beginning with One Syllable, and Proceeding by Degrees to Eight . . .; to which is added, an Historical Account of Several Plots and Remarkable Passages, from Queen Elizabeth to this Present Time, lively represented in Copper Plates . . . (London: Printed for Langly Curtiss, 1681).

Edition: *The Whole Works of the Most Rev. James Ussher,* 17 volumes, edited by Charles Richard Elrington and James Henthorn Todd (Dublin: Hodges and Smith, 1847–1864).

James Ussher achieved the highest ecclesiastical office available in his native Ireland, serving as archbishop of Armagh from 1625 to 1656. His service to the English monarch and to the English church in its Irish guise was protracted and distinguished. Ussher's situation was both singular and complex. Heading the Irish Church at a time when the English Protestants he represented were a minority compared to the native Irish and English Catholics, Ussher presided over a church in which many of the ministers were actually Scottish. Nevertheless, Ussher earned the respect of men of all religious persuasions. At the same time his reputation as a man of letters, an erudite theologian and historian, spread throughout Europe. Consumed by a need for books and manuscripts to support his research, Ussher accumulated a vast collection of materials. The vicissitudes of his library, which was caught up in the tragedy of civil war, surpassed in intensity the travails of its owner. Ussher was always concerned with the fate of his alma mater, the University of Dublin, or, more specifically, Trinity College, Dublin, the repository for the bulk of his collection.

Because of Ussher's eminence and influence, the sources of information about him are abundant. Two of his chaplains provided reverential accounts of his life. Nicholas Bernard delivered Ussher's funeral sermon and then published an extended version with biographical information appended as *The Life & Death of the Most Reverend . . . Dr. James Usher* (1656). The second chaplin, Richard Parr, claimed to be the custodian of Ussher's papers and produced a post-Restoration work in 1686, *The Life of the Most Reverend Father in God, James Usher . . . With a Collection of Three Hundred Letters.* In the nineteenth century the first volume of a massive seventeen-volume collection of Ussher's writings, *The Whole Works of the Most Rev. James Ussher* (1847–1864), was a biography written by Charles Richard Elrington (1848); the fifteenth and sixteenth volumes in the set comprise Ussher's correspondence. In the twentieth century, noteworthy works include Robert Buick Knox's full-length biography, *James Ussher Archbishop of Armagh* (1967), and Amanda L. Capern's March 1996 study in *Historical Journal* of Ussher's position within the church, "The Caroline Church: James Ussher and the Irish Dimension."

Ussher's collection has also received attention. Hugh Jackson Lawlor's account, "Primate Ussher's Library Before 1641," appeared in *Proceedings of the Royal Irish Academy* in 1901. The best source for the later history of Ussher's library is Toby C. Barnard's "The Purchase of Archbishop Ussher's Library in 1657," an article published in *Long Room* in 1971. Bernard Meehan's "The Manuscript Collection of James Ussher" is included in *Treasures of the Library Trinity College, Dublin* (1986). Also, the library at Trinity College, Dublin retains various manuscript catalogues that list parts of Ussher's collection: Edward Bernard's *Catalogi librorum manuscriptorum Anglia et Hiberniae in unum collecti, cum indice alphabetico* (1697), Thomas Kingsmill Abbott's *Catalogue of the Manuscripts in the Library of Trinity College, Dublin* (1900), and Marvin L. Colker's *Trinity College Library, Dublin: Descriptive Catalogue of the Mediaeval and Renaissance Latin Manuscripts* (1991).

James Ussher was born in Dublin on 4 January 1581 into a prominent family. His father, Arland Ussher, was clerk of the Irish Court of Chancery and his mother, Margaret Stanihurst Ussher, was the daughter of the speaker for several Irish Parliaments. His uncle Henry Ussher was one of the founding fathers of Trinity College, Dublin; moreover, he served as archbishop of Armagh between 1595 and 1613. A maternal uncle Richard Stanihurst was a learned Catholic professor at the English College in Louvain.

While growing up in a staunchly Protestant household, Ussher, according to legend, was taught by two blind aunts who had committed the Scriptures to memory. Later his education was entrusted to two Scottish Presbyterian schoolmasters; under one of these, James Hamilton, Ussher continued to study when he matriculated at the fledgling Trinity College, Dublin in

Ussher's bookstamp

1594. Ussher gained an M.A. in 1600 or 1601 and, despite his father's preferring him to study law, he was ordained in December 1601 by his uncle the archbishop. In the early years Ussher's career was closely linked with his college: he was made a fellow in 1599; then he was appointed college catechist; and, after earning his B.D. in 1607, he was named professor of divinity at Trinity College, Dublin. He lectured there for fourteen years, becoming a doctor of divinity in 1612.

Biographers Bernard and Parr both recount a tale of the battle of Kinsale in 1601, after which the English army was said to be so jubilant that it raised a healthy sum to buy books to furnish the library of the University of Dublin. Parr writes, "And when the sum was raised, it was resolved by the benefactors, that Dr. Challoner, and Mr. James Ussher should . . . procure such books, as they should judge most necessary for the library, and most useful for advancement of learning." The two traveled to England in 1603 where they purchased the best books they could find and met Thomas Bodley, who was then also beginning to assemble a library. The trip initiated for Ussher a pattern of triennial visits to England that he continued into the early 1620s.

Elrington reports that in 1606 Ussher again visited England and purchased books for himself and for his college. An extant list in Ussher's hand of the books that he purchased at this time, partially annotated with prices, contains few edition dates. On the whole it reveals an attempt to build a collection around the church fathers and to include more recent continental and English Calvinist writings and representative samples of Catholic-Protestant debates. Such books as *An abrigement of that booke which the ministers of Lincoln diocess delivered to his Maiestie* . . . (1605), and *A triall of subscription by William Bradshaw* (1599), reflected an interest in the subscription crisis that ensued within the Church of England after the promulgation of the new canons of 1604. Canon 36 had required all ministers to give unqualified subscription to three articles. Also listed is *Catalogi Francofurt,* presumably a trade catalogue of the Frankfurt book fair.

Early in his career Ussher made the acquaintance of famous antiquaries and book collectors such as William Camden and Robert Cotton. His correspondence is rich with information about the libraries and research interests of these men and, later, of others such as the jurist John Selden and the librarians Thomas James, who was instrumental in the development of the Bodleian Library at Oxford, and Patrick Young, the royal librarian. Camden acknowledged Ussher's prowess with Irish antiquities in the preface to the 1607 edition of *Britannia.*

Ussher's interests, however, were not limited to antiquities. He maintained a correspondence with some of the leading theologians of the age and his church career held a firm and successful course. In 1605 Ussher was granted the chancellorship of St. Patrick's Cathedral in Dublin, which included the rectory of Finglass. When in Ireland he preached Sunday sermons at Finglass parish. In London in 1613 Ussher published his first book, *Gravissimae Quaestionis, de Christianarum Ecclesiarum, In Occidentis praesertim partibus, Ab Apostolicis Temporibus ad nostram usq; aetatem, Continua Successione Historica Explicatio,* which was designed to perpetuate Bishop Jewel's claim that Anglican doctrine was the true doctrine of the early church. Ussher's colleague Luke Challoner had wished Ussher to marry his daughter Phoebe. Challoner died in 1613 and within a year Ussher had fulfilled this request; the couple had only one child, a daughter named Elizabeth.

Ussher's anti-Catholic, pro-Calvinist leanings were evident early in his predominantly Catholic country. It was to refute the teachings of Catholics such as Cardinal Robert Bellarmine that he began his patristic and scriptural studies, which in turn spurred his fascination with chronology and antiquity. Ussher's influence on the convocation of Irish clergy in 1615 led the Irish Church to adopt the Lambeth Articles of 1595, which were in ways more Calvinist than the Thirty-Nine Articles of the English Church. The role he played later haunted him.

After being chosen vice-chancellor of Trinity College Dublin in both 1614 and 1617, early in January 1621 he was named bishop of Meath. Remaining in England for nearly three years to research the antiquities of the British Church, he was promoted to the archbishopric of Armagh by James I early in March 1625. While lodging at Jesus College and examining Oxford manuscripts in July 1626 Ussher was named a doctor of divinity at Oxford. After a period of serious illness, Ussher later that year returned to Ireland, where he stayed for many years.

Although sustaining an active interest in the affairs of his college, Ussher was able upon his return to concentrate his resources on amassing a rich library of his own. He had earlier acquired manuscripts from the sale of Henry Savile of Banke's library in 1617, more than thirty of which went to Trinity College Library as his gift. Many of Savile's manuscripts came from the dissolution of the monasteries in northern England. So also the collection of the scientist John Dee had benefited from the dissolution of religious houses. About a dozen of his manuscripts were acquired by Ussher before October 1626, one of the most interesting being a catalogue of St. Augustine's Abbey library. While he was no longer much of a traveler after 1626, Ussher was more than ever a scholar, and he depended upon correspondents to assist with buying books, to copy manuscripts, and to respond to his research queries.

Ussher cast a wide net in his search for materials. Because of his emphasis on religious textual studies, he concentrated on eastern manuscripts as well as on relevant northern antiquities. Two of his agents, Thomas Davies in Aleppo and Christopher Ravius in Constantinople, reacted heroically to Ussher's call for esoteric materials, overcoming great obstacles in dangerous regions of the world. In 1625 Davies reported to Ussher: "Amongst all the Chaldeans that lay in Mount Libanus, Tripoly, Sidon, and Jerusalem, there is but only one copy of the Old Testament in their language extant, and that in the custody of the patriarch of the sect of the Maronites, who hath his residence in Mount Libanus, which he may not part with upon any terms." A little later, while tracking down a grammar, chronicles, and calendar in Damascus, Davies wrote: "[I] could not obtain any of them, there being but one poor man of the Samaritan race left in Damascus, who is not able to satisfy me in any thing you desire. . . . I will not cease labouring . . . and I hope to prevail in some things, unless the troubles in and about Jerusalem do hinder the free passage of caravans this ensuing spring."

Exploiting the kindness of many friends when borrowing materials, Ussher was especially predatory with the private library of the acquiescent Cotton. Other lenders, however, were not so complaisant. Early in Ussher's career he received the following complaint from William Crashaw: "I lent you Josseline de Vitis Archiep. Cant. in Fol. which you said you lent Dr. Mocket and I believe it, yet I could never get it; and now I find my book at Mr. Edwards his shop, near Duke-Lane, and he saith he bought it with Dr. Mocket's library, but I cannot have it." Selden, writing in 1625, urged Ussher to return several items of his as well as some from the Cotton collection that Cotton now intended to lend to Selden.

Ussher sustained a voluminous correspondence with other religious scholars, historians, and even astronomers. His impressive exchanges with divines such as Samuel Ward of Cambridge reveal his sure grasp of information as well as his ability to remember individual books and manuscripts and specific libraries that contained these materials. Ward was one of those in his network who arranged for borrowing–in his case from Cambridge libraries. Ussher must have tried the patience of many as he continually borrowed materials, sought manuscript transcripts, and prevailed upon surrogates to consult sources for him. John Price, in Florence in 1653 as keeper of the medals to Grand Duke Ferdinand II, betrayed a witty sense of frustration as he tried to unearth a reference for Ussher with only scanty clues:

> Much search hath been made in this library, but as yet it appears not; and no great wonder, here being almost thirty volumes of that father, some of them without beginning, others without end; and some, like eternity, without beginning and end: if the Pluteus and number had been specified by your lordship, it would have facilitated the enterprize. . . . I will not count your business desperate; perhaps that piece of Chrysostom may be lighted upon in some other volume of promiscuous tractates; and what we could not by industry, we may obtain by good fortune.

Perhaps as a residual effect of all this collaboration, in the 1630s Ussher's publishing assumed a more rapid pace. He published three books in 1631, among them the Dublin-published *Gotteschalci, et Praedestinatianae Controversiae ab Eo Motae, Historia: una cum duplice ejusdem confessione,* in which he elaborated his belief in predestination in direct violation of Charles I's order forbidding all such discussions. In London he brought out his book on the ancient religions of the British, *A Discourse of the Religion Anciently Professed by the Irish and Brittish.*

In the Irish Convocation of 1634, the Irish articles of 1615 were effectually replaced by the English Thirty-Nine Articles–certainly a defeat for Ussher although he emerged with his reputation unscathed. Doctrinally opposed to the new archbishop of Canterbury, William Laud, Ussher nonetheless developed a congenial working relationship with him and with Laud's close associate in Ireland, Lord Lieutenant Thomas Wentworth, later earl of Strafford. Before the convocation met, Ussher was awarded primacy in the Irish Church.

In August 1639 Ussher published *Britannicarum Ecclesiarum Antiquitates. Quibus inserta est pestiferae adversus Dei gratiam a Pelagio britanno in ecclesiam inductae haereseos historia,* which he had begun nearly twenty years earlier at the request of King James. After preaching to the Irish Parliament in March 1640, Ussher set off for England to pursue his studies in London and Oxford. He never saw Ireland again. With the onset of the Irish rebellion in 1641 he lost most of his Irish properties and revenue. His chaplain and library keeper, Bernard, later wrote of the four-month siege of Drogheda, where he had remained with Ussher's library: "The Priests and Friers without, talked much of the prize they should have of it, but the barbarous multitude of burning it, and of me by the flame of the books, instead of the faggots under me; but it pleased God . . . to deliver us, and it out of their hands; and so the whole, with all his Manuscripts, were sent him that summer to Chester."

Meanwhile, a calamitous period was under way in England as well. Ussher returned from literary work at Oxford to try to exert a calming influence on religious affairs in London. His loyalty to the monarch and to the institution of episcopacy caused him to take sides and distance himself from some of his fellow Calvinists. At some point after Ussher refused to join the Westminster Assembly, which was called by the English Long Parliament to reform the Church of England, books and papers that he had stored in Chelsea College were confiscated by parliamentary order. Daniel Featley and Selden arranged to retrieve these materials, but nonetheless there were thefts before they were reclaimed.

To offset the loss of Ussher's Irish income, Charles I made him bishop of Carlisle, a weak reward as the area soon fell prey to enemy armies. In the end Ussher retreated with the royal party to Oxford, and, when threatened by parliamentary troops in 1645, fled to his daughter's home in Wales. Cardiff, the capital of Wales, was garrisoned under the command of Ussher's son-in-law, Timothy Tyrell. Several trunks of books and papers accompanied the archbishop so that he might continue his studies. These treasures were later ransacked by Welsh insurgents, an event that almost destroyed Ussher's spirit. Parr, as an eyewitness, quotes Ussher as speaking to his daughter of God's will: "He has thought fit to take from me at once, all that I have been gathering together, above these twenty years, and which I intended to publish for the advancement of learning, and the good of the church." In the end the local populace rallied and were able to gather up and restore much of Ussher's property to him. Ussher later, when unable to find some papers, feared that "they were plundered, among my other books and papers, by the rude Welsh in Glamorganshire."

Recovering his morale along with most of this collection, Ussher next spent some time at St. Donate's, where he worked away happily in the library of Edward Stradling. He found peace under the protection of Elizabeth Mordaunt the countess dowager of Peterborough, who in June 1646 offered him sanctuary in several of her homes. While in her London home Ussher served as preacher of Lincoln's Inn, one of the four Inns of Court, from 1647 until the loss of sight and teeth made such work impossible. He was granted space at Lincoln's Inn to try to reassemble his library.

In the early 1650s Ussher published parts one and two of his monumental annals of the Old Testament: *Annales Veteris Testamenti, a prima mundi origine deducti: una cum rerum Asiaticarum et Aegypticarum chronico, a temporis historici principio usque ad Maccabaicorum initia producto* (1650) and *Annalium Pars Posterior. In qua, praeter Maccabaicam et Novi Testamenti historiam, imperii Romanorum caesarum sub C. Julio & Octaviano ortus, rerumque in Asia & AEgypto gestarum continetur chronicon: ab Antiochi Epiphanis regni exordio, usque ad Imperii Vespasiani inita atque extremum templi & reipublicae Judaicae deductum* (1654). Ussher is famous for his influential work on biblical chronology; his dating of the creation of the universe at 4004 B.C. was widely accepted until the nineteenth century.

One of Ussher's last public appearances was to preach a sermon at the funeral of his old friend, Selden. Although Ussher had been plagued by nosebleeds and sciatica, the latter said to have been caused by working late in the library at the University of Dublin, in the end pleurisy claimed him. He passed away quietly in the home of the countess of Peterborough in Reigate on 21 March 1656. He had been allowed to live in peace during the Cromwellian period, and it was Oliver Cromwell himself who decreed that Ussher should be buried at Westminster Abbey. The published version of Bernard's funeral sermon is replete with accolades from some of Ussher's many admirers. "Mr. Selden saith this of him, 'The most reverend prelate James Ussher, Arch-Bishop of Armagh, a man of great piety, singular judgment, learned to a miracle, and born to the promoting of the more severe studies.'" Men of all countries and factions esteemed him for his impressive learning.

Although Ussher's collection contained important printed books, its main strength was in its medieval manuscripts. Notable in his own day, Ussher's manuscript collection contributes greatly to the research resources available at Trinity College, Dublin. Meehan cites as one of Ussher's most spectacular possessions a manuscript of St. Alban's hagiography done by the thir-

Tinted drawing of the martyrdom of St. Alban in the saint's life by Matthew Paris, a thirteenth-century manuscript that Ussher bought in 1626 (Ms. E.I.40, Trinity College, Dublin)

teenth-century English historian and artist Matthew Paris, which Ussher bought in 1626 from the library of John Dee. Another Ussher treasure bought from Dee are the annals from the Cistercian Abbey of Margam, Glamorgan, in the thirteenth century.

It is not always easy to determine provenance of the manuscripts Ussher owned because in the eighteenth century the antiquary John Lyon oversaw the dismantling of many volumes of manuscripts in order to rearrange them into new subjects. According to W. O'Sullivan in "The Eighteenth-Century Rebinding of the Manuscripts," published in the spring 1970 issue of *Long Room,* "Ussher's papers bore the brunt of this meddling." Lyon's actions also destroyed the usefulness of *Catalogi librorum manuscriptorum Anglia et Hiberniae in unum collecti, cum indice alphabetico.*

In addition to medieval manuscripts, Ussher acquired papers of churchmen of his own time. For example, some of the literary effects of Bishop Lancelot Andrewes had gone to Ussher; they in turn held papers of Richard Hooker. Because of his dependence on procuring transcripts of manuscripts for his study of oriental biblical texts, Ussher needed to know the contents of other collections, which explains his holdings of library catalogues. Colker lists catalogues of the Barocci Greek manuscripts, purchased by William Herbert, Earl of Pembroke, and of Thomas Roe's manuscripts–both annotated by Ussher. English correspondents faithfully reported to Ussher about these collections. In April 1628 the bookseller and importer Henry Fetherstone alerted Ussher to the valuable Barocci library in Venice, which he was acquiring and was soon to catalogue. He promised a copy of the catalogue to Ussher. Both collections were donated to the Bodleian Library in 1629.

Ussher's book collection has been absorbed by Trinity College Library and is difficult to reconstruct. In his 1901 article Lawlor makes a complicated comparison of different shelfmarks from several manuscripts thought to be catalogues of Ussher's books. One of the notable books that can be identified is an incunabulum, Cassiodorus's *Expositio in Psalterium,* printed by Johann Amerbach in Basel in 1491. Manuscript 4 at Trinity College, Dublin, assigned different dates over the years, was thought by Lawlor to represent Ussher's book collection when it was brought together at Lincoln's Inn. Although the list seems to be ordered by shelfmark, thus preventing access by author, and lacks most dates, it provides a good indication of the contents of Ussher's library after a lifetime of collecting.

Theology was predominant in the collection, with a strong representation of the Greek and Latin church fathers, Calvinist controversialists, and Catholic apologists. The works of many English Calvinist authors appear: John Brinsley, Thomas Cartwright, John Dod, William Gouge, Samuel Hieron, William Perkins, William Prynne, and John Sprint. Some of the writers, including Richard Bernard and Samuel Ward, were correspondents of Ussher. All is not theology, however. There are also titles by Aristotle and Sophocles, Dante

Alighieri and Niccolò Machiavelli, and English classics such as Geoffrey Chaucer's *Canterbury Tales*. Medical works such as Robert Burton's *Anatomy of Melancholy*, works on exploration such as the various parts of Samuel Purchas's *Pilgrims*, and books on mathematics and astronomy to support Ussher's study of time are also present.

Toby C. Barnard has chronicled the fortunes of Ussher's book collection following the collector's death. Originally intending to bequeath it to Trinity College, Dublin, Ussher found his finances to be in such disarray that his library was his major asset and so left it to his daughter Elizabeth Tyrell. The family sold the library to the English army in Ireland, and the collection of some ten-thousand books was stored for a time in Dublin Castle, where it was subject to ransacking and the ravages of time and an inappropriate environment. With the Restoration, Charles II decided to bestow the collection upon Trinity College, Dublin.

Biographies:

Nicholas Bernard, *The Life & Death of the Most Reverend . . . Dr. James Usher* (London: Printed by E. Tyler, 1656);

Richard Parr, *The Life of the Most Reverend Father in God, James Usher . . . With a Collection of Three Hundred Letters* (London: Printed for Nathanael Ranew, 1686);

Charles Richard Elrington, *The Life of the Most Rev. James Ussher* (Dublin: Hodges and Smith, 1848);

Robert Buick Knox, *James Ussher Archbishop of Armagh* (Cardiff: University of Wales Press, 1967).

Letters:

Charles Richard Elrington, ed., *The Whole Works of the Most Rev. James Ussher,* volumes 15, 16 (Dublin: Hodges and Smith, 1847–1864).

References:

Toby C. Barnard, "The Purchase of Archbishop Ussher's Library in 1657," *Long Room,* 4 (1971): 9–14;

Amanda L. Capern, "The Caroline Church: James Ussher and the Irish Dimension," *Historical Journal,* 39 (March 1996): 57–85;

Peter Fox, "They Glory Much in Their Library," in *Treasures of the Library Trinity College Dublin,* edited by Fox (Dublin: Royal Irish Academy, 1986), pp. 1–15;

Hugh Jackson Lawlor, "Primate Ussher's Library Before 1641," *Proceedings of the Royal Irish Academy,* series three, 6 (1901): 216–264;

William O'Sullivan, "The Eighteenth-Century Rebinding of the Manuscripts," *Long Room,* 1 (Spring 1970): 19–28;

Julian Roberts and Andrew G. Watson, eds., *John Dee's Library Catalogue* (London: Bibliographical Society, 1990);

P. G. Stanwood, "The Richard Hooker Manuscripts," *Long Room,* 11 (Spring–Summer 1975): 7–10;

Watson, *The Manuscripts of Henry Savile of Banke* (London: Bibliographical Society, 1969).

Papers:

The main repositories of James Ussher's papers are Trinity College, Dublin and the Bodleian Library, Oxford.

Robert Vaughan

(1592? - 16 May 1667)

Daniel Huws

CATALOGUES: J. Gwenogvryn Evans, "The Welsh Manuscripts at Peniarth, Towyn, Merioneth; the Property of William Robert Maurice Wynne," volume 1, parts 2 and 3 of his *Report on Manuscripts in the Welsh Language,* 2 volumes in 7 (London: Printed for Her Majesty's Stationery Office by Eyre & Spottiswoode, 1898–1910);

Handlist of Manuscripts in the National Library of Wales, National Library of Wales Journal, Supplement, series 2, volume 1 (Aberystwyth: National Library of Wales, 1943).

BOOK: *British Antiquities Revived; or, A Friendly Contest Touching the Soveraignty of the Three Princes of Wales in Ancient Times, Managed With Certain Arguments, Whereunto Answers are Applyed. To Which Is Added, the Pedegree of the Right Honourable the Earl of Carbery, Lord President of Wales, with a Short Account of the Five Royal Tribes of Cambria* (Oxford: Printed by Henry Hall for Thomas Robinson, 1662).

Robert Vaughan of Hengwrt is most esteemed not as an author (only one of his projected writings reached publication) nor as a scholar and antiquary–though, as such, he was among the most scrupulous and acute of his age–but, rather, as the collector of the most important library of Welsh manuscripts ever brought together by one person. In contrast to other seventeenth-century Welsh collections, his collection has, in large part, survived intact. By 1667 more than half of the medieval manuscripts in Welsh that survive today had been gathered in his study at Hengwrt, and of the surviving manuscripts that are generally regarded as preeminent in importance to Welsh literature or history, the collection contained about two-thirds. In effect, much as Sir Robert Cotton had done for England at Cotton House, Westminster, a decade or two earlier, Vaughan had created a national collection for Wales. Vaughan wrote of his antiquarian labors that it was "love of my countrey and our ancestors that drives me."

Despite the high regard in which Vaughan and his library were held during his lifetime, little is known about him. Few personal papers survive; the only extant material is some forty letters, or drafts of letters, from Vaughan, the earliest dated 1622, and a similar number of letters addressed to him, which were found haphazardly placed among his manuscripts.

Vaughan was born around 1592, the only legitimate son of Howell Vaughan of Gwengraig (or Y Wengraig), a house on the northern slope of Cader Idris, south of Dolgellau, Merionethshire, that had been owned by the Vaughan family for several generations. Vaughan's mother, Margaret, was a daughter of Edward Owen of Hengwrt, a house that was a mile to the north of Dolgellau. Owen's grandfather, Lewis Owen, a baron of the exchequer of North Wales, had been the victim of a notorious murder in 1555 at the hands of the *Gwylliaid Cochion Mawddwy,* a renowned band of brigands.

Vaughan entered Oriel College, Oxford, in 1612 but left without taking a degree. He married Catherine Nannau of Nannau, another ancient house near Dolgellau. Their eldest son, Howell, was born in 1617; in all, they had four sons and four daughters. Vaughan was living at Gwengraig as late as 1624, but by 1632 he had moved to Hengwrt, which remained his home for the rest of his life.

Apart from his activities as a scholar and collector of manuscripts, Vaughan led a life that was typical of an educated and conscientious member of the landowning gentry of his time. He was named to the Commission of the Peace for Merionethshire in 1618 and remained a justice until 1660. Surviving documents indicate that he was an active member of the bench and was influential in the administration of the county. One of his daughters, Jane, married Robert Owen of Dolserau, who was on the Parliamentary side during the Civil War period. Vaughan himself, just a year after the execution of King Charles I in 1649, compiled the pedigree of one of the executioners, Colonel John Jones, a Merionethshire man and distant relative. Unlike many of his fellow gen-

Hengwrt, the former home of Robert Vaughan in Merionethshire, Wales, as it appeared in 1793 (watercolor by John Ingleby; National Library of Wales)

try, he continued to serve as a justice of the peace under the Commonwealth. He evidently had an inclination toward Puritanism: he made copies of the letters of the great Welsh Puritan writer Morgan Llwyd, compiled a scriptural concordance, and kept a notebook of sermons that features several Puritan preachers.

Vaughan's interests and reading were wide, as the contents of his library show, but they came to focus on early British history and the history of the Welsh. Such subjects, in that age, were not taught at universities. Vaughan's inspiration seems to have come from an early association with a father and son, Rhys and Siôn Cain of Oswestry, who were members of the centuries-old order of professional Welsh bards. Writing to Siôn Cain in 1632 on questions of Welsh genealogy, Vaughan said that he had "gotten all my knowledge in that faculty from you and your father." Since Rhys Cain died in 1614, Vaughan must have spent time with the two bards in Oswestry, either before entering Oriel or soon afterward. It is likely that before going to Oxford, Vaughn attended the well-regarded grammar school at Oswestry–it would have been one of the most accessible schools to a boy from Dolgellau–and perhaps met the Cains there.

Genealogy always formed part of Welsh bardic instruction, but by the sixteenth century the closely allied science of heraldry figured alongside it. Bardic learning, which in earlier centuries had mostly been transmitted orally, was by then sustained by a strong manuscript tradition. Rhys Cain, a leading herald-bard of his day, was a pupil of William Llyn, the greatest Welsh poet of the later sixteenth century; Llyn, in turn, was a pupil of the famous teacher of bards, Gruffudd Hiraethog. After the death of Rhys Cain several notable Welsh manuscripts that had descended through the hands of these bards came into Vaughan's possession, among them the Hendregadredd Manuscript, written about 1300, which contains the chief corpus of court poetry of the Welsh princes. Vaughan had acquired this manuscript by 1617. Other manuscripts of Rhys Cain remained with his son until Siôn's death around 1650, when they, too, were acquired by Vaughan.

Fixed points in the chronology of Vaughan's collecting of manuscripts and the evolution of his scholarly interests are few. Clearly, however, his collecting urge and interests were both developed early. Two datable manuscripts in Vaughan's hand (now National Library of Wales [NLW] MS 9092 and Cardiff Central Library [CCL] MS 4.83) show that by 1616 he had made a transcript from the earliest text of *Brut y Tywysogion* (Chronicle of the Princes) and of an important chronological tract, *O oes Gwrtheyrn,* and that he had already taken a lively interest in the works of the earliest Welsh poets, *Cynfeirdd* and *Gogynfeirdd.* The scope of what he aspired to collect is suggested by a notebook he compiled, probably between 1615 and 1620 (NLW MS 5262), in which he lists nearly forty owners of Welsh manuscripts, with particulars of what they were said to possess. Several of these manuscripts later came to Hengwrt.

Although Rhys and Siôn Cain probably gave Vaughan his introduction to Welsh history and literature, another early influence was likely that of John Davies, rector of Mallwyd, some ten miles from Dolgellau. Davies was one of the greatest of the Welsh humanist scholars, author of a Welsh grammar and a Welsh dictionary, both of which remained authoritative for centuries. By 1617 Davies was making transcripts from some of Vaughan's manuscripts, and he became a lifelong friend.

Two pioneers of Welsh local history with whose unpublished work Vaughan was in part familiar were George Owen, the historian of Pembrokeshire, and Sir John Wynn of Gwydir, who wrote on the history of his family and of Caernarfonshire. Towering above all topographical writing of the time was William Camden's *Britannia* in its many editions (the first was published in 1586), a work read by generations of Welsh scholars with a mixture of admiration and irritation because of a perceived anti-Welsh prejudice. Camden was evidently the main inspiration for an early tract of Vaughan's, "The Survey of Merioneth," written around 1620 to 1624. Another early work, composed about 1622 in rebuttal to a tract by George Owen, was *British Antiquities Revived,* Vaughan's only writing to be published during his lifetime–and that not until 1662, when he referred to it as "the first fruits of my study in antiquities." In this work he correctly argues that Anarawd, the ancestor of the royal line of North Wales, and not Cadell, the ancestor of the royal line of South Wales, was the eldest son of Rhodri Mawr (Rhodri the Great), who died in 877.

In 1638, giving as security a bond of £200, Vaughan borrowed five volumes containing the most comprehensive contemporary compilation of North Wales pedigrees (two of the volumes survive as British Library [BL] Add. MSS 28033–28034) from the executors of their compiler, Peter Ellis, a Wrexham lawyer who had died the previous year. These volumes provided Vaughan with the basis and pattern for his own great genealogical compilation (now in the Peniarth Collection of the National Library of Wales as Peniarth MS 287). In 1646 he was still deeply involved in genealogy; in a letter to Siôn Cain he mentioned that he had labored for half a year compiling a collection of the pedigrees of South Wales.

The middle years of Vaughan's life do not seem to have yielded much original historical writing, but toward the end of the 1640s he was tempted into new fields. The earliest surviving correspondence between Vaughan and contemporary English antiquaries dates from 1648. The most regular and significant correspondent was James Ussher, archbishop of Armagh. Encouraged by Ussher's curiosity about Welsh historical sources, Vaughan produced for him a tract on Welsh chronology, an English translation of the early part of *Brut y Tywysogion,* and a pioneering study of that rich repertory of history and legend, *Trioedd ynys Prydein* (Welsh Triads). The last work occupied him from 1652 to 1658 but remained unfinished. During this period Vaughan spent much time researching Geoffrey of Monmouth's *Historia Regum Britanniae* (History of the Kings of Britain, written between 1135 and 1139). Like most early English antiquaries, Vaughan was reluctant to reject it wholesale, being aware that much of Geoffrey's material derived from earlier sources–notably, *Historia Brittonum* (British History), attributed to Nennius, an eighth-century Welsh scholar. With Ussher's help Vaughan made a careful study of *Historia Brittonum.* He was also working on a revised history of Wales based on David Powel's *The Historie of Cambria, Now Called Wales* (1584). A 128-page portion of this work was printed in 1663 and survives in this imperfect form in a few copies. Several of Vaughan's works written during the 1650s, including a Welsh biblical concordance, were probably compiled with an eye to publication, although none were ever printed.

Vaughan's unpublished writings were known, in part at least, to several of the most able antiquaries of succeeding generations. To Edward Lhuyd, Vaughan was "that learned and candid antiquary." Evan Evans said, "His labours are the best things in my collection, and throw more light upon the British history than all historians and antiquarians put together." Vaughan's technical skills as an interpreter of old texts, whether literary or archival, were well regarded. While his interests were always historical rather than literary–it was for their historical content that he studied poetry and legendary texts–his familiarity with early and medieval Welsh literature was on or above the level of the leading literary scholars of his day. He was equally well read in the classical writers on Britain, the Dark Age historians,

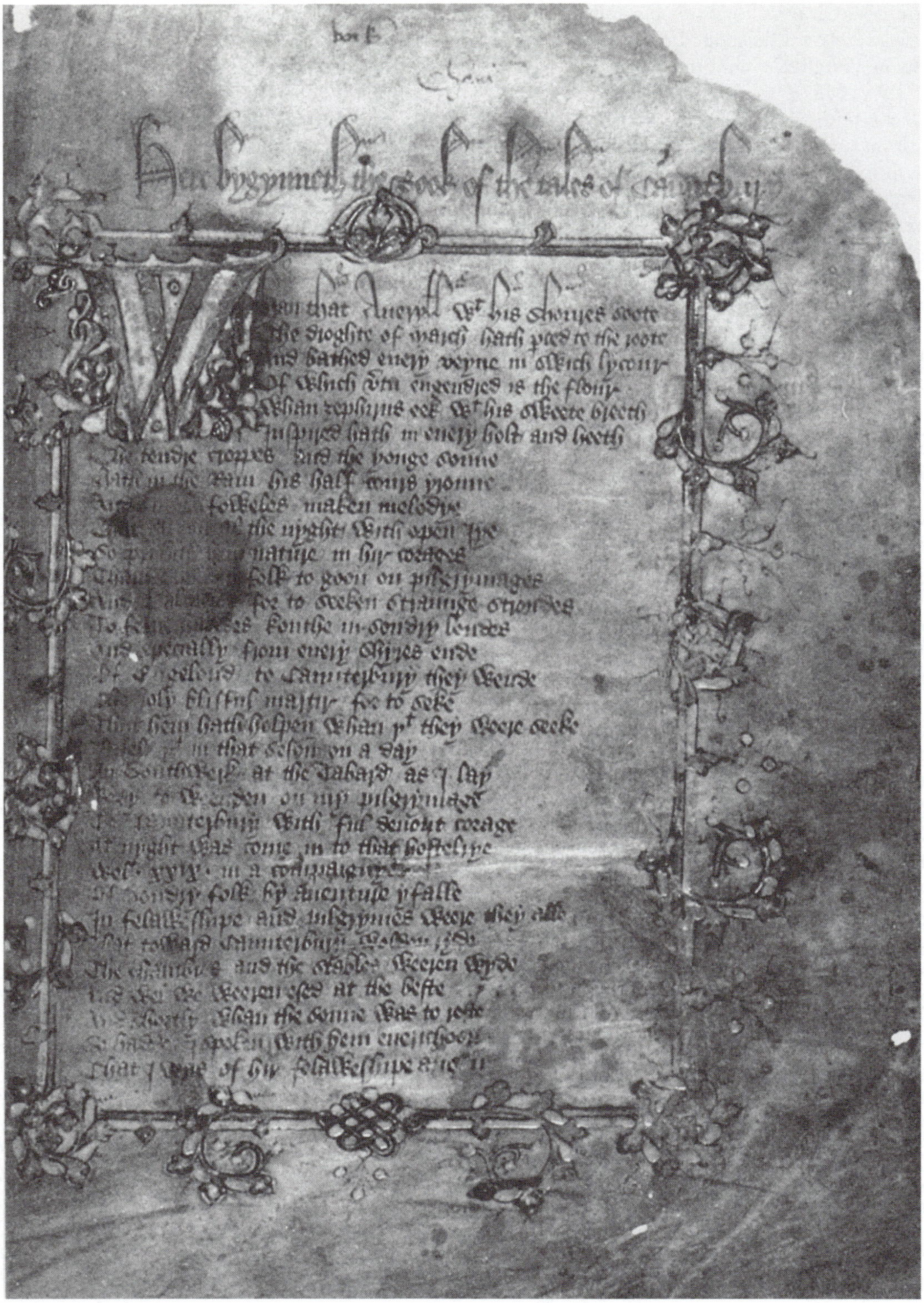

Page from the Hengwrt manuscript for Geoffrey Chaucer's The Canterbury Tales, *believed to be the earliest text of that work (National Library of Wales)*

and the medieval English chronicles. Like his great English antiquarian forerunners Camden and John Leland, and like George Owen, Vaughan had a keen archaeological eye; his evidence was not limited to books and manuscripts. Testimony to this skill is his 1648 transcription, the earliest known of the now largely eroded inscription on one of the key monuments of the Welsh Dark Ages, the Pillar of Eliseg, and the entries in a notebook that accompanied him on a journey to St. Davids, made about 1655.

Vaughan kept no contemporary records of accessions to his collection, at least none that has survived, and he seldom inscribed in his manuscripts any mark of ownership. While in the case of a few manuscripts it is possible to infer by what date they had reached his library, in general there is no firm guidance before 1658, the date of the earliest known catalogue of the collection. This catalogue, compiled by William Maurice, is known from several surviving manuscript copies deriving from more than one exemplar. In its original form it appears to have listed 158 manuscripts, including almost all the important ones, but it is demonstrably incomplete. A catalogue roughly contemporary with the one compiled by Maurice, in the hand of Vaughan himself, survives (NLW MS 9095); it is undated, but since it includes manuscripts of John Jones of Gellilyfdy, who died around 1658, it can be surmised that it was made about that year. It is a shelf list, arranged by press and shelf, evidently of the contents of the study at Hengwrt, and encompasses both manuscripts and printed books. Vaughan's catalogue includes nearly two thousand printed books and more than two hundred manuscripts, but it, too, falls short of being comprehensive. Some of the chief treasures of the collection that are included in Maurice's catalogue do not appear in Vaughan's; they may have been kept in a special cabinet and thus excluded from the shelf list. In 1678 Robert Owen, Vaughan's son-in-law, estimated the total number of books in the library to be "neere 3,000," which suggests that there were more books than those catalogued by their owner.

Vaughan's collection grew for almost fifty years. Among his most important acquisitions were several groups of manuscripts that had been owned or written by other scholars who were his contemporaries: Davies; Jaspar Gryffyth, who owned *Llyfr du Caerfyrddin* (Black Book of Carmarthen [Peniarth MS 1]) and *Llyfr Gwyn Rhydderch* (White Book of Rhydderch [Peniarth MSS 4 and 5]); John Lewis of Llynwene, from whom came an important group of manuscripts of southeastern Welsh provenance, including *Llyfr Taliesin* (Book of Taliesin [Peniarth MS 2]); Thomas Wiliems, the great lexicographer; John Jones of Gellilyfdy; and Meredith Lloyd. In the case of each except Lloyd, who outlived him, Vaughan seems to have acquired the manuscripts after the death of the owner, though in no case are the exact circumstances known, nor in any instance did the manuscript collections of these scholars pass in their entirety to Vaughan. Lloyd, a younger scholar, corresponded with Vaughan in the 1650s and supplied him with some manuscripts.

The single-mindedness with which Vaughan could pursue a particular manuscript is demonstrated in the case of *Llyfr Llandaff* (Book of Llandaff), the most important Welsh manuscript to survive from the twelfth century. This book had been removed from its rightful home in Llandaff Cathedral and appeared in the library of John Selden. After Selden's death Vaughan applied to one of the executors for the loan of the book, offering security for it. Four years later, in 1659, after protracted correspondence, he succeeded in borrowing it. Though he was approaching seventy and his sight was failing, Vaughan was still capable of making a handsome and accurate copy (now Peniarth MS 275) in a semblance of the original script, just as he had decades earlier, when he copied *Llyfr du Caerfyrddin.* His transcriptions, whether of Welsh literature or of Latin archives, are notable not only for their clarity but also for their accuracy.

To modern eyes, the principal glory of the Hengwrt collection of manuscripts lies in those that date from about 1250 to about 1350, the golden age of the production of manuscripts of vernacular Welsh literature. These include four of the five all-important codices of early Welsh poetry: *Llyfr du Caerfyrddin, Llyfr Aneirin* (Book of Aneirin [Cardiff MS 2.81]), *Llyfr Taliesin,* and the Hendregadredd Manuscript (NLW MS 6680); others from this period include *Llyfr Gwyn Rhydderch,* the earliest book to gather a large corpus of Welsh narrative, particularly the stories later known as "The Mabinogion"; the earliest texts of *Brut y Tywysogion;* and among the most important texts of *Brut y Brenhinedd* (the Welsh version of Geoffrey of Monmouth's *Historia Regum Brittaniae*) and *Caifreithiau Hywel Dda* (Law of Hywel the Good). Manuscripts of later medieval Welsh literature abound. But Vaughan's acquisitiveness was not limited to manuscripts from Wales or those that related to his particular areas of historical concern. His collection included fine English twelfth-century manuscripts of the Venerable Bede's *Historia Ecclesiastica* (Ecclesiastical History) and Henry of Huntingdon's *Historia Anglorum* (History of the English People); an important compilation by the Burton Abbey Chronicler (Peniarth 390), one of the few surviving medieval manuscripts in Cornish; a mystery play cycle (Peniarth 105); and, most famously perhaps, the "Hengwrt Chaucer" (Peniarth 392), now recognized as the earliest text of Geoffrey Chaucer's *Canterbury Tales.*

Vaughan died on 16 May 1667. A draft of a will, dated 1665, survives in which his son Howell is named as executor, and a bequest of the books, both written and printed, is made; the name of the beneficiary, however, is left blank. No evidence survives of a probate of will or grant of letters of administration, but from later documents it appears that Howell undertook administration of his father's estate and inherited the library. Howell died in 1676, leaving an infant heir, heavy debts, and an estate entangled with that of his father. Because of Howell's debts, it was proposed that the family sell the library, but views diverged and a legal battle ensued, tying up the possibility of a sale indefinitely. The possible sale of the collection had in the meanwhile excited the interest of other Welsh collectors. In 1676 an approach was made by Thomas Mostyn, later second Baronet Mostyn, who, before he died in 1692, assembled the most notable collection of manuscripts in Wales after that at Hengwrt. During 1677 and 1678 two of Robert Vaughan's fellow antiquaries, Maurice and Lloyd, were involved in negotiations with Vaughan's son-in-law Robert Owen to purchase the library on behalf of William Williams of Glasgoed, later of Llandforda, a prosperous lawyer who later came to fame in the House of Commons as "Speaker Williams." In 1678 Robert Owen mentioned to Maurice and Lloyd that some thought the value of the contents of the Hengwrt study to be £1,000, hinting that £300 might be an acceptable offer. Nothing came of these negotiations, however. In 1684 Mostyn, this time through Humphrey Humphreys, then dean of Bangor, made new overtures, again abortive. Later that year, Robert Owen immigrated to Pennsylvania.

After 1684 no more is heard of any possible sale of the Hengwrt library. For almost a hundred years the collection was neglected by Vaughan's descendants. The family's appreciation of the value of the manuscripts seems mostly to have resided in the idea that allowing them to be copied would reduce it: gaining access to the library was notoriously difficult. Lhuyd, one of the greatest Celtic scholars, managed in 1696 to spend enough time in the study at Hengwrt to make a perceptive list of the "old MSS" he found there, seventy-seven in number. He commented: "There are also a great many modern MSS, but it being a busy time with the gentleman that admitted me into the study, I was unwilling to detain him longer." Lhuyd's subsequent attempts to be allowed to borrow or copy some of the old manuscripts were rebuffed.

Two leading eighteenth-century scholars obtained access to the manuscripts at Hengwrt, though only briefly: Moses Williams in 1728 and Lewis Morris in 1738. Lhuyd had already referred to the library as having been "rifled," and Morris reported a story, probably ill founded, that Williams had borrowed many manuscripts that he never returned; but the losses from the library appear to have been on a small scale before the second half of the eighteenth century.

Hugh Vaughan inherited Hengwrt in 1750. His improvidence brought steadily increasing debts, and in 1778 he was declared bankrupt. His last years, until his death in 1783, were spent as a fugitive debtor. A description of the Hengwrt library in 1778 by the Reverend Richard Thomas refers to the damage caused by rats, rain, and negligence. Hengwrt was put up for sale in 1779, and although the sale of the house did not go through, the contents were sold. Prior to the sale, however, most of the library had secretly been removed to Nannau, which had recently been inherited by Hugh Vaughan. The purchaser of what remained of the library at Hengwrt, which included a small number of manuscripts, was John Lloyd, "the Philosopher," of Hafodunos and Wigfair. Contemporary reports refer to his having purchased "the wreck of the Hengwrt library" and of having "cleared the house of every book."

Among those who evidently had access to the Hengwrt library during these troubled years, whether at Hengwrt or at Nannau, were several local clergymen, including Thomas and a Dolgellau physician, Griffith Roberts. Roberts and four of the clergymen, including Thomas, lie under suspicion of having failed, intentionally or not, to return borrowed Hengwrt manuscripts. Items from the library that were never returned and survive elsewhere carry evidence of having passed through their hands. The two most spectacular items liberated from Hengwrt, both around 1780, were *Llyfr Aneirin* and the Hendregadredd Manuscript.

On the death of Hugh Vaughan in 1783 Hengwrt passed to his brother, Robert Howell Vaughan, a man of a more provident nature. When he died in 1793 the estate went to his son Colonel Griffith Vaughan. Gaining access to the library was still difficult and often had to be effected surreptitiously, but the colonel showed enterprise in trying to recoup some of the losses. In 1807 the library of Sir John Sebright was sold in London; it included a large part of Lhuyd's manuscript collection, and at least nineteen items were bought for Hengwrt. In 1808 Roberts died; soon afterward, if not before, his valuable manuscript collection, which included several items of Hengwrt provenance, was bought by Colonel Vaughan. And in 1816, at the sale of Lloyd's huge library, twenty manuscripts that had left Hengwrt in 1779 were bought back.

The first published catalogue of the Hengwrt manuscripts was made in 1824 by Aneurin Owen and printed in *Transactions of the Cymmrodorion or the Metropolitan Cambrian Institution* (1843). Owen's catalogue was

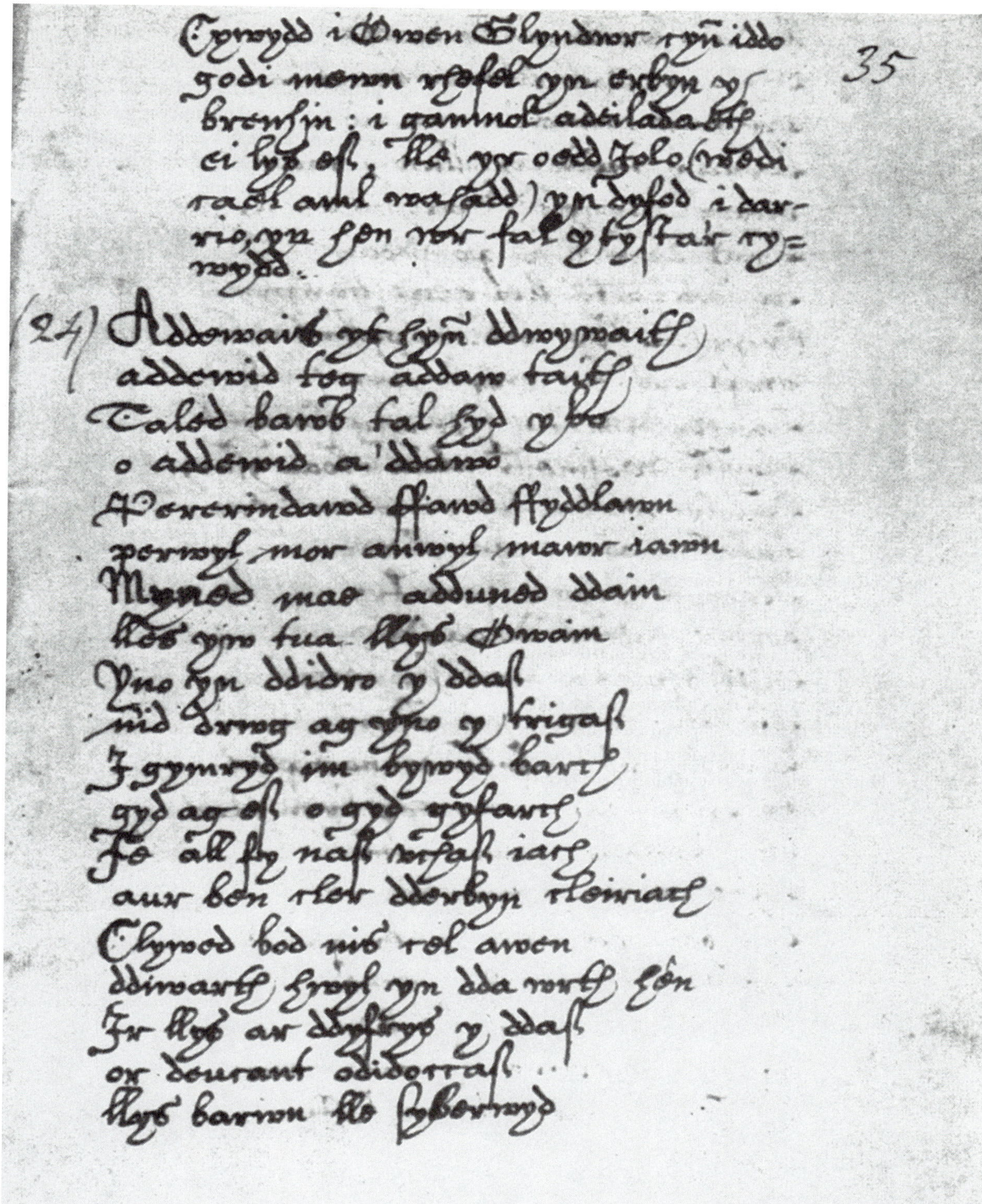

Cywydd i Owen Glyndwr cyn iddo
godi mewn rhyfel yn erbyn y
brenhin: i ganmol adeiladaeth
ei lys ef, lle yr oedd Iolo (medd-
rach aml wasadd) yn dyfod i dar-
rio, yn hen wr fal y tystia'r cywydd. 35

(24) Addewais yt hyn ddwywaith
addewid teg addaw taith
Taled bawb fal hyd y bo
o addewid a addawo
Pererindawd ffawd ffyddlawn
perwyl mor annwyl mawr iawn
Myned mae adduned ddain
lles yw tua llys Owain
Yno yn ddidro y ddaf
nid drwg ag yno y trigaf
I gymryd im bywyd barch
gyd ag ef o gyd gyfarch
Fo all fy naf uchaf ach
aur ben clêr dderbyn cleiriach
Clywed bod nid rôl awen
ddiwarth hwyl yn dda wrth hen
Ir llys ar ddyfrys y ddaf
or deuant odidocaf
llys barwn lle syberwyd

Page from a transcription of early Welsh poetry made by Vaughan (National Library of Wales)

based on that of Maurice, so far as the latter went, and was extended to include 361 manuscripts. No pressmarks corresponding to the Maurice and Vaughan catalogues were ever inscribed in the manuscripts themselves, apart from the numbers written on them by Lhuyd; the earliest Hengwrt pressmarks on the manuscripts are those associated with Owen's catalogue.

The last of the Hengwrt Vaughans, Sir Robert Williames Vaughan, was residing at Rhug, near Corwen, at the time of his death in 1859. He bequeathed his manuscript collection to the antiquary William Watkin Edward Wynne, who merged it with the much smaller collection already at his home, Peniarth. Wynne compiled a catalogue of the manuscripts that was published in *Archaeologia Cambrensis* (1869–1871). Wynne's catalogue, which corrected and added to Owen's, listed–including missing manuscripts–550 items. It was the last catalogue to identify the manuscripts by their Hengwrt numbers. At Peniarth the collection was renumbered in a single series by J. Gwenogvryn Evans in connection with his *Report on Manuscripts in the Welsh Language* (1898–1910). Most of the printed books were sold to the Bristol bookseller Thomas Kerslake, who listed them in two of his catalogues; in this way the greater part of Robert Vaughan's printed collection was scattered. The manuscripts remained at Peniarth until the death in 1909 of Wynne's last surviving son, who in 1904 had sold the reversion of the collection to Sir John Williams on behalf of the nascent National Library of Wales. Williams was the first president and chief benefactor of the library, which was established by royal charter in 1906; the major part of Vaughan's collection thus entered the National Library of Wales as its premier foundation collection. Since they became open to public use in 1909, the Hengwrt-Peniarth manuscripts have had as call numbers the numbers given to them at Peniarth by Evans. Robert Vaughan's activities as a book and manuscript collector truly benefited all of Wales by bringing together many of its greatest literary treasures.

Letters:

T. E. Parry, "Llythyrau Robert Vaughan Hengwrt (1592–1667), gyda rhagymadrodd a nodiadau," thesis, University of Wales, 1960.

References:

E. D. Jones, "Camden, Vaughan, and Lhuyd, and Merionethshire," *Cylchgrawn Cymdeithas Hanes a Chofnodion Sir Feirionydd,* 2 (1953–1956): 209–227;

Jones, "Robert Vaughan of Hengwrt," *Cylchgrawn Cymdeithas Hanes a Chofnodion Sir Feirionydd (Journal of the Merioneth Historical and Record Society),* 1 (1949–1951): 21–30;

Richard Morgan, "Robert Vaughan of Hengwrt (1592–1667)," *Cylchgrawn Cymdeithas Hanes a Chofnodion Sir Feirionydd,* 8 (1977–1980): 397–408.

Papers:

The main holdings of surviving papers of Robert Vaughan are in the National Library of Wales; some notebooks and papers are in the British Library and Cardiff Central Library.

Horace Walpole, fourth Earl of Orford

(24 September 1717 – 2 March 1797)

Virginia T. Bemis
Ashland University

See also the Walpole entries in *DLB 39: British Novelists, 1660–1800, Part 2* and *DLB 104: British Prose Writers, 1660–1800, Second Series.*

CATALOGUES: *A Catalog of the Classic Contents of Strawberry Hill Collected by Horace Walpole* (London: Printed by Smith & Robins, 1842);

Ædes Strawberrianæ; Names of Purchasers and the Prices to the Detailed Sale Catalogue of Books & Prints Withdrawn from Strawberry-Hill for Sale in London (London: J. H. Burn, 1842);

A Catalogue of Horace Walpole's Library, 3 volumes, edited by Allen T. Hazen (New Haven: Yale University Press, 1969).

BOOKS: *The Lessons for the Day. Being the First and Second Chapters of the Book of Preferment,* anonymous (London: Printed for W. Webb, 1742);

The Beauties. An Epistle to Mr. Eckardt, the Painter, anonymous (London: Printed for M. Cooper, 1746);

Epilogue to Tamerlane, on The Suppression of the Rebellion. Spoken by Mrs. Pritchard, in the Character of the Comic Muse, Nov. 4. 1746, anonymous (London: Printed for R. Dodsley & sold by M. Cooper, 1746);

A Letter to the Whigs. Occasion'd by the Letter to the Tories, anonymous (London: Printed for M. Cooper, 1747);

Ædes Walpolianæ; or, A Description of the Collection of Pictures at Houghton-Hall in Norfolk, the Seat of the Right Honourable Sir Robert Walpole, Earl of Orford (London, 1747 [i.e., 1748]); revised and enlarged edition (London: Dodsley, 1759);

The Original Speech of Sir William Stanhope, on the first reading of the Bill for appointing the Assizes at Buckingham, Feb. 19, 1748, as William Stanhope (London: Printed for W. Webb, 1748);

A Second and Third Letter to the Whigs, by the author of the First (London: Printed for M. Cooper, 1748);

The Speech of Richard White-Liver Esq.; in behalf of Himself and his Brethren. Spoken to the most August Mob at Rag Fair, as Richard White-Liver (London: Printed for W. Webb, 1748);

Horace Walpole, circa 1755 (portrait by John Giles Eckhardt; National Portrait Gallery, London)

A Letter from Xo Ho, a Chinese Philosopher at London, to His Friend Lien Chi at Peking, anonymous (London: Printed for N. Middleton, 1757);

A Catalogue of the Royal and Noble Authors of England, With Lists of Their Works, 2 volumes (Strawberry Hill, 1758);

Fugitive Pieces in Verse and Prose (Printed at Strawberry Hill, 1758);

A Dialogue between Two Great Ladies, anonymous (London: Printed for M. Cooper, 1760);

Catalogue of Pictures and Drawings in the Holbein-Chamber, at Strawberry-Hill (Strawberry Hill, 1760);

Anecdotes of Painting in England; With some Account of the principal Artists; And Incidental Notes on other Arts; Collected by the late Mr. George Vertue; And now digested and published from his original MSS., 4 volumes (Strawberry Hill: Printed by Thomas Farmer, 1762–1780);

The Opposition to the Late Minister Vindicated From the Aspersions of a Pamphlet, intitled, Considerations on the Present Dangerous Crisis, anonymous (London: Printed for William Bathoe, 1763);

The Castle of Otranto, A Story. Translated by William Marshal, Gent. From the Original Italian of Onuphrio Muralto, Canon of the Church of St. Nicholas at Otranto, as William Marshal (London: Printed for Tho. Lownds, 1765 [i.e., 1764]); as Walpole (London: Printed for William Bathoe & Thomas Lownds, 1765);

A Counter-Address to the Public, on the Late Dismission of a General Officer, anonymous (London: Printed for J. Almon, 1764);

An Account of the Giants Lately Discovered; in a Letter to a Friend in the Country, as S. T. (London: Printed for F. Noble, 1766);

Historic Doubts on the Life and Reign of King Richard the Third (London: Printed for J. Dodsley, 1768);

The Mysterious Mother. A Tragedy (Strawberry Hill, 1768);

Reply to Dean Milles (Strawberry Hill, 1770?);

Works, 2 volumes (Strawberry Hill: Printed by Thomas Kirgate, 1770);

A Description of the Villa of Horace Walpole, Youngest Son of Sir Robert Walpole, Earl of Orford, at Strawberry-Hill, near Twickenham: With an Inventory of the Furniture, Pictures, Curiosities, &c. (Strawberry Hill: Printed by Thomas Kirgate, 1774);

A Letter to the Editor of the Miscellanies of Thomas Chatterton (Strawberry Hill: Printed by T. Kirgate, 1779);

Hieroglyphic Tales (Strawberry Hill: Printed by T. Kirgate, 1785);

Postscript to The Royal and Noble Authors (Strawberry Hill, 1786);

The Works of Horatio Walpole, Earl of Orford, edited by Mary Berry as Robert Berry, 5 volumes (London: Printed for G. G. & J. Robinson & J. Edwards, 1798);

Notes to the Portraits at Woburn Abbey (N.p., 1800);

Memoires of the Last Ten Years of the Reign of George the Second, 2 volumes, edited by Lord Holland (London: John Murray, 1822);

Memoirs of the Reign of King George the Third, 4 volumes, edited by Sir Denis Le Marchant (London: Richard Bentley, 1845);

Journal of the Reign of King George the Third, from the Year 1771 to 1783, 2 volumes, edited by John Doran (London: Richard Bentley, 1859);

Notes on the Poems of Alexander Pope, edited by William Augustus Fraser (London: Printed at the Chiswick Press, 1871);

Journal of the Printing Office at Strawberry Hill, Now First Printed from the Ms. of Horace Walpole, edited by Paget Toynbee (London: Printed at the Chiswick Press for Constable and Houghton Mifflin, 1923);

The Duchess of Portland's Museum, edited by Wilmarth S. Lewis (New York: Grolier Club, 1936).

Editions and Collections: *The Last Journals of Horace Walpole During the Reign of George III, from 1771–1783* (London & New York: Lane, 1910); republished (New York: Garland, 1974);

The Castle of Otranto, edited, with an introduction, by Oswald Doughty (London: Scholartis, 1929);

Memoirs and Portraits, edited by Matthew Hodgart (London: Batsford, 1963);

The Castle of Otranto, edited by Lewis (London: Oxford University Press, 1969);

Historic Doubts on the Life and Reign of King Richard III: Including the Supplement, Reply, Short Observations and Postscript, introduction and notes by P. W. Hammond (Gloucester, U.K.: Sutton, 1974);

Hieroglyphic Tales, introduction by Kenneth W. Gross (Los Angeles: William Andrews Clark Memorial Library, 1982);

Memoirs of King George II, 3 volumes, edited by John Brooke (New Haven: Yale University Press, 1985).

Horace Walpole is known to literary scholars as the founder of a significant literary genre, the gothic novel, which he initiated with the publication of *The Castle of Otranto, A Story. Translated by William Marshal, Gent. From the Original Italian of Onuphrio Muralto, Canon of the Church of St. Nicholas at Otranto* (1764). Historians of the eighteenth century know him as a diarist and letter writer; art historians recognize him as a promoter of the Gothic in architecture; and students of publishing history and the history of the book know him as a book collector and a publisher.

Horatio Walpole was born 24 September 1717 (O.S.) at 17 Arlington Street, London. His parents were Sir Robert Walpole, later first Earl of Orford, and Catherine Shorter, daughter of John Shorter of Bybrook, Kent. Walpole was born into a famous political dynasty; his father served in Parliament and in the cabinet with distinction, becoming prime minister and the dominant political figure of his age. Walpole was christened Horatio after his uncle, Horatio Walpole, later Baron Walpole of Walterton, but disliked the

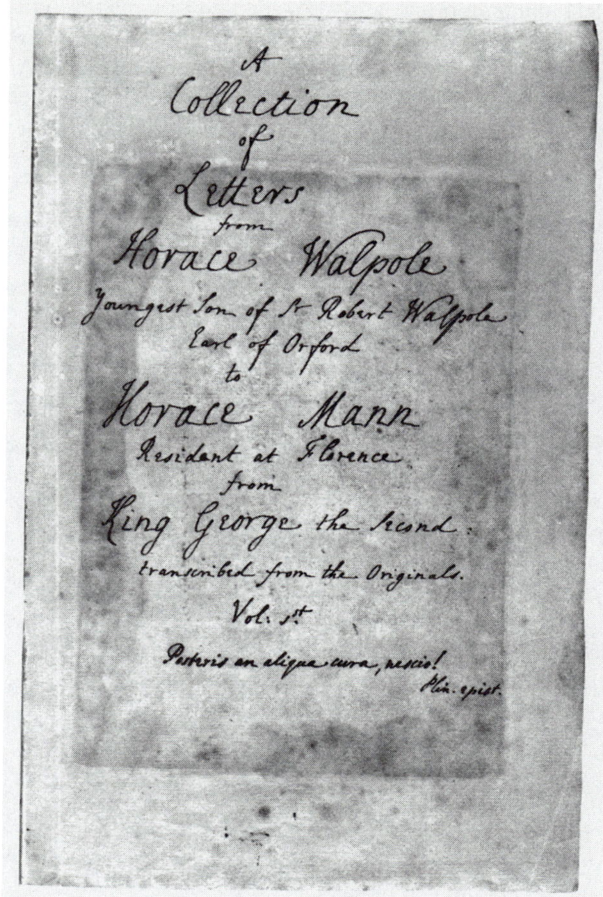
A Collection of Letters from Horace Walpole Youngest Son of Sr Robert Walpole Earl of Orford to Horace Mann Resident at Florence from King George the Second. transcribed from the Originals. Vol: 1st

Posteris an aliqua cura, nescio! Plin. epist.

Title page in Walpole's hand for a bound volume of his letters to his cousin Horace Mann (Lewis Walpole Library, Yale University, Farmington, Connecticut)

name and later anglicized it to Horace. Walpole was eleven years younger than his next sibling, and showed little resemblance to the rest of the family in either looks or interests. This lack of resemblance later lent some credence to rumors that he was actually the son of Carr, Lord Hervey, rather than of Sir Robert Walpole. These rumors, while scandalous, appear to be entirely unfounded, and Walpole himself, who wrote about his own life at great length, never showed any inkling of doubt as to his parentage.

Walpole spent most of his early years at his father's house near Chelsea College, a building later merged into the Royal Military Hospital. Some of his early schooling took place at Bexley, in Kent, under the supervision of the Reverend Edward Weston, son of the bishop of Exeter. Always one to want to be part of the great events of his day, Walpole records being taken in 1727, at his own request, to kiss the hand of George I, who was then nearing the end of his life. Walpole also began his book-collecting activities early. In 1725 he asked Lady Walpole to send him copies of John Banks's *The Unhappy Favourite; Or, the Earl of Essex; a Tragedy* (1682) and Nicholas Rowe's *The Tragedy of Jane Shore* (1714). These two works are the first books he is known to have owned, and they show, even at the age of eight, a strong interest in English history of earlier days and, with *Jane Shore,* the story of Edward IV's mistress, early stirrings of his intense interest in the era of Richard III. In 1728 he bought a copy of Andrew Michael Ramsay's *Travels of Cyrus* (2 volumes, 1727), which later came to rest in the University Library, Cambridge. His interest in books continued strong, and his library had grown to at least two hundred books by 1733. He formed the habit of writing inside each book both his name and the year he bought it. As well as standard textbooks on arithmetic, geography, French grammar, and the classics, he showed wider interests, buying a copy of Petronius's *Satyricon* when he was twelve. By the time he was thirteen he had begun to collect contemporary and near-contemporary authors, including Joseph Addison, Richard Steele, and William Congreve. One notable addition to his collection came when the duke of Brunswick gave him seventy-six volumes of the classics. This gift, an unusual one to make to a boy of about twelve, suggests that his tastes in reading were known, and also that the duke, who had been negotiating with Sir Robert Walpole over copies of George I's will, wanted to thank the prime minister for a satisfactory settlement.

Walpole went to Eton on 26 April 1727. His tutor was Henry Bland, the headmaster's eldest son. Walpole was not remarkable as a scholar, but formed friendships that were to influence his life. Particular among these was his friendship with Thomas Gray, who became a noted poet, and with George and Charles Montagu, Thomas Ashton, and William Cole, the antiquary. After leaving Eton on 23 September 1734, Walpole went to King's College, Cambridge. He had been entered at Lincoln's Inn as well, but never attended. While at Cambridge, beginning in March 1735, he studied civil law, anatomy, philosophy, and classics. He also tried to learn mathematics, traditionally highly valued at Cambridge, but after two weeks his instructor, Professor Saunderson, told him that he could not possibly learn the subject. Unwilling to acknowledge that there was anything he could not do, Walpole engaged a private tutor, but eventually he had to admit that mathematics defeated him entirely. He became skilled in French and Italian, but said that he was never much good at Greek. Shortly before the end of his time at Cambridge, Walpole's father appointed him an inspector of imports and exports in the custom house, a post he resigned in January 1738 when he became usher of the exchequer. With other minor political posts he accrued an income of about £1,200 a year. Such patronage was the typical practice of the day, and these political sinecures afforded him a comfortable income.

In 1739 Walpole left Oxford and went with Gray on the traditional Grand Tour of the Continent. They began in France and later journeyed to Italy, where Walpole nourished his taste for antiquities and soaked in the atmosphere that was later to prove so compelling in *The Castle of Otranto.* During his stay in Italy he became a connoisseur of art. Also during this time a quarrel with Gray resulted in a temporary cessation of their friendship. Walpole, in his memoirs, blamed himself for the entire misunderstanding. While in Florence, Walpole formed a friendship with Sir Horace Mann, a relative, who was then British minister to the court of Tuscany. Their tastes in art and literature were similar, and they became firm friends. They seldom met after Walpole left Italy, but they kept up a long and detailed correspondence until Mann's death in 1786. This was the first of the letter-writing relationships so characteristic of Walpole in later years, and the start of what was to prove a treasure trove for historians of the eighteenth century. Walpole's letters to Mann and others are a fount of information on events, gossip, styles, and politics, written in a witty, conversational style. At this time Walpole still hoped for fame as a poet or politician, but his letters and memoirs are his true claim to fame.

Walpole returned to England in the fall of 1741, having been elected as member of Parliament for Callington, in Cornwall. It was a family borough and, like the government posts, he had the seat because of his father's influence. The younger Walpole's political career was less distinguished than his father's. Horace Walpole was reelected at Callington in 1747, returned for Castle Rising, Norfolk, also a Walpole seat, and for King's Lynn in 1757 and 1761, retiring from active politics in 1768. He never held a cabinet position, rarely spoke in the House of Commons, and seems to have had little contact with his constituents. However, in 1761 the mayor of King's Lynn did present him with an illuminated book of the arms of the Knights of the Garter created by Richard III and Henry VII. The book, bound in red velvet, had once been owned by Elizabeth I.

Sir Robert retired as prime minister in 1742, and was created earl of Orford. Walpole lived with his father in London and at Houghton, in Norfolk, which had a fine picture gallery, a factor leading to his first major publication, *Aedes Walpolianæ; or, A Description of the Collection of Pictures at Houghton-Hall in Norfolk, the Seat of the Right Honourable Sir Robert Walpole, Earl of Orford* (1747), a catalogue and discussion of the works of art owned by his father.

Lord Orford died in 1744, leaving Walpole a house in London, £5,000, and an income of £1,000 a year from the position of collector in the custom house. For the next few years Walpole divided his time between London and Windsor, where he renewed his friendship with Gray and spent his time in writing. He was both a prolific and observant letter writer and an author of political memoirs. His letters form a chronicle of the history of his time, but it was in his memoirs that he was most consciously trying to leave a record for posterity. Using his letters and journals as resource materials and books in his collection as supplements, he produced a series of works on all the important events and figures of his day. While he had worked on earlier chronicles, his memoir-writing project began in earnest in 1751, and produced a history of that year and the nine just before it, *Memoires of the Last Ten Years of the Reign of George the Second* (2 volumes, 1822), edited by Lord Holland and published posthumously. Walpole continued writing his memoirs with varying degrees of

Walpole in his library at Strawberry Hill (drawing by John Henry Müntz; Collection of Commander Colin Campbell-Johnston)

energy, depending on what else was occupying his attention, for the next forty years.

In 1747 Walpole went to live at Twickenham, where he leased a small house. At this time Twickenham was still a quiet, rural area, whose most famous previous resident had been the poet Alexander Pope. By 1748 Walpole had become so fond of the area that be bought the property outright. This house became the famous Strawberry Hill, his home, art gallery, and major artistic creation. He devoted himself to reconstructing the house, attempting to create what he envisioned as "a little Gothic castle." Gothic design was already fashionable among the nouveaux riche, but Walpole brought it into the realm of taste. When he, as an acknowledged tastemaker and leader of fashion, adopted Gothic, Gothic became the mode. Strawberry Hill came to be extravagantly medieval, with arches and stained glass, ceilings derived from Westminster Abbey, all intended to reproduce what Walpole called "the gloomth of abbeys and cathedrals." He was more concerned with atmosphere than with archaeological accuracy, and blended motifs from various periods with modern carpets and "a thousand plump chairs, couches and luxurious settees." He later wrote that "I did not mean to make my house so Gothic as to exclude convenience and modern refinements in luxury. The designs of the inside and outside are strictly ancient, but the decorations are modern." Walpole finished the main house by 1754, but kept adding for forty more years as he got new ideas and as his collections of books and art expanded.

In 1753–1754 Walpole built a grand refectory with a library over it. In 1760–1761 he added a picture gallery, cloisters, and a round tower. These too were decorated with all sorts of Gothic detail, including pointed arches and painted glass windows. He then proceeded to fill his castle with pictures, statues, books, and art objects of all sorts. The particular joy of Strawberry Hill was the library, which housed his extensive collection of books and manuscripts. This was a working collection, gathered by a book lover who used his books and planned with an eye toward his own research. Walpole was not one to acquire a book simply because it was rare or expensive. The deciding factor for him was always how well it would fill a vacancy in his collection and whether it could be used in his studies. He had his own principles for choosing books, though these can only be deduced from looking at his collection. He worked with several booksellers, and may have had standing orders for contemporary works. Author and date notations on some contemporary treatises in his collection are in the handwriting of William Bathoe, a bookseller he favored. He also had a bookseller in France, and Mann and other friends on the Continent made purchases for him. In addition he watched auctions for items of interest, usually bidding through an agent, often Bathoe, though he sometimes went to a sale himself, once leaving a session in the House of Commons to attend a book sale.

Walpole often entered the publication date on his purchases of new works, and for anonymous works he had the habit of adding a note about the author, or his belief as to the author's identity. He also had many new works specially bound, some by James Campbell, others by John Robiquet and possibly by Christian Samuel Kalthoeber. He seems to have preferred to use British binders, even for his French purchases, and had items bound in morocco or calf, with his coat of arms on the sides. Walpole also had bookplates designed for him, and books from his library can be given approximate acquisition dates by looking at the plates. His first bookplate was designed early on, perhaps in 1732, by the noted engraver George Vertue and featured Walpole's coat of arms above the name "Mr. Horatio Walpole." From 1733 he used a bookplate rather than signing his name in his newly acquired books. He had so many bookplates printed that a new master had to be engraved in 1760 and retouched in 1780.

After Walpole became earl of Orford in 1791, he had a new bookplate designed, in a circular form, lettered "Sigillum Horatii Comitis de Orford." This plate was later copied with minor variations by Horatio William, fourth Earl of Orford of the second creation (1813–1894), whose seal is sometimes mistaken for that of his predecessor. Matters were made more confusing when Horatio William bought books Horace Walpole had owned and added his personal plate to one already there. The student of Walpole's collection can approximately date the book by examining the plate, and can also tell if the book is genuine. Imitations, or real plates switched from one book to another, do exist, with the spurious items being concocted in an effort to raise the price of a book by adding the cachet of Walpole's name.

Walpole had moved about one thousand books from his "bookery" in Arlington Street to Strawberry Hill, and kept few books in London. Those he did keep there were probably ones he was using in a current project or some duplicates. In 1753 he wrote to his friend Mann of two presses at Strawberry Hill in the room he called the Green Closet, containing "books of heraldry and antiquities, Mme Sevigne's letters, and any French books that relate to her and her acquaintance." Since his collection would certainly continue to expand, he decided to add a purposely designed library to Strawberry Hill. The addition of the Great Parlour and the library stemmed from his wish to keep his collection together and properly housed.

While the books and furniture are now dispersed, the library today remains much as originally planned. The room is twenty-eight feet long, seventeen-and-a-half-feet wide, and somewhat over fifteen feet high, making it one of the larger rooms at Strawberry Hill. The walls are lined with shelves divided into presses, with Gothic arches serving as doors. The design for the bookcases was of great concern to Walpole, who wanted something that would be both functional in a working library and suitably Gothic in style. The final result was based on an engraving of the arched side doors to the choir of Old St. Paul's, made somewhat wider and built of light wood, hinged to swing away for access to books normally hidden behind the carved doors.

Each of the twelve presses is lettered from *A* to *M,* as a means of helping in locating books. Since each press is ten-and-a-half-feet high, Walpole had to use a set of library steps to access books on the top shelves. The ceiling is painted with the arms and shields of the Walpole family and other ancestors, the FitzOsberts and Robsarts, painted by Jean-Francois Clermont from sketches drawn by Walpole. Walpole was sparing no expense to make his library exactly as he wished, and Clermont, painter to the duke of Marlborough and Frederick Louis, Prince of Wales, charged 70 guineas for the work.

By late 1754 the library was completed, and Walpole was able to shelve his cherished books in their permanent home. The first filled shelves held about two thousand books he already owned, and in the next ten years or so he bought about one thousand more. In this period he concentrated on the standard volumes that every library of the time needed, from the philosophical works of John Locke to a 1666 edition of the theologian Richard Hooker's *Of the Lawes of ecclesiasticall politie* (1594–1597). In his purchasing he tended to buy books for use rather than rarity. He could easily have afforded far more valuable editions of such writers as William Shakespeare, but he had only one copy of the Second

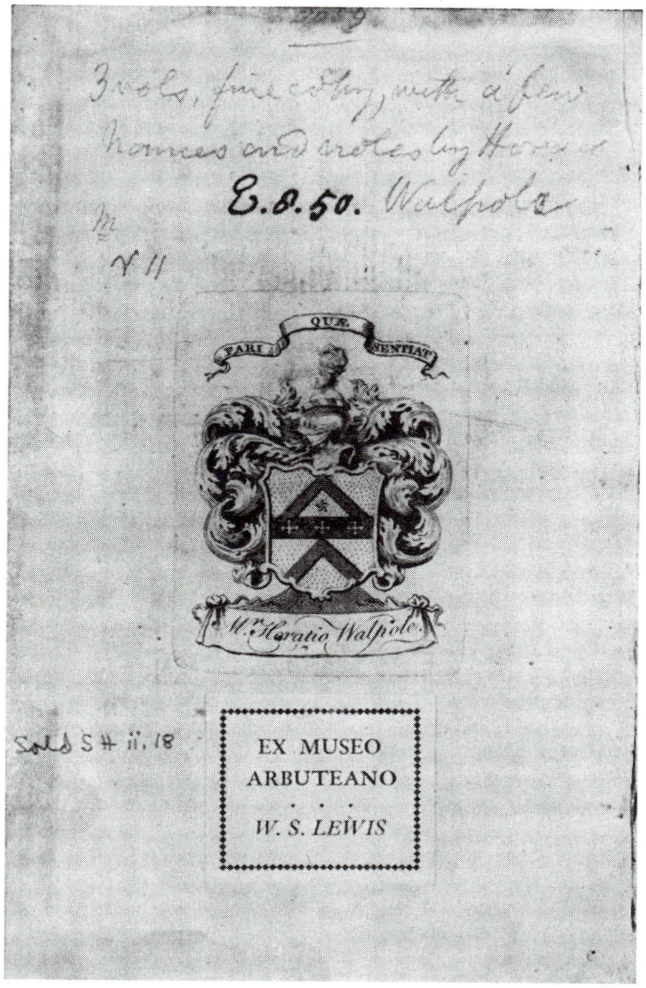

Flyleaf for Walpole's copy of Lady Mary Wortley Montagu's letters (1763), bearing the press number for Walpole's library, his second bookplate, and the bookplate for Walpole collector Wilmarth Sheldon Lewis (Lewis Walpole Library, Yale University, Farmington, Connecticut)

Folio of 1632 and no quartos. He did own several eighteenth-century editions and a fine copy of Shakespeare, but it was more valuable as an association copy, formerly owned by Alexander Pope, than as an intrinsic rarity. He preferred to buy later editions rather than the type of collector's gem one hesitates to use. By the end of Walpole's life the library held about eight thousand books, much less than other great libraries of the day, but Walpole was not consumed by the desire to own everything that overcomes so many collectors. He bought little in the sciences, law, or music. Instead, he specialized in literature and the arts, creating a personalized collection rather than a library in the modern sense. He had many duplicate copies, either because he had bought them in lots with other books or because he had forgotten that he already had a copy on his shelves.

Walpole did not feel the need for a catalogue until 1763, and then followed the standard practice of the day in having the books entered by author, location, and size. From that catalogue one can determine not only what he owned, but where in the library he kept it. Walpole continued cataloguing for three years, then abandoned the project and further entries were made only years later by Thomas Kirgate, secretary and printer of the press at Strawberry Hill. This catalogue thus lists only about half of the books Walpole owned at the end of his life, while the sale catalogue of 1842 is more comprehensive. The 1763 catalogue provides the size, author, title, place, and date of publication of each book, along with its press number, another standard practice of the time. Each book was assigned a letter and two numbers, one indicating the shelf, the second the place on the shelf. Walpole partly abandoned this inflexible and impractical system by discarding the second number, allowing placement of related books together on the same shelf regardless of order of accession. He still had difficulty using the catalogue, since the titles recorded in it sometimes did not match the main title on the book, and some were not entered at all, especially after 1766.

He wrote to John Henderson on 14 March 1782, "I was at Strawberry Hill yesterday, and hunted all over my library for *Palladis Tamia,* the book you wanted, but could not find it. I did not remember having it, nor is it in the catalogue of my books, though that is no certain rule, as I have bought a great many since the catalogue was made and have neglected to enter them. However I do believe Mr. Malone is mistaken in thinking I bought a book of which I have not the least idea . . ." Yet, he did own the book: Francis Meres's *Palladis Tamia; Wit's Treasury being the Second Part of Wits Commonwealth* (1598) was in the manuscript catalogue, under the title *Mere's Wit's Treasury.*

The first press, lettered *A,* held books by English royal and noble authors. It is likely that Walpole began to see books by the aristocracy as a collecting category while at work on *A Catalogue of the Royal and Noble Authors of England, With Lists of Their Works* (2 volumes, 1758). Press *B* held books on the arts and on numismatics, *C* and *D* held folios of European prints. In press *E* Walpole kept books in one of his favorite categories, English antiquities and topography. Eventually, he came to own about five hundred volumes on these subjects. Presses *F* and *G* held books in French, with a particular focus on the seventeenth century. He had an especial interest in the works of Marie de Sévigné, and also collected the works of Montesquieu, Bernard Le Bovier Fontenelle and Jacques Boileau. In press *H* was a miscellaneous collection of English letters and religious works. Walpole disliked discarding books once he purchased them, and in this press were many volumes of sermons he had acquired in younger days, followed by discussions of religious controversies he purchased later as his interests turned to less pious avenues. Press *I* held memoirs and biography of a miscellaneous character. Wilmarth S. Lewis reports that the fifth shelf held, in this order, lives of the eighteenth-century actress Anne Oldfield; Colonel James Gardiner; Bishop John Aylmer; James Butler, first Duke of Ormonde; Dr. Ralph Bathurst, one of the founders of the Royal Society; the seventeenth-century naturalist John Ray; the fourteenth-century warrior Edward, prince of Wales, known as the Black Prince; the sixteenth-century Spanish physician and theologian Miguel Serveto; John Churchill, who was created first Duke of Marlborough in 1702 for his victories over the French; the ninth-century king Alfred the Great; and the seventeenth-century poet John Milton. This haphazard assortment shows that Walpole was not a systematic historical enthusiast, but one with widely ranging interests. Press *K* contained English poetry, a favorite for Walpole. He had holdings in all the poets respected and popular in the day and many minor figures, now almost entirely forgotten. Their main value to a modern collector would be as association copies, having come from Strawberry Hill. Presses *H, I,* and *K* also held other material. The top of each press had a collection totaling 120 volumes of tracts printed before 1760, and *I* and *K* also held Walpole's contemporary collection. He had poems, plays, and tracts (by which he meant treatises, not pious and inspirational pamphlets) assembled in his own binding, with special title pages, as they appeared. Presses *L* and *M* contained Greek, Latin, and Italian books, but mainly books in Latin. Walpole did not care for Greek writers, and surprisingly for one whose masterwork, *The Castle of Otranto,* was set in Italy, was not fond of Italian writers either.

The one press without a letter was locked and provided with glass inserts rather than screens. It became known as the Glass Closet, and housed Walpole's favorite books and manuscripts, including those he felt were rare, gifts from special friends, and things he did not want the world to see. Here were found an early fifteenth-century manuscript collection of the York Mystery Plays, a copy of Thomas Lodge's *Rosalynd; Euphues Golden Legacie* (1604), two copies of George Puttenham's *Art of English Poesie* (1589), D'Eon's *Letters* (1764), and Walpole's complete set of the publications of the press at Strawberry Hill.

When he planned it, the library must have seemed more than adequate for Walpole's books and buying habits. Eventually he had to add extra shelves in *A* and *B,* and later had to set up additional library space as well. He created "The Little Library" in a room in a cottage in the garden, mainly to house manuscripts and prints, then a book room in his offices (built by James Wyatt in 1790) that held books he bought in the last thirty years of his life. This book room contained about 2,500 books, read and mainly annotated by Walpole, including such items as James Boswell's *Life of Samuel Johnson* (1791) and Gilbert White's *Natural History and Antiquities of Selborne* (1789). It was really an overflow library, housing items not in constant use, and it was Walpole's practice to send for any books he needed. The presses here were lettered from *N* to *V,* and subjects were arranged in a similar fashion to those in the main library. Many of the books were either in the original boards or unbound. In 1797 Walpole's heir, Anne Seymour Damer, moved the contents of the cottage library to the Offices as protection against damp and mold.

Walpole also made a print library in 1790 in a room in the Round Tower, and transferred to it many of the print volumes from presses *B, C,* and *D* of the main library. The presses in this room were lettered *A* to *Y,* with a closet not unlike the Glass Closet for special and extremely rare items. His prints included an extensive collection of the engravings of William Hogarth, three hundred Albrecht Dürer prints, many German and Flemish engravings, manuscripts, and drawings by Vertue, and Richard Bentley's drawings for Strawberry Hill along with his illustrations for Walpole's own memoirs and Gray's poems. Also in the Round Tower was Walpole's collection of Thomas Chatterton material.

Not content with collecting books, Walpole began to publish books in 1757. His printing press at Strawberry Hill, established in a cottage near his home, published his own works and the works of many noted writers of the day. The first publication was a book of the poetry of Walpole's friend Gray, *Odes by Mr. Gray,* in 1757. Other noteworthy publications included *Poems* (1764), by Anna Chamber, Countess Temple; and Hannah More's poem *Bishop Bonner's Ghost* (1789), the last major item the press produced. A full catalogue of the publications of Walpole's private press, *A Bibliography of the Strawberry Hill Press,* was compiled by Allen T. Hazen and published in 1942. Walpole's handwritten *Journal of the Printing Office at Strawberry Hill,* edited and published by Paget Toynbee in 1923, records the activities of what was the first private press in England. Each book was carefully designed, with Walpole taking an active editorial interest in illustration, type, and composition. He also had an engraved *flueron* (a printer's typographical ornament) designed for the books, featuring a design of leaves, his coat of arms, and a picture of Strawberry Hill.

Walpole was aided in this endeavor by printer and manager William Robinson, whom he dismissed in 1759. Several temporary printers succeeded him until Thomas Kirgate took up the job and stayed in it until Walpole's death. Kirgate was a skilled printer and also a thief who hoarded copies of the most rare works for later sale. He is known to have printed unauthorized copies late in Walpole's life and after his death and to have sold many of the reprints to collectors. These quasi forgeries account for some of the discrepancies among bibliographies of Walpoliana, in particularly some doubtful copies of *Odes by Mr. Gray.*

In 1764 Walpole had his literary masterpiece, *The Castle of Otranto,* published by Thomas Lownds in London. Although all copies of the book indicate that the work was published in 1765, it was actually published on 24 December 1764. This work, which Walpole described as a "Gothic romance" supposedly transcribed from an ancient manuscript, was an immediate success, blending the trappings of the supernatural with a modern adventure story. There have been well over a hundred editions of *The Castle of Otranto* since its first publication. Walpole can be credited with having established a literary genre, in which many imitators followed him with varying degrees of success. Notable among the successful followers of the time were Ann Radcliffe's *The Mysteries of Udolpho* (1794) and M. G. Lewis's *The Monk* (1796). The book influenced such notable later writers as Sir Walter Scott and Charlotte Brontë, and Gothic novels remain a best-selling type of fiction.

The Castle of Otranto was then and now Walpole's best-known book but he also had an extensive career as a political pamphleteer in the Whig interest and in defending friends of his father. As a writer and a behind-the-scenes political presence, Walpole enjoyed controversy and changed from faction to faction. He even wrote an anonymous series of articles in the opposition journals *Old England* and *The Remembrancer* between 1747 and 1749, apparently in the hope that assisting the Tories would bring him the office that had eluded him as a Whig. This effort was unsuccessful and he returned to his original alliances.

In 1765 Walpole took a long-planned trip to France, where he became friends with the sixty-eight-year-old Marie de Vichy-Chamand, Marquise du Deffand, a writer and society wit. He visited her many times and the two kept up a correspondence until her death in 1780, with Madame du Deffand buying books on Walpole's behalf and sending them to him in England. She apparently fell in love with Walpole, although he never reciprocated her passion. She bequeathed Walpole her manuscripts, which he kept in his Glass Cabinet with his other prized possessions, and copies of her published letters were featured in the Strawberry Hill sale of 1842. During this first Paris sojourn, he bought so many books and so much fine china and other art objects that twenty-two cases were needed to ship his new treasures back to London.

His stature and influence in the art world led many young writers and artists to approach Walpole, hoping for patronage. One of these young hopefuls was the young Chatterton, later to be known as one of the great literary hoaxers. In 1769 the sixteen-year-old Chatterton sent Walpole fragments of his prose and verse, supposedly written by a fifteenth-century Bristol priest, Thomas Rowley, and received an encouraging reply. After further correspondence, Walpole consulted Gray and Mason, who agreed that the fragments of ancient poems Chatterton claimed to have discovered and translated were, at best, of doubtful origin. Walpole ignored Chatterton's later requests for money, and eventually sent back all the letters and poems he had received.

Chatterton had indeed created the poems supposedly written by Rowley, and was later revealed as a hoaxer of considerable talent. He swore that he would get revenge on Walpole, and attacked him in periodicals, giving him the name of Baron Otranto. When Chatterton committed suicide by taking arsenic on 24 August 1770, Walpole was unfairly charged with having rejected a poet of talent and hence of causing the young man's death. Those who accepted the poems as authentic texts blamed Walpole, and the controversy continued for years, with Walpole refusing to defend himself publicly until 1779, when he published *A Letter to the Editor of the Miscellanies of Thomas Chatterton.* Walpole's studies of the writers of the Middle Ages had made him suspicious of the poems Chatterton had sent him, which indeed were later proved to be entirely spurious–Chatterton had even invented "Thomas Rowley," their purported author.

Walpole was no stranger to literary controversy. His *Historic Doubts on the Life and Reign of King Richard the Third* (1768) shows him as eager to take on established belief and to champion the historical underdog. His defense of Richard as a ruler and as innocent of the murders of his nephews, Edward V and Richard, Duke of York, countered the received image of Richard III that was largely shaped by Shakespeare's play *The Tragedy of King Richard III* (1597). Modern partisans of Richard's innocence trace their arguments in a direct line to Walpole's work, and mock trials of Richard are still held in law schools. The terms of the debate are still those Walpole set, although modern scholars find Walpole credulous and overly willing to disbelieve Thomas More simply because he supported the Tudors.

Walpole resigned his seat in Parliament in 1768, and spent the remainder of his life peacefully at Strawberry Hill. There he enjoyed his books, pictures, correspondence, and visits from friends, occasionally writing something of a more literary nature. As he said of himself in his posthumously published memoirs, "Arts, books, painting, architecture, antiquities, and those amiable employments of a tranquil life, to which in the warmest of his political hours he had been fondly addicted, assumed an entire empire over him."

A Description of the Villa of Horace Walpole, Youngest Son of Sir Robert Walpole, Earl of Orford, at Strawberry-Hill, near Twickenham: With an Inventory of the Furniture, Pictures, Curiosities, &c., appeared in 1774 and in a revised version in 1784. Walpole compiled it to give a history of his collection and the provenance of many items, from coins and curiosities to books and paintings. By this time Strawberry Hill and his collections were so well known that sightseers came from all over to see the house, and Walpole even had tickets printed up that allowed the bearer to tour the house and collections.

The Mysterious Mother. A Tragedy, was published in 1768, and a one-act comedy, *Nature Will Prevail,* written in 1773, was acted at the Haymarket in 1778 to some success. Another comedy, *The Fashionable Friends,* was attributed to him in 1802 but was actually written by his friend Mary Berry. Of his plays, *The Mysterious Mother* is the most interesting, as a Gothic play. It has many of the hallmarks of the genre, including castles, curses, incest, and secrets that reach beyond the grave, but lacks the development and fascination of *The Castle of Otranto.* It was never produced, for Walpole himself realized it was a poor effort.

On the death of his nephew in 1791, Walpole became the fourth (and last) earl of Orford. His nephew had left huge debts, added to those of his father and grandfather, and had sold the pictures at Houghton to Empress Catherine II of Russia to raise money. Walpole had tried to help his nephew with financial management during his lifetime and used his best efforts to restore the estate and protect the interests of the tenants once he became earl. He never took his seat in the House of Lords, having apparently abandoned all interest in politics save that of a keen observer.

In his old age, Walpole lived quietly at Strawberry Hill and in London, in frail health but enjoying his correspondence, books, and occasional visits from friends. He was still an eager book purchaser, buying fifty books at one sale in 1791, largely seventeenth-century books on natural history, the English countryside, and antiquities, all of which had long been among his great interests. He died at his London residence in Berkeley Square on 2 March 1797, and is buried in Houghton Church, with his father and brothers.

His later years were marked by the friendship with Agnes and Mary Berry, sisters whom he had met in 1789. They were accomplished and friendly, good at conversation, and filled his need for confidantes and correspondents. While their father, Robert Berry, was Walpole's literary executor, it was Mary Berry who actually did the work of preparing *The Works of Horatio Walpole, Earl of Orford,* which appeared in 1798, the year after Walpole's death. Walpole had left the works in such good order that she had little to do. In fact, as she said in her preface, "Lord Orford may still be considered as his own editor: every thing that he had selected is faithfully given to the public; and his arrangement . . . is in every respect strictly adhered to."

He also left his memoirs ready for publication, in a sealed chest, with instructions not to open it until the son of his niece, Lady Waldegrave, turned twenty-five. The chest was opened in 1818, and the memoirs were published in several volumes. The first two volumes,

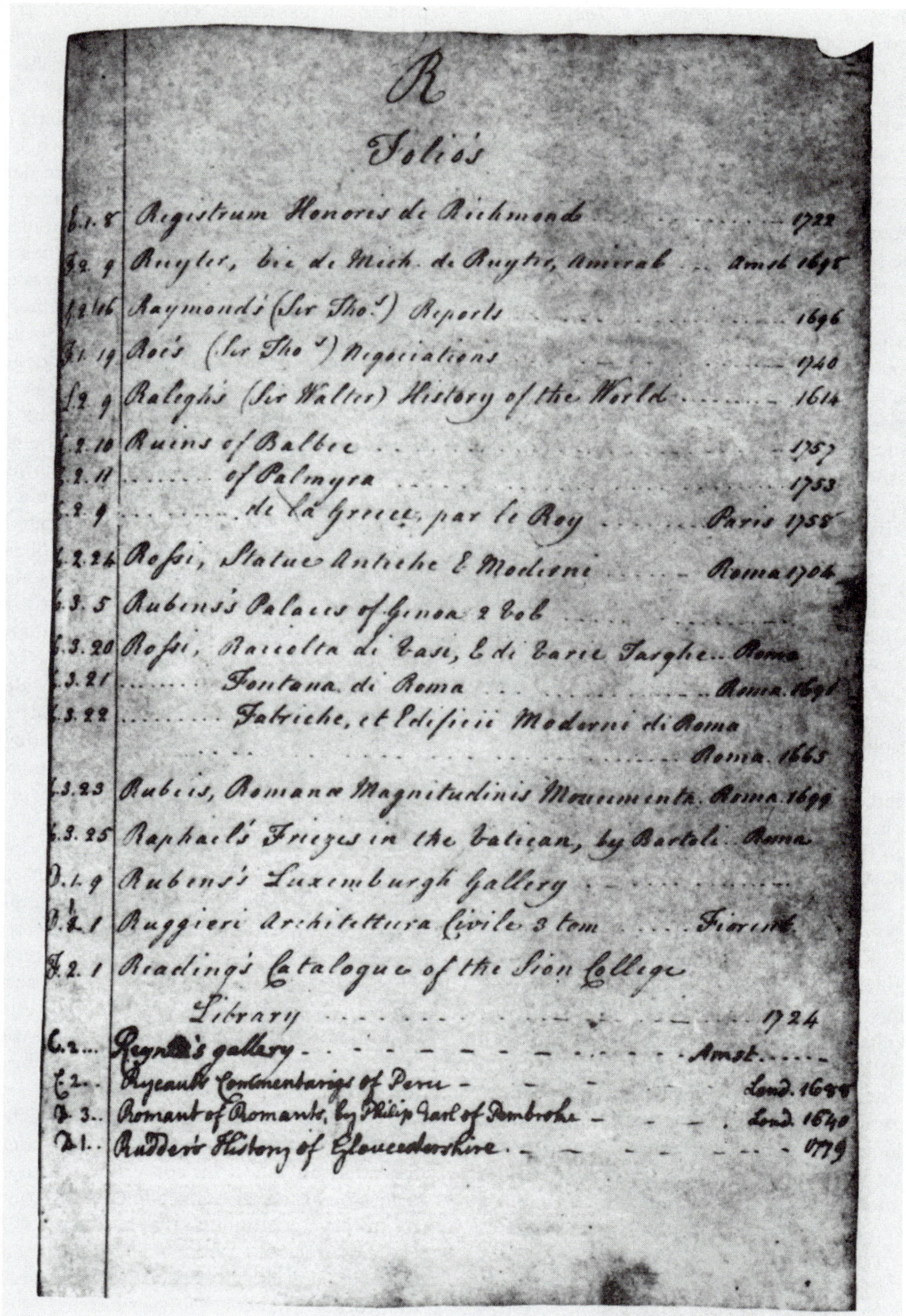

R

Folios

f.1.8 Registrum Honoris de Richmond 1722
f.2.9 Ruyter, Vie de Mich. de Ruyter, Amiral .. Amst 1698
f.2.16 Raymond's (Sir Tho.s) Reports 1696
f.1.19 Roe's (Sir Tho.s) Negociations 1740
f.2.9 Ralegh's (Sir Walter) History of the World 1614
f.2.10 Ruins of Balbec 1757
f.2.11 .... of Palmyra 1753
f.2.9 .... de la Greece, par le Roy .... Paris 1758
f.2.24 Rossi, Statue Antiche e Moderne .... Roma 1704
f.3.5 Rubens's Palaces of Genoa 2 vol ....
f.3.20 Rossi, Raccolta di Vasi, e di varie Targhe .. Roma
f.3.21 .... Fontana di Roma .... Roma 1691
f.3.22 .... Fabriche, et Edificii Moderni di Roma .... Roma 1665
f.3.23 Rubeis, Romanae Magnitudinis Monumenta. Roma 1699
f.3.25 Raphael's Friezes in the Vatican, by Bartoli. Roma
D.1.9 Rubens's Luxemburgh Gallery ....
D.2.1 Ruggieri Architettura Civile 3 tom .... Fiorenz.
E.2.1 Reading's Catalogue of the Sion College Library 1724
C.2... Reynst's gallery .... Amst. .....
C.2.. Rycaut's Commentaries of Peru .... Lond. 1688
[illegible] 3.. Romant of Romants, by Philip Earl of Pembroke .... Lond. 1640
D.1.. Rudder's History of Gloucestershire 1779

Page from the first catalogue of Walpole's library, begun in 1763 (Collection of Lord Walpole, Wolterton Park, Norfolk)

Memoires of the Last Ten Years of the Reign of George the Second, appeared in 1822, the four-volume *Memoirs of the Reign of King George the Third* in 1845, and the third part, *Journal of the Reign of King George III from 1771 to 1783,* was published in two volumes in 1859.

After his death, Walpole's library remained intact for some years. He had left Strawberry Hill to his cousin, Anne Seymour Damer, who did not add to the collection, but was concerned to keep it together. After her death the house and its contents went to the descendants of his favorite niece, Maria Walpole, Countess Waldegrave, later Duchess of Gloucester. In 1842 George Edward, seventh Earl of Waldegrave, decided to sell the books and other contents of Strawberry Hill. Tours of the mansion held before the sale showed that most visitors were interested in Walpole's art and furniture, or in such historical curiosities as a lock of Mary Tudor's hair, Cardinal Thomas Wolsey's hat, a bell embossed by Benvenuto Cellini, the spurs William III wore at the Battle of the Boyne, and a clock given to Anne Boleyn by Henry VIII as a wedding present. The sale catalogue, 250 pages long, is one of the main sources for information about Walpole's library. The first edition listed the books by lots, naming the first few and adding "and others," but later editions amplified the listings. The books and prints in the Round Tower were withdrawn from the sale and later recatalogued and sold separately.

Many of the noted collectors of the day attended the sale, including the eccentric Gothic novelist William Beckford, who bought the Sedan New Testament in Greek (1628) and the Sedan Horace (1627). Beckford had disliked Walpole, who had referred to him as a young man "who has just parts enough to lead him astray from common sense." Walpole had tried to ensure that none of his books or antiquities would go to Beckford, but Beckford outlived all of Walpole's direct heirs and thus had his revenge. In addition to a great many of Walpole's books and manuscripts, Beckford bought a small bronze bust of Emperor Caligula, with silver eyes, one of Walpole's greatest treasures.

Dealers acting as agents for many prominent collectors, including Sir Thomas Phillipps and Edward Smith-Stanley, thirteenth Earl of Derby, bid for various lots, with Lord Derby's agent paying 32 guineas for a set of Walpole's *Anecdotes of Painting in England; With some Account of the principal Artists; And Incidental Notes on other Arts; Collected by the late Mr. George Vertue; And now digested and published from his original MSS.* (4 volumes, 1762–1780). The manuscripts, prints, and drawings fetched the highest prices, however. The highest price was for an illuminated psalter, the work of Julio Clovio, which fetched £441. Lord Waldegrave bought it, seeming to want to keep it in the family. The next highest price was paid for a manuscript copy of the fourteenth-century York Mystery Plays, at 210 guineas. While Walpole's literary reputation was then in eclipse, his stature as a collector remained high, and book lovers were eager to own items from his collection. This demand led some unscrupulous dealers to remove Strawberry Hill book plates from genuine volumes that were damaged or in little demand and put the plates into other books, creating spurious Walpole holdings. Several of the books of prints were broken up immediately after the sale, following the deplorable habit of some art dealers, who want a greater profit by selling individual prints separately. Thus many separate leaves of prints exist and are genuine Walpoliana. The catalogues and the detailed research of Hazen have documented most of the books Walpole owned, and anything not on these lists is probably not authentic. When he gave the Sandars lectures on bibliography at Cambridge in 1958, Wilmarth S. Lewis estimated that about 3,300 items from Walpole's library had been located in various places. He suspected that 400 or so had been destroyed by accident or discarded by booksellers after the bookplates were removed, and that many of the rest were held by private collectors or libraries unaware of what they had.

Walpole has been a subject of considerable historical and artistic interest, with a revival of Walpolian scholarship coming in the twentieth century. The work of the Walpole scholar Lewis at Yale made Walpole's correspondence and much of his other works accessible to scholars. The Yale editions of Walpole, sometimes referred to as products of Lewis's "Walpole factory," have become the standards for students and teachers alike. Previous editions of Walpole's letters, while doing much to show Walpole as a correspondent, were incomplete and in some cases inaccurate. Greater time and access to modern techniques of textual scholarship has made the Yale edition of Walpole's correspondence the important resource Walpole would have wished it to be. Walpole was as eclectic a letter writer as he was a collector, writing on politics, fashion, society scandal, literature, antiquities, and what now would be known as social history. While they show his biases and tastes, the letters also show his concern for accuracy and keeping a true historical record. They also show the concern for history and antiquity that has inspired both the British and American Walpole Societies in their studies of old texts and efforts, especially in Britain, to republish the works of writers of former days.

Lewis was able to reconstruct much of Walpole's library, even determining what books were in which cases. From this reconstruction a portrait can be formed of a valuable working collection. Hazen's three-volume *A Catalogue of Horace Walpole's Library* (1969), which includes a reprint of Lewis's Sandars lectures on the subject, has the most complete extant list of Walpole's collection, checked and cross-checked against the manuscript catalogue, the 1882 sale catalogues, and internal reference points such as bookplates and press marks. Lewis assessed the Strawberry Hill library as "a conspectus of book-collecting during the past three hundred years." Between the noted collectors whose holdings Walpole acquired for their associations and the collectors of later days who bought books because Walpole had once owned them, Walpole is, Lewis said, "at the centre of a collecting web that joins in its shining strands a prime minister and a bootlegger of the Bronx."

Letters:

Letters from the Hon. Horace Walpole, to George Montagu, Esq. from the Year 1736, to the Year 1770, edited by John Martin (London: Printed for Rodwell & Martin and Henry Colburn, 1818);

Letters from the Hon. Horace Walpole, to the Rev. William Cole, and Others; from the Year 1745, to the Year 1782, edited by Martin (London: Printed for Rodwell & Martin and Henry Colburn, 1818);

Letters from the Honble. Horace Walpole, to the Earl of Hertford, during His Lordship's Embassy in Paris. To Which Are Added Mr. Walpole's Letters to the Rev. Henry Zouch, edited by John Wilson Croker (London: Printed for Charles Knight, 1825);

Letters of Horace Walpole, Earl of Orford, to Sir Horace Mann, British Envoy at the Court of Tuscany, 3 volumes, edited by Lord Dover (London: R. Bentley, 1833);

The Yale Edition of Horace Walpole's Correspondence, 48 volumes, edited by W. S. Lewis (New Haven: Yale University Press, 1937–1983).

Bibliographies:

Allen T. Hazen, *A Bibliography of Horace Walpole* (New Haven: Yale University Press, 1948);

Hazen, *A Bibliography of the Strawberry Hill Press* (New Haven: Yale University Press / London: H. Milford, Oxford University Press, 1942; revised edition, Folkestone & London: Dawsons of Pall Mall, 1973);

Peter Sabor, *Horace Walpole: A Reference Guide* (Boston: G. K. Hall, 1984).

Biography:

R. W. Ketton-Cremer, *Horace Walpole: A Biography,* third edition (London: Methuen, 1964; Ithaca, N.Y.: Cornell University Press, 1964).

References:

Wilmarth S. Lewis, *A Guide to the Life of Horace Walpole (1717–1797)* (New Haven: Yale University Press, 1973);

Lewis, *Horace Walpole* (New York: Pantheon, 1961);

Lewis, *Horace Walpole's Library* (Cambridge: Cambridge University Press, 1958);

Lewis, *Rescuing Horace Walpole* (New Haven: Yale University Press, 1978);

Warren Hunting Smith, ed., *Horace Walpole: Writer, Politician and Connoisseur, Essays on the 250th Anniversary of Walpole's Birth* (New Haven: Yale University Press, 1967).

Papers:

The Lewis Walpole Library, Yale University, at Farmington, Connecticut, has a collection of manuscript material by and relating to Horace Walpole. The core of the collection consists of roughly half of Walpole's extant correspondence: 1,478 letters from him and 1,573 to him, a total of 3,051 originals. These are supplemented by photocopies of all the remaining 3,701 traceable letters. In addition to holding many of Walpole's original manuscripts, the library has photocopies of all other known Walpole manuscripts and fragments not in its possession.

Izaak Walton

(September? 1593 – 15 December 1683)

Sandra Naiman
Elmhurst College

See also the Walton entry in *DLB 151: British Prose Writers of the Early Seventeenth Century.*

Izaak Walton (after the painting by Jacob Huysman)

BOOKS: *The Compleat Angler, or the Contemplative Man's Recreation. Being a Discourse of Fish and Fishing, Not unworthy the perusal of most Anglers* (London: Printed by T. Maxey for Richard Marriot, 1653); revised as *The Compleat Angler, or the Contemplative Man's Recreation. Being a Discourse of Rivers, and Fish-Ponds, and Fish, and Fishing. Not unworthy of the perusal of most Anglers* (London: Printed by T. Maxey for Richard Marriot, 1655); revised as *The Compleat Angler, or the Contemplative Man's Recreation. Being a Discourse of Rivers, Fish-Ponds, Fish and Fishing. To which Is added The Laws of Angling: with a new Table of the Particulars in this Book* (London: Printed by J. G. for Richard Marriot, 1661); revised in *The Universal Angler, Made so, by Three Books of Fishing. The First Written by Mr. Izaak Walton; The Second by Charles Cotton, Esq; The Third by Col. Robert Venables. All which may be bound together, or sold each of them severally* (London: Printed for Richard Marriot, 1676);

The Life of John Donne, Dr. in Divinity, and Late Dean of Saint Pauls Church London (London: Printed by J. G. for Richard Marriot, 1658)–revised from "The Life and Death of Dr Donne, Late Deane of St Pauls London," in *LXXX Sermons preached by that learned and reverend divine, Iohn Donne, D^r^ in Divinity, Late Deane of the Cathedrall Church of S. Pauls London* (London: Printed for Richard Royston & Richard Marriot, 1640);

The Life of Mr. Rich. Hooker, The Author of those Learned Books of the Laws of Ecclesiastical Polity (London: Printed by J. G. for Richard Marriot, 1665); revised in *The Works of Mr. Richard Hooker* (London: Printed by Thomas Newcomb for Andrew Crooke, 1666);

The Life of Mr. George Herbert (London: Printed by Thomas Newcomb for Richard Marriot, 1670); revised in *The Temple. Sacred Poems and Private Ejaculations,* by Herbert, tenth edition (London: Printed by W. Godbid for R. S. & John Williams, 1674);

The Lives of D^r^. John Donne, Sir Henry Wotton, M^r^. Richard Hooker, M^r^. George Herbert. To which are added some Letters written by Mr. George Herbert, at his being in Cambridge: With others to his Mother, the Lady Magdalen Herbert, written by John Donne, afterwards Dean of St. Pauls (London: Printed by Thomas Newcomb for Richard Marriot, 1670; revised edition, London: Printed by Thomas Roycroft for Richard Marriot, 1675)–life of Wotton revised from "The Life of Sir Henry Wotton," in *Reliquiae*

Wottonianae, edited by Walton (London: Printed by Thomas Maxey for Richard Marriot, 1651; revised edition, London: Printed by T. Roycroft for Richard Marriot, 1672);

The Life of Dr. Sanderson, Late Bishop of Lincoln. To which is added, some Short Tracts or Cases of Conscience, written by the said Bishop (London: Printed for Richard Marriot, 1678); revised in *XXXV Sermons,* by Robert Sanderson, seventh edition (London: Printed for Benjamin Tooke, 1681);

Love and Truth: in two modest and peaceable letters, concerning the distempers of the present times. Written from a quiet and conformable Citizen of London, to two busie and factious Shopkeepers in Coventry, anonymous (London: Printed by M. C. for Henry Brome, 1680).

Editions: *The Lives of Dr. John Donne; Sir Henry Wotton; Mr. Richard Hooker; Mr. George Herbert; and Dr. Robert Sanderson. By Isaac Walton. With Notes, and the Life of the Author,* edited by Thomas Zouch (York: Printed by Wilson, Spence & Mawman, 1796);

The Complete Angler, or The Contemplative Man's Recreation; Being a Discourse of Rivers, Fish-Ponds, Fish and Fishing, Written by Izaak Walton, and Instructions How to Angle for a Trout or Grayling in a Clear Stream, by Charles Cotton, 2 volumes, edited by Sir Harris Nicolas (London: Pickering, 1836);

The Complete Angler; or, The Contemplative Man's Recreation, by Isaac Walton. And Instructions How to Angle for a Trout or Grayling in a Clear Stream, by Charles Cotton. With Copious Notes, for the Most Part Original, a Bibliographical Preface, Giving an Account of Fishing and Fishing-Books, from the Earliest Antiquity to the Time of Walton, and a Notice of Cotton and His Writings, by the American Editor. To Which Is Added an Appendix, Including Illustrative Ballads, Music, Papers on American Fishing, and the Most Complete Catalogue of Books on Angling, etc., Ever Printed, edited by George Washington Bethune (New York & London: Wiley & Putnam, 1847);

Waltoniana: Inedited Remains in Verse and Prose of Izaak Walton, edited by Richard Herne Shepherd (London: Pickering, 1878);

The Compleat Angler, or The Contemplative Man's Recreation Being a Discourse of Rivers Fish-Ponds Fish and Fishing Written Izaak Walton, and Instructions How to Angle for a Trout or Grayling in a Clear Stream by Charles Cotton, 2 volumes, edited by R. B. Marston (London: Sampson Low, Marston-Searle & Rivington, 1888);

The Compleat Angler, or The Contemplative Man's Recreation, Being a Discourse of Rivers, Fish Ponds, Fish & Fishing, Written by Izaak Walton, and Instructions How to Angle for a Trout or Grayling in a Clear Stream, by Charles Cotton, 2 volumes, edited by George A. B. Dewar (London: Freemantle, 1902);

The Lives of John Donne, Sir Henry Wotton, Richard Hooker, George Herbert and Robert Sanderson, edited by George Saintsbury (London & New York: Oxford University Press, 1927);

The Compleat Walton, edited by Geoffrey Keynes (London: Nonesuch Press, 1929);

The Lives of John Donne, Sir Henry Wotton, Richard Hooker, George Herbert & Robert Sanderson, edited by S. B. Carter (London: Falcon Educational Books, 1951);

The Compleat Angler 1653–1676, edited by Jonquil Bevan (Oxford: Clarendon Press, 1983).

OTHER: "An Elegie upon D^r^. Donne," in *Poems, By J. D. with Elegies on the Authors Death* (London: Printed by M. F. for John Marriot, 1633; revised, 1635);

"To my ingenious Friend Mr. Brome, on his various and excellent Poems: An humble Eglog. Daman and Dorus. Written the 29. of May, 1660," in *Songs And Other Poems,* by Alexander Brome (London: Printed for Henry Brome, 1661);

Thealma and Clearchus, a Pastoral History, in smooth and easie Verse. Written long since, By John Chalkhill, Esq; an Acquaintant and Friend of Edmund Spencer, preface by Walton (London: Printed for Benjamin Tooke, 1683).

Izaak Walton has the distinction of having written not just one book that the world would not willingly let die, as John Milton aspired to do, but two. His treatise on fishing, *The Compleat Angler, or the Contemplative Man's Recreation. Being a Discourse of Fish and Fishing, Not unworthy the perusal of most Anglers* (1653), has been reprinted at an average rate of once a year since his death. Only the Bible and the *Book of Common Prayer* have been reprinted more often. Although Walton's biographies, several of which were collected as *The Lives of D^r^. John Donne, Sir Henry Wotton, M^r^. Richard Hooker, M^r^. George Herbert. To which are added some Letters written by Mr. George Herbert, at his being in Cambridge: With others to his Mother, the Lady Magdalen Herbert, written by John Donne, afterwards Dean of St. Pauls* (1670), have not reappeared with anything like that frequency, they have been immensely popular. Samuel Johnson, not easily impressed, counted *The Lives* among his favorite books.

Johnson thought it "wonderful that Walton, who was in a very low situation in life, should have been familiarly received by so many great men, and that at a time when the ranks of society were kept more separate than they are now." Although Walton was trained to be a tradesman rather than a literary man, throughout his long life he made friends among the high and the mighty, especially bishops. All the commentators on his life agree that he had a genius for friendship. Several of the extant books from Walton's library were given to him by friends.

Many of Walton's friends were bookmen. The most notable was probably the Anglican preacher John Hales, who acquired a library that cost £2,500, most of which he had to sell for £700 after he was deprived of his fellowship during the civil war. Walton knew Hales when he was a fellow at Eton. His other notable friends included Henry Wotton, who bequeathed his books and manuscripts to the library of Eton College; Thomas Barlow, bishop of Lincoln, whose library benefited Queen's College and the University of Oxford; Richard Holdsworth, who left books to his college, St. John's, as well as to Cambridge University and Emmanuel College; and Bishop Morley of Winchester, who established the cathedral library at Winchester by his will and left it a fine collection of Bibles.

Walton's writings make it obvious that he considered a man's library to be an index of his character. His *The Life of John Donne, Dr. in Divinity, and Late Dean of Saint Pauls Church London* (1658) is the primary source of information about Donne's library, which included "1,400 authors, most of them abridged and analysed in his own hand," as well as "six score of his sermons and a great collection of business documents." In *The Life of Mr. Rich. Hooker, The Author of those Learned Books of the Laws of Ecclesiastical Polity* (1665) Walton reports that Hooker, upon learning that his house had been robbed, was most concerned about his library: "Are my books and written papers safe? . . . then it matters not, for no other loss can trouble me." Hooker's library was substantial, for when he died he left an estate of £1,092, "a great part of it . . . in books."

That Walton read many more books than have been accounted for in his personal library is clear from the many quotations, allusions, and unacknowledged borrowings that have been identified in his writings. Whether he acquired whatever learning he had from books, from conversations with learned friends, or from both is not clear. Walton was a noted biographer, but the documentary evidence of his own life is meager.

Walton's father, Gervase, was a Staffordshire innkeeper who died when Izaak, who was baptized in Stafford on 21 September 1593, was three years old. His mother, Anne, married again in 1598, and his stepfather later became a burgess of the town. Sometime before 1618 Walton moved to London, where he apparently lived with his sister Anne, who was married to a prosperous linen draper, Thomas Grinsell. Walton was apprenticed to Grinsell and followed him in his trade.

Grinsell put Walton up for membership in the Ironmongers Company, to which Walton was admitted on 12 November 1618. Walton must have been an atypical ironmonger, however, for already a poem had been dedicated to him in lines that seemed to imply that Walton himself was a poet. Writing "To My Approved and Much Respected Friend, Iz. Wa.," the poet, "S.P.," claims sole responsibility for the "bad" verse: "No ill thing can be clothed in thy verse. / Accept them then, and where I have offended, / Rase thou it out, and let it be amended." Nevertheless, in his license to marry Rachel Floud, dated 27 December 1626, Walton is described as an ironmonger of the city of London.

Walton's wife was the daughter of William Floud of Kent and his wife, Susanna, who was related to Archbishop Thomas Cranmer. After his marriage Walton became close to the Cranmers and remained friends with them throughout his long life. Conversations with them provided some of the material for his books, notably *The Life of Mr. Rich. Hooker*.

Walton and his wife settled in the London parish of St. Dunstan's-in-the-West, where John Donne was vicar from 1624 until his death in 1631. St. Dunstan's was an upscale community with gardens and orchards, surrounded by the Inns of Court. Its fashionable residents could afford luxurious fabrics sold by a draper such as Walton, whose business evidently prospered. Walton held various church offices in the parish and thus came to know Donne, with whom he must have been intimate, for he describes himself as present at Donne's deathbed.

Donne's death on 31 March 1631 served as a catalyst to transform the successful linen draper into a popular author. For the posthumous edition of Donne's sermons of 1640 Sir Henry Wotton was to furnish an account of the poet's life. Walton collected notes for Wotton, but when Wotton died before writing Donne's life, Walton hastily used the notes himself to compose a memoir. Walton's wife died in 1640, the same year as "The Life and Death of Dr Donne, Late Deane of St Pauls London" was published in *LXXX Sermons preached by that learned and reverend divine, Iohn Donne, D^r^ in Divinity, Late Deane of the Cathedrall Church of S. Pauls London;* two years later the only survivor among their seven children died. Walton gave up his business and residence in St. Dunstan's and began acquiring farm property in the vicinity of Stafford.

In 1646 Walton married Anne Ken, whose much younger half brother, Thomas Ken, later became the bishop of Bath and Wells. Anne and Izaak Walton had two children who survived to adulthood: Anne, born in 1647 or 1648, married William Hawkins, a prebendary of Winchester; and Isaac, born in 1651, became canon of Salisbury Cathedral and probably placed the books he inherited from his father in the library of the cathedral. The Waltons may also have raised Thomas Ken after his parents died. In the same year his son was born, Walton's literary career received a fresh stimulus when Wotton's literary remains required a life to accompany them. Walton, who had often fished with Wotton, supplied "The Life of Sir Henry Wotton" for *Reliquiae Wottonianae* (1651), a motley assortment of poems, letters, and tracts.

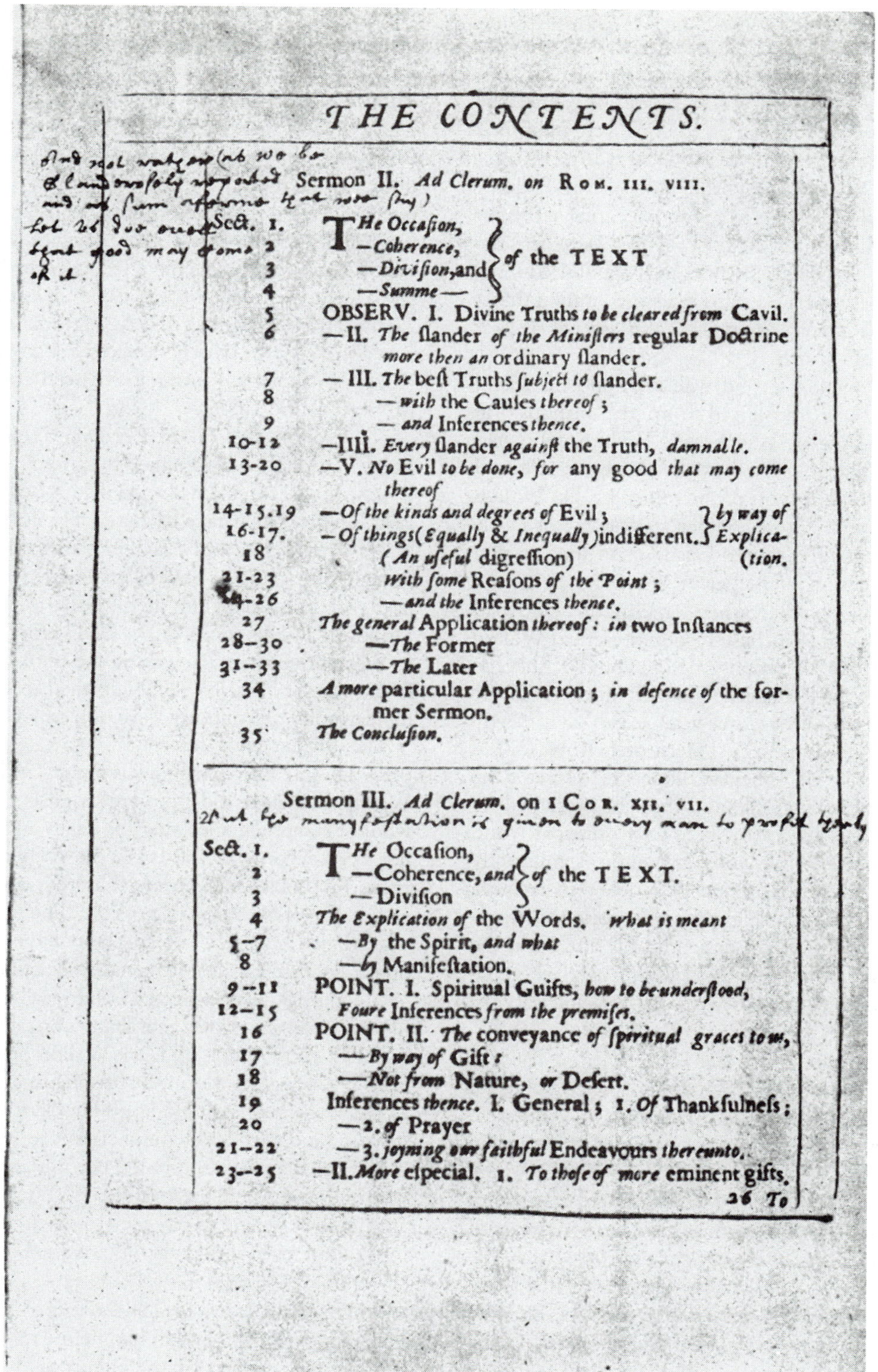

THE CONTENTS.

Walton's notes on a contents page in his 1656 copy of Robert Sanderson's Twenty Sermons formerly Preached *(Maggs Bros. Ltd.,* Three Centuries of English Literature and History, *catalogue 643, 1937)*

In 1653 Walton became the patron saint of fishermen by publishing his first book, *The Compleat Angler, or the Contemplative Man's Recreation. Being a Discourse of Fish and Fishing, Not unworthy the perusal of most Anglers.* He revised the work repeatedly. Four subsequent editions were published during his lifetime, in 1655, 1661, 1668, and 1676.

In 1658 Walton's publisher and friend Richard Marriot prevailed upon him to revise his earlier work on Donne without the sermons. *The Life of John Donne* was the first of Walton's biographical works to be published independently, and he took such pains in its preparation that it became, as David Novarr asserts in *The Making of Walton's Lives* (1958), a work of art.

In 1662 Walton's second wife died and his friend George Morley was transferred from the bishopric at Worcester to the see of Winchester. Walton, who had acted as Morley's personal steward at Worcester, followed him to Winchester. For most of the rest of his life Walton apparently lived with Morley, either at Winchester in the episcopal residence at Farnham Castle or in the London episcopal headquarters in Chelsea.

Gilbert Sheldon, the bishop of London, who had transferred Morley to Winchester, soon presented Walton with the assignment of writing a biography of the sixteenth-century divine Richard Hooker, for which he received from Sheldon a forty-year lease of a newly erected building in London's Paternoster Row for an annual rent of only 40s. Sheldon hoped to discredit the interpretation of Hooker's life and thought presented by John Gauden in his edition of Hooker's principal work, *Laws of Ecclesiastical Polity* (1662). Walton significantly altered Gauden's characterization of Hooker to create a portrait of a more admirable and more consistent personality, but he reserved for an appendix his attack on the authority of Gauden's text of *Ecclesiastical Polity,* where he impugned its authenticity as well as the integrity of Hooker's wife.

Walton also attached to *The Life of Mr. Rich. Hooker* a letter to Hooker from George Cranmer, which opens an interesting window on Walton's use of sources. Dated February 1598, Cranmer's letter was first printed at Oxford in February 1642 with the title *Letter Concerning the New Church Discipline.* John Keble, Hooker's editor in the nineteenth century, thought that Walton must have been unaware of the 1642 publication of the letter because of what Keble called the "remarkable" differences between its first printing and the version Walton offered. In fact, however, Walton owned a copy of *Letter Concerning the New Church Discipline;* it is one of the books that survived from his library and, according to Jonquil Bevan, was bought at Christie's on 19 April 1967 for £4. Novarr, a student of Walton's methods of composition, attributes the differences between the versions of the letter to Walton's habit of reworking his sources to suit his purpose. Although Novarr sees Walton's improvements on the dull letter as evidence of his conscious artistry, it must be noted that such a practice does not show a disinterested love of the truth or respect for the accuracy of a text.

Walton wrote two more biographies. His *The Life of Mr. George Herbert* (1670) was a labor of love. While he did not know Herbert, whom he portrays as the ideal country parson, he was obviously familiar with the poet's writings. No copies of Herbert's works, however, were among the extant books known to have belonged to Walton. At the age of eighty-five Walton published his last biography: *The Life of Dr. Sanderson, Late Bishop of Lincoln. To which is added, some Short Tracts or Cases of Conscience, written by the said Bishop* (1678). Walton had been introduced to Sanderson by Morley around 1638.

Walton died on 15 December 1683 at the age of ninety, leaving a will in which he carefully disposed of his books. To his son-in-law Dr. Hawkins he left Donne's *Sermons.* To his son he gave Richard Sibbes's *Soules Conflict* and to his daughter Sibbes's *Brewsed Reide,* "desiring them to reade them so, as to be well acquainted with them." He also gave to his daughter all his books at Winchester and Droxford and his copies of Dr. Hall's works that were then at Farnham Castle. The rest of the books at Farnham he left to his son. Finally, he bequeathed to John Darbishire the sermons of Anthony Farindon or of Dr. Sanderson, "which my executor thinks fit."

Despite his regard for his library and its disposition, Walton evidently did not care to ensure that his books would be kept together after his death and apparently did not keep records of the books he owned. Through the years his books have been scattered, and no complete recounting of his library is possible. The problem has been exacerbated because book collectors have often valued his books because of their personal association with Walton. Writing in 1904, W. Carew Hazlitt recalls seeing a copy of Donne's *Sermons* "with a brilliant portrait of the author, and a long inscription by Izaak Walton presenting the volume to his aunt. It was in the pristine English calf binding, as clean as when it left Walton's hands *en route* for his kinswoman, and such a delightful signature . . . An American gentleman acquired it, tore the portrait and leaf of inscription out, and threw the rest away!" Book collectors have always been willing to pay generously for books inscribed by Walton, even if they then threw the books away.

The 1836 edition of *The Complete Angler; or The Contemplative Man's Recreation* included more biographical information about Walton than had before appeared as well as annotations supplied by the editor, Sir Harris Nicolas. It was published by William Pickering, who was an avid collector of Waltoniana. According to the author of an article in the *Dublin University Magazine* in 1842, "Mr. Pickering, who is not ashamed to be a man of taste in addition to his excellent habits of business, possesses the following interesting memorials of the author of *The Compleat Angler:* A copy of this work with Izaak's autograph; Walton's prayer book with the register of his family in autograph; The copy of Donne's sermons, which Walton gave to his 'most deare ante Cranmer'; His copy of Sanderson's sermons with the texts in his own hand; His copy of Hooker's polity; Presentation copies of all his lives and works." When Pickering's publishing business encountered financial difficulties, he was forced to sell his possessions, including his personal library, to meet the demands of creditors. Bevan reports that many of the Walton books that Pickering owned have not reappeared since they were sold in his sale of 7 August 1854.

Among Sir Harris Nicolas's notes in the Pickering edition of *The Compleat Angler* was a list of books identified as Walton's by the librarian of the Salisbury cathedral. The list of twenty books was reprinted in some subsequent editions of *The Compleat Angler,* although the Winchester edition of 1902 included a letter dated 23 March 1901 from a later librarian of the cathedral giving a list of Walton's books in that library that differed somewhat from the list given by Nicolas.

Nicolas's list includes a folio edition of the *Works* of James I (1616) and an undated quarto edition of Pierre Charron's popular system of moral philosophy, *Of Wisdom* (1608), with Walton's note that he purchased it secondhand for 4s. 6p. on 17 November 1652. Two books were by the English historian and High Church controversialist Peter Heylyn: *Microcosmus* (1621) and *Parable of the Tares* (1659), the latter with Walton's note, "Given me may 28:1659 by Mr. Rich Marryot." Edward Reynolds, a moderate Anglican bishop who published many popular sermons and short religious works in the seventeenth century, is represented by *A Treatise of the Passions and Faculties of the Soule* (1640). Other devotional works include Josiah Shute's *Divine Cordials* (1644), Thomas Fuller's *Abel Redivivus* (1651), and Henry Hammond's *The Christian's Obligation to Peace and Charity* (1649). The text by Hammond is a sermon he preached before Charles I. According to Bishop John Fell, Hammond's first biographer, Hammond "had the disposal of treat charities reposed in his hands, as being the most zealous promoter of almsgiving that lived in England since the change of religion."

A copy of *Living Librarie* (1621) by Philip Camerarius contains Walton's note "given mee by my very good friend, Mr. Henry Field, July 29, 1634." A folio edition of Richard Sibbes's *The Saint's Cordiale* (1658), a collection of sermons by the Puritan divine, bears the date 1682 in Walton's hand. Patrick Symson's *Historie of the Church* (1624) is a corrected edition of two earlier works by that church historian and divine, *A Short Compend of the History of the First Ten Persecutions moved against Christians* (1613–1616) and *A Short Compend of the Growth of the Heresies of the Roman Anti-Christ* (1616). *A Worke Concerning the Truenesse of Christian Religion* (1617) was a popular book by Philippe Duplessis-Mornay, the French Huguenot leader who appealed for religious tolerance and ecumenicism; Walton dated it "July 5, 1621."

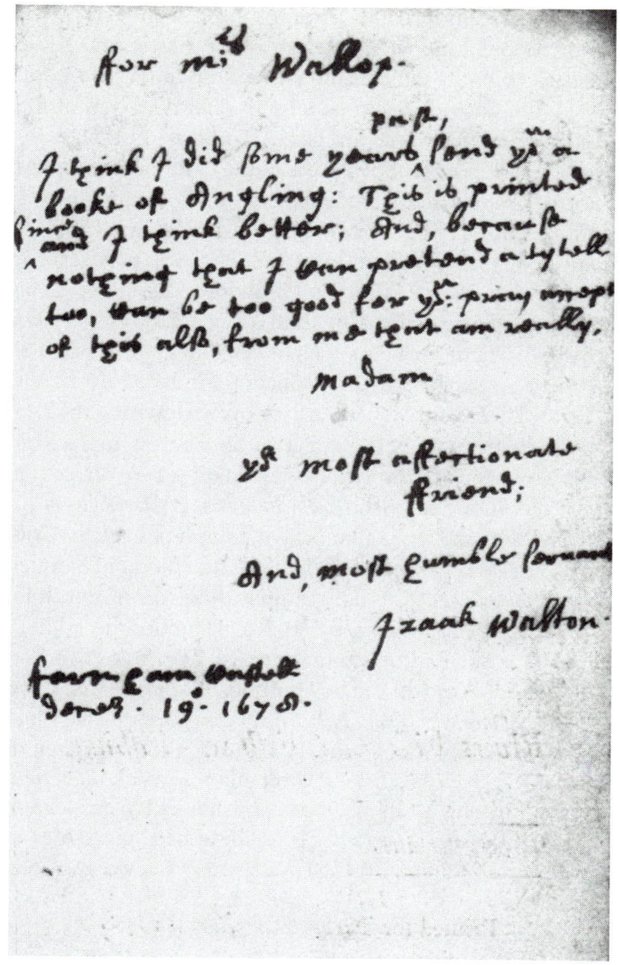
For mrs Wallop.
past,
I think I did some yeares send yu a
booke of Angling: This is printed
since and I think better; And, because
nothing that I can pretend a tytell
too, can be too good for yu: pray accept
of this alse, from me that am really,
Madam
yr most affectionate
friend;
And, most humble servant
Izaak Walton.
Farnham Castell
Decem. 19. 1678.

Walton's inscription to Mrs. Dorothy Wallop in a copy of the 1676 edition of The Universal Angler *(British Library)*

Other titles on the list are John Donne's *Letters* (1651) and *LXXX Sermons* (1640), a folio edition of Hooker's *Of the Laws of Ecclesiastical Polity* (1666), and a quarto edition of *Heaven Opened* (1613) by William Cowper, bishop of Galloway. There is also a folio edition of Abraham Cowley's *Works* (1674), dated 1682 by Walton. In a folio edition of George Sandys's translation of Ovid's *Metamorphoses* (1622) Walton notes he paid 5s. for the book. A folio edition of *Ecclesiastical Histories* by Eusebius, Socrates, and Evagrius (1636) contains twenty lines of notes Walton made for his biography of Donne. On the title page of Sibbes's *Returning Backslider* (1650) Walton has written a couplet: "Of this blest man let this just praise be given, / Heaven was in him, before he went to heaven."

In September 1980 Bevan published in *The Library* "Some Books from Izaak Walton's Library," in which she listed as being in the Salisbury cathedral library, in addition to the books on Nicolas's list, a quarto edition of the *Meditations* of Marcus Aurelius Antoninus translated by Meric Casaubon (1635) and a quarto edition of Francis Bacon's *Essayes* (1625), a translation by Thomas Norton of John Calvin's *The Institution of Christian Religion* (1582), a quarto edition of William Denton's *The Burnt Child* (1675), a quarto edition of Thomas Godwyn's *Moses and Aaron* (1628), a quarto edition of John King's *Lectures on Jonas* (1618), William Perkins's *The Whole Treatise of the Cases of Conscience* (quarto, 1619), William Pindar's *A Sermon* (quarto, 1677), and Sibbes's *Bowels Opened* (quarto, 1648).

Bevan also describes several books now owned by Yale University Library as having belonged to Walton: a folio edition of Elias Ashmole's *Institution & Ceremonies of the Order of the Garter* (1672), an octavo edition of Charles Cotton's *Wonders of the Peake* (1681), a quarto edition of Samuel Daniel's *Civile Warres* (1609), a quarto edition of Ben Jonson's *Execration against Vulcan* (1640), a duodecimo edition of Sir John Skeffington's translation of *The Heroe of Lorenzo* (1652), and a copy of the posthumous *Golden Remains of the Ever Memorable Mr. John Hales* (1659) inscribed "Izaak Walton. given me by Mr. Paulet." Charles Cotton, a poet and translator as well as a fishing companion to Walton, is represented among Walton's surviving books by an octavo edition of *Wonders of the Peake* (1681) inscribed "given me by Mr. Cotton, August 30.1681." It is also owned by Yale University.

The only copy of *The Compleat Angler* owned by its author that Bevan was able to identify is of the fifth edition, *The Universal Angler, Made so, by Three Books of Fishing. The First Written by Mr. Izaak Walton; The Second by Charles Cotton, Esq; The Third by Col. Robert Venables. All which may be bound together, or sold each of them severally* (1676), which is in the National Library of Scotland.

Seven of the books from Walton's personal library are by Donne: a 1627 quarto edition of *A Sermon in Commemoration of the Lady Davers,* said by Bevan to belong to R. H. Taylor of Princeton; a 1633 quarto edition of *Deaths Duell* bound with a 1634 quarto edition of *Six Sermons* (as well as "five other Donne Sermons, 1622–6, none of which gives evidence of ownership by Walton") in the collection of Pembroke College, Cambridge; the 1640 edition of *LXXX Sermons* in which Walton's biography of Donne first appeared, with many markings and three alterations in ink, now in Salisbury cathedral library; an octavo 1650 edition of *Poems; With Elegies on the Author's Death* with Walton's note: "Given me by Mr. Marryot the 7th of november 1650," owned by Harvard University Library; a duodecimo 1651 edition of *Essayes in Divinity,* said by Bevan to belong to R. S. Pirie of Hamilton, Massachusetts; and a 1651 quarto edition of *Letters* in the Salisbury cathedral library. Donne's son John bequeathed to Walton, in a will dated 21 July 1657, "all my writings under my father's hand, which may be of some use to his son, if he makes him a scholar."

Bevan also found in sale catalogues books described as having belonged to Walton, including a quarto edition of Bacon's *Two Bookes of the . . . Advancement of Learning* sold at Anderson Galleries 10 November 1919 for $37. A copy of *Reliquiae Wottonianae* with a presentation inscription to Dr. Thomas Gamble, prebendary of Winchester in 1661, which has been crossed out; and an added inscription of the younger Izaak Walton, was sold at Sotheby's 16 June 1964.

Among the books advertised as Walton's in the catalogue of the Pickering sale of 7 August 1854 were Edward Chamberlayne's *Anglia Notitia, or the Present State of England* (1682), a popular duodecimo handbook describing contemporary social and political conditions and providing a directory of public officials and various statistics, Martin Chemnitz's *Exposition of the Lord's Prayer* (1598), and an octavo edition of Thomas Flatman's *Poems and Songs* (1682) with Walton's note "Izaak Walton, July 3 1682, given me by the author." Another book from Walton's library that was owned by the publisher was an annotated edition of Bishop Sanderson's *Twenty Sermons* (1656) and his *Fourteen Sermons* (1657) bound together, which Walton purchased secondhand on 25 June 1658 for 15s., according to the notes in the book. Walton wrote at the end of the preface: "This Preface is an humble and bold challenge to the dissenting brethren of the Clergy of England: And was writ by that humble and good man the author, in the times of persecution and danger."

To the books identified as Walton's from sale catalogues belong an octavo edition of Samuel Herne's *Domus Carthusiana* (1677), listed in a sale at Parke-Bernet 4 March 1946; a folio edition of Adam Littleton's *Sixty One Sermons* (1680) "given by Mr. Marryot January 1679," according to the catalogue of Sotheby's sale of 17 July 1933 and bought by Dobell for £5; Walton's amended copy of the octavo edition of his *The Life of Mr. Rich. Hooker* (1665), listed at Sotheby's 30 November 1898; Walton's copy of the first collected edition of his *The Lives of Dr. John Donne, Sir Henry Wotton, Mr. Richard Hooker, Mr. George Herbert,* listed at Parke-Bernet 7 May 1945; a folio edition of John Spottiswoode's *History of the Church of Scotland* (1655) annotated: "Izaak Walton given me by my honored and Reverend friend, my Lord the: Bishop of Salisbury who wrote the authors life," listed as being at Parke-Bernet, 14 October 1946; a folio edition of Thomas Fuller's *Church History of Britain* (1656) that was in the Gott sale of 1907; *New Distemper, or the Dissenters Usual Plea for Comprehension, Toleration and the renouncing of the Covenant* (1680), described by Bevan as having been in both the Pickering sale and the

Gott sale of 1907; and the letter from George Cranmer to Richard Hooker that sold at Christie's 19 April 1967. A copy of *The Life of Mr. Rich. Hooker* said to have been Walton's sold at Sotheby's 30 November 1898.

Bevan also identifies as having belonged to Walton a folio edition of the *Book of Common Prayer* (1639) with his record of the births and deaths of members of his family, owned by the British Library; an octavo edition of *Poems* by William E. of Pembroke and Benjamin Ruddier (1660) and a duodecimo edition of John Raymond's *An Itinerary* (1648), both owned by the Bodleian; a quarto edition of John Denham's popular poem, *Cooper's Hill* (1642), owned by the Huntington Library; Paolo Sarpi's *The Historie of the Councel of Trent* in a folio edition of 1629, annotated "Izaak: Walton given me by Mr. John King September 12th. 1669," owned by Wells Cathedral Library; and an octavo copy of Gregory the Great's *De Cura Pastorali* (1629) owned by the William Salt Library in Stafford. Peter Walsh's octavo edition of *Prospect of the State of Ireland* (1682), annotated: "given me June. 28. by the Author Mr. Peter Welch," was owned by the American Art association 26 January 1922, Bevan says, and James Wadsworth's *Copies of Certaine Letters* (quarto, 1624) is owned by Christ Church, Oxford. Richard Montagu's *A Gagg for the New Gospell?* (quarto, 1624) is owned by R. S. Pirie of Hamilton, Massachusetts, according to Bevan, and a folio edition of Florio's translation of Montaigne's *Essays* (1613) is owned by Michael Phillips of Edinburgh.

Bevan's list inspired a spirited but inconclusive exchange of correspondence with I. A. Shapiro, published in the September 1982 issue of *The Library,* in which Shapiro suggested that some of the inscriptions Bevan attributed to Walton were forgeries. There is interest in the argument partly because it involves the amiable Walton, whose intimations of his life of quiet contentment and simple piety have endeared him to generations of readers.

Walton's books provide a microcosm of the seventeenth century in England. Almost all of the books treat religious concerns; in this they are typical not only of English private libraries in Walton's lifetime but of the country as a whole. Religious books dominated the seventeenth century book trade in England, and religious controversy was the most pressing issue of the time. Despite Walton's staunch support of the monarchy and the episcopacy, his library contains the whole spectrum of religious opinion: books by Puritan divines, Anglican divines, broad churchmen, Catholics, a Huguenot and hermetic philosopher (Duplessis-Mornay), as well as the founder of modern secularism (Pierre Charron). There is also a book of travel; two books by the putative father of English science; two translations of classics; some history; some poetry; Thomas Fuller's *Church History of Britain,* and Florio's translation of Montaigne's essays. There, for someone looking for a short course, is the literary history of England in the seventeenth century.

Bibliographies:

Peter Oliver, *A New Chronicle of The Compleat Angler* (New York: Paisley / London: Williams & Norgate, 1936);

Bernard S. Horne, *The Compleat Angler 1653–1967: A New Bibliography* (Pittsburgh: University of Pittsburgh Press, 1970);

Rodolphe L. Coigney, *Izaak Walton, A New Bibliography, 1653–1987* (New York: J. Cummins, 1989).

Biographies:

Anthony à Wood, *Athena Oxonienses: A New Edition, with Additions, and a Continuation by Philip Bliss,* 4 volumes (London: Printed for F. C. & J. Rivington, 1813–1820), I: 693–700;

Arthur M. Coon, "The Life of Izaak Walton," dissertation, Cornell University, 1938.

References:

Jonquil Bevan, "Some Books from Izaak Walton's Library," *Library,* sixth series, 2 (September 1980): 259–263;

Bevan and I. A. Shapiro, "Donne and the Walton Forgeries: A Correspondence," *Library,* sixth series, 4 (September 1982): 329–339;

Tucker Brooke, "The Lambert Walton-Cotton Collection," *Yale University Library Gazette,* 17 (April 1943): 61–65;

John Butt, "Izaak Walton's Collections for Fulman's Life of John Hales," *Modern Language Review,* 29 (July 1934): 267–273;

Raoul Granqvist, "Izaak Walton's *Lives* in the Nineteenth and the Early Twentieth Century: A Study of a Cult Object," *Studia Neophilologica,* 54, no. 2 (1982): 247–261;

W. Carew Hazlitt, *The Book Collector* (London: John Grant, 1904);

Stapleton Martin, *Izaak Walton and His Friends* (London: Chapman & Hall, 1903);

David Novarr, *The Making of Walton's Lives* (Ithaca, N.Y.: Cornell University Press, 1958);

Peter Oliver, *A New Chronicle of the Compleat Angler* (New York & London: Paisley Press/Williams & Norgate, 1936).

Papers:

Izaak Walton's few papers survive in widely scattered locations, including the British Library and the Public Record Office in London, the Bodleian Library and Corpus Christi College Library in Oxford, and Harvard University Library.

Humfrey Wanley

(21 March 1672 – 6 July 1726)

Clare A. Simmons
Ohio State University, Columbus

BOOKS: *Wanley's Catalogue of Ancient Northern Literature in English Libraries (H. Wanleii Librorum Vett. Septentrionalium, qui in Anglicae Bibliothecis extant),* published as the second volume of George Hickes's *Historico-Critical Dictionary of the Ancient Northern Languages (Linguarum Vett. Septentrionalium Thesaurus),* 2 volumes (Oxford: E. Sheldonian Theatre, 1703–1705);

A Catalogue of the Harleian Collection of Manuscripts, begun by Wanley and continued by others (Oxford: E. Sheldonian Theatre, 1759);

The Diary of Humfrey Wanley, 1715–1726, 2 volumes, edited by C. E. Wright and Ruth C. Wright (London: Bibliographical Society, 1966); introduction republished as *Humfrey Wanley and the History of the Harleian Library* (London: Bibliographical Society, 1966).

OTHER: *Anglo-Saxon Chronicle (Chronicon Saxonicum),* edited by Wanley (Oxford: E. Sheldonian Theatre, 1692);

"Description of the Harleian Library," in William Nicolson, *English Historical Library . . . or a Short View and Character of Most of the Writers . . . Which may be Serviceable to the undertakes of a General History of This Kingdom,* 3 parts (London: A. Swall & T. Child, 1696–1699);

Edward Bernard, *Catalogi librorum manuscriptorum Anglicae et Hiberniae in unum collecti, cum indice alphabetico,* with contributions and indexes by Wanley (Oxford: E. Sheldonian Theatre, 1697);

Jean F. Osterwald, *The Grounds and Principles of the Christian Religion, Explain'd in a Catechetical Discourse,* translated into English by Wanley (London: Printed by W. Sayes for William Hawes, 1704);

The Will of King Henry VII, edited, with a preface, by T. Astle and with an appendix by Wanley (London: Printed for T. Astle, 1775).

Humphrey Wanley in 1722 (portrait by Thomas Hill; British Library)

SELECTED PERIODICAL PUBLICATIONS–UNCOLLECTED: "Some Observations concerning the Invention and Progress of Printing, to the Year 1465," *Philosophical Transactions,* 288 (November–December 1703): 1507–1516; republished by L. Hanson, *Bodleian Library Record,* 6 (1957–1961): 106–112;

"Part of a Letter, written to a Most Reverend Prelate, in answer to one written by his Grace, judging of the Age of MSS., the Style of Learned Author, Painters, Musicians, &c.," *Philosophical Transactions,* 300 (June 1705): 1993–2008;

"An Essay on the Invention of Printing, by Mr. John Bagford; with an Account of his Collections for the same, by Mr. Humfrey Wanley, F. R. S., Communicated in two Letters to Dr. Hans Sloane, R. S.

Secr.," *Philosophical Transactions,* 310 (April–June 1707): 2397–2410;

"Proposal for a Palaeographical Survey of English Hands from the Earliest Times," partly published by Nichols, in *Literary Anecdotes* (London: Printed by P. L. Heyworth, 1812);

"Description of St. Mary's Hall, Coventry," in Joan C. Lancaster, *Official Guide to St. Mary's Hall* (Coventry: City of Coventry, 1948);

"Collecting Pastedowns from Bodleian Books," published by Milton C. McGatch as "Humphrey Wanley's Proposal to the Curators of the Bodleian Library on the Usefulness of Manuscript Fragments from Bindings," *Bodleian Library Record,* 11 (1982–1985); and by P. L. Heyworth in *The Letters of Humfrey Wanley, Palaeographer, Anglo-Saxonist, Librarian, 1672–1726* (Oxford: Clarendon Press, 1989).

Although his name is often written as Humphrey Wanley, Wanley himself was insistent that it should be spelled Humfrey Wanley: writing to his friend Arthur Charlett in 1705, Wanley noted of the Bodleian catalogue, "In reading the Paper, I could not but smile, percieving [sic] that my name *Humfrey* which is a Saxon name, and which I as the Saxons did, do always write with an f, should there be printed with *ph,* as if I knew no better . . .". Wanley's urge to identify himself with the Saxons is typical of his character; one of the earliest serious scholars of the Anglo-Saxon language, through his cataloguing work and paleographical research, Wanley helped lay the ground for the study of early English literature and culture. He also provides an unusually well-documented example of a professional librarian and bibliographer of the eighteenth century.

Wanley was born in Coventry on 21 March 1672. His father was Nathaniel Wanley, Vicar of Trinity Church, Coventry, and the author of many works, notably *The Wonders of the Little World, Or a General History of Man* (1678) and some poetry, which was rediscovered by Leonard C. Martin in the 1920s. His mother, Ellen, who lived until 1719, was the daughter of Humfrey Burton, Clerk to the Coventry Council. Wanley was one of five children, although his two brothers died young and the only sibling to whom he often refers in his correspondence is his sister Ellen.

Wanley's early life was shaped by a struggle for the income and patronage he needed to pursue his interests. His father died when he was eight, and about 1687 he was apprenticed to a linen draper. Although he stayed with Wright the draper until 1694, a visit to Oxford in 1692 seems to have inspired in him a desire to study, and he spent his spare time studying old books and particularly handwriting, thus becoming a self-taught paleographer. His talents became known to some of the scholars of the time, including Thomas Tanner, who claimed credit for taking Wanley from the draper's shop, and William Lloyd, bishop of Lichfield, who was more directly responsible. Lloyd helped Wanley enter St. Edmund Hall, Oxford, in 1694, where he seems to have supported himself by assisting other scholars in their researches. He also came under the patronage of Arthur Charlett, Master of University College, Oxford, and after his first year Wanley moved into accommodation at University College provided by Charlett. Charlett also helped Wanley obtain the post of assistant librarian at the Bodleian Library at a salary of £12 a year; the library was, however, sufficiently satisfied with his services to pay him some substantial bonuses.

Wanley's first major cataloguing work was his contribution to Edward Bernard's *Catalogi librorum manuscriptorum Anglicae et Hiberniae in unum collecti, cum indice alphabetico* (Catalogue of English and Scottish Manuscripts, 1697); Wanley compiled some entries from collections in his home city of Coventry and also produced the index. He worked at increasing the collections of the Bodleian Library by encouraging writers to donate copies of their books and by helping to acquire manuscripts; for example, he negotiated the purchase of Bernard's library for the Bodleian. Wanley's advancement at Oxford was, however, impeded by his having no degree, a fact that made him ineligible for promotion to head librarian. Charlett offered Wanley much (presumably unsolicited) advice about how he should show respect to his social superiors: for example, when in 1698 Wanley wrote from London telling Charlett that the antiquary Peter Le Neve had shown him some important historical documents at the Exchequer and had invited him out that evening, although Wanley had excused himself, his mentor's response was that

> such Gentlemen are to be treated with great Exactness and Deference, if you put yourself on equal Terms with them, you will find theyr Company very expensive. Remember the advice I gave You of keeping only such Company, as will pay your Reckoning. You must Learn the Act of complaining of Want.

Charlett seems to have proposed that Wanley fulfill his degree requirements by taking up residence at Oxford as a servitor, advice that Wanley refused, although he recovered from his initial indignation at Charlett's suggestion. After a chance for a fellowship at Worcester College also came to nothing, Wanley finally left Oxford about 1699. His initial hope was for an appointment with the Royal Library, but when he was unsuccessful in attaining it, he took the post of assistant to the secretary of the Society for Promoting Christian Knowledge at a salary of £40 a year; fifteen months later, in March 1702, he became secretary, and his annual salary was increased to £70. He was also working for Sir Hans Sloane, Secretary of the Royal Society.

Wanley returned temporarily to Oxford in 1702 during a visit by the future Queen Anne; according to Thomas Hearne, Wanley later claimed "that he was sent for at the time on purpose in order to shew the queen the curiosities of the Bodleian Library, had she went up thither, but she had not. Thus the vain coxcomb." While Hearne is a far from impartial witness, Wanley was certainly ambitious, and his ambitions were still directed toward librarianship. When the Cottonian Library was bequeathed to the nation by Sir John Cotton in 1702, Wanley applied to become its keeper, asking for help from influential friends such as Samuel Pepys. Although again Wanley was frustrated in his hopes, he was employed as part of a commission to report on the Cottonian collection in 1703, when he recommended recataloguing the collection.

By this time Wanley was friends with George Hickes; his early letters to Hickes are written in florid Latin but include interesting discussions of Anglo-Saxon studies, while others show indications of a genuine warmth between the two men. In 1699 Wanley confided in Hickes, for example, a plan for gaining financial independence by marrying his cousin Elizabeth Phillipps, who had inherited some property: he describes her as "young, well-bred, vertuous, honest, good-humor'd, & not very ugly." The scheme suggests a certain lack of romantic feeling on Wanley's part, and scarcely surprisingly, his cousin seems to have refused him. Wanley did marry on 1 May 1705, to Anna, daughter of Thomas Bourchier of Newcastle-upon-Tyne and widow of Bernard Martin Berenclow, who had several children from her first marriage; the marriage was conducted by another Anglo-Saxonist, William Elstob. Wanley and his wife had three children, but none survived infancy. His letters mention her with affection but imply that she suffered from ill health and possibly depression, and that she found his absences from her on business difficult to endure.

Wanley assisted Hickes in the paleographical research for his monumental thesaurus of the ancient northern languages. Throughout his life Wanley seems to have contemplated a major work on paleography, but although he wrote a prospectus and notes for such a book, it was never actually published. Wanley probably knew more about Latin, Greek, and early English hands than any of his contemporaries, and from employing as a source of reference the hands in manuscripts of which the dates were known, he was able to use the techniques of paleography to date other manuscripts. John Bagford reported that Wanley owned "thousands of fragments of old writings," which he used as reference sources in his paleography. Nevertheless, not all of his assumptions regarding styles and dating have stood the test of time. In particular, although they conceded that Anglo-Saxon writing was derived from Roman script, Wanley and Hickes insisted that many letters of the Anglo-Saxon alphabet–not merely *thorn, eth, yodh,* and *wen*–should be printed differently from Roman type. Wanley supervised the preparation of an elegant Anglo-Saxon font that was used for the thesaurus and other books printed at the Sheldonian Theatre at Oxford. Other scholars, however, did not have access to the font, and so this assumption may have limited the number of Anglo-Saxon works that were printed, scholars with fewer resources such as William and Elizabeth Elstob being constricted by their belief that a special font was necessary for Anglo-Saxon texts.

Hickes, moreover, employed Wanley to compile a catalogue of Anglo-Saxon manuscripts extant in English collections, which forms the second volume of the thesaurus. Although Hickes himself had previously listed the Anglo-Saxon manuscripts in the Bodleian collection, Wanley's work is important as the most complete compilation of Anglo-Saxon works then extant, mentioning books in some three dozen libraries, churches, and private collections, many of which had never been described in detail before. Wanley's usual method is to give the location and catalogue number of the manuscript (his objective was, he states, to help future scholars), then to transcribe the opening and the conclusion of each work, usually adding a brief Latin synopsis of the contents and describing the hand according to his own system of paleography. Almost half the total number of Anglo-Saxon manuscripts were in the Cottonian Library, and Wanley spent much time examining and describing them–a particularly important accomplishment since he saw the manuscripts before some were lost or damaged in the fire of 1731. He was the first person ever to draw attention to the poem now known as *Beowulf:* Junius had previously noted the existence of *Judith,* in the same manuscript, but until Wanley described *Beowulf,* no one seems to have been aware that it was indeed a substantial poem. Wanley told Thomas Tanner in 1695 that he had transcribed "almost a leaf & a half of the fragment of Judith" and that he hoped to copy the rest: that he apparently did not is a loss, since the manuscript was later among those manuscripts to suffer fire damage. His description of *Beowulf,* which translated into English reads "In this book, which is a splendid example of Anglo-Saxon poetry, there seem to be described the wars that Beowulf, a certain Dane, descended from the kings of

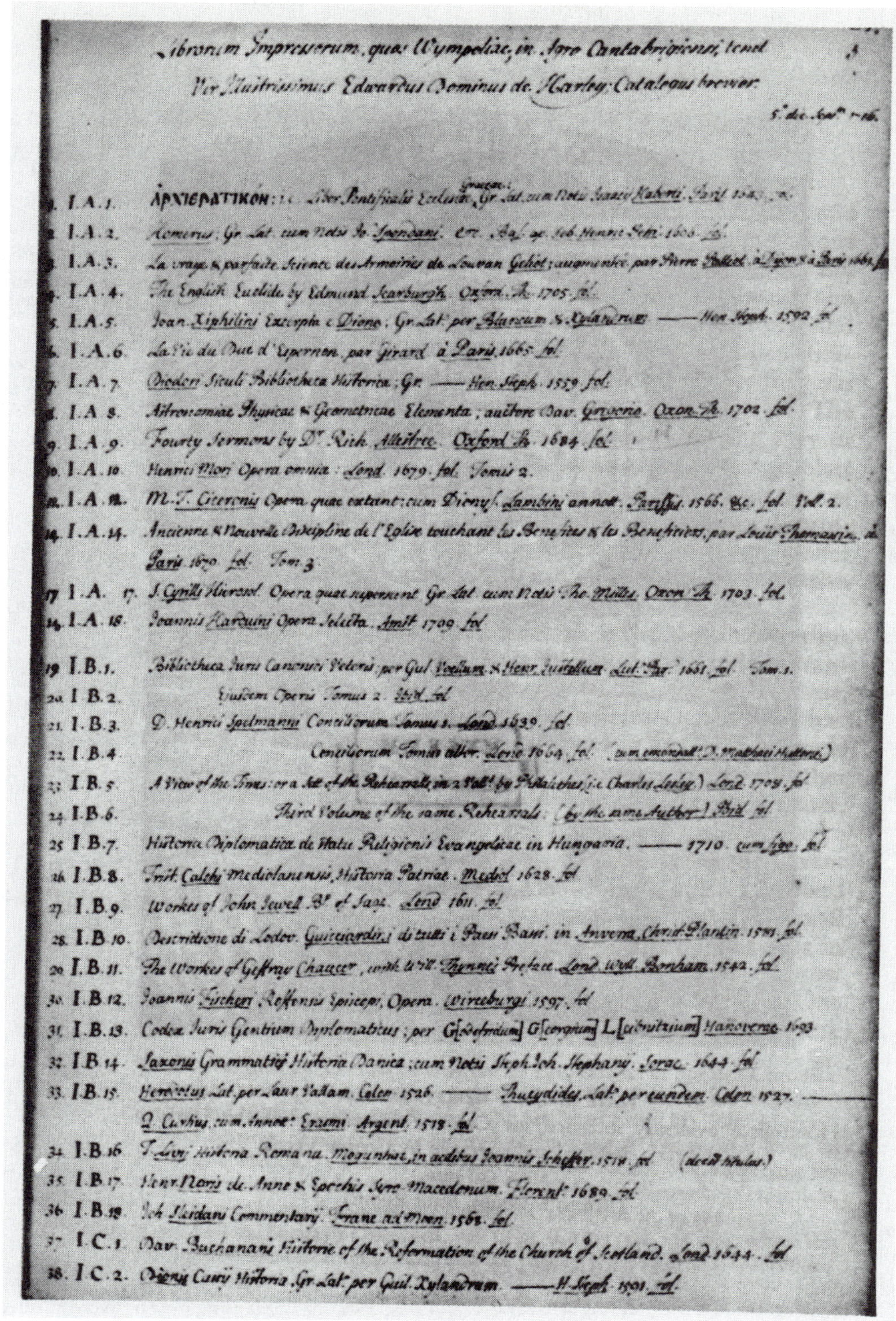

Librorum Impressorum, quos Wympoliae, in Agro Cantabrigiensi, tenet
Vir Illustrissimus Edwardus Dominus de Harley; Catalogus brevior.

5. die Jan[illegible]

1.	I.A.1.	ΑΡΧΙΕΡΑΤΙΚΟΝ: i.e. Liber Pontificalis Ecclesiae Graecae; Gr. Lat. cum Notis Isaaci Haberti. Paris [illegible]
2.	I.A.2.	Homerus; Gr. Lat. cum Notis Jo. Spondani. [illegible] Bas. [illegible] Henrici Petri. 1606. fol.
3.	I.A.3.	La vraye & parfaite Science des Armoiries de Louvan Geliot; augmentée par Pierre Palliot. à Dijon & à Paris 1661 fol.
4.	I.A.4.	The English Euclide by Edmund Scarburgh. Oxford. Th. 1705. fol.
5.	I.A.5.	Joan. Xiphilini Excerpta e Dione; Gr. Lat. per Blancum & Xylandrum —— Hen. Steph. 1592 fol.
6.	I.A.6.	La Vie du Duc d'Epernon, par Girard à Paris, 1665 fol.
7.	I.A.7.	Diodori Siculi Bibliotheca Historica; Gr. —— Hen. Steph. 1559 fol.
8.	I.A.8.	Astronomiae Physicae & Geometricae Elementa; auctore Dav. Gregorio. Oxon. Th. 1702 fol.
9.	I.A.9.	Fourty Sermons by Dr. Rich. Allestree. Oxford Th. 1684 fol.
10.	I.A.10.	Henrici Mori Opera omnia: Lond. 1679. fol. Tomis 2.
[illegible]	I.A.[illegible]	M. T. Ciceronis Opera quae extant; cum Dionys. Lambini annot. Parisiis. 1566. &c. fol. Vol. 2.
14.	I.A.14.	Ancienne & Nouvelle Discipline de l'Eglise touchant les Benefices & les Beneficiers, par Louis Thomassin. à Paris 1670. fol. Tom. 3.
17	I.A.17.	S. Cyrilli Hierosol. Opera quae supersunt. Gr. Lat. cum Notis Tho. Milles. Oxon. Th. 1703. fol.
1[illegible]	I.A.18.	Joannis Harduini Opera Selecta. Amst. 1709. fol.
19	I.B.1.	Bibliotheca Juris Canonici Veteris; per Gul. Voellum & Henr. Justellum. Lut. Par. 1661. fol. Tom. 1.
20.	I.B.2.	Ejusdem Operis Tomus 2. Ibid. fol.
21.	I.B.3.	D. Henrici Spelmanni Conciliorum Tomus 1. Lond. 1639. fol.
22.	I.B.4.	Conciliorum Tomus alter. Lond. 1664. fol. (cum emendat. D. Mathaei Hutton)
23.	I.B.5.	A View of the Times; or a Set of the Rehearsals, in 2 Vol. by Philalethes (i.e. Charles Lesley) Lond. 1708. fol.
24.	I.B.6.	Third Volume of the same Rehearsals: (by the same Author) Ibid. fol.
25	I.B.7.	Historia Diplomatica de Statu Religionis Evangelicae in Hungaria. —— 1710. cum fig. fol.
26.	I.B.8.	Trist. Calchi Mediolanensis, Historia Patriae. Mediol. 1628. fol.
27.	I.B.9.	Workes of John Jewell B. of Sar. Lond. 1611. fol.
28.	I.B.10.	Descrittione di Lodov. Guicciardini di tutti i Paesi Bassi. in Anversa, Christ. Plantin. 1581. fol.
29.	I.B.11.	The Workes of Geffray Chaucer, with Will. Thynne's Preface. Lond. Will. Bonham. 1542. fol.
30.	I.B.12.	Joannis Fischeri Roffensis Episcopi, Opera. Wirceburgi. 1597. fol.
31.	I.B.13.	Codex Juris Gentium Diplomaticus; per G[odefridum] G[uilielmum] L[eibnitzium] Hanoverae. 1693
32.	I.B.14.	Saxonis Grammatici Historia Danica; cum Notis Steph. Joh. Stephanii. Sorae. 1644. fol.
33.	I.B.15.	Herodotus Lat. per Laur. Vallam. Colon. 1526. —— Thucydides Lat. per eundem. Colon. 1527. —— Q. Curtius, cum Annot. Erasmi. Argent. 1518. fol.
34.	I.B.16.	T. Livii Historia Romana. Moguntiae, in aedibus Joannis Scheffer. 1518. fol. ([illegible])
35.	I.B.17.	Henr. Noris de Anno & Epochis Syro-Macedonum. Florent. 1689. fol.
36.	I.B.18.	Joh. Sleidani Commentarii. Franc. ad Moen. 1568. fol.
37.	I.C.1.	Dav. Buchanan's Historie of the Reformation of the Church of Scotland. Lond. 1644. fol.
38.	I.C.2.	Dionis Cassii Historia, Gr. Lat. per Guil. Xylandrum. —— H. Steph. 1591. fol.

Page from Wanley's catalogue of printed books at Wimpole (Lansdowne MS 816.f.3, British Library)

the Scyldings, fought against the rulers of the Sueciae," suggests that Wanley probably did not decipher the whole poem. The catalogue, for which Wanley prepared six separate indexes, represents an important step forward in Anglo-Saxon bibliography. Wanley has been accused of undertaking such a huge project in undue haste, but, in fact, he was under time pressure from Hickes, since Wanley's contribution was holding up the publication of the thesaurus: the entire work, parts of which had been printed for two years, finally appeared in 1705.

As secretary of the Society for Promoting Christian Knowledge, Wanley compiled minutes for meetings and conducted other business. To Charlett he described the business of the society as "to stop the Current of Debauchery and Profaneness, & promote the Salvation of Men's Souls; and that by several Prudent Methods; some whereof, are the Printing Good Books, and Founding Charity-Schools, &c. . . ." Wanley himself translated Jean F. Osterwald's *The Grounds and Principles of the Christian Religion, Explain'd in a Catechetical Discourse* (1704) for the society. With his friend John Bagford and others, Wanley was involved in the founding of a seemingly short-lived antiquarian society in 1707–1708 and also contributed articles on paleography to *Philosophical Transactions.*

During his first years in London, Wanley continued to consult with scholars and bibliophiles on manuscripts and research sources. Hickes introduced him to Robert Harley, first Earl of Oxford, on 23 April 1701, and from time to time Wanley seems to have assisted him in questions related to his remarkable collections of books, manuscripts, and antiquities–notably in negotiations over the purchase of the collection of Sir Simonds D'Ewes, whose estate Wanley described in detail in a letter to Harley in 1703. A letter to John Strype dated 14 January 1707 indicates that by that time Wanley was working in some capacity for Harley's library, and he took over the position of full-time librarian for a salary of £3 a week in June 1708 when he resigned from the Society for Promoting Christian Knowledge.

Wanley kept this position for the rest of his life, working first directly for Harley but then increasingly with Harley's son Edward, who seems to have taken over the principal charge of the collection by about 1715. Through the Harleys' influence Wanley gained privileges of which other bibliophiles, including his contemporary Hearne, could scarcely have dreamed: in 1713, for example, he worked on obtaining a warrant from Queen Anne "commanding all Keepers of Her Majesties Records & Libraries, to suffer Mr Wanley to peruse and transcribe what he shall think fit without paying fees." The warrant, probably drafted by Wanley himself, presents the study and transcription of ancient manuscripts as "a work which lends so much to the Honor of this our Kingdom, & the public benefit of learning."

Apparently at the Harleys' request, between March and August 1715 and January 1720 until the end of his life (the gap may possibly be because of political uncertainties regarding the Harleys), Wanley kept a "diary," which is really a logbook of his activities in their library that presumably provided a convenient reference source by which the Harleys could keep themselves informed of their librarian's work and what was happening in the library. The diary was first published in its entirety in 1966 as *The Diary of Humfrey Wanley, 1715–1726* under the editorship of C. E. and Ruth C. Wright, although extracts had appeared in earlier publications.

The diary provides an invaluable source as to the precise duties of an eighteenth-century librarian–or at least, of an exceptionally knowledgeable and industrious one. Wanley kept his employers apprised of possible sources of new acquisitions, such as the deaths of collectors or merchants from overseas. He negotiated with the representatives of such collections, with individuals selling items, and with dealers, although in general he seems to have sought Edward Harley's approval before closing on a bargain. Once the items were acquired, Wanley established their correct titles and descriptions, employing help if the documents were outside his own expertise. Wanley was fluent in Latin, Greek, French, Anglo-Saxon, and probably Italian, but he employed experts to help him with Gaelic, Hebrew, Arabic, and other Middle Eastern languages. He then provided bookbinders with the manuscripts, the titles, and usually Harley's own special leather with which to bind the volumes. On the return of the books, he inspected them according to his own exacting standards and catalogued them if this process was not already complete.

In addition, Wanley supervised the daily operation of the library, noting in his diary when scholars came to read or consult volumes. Occasionally, scholars were permitted to borrow from the collection, and Wanley ensured that the items were properly returned. The collection is best remembered for its manuscripts, which were sold to the British Museum in 1753 for £10,000, but also included printed books and a large number of antiquities, principally coins, about which Wanley also was remarkably well informed. In antiquities, also, his bargaining powers were shrewd; for example, he recorded his acquisition at auction of a comb believed to have belonged to the Saxon queen Bertha:

> Mr Howard said that a certain Gentleman of a considerable Estate had read the inscription on Queen Ber-

> tha's Comb, & that he would bid for it, as would several others, and among them his own Lady. Upon this, I prevailed with him to take-off Mrs. Howard; & went after Mr Pownhall [a jeweller who assisted in such matters] to see if he was come to Town, & to direct him a little; which I did accordingly.

In 1716–1717 Wanley was working on a catalogue of Harley's collection and spent some time in Cambridge consulting with experts, such as the antiquary Thomas Baker, notably on the question of anonymous and pseudonymous authors.

Wanley's diary and other sources suggest that he drove a hard bargain: even though the money was his patrons' rather than his own, he was reluctant to pay more than he considered the items were worth, the political influence of the Harley family doubtless aiding them in pressuring sellers to give up their books at reasonable prices. A letter to John Strype dated 25 July 1708, for example, reads:

> Reverend Sir,
> I have not yet had the opportunity of mentioning to Mr Harley the Sum you insist upon, for your eleven books, being fourty Guineas. I think it a great deal of money for so small a number; but since we have had so much communication about it, and you have taken so much pains about the Catalogue, &c: I will venture to Agree with you for them at that price, tho' it is the dearest bargain I ever bought.
> But in Order to shield me from any displeasure which may be conceived against me for my facility; and also for your own Sake, who may oblige a worthy and powerfull Friend thereby; I would desire you to throw in something farther, any thing that you can spare, be it Manuscript or Printed, or Letters or other loose papers of what kind so ever.

Wanley resented the book-buying extravagance of the Harleys' chief rival as a bibliophile–Charles Spencer, third Earl of Sunderland–and noted that

> by Reason of his Decease, some benefit may accrue to this Library, even in Case his Relations will part with none of his Books. I mean, by his raising the Price of Books no higher now; So that, in Probability, this Commodity may fall in the Market; and any Gentleman be permitted to buy an uncommon old Book for less than fourty or fifty Pounds.

He was often dealing with sums of money far larger than his own annual salary, even after it was increased to £3.10s. a week (Harley seems also to have provided Wanley and his first wife with accommodation), and was clearly trusted for his honesty, although the pointed statement in his diary that he never accepted gratuities may be more for Harley's benefit than a literal statement, letters suggesting that at least early in his life, Wanley expected prompt payment for copying and research work. By the end of his life, he still never forgot a debt but could afford to be generous; a letter from October 1721 notes that about twenty years before he had helped the Bodleian Library acquire books from Sir Hans Sloane by collating their catalogues,

> which Services I then valued at Seven Pounds & Ten Shillings, which money remaineth still due to me . . . ; it is my Desire that the said Seven Pounds & Ten Shillings be imployed in the procuring of some one or more good & useful Book or Books to be put into the said Library, wherein I have Served to my great Benefit (both of Information & Maintenance) without the trouble of any entrance into the Benefaction-book.

He also donated a fourteenth-century Latin manuscript Bible from his personal collection. Bagford informed Harley in the early 1700s that Wanley had a library of his own, his specialty being

> collecting books relating to the Service of the Church. The several Versions and Impressions of the Holy Bible in English and Latin, Psalters, Primers, and Common Prayer-Books. It will soon be the best of that kind in the kingdom; from whence in time we may expect his critical observations of the several Versions of Holy Writ into English, a work that hath been attempted by some.

After Wanley's death, this collection was acquired by the dean and chapter of St. Paul's.

Wanley's first wife (often referred to in his letters as "my poor Wife") died in January 1722. Wanley married again in the last year, or, according to Hearne, the last month, of his life, but died of dropsy at his "new Lodging" at Clarges Street, Piccadilly, on 6 July 1726 and was buried at Marylebone Church. His third wife, Anne, who Hearne claimed was "a very young Creature, who had been his Whore," inherited his property. Portraits of Wanley by Thomas Hill are still extant, revealing that in appearance he was dark browed, broad nosed, and heavily pockmarked. In his younger years he wore an elaborate wig. In addition to his extensive interests in librarianship, books, manuscripts, antiquities, and paleography, he was also an enthusiastic musician. He frequently suffered from ill health. Although Wanley has been hailed by British bibliographers as the father of their discipline–Thomas Frognall Dibdin, for example, calls him "as honest a man, and as learned a librarian, as ever sat down to morning chocolate in velvet slippers" and "a rare *Book-wight*" in his way–he was not universally liked among his contemporaries. In particular, Thomas Hearne resented Wanley's air of superiority to him and was indignant when Wanley asked him to provide a guarantee for the return of a book. Hearne claimed that Wanley was a womanizer and had drunk himself to death; letters such as one dated 11 September 1717 that begins "By drinking bad wine, after I went from the Genoa-Armes the last night, I have found my self much disorder'd in my Head this day" suggest that Wanley may indeed have liked his wine. References in letters by Pope, Hickes, and others implying that Wanley assisted them in obtaining wine have given rise to the conjecture that he had a second line of business as a wine merchant. Many notes survive in Wanley's beautiful, minute handwriting, outlining ambitious antiquarian projects that he never completed.

If in personality he often seemed obsequious, one must remember that Wanley's achievements were made entirely without personal advantages and on the strength of his own abilities. A 1701 letter to John Jackson, a nephew of Wanley's patron Samuel Pepys, who was about to set off on travels abroad, asks:

> Only one thing I would beg of you, that as you happen to see or hear of any Person whatsoever, who from a mean Birth & Extraction, ha's by his proper Merit, risen to an extraordinary degree of Eminence in his particular Way; that you would take the trouble to inform your self of the strength of that mans Genius, what Improvements he made to his Natural Endowments, what Methods he took in order to gain those Improvements, and what Advantages have accrued to the Public thereby.

Wanley was undoubtedly thinking of a man like himself and what he had accomplished by his own dedication and hard work. His work for Hickes's thesaurus survives as the foundation of Anglo-Saxon bibliography, while his catalogue of the Harleian manuscripts has continued to be the basis of one of the foundation manuscript collections of the British Library.

Letters:

P. L. Heyworth, ed., *Letters of Humfrey Wanley, Palaeographer, Anglo-Saxonist, Librarian, 1672–1726* (Oxford: Clarendon Press, 1989).

Biographies:

Thomas Hearne, *Chronicon, Sive Annales Prioratus de Dunstaple,* 2 volumes (Oxford, 1733)–the preface includes a sixty-page Latin life of Wanley;

P. L. Heyworth, "Thomas Smith, Humfrey Wanley and the Cottonian Library," *TLS,* 31 August 1962, p. 660;

Heyworth, "Humfrey Wanley and 'Friends' of the Bodleian, 1695–1698," *Bodleian Library Record,* 9 (1973–1978): 219–220.

References:

Michael Murphy, "Humfrey Wanley on How to Run a Scholarly Library," *Library Quarterly,* 52, no. 2 (April 1985): 145–155;

Kenneth Sisam, "Humfrey Wanley," in *Studies in the History of Old English Literature* (Oxford: Clarendon Press, 1953);

C. E. Wright, "Humfrey Wanley: Saxonist and Library-Keeper," *Proceedings of the British Academy,* 46 (1961): 99–129.

Papers:

The "Welbeck Wanleyana," on loan to the British Library from the duke of Portland's Harley Papers formerly in Welbeck Abbey, includes letters both to and from Humfrey Wanley and drafts of other works. Many other notes, transcriptions, and drafts of works are in the Harleian collection in the British Library; of especial note are Harleian 7055 and 6030, his commonplace book. The Lansdowne collection also includes important works, notably letters and the diary. P. L. Heyworth's edition of Wanley's letters includes a list of their locations.

Anthony à Wood

(17 December 1632 - 29 November 1695)

S. A. Baron
George Washington University

CATALOGUE: William Huddesford, *Catalogus librorum manuscriptorum viri clarissimi Antonii a Wood. Being a minute catalogue of each particular contained in the manuscript collections of Anthony à Wood . . .* (Oxford: Printed at the Clarendon Press, 1761).

BOOKS: *Historia et antiquitates universitatis Oxoniensis: duobus voluminibus comprehensae,* 2 volumes, translated into Latin by Richard Peers and Richard Reeve under the direction of John Fell (Oxford: E Theatro Sheldoniano, 1674); rewritten in English by Wood and published as *The History and Antiquities of the University of Oxford,* 2 volumes, edited, with additions, by John Gutch (Oxford: Printed for the editor at the Clarendon Press, 1786, 1790);

Athenæ Oxonienses. An exact History of all the Writers and Bishops who have had their education in the most ancient and famous University of Oxford, from the fifteenth year of King Henry the Seventh, Dom. 1500, to the end of the year 1690. Representing the birth, fortune, preferment, and death of all those authors and prelates, the great accidents of their lives, and the fate and character of their writings: to which are added, the Fasti, or, Annals, of the said university, for the same time . . . , 2 volumes (London: Printed for Thomas Bennet, 1691, 1692; second edition, enlarged, London: Printed for R. Knaplock, D. Midwinter & J. Tonson, 1721);

The Antient and Present State of the City of Oxford, edited, with additions by J. Peshall (London: Printed for J. & F. Rivington, 1773); republished from the original manuscript as *Survey of the Antiquities of the City of Oxford,* 3 volumes, edited by Andrew Clark, Oxford Historical Society Publications, volumes 15, 17, and 37 (Oxford: Printed for the Oxford Historical Society at the Clarendon Press, 1889–1899);

The life and times of Anthony Wood, antiquary, of Oxford, 1632–1695, described by himself, 5 volumes, edited by Andrew Clark, Oxford Historical Society Publications, volumes 19, 21, 26, 30, and 40 (Oxford: Printed for the Oxford Historical Society at the Clarendon Press, 1891–1900).

Anthony à Wood at age forty-five (watercolor copy of a bust; Bodleian Library, Oxford)

OTHER: Edward Wood, *Γνωστὸν τοῦ Θεοῦ, καὶ Γνωστὸν τοῦ Χριστοῦ, or, That which may be known of God by the Book of Nature, and the excellent Knowledge of Jesus Christ by the Book of Scripture. Delivered at St. Mary's in Oxford, Published since his death by his brother A. W.,* edited by Anthony à Wood (Oxford: Printed by H. H. for Jos. Godwin & Edw. Forrest, 1656);

Modius Salium, a Collection of such Pieces of Humour as prevailed at Oxford in the time of Mr. Anthony à Wood, collected by Wood, edited by Thomas Warton (Oxford: Printed for R. Clements, 1751).

Anthony à Wood was well known to his contemporaries as an antiquary and historian and continues to be recognized in the twentieth century for his work in those fields. As an historian, Wood was particularly interested in collecting works about the city and University of Oxford, but as a reader his taste was more cosmopolitan. At his death in 1695 his collection of books and manuscripts totaled more than 6,000 printed items–including many pamphlets and news books–bound in 959 volumes. It included many books not found in any other contemporary Oxford library. Furthermore, Wood collected more than 500 ballads, some of which, as Nicolas Kiessling has shown, constitute the two renowned modern collections of seventeenth-century ballads, the Roxburghe Ballads and most of the ballads in the Harleian Manuscripts in the British Library.

The son of Thomas Wood and his second wife, Mary Petty, Anthony Wood was born in Oxford on St. Lazarus Day, 17 December 1632. (Wood added the "à" to his name as an adult.) His family leased an "ancient stone house" known as Postmaster's Hall opposite the gate of Merton College. The Wood family had London merchant ties as well as Oxford city and university connections. Wood's mother was a member of an old, extensive Oxfordshire family, the Pettys. Having learned to read by the age of five and having received a good early education, Wood chose the academic life as his profession, a sensible choice for a younger son of a second wife. He matriculated at Merton (where his older brother Edward was a fellow) on 26 May 1647, undoubtedly through his family's long connection with the college and its familiarity with the warden, fellows, and students who frequented the Woods' inn, the Fleur-de-Lys, and its tennis court. Despite his academic inclinations, Wood took five years to obtain a B.A. and was awarded an M.A. three years later. Even as a young university student, Wood was already noted for his lifelong irascibility, and the author of the *Dictionary of National Biography (DNB)* entry on Wood believes it was this quality more than his mediocre scholarship that kept him from receiving a Merton fellowship.

It is not possible to pinpoint the precise date when Wood began to collect printed materials, although it was probably early in his years as a Merton student. His books include many published before his birth. Andrew Clark ventured that Wood began to collect ballads in 1640, when he first attended Latin grammar school, and that, when he matriculated at Merton in 1647, he purchased a 1635 edition of the Oxford statutes for undergraduates as well as the regulations concerning fines for nonattendance at university lectures and the 1643 edition of *Quadratura circuli studionum.* It appears that the events of the civil wars (1642–1646 and 1648–1652), many of which centered on Oxford, as well as subsequent political events, had the greatest impact on Wood's book collecting as well as on his life. The civil wars undoubtedly first drew Wood's attention to politics. Sir John Colepeper, the king's master of the rolls, commandeered the Wood house for his residence while the Royalists were garrisoned at Oxford. When he departed, Colepeper left behind the 1644 edition of *The Psalter of David* (Oxford: Printed for Leonard Litchfield), which Wood preserved in his library. Charles I confiscated Anthony Wood's christening plate to help finance the Royalist war effort and Wood's eldest brother, Thomas, was a soldier in the Royalist army. When the city of Oxford seemed likely to be besieged, Anthony and his younger brothers were sent to live in safety with relatives at Tetsworth and later Thame. Wood acquired runs of many civil-war era news books, nine volumes of other materials covering the war years, about fifty items relating specifically to Charles I, Thomas Wentworth, Earl of Strafford, and William Laud, Archbishop of Canterbury, as well as many items concerning the regicide, parliamentary government, and the Restoration.

After the completion of his university studies, Wood moved into the garrets of the family house by Merton gate, the lease of which had passed to his eldest brother, Robert, on the death of their father in 1643. Wood spent the rest of his life in these rooms, studying, researching, and collecting. He devoted himself to private study of genealogy and heraldry, music, good living in good company, and buying almanacs, books, ballads, pamphlets, a few plays, and many news books. In 1652 he began heraldic and genealogical research in the public library of Oxford, and in 1653, he took up his other grand passion: playing the violin. Wood published a collection of his brother Edward's sermons in 1656, a volume to which he referred frequently over the years and which he apparently viewed with some sense of pride and accomplishment.

Beginning in 1657, Wood kept a sort of financial diary in the pages of the almanacs that he purchased religiously. In this diary he recorded the books he bought and had bound, from whom and by whom, and the sums he spent in these activities. For example, Wood recorded on 9 June 1657 that he purchased Harrington's "*Church State*" from Blagrave for ten pence and had William Camden's "*Remaines*" bound by Beckford for six pence. Wood maintained charge accounts or "scores" with several booksellers and bookbinders in Oxford (some of whom were women), especially for acquiring news books. Wood also received print publications regularly by carrier from London. In addition he was an avid buyer of books from the libraries of deceased relatives and Oxford scholars, and he was eager to obtain books from the libraries of famous people. In 1661, for example, he acquired a volume that had belonged to Charles I as Prince of Wales, as well as volumes autographed by Thomas Bodley and Thomas Fortescue. The many entries in Wood's diary for the binding, sewing, and rebinding of his books illustrate his concern for their physical state and preservation. On one occasion in 1674 he had "7 paper books with stained covers" rebound. Four years later he spent a small legacy left to him by an Oxford fellow to bind many of his loose news books into volumes. The diaries show that Wood avidly engaged in selling, trading, borrowing, and lending books with others in the Oxford academic community as well as with his intellectual contacts outside of Oxford.

Wood sometimes recorded his occasional concerns over the availability, pricing, and circulation of printed matter. In July 1658, for example, he noted that the vice chancellor of the university had forbidden the booksellers in Oxford to sell the works of Francis Osborne. In June of 1660 Wood recorded that copies of the works of John Milton and John Goodwin, most of which were also in Wood's personal library, were taken out of the libraries of Oxford and burned. Wood's diaries show that in the aftermath of the Great Fire of London in 1666 "the price of books and paper rise. That which you bought for 3 [d.] was almost as much againe." He was also distressed over the loss of large numbers of books, both ancient and modern, in the fire. In the wake of the Popish Plot controversy of 1678, Wood's diary indicates that "nothing but pamphlets are taken into scolar's hands and they buy nothing else. Serious books and books of matter are neglected." In the summer of 1683 Wood wrote that the vice chancellor of the university had ordered books considered seditious to be publicly burned in a college quadrangle. Wood obtained a printed copy of the vice chancellor's order, which he annotated with a list of the books destroyed. The list includes George Buchanan's *De jure regni apud Scotos* (1579), Thomas Hobbes's *Leviathan* (1651), and Richard Baxter's *Holy Commonwealth* (1659). Among the Wood manuscripts in the Bodleian Library is a volume of Wood's notes on books and authors, perhaps indicating his interest in writing an historical work about books and the book trade.

In July 1658 Wood was formally admitted as a reader in the Bodleian Library of Oxford University. His studies attracted the attention of the head of the library, who occasionally asked Wood to assist with cataloguing and arranging newly acquired collections,

Wood's bookplate

such as that of John Selden, which came to the Bodleian in 1659. Wood's own library includes sale catalogues for book collections such as that of Sir Kenelm Digby, which went on the block in 1680; all the books printed in England for particular spans of years; all books printed in London; the libraries of various Oxford colleges; and a catalogue of writers on heraldry. At least one entry in his diary shows that he had a technical interest in organizing libraries: "Is it not a simple thing for a man to make a catalogue of books and not to set downe the Xtian names of the authors? for there be severall authors that have the same surname." Wood occasionally catalogued libraries for private individuals as well. Between 1677 and 1680, for example, he catalogued the library of Ralph Sheldon, a fellow antiquary who had agreed to subsidize the publication of Wood's life work, the *Athenæ Oxonienses* (1691, 1692). According to his diary, Wood "numbered [Sheldon's books] within side, and without by papers stuck upon the dorse; made a catalogue of them as they stand, . . . made another catalogue in alphabet with very great paines and industry. . . [and] pasted his arms in every book." Wood also catalogued the printed books in Elias Ashmole's collection in the Ashmolean Museum. Wood's own collection was well organized, listed in seven different catalogues that he made over the years. Wood also cross-referenced his printed books with his diaries and recollections for a planned autobiography. Wood's collection was a working library, and he frequently annotated his printed volumes, especially those with which he disagreed, such as the works of Hobbes. He also made notes in printed volumes preparatory to writing the *Athenæ Oxonienses* and a book on the lives of English musicians.

In June 1667 Wood made his first trip to London to research the history of Oxford. He negotiated with William Prynne, the keeper of records at the Tower of London and a notorious Puritan pamphleteer whose works Wood owned, to gain access to the ancient records there. Wood was also able to use Sir Robert Cotton's renowned library on this and other occasions. On his many visits to London, Wood bought books often written by famous people he had encountered while in the capital.

In the fall of 1667 Wood first made the acquaintance of another aspiring historian and antiquary, John Aubrey, who visited Wood in Oxford. It appears Wood had a reputation as a bibliophile and Aubrey knew of Wood's appetite for books because he brought him a gift of books on the occasion of their first meeting and continued to send him volumes for his library over the course of their friendship.

Wood's life work was collecting material for writing books about the history of the university and city of Oxford, a plan modeled on Sir William Dugdale's great antiquarian study of Warwickshire (1656) and the collections of Brian Twyne in the University library. Wood's experiences with publication were traumatic. His first published work was to be *The History and Antiquities of the University of Oxford.* However, Wood ran afoul of John Fell, dean of Christ Church College, whose funding he needed for publication of the book. Fell decided that, if the book were to be published by the university press, it should be published in Latin and had two undergraduates translate the book. Wood recorded in his diary that the translators made many mistakes and that Fell altered many passages in the manuscript, changing the fundamental character of the work. The book was published in Latin by the university press in 1674, and Wood worked the rest of his life on an English version to correct what he considered Fell's mutilation of his work. This second version did not appear until more than a century after Wood's death.

After 1682 the number of notes in Wood's diaries about purchasing and binding books noticeably decline. Wood continued to acquire books, however, right down to a few days before his death. During his later years his diary was devoted to political events at the national and local levels as well as intrauniversity and college politics. Much of this material was recorded with an eye to continuing and expanding his work on his *Athenæ Oxonienses,* as well as other planned histories, such as one on the city of Oxford.

On 18 June 1691 the first volume of Wood's *Athenæ Oxonienses* was published in London. Within a week news had reached Wood through the special efforts of Arthur Charlett, the master of University College who had provided Wood with much information for the *Athenæ Oxonienses,* that many people had begun to take exception to the information included in the book. For the next month, Wood's book about Oxford graduates was the talk of the university and the town. The bachelors and undergraduates regarded it with more favor than the fellows and heads of houses, many of whom thought it inclined toward popery. Wood was informed that the master of Balliol College considered it not "fit to wipe one's arse with." Richard Bathurst of Trinity College asserted that the book displayed "bad sense in very many places." Wood was confused about the reaction to his book, which he believed to be based on factual research. His diaries and recollections are filled with acerbic characterizations of people whom Wood considered both friend and enemy. He believed he perceived the truth about people and that there was nothing wrong with expressing it.

Almost one year later, the second volume of *Athenæ Oxonienses* was published. Wood received his copy by wagon from London on 18 July 1682. Two days later, Charlett informed him that John Wallis was angry over what Wood had said about him in the book and planned to file charges against Wood. Wood's second volume "set all Oxford in a flame" even more than the first. A mere six days after Wood received his copy, he recorded in his diary the fear that it would be confiscated from the booksellers and publicly burned. He also wrote in his diary of his own confusion about people who seemed to look only for the negative things in his book and not the positive. The second volume was also thought to be too preferential to the papists, and it was described as speaking favorably of nonjurors and speaking ill of Presbyterians and independents. In November 1692 Wood, with the assistance of his nephew Thomas Wood, answered charges of libel brought against him by Henry Hyde, second Earl of Clarendon, in the vice chancellor's court. The case dragged on through July 1693, when the court ruled against Wood and his book. On 31 July copies of volume two of the *Athenæ Oxonienses* were called in and burned in the courtyard of the Sheldonian Theater. The following December the ruling against Wood was entered in the black book of the university, and he was expelled. There is remarkably little mention of this situation in Wood's diaries despite the importance of the university in his life and his affection for the academy. Wood continued to fight against the ruling, however, and in May 1695 he was granted a pardon, which restored to him use of the library and the rights to wear a gown and participate in convocations. In October 1695, when Wood was already ill with what would

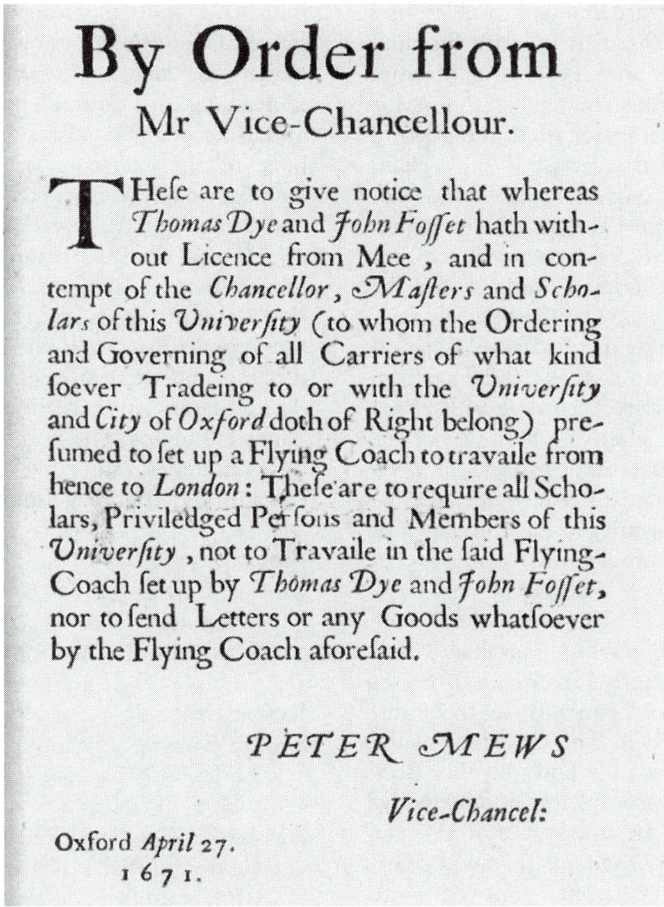

By Order from
Mr Vice-Chancellour.

THeſe are to give notice that whereas *Thomas Dye* and *John Foſſet* hath without Licence from Mee, and in contempt of the *Chancellor*, *Maſters* and *Scholars* of this *Univerſity* (to whom the Ordering and Governing of all Carriers of what kind ſoever Tradeing to or with the *Univerſity* and *City* of *Oxford* doth of Right belong) preſumed to ſet up a Flying Coach to travaile from hence to *London*: Theſe are to require all Scholars, Priviledged Perſons and Members of this *Univerſity*, not to Travaile in the ſaid Flying-Coach ſet up by *Thomas Dye* and *John Foſſet*, nor to ſend Letters or any Goods whatſoever by the Flying Coach aforeſaid.

PETER MEWS

Vice-Chancel:

Oxford *April* 27.
1671.

One of the many ephemeral broadsides in Wood's collection (Bodleian Library, Oxford)

prove his fatal ailment, he heard that Clarendon was in Oxford and rushed out at eight o'clock in the morning to confront him over the libel charges. They argued bitterly, but Clarendon refused to acknowledge any wrong on his part.

One historian described Wood as "an uneasy, bad-tempered man. . . . at odds with almost everyone with whom he came in contact." A contemporary said of him: "God and nature designed that fellow rather for a bricklayer than a historian." Yet, for all his legendary irascibility–and his deafness–Wood was an Oxford socialite. He socialized with many members of the book community and the city and university music community. He spent several evenings a week in some tavern, eating, drinking, playing music, and discussing music. He also had wide contacts among contemporary antiquaries. For example, after Aubrey visited Wood in Oxford in 1657, they were friends and collaborators for twenty-five years, despite Wood's description of Aubrey as "a shiftless person, roving and magotie-headed." Aubrey sent Wood a great deal of information for the *Athenæ Oxonienses,* and it was at Wood's suggestion that Aubrey wrote his *Brief Lives.*

There may have been another crucial aspect of Wood's character that colored his interpersonal relations: religious preference. He is noncommittal about his beliefs in his writings, diaries, and recollections; yet, his diaries record his fear that he would be arrested in the investigations surrounding the Popish Plot in December 1678. Ashmole believed Wood was a papist and feared his library and collections would be seized and destroyed by the government. Wood also conducted a lengthy correspondence with the recusant antiquary Thomas Blount. Much of the dissatisfaction with the *Athenæ Oxonienses* stemmed from the fact that it was considered too favorable toward Catholics, but there is no firm indication of Wood's religious preferences in his writings.

Wood continued to acquire books through September 1695. In the following month he experienced an acute attack of the kidney disease that had troubled him for some years. The physicians had no cure for him. Although he was apparently in a great deal of pain, Wood was up and about in his rooms, continuing his research and writing. The last major event recorded in his diary is a description of the reception of William and Mary at Oxford in early November 1695. News of Wood's illness spread in Oxford and on 22 November, Wood was visited by Charlett, who urged him to put his books, papers, and manuscripts in order before he died and to leave them in the care of the budding antiquary Thomas Tanner. Despite the distrust of Charlett that he had developed during the *Athenæ Oxonienses* controversy, Wood took his advice. According to Richard Rawlinson and Wood's nephew Robert, however, Wood burned quite a few things in the process of ordering his collection. In a will dated 24 November 1695 he left all his manuscripts and writings to the University of Oxford to be kept in the Ashmolean Museum, except for such papers and books as he had already given or sold to the Bodleian Library. He also bequeathed to the university all his "printed books, pamphlets, and papers," which were to be handed over to a group of trustees–Charlett, Tanner, and James Bisse–to be disposed of as decreed by the will. The executors of the will were the young daughters of Wood's brother Robert, who appear to have been completely dominated by Charlett and the trustees in the disposition of Wood's collections, which was not carried out in good faith. The trustees, in particular Charlett, removed large numbers of items, especially manuscript material, from the Wood collection, much of which made its way into the Bodleian Library over the next century and a half through the bequests of several antiquaries. In this fashion many of Wood's papers ended up in other collections, such as the Rawlinson and Tanner Manuscripts in the Bodleian Library. Other materials, however, completely vanished and remain unlocated.

Of the material that made it to the Ashmolean Museum, the manuscripts were considered the most important, and only they were catalogued. No catalogue of the printed material was made until 1761, by which time many volumes had disappeared. The Ashmolean deposit, although in the custody of the museum and its keepers, was also subject to abuse and theft. The bulk of the collection came to the Ashmolean in wooden boxes. Many people had access to these boxes and seem to have borrowed liberally from both the manuscripts and the printed books. In October 1859 the Ashmolean Museum board of visitors offered the books, manuscripts, coins, medals, and antiquities in the Wood collection to the Bodleian as part of a reorganization and expansion of their building to accommodate a manuscript collection bequeathed to them by Sir Thomas Phillips. The Bodleian accepted everything but the antiquities, and the bulk of Wood's collection remains in that library today.

Biography:

Richard Rawlinson, *The Life of Mr. Anthony à Wood, Historiographer of the Most Famous University of Oxford* (London: Printed for the Author, 1711).

References:

Stanley Gillam, "Anthony Wood's Trustees and Their Friends," *Bodleian Library Record,* 15 (October 1995): 187–210;

Nicolas K. Kiessling, "The Location of Two Lost Volumes of Ballads, Wood 399 and Wood 400," *Bodleian Library Record,* 15 (April 1996): 260–291.

Papers:

The bulk of Anthony à Wood's manuscripts and papers are in the Bodleian Library. Wood's lengthy correspondence during the composition of the *Athenæ Oxonienses,* including most of the correspondence with John Aubrey and Sir William Dugdale, are in this Wood Manuscripts collection. Some of Wood's papers are also in the Ballard, Rawlinson, and Tanner Manuscripts at the Bodleian Library.

Sir Christopher Wren

(20 October 1632 - 25 February 1723)

Sandra Naiman
Elmhurst College

CATALOGUE: "A Catalogue of the Curious and Entire Libraries of that Ingenious Architect Sir Christopher Wren, Knt. and Christopher Wren, Esq; his Son, late of Hampton Court, Both Deceas'd; consisting of Great Variety of Books of *Architecture, Antiquities, History,* &c. in Greek, Latin, French, and English; *together with some few lots of* Prints," in *Architects,* volume 4 of *Sale Catalogues of Libraries of Eminent Persons,* edited by D. J. Watkin (London: Mansell, 1972?), pp. 1–39.

Sir Christopher Wren, circa 1711 (portrait by Sir Godfrey Kneller)

BOOKS: *Elevations, Plans and Sections of Fifty Churches Designed and Built under the Direction of Sir Christopher Wren* (1680);

The Case of the Surveyor Concerning the Fabrick of St. Paul's (London, 1697);

A Catalogue of the Churches of the City of London; Royal Palaces, Hospitals, and Public Edifices; Built by S^r. Christopher Wren, K^t. Surveyor General of the Royal-Works during Fifty Years: vizt from 1668, to 1718 (London: Printed for S. Harding and others, 1719);

'Tom Tower', Christ Church, Oxford. Some letters of Sr Christopher Wren to John Fell, Bishop of Oxford, Hitherto Unpublished, Now Set Forth and Annotated by Douglas Caröe . . . With a Chapter by H. H. Turner . . . and another, by Arthur Cochrane . . . (Oxford: Clarendon Press, 1923);

St. Paul's Cathedral: Original Wren Drawings from the Collection at All Souls College, Oxford, volume 1 of the Wren Society publications, edited by Arthur Thomas Bolton and Harry Duncan Hendry (Oxford: Printed for the Wren Society at the University Press, 1924);

St. Paul's Cathedral: Original Wren Drawings from the Collection in the Library of St. Paul's Cathedral, volumes 2 and 3 of the Wren Society publications, edited by Bolton and Hendry (Oxford: Printed for the Wren Society at the University Press, 1925, 1926);

Hampton Court Palace, 1689–1702: Original Wren Drawings from Sir John Soane's Museum and All Souls College, Oxford, volume 4 of the Wren Society publications, edited by Bolton and Hendry (Oxford: Printed for the Wren Society at the University Press, 1927);

Designs of Sir Chr. Wren for Oxford, Cambridge, London, Windsor, etc.: Original Wren Drawings from All Souls, Hans Soane, and Sir John Soane's Collections, volume 5 of the Wren Society publications, edited by Bolton and Hendry (Oxford: Printed for the Wren Society at the University Press, 1928);

The Royal Hospital for Seamen at Greenwich, 1694–1728; Original Drawings by Sir Christopher Wren, Sir John Vanbrugh, Nicholas Hawksmoor, John James, from the Collections at the Bodleian, All Souls College, Worcester College, Sir John Soane's Museum, Royal Naval Museum, Greenwich, R. I. B. A. Library, volume 6 of the Wren Society publications, edited by Bolton and Hendry (Oxford: Printed for the Wren Society at the University Press, 1929);

The Royal Palaces of Winchester, Whitehall, Kensington, and St. James's, Sir Christopher Wren, Architect for Their Majesties King Charles II, King James II, King William III and Queen Mary II, and Queen Anne, 1660–1715; to which are added Some Additional Designs for Hampton Court Palace supplementary to Vol. IV, together with an Account of Marlborough House, St. James's Park and Two Plans of Buckingham House; Original Drawings by Sir Christopher Wren and Sir John Vanbrugh. From the Collections at All Souls College, Pepys's Library, British Museum, Sir John Soane's Museum, H. M. Office of Works, R. I. B. A. Library, volume 7 of the Wren Society publications, edited by Bolton and Hendry (Oxford: Printed for the Wren Society at the University Press, 1930);

Thirty-two Large Drawings for Whitehall, Windsor, and Greenwich, 1694–1698, Original Wren Drawings, purchased by Dr. Stack, F. R. S., in 1749, being now Volume V in the Collection at All Souls, volume 8 of the Wren Society publications, edited by Bolton and Hendry (Oxford: Printed for the Wren Society at the University Press, 1931);

The Parochial Churches of Sir Christopher Wren, 1666–1718 . . . , volumes 9 and 10 of the Wren Society publications, edited by Bolton and Hendry (Oxford: Printed for the Wren Society at the University Press, 1932, 1933);

Designs of Sir Chr. Wren for Westminster Abbey, the New Dormitory, Westminster School, Works at Westminster Palace for the Houses of Parliament, and the House, Library and Garden of Sir John Cotton; also for Sir John Moore's School at Christ's Hospital, Newgate Street, and for his School at Appleby in Leicestershire; Original of Wren Drawings from the All Souls Collection, the Library of Westminster Abbey, and the Gough collection at the Bodleian, volume 11 of the Wren Society publications, edited by Bolton and Hendry (Oxford: Printed for the Wren Society at the University Press, 1934);

Miscellaneous Designs and Drawings by Sir Chr. Wren and Others, including James Gibbs and Nicholas Hawksmoor, for Houses, Public Buildings and Decorations, with the Plans for the Rebuilding of the City of London after the Fire; Original Drawings from the All Souls Collection, Sir John Soane's Museum, the Gough Collection at the Bodleian, and Arbury in Warwicksire, volume 12 of the Wren Society publications, edited by Bolton and Hendry (Oxford: Printed for the Wren Society at the University Press, 1935);

Designs and Drawings by Sir Christopher Wren for St. Paul's Cathedral, the Residentiaries' Houses, and the Deanery; Original Drawings from the All Souls Collection, the Library of St. Paul's, the Surveyor's Office, the Public Record Office, and the Gibbs Collection at the Ashmolean Museum, volume 13 of the Wren Society publications, edited by Bolton and Hendry (Oxford: Printed for the Wren Society at the University Press, 1936);

Engravings of St. Paul's Cathedral and Part II of the Building Accounts for the Years 1685–95 . . . , volume 14 of the Wren Society publications, edited by Bolton and Hendry (Oxford: Printed for the Wren Society at the University Press, 1937);

Photographic Supplement of St. Paul's Cathedral and Part III of the Building Accounts from October 1st, 1695 to June 24th, 1713. Also the Chapter House Accounts, 1712–14 and Outline of Cathedral Accounts, 1714–25, volume 15 of the Wren Society publications, edited by Bolton and Hendry (Oxford: Printed for the Wren Society at the University Press, 1938);

Designs and Drawings Supplementary to Volume XII. 1935. The Work of Sir Chr. Wren, Sir John Vanbrugh, William and John Talman . . . Originals from Welbeck; Chatsworth; Castle Howard; Sir John Soane's House and Museum; the Bull Collection; British Museum; Gough Collection, Bodleian; Gibbs Collection, Ashmolean . . . With Appendices: The Domestic Work of Sir Chr. Wren, 1674–1702; Fawley Court, Winslow Hall, and Lichln Cathedral Library, Measured Drawings, contracts, and Building Accounts, volume 17 of the Wren Society publications, edited by Bolton and Hendry (Oxford: Printed for the Wren Society at the University Press, 1940);

The Wren Ms. 'Court Orders' with a Supplement of Official Papers from the Public Record Office, Welbeck Abbey, &c. A Biographical Note on Sir Chr. Wren's Visit to Paris 1665 and his Death and Funeral in 1723. Together with Some Account of Thomas White of Worcester, Sculptor and Architect, reputed pupil of Sir Chr. Wren. Engravings, Drawings, Photographs, volume 18 of the Wren Society publications, edited by Bolton and Hendry (Oxford: Printed for the Wren Society at the University Press, 1941);

The City Churches, Vestry Minutes and Churchwarden's Accounts; St. Mary's, Igestre, Staffordshire; All Saints' and Sessions House, Northampton; the Royal Hospital, Chelsea; the Church and Almshouses, Farley, Wiltshire; the Sheldonian Theatre and Tom Tower, Oxford; the

Market House, Abingdon, Berkshire; the Bridge, St. John's College, Cambridge; the New School, Eton; Kensington Palace; the Royal Observatory, Greenwich; Morden and Bromley Colleges; and the Five Tracts on Architecture by Sir Chr. Wren. Drawings, Engravings and Photographs, volume 19 of the Wren Society publications, edited by Bolton and Hendry (Oxford: Printed for the Wren Society at the University Press, 1942);

Catalogue of Sir Chr. Wren's Drawings at All Soul's, St. Paul's Library, Sir John Soane's Collection . . . Index to Volumes I–XIX. List of Members, volume 20 of the Wren Society publications, edited by Bolton and Hendry (Oxford: Printed for the Wren Society at the University Press, 1943).

OTHER: Thomas Willis, *Cerebri Anatome: cui accessit nervorum descriptio et usus,* illustrations by Wren (London: Printed by Tho. Roycroft for Jo. Martyn & Ja. Allestry, 1664).

Sir Christopher Wren epitomizes the Renaissance man. Adept in languages, adroit in personal relationships, and a brilliant mathematician, he became–with no architectural training–the greatest English architect of his day. The classical sources of his inspiration are clearly illustrated by the titles in his personal library.

Christopher Wren was born on 20 October 1632 in the county of Wiltshire at the rectory of East Knoyle, where his father, also named Christopher, served as rector. His mother, Mary, died when he was still young though records show that she lived for at least the first two years of her son's life. On 4 April 1635 his father was appointed dean of Windsor and registrar of the Order of the Garter by Charles I. The deanery had been vacated by the elder Wren's brother Matthew, who became the bishop of Ely in 1636. The Wrens enjoyed several years of prosperity until the outbreak of the civil war uprooted them in 1642. They moved to Bristol, a royalist stronghold, but that city was surrendered in 1645. The family found refuge with Wren's older sister Susan, who had married William Holder, the rector of Bletchingdon, a small Oxfordshire village near Bicester.

Several adults played important roles in Wren's development. Susan Holder was Wren's favorite sister and possibly a surrogate for his dead mother. Her husband, a virtuoso in both music and mathematics, became young Wren's mentor. Another significant mentor was Charles Scarborough, a mathematician and a surgeon-physician to whom one of Abraham Cowley's odes is addressed. Scarborough later became the knighted physician to Charles II, James II, and Queen Anne. He assembled what a 1694 sale catalogue

Wren's monogram on the spine of one of the books he gave to the library of the Savilian professors at Oxford (Bodleian Library, Oxford)

described as an "incomparable" library containing "almost a complete collection of Greek books in all faculties, with a large collection of mathematics and physics." Young Wren may well have become familiar with Scarborough's collection.

Under Scarborough's guidance Wren wrote a treatise on spherical trigonometry by a new method and pleased his mentor by engraving it on a tiny brass plate. He became Scarborough's assistant in his anatomical experiments, building models that the doctor used to illustrate his lectures. Perhaps at Scarborough's suggestion, Wren translated into Latin a tract of William Oughtred's *Clavis Mathematicae* (1631) that the author used, and later acknowledged, in the third edition of his famous work (1652).

When Wren went to Oxford at the age of seventeen, he was accustomed to relating to his elders as a peer. Instead of his father's college, St. John's, he chose Wadham College. The warden there, John Wilkins, made his college a magnet for brilliant young men interested in experimental science. Wren managed to take his bachelor of arts degree in two years instead of four, and by 1653, at the age of twenty-one, he earned his master of arts degree and become a fellow of All Souls College.

Soon after moving to All Souls, Wren designed a large sundial for the wall of the chapel (which can still be seen on the wall of the college library) and began a study of the planet Saturn which he pursued for many years. He also initiated and carried through an impressive series of experiments that anticipated the techniques of modern blood transfusions and the use of what is now called the hypodermic needle. In June of 1654 John Evelyn met "that miracle of a youth Mr. Christopher Wren," and they dined together with Wilkins at Wadham, where Evelyn was shown the Warden's collection of scientific specimens and models to which Wren, that "prodigious young scholar," had made many contributions.

At Oxford, Wren became devoted to the new fashion of drinking coffee in coffeehouses, a pleasure he shared through the years with his lifelong friend Robert Hooke. A physicist, Hooke was a great collector of books on architecture, which he may have shared with Wren. Both men were enthusiastic members of an Oxford club devoted to experimental science that formed the nucleus of what later became the Royal Society, founded officially in 1662. (Wren was elected its president in 1681.)

In 1657, at the age of twenty-five, Wren accepted the chair of astronomy at Gresham College in London. Four years later he was elected to succeed his former professor and friend Seth Ward as Savilian professor of astronomy at Oxford, and the same year he received doctor of law degrees from both Oxford and Cambridge. His experiments for the Royal Society attracted the attention of Charles II, who invited him to survey and direct the work of fortifying the Moroccan port of Tangier, which Charles had acquired by marrying the Portuguese princess Catherine of Braganza in 1662. Wren managed to decline this appointment without offending the king on the grounds that his health was delicate.

Shortly after turning down the Tangier appointment, Wren was invited by an old friend, Gilbert Sheldon, to design a building at Oxford where the ceremony of awarding degrees could appropriately take place. Sheldon, the bishop of London, was a rich man, a loyal Oxonian, and an astute politician who became the archbishop of Canterbury. Inspired by Sebastiano Serlio's descriptions in *Tutte l'opere d'architettura, et prospetiva* (1537–1575) of the theater of Marcellus, Wren designed the Sheldonian Theatre as his first building; it housed the Oxford Press for many years and is still used for conferring degrees. While the Sheldonian Theatre was being built, Wren accepted another architectural commission, this one from his uncle, Matthew Wren. During his eighteen years of imprisonment in the Tower of London by the Puritans, the bishop had vowed that upon his release he would present his old college of Pembroke, Cambridge, with a new chapel, which he asked his nephew to design.

When the Pembroke chapel was completed in 1665, Christopher Wren made his only trip outside England. He went to France for several months, to see the new French architecture and meet the French and Italian architects working in Paris. Wren was fortunate in his timing for he missed the worst of the outbreak of the Great Plague and returned at a propitious moment for an architect, for within months most of the city of London was leveled by the Great Fire of September 1666. Wren and Hooke were among the six men Charles II named as commissioners for the rebuilding of the city.

Three years later the king appointed Wren His Majesty's Surveyor-General of Works and Buildings, passing over other applicants with more experience. The position was the chief architectural office in England, entailing the responsibility of maintaining and repairing all palaces and other royal buildings. Its perquisites included a large house in Scotland Yard. Evidently the appointment made Wren feel secure, for later that year he married Faith Coghill, daughter of Sir Thomas Coghill of Bletchingdon, where Wren had spent much of his youth.

Wren was less fortunate in his personal life than in his professional life. In 1673 he was knighted by Charles II, but his first son died six months later, and two years after that his wife died of smallpox. The following year Wren married a second time. His wife, Jane Fitzwilliam, the daughter of William, Lord Fitzwilliam

Trinity College Library, Cambridge, which Wren designed for his friend Isaac Barrow

of Lifford, died in less than four years, after which Wren never remarried. His boon companion was his daughter Jane, the child of his second marriage. Her death preceded her father's by two decades. Wren's second son by his first marriage, Christopher, survived his father and cared for Wren's third son, Edward, who was born mentally retarded in 1679.

Despite personal woes, Wren flourished as an architect, successfully surviving political and religious vicissitudes under various monarchs. During the reign of Charles II he began work on St. Paul's Cathedral and sixty parish churches to replace the churches lost in the fire. He also designed for Charles II the first royal observatory to be built in England, Flamsteed House, the Royal Hospital in Chelsea, and Winchester Palace, which did not survive. For James II he designed a new royal chapel and a new privy gallery at the Palace of Whitehall. For William of Orange and Queen Mary II, Wren designed a new palace at Hampton Court. For his old friend Isaac Barrow, who became the master of Trinity College, Cambridge, Wren designed Trinity College Library.

Queen Anne also liked Wren and gave him the lease of a small house on Hampton Green, near the gates of Hampton Court Palace. It was only when Wren's decades of labor on St. Paul's Cathedral were nearly finished, at what might have been the sublime culmination of his career, that his good fortune unraveled. In 1712 a pamphlet titled "Frauds and Abuses at St. Paul's" he and his associates were maliciously accused of dishonesty. Subsequently, the commissioners ordered decorative changes at St. Paul's without Wren's approval, and in 1718 King George I deprived Wren of his life appointment as Surveyor-General, appointing in his stead a Whig politician named William Benson. The eighty-six-year-old Wren retired to the house on Hampton Green. He died in his house in London on St. James Street at the age of ninety on 25 February 1723.

Wren's son Christopher collected the Wren family papers, which were subsequently published by his son Stephen as *Parentalia; or, Memoirs of the Family of the Wrens; viz. of Mathew Bishop of Ely, Christopher Dean of Windsor, etc., but chiefly of Sir C. Wren* in 1750. The younger Christopher Wren died in 1747. On 24 October 1748 and the next three evenings, an auction was held at Mr. Cock's in the Great Piazza, Covent Garden. An annotated copy of the auction catalogue–"A Catalogue of the Curious and Entire Libraries of that Ingenious Architect Sir Christopher Wren, Knt. and Christopher Wren, Esq; his Son, late of Hampton Court, Both Deceas'd; consisting of Great Variety of Books of *Architecture, Antiquities, History,* &c. in Greek, Latin, French, and English; *together with some few lots of* Prints"–is owned by the Bodleian Library and is reproduced in the series *Sale Catalogues of Libraries of Eminent Persons,* under the general editorship of A. N. L. Munby. The architectural drawings of Sir Christopher Wren were part of a second sale in early April 1749 that featured the younger Wren's collection of medals and medallions, "antique marble statues, busts, urns and inscriptions, bronzes, gems, and other curiosities."

The catalogue of Sir Christopher Wren's library affords no intimate revelations. The only titles that do not readily fit into the major classifications are Thomas Salmon's *Essay on Marriage,* treating marriage, divorce, and prenuptial contracts, and a book on venereal disease published after the architect's death. Both books may have belonged to his son. The younger Wren was a coin collector, so it is not surprising that there were books about numismatics in the family library. The collection included Filippo Buonanni's *Numismata summorum pontificum templi Vaticani fabricam . . .* (1700), about papal medals, and Jean Foy-Vaillant's book about Syrian history and numismatics, *Seleucidarum imperium sive historia regum Syriae . . .* (1681) as well as his catalogue of Roman coins, *Selectiora numismata . . .* (1694). The son also owned Jean Hardouin's *Nummi antiqui* (1684), Enrico Noris's *Annus et epochae Syromacedonum in vetustis urbium Syriae nummis praesertim mediceis expositae* (1696), Count Costanzo Landi's *In veterum numismatum Romanorum miscellanea explicationes* (1695), Jacob de Wilde's *Selecta numismata antiqua* (1692), and John Evelyn's *Numismata* (1697).

Wren's is the library of a well-educated, well-to-do Renaissance gentleman with a variety of interests and a solid training in the classics. It is not the library of a thoroughgoing book collector. There are twenty-one books about architecture, for example, but these are not all the books about architecture that existed; Nicholas Hawskmoor, Wren's contemporary, owned architectural books that were not in Wren's library. Likewise, while there are books on astronomy, mathematics, and science, Wren clearly did not try to acquire all the available books on any of those subjects, and, in fact, there are more books of travel than books about those subjects.

The sale included more than six hundred books. Because of the way the auctioneer grouped the books in lots for the sale in 1748, it is impossible to make a definitive analysis of the content of Wren's library. The difficulty in assessing the library is suggested by the names given to the first 4 of the 570 lots listed: "Euclidis Elementa, J. Barrow [i.e., Isaac Barrow], and 17 Lat."; "Menagii Poemata, and 17 Lat."; "Quinte Curce, and 11 French"; "Histoire de la Chine, and 11 French." One lot consisted entirely of seventy-nine prints and drawings relating to ancient architecture; other lots were titled "a collection of fine Heads," "a collection of coins, neatly engraved," "a miscellaneous collection of Prints, of Palaces, Views, Ruins, &c.," "drawings of fortifications," and "Antique Statues." In addition and separate from the 570 lots there were 29 lots of prints.

Wren's books were obviously acquired for study rather than display. Fewer than ten lots have remarks about the appearance of the books and they may have been gifts. A 1525 edition of Jean Froissart's *Chronicle,* almost the oldest book in the collection, is described as being "black letter" (in Gothic script). Several volumes by Edward Stillingfleet are noted in the catalogue for their bindings. A 1665 edition of *Rational Account* is listed as being in large paper and "bound in Morocco"; *Origines Sacrae* and a four-volume set of *Pieces* are bound "in Turkey" (leather prepared from goatskins). *Rational Account* and *Origines Sacrae* are the same title: *Origines sacrae, or a Rational Account of the Christian Faith as to the Truth and Divine Authority of the Scriptures and the Matters therein contained.* First published in 1662, it was the engine of Stillingfleet's upward mobility as a divine. Associated with Wren in the 1660s and 1670s, Stillingfleet was successively prebendary of St. Paul's, chaplain to Charles II, and canon residentiary and dean of St. Paul's. Wren also owned Stillingfleet's *Origines Britannicae, or Antiquities of the British Church* (1685), which has been described as "a strange mixture of critical and uncritical research." Stillingfleet was widely respected by his contemporaries for his vast learning, and he possessed one of the best personal libraries in England. After his death in 1699 his manuscripts were bought by Robert Harley, later the earl of Oxford, and his books by Narcissus Marsh, archbishop of Armagh.

James Hodgson's *Navigation* and John Tillotson's *The Rule of Faith* are advertised as "bound in Morocco." Hodgson was a fellow of the Royal Society and wrote several papers for the society's publication *Philosophical Transactions.* Twelve volumes of the *Transactions,* one of the earliest periodicals, were in Wren's library. So were five volumes of *Acta Eriditorum* (Deeds of Distinguished Men), an international scientific journal that began publication in 1682.

Gottfried Wilhelm Leibniz's invention of calculus became known through the publication of his results in this journal in 1684. Wren must have known Archbishop John Tillotson as well; he became dean of St. Paul's around 1690. His pamphlet on *The Rule of Faith* was an answer to John Sergeant's *Sure Footing in Christianity, or Rational Discourses on the Rule of Faith.*

Wren's copy of Tillotson's *The Rule of Faith* was apparently a first edition (1666), though there is no indication from his library that Wren was interested in first editions per se. Wren's copy of John Evelyn's English translation of Roland Freart's *Parallele de l'architecture antique avec la moderne* (1664) was a third edition (1707) even though the book was dedicated to Wren. In the description of Wren's library that follows the date listed in the sale catalogue is given if there was one; otherwise the date in parentheses is the putative date of the first edition.

The only manuscript listed in the catalogue of Wren's library is a psalter "on vellum, with initial letters finely illuminated." The psalter brought £1 4s. at the auction, according to the annotator's notes, whereas Wren's copies of *Philosophical Transactions* brought £1 7s. The manuscript might have belonged to Wren's father or his uncle; both of them, as was typical of learned clergymen of the seventeenth century, owned libraries. Wren's father gave twelve printed books to St. John's College, Oxford, and the bishop of Ely gave six manuscripts and forty-nine printed books to Pembroke College, Cambridge. He also gave Pembroke its benefactors' book and wrote many of the entries himself, including all the entries on folios 1–30. The bishop, unlike his nephew who did not mark his books, identified his books with his motto: "Moriendo ViVam," always capitalizing the *V*s to suggest his initials, *MW.*

There were two manuscript catalogues in Wren's library: Thomas Smith's 1696 catalogue of the manuscripts in the Cotton library and David Casley's catalogue of the manuscripts of the king's library (1724). In addition Wren owned Bernard de Montfaucon's *Diarium italicum,* an account of the principal libraries of Italy and their contents published in Paris in 1702.

The oldest book in the Wren library is on architecture, a Latin edition of *De Re Aedificatoria* by Leon Baptista Alberti. It was first printed in Florence in 1485, but Wren's copy was published in Paris in 1512. The twenty sixteenth-century books Wren owned include N. T. Brisciana's Latin translation of Euclid's works (Venice, 1565); Terence's comedies with commentary (Venice, 1564) and another edition of Terence's works, *Il Terentio Latino, Commentato in Lingua Toscana,* a Latin text that includes a word-by-word translation into Italian, published in Venice in 1580; Robert Stephanus's edition of Cicero's *Orations* (Paris, 1539); Henri Stephanus's edition of Herodotus's *History* in Latin and Greek (1592); A. Loeschero's translation of Pausanias's description of Greece (Basel, 1551); an edition of Seneca's works published in Paris in 1591; a two-volume edition of Boethius's works (Basel, 1570); a Greek and Latin edition of Xenophon's *History* published in France in 1596; and the collected works of the Spanish humanist Juan Luis Vives (Basel, 1555), whose career at the English court had flourished until he opposed the divorce of Henry VIII. An anomaly in this group is a New Testament in Spanish (1556). Perhaps it belonged to the architect's father, or perhaps Wren meant to learn Spanish. He owned Sieur de Veneroni's description of a new way to learn Italian, published in Paris in 1678, and several language dictionaries.

The overwhelming majority of the books in Wren's library were published during his lifetime. Approximately one-sixth of the collection was published after his death. Probably the collection is most usefully regarded as belonging to the Wren family. An analysis of the publication years given in the catalogue shows that the number of books climbs steadily over the decades, except in the 1690s, reaching sixty-five in the first decade of the eighteenth century and sixty-four in the second, and then begins falling off: to fifty-three in the 1720s, thirty-four in the 1730s, and eleven in the 1740s; this is the pattern one would expect to find of a collection built by both father and son, as the peak period of 1700–1720 coincides with the adulthood of the son.

Since both Wrens held public office, it is not surprising that some of the books are accounts of contemporary events. These include Thomas Osborne's *Memoirs Relating to the Impeachment of Thomas, Earl of Danby, in the Year 1678* (1710); Sir Philip Warwick's *Memoires of the Reign of King Charles I, with . . . King Charles II* (1701); Charles Davenant's *Essays* on peace and war (1701 and 1704); Simon DuCros's *Letter . . . being an Answer to Sir Wm. Temple's Memoirs concerning What Passed from the Year 1672 until the Year 1679* (1693); Sir William Dugdale's *Short View of the Late Troubles in England* (1681); *The Memoirs of Lieutenant General Ludlow* (1698), one of the landmarks of British republicanism, which criticized both Cromwell and Charles I; Bulstrode Whitelocke's *Memorials of the English Affairs from the Accession to the Restoration* (1682); Father Pierre Joseph d'Orleans's *The History of the Revolutions in England under the Family of the Stuarts* (1711?); and a fifth edition of Guy Miege's *The Present State of Great Britain* (1723), plagiarized from Edward Chamberlayne's *Anglia Notitia.*

The Wrens also owned Arrigo Davila's *Historie of the Civil Warres of France* (1647); John Rushworth's *Historical Collections of Private Passages of State, Weighty Matters in Law, Remarkable Proceedings in Five Parliaments* (1659–1701), the first great collection of English state papers; John Dryden's translation of Louis Maimbourg's history of the Holy League (1684), done at the king's command; a French translation of Father Martinus Martini's Latin history of the Tatar conquest of China (1692); Josiah Burchett's *Memoirs of Transactions at Sea during the War with France, 1688–1697* (1703); *The Memoirs of the Marquess de Langallerie: Containing an Account of the Most Secret Intrigues of the French, Spanish, and Bavarian Courts* (1708); Daniel Defoe's *Minutes of the Negotiations of Monsr. Mesnager at the Court of England* (1717); Simon Ockley's *History of the Saracens* (1708); John Perry's *State of Russia* (1716); as well as many tracts, pamphlets, and state papers.

Some of the books on contemporary history were published after the architect's death, such as Gilbert Burnet's *History of His Own Time,* published in 1724 and 1734; Bevil Higgons's *Historical and Critical Remarks on Bp. Burnet's History of His Own Time* (1725); John Oldmixon's *Critical History of England* (1730); Paul de Rapin-Thoyras's *Acta Regia: or, an Account of the Treaties, Letters and Instruments between the Monarchs of England and Foreign Powers* (1726); Bruno Ryves's *Mercurius Rusticus, or, the Countries Complaint of the Barbarous Outrages Committed by the Sectaries of this Late Flourishing Kingdom* (1685), listed as a 1732 edition; Bishop Samuel Parker's *History of His Own Time* in both Latin (1726) and English (1728) editions; John Braithwaite's *History of the Revolutions in the Empire of Morocco* (1729); *The History of the Life and Actions of That Great Captain of his Age the Viscount de Turenne* (1686), listed as a 1735 edition; Thomas Corbett's *Account of the Expedition of the British fleet to Sicily . . . under the Command of Sir George Byng* (1739); and James Taylor's *Remarks on the German Empire* (1745).

Wren was also interested in biographies. His library includes Humphrey Prideaux's *Life of Mahomet* (1715), John Le Neve's *Lives and Characters of All the Protestant Bishops of the Church of England since the Reformation* in a large-paper edition of 1720, John Toland's life of Milton (1698), Francis Brokesby's *Life of Mr. Henry Dodwell, with an Account of His Work* (1715), Alexander Gordon's *The Lives of Pope Alexander VI and his son Caesar Borgia* (1729), and lives of Signior Rozelli, James V of Scotland, the earl of Leicester, Sir Thomas More, Lord Halifax, Louis XIII, and the earl of Warwick, "surnamed the kingmaker." To this class belongs the *Memoirs of John Ker of Kersland* (1726). Ker witnessed Gottfried Leibniz's funeral and wrote that "he was buried more like a robber than what he really was, an ornament of his country."

The Wren library contained the spirited correspondence between Leibniz and the English divine Samuel Clarke, carried on at Queen Caroline's instigation and published in 1717, and Voltaire's *Lettres Philosophiques sur les Anglais,* which savaged the French establishment and was ordered to be burned after it appeared in 1733. The Wrens also owned what the sale catalogue called the "best" edition of Francis Sandford's *A Genealogical History of the Kings and Queens of England,* by Samuel Stebbing (1707), and an account of "the families," presumably the royal families, of Austria and Bourbon, as well as the so-called *Memoirs of the Duke of Ripperda*–really a "Grubstreet tale of adventure published at Amsterdam in 1740." An anomaly is Laurent Bordelon's *A History of the Ridiculous Extravagancies of Monsieur Oufle; occasion'd by his Reading Books treating of Magick, the Black Art, Dæmoniacks, Conjurers, of Elves, Fairies, of Dreams, the Philosopher's-stone, Judicial Astrology* (1711).

The Wrens owned Peter Barwick's *Life* of his brother John in both Latin (1704) and English (1724), perhaps indicating that the younger Wren's facility in Latin did not equal his father's. The architect probably knew the Barwicks. John was dean of St. Paul's at the end of his life, and Matthew Wren appointed Peter to the fellowship at St. John's, though he was not be admitted because of the politics of the civil war.

One of the popular books Wren owned was Thomas Burnet's *Sacred Theory of the Earth.* Originally published in Latin as *Telluris Theoria Sacra* in 1681, it attracted so much attention that it was almost immediately translated into English (1684–1689), although Wren's copy is dated 1719. Of this work Samuel Johnson wrote in *Lives of the English Poets,* "the critick ought to read for elegance, the philosopher for its arguments, and the saint for its piety." Wren also owned William Whiston's *New Theory of the Earth* (1696) and his *Astronomical Principles of Religion* (1717). *New Theory of the Earth,* though it had no scientific basis, was praised by both Sir Isaac Newton and John Locke. The latter classified Whiston as one of the authors who, if they do not add much to our knowledge, "at least bring some new things to our thoughts."

Several of the titles Wren owned were by Oxford dons who had been his professors and became his friends. In this group are several books by John Wallis: a treatise on algebra (1685), his *Mechanica five de Motu* (1670), *Institutio Logicae ad communes usus accommodata* (1687), of *Claudii Ptolemaei Harmonicorum* (1682), and *Opera Mathematica* (1656). John Wilkins, warden of Wren's alma mater, is also represented by several books: *A Discourse concerning the Gift of Prayer ... [and] ... A Discourse concerning the Gift of Preaching* (1690?); a large-paper edition of his main work, *Essay toward a Real Character and a Philosophical Language* (1668), in which he proposes a new universal language for philosophers to use; and his *Mathematical and Philosophical Works* (1708), including several essays that had been published earlier, such as "The Discovery of a New World; or, a Discourse Tending to Prove, that 'tis Probable there may be another Habitable World in the Moon, with a Discourse of the Possibility of a Passage Thither," originally published in 1638 and 1640; "Mercury; or The Secret and Swift Messenger, shewing how a Man may with Privacy and Speed Communicate his Thoughts to a Friend at any Distance" (1641); and "Mathematical Magick: or the Wonders that may be Perform'd by Mechanical Geometry" (1648). Sir Robert Boyle, who was at Oxford when Wren studied there, is represented by *A Defence of the Doctrine Touching the Spring and Weight of the Air* (1662), *Some Considerations Touching the Usefulness of Experimental Natural Philosophy* (1663), and miscellaneous works.

Wren owned other works by his friends, including Thomas Sprat's *Observations upon Monsieur de Sorbier's Voyage into England* (1665), a satirical reply to the book by that name, and his *History of the Royal Society of London* (1667); engraved editions of Sir Robert Hooke's *Micrographia* (1665) and his *Posthumous Works* (1705); and several books by Thomas Willis, including his *Practice of Physick* (1685); *Cerebri Anatome Nervorumque descriptio et usus* (1664), containing the most detailed description of the nervous system so far made, and illustrated with drawings by Wren; *De Anima Brutorum* (1672); and *Pharmaceuticae Rationalis* (1674), in which Willis described diabetes mellitus. A fellow of the Royal Society, Willis dissected many brains of both men and animals, and he identified an anastomosis at the base of the brain which is still known as the circle of Willis.

Two striking features of Wren's library are the large number of books about travel and the preponderance of books relating to the ancient world, most of them in foreign languages. The books about travel can be explained partly by the fact that Wren became England's greatest Renaissance architect without ever having visited Italy, from which he drew so much inspiration for his buildings. Obviously, he had to do a great deal of armchair traveling to compensate for his lack of the real experience, and this can account for the many engraved books he owned about travel in Italy and Roman antiquities, such as Antonio Bosio's book about Roman cemeteries, *Roma Sotterranea* (1632); Bonaventura van Oberbeke's *Reliquiae Antiquae Urbis Romae; Scheuchzeri Itinerae Alpinae* (1708); an illustrated edition of Sieur de Rogissart's *Delices of Italie* (Leiden, 1706); and Jacob Spon's *Voyage d'Italie, de Grece, et du Levant* (1679).

Wren's travel interests, however, were not confined to Italy. His varied travel narratives include Charles Patin's *Travels thro' Germany, Bohemia, Swisserland* (1696); *The Voyage of Francois Leguat,* a trip by the author to the Mascarene Islands (1708?); Simon Ockley's *Account of South-west Barbary,* describing Morocco (1713); Melchisedech Thevenot's narrative of his voyages in the Levant (1687); engraved editions of Charles Le Brun's travels in the Levant (1702) and Joseph Pitton de Tournefort's voyages in the Levant (1717); Ogier Ghislain de Busbecq's *Four Epistles . . . concerning His Embassy into Turkey* (1633); Sir George Wheler's *A Journey into Greece . . . in Company of Dr. Spon of Lyons* (1682), in six books, "with variety of sculptures"; Martin Lister's description of his journey to Paris in 1698 (1709); Jacob Tollius's *Epistolae* describing his travels in Germany, Austria, and Hungary (1700); John Ogilby's *Africa* (1670); Charles Ferriol's *Explication des Cent Estampes Qui Representent Differentes Nations du Levant* (1715), illustrating Middle Eastern costumes; Willem Bosman's *A New and Accurate Description of the Coast of Guinea* (1705); John Norden's *Speculum Britanniae* (1723), containing an historical and chorographical description of Middlesex and Hartfordshire; William Hacke's edition of *A Collection of Original Voyages* (1683); William Dampier's *A Voyage to New Holland, &c., in the Year 1699, wherein are Described the Canary-Islands* (1703?); Edward Wright's *Certaine Errors in Navigation* (1657); the *Voyage du sieur Paul Lucas, Fait par Ordre du Roy dans la Grece, l'Asie Mineure, la Macedoine et l'Afrique* (1712); John Breval's *Remarks on Several Parts of Europe* (1726); John Windus's *A Journey to Mequinez* (1725); Captain Edward Cooke's *A Voyage to the South Sea and Round the World 1708–11* (1712); Amedee Francois Frezier's *A Voyage to the South-Seas and along the Coasts of Chile and Peru in 1712–14* (1717); Captain Woodes Rogers's *A Cruising Voyage round the World 1708–11* (1712); M. DuPerier's *A General History of All Voyages and Travels* (1708); Sir John Chardin's *Travels,* detailing Persia and the East Indies (1686) in an illustrated French edition; *Travels* by George Sandys, describing Turkey, Greece, Egypt, the Holy Land, and Italy (1615), listed as a 1670 edition; and Sir John Mandeville's *Travels,* which focus on the Holy Land, in a large-paper edition of 1725. Additionally, the Wren library contained unidentified accounts of travels to Naples, Constantinople, Spain, Livonia, Prussia and Hanover, Switzerland, Borneo, Buenos Aires, Denmark, the Dutch East Indies, and America, as well as many books about British antiquities. The younger Christopher Wren obviously shared his father's interests in antiquities, for several of the books about them were published after the architect's death, such as an illustrated *Antiquitates Middletonianae* (1745) and Alexander Gordon's *Itinerarium Septentrionale: or, A Journey thro' Most of the Counties of Scotland and Those in the North of England* (1726).

One remarkable characteristic of Wren's library is its lack of Elizabethan, metaphysical, and Restoration literature. Two of the few such writers that are represented are Francis Bacon and John Selden. Bacon is represented by a Latin edition of his complete works published in France in 1665, an undated edition of his *Natural History* "with large ms. notes," and his *Remains.* Wren owned Selden's edition of six books of Eadmer, describing the courts of the first two Williams and the first Henry (1623), and perhaps other Latin books as well that are not named in the sale catalogue.

During Christopher Wren's lifetime England had the greatest number of good poets it has ever had, but that is not reflected in the catalogue of his library. He owned no poems by John Donne, George Herbert, Andrew Marvell, or Richard Crawshaw. In this he was not different from most of his contemporaries, but that fact is not insignificant. He did not own the sermons of Donne, Lancelot Andrewes, or Jeremy Taylor. He owned the poems of Catullus in Latin, but not the poems of Ben Jonson or Robert Herrick. The Wren library had George Buchanan's Latin translation of Euripedes' plays (1694), and Laurence Echard's English translation of Plautus's comedies (1694) but no plays by William Shakespeare, Christopher Marlowe, John Webster, or their contemporaries. Wren owned a Greek and Latin edition of the comedies of Aristophanes but no Restoration drama. He owned several editions of Virgil's works, yet John Milton, arguably the greatest English poet of the seventeenth century, is only represented in Wren's library by *Eikonoklastes* and *Defensio Populi Anglicani.*

He owned some Latin poems of Abraham Cowley, but then, Cowley was an early candidate for membership in the Royal Society, and Wren's friend Thomas Sprat was Cowley's executor. He owned deluxe editions of the poems of Edmund Waller and John Denham, whom Douglas Bush described in *English Literature in the Seventeenth Century* (1945) as "the mediocre pair who happened to lead the return to the main tradition of European neoclassicism," but that was probably because both men were members of the Royal Society. Members of the Royal Society are heavily represented in Wren's library. For example, he owned almost all the works of the English naturalist and physician Martin Lister, who became a fellow of the Royal Society in 1671. Lister specialized in conches, and Wren owned his *Historiae Conchyliorum* (1694), his *Conchyliorum Bivalvium* (1696), his work on the anatomy of mollusks, *Martini Lister exercitatio anatomica altera* (1695), his work on chronic diseases, *Sex Exercitationes Medicinales de Quibusdam Morbis Chronicis* (1694), the previously mentioned *Journey to Paris,* and Lister's English translation of *Johannes Godartius Of Insects,* with Lister's notes and with copper etchings (1682). Of course, Wren owned Newton's books.

Sir Christopher Wren was perhaps a collector of pictures as much as he was a collector of books. His success as an architect, of course, suggests his visual acuity. His orientation toward the visual is also evident in the books he owned–the unusual number of travel books, the preponderance of illustrated books, and the prints and drawings listed in the catalogue of his library.

Biographies:

Christopher Wren, *Parentalia; or, Memoirs of the Family of the Wrens; viz. of Mathew Bishop of Ely, Christopher Dean of Windsor, etc., but chiefly of Sir C. Wren* (London: T. Osborn and R. Dodsley, 1750);

Harold E. Hutchison, *Sir Christopher Wren: A Biography* (New York: Stein & Day, 1976).

References:

Arthur H. Booth, *Sir Christopher Wren* (London: Muller, 1967);

Paul Waterhouse and others, *Sir Christopher Wren 1632–1723* (London: Architectural Press, 1923);

Margaret Whinney, *Christopher Wren* (New York: Praeger, 1971).

Books for Further Reading

Balsamo, Luigi. *Bibliography: History of a Tradition,* translated by William A. Pettas. Berkeley, Cal.: Rosenthal, 1990.

Basbanes, Nicholas A. *A Gentle Madness: Bibliophiles, Bibliomanes, and the Eternal Passion for Books.* New York: Holt, 1995.

Beadle, Richard, and Alan Piper, eds. *New Science Out of Old Books: Studies in Manuscripts and Early Printed Books in Honour of A. I. Doyle.* Aldershot, U.K.: Scolar, 1995.

Bowers, Fredson. *Principles of Bibliographical Description.* Princeton: Princeton University Press, 1949. Republished, with an introduction by G. Thomas Tanselle. New Castle, Del.: Oak Knoll Press, 1994.

Cabanne, Pierre. *The Great Collectors.* London: Cassell, 1963.

Carley, James P., and Colin G. C. Tite, eds. *Books and Collectors, 1200–1700: Essays for Andrew Watson.* London: British Library, 1996.

Carter, John. *ABC for Book Collectors.* London: Hart-Davis, 1952. Seventh edition, with corrections, additions, and an introduction by Nicolas Barker. New Castle, Del.: Oak Knoll Press, 1995.

Carter. *Books and Book Collectors.* Cleveland: World, 1957.

Carter. *Taste and Technique in Books: A Study of Recent Developments in Great Britain and the United States.* Cambridge: Cambridge University Press, 1948. Revised edition. London: Private Libraries Association, 1970.

Carter, ed. *New Paths in Book Collecting: Essays by Various Hands.* London: Constable, 1934.

Chapman, R. W., John Hayward, John Carter, and Michael Sadleir. *Book Collecting, Four Broadcast Talks.* Cambridge: Bowes & Bowes, 1950.

Clay, C. G. A. *Economic Expansion and Social Change: England, 1500–1700;* volume 1: *People, Land, and Towns.* Cambridge: Cambridge University Press, 1984.

Cooper, Douglas, ed. *Great Private Collectors.* London: Readers Union, 1963.

De Hamel, Christopher. *A History of Illuminated Manuscripts.* Boston: Godine, 1986.

De Ricci, Seymour. *English Collectors of Books and Manuscripts (1530–1930) and Their Marks of Ownership.* Cambridge: Cambridge University Press, 1930.

Drogin, Marc. *Biblioclasm: The Mythical Origins, Magic Powers, and Perishability of the Written Word.* Savage, Md.: Rowman & Littlefield, 1989.

Eighteenth-Century English Books Considered by Librarians, Booksellers, Bibliographers, and Collectors: Proceedings of a Conference Held at San Francisco, June 25–28, 1975. Chicago: Association of College and Research Libraries, 1976.

Eisenstein, Elizabeth. *The Printing Press as an Agent of Change: Communications and Cultural Transformations in Early-Modern Europe.* Cambridge: Cambridge University Press, 1979.

Elsner, John, and Roger Cardinal, eds. *The Cultures of Collecting.* London: Reaktion Books, 1994.

Febvre, Lucien, and Henri Jean Martin. *The Coming of the Book: The Impact of Printing, 1450–1800.* London: New Left Books, 1976.

Fletcher, William Younger. *English Book Collectors.* London: Kegan Paul, Trench, Trübner, 1902.

Francis, F. C. and others. *The Bibliographical Society, 1892–1942: Studies in Retrospect.* London: Bibliographical Society, 1949.

Freeman, Arthur, and Janet Ing Freeman. *Anatomy of an Auction: Rare Books at Ruxley Lodge, 1919.* London: The Book Collector, 1990.

Gaskell, Philip. *A New Introduction to Bibliography.* Oxford: Clarendon Press, 1972.

Greetham, D. C., *Textual Scholarship: An Introduction.* New York & London: Garland, 1992.

Greetham. ed. *Scholarly Editing: A Guide to Research.* New York: Modern Language Association of America, 1995.

Gregg, Pauline. *Black Death to Industrial Revolution: A Social and Economic History of England.* London: Harrap, 1976.

Griffiths, Tom. *Hunters and Collectors: The Antiquarian Imagination in Australia.* Cambridge: Cambridge University Press, 1996.

Hazlitt, William Carew. *The Book Collector.* London: Grant, 1904.

Herrmann, Frank. *The English as Collectors.* London: Chatto & Windus, 1972.

Hill, Richard L. *Papermaking in Britain, 1488–1988: A Short History.* London: Athlone Press, 1988.

Hunt, Arnold, Giles Mandelbrote, and Alison Shell, eds. *The Book Trade and Its Customers, 1450–1900: Historical Essays for Robin Myers.* Winchester, U.K.: St. Paul's Bibliographies, 1997.

John Evelyn in the British Library. London: British Library, 1995.

Keeling, Denis F., ed. *British Library History: Bibliography,* volumes 1–5: 1962–1968, 1969–1972, 1973–1976, 1977–1980, 1981–1984. London: Library Association, 1975–1987; volume 6: 1985–1988. Winchester, U.K.: St. Paul's Bibliographies, 1991.

Ker, Neil Ripley. *Books, Collectors, and Libraries: Studies in the Medieval Heritage.* London: Hambledon, 1985.

Kraus, H. P. *A Rare Book Saga.* New York: Putnam, 1978.

Lowndes, William T. *The Bibliographer's Manual of English Literature,* 4 volumes. London: Pickering, 1834.

Maslen, K. I. D. *An Early London Printing House at Work: Studies in the Bowyer Ledgers.* New York: Bibliographical Society of America, 1993.

McKerrow, R. B. *An Introduction to Bibliography for Literary Students.* Oxford: Clarendon Press, 1927; revised, 1928. Republished, with an introduction by David McKitterick. New Castle, Del.: Oak Knoll Press, 1994.

Muensterberger, Werner. *Collecting: An Unruly Passion–Psychological Perspectives.* Princeton: Princeton University Press, 1994.

Munby, A. N. L. *Essays and Papers,* edited by Nicolas Barker. London: Scolar, 1978.

Munby. *Portrait of an Obsession: The Life of Sir Thomas Phillipps, The World's Greatest Book Collector,* adapted by Barker. New York: Putnam, 1967.

Munby, ed. *Sale Catalogues of Libraries of Eminent Persons,* 12 volumes. London: Mansell / Sotheby Parke-Bernet, 1971–1975.

Myers, Robin, and Michael Harris, eds. *Antiquaries: Book Collectors and the Circles of Learning.* Winchester, U.K.: St. Paul's Bibliographies, 1996.

Myers and Harris, eds. *A Genius for Letters: Booksellers and Bookselling from the Sixteenth to the Twentieth Century.* Winchester, U.K.: St. Paul's Bibliographies, 1995.

Myers and Harris, eds. *Pioneers in Bibliography.* Winchester, U.K.: St. Paul's Bibliographies, 1988.

Myers and Harris, eds. *Property of a Gentleman: The Formation, Organization, and Dispersal of the Private Library, 1620–1920.* Winchester, U.K.: St. Paul's Bibliographies, 1991.

Myers and Harris, eds. *Spreading the Word: The Distribution Networks of Print, 1550–1850.* Winchester, U.K.: St. Paul's Bibliographies, 1990.

Nixon, Howard M. *Five Centuries of English Bookbinding.* London: Scolar, 1978.

Norton, David Fate, and Mary J. Norton. *The David Hume Library.* Edinburgh: Edinburgh Bibliographical Society in association with the National Library of Scotland, 1996.

Parry, Graham. *The Trophies of Time: English Antiquarians of the Seventeenth Century.* Oxford: Oxford University Press, 1995.

Pearce, Susan M. *On Collecting: An Investigation into Collecting in the European Tradition.* London: Routledge, 1995.

Pearson, David. *Provenance Research in Book History: A Handbook.* London: British Library, 1994.

Pfaff, Richard W. *Montague Rhodes James.* London: Scolar, 1980.

Quaritch, Bernard, ed. *Contributions towards a Dictionary of English Book-Collectors,* 14 parts. London, 1892–1921; 1 volume. New York: Burt Franklin, 1968.

Rayward, W. Boyd. *Systematic Bibliography in England, 1850–1898.* Occasional Papers, no. 84. Urbana: University of Illinois Graduate School of Library Science, 1967.

Reitlinger, Gerald. *The Economics of Taste: The Rise and Fall of the Objets d'Art Market since 1750.* New York: Holt, Rinehart & Winston, 1965.

Rettig, James. *Distinguished Classics of Reference Publishing.* Phoenix: Onyx, 1992.

Roberts, Julian, and Andrew G. Watson. *John Dee's Library Catalogue.* London: Bibliographical Society, 1990.

Selwyn, David G. *The Library of Thomas Cranmer.* Oxford: Oxford Bibliographical Society, 1996.

Sherman, William. *John Dee: The Politics of Reading in the English Renaissance.* Amherst: University of Massachusetts Press, 1996.

Sowerby, E. Millicent. *Rare People and Rare Books.* London: Constable, 1967.

Stokes, Roy. *The Function of Bibliography.* London: Deutsch, 1969. Second edition. Aldershot, U.K.: Gower, 1982.

Taylor, Archer. *Book Catalogues Their Varieties and Uses.* Chicago: Newberry Library, 1957. Second edition, revised by William P. Barlow Jr. New York: Beil, 1987.

Thomas, Alan G. *Fine Books.* London: Weidenfeld & Nicolson, 1967.

Thomas. *Great Books and Book Collectors.* London: Weidenfeld & Nicolson, 1975.

Thornton, John L., and R. I. J. Tully. *Scientific Books, Libraries, and Collectors.* London: Library Association, 1954; third edition, revised, 1974; supplement, 1978.

Tribble, Evelyn B. *Margins and Marginality: The Printed Page in Early Modern England.* Charlottesville & London: University Press of Virginia, 1993.

Wright, C. J., ed. *Sir Robert Cotton as Collector: Essays on an Early Stuart Courtier and His Legacy.* London: British Library, 1996.

Contributors

Jill D. Barker . . . . . *University of Luton*
S. A. Baron . . . . . *George Washington University*
Virginia T. Bemis . . . . . *Ashland University*
Richard W. Clement . . . . . *University of Kansas*
Conal Condren . . . . . *University of New South Wales*
A. I. Doyle . . . . . *University of Durham*
John Gallagher . . . . . *Northern Illinois University*
Thomas N. Hall . . . . . *University of Illinois at Chicago*
Brian Hillyard . . . . . *National Library of Scotland*
Daniel Huws . . . . . *Aberystwyth, Wales*
Claudia Thomas Kairoff . . . . . *Wake Forest University*
Michelle Kingston . . . . . *University of Wales, Aberystwyth*
Frans Korsten . . . . . *University of Nijmegen*
K. A. Manley . . . . . *Institute of Historical Research, University of London*
Richard Maxwell . . . . . *Valparaiso University*
Muriel McCarthy . . . . . *Marsh's Library*
Anthony G. Medici . . . . . *Northern Illinois University*
Sandra Naiman . . . . . *Elmhurst College*
Richard Ovenden . . . . . *National Library of Scotland*
Emily Smith Riser . . . . . *Southwest Texas State University*
Joseph Rosenblum . . . . . *University of North Carolina at Greensboro*
Suzanne Rosenblum . . . . . *Greensboro, N.C.*
John C. Ross . . . . . *Massey University*
Robert A. Shaddy . . . . . *University of Toledo*
Clare A. Simmons . . . . . *Ohio State University*
David A. Stoker . . . . . *University of Wales, Aberystwyth*
Stephen Tabor . . . . . *William Andrews Clark Memorial Library, UCLA*
Suellen Mutchow Towers . . . . . *Folger Shakespeare Library*
Kimberly Van Kampen . . . . . *The Scriptorium: Center for Christian Antiquities*
Alexis Weedon . . . . . *University of Luton*

Cumulative Index

Dictionary of Literary Biography, Volumes 1-213
Dictionary of Literary Biography Yearbook, 1980-1998
Dictionary of Literary Biography Documentary Series, Volumes 1-19

Cumulative Index

DLB before number: *Dictionary of Literary Biography,* Volumes 1-213
Y before number: *Dictionary of Literary Biography Yearbook,* 1980-1998
DS before number: *Dictionary of Literary Biography Documentary Series,* Volumes 1-19

A

B

C

D

E

F

G

H

I

J

K

L

M

N

O

P

W

X

Y

Z

ISBN 0-7876-3107-8
90000
9 780787 631079